Contexts for Criticism

Contexts for Criticism

Fourth Edition

DONALD KEESEY

San Jose State University

Boston   Burr Ridge, IL   Dubuque, IA   Madison, WI   New York   San Francisco   St. Louis
Bangkok   Bogotá   Caracas   Kuala Lumpur   Lisbon   London   Madrid   Mexico City
Milan   Montreal   New Delhi   Santiago   Seoul   Singapore   Sydney   Taipei   Toronto

McGraw-Hill Higher Education

A Division of The **McGraw-Hill** *Companies*

CONTEXTS FOR CRITICISM

Published by McGraw-Hill, a business unit of The McGraw-Hill Companies, Inc., 1221 Avenue of the Americas, New York, NY, 10020. Copyright © 2003, 1998, 1994, 1987, by The McGraw-Hill Companies, Inc. All rights reserved. No part of this publication may be reproduced or distributed in any form or by any means, or stored in a database or retrieval system, without the prior written consent of The McGraw-Hill Companies, Inc., including, but not limited to, in any network or other electronic storage or transmission, or broadcast for distance learning.

Some ancillaries, including electronic and print components, may not be available to customers outside the United States.

This book is printed on acid-free paper.

1 2 3 4 5 6 7 8 9 0 DOC/DOC 0 9 8 7 6 5 4 3 2

ISBN 0-7674-2296-1
President of McGraw-Hill Humanities/Social Sciences: *Steve Debow*
Executive director for student success: *Sarah Touborg*
Senior marketing manager: *David S. Patterson*
Senior media producer: *Todd Vaccaro*
Project manager: *Diane M. Folliard*
Production supervisor: *Carol Bielski*
Freelance design coordinator: *Gino Cieslik*
Supplement associate: *Kate Boylan*
Cover design: *Gino Cieslik*
Cover photo: *René Magritté, "La Condition Humaine," photograph*
  © 2002 Board of Trustees, National Gallery of Art
Typeface: *9/11 Palatino*
Compositor: *ColorType, San Diego*
Printer: *R. R. Donnelley and Sons Co.*

Library of Congress Cataloging-in-Publication Data

Contexts for criticism / [compiled by] Donald Keesey. — 4th ed.
      p. cm.
    Includes bibliographical references and index.
    ISBN 0-7674-2296-1 (alk. paper)
      1. Criticism. 2. Literature — History and criticism — Theory, etc.
    3. English literature — History and criticism — Theory, etc. I. Keesey, Donald.
PN81 .C745 2003
801'.95 — dc21   2002071782

www.mhhe.com

BRIEF CONTENTS

CONTENTS

APPENDICES

PREFACE

This new edition of *Contexts for Criticism* offers several changes. Shakespeare's *The Tempest* remains, though with one new application essay; Keats's "Ode on a Grecian Urn" returns from the second edition, replacing Wordsworth's Intimations Ode; and Melville's novella "Benito Cereno" and Charlotte Perkins Gilman's short story "The Yellow Wallpaper" replace Kate Chopin's *The Awakening* as examples of prose fiction. The greatest change, then, is the inclusion of four rather than three target texts and thus a higher proportion of application essays, with each chapter presenting two theoretical essays and four essays applying the theory to the same four target texts. With the exception of the final chapter, where I have kept three theoretical essays to better suggest the diversity of that context, I believe the chapter introductions and two theory essays will give readers sufficient orientation to each approach. The four application essays can then offer more illustrations of the theory and more models for practical criticism. They also allow more choice for users who don't have time to cover all the essays. Again the target texts represent different periods and different genres—drama, lyric, and prose fiction. And the inclusion of *The Tempest*, "Benito Cereno," and "The Yellow Wallpaper" ensure that issues central to cultural criticism, post-colonialism, and feminism are well represented in the book, although none of these is a chapter heading in my organizing scheme.

In sum, users of the third edition will find much fresh material in this new edition. But despite the many changes in content, the book's purpose, and the structure that supports it, remain the same. That purpose is to help readers focus on the fundamental issues of literary interpretation, and the organization supports this end, first, by arranging competing theories in a clear and useful way, and second, by applying these theories to the same literary texts. The book begins with a general introduction setting forth its "contextual" organization. Each chapter then opens with an introductory essay that explains the assumptions and interests of the critics who work in that context, traces briefly the role the context has played in the history of criticism, and offers an assessment of its place in the contemporary scene. The emphasis in these introductory essays is on the general orientation that critics in each context share rather than on matters that divide them, for the first task is to get a clear view of the basic approach. Each chapter next presents two theoretical essays representing strong contemporary arguments for this way of looking at literature. The essays are written by well-known critics who are themselves committed to the approach, and they often exhibit a polemical stance, for I have tried to include essays that state the issues forcefully enough to provoke thought and clearly enough to give that thought some direction.

To further clarify the issues, each chapter concludes with four essays applying some version of the critical approach to the same four texts: *The Tempest*, "Ode on a Grecian Urn," "Benito Cereno," and "The Yellow Wallpaper." These widely studied works, representing different periods and genres, are rich enough to have inspired a variety of critical comment and short enough to be read and reread in conjunction with the critical essays. So, as readers see each theory applied to works they know well, they will better understand what that theory can do. Further, as they see the other approaches applied to the same four works, they can more accurately estimate the strengths and uses of each context. And they will be better equipped to make their own applications of the theories. Criticism, as this book seeks to show, is something one *does,* and when I use the book in classes, I find it works best to have each student choose yet another target text and develop one more set of applications as we work through the various contexts. In the process, they discover that they have always been making their own applications in at least one of these contexts, for there are no other ways to read. By systematically comparing the competing theories, readers will come to see what theories inform their own practice and what alternatives are available.

The application essays, then, provide a way to clarify and test the theories. And because the same target texts appear in all chapters, they open a dialogue between the contexts. For example, Sidney Kaplan's controversial reading of "Benito Cereno" is explicitly or implicitly challenged by most of the other essays on Melville's story. In the same way, Francis Barker and Peter Hulme's approach to *The Tempest* serves as a reference point, or even as a starting point, for critics who argue for other ways to read the play. The essays on "The Yellow Wallpaper" are especially cross-referential. Those by Annette Kolodny, Jean E. Kennard, and Sandra M. Gilbert and Susan Gubar are frequently cited by other critics, and Julie Bates Dock comments on each in her summary critique.

This dialogue is continued in the theoretical essays as well. E. D. Hirsch, for example, seizes on Cleanth Brooks's reading of a short Wordsworth poem to argue the primacy of authorial meaning; in the next chapter, Brooks offers that same reading to argue the primacy of textual meaning. In the reader-response context, Norman Holland defines his position with reference to Wolfgang Iser and other reader-response critics. Bernard Paris reasserts the claims of mimetic criticism in the face of structural and poststructural challenges; Northrop Frye explains how he developed an intertextual emphasis to remedy the deficiencies of mimetic and formal criticism; Jonathan Culler extends the intertextual argument in overtly structuralist terms; and Jacques Derrida deconstructs structuralism, ushering in what is sometimes called a "poststructural" era. In the final chapter, the insights and assumptions of formalism, structuralism, and poststructuralism are given a historicizing critique and redirection.

In these and other ways, the dialogue is carried on from essay to essay and from context to context. As a result, readers who work through the contexts in sequence will see how the focus of interest in literary theory has shifted from the mid-twentieth century to the present. We should remember, though, that despite these shifts in theoretical focus, each of these contexts remains the ground for much contemporary critical practice. We should remember, too, that while arguments about the fundamental issues of interpretation appear here in modern dress, the issues are indeed fundamental, and perennial. Because every reading is necessarily an interpretation, every reader has an important stake in these arguments. These are contexts *for* criticism, ways of reading, and I hope that users of this book will not merely follow the dialogue but actively join it, adopting each perspective in turn, applying it to particular works, comparing it with other approaches, and deciding what use they can make of it. The book is designed to invite this participation and to enable these operations.

Acknowledgments

A number of people helped to make this book. Several users of earlier editions offered suggestions, as did my colleagues Paul Douglass and Bill Wilson. Douglas Keesey once again provided invaluable advice and encouragement, and my students in several sections of "Modern Approaches to Literature" helped their teacher learn. Useful reviews were provided by:

Charles L. P. Silet, Iowa State University

Michael McClintock, University of Montana

Diva Daims, SUNY–Albany

Rick Henry, SUNY–Potsdam

Forest Pyle, University of Oregon–Eugene

Mike Moran, University of Georgia

Michael Krasny, San Francisco State University

Milan Panic, Governors State University

Thanks are due as well to Sarah Touborg, Renée Deljon, Diane Folliard, and the helpful staff at McGraw-Hill.

Contexts for Criticism

General Introduction

Some are bewilder'd in the Maze of Schools.
—Pope, *An Essay on Criticism*

Why study literary criticism? Even to students of literature the answer is not always clear, for I have heard students announce that they make it a principle to ignore "criticism," by which term they mean everything from the popular book review to the scholarly tome, and sometimes this attitude is encouraged by their instructors. No doubt the purpose of this principled ignorance is to keep "interpretation" from coming between the reader and the text. Critics, in this view, are specialists whose concerns are remote from the reader's interests or may even threaten those interests. For the belief is widespread that the reader should confront the work with no pre-conceptions and should achieve thereby an authentic, unmediated response.

But in fact there can be no unmediated response. In the first place, every reader must bring to a text at least a basic understanding of the work's language and there-fore must bring as well an extensive range of cultural experience that "understand-ing the language" presupposes. Only the reader who knew no English at all could have a truly unmediated response to a work in that language. In the second place, every reader must bring not only a knowledge of language but also a set of expecta-tions about "literature" that will cause that reader to emphasize, to value, even to perceive some features of the work rather than others.

In short, we must always read in some way, for every reading is an active process of making sense, an interpretation. And because "literary criticism" may be broadly defined as the art of interpreting literature, every reading is an act of criticism and every reader is a critic. Perhaps the best argument, then, for the study of literary criticism is the realization that critics are not other people. To read literature at all is to practice some type of criticism, to read in some way and not in some other. No reader has a choice about this. The only choice is to decide what kind of critic one will be: a critic who remains unaware of his or her own critical assumptions or one who has chosen a way of reading with full knowledge that it is a way of reading and after some careful study of the alternatives.

But how can such a study be most usefully conducted? If every reader is a critic, then the kinds of criticism must be many and various, and certainly the names for the types or "schools" of criticism are bewildering in their number and diversity.

1

We hear of old historians, new historians, and antihistorians, of Freudians, Jungians, and Lacanians, of Marxists and feminists, affectivists and geneticists, structuralists and poststructuralists, old New Critics and new New Critics. The list of labels can be extended to distressing lengths. To confuse matters further, these terms are not all built on the same principle. Some indicate a critic's philosophical assumptions, his or her view of the world or of the mind; some announce allegiance to a particular discipline or to a particular ideology; some suggest an interest or lack of interest in historical background or social concerns or biographical information. Small wonder that books attempting to survey the field of literary criticism offer a perplexing variety of labels and organizing schemes. And any number of these might be valid for descriptive purposes.

But not all are very helpful for systematic study. To devise a usable grammar for this Babel, we need a conceptual scheme that will include the many types of literary criticism and at the same time separate the competing voices in a way that will help us make useful comparisons. Our categories, then, must be parallel and not so multiple that they add to the confusion. The idea of critical contexts offers such a scheme. Consider the different answers that might be given to the deceptively simple question "Why is there a gravedigger's scene in *Hamlet?*" One type of critic will immediately translate this question to a historical context and explain that the stage traditions, or the presence of a similar scene in the source plays, or the audience's demand for a favorite clown would motivate Shakespeare to write the scene, and so sufficiently answer the question. A different critic in the same context will argue that the scene is designed to reveal further Hamlet's melancholy *adust,* especially that form deriving from sanguine humor, because his grave levity, his jesting with death, would be recognized by the Elizabethan playgoer as a standard symptom of that malady.

Operating in a different context, another critic will explain the scene in terms of its effects, pointing out that the comic interlude temporarily relieves, if only finally to heighten, the emotional tension in the audience. This is "why" the scene is in the play. Yet another critic will interpret our question as a call to explain how the scene fits with other parts of the play, how its diction, imagery, and action serve to develop the coherent structure we call *Hamlet.* And still a different critic will understand the question as a request to account for the scene on some imitative principle. Directing our vision to the world of experience, this critic will remind us that the comic and the tragic are often inextricably mixed in life and will praise the genius of Shakespeare for furnishing richer and truer representations than those found in the more monotonic Greek or French tragedies.

These answers do not exhaust the possibilities, but they reveal an important point about the process of interpretation: the first and crucial step in that process is to decide from what perspective or angle of vision we will view the work. To put it another way, we must decide in what context the work should be placed. Because each answer to our *Hamlet* question involves the choice of a different context, we get the impression—an impression we often get from critical debates—that the respondents are not really answering the same question, are not really debating the issue. This impression is understandable, but it points up the fact that the central issue in criticism is precisely the choice of context. Each of these answers represents an implicit argument that the context the interpreter has selected is the most useful, relevant, or illuminating context.

To study criticism systematically, we need to make these arguments explicit. And we need a conceptual scheme or organizing metaphor that will help us define, ana-

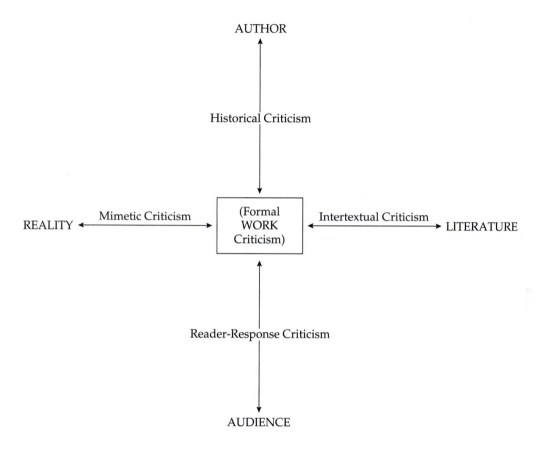

lyze, and compare the various contexts within which all particular interpretations are made. The scheme I use in this book may be visualized in the form of the accompanying diagram.

Because criticism usually involves the interpretation of a particular literary work, it is logical that the work in question should hold the central place in the diagram. The symmetrical arrangement of the various "contexts" around that work is, I should add, perfectly arbitrary and is designed, like the diagram itself, simply to help us think systematically about literary criticism. As presented here, a vertical axis unites the author and the audience and represents the basic communication line. Meanings, some semanticists are fond of saying, are in people, not in words, and many theories of interpretation are based on the belief that we must look either to the author or to the audience if we are to understand the meaning of the literary text. Types of criticism that see the author's conscious and unconscious intentions and, beyond these, his or her entire social, political, and intellectual milieu as the determiners of the poem's meaning are concerned to investigate the causal contexts of the work, and these represent forms of historical criticism. Other forms of criticism pursue the line in the opposite direction and focus on the work's effects rather than on its causes. Critics who adopt these approaches may argue that the study of causes is beyond our reach or merely beside the point, but they agree that the real "meaning" of literature results from the interaction of audience and work. For these critics, then, the reactions of the audience form the important context for the study of literary meaning, and they may be classed together as "reader-response" critics.

In the view of another group of critics, this tendency to look either to the author or to the audience causes us to overlook the very thing that unites them — the literary work itself. In the language of the communication model, these critics urge us to pay less attention to senders and receivers and more attention to poems, for they believe that meanings are, in fact, in words, and especially in the arrangement of words. In practice, their efforts are devoted largely to demonstrating the poem's coherence by showing how its various parts are integrated to create a complex but artistically unified whole. On their assumptions, the primary context for the study of literature is the completed work itself, and the parenthetical placement of "formal criticism" on the diagram represents the attempt of these critics to isolate the work from the other contexts, especially those labeled "historical" and "reader-response." Because they want to show how the various parts interrelate to create the complete poem, these critics are particularly concerned with the "form" of literary works, and "formal criticism" is a widely used label for this context.

The horizontal axis of the diagram cuts across the communication line and locates the work with reference to two very different contexts. One of these is that large, ill-defined, yet very important context we somewhat helplessly call "life" or "truth" or, as here, "reality." None of these terms is entirely satisfactory, and the context not only resists precise definition but also offers notorious philosophical puzzles. Despite these difficulties, forms of criticism that orient the work toward "reality" or "life as experienced outside of art" are at once the most venerable and the most popular. Because they are chiefly concerned with measuring the accuracy or "truth" of the characters and actions presented in literature, these approaches are traditionally labeled "mimetic." Unfortunately, no traditional or widely accepted label exists for those kinds of criticism that direct our attention away from reality and place the work instead in the context of literature as a whole. Because these approaches stress the artifice or conventionality of all literature and argue that any work must be understood by analogy with other works that employ similar conventions, I have called such approaches "intertextual" criticism.

Additional explanations for these and other terms will be developed in the introductions to the separate chapters. But the matter of terminology deserves some further comment here. First, we must face the troublesome fact that English has no synonym for the awkward "literary work"; consequently, the word "poem" must do double duty, denoting sometimes a verse composition and sometimes any work of literature in verse or prose. In this book I follow the usual practice and occasionally use "poem" in the general sense. So *The Tempest*, for example, and "Benito Cereno" are poems as well as the "Ode on a Grecian Urn," and "poetics" is the theory of "poetry" in this extended meaning. But I use "literary work" or "literary structure" when the situation requires the more cumbersome but less ambiguous term; and often I use "literary text," because in practice most of our concern is with the printed page, although we should remember that some poems have existed for centuries in purely oral form and that recitations or dramatic performances are not quite the same as written texts.

My effort to keep terminology simple is especially apparent in the very general definition I have given of "literary criticism" as "the art of interpreting literary works." Although this fairly bristles with ambiguities, attempts at this point to narrow our terms will only expand our confusions. There is, for example, no leakproof definition of a "literary" work. The adjective fits most of what we call lyrics, dramas, and fictional narratives in verse or prose, but what else it fits is a matter of endless debate. Similarly, "criticism" is usually thought to have both theoretical and practical aspects, as the arrangement of the essays in this book assumes, but it is often difficult and usually unnecessary to trace the fine line between them or to assign them different names. So I include under "criticism" all attempts to interpret literature as well as all arguments about how this can best be accomplished, however specific or general, *ad hoc* or theoretical. In the last analysis, clarity and precision may lie down easily together, but in this introductory text, which is far from the last analysis, I have tried to keep the distinctions few and functional. After the basic issues have become clear, further refinements can be made. Provisionally, then, "literary works" will mean what we usually mean by the phrase — that is, plays, lyrics, narratives, and things that resemble them — and attempts to interpret these are forms of "literary criticism."

The diagram of critical contexts and the conceptual map it supplies are also offered provisionally, not as the only valid way to classify types of criticism, but as a way that can help us understand some of the fundamental problems of interpretation. One result of this contextual organization is that critics who are usually classed together because they share a set of beliefs may be separated in this scheme according to the context in which they operate. So a Freudian critic who investigates an author's unconscious motivations is practicing a form of historical criticism, whereas a Freudian critic studying a reader's reactions is, in this plan, a reader-response critic. And because Freudian psychoanalysis claims to interpret human behavior in general, it also provides a mimetic model by which the truth or "realism" of a literary character's behavior can be measured. Feminist criticism, which has seen explosive growth in the last three decades, will pattern in the same way. So although "feminism" is absent from the table of contents, it is by no means absent from the book; on the contrary, feminist critics will be found in nearly every context. Other schools of thought and other psychological approaches could be similarly distributed. By cutting across these kinds of classifications, this book's contextual organization pushes to the background questions about the validity of these larger theories and focuses attention instead on the interpretive problems central to all forms of literary criticism. Whatever the critic's political or philosophical position, he or she will have to decide questions of meaning within one of the contexts we will be exploring.

The neatly symmetrical diagram is designed to aid that exploration. But such a spatial metaphor can be misleading if we forget that the diagram maps only the main terminals and not the often twisty routes that traffic between them. In practice, a single critic, sometimes in a single essay, may operate in two or more of these contexts. Furthermore, the contexts themselves tend to shade into each other as we move from their central to their peripheral concerns. Nevertheless, as the diagram may serve to remind us, the central position of each context represents a particular way of looking at literary meaning. As we try out these different perspectives and come to see what each can and cannot show us, we can learn something important about the art of reading literature. This is our goal; and this simple diagram is useful if it can help us think more clearly about the fundamental issues of interpretation.

This goal has guided my organization in other ways as well. The book is divided into seven chapters, each dealing with a separate critical context. Each chapter opens with an introductory essay that explains the basic assumptions and interests of the critics represented in that section. This essay traces briefly the role the context has played in the history of criticism, and it offers an assessment of its place and strength within the contemporary scene. But the main purpose of each prefatory essay is to show how those who adopt this perspective approach the literary work, what kinds of questions they ask, and what kinds of answers they offer.

After this introduction, each chapter presents two (in the last chapter, three) "theoretical" essays by well-known critics who are themselves committed to this approach. As readers try to come to terms with these wide-ranging and often polemical discussions, they should find that their understanding of the issues is considerably aided by the four "application" essays that conclude each chapter. Because we may at least provisionally assume that the proof of a critical theory is its ability to illuminate a literary work, readers must be continually testing any theory against the literature they know. Unfortunately, in most collections of critical essays they will face an accumulation of references to a bewildering number and variety of works, many of which they may not have read well, or recently, or at all. And even readers who manage to sort through the various examples may still complain that the arguments are difficult to compare because the theories are not brought to bear on the same literary texts. The application essays are included here to enable such comparisons. So, after the theoretical essays that explain and defend aspects of the general approach, often with references to various examples, each chapter offers four essays that apply some version of this approach to the same four literary works: Shakespeare's *The Tempest,* Keats's "Ode on a Grecian Urn," Melville's "Benito Cereno," and Gilman's "The Yellow Wallpaper."

Because these works are widely studied, chances are good that many readers will already be familiar with them. Because they are few and relatively brief, they can be read and reread along with the critical essays. And because they represent different literary forms and were written in different periods, they furnish useful test cases for theories that claim to illuminate literature of all types and times. Finally, each work is extraordinarily rich and complex, and each has inspired a large body of critical commentary representing the different perspectives. So, as readers see each theory applied to works they know well, they will be able to understand more fully what that approach can accomplish. Equally to the point, as they see the different approaches applied to the *same* works, they will be able to estimate more accurately their relative strengths and possible uses.

The arrangement of the chapters is designed to facilitate these comparisons. It is also designed to show how the major theoretical debates have shifted over the last half of the twentieth century. We begin with the formalist challenge to author-centered historical criticism, move on to the reader-response critics' challenge to formalism, pause to examine mimetic theories (these cannot be easily fixed in the sequence), take up the structural and semiotic approaches of the intertextual critics, look next at the poststructuralists' simultaneous continuation and deconstruction of structuralism, and end not quite where we began with a return to historical criticism, but a poststructural historicism different in many ways from traditional literary history.

We should remember, though, that although the theoretical debates have shifted in this roughly dialectic sequence, critical practice has maintained a more stable heterogeneity. That is to say, theorists may not be arguing much at the moment about authors' intentions, but studies of authors' lives and times, which assume the importance of intentions, continue to be published in large numbers. Formal concepts may not be at the center of today's theoretical controversies, but formal analysis is at the center of much published criticism and much classroom practice. And so with the other contexts. Each may be the focus of theoretical discussion for only a limited time, but all offer approaches that many sophisticated readers find useful, and all continue to be heavily cultivated grounds for practical criticism, as the recent dates for most of the application essays in this book will confirm. In short, although my chapters present a sequence of dialogues that approximates the shifting emphases in contemporary theory, contemporary critical practice might be better characterized as a polyphony — or cacophony — with all the voices still sounding loudly. The essays on *The Tempest* included here offer a clear confirmation on this point. Most of these first appeared in the nineties, after a decade in which "new historical" and cultural materialist approaches had come to dominate criticism of the play, and they show that "old historical" and formalist approaches, for example, are very much alive and very forcefully asserting their own claims against those of the cultural critics.

I should add, too, that I have further simplified matters by staging these debates from an Anglo-American perspective. Continental influences — and these have been very strong in recent decades — are acknowledged primarily as their impact is felt in the English-speaking world. If these dialogues were replayed from a European point of view, the chronology and the emphases would be different. But the basic questions, and the fundamental issues of interpretation, would be the same. These are what we want to get at, and it seems to me that for most readers of this book, the Anglo-American perspective offers the most direct way to get at them.

I have chosen a contemporary focus for the same reason. The "applications" included here are mainly of recent vintage, for I want to stress the point that although each of these contexts has a rich history, none is merely a historical curiosity; on the contrary, each is the basis for some vital contemporary criticism. At the same time, I have sought to include clear and forceful examples of each approach, and I have occasionally selected an earlier essay that met these criteria better than more recent examples. Similar concerns have controlled my choice of the "theoretical" essays. For the most part I have reprinted fairly recent writings because these can take into account current refinements and objections and reflect more directly the contemporary debate on these perennial issues. But we should always remember that these *are* perennial issues, and I have not hesitated to include an older essay if it seemed to set forth the basic arguments more clearly and more provocatively. Without clarity, we seldom think well; without provocation, we seldom think at all.

In fact, I am convinced that the reader who is provoked enough to enter actively into these debates will gain the most from this book. Throughout this introduction I have talked about "perspectives" and "approaches," and the book itself describes and illustrates different critical "contexts." It will be easy for the reader to assume that each context must have a special but limited validity and that the best literary criticism must be an eclectic combination of all contexts. Such a conclusion has some points to recommend it. It is consistent with the complexity of literature and with the diversity of critical practice; it acknowledges the difficulty of applying "outside" objections in some useful way to internally consistent systems; and it allows the eclectic critic to adopt an inclusive and tolerant, rather than an exclusive and combative, rhetorical stance. Besides, elementary logic suggests that no one of these contexts is likely to offer all the important truths about a literary work.

But by the same logic it is also unlikely that all contexts should offer equally valid or useful insights. To put it another way, although we may agree that there is no complete, definitive, and absolutely correct interpretation of a poem, it does not necessarily follow that there are no better or worse interpretations, interpretations more or less complete, more or less accurate, more or less approximating a "best" reading. At any rate, most of the writers included here will argue that their perspective offers a better way to read, and because all readers must confront the same problems of interpretation, all readers have a real stake in these arguments. If you are to come to an informed decision about them, you will need to analyze them carefully, compare them closely, and test them against specific literary works. This book is designed to make these operations easier. As my title is meant to suggest, these are contexts *for* criticism. Because to read at all is to read from one or another of these perspectives, the informed reader should at least know which he or she has chosen, and why.

Suggestions for Further Reading

Although this book aims to get at some of the perennial issues of literary interpretation through a reading of contemporary criticism, we should remember that these issues are indeed perennial and that discussion of them has a long and rich history. Many of the earlier discussions can be found in Hazard Adams, ed., *Critical Theory Since Plato* (2nd ed., 1992), which also includes a good collection of twentieth-century essays. An even larger collection is Vincent B. Leitch, ed., *The Norton Anthology of Theory and Criticism* (2001). M. C. Beardsley, *Aesthetics from Classical Greece to the Present: A Short History* (1966) and W. K. Wimsatt and Cleanth Brooks, *Literary Criticism: A Short History* (1957), are useful one-volume surveys, neither especially "short" except by reference to the size of the subject. That size is better gauged and the ground more thoroughly covered in the first four volumes of Rene Wellek's *A History of Modern Criticism* (1955–65), which discusses Western criticism from 1750 to 1900. Cambridge University Press is completing publication of the nine-volume *Cambridge History of Literary Criticism,* each volume containing essays by several contributors. For the twentieth century, Wellek has continued his monumental history from 1900 to 1950, devoting a volume each to Britain and the United States (1986), a third to Germany, Russia, and Eastern Europe (1991), and a fourth to France, Italy, and Spain (1993). For contemporary criticism, many books will be listed in the suggestions for reading that follow each chapter. But readers should know of two book-length bibliographies of recent critical theory: Leonard Orr, *Research in Critical Theory Since 1965* (1989) and Donald M. Marshall, *Contemporary Critical Theory: A Selective Bibliography* (1993). Michael Groden and Martin Keiswirth, eds., *The Johns Hopkins Guide to Literary Theory and Criticism* (1994) is an encyclopedic reference work with extensive bibliographies.

CHAPTER ONE

Historical Criticism I: Author as Context

In ev'ry Work regard the Writer's End,
Since none can compass more than they Intend.

— Pope, *An Essay on Criticism*

Most models of written communication posit an author and an audience. From the author's point of view, the task is to communicate meaning as effectively as possible. From the audience's perspective, the task is to interpret that meaning as accurately as possible. To ask what a poem means is, in this model, to ask what the author meant when he or she created it.

The poem's real meaning, it follows, is always in the past, even if sometimes in the very near past, and the search for that meaning is a search for the author's original intention. So even when we're dealing with contemporary writers, inquiry is seldom a simple matter. Not only are writers notoriously inclined to be reticent, evasive, or even deceptive when discussing the "meaning" of their works, but they are seldom in a position to know what they may have unconsciously intended, and in any case they must always talk about what they may have meant at some point in the past—last week, last year, three decades ago. Frequently, of course, the writers we're interested in are dead, making direct inquiry even less productive. But their works remain, and because it is the task of criticism to discover as fully as possible the meaning of those works, this can best be done by understanding as fully as possible the minds that created them.

The kinds of historical criticism that aim to supply this understanding, because they focus on the author as the cause of meaning, may be conveniently labeled "genetic." As we'll see, there are other kinds of historical criticism, and other places to center meaning. Our concern here is with those historical studies that ground the meaning of the poem in the mind of the poet at the time of creation.

Even with this limited focus, the genetic critic's job is formidable. To understand the author's mind at the time of creation means, in practice, to assemble and interpret all documents that may throw light on that mind, and these documents can be numerous. A writer's letters and library will be relevant certainly, earlier and later works probably, laundry lists possibly. Then there are the recorded comments of all those who knew the author well or casually. As we approach our own time, the number of available documents pertaining to a writer may become very large, and for a contemporary author, the enterprising biographer can supplement the written record with direct interviews.

Conversely, as we move back in time, the amount of information about authors rapidly diminishes; we know little about Marlowe, less about Virgil, nothing at all about "Homer." This state of affairs is naturally lamented by genetic critics who assume if we had more information about, say, Shakespeare's schooling or Chaucer's reading or Sophocles's religious views, we would be better able to understand their writings. But the lack of specifically biographical information does not fatally handicap genetic criticism. We may have no documentary evidence about Shakespeare's school days, but we can find out a good deal about what was studied and how in the schools available to someone of his age and station. We may not know exactly what Chaucer read, but we can discover what most educated people of his time were reading. We can never know with any precision what Sophocles's religious views were, but we can learn something about the forms of worship practiced in his day, what was considered orthodox, what was not.

By this logic the inquiry widens to include a great deal more than the strictly biographical. For the genetic critic, after all, is by definition a student of causes, and if a poem is the product of an author and the author is the product of an age, then nothing less than a full understanding of that age — the author's entire political, social, and intellectual milieu — is required if we are to fully understand that author's art. And, paradoxically, the need for this kind of information seems to grow as the author is more distant from us and the biographical information more scant. This explains why, although the known facts of Shakespeare's life will barely fill a page, the books about his life can easily fill a shelf. Add to these the many books treating Elizabethan religion, politics, economics, science, and all the other elements that make up the "life" of the "time," from sweeping generalizations about "worldviews" to the minutiae of numerology and pneumatology, and you have a sizable library.

And so with every writer and his or her "age." To be sure, not all these studies are examples of genetic criticism strictly defined; some don't even pretend to be. Just as a biography, even of a literary figure, can exist as biography and make no claim to supply interpretations of poems, so a study of Elizabethan psychology or seventeenth-century religious controversy or Victorian legal reforms may be written simply to cast light on that subject, and may use literary texts as part of its evidence, without making any claim to the status of literary criticism. In practice, however, most biographies of writers and most period studies with a literary cast do make such claims, at least implicitly. When we are offered an investigation of the sources of Blake's religious thought, of the background of the Battle of the Books, of the inadequacies of Keats's philosophy or Dryden's wife, we naturally expect that the investigator will get around to telling us something interpretive about poems. Sometimes this expectation is disappointed. Critical procedures using the life to explain the work can easily get entangled with biographical procedures using the work to explain the life, and the result may be a vast tautology. More often, scholars may be content simply to amass information about the writer's life or age on the assumption that somehow it will be critically useful to someone.

But this is merely to observe that not all historical studies manage to keep an unwavering critical focus. This observation does not undercut the historical critic's basic premise that literary meaning must be grounded in the author, and this premise is widely accepted. Inquiries into writers' intimate personal lives and into their social and intellectual backgrounds continue to be the focus of much classroom discussion, continue to be published both by academic and commercial publishers, continue to form the bulk of what is generally called "literary study." This state of affairs is so familiar at the start of the twenty-first century that we may be a little startled when we reflect that the immense industry devoted to historical study is a relatively recent phenomenon. Although the historical context has been the most heavily cultivated one in the past century, in the previous 23 it was the least. Aristotle, for instance, showed a lively interest in most of the contexts I have diagrammed, but he saw no reason for criticism to be much concerned with the maker of poems, and with few exceptions critics agreed with him on this point until well into the eighteenth century. So, despite the apparently axiomatic nature of the argument for genetic criticism, and despite its prominence in bibliographies and classroom instruction, the emphasis on the author and the period, on the circumstances of the poem's composition, is distinctly modern.

This emphasis seems to have come about largely as a result of two different but mutually reinforcing influences. The first was a gradual shift in the conception of a poem from something that reflected or imitated nature to something that reflected or expressed an individual, a unique mind. This shift, which had its chronological center somewhere near the beginning of the nineteenth century, was bound to focus attention on the life of the author, a kind of attention, not coincidentally, that some writers of the period seemed to invite. The second influence, which also had its roots in the eighteenth century but which did not become dominant until the nineteenth, was the sense of the *pastness* of the past, the idea that each "age" has different assumptions and different values, and hence that the art of any period can be understood only by someone specially trained to understand those assumptions and values.

These two ideas, then, one stressing the individuality of the poet, the other the individuality of the age, combined in the nineteenth century to turn literary study toward the biographical and the historical. And when, very late in the century, the graduate study of literature came into being, first in Germany and then in the United States and England, that study developed as a variation of the "scientific historicism" that dominated most academic disciplines at the time. Here the poetic value of a work might be assumed, could even occasionally be discussed in a warm "appreciation," but such discussions were "after hours," so to speak, and hopelessly "impressionistic." Real scholarship was concerned with the facts — that is to say, with the historical facts. And again this emphasis meant that at the inception of modern literary study on the academic level, the chief concern was with the circumstances of the poem's composition.

Thus, in the early decades of the twentieth century, various forms of historical criticism — the approach to the poem through the study of the life and times of its author — reigned virtually unchallenged in the universities. This historical criticism dealt in facts and required "research," like any solid academic discipline. It investigated the causes of things — something else that marked it as a legitimate field of study. And if, though few as yet raised the objection, the approach had no way to distinguish a poem from any other verbal construct, this inability was not necessarily a defect; any document could tell us something about the author or the age that produced it, and that knowledge in turn could be reflected back to illuminate any document. For the study of "literature," sometimes defined as anything written, was in its grandest conception nothing less than the study of cultural history. But even when more narrowly conceived as an inquiry whose end was the understanding of poems, the genetic approach had academic respectability: it was concerned with objective data; it employed "scholarship," and—not least important—it provided an easily understood and widely accepted scheme for organizing literary study.

Given the assumptions of genetic criticism, the proper context for such study was clearly the causal context. *Paradise Lost* may be an epic, *Lycidas* a pastoral elegy, and *Samson Agonistes* a drama, but to the genetic critic the fact of overriding importance is that they are all poems by John Milton. So the author, the most obvious cause of poems, becomes the first organizing focus of literary study. As one result, we have hundreds of books describing the lives and works of major and not-so-major writers, and few English curricula are considered complete if they lack separate courses devoted to, at the very least, Chaucer, Shakespeare, and Milton. But the writer, according to these same assumptions, is the product of an age, and that assumption suggests another causal principle: we should study the "Renaissance" writers together, and the "Victorians," the "Romantics," the "Augustans," and so on. The different sources implicit in these labels and the notoriously shifty boundaries between such "ages" may suggest that the problems of periodicity have never been fully resolved. But these difficulties are minor. The logic of historical criticism demands some period arrangement, just as the concern with causes further suggests that, as far as practical, we should study the writers within each period and the periods themselves in chronological order. Causes, after all, work through time and only in one direction.

In fact, despite the powerful and in some ways successful challenges to the dominance of historical criticism, the genetic categories of author, period, nation, and chronological sequence, which are the categories employed by Hippolyte Taine in the nineteenth century, remain nearly the only categories used to organize literary study in American universities. This conservatism shows partly the strength of the genetic position and partly that the other contexts have been unable to supply any alternative schemes. As a consequence, the organization of literary study often shows a historical basis even when some other forms of criticism are being practiced.

But genetic criticism continues to be much more than a framework for other kinds of studies. Many scholars accept all or part of the causal argument, teach comfortably within the period organization, and publish books and essays about the historical backgrounds of poems and authors. Biographical studies flourish, some employing the analytical tools of Freud and his followers and rivals to get at the author's unconscious meanings, others content to concentrate on more conscious and more fully documented intentions. And studies of the writer's "age," of the various aspects of the cultural milieu, continue to be published in large numbers.

Nevertheless, in contrast to the earlier decades of the twentieth century, genetic approaches no longer monopolize literary study. Other contexts are also heavily cultivated, and the story of their challenge to historical criticism is the opening chapter in the theoretical debates of the last half-century. It will be enough to sketch a few of the challengers' arguments to provide a context for the essays that follow.

Many of these arguments focus on the central but problematic concept of "cause," a concept especially problematic when causal explanations are offered for "effects" as complicated as poems. On the one hand, it seems reasonable to assume that the crucial experiences in a writer's life must leave some mark on his or her character and thought. On the other hand, it is often difficult to use specific pieces of biographical information to explain the meaning of a literary work. Information about the writer's period is similarly problematic. Even if we could discover what many or most Elizabethans believed about ghosts, and even if it turned out that they believed much the same things, we still wouldn't necessarily know what Shakespeare thought about the subject or what he might have meant in *Hamlet*, unless, that is, we were willing to assume that Shakespeare was a typical Elizabethan or that he expressed only typical beliefs in his plays. Such assumptions do seem to underlie many investigations of the writer's political, social, or intellectual milieu, but the assumptions are seldom clearly stated, and when they are, they look somewhat questionable. If the "age" does in fact make the writer, then we must admit that it sometimes makes him or her very different from their contemporaries. Furthermore, close examination generally shows that a historical "period" is fully as complex, unpredictable, and contradictory as the individuals it comprises. As it happens, different Elizabethans believed wildly different things about ghosts.

So here again we face a dilemma. On the one side, we have the plausible assumption that authors will be affected by the intellectual currents and social conditions that surround them. As we have noted, most literary study is organized on this assumption. On the other side, we have the argument that it is seldom easy in practice to make firm connections between (1) a knowledge of these currents and conditions and (2) the attitudes held by particular authors or—and this is not always the same thing—the attitudes expressed in particular poems.

By such arguments the objectors have sought to show that causal links between the period, the poet, and the poem are much more elusive, much more difficult to establish, than many genetic critics were willing to admit, and that to demonstrate them would require much more rigor and finesse than many historical studies were wont to show, if indeed they could be demonstrated at all. Most genetic critics today would probably admit that their task is more problematic than it had once appeared, that it demands not only wide knowledge but interpretive delicacy and tact. Naturally they would not agree that their difficulties are inherently insoluble or that the causal links can never be plausibly demonstrated.

A more radical challenge to historical criticism does not trouble to deny the possibility of the genetic task but denies instead its relevance. The entire genetic model, so this argument runs, is misleading. Poems are not like other documents. They are special verbal constructs that use language in a special way, and they do not relate to their authors the way other documents do. Formal critics have pursued this line of argument most vigorously, an argument based on a particular conception of a poem. For the formalist, such features as the tensive balance between different parts, the unity controlling a diversity of elements, and the resulting ambiguity, paradox, and irony are the defining features of poems, and it is with these that criticism must deal. Because a study of the circumstances of the poem's composition, no matter how carefully conducted, can never tell us much about these features, it can never lead to *critical* interpretation. The historians' tendency to treat the poem like any other kind of document, their failure to conceive of poetry as a special use of language, deflects attention to nonessential, "unpoetic" factors, and when historians do provide interpretations, they are likely to be reductive. That is, even if we could discover precisely what the poem meant to its author or its original audience, we still would not have discovered the full range of the "legitimate" meanings of the poem. In short, the "real" poem, in this argument, is not the poem in the author's mind at the moment of creation, so there is little point in searching for that mind or that moment.

We will leave to another section the discussion of the ways a poem may be thought to exist independently of its author or period. Here we simply note that such a conception undermines the foundation of all forms of genetic criticism. At the same time, by urging a definition of a poem that is also a description of a "good" poem, the formalist reminds us that it is difficult to develop a convincing theory of poetic value on strictly historical lines. Although values of a kind are apparently implied in many historical studies — this work is worth our attention because it is so thoroughly Jamesian, so typical of the Restoration, so representative of the Victorian concern with evolution — most often such reasons are advanced, if they are directly advanced at all, to justify the study of minor or second-rate works. And obviously a poem might just as easily be valued for the opposite reasons, for its lack of typicality. More to the point, the typicality of acknowledged masterpieces is seldom discussed, and we would think it odd if someone were to try to persuade us that *Oedipus Tyrannus* or *King Lear* was valuable simply because it was, or was not, a "representative" Greek or Elizabethan play.

Closely related to estimates of typicality but more promising as a basis for value is the argument of the historical relativist that our judgment of poems should be guided by period standards. Poets aim to excel under the terms and conditions of their times, and it is unfair to try their works by a different court. To judge accurately a medieval fabliau or an eighteenth-century satire, a Romantic ode or a Victorian novel, we have to condition ourselves to think and feel as their intended audiences did. This position seems defensible, and it has the further advantage of appealing to our sympathetic imagination. In practice, though, the advice may not hold in the crucial cases. We are inclined to say that the "Miller's Tale" or *Gulliver's Travels,* "Ode on a Grecian Urn" or *Middlemarch* are simply great works, and we probably feel little need to add that they were great by the standards of their own periods. Then, too, it is easy to find examples of works we value highly, such as Melville's novels or Blake's poems, which were largely unappreciated by their first audiences. And, from the other side, a check of publishing records from the eighteenth century to this week's bestseller list indicates that popular taste has rather consistently run toward what most serious students of literature would call the ephemeral. Historical relativists may object that they are really urging us to think like a discriminating Elizabethan playgoer, a perceptive Victorian reader. But this objection seems to beg the question.

The basic communication model suggests yet another value scheme. Every utterance is an attempt to express something — an idea, a feeling, a set of facts — and is successful to the extent that it effectively communicates what it set out to communicate. A poem, then, would be good if it achieved what its author intended. Surely it is pointless to complain about the presence of a chorus in a play by Aeschylus or about the absence of one in a play by Ibsen, to object that Donne's meter lacks the regularity of Pope's or that *Ulysses* is not structured like *Tom Jones.* It is foolish to condemn a work for lacking features the author never intended to supply. But in these and similar instances the argument is not really genetic. The evidence for "intention" is simply our understanding of the work itself. The procedure becomes genetic only when the evidence for what was intended, consciously or otherwise, is sought elsewhere, in letters, diaries, recorded conversations, in assumptions about what the "age" demanded or understood — in other words, only when "intention" is conceivably different from the achieved poem and independently knowable.

In such cases, we could compare what the author did with what he or she intended to do. But even this comparison might not give us a firm basis for judging poetic excellence. For example, if coherence is a value and a poem is judged to be incoherent, it is a weak defense of the poem to claim that it was meant to be incoherent. For similar reasons, apparent value terms such as "sincerity" or "authenticity," insofar as they refer to an alignment of achievement and intention, are of little help. A mawkish sonnet remains mawkish even if it perfectly expresses the sentiment of its creator, and a puerile satire is none the less puerile for accurately reflecting its author's mind. Indeed, the more the subject is examined, the clearer it becomes that the study of intention provides little basis for evaluating poems. If the ghost of Chaucer were to appear to us and swear that he saw nothing funny or ironic in the "Nun's Priest's Tale," we would have to revise our estimate, not of the poem, but of the critical sensibility of Chaucer's ghost.

But the fact that historical criticism continues to thrive shows that large numbers of critics do not find these objections overwhelming. For them, the failure to provide a historical ground for evaluating poems is probably the least troublesome charge. Not all critics are convinced that judging poems is a major part of the business of criticism and, in any event, it seems axiomatic that the full understanding of a poem must precede any sound evaluation of it. To the extent historical critics can claim to provide at least part of that understanding, they can concede their lack of value theory with a shrug. As to the inherent difficulty of their task, here again the historians can grant the point. We need, they argue, more and better information, more refined methodology, and more careful application. If psychoanalytical criticism of authors has often been clumsy, the remedy is not to abandon psychoanalysis but to apply it with more care and tact. If generalizations about, say, the "neoclassical" concern with restraint and reason are too simplistic or inaccurate to throw much light on writers such as Swift or Gay, the cure is not to abandon studies of the period but to pursue them with more intensity and rigor.

More radical objections that historical studies, no matter how carefully conducted, are doomed to fail in the nature of the case, are more difficult to address. To answer them directly, critics must step outside their own frame of reference far enough to examine and defend their most basic assumptions. If such defenders were rare when genetic studies were—and perhaps because they were—the only firmly established kinds of literary study, they are more plentiful now that strong rivals have entered the field. On the one side, these defenders stand opposed to the ahistorical view that we *should* read each poem as if it were essentially anonymous and contemporary, a verbal object to be understood by the public norms of language and judged by universal standards. On the other side, paradoxically, they confront the radically historical view that we *must* read each poem as if it were contemporary with us, for no matter how we try to transport ourselves to other places and periods, we inevitably carry our cultural perspective with us and remain twentieth-century readers. The radical historicist, in other words, applies the idea of historical relativism with a vengeance, and in such a way as to undercut the historicist's program. For if we can never lay aside our cultural blinders, then we are forced to read as the ahistorical critics say we should.

Against this odd alliance of forces, genetic theorists continue to maintain that we can, with much care and labor, reach an understanding of other periods that will allow us at least to approximate the perspective of the poem's original and intended audience. On this point they find the radical position simply too sweeping to be logically supportable. And furthermore, they argue, we *should* labor to gain such understanding. For these critics, the communication model remains the fundamental model, and it follows that to speak of meaning in any determinate sense is to speak of an author's meaning. Other contexts, they grant, can tell us what a work *may* mean, but only their own can tell us what it *does* mean. Without the knowledge of an author's character and culture that historical studies supply, there can be no useful check on the often "impressionistic," "anachronistic," "overly ingenious," and otherwise "irresponsible" interpretations that critics operating in other contexts are apt to produce. In short, only the historical context, they claim, can offer a stable meaning for "meaning."

Suggestions for Further Reading

Because this context includes many and diverse approaches, about all one can do is cite representative examples of some of the different kinds of "genetic" criticism. At the center is the very popular "critical biography." The form is discussed in Leon Edel, *Literary Biography* (1957), and it may be sampled in such exemplary works as Edel on Henry James (1953–1972), Edgar Johnson on Charles Dickens (1952), and Richard Ellmann on James Joyce (rev. ed., 1982). See also Ellmann's *Golden Codgers: Biographical Speculations* (1973). Sigmund Freud, *On Creativity and the Unconscious* (1958), shows some of the master's ideas; Frederick Crews, *The Sins of the Fathers: Hawthorne's Psychological Themes* (1966), shows one critic's use of Freud's concepts. If the author's life is the center of genetic studies, the elastic boundaries of his or her "times" or "milieu" form the circumference. The once-popular *Zeitgeist* or "spirit of the age" study is illustrated in E. M. W. Tillyard's *The Elizabethan World Picture* (1943); Eleanor Prosser, *Hamlet and Revenge* (2nd ed., 1971), shows how a scholar's wide reading in one aspect of a period can be focused to challenge our usual interpretations of a literary work. A classic example of source tracing is John L. Lowes, *The Road to Xanadu* (1927); an equally classic instance of the "history of ideas" approach is A. O. Lovejoy, *The Great Chain of Being* (1936). Both of these methods overlap a good deal with intertextual criticism, though they are based on quite different assumptions about the locus of literary meaning. Two attempts to formulate the internal dynamics of literary history are W. J. Bate, *The Burden of the Past and the English Poet* (1970), and Harold Bloom, *The Anxiety of Influence* (1973). E. D. Hirsch, *Validity in Interpretation* (1967), advances arguments for regarding the author as the ultimate source of meaning. Some of these arguments are further developed in P. D. Juhl, *Interpretation: An Essay in the Philosophy of Literary Criticism* (1980). Essays on both sides of this issue have been gathered in D. Newton-DeMolina, ed., *On Literary Intention* (1976). Robert D. Hume, *Reconstructing Contexts: The Aims and Principles of Archaeo-Historicism* (1999) argues the case for traditional literary history in the face of poststructural skepticism about our ability to reconstruct the author's perspective.

THEORY

Objective Interpretation

E. D. Hirsch, Jr.

*The central purpose of E. D. Hirsch's "Objective Inter-
pretation" is to make the search for the author's meaning once again the main business of literary study and
to provide for that study a closely argued rationale that
will allow it to stand as "a corporate enterprise and a
progressive discipline." In making his case, Hirsch directly disputes the contention of formal and intertextual
critics that the "public norms of language" are sufficient
to establish the meaning of a text without reference to
the author's probable intentions. Examining the Cleanth
Brooks–F. W. Bateson controversy over the meaning of
a Wordsworth poem, Hirsch seeks to show that such
"public norms" can support different, and even totally
opposed, interpretations. While he grants the relevance of
most formalist criteria for meaning, including the central
criterion of "coherence," Hirsch argues that "coherence"
is not an absolute quality. It depends on the context the
interpreter has invoked, and for an interpretation to be
valid "it is necessary to establish that the context invoked is the most probable context" [author's empha-
sis]. To establish this, we need to know all we can about
the intender of the meaning. Thus, although Hirsch
explicitly distinguishes between the "speaking subject"
and the biographical person, he sets forth a clear rationale
for intentionalist criticism. Unless we assume an author
whose probable meaning we can recover, he claims,
"meaning" itself can have no stable sense, "interpretation" cannot be objective, and literary commentary is in
danger of becoming a subjective and relativistic babble.*

*It is worth noting that although the direct targets
of Hirsch's arguments are formal critics like Cleanth
Brooks, the formalists agreed with Hirsch that literary
meaning is determinate; they simply disagreed about the
context in which it should be determined. In some ways,*

Reprinted by permission of the Modern Language Association of America from *PMLA* 75 (1960): 463, 470–79.
Copyright © 1960 by the Modern Language Association of
America. A part of the essay has been omitted, and the
notes have been renumbered.

then, Hirsch's essay may be read as opposing even more directly reader-response critics, poststructural critics, and cultural critics, many of whom are inclined to stress the indeterminacy of meaning and the irrelevance of authorial intention. Yet these approaches had scarcely been developed when Hirsch wrote his essay. Clearly, literary theory in the last forty years has taken not the direction Hirsch wished but the direction he feared.

The fact that the term "criticism" has now come to designate all commentary on textual meaning reflects a general acceptance of the doctrine that description and evaluation are inseparable in literary study. In any serious confrontation of literature it would be futile, of course, to attempt a rigorous banishment of all evaluative judgment, but this fact does not give us the license to misunderstand or misinterpret our texts. It does not entitle us to use the text as the basis for an exercise in "creativity" or to submit as serious textual commentary a disguised argument for a particular ethical, cultural, or aesthetic viewpoint. Nor is criticism's chief concern—the present relevance of a text—a strictly necessary aspect of textual commentary. That same kind of theory which argues the inseparability of description and evaluation also argues that a text's meaning is simply its meaning "to us, today." Both kinds of argument support the idea that interpretation is criticism and vice versa. But there is clearly a sense in which we can neither evaluate a text nor determine what it means "to us, today" until we have correctly apprehended what it means. Understanding (and therefore interpretation, in the strict sense of the word) is both logically and psychologically prior to what is generally called criticism. It is true that this distinction between understanding and evaluation cannot always show itself in the finished work of criticism—nor, perhaps, should it—but a general grasp and acceptance of the distinction might help correct some of the most serious faults of current criticism (its subjectivism and relativism) and might even make it plausible to think of literary study as a corporate enterprise and a progressive discipline.

No one would deny, of course, that the more important issue is not the status of literary study as a discipline but the vitality of literature—especially of older literature—in the world at large. The critic is right to think that the text should speak to *us*. The point which needs to be grasped clearly by the critic is that a text cannot be made to speak to us until what it says has been understood. This is not an argument in favor of historicism as against criticism— it is simply a brute ontological fact. Textual meaning is not a naked given like a physical object. The text is first of all a conventional representation like a musical score, and what the score represents may be construed correctly or incorrectly. The literary text (in spite of semi-mystical claims made for its uniqueness) does not have a special ontological status which somehow absolves the reader from the demands universally imposed by all linguistic texts of every description. Nothing, that is, can give a conventional representation the status of an immediate given. The text of a poem, for example, has to be construed by the critic before it becomes a poem for him. Then it is, no doubt, an artifact with special characteristics. But before the critic construes the poem it is for him no artifact at all, and if he construes it wrongly, he will subsequently be talking about the wrong artifact, not the one represented by the text. If criticism is to be objective in any significant sense, it must be founded on a self-critical construction of textual meaning, which is to say, on objective interpretation.

•　　•　　•

[In the section of the essay omitted here, Hirsch draws a distinction between the "meaning" of a text, "in and for itself," and the "significance" that can be given to that meaning when it is related to something else, such as contemporary issues, our present concerns, and so forth. "Meaning," which is relatively stable and unchanging through time, is the object of "interpretation"; "significance," which may change from reader to reader and from period to period, is the object of "criticism." Interpretation of textual meaning, then, is the logically prior task and the foundation for all criticism. But to what extent is "textual meaning" the same thing as "authorial meaning"? On this crucial question, Hirsch parts company with the New Critics. —ED.]

Determinateness of Textual Meaning

In the previous section I defined textual meaning as the "verbal intention" of the author, and this argues implicitly that hermeneutics must stress a reconstruction of the author's aims and attitudes in order to evolve guides and norms for construing the meaning of his text. It is frequently argued, however, that the textual meaning has nothing to do with the author's mind, but only with his verbal achievement, that the object of interpretation is not the author but his text. This plausible argument assumes, of course, that the text automatically has a meaning simply because it represents an unalterable sequence of words. It assumes that the meaning of a word sequence is directly imposed by the public norms of language, that the text as a "piece of language" is a public object whose character is defined by public norms.[1] This view is in one respect sound, since textual meaning must conform to public norms if it is in any sense to be verbal (i.e., sharable) meaning; on no account may the interpreter permit his probing into the author's mind to raise private associations (experience) to the level of public implications (content).

However, this basically sound argument remains one-sided. For even though verbal meaning must conform to public linguistic norms (these are highly tolerant, of course), no mere sequence of words can represent an actual verbal meaning with reference to public norms alone. Referred to these alone, the text's meaning remains indeterminate. This is true even of the simplest declarative sentence like "My car ran out of gas" (did my Pullman dash from a cloud of Argon?). The fact that no one would radically misinterpret such a sentence simply indicates that its frequency is high enough to give its usual meaning the apparent status of an immediate given. But this apparent immediacy obscures a complex process of adjudications among meaning-possibilities. Under the public norms of language alone no such adjudications can occur, since the array of possibilities presents a face of blank indifference. The array of possibilities only begins to become a more selective system of *probabilities* when, instead of confronting merely a word sequence, we also posit a speaker who very likely means something. Then and only then does the most usual sense of the word sequence become the most probable or "obvious" sense. The point holds true a fortiori, of course, when we confront less obvious word sequences like those found in poetry. A careful exposition of this point may be found in the first volume of Cassirer's *Philosophy of Symbolic Forms,* which is largely devoted to a demonstration that verbal meaning arises from the "reciprocal determination" of public linguistic possibilities and subjective specifications of those possibilities.[2] Just as language constitutes and colors subjectivity,

so does subjectivity color language. The author's or speaker's subjective act is *formally* necessary to verbal meaning, and any theory which tries to dispense with the author as specifier of meaning by asserting that textual meaning is purely objectively determined finds itself chasing will-o'-the-wisps. The burden of this section is, then, an attack on the view that a text is a "piece of language" and a defense of the notion that a text represents the determinate verbal meaning of the author.

One of the consequences arising from the view that a text is a piece of language — a purely public object — is the impossibility of defining in principle the nature of a correct interpretation. This is the same impasse which results from the theory that a text leads a life of its own, and indeed, the two notions are corollaries since any "piece of language" must have a changing meaning when the changing public norms of language are viewed as the only ones which determine the sense of the text. It is therefore not surprising to find that Wellek subscribes implicitly to the text-as-language theory. The text is viewed as representing not a determinate meaning, but rather a system of meaning-potentials specified not by a meaner but by the vital potency of language itself. Wellek acutely perceives the danger of the view: "Thus the system of norms is growing and changing and will remain, in some sense, always incompletely and imperfectly realized. But this dynamic conception does not mean mere subjectivism and relativism. All the different points of view are by no means equally right. It will always be possible to determine which point of view grasps the subject most thoroughly and deeply. A hierarchy of viewpoints, a criticism of the grasp of norms, is implied in the concept of the adequacy of interpretation."[3] The danger of the view is, of course, precisely that it opens the door to subjectivism and relativism, since linguistic norms may be invoked to support any verbally possible meaning. Furthermore, it is not clear how one may criticize a grasp of norms which will not stand still.

Wellek's brief comment on the problem involved in defining and testing correctness in interpretation is representative of a widespread conviction among literary critics that the most correct interpretation is the most "inclusive" one. Indeed, the view is so widely accepted that Wellek did not need to defend his version of it (which he calls "Perspectivism") at length. The notion behind the theory is reflected by such phrases as "always incompletely and imperfectly realized" and "grasps the subject most thoroughly." This notion is simply that no single interpretation can exhaust the rich system of meaning-potentialities represented by the text. *Ergo* every plausible reading which remains within public linguistic norms is a correct reading so far as it goes, but each reading is inevitably partial since it cannot realize all the potentialities of the text. The guiding principle in criticism, therefore, is that of the inclusive interpretation. The most "adequate" construction is the one which gives the fullest coherent account of all the text's potential meanings.[4]

Inclusivism is desirable as a position which induces a readiness to consider the results of others, but, aside from promoting an estimable tolerance, it has little theoretical value. For although its aim is to reconcile different plausible readings in an ideal, comprehensive interpretation, it cannot, in fact, either reconcile different readings or choose between them. As a normative ideal, or principle of correctness, it is useless. This point may be illustrated by citing two expert readings of a well-known poem by Wordsworth. I shall first quote the poem and then quote excerpts from two published exegeses in order to demonstrate the kind of impasse which inclusivism always provokes when it attempts to reconcile interpretations, and, incidentally, to demonstrate the very kind of interpretive problem which calls for a guiding principle:

> A slumber did my spirit seal;
>   I had no human fears:
> She seemed a thing that could not feel
>   The touch of earthly years.
>
> No motion has she now, no force;
>   She neither hears nor sees;
> Rolled round in earth's diurnal course,
>   With rocks, and stones, and trees.

Here are excerpts from two commentaries on the final lines of the poem; the first is by Cleanth Brooks, the second by F. W. Bateson:

1. [The poet] attempts to suggest something of the lover's agonized shock at the loved one's present lack of motion—of his response to her utter and horrible inertness. . . . Part of the effect, of course, resides in the fact that a dead lifelessness is suggested more sharply by an object's being whirled about by something else than by an image of the object in repose. But there are other matters which are at work here: the sense of the girl's falling back into the clutter of things, companioned by things chained like a tree to one particular spot, or by things completely inanimate like rocks and stones. . . . [She] is caught up helplessly into the empty whirl of the earth which measures and makes time. She is touched by and held by earthly time in its most powerful and horrible image.

2. The final impression the poem leaves is not of two contrasting moods, but of a single mood mounting to a climax in the pantheistic magnificence of the last two lines. . . . The vague living-Lucy of this poem is opposed to the grander dead-Lucy who has become involved in the sublime processes of nature. We put the poem down satisfied, because its last two lines succeed in effecting a reconciliation between the two philosophies or social attitudes. Lucy is actually more alive now that she is dead, because she is now a part of the life of Nature, and not just a human "thing."[5]

Now, if we grant, as I think we must, that both the cited interpretations are permitted by the text, the problem for the inclusivist is to reconcile the two readings.

Three modes of reconciliation are available to the inclusivist: (1) Brooks's reading includes Bateson's; it shows that any affirmative suggestions in the poem are negated by the bitterly ironical portrayal of the inert girl being whirled around by what Bateson calls the "sublime processes of Nature." (2) Bateson's reading includes Brooks's; the ironic contrast between the active, seemingly immortal girl and the passive, inert and dead girl is overcome by a final unqualified affirmation of immortality. (3) Each of the readings is partially right, but they must be fused to supplement one another. The very fact that the critics differ suggests that the meaning is essentially ambiguous. The emotion expressed is ambivalent, and comprises both bitter regret and affirmation. The third mode of reconciliation is the one most often employed, and is probably, in this case, the most satisfactory. A fourth type of resolution, which would insist that Brooks is right and Bateson wrong (or vice versa) is not available to the inclusivist, since the text, as language, renders both readings plausible.

Close examination, however, reveals that none of the three modes of argument manages to reconcile or fuse the two different readings. Mode (1), for example, insists that Brooks's reading comprehends Bateson's, but although it is conceivable that Brooks implies all the meanings which Bateson has perceived, Brooks also implies a *pattern of emphasis* which cannot be reconciled with Bateson's reading. While Bateson construes a primary emphasis on life and affirmation, Brooks emphasizes deadness and inertness. No amount of manipulation can reconcile these divergent emphases, since one pattern of emphasis irrevocably excludes other patterns, and, since emphasis is always crucial to meaning, the two constructions of meanings rigorously exclude one another. Precisely the same strictures hold, of course, for the argument that Bateson's reading comprehends that of Brooks. Nor can mode (3) escape with impunity. Although it seems to preserve a stress both on negation and on affirmation, thereby coalescing the two readings, it actually excludes both readings, and labels them not simply partial, but wrong. For if the poem gives equal stress to bitter irony and to affirmation, then any construction which places a primary stress on either meaning is simply incorrect.

The general principle implied by my analysis is very simple. The sub-meanings of a text are not blocks which can be brought together additively. Since verbal (and any other) meaning is a *structure* of component meanings, interpretation has not done its job when it simply enumerates what the component meanings are. The interpreter must also determine their probable structure, and particularly their structure of emphases. Relative emphasis is not only crucial to meaning (perhaps it is the most crucial and problematical element of all), it is also highly restrictive; it excludes alternatives. It may be asserted as a general rule that whenever a reader confronts two interpretations which impose different emphases on similar meaning components, at least one of the interpretations must be wrong. They cannot be reconciled.

By insisting that verbal meaning always exhibits a determinate structure of emphases, I do not, however, imply that a poem or any other text must be unambiguous. It is perfectly possible, for example, that Wordsworth's poem ambiguously implies both bitter irony and positive affirmation. Such complex emotions are commonly expressed in poetry, but if that is the kind of meaning the text represents Brooks and Bateson would be wrong to emphasize one emotion at the expense of the other. Ambiguity or, for that matter, vagueness is not the same as indeterminateness. This is the crux of the issue. To say that verbal meaning is determinate is not to exclude complexities of meaning but only to insist that a text's meaning is what it is and not a hundred other things. Taken in this sense, a vague or ambiguous text is just

as determinate as a logical proposition; it means what it means and nothing else. This is true even if one argues that a text could display shifting emphases like those Sunday supplement magic squares which first seem to jut out and then to jut in. With texts of this character (if any exist), one need only say that the emphases shift, and must not, therefore, be construed statically. Any static construction would simply be wrong. The fundamental flaw in the "theory of the most inclusive interpretation" is that it overlooks the problem of emphasis. Since different patterns of emphasis *exclude* one another, inclusivism is neither a genuine norm nor an adequate guiding principle for establishing an interpretation.

But aside from the fact that inclusivism cannot do its appointed job, there are more fundamental reasons for rejecting it and all other interpretive ideals based on the conception that a text represents a system of meaning-possibilities. No one would deny that for the interpreter the text is at first the source of numerous possible interpretations. The very nature of language is such that a particular sequence of words can represent several different meanings (that is why public norms alone are insufficient in textual interpretation). But to say that a text *might* represent several structures of meaning does not imply that it does in fact represent all the meanings which a particular word sequence can legally convey. Is there not an obvious distinction between what a text might mean and what it does mean? According to accepted linguistic theory, it is far more accurate to say that a written composition is not a mere locus of verbal possibilities, but, rather, a record (made possible by the invention of writing) of a verbal actuality. The interpreter's job is to reconstruct a determinate actual meaning, not a mere system of possibilities. Indeed, if the text *represented* a system of possibilities, interpretation would be impossible, since no actual reading could correspond to a mere system of possibilities. Furthermore, if the text is conceived to represent all the *actual* structures of meaning permissible within the public norms of language, then no single construction (with its exclusivist pattern of emphases) could be correct, and any legitimate construction would be just as incorrect as any other. When a text is conceived as a piece of language, a familiar and all too common anarchy follows. But, aside from its unfortunate consequences, the theory contradicts a widely accepted principle in linguistics. I refer to Saussure's distinction between *langue* and *parole*.

Saussure defined *langue* as the system of linguistic possibilities shared by a speech community at a given point in time.[6] This system of possibilities contains two distinguishable levels. The first consists of habits, engrams, prohibitions, and the like derived from past linguistic usage; these are the "virtualities" of the *langue*. Based on these virtualities, there are, in addition, sharable meaning-possibilities which have never before been actualized; these are the "potentialities." The two types of meaning-possibilities taken together constitute the *langue* which the speech community draws upon. But this system of possibilities must be distinguished from the actual verbal utterances of individuals who draw upon it. These actual utterances are called *paroles*; but they are *uses* of language, and actualize some (but never all) of the meaning-possibilities constituting the *langue*.

Saussure's distinction pinpoints the issue: does a text represent a segment of *langue* (as modern theorists hold) or a *parole*? A simple test suffices to provide the answer. If the text is composed of sentences it represents *parole*, which is to say the determinate verbal meaning of a member of the speech community. *Langue* contains words and sentence-forming principles, but it contains no sentences. It may be presented in writing only by isolated words in disconnection (*Wörter* as opposed to *Worte*). A *parole*, on the other hand, is always composed of sentences, an assertion corroborated by the firmly established principle that the sentence is the fundamental unit of speech.[7] Of course, there are numerous elliptical and one-word sentences, but wherever it can be correctly inferred that a text represents sentences and not simply isolated words, it may also be inferred that the text represents *parole*, which is to say, actual, determinate verbal meaning.

The point is nicely illustrated in a dictionary definition. The letters in boldface at the head of the definition represent the word as *langue*, with all its rich meaning-possibilities. But under one of the subheadings, in an illustrative sentence, those same letters represent the words as *parole*, as a particular, selective actualization from *langue*. In yet another illustrative sentence, under another sub-heading, the very same word represents a different selective actualization. Of course, many sentences, especially those found in poetry, actualize far more possibilities than illustrative sentences in a dictionary. Any pun, for example, realizes simultaneously at least two divergent meaning-possibilities. But the pun is nevertheless an actualization from *langue* and not a mere system of meaning-possibilities.

The *langue–parole* distinction, besides affirming the determinateness of textual meaning, also clarifies the special problems posed by revised and interpolated text. With a revised text, composed over a long period of time (*Faust*, for example), how are we to construe the *unrevised* portions? Should we assume that they still mean what they meant originally or that they took on a new meaning when the rest of the text was altered or expanded? With compiled or interpolated texts, like many books of the Bible, should we assume that sentences from varied provenances retain their original meanings, or that these heterogeneous elements have become integral components of a new total meaning? In terms of Saussure's distinction, the question becomes: should we consider the text to represent a compilation of diverse *paroles* or a new unitary *parole* "respoken" by the new author or editor? I submit that there can be no definite answer to the question, except in relation to a specific scholarly or aesthetic purpose, for in reality the question is not, "How are we to interpret the text?" but, "*Which* text are we to interpret?" Is it to be the heterogeneous compilation of past *paroles*, each to be separately considered, or the new, homogeneous *parole*? Both may be presented by the written score. The only problem is to choose, and having chosen, rigorously to refrain from confusing or in any way identifying the two quite different and separate "texts" with one another. Without solving any concrete problems, then, Saussure's distinction nevertheless confirms the critic's right in most cases to regard his text as representing a single *parole*.

Another problem which Saussure's distinction clarifies is that posed by the bungled text, where the author aimed to convey a meaning which his words do not convey to others in the speech community. One sometimes confronts the problem in a freshman essay. In such a case, the question is, does the text mean what the author wanted it to mean or does it mean what the speech community at large takes it to mean? Much attention has been devoted to this problem ever since the publication in 1946 of Wimsatt's and Beardsley's essay on "The Intentional Fallacy."[8] In that essay the position was taken (albeit modified by certain qualifications) that the text, being public, means what the speech community takes it to mean. This position is, in an ethical sense, right (and language, being social, has a strong ethical aspect): if the author has bungled so badly that his utterance will be misconstrued, then it serves him right when folk misunderstand him. However, put in linguistic terms, the position becomes unsatisfactory. It implies that the meaning represented by the text is not the *parole* of an author, but rather the *parole* of "the speech community." But since only individuals utter *paroles,* a *parole* of the speech community is a non-existent, or what the Germans call an *Unding.* A text can represent only the *parole* of a speaker or author, which is another way of saying that meaning requires a meaner.

However, it is not necessary that an author's text represent the *parole* he desired to convey. It is frequently the case, when an author has bungled, that his text represents no *parole* at all. Indeed there are but two alternatives: either the text represents the author's verbal meaning or it represents no *determinate* verbal meaning at all. Sometimes, of course, it is impossible to detect that the author has bungled, and in that case, even though his text does not represent verbal meaning, we shall go on misconstruing the text as though it did, and no one will be the wiser. But with most bungles we are aware of a disjunction between the author's words and his probable meaning. Eliot, for example, chided Poe for saying "My most immemorial year," when Poe "meant" his most *memorable* year.[9] Now we all agree that Poe did not mean what speakers of English generally meant by the word "immemorial"—and so the word cannot have the usual meaning. (An author cannot mean what he does not mean.) The only question, then, is: does the word mean more or less what we convey by "never-to-be-forgotten" or does it mean nothing at all? Has Poe so violated linguistic norms that we must deny his utterance verbal meaning or "content"?

The question probably cannot be answered by fiat. But since Poe's meaning is generally understood, and since the single criteria for verbal meaning is communicability, I am inclined to describe Poe's meaning as verbal.[10] I tend to side with the Poes and Malaprops of the world, for the norms of language remain far more tolerant than dictionaries and critics like Eliot suggest. On the other hand, every member of the speech community, and especially the critic, has a duty to avoid and condemn sloppiness and needless ambiguity in the use of language, simply in order to preserve the effectiveness of the *langue* itself. Moreover, there must be a dividing line between verbal meanings and those meanings which we half-divine by a supra-linguistic exercise of imagination. There must be a dividing line between Poe's successful disregard of normal usage and the incommunicable word sequences of a bad freshman essay. However, that dividing line is not between the author's meaning and the reader's, but rather between the author's *parole* and no *parole* at all.

Of course, theoretical principles cannot directly solve the interpreter's problem. It is one thing to insist that a text represents the determinate verbal meaning of an author, but it is quite another to discover what that meaning is. The very same text could represent numerous different *paroles,* as any ironic sentence discloses ("That's a *bright* idea!?" or "That's a bright *idea!*"). But it should be of some practical consequence for the interpreter to know that he does have a precisely defined task, namely to discover the author's meaning. It is therefore not only sound but necessary for the interpreter to inquire, "What in all probability did the author mean? Is the pattern of emphases I construe the author's pattern?" But it is both incorrect and futile to inquire, "What does the language of the text say?" That question can have no determinate answer.

Verification

Since the meaning represented by a text is that of another, the interpreter can never be certain that his reading is correct. He knows furthermore that the norms of *langue* by themselves are far too broad to specify the particular meanings and emphases represented by the text, that these particular meanings were specified by particular kinds of subjective acts on the part of the author, and that these acts, as such, remain inaccessible. A less self-critical reader, on the other hand, approaches solipsism if he assumes that the text represents a perspicuous meaning simply because it represents an unalterable sequence of words. For if this "perspicuous" meaning is not verified in some way, it will simply be the interpreter's own meaning, exhibiting the connotations and emphases which he himself imposes. Of course, the reader must realize verbal meaning by his own subjective acts (no one can do that for him), but if he remembers that his job is to construe the author's meaning, he will attempt to exclude his own predispositions and to impose those of the author. But no one can establish another's meaning with certainty. The interpreter's goal is simply this: to show that a given reading is more probable than others. In hermeneutics, verification is a process of establishing relative probabilities.

To establish a reading as probable it is first necessary to show, with reference to the norms of language, that it is possible. This is the criterion of *legitimacy:* the reading must be permissible within the public norms of the *langue* in which the text was composed. The second criterion is that of *correspondence:* the reading must account for each linguistic component in the text. Whenever a reading arbitrarily ignores linguistic components or inadequately accounts for them, the reading may be presumed improbable. The third criterion is that of *generic appropriateness:* if the text follows the conventions of a scientific essay, for example, it is inappropriate to construe the kind of allusive meaning found in casual conversation.[11] But when these three preliminary criteria have been satisfied, there remains a fourth criterion which gives significance to all the rest, the criterion of plausibility or *coherence.* The three preliminary norms usually permit several readings, and this is by definition the case when a text is problematical. Faced with alternatives, the interpreter chooses the reading which best meets the criterion of coherence. Indeed, even when the text is not problematical, coherence remains the decisive criterion, since the meaning is "obvious" only because it "makes sense." I wish, therefore, to focus attention on the criterion of coherence, and shall take for granted the demands of legitimacy, correspondence, and generic appropriateness. I shall try to show that verification by the criterion of coherence, and ultimately, therefore, verification in general, implies a reconstruction of relevant aspects in the author's outlook. My point may be summarized in the paradox that objectivity in textual interpretation requires explicit reference to the speaker's subjectivity.

The paradox reflects the peculiar nature of coherence, which is not an absolute, but a dependent quality. The laws of coherence are variable; they depend upon the nature of the total meaning under consideration. Two meanings ("dark" and "bright," for example) which cohere in one context may not cohere in another.[12] "Dark with excessive bright" makes excellent sense in *Paradise Lost,* but if a reader found the phrase in a textbook on plant pathology, he would assume that he confronted a misprint for "Dark with excessive blight." Coherence depends on the context, and it is helpful to recall our definition of "context": it is a sense of the whole meaning, constituted of explicit partial meanings plus a horizon of expectations and probabilities. One meaning coheres with another because it is typical or probable with reference to the whole (coherence is thus the first cousin of implication). The criterion of coherence can be invoked only with reference to a particular context, and this context may be inferred only by positing the author's "horizon," his disposition toward a particular type of meaning. This conclusion requires elaboration.

The fact that coherence is a dependent quality leads to an unavoidable circularity in the process of interpretation. The interpreter posits meanings for the words and word-sequences he confronts, and, at the same time, he has to posit a whole meaning or context in reference to which the sub-meanings cohere with one another. The procedure is thoroughly circular; the context is derived from the sub-meanings and the sub-meanings are specified and rendered coherent with reference to the context. This circularity makes it very difficult to convince a reader to alter his construction, as every teacher knows. Many a self-willed student continues to insist that his reading is just as plausible as his instructor's, and, very often, the student is justified; his reading does make good sense. Often, the only thing at fault with the student's reading is that it is probably wrong, not that it is incoherent. The student persists in his opinion precisely because his construction *is* coherent and self-sustaining. In such a case he is wrong because he has misconstrued the context or sense of the whole. In this respect, the student's hardheadedness is not different from that of all self-convinced interpreters. Our readings are too plausible to be relinquished. If we have a distorted sense of the text's whole meaning, the harder we look at it the more certainly we shall find our distorted construction confirmed.

Since the quality of coherence depends upon the context inferred, there is no absolute standard of coherence by which we can adjudicate between different coherent readings. Verification by coherence implies therefore a verification of the *grounds* on which the reading is coherent. *It is necessary to establish that the context invoked is the most probable context.* Only then, in relation to an established context, can we judge that one reading is more coherent than another. Ultimately, therefore, we have to posit the most probable horizon for the text, and it is possible to do this only if we posit the author's typical outlook, the typical associations and expectations which form in part the context of his utterance. This is not only the single way we can test the relative coherence of a reading, but is also the only way to avoid pure circularity in making sense of the text.

An essential task in the process of verification is, therefore, a deliberate reconstruction of the author's subjective stance to the extent that this stance is relevant to the text at hand.[13] The importance of such psychological reconstruction may be exemplified in adjudicating between different readings of Wordsworth's "A Slumber Did My Spirit Seal." The interpretations of Brooks and Bateson, different as they are, remain equally coherent and self-sustaining. The implications which Brooks construes cohere beautifully with the explicit meanings of the poem within the context which Brooks adumbrates. The same may be said of Bateson's reading. The best way to show that one reading is more plausible and coherent than the other is to show that one context is more probable than the other. The problem of adjudicating between Bateson and Brooks is therefore, implicitly, the problem every interpreter must face when he tries to verify his reading. He must establish the most probable context.

Now when the *homme moyen sensuel* confronts bereavement such as that which Wordsworth's poem explicitly presents he adumbrates, typically, a horizon including sorrow and inconsolability. These are for him components in the very meaning of bereavement. Sorrow and inconsolability cannot fail to be associated with death when the loved one, formerly so active and alive, is imagined as lying in the earth, helpless, dumb, inert, insentient. And, since there is no hint of life in heaven but only of bodily death, the comforts of Christianity lie beyond the poem's horizon. Affirmations too deep for tears, like those Bateson insists on, simply do not cohere with the poem's explicit meanings; they do not belong to the context. Brooks's reading, therefore, with its emphasis on inconsolability and bitter irony, is clearly justified not only by the text but by reference to universal human attitudes and feelings.

But the trouble with such a reading is apparent to most Wordsworthians. The poet is not an *homme moyen sensuel;* his characteristic attitudes are somewhat pantheistic. Instead of regarding rocks and stones and trees merely as inert objects, he probably regarded them in 1799 as deeply alive, as part of the immortal life of nature. Physical death he felt to be a return to the source of life, a new kind of participation in nature's "revolving immortality." From everything we know of Wordsworth's typical attitudes during the period in which he composed the poem, inconsolability and bitter irony do not belong in its horizon. I think, however, that Bateson overstates his case, and that he fails to emphasize properly the negative implications in the poem ("No motion has she now, no force"). He overlooks the poet's reticence, his distinct unwillingness to express any unqualified evaluation of his experience. Bateson, I would say, has not paid enough attention to the criterion of correspondence. Nevertheless, in spite of this, and in spite of the apparent implausibility of Bateson's reading, it remains, I think, somewhat more probable than that of Brooks. His procedure is also more objective. For even if he had botched his job thoroughly and had produced a less probable reading than that of Brooks, his method would remain fundamentally sound. Instead of projecting his own attitudes (Bateson is presumably not a pantheist) and instead of positing a "universal matrix" of human attitudes (there is none), he has tried to reconstruct the author's probable attitudes so far as these are relevant in specifying the poem's meaning. It is still possible, of course, that Brooks is right and Bateson wrong. A poet's typical attitudes do not always apply to a particular poem, although Wordsworth is, in a given period, more consistent than most poets. Be that as it may, we shall never be *certain* what any writer means, and since Bateson grounds his interpretation in a conscious construction of the poet's outlook, his reading must be deemed the more probable one until the uncovering of some presently unknown data makes a different construction of the poet's stance appear more valid.

Bateson's procedure is appropriate to all texts, including anonymous ones. On the surface, it would seem impossible to invoke the author's probable outlook when the author remains unknown, but in this limiting case the interpreter simply makes his psychological reconstruction on the basis of fewer data. For even with anonymous texts it is crucial to posit not simply some author or other, but a *particular* subjective stance in reference to which the construed context is rendered probable. That is why it is important to date anonymous texts. The interpreter needs all the clues he can muster with regard not only to the text's *langue* and genre, but also to the cultural and personal attitudes the author might be expected to bring to bear in specifying his verbal meanings. In this sense, all texts, including anonymous ones, are "attributed." The objective interpreter simply tries to make his attribution explicit, so that the grounds for his reading are frankly acknowledged. This opens the way to progressive accuracy in interpretation since it is possible, then, to test the assumptions behind a reading as well as the coherence of the reading itself.

The fact that anonymous texts may be successfully interpreted does not, however, lead to the conclusion that all texts should be treated as anonymous ones, that they should, so to say, speak for themselves. I have already argued that no text speaks for itself, and that every construed text is necessarily "attributed." These points suggest strongly that it is unsound to insist on deriving all inferences from the "text itself." When we date an anonymous text, for example, we apply knowledge gained from a wide variety of sources which we correlate with data derived from the text. This extrinsic data is not, however, read *into* the text. On the contrary, it is used to *verify* that which we read out of it. The extrinsic information has ultimately a purely verification function.

The same thing is true of information relating to the author's subjective stance. No matter what the source of this information may be, whether it be the text alone or the text in conjunction with other data, this information is *extrinsic* to verbal meaning as such. Strictly speaking, the author's subjective stance is not part of his verbal meaning even when he explicitly discusses his feelings and attitudes. This is Husserl's point again. The "intentional object" represented by a text is different from the "intentional acts" which realize it. When the interpreter posits the author's stance, he sympathetically reenacts the author's "intentional acts," but although this imaginative act is necessary for realizing meaning, it must be distinguished from meaning as such. In no sense does the text *represent* the author's subjective stance: the interpreter simply adopts a stance in order to make sense of the text, and, if he is self-critical, he tries to verify his interpretation by showing his adopted stance to be, in all probability, the author's.

Of course, the text at hand is the safest source of clues to the author's outlook, since men do adopt different attitudes on different occasions. However, even though the text itself should be the primary source of clues and must always be the final authority, the interpreter should make an effort to go beyond his text wherever possible, since this is the only way he can avoid a vicious circularity. The harder one looks at a text from an incorrect stance, the more convincing the incorrect construction becomes. Inferences about the author's stance are sometimes difficult enough to make even when all relevant data are brought to bear, and it is self-defeating to make the inferential process more difficult than it need be. Since these inferences are ultimately extrinsic, there is no virtue in deriving them from the text alone. One must not confuse the result of a construction (the interpreter's understanding of the text's *Sinn*)* either with the *process* of construction or with a validation of that process. The *Sinn* must be represented by and limited by the text alone, but the process of construction and validation involves psychological reconstruction and should therefore be based on all the data available.

Not only the criterion of coherence but all the other criteria used in verifying interpretations must be applied with reference to a psychological reconstruction. The criterion of legitimacy, for example, must be related to a speaking subject, since it is the author's *langue*, as an internal possession, and not the interpreter's, which defines the range of meaning-possibilities a text can represent. The criterion of correspondence has force and significance only because we presume that the author meant something by each of the linguistic components he employed. And the criterion of generic appropriateness is relevant only so far as generic conventions are possessed and accepted by the author. The fact that these criteria all refer ultimately to a psychological construction is

---

*Sinn: The work's unchanging "textual meaning," as opposed to the various types of "significance" that might be given to that meaning. —ED.

hardly surprising when we recall that to verify a text is simply to establish that the author probably meant what we construe his text to mean. The interpreter's primary task is to reproduce in himself the author's "logic," his attitudes, his cultural givens, in short his world. For even though the process of verification is highly complex and difficult, the ultimate verificative principle is very simple: the imaginative reconstruction of the speaking subject.[14]

The speaking subject is not, however, identical with the subjectivity of the author as an actual historical person; it corresponds, rather, to a very limited and special aspect of the author's total subjectivity; it is, so to speak, that "part" of the author which specifies or determines verbal meaning.[15] This distinction is quite apparent in the case of a lie. When I wish to deceive, my secret awareness that I am lying is irrelevant to the verbal meaning of my utterance. The only correct interpretation of my lie is, paradoxically, to view it as being a true statement, since this is the only correct construction of my "verbal intention." Indeed it is only when my listener has *understood* my meaning (presented as true) that he can *judge* it to be a lie. Since I adopted a truth-telling stance, the verbal meaning of my utterance would be precisely the same, whether I was deliberately lying or suffering from the erroneous conviction that my statement was true. In other words, an author may adopt a stance which differs from his deepest attitudes in the same way that an interpreter must almost always adopt a stance different from his own.[16] But for the process of interpretation, the author's private experiences are irrelevant. The only relevant aspect of subjectivity is that which determines verbal meaning, or, in Husserl's terms, "content."

In a sense all poets are, of course, liars, and to some extent all speakers are, but the deliberate lie, spoken to deceive, is a borderline case. In most verbal utterances the speaker's public stance is not totally foreign to his private attitudes. Even in those cases where the speaker deliberately assumes a role, this mimetic stance is usually not the final determinant of his meaning. In a play, for example, the total meaning of an utterance is not the "intentional object" of the dramatic character; that meaning is simply a component in the more complex "intention" of the dramatist. The speaker himself is spoken. The best description of these receding levels of subjectivity was provided by the scholastic philosophers

in their distinction between "first intention," "second intention," and so on. Irony, for example, always entails a comprehension of two contrasting stances ("intentional levels") by a third and final complex "intention." The "speaking subject" may be defined as the final and most comprehensive level of awareness determinative of verbal meaning. In the case of a lie the speaking subject assumes that he tells the truth, while the actual subject retains a private awareness of his deception. Similarly, many speakers retain in their isolated privacy a self-conscious awareness of their verbal meaning, an awareness which may agree or disagree, approve or disapprove, but which does not participate in determining their verbal meaning. To interpretation, this level of awareness is as irrelevant as it is inaccessible. In construing and verifying verbal meaning, only the speaking subject counts.

A separate exposition would be required to discuss the problems of psychological reconstruction. I have here simply tried to forestall the current objections to extrinsic biographical and historical information by pointing, on the one hand, to the exigencies of verification, and, on the other, to the distinction between a speaking subject and a "biographical" person. I shall be satisfied if this part of my discussion, incomplete as it must be, will help revive the half-forgotten truism that interpretation is the construction of *another's* meaning. A slight shift in the way we speak about texts would be highly salutary. It is natural to speak not of what a text says, but of what an author means, and this more natural locution is the more accurate one. Furthermore, to speak in this way implies a readiness (not notably apparent in recent criticism) to put forth a whole-hearted and self-critical effort at the primary level of criticism — the level of understanding.

Notes

1. The phrase, "piece of language," comes from the first paragraph of William Empson's *Seven Types of Ambiguity*, 3rd ed. (New York, 1955). It is typical of the critical school Empson founded.
2. *Vol. 1. Language*, trans. R. Manheim (New Haven, 1953). It is ironic that Cassirer's work should be used to support the notion that a text speaks for itself. The realm of language is autonomous for Cassirer only in the sense that it follows an

independent development which is reciprocally determined by objective *and* subjective factors. See pp. 69, 178, 213, 249–250, et passim.

3. René Wellek and Austin Warren, *Theory of Literature*, 3rd ed. (New York, 1956), p. 144.

4. Every interpretation is necessarily incomplete in the sense that it fails to explicate all a text's implications. But this kind of incomplete interpretation may still carry an absolutely correct system of emphases and an accurate sense of the whole meaning. This kind of incompleteness is radically different from that postulated by the inclusivists, for whom a sense of the whole means a grasp of the various possible meanings which a text can plausibly represent.

5. Cleanth Brooks, "Irony as a Principle of Structure," in M. D. Zabel, ed., *Literary Opinion in America*, 2nd ed. (New York, 1951), p. 736. F. W. Bateson, *English Poetry: A Critical Introduction* (London, 1950), p. 33 and pp. 80–81.

6. This is the "synchronic" as opposed to the "diachronic" sense of the term. See Ferdinand de Saussure, *Cours de linguistique générale* (Paris, 1931). Useful discussions may be found in Stephen Ullman, *The Principles of Semantics* (Glasgow, 1951), and W. von Wartburg, *Einführung in die Problematik und Methodik der Sprachwissenchaft* (Halle, 1943).

7. See, for example, Cassirer, p. 304.

8. *Sewanee Review*, 54, 1946. Reprinted by W. K. Wimsatt, Jr., *The Verbal Icon* (Lexington, Ky., 1954).

9. T. S. Eliot, "From Poe to Valéry," *Hudson Review*, 2, 1949, p. 232.

10. The word is, in fact, quite effective. It conveys the sense of "memorable" by the component "memorial," and the sense of "never-to-be-forgotten" by the negative prefix. The difference between this and Jabberwocky words is that it appears to be a standard word occurring in a context of standard words. Perhaps Eliot is right to scold Poe, but he cannot properly insist that the word lacks a determinate verbal meaning.

11. This third criterion is, however, highly presumptive, since the interpreter may easily mistake the text's genre.

12. Exceptions to this are the syncategorematic meanings (color and extention, for example) which cohere by necessity regardless of the context.

13. The reader may feel that I have telescoped a number of steps here. The author's verbal meaning or "verbal intention" is the object of complex "intentional acts." To reproduce this meaning it is necessary for the interpreter to engage in "intentional acts" belonging to the same species as those of the author. (Two different "intentional acts" belong to the same species when they "intend" the same "intentional object.") That is why the issue of "stance" arises. The interpreter needs to adopt sympathetically the author's stance (his disposition to engage in particular kinds of "intentional acts") so that he can "intend" with some degree of probability the same "intentional objects" as the author. This is especially clear in the case of *implicit* verbal meaning, where the interpreter's realization of the author's stance determines the text's horizon.

14. Here I purposefully display my sympathies with Dilthey's concepts, *Sichhineinfühlen* and *Verstehen*. In fact, my whole argument may be regarded as an attempt to ground some of Dilthey's hermeneutic principles in Husserl's epistemology and Saussure's linguistics.

15. Spranger aptly calls this the "cultural subject." See Eduard Spranger, "Zur Theorie des Verstehens und zur geisteswissenschaftlichen Psychologie" in *Festschrift Johannes Volkelt zum 70. Geburtstag* (Munich, 1918), p. 369. It should be clear that I am in essential agreement here with the American anti-intentionalists (term used in the ordinary sense). I think they are right to exclude private associations from verbal meaning. But it is of some practical consequence to insist that verbal meaning is that aspect of an author's meaning which is interpersonally communic- *able*. For this implies that his verbal meaning is that which, under linguistic norms, one *can* understand, even if one must sometimes work hard to do so.

16. Charles Bally calls this "dédoublement de la personalité." See his *Linguistique générale et linguistique française*, 2nd ed. (Bern, 1944), p. 37.

THEORY

Are Poems Historical Acts?

George Watson

Supplying a vigorous affirmative answer to his question, George Watson defends the practices of traditional literary history, practices which assume "a correspondence of some kind between what the poet and his age might reasonably be thought to have in mind, on the one hand, and the true meaning of the poem on the other." "The poet and his age" is the key phrase here. Taking the author's intention as the center of poetic meaning, Watson widens the argument to include the traditional concerns of literary history as they bear on that center. So, in addition to strictly biographical information, we need to consider, for example, genre (Hirsch's "generic appropriateness"), a subject with an important historical dimension. "When the literary historian identifies the lineage of poems whose pedigrees have fallen into oblivion . . . he is restoring to the consciousness of the reader knowledge of an indispensable kind." At an even more fundamental level, language itself is historically embedded. Those who would substitute the "norms of language" for authorial intention need to remember, says Watson, that the norms of language are historically contingent. "To speak of the norms of language is to concede, however unwittingly, the case for an historical discipline." The practitioner of this discipline, the literary historian, by reconstructing the philosophical, political, and linguistic horizons of the author's "age," constructs not only the author's probable intentions but also the limits of the author's possible meanings. Thus Watson's author-centered literary history, while a direct counterstatement to the formalists we'll meet in the next chapter, is also a counter to the very different historical approaches we'll meet in the final chapter.

Reprinted by permission of the author from George Watson, *The Study of Literature* (London: Allen Lane, 1969), 70–77.

The nagging doubt about literary history in the present century does, after all, have more than a semblance of an objection of principle and is something more than a mere intellectual fashion. It is based upon a persuasive scepticism about the status of a poem as an historical act. The scepticism needs to be seen in perspective. Nobody has ever doubted that poems were written in the past. But it does not plainly follow that a poem is an historical document in the sense that it derives its chief interest and value from the personality and purpose of its author in the historical conditions under which he wrote. The debate surrounding the "intentional fallacy" has been concerned with this larger issue — an issue in which "the poet's intention" is only one of the problems involved. To speak of the intentional fallacy at all was to react against an historical view of literature which, by the 1940s, had been dominant in the West for over a hundred years. And to accept it as a fallacy was to offer a view deeply subversive to literary history, as it was meant to be, since the literary historian is bound to assume a correspondence of some kind between what the poet and his age might reasonably be thought to have in mind, on the one hand, and the true meaning of the poem on the other. When the historian investigates the question whether the figure of Shylock in *The Merchant of Venice* represents an anti-Semitic view, for instance, he regards the question as hardly distinguishable from a question about what Shakespeare and his first audience would have thought of Shylock. If the literary historian is to be told that the play now exists independently of its creator, and that the modern reader or actor is entitled to make what sense he can of it, then he had better gather up his writing materials and go elsewhere. Such an atmosphere is not for him.

In the following discussion, which is offered among other things as a refutation of the claim that intentionalism is a fallacy, I shall deliberately widen the scope of the argument to include issues beyond the intention of the poet himself. This procedure is justifiable to the extent that the issue involved in contemporary controversy is genuinely wider than the protagonists have always fully realized. What is involved here, at its widest extent, is the momentous issue whether literature is primarily to be studied as a purposive activity or not. It was among the greatest achievements of nineteenth-century historiography to emphasize, perhaps even to exaggerate, the sense of purpose out of which a great poem is born. If this process is to be put into reverse, and if literature is now to be regarded as the first audiences for the Homeric poems perhaps regarded the *Iliad*, or as those who listen to pop-songs today regard what they hear — experiences involving curiosity about the performers, it may be supposed, rather than about the creators — then powerful reasons would be needed for supposing that such a reversal would represent a gain to civilized values. For most men who have valued the literary experience in the past century and more, literature is by contrast the supremely purposive activity: "an objective, a projected result," as Henry James once called it emphatically, adding sententiously: "it is life that is the unconscious, the agitated, the struggling, floundering cause."[1]

It was the Victorians themselves who raised the first protests against the prevailing obsession of their age with the pastness of the past. Robert Browning, who was perhaps the first Englishman to consider the issue in print, argued in a preface of 1852 on Shelley that, in the case of "objective" poets at least, biography may be dispensed with as "no more necessary to an understanding or enjoyment . . . than is a model or anatomy of some tropical tree to the right tasting of the fruit we are familiar with on the market-stall." Saintsbury sometimes claimed to believe — in his study of *Dryden* (1881), for example — that only the verbal analysis of poems can be defended in principle, though he practiced many other sorts himself. Matthew Arnold spent half a lifetime emphasizing the essential timelessness of great poetry. Oscar Wilde spoke of the work of art as having "an independent life of its own" which may "deliver a message far other than that which was put in its lips to say." Quiller-Couch, in his Cambridge lectures *On the Art of Writing* (1916), held that the greatest literature is always

> seraphically free
> From taint of personality.

E. M. Forster, in an essay of 1925 entitled "Anonymity," argued that "a poem is absolute," and that "all literature tends towards a condition of anonymity. . . . It wants not to be signed." Like so many campaigns against the Victorians, the campaign against literary history is itself Victorian in its origins. But the real reason for rehearsing these objections, which if placed beside the manifestoes of French "*l'art pour l'art*" and Proust's *Contre Sainte-Beuve* would make a massive dossier, is to emphasize the scope and variety of the campaign rather than its antiquity. And many of these issues are rightly associated, various as they are. If in the following account I attempt to refute the case point by point, it is rather in the hope of marshalling a lucid argument in favour of a new tradition of literary history than out of any inclination to convict others of muddle or equivocation.

First, there is the issue of evaluation by intention. I mention this here only for the sake of completeness, since no one, it may be supposed, has ever seriously held that a poem is good because its author intended it to be so. To deny, against Wimsatt and Beardsley, that an author's intention is properly "a standard for judging . . . success" is to consider a phrase that opens many issues: but so far as this one is concerned, it would be better to suppose that it had never existed.

The appeal to fulfilled intention, however, is a more serious matter, in the sense that it is a fallacy which is plausible enough to be believed. It is often suggested that a poet has done enough if he fully performs what he set out to do, and often objected that it is improper to demand of the author that he should have written a different book. But it is notable that good critics often demand of an author, and with good reason, that he should have written a different book. And it is not at all obvious that in principle they should not. When Dr. Johnson, in his Life of Dryden, complained of *Absalom and Achitophel* that

> the original structure of the poem was defective; allegories drawn to great length will always break; Charles could not run continually parallel with David,

he is certainly regretting that Dryden had not written a radically different poem, and to object that he should accept the poem for what it is amounts to a demand that he should abdicate his function altogether. But then to fulfill an intention, in literature as in life, is not necessarily to behave as one should. If a man sets out to shoot his mother-in-law, and does so, one may applaud his marksmanship but not the deed itself.

If these were the only uses to which the determination of authorial intention were put by critics, it would be easy to agree that intentionalism is a fallacy. But they are not. After all, there is the wide and distinct issue of the distribution of literature: not just in the way of mechanical improvements like the in-

vention of printing, but in matters which affect the literary experience at its deepest roots. It is of much less than decisive importance that Chaucer did not intend his poems to be printed, for instance; though the fact that he probably intended his poems to be heard rather than silently perused is a fact of real interest. To print is to multiply copies, and the world is evidently right to assume that Chaucer's intentions in the matter are of little concern now. But a new form of distribution might represent a more radical change of emphasis than this. Milton is unlikely to have intended *Samson Agonistes* for the stage; Shakespeare designed his plays altogether for performance, and is unlikely to have taken much interest in their publication. Again, nobody supposes such intentions to be decisive upon posterity; but equally, the probability that *Samson* was written for the study rather than for the stage is a major fact about *Samson*. Anyone who supposed that Milton was attempting a theatrical rival to Dryden's *Conquest of Granada,* for example, would probably prove an unreceptive reader of Milton's play. It is said that Tibetan tea, which is partly composed of rancid butter, is revolting to Western tastes if considered as tea but acceptable if considered as soup. When we ask of a poem questions on the order of "What did the poet intend it for?" — whether stage or study, whether court audience or popular — the answer seems in principle likely to be useful to the extent that it is accurate. This is surely a good question to ask, and anybody who objects at this point that the search for the author's intention is necessarily a fallacy should be sent about his business.

It seems likely, too, that the purposive property of literature is under unnecessary attack at this point. To concede, for instance, that a good stage-play could be written by someone who is not trying to write a stage-play at all is not only to concede something vastly improbable in itself. It is also to humiliate the status of literature as a human act. As Wordsworth put it, a poet is a man speaking to men. On the whole, we listen to those who address us in order to discover what they mean. It is also true that, in rare and memorable instances, people say remarkable things without meaning them. But anybody who conducted his social life on the principle that conversation is worth listening to only or mainly for the sake of such instances would be guilty of continuous discourtesy and, still more important, would find himself much the worse for the bargain. Freaks in creation exist: Musset, for example, is said to have written his plays with no thought for the stage, though in fact they succeed there. But freaks are exactly what such cases are.

A further support for the doctrine of the poem as an historical act seems to arise from the study of the literary kinds. This is an extension of the preceding argument concerning the distribution of literature, and one to be distinguished from it only with difficulty. Nobody, in all probability, has ever denied that on the whole a novel is a novel, or an elegy an elegy, because its author intended it to be so. But in the anti-historical atmosphere of the early twentieth century it was possible to protest that, since works usually bear the evidence of the kind to which they belong on their faces, the historical critic had little to contribute by "going outside the poem." This view is certainly mistaken. When a reader recognizes a novel to be such, or chooses it because it is such, he is certainly using evidence from outside the work as well as evidence from within. He is recognizing features in the novel he holds in his hand which resemble those in other novels he has read. The uncertainty that overhangs early and unestablished literary forms, such as the novel in early eighteenth-century England, and the hesitating attempts to confer dignity and status upon such forms, as in Fielding's formula of the "comic epic in prose," are examples of the problems that ignorance or uncertainty concerning the literary kinds can raise. And when the literary historian identifies the lineage of poems whose pedigrees have fallen into oblivion — when he identifies one of *The Canterbury Tales* as a beast-fable, for instance, and another as a romance of courtly love — he is restoring to the consciousness of the reader knowledge of an indispensable kind. But then the achievements of genre-identification seem among the most massive and incontestable triumphs of historical criticism over the past two hundred years. To demonstrate the complex relation between Spenser's *Faerie Queen*, for instance, and the Italian epics which in the sixteenth century dominated the mode of romantic epic throughout Europe, is to restore to the English poem the status and interest of a masterpiece and rescue it from the imputation of a work that might otherwise barely survive as a loose collection of occasional beauties.

If the wider problem of language is considered in the same light, the historical status of literature grows steadily and inescapably clearer. It was sometimes objected of historical criticism that it encouraged a chaos of romantic individualism on the part of the poets in their use of language, whereas the fashionable demand in the earlier years of the century was for continuity, order and "the tradition." Words, it was emphasized by the New Critics and others, need to be disciplined to fit the norms of language, so that the poem itself might ideally exist in a void of space or time, a formal object or "well wrought urn." "The work after being produced must continue to exist independently of the author's intentions or thoughts about it. The idiosyncrasies of the author must not be repugnant to the norm."[2] But certain celebrated literary effects, after all, *are* repugnant to the norms of language as established in their age. The obscenities of Swift are repugnant to the norms of polite language in the Augustan age, as they were meant to be, and it is just their repugnancy — in this case, their power to shock — that makes them tell. Some English poets are well known to have used linguistic devices — Milton's syntax, Dylan Thomas's diction — which deviate from any known use of language in their age, and the reader is meant to sense that a deviation or perversion of usage is happening. It is admittedly tempting to suppose that there must be some limit to the degree of repugnancy that is admissible in literature; and certainly there is a point beyond which language can only turn into nonsense. But then nonsense can be literature too, and sometimes is — a warning that, if there is a limit to be placed, it may be worth insisting that it should be placed at some remote point.

In any case, to speak of norms of language is to concede, however unwittingly, the case for an historical discipline. The poem itself is not the norm, after all, and in itself it cannot reveal what the norm is. In order to demonstrate the idiosyncrasies of Milton's syntax in *Paradise Lost*, it is of no use to confine the discussion to the poem itself: one must look at other documents by Milton and by his contemporaries. The oddities of Thomas's diction exist only in relation to mid-twentieth-century usages outside his poems. If we are anxious to pretend that poems could ever "exist independently of the author's intentions," we had better banish all idea of the norm. And in banishing that, it is easy to see, a great deal of significance must go too. A reader content to suppose that Milton's language was the ordinary language of his age would certainly miss much of the significance of *Paradise Lost*. To evade in all circumstances the study of the author's intentions, in fact, is at times to evade the meaning of the poem itself.

What does it mean to speak usefully of an author's intentions in his poem? I emphasize "usefully," since it is right to concede at once that such discussions need not be useful at all; and doctrines like "the intentional fallacy" probably represent an exaggerated reaction to this realization, obvious as it is. But then the historian, whether of literature or of anything else, is in no way committed to the view that everything about the past is of equal interest: in fact it is precisely the historian who is expected to show the greatest skill and experience in sorting the important evidence from the insignificant. That is his trade. When we have shown that much skilful and informed speculation about the poet's intention does not help in reading his poems — a charge sometimes levelled against J. L. Lowes's study of Coleridge, *The Road to Xanadu*, for example — nothing decisive has been said or shown against the nature of such enquiries in general. If it sometimes helps, it does not follow that it always helps. Equally, the historical critic need not allow himself to be committed to the view that his enquiry is utterly limited to the question of what the poet intended. It is notorious that Shakespeare would not understand much modern Shakespearean criticism. But then that, in itself, is hardly an objection to what the critics are doing. Newton, equally, would presumably not understand modern physics. It seems likely that one or the other, if he could return to life, might be trained in understanding and would prove an unusually apt pupil; but to demand of the historical critic that he should in all circumstances limit himself to seeing in a Shakespeare play only as much as the dramatist himself might have seen and in something like the very terms in which he would have seen it is to ask, in large measure, that literary studies should be stopped.

On the other hand, the historical criticism of literature imposes a limit of another and more reasonable kind than this. If it does not forbid elucidation beyond the point where the poet himself might cease to follow the argument, it commonly forbids explanations that run counter to what the poet could have thought or felt. The enlargement of "intended" to "thought or felt" is a safety-device in this argument, but an allowable one if it is conceded how much wider than the conscious and articulate intention of the poet the scope of the modern argument about the poet's intention has proved. To set out to show that Shakespeare was something like a Marxist, or that he had a horror of autocracy and the police-state, is to attempt to prove something that runs counter not only to the texts of the plays but, short of the remotest freak of intellectual history, counter to anything an Elizabethan could have believed. When one exclaims "But Shakespeare *can't* have thought that," the curtain that drops upon the line of argument is a curtain that has good reason to be there.

Notes

1. "The Lesson of Balzac" (1905), reprinted in *The House of Fiction*, edited by Leon Edel (London, 1957), p. 64.
2. Wimsatt and Beardsley, in *Dictionary of World Literature*, edited by Joseph T. Shipley (New York, 1942), p. 327.

Shakespeare and the Idea of Obedience: Gonzalo in *The Tempest*

Paul Yachnin

If we want to understand The Tempest, *Paul Yachnin argues, we need to see it at "the historical moment of its production and reception." Although we know little about Shakespeare aside from his works, we can discover much about the audience for whom those works were intended, and this will be the surest guide to their meaning. In the case of* The Tempest, *a lack of this historical knowledge frequently causes modern readers to mistake both the genre of the play and its main theme. Genre, as Watson and Hirsch remind us, has a historical dimension, and Yachnin locates the distinction between a "polemical" and a "literary" work in its specific historical context: "whether the work in question, at the historical moment of its production, seems more concerned with persuading readers with respect to an issue or more concerned with thinking about an issue." To see* The Tempest *as a literary work "does not necessarily foreclose the possibility of a particular political reading of the play: rather it simply requires that such a reading be grounded in a historically specific negotiation between the text and the normal political attitude of the theatre-audience."*

The "normal" attitude of the audience is the key. On this assumption, Yachnin takes issue with the numerous "new historical" and cultural materialist readings of The Tempest, *including those by Stephen Greenblatt and Barker and Holme, on the grounds that these attempts to historicize our understanding are not historical enough; that is, they "do not adequately come to terms with the normative 1611 reception of* The Tempest's *politics." In short, the closer we get to the concerns of the intended audience, the closer we get to Shakespeare's meaning. Yachnin argues that in* The Tempest *these concerns were domestic and European rather than colonial and, on the central and conflicted issue of obedience to political authority, weighted toward the conservative*

Reprinted by permission from *Mosaic: A Journal for the Interdisciplinary Study of Literature*, 24.2 (Spring 1991): 1–18.

side. *Modern readers, he concedes, have different concerns—hence, our tendency to mistake the play's original meaning.*

The question of how far subjects were obliged to obey their princes was prominently contested in the Renaissance.[1] During the Reformation, struggles between Protestants on one side and the Catholic Church on the other threw into high relief the often opposing claims of conscience and political obedience, and moved the question of obedience near the center of the polemical wars ongoing from the time of Luther to the time of Milton. Of course, Catholic and Protestant positions on the duty of obedience were by no means consistent through the period; on the contrary, positions on both sides tended to shift depending upon which side was dominant in whatever nation was in question.

English Protestants, for example, who during the Marian exile had extended the Calvinist argument for the right of active resistance to include the common people as well as lesser magistrates retreated to a far more quiescent position once the Protestant Elizabeth acceded to the throne (Greaves 23). To the same effect, the Catholic Church, which in most matters espoused the necessity of submitting to authority, nonetheless was able to enjoin English Catholics to murder the Queen of England on the grounds that she was a tyrant responsible for endangering her subjects' souls: "there is no doubt," Gregory XIII's secretary wrote in 1580, "that whosoever sends her out of the world with the pious intention of doing God service, not only does not sin but gains merit" (qtd. in Greaves 33).

The clarity and assurance of the various positions adopted on both sides throughout the period depended upon suppressing the contradictions attendant upon the role played by power. The effective Elizabethan controversialist had *not* to know, had to forget that he had known, that English people had been enjoined to resist during Mary's reign, but were commanded to submit under Elizabeth; equally, he had to maneuver around the fact that Protestants under Catholic rule were said to be justified in following the dictates of conscience, but that Catholics in Elizabethan England were "justifiably" subject to severe punishments for obeying *their* consciences. Further, the Elizabethan doctrine of non-resistance in the face of wicked rulers depended upon suppressing the fact that non-resistance—suffering rather than

rebelling—was often difficult to distinguish from complicity. That is, if a subject did not actively resist a wicked ruler, was not s/he in fact complicit with the ruler's wickedness, even if s/he refused to carry out wicked orders? This point was brought out by John Ponet, one of the Marian exiles. Who, Ponet asked, was to be blamed for Nero's crimes: "He for doing them, or others for flattrying him, or the Senate and people of *Rome* in suffring him? Surely there is none to be excused, but all to be blamed, and chiefly those that might have bridled him, and did not" (16).

In spite of these contradictions, however, it seems clear that the majority of the English people throughout the Elizabethan and Jacobean periods both espoused a doctrine of political obedience and renounced any idea of active resistance. The Elizabethan doctrine of obedience, it should be noted, did not entail "blind" obedience, since both ruler and subject were seen to be under the ultimate authority of God. The ruler, however, was answerable only to God, and the subject, if conscience enjoined non-obedience, was merely to suffer but never to resist. Elizabethan and Jacobean arguments in favor of obedience built upon the earlier Henrician linking of political and religious obligations, according to which loyalty to civic authorities constituted a Christian duty. This linking of spheres of obligation constituted an attempt to obliterate the distinction between the claims of conscience and the claims of obedience. The 1570 *Homily against Disobedience and Wilful Rebellion* undertook to inscribe the particular relations of power existing in Elizabethan England within the universal text of what—according to the Elizabethan authorities—had been ordained by God as natural, thus making rebellion a crime against the divine as well as against the political order:

> What shall subjectes do then? Shall they obey valiaunt, stoute, wyse and good princes, and contemne, disobey and rebell against chyldren beyng their princes, or against undiscrete and evyll governours? God forbid. For first what a perilous thing were it to commit unto the subjectes the judgement which prince is wyse and godly and his government good, and whiche is otherwise, as though the foote must judge of the head—an enterprise very heynous, and must needes breede rebellion. . . .
> How horrible a sinne against God and man rebellion is, can not possiblie be expressed according

unto the greatnesse therof. For he that nameth rebellion, nameth not a singular, or one only sinne . . .
but he nameth the whole poodle and sinke of all
sinnes against God and man. . . .

(*Certain Sermons* 213, 225)

Furthermore, Elizabethan and Jacobean arguments
for obedience were absolutist in the sense that they
based the obligation of obedience to the monarch on
a metaphysical, as opposed to a merely legal, legitimation of monarchical power (Sommerville 9–50). In
this view, the monarch's power was "absolute"—un-
conditional, independent, superior to all other civil
authority—deriving from God rather than from the
people. In the Elizabethan period, "absolutism" did
not imply "arbitrary" power, which is how it came to
be conceived during the Civil War period (Daly
228–48). Nonetheless, the absolutism of monarchical
power was productive of a dilemma which vexed the
question of obedience in the culture at large. Whereas
in resistance theory, the claims of the state and of conscience were distinct, since the power of the monarch
was normally seen to derive from the people rather
than from God, in terms of Elizabethan/Jacobean absolutism, the claims of the state and of conscience
were on an equal footing.

The Elizabethan/Jacobean idea of obedience also
derived support from what Jonathan Goldberg has
called "the absolutist trope of state secrets" (55–112,
230–39), a mystification of the commonsense idea
that the ruler has often to keep secret the reasons for
pursuing some course of action or for issuing some
command. This idea underlies Jonson's defense of
James's handling of the Spanish Marriage negotiations; Jonson's parliamentarian contemporary, Sir
Robert Phelips, conceded that members of Parliament "ought not to draw the veyles that princes are
pleased to sett between theyr secret ends and common eyes" (qtd. in Sharpe 16).

Shakespeare tends both to strengthen this defense
and also to put it in question by relating the argument for the necessity of secrecy to the wider issue of
epistemological uncertainty. Already broached, in a
truly dizzying fashion by Castiglione in *The Courtier*
(Strier 105–06), radical uncertainty in Shakespeare
is normally attendant on and supportive of positions
opposed to political resistance. John of Gaunt's refusal to punish Richard II for the murder of Thomas
of Gloucester is based on the conventional idea of
the king's absolute power, but also on his own un-

certainty with respect to the moral status of the murder itself:

> God's is the quarrel, for God's substitute,
> His deputy anointed in His sight,
> Hath caus'd his death, *the which if wrongfully,*
> Let heaven revenge, for I may never lift
> An angry arm against His minister.
> (*Richard II*, I.ii.37–41; emphasis mine)[2]

Finally, the Elizabethan/Jacobean doctrine of submission to divinely ordained civic authority derived
considerable urgency from Catholic arguments in favor of killing the English monarch. One example of
how Englishmen, especially during the Elizabethan
period and in the wake of the 1605 Gunpowder Plot,
came to identify the idea of active resistance with
"the Catholicke zeale to stab good Princes" is to be
found in James Cleland's 1607 courtesy-book, *The
Institution of a Young Noble Man*: "What man is hee
then so rash and unadvised to saie or mainetaine
that you shoulde not obay your Soveraigne if hee be
cruel or rigorous? Where finde you that Gods com-
maundements will suffer Kings to bee throwne out
of their thrones? . . . This is the Papists doctrine: this is
the Romane Religion I wish you to beware of: this
is the Catholicke zeale to stab good Princes" (116).

In spite of this commonplace adherence to the
idea of political obedience, however, many English
people must have felt unsettled and disturbed by the
sheer "shiftiness" of official positions with regard to
the subject's duty of obedience. The political and religious instability of England itself throughout the
sixteenth century seems to have engendered in many
people an increasing degree of political and religious
free-thinking and even skepticism. The deep rifts in
the ideological system made visible by the instability
of the period spawned doubt in the minds of many.
A subject who thought about the issue of obedience
hard enough might begin to find the government's
position burdened by contradiction and special
pleading. Someone like Donne, intensely engaged in
the wars between Protestantism and Catholicism,
seems to have adopted a "self-centered" position
which ostensibly preserved both the integrity of conscience and the duty of obedience, but only by putting
in question the connection between secular rule and
the divine authority which normally was seen to constitute its legitimation. In "Satyre III" (c. 1597; pub.
1633), Donne advised his reader,

Keepe the truth which thou hast found; men do not
  stand
In so ill case here, that God hath with his hand
Sign'd Kings blanck-charters to kill whom they hate,
Nor are they Vicars, but hangmen to Fate.   (139)

Donne's skeptical position remained unpublished
during his lifetime. Others, often those working in
more visible places, normally spoke in favor of the
subject's duty to obey over the demands of conscience. In *Neptune's Triumph for the Return of Albion*
(1624), written to whitewash the fiasco of the Spanish Marriage negotiations, Ben Jonson ruled out the
issue of doubts about a prince's intelligence or integrity. In response to popular skepticism and resentment aroused by both King James's ineffectual
management of the negotiations and by the negotiations themselves, Jonson suggested that James had in
fact been testing his subjects' loyalty:

It was no envious stepdame's rage,
Or tyrant's malice of the age
    That did employ him [Prince Charles] forth
But such a wisdom that would prove,
By sending him, their hearts and love,
    That else might fear his worth.

                                    (ll. 243–48)

It seems fair to say that the issue of political obedience was pursued in at least two distinct but per-
meable fields of discourse. The first is a "polemical"
field marked by clearly defined and univocal positions founded on both the suppression of contradiction and a clear idea of the constituency and
interpretive practices of the readership. The second
is what I will call a "literary" field; here political qui-
etism is coupled with a less constrained consideration of the problems attendant upon the opposing
claims of obedience and conscience; here there is a
willingness to allow the emergence of contradiction,
a less settled sense of the make-up and politics of the
readership, and far less authorial policing of the production of meaning.

The essential difference between the polemical and
the literary might be defined, roughly, as the difference between a discourse of power (or persuasion) on
the one hand, and a discourse of (powerless or non-
persuasive) imaginative freedom on the other. Literary scholars are familiar with the modern version of
this divided field, since the normal practice here is to
inscribe one's own discourse within a "polemical"
field and to locate the texts discussed within a "liter-

ary" field. The division of the universe of discourse in
this way gives the critic power to speak persuasively
for the literary texts which are thus constructed as unable to speak authoritatively for themselves. As Roger
Seamon has suggested, modern criticism tends to assume that the text itself is "dumb," and that the business of criticism is to "speak" for it (296). One of my
contentions is that many Renaissance texts constructed *themselves* as unable to speak authoritatively
or powerfully about politics, and that by marking
themselves as "dumb," such texts were freed from
censorship and thus able to represent political issues
in complex and candid ways ("Powerless Theater").

The polemical field includes works such as Jonson's *Neptune's Triumph* or the 1570 *Homily against
Disobedience and Wilful Rebellion;* but it also includes
works which argue for active resistance, such as
Christopher Goodman's *How Superior Powers Oght
to be Obeyd* (1558), and even openly subversive
pamphlets such as Thomas Scot's *Vox Populi* (1624).
The literary field includes works such as Thomas
More's *Utopia* (1516), Donne's "Satyre III" or Thomas
Browne's *Religio Medici* (1636; pub. 1642). Such cate-
gorization does not depend directly upon the formal
features of the work itself; rather, it depends upon
whether the work in question, at the historical moment of its production, seems more concerned with
persuading readers with respect to an issue or more
concerned with thinking about an issue. This distinction is often unstable, particularly with respect to
"literary" writing. Indeed interpretive instability and
changeability are two of the central features of the
literary field. For this reason, works such as *Utopia* or
Thomas Middleton's *A Game at Chess* (1624) or *Religio Medici* can be, and have been, inscribed within the
polemical field and, consequently, have been interpreted as politically purposeful texts.

I want to suggest that *The Tempest*, at the historical moment of its production and reception, should
be seen in terms of both the freedom to consider
vexed political issues and the freedom from authorial policing of the production of meaning which are
characteristic of texts inscribed in the literary field.
Such a starting-place assumes that *The Tempest* was,
largely, politically quiescent: free to "think" about
political issues because constructed as powerless to
speak authoritatively about such issues, powerless
because of its openness to differing, even opposing,
interpretations of its political meaning.

To locate *The Tempest* in the literary field does not necessarily foreclose the possibility of a particular political reading of the play; rather, it simply requires that such a reading be grounded in a historically specific negotiation between the text and the *normal* political attitude of the theater-audience. Such a political reading recognizes the instability and changeability of meaning, the fact that many Jacobean audience-members would have seen the play differently from how I will be suggesting it was normally seen; it also recognizes the fact that the meanings of *The Tempest* at the Globe in 1611 were not necessarily consonant with its meanings in London in 1674 (in Dryden's adaptation, *The Tempest,* or *The Enchanted Island*), or in Ernest Renan's 1878 adaptation (*Caliban: Suite de La Tempête*) in the wake of the Paris Commune, or at the 1988 meeting of the Shakespeare Association of America in Austin, Texas, where *The Tempest* was the focus of a special session on "Shakespeare and Colonialism." Furthermore, such a reading positions itself between left-wing and intentionalist interpretations of Shakespeare's politics (such as Curt Breight's recent interpretation of *The Tempest* as subversive or Richard Strier's similar study of *King Lear*) and Foucauldian readings of *The Tempest* as conservative and colonialist by scholars such as Stephen Greenblatt and Peter Hulme. These readings, while theoretically sophisticated, pay not enough attention to the centrality of the conscious activity both of writing on Shakespeare's part and of interpreting on the part of the Jacobean audience.

My reading of *The Tempest* as conservative, then, agrees with much new historicist and cultural materialist work on the play. I part company, however, from new historicist work by focusing on the European political scene in itself as central (as opposed to Europe in relation to the New World) and by insisting on the play's relative autonomy from determining discursive formations, whether discourses of colonialism, hierarchy or resistance. In particular, my emphasis on a conscious but never fully autonomous negotiation between author, players and audiences distinguishes my account of *The Tempest*'s meanings from Paul Brown's brilliant work on the play, since he sees the play's ideological complexity and instability as an effect of a conflicted discursive formation rather than as a product of the minds which had to respond to that discourse. Finally, my historicization of *The Tempest* differs from Kay Stockholder's recent psychoanalytic reading of what she sees as the play's conflicted figuration of power; she produces an effectively transhistorical authorial psyche by folding into the 1611 *Tempest* the conflicting readings which I want to see developing in history (197–232).

Accordingly, the supposed univocality of the political meaning of *The Tempest* must be seen to split along two separate axes — the first having to do with the heterogeneity of the political views of Shakespeare's contemporary audiences, the second having to do with the changing interpretations of *The Tempest* over time and in different cultural and political settings. My present discussion has to do only with the play as a conservative meditation, in 1611, on the necessity of political obedience over the demands of individual conscience in terms of the Reformation question of the subject's obligation to civil authority.

Such a focus disallows neither the view of *The Tempest* as subversive of domestic power relations (Breight) nor the "con-textualization" of the play in terms of its complicity with nascent colonialist discourse (Barker and Hulme; Brown; Erlich; Greenblatt; Hulme; Leininger). What I am suggesting, however, is that these views do not adequately come to terms with the normative 1611 reception of *The Tempest*'s politics — Breight's view because it is not sufficiently in tune with the play's affective structure (which invites identification with Prospero) and because it exaggerates popular disaffection with the monarchy; Barker and Hulme's view because it mistakes the particular range and contemporary import of the play's topical references. As Meredith Skura has argued recently, "colonialism" did not crystallize into a coherent discursive formation until after the first performances of *The Tempest* (52–57); consequently, one might argue that, in 1611, the play's allusions to the New World would have had reference primarily to Old World "domestic" concerns, rather than to the relationship between the Old and New Worlds. I would suggest, further, that such a domestic emphasis was equally in play in More's *Utopia* or in Montaigne's "Of the Caniballes," and even that European concerns in themselves constituted the determining emphasis for those works' early readers, a group which included Shakespeare. Equally, I would counter the new historicist view of the play as *automatically* supportive of colonialism's "euphemisation" of European exploitation of the New World, since such a view ignores both the constitutive function of the interpretation of "literary" texts and the differences of opinion which it is reasonable to assume existed between members of Shakespeare's original audiences.

• • •

The story of Gonzalo, the old counselor at the court of Alonso, lies at the center of the opposing claims of obedience and conscience in *The Tempest*. Although he is praised by Prospero, the play itself reveals — as Harry Berger pointed out in 1969 — that Gonzalo was Antonio's accessory in the usurpation of Prospero. Gonzalo was in command of those who carried Prospero and Miranda from Milan and who abandoned them at sea; Gonzalo gave the castaways some necessities of life but abandoned them to death. According to Prospero, the agents of the usurpation carried him and Miranda out of Milan, bore them out to sea, and cast them adrift in "A rotten carcass of a butt, not rigg'd . . . the very rats / Instinctively have quit it" (I.ii. 146–48). In answer to a question from Miranda, Prospero reveals that the master of this heinous design was Gonzalo:

> MIRANDA: How came we ashore?
> PROSPERO: By Providence divine.
>   Some food we had, and some fresh water, that
>   A noble Neapolitan, Gonzalo,
>   Out of his charity, who being then appointed
>   Master of this design, did give us, with
>   Rich garments, linens, stuffs, and necessaries,
>   Which since have steaded much. . . .
>
>   (I.ii.159–65)

Unlike "polemical" works such as Jonson's *Neptune's Triumph* or King James's *Trew Law of Free Monarchies* (1598), *The Tempest* does not produce an incontestable conservative meaning; instead, the play "covers" its conservatism, so that only the interpretive efforts of a cooperative audience-member will "discover" the play's political meaning. We could say that *The Tempest* poses the case of Gonzalo as an interpretive problem whose solution produces a political argument. Gonzalo's participation in the overthrow of Prospero calls into question the validity of Prospero's praise of Gonzalo as his savior, and beyond that, calls into question Prospero's practical intelligence, acuity and authority. The play invites us to solve the problem of Gonzalo along lines that are predetermined by the requirement of recuperating Prospero as an authoritative and sympathetic figure. If Prospero is to remain the focus of our respect and sympathy, we will want to explain why he chooses to praise the very man who oversaw his ouster.

The reader or audience-member is entitled, of course, to decline the play's invitation to solve the problem of Gonzalo along the lines of the play's affective structure. It is possible to argue instead that Prospero's praise of Gonzalo reveals Prospero's inadequacy, lack of real authority, limited practical intelligence. This is Harry Berger's interpretation, one which suits both modern skepticism about authority and the current preference for irony as an interpretive technique. Moreover, Berger's ironic and skeptical reading would no doubt have been available to anti-absolutists or skeptics in Shakespeare's audience. Such a group might well have welcomed Berger's reading of Prospero as a ruler who refuses "to look too closely at the actual state of affairs, and more generally, at the world [he] live[s] in" (265); such a group might also have applauded Breight's (similar but different) historicized ironic reading of Prospero as a diabolically clever and successful politician who manufactures the threat of treason in order to legitimate and mystify his own claim to power.

I suggest, however, that neither of these ironic readings would have been normative in 1611, since the overall political climate at that juncture tended to be royalist rather than anti-royalist. Nor am I here simply invoking the fact that *The Tempest* was performed by the "King's Men," and performed by that company at court; that the court undoubtedly viewed the play as royalist does not necessarily mean that this was the way it was perceived by a large, public audience. Much more important is the massive positive reassessment of King James's ability, reputation and relations with his subjects which has been undertaken by scholars such as R. C. Munden and Jenny Wormald. In particular, in debunking the Whig interpretation of history by building a compelling refutation of the notion that Jacobean Parliaments constituted an "opposition" to the monarchy, Conrad Russell and Kevin Sharpe remove the ground underlying Breight's and Strier's arguments for seeing Shakespeare as a subversive playwright. Russell explains:

> An opposition, as we know the term now, can hope to force changes of policy either by changing the government, or by appealing so eloquently to the public that the government is forced to change its ground. In this sense, opposition as we know the term now was impossible. It is also a characteristic of an "opposition" that it is united by some common body of beliefs, which it does not share with members of the government. This ideological gulf

between "government" and "opposition" is impossible to find in Parliament before 1640. There were many disagreements on policy, often profound ones, but these were divisions which split the Council itself. On none of the great questions of the day did Parliamentary leaders hold any opinions not shared by members of the Council. Men who depend on persuasion to get their way, and who hold no beliefs incompatible with office, cannot be described as an "opposition" without grossly misleading modern readers. (18)

Thus, when Annabel Patterson attempts to strengthen her left-wing interpretation of *Coriolanus* by alluding to a contemporary parallel drawn between the Roman tribunes and what she calls "the opposition leaders in the Commons" (123), she is depending upon a no longer tenable view of Jacobean parliamentary relations with the crown. Bright refers to "oppositional discourse" rather than to an "opposition," and attempts to inscribe *The Tempest* within that discursive field. The exemplary oppositional texts he adduces, however, consist in the Marprelate tracts and, especially, in the dissident Catholic propaganda produced throughout the period on the Continent (3–4). As a consequence, Bright effectively aligns Shakespeare against the dominant views of his popular audience.

The prevailing royalism of Shakespeare's audience for which I am arguing need not be seen to preclude the possibility of satirical and skeptical theatrical representations of either James himself or the operations of power in general. Indeed, plays such as *Troilus and Cressida* (1601–02), *Eastward Ho!* (1605) and *A Game at Chess* (1624) demonstrate the persistence of satire and skepticism as elements in the theater's depiction of power throughout the Jacobean period. The point is, however, that the play in question must itself be satirical or, as is the case with *Game at Chess*, must encourage an ironic reception (Yachnin "*Game*"). *The Tempest*, like any literary text, can be interpreted ironically; however, because of its strong drive toward identification with Prospero, such an ironic interpretation would seem to require a powerful bias on the part of the interpretive community. Such a bias was perhaps characteristic of American Shakespeareans in the late 1960s and may be characteristic of modern left-wing Shakespeareans aligned against what they see as the conservative bias of New Historicism, but it was unlikely to be typical of Shakespeare's 1611 audience.

Also relevant is the time of the play's performance. *The Tempest* was first performed before the death of the popular and militantly Protestant heir to the throne, Prince Henry, before the scandalous revelations surrounding the murder of Sir Thomas Overbury, and about seventeen months after the assassination of Henri IV, the Protestant ruler of France, an event which served to re-ignite English fears of Catholic subornation and treachery. Taken together with the revisionist account of the Jacobean political climate, these admittedly exemplary rather than decisive facts suggest that the first audiences of *The Tempest* would not have responded to the play against the bias of its affective structure.

In order to solve the problem of Gonzalo in a way which preserved Prospero's moral centrality and authority, Shakespeare's audience would have had to consider the contradictions and limitations attendant upon the idea of political obedience. The solution, that is, depends upon an endorsement of the idea of obedience *along with* an awareness of the moral and human costs that such obedience demands. Put another way, *The Tempest* invited the audience to formulate a critique of political obedience which demurred at the "obvious" next step of repudiation.

While the play's implicit support of obedience is uncongenial to modern readers, both because we value the rule of law and also because we have seen the heinous consequences of "following orders," it does not, of course, necessarily follow that Shakespeare's audience would have valued individual rights over the interests of the state, or would have associated political obedience with the abuses of fascism (as we do). Consequently, we have no reason to think either that *The Tempest* "fails" to repudiate the idea of obedience, or that the play does not repudiate obedience because Shakespeare lacked either courage or imagination. We can see, instead, that the subversion of and yet containment by the idea of political obedience is the effect of a negotiation between, on the one side, the powerless freedom itself of "literary" discourse and, on the other, a predominantly royalist audience, at a particular juncture in English history when resistance-theory tended to be identified with Catholic polemics against Protestantism and when actual opposition to authority tended to be identified with Catholic fifth-column activity.

The question of the opposing claims of obedience and conscience is also represented in *The Winter's Tale*. Written within a year of *The Tempest*, *The Win-*

ter's Tale provides two test cases which seek to emphasize the moral costs of political obedience and the value of obeying an absolute moral standard. That is, *The Winter's Tale* seeks to resolve the problem of obedience by pursuing a radical perspective and fails to do so because its nascent radicalism cannot be articulated in the absolutist terms dominant in the play. In the play, Camillo and Antigonus, two Sicilian lords in the Court of Leontes, respond in opposite ways to commands which each finds morally repugnant. Camillo, the first courtier, is commanded by Leontes to murder the innocent Polixenes. Camillo merely feigns compliance, and instead spirits Polixenes out of Sicilia. Antigonus, the second courtier, suppresses his moral repulsion in order to obey his prince. He obeys Leontes's wicked command to expose the baby, Perdita. Like Camillo, Antigonus carries an exile from Sicilia across the sea to Bohemia. Where Camillo's life-saving dereliction of duty is vindicated and rewarded, however, Antigonus's life-threatening obedience is punished by the aggregate forces of Nature, figured by the storm and by the bear which "mocks" him to death.

Gonzalo in *The Tempest* is closer to the bad example of Antigonus than he is to the good example of Camillo. Both Antigonus and Gonzalo are obedient to their princes; both are "throwers-out" of innocent victims; both are "masters of the design." Both are charitable in the commission of an evil act: Antigonus abandons Perdita with both a kind word and a small fortune in gold; Gonzalo abandons Prospero and Miranda with "some food," "some fresh water," "Rich garments, linens, stuffs, and necessaries," and Prospero's overprized books. Shakespeare arranges the details in order to make Gonzalo's act less clearly tantamount to murder; however, as Prospero suggests, their lives were saved by Providence, not by Gonzalo. In essence, therefore, the acts of Antigonus and Gonzalo are virtually identical.

If Prospero applied to his own situation the moral standard which serves to legitimate Antigonus's dismemberment in *The Winter's Tale*, he would not be able to praise Gonzalo. Moreover, if this moral standard were seen to obtain in general in *The Tempest*, we would have to conclude that Prospero is either a fool or a self-deceiver. As I want to argue, however, the moral standard of *The Winter's Tale* does not adequately cover events in *The Tempest*. Both plays adopt an absolutist paradigm, but *The Tempest*'s analysis of political acts and relations articulates the contradic-

tions which remain unarticulated in *The Winter's Tale*. Camillo's decision against murder is morally correct, Antigonus's decision in favor of the exposure of Perdita is immo41ral; but both courtiers' reasons for acting as they do are burdened by their inability to separate morality from political obedience. In contrast, Gonzalo's morally incorrect decision to obey Alonso's command to cast Prospero adrift is seen to have been undertaken in the knowledge that obedience requires culpable action.

When Camillo considers Leontes's regicidal command, the obvious moral objection to the murder of an innocent man is present in his mind, but his soliloquy swerves away from an articulation of the claims of morality as opposed to those of political hierarchy. As I have already suggested, Camillo turns away from the moral objection because the absolutist paradigm dominant in the play precludes the separation of political and religious spheres of obligation (just as in the 1570 *Homily against Disobedience*). Camillo is unable to say something like the following: "Poisoning Polixenes is morally wrong and therefore I will not do it." On the contrary, Camillo must think through his dilemma tortuously: "Poisoning Polixenes is morally wrong; my only reason to do it consists in my obedience to Leontes; but he is 'in rebellion with himself'; on the other hand, I might advance my career by doing it; but now that I think of it, I cannot recall hearing of anyone who has prospered by committing regicide; therefore I will not do it (and would not do it even if I were a villain [which I am not]; indeed, since I lose either way [does this entail moral or political loss?], I will do nothing—I will run away":

> What case stand I in? I must be the poisoner
> Of good Polixenes, and my ground to do't
> Is the obedience to a master; one
> Who, in rebellion with himself, will have
> All that are his so too. To do this deed,
> Promotion follows. If I could find example
> Of thousands that had struck anointed kings
> And flourish'd after, I'd not do't; but since
> Nor brass nor stone nor parchment bears not one,
> Let villainy itself forswear't. I must
> Forsake the court. To do't, or no, is certain
> To me a break-neck.   (I.ii.351–62)

In a sense, *The Winter's Tale* achieves both its resolution of the problem of obedience and its preservation of hierarchy and morality by cheating. It must cheat, because to admit the full meaning of Camillo's disobedience would require not only a shift of the

primary ground of authority from the divinely appointed monarch on the one side to the Law and the
underlying principles of natural justice on the other;
it would also require the virtual dissolution of the divine legitimation of the ruler's power over and
against the state. Further, it would require Camillo to
become his own master, to become—in a metaphysical sense—free. Yet although Camillo disobeys his
master in Act I (for reasons he is unable fully to
define), he remains personally and feudally bound
to Leontes. The persistence of his fealty is token of
the stability of the absolutist paradigm which his
morally correct derogation has jeopardized. After fifteen years of serving Polixenes (whom he addresses
as "sir," in contrast to his use of "my lord" for
Leontes), he is called back home: "I desire to lay my
bones there. Besides, *the penitent King, my master, hath
sent for me*, to whose feeling sorrows I might be some
allay (or I o'erween to think so), which is another
spur to my departure" (IV.ii.6–9; emphasis mine).

The Tempest's account of the problem of obedience
forces into the open the contradictions which vex
absolutism's amalgamation of politics and religion.
Further, the recollection of the repressed differences
between political and religious spheres is made to
take place as an aspect of the process of interpretation. Once we realize that Gonzalo is guilty of
complicity in Prospero's overthrow, that he obeyed
Alonso's command to cast Prospero and Miranda
adrift, we will want to know why we should not
view him as a mere time-server. From Prospero's
viewpoint, Gonzalo's obedience to his master (even
though it has entailed Prospero's suffering and near-
death) is praiseworthy because political obedience
guarantees the stability of government. Prospero's
own experience with disobedient and treacherous
subjects (Antonio and Caliban) underlies his praise
of Gonzalo, whom he finds "good" both because
Gonzalo tempered his immoral act by charitably providing food and other necessities and because Gonzalo did not allow his charity to violate the terms of
his assignment:

O good Gonzalo,
My true preserver, and a loyal sir
To him thou follow'st!
(V.i.68–70)

This insight into the conditions of Prospero's
praise of Gonzalo would have allowed Shakespeare's
audience to see the politics of *The Tempest* as alto-

gether harsher and more reflective of the culpable
nature of all public action than the politics of *The
Winter's Tale*. For us as well, the idea that Gonzalo is
guilty of an act tantamount to murder means that he
is not what we have been used to thinking he was.
He might be either a time-server (Berger's view) or a
man who has subverted the integrity of conscience
rather than the integrity of obedience (my view).
What he cannot be is merely a doddering courtier—
insignificant in terms of the play as a whole. That
Prospero is aware of the guilt of the man he chooses
to praise as "Holy Gonzalo, honorable man" (V.i.62)
suggests the fullness of Prospero's acknowledgement
of the moral cost of preserving political hierarchy.

Gonzalo's guilt valorizes his conduct and speech.
His scorn of Antonio and Sebastian in II.i. has been
noted (Orgel II.i.180–82n), but not the way his scorn
shifts what would normally be the distribution of
ridicule in this kind of scene. Conventionally, when
two or more characters defame another character
in asides, the third bears the full weight of ridicule
(e.g., *Twelfth Night*, II.v; *Cymbeline*, I.ii; II.i). In *The
Tempest*, II.i, in contrast, Gonzalo hears and understands Antonio's and Sebastian's "asides" (Shakespeare signals this variation of the convention at
ll. 19, 166–70 [Orgel II.i.10–12n]). Therefore, instead
of being the butt of their mockery, Gonzalo is shown
as being tolerant and even contemptuous of their ineffectual cynicism:

ALONSO: Prithee no more; thou dost talk nothing to
me.
GONZALO: I do well believe your Highness, and did
it to minister occasion to these gentlemen, who
are of such sensible and nimble lungs that they
always use to laugh at nothing.   (II.i.171–75)

The "nothing" to which Gonzalo refers consists of
a passage borrowed from Montaigne's essay "Of the
Caniballes." His denigration of his own "golden age"
speech, of course, reveals his awareness of its naiveté
and so disarms Antonio's and Sebastian's ridicule.
More important, Gonzalo's self-consciously edenic
and egalitarian fantasy reflects the weight of the
crime which was required by his station in a hierarchical political culture. Interestingly, Gonzalo's main
additions to Montaigne consist in both an emphasis
on boundaries or borders and a catalog of weapons,
which together perhaps recall the "treacherous army"
(I.ii.128) that invaded Milan. Florio's 1603 translation of Montaigne (qtd. in Kermode 146) has "parti-

tion"—division of property—where Shakespeare has "Bourn, bound of land":

> I' th' commonwealth I would, by contraries,
> Execute all things; for no kind of traffic
> Would I admit; no name of magistrate;
> Letters should not be known; riches, poverty,
> And use of service, none; contract, succession,
> *Bourn, bound of land,* tilth; vineyard, none;
> No use of metal, corn, or wine, or oil;
> No occupation; all men idle, all;
> And women too, but innocent and pure;
> No sovereignty—
> . . . . All things in common nature should produce
> Without sweat or endeavor: treason, felony,
> *Sword, pike, knife, gun, or need of any engine,*
> Would I not have. . . .
> (II.i.148–63; emphasis mine)

Gonazlo's encomium to Providence toward the end of the play also registers the burden of his crime, and his rejoicing signals his surprise at the sudden recuperation of the moral integrity he had chosen to subvert "when he was not his own." The last two lines span the ideological poles of absolutism. On one side is obedience: no man is "his own" since each man is determined by his station (Kermode V.i.213n); and on the other side is conscience: each man *is himself* because each values himself according to the integrity of his conscience:

> Was Milan thrust from Milan, that his issue
> Should become kings of Naples? O, rejoice
> Beyond a common joy, and set it down
> With gold on lasting pillars: in one voyage
> Did Claribel her husband find at Tunis,
> And Ferdinand, her brother, found a wife
> When he himself was lost; Prospero his dukedom
> In a poor isle; and all of us, ourselves,
> When no man was his own.　　(V.i.205–13)

Gonzalo's commitment to political obedience is grounded as well on the problem of epistemological uncertainty. His skepticism with respect to the human capacity either to determine or to predict the consequences of actions is clear in his surprise at the happy ending of his own narrative, in his praise of the gods who "chalk'd forth the way / Which brought us hither" (V.i.203–04). Uncertainty about the ramifications of actions undermines evaluation of their moral status at a level above that of the motivation of the actor. For example, Henry's divorce from Katherine in *Henry VIII* is immoral at the motivational level because the king's desire for Anne Bullen

is at least as important as his wish to provide a male heir. In terms of consequences, however, the divorce is praiseworthy, since the offspring of Henry's marriage to Anne Bullen is the infant who will become Queen Elizabeth.

Both Gonzalo's suspension of judgment and his deference to higher powers indicate his acute sense of the limits placed upon action by uncertainty. He believes that the acts he performs cannot be meaningful in themselves (that is, that he cannot be certain of their meaning). He assumes that his acts have meaning only in terms of a larger hierarchical structure which includes the political, natural and cosmic worlds. The storm-scene (I.i.) provides a key instance of Gonzalo's hierarchical structuring of experience: in the face of imminent death which levels and demystifies conventional social categories (see the Boatswain's critique of hierarchy, ll. 16–27), Gonzalo preserves political order by enjoining the others to "assist" the king and prince at prayers. In contrast to the Boatswain's radically individualistic response to the threat of death—"None that I more love than myself"—Gonzalo draws a politically conservative lesson from the same threat—"The King and Prince at prayers, let's assist them, / For our case is as theirs" (ll. 54–55). Further, Gonzalo interprets the storm itself in terms of hierarchy, so that the wildness of nature which jeopardizes hierarchy (overturns it from the Boatswain's viewpoint) is seen to be merely an expression of hierarchy, an unwelcome but valorizing effect of divine agency whose import cannot be known but must be accepted nevertheless: "The wills above be done! but I would fain die a dry death" (ll. 67–68).

Political obedience is supported here by the conjoining of hierarchy with the uncertainty which undermines personal moral judgment. This does not mean that the moral implications of acts are of no consequence, but it does follow that the full moral import of any act cannot be known by the actor at the moment he or she performs it, and that the investiture of action with meaning must be projected into the future. To plot the movement of history along the lines of the "fortunate fall" (as Shakespeare does in *The Winter's Tale, The Tempest,* and *Henry VIII*) arrests time's unending motion toward futurity, providing an authoritative moment of closure which crystallizes the meaning of individual acts. The "fortunate" ending of *The Tempest* reveals the mixed nature of Gonzalo's participation in the overthrow of Prospero. The fact that

Prospero has regained his dukedom, that Gonzalo's charity was conducive to Prospero's survival, and that Gonzalo maneuvered in order to preserve political hierarchy, suggests that although Gonzalo's act was tragically culpable, it has nevertheless been redeemed by the providential ordering of history.

It is true that the "fortunate" ending of the play barely manages to contain the subversive energies which threaten it: Caliban's credibility as a subversive, the obduracy of Antonio and Sebastian, Prospero's bitterness, Gonzalo's crime itself, the fact that the marriage accomplishes the very Neapolitan takeover of Milan which Prospero has decried. The point, however, is that these energies, while not erased, are contained for audience-members inclined to take sides with authority. In terms of my argument, the fact that an astute modern critic such as Anne Barton has judged the *felix culpa* ending to be deliberately flawed by uncontrolled subversive energies (37–39) should be seen, again, to indicate the lack of authorial policing of the production of meaning, and the changeability and historical specificity of the meaning of works in the literary field.

The particular historical context of *The Tempest*'s implied argument for obedience consists in the foreign threat to English sovereignty posed by European Catholic powers during the sixteenth and early seventeenth centuries. The 1570 *Homily against Disobedience* followed upon the rising of Catholic forces in the north of England (a rebellion fomented by expectations of Spanish military assistance) and upon the papal excommunication of Elizabeth (MacCaffrey 330–71).

The absolutist implications of the "problem of Gonzalo" do not, therefore, reflect primarily a general state of anxiety concerning lower-class rebellion (as Gary Schmidgall has argued [171–214]); nor do they suggest the Hobbesian idea that the political order is fundamentally artificial, the state of nature being a "war of all against all" which must be controlled by unquestioning submission to a ruler (as has been suggested by Jan Kott [272–73]). On the contrary, *The Tempest*'s endorsement of political obedience constitutes, in the broadest terms, a nationalist reaction to a threat which was seen to be primarily foreign rather than primarily domestic, in particular the danger of Spanish Catholic subornation of disaffected elements within the English Protestant commonwealth. The central threat to political order and national sovereignty, both in *The Tempest* and in Elizabethan and Jacobean England, was seen to consist in the intervention by foreign powers through the agency of dissident elements within the nation. This is the pattern in *The Tempest* where Prospero's throne is usurped by Antonio in collusion with the King of Naples (a betrayal that costs Milan both its *de jure* ruler and its sovereignty), and where, even in extremely reduced circumstances, Prospero's rule is threatened a second time by the domestic malcontent Caliban in league with the foreign invaders Stephano and Trinculo. In both cases, the internal menace to the political order is essentially powerless until it is abetted by a foreign master.

The patterning of sedition, invasion and usurpation in *The Tempest* is homologous with the popular conception of England's geopolitical situation throughout the Elizabethan and Jacobean period, according to which the English were the embattled representatives of apostolic Christianity, surrounded and vulnerable to subornation by the antichristian empire of Spain and Rome (Haller *passim*). Accordingly, I would argue that the conventional identification of Catholic fifth-column activity with resistance theory constituted the central determining factor in Shakespeare's audience's interpretation of the political meaning of *The Tempest*. To suggest this, of course, is not to preclude the possibility of subversive interpretations of the play in Shakespeare's time; however, it does mean that the normative meaning of *The Tempest* for Shakespeare's audience would have been conservative. Shakespeare's audience would have solved the "problem of Gonzalo" in a way productive of an argument in favor of political obedience; and the ending of the play, while allowing for the continuing operation of subversive forces within the body politic, would nonetheless have redeemed and valorized Gonzalo's choice of obedience over morality.

Ariel's last image of Gonzalo is evocative of the costs attendant upon Gonzalo's choice of obedience over conscience. The image suggests how structure itself can produce shelter even out of materials which are inherently unsound. Gonzalo's beard is figured as a shelter fashioned out of reeds, with reeds also being the metaphor used to symbolize Ferdinand's moral weakness in the face of death: "Ferdinand, / With hair up-staring (then like reeds, not hair), / Was the first man that leapt" (I.ii.212–14):

> but chiefly
> 'Him that you term'd, sir, "the good old Lord Gonzalo,"
> His tears run down his beard like winter's drops
> From eaves of reeds.   (V.i.14–17)

The contradictions of English Renaissance political culture are figured in Gonzalo's face. Absolutism's enhancement of political obedience *as loyalty* provides shelter from "winter's drops," but the drops do not represent a "natural" affliction. Instead they represent Gonzalo's ideologically determined sorrow for culpable acts which were themselves determined by the idea of obedience. Finally, in terms of *The Tempest*'s interrogation and endorsement of political obedience in 1611, Gonzalo's weeping is earnest of his determination to persevere in the guilty business of government, and in this respect his attitude is like Prospero's bitter willingness to return into the world.[3]

Notes

1. For a brief overview of the issue of political obedience in the period, see Greaves; for a masterful survey of political theory in the period, see Skinner.
2. All Shakespeare quotations are from *The Riverside Shakespeare*.
3. An earlier version of this essay was presented at the CEMERS Renaissance Conference, 1987: I thank the members of that meeting for their instructive questions, and also my colleague Kay Stockholder for her valuable critique of a more recent version.

Works Cited

Barker, Francis, and Peter Hulme. "Nymphs and reapers heavily vanish: The Discursive Contexts of *The Tempest*." *Alternative Shakespeares*. Ed. John Drakakis. London: Methuen, 1985. 191–205.

Barton (Righter), Anne. "Introduction." *The Tempest*. Ed. Barton. Harmondsworth: Penguin, 1968.

Berger, Harry, Jr. "Miraculous Harp: A Reading of *The Tempest*." *Shakespeare Studies* 5 (1969): 253–83.

Breight, Curt. "'Treason doth never prosper': *The Tempest* and the Discourse of Treason." *Shakespeare Quarterly* 41.1 (1990): 1–28.

Brown, Paul. "'This thing of darkness I acknowledge mine': *The Tempest* and the Discourse of Colonialism." *Political Shakespeare: New Essays in Cultural Materialism*. Ed. Jonathan Dollimore and Alan Sinfield. Ithaca: Cornell UP, 1985. 48–71.

Certain Sermons or Homilies (1547) and A Homily against Disobedience and Wilful Rebellion (1570). Ed. Ronald B. Bond. Toronto: U of Toronto P, 1987.

Cleland, James. *The Institution of a Young Noble Man* (1607). Facsimile rpt. New York: Scholars, 1948.

Daly, James. "The Idea of Absolute Monarchy in Seventeenth-Century England." *Historical Journal* 21.2 (1970): 227–50.

Donne, John. *Poetical Works*. Ed. Herbert Grierson, 1912. Rpt. London: Oxford UP, 1966.

Erlich, Bruce. "Shakespeare's Colonial Metaphor: On the Social Function of Theatre in *The Tempest*." *Science & Society* 41.1 (1977): 43–65.

Goldberg, Jonathan. *James I and the Politics of Literature: Jonson, Donne, and Their Contemporaries*. Baltimore: Johns Hopkins UP, 1983.

Greaves, Richard L. "Concepts of Political Obedience in Late Tudor England: Conflicting Perspectives." *Journal of British Studies* 22.1 (1982): 23–34.

Greenblatt, Stephen. "Learning to Curse: Aspects of Linguistic Colonialism in the Sixteenth Century." *First Images of America: The Impact of the New World on the Old*. Ed. Fredi Chiappelli et al. 2 vols. Berkeley: U of California P, 1976. 2: 561–80.

Haller, William. *Foxe's Book of Martyrs and the Elect Nation*. London: Cape, 1963.

Hulme, Peter. *Colonial Encounters: Europe and the Native Caribbean, 1492–1797*. London: Methuen, 1986.

Jonson, Ben. *Neptune's Triumph for the Return of Albion. The Complete Masques*. Ed. Stephen Orgel. New Haven: Yale UP, 1969.

Kermode, Frank, ed. *The Tempest*. Arden Shakespeare. Cambridge: Harvard UP, 1958.

Kott, Jan. *Shakespeare Our Contemporary*. Trans. Boreslaw Taborski. New York: Anchor, 1966.

Leininger, Lorie Jerrell. "Cracking the Code of *The Tempest*." *Bucknell Review* 25 (1980): 121–31.

MacCaffrey, Wallace. *The Shaping of the Elizabethan Regime*. Princeton: Princeton UP, 1968.

Munden, R. C. "James I and 'the growth of mutual distrust': King, Commons, and Reform, 1603–1604." *Faction and Parliament: Essays on Early Stuart History*. Ed. Kevin Sharpe. Oxford: Clarendon, 1978: 43–72.

Orgel, Stephen, ed. *The Tempest*. The Oxford Shakespeare. Oxford: Clarendon, 1987.

Patterson, Annabel. *Shakespeare and the Popular Voice*. Oxford: Blackwell, 1989.

Ponet, John. *A short treatise of politike power, and of the true obedience which subjects owe to Kings and other civill Governours*, 1556. Rpt. [London], 1649.

Russell, Conrad. "Parliamentary History in Perspective 1604–1629." *History* 61 (1976): 1–27.

Schmidgall, Gary. *Shakespeare and the Courtly Aesthetic.* Berkeley: U of California P, 1981.

Seamon, Roger. "Poetics against Itself: On the Self-Destruction of Modern Scientific Criticism." *PMLA* 104.3 (1989): 294–305.

Shakespeare, William. *The Riverside Shakespeare.* Ed. G. Blakemore Evans. Boston: Houghton, 1974.

Sharpe, Kevin. "Parliamentary History 1603–1629: In or Out of Perspective?" *Faction and Parliament: Essays on Early Stuart History.* Ed. Sharpe. Oxford: Clarendon, 1978. 1–42.

Siegel, Paul N. "Historical Ironies in *The Tempest.*" *Shakespeare Jahrbuch* 119 (1983): 104–11.

Skinner, Quentin. *The Foundations of Modern Political Thought.* 2 vols. Cambridge: Cambridge UP, 1978.

Skura, Meredith Anne. "Discourse and the Individual: The Case of Colonialism in *The Tempest.*" *Shakespeare Quarterly* 40.1 (1989): 42–69.

Sommerville, J. P. *Politics and Ideology in England, 1603–1640.* London: Longman, 1986.

Stockholder, Kay. *Dream Works: Lovers and Families in Shakespeare's Plays.* Toronto: U of Toronto P, 1987.

Strier, Richard. "Faithful Servants: Shakespeare's Praise of Disobedience." *The Historical Renaissance: New Essays on Tudor and Stuart Literature and Culture.* Ed. Heather Dubrow and Richard Strier. Chicago: U of Chicago P, 1988: 104–33.

Wormald, Jenny. "James VI & I: Two Kings or One?" *History* 68.223 (1983): 187–209.

Yachnin, Paul. "*A Game of Chess:* Thomas Middleton's 'Praise of Folly.'" *Modern Language Quarterly* 48.1 (1987): 107–23.

———. "The Powerless Theater." *English Literary Renaissance,* forthcoming.

APPLICATION

Allen C. Austin's essay is doubly useful: it gives us a survey of the various readings of Keats's ode, and it gives us a direct application of one carefully argued historical approach to literature. After describing and classifying many different interpretations of the last lines of the ode, Austin offers to resolve the long-standing controversies by applying E. D. Hirsch's concepts of "coherence" and "correspondence" to determine which interpretation is most probably "valid." (Since these terms are used differently elsewhere in my book, it is well to note that here "correspondence" refers to the fit between the interpretation and the parts of the poem, whereas "coherence" relates the interpretation to the author's "psychological and philosophical stance.") As Austin demonstrates, several different and even opposing interpretations may "correspond" to the poem in that they can explain all of the poem's parts. This is the formalist's criterion, and Austin, echoing Hirsch, points out that this criterion gives us no way to choose between opposing but equally possible meanings. But when we ask which of these meanings John Keats is most likely to have meant, the number of possibilities diminishes rapidly. Thus Austin adopts Hirsch's fundamental assumptions, which are also the fundamental assumptions of Watson and most traditional literary historians: literary meaning can be determined, and it is finally determined by reference to the author's probable intentions. These are in turn determined by careful examination of the documentary evidence surrounding the poem's composition. In this case, Austin refers extensively to Keats's letters and his other poems to reconstruct the author's typical "psychological and philosophical stance" as he builds a case for claiming that only one of many possible meanings is also Keats's probable meaning and therefore the most "valid" interpretation.

Toward Resolving Keats's Grecian Urn Ode

Allen C. Austin

Reprinted by permission from *Neophilologus* 70 (1986): 615–29. Copyright © 1986 by *Neophilologus*.

The conclusion of Keats's "Ode on a Grecian Urn" remains a much-disputed literary crux, one that invites a discussion of critical methodology. The hundreds of explicators the poem has attracted—many of them concentrating on the last lines—continue to search out exactly what the urn is counseling, what the tone of its counsel is and how that counsel figures into the ode it concludes. Analyses of the final stanza fall into half a dozen seemingly irreconcilable schools or types. How do we judge among these contending interpretations? What makes one more valid than another? These are issues that pertain not only to the Grecian Urn ode, but to the processes and judgments of criticism as well.

E. D. Hirsch offers an effective way of approaching such dilemmas. In *Validity of Interpretation*, he suggests, reasonably enough, when "interpretive disagreements . . . occur, genuine knowledge is possible only if someone takes the responsibility of adjudicating the issue in the light of all that is known."[1] This involves determining a general standard of critical sanity or sensibleness, identifying the various interpretations (in this case, of Keats's lines), examining the evidence relating to each (including biographical and historical), and then judging which interpretation is most probably valid.

In order to compare and judge contending interpretations, we need a standard on which to base our judgments. If we propose "what the text says," we have a standard, but a rather loose one. Any sequence of words, such as "Beauty is truth," can be interpreted in a number of different ways, all equally plausible. In an attempt to set up a more reliable standard of interpretation, one based on the actual linguistic situation of shared meanings, Hirsch proposes the standard of "coherence"—the relationship of meaning to the author's psychological and philosophical stance, to what the author is likely to mean under a particular set of circumstances. Hirsch's second major criterion is "correspondence"—an accounting for all the parts of the work and their relationship to the whole. In weighing contending interpretations, the critic should first examine the evidence in relation to coherence and correspondence. He should then conclude that one of the interpretations is probably valid or that not enough evidence exists to resolve the issue.

Although there are numerous interpretations of the concluding lines of Keats's Ode, each of them expresses one of six contending perspectives: that beauty and truth are the same (1) in life, (2) in Keats's dream world, (3) in some Platonic or Absolute reality, (4) in the world of the Urn, (5) in imaginative or artistic perception, and (6) in eternity.[2]

Critics of the late nineteenth and early twentieth centuries who maintained that beauty refers to truth in life judged such a belief as false or "immature." But recently, advocates of this interpretation argue that this belief represents the mature Keats, who directly confronts life, rejecting the substitution of a dream world for the real world. Keats, they point out, states that "a World of Pains and troubles" is necessary "to school an Intelligence and make it a soul."[3] Although in the "Ode on a Grecian Urn" he represents a happy make-believe world of love and music, it is a frozen and static world. Like Wallace Stevens, Keats implies that process, involving decay and death, is necessary to beauty; the only beauty of genuine and lasting satisfaction is a truth that includes the fact of mutability.

The opposite of this view is the belief that the lines refer to Keats's dream world. E. C. Pettet describes this attitude:

> out of his own actual unhappiness he is indulging in a dream of supreme felicity, and the constituents of this are such as no true mystic would for a moment accept: sexual passion, undecaying physical beauty, and an eternity of songs and poesy . . . The arrested moment is a necessary condition of his vision because happiness, as here conceived, is a fresh throbbing state of expectancy, and unhappiness the exhaustion and disillustionment of consummation.[4]

The euphoric scenes are imagined; the unheard melodies are sweeter than heard melodies; and imagined love is superior to actual love ("For ever painting, and for ever young; / All breathing human passion far above"). Keats frequently expresses the idea that imagination is superior to reality: "Ever let the fancy roam, / Pleasure never is at home." The Ode, then, expresses his belief that an imagined world of "beauty and sensuous life" is far above "the poor harsh real world of everyday life."[5]

Similar to the idea that the Ode portrays a dream world is the idea that it is Platonic; the world set apart from the real world is representative of absolute reality: "Beauty is eternal; in its concrete reality it is a symbol, a 'shadow' of the absolute; its tangible, visible being is merely a mode of revealing divine, ideal, immutable truth."[6] In the world of the Absolute, "Beauty is truth, truth beauty." That is all that Man knows or needs to know on earth.

A view that concentrates on "all ye need to know" is the interpretation that beauty and truth are the same (only) in the world of the Urn. The ideal world portrayed by the Urn is contrasted to the real world of pain. When the Urn, from its limited perspective, states that "Beauty is truth, truth beauty," the poet responds that that is all the Urn or the figures on the Urn know or need to know. Man, in the world of struggle, needs to know many things, but the Urn or the figures need to know only that beauty and truth are the same.

The interpretation that has gained the widest acceptance is that the Ode implies that "imaginative insight . . . embodies the basic and fundamental perception of man and nature." Accordingly, the Ode is a "parable of the nature of poetry, and of art in general," the scenes on the Urn reflecting "an imaginative perception of essentials."[7] As a pastoral "historian," the Urn expresses truth, exemplifying the esthetic principle that beauty and truth are one in art. This is the only knowledge that Man is likely to get on earth, and it is the only knowledge that he *has* to have. (Some interpreters who hold this view maintain that this message, stated from the Urn's limited perspective, is to Keats false. The Urn says that in its world of art, beauty and truth are one. From the Urn's perspective, that is all that Man knows on earth and all he needs to know.)

The sixth and last interpretation of the Ode is that the Urn is a symbol of eternity, where beauty and truth are one. The major external support of this interpretation is Keats's "Adam's dream" letter to Benjamin Bailey—in which Keats states his belief that the imaginative perception of beauty is a reflection of eternity and that earthly happiness is repeated in eternity in a "finer tone." In four other letters, Keats states his belief or his desire to believe in eternity, particularly an eternity of sexual love. Much of Keats's poetry, including his longest poem, *Endymion,* also deals with eternity or eternal love. In "Ode on a Grecian Urn," the Urn doubly portends eternity because as a product of the imagination it reflects eternity and as a narrator ("historian") it depicts scenes of eternity. The Urn is a friend to Man, consoling him with its message that beauty in eternity is truth; that is all that Man knows or needs to know of eternity.

All these interpretations have some merit, but each faces problems that make validity difficult to establish. Critics who defend the idea that beauty refers to life put the emphasis on "truth," interpreting the concluding lines to mean that truth—the accurate representation of reality—is beauty, or the beautiful; truth, or a true rendering of the world, is necessary for genuine beauty. This interpretation is based on a valid assumption—that Keats is not an escapist living in a pleasant dream world. But it fails to demonstrate that Keats also believes that representing natural process is essential to artistic beauty. On the contrary, "Ode on a Grecian Urn" presents imagined melodies as superior to actual ones. Keats ends the Ode, according to the "life" interpretation, by denigrating the world of the Urn, of the false artificial pastoral. "O Attic shape," for example, is not then an apostrophe praising the Urn but a sign of Keats's disenchantment. Even if it could be established that Keats believes that natural process is necessary to beauty, there is no evidence that he believes that Man knows and needs to know *only* that truth is beauty.

The second interpretation, that the Ode portrays a dream world, is convincing up to its treatment of the concluding lines. E. C. Pettet, in his analysis, points out aspects of the poem that have generally been ignored—that Keats's ideal is not a consummation but anticipation: "happiness . . . is a fresh, throbbing state of expectancy." But the "dreamworld" interpretation fails to give a satisfactory explanation of the concluding lines. As numerous commentators have noted, Keats fully commits himself to life, extolling both philosophical knowledge and ethical action (*Letters,* II, 139, 146). He would have rejected the idea that a dream world is all that Man knows or needs to know.

The Platonic interpretation provides a more logical explanation of the Ode's concluding lines: beauty is truth, and truth is beauty in the ideal world of the Absolute. According to this interpretation, what seems to be a paradox, the oneness of beauty and truth, is not a paradox. The problem, however, is that there is no evidence that Keats, although familiar with Platonism, was himself a Platonist. In fact, the sensuous and sexual life he portrays in the Ode is not suggestive of Platonism. And even if it could be demonstrated that Keats was a Platonist, it is not likely that he would have believed that Platonic truth is all that Man knows or needs to know.

In some ways, the most satisfactory explanation of the concluding lines is provided by the interpretation that beauty and truth are the same in the world of the Urn. There is then no contradiction in "all / Ye know . . . and all ye need to know"; the figures in the ideal world of the Urn know only beauty and need to know nothing else. This interpretation, however, faces major difficulties. First, it cannot account for the phrase "on earth," which is not likely to refer to the figures on the Urn. Throughout the poem, Keats stresses that the figures inhabit a world that is entirely different from the world of woe. Second, "that is all / Ye know on earth and all ye need to know" appears in this interpretation to be a postscript. The Urn, a friend to Man, proclaims, "Beauty is truth, truth beauty," and then the poet adds, like an afterthought, that that is all the figures know or the Urn knows or needs to know. The Urn's statement, logically a part of its role of providing consolation, would not be a consolation, but a reminder to Man that he himself lives in a world of woe. Finally, such a statement to the Urn or the figures is inappropriate. The last stanza is totally devoted to enthusiastic praise addressed to the Urn. If the poet at the end addresses the figures, then he makes an abrupt shift from the Urn to the figures. If he addresses the Urn, he makes an abrupt shift in tone. In either case, he turns from praise to evaluation, delivering a lecture on what is obvious: the Urn or the figures need to know only that beauty is truth.

The fifth interpretation, that beauty refers to imaginative or artistic perception, is based on the valid idea that Keats places great value on the power of imagination. As he states in the Bailey letter, he has more confidence in imagination than in consecutive reason. Although he never fully makes up his mind on the place of art in society, he is convinced of its great value. Whatever his occasional doubts, he knew that poetry was the center of his life, and he hoped that it would do some good in the world. Could not poetry be a moral force in the sense of giving Man insight and raising his spirits? In the Ode, he takes the position, as Cleanth Brooks argues, that the Urn in some sense gives Man insight. Could Keats, then, be saying that beauty is truth in art and that that is all Man knows or needs to know? Although Keats may have believed that in art truth to human emotions is beauty or value (his position on this issue has not been precisely determined), he did not believe that this knowledge is all that Man needs. Only an uncompromising esthete would assert that art is Man's only intellectual necessity, and few interpreters would maintain that this was Keats's stance.

The view that beauty refers to art but that the Urn utters what Keats believes is a false philosophy detracts from the Urn as a consolation to Man. If the Urn's message is false, then the Urn is a false guide. If the view that the Urn erroneously says that beauty is truth depended solely on the characterization of the Urn, it might have validity. But we cannot ignore the role of the poet, who feels that the Urn and the message it implies is a consolation to Man. What the Urn says is in some sense true to Keats, whatever it may be to anyone else.

The final interpretation, that beauty refers to eternity, is based on the proposition that imagination reflects eternity and that eternity is the repetition in a "finer tone" of earthly happiness. The Urn, as a product of imagination (explained in the Bailey letter), and the scene of love and happiness symbolize and portend eternity. Keats compares the Urn to eternity, which he perceives as not subject to reason, only intuition. As he contemplates the Urn, feeling that he is "mounted on the Wings of Imagination," he becomes convinced, at least for the moment, that beauty is the truth of eternity.

This interpretation views not only the Urn but also the two scenes as symbols of eternity. Only one scene, however, is portrayed as eternal happiness, the scene of love and music. The other scene of eternity is one of desolation. Throughout the Ode, Keats views the figures in two different ways: as representative of idealized life (lines 5–10, Stanza I, and lines 1–7, Stanza IV) and as symbols of eternity (lines 5–10, Stanza II, lines 1–7, Stanza III, and lines 8–10, Stanza IV). In the last part of Stanza I and the first part of Stanza IV, Keats does not know precisely what life is being represented, except that it is Grecian. He looks at the "leaf-fring'd legend" as he would look at a painting. What life is being portrayed? He does not answer this question, except to say that the first scene is "wild ecstasy" and the second, "pious" worship. In Stanza II and the last three lines of Stanza IV, he transforms the figures into symbols of eternal life, of ecstasy and of desolation. In this attitude toward the Urn itself, however, Keats is consistent. Keats does not think of the Urn as being itself permanent but as symbolizing permanence—that is, eternity. Thus, even though Stanza IV portrays an eternity of desolation, the Ode, with its scene of ecstatic love, emphasizes eternal happiness. This interpretation, like the others, faces the problem of the meaning of "all," for Keats could not have believed that knowledge of eternity is all the knowledge Man has or needs.

Each of the interpretations assumes that beauty refers to life or Keats's dream world or Platonic reality or the world of the Urn or the imaginative perception or eternity. Those who maintain that the poet speaks the last line and a half to the Urn could argue that Keats does not believe that any of these propositions is all that Man needs to know. This argument cannot be refuted unless we can show that there is an implied phrase after "on earth":

> When old age shall this generation waste,
> Thou shalt remain, in midst of other woe
> Than ours, a friend to man, to whom thou say'st,
> "Beauty is truth, truth beauty," — that is all
> Ye know on earth, and all ye need to know.

If the poet speaks the last part of the concluding lines to the Urn or the figures, the problem of the meaning of "all" is solved, but we are left with the contradictory phrase "on earth" (not to mention the other objections to this interpretation). If Keats, however, is referring to eternity, the Urn could be saying that in its world, which is an emblem of the world of eternity, beauty is truth. The line could then read, "that is all/Ye know *on earth*" of eternity. What else could be Keats's purpose in using "on earth" except to imply a life opposite to life on earth? That beauty is truth is all Man knows on earth of eternal life, but apparently he would learn more when he experienced it. At the time Keats was writing, transcendent ideas were common, discussed, for example, by both the conventional Benjamin Bailey, Keats's friend studying for the clergy, and the unorthodox Leigh Hunt, who urges belief in an afterlife.[8] It seems reasonable to conclude that Keats entertains such ideas in the Ode, as he does in the Bailey letter and in *Endymion*.

Even if Keats were not convinced of the validity of this idea, he could write as if he thought, at least for the moment, that it were true. Could he not be saying that the Urn is a friend to Man in a world of woe, offering the consolation that beauty is truth in eternity? That is all that Man knows on earth of eternity and all that he needs to know. This reading, requiring an implied "of eternity," offers less difficulty than the reading that Keats speaks to the marble figures on the Urn as if they were on earth. It also encompasses all the other readings except the first (that beauty refers to life). Keats's dream world is what he imagines eternity to be. Also, this world is "Platonic" in the sense that it represents for Keats, at least as a speculation, the core of reality. Most important of all, the world of the Urn itself is a symbol of eternity. Finally, Keats's mode of apprehending eternity is through imaginative perception; therefore, the idea of eternity encompasses this perception.

The question that arises is how Keats could have expected the reader to understand that following "on earth" is an implied "of eternity." Keats could have had such an expectation if in his own mind the Urn is clearly a symbol of eternity. Throughout the poem, he concentrates on eternity, explicitly comparing the Urn to eternity. According to the Bailey letter, beauty ("What the imagination seizes as Beauty") is truth ("must be truth"). This truth, as the letter makes clear, is the truth of eternity. By giving "truth" this special meaning, Keats requires of the reader an understanding of the content of the poem. Under the inspiration of the moment, "mounted on the Wings of Imagination so high," Keats wrote, as in the Bailey letter, what he felt, without concerning himself with the problem of clarity. If the reader, however, understands that "truth" refers to eternity, he can understand an implied "of eternity" after "on earth." A reader who considers Keats's poems and letters knows that Keats would not under any circumstances mean that knowledge of eternity is the only knowledge that Man needs. Keats would have had to mean that earthly intimations of eternity are all the knowledge of *eternity* that Man needs.

This interpretation fully meets the criterion of coherence (relating meaning to the author's psychological and philosophical stance). Although we cannot establish that Keats believed consistently in eternity, we can establish that he tentatively proposes the idea and that he undoubtedly hoped for the kind of eternity he imagines. In his letter to Bailey (Nov. 1817), he sets forth in detail his concept of the nature of eternity and its relationship to imagination:

> I am certain of nothing but of the holiness of the Heart's affections and the truth of Imagination — What the imagination seizes as Beauty must be truth — whether it existed before or not — for I have the same Idea of all our Passions as of Love they are all in their sublime, creative of essential Beauty —

In a Word, you may know my favorite Speculation by my first Book and the little song I sent in my last [letter]—which is a representation from the fancy of the probable mode of operating in these Matters.

"What the imagination seizes as beauty must be truth" applies to both natural and artistic beauty. But in his examples, Keats chooses the beauty of the content of art, comparable to any product of the imagination, such as an imaginary face, to which he later alludes. The first example Keats gives, Book I of *Endymion,* is a dream of eternal love; the second, the song "O Sorrow," sent in Keats's previous letter to Bailey (Nov. 3) and included in Book IV of *Endymion* (146–181), is of the creation by sorrow of natural beauty, such as "white Rose bushes," "the glow worm Light," or the song of the nightingale. What the imagination perceives or creates as beauty—whether or not it exists in life—is truth:

> The Imagination may be compared to Adam's dream—he awoke and found it truth. I am the more zealous in this affair, because I have never yet been able to perceive how any thing can be known for truth by consequutive reasoning—and yet it must be—Can it be that even the greatest Philosopher ever arrived at his goal without putting aside numerous objections—However it may be, O for a Life of Sensations rather than of Thoughts! It is 'a Vision in the form of Youth' a Shadow of reality to come—and this consideration has further conv[i]nced me for it has come as auxiliary to another favorite Speculation of mine, that we shall enjoy ourselves here after by having what we called happiness on Earth repeated in a finer tone and so repeated.

Just as Adam in *Paradise Lost* (VIII, 452–490) awoke from a dream of Eve and found her real, man will awake in eternity to find that imagination is prophetic. Keats more zealously embraces this belief because he has more confidence in intuition than in "consequutive" reasoning, although he concedes that a philosopher, after "putting aside numerous objections," may discover truth. Keats himself desires a life of sensations rather than of thought. A life of sensations is an anticipation, a "Shadow of reality to come—a consideration" that has further convinced him of the truth of imagination because it has occurred in conjunction with another speculation, that eternity is a refinement of earthly happiness: "we shall enjoy ourselves here after by having what we called happiness on Earth repeated in a finer tone and so repeated." Keats elaborates in the letter:

Adam's dream will do here and seems to be a conviction that Imagination and its empyreal reflection is the same as human Life and its spiritual repetition. But as I was saying—the simple imaginative Mind may have its rewards in the repeti[ti]on of its own silent Working coming continually on the spirit with a fine suddenness—to compare great things with small—have you never by being surprised with an old Melody—in a delicious place—by a delicious voice, fe[l]t over again your very speculations and surmises at the time it first operated on your soul—do you not remember forming to yourself the singer's face more beautiful than it was possible and yet with the elevation of the Moment you did not think so—even then you were mounted on the Wings of Imagination so high—that the Prototype must be here after—that delicious face you will see. (I, 184–185)[9]

The dream of eternity, like Adam's dream, suffices on earth: its existence is evidence that the relationship between the imagination and eternity is the same as the relationship between refined earthly beauty, a product of the imagination, and its repetition in eternity. The beauty created by imagination is the same as the beauty of eternity. We may imagine the extraordinarily beautiful face of a singer of an old melody, and this imaginative act may be continually repeated. If we hear the song, our imagination is reactivated. Such a continual dream of a beautiful face, like Adam's or Endymion's dream of supreme beauty, is "proof" of the existence of this face in eternity—"the Prototype . . . here after—that delicious face you will see."

Keats discusses immortality in four other letters. The first letter was written just after the death of his brother Tom in December of 1818: "I have scarce a doubt of immortality of some nature or other—neither had Tom" (II, 4). Later in the same letter he says, "That will be one of the grandeurs of immortality—there will be no space and consequently the only commerce between spirits will be by their intelligence of each other—when they will completely understand each other" (II, 5). In his "Soul-making" letter (April 1819), he assumes the existence of immortality: "I am speaking now in the highest terms for human nature admitting it to be immortal" (II, 102).

Keats's final statements on immortality were made after he had become ill. In a highly emotional letter to Fanny Brawne in June 1820, he expresses his desire for an immortality of love: "I long to believe in immortality I shall never be ab[le] to bid you an entire farewell. If I am destined to be happy with you here — how short is the longest Life — I wish to believe in immortality — I wish to live with you for ever" (II, 293). Finally, a few months before his death, in a letter to Charles Brown, he expresses his despair at leaving her: "The thought of leaving Miss Brawne is beyond every thing horrible — the sense of darkness coming over me — I eternally see her figure eternally vanishing ... Is there another Life? Shall I awake and find all this a dream? There must be we cannot be created for this sort of suffering" (II, 345–346).

Keats also expresses hopes of immortality in his poetry. In *Endymion* a man dreams of immortal love and finally achieves it, asserting that love is Man's highest good, not only as an earthly joy but also as a portent of heaven, love having the power "to make / Men's being mortal, immortal" (I, 843–844). The goddess Cynthia promises Endymion "endless heaven" (III, 1027), which he achieves through his love of an Indian maid, who is Cynthia in disguise. In "Epistle to J. H. Reynolds," the "material sublime," an object of beauty such as a sunset, portends eternity. In "Ode to Psyche," love is substituted for religion, and in "Ode to a Nightingale," the Nightingale represents eternity, although Keats is uncertain of the validity of his vision. In *The Fall of Hyperion,* Keats says that everyone "whose soul is not a clod" (I, 13) has visions of eternity, which the poet expresses and thus saves "Imagination from the sable chain / And dumb enchantment" (I, 9–11).

The "eternity" interpretation of the concluding lines of the Ode also meets the criterion of correspondence (accounting for all the parts of the work and their relationship to the whole). As has been frequently noted, Keats in *Endymion* says that heavenly Powers, who seldom reveal themselves to Man, "keep religious state, / ... And silent as a consecrated urn, / Hold sphery sessions for a season due" (III, 30–33). Grecian urns were, in fact, consecrated, originally used to preserve the ashes of the dead and to depict scenes of vibrant life. As S. R. Swaminathan points out, Leigh Hunt in 1817 published an article on Grecian urns in *The Round Table,* a publication with which Keats was familiar (*Letters,* I, 166). Hunt says that on the urns "were painted the most cheerful actions of the person departed, ... which seemed to keep up the idea of a vital principle, and to say, 'the creature who so did and so enjoyed itself cannot

be all gone.' The image of a vital principle and of an after-life, was, in fact, often and distinctly repeated on these vessels."[10]

The Urn's freshness and purity are stressed in the opening line of the Ode, in the metaphor "unravish'd bride of quietness," which has been interpreted, on the one hand, as praise of the Urn, and on the other, as to some extent a denigration, as an allusion to the Urn's limitations because an actual unravished bride would be in a state of unfulfillment. If, however, we view the terms of Keats's metaphor as applying in only one respect, then it is praise of the Urn: the Urn is ancient but as fresh and young looking as when it was created, a point about both the Urn and its scene of eternal love that Keats stresses. The interpretation of "unravish'd bride" as denigrating is based on the idea that Keats is ambivalent toward the Urn, that although he sees it as beautiful and eternal, he is aware that it is cold and lifeless. According to this view, the Urn in not being a part of the dynamic process of life is separated from both life's suffering and joy.

The idea that Keats is ambivalent toward the Urn is based on the argument that Keats contrasts eternal static love to transient dynamic love. But this is not what Keats does. In Stanza I, when he directs his attention to the figures, he views them as representative of some kind of idealized life, "Of deities or mortals, or of both, / In Tempe or the dales of Arcady." In Stanza II, when he addresses the figures, he transforms them into symbols of a special kind of eternity. He asks himself what life would be like if it were eternal but static. Contrary to what has usually been said about the Ode, he comes to the conclusion that such an eternally motionless life would be far superior to actual life; although the Lover cannot kiss, his love will always be fair. But even if Keats had found this life wanting, there would be no justification for saying that he denigrates the Urn. Although the figures are represented by the Urn, they are not symbols of art, but of a special kind of eternal life. Keats does not think of art in Stanzas II and III, much less speak unfavorably of it. When he does speak of the art of the Urn in Stanza I, he bestows the highest praise: the Urn can "express / A flowery tale more sweetly than our rhyme."

Keats's imagination imposes the limitations (from the standpoint of most readers) of immobility on eternal life, for if he can imagine the figures as alive, he can also imagine them as mobile. He begins in

Stanza II to find this motionless life appealing. In Stanza III, he becomes ecstatic, repeating "happy" six times in his enthusiastic praise of it. But we have often been told that such a life, without consummation, would not be satisfying, even though Keats imagines that it would be:

> More happy love! more happy, happy love!
> For ever warm and still to be enjoy'd,
> For ever panting, and for ever young.

For readers to say that such a state would not be pleasurable is irrelevant. Keats imagines that it would be and gives himself wholly to it; as E. C. Pettet says, Keats's ideal is one of eternal anticipation. The limitations of this ideal to others is beside the point.

The interpretation that there is consolation in the consummation of earthly as contrasted to eternal love cannot be justified on the basis of what the poem says:

> All breathing human passion far above,
> That leaves a heart high-sorrowful and cloy'd,
> A burning forehead, and a parching tongue.

Consummation or non-consummation is not relevant to these lines. Keats's point is that to him earthly love is painful, having nothing to recommend it, not even consummation. But we should not conclude that it is painful because it is consummated. The lines could, in fact, be a description of longing and frustration, of unsatisfied passion, that leaves a heart high sorrowful and cloyed (in the sense of being filled to bursting). A "burning forehead, and a parching tongue" is a vivid description of such a state. At any rate, Keats finds no consolation in earthly love. As unsatisfactory as this attitude may be to the reader, it *is* Keats's attitude. Keats imagines an eternal love of perfect bliss, whose very changelessness appeals to him—the steadfastness of a star, "pillow'd upon my fair love's ripening breast, / Awake for ever in a sweet unrest," a sharp contrast to a world "Where youth grows pale, and spectre-thin, and dies." Keats in no way sees this love of eternal anticipation as lifeless; his imagination transforms it into eternal euphoria. Although an eternity of sexual love is not commonly imagined, it is a natural and logical ideal for Keats, who devotes his longest poem to eternal sexual love and who idealizes sexual love in "The Eve of St. Agnes," "Bright Star," and "Ode to Psyche."

Keats does not delude himself that he is speaking of actual marble figures; he is not concerned with the permanence and lifelessness of art, but with the everlasting newness and freshness of eternity. For the moment, carried away on the "Wings of Imagination," he creates an eternal world of perfect bliss, contrasted to the world of suffering. Keats may not be consistent or remain long in this state, but he is at the time constructing a world of eternity that he finds attractive.

His eternity is one shaped according to his own desire, like the eternities he describes in Endymion:

> Anon they wander'd, by divine converse,
> Into Elysium; vieing to rehearse
> Each one of his own anticipated bliss.
> One felt heart-certain that he could not miss
> His quick gone love, among fair blossom'd boughs.
>
>   •   •   •
>
> Another wish'd, mid that eternal spring,
> To meet his rosy child, with feathery sails.
>
>   •   •   •
>
> Some were athirst in soul to see again
> Their fellow huntsmen o'er the wide champaign
> In times long past.   (I, 371–387)

The idea that the eternal love in the Ode is "not human" because "it is *above* all breathing passion" (Brooks, p. 146), "far above" being read as "separated from" rather than "superior to," is not justified by the context. Keats in Stanza I wonders what kind of life the figures represent. In Stanza II he imagines that they are humans in a life of eternity but they are immobile. His first reaction is to view this immobility as deprivation: "Bold Lover, never, never canst thou kiss." But on second thought, he views the situation of the Lover, whose love will remain forever young and fair, as an advantage. Readers, however, often respond as if Keats's initial reaction is maintained throughout. Cleanth Brooks asserts that Keats "is being perfectly fair to the terms of his metaphor" (p. 144). But why is Keats's choice of immobility fairness to the terms of his metaphor? Is he being unfair in lines 5–10, Stanza I, and lines 1–7, Stanza IV, when he imagines the figures as mobile? The fixed marble figures naturally suggest to him the idea of immobility, but since he views the figures as alive, his imagination is not restricted by the Urn. The situation is not determined by the Urn but by Keats's imagination. At the time that Keats wrote the Ode, his life was uncertain and unhappy. It is not surprising that he imagines an eternal love that has to him none of the disadvantages of earthly love. The eternal love of expectancy that he desires, as E. C. Pettet points out, is one that no mystic or idealist had imagined. But it is the one Keats chooses. To say that Keats's ideal is "not human" is true in the sense that it is eternal and unconsummated but untrue in the sense that it is lifeless or unsatisfying to Keats.

In the Stanza following the love scene, Keats shifts his vision, returning to the perspective of Stanza I, viewing the marble figures as representative of idealized life. He again addresses the Urn ("Who are these coming to the sacrifice?") and then the marble figures: "To what green altar, O mysterious priest, / Lead'st thou that heifer lowing at the skies . . .?" The scene Keats portrays is a communal religious experience, paralleling an example of the "material sublime" in his "Epistle to J. H. Reynolds": "Some Titian colours touch'd into real life," a religious ceremony involving the sacrifice of a "milkwhite heifer," witnessed by mariners who join in "hymn with those on land" (20–25). The scene in the Ode of the priest leading the heifer to sacrifice recalls the "happy pieties" of an earlier religious Age, with its "fond believing lyre, / When holy were the haunted forest boughs" ("Ode to Psyche"). The religious scene in the Ode is associated in Keats's mind with Man's concern for eternity. In *Endymion*, for example, Keats describes a scene in which worshipers gather and a priest prays to Pan as one who can give knowledge of eternity:

> Dread opener of the mysterious doors
> Leading to universal knowledge—see, . . .
> The many that are come to pay their vows
> With leaves about their brows. (I, 288–292)

Whatever may be the response of modern taste to the scene of the heifer being led to sacrifice, Keats views it as a scene of religious communion, of the "happy pieties" of a believing Age.

In the last three lines of the Stanza, however, Keats introduces a disturbing note, picturing the eternally desolate town from which the worshipers have come, shifting his perspective to the figures as representative of eternal life. But instead of concentrating on the "happy pieties" of the worshipers, paralleling the ecstasy of the motionless Lover in Stanza III, he imagines the figures as eternal exiles and their town as forever desolate. Whereas the eternity of Stanza III is one of ecstasy, the eternity of Stanza IV is one of desolation. The scene of the happy worshipers is suddenly transformed into the vision of the desolate town—similar to his response in "Ode to a Nightin-

gale," when, just as it seems to him that it would be "rich to die," he is jolted into an awareness that were he to die, he would "have ears in vain," becoming to the bird's "high requiem . . . a sod." Perhaps eternity is, after all, only emptiness, a silent desolation. Even in a moment of inspiration, when he is "mounted on the Wings of Imagination so high," his doubts assert themselves.

In Stanza V, however, he thoroughly recovers his vision. As he beholds the Urn's form and the scenes it depicts, he compares it to eternity, to which Man must respond intuitively, not intellectually (it "dost tease us out of thought / As doth eternity"). Keats says in the Bailey letter that he does not understand "how anything can be known for truth by consequitive reasoning" and states his preference for a "Life of Sensations," which intuition tells him is a "Shadow of reality to come" (I, 185). In "Epistle to J. H. Reynolds," he complains that although he has tried to philosophize, he finds that the deepest questions cannot "to the will / Be settled, but they tease us out of thought" (76–77). To try to understand eternity rationally, to philosophize, like his friend Bailey, is for him useless. The silent Urn, like his Life of Sensations, intuitively suggests to him that an eternity of beauty exists.

The paradox "Cold Pastoral" following the comparison of the Urn to eternity has generally been interpreted as a literal description, as a pastoral that should be warm but is cold. Keats, however, has consistently praised the Urn as an object of beauty and as a narrator of tales, "more sweetly" told than those of poetry. "Cold Pastoral" is an expression of his amazement that such a resistant medium as cold marble is able to portray so vividly the vibrance and warmth of summer scenes. A reader objecting to this interpretation might argue that Keats has had a lapse as in Stanza IV particularly since "Cold Pastoral" directly follows "eternity." What makes this interpretation unlikely is that Keats has not changed his vision of the ecstatic scene of love in Stanza III nor his opinion of the artistic power of the Urn, which can "express / A flowery tale more sweetly than our rhyme." If the Urn portrays a pastoral that is cold, it cannot be said to surpass the power of poetry. But if cold marble portrays a warm pastoral, then Keats's praise of the Urn's power is justified. Since Keats in the last five lines of the Stanza is enthusiastic in his admiration of the Urn, it is likely that "Cold Pastoral" is intended as an accolade.

The final lines of the Ode raise the problem not only of the meaning of "Beauty is truth" but also of the way in which the urn is a "friend to man." If we say that the Urn is a friend because it is art, we give a partial answer, but we do not convey the sense of the whole passage: the Urn remains "in midst of other woe" and delivers to Man a message of significance. The urn's role as a friend is dependent at least partially on what it says. If the Urn utters the falsehood, in Keats's view, that art is all that Man needs to know, then in this respect it is not a friend. What it says sustains Man in a world of woe. Since the Urn as both a work of art and narrator ("historian") portends eternity, what it says is likely to relate to its role: beauty in its world, an emblem of eternity, is truth.

This interpretation is supported by the statement that occurs at the beginning of Stanza II: "Heard melodies are sweet, but those unheard / Are sweeter." This praise of the power of imagination is an echo of an idea expressed in the Bailey letter—that an imagined face, a "Prototype" of the hereafter, is more beautiful than an actual face. An imagined melody, like the imagined love of Stanza III, far surpasses reality. The imagination creates what is most beautiful and its creations are a reflection of eternity: "What the imagination seizes as Beauty must be truth." Far from being a blemish on the poem, the concluding lines contribute to its power, climaxing Keats's celebration of eternity.

The Ode as a whole is more concerned with eternity than with art, itself a symbol of eternity. The first four lines of Stanza I and the first five of Stanza V are devoted to the Urn as art. The last six lines of Stanza I and the first seven of Stanza IV portray the figures as representative of some kind of idealized life. The first four lines of Stanza II, praising the power of imagination, are transitional, moving from the figures as representative of life to the figures as symbols of eternal life. The last six lines of Stanza II, the first seven of Stanza III (a contrast to the final three lines on earthly love), and the last three of Stanza IV portray the figures as symbols of eternity. The final five lines of Stanza V imply that the Urn's function transcends its role as a work of art.

This interpretation provides a logical explanation of the phrases "on earth" and "all ye need to know." The phrase "on earth" is not mere filler, but is substantive, implying a contrast between earthly and transcendent life, at a time when such ideas were

common. Keats discussed the question of eternity in the fall of 1817 with Bailey and stated that he prefered his intuition of eternity to Bailey's abstract and traditional concept. Although he may not have held firmly the belief that beauty or earthly happiness refined is the nature of eternity, he intensely desired such an eternity. The Ode implies that this eternity exists and that awareness of its existence is a consolation to Man.

As Hirsch says in *Validity in Interpretation*, the aim of interpretation is not certainty, but probability. This is the principle on which I base my argument. Of the six interpretations, the one relating beauty and truth to eternity is, on the basis of the evidence, most probably valid. Without wrenching the syntax, we can read the final lines as "Beauty is truth, truth beauty" in eternity—that is all you know or need to know on earth of eternity. The Ode interpreted in this way becomes a coherent and powerful work, with the concluding lines fully integrated into the poem as a whole.

Notes

1. E. D. Hirsch, *Validity in Interpretation* (New Haven and London: Yale Univ. Press, 1967), p. 171.
2. As a matter of general interest, I give the results of my survey. I examined 158 interpretations (extending from the mid-nineteenth century to the present) of "Ode on a Grecian Urn." Fifty-four of them either did not discuss the concluding lines or did not state a viewpoint. The remaining 104 (56 of which are excerpted in Harvey Lyon's *Keats' Well-Read Urn* [New York: Henry Holt, 1958]) are divided as follows: 7, in life; 9, in Keats's dream world; 5, in Platonic reality; 10, in the world of the Urn; 61, in imaginative or artistic perception; and 12, in eternity. A surprisingly low figure is that for Platonic reality. Not all interpreters who use the word "Platonism" are in fact committed to that view. I have included no interpretation that is not definitely committed to one of the views I have listed. But an interpretation might, for example, concentrate on Keats's dream world, yet interpret the concluding lines as referring to imaginative or artistic perception.
3. *The Letters of John Keats*, ed. Hyder Edward Rollins (Cambridge, Mass.: Harvard Univ. Press, 1958), I, p. 102. Hereafter cited in the text. An example of the view that beauty refers to life is Pratap

Biswas's "Keats's Cold Pastoral," *UTQ*, 47 (Winter, 1977–78), pp. 95–111.

4. E. C. Pettet, *On the Poetry of Keats* (Cambridge: Cambridge Univ. Press, 1957), p. 333.

5. Christopher Caldwell, *Illusion and Reality* (New York: International Publishers, 1947), p. 94.

6. Martha Shackford, "The *Ode on a Grecian Urn*," *KSJ*, 4 (Winter 1955), p. 12.

7. Cleanth Brooks, *The Well-Wrought Urn* (New York: Reynal and Hitchcock, 1947), pp. 150, 140, 150.

8. In "Death and Burial," *The Round Table*, 1817 and "Life after Death," *The London Journal*, 1834. Quoted by S. R. Swaminathan, "The Odes of Keats," *KSMB*, 12 (1961), pp. 45–46.

9. The most thorough and helpful interpretation of the Adam's dream letter is Newell Ford's in *The Prefigurative Imagination of John Keats* (Hamden, Conn.: Archon Books, 1966), pp. 20–38.

10. In "Death and Burial." Quoted by Swaminathan, pp. 45–46.

APPLICATION

In seeking the "meaning" of Benito Cereno, *Sidney Kaplan agrees with Hirsch, Watson, and other traditional literary historians that we need to place the work in its original setting and to reconstruct the author's probable intentions. Our failure to do this has led to fundamental disagreements about the story's meaning. "To begin with, it seems highly improbable that Melville in writing* Benito Cereno *was not thinking within the framework of the cultural concerns of his time as well as in a time-less region of universal truth." When we read the story in the context of the 1850s with its slave insurrections, slave-ship mutinies, and increasing national tensions over the issue of slavery, we must assume, Kaplan argues, that slavery is central to the work. But even critics who grant this point, and who further agree that the portrait of Delano is satiric, disagree profoundly about the story's ultimate meaning. One side finds the obtuse Delano oblivious to the rebels' heroic fight for freedom; the other side finds the naïve Delano blind to the muti-neers' innate evil. Thus Kaplan isolates an interpretive crux: "Which side is right? What did Melville mean?" And like E. D. Hirsch adjudicating the Brooks-Bateson disagreement, Kaplan offers to solve the problem by dis-covering the author's probable intention. He does this chiefly by comparing Melville's story with his source, and he finds that in nearly every instance, Melville chose to make the white figures more benign, the black figures more evil. Thus he is forced to conclude—very reluc-tantly—that "the image of Melville as subtle abolition-ist in* Benito Cereno *may be a contribution of generous wish rather than hard fact." It is the task of the literary historian, however, to discover not what the reader may want the story to mean, but what its author meant.*

Herman Melville and the American National Sin: The Meaning of "Benito Cereno"

Sidney Kaplan

Reprinted by permission from the *Journal of Negro History* 57 (1957): 12–27. Copyright © 1957 by the Association for the Study of Afro-American Life and History. Parts of the essay have been omitted and the notes have been renumbered.

Reluctantly, very reluctantly—for it is with a . . . special sadness that we are forced to repudiate any portion of the "usable past" in the classic figures of our American Renaissance—it must be ventured that the image of Melville as subtle abolitionist in *Benito Cereno* may be a construction of generous wish rather than hard fact. Just as Melville cautioned his readers that they must discriminate between what was indited as Pierre's and what was indited concerning him, so here care must be had to discriminate the thoughts that Melville indites in *Benito Cereno* from what the reader may hope these thoughts to be. The events of a story by themselves do not always clearly reveal the writer's judgment on those events; bare plot does not mechanically provide its interpretation.

As Melville once wrote to Hawthorne, he liked "a skeleton of actual reality to build about with fulness & veins & beauty." Now, Delano's *Narrative* was such "a skeleton of actual reality." Taken as incident, as a news-item reported with horror by a pro-slavery writer in the Southern press, to a John Brown or Ralph Waldo Emerson the revolt of the Negroes against their white masters of the *San Dominick* might seem a healthy and heartening thing (indeed, the *Liberator* is full of such joyful items); conversely, reported by a Frederick Douglass or a Sojourner Truth in the abolitionist press of the North, to a Calhoun, a Simms or a Poe the same revolt would be an illustration of the last evil. Thus, Glickberg's query— "If they went to extremes of butchery in their desperate bid for freedom, who shall presume to pass final judgment upon them?"—is in a sense a meaningless one; nor is Schiffman to the point when he contends that the anti-slavery intention of *Benito Cereno* is shown by Melville's mere choice of the *subject* of slave-revolt, even at a time when pro-slavery novelists, in order to rebutt Mrs. Stowe, were busy turning out caricatures of contented slaves. The fact is that Melville's intention must be determined mainly by what he did with his plot, how he veined and fleshed it, and in part how he manipulated his source. His mere telling of the story, while it will reveal something about that intention, will not by its bare outline establish Babo as hero or Cereno as villain.

Let us try to clarify this point. To begin with, it seems highly improbable that Melville in writing *Benito Cereno* was not thinking within the framework of the cultural concerns of his time as well as in a timeless region of universal truth. His technique was often to expand a current and concrete context into eternal abstractions, but this technique rarely excluded judgment on the concrete. Now, *Benito Cereno* was written at the mid-point of the hottest decade of the anti-slavery struggle prior to the Civil War, when to many the conflict seemed both irrepressible and impending. Nor was it a struggle fought solely in legislative halls, in the press, in the lyceum circuit, in the pulpit. The threat of a black Spartacus waiting to rise in the South pervaded the decade of the fifties; it was John Brown's idea precisely to raise up such leaders. The names of Gabriel, Vesey, Turner and Douglass were familiar names in American households. One modern historian, Harvey Wish, looking back on the period, has written of what he calls "the slave insurrection panic of 1856"—the year that *The Piazza Tales* came off the press.[1]

Nor were slave revolts on the plantations of the South the only items of Negro unrest that Americans could read about either in their daily press or in the pamphlet literature of the slavery controversy. Black mutiny on the high seas was also a familiar thing. Although by the mid-century, Captain Amasa Delano's original *Narrative* was apparently unknown to contemporary readers of *Benito Cereno,* the mutiny described in it was no antique chronicle either for them or for Melville. Such mutinies, a part of the living tissue of American life, had probably begun not long after Captain John Hawkins had pioneered the slave trade in his good ship, *The Jesus.*[2]

In Melville's young manhood, two famous slave mutinies filled the press—the first on the Spanish blackbird *Amistad* in the summer of 1839, the second on the brig *Creole* two years later. Four nights out of Havana en route to Port Principe the fifty-four slaves on the *Amistad* murdered its captain, sailed the ship north and ultimately surrendered to the authorities at Montauk Point after ascertaining that they were in a "free country." As described in New York and New England newspapers, the appearance of the *Amistad* is strangely reminiscent of the *San Dominick's*:

> Her sides were covered with barnacles and long tentacles of seaweed streamed from her cable and her sides at the water line. Her jibs were torn and big rents and holes appeared in both foresale and mainsail as they flapped in the gentle breeze. Most of the paint was gone from the gunwails and rail— over which [peered] coal-black African faces.

The *Amistad* case became a *cause célèbre* of the abolitionists, who hired Rufus Choate to defend the

Negroes against the claims of the Spaniards. Kali, one of the mutineers, travelled throughout the North on a speaking tour, while on the New York stage the event was dramatized in *The Black Schooner*, whose protagonist was Joseph Cinquez, leader of the mutiny. Cinquez, reported to be the son of an African prince, "of magnificent physique, commanding presence, forceful manners and commanding oratory," reminds one of Atufal, a prince in his own country.

Every step in the progress of the case was followed by the Northern press. The abolitionist campaign was a strong one, and two years later, as Melville was shipping for the South Seas, Justice Story delivered the opinion of the Supreme Court—a historic decision which stated legally for the first time that black men, carried from their homes as slaves, had the right, when seeking liberty, to kill anyone who tried to deprive them of it. In the North there was great sympathy for the mutineers of the *Amistad* and much hostility against the Spaniards who, claiming indemnity for their lost slaves, called them "pirates who, by revolt, murder, and robbery, had deprived" owners of their property.

The case of the *Creole* received even wider publicity. In the fall of 1841, the brig had set sail from Hampton Roads for New Orleans with a cargo of tobacco and 135 slaves. One Sunday night nineteen of the slaves led by one Madison Washington—a fugitive who had returned from Canada to rescue his wife, had been captured, and was being returned to bondage—rose up, killed a slavedealer on board, wounded the captain, cowed the passengers, and forced the crew to sail the ship to free Nassau. There, although the British authorities held the nineteen on charges of mutiny, the rest, despite the protest of the American consul, were freed. The indignation of the Southerners in Congress was violent, and Daniel Webster, then Secretary of State, supported them, for which action Garrison, Channing and Sumner excoriated him. For a dozen years the case was in and out of the papers, and it was only two years before *Benito Cereno* was written that the quarrel between the Americans and the British was finally arbitrated by the Englishman, Joshua Bates, whom Melville had dined with in London in 1849. Some years later, Frederick Douglass wrote a short story, whose hero was Madison Washington.

It was in the atmosphere of the slave insurrection panic of the middle fifties, of the mounting tension of the slavery controversy (in which Melville's rela-

tives and friends took varying positions), of the *Amistad* and *Creole* mutinies, that *Benito Cereno* was conceived and written.

Is it credible, then, that Melville meant *Benito Cereno* to have little or nothing to do with slavery and rebellion, or with the character of the Negro as slave and rebel? Given the Melville we have described and his times, such an opinion seems hardly tenable. Yet to argue thusly, is not, as we shall see, wholly to accept the view of Brown, Schiffman and Glicksberg. Let us turn once more to the text itself.

The most central and completely described character of *Benito Cereno* is Amasa Delano, through whose temperament filters most, although not all, of the action of the tale. On Delano both schools of interpretation concur in at least one respect: in the Yankee captain Melville meant to paint a satiric portrait. An important question, however, still remains to be answered: What is satirized? What in Delano is the target of Melville's irony? That the duped Delano was meant to be simple, even stupid, both schools agree. It is at the point where agreement stops and divergence begins that we find the crux of the problem of *Benito Cereno*, for whereas one school holds that Delano was naive because he could not discern the motiveless malignity in Babo and his fellows, it is the contention of the other that his stupidity lay in his blindness to the innate and heroic desire of the Negroes for freedom, to their dignity as human beings.

Which side is right? What did Melville mean?

The major premise for the development of Delano's character is given quite clearly in Melville's first assessment of it: Delano was "a person of a singularly undistrustful good-nature, not liable, except on extraordinary and repeated incentives, and hardly then, to indulge in personal alarms, any way involving the imputation of malign evil in man." Thus Melville declares that Delano is blind—not to goodness or courage or the love of freedom in anybody—but to the "malign evil in man." Delano is trusting. Is he intelligent? Not at all. That he is a good-natured fool Melville points up in the ironic sentence that follows: "Whether, in view of what humanity is capable, such a trait implies, along with a benevolent heart, more than ordinary quickness and accuracy of intellectual perception, may be left to the wise to determine." Now, the tale that follows is precisely the parable by which the wise may so determine; by it readers are to be educated; in it Captain Delano is to be educated. Yet, as we shall see, the final truth that Delano will learn is that Babo is the embodiment of "malign evil," Cereno of goodness maligned. For Delano to learn this new truth, he must unlearn the old errors of his period of delusion.

What are these old errors about Negroes in general and about those of *San Dominick* in particular that Delano must unlearn? He thinks that they are all jolly, debonair, "sight-loving Africans," who invariably love bright colors and fine shows; that their gentleness peculiarly fits them to be good body servants and that they possess the "strange vanity" of faithful slaves; that they sing as they work because they are uniquely musical; that they are generally stupid, the white being the shrewder race; that mulattoes are not made devilish by their white blood and that the hostility between mulattoes and blacks will not allow them to conspire against whites; that yellow pirates could not have committed the cruel acts rumored of them. And of all these beliefs he is disabused. He is a man who has had "an old weakness for negroes"; who has always been "not only benign, but familiarly and humorously so" to them; who has been fond of watching "some free men of color at work or play," and if on a voyage he chanced to have a black sailor, had inevitably been on "chatty and half-gamesome terms with him." He is a man who, "like most men of good, blithe heart . . . took to negroes, not philanthropically, but genially, just as other men to Newfoundland dogs," and who on the *San Dominick* speaks a "blithe word" to them; who admires the "royal spirit" of Atufal and pities his chains; who suspects that Don Benito is a hard master and that slavery breeds ugly passions in men—and in every item he will be proven blind.

To Delano, in short, Negroes are jolly primitives, uncontaminated nature, simple hearts, people to be patronized. The "uncivilized" Negro women aboard the *San Dominick* are "tender of heart"; as the "slumbering negress" is awakened by her sprawling infant, she catches the child up "with maternal transports," covering it with kisses. "There's naked nature, now; pure tenderness and love," thinks Captain Delano, "well pleased." Gazing at the kindly sea and sky, he is sorry for betraying an atheist doubt about the goodness of Providence.

All these things Delano has believed—and they are all to be proven false in fact, masquerades behind which lurk "ferocious pirates," barbarous sadists, both male and female, shrewd wolves, devilish mulattoes. In the course of events he must learn what

Cereno already knows, and Cereno it is who rams the lesson home, generalizing what the obtuse Yankee has been constitutionally unable to comprehend. His last words are, "The negro." Delano has no answer; it is the silence of agreement. "You were undeceived," Cereno had said to him, "would it were so with all men." Delano has been stripped of his delusions; he is wiser. But wiser in what respect? In that he now knows that Negroes are courageous lovers of freedom? Not at all; rather wiser in that he has at last discerned the blacks to be wolves in the wool of gentle sheep.

The shock of recognition makes brothers of Delano and Cereno; they now can speak with "fraternal unreserve"; indeed, there was never any real basic opposition between them. Delano was no philanthropic abolitionist; he was not even anti-slavery—he offered to buy Babo; for him the *San Dominick* carries "negro slaves, amongst other valuable freight"; he intends his sugar, bread and cider for the whites alone, the wilted pumpkins for the slaves; he orders his men to kill as few Negroes as possible in the attack, for they are to divide the cargo as a prize; he stops a Spanish sailor from stabbing a chained slave, but for him the slaves are "ferocious pirates" and he says no word against their torture and execution, far more cruel than the machinations of Babo. Like Cereno he too has been "a white noddy, a strange bird, so called from its lethargic, somnambulistic character, being frequently caught by hand at sea." No more will he be a somnambulist in the presence of evil. Meeting another *San Dominick* he will not again be duped.

And Cereno? He is the good man, the religious man, whose nobility may be seen in his hidalgo profile, in health, perhaps, something like the graceful Spanish gentry who listened to Ishmael tell his Town-Ho story, the real aristocrat that the superficial democrat, Delano, had wrongly suspected. Everywhere Melville pruned the Cereno of Delano's *Narrative* to vein and flesh him with altruism and goodness. In life, he was a swindler, a liar, the scorn of his friends, the stabber of a helpless Negro slave; as Lewis Mumford justly declares, in the original narrative, Cereno is "far more cruel, barbarous, and unprincipled than the forces he contends against." All this is gone in the tale. Pathetic and beaten he is, done to death by his experience, but only because he has been an altruist and trusted the slaves as tractable; the good man's illusions of goodness have been fatally overthrown. At the last Cereno reminds one of Bartleby the scrivener, who has rejected life as a black and monstrous wall he cannot pierce. Whereas in *Bartleby* the wall is the enigma of life, in *Cereno* it is Babo.

And what of Babo? Let us forget that objectively he is a maritime Nat Turner. What was he for Melville—for the tale? He is the "malign evil" that Delano at first cannot comprehend—and all his brothers and sisters are that evil too. The fact that for *us*, the heirs of Lincoln, his cunning ruthlessness is worthily motivated is not an issue *within the story;* to Melville "faithful" Babo is an "honest" Iago[3]; to Delano and Cereno he is a ferocious pirate, not a black David. A pirate has motives; his motives are malign—a fact not necessary to discuss.

Babo is more like a minor character of *Omoo*, one Bembo, than like Jackson or Bland. Did Melville, finding Babo in Delano's *Narrative,* remember the "swart" Mowree Bembo, harpooner of the *Julia?* "Unlike most of his countrymen," Bembo was short and "darker than usual." It was whispered that he was a cannibal, so fearless and blood-thirsty was he in his desire to kill whales. Extremely sensitive to slight, he would not tolerate joshing from Sydney Ben: "Bembo's teeth were at his throat." Thrown down on the deck by Ben's friends, Bembo was "absolutely demoniac; he lay glaring, and writhing on the deck without attempting to rise." In revenge he plots to wreck the ship. Thwarted, Bembo "never spoke one word. . . . His only motive could have been a desire to revenge the contumely heaped upon him the night previous, operating upon a heart irreclaimably savage, and at no time fraternally disposed toward the crew."

True Melville found the name Babo in Delano's *Narrative,* but the Babo of *Benito Cereno* is actually a composite of two characters in the source, Babo and Mure. Melville chose Babo—the baboon, ring-leader of the Negroes who are primitives, beasts.[4] The imagery connected with Babo and the other Negroes throughout the tale is strictly from the bestiary. The *San Dominick*'s headpiece is a dark satyr in a mask, trampling the neck of a writhing figure, likewise masked. It is, of course, Babo trampling on Don Benito: Babo is the satyr, a lecherous sylvan deity, sensual, part beast. He is the "lion rampant" in the white field of the flag of Spain. The four grizzled junk-into-oakum pickers are "sphynx like"—silent, inscrutable,

anti-human, part beast; the "ebon flights of naked boys and girls, three or four years old, darting in and out of the den's mouth," are "like a social circle of bats, sheltering in some friendly cave. . . ." Babo "snakishly writhes" to kill Benito—the image is Satanic and is associated with Babo's "central purpose." The Negro women are leopardesses, the nursing mother a doe whose fawn sprawls at its dam's lapped breasts, its paws searching, its mouth and nose rooting for the mark, while it grunts. As the *San Dominick* gives way before the onslaught of the *Bachelor's Delight*, the retreating Negroes are "cawing crows"; during the fight on deck, they are "blackfish" among which swordfish run amok; their "red tongues drool wolf-like from their black mouths" (while the white sailors fight with pale set faces); to the source account Melville adds a strong hint that Aranda's skeleton has been cannibalistically prepared. Most of these are Melville's direct images—not Delano's. Moreover, to show that neither Christianity nor white blood can redeem this beastliness there is the "mulatto, named Francesco, the cabin steward, of a good person and voice, having sung in the Valparaiso churches"—all this added by Melville to Cereno's original deposition. It is Francesco, "just before a repast, in the cabin," who proposes "to the negro Babo, poisoning a dish for the generous Captain Amasa Delano."[5]

Is their anything in the color imagery of *Benito Cereno* to refute this analysis of character and plot? Schiffman maintains that the reversal of conventional black-white symbolism in *Moby-Dick* is applied also in *Benito Cereno* and is proof positive that white Cereno is an image of evil. The opposite is the case. In *Moby-Dick,* the traditional equation is rejected so that in the new equation black may equal virtue and white evil. In *Benito Cereno* the traditional equation is merely transposed so that black (delusively virtuous or harmless to early Delano) may equal blacker (incarnate iniquity to later Delano), while white (delusively evil and suspiciously malign to early Delano) may equal whiter (tragically victimized virtue to later Delano). Beyond this, within the color schema of *Benito Cereno* wherever black and white are used for ambiguous or foreboding effects, the aim is simply conventional deception that builds up wrong leads in order to contrive mechanical suspense and a trick finale. Is Cereno's *real* whiteness (conventional) anything like the whiteness of the

slaver lost forty of its Negroes in an insurrection. The trials of the conspirators in the Denmark Vesey plot of 1822 revealed that they had sent a letter asking for help to the president of the Republic of San Domingo. The letter was carried by a Negro cook on board a Northern schooner. The press of the 1850s is full of reports of battles between slave-runners and the authorities; such battles were the frequent subjects of popular juvenile and adult literature.

3. Arthur L. Vogelback ("Shakespeare and Melville's *Benito Cereno*" [*Modern Language Notes* 67 (1952): 113–16]) has noted the Babo-Iago resemblance in detail.

4. Is there an echo here too of Baubo, obscene leader of the witches in Goethe's *Faust,* which Melville possibly was reading while writing his story? And was a writer in the issue of *Putnam's* that carried the final installment of *Benito Cereno* alluding to Babo when in an article "About Niggers" he had this to say: "But with all this charming jollity and waggishness, the nigger has terrible capacities for revenge and hatred (which opportunity may develope, as in St. Domingo), and which ought to convince the skeptic that he is a man, not a baboon . . . our Southern partners will learn that they are no joke. The nigger is no joke, and no baboon; he is simply a black man, and I say: Give him fair play and let us see what he will come to."

5. Note also Dago, another invention, "who had been for many years a grave-digger among the Spaniards. . . ." Was Melville reversing his conception of Daggoo in *Moby-Dick,* who was ready to dig a grave for his Spanish tormenter? As we have pointed out, there is more than a hint in the forecastle tableau of *Moby-Dick* that Melville's choice of the Spanish sailor to quarrel with Daggoo was based on the old conflict between Spaniard and Moor.

6. That Melville, on the concrete level at least, meant "The negro" to mean Babo, may be seen in a re-

dundant sentence he deleted from the penultimate paragraph of the first printing: "And yet the Spaniard could, upon occasion, verbally refer to the negro, as has been shown; but look upon him he would not, or could not."

7. Among others, Yvor Winters—and T. E. Sil'man (as John C. Fiske points out) in *Istoria amerikanskoi literatury* (Moscow-Leningrad, 1947).

8. Matthiessen continues: "Although the Negroes were savagely vindictive and drove a terror of blackness into Cereno's heart, the fact remains that they were slaves and that evil had thus originally been done to them. Melville's failure to reckon with this fact within the limits of his narrative makes its tragedy, for all its prolonged suspense, comparatively superficial." Matthiessen's judgments on *Benito Cereno* are curiously contradictory. Our point, of course, is that Melville did "reckon with this fact within the limits of his narrative." [*American Renaissance: Art and Expression in the Age of Emerson and Whitman* (New York: Oxford University Press, 1941), 508.]

9. It should be clear by now that although our findings reject the Brown-Schiffman-Glicksberg thesis, we in no manner share the admiration for the allegedly profound "truth" that Feltenstein, et al., discover in the meaning of *Benito Cereno*. Nor do we take part in the praise given the tale by current worshippers of the art of ambiguity. Where *Benito Cereno* is ambiguous—and it is only rarely so— it is the shell-game ambiguity of *The Lady or the Tiger*. Our view of *Benito Cereno* is nearer that of John Howard Lawson, whose brief page of analysis in his *The Hidden Heritage* [New York: Citadel Press, 1950] seems long in insight. For Lawson the tale exhibits a "tragic decline" of Melville's talent, a "cheap melodrama, a distortion of human and moral values . . . a pitiful attempt to accomplish the task which Shelley rejected—to reconcile 'the Champion with the Oppressor of mankind.'"

"The Yellow Wallpaper"

Denise D. Knight

Denise D. Knight's recent biographical reading of The Yellow Wallpaper *illustrates the enduring popularity of author-centered criticism. While she is fully aware of the variety of critical approaches to the story that have appeared since 1970, and while she grants that the story "stands apart" from Gilman's other work for "artistry and execution," Knight nevertheless finds knowledge about the author's life, and especially about Gilman's first marriage, an important key to the story's meaning. After describing the parallels between figures and events in the story and those in Gilman's life at the time of the story's creation, Knight remarks, "Although Gilman fared better than her fictional protagonist, the biographical dimension, particularly as regards her oppressive first marriage to Walter Stetson, is nevertheless instrumental in understanding the power of the story." Though Gilman herself claimed the story was aimed at S. Weir Mitchell, Knight argues that by examining the story's dominant images and "by exploring the applications of these images in Gilman's own life, the reader can clearly see that Walter Stetson is implicated along with Mitchell in the intricate patterns encoded in the text." Drawing on the author's diaries and other biographical information, Knight proposes to illuminate the real meaning of these patterns.*

Just six months prior to her May 2, 1884, wedding to Rhode Island artist Charles Walter Stetson, Charlotte Anna Perkins remarked in her diary that one of the things she had done that day was to "Paint [a] lugubrious picture of 'The Woman Against The Wall.'"[1] When she showed the painting to Stetson a few days later, he recognized the work as a troubling

Reprinted by permission of the Gale Group from Denise D. Knight, *Charlotte Perkins Gilman: A Study of the Short Fiction,* New York: Twayne Publishers, 1997: 7–17. A part of the chapter has been omitted, notes have been renumbered, and a Works Cited list has been added where deletions have created notes with incomplete information.

self-portrait of his bride-to-be. *His* diary entry described the painted figure as "a wan creature," a "worn-out" woman facing "an insurmountable wall which extended around the earth." Stetson characterized the artwork as "powerful" and "a literal transcript of her mind" (*Endure*, 244). More than 40 years later, near the end of a highly visible career, Gilman searched for that painting, hoping to reproduce it in her forthcoming autobiography.[2] She never found it. But worn-out women and wall imagery would be forever associated with Gilman as a result of her most famous short story, "The Yellow Wallpaper," a chillingly realistic depiction of a nervous breakdown.

"The Yellow Wallpaper" was written in the summer of 1890, during Gilman's "first year of freedom" (*Living*, 111), shortly after her permanent separation from Walter Stetson. It was composed over a two-day period in Pasadena, California, during a heat wave that sent the thermometer soaring to 103 degrees.[3] In August, Gilman sent the story to William Dean Howells, who had written earlier that year to praise her poem "Similar Cases," which appeared in the April 1890 edition of the *Nationalist*. Howells passed the story on to Horace Scudder, editor of *Atlantic Monthly*, who returned it to Gilman with a curt reply: "I am returning herewith the manuscript of 'The Yellow Wallpaper.' I should never forgive myself if I made other people as miserable as reading your story has made me" ("History").[4] Gilman persisted in her efforts to publish the story, placing it with a literary agent in the fall of 1890. Finally, in January 1892, "The Yellow Wallpaper" appeared in *New England Magazine*. A chapbook edition was published in 1899 by Small, Maynard, and Co., and in 1973 the Feminist Press issued a reprint edition. Since 1973, "The Yellow Wallpaper" has been widely anthologized.

Based loosely on her experiences in undergoing the rest cure for neurasthenia but with "embellishments and additions,"[5] "The Yellow Wallpaper" was Gilman's attempt to document what might have been the "inevitable result, progressive insanity" (*Living*, 119), had she not cast her doctor's "advice to the winds" (*FR*, October 1913). That doctor, the noted nerve specialist Silas Weir Mitchell of Philadelphia, treated the 26-year-old Gilman during the spring of 1887, after she had struggled with severe postpartum depression for more than two years following the birth of her daughter Katharine. Mitchell greeted his patient with open contempt, citing the self-recorded

"history of the case" that she prepared for his review as evidence of "self-conceit" (*Living*, 95). He also confessed his "prejudice against the Beechers," having previously treated two of her female relatives (p. 95).

After she had undergone several weeks of bed rest, Mitchell concluded that "there was nothing the matter" with his young patient and sent her back to Providence, Rhode Island, with the following prescription: "'Live as domestic a life as possible,'" which included having the baby with her at all times; "'have but two hours' intellectual life a day. And never touch pen, brush or pencil as long as you live.'" (*Living*, 96). For three months following her return home, Charlotte Stetson tried to follow Mitchell's advice. In doing so, she came perilously close to the "utter mental ruin" that claimed her fictional narrator (*FR*, October 1913). Clearly, her temperament—and particularly her desire to work—was ill-suited for such radical restrictions as Mitchell prescribed.

The "real purpose" of "The Yellow Wallpaper," Gilman insisted, "was to reach Dr. S. Weir Mitchell, and convince him of the error of his ways" in treating nervous prostration (*Living*, 121). The story "is a description of a case of nervous breakdown beginning something as mine did," Gilman wrote (pp. 118–19). But she never experienced "hallucinations or [had] objections to [her] mural decorations" (*FR*, October 1913), and the end of the story is strikingly different from her own ordeal. Although Gilman suffered prolonged "mental agony" and "profound distress" (*Living*, 96), she ultimately garnered enough emotional strength to reclaim her independence, leave an unhappy marriage, and carve out a successful career. Her fictional narrator, on the other hand, goes insane.

Despite its implicit didacticism—the common element in nearly all of Gilman's fiction—the story stands apart from the others in her vast oeuvre. In artistry and execution, it is superior to any of her other literary works. As Elaine Hedges documents in her historical overview "'Out at Last'? 'The Yellow Wallpaper' after Two Decades of Feminist Criticism," the collective criticism of the story offers "a dazzling and significantly disparate array of interpretations."[6] Indeed, critics have disagreed vehemently over the meaning of the story, variously arguing the significance of everything from linguistic cues and psychoanalytic interpretations to historiographical readings.

While some critics have hailed the narrator as a feminist heroine, others have seen in her a maternal failure coupled with a morbid fear of female sexuality. Some have viewed the story as an exemplar of the silencing of women writers in nineteenth-century America; others have focused on the gothic elements, comparing the story to some of "the weird masterpieces of Hawthorne and Poe," which critic Amy Wellington dismissed as "only a lazy classification for a story which stands alone in American fiction."[7] Undoubtedly, because the story is so unusual and provocative, it will continue to engender debate and controversy with the passage of time.

The opening of "The Yellow Wallpaper" quickly establishes the narrator's circumstances.[8] She is spending the summer in "a colonial mansion" with her husband, John, a "physician of high standing" who "is practical in the extreme (*YW*, 10, 9). She is suffering from an illness, which John dismisses as "temporary nervous depression—a slight hysterical tendency" (p. 10). As part of her treatment, she is "absolutely forbidden 'to work,'" a remedy with which she strenuously disagrees. "Personally, I believe that congenial work, with excitement and change, would do me good. But what is one to do?" the narrator muses (p. 10). Along with his sister/housekeeper Jennie, John appropriates all of his wife's power, providing her with "a schedule prescription for each hour of the day" and taking "all care" from her (p. 12). Writing of any kind is prohibited, since John has cautioned her "not to give way to fancy in the least" (p. 15). But the narrator, Jane, is convinced that writing might prove therapeutic. "I think sometimes that if I were only well enough to write a little it would relieve the press of ideas and rest me. . . . It is so discouraging not to have any advice and companionship about my work" (p. 16). Despite John's admonitions, however, the narrator does write, recording her impressions in a secret diary.

Through these diary entries, which comprise the text of the story, the reader learns much about the narrator's state of mind. As the story unfolds, it becomes apparent that she is suffering an acute form of postpartum depression, a condition acknowledged neither by John nor by the late-nineteenth-century medical community of which he is a part. "John does not know how much I really suffer," the narrator confides. "He knows that there is no *reason* to suffer, and that satisfies him" (p. 14). Since pragmatism and reason are fundamental aspects of John's personality, he instructs the narrator to simply use "will and self-control" to make herself well (p. 22). If she doesn't show rapid improvement, John warns, "he shall send [her] to Weir Mitchell in the fall" (p. 18), a scenario she clearly wants to avoid.

So extreme is the narrator's depression that the care of the new baby has been assumed by a nursemaid, Mary. "Such a dear baby! And yet I *cannot* be with him, it makes me so nervous," the narrator confesses (p. 14). Deprived of the freedom to write openly and relinquishing care of the infant to a nanny, the narrator gradually shifts her attention to the wallpaper in the attic nursery where she spends most of her time. The paper is the worst she has ever seen, depicting "one of those sprawling flamboyant patterns committing every artistic sin," and "the color is repellant, almost revolting; a smouldering unclean yellow," she writes (p. 13). Soon she begins to detect a subpattern in the wallpaper, "a strange, provoking, formless sort of figure" that "gets clearer every day" (pp. 18, 22). Eventually, the dim shape crystallizes into the image of a woman attempting to escape from behind the wallpaper, on which the narrator gradually begins to discern prisonlike bars. The entrapped woman tries to break free and "takes hold of the bars and shakes them hard" (p. 30). As the woman behind the wallpaper becomes increasingly desperate to effect an escape, the narrator comes to her aid. "I got up and ran to help her. I pulled and she shook, I shook and she pulled, and before morning, we had peeled years off that paper," she writes (p. 32). Eventually, the narrator's own identity becomes merged with that of the entrapped woman, and she begins to collaborate in her own escape. Having tolerated enforced rest for weeks, the narrator reclaims her right to "work" by joining her symbolic sister in bondage in vigorously stripping the walls of its paper with the "strangled heads and bulbous eyes and waddling fungus growth just shriek[ing] with derision!" (p. 34). At the end of the story, John breaks into the locked room, discovers his wife crawling on the floor, and faints "right across my path by the wall, so that I had to creep over him every time!" (p. 36).

Although Gilman fared better than her fictional protagonist, the biographical dimension, particularly as regards her oppressive first marriage to Walter Stetson, is nevertheless instrumental in understanding the power of the story. Obscuring the biographical link, however, is Gilman's own disclaimer: her insistence that the "real purpose" of "The Yellow Wallpaper" was to convince Dr. S. Weir Mitchell that his rest cure treatment, albeit well intended, was not only misguided but dangerous. By examining the three primary metaphors embedded in the text, however — the color yellow, the insurmountable walls that entrap, and the various functions of the paper itself — and by exploring the applications of these images in Gilman's own life, the reader can clearly see that Walter Stetson is implicated along with Mitchell in the intricate patterns encoded in the text.

While the various theoretical approaches to the text — psychoanalytical, linguistic, new historicist, deconstructionist, reader response, and the like — open endless debates about infantile regression, referentiality, and triumph or defeat, the process of creating it was, for Gilman, a major act of empowerment, an act both defiant and personally triumphant. Whether Jane is victorious or defeated at the story's end is perhaps not as significant as the fact that Gilman succeeded in providing an exposé about the devastating effects of work deprivation on intelligent women. It is unlikely that Gilman would have written the story merely to condemn the treatment of her illness, or even the practitioner who prescribed it, without also intentionally exposing one of the primary sources of that illness. While Mitchell's involvement in Gilman's life lasted only a few weeks — he is mentioned only briefly in the story — her marriage to Walter Stetson lasted 10 years, and the imbalance of power in their marriage is as much at issue in the cause of the illness as are the dangers of the "cure."

Walter Stetson understood Charlotte Perkins's reluctance to marry; she constantly articulated her fear that wedlock would require a total subordination of her life's work. "Were I to marry, my thoughts, my acts, my whole life would be centered in husband and children. To do the work that I planned I must be free," she told Stetson early in their relationship (*Endure*, 32). A few weeks later, she was even more adamant: "As much as I love you I love *WORK* better, & I cannot make the two compatible" (p. 63). Stetson persuaded her, however, that should she consent to be his wife, he would not object to her earning an income through writing (p. 69). As if to reinforce his commitment, Stetson occasionally presented his future wife with small gifts — including tablets of paper and stylograph pens — to encourage her writing. But his promises, however well intended, were short-lived, and his gifts of blank paper became an ominous reminder of Gilman's forfeiture of self — a symbol recalling her failure to produce meaningful

work and to serve humanity. As various critics of "The Yellow Wallpaper" have observed, deprived of the freedom to write, the narrator symbolically inscribes her "text" onto the wallpaper in that large attic nursery.[9] Through her fictional alter ego, Gilman projects the trauma of her own first marriage onto the substitute text in a bizarre configuration that "slaps you in the face, knocks you down, and tramples upon you. It is like a bad dream," the narrator writes (*YW*, 25). Moreover, we are told that the paper is "hideous," "unreliable," "infuriating," and "the pattern is torturing" (p. 25), descriptors that can all be applied to Gilman's marriage to Stetson. The protagonist also asserts that "there are things in that paper that nobody knows but me, or ever will" (p. 22). Indeed, the barred paper is at once both a nagging reminder of her silencing in marriage and a frightening tableau depicting the narrator's torment under the care of her physician/husband. Her statement that "there are things . . . that nobody knows" is ultimately untrue, since Gilman makes certain through the discourse of the text that the community of readers will know the details of her marital entrapment. The remark is also strikingly similar to an entry that Gilman recorded in her diary the day before she left Providence to seek the rest cure from Dr. Mitchell: "No one can ever know what I have suffered in these last five years. Pain pain pain, till my mind has given way." Then follows a revealing passage in which Walter Stetson is directly addressed: "I leave you — O remember what, and learn to doubt your judgement before it seeks to mould another life as it has mine" (*Diaries*, 18 April 1887). Just as John attempted to exert control over the narrator's life, Walter Stetson apparently sought to "mould" his young wife.

On the day that Charlotte Stetson left for Mitchell's sanitarium, she first took her young daughter to her friend Mary Phelon, who occasionally served as Katharine's caretaker (significantly, the nursemaid in the story is also named Mary), and returned home to find herself locked out of the house. "Doors locked. No key to be found. Struggle in at bay window with much effort. . . . Begin to write an account of myself for the doctor" (*Diaries*, 19 April 1887). In an ironic reversal in "The Yellow Wallpaper," the oppressive physician/husband is locked out at the end of the story and has difficulty finding the key that will allow him entrance to the attic room. Gilman's fictional narrator appropriates power, in part, by rendering her physician/husband more marginal than even she is at the story's end; he is on the outside trying in vain to get in while she creeps around the perimeter of the room. If, as critics such as Jeffrey Berman, Mary Jacobus, William Veeder, and Linda Wagner-Martin argue, the narrator's fear of sexuality contributes to her breakdown, then the final scene, in which John urgently attempts to gain entrance, has added significance. When he does finally enter the room, Gilman has him faint, effectively reducing him to a prone and impotent lump on the floor. Significantly, however, he is still blocking his wife, literally and symbolically obstructing her path so that she has to "creep over him every time" (*YW*, 36).

While the diary, of course, was a private document in which Stetson is directly implicated, "The Yellow Wallpaper" was created for a public audience and thus invites the reader to interact with the text. The narrator's assertion, then, that "there are things in that paper that nobody knows but me" actually entices the reader into exploring further that particularly enigmatic statement and into reading the patterns in the wallpaper. It is at this point in the story that color imagery, walls, and paper—and the significance of the three in Gilman's own life—begin to coalesce.

The color yellow—lurid and revolting—has been variously interpreted as the narrator's sexual repression, her sexual fear, her disgust of sexuality. Indeed, the yellow in the story exemplifies the negative. It is "not beautiful . . . like buttercups"; rather, it reminds the narrator of "old foul, bad yellow things" (p. 28), and it is "smouldering," "unclean," "repellant" (p. 13). Moreover, in the original manuscript of "The Yellow Wallpaper," Gilman includes a sentence that describes the color as "a sickly penetrating suggestive yellow," a descriptor that doesn't appear in published versions of the story until 1994 and that reinforces the narrator's fear of sexuality as posited by various critics.[10] The color also has extratextual relevance. Less than two months prior to her wedding, Charlotte Perkins cheerfully attempted to play the role of attentive wife-to-be at an opening-night reception honoring her fiancé's latest art exhibition. In dressing for the evening, she virtually swathed herself in yellow, adorning herself with "yellow ribbons, yellow beads, [a] gold comb, [an] amber bracelet, [a] yellow bonnet, [and] yellow flowers" (*Diaries*, 4 March 1884). Unlike Kate Chopin's protagonist in *The Awakening*, Edna Pontellier, who casts aside society's expectations in an effort to formulate an independent identity, Charlotte Perkins was attempting to appropriate "that fictitious self which we assume like a garment with which to appear before the world."[11] She was exceedingly ill at ease in the role, however: rather than feeling exhilarated at the success of Stetson's exhibition, she complained of feeling "strangely tired," and within days was "lachrymose," praying that her "forebodings of future pain. . . be untrue" (*Diaries*, 9 March 1884). Unfortunately, her worst fears about marriage and motherhood were confirmed.

In his essay "Who Is Jane? The Intricate Feminism of Charlotte Perkins Gilman," William Veeder traces "the intricate dramatization of conjugality" between Gilman's biography and "The Yellow Wallpaper."[12] Using a psychological model exploring ego boundary and object-relations theories, Veeder offers an extended analysis of the color yellow, arguing that "the peculiar yellow odor suggests urine and that the permeated wallpaper represents—among other things—the saturated diaper of childhood" (p. 48). Likewise, Ann J. Lane posits that the foul odor is "a smell, perhaps, of a child's feces."[13]

There is evidence in Gilman's diaries to corroborate the theories of Veeder, Lane, and others who have suggested that the yellow color and smell of the wallpaper might variously be associated with urine, with the narrator's fear of motherhood, and with her regression to an infantile state that finds her creeping around on the attic floor. Gilman's own early experiences with maternity left her nervous, exhausted, and despondent, particularly after Katharine became chronically ill with "bad diaper," Gilman's euphemism for diarrhea (*Diaries*, 6 May 1885). Not only did Katharine's frequent illnesses cause Gilman to question her maternal competence, but her own mother's ease and pleasure in caring for Katharine reinforced Gilman's insecurities. "Mother . . . takes all the care of the baby . . . with infinite delight. I fear I shall forget how to take care of the baby," she confided to her diary (10 May 1885). She was also still desperately anxious to engage in meaningful work. When Katharine was just five months old, Gilman expressed resentment that she had been "forced to be idle and let things drift. Perhaps now I can pick up the broken threads again and make out some kind of a career after all" (*Diaries*, 5 August 1885).

Gilman became increasingly angry at her husband, who not only failed to honor his prenuptial pledge to allow his wife the freedom to write but also imposed a two-week moratorium against her reading anything "about the woman question."[14] In his own diaries, he reviled the drudgeries of housework and engaged in a double standard that mimics the source of much of the tension found in "The Yellow Wallpaper":

> There is housework to do and though [Charlotte] does what she can, I find enough to tire me and make me feel sometimes that I am wasting my energy, power that should be applied to my art. For love's sake, one must bear all things. . . . But I feel certain that other work is not so well done because of it. I cannot let my mind roam in sweet fancy's field now. It is utterly impossible. . . . I cannot afford, nor would it be right for me, to give up all my time and strength to such things [as housework].
> (*Endure*, 276)

Not surprisingly, Gilman's own sentiments toward the need to indulge *her* fancies—toward her need to accomplish "meaningful" work—mirrored those recorded in her husband's diary. The theme of work, and the earnest desire to indulge the "need" to work, is foregrounded in "The Yellow Wallpaper." The narrator laments that she is "absolutely forbidden to 'work' until well" and vehemently "disagree[s] with [her husband's] ideas" (*YW*, 10). Near the end of the story, the narrator temporarily assumes control by asserting, "I must get to work" (p. 34), effectively subverting what John had "prescribed" for her. The narrator echoes Gilman's sentiments about the importance of work, that "first duty of a human being" (*Living*, 42). Like the fictional John, Walter Stetson seemed not to recognize the importance of work to his future wife's well-being. Stetson's diary entry for March 13, 1884, is telling: "My love is . . . depressed. *I* think she is unwell." And, like John, he offers his own prescription: "I think a cure will come with marriage and *home*" (*Endure*, 256). Home, for Charlotte Stetson, was analogous to prison. By tearing down the paper, her narrator symbolically destroys the walls that have kept her bound and entrapped—walls Gilman alluded to in her landmark feminist treatise *Women and Economics*, which advocates economic independence and employment for women, "the very walls of [the subordinate woman's] prison" (p. 133).

Although Walter Stetson tried to accommodate his fiancée's desire "to make a name for herself in the world by doing good work," (*Endure*, 144) he paradoxically viewed it is as sinful: "It is sin—surely sin: anything that takes woman away from the beautifying and sanctifying of home and bearing children must be sin," he rationalized (pp. 144, 148). Stetson was exceedingly conventional in his advocacy of a gender-based division of labor, a practice Gilman emphatically rejected on both philosophical and ideological grounds. (It is likely that Gilman's outrage at Stetson's conventional notions helped to inspire *Women and Economics*, published just four years after their divorce became final.) "The Yellow Wallpaper," then, actually became a vehicle through which Gilman could encode her rage toward Stetson over a host of matters: his broken promises, the loss of her personal freedom following Katharine's birth, her enforced economic dependence, her obsequious status and entrapment in marriage, and even the pressure Stetson exerted on her to marry while she was still obviously mourning the loss of her longtime friend Martha Luther Lane.[15]

Gilman's resentment at being coerced into assuming the role of wife and mother not only emerges in diary entries and in the painting depicting a defeated woman literally up against a wall—a potent symbol of her unattainable quest to serve humanity should she marry—but is embedded deep within the framework of "The Yellow Wallpaper." The arbitrary restrictions that John imposes on his wife—particularly forbidding her to write—symbolize artificial walls between the narrator and the work she aspires to perform.

One of the basic requirements of the rest cure was that the patient be denied liberties of all kinds, including the freedom to write. Again, an intriguing bit of extratextual evidence sheds light on Gilman's distress at being forbidden to write. In the diary entry made the day before she left for S. Weir Mitchell's sanitarium, she writes, "I have kept a journal since I was fifteen, the only blanks being in these last years of sickness and pain. I have done it because it was useful. Now I am to go away for my health, and shall not try to take any responsibilities [*sic*] with me, even this old friend" (*Diaries*, 18 April 1887). Charlotte Stetson obviously resented the forced abandonment of her "old friend"; hence, she creates a fictional narrator who outwits her husband by hiding a secret diary in which she documents the cause of her gradual descent into madness.

Perhaps one of the most crucial links between Gilman's biography and "The Yellow Wallpaper" lies in the narrator's enigmatic assertion at the end of the story: "'I've got out at last,' said I. . . . 'And I've pulled off most of the paper, so you can't put me back!'" (*YW*, 36). In looking for a parallel to this declaration of independence in Gilman's own life, we are reminded of the pivotal moment when, after "crawl[ing] into remote closets and under beds—to hide from the grinding pressure of that profound distress" (*Living*, 96), she "recovered some measure of power" by reclaiming an identity independent of that thrust on her by Walter Stetson (*FR*, October 1913). "Coming out of the closet," which evokes images of suffocation, constraint, and secrecy, involves a public disclosure of one's formerly concealed identity and breaking the silence—exposing to the world the truths about one's life.

Although Gilman deflected direct blame from Stetson by instead implicating Mitchell and "the error of his ways," there is little doubt that Stetson recognized in John of "The Yellow Wallpaper" a thinly disguised portrait of himself. But even though (or perhaps because) he was disconcerted by what he read, Gilman seemed smugly satisfied by his reaction. In a letter to Martha Luther Lane, she urged: "When my awful story 'The Yellow Wallpaper' comes out, you must try & read it. Walter says he has read it *four* times, and thinks it is the most ghastly tale he ever read. . . . But that's only a husband's opinion."[16] As an unintended but ironic commentary on their relationship, Gilman described the story to Lane as one that was "highly unpleasant." But to openly state that the purpose of the story was to paint Walter Stetson as a villain would have been needlessly cruel, as Gilman undoubtedly recognized. She was, after all, still married to Stetson when the "The Yellow Wallpaper" was first published, and an open indictment would have proved personally embarrassing to him. In her essay "Why I Wrote The Yellow Wallpaper?" Gilman states that casting aside Mitchell's advice and returning to work enabled her to recover "some measure of power" (p. 271). And loss of power was precisely the issue around which much of her apprehension toward marriage was originally focused. The act of writing an exposé of her breakdown—the price exacted for succumbing to the pressure to marry—helped to restore her sense of control.

Gilman's indictment of S. Weir Mitchell is, in part, a psychological maneuver: by deflecting criticism from Walter Stetson, she also avoided confronting the vulnerable part of herself that had reluctantly submitted, against her better judgment, to a marriage of servility.[17] It also served a therapeutic purpose. She could simultaneously retaliate against her oppressor, restore a sense of power, and ultimately practice the very craft she had been for so long denied. Regrettably, although she remained remarkably prolific, she would never again write a story that rivaled the power and poignancy of "The Yellow Wallpaper."

Notes

1. Diary entry dated 9 November 1883. Denise D. Knight, ed., *The Diaries of Charlotte Perkins Gilman*, vol. 1 (Charlottesville: University Press of Virginia, 1994), 233. Hereafter, *Diaries*.

2. In a collection of miscellaneous notes titled "Thoughts and Figgerings, 1920–1935," Gilman makes two undated references to the painting "The Woman Against The Wall" in conjunction with her plans for writing her autobiography. In her notes for the chapter titled "The Breakdown," Gilman wrote: "The degree of weariness. Those *pictures*. The Woman by the Wall . . . & that ghastly photo." On another scrap of paper, she wrote herself a reminder: "To Put In [the autobiography] . . . Photographs—all the way up. If I can, find that picture of the Woman by the Wall." Folder 17, Gilman Papers, Schlesinger Library, Radcliffe College. Quoted by permission.

3. "'The Yellow Wall Paper'—Its History & Reception." Undated typescript, box 17, folder 221, Gilman Papers, Schlesinger Library, Radcliffe College. Quoted by permission. Hereafter, "History."

4. Gilman's language in the undated transcript (cf. note 3) is somewhat different from the language in her memoirs. See part 2.

5. Gilman, "Why I Wrote 'The Yellow Wallpaper'?" *Forerunner* 4 (October 1913): 271. Hereafter, *FR*.

6. Elaine Hedges, "'Out at Last'? 'The Yellow Wallpaper' after Two Decades of Feminist Criticism," in *The Captive Imagination: A Casebook on The Yellow Wallpaper*, Catherine Golden, ed. (New York: Feminist Press, 1992), 319–33. Reprinted in *Critical Essays on Charlotte Perkins Gilman*, Joanne B. Kar-

pinski, ed. (New York: G. K. Hall, 1992), 222–33. Reprinted in part 3 of this [Twayne] edition.

7. Amy Wellington, "Charlotte Perkins Gilman," in *Women Have Told: Studies in the Feminist Tradition* (Boston: Little, Brown, 1930), 118.

8. Gilman, "The Yellow Wallpaper," *New England Magazine* (January 1892): 647–56; rpt., with an afterword by Elaine Hedges (Old Westbury: Feminist Press, 1973), 9. Page numbers in the text refer to the 1973 reprint edition. Hereafter, *YW*.

9. See for example Annette Kolodny's "A Map for Rereading: Or, Gender and the Interpretation of Literary Texts," *New Literary History* 11, no. 3 (1980): 451–67. Reprinted in *The Captive Imagination: A Casebook on The Yellow Wallpaper*, Catherine Golden, ed. (New York: Feminist Press, 1992), 149–67.

10. See Denise D. Knight, ed., *"The Yellow Wall-Paper" and Selected Stories of Charlotte Perkins Gilman* (Newark: University of Delaware Press, 1994) for the original manuscript version of the story. Hereafter, *Yellow*.

11. Kate Chopin. *The Awakening* (New York: Norton, 1976), 57.

12. William Veeder, "Who is Jane? The Intricate Feminism of Charlotte Perkins Gilman," *Arizona Quarterly* 44 (Autumn 1988): 40–79.

13. Ann J. Lane, *To "Herland" and Beyond: The Life and Work of Charlotte Perkins Gilman* (New York: Pantheon, 1990), 129.

14. In her diary entry for 5 February 1887, Gilman noted that she had resumed her "course of reading" after a two-week break, in order "to oblige" Walter. Stetson wrote in his diary on 9 February 1887 that "Charlotte of late has been so absorbed in the woman question—suffrage, other wrongs, that she has tired me dreadfully with it" (*Endure*, 331).

15. Martha Luther was Charlotte's longtime girlhood friend, with whom she "knew perfect happiness" (*Living*, 78). When Luther decided to marry Charles A. Lane, from Hingham, Massachusetts, Charlotte was devastated. "It was the keenest, the hardest, the most lasting pain I had yet known," she wrote (p. 80).

16. Gilman to Martha Luther Lane, 27 July 1890, Rhode Island Historical Society.

17. Significantly, in a poem titled "Locked Inside," first published in *Forerunner* 8 (January 1910) and later reprinted in *Woman's Journal* and *Suffrage Songs and Verses*, Gilman seems to concede that she possessed the power to effect change all along. The poem reads:

> She beats upon her bolted door,
> With faint weak hands;
> Drearily walks the narrow floor;
> Sullenly sits, blank walls before;
> Despairing stands.
>
> Life calls her, Duty, Pleasure, Gain—
> Her dreams respond;
> But the blank daylights wax and wane,
> Dull peace, sharp agony, slow pain—
> No hope beyond.
>
> Till she comes a thought! She lifts her head,
> The world grows wide!
> A voice—as if clear words were said—
> "Your door, o long imprisoned,
> Is locked inside!"

Works Cited

Hill, Mary A., ed. *Endure: The Diaries of Charles Walter Stetson*. Philadelphia: Temple University Press, 1985.

Gilman, Charlotte Perkins. *The Living of Charlotte Perkins Gilman*. New York: Appleton-Century, 1935; rpt. Madison: University of Wisconsin Press, 1990.

CHAPTER TWO

Formal Criticism: Poem as Context

'Tis not a Lip, *or* Eye, *we Beauty call,*
But the joint Force and full Result *of all.*

　　　—Pope, *An Essay on Criticism*

Historical critics argue that if we want to understand poems, we must look to their causes; reader-response critics insist we must look to their effects. Formal critics complain that both these views tend to overlook the poem itself, the central object that unites authors and readers and that offers a basis for an "objective" study of poetic art free from the difficulties and irrelevancies of author and reader psychology.

This argument tells us something about the way Anglo-American criticism has developed in our century. A simplified sketch of that development might well begin with the formalist challenge to the then-dominant historical criticism. It would trace the gradual progress of that challenge as the formalist argument found converts and the formalists themselves found prestigious academic positions. It might mark the 1950s as the apogee of the movement. This decade saw the formal approach established on nearly equal footing with historical studies in many graduate schools, and on more than equal footing in several critical journals. Even more telling, perhaps, the decade saw formal criticism also well established in hundreds of undergraduate classes in literature. If the sketch were then continued to the present day, it would show the last four decades dominated by attempts to challenge in turn the new formalist orthodoxy. Reader-response and historical approaches have found new defenders while other theorists have labored to revise formal methodology on formal principles and still others have argued that we must go "beyond" formalism in new directions.

In other words, the formal context holds a central position in modern Anglo-American criticism. To chart its development from the early writings of I. A. Richards and T. S. Eliot (though neither should be called simply a "formalist") through the important theoretical essays of such critics as John Crowe Ransom and Allen Tate to the widely influential critiques and textbooks by Cleanth Brooks and Robert Penn Warren and the inclusive and systematic theorizing of Austin Warren, René Wellek, and W. K. Wimsatt is to name a number of the important figures in mid-twentieth-century criticism. To recount the debates between these writers and others who were themselves essentially formalists, such as R. P. Blackmur, Kenneth Burke, Yvor Winters, and the "Chicago Critics" led by R. S. Crane, Richard McKeon, and Elder Olson, is to name still more.

At the same time, it would be misleading to suggest that formal criticism represents a new or peculiarly modern approach. This approach is at least as old as Aristotle, who asserted a basic formal axiom when he declared that skill in the use of metaphor was the true mark of poetic genius, and when Aristotle showed how his six tragic elements should relate to each other, how they must work together to achieve the ideal tragedy, he was performing a formal analysis. A more frequently cited father figure is Coleridge, who defined a poem as that species of composition that "proposes to itself such delight from the whole as is compatible with the distinct gratification from each component part," and who provided a very influential phrasing of formal principles when he declared that the poetic imagination revealed itself "in the balance or reconciliation of opposite or discordant qualities: of sameness, with difference; of the general, with the concrete; the idea, with the image; the individual, with the representative . . . a more than usual state of emotion, with more than usual order" (*Biographia Literaria*, 1817). Indeed, whenever the critic looks closely at the artistic design and devices of poems, whenever theory stresses the unity and coherence of the work of art, formal concepts are involved. In this sense, it is correct to say that the formal approach has been an important part of literary criticism from Aristotle's time to our own.

But only in our own century has the approach attained a well-developed theoretical base, and only in our own time has it achieved such popularity that it has become the central position against which other theories have had to define themselves. Because this popularity is sometimes obscured by the fact that not all analyses I here call "formal" are presented under that name, it will be useful to examine briefly some alternative labels, for each reveals something about the formalist's chief concerns.

The "New Criticism" is one of these labels, though one of the least helpful. The phrase was employed by John Crowe Ransom to refer to the work of Richards, Eliot, and others in the 1920s, but it was soon used to describe Ransom's own approach and that of his followers, and it has remained in the critical lexicon ever since to denote, and sometimes to dismiss, any formal analysis. The term was of doubtful value even when Ransom used it, and now that formal theories have been the center of critical discussion for several decades, the word "new" has taken on a distinctly ironic cast. But it does at least remind us that modern formalism developed first outside the established academic hierarchy and in opposition to the prevailing historical approaches. Because defenders of a position often define that position with reference to the most conspicuous opposition, this point is worth remembering.

A better descriptive term is "objective" criticism. The phrase is potentially misleading because it may call to mind a kind of scientific detachment or a dispassionate, methodical approach very far from the critic's actual purpose or practice. But the virtue of the term "objective" is that it stresses the "objectness" of the poem. The status of the poem as an "object," as something that exists independently of its creator and independently of any of its readers, is a key concept in formal theory. This concept implies, on the one hand, that we can have access to the poem quite apart from the mind of its creator or the circumstances of its creation and, on the other, that any reader's interpretation can be measured against and corrected by the "objective" standard of the poem itself, even if that reader should happen to be the author.

This view of the poem as independent "object," then, frees the formalist from the chief difficulties of the historical and affective contexts. When Ransom advertised for an "ontological" critic, he was asking for "objective" criticism in this sense. But the conception of the "objectness" of the poem has further implications. Poetry is a verbal art, which means that we must apprehend it first as a process while our eyes move down the page or the syllables fall on the ear. But the formal emphasis on the wholeness of the poem, on its "structure," on its "organic unity," on its "patterns" of images or motifs, inevitably suggests a spatial rather than a temporal mode of perception. This emphasis is apparent in the titles of such famous formalist works as Cleanth Brooks's *The Well Wrought Urn* or W. K. Wimsatt's *The Verbal Icon,* and it is implied in the formalist's belief that through many careful readings we can come to see the poetic object steadily and to see it *whole.*

This concern for the wholeness of the poetic object is an important characteristic of formalism, for the goal of formal analysis is to show how the various elements in the poem fit together, how the parts cohere to produce the whole, and how our understanding of the whole conditions our understanding of the parts. Such an analysis illustrates the central formal axiom that the primary context for the understanding of any part of the poem is the poem itself. Consider, as a brief example, the opening lines of William Blake's short poem "London": "I wander through each charter'd street / Near where the charter'd Thames does flow." (The complete poem appears in Jonathan Culler's essay in the Intertextual chapter.) Suppose we want to discover the meaning of the word "charter'd" in these lines. A large dictionary will give us several possible meanings for the word. A historical dictionary will give us the range of meanings generally known to Blake's contemporaries. A study of all of Blake's writings will tell us the various ways he used the word on other occasions. But none of these, says the formalist, will tell us exactly what the word means in the lines in question. Only a full understanding of their immediate context—that is, of the poem itself—will tell us that.

Thus, of the several recorded meanings of "charter'd," only some will fit the particular context that is this poem. But contextual pressures can create meanings as well as eliminate them. Whatever a "charter'd Thames" may mean in, say, nautical terms, when the phrase appears in juxtaposition with "charter'd streets" and with the thickly clustered imagery of bondage, restraint, and repression developed throughout the poem, it takes on a sinister resonance far beyond any recorded legal or cartographic senses. Such is the power of context to create connotations, overtones, implications, in brief, "meanings," beyond those cited in even the largest dictionaries. And the principle applies to all elements in the poem. What is the meaning of an image, a motif, a symbol, of a character or a pattern or a scene? In each case we must see how the element fits its context, how it functions in the poem. To investigate these relationships and the meanings they produce is the chief task of formal analysis.

"Formal criticism," then, is an accurate label for this context, as well as the most popular one. For when we consider the formalists' quarrel with the historical and reader-response approaches, their conception of the objective status of the poem, and their insistence that the context formed by the poem itself is the ultimate determiner of meaning, we see that their main concern is always with the unique verbal construct before them, with these particular words in this particular order. To put it another way, formalists refuse to separate form from content.

Other types of criticism fail, they argue, because they make that separation. Thus, the psychoanalytic critic or the myth critic, who may locate a poem's appeal in the latent content or underlying patterns it shares with other poems and with our dreams, is apt to overlook those specifically formal features that set poems apart from dreams and one poem apart from another. And biographical critics, in their concern with causes, are equally likely to ignore poetic form. Representatives of these other schools may regard this charge as minor as long as they can still claim to increase our understanding of the poem's meaning. But the formalists won't accept this separation. There is, they insist, no poetic meaning apart from poetic form.

This is the fundamental principle of formal criticism, and it leads directly to the formalist's famous distrust of the "paraphrase" on the grounds that too many readers are inclined to confuse the poem's paraphrasable content with its "meaning," an inclination encouraged, the formalist would argue, by other critical approaches. In reaction, formal critics are inclined to reverse the emphasis and locate poetic meaning in what can't be paraphrased. The goal of their analyses is to get us back to the poem itself, to show how it differs from the paraphrase, to point out those formal elements that make it a poem, and that particular poem, and not some other thing. By pointing to these formal elements, the formalist undertakes to show us not so much *what* the poem means, as "meaning" is usually understood in discursive contexts, but *how* it means. In large and complex structures like *Hamlet,* for instance, one critic may demonstrate a consistent image pattern, a second may remark the fitting of speech to character, a third may illuminate structural parallels, a fourth call attention to repeated motifs, and so on. In each case, the goal is to send the reader back to the play better equipped to see all the elements working together to create a verbal structure at once richly complex and highly coherent. Readers whose vision is thus armed will see that *how* a poem means is the same thing as *what* it means. They will understand that form is meaning.

Form is also value, the formalists argue. For we should value a thing for what it does essentially and always, not for what it does incidentally and occasionally. A poem may or may not heal or reveal its author's psychic wounds; it may or may not depict accurately the social or political conditions of its time; it may or may not do all or any of the many things that nonpoetic constructs do. But to be a poem at all, say the formalists, it must be a verbal structure possessing a high degree of complexity and coherence. Since it is the purpose of formal analysis to explicate these very qualities, we can understand the formalists' contention that such explication is in itself a demonstration of the poem's value as well as of its meaning. Explication *is* criticism.

This is a cogent argument, and it has persuaded many. The formalists claim to deal directly with poems and in poetic terms. They detach the poem from what they consider secondary contexts in order to concentrate on the poem itself, and they undertake to illuminate both poetic meaning and poetic value by the same kind of analysis. Even critics who remain skeptical are likely to concede that the formalist argument has had the salutary effect of forcing all types of critics to look more carefully at poems and to try to explain more fully the relevance of any information they offer about them. The formal approach also places interpreters in a somewhat different relationship to their audience. Whereas historical critics, for example, usually appear as experts who are supplying information obtained through months or years of research into an author's life or times, formal critics appear to be simply pointing to features or patterns in the poem that we might have overlooked. They seem to claim no special expertise beyond well-developed powers of observation and a sharpened sense of what to look for. And we can all play the game. We test their reading against the poem and accept, reject, or modify that reading as our own understanding of the text demands. Indeed, we *must* all play the game, for the analysis never substitutes for the poem. The critics can tell us only where to look and what to look for; we have to see for ourselves.

In a way, then, and despite the formalists' belief that we can and should approach a "best" reading, formal theory appears to democratize literary criticism. And this may in part account for the popularity of formal analysis as a classroom technique at many levels of instruction. At any rate, there seems to be no reason why the untrained reader equipped only with a sharp eye and a large dictionary should not explicate a given poem as well as the most experienced critic. That in practice the untrained reader can seldom do this is a phenomenon for which formal theory offers no clear explanation.

And here we touch on one of the perennial objections to the formal approach. Formal analysis, so this argument runs, is often better than formal theory because that analysis is actually based on knowledge imported from other contexts. In other words, the claim is that formalists do not in practice really isolate the poem. A more forceful form of this objection, as we have seen, insists that they dare not isolate it, and especially not from the historical context, because the idea of authorial meaning provides the only valid check against misinterpretation. Without it, the poem becomes either a truly closed system impervious to analysis, or an isolated verbal object open to any number of equally coherent readings but providing no valid way to choose among them. To this, formal critics reply that we can and should establish what the poem "means" apart from what the author might have "meant," and that the public nature of language and our knowledge of its norms and conventions guarantee the validity of this distinction. At this point the intertextual critics enter the debate, insisting that to talk of norms and conventions does indeed circumvent the genetic context, but only by placing the poem in the larger context of literature as a whole. This line of argument will be developed in another chapter. Here we should simply note that the concept of the poem as an object of determinate meaning existing apart from author or audience remains a central, and much contested, concept in formal criticism.

The formal theory of poetic value is also much contested. That formal analysis is designed to demonstrate the degree of complexity and coherence a poem possesses is clear; that such an analysis is therefore a demonstration of value can follow only if we are willing to accept complexity and coherence as the appropriate value terms. Some readers are reluctant to do so, and one frequent charge against formal criticism is that it ignores direct and simple literary works to concentrate instead on those special kinds of poems that allow considerable scope for critical ingenuity. Furthermore, even if it can be demonstrated that "tension," "irony," "paradox," and "ambiguity" are qualities of even apparently simple poems, it is still not clear why such forms of "complexity" as these should be considered valuable.

Now I. A. Richards, as we will see, had also been concerned to demonstrate the complexity and coherence of poems, and Richards was a strong influence on formal criticism. But Richards had grounded these terms in his affective theory of value. The complex poem is better than the simple poem because it appeals to a greater number of our desires and aversions. And a coherent poem is better than an incoherent poem because in organizing its diverse elements, it also organizes the reader's psyche. In this way, Richards furnished a cogent defense of complexity and coherence as value terms on strictly affective grounds. But most formal critics, though not necessarily denying that poems have the potential to do something like this for certain readers, rejected the entire reader-response approach as largely irrelevant. The poem, they argued, is not your experience or my experience; it is only a potential cause of experiences, and the adequacy of any subjective response must be tested against the "objective" poem itself. This argument eliminates some of the problems that trouble affective theories, but it also eliminates the affective defense of complexity and coherence as poetic values.

Indeed, as long as the poem is supposed to exist in isolation from other contexts, it is difficult to see how the formal critic can find a basis for any value scheme at all. But in practice most formalists do not really isolate the poem so completely. Part of the difficulty is simply a matter of rhetorical emphasis. Developing their views in opposition to the once more popular genetic and affective approaches, the formalists often insisted on the separateness of the poetic "object," but they chiefly meant its separateness from those particular contexts, from its possible causes or its possible effects. Some objectors, taking them literally, have charged that the formalists advocate "art for art's sake," that they wish to isolate the poem from "life," from "human significance." But this charge reveals a serious misunderstanding of the formalist position. Far from urging the poem's isolation from experience outside art, Anglo-American formal theory has usually insisted that the real function of poetry is to tell us the truth about that experience.

At the same time, the formalists, like many other modern critics, were unwilling to concede that the "scientific" model for truth is the only or the most adequate model. To be sure, the scientific picture of the world possesses a kind of truth. But the very nature of scientific inquiry dictates that this picture will be highly abstract and skeletal. The atomic physicist's conception of my desk, for example, which tells me that the desk is mainly space, or a time–space event, may well be true, but it doesn't appear to describe the knuckle-rapping, shin-barking solidity that is my experience of the desk. The world presented in literature seems to have more of this kind of concreteness. It describes more nearly the world as we experience it. It puts flesh on the scientist's skeletal picture and gives us, in Ransom's phrase, the "world's body."

And it does more. By presenting complex characters in complex situations, it offers us a world of actions with emotional and moral significance. For the poem, through the magic of the concrete symbol, mediates between the abstract world of the philosophic and moral precept and the solid but chaotic world of felt experience. It provides for the first a specific illustration, for the second, a significant form. If the poem is, as Aristotle said, a more philosophical thing than history, it is also, as he did not say, a more concrete thing than philosophy. Philosophy, like science, tends toward the abstract and the systematic. But these qualities are achieved only by simplification; life as we experience it remains multifaceted and contradictory. And poetry offers to deal with, to assimilate, all of it: Desdemona and Iago, Falstaff and Hotspur, Edgar and Edmund. This is why good poems must be "multivalent," "ambiguous," "paradoxical," and all the other things formal critics say they are, because these are the salient characteristics of the life poems seek to describe. These are all forms of complexity, and the good poem is complex because, more than any other kind of discourse, it deals faithfully with our complex experience of the world. It tells us the truth about that experience.

In other words, many formal critics ultimately ground their value theory in the mimetic or "imitative" context. And they do this so consistently that we might properly speak of the "formal-mimetic" critic. This phrase is rather awkward and hardly anyone uses it, but it has the virtue of being reasonably accurate, and its use would remind us that the formalists actually make very large claims for poetry. It might also remind us that very few critics are really "pure" formalists, perhaps for the simple reason that the poem "in itself" supplies no base for a theory of value. The mimetic context, on the contrary, offers the oldest and most popular value criterion, the appeal to truth. Of course, this criterion is not without its own difficulties, and it will be the business of another section to explore some of these. Here we should simply notice that if the formal critics are seldom "pure" formalists, neither are they "pure" mimeticists. Their concern for poetic form remains the defining feature of their criticism and the mainstay of their claim that their type of analysis is centrally relevant to poetry.

Now, because the term "form" seems to refer most directly to such elements as rhythm and repetition, to those patterns and structural devices that chiefly provide the poem's coherence, the formal critic is faced with a rather puzzling problem. Complexity, we saw, can be justified as a value on mimetic grounds. The complex poem is "congruent" with reality as we experience it and therefore "true." But it is not clear that "coherence" can be similarly explained. For many readers, in fact, reality as we experience it seems conspicuously to lack satisfactory design, to lack precisely that formal coherence we find in the poem. To be sure, in some philosophical systems—Plato's for one, and perhaps Aristotle's—there is no ultimate conflict between coherence or formal order and congruence or imitative accuracy, but the number of contemporary readers deeply committed to these or similar systems is small. For many of us, the claims of congruence are not easily reconciled with those of coherence. And while we may wish to assent to the argument that art, by selecting and arranging the material of ordinary experience, gives that material extraordinary intensity and significance, our empirical premises lead us to suspect that any selecting and arranging is necessarily a kind of falsification, a diminution of complexity, and that therefore coherence is a value different from and opposed to congruence.

It is this apparently polar opposition that causes our perplexity. As certain features of a prose narrative, for example, move toward the pole of congruence, as the characters and their actions take on the endless complication and apparent randomness of people and actions outside of art, our sense of shape and point diminishes. Only chaos truly mirrors chaos. But as we move toward the opposite pole, as the characters become simpler, the actions more directed, the plot more symmetrical, our sense of the incongruity of life and art increases. Perhaps the magic of great poetry lies in its ability to have it both ways, to reconcile the apparently rival claims of coherence and congruence in the same way it is said to combine the concrete and the universal. As W. K. Wimsatt, one of the most influential formal theorists, has put it, "poetry is that type of verbal structure where truth of reference or correspondence reaches a maximum degree of fusion with truth of coherence—or where external and internal relations are intimately mutual reflections" (*The Verbal Icon* 149). Perhaps so. Yet it is difficult to avoid the feeling that formal criticism insists finally on two opposing principles of value—the mimetic principle of congruence and the formal principle of coherence—and that these are not easily reconcilable under one theory of value.

And this problem leads to a further difficulty, a difficulty inherent in the term "form" itself. We use this term in a number of senses, two of which are of particular interest here. When formal critics speak of "form," they mean nearly everything about the poem, these particular words in this particular order. In this sense, every poem is a unique form. But we also speak of form when we say this poem is a sonnet, a villanelle, a rondeau, or when, with less precision but more significance, we describe a work as a satire or a tragedy, an epic or a pastoral. That is, we also use the term "form" to suggest that this particular poem is a certain kind of poem.

These two senses of "form," then, are really quite different. One stresses the singularity or uniqueness of the poem, the other calls attention to features it shares with similar poems. "Formal" critics are very much concerned with form in the first sense, very little with form in the second. Indeed, they are often impatient with discussions of genre, feeling that the distinctions such discussions seek to draw are problematic, arbitrary, and generally irrelevant. Studies that attempt to show that *Hamlet* is or is not a "real" tragedy, that *Paradise Lost* is or is not a "true" epic, reveal more, the formalists think, about definitions than they do about poems. And like all "irrelevant" contexts, such studies distract our attention from the unique form that is the particular poem in question. So, for many formal critics, classifications such as "tragic novel" or "pastoral elegy" are similar to the historical categories "a Conrad novel" or "a seventeenth-century poem." Formalists may find it convenient to use the terms, but they have little use for the contexts these terms imply. Their task is to explicate the unique verbal object before them, and the poem, whether others call it tragic or comic, elegiac or satiric, will be good to the extent that it possesses a high degree of complexity and coherence. On these grounds, a good poem, regardless of its period or type, is simply a good poem, and the judgment needs no historic or generic qualification.

As we have seen, this "absolute" standard of value is ultimately grounded in the mimetic context. The more complex poem is better because it more adequately "imitates" complex reality. But can we account for poetic form on this ground? As long as we think primarily of the characters or plots of "realistic" plays or novels, we might be inclined to feel that these forms present imitations of human actions. And in a sense even a lyric poem is a small drama. The speaker is a character who undergoes emotional changes as the "plot" of the poem moves from mood to mood, from statement to counterstatement, from problem to solution. So even a Petrarchan sonnet may be said to possess character and plot and to imitate action. On the other hand, it also possesses an octave, a sestet, and five iambic feet per line, and in these respects it imitates nothing in the world at all—except other Petrarchan sonnets. Working back, then, from this point, we may be moved to argue that even the most "realistic" novel has a degree of conventionality and stylization, in short, a formal order that causes it to resemble more nearly a sonnet than it does the apparent formlessness of experience outside of art. It most resembles, of course, other "realistic" novels. In this way the opposition between congruence and coherence returns to haunt the key term "form" and makes it very difficult to account for literary form on mimetic grounds. Thus, to push the point to its paradoxical conclusion, to the extent that they have developed their evaluative principles on those grounds, "formal" critics can deal with nearly everything in the poem except its "form."

Here again formal practice has often been more flexible than its supporting theory, and admittedly I am highlighting only one of the several senses of the word "form." But it is an important sense, and the failure of formal theory to account for the formal principles of literature must be considered a deficiency. As we will see, intertextual critics offer to make good precisely this deficiency. But to do so, they must abandon some of the central tenets of the formalist position. So the debate between these two critical schools centers on their different conceptions of literary form. Meanwhile, many historical and reader-response critics remain unconvinced by the formalists' attempts to isolate the poem from its historical causes or its particular effects. And, to repeat, there is the central problem within formal theory of how to reconcile the conflicting claims of coherence and congruence, formal unity and imitative fidelity. So the formalists, holding their central position, find themselves open to challenges from all sides.

In part, these challenges are simply the price of success, and they remind us that in the past century the formal context has been central historically as well as conceptually. And while formalists sometimes claim that other perspectives are irrelevant to the main business of criticism, their own position is largely immune to that charge. Objectors may find formal theory limited, but they can't seriously claim that the formalists' concentration on the poem is irrelevant. In fact, even the most committed opponent will probably admit that the formalists' abiding concern with the poem—with these particular words and the specific pattern they make—has taught critics of all persuasions the value of close, careful reading. Furthermore, and despite the very real difficulties in formal theory, many "revisionists" have discovered that it is one thing to point out some problems with the formalists' key concepts, but quite another thing to try to do without them. The most basic of these concepts is the insistence that poetic form and poetic meaning are inseparable, are, in fact, one and the same thing, and that all relevant criticism must start from this principle. This concept will inevitably lead critics into some puzzling theoretical difficulties. But it also promises to lead them toward the central mysteries of the art of poetry. This promise is the strongest reason that formal criticism, under its various labels and adaptations, continues to thrive.

Suggestions for Further Reading

Formal criticism in its Anglo-American versions (still often called "New Criticism") is displayed in a group of central texts: William Empson, *Seven Types of Ambiguity* (rev. ed., 1947), John Crowe Ransom, *The World's Body* (1938), Cleanth Brooks, *The Well Wrought Urn* (1947), René Wellek and Austin Warren, *Theory of Literature* (3rd ed., 1956), and W. K. Wimsatt, Jr., *The Verbal Icon* (1954). Critics who share many of the formalists' basic assumptions include Kenneth Burke, *The Philosophy of Literary Form* (1941), R. P. Blackmur, *Language as Gesture* (1952), and the "Chicago" or "neo-Aristotelian" group represented by R. S. Crane, ed., *Critics and Criticism* (1952), and Wayne Booth, *The Rhetoric of Fiction* (rev. ed., 1982). Some attempts to restate and defend the formalist position are Monroe Beardsley, *The Possibility of Criticism* (1970), John Ellis, *The Theory of Literary Criticism* (1974), and Murray Krieger, *Theory of Criticism* (1976). Krieger's *The New Apologists for Poetry* (1956) is a sympathetic and insightful analysis of main-line Anglo-American formalism. Victor Erlich, *Russian Formalism* (2nd ed., 1965), describes the sometimes similar but largely unrelated Russian movement. Some of the key essays in that movement are translated in Lee Lemon and Marion Reis, *Russian Formalist Criticism* (1965). William J. Spurlin and Michael Fisher, eds., *The New Criticism and Contemporary Literary Theory* (1995) reprints some classic formalist essays and adds some recent evaluations of the movement.

Irony as a Principle of Structure

Cleanth Brooks

Cleanth Brooks was one of the leading figures in Anglo-American formal criticism, and his essay "Irony as a Principle of Structure" illustrates several of the formalists' key ideas. One of these is the insistence that poetry is radically metaphorical—its meaning is bound to the particular, the concrete, and no paraphrase can carry the same meaning. Another key idea is that the parts of a good poem are "organically" related, so each part can have meaning only within the "context" of the work as a whole. As Brooks examines the contextual pressures exerted in a few short poems, he discovers that in each case these pressures produce a kind of "irony," and this is the mark of a mature or complex vision that takes in more than the simple or single vision. Good poetry, then, is congruent with experience (complex, ironic), but at the same time, unified and "coherent"; it is "a poetry which does not leave out what is apparently hostile to its dominant tone and which, because it is able to fuse the irrelevant and discordant, has come to terms with itself and is invulnerable to irony." To illustrate his points, Brooks explicates a few short poems, among them Wordsworth's "A slumber did my spirit seal." It is this explication that E. D. Hirsch found consistent with Wordsworth's text, but probably inconsistent with Wordsworth's meaning. Can the poem provide its own context? On this question the formal and the historical critics divide.

One can sum up modern poetic technique by calling it the rediscovery of metaphor and the full commitment to metaphor. The poet can legitimately step out into the universal only by first going through the narrow door of the particular. The poet does not select an abstract theme and then embellish it with concrete details. On the contrary, he must establish the details, must abide by the details, and through his realization of the details attain to whatever general meaning he can attain. The meaning must issue from the particulars; it must not seem to be arbitrarily forced upon the particulars. Thus, our conventional habits of language have to be reversed when we come to deal with poetry. For here it is the tail that wags the dog. Better still, here it is the tail of the kite—the tail that makes the kite fly—the tail that renders the kite more than a frame of paper blown crazily down the wind.

The tail of the kite, it is true, seems to negate the kite's function: it weights down something made to rise; and in the same way, the concrete particulars with which the poet loads himself seem to deny the universal to which he aspires. The poet wants to "say" something. Why, then, doesn't he say it directly and forthrightly? Why is he willing to say it only through his metaphors? Through his metaphors, he risks saying it partially and obscurely, and risks not saying it at all. But the risk must be taken, for direct statement leads to abstraction and threatens to take us out of poetry altogether.

The commitment to metaphor thus implies, with respect to general theme, a principle of indirection. With respect to particular images and statements, it implies a principle of organic relationship. That is, the poem is not a collection of beautiful or "poetic" images. If there really existed objects which were somehow intrinsically "poetic," still the mere assemblage of these would not give us a poem. For in that case, one might arrange bouquets of these poetic images and thus create poems by formula. But the elements of a poem are related to each other, not as blossoms juxtaposed in a bouquet, but as the blossoms are related to the other parts of a growing plant. The beauty of the poem is the flowering of the whole plant, and needs the stalk, the leaf, and the hidden roots.

If this figure seems somewhat highflown, let us borrow an analogy from another art: the poem is like a little drama. The total effect proceeds from all elements in the drama, and in a good poem, as in a good drama, there is no waste motion and there are no superfluous parts.

In coming to see that the parts of a poem are related to each other organically, and related to the total theme indirectly, we have come to see the importance of *context*. The memorable verses in poetry—even those which seem somehow intrinsically "poetic"—show on inspection that they derive their poetic quality from their relation to a particular context. We may, it is true, be tempted to say that Shakespeare's "Ripeness is all" is poetic because it is a sublime thought, or because it possesses simple eloquence; but that is to forget the context in which the passage appears. The proof that this is so becomes obvious when we contemplate such unpoetic lines as "vitality is all," "serenity is all," "maturity is all,"—statements whose philosophical import in the abstract is about as defensible as that of "ripeness is all." Indeed, the commonplace word "never" repeated five times becomes one of the most poignant lines in *Lear*, but it becomes so because of the supporting context. Even the "meaning" of any particular item is modified by the context. For what is said is said in a particular situation and by a particular dramatic character.

The last instances adduced can be most properly regarded as instances of "loading" from the context. The context endows the particular word or image or statement with significance. Images so charged become symbols; statements so charged become dramatic utterances. But there is another way in which to look at the impact of the context upon the part. The part is modified by the pressure of the context.

Now the *obvious* warping of a statement by the context we characterize as "ironical." To take the simplest instance, we say "this is a fine state of affairs," and in certain contexts the statement means quite the opposite of what it purports to say literally. This is sarcasm, the most obvious kind of irony. Here a complete reversal of meaning is effected: effected by the context, and pointed, probably, by the tone of voice. But the modification can be most important even though it falls far short of sarcastic reversal, and it need not be underlined by the tone of voice at all. The tone of irony can be effected by the skillful disposition of the context. Gray's *Elegy* will furnish an obvious example.

> Can storied urn or animated bust
> Back to its mansion call the fleeting breath?
> Can Honour's voice provoke the silent dust,
> Or Flatt'ry soothe the dull cold ear of death?

In its context, the question is obviously rhetorical. The answer has been implied in the characterization of the breath as fleeting and of the ear of death as dull and cold. The form is that of a question, but the manner in which the question has been asked shows that it is no true question at all.

These are obvious instances of irony, and even on this level, much more poetry is ironical than the reader may be disposed to think. Many of Hardy's poems and nearly all of Housman's, for example, reveal irony quite as definite and overt as this. Lest these examples, however, seem to specialize irony in the direction of the sardonic, the reader ought to be reminded that irony, even in its obvious and conventionally recognized forms, comprises a wide variety of modes: tragic irony, self-irony, playful, arch, mocking, or gentle irony, etc. The body of poetry which may be said to contain irony in the ordinary senses of the term stretches from *Lear,* on the one hand, to "Cupid and Campaspe Played," on the other.

What indeed would be a statement wholly devoid of an ironic potential—a statement that did not show any qualification of the context? One is forced to offer statements like "Two plus two equals four," or "The square of the hypotenuse of a right triangle is equal to the sum of the squares on the two sides." The meaning of these statements is unqualified by any context; if they are true, they are equally true in any possible context.[1] These statements are properly abstract, and their terms are pure denotations. (If "two" or "four" actually happened to have connotations for the fancifully minded, the connotations would be quite irrelevant: they do not participate in the meaningful structure of the statement.)

But connotations are important in poetry and do enter significantly into the structure of meaning which is the poem. Moreover, I should claim also—as a corollary of the foregoing proposition—that poems never contain abstract statements. That is, any "statement" made in the poem bears the pressure of the context and has its meaning modified by the context. In other words, the statements made—including those which appear to be philosophical generalizations—are to be read as if they were speeches in a drama. Their relevance, their propriety, their rhetorical force, even their meaning, cannot be divorced from the context in which they are imbedded.

The principle I state may seem a very obvious one, but I think that it is nonetheless very important. It may throw some light upon the importance of the term *irony* in modern criticism. As one who has certainly tended to overuse the term *irony* and perhaps, on occasion, has abused the term, I am closely concerned here. But I want to make quite clear what that concern is: it is not to justify the term *irony* as such, but rather to indicate why modern critics are so often tempted to use it. We have doubtless stretched the term too much, but it has been almost the only term available by which to point to a general and important aspect of poetry.

Consider this example: The speaker in Matthew Arnold's "Dover Beach" states that the world, "which seems to lie before us like a land of dreams . . . hath really neither joy nor love nor light. . . ." For some readers the statement will seem an obvious truism. (The hero of a typical Hemingway short story or novel, for example, will say this, though of course in a rather different idiom.) For other readers, however, the statement will seem false, or at least highly questionable. In any case, if we try to "prove" the proposition, we shall raise some very perplexing metaphysical questions, and in doing so, we shall certainly also move away from the problems of the poem and, finally, from a justification of the poem. For the lines are to be justified in the poem in terms of the context: the speaker is standing beside his loved one, looking out of the window on the calm sea, listening to the long withdrawing roar of the ebbing tide, and aware of the beautiful delusion of moonlight which "blanches" the whole scene. The "truth" of the statement, and of the poem itself, in which it is imbedded, will be validated, not by a majority report of the association of sociologists, or a committee of physical scientists, or of a congress of metaphysicians who are willing to stamp the statement as proved. How is the statement to be validated? We shall probably not be able to do better than to apply T. S. Eliot's test: does the statement seem to be that which the mind of the reader can accept as coherent, mature, and founded on the facts of experience? But when we raise such a question, we are driven to consider the poem as drama. We raise such further questions as these: Does the speaker seem carried away with his own emotions? Does he seem to oversimplify the situation? Or does he, on the other hand, seem to have won to a kind of detachment and objectivity? In other words, we are forced to raise the question as to whether the statement grows properly out of a context; whether it acknowledges the pressures of the context; whether it is "ironical"—or merely callow, glib, and sentimental.

I have suggested elsewhere that the poem which meets Eliot's test comes to the same thing as I. A. Richards's "poetry of synthesis"—that is, a poetry which does not leave out what is apparently hostile to its dominant tone, and which, because it is able to fuse the irrelevant and discordant, has come to terms with itself and is invulnerable to irony. Irony, then, in this further sense, is not only an acknowledgment of the pressures of a context. Invulnerability to irony is the stability of a context in which the internal pressures balance and mutually support each other. The stability is like that of the arch: the very forces which are calculated to drag the stones to the ground actually provide the principle of support — a principle in which thrust and counterthrust become the means of stability.

In many poems the pressures of the context emerge in obvious ironies. Marvell's "To His Coy Mistress" or Raleigh's "Nymph's Reply" or even Gray's "Elegy" reveal themselves as ironical, even to readers who use irony strictly in the conventional sense.

But can other poems be subsumed under this general principle, and do they show a comparable basic structure? The test case would seem to be presented by the lyric, and particularly the simple lyric. Consider, for example, one of Shakespeare's songs:

Who is Silvia: what is she
    That all our swains commend her?
Holy, fair, and wise is she;
    The heavens such grace did lend her,
That she might admired be.

Is she kind as she is fair?
    For beauty lives with kindness.
Love doth to her eyes repair,
    To help him of his blindness
And, being help'd, inhabits there.

Then to Silvia let us sing,
    That Silvia is excelling;
She excels each mortal thing
    Upon the dull earth dwelling:
To her let us garlands bring.

On one level the song attempts to answer the question "Who is Silvia?" and the answer given makes her something of an angel and something of a goddess. She excels each mortal thing "Upon the dull earth dwelling." Silvia herself, of course, dwells upon that dull earth, though it is presumably her own brightness which makes it dull by comparison. (The dull earth, for example, yields bright garlands, which the swains are bringing to her.) Why does she excel each mortal thing? Because of her virtues ("Holy, fair, and wise is she"), and these are a celestial gift. She

is heaven's darling ("The heavens such grace did lend her").

Grace, I suppose, refers to grace of movement, and some readers will insist that we leave it at that. But since Silvia's other virtues include holiness and wisdom, and since her grace has been lent from above, I do not think that we can quite shut out the theological overtones. Shakespeare's audience would have found it even more difficult to do so. At any rate, it is interesting to see what happens if we are aware of these overtones. We get a delightful richness, and we also get something very close to irony.

The motive for the bestowal of grace — that she might admired be — is oddly untheological. But what follows is odder still, for the love that "doth to her eyes repair" is not, as we might expect, Christian "charity" but the little pagan god Cupid ("Love doth to her eyes repair, / To help him of his blindness"). But if Cupid lives in her eyes, then the second line of the stanza takes on another layer of meaning. "For beauty lives with kindness" becomes not merely a kind of charming platitude — actually often denied in human experience. (The Petrarchan lover, for example, as Shakespeare well knew, frequently found a beautiful and *cruel* mistress.) The second line, in this context, means also that the love god lives with the kind Silvia, and indeed has taken these eyes that sparkle with kindness for his own.

Is the mixture of pagan myth and Christian theology, then, an unthinking confusion into which the poet has blundered, or is it something wittily combined? It is certainly not a confusion, and if blundered into unconsciously, it is a happy mistake. But I do not mean to press the issue of the poet's self-consciousness (and with it, the implication of a kind of playful irony). Suffice it to say that the song is charming and delightful, and that the mingling of elements is proper to a poem which is a deft and light-fingered attempt to suggest the quality of divinity with which lovers perennially endow maidens who are finally mortal. The touch is light, there is a lyric grace, but the tone is complex, nonetheless.

I shall be prepared, however, to have this last example thrown out of court since Shakespeare, for all his universality, was a contemporary of the metaphysical poets, and may have incorporated more of their ironic complexity than is necessary or normal. One can draw more innocent and therefore more convincing examples from Wordsworth's Lucy poems.

She dwelt among the untrodden ways
    Beside the springs of Dove,
A maid whom there were none to praise
    And very few to love;

A violet by a mossy stone
    Half hidden from the eye!
Fair as a star, when only one
    Is shining in the sky.

She lived unknown, and few could know
    When Lucy ceased to be;
But she is in her grave, and, oh,
    The difference to me.

Which is Lucy really like—the violet or the star? The context in general seems to support the violet comparison. The violet, beautiful but almost unnoticed, already half hidden from the eye, is now, as the poem ends, completely hidden in its grave, with none but the poet to grieve for its loss. The star comparison may seem only vaguely relevant—a conventional and here a somewhat anomalous compliment. Actually, it is not difficult to justify the star comparison: to her lover's eyes, she is the solitary star. She has no rivals, nor would the idea of rivalry, in her unselfconscious simplicity, occur to her.

The violet and the star thus balance each other and between themselves define the situation: Lucy was, from the viewpoint of the great world, unnoticed, shy, modest, and half hidden from the eye, but from the standpoint of her lover, she is the single star, completely dominating that world, not arrogantly like the sun, but sweetly and modestly, like the star. The implicit contrast is that so often developed ironically by John Donne in his poems where the lovers, who amount to nothing in the eyes of the world, become, in their own eyes, each the other's world—as in "The Good-Morrow," where their love makes "one little room an everywhere," or as in "The Canonization," where the lovers drive into the mirrors of each other's eyes the "towns, countries, courts"—which make up the great world; and thus find that world in themselves. It is easy to imagine how Donne would have exploited the contrast between the violet and the star, accentuating it, developing the irony, showing how the violet was really like its antithesis, the star, etc.

Now one does not want to enter an Act of Uniformity against the poets. Wordsworth is entitled to his method of simple juxtaposition with no underscoring of the ironical contrast. But it is worth noting that the contrast with its ironic potential is there in his poem. It is there in nearly all of Wordsworth's successful lyrics. It is certainly to be found in "A slumber did my spirit seal."

A slumber did my spirit seal;
    I had no human fears:
She seemed a thing that could not feel
    The touch of earthly years.

No motion has she now, no force;
    She neither hears nor sees,
Rolled round in earth's diurnal course,
    With rocks, and stones, and trees.

The lover's insensitivity to the claims of mortality is interpreted as a lethargy of spirit—a strange slumber. Thus the "human fears" that he lacked are apparently the fears normal to human beings. But the phrase has a certain pliability. It could mean fears *for* the loved one as a mortal human being; and the lines that follow tend to warp the phrase in this direction: it does not occur to the lover that he needs to fear for one who cannot be touched by "earthly years." We need not argue that Wordsworth is consciously using a witty device, a purposed ambiguity; nor need we conclude that he is confused. It is enough to see that Wordsworth has developed, quite "normally," let us say, a context calculated to pull "human fears" in opposed directions, and that the slightest pressure of attention on the part of the reader precipitates an ironical effect.

As we move into the second stanza, the potential irony almost becomes overt. If the slumber has sealed the lover's spirit, a slumber, immersed in which he thought it impossible that his loved one could perish, so too a slumber has now definitely sealed *her* spirit: "No motion has she now, no force; / She neither hears nor sees." It is evident that it is her unnatural slumber that has waked him out of his. It is curious to speculate on what Donne or Marvell would have made of this.

Wordsworth, however, still does not choose to exploit the contrast as such. Instead, he attempts to suggest something of the lover's agonized shock at the loved one's present lack of motion—of his response to her utter and horrible inertness. And how shall he suggest this? He chooses to suggest it, not by saying that she lies as quiet as marble or as a lump of clay; on the contrary, he attempts to suggest it by imagining her in violent motion—violent, but imposed motion, the same motion indeed which the very stones share, whirled about as they are in earth's diurnal course. Why does the image convey so powerfully the sense of something inert and helpless? Part of the effect, of course, resides in the fact that a dead lifelessness is suggested more sharply by an object's being whirled about by something else than by an image of the object in repose. But there are other matters which are at work here: the sense of the girl's falling back into the clutter of things, companioned by things chained like a tree to one particular spot, or by things completely inanimate, like rocks and stones. Here, of course, the concluding figure leans upon the suggestion made in the first stanza, that the girl once seemed something not subject to earthly limitations at all. But surely, the image of the whirl itself is important in its suggestion of something meaningless—motion that mechanically repeats itself. And there is one further element: the girl, who to her lover seemed a thing that could not feel the touch of earthly years, is caught up helplessly into the empty whirl of the earth which measures and makes time. She is touched by and held by earthly time in its most powerful and horrible image. The last figure thus seems to me to summarize the poem—to offer to almost every facet of meaning suggested in the earlier lines a concurring and resolving image which meets and accepts and reduces each item to its place in the total unity.

Wordsworth, as we have observed above, does not choose to point up specifically the ironical contrast between the speaker's formal slumber and the loved one's present slumber. But there is one ironical contrast which he does stress: this is the contrast between the two senses in which the girl becomes insulated against the "touch of earthly years." In the first stanza, she "could not feel / The touch of earthly years" because she seemed divine and immortal. But in the second stanza, now in her grave, she still does not "feel the touch of earthly years," for, like the rocks and stones, she feels nothing at all. It is true that Wordsworth does not repeat the verb "feels"; instead he writes "She neither *hears* nor *sees*." But the contrast, though not commented upon directly by any device of verbal wit, is there nonetheless, and is bound to make itself felt in any sensitive reading of the poem. The statement of the first stanza has been literally realized in the second, but its meaning has been ironically reversed.

Ought we, then, to apply the term *ironical* to Wordsworth's poem? Not necessarily. I am trying to account for my temptation to call such a poem ironical—not to justify my yielding to the temptation—least of all to insist that others so transgress. Moreover, Wordsworth's poem seems to me admirable, and I entertain no notion that it might have been more admirable still had John Donne written it rather than William Wordsworth. I shall be content if I can make a much more modest point: namely, that since both Wordsworth and Donne are poets, their work has at basis a similar structure, and that the dynamic structure—the pattern of thrust and counterthrust—which we associate with Donne has its counterpart in Wordsworth. In the work of both men, the relation between part and part is organic, which means that each part modifies and is modified by the whole.

Yet to intimate that there are potential ironies in Wordsworth's lyric may seem to distort it. After all, is it not simple and spontaneous? With these terms we encounter two of the critical catchwords of the nineteenth century, even as *ironical* is in danger of becoming a catchword of our own period. Are the terms *simple* and *ironical* mutually exclusive? What after all do we mean by *simple* or by *spontaneous?* We may mean that the poem came to the poet easily and even spontaneously: very complex poems may—indeed have—come just this way. Or the poem may seem in its effect on the reader a simple and spontaneous utterance: some poems of great complexity possess this quality. What is likely to cause trouble here is the intrusion of a special theory of composition. It is fairly represented as an intrusion since a theory as to how a poem is written is being allowed to dictate to us how the poem is to be read. There is no harm in thinking of Wordsworth's poem as simple and spontaneous unless these terms deny complexities that actually exist in the poem, and unless they justify us in reading the poem with only half our minds. A slumber ought not to seal the *reader's* spirit as he reads this poem, or any other poem.

I have argued that irony, taken as the acknowledgment of the pressures of context, is to be found in poetry of every period and even in simple lyrical poetry. But in the poetry of our own time, this pressure reveals itself strikingly. A great deal of modern poetry does use irony as its special and perhaps its characteristic strategy. For this there are reasons, and compelling reasons. To cite only a few of these reasons: there is the breakdown of a common symbolism; there is the general skepticism as to universals; not least important, there is the depletion and corruption of the very language itself, by advertising and by the mass produced arts of radio, the moving picture, and pulp fiction. The modern poet has the task of rehabilitating a tired and drained language so that it can convey meanings once more with force and with exactitude. This task of qualifying and modifying language is perennial; but it is imposed on the modern poet as a burden. Those critics who attribute the use of ironic techniques to the poet's own bloodless sophistication and tired scepticism would be better advised to refer these vices to his potential readers, a public corrupted by Hollywood and the Book of the Month Club. For the modern poet is not addressing simple primitives but a public sophisticated by commercial art.

At any rate, to the honor of the modern poet be it said that he has frequently succeeded in using his ironic techniques to win through to clarity and passion. Randall Jarrell's "Eighth Air Force" represents a success of this sort.

> If, in an odd angle of the hutment,
> A puppy laps the water from a can
> Of flowers, and the drunk sergeant shaving
> Whistles *O Paradiso!*—shall I say that man
> Is not as men have said: a wolf to man?
>
> The other murderers troop in yawning;
> Three of them play Pitch, one sleeps, and one
> Lies counting missions, lies there sweating
> Till even his heart beats: One; One; One.
> *O murderers!* . . . Still, this is how it's done:
>
> This is a war. . . . But since these play, before they die,
> Like puppies with their puppy; since, a man,
> I did as these have done, but did not die—
> I will content the people as I can
> And give up these to them: Behold the man!
>
> I have suffered, in a dream, because of him
> Many things; for this last saviour, man,
> I have lied as I lie now. But what is lying?
> Men wash their hands, in blood, as best they can:
>   I find no fault in this just man.

There are no superfluous parts, no dead or empty details. The airmen in their hutment are casual enough and honest enough to be convincing. The raw building is domesticated: there are the flowers in water from which the mascot, a puppy, laps. There is the drunken sergeant, whistling an opera aria as he

shaves. These "murderers," as the poet is casually to call the airmen in the next stanza, display a touching regard for the human values. How, then, can one say that man is a wolf to man, since these men "play before they die, like puppies with their puppy." But the casual presence of the puppy in the hutment allows us to take the stanza both ways, for the dog is a kind of tamed and domesticated wolf, and his presence may prove on the contrary that the hutment is the wolf den. After all, the timber wolf plays with its puppies.

The second stanza takes the theme to a perfectly explicit conclusion. If three of the men play pitch, and one is asleep, at least one man is awake and counts himself and his companions murderers. But his unvoiced cry "O murderers" is met, countered, and dismissed with the next two lines: ". . . Still this is how it's done: / This is a war. . . ."

The note of casuistry and cynical apology prepares for a brilliant and rich resolving image, the image of Pontius Pilate, which is announced specifically in the third stanza:

> I will content the people as I can
> And give up these to them: behold the man!

Yet if Pilate, as he is first presented, is a jesting Pilate, who asks "What is truth?" it is a bitter and grieving Pilate who concludes the poem. It is the integrity of Man himself that is at stake. Is man a cruel animal, a wolf, or is he the last savior, the Christ of our secular religion of humanity?

The Pontius Pilate metaphor, as the poet uses it, becomes a device for tremendous concentration. For the speaker (presumably the young airman who cried "O murderers") is himself the confessed murderer under judgment, and also the Pilate who judges, and, at least as a representative of man, the savior whom the mob would condemn. He is even Pilate's better nature, his wife, for the lines "I have suffered, in a dream, because of him, / Many things" is merely a rearrangement of Matthew 27:19, the speech of Pilate's wife to her husband. But this last item is more than a reminiscence of the scriptural scene. It reinforces the speaker's present dilemma. The modern has had high hopes for man; are the hopes merely a dream? Is man incorrigible, merely a cruel beast? The speaker's present torture springs from that hope and from his reluctance to dismiss it as an empty dream. This Pilate is even harder-pressed than was the Roman magistrate. For he must convince himself of this last savior's innocence. But he has lied for him before. He will lie for him now.

> Men wash their hands, in blood, as best they can:
> I find no fault in this just man.

What is the meaning of "Men wash their hands, in blood, as best they can"? It can mean: Since my own hands are bloody, I have no right to condemn the rest. It can mean: I know that man can love justice, even though his hands are bloody, for there is blood on mine. It can mean: Men are essentially decent: they try to keep their hands clean even if they have only blood in which to wash them.

None of these meanings cancels out the others. All are relevant, and each meaning contributes to the total meaning. Indeed, there is not a facet of significance which does not receive illumination from the figure.

Some of Jarrell's weaker poems seem weak to me because they lean too heavily upon this concept of the goodness of man. In some of them, his approach to the theme is too direct. But in this poem, the affirmation of man's essential justness by a Pilate who contents the people as he washes his hands in blood seems to me to supply every qualification that is required. The sense of self-guilt, the yearning to believe in man's justness, the knowledge of the difficulty of so believing—all work to render accurately and dramatically the total situation.

It is easy at this point to misapprehend the function of irony. We can say that Jarrell's irony pares his theme down to acceptable dimensions. The theme of man's goodness has here been so qualified that the poet himself does not really believe in it. But this is not what I am trying to say. We do not ask a poet to bring his poem into line with our personal beliefs—still less to flatter our personal beliefs. What we do ask is that the poem dramatize the situation so accurately, so honestly, with such fidelity to the total situation that it is no longer a question of our beliefs, but of our participation in the poetic experience. At

his best, Jarrell manages to bring us, by an act of imagination, to the most penetrating insight. Participating in that insight, we doubtless become better citizens. (One of the "uses" of poetry, I should agree, is to make us better citizens.) But poetry is not the eloquent rendition of the citizen's creed. It is not even the accurate rendition of his creed. Poetry must carry us beyond the abstract creed into the very matrix out of which, and from which, our creeds are abstracted. That is what "The Eighth Air Force" does. That is what, I am convinced, all good poetry does.

For the theme in a genuine poem does not confront us as abstraction—that is, as one man's generalization from the relevant particulars. Finding its proper symbol, defined and refined by the participating metaphors, the theme becomes a part of the reality in which we live—an insight, rooted in and growing out of concrete experience, many-sided, three-dimensional. Even the resistance to generalization has its part in this process—even the drag of the particulars away from the universal—even the tension of opposing themes—play their parts. The kite properly loaded, tension maintained along the kite string, rises steadily *against* the thrust of the wind.

Note

1. This is not to say, of course, that such statements are not related to a particular "universe of discourse." They are indeed, as are all statements of whatever kind. But I distinguish here between "context" and "universe of discourse." "Two plus two equals four" is not dependent on a special dramatic context in the way in which a "statement" made in a poem is. Compare "two plus two equals four" and the same "statement" as contained in Housman's poem:

   > —To think that two and two are four
   >   And neither five nor three
   > The heart of man has long been sore
   >   And long 'tis like to be.

The Relevant Context of a Literary Text

John M. Ellis

John Ellis agrees with E. D. Hirsch that "it is necessary to establish that the context invoked is the most probable context." *But he disagrees about what that context should be. In the excerpts below from Chapter 5 of* Theory of Literature: A Logical Analysis, *Ellis begins by repeating a central point he had made in an earlier chapter: rather than trying to define a literary work by identifying inherent qualities that require us to read the work in a particular way (a futile procedure, he feels), he proposes to reverse the process and argue that works become "literary" only because we decide to treat them as such. A defining feature of such treatment is our willingness to see the work as transcending the circumstances of its creation. From this premise, Ellis offers an uncompromising argument against intentionalism specifically and against most forms of literary history. For on Ellis's view, all attempts to historicize a text will involve us in distracting irrelevancies; worse, they will ultimately serve to trivialize the text. "Concentration on [historical] factors makes our understanding more localized, and hence more superficial." The point is, not all knowledge about texts is relevant to our understanding of these texts as "literature." That which is likely to be most relevant is the kind supplied by formal-mimetic analysis, rather than that supplied by historical research. To the charge that divorcing the work from its original social and political contexts cuts it off from "life," Ellis counters that "The context of a work of literature is that of the whole society for which it is a literary text, and which has made it such; its purpose is precisely that use; and its relation to life is to the life of the whole community. If we insist on relating the text primarily to the*

---

context of its composition and to the life and social context of its author, we are cutting it off from that relation to life which is the relevant one, and substituting for it another that is greatly restricted." Thus, while Ellis explicitly addresses Hirsch, Watson, and other traditional literary historians, his arguments oppose with equal vigor the newer historians we will meet in the final chapter.

From my discussion of the definition of literary texts, it will be remembered that the defining point for these texts is the use made of them, and the way in which they are treated; and further, that this use was centrally a matter of not taking them as part of the context of their origin in the way in which we normally treat pieces of language. Literary texts are not treated as part of the normal flow of speech, which has a purpose in its original context and is then discarded after that purpose is achieved, and they are not judged according to such limited purposes. These texts are defined as those that outgrow the original context of their utterance, and which function in the community at large. They do not function in that original context, are not dependant on that context for meaning, and are not judged according to their appropriateness or success in achieving what was to be achieved there. Therefore, when we decide to treat a piece of language as literature, that decision is in itself a decision not to refer the text to its originator nor to treat it as a communication from him.[1] Literary texts can be converted into nonliterary texts quite simply: since the use made of the one is quite different from the use made of the other and, since it is this use (not properties of the texts) which is defining, we can make a poem not a poem by so treating it. We can treat a poem of Goethe as a letter from him to Friederike Brion. It may well have functioned that way in its context of origin; and there is nothing logically wrong in doing this. But we must be clear about our aim in doing so: it is not the aim of literary study. If our inquiry is to be a meaningful one, and not the wholly meaningless one of "statements about this text," we must think of these possible uses of the text as belonging to distinct activities, with their own very different rationales and criteria of relevance.

The one thing that is different about literary texts, then, is that they are not to be taken as part of the contexts of their origin; and to take them in this way is to annihilate exactly the thing that makes them literary texts. I am not making the point that this use is

an inappropriate one, but the stronger point that the texts are actually made into something different by this use: they are not just literature misused, they are no longer literature at all. The process of a text becoming a literary text involves three stages: its originating in the context of its creator, its then being offered for use as literature, and its finally being accepted as such. In the final step, society makes the text into literature. The biographical approach returns the text to its former status, and reverses the process of its becoming a literary text.

This, it appears to me, is the most radical and accurate argument against intentionalism that can be made. Yet, so far, it is a theoretical argument, which shows that intentionalism is in theory injurious to literary texts. It may not seem to speak to all of those practical situations in which critics have information derived from the context of origin of a literary work, and have the psychological conviction that that knowledge has been helpful to them. For this reason I shall go beyond the general logical argument to discuss the various kinds of practical arguments for intentional knowledge in the light of both the logical problems peculiar to each one and of the general logical argument that I have already set out.

There is, first of all, a general claim that it can do no harm to know more about literary texts, but one answer to that will already, after my discussion of the aims of criticism, be clear enough: if something is irrelevant, it always deflects attention from what is relevant, and weakens the investigation in the process. But there is also in this case a more specific answer: when we examine carefully the way in which biographical or intentional information is used, it turns out to be the case that such information is directly harmful. Typical uses of such information interfere with and are even destructive of our relation to literary texts. Far from deepening that relation with the texts (as is frequently claimed), such statements tend to make it more superficial.

In being taken back to its original context, a poem is made more specific, and (as the arguments for and against this operation can both agree) something additional is brought to the poem. But that specificity is a loss, not a gain; what is taken away is the level of generality possessed by the text as a literary text. Let us assume, for example, that the process of a poet's composing his poem involved as a starting point a situation that he himself experienced; we can immediately see that it must have had much more detail than was eventually put into the text itself. To that extent, much of the original situation was left out. On the other hand, detail and emphasis may have been added which were not in the original situation. There is, then, both more and less in the text than in the original situation and the impact of the text is different from the original situation to the degree that those changes have occurred. To replace everything in the work that was there in the original situation is, in fact, to reverse the process of composition. The work became a work of literature after having been changed from the original situation, so that to put back all that the poet thought was irrelevant and therefore left out is to destroy the structure of the finished work by virtue of which it has its artistic impact and meaning; that meaning was created precisely by the selective operation that so many critics seem to be at pains to reverse and remove. This, then, is the sense in which knowing more, that is, putting back into the work what has been kept out of it, is to end up with less — with a work whose meaning has been made too local, whose controlled emphases have been removed, and which has been given a kind of specificity that it should not have. To do all this is to have forced the text to function in a limited situation in the life of one individual, instead of in the life of the community. This is all nothing less than the demolition of a literary structure.[2]

• • •

I now turn to the wider question of the relevance of the social and historical context of literary texts. Once more the guiding principle must be invoked that not everything that can be said about a text is relevant to a literary investigation, and that our grasp on what we are doing must not be weakened by the vague idea that the more we know the better,[3] whatever its character.

We are here involved in one of the most difficult and persistent clashes of viewpoint in literary theory; it is on this ground that the case for *art engagé* as opposed to art for art's sake is argued out. One side may stress the timelessness of art, the other its being a very direct social act at a particular time;[4] while the charge of "empty formalism" is countered with one of "historical reductionism."

The analysis of this issue begins in the same way as does that for the case of biographical context, though some complications will emerge at a later stage. The use of texts in such a way that they are not regarded as limited to and functioning within the original circumstances of their origin is defining for

literary texts; therefore, to refer them back to that original context in order to treat them as functioning primarily in that context is to make them no longer literary texts. Literary historians commonly insist that knowledge of the original historical circumstances that gave rise to a work deepens our appreciation;[5] but the reverse is true. Concentration on such factors makes our understanding more localized, and hence more superficial; in taking this path we have again reversed the process of a text becoming literature. The same genetic arguments occur in this sphere as in that of biographical criticism, and with the same analysis; to speak of understanding the origin of a work of literature is not the same thing as speaking of understanding its meaning, and only the confusion of the different uses of the word "understand" can make genetic explanation seem to be part of the statement of the meaning of the text. As before, it must be noted that an understanding of the meaning of the text is necessary before its genesis can be investigated, and that limitations in understanding the text will make one's ability to understand its genesis limited in exactly the same way.

Literary historians commonly use the trick of argument to which I referred at the beginning of this chapter — that of offering a choice between two views, one of which is their own, and the other an absurd alternative to it. But the alternatives offered reveal a good deal about their misconceptions concerning both their own views and the real nature of the objections to taking works of literature primarily in their historical context. For example, Spiller offers us the alternatives of either seeing the work in its historical dimension or reducing it to "a static and causeless existence"; Colie, that we either concern ourselves with the history of a work or commit ourselves to viewing it as existing only "an sich"; R. Hall, that we either take literature together with its cultural background and author's life history or take it to exist in a vacuum; and so on.[6] An even more common view is the simple one that to divorce a text from its historical context is to divorce literature from life.[7]

Clearly, no one would wish to divorce literature from life, to treat it in a vacuum, or to reduce it to something static. The question is this: Are these adequate characterizations of what a nonhistoricist criticism involves? My view is that they are, if anything, nearer to characterizing the historicist position itself than its opposite.

No activity that involves large numbers of people in the way that a concern with literary texts does can ever be thought of as cut off from life; likewise, there is no example of language activity that does not have some context and purpose. The critical question is one of what kind of relation to life, what context, and what purpose. The context of a work of literature is that of the whole society for which it is a literary text, and which has made it such; its purpose is precisely that use; and its relation to life is to the life of the whole community. If we insist on relating the text primarily to the context of its composition and to the life and social context of its author, we are cutting it off from that relation to life which is the relevant one, and substituting for it another that is greatly restricted. Far from stressing the social importance of literature, this approach undervalues the social importance of literature by construing its relation to society in too limited a way. The result is a simplification of the issues of the text down to those relevant to one particular social situation only;[8] but the literary value of the text resides precisely in the fact that this limited social situation was outgrown. Such a view of literature might with some justice be described as a "static" one.

The opposed viewpoints of art for art's sake and *art engagé* represent a typical misconceived opposition, and it is one that has been extremely persistent; the latter view has often been identified with the historicist viewpoint, the former as antihistoricist. But the opposite of taking art in the author's immediate social context of his time is not to take it as pure enjoyment, any more than the opposite of treating art as art is to treat it as socially relevant.[9] It is when we treat art as relevant to the whole society for which it is art that we treat it as art; when we do not do this we are neither treating it as art, nor are we dealing with its social relevance.

Satire is a case most often advanced to show the necessity of considering the original historical context of a literary text, and it will therefore be peculiarly appropriate to show how satire proves the reverse to be true. It is generally argued that without a knowledge of the local situation that was being satirized, we have only a vague apprehension of the humor and the issues involved; but when the shadowy figures who inhabit the text in an often two-dimensional form are identified as real people who once lived, and when they are given names and characteristics, then the whole situation becomes alive; the "satire cuts far deeper."[10] And so figures in the text are equated with real-life figures and the real-life situation is expounded and explained.

A kind of gain from this procedure is readily appreciated; but there has also been a loss. Suppose that we ask the question: What distinguishes the satire that has survived its original context from the satire that continually appears from time to time in newspapers and journals and is soon forgotten? The difference must lie in the fact that the former has something to say to people outside the original situation. Swift's *A Modest Proposal*, for example, survives and still plays a great role in the life of the English-speaking community. Now this does not happen because the contemporary Irish situation is still of interest to us from a historical point of view, or because Swift made some clever remarks about it; the social significance of his work is much wider than this, and to identify actual historical personages in his texts is to ignore the fact that they are not uniquely the people known to Swift—they are still with us. *A Modest Proposal* may well now make a great impact on a modern reader in the context of the war in Vietnam; it is a remarkable satire on the kind of technical solution to human problems that forgets about people, and of the insanity that bureaucratic talk can easily embody. And so even satire proves the point I have argued: to be concerned to find out the historical source is not to deepen, but to trivialize the meaning of the satire, to prevent ourselves from thinking about its relation to life in the deepest sense, to move from central issues to irrelevances. Even in a satire, those "scarcely concealed identities"[11] of actual historical figures are not the same as those of the figures in the text; and for the modern reader, his own experience is the important thing that he can bring to Swift's satire in order to grasp the depth of Swift's meaning.

The distinction between a kind of criticism that concerns itself with the original context of a literary text and one that does not is often spoken of as the difference between one that goes beyond the text and one that considers the text in itself. But this opposition, too, distorts the issue, and misses the most important aspect of the difference between the two positions. We might just as well put the matter the other way round, and think of the former as one that considers the original context in itself, and the latter as one that goes beyond the original context. But the most important issue raised by this opposition of views is a linguistic one.

In the case of any piece of language, the question of meaning takes us outside the text: the text only exists by virtue of its being part of a linguistic system, and the meaning of the words used derives in every aspect (whether thought of as denotation and connotation, or in the terms of any other view of meaning) from that system. The notion of "the text and nothing but the text" is either right or wrong by definition, depending on how we understand the word "text." If we exclude everything but the signs on the paper, it is wrong and foolish; while if we include all that the text includes in whatever sense, we must be right, but at the cost of saying nothing. The question, then, still remains: What does the text imply, and what kind of evidence or material do we need to show it? Common to almost all critical positions is the use of information from outside the text to interpret the text, and the crucial question is that of the characterization of that information, not of whether we are entertaining any information at all — for clearly we are.

A better and more relevant distinction here is that between the shared meanings and associations of words in the linguistic community, on the one hand, and the local features of the original context of the composition of the text on the other. This distinction focuses the issue in a more useful way than does that between "textual" and "extratextual," and it allows us to see that ignoring what is "extratextual" (in the historicist's sense) is by no means to take the text in isolation; on the contrary, it is to refer it to a wider context, and even to use more information to interpret it.

The problem of allusion, for example, is much more easily dealt with in this framework; biblical allusions can be a meaningful part of a literary text only because the Bible is part of the shared experience of a given community, not because the author of that text in particular has read it.[12] Cultural allusions,[13] too, must be viewed as part of the stock of the linguistic community,[14] and so must allusions to historical situations that are sufficiently part of the consciousness of the community to present distinct images to its members. That is to say, the details of historical fact may not be relevant, but any part of history that has become in a sense legendary will be part of the available stock of the community's shared ideas, and therefore part of its system of communication.

Literary criticism that proceeds by means of explanation of historical circumstances has the apparent advantage that it makes the work seem more accessible and more easily graspable to the reader from another age. But this advantage is indeed only

apparent. Not only is this kind of assistance to the reader deceptive and dangerous in its substituting an acquaintance with some simple facts for the need to respond to the texts, but the degree of success of this procedure often has nothing to do with the historical localization at all. For the historical situations invoked most frequently are only graspable in terms of notions with which the reader is quite familiar from his own age, and which do not need the local historical situation to exemplify them. For example, the challenge to a rigid social system by a younger group which finds it restrictive, is a recurring situation in Western society, and a reader urged by a historical critic to feel his way back into a particular historical situation to understand a work that had this kind of situation as its original context has no need to do so; indeed, if he understands the historical situation at all, it is precisely in terms of his own experience. And so the historical critic's way of looking at this situation is the reverse of what is really happening; the reader is not understanding the work through knowledge of history, but understanding history by a knowledge from his own experience of the issues raised in the work. Shaw's blasphemy in *Pygmalion* will not be understood by any explanation of the social situation and the status of the word "bloody" at that time; it will be understood because the context of the work suggests that the word is tabu, and by the modern reader's understanding the concept of "tabu" words, even though nowadays different actual words or acts would exemplify it.

• • •

One more cause of the general tendency to think the modern reader's relation to a literary text in an idiom different from his own an unduly problematic one lies in the fact that the degree to which a text "mirrors" its historical context is generally much overestimated. The medieval knight in shining armor was a conventional image then, as now, and our interest in it now is only more obviously a matter of its value as an image. Similarly, Victorian melodrama evidently represented a convention, and it will always remain a possible convention, irrespective of what that society was in fact like. It is, no doubt, useful for historians to stress the differences between medieval man and modern man, and there are evidently differences; but the literary analyst is in a very different position. The continuity of a given culture must be the focus of his attention, and his analysis must always be turned toward questions of the shared experiences of members of that culture, and the meaning of its images of experience for any of its members, even though some of those images may have arisen in a particular historical or geographical part of the culture. The issues raised in the texts must be thought of as relevant throughout the community; that is why they are found in the community's literary texts. If they are thought of primarily as the experiences of another age, to which a modern reader is an onlooker, then by definition, the texts concerned are being treated not as the literary texts of his culture at all, but only as historical documents and the property of a culture foreign to him.

It is entirely possible, within the framework that I have outlined, to speak of "literary tradition" as being part of the source of meaning of a literary text, but only in the sense that a work can invoke the community's shared associations which reside in its literary texts. Yet this legitimate concern with literary tradition must be distinguished from the narrowly bookish view of those critics who see the modification of tradition almost as an end in itself. This kind of approach15 sees the reason for literary works in terms of preceding literary works, and their meaning as being determined by their relation to those preceding works; at its most extreme, it views the writing of books as an activity that is above all about writing books. That kind of concern with literary tradition would, once more, remove literary texts from their relevant context. The dependence of literary texts upon all other literary texts is grossly exaggerated by adherents of such a view, which has evidently lost sight of the fact that literary texts relate primarily to the life of the community and not simply to that of literary scholars. Taking the literary text as functioning primarily in the limited context of a small group of writers and students of writers is fully analogous to the more common reduction of the text's context to a local biographical and historical one; and the same trivialization occurs in both cases.

Notes

1. Cf. D. G. Mowatt, "Language, Literature, and Middle High German," *Seminar: A Journal of Germanic Studies* 1 (1965): 72, for a related point.
2. Edel, in "Literature and Biography," misconceives this kind of objection in his answers (p. 69) to the charge that biographical criticism is reductive. He replies that it may seem to reduce the mystery of works of literature, but replaces that with knowledge and insight. This is not what the objections to biographical criticism are about: they are generally about the introduction of irrelevant instead of relevant knowledge, and the reduction of the possible meanings of a literary text which occurs as a result.
3. An entirely different and legitimate use of "the more we know the better" refers to the general preparation of the reader of a literary text. The more he brings to a text in personal experience, including experience of diverse situations in his life and also experience of a variety of literary texts, the more he will be open to the experience that a literary text offers. This is, of course, nothing to do with the question under discussion, which concerns specific information about a particular text, not general receptivity to literary texts.
4. It is perhaps at this point in their book that Wellek and Warren seem most content to state the issues and leave them unresolved. See, for example, their Chapter 9.
5. Colie ("Literature and History") argues this way, e.g., pp. 10 and 13.
6. Spiller, "Literary History," p. 51; Colie, "Literature and History," p. 1; R. A. Hall, Jr., *Cultural Symbolism in Literature* (Ithaca, 1963), p. 9. Cf. Ellis, Mowatt, and Robertson, "A Closer Look at 'Aims and Methods,'" for an analysis of Spiller's argument.
7. E.g., Sutton, *Modern American Criticism*, chapter 9. See here the argument against Sutton by Adams (*The Interests of Criticism*, p. 116) who rightly claims that Sutton does not argue the real issue raised by the New Critics, but treats them and their descendants as if they could be viewed as nineteenth-century aesthetes.
8. This theoretical statement of the implications of historicist criticism is not at variance with the practical results of such criticism; historicist critics are in general very slow to respond to the human significance of a literary work, and tend to use the local historical situation upon which they dwell as a substitute for such a response to the text. And it seems also to be the case that literary historians, in spite of their professed desire to explain the causes of literature, never study the most relevant cause of a work becoming literature — its structure and meaning.

9. See also Watson's espousal of the historicist viewpoint, and his description of the opposing views as anticognitive (*The Literary Critics*, p. 221); there is no reason whatever to oppose these two viewpoints, and so Watson's argument is also one of those that adduces support from an irrelevant and caricatured opposition. The name most often (and rightly) associated with the idea that the reader might come to terms with the challenge of the text without the safety of a limited historical context is that of I. A. Richards; see his *Practical Criticism* (London, 1929). The orthodox historicist reduction still flourishes even in work by contemporary linguists, e.g., M. Gregory and J. Spencer, "An Approach to the Study of Style," in *Linguistics and Style*, ed. J. Spencer (London, 1964). Only Firthian terminology, not Firth's sense of the different ways in which language could function, could be involved in the view that "A literary text may be said to have a context of situation in the sense in which it was understood by Firth" (p. 100). Gregory and Spencer make no distinction between literature and ordinary utterances as far as their relation to a context of origin is concerned.

10. Colie, p. 13.

11. Again the practice of historicist scholarship confirms the theoretical point: the historical footnotes which are thought to be vital for a deeper understanding of satire remain historical footnotes and testify only to the historian's fascination with such footnotes.

12. Juhl (p. 22) argues that to judge any part of one literary work as an allusion to another work, we must know that the author could have alluded to it. Even if we were to grant all its biographical premises, this argument would still be self-destructive; to demonstrate a negative of the order "Y never read nor heard of X" is virtually impossible. Since the most that could be shown is that there is no known evidence that Y read or heard of X, it must always be possible that the author could have alluded to the work in question; and so, Juhl's test creates no means of distinguishing one case from another.

13. Linguists often try to exclude cultural allusion from their field of inquiry. But there can be no reason to restrict the field of linguistics in this way: the study of language should not be anything less than the whole system of communication of a linguistic community.

14. It is probably best to view such phenomena as Goethe's references to his own work in this light; e.g., not as biographical information (reached by knowledge of Goethe's other work) but as the exploitation of the community's shared associations. His *Die Leiden des jungen Werthers* had become a cultural document by the time he referred directly to it in such poems as the "Trilogie der Leidenschaft" and the ode "Klein ist unter den Fürsten Germaniens. . . ."

15. This fallacy is frequent enough, and destructive enough, to warrant a name to make it comparable to the "Intentional Fallacy" and the "Affective Fallacy"; I propose the "Bookish Fallacy." A recent example is J. Fletcher, "The Criticism of Comparison: The Approach through Comparative Literature and Intellectual History," in *Contemporary Criticism*, eds., M. Bradbury and D. Palmer, Stratford-upon-Avon Studies 12 (New York, 1971). See, for example, p. 128: ". . . nothing springs *ex nihilo*, but from a corpus of books." Note, once more, the use of alternatives that are not in contrast with each other, and one of which is an absurdity, to force the right conclusion.

Works Cited

Adams, Hazard. *The Interests of Criticism*. New York, 1969.

Colie, Rosemarie L. "Literature and History." In *Relations of Literary Study*, ed. Thorpe, pp. 1–26. New York, 1967.

Edel, Leon. "Literature and Biography." In *Relations of Literary Study*, ed. Thorpe, pp. 57–72. New York, 1967.

Juhl, Peter D. "Intention and Literary Interpretation." *Deutsche Vierteljahrsschift für Literaturgeschicte und Geisteswissenschaft* 6 (1971): 1–23.

Spiller, Robert E. "Literary History." In *The Aims and Methods of Scholarship in Modern Languages and Literatures*, ed. Thorpe, pp. 43–55. New York, 1963.

Sutton, Walter. *Modern American Criticism*. Englewood Cliffs, N.J., 1963.

Wellek, René and Warren, Austin. *Theory of Literature*. 2nd ed. New York, 1956.

APPLICATION

*Like Paul Yachnin, Russ McDonald takes issue with
many of the recent new historical and cultural materialist interpretations of* The Tempest, *but while Yachnin
faults these for not paying enough attention to Shakespeare's time, McDonald faults them for not paying
enough attention to Shakespeare's text. Citing the essay
by Barker and Hulme, among others, McDonald notes
that many political readings do not simply ignore formal
features but are even "deliberately anti-aesthetic," fearful
that concentration on poetic features will distract our attention from the text's political implications. The result,
according to McDonald, is interpretations as one-sided
as the earlier readings they claim to correct.*

*The true corrective in either case is close, careful
analysis with attention to "the most minute formal details." Such a reading discovers a more complex, ambiguous, and subtly nuanced text. "In* The Tempest, *as in
late Shakespeare generally, the effect of the poetry is to
promote uncertainty and to insist upon ambiguity, and
attention to the verse makes one increasingly dubious
about the bluntness of most political interpretation."
Some of the New Critics, McDonald acknowledges,
may have had their own ideological agendas, but formal
analysis is not itself an ideology. It is, rather, the surest
method to discover the true politics of a text. And despite
his reservations about the New Criticism, McDonald's
description of* The Tempest *sounds very much like
Cleanth Brooks's "Irony as a Principle of Structure":
"The play valorizes ambiguity and irony, ironizing its
own positions and insisting upon the inconclusiveness
of its own conclusions. The new orthodoxy, which exalts
the colonized, is as narrow as the old, which idealizes
and excuses the colonizer." In short, by failing to see
how the text means, we fail to see what it means.*

Reading
The Tempest

Russ McDonald

Reprinted by permission of Cambridge University Press
and the author from *Shakespeare Survey* 43 (1991): 15–28.

M y subject is *The Tempest*—how it has been read recently and how it might be read otherwise. My vehicle for approaching this subject is the poetic style, its most minute formal details. My immediate purpose is to read *The Tempest* in a way that offers an alternative to, and an implicit critique of, certain readings produced by American New Historicism and British Cultural Materialism. My larger aim is to discover uses for stylistic criticism that will reassert the value of textuality in a nontextual phase of criticism and that may contribute to the reconciliation of text and context, the aesthetic and the political.

I

It will come as no surprise to anyone who has followed developments in Renaissance studies that treatments of *The Tempest* seldom concern themselves with the verse. Recent criticism looks beyond textual details and formal properties to concentrate on cultural surroundings, addressing the play almost solely in terms of social and political contexts, particularly its relation to colonial discourse. The essay by Francis Barker and Peter Hulme in John Drakakis's *Alternative Shakespeares* is typical: 'The ensemble of fictional and lived practices, which for convenience we will simply refer to here as "English colonialism," provides *The Tempest*'s dominant discursive "contexts." We have chosen here to concentrate specifically on the figure of usurpation as the nodal point of the play's imbrication into this discourse of colonialism.'[1] If American New Historicists seem slightly less virulent than British Cultural Materialists, their concerns are scarcely less political and their methods similarly contextual.[2] The Virginia pamphlets, Shakespeare's personal association with contemporary colonial projects, Montaigne on cannibals, twentieth-century racism and political oppression and their relation to Caliban—these are the contexts that have dominated recent treatments of this text.[3]

Many of the readings that regard *The Tempest* primarily as what Paul Brown calls an "intervention" in European colonial history are tendentious in conception and narrow in scope. In disputing them, however, I do not wish to neglect their nuances nor to suppress the differences among them: Greenblatt's 1976 essay, "Learning to Curse: Aspects of Linguistic Colonialism in the Sixteenth Century," for example, contextualizes *The Tempest* in a way that is balanced and sensitive to ambiguity,[4] but recent readers have become increasingly single-minded and reductive,

often adopting a censorious and shrill tone in delineating the text's relation to the problems of cultural tyranny, political freedom, and exploitation. One of the most notable of these discussions, Paul Brown's "'This thing of darkness I acknowledge mine': *The Tempest* and the discourse of colonialism," printed in Dollimore and Sinfield's *Political Shakespeare*, states its purpose in a way that fairly represents the revisionist reading. "This chapter seeks to demonstrate that *The Tempest* is not simply a reflection of colonialist practices but an intervention in an ambivalent and even contradictory discourse. This intervention takes the form of a powerful and pleasurable narrative which seeks at once to harmonise disjunction, to transcend irreconcilable contradictions and to mystify the political conditions which demand colonialist discourse. Yet the narrative ultimately fails to deliver that containment and instead may be seen to foreground precisely those problems which it works to efface or overcome."[5] Something like this point of view is expressed more succinctly by Walter Cohen: "*The Tempest* uncovers, perhaps despite itself, the racist and imperialist bases of English nationalism."[6] And some critics decline to treat the work at all. Richard Strier, for example, considers *The Tempest* "more conservative than the plays, from *Hamlet* on, which precede it,"[7] and the adjective is not intended as a compliment.

As these remarks show, a basic argumentative move on the part of many poststructuralist critics has been to attack the play's sophistication. This gambit follows an earlier one, a critical usurpation of the dramatic sovereignty of Prospero and a concomitant attack on the idealist reading set forth in Frank Kermode's Introduction to the Arden edition.[8] Having cast the benevolent Prospero out to sea, New Historicists and Cultural Materialists have sought to exert their hegemony over the text (and interpretation of it) by urging the claims of discourse, usually asserting that *The Tempest* cannot be aware of its own participation in the language of oppression and colonial power.[9] Such readings are not simply uninterested in the contribution of poetic texture; in fact, much criticism of *The Tempest*, like much political reading in general, is deliberately anti-aesthetic. The verbal harmonics can too easily be considered a means of textual mystification, a tool in Prospero's magic trunk contributing to the "enchantment" that has made this play especially appealing and thus especially dangerous, made it "a powerful and pleasurable narrative." Some voices have been raised against the tendentious and monochromatic quality of much interpretation of *The Tempest*: Meredith Anne Skura, for example, in a persuasive psychological essay, argues that "recent criticism not only flattens the text into the mold of colonialist discourse and eliminates what is characteristically 'Shakespearean' in order to foreground what is 'colonialist,' but it is also—paradoxically—in danger of taking the play further from the particular historical situation in England in 1611 even as it brings it closer to what we mean by 'colonialism' today."10 Despite this and a few other protests, the colonialist reading in the past decade has demonized Prospero, sentimentalized Caliban, and tyrannized conferences and journals with a new orthodoxy as one-sided as that which it has sought to replace.

Sensitivity to the verse offers an alternative to both of these restrictive interpretations. In the first place, awareness of the poetic complexity of *The Tempest* suggests that the play is considerably more self-conscious than the recent demystifiers will allow. Repetition—of vowels and consonants, words, phrases, syntactical forms, and other verbal effects—is a fundamental stylistic turn in *The Tempest*; these aurally reiterative patterns serve to tantalize the listener, generating expectations of illumination and fixity but refusing to satisfy those desires. Such poetic echoes function in concert with the open-endedness of the romance form and with the reappearance of a host of familiar Shakespearian topoi: verbal and ideational patterns entice the audience by promising and withholding illumination, demonstrating the impossibility of significational certainty and creating an atmosphere of hermeneutic instability.

Moreover, the style and form of *The Tempest* engage the audience textually with the same issues of control and mastery—the problem of power—that are brought into sharp focus by considerations of historical context. The tendency of words and phrases to repeat themselves may be linked to the play's profound concern with reproduction, in various senses from the biological to the political. Versions of this very broad topic appear especially in those episodes that have appealed to recent critics: the story of the deceased Sycorax, the absent wife of Prospero, Antonio's usurpation, Prospero's taking the island from Caliban, the attempt of the "savage" to rape Miranda, the enslavement of Ariel, the political ambitions of Stephano and Trinculo, the arranged marriages of Claribel and Miranda, the masque's concern with fertility and succession, the problem of dynasty, the effort to re-

produce the self through art. I shall argue that the stylistic implications of repetition offer a way of treating these political topics that is considerably more nuanced than most recent discussions of the play, more responsive to its balances and contradictions. The repetitions of the dramatic poetry help to expose the problems inherent in the art of cultural recreation and to magnify their complexity, not to supply answers. Virgil Thomson described "structural elements" in music as "expressive vocabularies, . . . repertories of devices for provoking feelings without defining them."11 In *The Tempest*, as in late Shakespeare generally, the effect of the poetry is to promote uncertainty and to insist upon ambiguity, and attention to the verse makes one increasingly dubious about the bluntness of most political interpretation.

II

Repetition becomes a prominent figure in Shakespeare's late style generally, and *The Tempest* in particular derives much of its poetic power from phonetic, lexical, and syntactical reiteration.12 From the confused echoes of the first scene ("We split, we split!") through Prospero's re-creation of the past ("Twelve year since, Miranda, twelve year since") to the pleasing assonantal chiming of the Epilogue, aural patterns impart a distinctive texture to this text. And yet *The Tempest* is something of a stylistic paradox, being simultaneously one of the most pleonastic and one of the briefest plays in the canon. The incantatory tone is in turn reinforced by the ellipses that represent a complementary and equally prominent feature of the late verse. But the repetition of sounds and words is only one type of larger and more frequently discussed modes of iteration, to which Jan Kott in particular has directed our notice: the replicated actions of usurpation and assassination, the structural mirroring of the aristocratic and the servant plots, the allusion to and reproduction of major motifs from *The Aeneid*, the creation of a masque within the play, and Shakespeare's representation of some of his own most familiar dramatic actions and topics.13 Likewise, omission makes itself felt narratively as well as stylistically. By this stage of his career Shakespeare has told the story of, say, regicide so many times that he now presents it in its most abbreviated and indicative fashion. Such a mimetic approach might be called abstract: the artist is sufficiently confident of his ability to tell a story and of his audience's capacity to receive it that he is able to signal an action rather than develop it in detail.[14] We are in the realm of the comedian performing at a convention of co-medians: since everybody knows the jokes, he need only refer to a gag by number, and the house breaks into laughter.

Presence being easier to demonstrate than ab-sence, I shall concentrate on figures of repetition, but a few words are in order about Shakespeare's im-pulse to omit. The gestural approach to storytelling corresponds to the poet's attempt at concentration and density throughout the last plays: Shakespeare strives for power of expression not only by contract-ing words and skipping over nonessential syllables, but also by discarding participles, pronouns (espe-cially relative pronouns), conjunctions, and even nouns and verbs. Asyndeton appears about as fre-quently as in *King Lear* and *Antony and Cleopatra*, two plays of much greater length.[15] And the play is re-plete with verbless constructions: "Most sure the goddess / On whom these airs attend" (1.2.425–6); "No wonder, sir, / But certainly a maid" (1.2.431–2). Participles often do the work of longer noun/verb phrases, thus accelerating the tempo: "I, not remem-b'ring how I cried out then, / Will cry it o'er again" (1.2.133–4). Anne Barton, in a brilliant discussion of this stripping away of nonessentials, points out that the vocabulary of *The Tempest* is spiked with spon-taneous compounds ("sea-change," "cloud-capped," "hag-seed," "man-monster"), proposing that such phrases "seem to be driving towards some ultimate reduction of language, a mode of expression more meaningful in its very bareness than anything a more elaborate and conventional rhetoric could de-vise." She groups Shakespeare's urge towards lin-guistic compression with his disjunctive approach to characterization, observation of the unities, and re-luctance to supply apparently pertinent details, all strategies by which *The Tempest* "continually gives the impression of being much bigger than it is."[16]

For all its compression and abbreviation, however, it is also pleonastic and reiterative—phonetically, rhythmically, lexically, syntactically, and architecton-ically. Although the structural and narrative replica-tions are more likely to be the subject of critical interest than the aural, most listeners find them-selves beguiled by the musical repetition of vowels and consonants, reduplication of words, echoing of metrical forms, and incantatory effect of this musical design. Even enthusiasts of prosody, however, are apt to weary of the repetitions of my close analysis, and

so I beg the reader's indulgence as I lay the ground-work for the demonstration, in the second half of this essay, of how these effects function ideologically.

One of the play's most distinctive stylistic prop-erties is the interlocking of aural effects in a way that recalls the etymology of *text* in weaving. Instances of consonance and assonance call attention to them-selves in virtually every line: in a phrase such as "There's nothing ill can dwell in such a temple," "ill" is glanced at in "dwell," then both are altered with the repetition of the *e* and *l* in "temple," and these harmonies are augmented by the reiteration of the *th* and *n* sounds. Such interweavings are audible in lines that seem merely declarative ("For thou must now know farther") as well as in the obviously mu-sical ("Wound the loud winds, or with bemocked-at stabs / Kill the still-closing waters"). They dominate Prospero's recitation of Ariel's history:

> within which rift
> Imprisoned thou didst painfully remain
> A dozen years, within which space she died
> And left thee there, where thou didst vent thy
>   groans
> As fast as mill-wheels strike. Then was this
>   island—
> Save for the son that she did litter here,
> A freckled whelp, hag-born—not honoured with
> A human shape.   (1.2.279–86)

To begin with the smallest units, a series of vowel sounds spin themselves out to almost absurd lengths ("within which rift / Imprisoned thou didst painfully remain"); pairs of long vowels alternate with short ("she did litter here"): consonants can be repeated in-dependently and then combined and split apart (in "put thyself / Upon this island as a spy," the *p, s,* and *i* sounds establish themselves separately and then coalesce in "spy"). This practice of joining and split-ting phonemes creates what Stephen Booth has called "pulsating alliteration," a sensation of expan-sion and contraction that implies density and activ-ity, making the text effectively "poetic" even when it may not sound conventionally so.[17]

Lexical repetition is largely responsible for the incantatory appeal of *The Tempest,* and thus for some of the most memorable passages in the play. Even in the prose of the opening shipwreck—"All lost! To prayers, to prayers! All lost!"; "'We split, we split, we split!'"—the confused shouts of desperation take a reiterative form that functions poetically in the early speeches of Prospero and then throughout the work.

Here, for instance, is a seven-line passage from the beginning of the play.

> PROSPERO: . . . Tell your piteous heart
> There's no *harm done.*
> MIRANDA: O woe the day!
> PROSPERO: *No harm.*
> I have done nothing but in care *of thee,*
> *Of thee, my* dear one, *thee, my* daughter, who
> *Art* ignorant of what thou *art,* naught knowing
> Of whence *I am,* nor that *I am* more better
> Than Prospero, master of a full poor cell
> And thy no greater father. (1.2.14–21)[18]

In addition to the italicized repetitions, the passage echoes with phonetic duplication: "heart . . . harm," "O, woe," "my dear . . . my daughter," "naught . . . daughter," "naught knowing," "full . . . cell," and "greater father." (Our uncertainty about Elizabethan pronunciation may limit but surely does not invalidate speculation about such phonetic echoes.) The regularity of certain metrical patterns and the isocolonic arrangement of clauses intensify the effect of the repeated words, notably "thee, my dear one, thee, my daughter" and "Of whence I am, nor that I am." And then there are all the negatives: "No," "no," "nothing," "naught," "knowing," "nor," "no."

To catch the repetitive flavour of Prospero's narrative to Miranda is to learn how to hear the language of the text as a whole; the following examples are taken from the first two hundred lines of the long second scene:

> Which thou heard'st cry, which thou saw'st sink.
> Sit down,
> For thou must now know farther.

> If thou remember'st aught ere thou cam'st here,
> How thou cam'st here thou mayst.

> Twelve year since, Miranda, twelve year since

> What foul play had we that we came from thence?
> Or blessed was't we did?
> Both, both, my girl.
> By foul play, as thou sayst, were we heaved thence,
> But blessedly help hither.
> *how to* grant suits,
> *How to* deny them, *who t'*advance and *who*
> *To* trash for over-topping, new *created*
> The *creatures* that were mine, I say — or changed 'em
> Or else new formed 'em; having both the key
> Of *officer* and *office,* . . .

> no screen between this part he
> played
> And him he played it for

Which now's upon's, without the which this story
To cry to th'sea that roared to us, to sigh
To th'winds, whose pity, sighing back again

Sit still, and hear the last of our sea-sorrow.
Here in this island we arrived, and here
Have I, thy schoolmaster . . .

Since stylistic criticism often founders in an elaborate summation of what its examples have already disclosed, I leave it to the reader to note the poetic and rhetorical details, the instances of assonance, alliteration, epanalepsis, isocolon, several species of paronomasia (polyptoton, syllepsis, antanaclasis), not to mention the fundamental pleasures of the repeated sounds. The various kinds of verbal play impart energy and motion to what is dramatically a notoriously static scene.

That such echoing patterns are not confined to the protasis or to the protagonist but resound throughout the work is apparent by a glance at the episode in which Antonio seeks to inveigle Sebastian into fratricide, the temptation scene (2.1.204–311). The villain begins his scheme by priming his partner with anaphoric and rhythmic restatement: "They fell together all, as by consent; / They dropped as by a thunder-stroke" (2.1.208–9). He continues by arguing that Ferdinand's disappearance is Sebastian's good fortune, demonstrating the transformation linguistically:

> SEBASTIAN: I have *no hope*
> That he's undrowned.
> ANTONIO: O, out of that *"no hope"*
> What *great hope* have you! *No hope* that way is
> Another way *so high a hope* that even
> Ambition cannot pierce a wink beyond,
> But doubt discovery there. (2.1.243–8)

Apart from the obvious echoes, the passage rings with assonance and consonance; in addition to the aural repetition, we also catch the relentless negatives characteristic of Shakespeare's villains; the glance at sleep imagery ("wink") to which the dramatic atmosphere of the scene and the island has acclimated us; and the self-conscious worrying of words that extends the game begun earlier, when the conspirators toy with the metaphor of "standing water" (226). As is often the case in *The Tempest,* language emerges as a subject itself, as speakers play with it, take pleasure in it, test its capacities, and misuse it consciously and unconsciously, sometimes, as here, at the same time.[19]

Antonio's principal trick is structural recapitulation, the stringing together of formally similar clauses. Consider his appositional elaboration of Sebastian's one-word speech, "Claribel":

> She that is Queen of Tunis; she that dwells
> Ten leagues beyond man's life; she that from Naples
> Can have no note—unless the sun were post—
> The man i'th'moon's too slow—till newborn chins
> Be rough and razorable; she that from whom
> We all were sea-swallowed, though some cast
>   again—
> And by that destiny, to perform an act
> Whereof what's past is prologue, what to come
> In yours and my discharge.   (2.1.251–9)

This string of clauses—the reader will have noticed that it is not even a sentence—is calculated to inveigle the auditor into rhythmic sympathy with and, finally, assent to the speaker's claims. It depends for its seductive power on the reiterative disposition of phrases, specifically on the pattern known as *conduplicatio*, the repetition of words in succeeding clauses. Antonio/Shakespeare strives for a kind of hypnosis with simplicity of diction, at least in the first half, where until "razorable" no word is longer than two syllables and most are monosyllabic; with regular disruption of the normal metrical structure, each of the "she that" phrases being a trochee substituted for an iamb;[20] and with syntactical recapitulation. Even those qualifying clauses that violate the pattern of "she that" develop their own rhythmic echo: "unless the sun were post" and "The man i'th'moon's too slow" are identical in length and regularity, similar in the importance of consonance and assonance, and completed with the repeated "o" sound. In these dramatic circumstances, Antonio's periphrastic style amounts to verbal overkill, as even the dim Sebastian seems to perceive in his response to the "Claribel" speech: "What stuff is this?" But the local effect is less important than the overriding dramatic goal: Antonio and Sebastian are merely the agents of a playwright seeking to seduce his audience with words.[21]

So it goes through other scenes and with other speakers. Some of the richest passages in the text depend upon such lexical and sonic echo. One of the play's axiological cruces, for example, the complex relation between biology and culture, is set forth in an aurally pleasing and complex frame:

> A devil, a born devil, on whose nature
> Nurture can never stick; on whom my pains,
> Humanely taken, all, all lost, quite lost.
>   (4.1.188–90)

"Full fathom five thy father lies," "Where the bee sucks, there suck I"—the power of the play's songs is at least partly attributable to various kinds of echo. Finally, the notorious mystery surrounding Gonzalo's "Widow Dido" has been examined in almost every context except, I think, that of aural identity, simple rhyme. Is it perhaps just another case of internal rhyme that sounds as if it ought to mean more than it does? Such density and concentration are essential to the sense of pregnancy upon which *The Tempest* depends.

III

Verbal patterns are congruent with and supported by larger networks of reiteration, most of them narrative and structural. Internal repetition of action has been a staple of Shakespearian dramatic structure since the early 1590s, the double wooing of Katherine and Bianca in *The Taming of the Shrew* being perhaps the most illustrative case. But rarely are the symmetries and parodic constructions made so obvious—or so obviously the subject of comment—as in *The Tempest*. The play is famous for the density and congruity of its mirrored actions.[22] To mention only those events associated with the celebrated example of usurpation, "the nodal point" of colonialist readings: Antonio's prompting Sebastian to regicide and fratricide seeks to repeat in Naples his own theft of power in Milan and re-enacts Prospero's seizure of the island and enslavement of Caliban, and all are burlesqued in "that foul conspiracy / Of the beast Caliban and his confederates / Against [Prospero's] life" (4.1.139–41). This reticulum of stories contributes to a dramatic design that seems both familiar and wonderful.

But the pattern of narrative and thematic recapitulation goes far beyond this text. *The Tempest* is flagrantly intertextual, and the cluster of echoes is especially audible, again, in the temptation scene. As commentators since Coleridge have noticed, both in general structure and particular details—Antonio's hectoring Sebastian about "What thou shouldst be," the image of the crown, the sleep imagery implying failure to understand or to act, the suppression of conscience, even the image of the hungry cat (although it is used differently)—the episode restages the scene between the Macbeths before the killing of Duncan.[23] Everywhere in the scene Shakespeare is repeating himself, unashamedly gazing back over his entire *oeuvre* and summoning up scenes, persons, themes, metaphors, bits of vocabulary, and other minor theatrical strategies, so much so that the personal allegorists can hardly be blamed for the vigour with which they have approached this text. The re-created actions and speeches function as all allusions do, giving pleasure by exercising the mind and flattering veteran spectators on their perspicacity; and this audacious kind of authorial self-cannibalism contributes another layer of complexity, another apparently meaningful pattern of familiar and yet rearranged material. The duplication which constitutes the original source of meaning and pleasure, and which contains all the other patterns I have mentioned, is the troping by the play of the actual world: reality is (re)presented on the stage.24 This act of repetition is the most general instance of the process I have been describing in little, in that the relationship of play to life would seem to amount to a meaningful pattern, and yet it is immensely difficult to articulate that meaning. As Stanley Wells puts it, "The enchanted island reverberates with sounds hinting at tunes that never appear fully formed."25

IV

The prominence of the figure of repetition in both the verbal style and dramatic structure of *The Tempest* leads perforce to the question of its importance — what does the figure import through the text to the audience? what is its function? how does it mean? Although for the most part I would decline to assign specific stylistic functions to particular sounds, certain aural configurations do undeniably accomplish certain small tasks of characterization and tone.26 The hieratic style suggested by Prospero's repetitions is clearly appropriate to his vatic persona and elegiac frame of mind, it is a commonplace that some of his poetically knotted reiterations attest to his agitation at narratively re-creating his deposition, and Caliban's exultant "Freedom, high-day! High-day, freedom! Freedom, high-day, freedom!" ironically establishes his personal entrapment, his exchange of one master for another. But for the most part these and other such instances of functional echo constitute special cases. There is small profit in seeking "meaning" in Miranda's antanaclastic quibble on "your reason / For raising this sea-storm," in the vowels and consonants of Gonzalo's "If I should say I saw such islanders," or in most other lines.

I would argue that the operation of these acoustic and lexical echoes is musical, and that this music is only indirectly functional. The mutual effect of con-

centration and repetition creates a poetic counterpoint that challenges and exhilarates the auditor — Jan Kott describes *The Tempest* as a fugue27 — and this contrapuntal effect induces aurally a sense of wonder corresponding to the aims and effects of the romantic or tragicomic mode. The operation of these verbal patterns is thus paradoxical, their greatest significance being precisely their ostensible significance combined with their refusal to signify. The effect is dream-like.28 The verbal music is related to the oneiric and unreal atmosphere that attends and complicates the action of Shakespeare's late romantic forms; it promises much and delivers little, and I propose that it is just this dynamic that makes *The Tempest* uncommonly meaningful.

The insistent poetic reiterations interact with the elliptical verse style to mystify the audience about a function that never manifests itself. The play encourages its audience to scrutinize the linguistic and structural patterns for meaning, but it stoutly refuses to yield those meanings easily or fully. Eager to satisfy the desire for comprehension, we find ourselves both stimulated and frustrated. On the one hand, the repeated sounds or phrases in a brief and complicated text offer a kind of aural comfort: specifically, they create a richness of texture that seems to promise profundity. On the other, the text never fulfils the expectations of clarity which the discovery of such patterns engenders: in the rapid flow of the dialogue the repetitions themselves are succeeded by more repetitions which seem equally promising and equally unyielding. Such a strategy tantalizes the audience with the hope of clarification and fixity that art seems to promise, but it also demonstrates the difficulty and perhaps, finally, the impossibility of attaining them. Since order and comprehension seem always available but never thoroughly realized, the audience participates directly in the atmosphere of evanescence vital to this play.

The Tempest thus addresses itself directly to the problem of language and meaning, about which it registers extremely serious doubts. Denied or delayed communication becomes a minor but explicit motif as the action proceeds: numerous acts of communication (a speech, a song, a banquet, a masque) are broken off or delayed or redirected. Our position is something like that described by Caliban in his most memorable speech:

> Be not afeard. The isle is full of noises,
> Sounds, and sweet airs, that give delight and
>   hurt not.

> Sometimes a thousand twangling instruments
> Will hum about mine ears, and sometimes voices
> That if I then had waked after long sleep
> Will make me sleep again; and then in dreaming
> The clouds methought would open and show riches
> Ready to drop upon me, that when I waked
> I cried to dream again.   (3.2.138–46)

Often cited as evidence of natural sensitivity or of the magical atmosphere of the setting, these lines are most helpful as a statement of how the music of *The Tempest* impresses an audience. Robert Graves has shown that the confusion of tenses contributes to a feeling of arrested time;[29] lovely sounds "hum" about our ears; we seem to be about to receive the riches of meaning which remain forever elusive. The desired unity and gratification are contradicted by the brevity and compression of the text, and thus we find ourselves in what A. D. Nuttall has called an "atmosphere of ontological suspension" that pervades *The Tempest*, a region midway between promise and fulfilment.[30] And lest this seem too solemn let me add that this state of expectancy is also the source of immense pleasure. At this point one of my old teachers would have said, "You know. The Keats thing."

V

Tantalization is also one of the principal effects of the new mode of romance or tragicomedy that Shakespeare adopted in the late phase of his career, and the structure of the drama reinforces the fundamental erotic appeal of the verse by protracting but never seeming to supply the imminent resolution. Peter Brooks, commenting on an essay of Freud's, "Creative Writers and Day-Dreaming," writes about the aesthetic values of literary form, specifically what Freud calls "forepleasure."

> The equation of the effects of literary form with forepleasure in this well-known passage is perhaps less trivial than it at first appears. If *Lust* and *Unlust* don't take us very far in the analysis of literary texture, *Vorlust*—forepleasure—tropes on pleasure and thus seems more promising. Forepleasure is indeed a curious concept, suggesting a whole rhetoric of advance toward and retreat from the goal or the end, a formal zone of play (I take it that forepleasure somehow implicates foreplay) that is both harnessed to the end and yet autonomous, capable of deviations and recursive movements. When we begin to unpack the components of forepleasure, we may find a whole erotics of form, which is perhaps what we most need if we are to make formalism

serve an understanding of the human functions of literature. Forepleasure would include the notion of both delay and advance in the textual dynamic, the creation of that "dilatory space" which Roland Barthes, in *S/Z*, claimed to be the essence of the textual middle. We seek to advance through this space toward the discharge of the end, yet all the while we are perversely delaying, returning backward in order to put off the promised end and perhaps to assure its greater significance.[31]

This suggestive paragraph is relevant to the way that Shakespeare's late style functions in, and in concert with, the voguish new dramatic mode. A more or less contemporary description of the process of narrative teasing is found in William Cartwright's prefatory verses in the 1647 Beaumont and Fletcher Folio:

> None can prevent the fancy, and see through
> At the first opening; all stand wondering how
> The thing will be, until it is; which hence
> With fresh delight still cheats, still takes the sense;
> The whole design, the shadow, the lights such
> That none can say he shews or hides too much.

The titillating diction of Cartwright's description is given special meaning in light of Brooks's plea for a textual erotics, for both capture the gamesome or sportive quality of romance or tragicomedy.[32]

Narrative progress towards the satisfactions of complete understanding, or closure, is indirect and irregular, and the chief pleasure rests in the delay and the circuitousness of the journey. Romance depends upon suspense, secrets, surprises, discoveries, peripeties, awakenings, revelations. Thus it automatically raises questions of epistemology but almost invariably leaves them open. It is a knowing form, a self-conscious mode reliant upon the audience's familiarity with conventions of tragic and comic storytelling and its willingness to be teased by the playwright's manipulation of generic signals. For similar reasons it is an ironic form in flattering the audience with privileged information; yet it deals in double ironies when it betrays this cosy relationship by a sudden reversal or surprise. Suspense and irony constitute only one pair of several antitheses inherent in tragicomic form (and implicit in its name); these have been described by Philip Edwards as "the pleasure of being kept out of the secret and the pleasure of being let into the secret."[33] Brooks's account of formal erotics is especially pertinent to the gestural narrative style of *The Tempest* and of the mode of romance generally.[34] Although the formal divagations are perhaps not as easy to discern in a compact work such as *The Tempest* as they are in *Cymbeline*, they are present none the less, and they recapitulate on a larger scale the sense of promise and profundity fostered by the texture of the verse.

VI

The sophisticated effects of form and style bespeak a degree of self-consciousness considerably greater than most recent political readings can admit, a self-awareness that comprehends the issues of politics and power central to the colonialist argument. The poetic and structural figures of repetition become directly pertinent to the critical debate over the European colonial impulse when that will to power is regarded as an effort to re-create the self in a new environment. Therefore the episodes and topics political critics have chosen to stress—the proprietary claims of the deceased Sycorax and her legacy to Caliban, Prospero's usurpation of the island from him, the enslavement of Ariel, the dynastic marriages of Claribel and Miranda—all these attest to the play's profound concern with reproduction, in various senses from the biological to the political to the aesthetic. Throughout its narrative *The Tempest* raises disturbing questions about the act of reproduction, not only the genetic possibilities ("Good wombs have borne bad sons") but also the difficulties of re-creating society, beginning afresh, repairing in the new world the errors of the old, and it does so in a style that refuses to cease re-creating itself.

The opening scene introduces the problem of sovereignty ("What cares these roarers for the name of king?"); Prospero's epilogue begs for remission and release ("let your indulgence set me free"): from beginning to end the playwright gives prominence to the problems of dominion, freedom, political failure, and the repetition of the past. Prospero's expository recital of how he lost control of himself and his dukedom is inflected with multiple variations on political failure and the repetition of past errors. He begins with a consideration of Miranda's memory, her ability to re-create the past imaginatively—"Of anything the image tell me that / Hath kept with thy remembrance" (1.2.43–4)—and the dimness of that memory prompts his rehearsal of the usurpation. Moreover, the daughter's piteous reaction to the tale reproduces emotionally the ordeal of banishment: she "will cry it o'er again" (1.2.134). His lecture reviews Antonio's seizure of power and renovation of the court, and, as Stephen Orgel points out, "this

monologue is only the first of a series of repetitions."[35] Antonio encourages Sebastian to repeat the crime of deposing his brother; Prospero seeks to repair political division by arranging the dynastic marriage of Miranda and Ferdinand; Alonso is desperate at the loss of his son, which is the end of the biological line and the forfeiture of his future, Claribel being "lost" to him as well; Stephano, Trinculo, and Caliban seek to establish their own kingdom, taking power from Prospero who has himself seized the island from Caliban; Caliban has tried to reproduce himself by raping Miranda ("I had peopled else / This isle with Calibans"); the masque of Ceres dramatizes the importance of fertility, agriculture, and orderly succession; Prospero has sought by his magical art to remake his kingdom; and Shakespeare has sought by his theatrical art to reconstruct the material world. Looked at from one point of view, colonialism becomes a form of political and cultural reproduction congruent with the effort to transcend time through art, and both of these represent versions of the defence against death.

Considerations of political and artistic re-creation lead us back to the poetry of *The Tempest,* for the stylistic and structural repetitions engage the audience textually with the same problems of authority and power that dominate political interpretation. The tendency of words and phrases to repeat themselves is a case of stylistic reproduction that creates, as I have shown, an atmosphere in which control of meaning remains necessarily elusive. The effect of the style throughout is to place the auditor in an intermediate state, and that region of indeterminacy is a version of the various other kinds of liminality associated with this text: the island is located midway between Africa and Europe; it apparently partakes of, or is hospitable to, the natural and supernatural realms; Miranda stands between childhood and maturity, Caliban between demon and human, Prospero between vengeance and mercy; even time seems arrested ("what's past is prologue"). The poetry seduces the audience into a state of stylistic suspension, an intuitive zone between sleep and wake, "a strange repose" like that felt by Sebastian (2.1.218) or that described in Caliban's lyric. It is a marginal condition between expectation and understanding, affirmation and scepticism, comedy and tragedy.

Poetic indeterminacy shows us how to evaluate the appropriation of the play by those who see it as a political act in the colonialist enterprise. It helps to complicate the ideology of *The Tempest,* indicating that the political ideas are more subtle and difficult than recent readings would suggest. Pleas for interpretative caution are often attacked as retrogressive politics, but the recognition that this is one of the most knowing, most self-conscious texts in the canon should warn us about pretensions to ideological certainty. On the very issues that have most deeply concerned materialist critics and their American cousins—power, social and political hierarchy, the theatre as a political instrument, freedom of action, education, and race—*The Tempest* is at its most elusive and complicated. The play valorizes ambiguity and irony, ironizing its own positions and insisting upon the inconclusiveness of its own conclusions. The new orthodoxy, which exalts the colonized, is as narrow as the old, which idealizes and excuses the colonizer.[36]

This stylistic interpretation is not, however, merely another version of New Criticism, a retreat, that is, into the restful shadows of irony and ambiguity. The difference is that this reading of *The Tempest* admits the importance of contextual study and historical location, just as it recognizes the inescapable affiliation of the political and the aesthetic. I acknowledge the capacity of new modes of criticism to identify and promote ideological issues and other points of departure that more traditional forms of criticism have neglected or deliberately suppressed. But I also seek to balance those virtues with a sensitivity to the claims of the text. It needs to be pointed out that as students and teachers of literature we are professionally concerned with political issues not just in themselves but as they are embodied in aesthetic forms. The dismissal of verse is dangerous, especially if the subject of inquiry is verse drama. In reaction to the excesses and orthodoxies of New Criticism, our own critical practice is moving farther and farther away from the text, and in reading this play stylistically I register a mild protest against the implicit cheapening of textuality. The poetry of *The Tempest* alerts us to the delicate relation between literature and ideology.

Which is what, according to Kenneth Burke, art ought to do. In an essay on the fictional uncertainties of Mann and Gide, he identifies the pleasures of the unfixed:

> so long as we feel the need of certitude, the state of doubt is discomforting, and by its very prolongation can make for our hysterical retreat into belief, as Hans Castorp descended from his mountain to

the battlefield. But why could one not come to accept his social wilderness without anguish, utilizing for his self-respect either the irony and melancholy of Mann, or the curiosity of Gide? One need not suffer under insecurity any more than an animal suffers from being constantly on the alert for danger. In the unformed there are opportunities which can be invigorating to contemplate. This state of technical apprehension can be a norm, and certainly an athletic norm.[37]

The Tempest promotes in its audience a kind of moral and imaginative athleticism, an intellectual fitness that much recent interpretation, by relaxing—or stiffening—into a single mode of reading, has evaded. The play's epistemological sophistication is inconsistent with the baldness of a single-mindedly ideological interpretation. To listen to its language is to become deeply sceptical about the operation of all kinds of power—poetic, political, and critical too.

Notes

1. "'Nymphs and reapers heavily vanish': the Discursive Con-texts of *The Tempest*," *Alternative Shakespeares*, ed. John Drakakis (London and New York: Methuen, 1985), pp. 191–205.

2. Recent British readers seem especially unsympathetic to the play, perhaps because, as Walter Cohen suggests, their response to its colonial associations undermines an otherwise unified vision of Shakespeare's political progressivism. See "Political Criticism of Shakespeare," in *Shakespeare Reproduced: The Text in History and Ideology*, ed. Jean E. Howard and Marion F. O'Connor (London: Methuen, 1987), p. 37.

3. Some of the essays that make the topic of colonialism their central theme are the following: Paul E. Brown, "'This thing of darkness I acknowledge mine': *The Tempest* and the Discourse of Colonialism," in *Political Shakespeare*, ed. Jonathan Dollimore and Alan Sinfield (Ithaca: Cornell University Press, 1985); Paul N. Siegel, "Historical Ironies in *The Tempest*," *Shakespeare Jahrbuch*, 119 (1983), 104–11; Thomas Cartelli, "Prospero in Africa: *The Tempest* as Colonialist Text and Pretext," in Howard and O'Connor, *Shakespeare Reproduced*, pp. 99–115; Terence Hawkes, "Swisser-Swatter: Making a Man of English Letters," in Drakakis's *Alternative Shakespeares*, pp. 26–46; Stephen Orgel, "Prospero's Wife," *Representations*, 8 (1985), 1–13,

and "Shakespeare and the Cannibals," in *Witches, Cannibals, Divorce: Estranging the Renaissance,* Selected Papers from the English Institute, NS II, ed. Marjorie Garber (Baltimore: Johns Hopkins University Press, 1986), pp. 40–66; Stephen Greenblatt, "Martial Law in the Land of Cockaigne," in *Shakespearean Negotiations: The Circulation of Social Energy in Renaissance England* (Berkeley: University of California Press, 1988), pp. 129–63.

4. The essay is printed in *First Images of America: The Impact of the New World on the Old,* ed. Fredi Chiappelli, 2 vols. (Berkeley: University of California Press, 1976), pp. 561–80.

5. (Ithaca: Cornell University Press, 1985), p. 48.

6. *Drama of a Nation: Public Theater in Renaissance England and Spain* (Ithaca: Cornell University Press, 1985), p. 401.

7. "Faithful Servants: Shakespeare's Praise of Disobedience," in *The Historical Renaissance: New Essays on Tudor and Stuart Literature and Culture,* ed. Heather Dubrow and Richard Strier (Chicago: University of Chicago Press, 1988), p. 133 n. 81.

8. *The Tempest,* ed. Frank Kermode (London: Methuen, 1954). Other studies now considered limited for their neglect of political issues would include those of G. Wilson Knight, *The Crown of Life* (Oxford: Clarendon Press, 1947), pp. 203–55; Reuben A. Brower, "The Mirror of Analogy: *The Tempest,*" in *The Fields of Light: An Experiment in Critical Reading* (New York: Oxford, 1951), pp. 95–122; Northrop Frye, Introduction to *The Tempest* in *The Complete Pelican Shakespeare,* gen. ed. Alfred Harbage (Baltimore: Penguin, 1969); D. G. James, *The Dream of Prospero* (Oxford: Clarendon Press, 1967); Harry Levin, "Two Magian Comedies: *The Alchemist* and *The Tempest,*" *Shakespeare Survey* 22 (1969), 47–58; Derek Traversi, *Shakespeare: The Last Phase* (London: Hollis and Carter, 1954); Harry Berger, "Miraculous Harp: A Reading of Shakespeare's *Tempest,*" *Shakespeare Studies,* 5 (1969), 253–83; Howard Felperin, *Shakespearean Romance* (Princeton: Princeton University Press, 1972); Joseph H. Summers, "The Anger of Prospero," in *Dreams of Love and Power: On Shakespeare's Plays* (Oxford: Clarendon, 1984).

9. For a fascinating commentary on this kind of critical power struggle, see Anthony B. Dawson, "*Tempest* in a Teapot: Critics, Evaluation, Ideology," in *Bad Shakespeare: Revaluations of the Shakespeare Canon,* ed. Maurice Charney (Rutherford, NJ: Fairleigh Dickinson University Press, 1988), pp. 61–73. Dawson is especially eloquent on "the way 'materialist' critics expose the hidden biases of traditional criticism . . . but fall into some of the same traps, particularly in the vexed area of evaluation and the ideological assumptions that the act of evaluating often makes plain" (71).

10. "Discourse and the Individual: The Case of Colonialism in *The Tempest,*" *Shakespeare Quarterly,* 40 (1989), 47. One of the earliest complaints about the excesses of recent political criticism was Edward Pechter's "The New Historicism and Its Discontents: Politicizing Renaissance Drama," *PMLA,* 102 (1987), 292–303. On the other hand, Carolyn Porter has attacked New Historicists for being insufficiently historical and insufficiently political: see "Are We Being Historical Yet?," *South Atlantic Quarterly,* 87 (1988), 743–86.

11. "Music Does Not Flow," *New York Review of Books,* 17 December 1981, p. 49.

12. Although everyone agrees that the poetry of the last plays is difficult and different from the earlier verse, surprisingly little has been written about it. See F. E. Halliday, *The Poetry of Shakespeare's Plays* (London: Duckworth, 1954); J. M. Nosworthy's Introduction to the Arden edition of *Cymbeline* (London: Methuen, 1955), lxii–lxxiii; N. F. Blake, *Shakespeare's Language: An Introduction* (London: Methuen, 1983); John Porter Houston, *Shakespearean Sentences: A Study in Style and Syntax* (Baton Rouge: Louisiana State University Press, 1987); and George T. Wright, *Shakespeare's Metrical Art* (Berkeley: University of California Press, 1988). In preparing this essay I have also profited from Cyrus Hoy's "The Language of Fletcherian Tragicomedy," in *Mirror up to Shakespeare: Essays in Honour of G. R. Hibbard,* ed. J. C. Gray (Toronto: University of Toronto Press, 1984), pp. 99–113.

13. "*The Tempest,* or Repetition," in *The Bottom Translation: Marlowe and Shakespeare and the Carnival Tradition,* tr. Daniela Miedzyrzecka and Lillian Vallee (Evanston: Northwestern University Press, 1987).

14. For an intelligent discussion of the "abstract" qualities of Shakespeare's late work, see Marion Trousdale, "Style in *The Winter's Tale,*" *Critical Quarterly,* 18 (1976), 25–32.

15. On this and many points of stylistic criticism, I have been aided by the analysis of John Porter Houston in *Shakespearean Sentences.*

16. Introduction to *The Tempest* (Harmondsworth: Penguin, 1968), pp. 13–14.

17. *An Essay on Shakespeare's Sonnets* (New Haven: Yale University Press, 1969), pp. 87–88. Booth's comments on how poetic effects function in individual sonnets are extremely stimulating and applicable beyond their immediate subject. See also the essay by Kenneth Burke, "On Musicality in Verse," in which he demonstrates the complex effects of assonance and consonance in some poems of Coleridge: *The Philosophy of Literary Form* (Berkeley: University of California Press, rpt. 1973), pp. 369–79.

18. Here, as in a few other passages, I have added emphasis to illustrate certain poetic effects.

19. See Anne Barton, "Shakespeare and the Limits of Language," *Shakespeare Survey* 24 (1971), 19–30.

20. On the expressive possibilities of this tactic, see Wright's *Shakespeare's Metrical Art*, especially chapter 13, "Trochees."

21. On the relative importance of specific and general effects in the last plays, see Anne Barton, "Leontes and the Spider: Language and Speaker in the Last Plays," *Shakespeare's Styles: Essays in honour of Kenneth Muir,* ed. Philip Edwards, G. K. Hunter, and Inga-Stina Ewbank (Cambridge: Cambridge University Press, 1980), pp. 131–50.

22. See, for example, Joan Hartwig, *Shakespeare's Analogical Scene: Parody as Structural Syntax* (Lincoln: University of Nebraska Press, 1983), chapter 8; Brower's *The Fields of Light*; and Knight's *The Crown of Life.*

23. For an excellent discussion of the densely allusive quality of this scene, see Paul A. Cantor, "Shakespeare's *The Tempest:* The Wise Man as Hero," *Shakespeare Quarterly,* 31 (1980), 64–75.

24. See Ruth Nevo's comments on this metatheatrical device: "The embedding of play within play dissolves representational boundaries so that the audience is required to suspend its attention, to negotiate a constant interchange between fictional reality and fictional illusion," *Shakespeare's Other Language* (London: Methuen, 1987), p. 136. This point of view is consistent with Shakespeare's late attitude toward a device that had served him well from the beginning, as Anne Barton points out: "On the whole, efforts to distinguish the fictional from the 'real,' art from life, tales from truth, come in the Romances to replace the older, moral concern with identifying hypocrisy and deceit." "Leontes and the Spider," p. 147.

25. "Shakespeare and Romance," in *Later Shakespeare,* ed. John Russell Brown and Bernard Harris, Stratford-upon-Avon Studies, 8 (London: Edward Arnold, 1966), p. 75.

26. From time to time aural echoes function as images do, pointing up crucial words and the ideas they raise. Consider the effect of "be" in the following exchange:

> ALONSO: Whe'er thou beest he or no,
> Or some enchanted trifle to abuse me,
> As late I have been, I not know: Thy pulse
> Beats, as of flesh and blood; and, since I saw thee
> Th'affliction of my mind amends, with which
> I fear a madness held me. This must crave—
> An if this be at all—a most strange story.
> Thy dukedom I resign, and do entreat
> Thou pardon me my wrongs. But how should Prospero
> Be living and be here?
> PROSPERO (*to Gonzalo*): First, noble friend.
> Let me embrace thine age, whose honour cannot
> Be measured or confined.
>   *He embraces Gonzalo*
> Gonzalo: Whether this be,
> Or be not, I'll not swear.   (5.1.113–24)

The hammering of the verb underscores the problem that Alonso and finally the audience must confront, the ontological status of what we are witnessing.

Stanley Fish has written brilliantly on the logical dangers of such interpretation, specifically on the circularity of thematic stylistics: "formal patterns are themselves the products of interpretation and . . . therefore there is no such thing as a formal pattern, at least in the sense necessary for the practice of stylistics: that is, no pattern that one can observe before interpretation is hazarded and which therefore can be used to prefer one interpretation to another." *Is There a Text in This Class?: The Authority of Textual Communities* (Cambridge, Mass.: Harvard University Press, 1980), p. 267. See also John Hollander, "The Metrical Frame," in *The Structure of Verse: Modern Essays on Prosody,* ed. Harvey Gross, rev. ed. (New York: Ecco Press, 1979), pp. 77–101.

27. *The Bottom Translation*, p. 97.
28. Of the many studies of the oneiric qualities of *The Tempest*, the most recent is found in Ruth Nevo's *Shakespeare's Other Language*, especially pp. 136–43.
29. *The White Goddess* (London: Farrar, 1948), p. 425.
30. *Two Concepts of Allegory: A Study of Shakespeare's "The Tempest" and the Logic of Allegorical Expression* (New York: Barnes and Noble, 1967), p. 158.
31. Peter Brooks, "The Idea of a Psychoanalytic Literary Criticism," *Critical Inquiry*, 13 (1987), 339.
32. Although I am sensitive to the various differences between the two kinds known as "romance" and "tragicomedy," it will be agreed that the forms share a number of fundamental features, and it is those similarities on which I am concentrating here.
33. "The Danger Not the Death: The Art of John Fletcher," in *Jacobean Theatre*, edited John Russell Brown and Bernard Harris (London: Edward Arnold, 1960), p. 164.
34. Patricia A. Parker brilliantly develops some of the same ideas as Brooks: "The suspensions which for Barthes become part of an erotics of the text recall not only the constant divagations of romance and its resistance to the demands of closure, but also the frustration in Ariosto of what Barthes calls the teleological form of vulgar readerly pleasure—the desire to penetrate the veil of meaning or to hasten the narrative's gradual striptease—by a continual postponement of revelation which leaves the reader suspended, or even erotically 'hung up.'" *Inescapable Romance: Studies in the Poetics of a Mode* (Princeton: Princeton University Press, 1979), pp. 220–221.
35. Introduction to his edition of *The Tempest*, p. 15.
36. See Skura, "The Case of Colonialism," in which she argues that new historicism "is now in danger of fostering blindness of its own. Granted that something was wrong with a commentary that focused on *The Tempest* as a self-contained project of a self-contained individual and that ignored the political situation in 1611. But something seems wrong now also, something more than the rhetorical excesses characteristic of any innovative critical movement" (pp. 46–47).
37. *Counter-statement* (rpt. Berkeley: University of California Press, 1968), p. 106.

APPLICATION

On the Third Stanza of Keats's "Ode on a Grecian Urn"

David A. Kent

David A. Kent's essay "On the Third Stanza of Keats's 'Ode on a Grecian Urn'" asks a characteristic formalist question: what is the function of a "part" of a literary work? And it provides a characteristic formalist answer: it explains the part in terms of the whole, thereby demonstrating the coherence of the work. The "part" may be a technique, an image pattern, a character, a scene, or as here, a formal unit—the third stanza. Kent begins by identifying an interpretive problem, noting the different ways critics have described the stanza's function and variously rated its success. His proposed solution is to read the stanza with even closer attention to the "very forms of language" used throughout the poem. "In short, to appreciate the place of the stanza in the poem's development, we need to attend to the poet's grammar and rhetoric." In the analysis that follows, Kent finds a tension between the grammatical and rhetorical effects and a paradoxical role for the stanza within this paradoxical poem. But the tension is carefully contrived, the paradox is the precise result of the artistic form, and grammar and rhetoric are ultimately reconciled on the thematic level. (Compare the discussion of grammar and rhetoric in the essays by Paul de Man and Barbara Jones Guetti in chapter 6.) In the end, the stanza is seen to function as a coherent part of a coherent whole. "Looking both backward and forward, acting as climax to the first two stanzas and as prophetic of the fourth stanza's discovery, the third stanza occupies a pivotal position in the ode's entire dramatic trajectory."

In the commentaries on Keats's "Ode on a Grecian Urn," the function of stanza three in the poem has been variously described. First, on the critical side, in it Cleanth Brooks detected "a falling-off from the delicate but firm precision of the earlier stanzas" and thought the stanza (rather than the last) "the blemish

Reprinted by permission from the *Keats-Shelley Journal* 36 (1987): 20–25.

on the ode," if one were to be identified. Rayan has more recently claimed that the repetitions in the stanza charm the reader "into forgetting the main argument" of the ode. More often, however, the third stanza has been perceived as central to the ode's structure and development. For example, Kenneth Burke described it as "the fulcrum" in the poem's "swing." In any reading that finds the poem as involving an experience of (to use Stuart Sperry's words) "imaginative engagement and disengagement," the third stanza must be pivotal. Indeed, Morris Dickstein locates the ode's crucial "turn" immediately after the ecstatic "More happy love! more happy, happy love!", a hyperbolic utterance that seems effectively to preclude further elaboration.[1] It is, for Earl Wasserman too, a "climatic" stanza. And yet, in spite of its generally acknowledged centrality, the exclamatory manner of the stanza has been characterized by still other critics as "a form of babble" or dismissed as "excessive" and "strained."[2] The repetitions, hyperbole, and babble observed by these critics may suggest that the very forms of language employed by Keats need closer scrutiny. In short, to appreciate the place of the stanza in the poem's development, we need to attend to the poet's grammar and rhetoric.

When the language of Keats's "Ode on a Grecian Urn" as a whole is examined, we find that it is essentially characterized by interrogative, exclamatory, and phrasal forms. Each of these rhetorical and grammatical modes takes its dramatically appropriate place in the poem's "plot" (to borrow Keats's apposite pun from "Ode to a Nightingale"). Taken together, these modes confirm the ode, first, as a poem of intense involvement (for both speaker and reader) leading, it would appear, to a revelatory discovery; and yet, second, as a poem in which the reader vainly searches for statements which contain or point to some verifiable meaning. In the ode, in fact, there is a discernible absence of independent clauses, i.e., of complete, declarative statements. When independent statements do occur (for example, at the beginning and end of the second stanza), they are used to push the poem forward or to state conclusions (as at the end of the fourth stanza). This same function is more ambiguously employed in the grammar of the ode's final five lines where three consecutive compound sentences appear. However, the best known of these sentences has been reduced to an elliptical aphorism ("'Beauty is truth, truth beauty'") once described by T. S. Eliot as "grammatically meaningless."[3]

More specifically, Keats's ode features an abundance of apostrophes (see the opening three definitions of the urn in the first stanza), of questions (to express the excitement of speculation in the first stanza; to convey a more searching and troubled attitude in the fourth stanza), of imperatives (as in the second stanza), and of exclamations (to express a mounting ecstasy in the second and third stanzas). The initial apostrophes postulate metaphorical definitions of the urn as a prelude to more intimate engagement, while the apostrophe at the start of the concluding stanza ironically testifies to the fact that, by this point, the urn has been emptied of metaphorical value and that such value, in any case, is not intrinsic but had been imputed to the urn by the poet. The imperative forms appear in the second stanza as the poet urges his imagination to animate the figures on the urn, an undertaking closely allied to the traditional activity of the figure of apostrophe itself. Other forms combine with the vocative in the second, fourth, and fifth stanzas—a verbal mood perhaps understandable in a poem juxtaposing poetry and the visual arts but in which all the aesthetic activity is necessarily recorded in language. Earl Wasserman remains one of the few critics to have given sustained attention to Keats's grammar and rhetoric in the ode. While he does observe a "disintegration of the syntax" in the third stanza of the ode, his analysis of the poem is largely in the service of a schematic, transcendentalist thesis with which few readers are still in sympathy.[4] In the brief analysis which follows, I wish to focus attention on the grammatical and rhetorical elements Keats deploys in the third stanza and so to clarify the function of the stanza within the development of the ode.

> Ah, happy, happy boughs! that cannot shed
> Your leaves, nor ever bid the spring adieu;
> And, happy melodist, unwearied,
> For ever piping songs for ever new;
> More happy love! more happy, happy love!
> For ever warm and still to be enjoy'd,
> For ever panting, and for ever young;
> All breathing human passion far above,
> That leaves a heart high-sorrowful and cloy'd,
> A burning forehead, and a parching tongue.

The third stanza evokes the contradictory critical reactions cited above because its role in the ode's development is a paradoxical one. In the first place, the assertions in the stanza are largely generated by repetition, but these assertions, taken cumulatively, call themselves into question; the reader begins to think that the poet protests too much. The most evident repetition is of the word "happy" and of the phrase "for ever." The word "happy" occurs six times in the first five lines of the stanza. The phrase "for ever" appears five times in the stanza, with an additional "ever" used in the second line. Walter Jackson Bate suggests that the fact of repetition may spring from the poet's envy of the happiness the figures on the urn appear to be experiencing, although "envy" is precisely what Keats repudiates as a motive in the similarly empathic experience of the companion "Ode to a Nightingale" ("'tis not through envy of thy happy lot," line 5).[5] Certainly the repetition conveys a sense of strain and desperation. Yet the repetition equally suggests a poverty or inadequacy in language itself, perhaps implying that the poet has reached the upper limits of his power to articulate his experience. The appearance of "happy" three times in a single line, the fifth, and in conjunction with the comparative ("More . . . more"), does affirm life on the urn as having a superior status, but the very fact of comparison also implies that reality has already begun to impinge on the idealized vision the poet has projected onto the urn. In effect, the rhetoric of repetition destabilizes the assertion of happiness.

Secondly, besides the use of repetitions, Keats exploits present participles in the second half of the stanza ("panting," "breathing," "burning," and "parching"). These participles focus attention on the activity denoted by each verb and seek to prolong the identification with the urn that the speaker has been at pains to effect. Nevertheless, as with Keats's use of repetition, the participles simultaneously betray the futility of this endeavour by inexorably dragging the poet back to life—aptly summarized in the phrase "all breathing human passion." "For ever warm" may initially appeal to the imagination but "for ever panting," on reflection, rapidly loses its appeal. As Dickstein observes, the "breathing" of "human passion" becomes "more unambiguously desirable" than the lovers' apparently perpetual state of hyperventilation.[6] Similarly, the "still" in "still to be enjoy'd" receives a heavy rhythmical stress that emphasizes the endless and static wait for fulfillment in which the figures on the urn are trapped. This suggested meaning marks a significant shift from the richly ambiguous "still" of the ode's first line.

Thirdly, the poet's assertive praise for the urn in this stanza is also, paradoxically, framed in negatives. The boughs "cannot shed" their leaves. Even the fracturing of the line (between "shed" and "leaves") conveys a subtle awareness of the unnaturalness of this elaborately fabricated "Bower of Bliss." Concentrating synecdochally on the leaves as unnatural and emblematic artifacts only further underlines the odd, perhaps ultimately perverse, insistence marking the subsequent lines of the stanza. The inability to "shed" thus points directly to another, more "telling" liability: nor can the leaves "ever bid the Spring adieu." Life on the urn is not, however, bilingual as this French word might fancifully suggest; as Keats discovers, this life is not even unilingual. The urn's life is beyond, or possibly below, language. The melodist may be "unwearied" but "the weariness, the fever, and the fret" (Ode to a Nightingale," line 23) lurk just behind the urn. To pipe songs "for ever" would seem, logically, to deny that these songs could be "forever new" except in some almost grotesque fantasy of infinite creative fecundity. Here, then, is one of the idealist's perennial dilemmas: having to describe the ideal in terms of the real. In the ode the ideal is implicitly distanced and made alien from human life even as "for" modulates to "far"; and just how "far" is underlined by "All" and "human."

Repetition, participles, praise: the activity of language in the rhetoric of the stanza's assertiveness has masked one final (and perhaps most significant) grammatical fact. Earlier I noted the general absence of independent clauses in the ode; the third stanza does not contain a single independent clause. Composed merely of phrases and subordinate clauses, it stands as a fragment, incomplete and dependent, though its dependence ironically proclaims a delusive independence. One of its key phrases, moreover ("All breathing human passion far above"), is itself isolated, disconnected, and formally "dangling."[7] The dependent grammatical status of the stanza, however, directly supports one of the urn's major themes and marks the climax in a subplot initiated in the first stanza (the urn as "Sylvan historian" expressing a "tale more sweetly than our rhyme," lines 3–4) and reiterated in the second ("those unheard / Are sweeter," lines 11–12). In these opening two stanzas silence is proposed as superior to language, the art of the urn to the art of the poet, life on the urn to life on earth. On the other hand, the poem subsequently records the implications generated by the forms of language in the third stanza: the discovery that the urn is incomplete, lifeless, its empty town abandoned by human folk and therefore deprived of articulation. No one is left to "tell" (line 39), to explain. This radical insufficiency (also prefigured by the "cannot . . . bid" [lines 21–22] in the third stanza) is now perceived as just that. Silent inexpressiveness is no asset but an inhuman deficiency. The perpetual "leaves" (line 22) also, in retrospect, anticipate the "leaves" of line 29 in which the intimation of residue or aftermath is precisely the urn's legacy to the fantasizing poet who must face the inevitable leave-taking. It is, finally, no accident that Keats has placed the words "art" and "desolate" side by side in the fourth stanza (line 40). Art is found to be, in part at least, a desolation.[8]

If the desolation of art involves its ultimate dependence, that dependence in turn allows Keats to discover art's corresponding usefulness, why it is "a friend to man." And, of course, Keats implicitly includes his own urnlike ode in his reflection on this issue; he has, after all, fashioned his poem with a circular structure, with a predominance of 'o' sounds, and with a riddling, endlessly circling motto as its ultimate statement.[9] Both urn and ode are finally dependent on a beholder, a reader, to give life to image and typographical symbol—to animate by imagination. The bride of art requires its devoted, courting bridegroom. This dependency is only temporarily erased in the brief experience of conjunction, the joining of subject and object (reflected, perhaps, in the enigmatic formula of the closing lines where the copula verb is initially explicit—"Beauty is truth"— and then is erased as the terms merge in unity— "truth beauty"). But that joining cannot be sustained and to prefer art to life involves, for Keats, a "sacrifice" (line 31) that is really suicide, the discovery also recorded in "Ode to a Nightingale." All art is, finally, dependent.

The grammatical dependence at the heart of "Ode on a Grecian Urn"—together with such other rhetorical phenomena as repetition, the exploitation of participles, and the use of negatives in praise—all join to subvert the ostensible assertions the language contains. The lifeless desolation of art uncovered by the ode's fourth stanza is thus already implied by the grammatical and rhetorical elements of the third stanza and, in particular, by its dependent quality. The third stanza of Keats's poem is not then a "digression," as Bate once observed.[10] Looking both backward and forward, acting as climax to the first two stanzas and as prophetic of the fourth stanza's discovery, the third stanza occupies a pivotal position in the ode's entire dramatic trajectory.

Notes

1. Cleanth Brooks, "Keats's Sylvan Historian" in *John Keats, Odes: A Casebook,* ed. G. S. Fraser (London: Macmillan, 1971), p. 138; Krishna Rayan, "The Grecian Urn Re-Read," *Mosaic,* 11 (1977–78), 17; Kenneth Burke, "Symbolic Action in a Poem by Keats," in Fraser, *Casebook,* p. 110; Stuart M. Sperry, *Keats the Poet* (Princeton: Princeton University Press, 1973), p. 270; Morris Dickstein, *Keats and His Poetry: A Study in Development* (Chicago: University of Chicago Press, 1971), p. 224; all references to Keats's poetry are from *The Poems of John Keats,* ed. Jack Stillinger (Cambridge: Harvard University Press, 1978).

2. Earl Wasserman, *The Finer Tone: Keats' Major Poems* (1953; rpt. Baltimore: The Johns Hopkins Press, 1967), p. 36; Helen Vendler, *The Odes of John Keats* (Cambridge: Harvard University Press, 1983), p. 138; W. J. Bate, *The Stylistic Development of Keats* (1945; rpt. New York: Humanities Press, 1962), p. 140; Dickstein, *Keats and His Poetry,* p. 224.

3. T. S. Eliot, "Dante" in *Selected Essays,* 3rd ed. (1932; rpt. London: Faber and Faber, 1969), p. 270.

4. Wasserman, *The Finer Tone,* p. 41.

5. W. J. Bate, *John Keats* (London: Oxford University Paperbacks, 1967), p. 513.

6. Dickstein, *Keats and His Poetry,* p. 225. It should also be noted here that Keats manages to embody his theme dramatically by forcing the reader to "pant" and strain in the act of reading the stanza aloud.

7. See Susan Wolfson, "The Language of Interpretation in Romantic Poetry: 'A Strong Working of the Mind,'" in *Romanticism & Language,* ed. Arden Reed (Ithaca: Cornell University Press, 1984), pp. 42–43.

8. I am indebted to Paul Read for this observation.

9. The two "contestants" in the ode are not life and art but rather two art forms. See the detailed discussion of this approach in John J. Teunissen and Evelyn Hinz, "'Ode on a Grecian Urn': Keats's 'Laocoon,'" *English Studies in Canada,* 6 (1980), 181, and *passim.* For comments on the "self-sufficient circularity of the urn," see Darrel Mansell, "Keats's Urn: 'On' and On," *Language and Style,* 7 (1974), 244.

10. *John Keats,* p. 514.

APPLICATION

Taking seriously the formalist claim that "how" the poem means is "what" it means, R. Bruce Bickley, Jr. focuses his analysis on Melville's narrative techniques, especially his handling of point-of-view and imagery. Melville "sought a method for hinting at Delano's incomplete view of reality, yet at the same time he wanted to preserve the immediacy and familiarity of the first-person technique, which had proven itself artistically seaworthy in his previous writings. What he settled on was a limited-omniscient narrator, one privileged to enter Delano's mind alone, but also permitted to draw partially aside the masks that conceal the identities of Babo and Cereno." By telling the story from this point of view, Melville forces the reader to experience the ironies and uncertainties of a very complex reality. Indeed, as Bickley's analysis shows, there are layers upon layers of irony in Melville's tale; so much so that Cleanth Brooks's title, "Irony as a Principle of Structure," might serve as well for Bickley's essay. And for the same reason: irony functions to convey the complexity of the artist's vision. In addition to point of view, Bickley also analyzes the imagery of the story, and again with an eye to its thematic implications: "In its basic form the tale is a meditation upon the texture of reality," and imagery is Melville's vehicle for representing that texture. In short, the good prose narrative is as carefully wrought as the compressed lyric poem and must be just as carefully read with attention to how its formal features function to reveal meaning.

The Method of Melville's Short Fiction: "Benito Cereno"

R. Bruce Bickley, Jr.

Chapter 18 of Captain Amasa Delano's *Narrative of Voyages and Travels*[1] reported an incident that, to Melville's literary imagination, must have seemed fraught with a "suggestiveness" equal to that in the *Agatha material. Delano had for several hours given personal assistance to a Spanish slave trader that was short of water and supplies; the whole time he was on board, however, he was unaware that the slaves had rebelled and, even before his eyes, were holding the Spanish captain and crew in brutal subjection. Furthermore, Melville's source provided him with a compelling cast of characters. Like Agatha and Robertson, Captain Delano, Benito Cereno, and his black attendant were prototypes from real life; given careful psychological and emotional development, they would readily serve the tale's larger metaphysical themes.

In re-creating his source materials as art, Melville worked a variation on his characteristic rhetorical mode, first-person ironic narration. He sought a method for hinting at Delano's incomplete view of reality, yet at the same time he wanted to preserve the immediacy and familiarity of the first-person technique, which had proven itself artistically seaworthy in his previous writings. What he settled on was a limited-omniscient narrator, one privileged to enter Delano's mind alone, but also permitted to draw partially aside the masks that conceal the identities of Babo and Cereno. Melville conceived his tale as an interior psychological portrait of the American captain, counterpointed by an alternately increasing and decreasing atmospheric pressure of suspense as Delano wavers between uneasiness and restored confidence. Also, Delano's responses to the enigmatical and disconcerting figure of Cereno, like the lawyer's to his scrivener, vary in both pitch and intensity: from objective deliberation (the ship's misfortune has resulted in an unusual state of affairs on board), to irritation and petulance (Cereno's impoliteness and reserve are an insult to a fellow sea-officer), to worldly-wise indulgence (Cereno is merely an incompetent), to near-panic (Cereno is a plotting pirate only waiting for an opportune moment to call his armed men out of the hold), to self-reproach (the poor fellow has suffered greatly, after all; the idea of a plot is absurd).

The tale thus moves with a studied uncertainty towards its climax, as the narrator explores Delano's subjective responses to Cereno and to the scenes which shape and reshape themselves before his eyes. As Berthoff explains, the story is a kind of riddle that the reader, no less than Delano, must solve: "The states of mind Captain Delano passes through are not, after all, essentially different from the ordinary ways by which we move, more or less blindly, through our works and days. So the story can fairly be seen as composing a paradigm of the secret ambiguity of appearances—an old theme with Melville—and, more particularly, a paradigm of the inward life of ordinary consciousness, with all its mysterious shifts, penetrations, and side-slippings." Melville's emphasis on Delano's thought processes and states of mind, rather than on dramatic action or event, is his way of stating, indirectly, that this is a world in which "ambiguity of appearances is the baffling norm."[2]

Another Melvillean "bachelor," good-natured Delano is naively confident about the world, and about his own God-given potentialities as a leader of men of will and benefactor of those weaker than himself. Out of his naiveté arises both a sense of superiority and a conviction that one is treated as he treats others. But Delano is also perceptually obtuse: he is unwilling and unable to allow his intuitive glimpses of the truth to overturn his preconceived notions about reality and human nature. The historical Delano had seen the central irony in his own experiences with the slaves, and Melville would follow it up in his story: "[The slaves] all looked up to me as a benefactor; and as I was deceived in them, I did them every possible kindness. Had it been otherwise there is no doubt I should have fallen a victim to their power. It was to my great advantage, that, on this occasion, the temperament of my mind was unusually pleasant. The apparent sufferings of those about me had softened my feelings into sympathy, or, doubtless my interference with some of their transactions would have cost me my life."[3] Both Delano and Melville were struck by the fortune that can sometimes attend incomplete vision. Too thorough an understanding of reality can precipitate dangerous reflex actions; in Delano's obtuseness lies his salvation, and, for the moment at least, Don Benito's as well.

In retrospect, Captain Delano seems an almost transparently ironic figure and we are surprised at our own failure to see "around" him earlier than we

---

*"Agatha material"—other real-life experiences used in Melville's fiction. —Ed.

do. The American captain is "blunt-thinking," "a man of such native simplicity as to be incapable of satire or irony," and "a person of singularly undistrustful good nature, not liable, except on extraordinary and repeated incentives, and hardly then, to indulge in personal alarms, any way involving the imputation of malign evil in man" (*SW, p. 256). Melville also plays more subtle variations on his rhetorical method, giving Delano ironic thoughts or having him make ironic statements to poor Cereno. At one point, for instance, Delano observes to himself that the Spanish captain's authority over the Negro slaves seems to have been impaired. Delano's conclusion is in fact correct, but his reasoning is faulty: he assumes that lack of water and long-continued suffering brought on the misrule aboard ship. Or, when the psychologically and physically debilitated Don Benito collapses into the arms of ever-present Babo, Delano exclaims, "'Faithful fellow! . . . Don Benito, I envy you such a friend; slave I cannot call him!'" Again, the good-natured captain speaks more than he knows. Delano's musings on the tableau before him further compound the irony: "As master and man stood before him, the black upholding the white, Captain Delano could not but bethink him of the beauty of that relationship which could present such a spectacle of fidelity on the one hand and confidence on the other" (SW, p. 270).

Melville's narrative method carefully prepares the reader for the culminating irony of the story. In spite of what they have experienced together, Delano understands as little about Cereno's spiritual and psychological state at the end as he did at the beginning of their relationship. To the last Delano remains an innocent, for even after learning of Babo's atrocities he fails to see why the broken-spirited Don Benito cannot forget the past. In the final conversation between the two captains, Delano's comments on the natural landscape not inappropriately echo the lawyer's when he visited Bartleby in prison and tried to lift his spirits by pointing out the sky and the grass:

> "But the past is passed; why moralize upon it? Forget it. See, yon bright sun has forgotten it all, and the blue sea, and the blue sky; these have turned over new leaves."

*SW—Selected Writings of Herman Melville, Modern Library, New York, Random House, 1952.—ED.

> "Because they have no memory," he dejectedly replied; "because they are not human."
> "But these mild trades that now fan your cheek, do they not come with a human-like healing to you? Warm friends, steadfast friends are the trades."
> "With their steadfastness they but waft me to my tomb, Señor," was the foreboding response.
> "You are saved," cried Captain Delano, more and more astonished and pained; "you are saved: what has cast such a shadow upon you?"
> "The negro."   (SW, pp. 351–52)

And Melville terminates the dialogue fittingly: "There was no more conversation that day." Don Benito Cereno died a short time after this meeting, psychologically annihilated, and Melville suggests that the "steadfastness" of Delano's incomprehension also helped to waft the pale Spaniard to his tomb.

The imagery of "Benito Cereno" counterpoints Delano's interior monologue: Melville's images establish and reinforce mood, while they also symbolize the disintegrated psyche of the Spanish captain. In its basic form the tale is a meditation upon the texture of reality. For Delano reality is a flux of ambiguous images, but for Benito the images of reality are static, their meaning horribly apparent. As Berthoff explains Melville conveys the images of "Benito Cereno" in a succession of tableaux, or descriptive set-pieces.[4] The images that compose these tableaux fall into two patterns. Motifs of ambiguity and unreality dominate Delano's field of vision and probably the reader's as well, his first time through the tale; at the same time, images of physical deterioration, brutality, and death inject into the tale's ambiguousness a disquieting sense of pending violence and destruction. It is these images of decay and physical violence that come to represent the tormented consciousness of Don Benito.

The most celebrated of Melville's tableaux opens the narrative and suggests the forthcoming ambiguities and veiled tensions between blackness and whiteness. On the morning that marked Delano's encounter with the Spanish slave ship, "everything" was mute, calm, and gray: "The sea, though undulated into long roods of swells, seemed fixed, and was sleeked at the surface like waved lead that has cooled and set in the smelter's mold. The sky seemed a gray surtout. Flights of troubled gray fowl, kith and kin with flights of troubled gray vapors among which they were mixed, skimmed low and fitfully over the waters . . ." (SW, p. 255). Melville closes his description with the pithy aside, "Shadows present, foreshadowing deeper shadows to come."

Having set the stage generally with a mood of ambiguity and uncertainty, Melville reinforces his theme through more specific scenes. For instance, Delano's glimpse of the noisy throng of blacks and whites as he steps over the *San Dominick's* bulwarks has "the effect of enchantment": "The ship seems unreal; these strange costumed, gestures, and faces, but a shadowy tableau just emerged from the deep . . ." (*SW*, p. 260). Two elements from this tableau, the four black oakum-pickers and the six hatchet-polishers, are pictured again at later points in the story. The artificial disposition of these figures, and the awkward playacting of Babo and Cereno, make Delano vaguely apprehensive; he senses that he is viewing a masquerade, arranged for some deceitful purpose. Delano is right, of course, but he is a man reluctant to yield his "reason" to his intuition.

Motifs of decay, brutality, and death — the second major pattern of imagery — augment the threatening quality of the atmosphere, but they also help to generate additional levels of meaning in the story. The Negroes aboard the *San Dominick* are compared to the Black Friars, the Dominicans who conducted the Inquisition; mastering both the mind and the body of Cereno, they even extract "false confessions" from him, for Delano's benefit. Cereno's vessel, furthermore, is likened to the monastery to which Charles V of Spain retired, and it serves as a fitting symbol of the faded glory and strength of the Spanish empire. Melville's story thus becomes a kind of allegory on the confrontation of primitive Africa, civilized Europe, and native America, and on the destruction and spiritual loss attendant upon political and religious upheaval.

More specifically, however, these images represent the horribly debilitating effects of Cereno's experience. The *San Dominick* itself is the most dramatic symbol of her captain's suffering: "Battered and mouldy, the castellated forecastle seemed some ancient turret, long ago taken by assault, and then left to decay." In an allusion to the decline of both the Spanish empire and Cereno's authority, Melville adds: "the principal relic of faded grandeur was the ample oval of the shield-like stern-piece, intricately carved with the arms of Castile and Leon, medallioned about by groups of mythological or symbolic devices; uppermost and central of which was a dark satyr in a mask, holding his foot on the prostrate

neck of a writhing figure, likewise masked" (*SW*, pp. 258–59). The stern-piece is an appropriately ambiguous symbol of the story's various "masked" characters, both conquered and conquering. Cereno and Babo wear "masks," although Babo is the real "dark satyr," Cereno's malevolent conqueror. Of course, Delano is the figure who, in a very literal sense, comes to hold Babo underfoot and "prostrate," when the Negro tries to kill Cereno aboard the American's longboat.

The tableau of the cuddy, like the ship itself, symbolizes the psychological torture that Cereno has undergone. In this chamber, where the Spanish captain was kept prisoner, is a "claw-footed old table" underneath which lie "a dented cutlass or two" and a "hacked harpoon." Nearby are "two long, sharp-ribbed settees . . . uncomfortable to look at as inquisitors' racks," and "a large, misshapen arm-chair, which, furnished with a rude barber's crotch at the back, working with a screw, seemed some grotesque engine of torment" (*SW*, p. 305). While making Cereno's suffering more "visible," these motifs also reinforce in the story a mood of threatening violence and psychic horror.

Motifs of death and incarceration serve two aesthetic and rhetorical purposes. They provide, in retrospect, a continual reminder of the slaughter that has taken place aboard the *San Dominick,* even as they foreshadow Don Benito's incarceration in the monastery and, finally, his death. Appropriately, then, Melville describes the sea-grass draping the vessel as "mourning weeds" and notes the "hearse-like roll of the hull" (*SW*, p. 259). Built into the cabin wall, furthermore, are "small, round dead-lights — all closed like the coppered eyes of the coffined," and the cabin door is "calked fast like a sarcophagus lid."

In the tableau that concludes the tale, Melville turns again to a motif in his source. Among the documents pertaining to the trial is the official court sentence, pronouncing that the heads of the leaders of the murderous rebellion be "fixed on a pole" in the town square and their bodies burned. In Melville's story black Babo, symbol of depravity and hatred, receives the same judgment. The Black had cast his shadow over Don Benito, and it drove the Spanish captain to his grave. Yet even though the Negro, too, found his own "voiceless end," his blackness lived on as a force for deception and evil. Babo's head, "that hive of subtlety, fixed on a pole in the Plaza, met, unabashed, the gaze of the whites" and looked toward the monastery where Cereno soon died. In his final ironic gesture Melville implies that Babo, even after death, remains the master of man's spirit and fate. His dead head looks out over the world and his inhumanity somehow still arranges the events of the universe.

Notes

1. *A Narrative of Voyages and Travels, in the northern and southern hemispheres: comprising three voyages round the world, together with a voyage of survey and discovery in the Pacific Ocean and Oriental Islands,* 2nd ed. (Boston: E. G. House, 1817), pp. 318–53. Harold H. Scudder, in "Melville's *Benito Cereno* and Captain Delano's *Voyages,*" *PMLA,* 43 (June 1928), 502–32, documented Melville's use of his source. Melville's story, Chapter 18 of Delano's narrative, pertinent critical essays, and a list of textual variants have been collected in John P. Runden, ed., *Melville's "Benito Cereno"* (Boston: D. C. Heath, 1966).

2. *The Example of Melville,* p. 153. John Seelye has noted that there are some one hundred and fifteen "conjectural expressions" in "Benito Cereno" (*Melville: The Ironic Diagram,* p. 105).

3. Runden, *Melville's "Benito Cereno,"* p. 80.

4. *The Example of Melville,* p. 69.

"Too Terribly Good To Be Printed": Charlotte Gilman's "The Yellow Wallpaper"

Conrad Shumaker

Citing essays by Annette Kolodny and Jean F. Kennard (see chapters 3 and 5), Conrad Shumaker acknowledges the polemical intent and effects of "The Yellow Wallpaper" but claims that the story "transcends its author's immediate intent, and my experience in teaching it suggests that it favorably impresses both male and female students, even before they learn of its feminist context or of the patriarchal biases of nineteenth-century medicine." Despite Gilman's protests that she didn't write "literature," Shumaker finds the story a "strikingly effective work of literature" precisely because here Gilman's fictional techniques, her "masterly use of association, foreshadowing, and even humor" and her "skillful handling of the narrative voice" serve to discover the story's exploration of a large and still-current question: "What happens to the imagination when it's defined as feminine (and thus weak) and has to face a society that values the useful and the practical and rejects anything else as nonsense?" But as Cleanth Brooks argues, "the poet can legitimately step out into the universal only by first going through the narrow door of the particular," and only those who read with careful attention to the story's artistry will fully understand its larger meanings. In Shumaker's reading, the story emerges as a "complex work of art as well as an effective indictment of the nineteenth-century view of the sexes and the materialism that underlies that view." Indeed, it is an effective indictment because it is a complex work of art.

In 1890 William Dean Howells sent a copy of "The Yellow Wallpaper" to Horace Scudder, editor of the *Atlantic Monthly*. Scudder gave his reason for not publishing the story in a short letter to its author, Charlotte Perkins Stetson (later to become Charlotte

Reprinted by permission from *American Literature* 57:4 (December 1985): 588–99. Copyright 1985 by the Duke University Press. All rights reserved.

Perkins Gilman): "Dear Madam, Mr. Howells has handed me this story. I could not forgive myself if I made others as miserable as I have made myself!"[1] Gilman persevered, however, and eventually the story, which depicts the mental collapse of a woman undergoing a "rest cure" at the hands of her physician husband, was printed in the *New England Magazine* and then later in Howells's own collection, *Great American Stories*, where he introduces it as "terrible and too wholly dire," and "too terribly good to be printed."[2] Despite (or perhaps because of) such praise, the story was virtually ignored for over fifty years until Elaine Hedges called attention to its virtues, praising it as "a small literary masterpiece."[3] Today the work is highly spoken of by those who have read it, but it is not widely known and has been slow to appear in anthologies of American literature.

Some of the best criticism attempts to explain this neglect as a case of misinterpretation by audiences used to "traditional" literature. Annette Kolodny, for example, points out that though nineteenth-century readers had learned to "follow the fictive processes of aberrant perception and mental breakdown" by reading Poe's tales, they were not prepared to understand a tale of mental degeneration in a middle-class mother and wife. It took twentieth-century feminism to place the story in a "nondominant or subcultural" tradition which those steeped in the dominant tradition could not understand.[4] Jean F. Kennard suggests that the recent appearance of feminist novels has changed literary conventions and led us to find in the story an exploration of women's role instead of the tale of horror or depiction of mental breakdown its original audience found.[5] Both arguments are persuasive, and the feminist readings of the story that accompany them are instructive. With its images of barred windows and sinister beadsteads, creeping women and domineering men, the story does indeed raise the issue of sex roles in an effective way, and thus anticipates later feminist literature.

Ultimately, however, both approaches tend to make the story seem more isolated from the concerns of the nineteenth-century "dominant tradition" than it really is, and since they focus most of our attention on the story's polemical aspect, they invite a further exploration of Gilman's artistry—the way in which she molds her reformer concerns into a strikingly effective work of literature. To be sure, the polemics are important. Gilman, an avowed feminist and a rel-

ative of Harriet Beecher Stowe, told Howells that she didn't consider the work to be "literature" at all, that everything she wrote was for a purpose, in this case that of pointing out the dangers of a particular medical treatment. Unlike Gilman's other purposeful fictions, however, "The Yellow Wallpaper" transcends its author's immediate intent, and my experience teaching it suggests that it favorably impresses both male and female students, even before they learn of its feminist context or of the patriarchal biases of nineteenth-century medicine. I think the story has this effect for two reasons. First, the question of women's role in the nineteenth century is inextricably bound up with the more general question of how one perceives the world. Woman is often seen as representing an imaginative or "poetic" view of things that conflicts with (or sometimes complements) the American male's "common sense" approach to reality. Through the characters of the "rational" doctor and the "imaginative" wife, Gilman explores a question that was—and in many ways still is—central both to American literature and to the place of women in American culture: What happens to the imagination when it's defined as feminine (and thus weak) and has to face a society that values the useful and the practical and rejects anything else as nonsense? Second, this conflict and the related feminist message both arise naturally and effectively out of the action of the story because of the author's skillful handling of the narrative voice.

One of the most striking passages in Gilman's autobiography describes her development and abandonment of a dream world, a fantasy land to which she could escape from the rather harsh realities of her early life. When she was thirteen, a friend of her mother warned that such escape could be dangerous, and Charlotte, a good New England girl who considered absolute obedience a duty, "shut the door" on her "dear, bright, glittering dreams."[6] The narrator of "The Yellow Wallpaper" has a similar problem: from the beginning of the story she displays a vivid imagination. She wants to imagine that the house they have rented is haunted, and as she looks at the wallpaper, she is reminded of her childhood fancies about rooms, her ability to "get more entertainment and terror out of blank walls and plain furniture than most children could find in a toy store."[7] Her husband has to keep reminding her that she "must not give way to fancy in the least" as she comments on her new surroundings. Along with her vivid imagination she has the mind and eye of an artist. She begins to study the wallpaper in an attempt to make sense of its artistic design, and she objects to it for aesthetic reasons: it is "one of those sprawling, flamboyant patterns committing every artistic sin" (p. 13). When her ability to express her artistic impulses is limited by her husband's prescription of complete rest, her mind turns to the wallpaper, and she begins to find in its tangled pattern the emotions and experiences she is forbidden to record. By trying to ignore and repress her imagination, in short, John eventually brings about the very circumstance he wants to prevent.

Though he is clearly a domineering husband who wants to have absolute control over his wife, John also has other reasons for forbidding her to write or paint. As Gilman points out in her autobiography, the "rest cure" was designed for "the business man exhausted from too much work, and the society woman exhausted from too much play."[8] The treatment is intended, in other words, to deal with physical symptoms of overwork and fatigue, and so is unsuited to the narrator's more complex case. But as a doctor and an empiricist who "scoffs openly at things not to be felt and seen and put down in figures," John wants to deal only with physical causes and effects: if his wife's symptoms are nervousness and weight loss, the treatment must be undisturbed tranquility and good nutrition. The very idea that her "work" might be beneficial to her disturbs him; indeed, he is both fearful and contemptuous of her imaginative and artistic powers, largely because he fails to understand them or the view of the world they lead her to.

Two conversations in particular demonstrate his way of dealing with her imagination and his fear of it. The first occurs when the narrator asks him to change the wallpaper. He replies that to do so would be dangerous, for "nothing was worse for a nervous patient than to give way to such fancies." At this point, her "fancy" is simply an objection to the paper's ugliness, a point she makes clear when she suggests that they move to the "pretty rooms" downstairs. John replies by calling her a "little goose" and saying "he would go down to the cellar if she wished and have it whitewashed into the bargain" (p. 15). Besides showing his obviously patriarchal stance, his reply is designed to make her aesthetic objections

seem nonsense by fastening on concrete details — color and elevation — and ignoring the real basis of her request. If she wants to go downstairs away from yellow walls, he will take her to the cellar and have it whitewashed. The effect is precisely what he intends: he makes her see her objection to the paper's ugliness as "just a whim." The second conversation occurs after the narrator has begun to see a woman behind the surface pattern of the wallpaper. When John catches her getting out of bed to examine the paper more closely, she decides to ask him to take her away. He refuses, referring again to concrete details: "You are gaining flesh and color, your appetite is better, I feel really much better about you." When she implies that her physical condition isn't the real problem, he cuts her off in midsentence: "I beg of you, for my sake and for our child's sake, as well as for your own, that you will never for one instant let that idea enter your mind! There is nothing so dangerous, so fascinating, to a temperament like yours. It is a false and foolish fancy" (p. 24). For John, mental illness is the inevitable result of using one's imagination, the creation of an attractive "fancy" which the mind then fails to distinguish from reality. He fears that because of her imaginative "temperament" she will create the fiction that she is mad and come to accept it despite the evidence — color, weight, appetite — that she is well. Imagination and art are subversive because they threaten to undermine his materialistic universe.

Ironically, despite his abhorrence of faith and superstition, John fails because of his own dogmatic faith in materialism and empiricism, a faith that will not allow him even to consider the possibility that his wife's imagination could be a positive force. In a way John is like Aylmer in Hawthorne's "The Birthmark": each man chooses to interpret a characteristic of his wife as a defect because of his own failure of imagination, and each attempts to "cure" her through purely physical means, only to find he has destroyed her in the process. He also resembles the implied villain in many of Emerson's and Thoreau's lectures and essays, the man of convention who is so taken with "common sense" and traditional wisdom that he is blind to truth. Indeed, the narrator's lament that she might get well faster if John were not a doctor and her assertion that he can't understand her "because he is so wise" remind one of Thoreau's question in the first chapter of Walden: "How can he remember his ignorance—which his growth requires—who has so often to use his knowledge?" John's role as a doctor and an American male requires that he use his "knowledge" continuously and doggedly, and he would abhor the appearance of imagination in his own mind even more vehemently than in his wife's.

The relationship between them also offers an insight into how and why this fear of the imagination has been institutionalized through assigned gender roles. By defining his wife's artistic impulse as a potentially dangerous part of her feminine "temperament," John can control both his wife and a facet of human experience which threatens his comfortably materialistic view of the world. Fear can masquerade as calm authority when the thing feared is embodied in the "weaker sex." Quite fittingly, the story suggests that American is full of Johns: the narrator's brother is a doctor, and S. Weir Mitchell—"like John and my brother only more so!"—looms on the horizon if she doesn't recover.

As her comments suggest, the narrator understands John's problem yet is unable to call it his problem, and in many ways it is this combination of insight and naiveté, of resistance and resignation, that makes her such a memorable character and gives such power to her narrative. The story is in the form of a journal which the writer knows no one will read— she says she would not criticize John to "a living soul, of course, but this is dead paper"—yet at the same time her occasional use of "you," her questions ("What is one to do?" she asks three times in the first two pages), and her confidential tone all suggest that she is attempting to reach or create the listener she cannot otherwise find. Her remarks reveal that her relationship with her husband is filled with deception on her part, not so much because she wants to hide things from him but because it is impossible to tell him things he does not want to acknowledge. She reveals to the "dead paper" that she must pretend to sleep and have an appetite because that is what John assumes will happen as a result of his treatment, and if she tells him that she isn't sleeping or eating he will simply contradict her. Thus the journal provides an opportunity not only to confess her deceit and explain its necessity but also to say the things she really wants to say to John and would say if his insistence on "truthfulness," i.e., saying what he wants to hear, didn't prevent her. As both her greatest deception and her attempt to be honest, the journal embodies in its very form the absurd contradictions inherent in her role as wife.

At the same time, however, she cannot quite stop deceiving herself about her husband's treatment of her, and her descriptions create a powerful dramatic irony as the reader gradually puts together details the meaning of which she doesn't quite understand. She says, for instance, that there is "something strange" about the house they have rented, but her description reveals bit by bit a room that has apparently been used to confine violent mental cases, with bars on the windows, a gate at the top of the stairs, steel rings on the walls, a nailed-down bedstead, and a floor that has been scratched and gouged. When she tries to explain her feelings about the house to John early in the story, her report of the conversation reveals her tendency to assume that he is always right despite her own reservations:

> . . . there is something strange about the house—
> I can feel it.
> I even said so to John one moonlight evening,
> but he said what I felt was a *draught*, and shut the
> window.
> I get unreasonably angry with John sometimes.
> I'm sure I never used to be so sensitive. I think it is
> due to this nervous condition.   (p. 11)

As usual, John refuses to consider anything but physical details, but the narrator's reaction is particularly revealing here. Her anger, perfectly understandable to us, must be characterized, even privately, as "unreasonable," a sign of her condition. Whatever doubts she may have about John's methods, he represents reason, and it is her own sensitivity that must be at fault. Comments such as these reveal more powerfully than any direct statement could the way she is trapped by the conception of herself which she has accepted from John and the society whose values he represents. As Paula A. Treichler has pointed out, John's diagnosis is a "sentence," a "set of linguistic signs whose representational claims are authorized by society," and thus it can "control women's fate, whether or not those claims are valid." The narrator can object to the terms of the sentence, but she cannot question its authority, even in her own private discourse.[9]

To a great extent, the narrator's view of her husband is colored by the belief that he really does love her, a belief that provides some of the most striking and complex ironies in the story. When she says, "it is hard to talk to John about my case because he is so wise, and because he loves me so," it is tempting to take the whole sentence as an example of her naïveté. Obviously he is not wise, and his actions are not what we would call loving. Nevertheless, the sentence is in its way powerfully insightful. If John were not so wise — so sure of his own empirical knowledge and his expertise as a doctor — and so loving — so determined to make her better in the only way he knows — then he might be able to set aside his fear of her imagination and listen to her. The passage suggests strikingly the way both characters are doomed to act out their respective parts of loving husband and obedient wife right to the inevitably disastrous end.

Gilman's depiction of the narrator's decline into madness has been praised for the accuracy with which it captures the symptoms of mental breakdown and for its use of symbolism.[10] What hasn't been pointed out is the masterly use of association, foreshadowing, and even humor. Once the narrator starts attempting to read the pattern of the wallpaper, the reader must become a kind of psychological detective in order to follow and appreciate the narrative. In a sense, he too is viewing a tangled pattern with a woman behind it, and he must learn to revise his interpretation of the pattern as he goes along if he is to make sense of it. For one thing, the narrator tells us from time to time about new details in the room. She notices a "smooch" on the wall "low down, near the mopboard," and later we learn that the bedstead is "fairly gnawed." It is only afterwards that we find out that she is herself the source of these new marks as she bites the bedstead and crawls around the room, shoulder to the wallpaper. If the reader has not caught on already, these details show clearly that the narrator is not always aware of her own actions or in control of her thoughts and so is not always reliable in reporting them. They also foreshadow her final separation from her wifely self, her belief that she is the woman who has escaped from behind the barred pattern of the wallpaper.

But the details also invite us to reread earlier passages, to see if the voice which we have taken to be a fairly reliable though naive reporter has not been giving us unsuspected hints of another reality all along. If we do backtrack we find foreshadowing everywhere, not only in the way the narrator reads the pattern on the wall but in the pattern of her own narrative, the way in which one thought leads to another. One striking example occurs when she describes John's sister, Jennie, who is "a dear girl and so careful of me," and who therefore must not find out about the journal.

> She is a perfect and enthusiastic housekeeper, and hopes for no better profession. I verily believe she thinks it is the writing which made me sick!
>
> But I can write when she is out, and see her a long way off from these windows.
>
> There is one that commands the road, a lovely shaded winding road, and one that just looks off over the country. A lovely country too, full of great elms and velvet meadows.
>
> This wallpaper has a kind of sub-pattern in a different shade, a particularly irritating one, for you can only see it in certain lights, and not clearly then.
>
> But in the places where it isn't faded and where the sun is just so — I can see a strange, provoking, formless sort of figure, that seems to skulk about behind that silly and conspicuous front design.
>
> There's sister on the stairs!   (pp. 17–18)

The "perfect and enthusiastic housekeeper" is, of course, the ideal sister for John, whose view of the imagination she shares. Thoughts of Jennie lead to the narrator's assertion that she can "see her a long way off from these windows," foreshadowing later passages in which the narrator will see a creeping woman, and then eventually many creeping women from the same windows, and the association suggests a connection between the "enthusiastic housekeeper" and those imaginary women. The thought of the windows leads to a description of the open country and suggests the freedom that the narrator lacks in her barred room. This, in turn, leads her back to the wallpaper, and now she mentions for the first time the "sub-pattern," a pattern which will eventually become a woman creeping behind bars, a projection of her feelings about herself as she looks through the actual bars of the window. The train of associations ends when John's sister returns, but this time she's just "sister," as if now she's the narrator's sister as well, suggesting a subconscious recognition that they both share the same role, despite Jennie's apparent freedom and contentment. Taken in context, this passage prepares us to see the connection between the pattern of the wallpaper, the actual bars on the narrator's windows, and the "silly and conspicuous" surface pattern of the wifely role behind which both women lurk.

We can see just how Gilman develops the narrator's mental collapse if we compare the passage quoted above to a later one in which the narrator once again discusses the "sub-pattern," which by now has become a woman who manages to escape in the daytime.

> I think that woman gets out in the daytime!
> And I'll tell you why—privately—I've seen her!
> I can see her out of every one of my windows!
> It is the same woman, I know, for she is always creeping, and most women do not creep by daylight.
> I see her on that long road under the trees, creeping along, and when a carriage comes she hides under the blackberry vines.
> I don't blame her a bit. It must be very humiliating to be caught creeping by daylight!
> I always lock the door when I creep by daylight!
> (pp. 30–31)

Here again the view outside the window suggests a kind of freedom, but now it is only a freedom to creep outside the pattern, a freedom that humiliates and must be hidden. The dark humor that punctuates the last part of the story appears in the narrator's remark that she can recognize the woman because "most women do not creep by daylight," and the sense that the journal is an attempt to reach a listener becomes clear through her emphasis on "privately." Finally, the identification between the narrator and the woman is taken a step further and becomes more nearly conscious when the narrator reveals that she too creeps, but only behind a locked door. If we read the two passages in sequence, we can see just how masterfully Gilman uses her central images—the window, the barred pattern of the paper, and the woman—to create a pattern of associations which reveals the source of the narrator's malady yet allows the narrator herself to remain essentially unable to verbalize her problem. At some level, we see, she understands what has rendered her so thoroughly powerless and confused, yet she is so completely trapped in her role that she can express that knowledge only indirectly in a way that hides it from her conscious mind.

In the terribly comic ending, she has destroyed both the wallpaper and her own identity: now she is the woman from behind the barred pattern, and not even Jane—the wife she once was—can put her back. Still unable to express her feelings directly, she acts out both her triumph and her humiliation symbolically, creeping around the room with her shoulder in the "smooch," passing over her fainting husband on every lap. Loralee MacPike suggests that the narrator has finally gained her freedom,[11] but that is true only in a very limited sense. She is still creeping, still inside the room with a rope around her waist. She has destroyed only the front pattern, the "silly and conspicuous" design that covers the real wife, the creeping one hidden behind the facade. As Treichler suggests, "her triumph is to have sharpened and articulated the nature of women's condition,"[12] but she is free only from the need to deceive herself and others about the true nature of her role. In a sense, she has discovered, bit by bit, and finally revealed to John, the wife he is attempting to create—the woman without illusions or imagination who spends all her time creeping.

The story, then, is a complex work of art as well as an effective indictment of the nineteenth-century view of the sexes and the materialism that underlies that view. It is hard to believe that readers familiar with the materialistic despots created by such writers as Hawthorne, Dickens, and Browning could fail to see the implications. Indeed, though Howells's comment that the story makes him "shiver" has been offered as evidence that he saw it as a more or less conventional horror story, I would assert that he understood quite clearly the source of the story's effect. He originally wrote to Gilman to congratulate her on her poem "Women of Today," a scathing indictment of women who fear changing sexual roles and fail to realize that their view of themselves as mothers, wives, and housekeepers is a self-deception. In fact, he praises that poem in terms that anticipate his praise of the story, calling it "dreadfully true."[13] Perhaps the story was unpopular because it was, at least on some level, understood all too clearly, because it struck too deeply and effectively at traditional ways of seeing the world and woman's place in it. That, in any case, seems to be precisely what Howells implies in his comment that it is "too terribly good to be printed."

The clearest evidence that John's view of the imagination and art was all but sacred in Gilman's America comes, ironically, from the author's own pen. When she replied to Howells's request to reprint the story by saying that she did not write "literature," she was, of course, denying that she was a mere imaginative artist, defending herself from the charge that Hawthorne imagines his Puritan ancestors would lay at his doorstep: "A writer of storybooks!—what mode of glorifying God, or being serviceable to mankind in his day and generation—may that be? Why, the degenerate fellow might as well have been a fiddler!"[14] One wonders what this later female scion of good New England stock might have done had she been able to set aside such objections. In any case, one hopes that this one work of imagination and art, at least, will be restored to the place that Howells so astutely assigned it, alongside stories by contemporaries such as Mark Twain, Henry James, and Edith Wharton.

Notes

1. Quoted in Charlotte Perkins Gilman, *The Living of Charlotte Perkins Gilman: An Autobiography* (1935; rpt. New York: Arno, 1972), p. 119.

2. *The Great Modern American Stories: An Anthology* (New York: Boni and Liveright, 1920), p. vii.

3. Afterword, *The Yellow Wallpaper* (New York: Feminist Press, 1973), p. 37.

4. "A Map for Rereading: Or, Gender and the Interpretation of Literary Texts," *New Literary History,* 11 (1980), 455–56.

5. "Convention Coverage or How to Read Your Own Life," *New Literary History,* 13 (1981), 73–74.

6. Gilman, *Living,* p. 95.

7. *The Yellow Wallpaper* (New York: Feminist Press, 1973), p. 17. Page numbers in the text refer to this edition.

8. Gilman, *Living,* p. 95.

9. "Escaping the Sentence: Diagnosis and Discourse in 'The Yellow Wallpaper,'" *Tulsa Studies in Women's Literature,* 3 (1984), 74.

10. See Beate Schöpp-Schilling, "'The Yellow Wallpaper': A Rediscovered 'Realistic' Story," *American Literary Realism,* 8 (1975), 284–86; Loralee MacPike, "Environment as Psychopathological Symbolism in 'The Yellow Wallpaper'" *American Literary Realism,* 8 (1975), 286–88.

11. MacPike, p. 288.

12. Treichler, p. 74.

13. Quoted in Gilman, *Living,* p. 113.

14. *The Scarlet Letter* (Columbus: Ohio State Univ. Press, 1962), p. 10.

CHAPTER THREE

Reader-Response Criticism: Audience as Context

'Tis with our Judgments *as our* Watches, *none*
Go just alike, *yet each believes his own.*

    —Pope, *An Essay on Criticism*

While genetic critics ground their approach on the firm fact that poems have authors, reader-response critics claim the equally solid ground that they also have audiences. By starting at this end of the communication line, they avoid most of the difficulties that trouble historical criticism. Certainly a poem is caused to exist at a particular time, but it continues to exist long after its causes have vanished. Authors grow old and die, and the circumstances of the poem's creation are soon lost in the irrevocable past. But the poem, a foster child of silence and slow time, remains for us in the perpetual present.

For reader-response critics are most often concerned with the present audience. There are, it should be noted, audience-oriented critics with a historical bent who study the reception of poems over time. And there have long been studies focused on the poem's original audience. But the latter are really forms of historical criticism that assume if we could learn to think like the intended audience, we could recover the author's intended meaning. Most reader-response critics have little interest in authors or intended meanings. The poem exists now. It affects us now. These, they claim, are the crucial facts, and any relevant criticism must be built on them.

Not only do poems exist independently of their authors, they are almost always valued independently of their original contexts. Even historical criticism must start from this point. Milton's biography has received more attention than Cowley's because we have judged Milton's poems, not his life, to be more important than Cowley's. We may try to become Elizabethans to understand *The Tempest*; we do not read *The Tempest* to become Elizabethans. That is, we must first respond to the power of poems before we trouble to investigate their causes. What is that power, and what is the nature of our response to it? What happens when we read a novel, hear a poem, see a play? What is this interaction between audience and work without which that work would have no meaningful existence and certainly no value?

The study of these questions, says the reader-response critic, is the chief business of literary criticism.

But before we consider what such study entails, we need to make some distinctions. Everyone agrees that we are affected by literature—delighted, disturbed, sometimes even instructed. Concern with the effects of poetry is as old as Aristophanes and as recent as the latest censorship case; and the long-playing debate about the moral and educative value of poetry has occasionally produced an attack, like Plato's, or a defense, like Shelley's, which are important documents in the history of literary criticism. But only very occasionally. Similarly, the sort of affectiveness found in numerous impressionistic essays that tell us how the critic felt while reading may seldom contribute directly to our general understanding of literature. In other words, while a good deal of the talk about literature has always been loosely affective, significant attempts to develop a consistent theory along these lines have been few, and most of these are quite modern.

There is, to be sure, the long and strong "rhetorical" tradition, which includes Aristotle, Horace, Cicero, Quintilian, and their legions of followers in Renaissance and post-Renaissance Europe. Certainly the language of this tradition is heavily "affective," stressing the ways authors can persuade or otherwise work upon their audiences. But in practice the rhetorical approach, especially when it was applied to poetry and drama, concentrated on the formal arrangement of elements within the work. It was assumed that these arrangements would produce certain effects, but little attempt was made to demonstrate this assumption or to study the responses of actual audiences. Consequently, the real heirs of this tradition have been the modern formalists who found they could use the well-developed terminology of the rhetoricians in their analyses while paying scant attention to the study of audience response.

But such study has become the focus of several other schools of modern criticism, and especially of those based on some form of psychology, for the very conception of the reader–poem context invites a psychological investigation. In fact, there are probably as many different approaches as there are different kinds of psychology. Experimental psychologists, for example, have wired readers to galvanometers, with sometimes hilarious results, and some other schools of psychology have appeared only slightly less clumsy when they have tried to deal with the subtleties of poetry. But two psychological theories, the Freudian and the Jungian, have seemed to hold a special promise to illuminate our reactions to literature. In the Freudian view, the poem, like the dream, has its manifest and latent content. Like the dream, it works for the reader's psyche. And like the dream, it yields its real meaning only to the critic trained in the proper psychoanalytic techniques. Until fairly recently, though, the reader-response applications of Freudian psychology have been less fully developed than the genetic or mimetic applications. The theories of Carl Jung, on the other hand, have been most frequently employed in the affective context to account for the power of poetry. Jung's model of the different facets of the human psyche, his idea of the "collective unconscious," and above all his conceptions of "symbol" and "archetype" have seemed to many critics directly applicable to our experience of literature.

Jungian ideas have strongly influenced a number of studies usually classed under the label "myth criticism." Such studies may show as well the influence of mythographers like G. S. Frazer, Gilbert Murray, and Joseph Campbell. As this diversity of influences suggests, "myth criticism" is not a single approach or a unified school, and in terms of the organization of this book "myth critics" can be found in most of our contexts. But they are found most often in the affective context for, whether they base their readings on Jung or on some other model of the human psyche, they agree that the power of literature chiefly resides in its presentation of special symbols, characters, and patterns of action to which we respond at the deepest levels of our being.

Great literature, in this view, is not great because it possesses complex verbal texture, realistic characters, fidelity to historical fact, or formal symmetry. A poem can have all these qualities and still be second-rate. Conversely, it can be marred by textual lacunae, as is the *Oresteia*, or by structural flaws, as is *Moby Dick*, and still succeed brilliantly. For in the imagery and characters of great works, in the green gardens and wintery wastelands, in the questing heroes and menacing villains, and in the archetypal patterns of their actions that form analogies to rites of spring and rites of passage, to cycles of death and rebirth, we recognize, usually at some subconscious level, the images and actions that haunt our dreams and that form the substance of our psychic lives. Here, too, as in the Freudian model, the poem is seen to have levels of meaning, a surface level available to formal or rhetorical analysis and a deeper level that can be explained only by those armed with the insights of psychological theory. Unarmed readers may believe they are responding to the surface level, but they are really being affected by the underlying patterns of archetypal symbolism.

But not all sophisticated forms of affective criticism depend on a type of depth psychology. In the third decade of this century, I. A. Richards, whose bent was empirical and behavioristic, developed an influential line of reader-response criticism, a line that included a fully argued theory of affective value. Because the strengths and the weaknesses of Richards's theory are in many respects representative, it will be worthwhile to examine his argument. Richards, an aesthetician, a psychologist, and a pioneering semanticist as well as a man well read in ancient and modern literature, differed from many twentieth-century critics in his willingness to concede that the scientific conception of truth is correct. Science provides accurate statements about the world; poems supply only "pseudo-statements." At the outset, then, Richards abandoned the traditional mimetic justifications for literature. With equal nonchalance, he abandoned the genetic researches so vigorously pursued by historical critics. The study of the circumstances of the poem's creation is simply not very relevant.

We are left, then, with some artfully constructed "pseudo-statements" and their readers. This may not look like a very promising basis for a defense of poetry. But people, Richards reminds us, do not live by scientific truth alone. Indeed, they live very little by it. Human beings are essentially bundles of desires and aversions, of "appetencies," to use Richards's term. Our lives consist of trying to satisfy as many of these appetencies as we can. And this task is not simple. The universe seldom seems designed to our purposes, other people's desires frequently contend with ours, and—perhaps most troublesome—our own appetencies are often in conflict.

Yet our psychic health depends entirely on our ability to harmonize and satisfy these appetencies. The desire for truth is only one appetency, and in awarding its satisfaction to science, Richards was not awarding so much as it might seem. For people have many other needs, one of the most important being a need to construct a vision of the world in which we can feel at home. Religion used to supply this vision, but since we moderns have largely lost our religious beliefs without losing the wants they used to satisfy, it will fall to poetry to fill their place, just as Matthew Arnold had predicted. More accurately, we now see from this perspective that religion, myth, and poetry are functionally the same thing. They are all imaginative constructs. The mistake was to think of them as offering "truth" in the scientific sense. The real purpose of art is to answer the human need for an intelligible and satisfying vision of the universe and our place within it and to answer as well our many other psychic wants, few of which can be met by scientific truth or the brute facts of experience. And poetry, because it operates through language, the most potent and flexible artistic medium, can encompass the greatest part of our psychic life, can appeal to and harmonize the greatest number of our appetencies. Poetry is art *par excellence.*

One advantage of Richards's view is that it offers to account for all features of the literary work. As we noticed, the depth psychologists' attempts to explain the power of poems sometimes produce analyses that strip away the verbal texture and rhetorical structure of the work to reveal its underlying patterns, its embodiment of the dream or the myth that carries its true appeal. This focus on the latent content opens these methods to the charge that they are reductive, that they fail to deal with the art of poetry, and that, in their search for the mythic patterns or psychological mechanisms that inform many poems, such methods ignore the unique poem before them. If the oedipal conflict is the heart of *Hamlet,* in what ways does Shakespeare's play differ from an analyst's case history? If all tragedies embody the death–rebirth cycle, then why does *King Lear* affect us more strongly than *Alcestis* does, and why is a performance of *Oedipus Tyrannus* more powerful than a summary of its plot? These charges do not apply to Richards's approach. The orderly structure and rich verbal texture of literary works, their networks of images and motifs, their symmetrical designs, their tricks and tropes, their rhythms and rhymes are not decorative excrescences—they are in themselves important sources of our satisfaction. For art, to repeat, appeals to many of our appetencies. Poetry allows us the chance to experience, and to experience more fully, more of life's possibilities than our nonverbal existence ordinarily affords, and a great poem, like *Hamlet,* is great because it deals with a wider range of human experiences than does a lesser poem. This is why "complexity" is a value in art; the complex poem appeals to more appetencies than a simple poem does.

But complexity is only part of the effect. In ordinary existence, appetencies are often in conflict. In art, however, the formal unity of the artistic structure arranges and contains this complexity; it subdues even the painful and the ugly; it holds the disparate elements in a tensive balance; and it offers not the chaotic fragment but the harmonious whole. The more we look at *Hamlet,* the more we see that all its elements from the smallest to the largest, all its special and local effects, are working together. It takes in much more than a carefully wrought sonnet, but it is just as superbly organized, in fact, more superbly because there is more to organize. And when we read a great poem, as so many of our desires and aversions are brought skillfully into play, they are also brought—as they almost never are in experiences outside of art—into harmonious balance. The harmony in the poem becomes a harmony in the reader's psyche. This is why human beings need poetry. It is indispensable to our psychic health.

Thus, Richards constructs an ambitious and cogent defense of art on affective grounds, a defense that promises to deal with both the complexity and the coherence of poems and to account for each in terms of a fully articulated affective theory of value. Having explained his theory in *Principles of Literary Criticism* (1925), Richards went on to study the actual responses of readers in *Practical Criticism* (1929). He gave some Cambridge students several short poems that he felt varied widely in poetic quality. To eliminate any interference from preconditioned effects, he deleted all references to authors and dates, and he asked the students to read the poems as often as they wished and to record their reactions and evaluations. The widely disparate readings that resulted seemed to Richards to indicate that most people are poor readers of poetry. So Richards set about arranging, classifying, and analyzing the various ways his readers' responses had gone awry, and in the process he supplied his own analyses of the poems. Ironically, his analytical techniques were to be widely imitated in the next decades by many formalist critics who raised, at the same time, serious questions about his underlying affective theory.

The first and fundamental question is exactly whose response are we going to talk about? It is easy to speak in general terms about what "people" do, about the behavior of "audiences" or the reactions of "readers," but as Richards's research showed, and as a moment's reflection will confirm, different people react very differently to the "same" poem. Some see superficiality where others find profundity; some praise uplifting sentiments where others complain of clichés; some discover coherence where others see only chaos.

Is there any way to tell which of several responses is the best one? Richards thought there was, for he classified the various ways his respondents had deviated from the "right" or "more adequate" reading. And to illustrate that better reading, he appealed to "the poem itself." He pointed out what the words meant, how the sentiments expressed in the poem were or were not appropriate to the fictive speaker and situation, how the imagery developed consistently or inconsistently, how the parts fit or failed to fit together. In short, claims the formalist critic, Richards furnished a formal analysis, an analysis not of readers but of texts. Without this or some other standard, no way exists to decide if one response is better than another. In fact, without some standard there appears to be no alternative to complete relativism. For if, as many reader-response critics argue, the poem truly exists only when it is apprehended, then we seem to be driven toward the conclusion that there are as many *Hamlets* as there are readers of *Hamlet*. More accurately, there are as many *Hamlets* as there are readings, for our responses change from year to year, or even from day to day.

So this variability gives rise to one set of problems: How can reader-response critics avoid the conclusion, and the total relativism it entails, that a new poem is created with every reading? How can they establish a standard to measure the adequacy of any particular reading without assuming the stability of the text and importing that standard from some other context—in other words, without grounding meaning in the text, or the author, or the structure of language? And if reader-response critics do import a standard from some other context, how can they keep the discussion from shifting to that context, thus leaving behind as irrelevant the whole question of the responses of actual readers? In short, how can they talk *critically* about the poem–audience relationship?

These are problems, of course, only so long as the "better" interpretation is seen, as it usually has been seen, as the goal of literary criticism. For some reader-response critics, this goal is neither attainable nor even especially desirable. And they contend that our responses to literature are in themselves a subject of sufficient psychological interest as to require no further justification. Without disputing this contention, we should at least notice that the work of these critics differs in a fundamental way from that produced by critics working in other contexts. When historical critics, for example, offer us information about the author's life or intellectual background, they are claiming that this information will alter our understanding of poems, that it will confirm or eliminate certain interpretations. When formal critics point to a cluster of images or a pattern of motifs, they are claiming to show us something important that we may have overlooked, something that, now that we see it, will allow us to better understand and evaluate the poem. So they, too, are offering to confirm or eliminate readings. Reader-response critics who abandon this normative function (and certainly not all reader-response critics do abandon it) are simply not performing a parallel function. The claim to describe or even to explain the reactions of specific readers is a very different thing from the claim to supply insights that will alter or correct reactions. In each case, critics stand in quite a different relationship to the reader and the poem. Not until reader-response critics go beyond describing and analyzing responses and begin to tell us how and why we should respond do their statements really parallel those of critics in other contexts. And at exactly this point, of course, the critics encounter the first problem we discussed: how can they find, in the affective context, a normative standard for measuring the adequacy of any reading?

Some serious conceptual problems, then, face critics who work in this context. Even so, audience response seems to many critics so obviously central to the business of literature that the affective context has remained one of criticism's perennial interests. Especially in the 1970s and 1980s and partly in reaction to the dominance of formalist criticism, that interest flourished. Practice in this context goes under a variety of names—"phenomenological" criticism, "speech-act" criticism, "transactive" criticism, "subjective" criticism, "rhetorical" criticism—but "reader-response" criticism continues to be the most popular label. And though all critics in this context are centrally concerned with the interaction between the audience and the literary work, they differ in the way they distribute their interest between these two poles, some keeping their focus near the text and only occasionally nodding toward actual readers, others concentrating on the responses of specific readers while paying scant attention to the text as a separable entity. Since this brief introduction can cite only a few representative examples of contemporary affective or reader-response criticism, it will be helpful to think of our exemplary critics as occupying a series of points along the imaginary line connecting the work and the reader.

Louise Rosenblatt, for instance, has a position near the textual terminus of that line. Although she has long argued that contemporary critical theory has given too little attention to the role of the reader, she is wary of "aggressively subjective" approaches that analyze responses but not texts, and she often remarks the need to distinguish "relevant" from "irrelevant" responses. Nevertheless, her "transactional" theory puts her well within the affective context. In her terminology, a "text" may exist independently of a reader, but a "poem" exists only when a reader "compenetrates" a text; that is, when he or she chooses to read it "aesthetically." Whether that choice is entirely free is not quite clear because Rosenblatt implies that some texts have features that invite an aesthetic reading and others—a newspaper article, for example—have features that do not. But this very ambiguity is consistent with her view that both the nature of the text and the nature of the reader determine the "poem as event," which is the "transaction" in her transactional theory.

A little further down the line, but still very much toward the textual end, we reach the position of Wolfgang Iser, a German critic whose work is well known in the United States. Iser shares with many other Continental critics a strong interest in phenomenology, a philosophy that stresses the perceiver's role in perception and that insists it is difficult to separate the thing known from the mind that knows it. Other European critics who share these assumptions include Roman Ingarden,

Gaston Bachelard, and the "Geneva Critics" or "Critics of Consciousness," as they are sometimes called, of whom the best known to English readers is Georges Poulet. But whereas Bachelard, for example, is willing to follow at great length a train of personal associations set in motion by an image in the text, and whereas Poulet is often struggling to merge his "consciousness" with the "consciousness" of the author as that consciousness is revealed not only in a particular work but in everything the author has written, Iser's uses of phenomenology keep him much closer to the text. From another direction, although he has ties with the movement, he distances himself from the practitioners of "reception aesthetics," a line of inquiry that studies the history of a text's reception. Iser's concern is not with "actual readers"; he is interested, instead, in the "implied reader," a reader who "embodies all those predispositions necessary for a literary work to exercise its effect — predispositions laid down, not by an empirical outside reality, but by the text itself. Consequently, the implied reader as a concept has its roots firmly planted in the structure of the text; he is a construct and in no way to be identified with any real reader" (*The Act of Reading* 34).

Clearly, then, Iser wants to stay near the textual pole of our diagram. But he keeps a distance between himself and the formalist position as well. There can be no single best meaning that all readings must strive to approximate. The idea of a single meaning is not only at odds with Iser's phenomenological assumptions, but it is equally inconsistent with his view of our experience of literature and of the value of that experience. Much of that value lies exactly in the "indeterminacy" of the text. The text, for Iser, doesn't "contain" the meaning of the poem. Rather, we must "assemble" that meaning from the perspectives the text provides. In a complex novel such as Joyce's *Ulysses,* these perspectives are so many and varied that reconstructing the novel's meaning is like reconstructing reality itself. And our reconstructions always remain various because they always depend more on what the reader brings to the text than the formalist's model allows. It is true, and here Iser would agree with the intertextual critic, that readers must bring to the text a knowledge of the appropriate conventions or codes that will allow them to decode the poem. But here again Iser would insist on the poem's ability to transcend the code, to violate the conventions. It does so by presenting readers with "gaps" or "blanks" that they must bridge; in the process they have to construct, from the conventions they bring, new and unconventional meanings. So the text does offer a broad base of determinate meaning, as the formalist argues, and the "implied reader" brings to it a knowledge of the relevant conventions, as the intertextual critic claims, but the "poem itself" exists only in the interaction of the text and the reader, and the meaning that results is reducible neither to the conventions the reader has brought nor to the text.

Iser's position, then, allows for more "openness" in the text and more variability in our responses than critics operating in other contexts will usually admit. Equally to the point, Iser finds the value of literature largely in those indeterminacies that force readers to transcend the received codes as they construct, from their interaction with the text, new meanings. We should remember, though, that this value is most available to the "implied reader." Actual readers, who may lack the implied reader's mastery of the appropriate conventions and who may overlook important textual cues, will be more likely to misinterpret the text and to produce readings outside Iser's vaguely defined but certainly fairly narrow range of permissible "meanings."

A very different emphasis appears in the work of Norman Holland, who usually operates at a considerable distance from the textual end of our line. More accurately, he has operated at different distances over the years as his focus has moved ever closer to an exclusive concentration on the responses of actual readers. In his 1964 book *Psychoanalysis and Shakespeare,* Holland applied to Shakespeare's plays the terms and concepts of Freudian analysis. While he granted the usefulness of these concepts in the genetic and mimetic contexts, he thought their application in the reader-response context held the greatest potential for literary criticism, a potential that, aside from a few studies such as the pioneering work of S. O. Lesser, had remained largely unexplored. Holland continued to explore that potential with reference to a variety of texts in *The Dynamics of Literary Response* (1968). Here the text itself was seen as embodying various fantasies and their transformations. Readers "participate" in these to the extent that their own psychic imperatives allow, and to this extent the poem can "work" for them.

In his later writings, though, Holland has been more impressed by the reader's share in the transaction. In *Poems in Persons* (1973), in *5 Readers Reading* (1975), and in several later works, he has argued that an individual reader's psychic needs — more specifically, his or her "identity theme" — dictate that reader's perception of the text:

> By means of such adaptive structures as he has been able to match in the story, he will transform the fantasy content, which he has created from the materials of the story his defenses admitted, into some literary point or theme or interpretation. . . . He will, finally, render the fantasy he has synthesized as an intellectual content that is characteristic — and pleasing — for him. (*5 Readers Reading* 121–22).

By now the reader's share in the transaction has become almost total, and we are very close to the view that a new poem is created with every reading. If two or more readers should happen to agree about an interpretation, this agreement could only arise because their "identity themes" were so similar to begin with that they created very similar poems as they read. All that remains, then, is to study readers reading.

Holland is not alarmed by this conclusion, but he is occasionally nagged by the difficulty of talking about a largely one-sided transaction. "The literary text may be only so many marks on a page — at most a matrix of psychological possibilities for its readers. Nevertheless only some possibilities truly fit the matrix" (12). This comment suggests that the text does set some boundaries to interpretation. But as soon as we try to measure these boundaries, the problem returns from the other direction. "A reader reads something, certainly, but if one cannot separate his 'subjective' response from its 'objective' basis, there seems no way to find out what that 'something' is in any impersonal sense. It is visible only in the psychological process the reader creates in himself by means of the literary work" (40). But neither is there any compelling need to find out what that "something" is, for the focus of study now is precisely this psychological process. As we study readers reading and see the various defenses and adaptations they adopt as they confront the text, we can hope to learn something about defenses and adaptations in general — our own and others' — in all kinds of situations.

Although we seem at this point to be very near the reader's end of the line, we are not quite near enough to suit David Bleich. While Bleich agrees in most respects with Holland's emphases (though not necessarily with his psychoanalytic terminology), he complains that Holland's refusal to distinguish between the "objective" and the "subjective" merely confuses the argument, and he suspects that Holland is really trying to find his way back to "objectivity." In Bleich's view, criticism has labored too long on the mistaken assumption that the poem can be profitably considered as an "object" independent of the perceiving "subject":

> The assumption derived from the objective paradigm that all observers have the same perceptual response to a symbolic object creates the illusion that the object is real and that its meaning must reside in it. The assumption of the subjective paradigm is that collective similarity of response can be determined only by each individual's announcement of his response and subsequent communally motivated negotiative comparison. . . . The response must therefore be the starting point for the study of the aesthetic experience (*Subjective Criticism* 98).

What the end point of such a study must be is not so clear. It could not be a progressively brighter illumination of the text, because this goal is ruled out from the start by Bleich's epistemology. But presumably "communally motivated negotiative comparison" could throw light on our motives and strategies for reading. By honestly and tolerantly exchanging information about our responses to literature, we might begin to understand our own psyches, and this self-knowledge, for Bleich, is the larger and more important goal, for "each person's most urgent motivations are to understand himself" (298).

Finally, then, though he endorses no particular school of psychology, Bleich shares with Holland a psychological emphasis and a nearly exclusive focus on the responses of actual readers. Assuming, as both critics do, that the poem as independent object is beyond our reach, they argue with some force that no other focus is really available. Even so, the wary reader may wonder why their extreme skepticism about our ability to understand poetic objects should seem so relaxed when it comes to our ability to understand perceiving subjects. For in such studies, readers must become, in turn, perceived objects, and objects quite as complex as poems.

A last representative critic, and one who threatens to undermine my scheme of placing affective critics at neat intervals on the line between text and reader, is Stanley Fish. When Fish first displayed his "affective stylistics," his position seemed to be somewhere near Iser's. Like most recent reader-response critics, he was rebelling against the formalist's doctrine that the poem "in itself" provided an objective standard of meaning, but he was rebelling more strongly against the formalists' view of the poem as a static object, something to be grasped as a whole. Instead, he argued, we really experience the poem as a sequence of effects. Analyzing *Paradise Lost* and several other seventeenth-century poems on this premise, Fish sought to show how the poem worked on the reader, setting up a pattern of responses or a set of expectations that it later violated or undercut. Our experience of the poem was sequential and dynamic. The focus here was clearly on the reader, but Fish was careful to point out that he had in mind a specially qualified reader, someone trained, as Fish himself was, in the conventions of seventeenth-century poetry. Such a figure is in some ways like Iser's "implied reader," the reader the text seems to require.

But as Fish continued to explore the problems of interpretation, he came to feel it was really inaccurate to speak of the text as directing the reader's response. It would be more precise to say that the reader creates the poem in the very act of perceiving it, and what we call "interpretation" is a more elaborate process of creation in which the formal features the reader claims to "find" in the text are "(illegitimately) assigned the responsibility for producing the interpretation which in fact produced them" (*Is There a Text in This Class?* 163). Fish is willing to push this argument to its logical conclusion: each reading is a new creation, and the poem that results is the creature of whatever "interpretive strategies" the reader has employed. The poem "in itself" has quite disappeared.

What, then, is the interpreter interpreting? "I cannot answer that question," Fish admits, "but neither, I would claim, can anyone else." The illusion that we are reading the "same" poem seems to derive support from the fact that many readers can agree about the text's meaning, and even more support from the fact that some readers will allow their readings of a poem to be "corrected." But this support is itself illusory, argues Fish. Readers can agree when they are members of the same "interpretive community"; that is, when they share the same "interpretive strategies." And when readings are "corrected," they are simply brought into line with those agreed-upon strategies, not with the poem "itself." In Fish's later view, then, his own "affective stylistics," a way of reading that would place him nearer the textual end of our line than either Holland or Bleich, is simply one more arbitrarily chosen method, a method no more authorized by his theory than any other.

Fish's concept of interpretive communities has far-reaching implications, some of which we will consider in a later section. Most reader-response critics, though, continue to hold that they have very sound reasons for placing their focus where they do, and they are willing to argue that the nature of the poem, the nature of readers, or both combined dictate where the critics' emphasis should be if they are going to do justice to the literary experience. They differ, as we have seen, in their placement of that emphasis. Although no reader-response critic gives the text the autonomy that the formal critic would give it, some do see the text as considerably restricting the range of readings they will accept. So these critics must construct some hypothetical reader whose responses will be in conformity with the text's clues, and they show, consequently, little interest in the responses of actual readers. Other reader-response critics largely reverse this emphasis. We must start with the responses of actual readers, they argue, because that is all we can directly discover. So they complain that the first group is often practicing a type of disguised formalism and giving the text an illusory "objectivity." The first group, in turn, complains that the second, while showing us what some readers do, can never show us what they should do. So the various kinds of reader-response critics find much to argue about. But they agree on one main point: since the "poem" exists only when the reader (however defined) encounters the text, literary criticism must focus on that encounter.

Suggestions for Further Reading

The variety of contemporary reader-response criticism can be sampled in such collections as Susan Suleiman and Inge Crosman, eds., *The Reader in the Text* (1980), and Jane Tomkins, ed., *Reader-Response Criticism* (1980); both contain useful introductions and full bibliographies. The intersections of gender theory and reader-response criticism are explored in Elizabeth Flynn and P. P. Schweickart, eds., *Gender and Reading: Essays on Readers, Texts, and Contexts* (1986). See also Charles R. Cooper, ed., *Researching Responses to Literature and the Teaching of Literature: Points of Departure* (1985), Elizabeth Freund, *The Return of the Reader: Reader-Response Criticism* (1987), and Diane P. Freedman, Olivia Frey, and Frances Murphy Zauhor, eds., *The Intimate Critique: Autobiographical Literary Criticism* (1993). Since many "myth critics," and especially those influenced by Jung, are more concerned with literature's effect on the reader than with other contexts, they may be classed under this heading. John B. Vickery, ed., *Myth and Literature* (1966), provides the most convenient collection of essays on this large topic. Some representative books are Carl Jung, *Psyche and Symbol* (1958), Maud Bodkin, *Archetypal Patterns in Poetry* (1934), Joseph Campbell, *The Hero with a Thousand Faces*

(1949), and Richard Chase, *Quest for Myth* (1949). I. A. Richards, in *Principles of Literary Criticism* (1925), makes a pioneering twentieth-century attempt to construct an affective poetics. Simon O. Lesser, in *Fiction and the Unconscious* (1957), offers one of the first books systematically to apply Freudian concepts to explain reader response. Norman Holland has continued work in that direction in *The Dynamics of Literary Response* (1968) and, more radically, in *5 Readers Reading* (1975). Versions of continental phenomenological approaches are represented by Gaston Bachelard in *The Poetics of Reverie* (1960); by the Geneva Critics, handily described by Sarah Lawall in *Critics of Consciousness* (1968); and by Wolfgang Iser in *The Act of Reading* (1976). Reception aesthetics remains chiefly a German interest, and its historical emphasis might place it as logically in the last chapter of this book. The work of Hans Robert Jauss, represented by *Toward an Aesthetics of Reception* (1982), is central. The movement is described in Robert C. Holub, *Reception Theory: A Critical Introduction* (1984). Stanley Fish, *Self-Consuming Artifacts* (1972), and Louise Rosenblatt, *The Reader, The Text, The Poem* (1994), use reader-oriented approaches that see the text as largely controlling the reader's responses. Near the opposite pole is David Bleich, *Subjective Criticism* (1978), where the subject is the main object.

Readers and the Concept of the Implied Reader

Wolfgang Iser

In this chapter from The Act of Reading, *Wolfgang Iser explains his concept of the "implied reader." As Iser notes, reader-response critics can be divided into two groups: those who study the documented responses of "real" readers, and those who construct a "hypothetical" reader, "upon whom all possible actualizations of the text may be projected." One such hypothetical reader Iser calls the "ideal" reader. "It is difficult to pinpoint precisely where he is drawn from, though there is a good deal to be said for the claim that he tends to emerge from the brain of the philologist or critic himself." In fact, Iser argues, the ideal reader cannot exist because the concept denotes a reader who could "realize in full the meaning potential of the fictional text." The ideal reader, then, is a fiction, but often a useful fiction: "as a fiction he can close gaps that constantly appear in any analysis of literary effects and responses." Iser then proceeds to critique some of the ideal readers that other reader-response critics have constructed, among them Michael Riffaterre's "superreader," Stanley Fish's "informed reader," and Erwin Wolff's "intended reader." As a more adequate model of the reading process, Iser offers his own hypothetical reader, the "implied reader," a reader who "embodies all those predispositions necessary for a literary work to exercise its effect—predispositions laid down, not by an empirical outside reality, but by the text itself. Consequently, the implied reader as a concept has his roots firmly planted in the structure of the text; he is a construct and in no way to be identified with any real reader." But neither is the implied reader the same as the "fictitious reader," which is merely one of the perspectives offered by the fictional text. The convergence of all the textual perspectives—those of the narrator, the characters, the plot, and the fictitious reader—produce the "meaning" of the text, and this convergence must be*

---

visualized from a standpoint outside the text. "Thus the reader's role is prestructured by three basic components: the different perspectives represented in the text, the vantage point from which he joins them, and the meeting place where they converge." Unlike the various forms of the "ideal reader," Iser claims, the implied reader is not an abstraction from any real reader but a construction from the text. The concept denotes "the role of the reader, which is definable in terms of textual structure and structured acts." As such, the concept of the implied reader "offers a means of describing the process whereby textual structures are transmuted through ideational activities into personal experiences."

Northrop Frye once wrote: "It has been said of Boehme that his books are like a picnic to which the author brings the words and the reader the meaning. The remark may have been intended as a sneer at Boehme, but it is an exact description of all works of literary art without exception."[1] Any attempt to understand the true nature of this cooperative enterprise will run into difficulties over the question of which reader is being referred to. Many different types of readers are invoked when the literary critic makes pronouncements on the effects of literature or responses to it. Generally, two categories emerge, in accordance with whether the critic is concerned with the history of responses or the potential effect of the literary text. In the first instance, we have the "real" reader, known to us by his documented reactions; in the second, we have the "hypothetical" reader, upon whom all possible actualizations of the text may be projected. The latter category is frequently subdivided into the so-called ideal reader and the contemporary reader. The first of these cannot be said to exist objectively, while the second, though undoubtedly there, is difficult to mould to the form of a generalization.

Nevertheless, no one would deny that there is such a being as a contemporary reader, and perhaps an ideal reader too, and it is the very plausibility of their existence that seems to substantiate the claims made on their behalf. The importance of this plausible basis as a means of verification can be gauged from the fact that in recent years another type of reader has sometimes been endowed with more than merely heuristic qualities: namely, the reader whose psychology has been opened up by the findings of psychoanalysis. Examples of such studies are those by Simon Lesser and Norman Holland, to which we

shall be referring again later. Recourse to psychology, as a basis for a particular category of reader in whom the responses to literature may be observed, has come about not least because of the desire to escape from the limitations of the other categories. The assumption of a psychologically describable reader has increased the extent to which literary responses may be ascertained, and a psychoanalytically based theory seems eminently plausible, because the reader it refers to appears to have a real existence of his own.

Let us now take a closer look at the two main categories of readers and their place in literary criticism. The real reader is invoked mainly in studies of the history of responses, i.e., when attention is focused on the way in which a literary work has been received by a specific reading public. Now whatever judgments may have been passed on the work will also reflect various attitudes and norms of that public, so that literature can be said to mirror the cultural code which conditions these judgments. This is also true when the readers quoted belong to different historical ages, for, whatever period they may have belonged to, their judgment of the work in question will still reveal their own norms, thereby offering a substantial clue as to the norms and tastes of their respective societies. Reconstruction of the real reader naturally depends on the survival of contemporary documents, but the further back in time we go, beyond the eighteenth century, the more sparse the documentation becomes. As a result, the reconstruction often depends entirely on what can be gleaned from the literary works themselves. The problem here is whether such a reconstruction corresponds to the real reader of the time or simply represents the role which the author intended the reader to assume. In this respect, there are three types of "contemporary" reader—the one real and historical, drawn from existing documents, and the other two hypothetical: the first constructed from social and historical knowledge of the time, and the second extrapolated from the reader's role laid down in the text.

Almost diametrically opposite the contemporary reader stands the oft quoted ideal reader. It is difficult to pinpoint precisely where he is drawn from, though there is a good deal to be said for the claim that he tends to emerge from the brain of the philologist or critic himself. Although the critic's judgment may well have been honed and refined by the many texts he has dealt with, he remains nothing more than a cultured reader—if only because an ideal reader is a structural impossibility as far as literary communication is concerned. An ideal reader would have to have an identical code to that of the author; authors, however, generally recodify prevailing codes in their texts, and so the ideal reader would also have to share the intentions underlying this process. And if this were possible, communication would then be quite superfluous, for one only communicates that which is *not* already shared by sender and receiver.

The idea that the author himself might be his own ideal reader is frequently undermined by the statements writers have made about their own works. Generally, as readers they hardly ever make any remarks on the impact their own texts have exercised upon them, but prefer to talk in referential language about their intentions, strategies, and constructions, conforming to conditions that will also be valid for the public they are trying to guide. Whenever this happens, i.e., whenever the author turns into a reader of his own work, he must therefore revert to the code, which he had already recoded in his work. In other words, the author, although theoretically the only possible ideal reader, as he has experienced what he has written, does not in fact *need* to duplicate himself into author and ideal reader, so that the postulate of an ideal reader is, in his case, superfluous.

A further question mark against the concept of the ideal reader lies in the fact that such a being would have to be able to realize in full the meaning potential of the fictional text. The history of literary responses, however, shows quite clearly that this potential has been fulfilled in many different ways, and if so, how can one person at one go encompass all the possible meanings? Different meanings of the same text have emerged at different times, and, indeed, the same text read a second time will have a different effect from that of its first reading. The ideal reader, then, must not only fulfill the potential meaning of the text independently of his own historical situation, but he must also do this exhaustively. The result would be total consumption of the text—which would itself be ruinous for literature. But there are texts which can be "consumed" in this way, as is obvious from the mounds of light literature that flow regularly into the pulping machines. The question then arises as to whether the reader of such works is really the one meant by the term "ideal reader," for the latter is usually called upon when the text is hard to grasp—it is hoped that he will help to unravel its mysteries and, if there are no mysteries, his presence

is not required anyway. Indeed, herein lies the true essence of this particular concept. The ideal reader, unlike the contemporary reader, is a purely fictional being; he has no basis in reality, and it is this very fact that makes him so useful: as a fictional being, he can close the gaps that constantly appear in any analysis of literary effects and responses. He can be endowed with a variety of qualities in accordance with whatever problem he is called upon to help solve.

This rather general account of the two concepts of ideal and contemporary readers reveals certain presuppositions, which frequently come into play when responses to fictional texts are to be assessed. The basic concern of these concepts is with the results produced rather than with the structure of effects, which causes and is responsible for these results. It is time now to change the vantage point, turning away from results produced and focusing on that potential in the text which triggers the recreative dialectics in the reader.

The desire to break free from these traditional and basically restrictive categories of readers can already be seen in the various attempts that have been made to develop new categories of readers as heuristic concepts. Present-day literary criticism offers specific categories for specific areas of discussion: there is the superreader (Riffaterre),[2] the informed reader (Fish),[3] and the intended reader (Wolff),[4] to name but a few, each type bringing with it a special terminology of its own. Although these readers are primarily conceived as heuristic constructs, they are nevertheless drawn from specific groups of real, existing readers.

Riffaterre's superreader stands for a "group of informants,"[5] who always come together at "nodal points in the text,"[6] thus establishing through their common reactions the existence of a "stylistic fact."[7] The superreader is like a sort of divining rod, used to discover a density of meaning potential encoded in the text. As a collective term for a variety of readers of different competence, it allows for an empirically verifiable account of both the semantic and pragmatic potential contained in the message of the text. By sheer weight of numbers, Riffaterre hopes to eliminate the degree of variation inevitably arising from the subjective disposition of the individual reader. He tries to objectify style, or the stylistic fact as a communicative element additional to the primary one of language.[8] He argues that the stylistic fact stands out from its context, thus pointing to a density within the encoded message, which is brought to light by intratextual contrasts that are spotted by the superreader. An approach like this bypasses the difficulties inherent in the stylistics of deviation, which always involves reference to linguistic norms that lie outside the text, in order to gauge the poetic qualities of a text by the degree it deviates from these presupposed extratextual norms. This argument, however, is not the core of Riffaterre's concept; the most vital point is that a stylistic fact can only be discerned by a perceiving subject. Consequently, the basic impossibility of formalizing the intratextual contrasts manifests itself as an effect that can only be experienced by a reader. And so Riffaterre's super-reader is a means of ascertaining the stylistic fact, but owing to its nonreferentiality this concept shows how indispensable the reader is to the formulation of the stylistic fact.

Now even the superreader, as a collective term for a group of readers, is not proof against error. The very ascertaining of intratextual contrasts presupposes a differentiated competence and is dependent not least on the historical nearness or distance of the group in relation to the text under consideration. Nevertheless, Riffaterre's concept does show that stylistic qualities can no longer be exclusively pinpointed with the instruments of linguistics.

To a certain degree this also holds true of Fish's concept of the informed reader, which is not so much concerned with the statistical average of readers' reactions as with describing the processing of the text by the reader. For this purpose, certain conditions must be fulfilled:

> The informed reader is someone who 1.) is a competent speaker of the language out of which the text is built up. 2.) is in full possession of "semantic knowledge that a mature . . . listener brings to this task of comprehension." This includes the knowledge (that is, the experience, both as a producer and comprehender) of lexical sets, collocation probabilities, idioms, professional and other dialects, etc. 3.) has *literary* competence. . . . The reader, of whose responses I speak, then, is this informed reader, neither an abstraction, nor an actual living reader, but a hybrid—a real reader (me) who does everything within his power to make himself informed.[9]

This category of reader, then, must not only possess the necessary competence, but must also observe his own reactions during the process of actualization[10] in order to control them. The need for this self-observation arises first from the fact that Fish developed his concept of the informed reader with close reference to generative-transformational grammar, and second from the fact that he could not take over some of the consequences inherent in this model. If the reader, by means of his competence, structures the text himself, this implies that his reactions will follow one another in time, during the course of his reading, and that it is in this sequence of reactions that the meaning of the text will be generated. To this extent Fish follows the model of transformational grammar. Where he diverges from this model is in his evaluation of surface structure: "It should be noted however that my category of response, and especially of meaningful response, includes more than the transformational grammarians, who believe that comprehension is a function of deep structure perception, would allow. There is a tendency, at least in the writings of some linguists, to downgrade surface structure—the form of actual sentences—to the status of a husk, or covering, or veil; a layer of excrescences that is to be peeled away or penetrated or discarded in favor of the kernel underlying it."[11]

The sequence of reactions aroused in the reader by the surface structure of a literary text is often characterized by the fact that the strategies of that text lead the reader astray—which is the prime reason why different readers will react differently. The surface structure sets off in the reader a process which in fact would grind to an almost immediate halt if the surface structure were meant only to unveil the deep structure. Thus, Fish abandons the transformational model at a point that is vital both for it and for his concept. The model in fact breaks down just when it reaches one of the most interesting tasks of all: clarifying the processing of literary texts—an act that would be grotesquely impoverished if reduced to terms of mere grammar. But it is also at this point that the concept of the informed reader loses its frame of reference and changes into a postulate that, for all the plausibility of its premises, is very difficult to consolidate. Fish himself is aware of the difficulty, and at the end of the essay he says of his concept: "In a peculiar and unsettling (to theorists) way, it is a method which processes its own user, who is also its only instrument. It is self-sharpening and what it sharpens is *you*. In short, it does not organize materials, but transforms minds."[12] The transformation, then, no longer relates to the text, but to the reader. Viewed from the standpoint of generative-transformational grammar, the transformation is just a metaphor, but it also shows clearly the limited range of the generative-transformational model, as there is no doubt that processing a text is bound to result in changes within the recipient, and these changes are not a matter of grammatical rules, but of experience. This is the problem with Fish's concept — it starts out from the grammatical model, justifiably abandons the model at a particular juncture, but can then only invoke an experience which, though indisputable, remains inaccessible to the theorist. However, we can see even more clearly from the concept of the informed reader than from that of the superreader that an analysis of text processing requires more than just a linguistic model.

While Fish concerns himself with the effects of the text on the reader, Wolff — with his intended reader — sets out to reconstruct the idea of the reader which the author had in mind.[13] This image of the intended reader can take on different forms, according to the text being dealt with: it may be the idealized reader,[14] or it may reveal itself through anticipation of the norms and values of contemporary readers, through individualization of the public, through apostrophes to the reader, through the assigning of attitudes, or didactic intentions, or the demand for the willing suspension of disbelief.[15] Thus the intended reader, as a sort of fictional inhabitant of the text,[16] can embody not only the concepts and conventions of the contemporary public but also the desire of the author both to link up with these concepts and to work on them — sometimes just portraying them, sometimes acting upon them. Wolff outlines the history of the democratization of the "reader idea," the definition of which, however, demands a relatively detailed knowledge of the contemporary reader and of the social history of the time, if the importance and function of this intended reader are to be properly evaluated. But, in any case, by characterizing this fictitious reader it is possible to reconstruct the public which the author wished to address.

There can be no doubting the usefulness, and indeed necessity, of ascertaining this figure, and equally certain is the fact that there is a reciprocity between the form of presentation and the type of reader intended,[17] but the question remains open as to why, generations later, a reader can still grasp the meaning (perhaps we should say *a* meaning) of the text, even though he cannot be the intended reader. Clearly, the historical qualities which influenced the author at the time of writing mould the image of the

intended reader — and as such they may enable us to reconstruct the author's intentions, but they tell us nothing about the reader's actual response to the text. The intended reader, then, marks certain positions and attitudes in the text, but these are not yet identical to the reader's role, for many of these positions are conceived ironically (frequently the case in novels), so that the reader is not expected to accept the attitude offered him, but rather to react to it. We must, then, differentiate between the fictitious reader and the reader's role, for although the former is present in the text by way of a large variety of different signals, he is not independent of the other textual perspectives, such as narrator, characters, and plotline, as far as his function is concerned. The fictitious reader is, in fact, just one of several perspectives, all of which interlink and interact. The role of the reader emerges from this interplay of perspectives, for he finds himself called upon to mediate between them, and so it would be fair to say that the intended reader, as supplier of *one* perspective, can never represent more than one aspect of the reader's role.

The three concepts of reader that we have dealt with start out from different assumptions and aim at different solutions. The superreader represents a test concept which serves to ascertain the "stylistic fact," pointing to a density in the encoded message of the text. The informed reader represents a self-instructing concept that aims at increasing the reader's "informedness," and hence his competence, through self-observation with regard to the sequence of reactions set off by the text. The intended reader represents a concept of reconstruction, uncovering the historical dispositions of the reading public at which the author was aiming. But for all the diversity of their intentions, these three concepts have one common denominator: they all see themselves as a means of transcending the limitations of (1) structural linguistics, (2) generative-transformational grammar, or (3) literary sociology, by introducing the figure of the reader.

It is evident that no theory concerned with literary texts can make much headway without bringing in the reader, who now appears to have been promoted to the new frame of reference whenever the semantic and pragmatic potential of the text comes under scrutiny. The question is, what kind of reader? As we have seen, the different concepts, of real and of hypothetical readers, all entail restrictions that inevitably undermine the general applicability of the theories to which they are linked. If, then, we are to try and understand the effects caused and the responses elicited by literary works, we must allow for the reader's presence without in any way predetermining his character or his historical situation. We may call him, for want of a better term, the implied reader. He embodies all those predispositions necessary for a literary work to exercise its effect—predispositions laid down, not by an empirical outside reality, but by the text itself. Consequently, the implied reader as a concept has his roots firmly planted in the structure of the text; he is a construct and in no way to be identified with any real reader.

It is generally recognized that literary texts take on their reality by being read, and this in turn means that texts must already contain certain conditions of actualization that will allow their meaning to be assembled in the responsive mind of the recipient. The concept of the implied reader is therefore a textual structure anticipating the presence of a recipient without necessarily defining him: this concept prestructures the role to be assumed by each recipient, and this holds true even when texts deliberately appear to ignore their possible recipient or actively exclude him. Thus the concept of the implied reader designates a network of response-inviting structures, which impel the reader to grasp the text.

No matter who or what he may be, the real reader is always offered a particular role to play, and it is this role that constitutes the concept of the implied reader. There are two basic, interrelated aspects to this concept: the reader's role as a textual structure, and the reader's role as a structured act. Let us begin with the textual structure. We may assume that every literary text in one way or another represents a perspective view of the world put together by (though not necessarily typical of) the author. As such, the work is in no way a mere copy of the given world—it constructs a world of its own out of the material available to it. It is the way in which this world is constructed that brings about the perspective intended by the author. Since the world of the text is bound to have variable degrees of unfamiliarity for its possible readers (if the work is to have any "novelty" for them), they must be placed in a position which enables them to actualize the new view. This position, however, cannot be present in the text itself, as it is the vantage point for visualizing the world represented and so cannot be part of that world. The

text must therefore *bring about* a standpoint from which the reader will be able to view things that would never have come into focus as long as his own habitual dispositions were determining his orientation, and what is more, this standpoint must be able to accommodate all kinds of different readers. How, then, can it evolve from the structure of the text?

It has been pointed out that the literary text offers a perspective view of the world (namely, the author's). It is also, in itself, composed of a variety of perspectives that outline the author's view and also provide access to what the reader is meant to visualize. This is best exemplified by the novel, which is a system of perspectives designed to transmit the individuality of the author's vision. As a rule there are four main perspectives: those of the narrator, the characters, the plot, and the fictitious reader. Although these may differ in order of importance, none of them on its own is identical to the meaning of the text. What they do is provide guidelines originating from different starting points (narrator, characters, etc.), continually shading into each other and devised in such a way that they all converge on a general meeting place. We call this meeting place the meaning of the text, which can only be brought into focus if it is visualized from a standpoint. Thus, standpoint and convergence of textual perspectives are closely interrelated, although neither of them is actually represented in the text, let alone set out in words. Rather they emerge during the reading process, in the course of which the reader's role is to occupy shifting vantage points that are geared to a prestructured activity and to fit the diverse perspectives into a gradually evolving pattern. This allows him to grasp both the different starting points of the textual perspectives and their ultimate coalescence, which is guided by the interplay between the changing perspectives and the gradually unfolding coalescence itself.[18]

Thus, the reader's role is prestructured by three basic components: the different perspectives represented in the text, the vantage point from which he joins them together, and the meeting place where they converge.

This pattern simultaneously reveals that the reader's role is not identical to the fictitious reader portrayed in the text. The latter is merely one component part of the reader's role, by which the author exposes the disposition of an assumed reader to interaction with the other perspectives, in order to bring about modifications.

So far we have outlined the reader's role as a textual structure, which, however, will be fully implemented only when it induces structured acts in the reader. The reason for this is that although the textual perspectives themselves are given, their gradual convergence and final meeting place are not linguistically formulated and so have to be imagined. This is the point where the textual structure of his role begins to affect the reader. The instructions provided stimulate mental images, which animate what is linguistically implied, though not said. A sequence of mental images is bound to arise during the reading process, as new instructions have continually to be accommodated, resulting not only in the replacement of images formed but also in a shifting position of the vantage point, which differentiates the attitudes to be adopted in the process of image-building. Thus the vantage point of the reader and the meeting place of perspectives become interrelated during the ideational activity and so draw the reader inescapably into the world of the text.

Textual structure and structured act are related in much the same way as intention and fulfillment, though in the concept of the implied reader they are joined together in the dynamic process we have described. In this respect, the concept departs from the latest postulate that the programmed reception of the text be designated as *"Rezeptionsvorgabe"* (structured prefigurement).[19] This term relates only to discernible textual structures and completely ignores the dynamic act which elicits the response to those structures.

The concept of the implied reader as an expression of the role offered by the text is in no way an abstraction derived from a real reader, but is rather the conditioning force behind a particular kind of tension produced by the real reader when he accepts the role. This tension results, in the first place, from the difference

> between myself as reader and the often very different self who goes about paying bills, repairing leaky faucets, and failing in generosity and wisdom. It is only as I read that I become the self whose beliefs must coincide with the author's. Regardless of my real beliefs and practices, I must subordinate my mind and heart to the book if I am to enjoy it to the full. The author creates, in short, an image of himself and another image of his reader; he makes his reader, as he makes his second self, and the most successful reading is

one in which the created selves, author and reader, can find complete agreement.[20]

One wonders whether such an agreement can really work; even Coleridge's ever popular demand for a "willing suspension of disbelief" on the part of the audience remains an ideal whose desirability is questionable. Would the role offered by the text function properly if it were totally accepted? The sacrifice of the real reader's own beliefs would mean the loss of the whole repertoire of historical norms and values, and this in turn would entail the loss of the tension which is a precondition for the processing and for the comprehension that follows it. As M. H. Abrams has rightly stressed: "Given a truly impassive reader, all his beliefs suspended or anesthetized, (a poet) would be as helpless, in his attempt to endow his work with interest and power, as though he had to write for an audience from Mars."[21] However, the suggestion that there are two selves is certainly tenable, for these are the role offered by the text and the real reader's own disposition, and as the one can never be fully taken over by the other, there arises between the two the tension we have described. Generally, the role prescribed by the text will be the stronger, but the reader's own disposition will never disappear totally; it will tend instead to form the background to and a frame of reference for the act of grasping and comprehending. If it were to disappear totally, we should simply forget all the experiences that we are constantly bringing into play as we read — experiences which are responsible for the many different ways in which people fulfill the reader's role set out by the text. And even though we may lose awareness of these experiences while we read, we are still guided by them unconsciously, and by the end of our reading we are liable consciously to want to incorporate the new experience into our own store of knowledge.

The fact that the reader's role can be fulfilled in different ways, according to historical or individual circumstances, is an indication that the structure of the text *allows* for different ways of fulfillment. Clearly, then, the process of fulfillment is always a selective one, and any one actualization can be judged against the background of the others potentially present in the textual structure of the reader's role. Each actualization therefore represents a selective realization of the implied reader, whose own structure provides a frame of reference within which individual responses to a text can be communicated to others. This is a vital function of the whole concept of the implied reader: it provides a link between all the historical and individual actualizations of the text and makes them accessible to analysis.

To sum up, then, the concept of the implied reader is a transcendental model which makes it possible for the structured effects of literary texts to be described. It denotes the role of the reader, which is definable in terms of textual structure and structured acts. By bringing about a standpoint for the reader, the textual structure follows a basic rule of human perception, as our views of the world are always of a perspective nature. "The observing subject and the represented object have a particular relationship one to the other; the 'subject-object relationship' merges into the perspective way of representation. It also merges into the observer's way of seeing; for just as the artist organizes his representation according to the standpoint of an observer, the observer—because of this very technique of representation—finds himself directed toward a particular view which more or less obliges him to search for the one and only standpoint that will correspond to that view."[22]

By virtue of this standpoint, the reader is situated in such a position that he can assemble the meaning toward which the perspectives of the text have guided him. But since this meaning is neither a given external reality nor a copy of an intended reader's own world, it is something that has to be ideated by the mind of the reader. A reality that has no existence of its own can only come into being by way of ideation, and so the structure of the text sets off a sequence of mental images which lead to the text translating itself into the reader's consciousness. The actual content of these mental images will be colored by the reader's existing stock of experience, which acts as a referential background against which the unfamiliar can be conceived and processed. The concept of the implied reader offers a means of describing the process whereby textual structures are transmuted through ideational activities into personal experiences.

Notes

1. Northrop Frye, *Fearful Symmetry. A Study of William Blake* (Boston, 1967), pp. 427f.
2. Michael Riffaterre, *Strukturale Stilistik*, transl. by Wilhelm Bolle (Munich, 1973), pp. 46ff.
3. Stanley Fish, "Literature in the Reader: Affective Stylistics," *New Literary History* 2 (1970): 123ff.
4. Erwin Wolff, "Der intendierte Leser," *Poetica* 4 (1971): 141ff.
5. Riffaterre, *Strukturale Stilistik*, p. 44.
6. Ibid., p. 48.
7. Ibid., p. 29, passim.
8. See also the critique by Rainer Warning, "Rezeptionsästhetik als literaturwissenschaftliche Pragmatik," in *Rezeptionsästhetik. Theorie und Praxis* (UTB 303), Rainer Warning, ed. (Munich, 1975), pp. 26ff.
9. Fish, "Literature in the Reader," p. 145.
10. Ibid., pp. 144–46.
11. Ibid., p. 143.
12. Ibid., p. 160f.
13. Wolff, "Der intendierte Leser," p. 166.
14. Ibid., p. 145.
15. Ibid., pp. 143, 151–54, 156, 158, 162.
16. Ibid., p. 160.
17. Ibid., pp. 159f.
18. For a more detailed discussion, see Part II, Chap. 4, pp. 96–99.
19. See Manfred Naumann et al., *Gesellschaft—Literatur—Lesen. Literaturrezeption in theoretischer Sicht* (Berlin and Weimar, 1973), p. 35, passim; see also my critique of this book, "Im Lichte der Kritik," in Warning's *Rezeptionsästhetik*, pp. 335–41, as well as that of H. R. Jauss, ibid., pp. 343ff.
20. Wayne C. Booth, *The Rhetoric of Fiction* (Chicago, 1963), pp. 137f.
21. M. H. Abrams, "Belief and Suspension of Disbelief," in *Literature and Belief* (English Institute Essays, 1957), M. H. Abrams, ed. (New York, 1958), p. 17.
22. Carl Friedrich Graumann, *Grundlagen einer Phänomenologie und Psychologie der Perspektivität* (Berlin, 1960), p. 14.

The Miller's Wife and the Professors: Questions about the Transactive Theory of Reading

Norman Holland

In contrast to Wolfgang Iser, who puts much of his emphasis on the ways the text controls the reader's responses, Norman Holland is more concerned with the ways actual readers control the text. Thus, while Iser offers a reader-response theory that explains why we should have similar reactions to the same text, Holland offers one that explains why we very often do not. Basing his literary theory on a psychoanalytic view of readers rather than on a phenomenological view of reading, Holland claims that each reader will impose his or her "identity theme" on the text, to a large extent re-creating that text in the reader's image. And this process can be illustrated, Holland argues, even when the readers are professional literary analysts. This argument inevitably raises questions about the relative weight of "subjective" and "objective" data, about the possibility of "misreadings," and about the need to account for a reader's changing interpretations, questions that Holland undertakes to answer as he sets forth his own "transactive" theory of reading and defines his position with reference to several other reader-response critics.

The scene: spring at a large midwestern university, 10:15 A.M. A seminar room. Around the long table and in outer rows of seats are gathered a score or so of professorial-looking types from the English department, some senior, some junior. About a quarter are women, some of them, it turns out, faculty wives. They have assembled for a "Working Teach-shop" by the Visiting Fireman.

It is the morning after the lecture and party the night before. People are gearing up for the day or, having taught 9:00s, gearing down. Those seated at the table are holding photocopies of a poem. As they banter, they seem to be approaching the morning's

Reprinted by permission of the publisher from *New Literary History* 17 (1986): pp. 423–47. Copyright © 1986 by The Johns Hopkins University Press.

exercise in a spirit of curiosity. Let's play the VF's game and see what happens.

The VF himself, neatly dressed if slightly hung over, sits in the middle of one long side. He speaks in a friendly but hesitant voice, feeling his way with this group, new to him. He begins by reading the poem aloud:

The Mill

The miller's wife had waited long,
    The tea was cold, the fire was dead;
And there might yet be nothing wrong
    In how he went and what he said;
"There are no millers any more,"
    Was all that she had heard him say;
And he had lingered at the door
    So long that it seemed yesterday.

Sick with fear that had no form
    She knew that she was there at last;
And in the mill there was a warm
    And mealy fragrance of the past.
What else there was would only seem
    To say again what he had meant;
And what was hanging from a beam
    Would not have heeded where she went.

And if she thought it followed her,
    She may have reasoned in the dark
That one way of the few there were
    Would hide her and would leave no mark:
Black water, smooth above the weir
    Like starry velvet in the night,
Though ruffled once, would soon appear
    The same as ever to the sight.

"The Mill" is by Edwin Arlington Robinson, 1920. This morning's consensus is: Not a great poem, but good. One senior man in American literature gravely opines that Robinson is "much underrated."

The VF remarks that he picked this particular poem because part of his lecture the night before dealt with Robert Frost's comments on it. He therefore thought the assembled company might find this poem a useful starting point. This morning, as advertised, he would like to consider how one might apply the theoretical ideas developed in the lecture (the transactive theory of reading, identity theory, feedback networks, cognitive psychology, the architecture of the brain) to something more practical, the teaching of literature. Would the professors be so kind as to fill in answers to the following five questions?

Actually, of course, the VF has a hidden agenda. As he goes to and fro on the earth, from campus to campus, explaining his devilish ideas about reading,

he gets the same questions over and over. Last night's lecture was no exception. Three questions, in particular, always arise:

> Doesn't this make every reading totally subjective, so that any one reading is as good as any other?
>
> In teaching what do you do about misreadings?
>
> Don't people change their readings? I know I read *Huckleberry Finn* differently now from the way I did when I was a child.

In answer, the VF has stated his views, his transactive theory of reading, many times. Although there are (obviously!) shared elements in the reading situation, we can represent someone's reading a poem or a story as a personal transaction—as an expression of character or identity. The VF is not abandoning the text or techniques of interpretation or the social situation within which interpretation takes place. He is not saying that a reading is not *also* a function of these things. Quite the contrary! he says. He is simply claiming that we *can* understand someone's reading as a function of personal identity.[1]

Sadly, however, the VF feels deep down inside him that no matter how clearly he says these, by now, to him, palpable truths, he will hear these same questions over and over again. To elicit them and discuss them and perhaps even lay to rest these recurring questions he has put together some materials for a workshop for professors of literature. If he coalesces several occasions on which he got groups of professors to work on his materials, he comes up with the scene with which this article began.

Meanwhile, back in that seminar room, the VF, ever hopeful, hands out questionnaires. He promises to hand out his own answers in exchange for their candor, but even so, the professors assembled around the seminar table are a little reluctant, a little shy, a little tested in their professional mettle.

1. To what does the clause "what was hanging from a beam" refer? _____
_____

2. To what does the clause "What else there was" refer? _____
_____

3. What is the most important single word in the poem? _____
Why? _____
_____

4. What does the miller's wife look like (features, build, clothing, etc.)? _____

_____

5. Whom does she remind you of, and why?

_____

_____

The questions artfully span a gamut from the most "objective" to the most "subjective." That is, question 1 asks a grammatical question which I think most professional readers would agree has one "right" and various "wrong" answers.

Question 2 looks like 1, but there probably is no definitely right answer. Still, some answers would be clearly wrong ("the wife," say) while a number of others would be acceptable and, in that sense, "right." I had in mind here Stanley Fish's concept of an "interpretive community." When we ask a grammatical question of a poem, we apply the procedures and conventions of the community of university readers, professors, and students to answer it. We use "interpretive strategies" that we learned from an "interpretive community." These, says Fish, "enable," "constitute," "make available" such ideas as a clause's referring to something.[2] Would the professors' answers demonstrate Fish's claim?

Question 3 asks for a more freely imaginative response. There are no "wrong" answers except (I suppose) words that do not occur in "The Mill." I took the question from David Bleich's book on "subjective" pedagogy in which the author says an answer to this question "begins in complete subjectivity and is then transformed into judgments that appear to be objective."[3]

Question 4 asks for even more projection, since the poem does not describe the wife at all. I wrote this question hoping to test Wolfgang Iser's model of response in which the text leaves gaps (here, the wife's appearance) which the reader feels impelled to fill.[4]

Question 5 admits a wholly personal response. That is, anyone would comprehend a description answering 4 (thin, gaunt, even "like an Eskimo"), but no one else in the room but the answerer could understand some of the answers possible for 5: my mother-in-law; a woman I saw once. Thus 5 calls for a "very subjective" and 1 for a "very objective" answer, and indeed the responses came out accordingly.

Most readers gave the "right" answer to question 1:

The miller
the miller's body

The miller's corpse
the miller
THE DEAD MILLER
refers to a new subj. serving as gr. subj. of verb "could not have heeded." serves as antecedent of "it" — applies to hanged miller.

Inevitably, there were a few who arrived at special results:

fear or the fear of what the future holds
I have no idea.
Seems something dead, fearful, underscoring her fright.

Question 2, allowing more leeway, elicited more varied answers and varied wording:

THE DEAD MILLER
Again it is referentially the hanged body of No. 1.
This also refers to the hanging body of the miller.
Various possibilities: Hanged miller — smell of hanged miller (bowels loosening, etc. — in contrast to pleasant "fragrance"), what was "there" beside the fear, finally given form — the scene & situation —

Maybe those who said in answer to 2 the miller's body (incorrect, in my reading) had some sort of carryover from question 1. They tended to use more language in answering question 2, possibly expressing uncertainty about their answers.

Some people wrote down what seems to me, at least, the "right" answer, namely, other things that embody the miller's outmoded craft:

The other reminders in the mill of the dead occupation.
Everything in the mill that reminds the wife of the Miller's life & that Millers are now unnecessary.

Still others suggested vague fears or futures or failures:

"what else there was" refers to "what he had meant" and "what was hanging from the beam." The referents are nonspecific and what floats around is the phantom of fear, or doubt or distrust — something that has no form.
It refers to that "something" that pervades the room, fills it with suspense. Not knowing what that something is is half the reason for its powerful effect.

It refers to the *non*-reassuring aspects of the mill—what speaks to her fears (of the future), not to her knowledge of the past. Fear directs itself toward the future.

Questions 1 and 2 should surely evoke the effects of Stanley Fish's interpretive communities. And they do. Clearly the professors were drawing on a common store of syntactic knowledge and shared principles of reading. On the other hand, there was no great unanimity. The idea of interpretive communities may be necessary, but it is not sufficient to explain these responses.

Question 3 elicited (as I had expected) a wide variety of answers:

dead. is right at beginning of poem & puts weight on everything that follows

"dead." It suggests what happens.

fear: Because of her first phrase "There are no millers anymore" which is, it appears, the point of her fear of economic downfall. Such things as yesterday, past, linger

Fear. It colors all responses to her encounters in the mill

hanging   Because he's hanging (the miller) in a society that no longer needs him.

hanging—everything in the poem seems to hang, be suspended, the wife waiting, the miller, no need, the dead miller, hope, etc.

Some said there was *no* most important word, leaving the question blank or fussing with it:

There isn't one. To answer, though: dead so much death, everywhere—no more millers (other words seem to say again what it had meant).

I'm uncomfortable choosing—each word seems to be dependent on the others. "There" is used many times in different ways—as a place—as a nonplace—The poem draws attention to *place* (The Mill) as determining action.

Others showed remarkable ingenuity:

Same.   The irony that there are no millers anymore—and yet no change, no mark, everything still appears the same.

what   brings reader in

"No"   that which *is* disappears; connects to "nothing," "no millers," "no form," would not, "no mark."

MIL   The assonant found in "meal" & "miller"—it ties the entire poem together—especially in "mealy fragrance"

mealy?   pleasant, warm ground-down grain, devastated people, "mealy-mouthedness" of the probably—uncomplaining wife to the miller, & miller to anyone who might have heard or understood.

yet   she does not know—yet—and so the poem hangs in the moment before knowing, when she suspects, doesn't know, doesn't want to believe

And, of course, there was a joker. The most important word? "'Hangs.' It jars you."

Surely one could say with Bleich that these answers begin in subjectivity and end in objectivity, but does that statement do more than describe what is taking place? Surely these answers are, finally, "subjective," yet they mark various "objective" appeals to the poem. There must be more helpful metaphors than "begins" and "ends" for developing the relation.

Asked in question 4 to project visually, some hesitated, agreed to make an image, but insisted they did not know for sure:

I remember nothing of her appearance. She seems an image—abstract—of domesticity.

She is not described at all, of course, and the poem seems to convey a sense of formlessness. There is a sense of evasion, of dimly making out the forms and outlines of things. Yet I see her as a heavy set woman, with a pale face, broad features, a woman who has worked hard all her life.

No clue in poem—probably small, plain, calico & gingham—anything but velvet

Others tried to reason an image into being:

? young?

She is *probably* short, as she must look up at the beam where he is hanging

Apron (tea). White face in fear, Hands red with hard work. Slightly overweight = the diet of poor people who eat a lot of starch.

Some simply went ahead and described her:

Older woman, motherly, has known hard time

apron, thin, long hands & fingers, gaunt cheeks

Slightly over-weight, plain, middle-aged woman—wearing work clothes (housedress)

like a fat Russian peasant-woman in late middle-age

Others resorted to pictures and analogies:

not described—we are free to create our own image—I see a Brueghel.

Like a weaker version of the woman in Grant Wood's "American Gothic"

Several possibilities: the mother in the Katzen-jammer Kids strip (older, obese/sturdy/hard-farm working immigrant with apron)—in this case suicide results of economy, *or* Nastasia Kinsky (grey peasant dress unbuttoned at the top showing inner breast & chest wall, hair seductively falling over left eye, pushed back, falls again)—then suicide due to jealousy, etc.

The variability in these pictures suggests to me a number of things about Iser's model. For one thing, Iser writes as though the bulk of the response were controlled by the poem and the reader simply fills in some inessential gaps. The poems these people describe, however, are *so* different (Grant Wood, Brueghel, thin, fat) that the balance seems rather the other way. Also, the answers to questions 1 and 2 suggest that, even in simple grammatical matters, readers are not constrained or limited. Third, it is not clear to me that readers are "impelled" to fill in gaps. Several of these professors simply refused.

To the last and most projective question of the five, there were the predictable blanks and responses like

no one

I can't think of anyone right now

—Can't think of a literary character just now

As in that last response, most of these professors of literature assumed, more or less automatically, that what was called for was a literary association, and most provided one. Some were predictable, others quite ingenious:

Chaucer—connotations of famous Miller?

The Wife in "Death of a Salesman"

Tristan, Romeo

Women in the Death of the Hired Man, Hedda Gabler

the old peasant woman whose shoes Heidegger writes about in "The Origin of Art"—because she seems to have been totally and unreflec-

tively absorbed in her work (or her husband's) until the event which precipitates the poem occurs. Then, she is incapable of going on.

Others did what I had hoped for the purposes of my demonstration:

An old woman I saw once.

My grandmother—because she was old world & full of care & overworked

My Aunt Betty, who discovered her husband dead on his workshop floor

A former girlfriend, a timorous and dependent person, who gave meaning to her own life by identification with others—an identification with me I couldn't tolerate in the end.

They recalled figures entirely personal to themselves, people no one else in the room would know—except for

She does not remind me of anyone I know. In her fear that something may have happened to hurt a loved one, she reminds me of me.

Others turned to works of art or places, personal recollections but not entirely personal:

Woman figure in Dorothea Lange's depression photo. Sense of being lost, bereft, nowhere, empty.

Any Iowa farmer's wife, perhaps from a photo in the depression, black & white

I saw many working women in England who had that stoical air about them; they were worn by life, not very "well cared for" but still cheery and tough.

She's probably like that only without much fight left in her. Her ending seems so quiet and un-dramatic—just a bowing to the inevitable.

Finally others *imagined* a person to be reminded of:

She reminds me of someone who someone wants taking a less active role—content to let things happen "They also serve who stand & wait" She is unaffected by what's happening & partly paying no attention

And, of course, there was a joker. "Whom does she remind you of?" "The miller."

So far, we have been looking at answers by many different people to one question. Although these are skilled professional readers, although they are part of an interpretive community—American university teachers of literature—although most are drawing on an essentially similar "New Critical" training, their answers vary all over the place. Question 1 has "right" and "wrong" answers, but after that, responses go every which way.[5]

When we look at many answers to single questions, we can trace some rather vague patterns, but the whole picture is rather a jumble. We can get more coherence, however, if, instead of comparing everyone's answer to one question, we look at one person's answers to all five questions. For example:

1. body hanging there
2. the only thing that was left was his found body—
3. fear—gives feeling of dread
4. no idea—housewife—heavy set; placid air of waiting—doesn't pay much attention Keeps on with her
5. She reminds me of someone who someone wants taking a less active role—content to let things happen "They also serve who stand & wait" She is unaffected by what's happening & partly paying no attention

In these five answers by someone I'll call Professor One, I can read back from the last to the first and perceive a pattern. Answer 5 has a mistake: the repeated "someone," as if the final clause could stand alone, "Someone wants taking a less active role," as if the final clause could apply to Professor One herself as well as to the miller's wife. (Evidently she felt rushed—see 4.) To 5, the most projective of the questions, the one that allows most room, for individual feelings and associations, she speaks of someone "less active," who only stands and waits, who is partly paying no attention.

I see the same theme in her answer to question 4: placid, waiting, not paying attention. Again, as though what Professor One was saying applied equally to the miller's wife and to herself, she does not finish her last clause in 4. Perhaps she as well as the miller's wife is not paying attention. Perhaps she has identified herself with the wife.

In 3, she names "fear" as the most important word because it "gives feeling of dread." Again the phrasing is both passive and vague: the word *does something* to One, something vague. It "gives feeling." The verbs in 2 are exaggeratedly passive: "The only thing that was left was his found body." Finally, in 1, "body hanging there," we get a "correct" answer to this "objective" question, but stated so as to

emphasize the theme of passivity ("hanging") and vagueness ("there") that I find more obvious in her longer, more projective responses.

In tracing these themes, of course, I am primarily talking about her responses, only secondarily, inferentially about her. The distinction is essential, for two reasons. First, one cannot infer from One's writing alone what the relation is between her responses and her personality. The passivity I see in this specimen of her writing might be an overreaction by an intensely active person, or it might be a special frame of mind for reading, or it might simply be the result of the party the night before. Second, my reading of her response is as much a function of my identity as her reading of the poem is of hers. My conclusions, like hers, express me as well as what I am reading. Hence, what I am describing is a mutual interpretation. She reads the poem and the poem, so to speak, reads her. I read her response and her response, so to speak, reads me. My reading is my attempt to represent that systematically elusive process in words.

Possibly these interrelations will become clearer if we contrast One's reading with Professor Two's set of five responses:

1. refers to a new subj. serving as gr. subj. of verb "could not have heeded." serves as antecedent of "it"—applies to hanged miller.
2. 2d attribution of something in the mill—1st thing being "fragrance"
3.
4. Unspecified—yet implied she follows, by drowning, her husband's departure by hanging.
5. Tristan, Romeo

Two is reluctant to project at all: he leaves 3 blank and insists in 4 that the wife's looks are "Unspecified." He makes up the lack by a process of inference which he attributes to the poem: the poem "implied" she drowned. Similarly, in 5, he pointed out by way of explanation, Tristan and Romeo fit in a sort of logical way. Each is a literary figure who dies in a double suicide or mutual love-death. His appeal to logic and observable behavior (as in 4) outweighed the woman's sex: very few respondents to 5 were reminded of men by the miller's *wife*.

The wife reminded him of literary figures, Tristan and Romeo, and he showed in 1 and 2 a similar focus on language (at the expense of the physical world). In 1 he spelled out a grammatical answer to a grammatical question exactly, almost fussily. In 2 he provided a grammatical answer—two grammatical answers—to a question that most people answered by an appeal to the events. In 4 he phrased the distressing facts of the poem in tangled euphemisms, "departure" for death or suicide, "follows" for the second death. From merely these brief responses, I can phrase a pair of themes that will unify Two's responses for me: displacement to logic, language, or demonstrable surface behavior; conversely, a reluctance to imagine what is not directly observable.

Young Professor Three was unusual in being witty:

1. The husband (miller) who has hanged himself. Poem draws attention to, depicts the transformation of person → object ("it" followed her); woman submerged beneath water, which then heals itself.

2. Various possibilities: Hanged miller—smell of hanged miller (bowels loosening, etc.—in contrast to pleasant "fragrance"), what was "there" beside the fear, finally given form—the scene & situation—

3. I'm uncomfortable choosing—each word seems to be dependent on the others. "There" is used many times in different ways—as a place—as a non-place—The poem draws attention to *place* (The Mill) as determining action.

4. We don't know; the poem doesn't tell us. Wet.

5. The miller.

She, too, is reluctant to project in 4 and 5. Her jokes in 4 and 5 serve as an evasion of the imagining the questionnaire asked her for. Her jokes take us, like Professor Two's focus on language, somewhat stubbornly back to what is demonstrable and obvious. Other themes: smells (2), body wastes (2) being "wet" (2,4), autonomy and dependency both for herself and for the words (3), persons as inanimate objects (1) and vice versa (1), delivering a precise and "professional" reading of the poem even if not called for (1). A psychoanalytic critic might well call this cluster of themes of self-rule and rule by others, obsessional, or, in a bodily terminology, "anal" themes. That is, to make a unity of this reading, I draw (from *my* interpretive community) psychoanalytic accounts of the kind of conflict parents and children have over who is autonomous and who is dependent. Whose rules will be followed, particularly about delivering from one's body something that may or may not be a living part of oneself? Possibly that question applies to Professor Three's relation to this questionnaire as much as to the two-year-old on the potty.

I will call the next reader Professor Four, although I am not sure whether this woman was a professor or a graduate student.

1. fear or the fear of what the future holds

2. millers who are no more

3. fear: Because of her first phrase "There are no millers anymore" which is, it appears, the point of her fear of economic downfall. Such things as yesterday, past, linger

4. Older woman, motherly, has known hard times

5. poverty of a woman on the brink of it.

The themes that come across to me are fear—the word occurs four times—loss, and deprivation of poverty, specifically in an economic sense (2,3,4,5). In her metaphors, the future is a container that holds something to fear (1). Poverty is a pit one can fall into (5). She gives graphic versions to psychosocial deprivation from a "primary caretaker." I would call the container and pit symbols for what Four calls "motherly." The ultimate fear (in psychoanalytic theory) is annihilation at the hands of such a failing caretaker, and Four repeats that threat twice (2,3): one is no more, and she attributes the phrase to the wife. What defense Four expresses against this fear seems to be simply to face the danger, as the analysts might say, counterphobically: to fear the future, to know hard times, to be on the brink. If the choice is fight or flight, Four says fight: accept the fear and live with it.

The dominant motif in Professor Five's responses is also fear, but with a somewhat different tone:

1. The miller's wife's fears of her husband's suicide: she sees him *as if* hung

2. It refers to the *non*-reassuring aspects of the mill—what speaks of her fears (of the future), not to her knowledge of the past. Fear directs itself toward the future.

3. "Dead"

    The "dead" fire suggests the failures—and fears—which haunt the poem.

4. I remember nothing of her appearance. She seems an image—abstract—of domesticity.

5. She does not remind me of anyone I know. In her fear that something may have happened to hurt a loved one, she reminds me of me.

Five's last, candid answer suggests how his whole set of responses may reflect his own anxiety, leading to his error in the "objective" question, 1. The other answers suggest he may have a characteristic way of speaking about that fear: saying it applies to the unknown rather than the known, a kind of denial. The miller is only "as if" hung (1). Something "may have happened" (5). Fears apply to the necessarily unreadable future (2) and to abstractions, the "*nonreassuring aspects*" of a mill (2), or the "nothing" of an abstract image of domesticity (4). Five moves from relatively concrete images — "mill," "fire" — to abstractions — fear, failure, domesticity, future. The hanged man is only "as if" hung. He thus wards off literal fear: "She does not remind me of anyone I know." But he does make a mistake in 1.

Professor Six's responses somewhat resemble Five's:

1. The miller
2. His absence
3. "No" That which is disappears; connects to "nothing," "no millers," "no form," would not, "no mark."
4. apron, thin, long hands & fingers, gaunt cheeks
5. Woman figure in Dorothea Lange's depression photo. Sense of being lost, bereft, nowhere, empty.

If Five was defending against anxiety, Six was warding off a sense of absence, emptiness, or depression, as she (like Five) frankly says in her last response. She chooses "no" for the most important word, coupling it with phrasings of absence. In 2 she speaks of absence directly, and in 4 she imagines thinness and gauntness and, first of all, an apron obscuring the woman's body. In 1, perhaps one can find a significance in her speaking of "the miller" who is absent instead of "the miller's body" which is present.

In short, if I look at all the answers by one person, I can trace a theme or themes that permeate all five:

Professor One: being passive and vague

Professor Two: displacement to language

Professor Three: "anal" themes

Professor Four: loss from a mother

Professor Five: fear of loss, displacement to the unknown

Professor Six: depression at absence; painful acceptance.

If these themes permeate *all* of one person's answers, then they have entered into the answer to 1 just as

much as the answer to 5. In other words, identical answers can be based on very different underlying concerns.[6] If we were to judge by the answers to questions 1 and 2 alone, we might very well say most of the professors were reading the same text in more or less the same way. We might conclude the text was constraining or limiting their responses. We might say they were applying the canons of an interpretive community. We might say they were constrained another way, by the workshop we were all engaged in.

Having the answers to questions 3–5 as well, though, we can see that they were reading the same text in very different ways. Some were concerned with realism, some with logic, some with language, some with literary form. Some were concerned with fear, others with loss, and others with deprivation.

Question 1 asked an "objective" question with "right" and "wrong" answers. The "right" answers all look more or less alike. Since question 5 asked each person to imagine or remember in a very personal way, people's answers to question 5 look very different. Behind the answers to both 1 and 5, however, is the same personal process, although it may be visible only in the answers to question 5 (or 4 or 3), and invisible in the answers to question 1 (or visible only as capitals or lower case or such slight differences in phrasing as "the miller," "the miller's body," "the miller's corpse," and so on). The "objective" and "subjective" answers draw on the same internal process in which themes of interest or concern to the answering professors shaped the way they worked with the text which was the same for all of them. *Both objective and subjective responses emerge from a process in which subjectivity shapes objectivity.*

The transactive theory of reading models this process as a person, with a certain identity, *using* (as an artist or a craftsman uses) the poem and the various codes, strategies, and settings to achieve a reading that *feels right.* For example, Professor Three was concerned with the relationship between person and thing. Her interest enabled her to *use* familiar interpretive techniques to read the poem as transforming persons to objects, for example, to understand the phrase "would soon appear / The same as ever to the sight" as "heals itself." Persons becoming objects also reflected some aspects of her personality or identity (as I read it). Her overall concern guided her use of shared techniques toward a particular reading that felt "right" to her. She was using the techniques many critics share with her, but using them to suit her unique identity. In the same way, Professor Six used them to suit her unique identity. In the same way, Professor Five used a critic's skill with ambiguity to manage his anxiety. Professor Two used a displacement to language that many critics would applaud, and he used it to serve his defensive needs as well as to interpret the poem. And so do we all.

I suggest that we all, as readers, use shared techniques to serve highly personal, even idiosyncratic, ends. We put hypotheses out from ourselves into the text. Indeed, the psychologists tell us this is the way we see and hear any chunk of the world.[7] Then we perceive *and feel* a return from the text. The poem seems delightful, pleasing, anxiety-arousing, incoherent, frustrating, satisfying, or whatever. Both emotionally and cognitively, then, both as a whole and part by part, we *feel* the poem responding to the hypotheses we bring to it.

For example, a VF hands us a questionnaire. It asks, "To what does the clause 'what was hanging from a beam' refer?" Those who have agreed to fill in the blanks approach the poem with hypotheses about grammar and antecedents. Within those hypotheses, the text enables us to arrive at some image of the miller's body which feels (emotionally and cognitively) like a satisfactory response to the VF's question. "To what does the clause 'What else there was' refer?" Here, the text does not give so clear a feedback to our hypotheses, and we respond differently. To some of us, flour bags and mice felt "right," to others the miller's body, and so on.

In other words, "The Mill," did not, on its own initiative, so to speak, cause what we saw. "The Mill" did not "constrain" a certain response among these professors. Rather, what the poem "did" depended on what we asked it to do. That in turn depended on what we brought to it: what questions, what expectation, what prejudices, what stock responses, what trust, what codes and rules. "The Mill" made a certain reading easy or difficult relative to the hypotheses *we* brought, hypotheses (in this instance) from the VF's questionnaire. If we had not been looking for antecedents for "what," we would not have seen the text the way we did.

That spring morning, the VF supplied the hypotheses. In the more usual situation, we supply our own. We may derive them from what we have been taught, from our culture (our "interpretive community"), or from the situation in which we find ourselves (a classroom, for example, or a theater). We may simply invent our own expectations for a poem.

We always hypothesize, however, for that is the way we perceive not only poems and stories but everything. Hence, we perceive the text *only* as it responds to the hypotheses we bring to bear. The text can only affect our re-creation reactively, the way the transparency of watercolors affects what a painter can do.

According to the transactive theory, then, reading is a creative process in which (one might say) subjectivity questions objectivity, thereby enabling objectivity to respond to and shape subjectivity. But that appealing paradox, obviously, does not provide a precise phrasing. We can imagine the reading of "The Mill" more rigorously, as a processing of information described by a feedback diagram (see Fig. 1).

While the appeal to a feedback model makes more precise various philosophical ways of stating the process (as dialectical, for example, or as deconstructive, perhaps), it has the further advantage of linking this account of reading to Piaget's idea of development, to theories of artificial intelligence, to brain physiology, to cognitive science, and to various psychological accounts of perception, symbolization, and memory.

In thinking through this picture (my students call it the "lima bean diagram") and the results of the questionnaire, however, it is essential to keep in mind a rather formal threefold definition of identity.[8] Identity is ARC—agency, representation, and consequence. That is, a person's identity is what initiates the feedback loops which are the way we sense and act on not only poems, but everything. In that sense, identity is an *agency:* it puts out hypotheses from our bodies into the world. The world (or a text) in turn gives back answers to those hypotheses, in a form which is ultimately sensory, and the way we feel about those answers determines the success or failure of the hypotheses. Identity is also therefore the cumulating *consequence* of those perceptions and actions. We are the history of what we have experienced. Finally, however, and this is most important, identity is somebody's *representation* of that identity, just as a history is not just events but somebody's narrative of those events. In representing identity, I have urged the use of a theme and variations which I find most telling. Identity then becomes *the history of an identity theme and its variations.*

Evidently, if Professor Two's reading of "The Mill" is a function of his identity, my reading of Professor Two's identity and its recreation in his reading of the poem is a function of mine. In effect, the lima

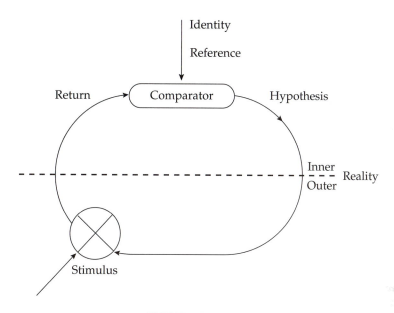

FIGURE 1 Perception

bean diagram is itself the loop in somebody else's lima bean diagram. If this is a schematic of Professor Two responding to "The Mill," one has to imagine another identity (mine) over to one side of this one hypothesizing this process of Two's and forming a narrative of it (see Fig. 2).

To use this concept of identity effectively, one has to keep all three components of this definition in mind at once, particularly the third. Omitting one or another leads to the common misunderstandings of the theory. In particular, if one neglects the idea of identity as representation, the concept becomes excessively deterministic. Unless one remembers identity is ARC, all three, the theory says that we have identity themes imposed on us in early childhood and we can never ever change them.[9]

Thus, one finds people asking: "Don't people change their readings? I know I read *Huckleberry Finn* differently now from the way I did when I was a child." Yes, of course people change their readings, and it would be the task of a person phrasing an identity to represent those changes. That would involve showing *both* the sameness *and* the differences in someone's readings of *Huckleberry Finn*, since one recognizes difference against a pattern of sameness and sameness against a flow of differences. Putting these samenesses and differences into words neither causes nor limits them. It is not the phraser who can

affect an AC-identity but the person with an AC-identity who can affect its phrasing (R).

For theories of reading, a feedback model is useful because it provides for *both* the reader's expression of self *and* the reader's use of semantic codes, taught techniques, interpretive communities, or, in general, the social, cultural, interpersonal, or transpersonal features of reading. One is not forced to such extreme claims as, "My language is not mine, just as my unconscious is not mine."[10]

Identity (loosely, "the subjective") enters the feedback loop in at least four different ways. First, identity was the agent. Each professor adapted from my questionnaire the hypotheses with which to approach the poem, doing so in as individual a style as they would later write their answers. Second, the poem did not simply "return" an answer. Each of us *heard* an answer, and we heard it with our own set of ears, our own linguistic usage, our own inner sentences, and all the rest. That is, we heard the questionnaire, and we heard "The Mill" answer the questions we asked of it—both in the idiom of our identities.

Third, what sounded "right" or satisfying or incoherent to each of us in the poem's answers to those hypotheses depended on the standards each of us applied. What seems coherent to you may not seem coherent to me. What pleases passive Professor One may not please fearful Professor Five. What suits

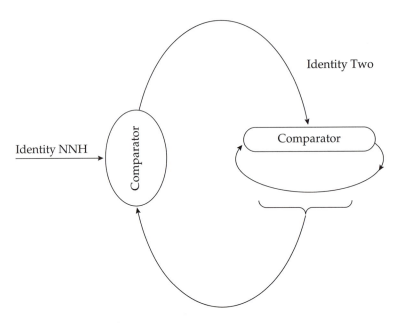

FIGURE 2 Perception of an Identity

Four as an answer to question 1 may not suit Two's more finely honed sense of grammar. All these criteria in turn are aspects of personality.

More precisely, they are the kinds of things we think about when we put someone's identity into words. When I say "fearful Professor Five," I am phrasing *my* reading of his standards for apprehending loss and anxiety, inferring them from the answers he wrote down and phrasing them in the light of my own standards and hypotheses. Hence we need to imagine another identity in the lima bean diagram, one who is representing the identity of the reader under discussion.

Identity thus enters the feedback picture in at least four points. Identity frames the hypotheses, identity hears the return, and identity *feels* the discrepancy between that return and one's inner standards. Finally, *my* identity phrases the identity which does these things. Moreover, to avoid confusion, it is important to distinguish between different kinds of hypotheses an identity can put out into the text. Some are physiological. How fast can my eyes scan this novel? How fast can I absorb it? How much of the wording of this poem can I remember as I start the next page? How will the page division affect my reading? The answers to such questions would appear at the bottom of the feedback picture. They af-

fect the answers the reader gets from his hypothesis in quite literal, physical ways.

Other hypotheses make use of cultural or semiotic codes. I intend "code" in the strict sense: a rule that makes a message possible.[11] I mean letters of the alphabet, numbers, grammar, dictionary meanings, and other things which have relatively fixed significations to all people in a given culture. For example, I see an *A* as an *A*. It would be very difficult for me to interpret it any other way. Indeed I learned this code so young and used it so often it would be well-nigh impossible for me to unlearn it. I could live for fifty years in Ulan Bator, reading nothing but Khalkha Mongol, and still, if I saw *A*, I would very likely think *A*.

Such codes are indispensable, enabling and constraining almost in the same sense as our bodies. We put them as hypotheses into the poem in order to read words, construe sentences, and arrive at meanings, and we do so automatically. The whole process is so fast and unconscious, we scarcely notice it unless we are dealing with a strange language. The only such code the questionnaire overtly used was syntax, in questions 1 and 2.

The other codes a professor uses to read a poem are of an entirely different order. We have seen our six readers seek unity in the poem ("each word . . .

dependent on the others"). We have seen professors resist the idea of imagining either the look of the miller's wife or a private association to her. They are, I take it, tacitly following a rule: stick to the words on the page. I hear professors reaching for themes that go far beyond the immediate story of the poem, themes like irony, love–death, social determinism (Four), or negativity (Six).

Any one reader uses both kinds of rules, semiotic codes and interpretive canons, putting them out as hypotheses into the poem. The two kinds of rules are quite different, however. One can put aside a search for unity and start deconstructing as easily as one can drop the Odd Fellows and join the Elks.12 One cannot so easily abandon seeing *A* as *A* or thinking in terms of subject–verb. One kind of rule, the interpretive canon, is chosen. The other, the cultural or semiotic code, is learned willy-nilly and can hardly be unlearned.

The "subjective" individual—an identity—puts forth these "objective" codes as hypotheses with which to read the text. The text in turn rewards some hypotheses and defeats others. As a result, the person senses both a cognitive and an emotional return from the text. The poem may feel delightful, moderately pleasing, anxiety-arousing, incoherent, frustrating—whatever. These sensations come about as we readers compare the return we get from the text with our inner standards for, perhaps, coherence, complexity, unity, or intensity. These inner standards are in turn functions of any one reader's personality or, better, identity. They may, of course, be learned. We first apply them as the hypotheses we put forward (but those hypotheses may also be our use of convention, an interpretive community, a semiotic code, or even our physiology). We apply these standards to judge the return our hypotheses yield. These standards provide the language—the terms of the contract, so to speak—in which we hear the return from the text.

In short, a person—an identity—*uses* hypotheses with which to sense the poem. The poem responds to those hypotheses, and the individual *feels* whether it is a favorable or unfavorable response and so closes the loop, preparatory to sending another hypothesis out around it. This is the model that has been so closely questioned.13

"Doesn't all this make every reading totally subjective, so that any one reading is as good as any other?" That is the one question people most commonly ask me. What I can answer, on the basis of the identity-cum-feedback model, is that every reading inextricably combines subjective and objective aspects to the point where those words cease to be useful terms with which to address the problem. Merely to use those words is to assume that one could separate reading into subjective and objective parts, as though one could separate the process of painting into one part from the medium and another part from the artist, or a hammering into part from the carpenter and part from the hammer.

The metaphor hidden in "totally" raises the problem. It assumes that a reading can be "totally" or "more" or "less" subjective, as though it were addable parts. By my feedback picture, I am suggesting that we need to think of identity as *using, working with, building on, creating from* various hypotheses projected into the world. The world and the hypotheses are, in a manner of speaking, "objective." One cannot separate them from the hypothesizer and perceiver, however, any more than in a sculpture one can sort out the sculptor's subjectivity from the objectivity of the bronze.

One would quite lose sight of the process of sculpting by asserting this sculpture is less subjective than that. It is equally falsifying to assume that a reading could be totally subjective or more subjective than another reading, as the question does. Hence, there is no way to answer such a question. Properly, I am not saying all readings are equally or totally or even partially subjective. I am claiming that one cannot characterize readings as subjective or objective at all.14

The next most common question follows from the first. "In teaching, what do you do about misreadings?" Or sometimes, "If all readings are 'subjective,' what's the good of teaching reading?" One purpose of the identity-and-feedback model is precisely to enable us to sort out what we *are* doing when we teach people how to read. That was the reason I addressed a group of professors with it. That is, the model enables us to get beyond the old opposition of objective and subjective, and ask ourselves more tellingly what we are doing by any given classroom move. For example, some teaching consists simply of exposing the student to the world of letters: "Read Chapters 20–30 of *A Tale of Two Cities* by Wednesday." In terms of the model, that move simply places students in contact with what is labeled "Outer Reality." We expect the students to use the hypotheses they already have for addressing a text, the ability to put shapes together to form letters, letters to form words, words to form sentences, sentences to form plot, characters, setting—and so on. If one goes further, if one poses (in the manner of many textbooks) "Study Questions," one provides the student with ready-made hypotheses to try out on that (as did my questionnaire).

Just as a beginning reader learns how to use hypotheses to find the sound or meaning of an unknown word, so a more sophisticated reader learns how to use hypotheses to interpret a whole text. Higher level teaching tries to provide the student with hypotheses with which to address *any* text or, even better, the ability to hypothesize hypotheses which will give the best return from this particular text.

In general, then, the familiar modes of teaching literature address the *hypotheses* a student brings to a text, hypotheses like: You will be able to read the poem as referring to more than its ostensible subject (the obsolescence of millers). You will be able to shape the poem into a unity. Once you have done so, you will not be able to find an unnecessary word in this poem. Any changes you make in details will change the whole, probably for the worse. You will probably be able to find an irony crosscutting the poem, complicating it ("velvet," for example). You will probably be able to find a reference in the poem to its own creation; often such a reference will seem to deconstruct or cut across the ostensible sense of the poem.

At any given moment a teacher may be giving a student hypotheses or hypotheses for finding hypotheses or may be carrying a hypothesis through its testing to sense the return. All these are familiar strategies in teaching. All use the students' responses but seek a homogeneity of response. Typically this kind of teaching uses only those responses that can be generalized, shared, or otherwise made available to all the students. Like question 1 in the Visiting Fireman's questionnaire, they look objective because one is providing a pigment or a canvas for the picture of the poem the reader will paint. In fact, however, the identity of the artist will govern the use made of the hypothesis the teacher gives. Ultimately, whether the hypothesis is used at all or whether any given application feels right will depend on the response of the reader—his or her identity.

In recent years, another kind of response-centered teaching has grown up which addresses the nature of the reading process itself instead of some particular hypotheses associated with one or another school of criticism. Such teaching strives to make explicit the experience—the feelings—the student has in addition to or instead of the interpretive strategies. In terms of the model, the teacher does not talk about the hypotheses coming out of the right side of the student "comparator," so much as the "return" on the left. He asks students to be aware specifically of how a given return *feels* (as opposed to "fits"). The teacher may (but need not) go further and explore how a given hypothesis or return fits the identity of the reader in question so far as it has appeared in the classroom.[15] In terms of the model, this is a process quite distinct from examining the right and wrong applications of hypotheses.

In my experience, the two kinds of teaching are essentially independent (except that they cast one teacher in contrary roles, permissive and corrective). The familiar teaching of how-to-read-literature, by addressing the hypotheses by which one reads, directs attention away from the person applying the hypotheses. Reader-response teaching addresses the person as an applier of hypotheses, how that person feels, and what that person says when those hypotheses are applied. Hence reader-response teaching points away from a critique of the hypotheses themselves or the ways they are applied.

I cannot find any reason, however, why two teachers or even one could not apply both methods as they seemed appropriate. One could do the regular teaching only, as most teachers do. One could concentrate on responses only, as reader-response teachers do. Or one could consider the response as a function of both the person and the hypotheses chosen and applied. In that sense, a misreading would correspond to a wrong hypothesis or a wrong application of a right hypothesis. But it is not true that the transactive model of reading eliminates the idea of a misreading. It does ask, however, that the one who proclaims a misreading make the rule or context explicit that makes the reading a misreading. Too often teachers take it for granted—as part of a residual belief, I think, that modes of reading are self-evident, not to be questioned, eternal verities, linguistic competences, objective.

By contrast, the psychological theory of identity and the transactive model of reading let us tell a more coherent story of reading. I believe that, using these theories, we have obtained good evidence, both from these workshops on "The Mill" and earlier work with individual readers, for the proposition that each of us reads a poem or a story as a personal transaction. We, as individuals with individual styles, create literary experiences within those styles. In doing so, we *use* the text. We *use* the methods we have learned in school. We *use* the classroom or reading room or theater or learned conference in which we are responding. We *use* the canons of the interpretive community to which we have allied ourselves. And in reading, in using all these things, we recreate our personal identities (understood as the agency, consequence, and representation—ARC—of our own continuity in time).

It is too simple to say texts impose meanings or control responses. It is too simple to say there is a subjective part of reading and an objective part. Rather, we need to understand the text, the interpersonal situation, or the rules for reading, as all interacting with a self in a feedback (like painter's pigments) *in which the self is the active, creative element*. The interpretive community, the armchair or theater or classroom, even the text itself, affect our recreation only *re*actively, the way a chisel acts back on a carpenter's plans or as bronze both enables and limits a sculptor. The text, the rules, the codes are like musical instruments with which we play variations on our identity themes.[16]

In short, reading is an art like any other art. It has its medium, its techniques, its failures, and its successes. Above all, it has its mysteries. The three questions with which I began, however, are not among them.

Notes

1. I have expounded these theories through all too many years and stages of development. See *Poems in Persons: An Introduction to the Psychoanalysis of Literature* (New York, 1973); *5 Readers Reading* (New Haven, 1975); and *Laughing: A Psychology of Humor* (Ithaca, 1982).
2. Stanley Fish, *Is There a Text in This Class? The Authority of Interpretive Communities* (Cambridge, Mass., 1980), pp. 357, 338, 366, and passim.
3. David Bleich, *Readings and Feelings: An Introduction to Subjective Criticism* (Urbana, Ill., 1975), p. 49.
4. Wolfgang Iser, *The Act of Reading: A Theory of Aesthetic Response* (Baltimore, 1978).
5. In designing my questions, I now realize I had met some objections raised by Jonathan Culler to

my work at an English Institute panel on reading. See his "Prolegomena to a Theory of Reading," in *The Reader in the Text: Essays on Audiences and Interpretation,* ed. Susan R. Suleiman and Inge Crosman (Princeton, 1980), pp. 46–66, esp. pp. 53–56. He objected to studying reading through the free associations of undergraduate readers on the grounds they were not competent, that the search for free associations will hide the agreement of "ninety-three out of a hundred" readers, and so on. Here, the readers are professors, committed to professional techniques in reading. The occasion was public, not a private interview. The questions pointed to the text rather than seeking associations "away" from the text. I believe this article shows that the conclusions of *5 Readers Reading* hold in this situation, *pace* Culler, as well as for undergraduate free associations.

6. Obviously, realizing this more complex process is important in basing psychological or literary research on questionnaires. The same answer may not express the same underlying process at all. If one is simply counting deodorant users or Democrats, that may not matter. If one is studying reading, it may matter very much. For example, I think my caveat is important for using such valuable survey work as the IEA (International Association for the Evaluation of Educational Achievement) data bank or the 3rd National Assessment of Reading and Literature. See Alan C. Purves, "Using the IEA Data Bank for Research in Reading and Response to Literature," *Research in the Teaching of English,* 12 (1978), 289–96 and Anthony R. Petrosky, "The 3rd National Assessment of Reading and Literature versus Norm- and Criterion-Referenced Testing," paper presented at the Annual Meeting of the International Reading Association, May 1–5, Houston, 1978, ERIC Document No. 159599.
7. A brief, lucid, and authoritative introduction to modern perceptual theory is Edwin Land's "Our 'Polar Partnership' with the World Around Us," *Harvard Magazine,* 80 (1978), 23–26.
8. I have spelled out this concept of identity in detail most recently in my *Laughing: A Psychology of Humor,* chs. 9 and 11.
9. For instance, David Bleich can claim that with this theory "the idea of novelty loses its meaning altogether." See *Subjective Criticism* (Baltimore, 1978), p. 121. The theory, however, claims no more than

that *one can trace* a consistent pattern in a person's behavior beginning in early childhood. Obviously, neither one's ability to trace nor a mere consistency implies that novelty drops out of human experience.

10. Culler, "Prolegomena," p. 56. One might ask with Freud, "Whose is it then?" "Unless the content of the dream . . . is inspired by alien spirits, it is a part of my own being." Sigmund Freud, "Moral Responsibility for the Content of Dreams," from "Some Additional Notes on Dream-Interpretation as a Whole" (1925), in *The Standard Edition of the Complete Psychological Works of Sigmund Freud,* tr. and ed. James Strachey et al. (London, 1961), XIX, 133.

11. I find conceptual difficulties in the loose sense of "code" some semioticians use. They announce what is no more than a personal interpretation as a code. In this sense, the famous Dorothea Lange photograph of the Depression farm wife to which several readers referred would be a "code" for poverty, obsolescence, or depression. Why not a code for the oppression of women? For aprons? For thinness? A code in this sense simply decrees a single, universal meaning for what is patently variable.

12. Jonathan Culler, however, has called these interpretive rules, the conventional procedures of teachers of literature today, "literary competence," analogizing to Chomsky's idea of grammatical competence. His metaphor equates the deliberate, studied practice of a small group of people in universities with the syntactic rules an entire speech community is born into, acquires almost intuitively, without study, as children, and continues to live by. See Culler's "Literary Competence," in *Reader-Response Criticism: From Formalism to Post-Structuralism,* ed. Jane P. Tompkins (Baltimore, 1980), pp. 101–17, esp. 108–15.

13. The model, I find, bears some similarity to the "three worlds" hypothesis derived from studies of the brain by Sir Karl Popper and Sir John Eccles. Basically, World 2 (self-conscious mind), acting through World 3 (mental products such as language, arts, or theories), governs and is governed by World 1 (physical reality). See Karl Popper and John C. Eccles, *The Self and Its Brain* (Berlin and New York, 1977).

14. Working from a different point in the transactions, the interpretive community or cultural code, Stanley Fish comes to the same conclusion. See *Is There a Text in This Class?,* pp. 332, 336.

15. I have discussed this procedure as a Delphi ("know thyself") seminar. See Norman H. Holland (with Murray M. Schwartz), "The Delphi Seminar," *College English,* 36 (1975), 789–800; Norman H. Holland, "Transactive Teaching: Cordelia's Death," *College English,* 39 (1977), 276–85; and Norman N. Holland (with the members of English 692, Colloquium in Psychoanalytic Criticism), "Poem Opening: An Invitation to Transactive Criticism," *College English,* 40 (1978), 2–16.

16. You could, of course, in the manner of some deconstructionists, choose to read this feedback upside down. You could say *we* are the instruments on which the poem, the rules of interpretation, or the semiotic codes play out variations on *their* identities. That seems, however, a perversely difficult way of thinking about human perception.

APPLICATION

Anachronistic Themes and Literary Value: *The Tempest*

Ole Martin Skilleås

The responses of readers may vary not only from individual to individual, as Holland shows, but from group to group. Feminist critics, for example, and critics who focus on the dynamics of race and class have documented the differing reactions among these different "interpretive communities." Do readers of a particular era form a large interpretive community? Ole Skilleås argues that they do and illustrates his case with a "modern" reading of The Tempest in which Prospero's powers are seen to represent the powers of the modern scientist to an audience familiar with the amazing benefits of scientific knowledge but also fearful of instant annihilation from nuclear war and slow death from ecological poisoning. This theme was, of course, unavailable to the original audience, or to the author. Conversely, the philosophical and ethical problems of white and black magic that concerned the Elizabethans are largely unavailable to modern readers, most of whom do not believe in magic of any kind.

Skilleås concedes that these very different "topical" themes can be reconciled at a higher level of generality, but he maintains that "the change in the way the modern audience conceives of Prospero is profound." In fact, "it is arguable that The Tempest is a play more relevant to the present audience than to Shakespeare's contemporary audience." This claim raises some large questions of interpretive theory. Does a literary work have a stable meaning through time, as Hirsch and others have argued? If so, will Hirsch's distinction between unchanging "meaning" and shifting "significance" dispose of the problems raised by Skilleås's "anachronistic" themes? Or is it rather the case, as many reader-response theorists assume, that different groups of readers will inevitably confer different meanings on a text? Or is there an intermediate possibility: are some texts, particularly those we call "classics," so constructed that they possess a special kind of "openness" to interpretation that makes them

Reprinted by permission of Oxford University Press from the *British Journal of Aesthetics* 31:2 (April 1991): 122–33.

seem highly relevant to the different concerns of different eras?

In the second part of his essay, Skilleås explores these questions and, drawing on the work of Hans-Georg Gadamer, suggests a tentative reconciliation between "topical" and "perennial" themes. But he ends by posing an even larger question: is there an element of creativity or play in interpretation and are some literary works more valuable because they offer more scope for this play?

The primary concern of this paper is to explore how the concerns of the period in which a literary work is read and the concerns of the individual interpreter in that period influence interpretation. It would seem that if constructive activity beyond the level of determining sentence-meaning is involved in interpreting literature, then the assumptions and concerns of the interpreter, and consequently of the historical moment in which he or she lives, will play a part in determining which elements of the work are regarded as important, how they are related to each other by the interpreter and, more generally, how they are understood.

In order to provide an appropriate context for the discussion of this issue, part I of the paper provides a reading of *The Tempest*[1] which focuses on the role of Prospero as "prime mover," with particular reference to his "art" not only in steering the course of events, but also in the manipulation of the natural environment. This modern interpretation acknowledges that the concerns of today embrace an awareness of the power of modern science and technology to destroy the natural environment, and proposes that Prospero's position in the play with regard to his power on the island can be seen to be analogous to the power of the scientist to manipulate the environment in the present day.

It is plausible to suppose that the reader/spectator of today will approach Prospero's powers over the natural environment of the island through his "art" with an awareness of the powers of science over the natural environment of the earth. I shall argue that in the context of the play it is possible that a reflecting modern audience[2] will see Prospero's "art" as suggestive of the powers of today's science over the environment, be it through its most dramatic manifestation, nuclear weapons, or through other means devised by science to modify the natural environment. I shall further argue that the topicality of the connection between Prospero and modern science

can lead to an identification of Prospero with humanity as a whole in a way that would not be plausible before, say, this century, because of the way our self-conception has changed with regard to our position in relation to nature. Only with the now almost boundless powers of knowledge, in the form of science, can this connection between Prospero and humanity be made. Thus, I argue, the topical theme of ecology leads easily into the perennial themes of "nature versus nurture," and/or "revenge and restraint." My discussion of *The Tempest* in the first part of this paper will therefore focus on the formation of such themes with close reference to the text of the play.[3] The theoretical soundness or otherwise of such moves, as well as the theoretical issues relating to theme formation, will be taken up in the latter part of the paper.

I

The central issue in any attempt to elicit *The Tempest*'s "ecological theme" is the nature of Prospero's command over the course of events in *The Tempest*. It seems that his powers do not go beyond the vicinity of the island:

> By accident most strange, bountiful
> Fortune . . . hath mine enemies
> Brought to this shore.[4]

As it is, his powers of manipulation on the island seem extensive. He creates the tempest, saves all the passengers from drowning, and has them stranded at different spots on the island's shore with their garments restored, and finally with the ship intact.

From the second scene of the first act the text emphasizes the importance of Prospero's powers, from the visual presence of his "magical garment"[5] to Miranda's plea that:

> If by your Art, my dearest Father, you have
> Put the wild waters in this roar, allay them.[6]

The scenes conjured up by Miranda's colourful imagination in the lines following this quotation bring home to the modern audience the fearful consequences the exercise of Prospero's powers could have. The world of the play, we are reminded, can be brought to the most terrible end by the powers of this man. The modern audience is unlikely to see or read this, and reflect,[7] without bringing knowledge of the present predicament to bear on the interpretation of the play. The development of physics, for example, has given us nuclear fission. With a power source of such immense force, anyone who possesses it holds a destructive potential over the real world of a magnitude at least matching that of Prospero's over his island.

Prospero, very modestly, calls himself "master of a full poor cell."[8] The discrepancy between this self-description and the power he has wielded to bring about the tempest borders on the self-deflatory as it is clear that the cell is where he keeps his books, which are the very source of his power. That it is a source is brought out by Prospero saying that:

> I'll to my book;
> For yet, ere supper-time, must I perform
> Much business appertaining.[9]

From this it is clear that the book (or books) is the source of his power, which in the fifth act is vindicated by his pledge to abjure his power[10] and consequently drown his book deep in the sea.[11] It is therefore less ironic when Prospero later refers to his "poor cell"[12] if he makes good his pledge.

The book, of course, should only strengthen the link the modern audience makes between Prospero and the notion of this character as a proto-scientist. A production might very well strengthen this link by showing the cell with book(s).

Much has been made of Prospero as magician, even "white magician" in contrast to Sycorax's black magic.[13] However, no matter what colour one attributes to his magic, it cannot be expected of the modern audience that it will interpret the character of Prospero in this way. The thought-world in which magic is a serious option is one which it takes great mental effort to enter. To relate to the powers of Prospero, and appropriate the themes of the play for present concerns, it seems more fruitful to see him as the proto-scientist suggested earlier.[14]

The modern audience may also note that the relation between Prospero and his powers is a role he can enter or leave at will, thus providing a further analogy to the modern scientist, who typically is a scientist by profession not vocation. The character of Prospero sanctions such an interpretation, since after Miranda had taken off his "magic garment" he addresses it: "Lie there, my Art." The modern popular conception of the scientist as a person in a white robe with a test tube in hand does nothing to undermine the plausibility of this connection.

An example of how the reception situation of *The Tempest* today gives us access via a topical to a perennial theme, that was not as readily available before, is the conflict of "revenge versus restraint."

With regard to the nature of Prospero's "art," it seems that his powers are significantly contrasted with the baser instincts of mankind, since his "art" does not stick on "the beast Caliban":

> A devil, a born devil, on whose nature
> Nurture can never stick; on whom my pains,
> Humanely taken, all, all lost, quite lost;
> And as with age his body uglier grows,
> So his mind cankers. I will plague them all,
> Even to roaring.[15]

It is evident here that Prospero's impotence in the face of unyielding nature torments him to distraction. He is quite clearly not omnipotent in the contest with stupid primitivity, represented by Caliban.[16] Prospero's inclination to take out his frustration on Caliban illustrates the conflict between the "Art" and the emotional immaturity of mankind, since the powerful Prospero does not automatically act virtuously despite all his knowledge and learning.

Knowing what we do about the probable effects of thermo-nuclear warfare, Prospero's battle with his own emotions is indeed a highly topical theme. It is natural to worry about what would happen if the power inherent in scientific knowledge was exercised by an over-heated brain. In *The Tempest* Prospero fights this battle within himself. The desire is for revenge over his brother, who usurped his political powers in Milan, and he battles with his rage against the obdurate ignorance of Caliban and the plot hatched by him and the drunkards. In the last act the "good" prevails[17] as he says:

> Yet with my nobler reason 'gainst my fury
> Do I take part: the rarer action is
> In virtue than in vengeance.[18]

Both in our world and in that of the play, power to command nature and power to command men are independent. In the play Prospero's powers to integrate them are at issue. He ends having shown his capacity to rule wisely. In our world, we hope against hope for a similar outcome.

A further, related, example of how the reception situation changes the theme of the interpretation is the new content the modern audience can give to the perennial theme of "nature versus nurture." "Nature," in this context, is understood in contrast to the socially conveyed virtues of "nurture." The fundamental change comes with the perception of Prospero as the scientist. The concept of "The Mage" implied a certain type of virtue, because the superior knowledge of "The Mage" made him wise. This connection is now missing, given the identification of Prospero with the scientist and the modern awareness that power and intelligence do not entail wisdom. The ability to react maturely to social and emotional conflicts and crises, we know, has not kept pace with the improvements in humanity's scientific knowledge. The awareness of the modern audience of this characteristic of the present situation highlights those aspects of the play that deal with similar situations. The failure of Prospero to improve the nature of Caliban is made all the more serious by the fact that Caliban is easily led by the drunkards Stephano and Trinculo.[19] Without the link between knowledge, power and virtue provided by the concept of "The Mage," the plot hatched by Caliban, Trinculo and Stephano[20] puts before us the possibility of a "Caliban mind" with "Prospero power."[21] In other words, the current situation makes it more likely that the modern audience will see these connections in the play. The concerns of the modern audience give a content to the theme of nature versus nurture that is different from any available to Shakespeare's contemporary audience.

So, if the modern audience looks for a fictional treatment of humanity's predicament of having the power to destroy the earth as we know it, yet still being immature in ability to resolve emotional conflicts, Prospero's dilemma with regard to revenge against his treacherous brother, his frustration with the unyielding nature of Caliban and the plot to oust him, offers scope for these themes. The conflicts fortunately also have happy endings. By the time Prospero is prepared to choose "virtue," he has more or less achieved his objectives and successfully fought the urge to take revenge—so graphically described in his rage against Caliban in the preceding act.[22]

Thus, for the modern audience Prospero resembles a symbol of modern science: frail in the face of evil and humanity's emotional immaturity, yet with a power that can, if injudiciously applied, be horrible in its consequences, and that on a scale far larger than Prospero's revenge. On the other hand, we also see that Prospero can use his "art" to please, not only manipulate for his own ends, as is shown in the masque he puts on for Miranda and Ferdinand:

> I must
> Bestow upon the eyes of this young couple
> Some vanity of mine Art; it is my promise,
> And they expect it from me.[23]

This contrast between the "revenge and reconciliation" aspects of his "art" is only resolved in the last act of the play in the soliloquy where he lists the various destructive and fiercely manipulative powers of his "so potent Art":

> But this rough magic
> I here abjure; and, when I have requir'd
> Some heavenly music,—which even now I do,—
> To work mine end upon their senses, that
> This airy charm is for, I'll break my staff,
> Bury it certain fadoms in the earth,
> And deeper than did ever plummet sound
> I'll drown my book.[24]

This is where Prospero relinquishes his powers. In his last act before breaking his staff and drowning his book he uses the power to give heavenly music to the senses of the people he manipulates.[25]

Having established the nature of Prospero's art and that it is confined to the island and its vicinity, the next step in an interpretation that tries to relate the play to the power of science over nature must be to inquire into the status of the island within such an interpretation.

In his *Shakespeare Our Contemporary* Jan Kott claimed that for the Elizabethans "the stage was the world, and the world was the stage."[26] Now, even if we do not accept this claim, or deem it irrelevant on the grounds that the modern audience will not bring Elizabethan assumptions to bear even on an interpretation of a play from that particular epoch, it still remains the case that for any audience the phenomenological character, in a certain sense of the term, of the spectator situation *makes* the world of the play to all intents and purposes appear to be the real world.

Both in our world and in that of the play, power to command nature and power to command men are independent. In the play Prospero's powers to integrate them are at issue. He ends having shown his capacity to rule wisely. In our world, we hope against hope for a similar outcome.

II

Given contemporary concern with the environment, and the quite recent realization that we might be in the process of destroying the basis of our way of life by the effects of the very same way of life, the "ecological theme" of *The Tempest* that I have outlined above is indeed topical.

It is maintained by most theorists who have discussed the nature and value of theme formation in literary criticism that topical themes are particularly fragile when put through the test of time.[27] They argue that it is the perennial themes which define great literature, and that the treatment of topical themes is the mark of ephemeral works. The interpretation of *The Tempest* proposed above can be seen to offer a new angle on this discussion.

For earlier critics Prospero has been "The Mage." With the modern, topical and anachronistic conception of Prospero as the scientist proposed in this essay, we can see that a new interpretation of the play is available to us that could not have been available to an earlier audience. This possibility arises from mankind's changing self-conception.

It is arguable that we live in "the age of science." The role of humanity has changed in important respects in a short period of time. The realm of the possible has expanded beyond the wildest dreams of earlier generations, and our daily lives have been radically transformed. If there is a single concept which represents the forces that have caused this momentous change it must be "science." It is thus plausible to claim that the present-day conception of humanity, our "self-conception," is that of "scientific man," and that this self-understanding has wide currency in present-day western societies. The next step, then, is to suggest that the topical interpretation of *The Tempest* in this paper implies that "Prospero the scientist" represents humanity as a whole. This transformation does not have to be at all abrupt in order for this relation to be productive in the understanding of the play. The transformation of Prospero the arch-scientist to Prospero as representing humanity happens just because of the change in self-conception which has occurred, in a historical perspective, quite recently.

Thus, the transformation of the role of Prospero from "Mage" to "Scientist" is brought about by the topicality of ecology and our manipulation of nature, and by our new self-conception. The further transformation of the character into a representative of humanity as a whole would appear to be virtually inevitable because of the present situation of the whole of humanity, posing a possible threat to ourselves by the power wielded by knowledge under the mantle of science. The upshot of these considerations is that the reception situation of today can change our interpretation of the play in a way previously impossible. At a higher level of generality the situation problematized by this interpretation is that of the perennial dilemmas of "revenge and restraint," and "nature versus nurture."[28] These are perennial themes which previous generations of interpreters may have arrived at through different topical themes, or not at all.

However, despite the possible identity of themes at a higher level of generality, the change in the way the modern audience conceives of Prospero is profound. As "Mage" Prospero is set apart from the modern audience by the mystical and esoteric nature of his knowledge. The "Mage" was further a marginal figure in the eyes of Elizabethan society as a whole. On the other hand, Prospero as "Scientist" brings him closer to the modern audience by the public nature of his "art," which also makes it much easier for the modern audience to identify with him. The powers of science are the powers of society. Despite the long initiation process, there is nothing inherently secret about the powers of science, and science is embraced by society. So much so, that I have argued that modern society may well be said to conceive of itself as "scientific society." Thus, it can be said that changes in society have brought Prospero from the elevated and esoteric level of the "Mage" down to the public in a way that was previously unthinkable. In terms of this background it is arguable that *The Tempest* is a play more relevant to the present audience than to Shakespeare's contemporary audience.

This raises the question how such a move can be justified in the face of interpretations more plausible from the point of view of readings rooted in the Elizabethan era.

Since the interpretation I have suggested here is based on assumptions about the concerns of the modern audience with topical questions, this is to enter upon a continuing debate about topical and perennial themes in literary works. The critic and theorist Frank Kermode seems to favour openness to topical themes:

> It seems that on a just view of the matter the books we call classics possess intrinsic qualities that endure, but possess also openness to accommodation which keeps them alive under endlessly varying dispositions.[29]

The more "austere" view is held by, among others, Stein Haugom Olsen.[30] He defines a topical theme as:

> a formulation of problems and issues of particular interest to a group of people (a society, a class, . . .) for a certain period. These problems and issues are related to specific situations in which that group of

people sees itself or society/mankind as a whole as being, at that particular time.[31]

On this account the topical theme is transitory and cannot be used to explain how it is that the great works have survived over the ages to delight and enrich the lives of new generations. The austerity of his view is brought out by his strict definition of "literature" according to which, "it is necessary for a piece of discourse to invite construal in thematic terms if it is to merit the label 'literary work.'"[32] The only valuable themes are perennial ones: "Literary appreciation . . . always involves an attempt to apprehend the theme of a work using such thematic concepts as come closest to being perennial thematic concepts."[33] Olsen defines perennial themes in opposition to topical ones, such that, "a perennial theme differs from a topical theme in two respects: in the nature of the concepts which are used to define it, and in its lack of connection with a specific social/historical situation."[34] According to Olsen perennial concepts describe aspects of human nature and existence which have given rise to existential and metaphysical problems that we have not been able to solve, and which remain of continuing human interest.

However, it need not be the case that the views of Kermode and Olsen are irreconcilable. It can be argued that the great themes are the meta-level of more topical themes, and that the relation between them resembles that between type and token. Indeed, Olsen concedes that topical themes can constitute an element in the development of a perennial theme.[35] It is far from clear, however, whether this modification changes the general picture significantly. The most problematic element in Olsen's account lies in his assumption that thematic concepts and themes are *there* in the literary works.[36] It is an empirical fact that interpretations of literary works reach different results, and even if some of the interpretations are good and others bad, it does not follow that the demarcation criterion we employ is whether the interpreter has got *the* perennial theme right.

A common assumption underlying the various theories which assume that there is a single theme in a literary work is that the interpreter has no role to play other than eliciting whatever is there already. The assumption is, however, implausible, and Hans-Georg Gadamer's theory of understanding, his hermeneutics, helps us to see how it may be coherently rejected.

Gadamer offers a theoretical account of the relationship between text, reader and the situation of reception that takes account of the fact that in the process of understanding all three elements interact. One of the more provocative elements of his theory is that one's "prejudices" are the productive ground of understanding. "The overcoming of all prejudices, this global demand of the enlightenment, will prove itself to be a prejudice."[37] Gadamer is concerned to "rescue" the term from the enlightenment's discrediting account of it by pointing out that rather than impede understanding, the judgements one makes before encountering a phenomenon are preconditions for understanding the phenomenon. This is because "the prejudices of the individual, far more than his judgments, constitute the historical reality of his being."[38] This is because understanding takes place in a situation, and "the very idea of a situation means that we are not standing outside it and hence are unable to have any objective knowledge of it."[39] This rules out any purely "objective" conception of literary interpretation, since prejudices, in Gadamer's sense, will always be with the interpreter. In other words: prejudice is the very stuff understanding is made of.

Gadamer emphasizes "application" of the issues discussed to the situation of the interpreter as the very nature of hermeneutics, since the interpreter's situation and concerns are unavoidable elements in the process of understanding. Gadamer's model for the role of application in understanding is *legal* hermeneutics. The meaning of a law is not fixed by the original statement of the law, but is realized, expanded and modified, within limits, by its application to ever new situations which are seen to be governed by the law. The phenomenon of understanding a text works in a corresponding way: it is by applying the text to one's own situation that its meaning can be understood. This is part of the background for Gadamer's notorious claim that "we understand in a different way, if we understand at all."[40] However, to use Gadamer's term, the interpreter's relation to the text is one of "dialogue." As well as inviting discussion of a *Sache* (subject-matter), the text "speaks to you." This should be emphasized, since one can be misled by a relativist euphoria when encountering Gadamer for the first time. So, one's prejudices may well be confounded. However, the notion of *Sache* is problematic in literary interpretation. The reason may well be that Gadamer's hermeneutics is developed in response to questions that have arisen in the interpretation of philosophical, legal, theological and historical documents, but not specifically of literary works. One way to bring out this deficiency is to ask what the "sache" is in, for instance, Joseph Conrad's *Heart of Darkness*. Is it imperialism? Is it Conrad's own journey up the Congo? Can it be the nature of evil? The importance of moral restraint in the absence of social cohesion? The moral effects of culture shock? It is a good deal easier to answer questions about the *Sache* of different laws, Kant's *Kritik der reinen Vernunft* and Adam Smith's *Wealth of Nations*; the difference stems from the "openness" of literary works, their ability to address different issues and concerns. But there is one limiting factor at work in determining which issues or subject matters we take the literary works to address: the tradition which transmits preconceptions about the works through previous generations' encounters with them.[41] In Gadamer's terminology this is *wirkungsgeschichtliches Bewusstsein* (effective-historical consciousness).

The most important of these preconceptions or prejudices in the interpretative situation is that we deem the object for interpretation interesting. To do that we have to pre-judge the object to be worthy of our interest. The main class of objects which are judged worthy of interest for us by the culture in which we live are the classical works.

This is where we return to Kermode's claim about the intrinsic qualities of the text and its openness to accommodation. Gadamer's account allows for the possibility that the intrinsic qualities, the beautiful form, entertainment and the eternal truths[42] it contains are, along with its openness to accommodation, the reasons why ever new generations return to the same texts. It can be argued that the spectacle and beauty, as well as the profundity of the soliloquies, are the main reasons for *The Tempest's* standing. So we may not need to postulate treatment of perennial themes as the reason for the survival over the ages of the canonical, or great, works. This implies that we have an alternative conception to Olsen's, and that his view that: "a formulation of theme which does not go beyond the level of topical thematic concepts aborts the aesthetic significance of the work and is therefore unsatisfactory"[43] is itself unsatisfactory.

It is by reference to this broad theoretical background that I would claim theoretical validity and plausibility for the interpretation of *The Tempest* that I have presented above. The rationale for interpreting *The Tempest* in the way I have outlined is that it displays the play's relevance to the concerns of the modern audience, in a way that provides a fictional playing out through this great work of those concerns in a dialogue between the text/performance[44] and the concerns of the lives of the interpreters. I suggest that interpreters, in the constructive effort involved in interpretation, apply concepts and concerns from their own lives in a way that my interpretation illustrates. The question, then, is more specifically what *kind* of application this is.

In the interpretation of *The Tempest* provided above, for example, one can hold that on the one hand Prospero represents the scientist's power over the environment, enacting humanity's dilemma of the power we have and the frail character of the ecological status quo—the topical theme built around ecological concerns in the broad sense—and on the other hand that the play deals with the perennial themes of "revenge and restraint," and/or "nature versus nurture." The latter are only a more general description of the former and may not be available for the modern audience save through the topical theme and the topical thematic concepts which lead up to it. On this account, the relation between topical and perennial themes is such that the former provides access to the latter, and divining the perennial theme of one particular work is a creative and not a recreative activity. It also suggests that we can do without the added level of generality to explain why literary works survive over the ages.

However, it may also well be that one literary work can be interpreted as addressing different topical themes for different audiences, and that all of these can be seen at a higher level of generality to be perennial because the *types* of conflict, or comparable themes, are inherent in the human predicament. A consideration which supports Kermode's claim that "openness to accommodation" is a criterion for literary survival.

This leads us to a final question, which I shall only pose in this paper. It relates to the cognitive status of literary interpretation. Is there a rationale for reading and interpreting literature beyond entertainment and improving the performance of one's cerebral cortex?

My own emphasis in this paper has been on the creative activity of interpretation, an activity which can be seen as similar to children's play. It can be argued that children play, not in order to represent the world as it is, but to try out various ways it *could* be. Similarly, by interpreting literary works as addressing their own concerns, or those "of the age," the readers/spectators may add to the understanding of their world, and the various ways it could be. My suggestion is that the possibilities some literary works have for "application" to different concerns, and the "dialogue" with the audience that this feature invites are an important element in the value of literature. It is time that literary aesthetics took account of this quality.[45]

Notes

1. My references to *The Tempest*, given with act, scene and line number(s), are to the edition in The Arden Shakespeare, edited by Frank Kermode (London: Macmillan, 1954).
2. I shall use "the modern audience" in a more restricted sense than to mean just any contemporary audience or readership. I assume a higher degree of theatrical and literary knowledge and sophistication than one might expect from, say, picking a contemporary audience at random in London's West End.
3. Part I does not attempt to draw all the interrelated elements of the play together into a comprehensive interpretation. Rather, it is "a reading" in the sense that it presents a way of viewing a selection of aspects the modern audience may foreground when seeing or reading the play. This foregrounding does not entail blotting out other aspects of the play, such as the political themes, but is an expansion rather than an alternative. Literary aesthetics has all too often taken for granted that the way critics present their papers is the way readers make sense of literary works. In my view this is a serious mistake.
4. I,ii,178–180.
5. I,ii,24.
6. I,ii,1–2.
7. The importance of reflection should be stressed, since interpretation is an activity which requires constructive activity. It is all too tempting for the theorist to assume that any audience will respond with a high degree of sophistication.
8. I,ii,20.
9. III,i,94–96.
10. V,i,50–51.
11. V,i,56–57.
12. In V,i,301.
13. See Frank Kermode's Editor's Introduction to the Arden Shakespeare, William Shakespeare, *The Tempest, The Arden Shakespeare* (London: Macmillan, 1954), for the distinction between Sycorax's and Prospero's magic, pp. xl–xli, and the nature of Prospero's magic, pp. xlvii–li.
14. "Magic sought power over nature; astrology proclaimed nature's power over man. Hence the magician is the ancestor of the modern practicing or 'applied' scientist, the inventor/ . . ." C. S. Lewis, *Studies in Medieval and Renaissance Literature,* collected by Walter Hooper (Cambridge U.P., 1966), p. 56.
15. IV,i,188–193.
16. Note how the location of the island, between "primitive" Africa and Renaissance Italy, is also relevant in this conflict.
17. But they have suffered for their treason: IV,i,258–262.
18. V,i,26–28.
19. See the end of II,ii.
20. VI,i.
21. Cosmo Corfield, in "Why Does Prospero Abjure His 'Rough Magic'?" *Shakespeare Quarterly,* 36 (1985), pp. 31–48, argues that the opposition between Ariel and Caliban is an allegory of Prospero's mind. That would make "Prospero power with Caliban mind" a real alternative in the play.
22. VI,i,188–193.
23. IV,i,39–42.
24. V,i,50–57.
25. These now include the audience since they also will hear the music.
26. Jan Kott, *Shakespeare Our Contemporary*, translated by Boleslaw Taborski, second edition (London: Methuen, 1967), p. 250.
27. See in particular Anthony Savile, *The Test of Time: An Essay in Philosophical Aesthetics* (Oxford: Clarendon Press, 1982) and Stein Haugom Olsen, "Thematic Concepts: Where Philosophy Meets Literature," in *Philosophy and Literature*, edited by A. Phillips Griffiths (Cambridge U.P., 1984), pp. 75–93, and "Topical Themes and Literary Value," in *Forskningsprosjektet KRITIK och KONST,* edited by Goran Sorbom (Uppsala: Institutionen for Estetik, 1986), pp. 46–64.
28. At an even higher level of generality these two dilemmas can, I think, be unified in one theme. I shall not attempt to do so here, and it is in any case doubtful if such a move would serve any purpose.
29. Frank Kermode, *The Classic* (Cambridge, Massachusetts: Harvard U.P., 1983), p. 44.
30. Olsen is influenced by Savile.

31. Olsen in Sorbom, p. 54.

32. Stein Haugom Olsen, "Thematic Concepts: Where Philosophy Meets Literature," in *Philosophy and Literature,* edited by A. Phillips Griffiths, (Cambridge U.P., 1984), p. 81.

33. Olsen in Phillips Griffiths, p. 86.

34. Olsen in Sorbom, p. 58.

35. Olsen in Sorbom, p. 59.

36. Witness that he stresses that the correct description of the literary response to a literary work is "imaginative *reconstruction* of its literary aesthetic features" (my emphasis). Stein Haugom Olsen, *The End of Literary Theory* (Cambridge U.P., 1987), p. 16.

37. Hans-Georg Gadamer, *Truth and Method,* trans. by William Glen-Doepel, ed. by John Cumming and Garrett Barden from the second German ed. (1965) of *Wahrheit und Methode,* second English ed. (London: Sheed and Ward, 1979), p. 244.

38. Gadamer, p. 245.

39. Gadamer, p. 269.

40. Gadamer, p. 264.

41. Gadamer, p. 268.

42. What I mean by "eternal truths" is more like the statements of the text, such as "we are such stuff as dreams are made on"; and "our little life is rounded with a sleep," than the "perennial themes" Olsen argues for. The former may form part of the latter, but the "perennial themes" are at a higher level of generality and stand in relation to several elements of the work.

43. Olsen in Phillips Griffiths, p. 87.

44. I do not suggest that these modes of representation of *The Tempest* are similar, only that they in this respect play a corresponding role as the source for reflection and interpretation.

45. I am indebted to Dr. Michael Bell, Helge Hoibraaten, Professor Stein Haugom Olsen and, in particular, Martin Warner for comments and discussions on drafts of this paper. Responsibility for remaining shortcomings is mine alone.

Reading the Urn: Death in Keats's Arcadia

Douglas B. Wilson

Remarking the tendency of reader-response critics to argue about the degree of control the text exerts over the reader, Douglas B. Wilson aligns himself with critics such as Iser, who stress that the poem "contains signals for its own reading." So in the story of reading that Wilson recounts, his reader is more like Iser's "implied reader" than like Holland's idiosyncratic "actual" reader. But even the implied reader must be an active pursuer of the text's clues, and all the more active when the text is indeterminate and the reader is compelled to "complete the picture."

Wilson argues that "Ode on a Grecian Urn" is especially suited to an approach that emphasizes the agency of the reader because the poem dramatizes the struggle of a mind trying to come to terms with oscillating polarities—sound and sight, reality and ideality, life and art. For Wilson, the poem's speaker illustrates the divided consciousness described both in Schiller's contrast between the naive and the sentimental artist and in the tensions of Schlegel's "romantic irony." But the real theater for this drama, Wilson claims, is not the mind of the speaker but the mind of the reader, where the speaker's struggle is not only replayed but differently resolved. Finally, the reader is able to go beyond the speaker's perspective and to achieve a more inclusive understanding.

Like Blake's "Mental Traveler" and so many other Romantic poems, "Ode on a Grecian Urn" invites the reader into a landscape of consciousness. As S. T. Coleridge puts it, the primary function of the poetic work, like the visual language of painting, is "to instill energy into the mind, which compels the imagination to complete the picture." The "Grecian Urn" provided an exemplary model of a greater Romantic lyric whose interpretation both calls for a rhetorical focus upon the agency of the reader and exacts the

Reprinted by permission of *SEL: Studies in English Literature 1500–1900*, 25, 4 (Autumn 1985).

strengths of this critical mode. The sense of audience implicit or explicit in Keats's ode, which contains signals for its own reading, governs the relations between text and reader. The ode's speaker responding to an imaginary urn conjures up, as part of a mental drama, the underside of a vanished culture that created such urns. It is the speaker's divided mind that provides the model for the act of reading and creates the opposing poles of romantic irony: his alienated awareness begets a dialectic between the permanence of an urn and the absent life implied by its imitative forms. The concept of romantic irony, articulated by a German philosophical tradition unknown to Keats, affords a theoretical frame that usefully illuminates the ode's poetic action. Recognition of the fictional role of the reader, inferred from the "Ode on a Grecian Urn," yields a fresh critical perspective. By addressing Keats's own ironic practice—his speaker's final inability "to complete the picture"—the implied reader goes beyond the speaker's dilemma and thus forestalls an either/or choice between sculptured marble and mortal life.[1]

I

This ode, the action of which is a progression in the speaker's mind, suggests a reader-response critical approach because its very subject is the responding mind engaged in the interpretive process. Reader criticism has shown a tendency to split into factions: it frequently refuses any consideration at all of the author's role; at times it begrudges the text its power to govern the act of reading; often it denies virtually any restraint upon the reader's subjective response.[2] Yet the "Ode on a Grecian Urn" itself requires an awareness of the entire communication process: poet, poem, and reader all inextricably play their parts in the reading act. Romantic lyrics are notorious for calling attention to the poet himself and ignoring the audience: Shelley's comparison of the poet to a nightingale—"who sits in darkness and sings to cheer its own solitude with sweet sounds"—readily comes to mind. Keats's "Ode on a Grecian Urn," however, with its courteous invitation to join in its play, manifests an urbane sensitivity for its reader. Walter J. Ong, in describing the flexibility demanded of readers of prose fiction, provides an apt introduction to Keats's demands upon his audience:

> Readers over the ages have had to learn the game of literacy, how to conform themselves to the pro-

jections of the writers they read, or at least how to operate in terms of these projections. They have to know how to play the game of being a member of an audience that "really" does not exist. And they have to adjust when the rules change, even though no rules thus far have even been published and even though the changes in the unpublished rules are themselves for the most part only implied.[3]

In the "Ode on a Grecian Urn," Keats signals the reader to conform to the speaker's projections and to make strategic adjustments to its demands of fictional play. By seeing through the imaginative eye of the ode's speaker, the reader is charmed into exploring an imaginary Greek artifact. The reader's relation to the ode is analogous to the speaker's relation to the urn but, as will later become clear, the reader must subtly distinguish between urn and poem. Keats makes this analogy clear at the outset by tactfully allowing the urn—which can "thus express / A flowery tale more sweetly than *our* rhyme"—to upstage the poem. The pronoun "our" serves mainly as a plural for Keats as writer, yet it also urbanely endows us as readers with part-ownership in the ode. The urn's greater sweetness of expression hints, by way of foresight, at the less than sweet undersong of the poem. In "the struggle to escape" of the "maidens loth," a trace of violence appears which contradicts even the urn's sweetness. In the telling phrasing of the following question, Keats gives the reader a cue to participate in an act of interpretive consciousness: "What leaf-fring'd legend *haunts* about thy shape"?[4] The responding mind of the speaker goes beyond the marble detail: the mental activity in the verb "haunts" reminds us both that the urn's message comes from the dead and that the poem's action is taking place in consciousness.

The seven tantalizing questions that conclude the ode's first stanza might appear at first glance to be rhetorical, yet they are actually open questions. Their boldness of voice functions as an imperative mood, yet their very indeterminacy whets our curiosity. As Wolfgang Iser reminds us, we tend to reject a baldly prescriptive text as tedious, and we learn to recognize indeterminacy as a cause of our active participation in the act of reading.[5] By sharing the enigma of the speaker's searching questions, we become fictionalized before we are aware of it. We too must infer the absent element. Since Keats does not tell us what to think, we trust his poise and we consent to join his quest for meaning in the urn's silent detail.

He makes his reader an accomplice, just as E. H. Gombrich describes the modern artist who gives the "beholder increasingly 'more to do,'" drawing "him into the magic circle of creation and allow[ing] him to experience something of the thrill of 'making' which had once been the privilege of the artist."[6]

The reader who first encounters the second stanza of the "Grecian Urn" is already prepared for its paradoxical silent music. As a "bride of quietness" and "foster-child of silence," the urn can never address the "sensual ear" with literal sound. Yet the piper in low relief plays his "soft pipes" to the attuned ear of spirit. Keats's letter on "the greeting of the Spirit" helps us to grasp just how the piper's music in "Ode on a Grecian Urn" implies an allegory of its own reading. Taking a cue from the speaker, in the act of half-creating, half-perceiving an imaginary urn, the reader engages in the process of greeting "semireal" marble "things": "Ethereal thing[s] may at least be thus real, divided under three heads—Things real—things semireal—and no things—Things real—such as existences of Sun Moon & Stars and passages of Shakespeare—Things semireal such as Love, the Clouds &c which require a greeting of the Spirit to make them wholly exist—and Nothings which are made Great and dignified by an ardent pursuit."[7] In making the piper strike the keynote for our role as reader, Keats beguiles us into sharing a quest for his imaginary urn. Our participatory greeting of marble detail governs our interpretive responses acting upon urn and poem at the same time. Yet as will become clear, the piper is an allegory for the naive realm of artistic permanence as symbolized by the urn, and the reader's imaginative greeting includes the shadows of an absent depth lurking beneath the marble surface.[8] A psychocritical reading of the ode induces a dialogue in the reader's consciousness between the urn's exterior figures and their implicit ghosts.

Keats's letter on the "greeting of the Spirit," expressed as thinking aloud, more than likely derives from his reading of *Antony and Cleopatra*. Not only the inclusion of *clouds* and *love* supports this inference, but also the subjective overvaluation implicit in Cleopatra's dream of Antony. The letter also brings to mind Antony's projection of his own identity upon the dislimning images that he discovers in the sunset clouds of Alexandria, as he prepares to accept the outcome of his effeminate generalship and to seek his own death in the face of Cleopatra's apparent infidelity.[9] Whether we are reading the language of the "Ode on a Grecian Urn" or the language of art, our act of *greeting* (like the imagination of Shakespeare's lovers) augments the artists's canvas as it does the piper's music. Wolfgang Iser discerns just such "an allegory of the reader's task in the novel" *Vanity Fair* as we have seen represented by Keats's vignette of the piper.[10] Though the piper allegorizes the ideal dimension of Grecian art, by an analogous act of greeting marble detail, the speaker infers the vestiges of a culture that has expired. Our response to the ode, then, goes beyond the ideal strains of the piper, yet his music remains a paradigm for the larger task of the reader.

As Keats's speaker shifts his focus from the figure of the piper to the "bold lover" and the reluctant maiden, his imaginative greeting humanizes the urn's figures with poetic license as if they were alive. Keats thus makes the reader an accomplice in the action of the speaker's surmising: he must vicariously intuit the counterparts in ancient life that are imitated in attitudes of peak intensity upon the lifeless marble. The lover in stanza three is first consoled for never achieving his kiss: "yet, do not grieve; / She cannot fade, though thou hast not thy bliss, / For ever wilt thou love, and she be fair!" But the reader cannot avoid the reflex awareness: though kisses take place in live experience, love and beauty must also endure the blighting shadow of change. From the speaker's limited point of view, the progression of "Ode on a Grecian Urn" is only intelligible "as a series of movements within a single (though divided) consciousness."[11] But for the reader, who sees beyond the self-division of the speaker, both sides of this oscillating polarity between art and life become a dialectical disclosure of the entire artistic process. A moment's reflection triggers the recognition that not only the marble ideal of love, itself a fiction, but also the anxious condition of living lovers owe their fictional existence to the imagination of the speaker. The reader's empathic response to the speaker's divided consciousness discovers the flawed permanence of marble urns in addition to the contrary liabilities of mutable human life. Yet the unpleasant reality implicit in this mutual discovery of shortcomings does not inhibit art and life from disclosing vital energies emerging from their polar interaction.

Since the poem's action occurs within the divided consciousness of the speaker, the reader might succumb to the prevalent critical tendency to privilege either sculptured art or passionate life. Yet we mistake the poem for the urn if we opt for either side and read the ode merely as a dualistic debate. The allegory of the piper's imaginative appeal to the spirit might warrant valuing the ideal of permanence over the harsh realities of life. Yet if we grant our empathy to the speaker's fertile dilemma of contrariety, we can still recognize his sentimental voice as generating a dialectic between his own alienated condition and his ideal longing for the naive songs of the piper. When marble urn and passionate experience exist in such energetic polarity, as we have seen, they mutually reinforce their opposing delights and deficiencies. Their beauty includes this dark truth. Just as Blake's contrary poems of innocence and experience cannot be read separately without sacrificing their full meaning, so Keats's contraries also both nourish and satirize each other. From this perspective in the reader's superior consciousness, in response now to the poem, not merely to the urn, the subject is no less than the creation of and response to art and poetry.

II

Part of the indeterminacy encountered by the reader comes from the historic gap between Keats and the Hellenic culture when such urns were made. Since Keats makes us aware of his own moment in history, and since the imaginary urn derives from an ancient civilization, our temporal distance from him complicates our reading of his temporal distance from the urn. Keats had seen historic prototypes for his Grecian urn (as Sir Sidney Colvin and Ian Jack have demonstrated) in a variety of burial urns, in their Wedgwood imitations, and even in the Parthenon friezes among the Elgin marbles. After considering something like the Portland Vase, made of "dark glass," as a possible source for Keats, Jack writes, "But the more obvious supposition is that he is thinking of one of the large neo-Attic urns made in Rome between c. 50 B.C. and c. A.D. 50. These urns . . . were intended either as funerary caskets or as purely decorative objects."[12] Though no single original has yet been identified for Keats's urn, his very selection of detail from a variety of ancient art leaves an imprint of Hellenic history if only in the signature of its style.

Against Leo Spitzer who decides in favor of the aesthetic mode over the urn's unknowable history,"[13] Lionel Trilling makes a strong case for historicity: "Actually . . . the poem may be said to assimilate the

two modes to each other in that it conceives the essence of the aesthetic object as having *pastness* as one of its attributes. The aesthetic essence of what is depicted on the urn is that it will never proceed into the future; the culture of the little hillside town is no longer in process." As the reader contemplates these lovers in an "eternal present," their frozen attitude presents a historic gap between them and a succession of later readers in changing periods of historical time. "In the comparison which the poem institutes between them and actual persons, they are represented as lacking in certain of the attributes of life, as being in some degree or in some sense *dead,* and it is in their being so that we find their significance."[14] Of course Keats's sylvan history is largely indistinguishable from myth because the temporal gap between Keats and ancient Greece helps to create the mythical. Yet the reader, who responds to the speaker's sentimental dilemma, discovers historic mortality crystallizing out the mythic at dramatic moments in the poem's progression. The absent town, for instance, inferred behind the priest and heifer moving in procession to the sacrifice, injects just such a moment of historic desolation when the gap emerges with vivid force. The historicity of the urn may largely elude the reader, yet confronting vestiges of an archaic style imposes the double labor upon him of differentiating that temporal level from the moment in time of the ode written by Keats.

The gap between Keats's early nineteenth-century moment and his Hellenic urn presents the reader with one of the most complex problems in fathoming the ode. One source of the high degree of critical controversy over the "Ode on a Grecian Urn" stems from the indeterminacy generated by the complex interplay of these two historic times. Since the reader must "build his own bridges" between these temporal levels, "gaps are bound to open up, and offer a free play of interpretation for the specific way in which the various views can be connected with one another" (Iser, "Indeterminacy," p. 11). Far from mere antiquarianism, this ode reflects a large amount of Keats's own personal symbolism. Like the nightingale's song in the companion ode, the Grecian urn "is manipulated willfully, because it is a symbolic projection of his own mind, an externalization against which another part of his mind can locate itself" (Dickstein, p. 196). The very urgency inherent in Keats's repetition of the word "happy," in his third stanza, often faulted by critics as betraying signs of strain, functions subtly in the context of the poet's own contemporary needs. The speaker's frequent repetition of the epithet "happy," first in relation to his eternal boughs, then to his untiring melodist, and finally to his lover, implies a contrary reality unlike this idealized pastoral permanence. Real boughs shed their leaves; living pipers grow weary of their melodies; actual lovers suffer decline in their passionate ardor. As in the "Ode to a Nightingale," "Where but to think is to be full of sorrow / And leaden-eyed despairs," Keats's speaker is departing from the anxiety of modern consciousness and seeking an ideal beyond ordinary fret. Though some readers will continue to censure this repetition as poetic softness, this overstatement betrays Keats's need to counter the alienated consciousness.[15]

In the historic climate of Keats's time, the word *consciousness* commonly tends to imply self-division and the divided mind: it may even be redundant to gloss this word with these qualifiers. This sense of inner alienation, though introduced with restraint, often makes up the underlying ground of Keats's poetry. His sonnet "To Sleep," for instance, builds upon a contrast between the "lulling charities" of sleep as an opiate and the insomniac's "curious conscience, that still hoards / Its strength for darkness, burrowing like the mole." In the "Ode to a Nightingale," he contrasts the clinical reality of youth growing "pale, and spectre-thin," and dying with the ecstatic release symbolized by the nightingale's song. Indeed the stark unsanitary conditions that Keats encountered during his four years of apprenticeship to Thomas Hammond at Edmonton (1811–1815) and his further study of surgery at Guy's Hospital (October 1815–July 1816) are essential biographical facts (Bate, pp. 42–43). They loom larger in forming Keats's reality principle than is often recognized. In the "Ode to Psyche," Keats capitalizes upon the ancient neglect of the goddess Psyche to revive in his own individual consciousness a new worship befitting a poetics of interiority. In this ode he injects a strong contrast between Psyche's mythic world and his own iron time, "those days so far retir'd / From happy pieties." These recurrent polarities provide insight into the ongoing generations wasted by old age, "in midst of other woe / Than ours," as contrasted with the permanence of art in "Ode on a Grecian Urn." Unlike Schiller's stressing of the free play of artistic imagination at the expense of sensory reality, Keats's idealisms or mythic constructs increasingly abide the testing of the real.

III

Let us now explore the concept of romantic irony as it arises within the tradition of German philosophy. Friedrich von Schiller reveals the guilt and alienation attendant upon the growth of artistic consciousness as it emerges in Romantic poetry, and as we have already seen it taking shape in the Keatsian canon. Schiller affords an apt diagnosis of an alienation which is so often the subtext of Keats's poems. As a near contemporary working independently of Keats, Schiller precisely articulates the historical climate that pervades Keats's thought:

> Once the increase of empirical knowledge, and more exact modes of thought, made sharper divisions between the sciences inevitable, and once the increasingly complex machinery of State necessitated a more rigorous separation of ranks and occupations, then the inner unity of human nature was severed too, and a disastrous conflict set its harmonious powers at variance. The intuitive and the speculative understanding now withdrew in hostility to take up positions in their respective fields, whose frontiers they now began to guard with jealous mistrust.[16]

In this analysis of the alienating consequences of civilization, mankind is destined to separation from an earlier wholeness — either fictional or real — often associated with lost childhood and unity with nature. Schiller's naive poet, like Homer or Shakespeare, directly renders the presence of objective nature, without calling attention to the self-conscious filter of the poet's imagination. The modern sentimental poet deliberately filters his subject through his reflective consciousness, disclosing nostalgia and melancholy as byproducts of his disunity and inner division.[17] The fragmented self of Keats's speaker evokes an image of his own desire for naive wholeness as symbolized by the piper's music, yet this ideal music elicits, in turn, an answering chord of estrangement in the sentimental consciousness of both speaker and reader.

Strongly influenced by the spirit of Kant's *Critique of Judgement*, Schiller seeks to escape from the categorizing understanding of Kant and its passive determinism by the senses: "Man in his physical state merely suffers the dominion of nature; he emancipates himself from this dominion in the aesthetic state, and he acquires mastery over it in the moral" (*Aesthetic Education*, p. 171). Kant derives his aesthetic judgments from a play of faculties rather than the categorical intellect that functions as a clearing house for sensory data. Building upon this Kantian foundation, Schiller erects his own idea of freedom as aesthetic play. In the liberating realm of play, the artist, no longer passively determined by the senses, subjects the stuff of matter to his own sense of form. Though Schiller maintains a stronger grip upon the actual than is often recognized, his bias against sensuality leads him to favor the ideal over the chaos of civilized reality. In his early poetry, Keats shares this bias toward the ideal as an escape from unpleasant reality, but as his poetry matures, in keeping with the reality principle, he pays more and more heed to the alienated consciousness.

An even closer contemporary model than that of Schiller for elucidating the dialectical progression in the "Grecian Urn" may be found in Friedrich Schlegel's fragments on romantic irony, evolved under the influence of Kant and Schiller. Instead of triumphing like Schiller in aesthetic play over phenomenally determined consciousness, Schlegel adapts the idea of play to ironic participation in becoming: "the Romantic type of poetry is still becoming; indeed, its peculiar essence is that it is always becoming and that it can never be completed."[18] From this inexhaustible abundance (*Fülle*) in nature's becoming, Schlegel discovers a means of overcoming the Kantian dualism between noumena and phenomena. Whereas for Kant our knowledge applies merely to appearances and noumena remain unknowable, Schlegel defines noumena as part of the process of becoming and maintains that the infinite can be experienced through the finite. Though human consciousness is of course limited, it participates in the contradictory vitality of becoming. Because of its limits the mind can never fully experience the noumenal but, as Anne K. Mellor explains Schlegelian romantic irony, consciousness hovers between the ongoing productive flux of becoming and the mind's own bounds:

> The artist who conceives the universe as an infinitely abundant chaos, who sees his own consciousness as simultaneously limited and yet involved in an on-going process of growth or becoming, who therefore enthusiastically engages in the difficult but exhilarating balancing between self-creation and self-destruction, and who then articulates this experience in a form which simultaneously creates and de-creates itself is producing that literary mode Schlegel called romantic irony.[19]

By definition romantic irony keeps alive in dynamic interplay two opposing ideas that do not cancel each other out. Coleridge defines imagination, in part, as a "balance or reconciliation of opposite or discordant qualities"; rather than neutralizing the energies of these opposites, he infers a dynamic interchange similar in function to that of romantic irony. In the very first line of "Ode on a Grecian Urn," the punning ambiguity on the word "still" illustrates this Schlegelian irony. As a "still unravish'd bride," is the urn an image of motionless stillness, or is it eventually going to be despoiled by "slow time"? A third Elizabethan meaning of "still" as "always" plays off against the sense of "as yet unravished." All three meanings are operative, and none cancels out its opposing counterpart. This dialectical encounter between the permanent and the mutable—a pattern repeated again and again in the progress of the poem—nowhere reveals itself more clearly than in the lover captured forever in anticipation of a kiss. The impassioned pastoral of this sculptured lover immediately suggests the feverish actuality of love in the world of process. The ancient Greek lover initially seeking to possess a reluctant maiden, even by force, leads later in the poem to the distinctly un-Greek, more clinical portrayal of a fevered lover by the speaker. Though of course the marble lover represents a timeless attitude, Keats's intense greeting of the spirit ironically discloses a high valorization of physical passion even as it is attributed to a marble surface. In the very ambiguity of this lover, "All breathing human passion far above," Keats reveals a dynamic interchange between the ideal form and the actual. The line may either mean an eternal love beyond the passionate breathing of human flesh or, in contrast, a lover breathing a heightened passion in some timeless world. Yet the marble reality of this lover ironically obtrudes to reduce such ideal love to a "bloodless emulation" of ordinary human passion. Actual human passion, on the other hand, inferred from its marble imitation, "leaves a heart high-sorrowful and cloy'd, / A burning forehead, and a parching tongue." These ambiguities of language, then, function as romantic irony: the ideal and the real mutually create and de-create each other in the unfolding progression of the ode.

IV

The passage in "Ode on a Grecian Urn" that, apart from its ending, has elicited the most critical controversy is stanza four. Imagination here achieves its fullest activity in the speaker's greeting of the ritual sacrifice, with the heifer bellowing like its counterpart on the Parthenon frieze in reaction to the smell of blood and fear of violence. At the very height of its progress into mythic place, the ode, as previously observed, now reveals its historic vacancy, the absence of an ancient culture. Critics who read life as corrosive upon art typically find that "In the *Grecian Urn,* the sensations evoked are almost wholly concerned with young love (the great fourth stanza is logically a digression)," and that Keats again "cannot convince himself that love and beauty on marble are better than flesh-and-blood experience, however brief and unhappy that may be" (Bush, p. 335). Any logical digression incurred by this sacrificial scene depends upon the questionable assumption that Keats intended to write a poem about "young love," but several different figures on the urn have suggested to the speaker's responding mind a counterpart in the world of process that goes beyond the experience of love. Since each low-relief detail adds to a microcosmic portrait of a Hellenic culture, the absent town may more usefully be seen as the fullest development in the poem of the speaker's greeting of the spirit. At this peak of mythic suggestiveness, the despoiling blight of history emerges naturally from the revealing pattern of romantic irony. Such irony does not really exist on the written page: it comes to life in the reader's consciousness where two opposing ideas may interact together at the same time.

For Bush the "Grecian Urn" purports to offer a consolation through art, but unconsciously reveals more about the loss of life. Kenneth Burke, on the other hand, makes no dualistic separation between these polarities, and provides insight into the act of reading:

> And finally, the poem, in the name of the Urn, or under the aegis of the Urn, is such a bond [i.e., a bond between a mortal and an immortal scene]. For we readers, by re-enacting it in the reading, use it as a viaticum to transport us into the quality of the scene which it depicts on its face (the scene containing as a fixity what the poem as act extends into a process). The scene *on* the Urn is really the scene *behind* the Urn; the Urn is literally the ground of this scene, but transcendentally the scene is the ground of the Urn. The Urn contains the scene out of which it arose.

By separating the spatial character of the visual scene on the urn from the temporal progression of reading the poem, Burke discerns the ode as an action in consciousness played off against the frozen, static quality of the urn. Yet paradoxically the sacrificial scene becomes for him the vehicle of mythic transcendence, and the reader's participation in a rite, a symbolic transition to a place that is the origin of myth. The ritual act of slaughter unifies the Hellenic community in a ceremonial act of violence. The reader's *rite de passage* into and beyond the sacrifice provides access into "the dead world of ancient Greece, as immortalized on an urn surviving from that period, [since it] is the vessel of this deathy-deathless ambiguity."[20] Clearly our encounter with mortality in reading the "Ode on a Grecian Urn" (first intimated by the verb "haunts" mentioned earlier) amounts to an encounter with death in Arcadia. By reading this symbolic action entirely on the transcendent level, Burke equates beauty with *poetry* and *act,* and truth with *science* and *scene,* and thus reconciles the normally incompatible science and poetry on the higher plane of myth. This reading validates the dark side of truth and, for him, abolishes "romanticism through romanticism" (Burke, p. 447). But as effective as his argument is, Burke does not allow for the full progression of romantic irony. In that mode the equation of truth and beauty occurs not only on the transcendent but also the mundane level.

At the end of the fourth stanza, Keats deplores the vacant citadel forever emptied on its folk, without a soul alive to tell why it is "desolate." The very plangency of this loss of life marks a change in the reader's role. Because of the uncertainty of the "little" town's location by river, sea, or mountain side (as is now a critical commonplace), it exists in the imagination of the speaker rather than as a visual presence on the urn. Yet the two poles of romantic irony — the pious procession and the absent town — remain like the positive and negative poles of a magnet in active opposition within the reader's consciousness. Alienation is the inevitable shadow of permanence. Having reached the height of imaginative greeting in conjuring up the desolate town, the speaker now breaks his empathic spell and redirects our attention to the outer shape and separate marble fact of the urn. At the onset of the final stanza, the ode's action ceases to function as a dialectic in the divided consciousness of the speaker, because this division emerges only in connection with his response to localized figures on the urn's curvature. Now he acknowledges that the marble artifact is after all a "Cold Pastoral." The "brede" of men carved in low relief and the maidens wrought upon the urn have actually acquired their passion from the speaker's responding mind. The puns on "brede" and "overwrought," including dimensions of both art and life, help the reader to disengage from a beholder's absorption and to see the marble object at a distance. Here wordplay, by its very duality, helps to silence the dialogue between art and life by withdrawing the action from the speaker's consciousness and modulating to the urn's separate existence apart from the reader. The reader's task—from this vantage point of detachment—now demands a response to the poem, not merely to an imaginary urn.

V

Rhetorical emphasis upon the reader, properly suited to the structure and interiority of "Ode on a Grecian Urn," now provides the key to the role of romantic irony in the closure of the ode. In reflecting upon the stages of lyric action that prepare for a resolution, the reader begins with the allegory of the piper as a model for partaking of an action in consciousness. Then the sentimental voice of the speaker's divided mind creates a dilemma between permanence and alienation. Finally, as an action in the reader's imagination, this dilemma becomes a dialectic of oscillating polarities that emerges as a progression of romantic irony. In her book on *Poetic Closure*, Barbara Herrnstein Smith briefly discusses this ode in a section on "Failures of Closure," even though paradoxically the ode contains almost all the traditional devices used to achieve successful endings. If Keats had set out "to construct the most securely closed poem ever written," he could scarcely have included more closural devices than appear in the "Grecian Urn": "They are all there: verbal repetitions, monosyllabic diction, metrical regularity, formal parallelism, unqualified absolutes, closural allusions, and the oracular assertion of an utter and ultimate verity. And yet it is an open question whether or not these lines offer a poetically legitimate or effective resolution to the thematic structure of the entire ode."[21] In discussing failures of closure, Smith concedes the variable factor of differing readers' temperaments: one reader's recall of the essential factors governing an ending will not be exactly the same as that of any other reader. Since many perceptive critics have found Keats's closing lines a blemish on the ode, her bold argument will doubtless find its advocates. For the moment let us suspend judgment upon the ode's concluding utterance until we examine Keats's final task for his reader.

At the close of the poem, after engaging in this dialectical disclosure of artistic process, the reader is as deftly restored to his own separate life as he was previously schooled in his role of fictional play. The chastening lines, "When old age shall this generation waste, / Thou shalt remain, in midst of other woe / Than ours," remind the reader of his own impending death along with the perfected death of Keats and his generation. The reader, who was at first included in part ownership of the ode, again encounters the pronoun "ours": now it admonishes him about his own brevity amid the woe of ongoing generations of men. The reader's passage from fiction to life must be a factor in judging the ode's closure.

Beyond her negative reaction to the closure of "Ode on a Grecian Urn," Smith raises another unsettling question for a poem written in the mode of romantic irony. She wonders "whether strong closure may not become, in certain styles, a violation of the style itself" (Smith, p. 195). Since romantic irony normally requires an open-ended or tentative ending, all the evidence points toward an unsuccessful closure of the "Grecian Urn." But the "oracular utterance," like that of this ode, was notorious for its ambiguity, and conveniently relied upon the interpreter for its validity. What Smith calls the "unqualified absolutes"—"Beauty is truth, truth beauty"—may now be explored in reader response—the crucible of romantic irony. First we must concede that this loaded equation is *not* all we need to know in this world. Instead, for this paradoxical aphorism to mean anything at all, the logic of the entire poem must govern its utterance.

I prefer Garrod's omission of the quotation marks around the first five words in the penultimate line of the ode:

> Beauty is truth, truth beauty,—that is all
> Ye know on earth, and all ye need to know.[22]

I would delete the quotation marks, in keeping with the version printed in the *Annals of the Fine Arts* (1820), because such a reading suggests that these two lines are addressed to mankind by the urn. This omission effaces the poet and more elegantly preserves a dialogue between speaker and reader. But perhaps the most sensible solution to the controversy as to whether poet or urn utters the last line and a third, "that is all / Ye know on earth, and all ye need to know," comes form Nathaniel Teich: "It makes little difference to the basic meaning of this type of interpretation whether one holds that the urn speaks the entire epigram, or that Keats as the narrator, speaks the last one and one-third lines. Either way, the basic meaning is clear: that the message of the urn is applicable to man's life on earth and his aesthetic experiences."[23] With or without quotation marks, then, the urn delivers this message to the reader. If the quotation marks are omitted, the speaker actually discloses the epigramatic utterance of the urn (the full two lines) as an indirect discourse—"to whom thou say'st." Yet the urn, under the aegis of the ode, is in fact the speaker because, as a work of art, it speaks from its "world" (Heidegger's term) to successive generations of new readers.

How can beauty *be* truth, or truth beauty? The following mode of reconciling Smith's "unqualified absolutes" typifies widespread critical practice (including the major essays by Brooks and Burke): art relieves the burden of earthy consciousness "by holding out to man the promise that somewhere—at heaven's bourne, where the woes of this world will be resolved—songs are forever new, love is forever young, human passion is 'human passion far above,' beauty is truth" (Wasserman, p. 61). Wasserman draws upon Keats's letter on Adam's dream, a text that does warrant such an absolute truth as a gloss on the ode's epigraph: "What the imagination seizes as Beauty must be truth—whether it existed before or not" (*Letters*, 1:184). No doubt the "Grecian Urn" renders things in a "finer tone" as compared with everyday life, but this transcendental reading takes no account of how beauty also includes the ugly truth, of how surface detail discloses turbulent depth, of how ideal and real beget their contraries in an oscillating polarity that precludes a dualistic reading. A condensed summary of the ode's progression reveals the accumulating pattern of romantic irony: the piper's barely audible music conjures up the flawed human ear; the ideal lover, ever anticipating a kiss, evokes a mortal counterpart with "a burning forehead and a parching tongue"; boughs that never shed their leaves imply a contrary cycle of seasonal decay; the sacrificial procession suggests a ruined culture that had created such funereal urns. The human vacancy disclosed by romantic irony does not finally de-create the world on the outer curvature of

the urn, nor does the marble carving obstruct the desolate vacancy of its imitated world. The paradoxical identity of beauty and truth, as contained in the urn's epigraph, preserves the dynamic interaction of opposites that emerges throughout the poem's progression. The "Grecian Urn"'s unfolding irony—itself in part created by the reader—governs and makes possible the precarious equation of truth and beauty. Only thus can we find a hermeneutic key to these otherwise empty abstractions.

Wasserman, Brooks, and Burke, who would reconcile beauty and truth on a higher level, correspond with Schiller's theory that isolates the poet's fictive world of language and play from the infection of reality. For the poet possesses his artist's prerogative, in Schiller's terms, his "sovereign right positively only in the *world of appearance*" and "the poet . . . steps outside his boundaries when he attributes existence to his ideal, and when he aims at some definite existence through it."[24] Tilottama Rajan—whose evidence used in discussing the "Grecian Urn" equally supports a conclusion contrary to her findings—finally places the ode on the border of Schiller's Romantic idealist discourse, but on the verge of breaking out of its mode. Where she resists the possibility of transparency between the Arcadian surface and its turbulent depth, I think her own evidence validates an opposite position. She applies Nietzsche's critique of Romantic idealism to "Ode on a Grecian Urn": for her the poem works within the Apollonian discourse of dream which represses the Dionysian knowledge that lurks beneath its surface. For this reason, the ode hovers on the brink "of redefining the semantics of aesthetic illusion":

> But such a redefinition, which would recognize that the aesthetic surface is related to the knowledge it encloses as a transparency rather than as a barrier, that aesthetic signs can represent but cannot banish the "world as will," does not occur *except perhaps in the mind of the reader*. Irrespective of who speaks them, the last lines of Keats's poem reaffirm the rhetoric of the surface and reduce questions to the flatness of statement and the urn itself to its merely decorative appearance.   (Rajan, p. 135, my italics)

My argument has demonstrated exactly how the mutual creation and de-creation of surface and depth in the ode can *only* exist in reader consciousness, not on the page as textual object. I think that the Apollonian surface is indeed transparent to the Dionysian depth in this ode, that sentimental surface begets a tragic depth, and that Keats *has* in fact redefined "the semantics of aesthetic illusion." Though the ode never loses its sense of fictional play so essential to romantic irony, the concluding lines, as we have seen, go beyond "the rhetoric of appearance." The urn alone might invite just such a rhetoric, but the real utterance of the poem must be inferred from the allegory of response in speaker and reader. Other readers will be fictionalized as we have been by the model reading derived from the speaker's divided mind. The turbulent depth is inseparable from its more tranquil surface.

By concluding at the end of the ode that "there is no reality to give depth and ambiguity to the fictive appearance," Rajan restricts the equation of truth and beauty to the level of appearance. By denying the historicity of the ode, she includes this poem within "the artifice of evasion": "To search beneath the surface, by seeking the historical Greece underlying the Arcadian fiction, would be to ask what becomes of the abstractions of idealism when they are incarnated in the real world and made the property of real men and lovers" (Rajan, pp. 133, 135). But, as we have seen, Keats creates a dialectic between a vanished historical culture and its imitative form upon an urn. As Rajan herself rightly infers, the reader's consciousness can accommodate the co-presence of such polarities as the surface detail of the sacrifice and the depth implicit in the absent town. Romantic irony, based upon Friedrich Schlegel's model, prevents this language of reality from deconstructing the ideal surface of the urn. Not the least of Keats's achievements in "Ode on a Grecian Urn" inheres in his creation of a dialectic between surface and depth. Keats's poem survives the Nietzschean criticism of Romantic idealism by exposing the Dionysian suffering through the transparency of the Apollonian dream.

A reader-oriented rhetoric both verifies the equation of truth and beauty and overcomes an apparent incompatibility between romantic irony and strong closure in the "Grecian Urn." This irony transforms our expectation of strong closure into an open-ended balancing of opposites, yet this ending is actually stronger for its not being writ in stone. These "unqualified absolutes" in Barbara Herrnstein Smith's summary of closural devices radically qualify each other. They derive their meaning, moreover, from the entire progression of romantic irony that subtends their precarious conjunction.[25] Although Smith recognizes the factor of reader response in all closure,

her summary tends to reify the poem's language as textual object and to ignore potential ironic action in consciousness. In sum, the full structure of the ode—with its allegory of its own reading that makes its surface transpicuous to its tragic depth—governs and vindicates the poem's ending. Although the speaker in fact delivers the indirect discourse of the ode's epigraph, the reader, now detached from previous empathy, accepts the fiction of a silent urn's acquiring language. "Ode on a Grecian Urn" carries Keats beyond the "barren dream" of romance into the Dionysian realm of Nietzsche's lyric voice.

Notes

1. It is a pleasure to thank the National Endowment for the Humanities for a stipend (Summer 1982) that made possible the writing of this article. Samuel Taylor Coleridge, *Shakespearean Criticism*, 2 vols., ed. T. M. Raysor (Cambridge, Mass.: Harvard Univ. Press, 1930), 2:174. For a critic who places the ideal of beauty above the woes of life, see Earl R. Wasserman, *The Finer Tone* (Baltimore: Johns Hopkins, 1953), p. 61. For critics who discover life as corrosive upon art, see Douglas Bush, "Keats and His Ideas," in *English Romantic Poets*, ed. M. H. Abrams (New York: Oxford Univ. Press, 1960), p. 335, and Morris Dickstein, *Keats and His Poetry* (Chicago: Univ. of Chicago Press, 1971), p. 226. For a critic who finds modified aestheticism in Keats's poem, see Jean-Claude Sallé, "The Pious Frauds of Art: A Reading of the 'Ode on a Grecian Urn,'" *SIR* 11 (1972): 92–93; and for a tragic religion of secular aestheticism, Ronald A. Sharp, *Keats, Skepticism, and the Religion of Beauty* (Athens: Univ. of Georgia Press, 1979), pp. 156–57. For a predominant affirmation of life in the face of mortality, see Charles I. Patterson, *The Daemonic in the Poetry of John Keats* (Urbana: Univ. of Illinois Press, 1970), p. 181. Tilottama Rajan, *Dark Interpreter: The Discourse of Romanticism* (Ithaca: Cornell Univ. Press, 1980), pp. 133–35, discusses the ode in the context of deconstruction. Helen Vendler, *The Odes of John Keats* (Cambridge, Mass.: Harvard Univ. Press, 1983), pp. 127–28, recognizes the claims of reality and the transforming factor of the artistic medium in the act of representation: "Keats has to affirm two wholly incompatible responses, never simultaneous, one always canceling the other, but both of them authentic,

both of them provided by the artifact, both of them 'aesthetic.'" Vendler validates both poles of art and life, yet as will later become clear, romantic irony more effectively unites these opposites in dynamic polarity.

2. *The Reader in the Text: Essays on Audience and Interpretation,* ed. Susan R. Suleiman and Inge Crosman (Princeton: Princeton Univ. Press, 1980). *Reader-Response Criticism: From Formalism to Post-Structuralism,* ed. Jane P. Tompkins (Baltimore: Johns Hopkins, 1980). George Poulet, "Phenomenology of Reading," *NLH* 1 (1969):56, explains how the reader becomes a subject of another's consciousness.

3. Walter J. Ong, "The Writer's Audience is Always a Fiction," *PMLA* 90 (1975):12. See also by Ong, *Interfaces of the Word* (Ithaca: Cornell Univ. Press, 1977), "From Mimesis to Irony," pp. 272–302; and "Beyond Objectivity: The Reader–Writer Transaction as an Altered State of Consciousness," *The CEA Critic* 40 (1977):10. On the intersubjectivity of texts, Ong writes, "For we mean by a text something that can be used by human consciousness so as to evoke sound which is not on the inscribed surface at all but is a product of consciousness working with and transmitting what it learns from sight."

4. Jack Stillinger, *The Poems of John Keats* (Cambridge, Mass.: Harvard Univ. Press, 1978), p. 372, my emphasis. Hereafter, unless otherwise noted, references to Keats's poetry are taken from this edition.

5. Wolfgang Iser, "Indeterminacy and the Reader's Response," in *Aspects of Narrative,* ed. J. Hillis Miller (New York: Columbia Univ. Press, 1971), p. 14.

6. E. H. Gombrich, *Art and Illusion* (Princeton: Princeton Univ. Press, 1972), p. 202.

7. *The Letters of John Keats,* ed. Hyder E. Rollins, 2 vols. (Cambridge, Mass.: Harvard Univ. Press, 1958), 1:242–43. Hereafter citations for this edition by volume and page will be indicated parenthetically in the text. Walter Jackson Bate remarks of "the greeting of the Spirit" that it is "as much a part of nature, or reality, as is its object," *John Keats* (Cambridge, Mass.: Harvard Univ. Press, 1963), pp. 517–18.

8. Rajan, p. 135. I use the expression "allegories of reading" in a sense contrary to Paul de Man's "allegories of the impossibility of reading," *Allegories of Reading* (New Haven: Yale Univ. Press, 1979), p. 205.

9. *Letters,* 1:265. Keats wrote his letter on "the greeting of the Spirit" to Bailey on 13 March 1818. Less than a month later he writes to Haydon, 8 April 1818, and mentions his empathy for *Antony and Cleopatra.* See also *A&C* (IV.xiv. 1–22).

10. Iser, "Indeterminacy," pp. 29–30, describes how Thackeray presents Becky Sharp in a moment of triumphant flirtation amid the *beau monde.* Suddenly the servants carrying ices and wafer-biscuits come on stage as allegorical embodiments of Discovery and Calumny. In these officious servants hovering behind Becky's chair and in the euphoria of her self-deception, the reader finds in epitome the social facade that he must be alert enough to penetrate in the novel as a whole. See also Gerald Prince, for whom the presence of the piper is tantamount to "the stance taken by the narrative with regard to its own communicability and readability, as an indication of how it ostensibly wants to be read," *The Reader in the Text,* p. 237.

11. Dickstein, p. 196, cites Wasserman as a source for this idea in *The Finer Tone,* pp. 13–62.

12. *Keats and the Mirror of Art* (Oxford: Oxford Univ. Press, 1967), pp. 217 and 214–17. Jack hoped to find a Wedgwood imitation of a Grecian urn that might have provided Keats's actual model. After finding some similarities to Keats's urn in Wedgwood vases, he concludes: "Even when his debt to a work of art is undeniable, [Keats] is almost certain to introduce details which are not to be found in his original, and as a rule he uses a painting or a work of sculpture as a springboard for his own imagination" (p. 221). See also a book of prints discovered in the Warburg Institute in London by Noel Machin, "The Case of the Empty-Handed Maenad," *Sunday Times Magazine* (London), 31 April 1965, pp. 11–12, who makes a strong case for Keats's use of a book of engraved plates by Henry Moses, *A Collection of Antique Vases, Altars, Patterae, Tripods, Candelabra, Sarcophagi, etc. from various museums and collections,* engraved in 170 plates (1814). Machin confirms Jack's Graeco-Roman hypothesis: Keats "was thinking of a large vase carved out of marble — the kind which Roman emperors used to keep in the gardens of their country villas. Machin's evidence is impressive: one of Keats's own drawings (now in the Keats-Shelley Memorial House in Rome) copies a marble vase with a

dancing maenad that almost certainly comes from Moses's book. In this collection of prints there are plates containing "leaf-fring'd legends," "pipes and timbrels," "maidens loth," and even a sacrifice, though it includes no "heifer lowering at the skies." I am indebted to Professor Anne K. Mellor for calling my attention to Machin's article.

13. Leo Spitzer, "The 'Ode on a Grecian Urn,' or Content Versus Metagrammar," *CL* 7 (1955):208 and 213.

14. Lionel Trilling, "Why We Read Jane Austen," *TLS*, 5 March 1976, p. 252. See also Ronald A. Sharp, pp. 114–58, for further support for Keats's historicism.

15. David Simpson, *Irony and Authority in Romantic Poetry* (Totawa, N.J.: Rowman and Littlefield, 1979), pp. 9–10, rightly stresses the ironic distance between Keats and his speaker, but I dissent from his view that Keats is exposing the pomposity of the speaker.

16. Friedrich von Schiller, *On the Aesthetic Education of Man*, trans. Elizabeth M. Wilkinson and L. A. Willoughby (Oxford: Oxford Univ. Press, 1967), p. 33. See also M. H. Abrams, *Natural Supernaturalism* (New York: W. W. Norton, 1973), pp. 201–17, for an excellent discussion of Schiller's position on the fragmented consciousness.

17. Friedrich von Schiller, *Naive and Sentimental Poetry and On the Sublime*, trans. Julias A. Elias (New York: Friedrick Ungar, 1980), pp. 22–23.

18. Friedrich Schlegel, *Dialogue on Poetry and Literary Aphorisms,* trans. Ernst Behler and Roman Struc (University Park: Pennsylvania State Univ. Press, 1968), p. 141.

19. Anne K. Mellor, "On Romantic Irony, Symbolism and Allegory," *Criticism* 21 (1979):229. See also Anne K. Mellor, *English Romantic Irony* (Cambridge, Mass.: Harvard Univ. Press, 1980). See also Janice L. Haney, "Shadow-Hunting': Romantic Irony, *Sartor Resartus,* and Victorian Romanticism," *SIR* 17 (1973):307–33. I am indebted to Janice Haney Peritz for incisive comments on this article. Stuart Sperry, "Toward a Definition of Romantic Irony in English Literature," in *Romantic and Modern: Revaluations of Literary Tradition,* ed. George Bornstein (Pittsburg: Univ. of Pittsburg Press, 1977), pp. 3–28, traces the emergence of romantic irony on English soil, its affinities with Keats's negative capability and Byron's mobility, and perceives its dominant characteristic as indeterminacy. Vendler, p. 133, gives full weight to both sides of Keats's polarity: we see it "with the eyes of sensation, seeing its beautiful forms as actual people," and we see it also "with the eyes of thought, seeing it, as the mind must see it, as marble inscribed by intentionality, the true made beautiful by form." For her these two visions alternate like the strobes of a lighthouse beam, but for me they function in dialectic polarity so that they are, in fact, inseparably bound together by romantic irony. Lilian R. Furst, *Fictions of Romantic Irony* (Cambridge, Mass.: Harvard Univ. Press, 1984), pp. 29–30, observes that the phrase "romantic irony" does not occur in Germany until 1850 as a critical term and that Friedrich Schlegel derives it from the practice of "Socrates, Petrarch, Dante, Cervantes, Shakespeare, Sterne and Diderot." The phrase "romantic irony" does, however, occur in Schelegel's "private literary notebooks which were not deciphered and published until 1957."

20. Kenneth Burke, *A Grammar of Motives* (Berkeley: Univ. of California Press, 1962), pp. 457–58.

21. Barbara Herrnstein Smith, *Poetic Closure: A Study of How Poems End* (Chicago: Univ. of Chicago Press, 1968), p. 195.

22. *The Poetical Works of John Keats,* 2nd ed., ed. H. W. Garrod (Oxford: Oxford Univ. Press, 1958), p. 260. Garrod included the quotation marks around the first five words of the penultimate line in his first edition (1939), but omitted them from his second edition (1956). Nathaniel Teich, "Criticism of Keats's *Grecian Urn,*" *PQ* 44 (1965):497, records Garrod's change of mind on this point. The actual printing of the ode's last two lines in the *Annals* (MDCCCXIX) is as follows: "Beauty is Truth, Truth Beauty.—That is all / Ye know on Earth, and all ye need to know." (Published c. January 1820). Jack Stillinger, *The Hoodwinking of Madeline* (Urbana: Univ. of Illinois Press, 1971), p. 167, supplies the proper printing and dating of the *Annals* reading.

23. Teich, p. 500. Jean-Claude Sallé notes an increasing critical tendency in favor of reading the last two lines of the ode as an address "to 'man' by the Urn" (p. 80, n. 7). Among critics who endorse this view are: C. M. Bowra, I. A. Richards, Kenneth Burke, Cleanth Brooks, Alvin Whitley, David Perkins, Douglas Bush, and Walter Jackson Bate. Stillinger writes that "the principal obstacle,

however, [to this reading] is the punctuation of the text in the *Lamia* volume." Since he concedes that "it seems better for the urn to tell us what we know and need to know than for the poet to do so" (*Hoodwinking*, p. 173), the quotation marks around the first five words of the penultimate line are actually the only impediment to this reading. What he ought to supply is a reading that carries more conviction by including these quotation marks than by excluding them. He has questioned the manuscript authority of the four transcripts (which all omit the quotation marks) by Charles Brown, Richard Woodhouse, George Keats, and Charles Dilke. Charles Brown, a notoriously inaccurate transcriber, was the source of Woodhouse, the most reliable transcriber, and might well have been the source of the other transcripts. Stillinger makes a strong case for this point, and also establishes that Keats did read proof on at least part of the *Lamia* volume (*Hoodwinking*, pp. 167–70). One must grant Stilinger's reasons for inclining toward the greater textual authority of the 1820 volume. If the quotation marks are included around the first five words of the penultimate line, perhaps the best reading is to take these five words as an "apothegm, motto, or sepulchral epigram" (Stillinger's phrase for a position taken by Raymond D. Havens, *MP* 24 [1926]:213, and Spitzer, pp. 220–21; *Twentieth Century Interpretations of Keats's Odes*, p. 114). Stillinger also raises here "the question of common sense meaning" as a further obstacle to the urn's addressing itself to the reader. If the quotation marks are omitted, my reading of the speaker's indirect discourse as presenting the urn's message to man does not violate any "common-sense meaning."

24. Friedrich von Schiller, *On the Aesthetic Education of Man*, trans. Reginald Snell (New York: Frederick Ungar, 1965), p. 128.

25. Cleanth Brooks, *The Well Wrought Urn* (New York: Harcourt Brace, 1947), p. 165, nicely discusses the progression of paradox which culminates in the urn's speaking silence, but his paradoxes remain exclusively in the rhetoric of the Apollonian surface. The phrase "barren dream" in the final sentence of my essay comes from "On Sitting Down to Read *King Lear* Once Again."

APPLICATION

Catharine O'Connell argues that disagreements about the meaning of "Benito Cereno" often turn upon the way the text is designed to structure the reader's responses. After viewing several ways other critics have interpreted this design, she offers her own analysis of the "inscribed reader" and that reader's relationship to the actual reader. At first glance, this "inscribed reader" appears to resemble Iser's "implied reader" and even more the various "ideal readers" that Iser discusses. But this is an ideal reader with a difference. "The story ironically inscribes an ideal reader who will not *initially get the story's full meaning." O'Connell's "inscribed reader" then ultimately resembles the reader in Stanley Fish's early work with "affective stylistics," a reader who "misreads" the text in exactly the way the text requires only to realize later a humbling enlightenment. So the ideal readers of* Paradise Lost, *for example, initially identify with Satan only finally to see that they have fallen, like Adam and Eve, into Satan's sin of pride. The poem doesn't simply reveal Satan's error, it forces the reader to replicate it. O'Connell sees Melville's text as operating in a similar way. Readers are invited to view Delano indulgently and to assume their superiority to him. But this invitation is a trap. "'Benito Cereno' structures and encourages misreadings so that the eventual discovery that one has been duped has the effect of revealing to the reader his or her complicity with Delano's most egregious and self-serving assumptions." The result is not merely intellectual enlightenment but a complex and powerful — if humbling — reader response. "Melville's reader may feel betrayed and misused . . . but there remains tremendous potential for the narrative integration of the inscribed reader to effect a strong reaction in the real reader."*

Reprinted by permission from Kevin Alexander Boon, ed., *Reading the Sea: New Essays on Sea Literature*. New York: Fort Schuyler Press, 1999, pp. 113–32. Copyright 1999 by the Fort Schuyler Press.

Narrative Collusion and Occlusion in Melville's "Benito Cereno"

Catharine O'Connell

When the narrator remarks well into the novella "Benito Cereno" that the story's protagonist and organizing consciousness, the American sea captain Amasa Delano, is "like most men of a good, blithe heart," it is Delano's tendency to see blacks as animalistic that earns him this apparent praise. The narrator notes approvingly that "like most men of a good, blithe heart, Captain Delano took to negroes, not philanthropically, but genially, just as other men to Newfoundland dogs" (213). What are we to make of the narrator's alliance with Delano through pernicious racial stereotyping, and even more striking, the narrator's efforts to implicate the reader by asserting a shared belief that such attitudes signal a good heart? Throughout "Benito Cereno," the narrator colludes with Delano to present his racist misunderstandings as natural and understandable. The narrative is not focalized through Delano so much as it is a defense of him and his constant misreadings. This defense is premised on the inclusion of the reader in the "conspiracy"; we are urged to confirm the essential goodness and rationality of Delano's delusions.

"Benito Cereno" is profoundly ironic, but the narrative presentation is such that the irony is initially occluded; virtually all critics of "Benito Cereno" note the necessity of a second reading to "get it." Why should Melville expend such narrative energy to obscure the irony of the text? Isn't the danger with irony that it might be missed? I argue that "Benito Cereno" employs an insidiously unreliable narrator to "set up" the reader, and that the reader is incorporated into the text in a subject position analogous or at least complementary to Delano's.

If an actual reader accepts the role scripted within the text, the power of the irony is greatly intensified. It is one thing to be able to look down with the narrator upon the object of the ironic gaze; it is quite another to suddenly realize that the gaze is directed at oneself. While the racial politics of "Benito Cereno" have long been a topic of critical concern, the way the text's narration relates to the problem of race and representation has not been fully explored, particularly the dynamic interaction structured between narrator and inscribed reader.

There is now critical agreement that the presentation of Delano is ironic: no longer are Delano's prejudices and ideological investment in racism conflated with Melville's: no longer do we have the possibility of seeing Delano as the "innocent" American. Where once Melville was seen as insensitive to the injustices of slavery, we now see Melville critiquing the insensitivity pervasive in antebellum American culture.[1] Melville, we can agree, is not on Delano's side. However, his narrator is; it is not just bad reading that made it so easy for so long to misunderstand the antislavery politics of the novella. "Benito Cereno" formulates its indictment of antebellum racial ideology through first structuring identification with, or sympathy for, the character of Amasa Delano, and later exposing the terrible moral, political, and epistemological implications of a willingness to accept Delano's premises.

"Shadows Present": The Ongoing Critical Debate over Ambiguity in "Benito Cereno"

The narrative structure of "Benito Cereno" works to confound rather than clarify, and there continues to be lively critical discussion about the meaning of this presentation.

At the beginning of the story, the narrator describes the setting by intoning: "Shadows present, foreshadowing deeper shadows to come." With this overstated and almost parodic verbal gesture, the narrator invites us to understand the story as fundamentally ambiguous. But what constitutes the "shadows"? The events on board the *San Dominick* are not, in the final analysis, all that ambiguous, except to the willfully blind Delano. The text's ambiguity is constituted primarily through the narrative's indeterminate and unstable allegiances. The critical history of "Benito Cereno" shows a range of responses to this instability, most recently concentrated on analyses of Melville's critique of contemporary ideology. I would suggest that looking in particular at the narrator/reader interaction helps to expand our understanding of this attribute of the text.

The most important of the recent (that is, post-New Critical) reinterpretations of "Benito Cereno" is James Kavanaugh's "'That Hive of Subtlety': 'Benito Cereno' and the Liberal Hero." Kavanaugh challenges readers that find the text's ambiguity evidence of the impossibility of ever gaining definitive understanding or moral certainty. Kavanaugh sets himself against those "critical elaborations [which] construe the text as leading the reader into an infinite maze of irony and ambiguity, if not moral and epistemological uncertainty" (355). Instead, Kavanaugh argues that "Benito Cereno" functions as an attack on the ideology represented by Amasa Delano, and that the presentation of Delano's perspective ultimately works to undermine it.

> "Benito Cereno" can be read as a discourse about discourse, about how the mind of a certain type of social subject *talks to itself* . . . "Benito Cereno" appears, then, to take as both its form of presentation and object of critique a peculiar American ideology that sets an imaginary relation to the world in which one can "feel" comfortable and innocent even while one is actively working to reproduce repressive social relations. (357)

Therefore Delano's self-delusion and the text's extensive engagement with it are essential to the argument the text advances.

Kavanaugh acknowledges that this narrative approach has the effect of placing the reader in an unstable position; we must spend time inside Delano's head and understand his conviction of innocence; yet if the text functions as critique, we must ultimately be able to distance ourselves from him, and ultimately to condemn him. For Kavanaugh, any useful engagement with the text is predicated on resisting or coming to dismiss the pull of identification with Delano's perspective that the text so insistently constructs:

> The analysis of "Benito Cereno" must begin by breaking absolutely the seductive grip of identification between the reader and Amasa Delano, a grip not even loosened by the seemingly negative judgments of the American Captain carried in phrases like "moral simplicity" and "weak-wittedness." (360)

Other critics join Kavanaugh in relying on a "critical reader" (another refers to a "careful reader" who will get what the "casual reader" or "naïve reader" will not).[2] If "Benito Cereno" is an anti-slavery novel, and most recent critical readers agree that it is, why should Melville run such a risk of the reader missing the point of the story? For Kavanaugh this "risk" results from Melville's own immersion in the ideology he critiques, an immersion Kavanaugh likens to "paralysis," an "inability to remain at ease within, or get definitively out of, a stifling ideology" (359).

John Haegert engages with the problem of the supposed "bad" reader, and argues that the narrative structures the kind of "misreading" critics so frequently identify as a problem. He argues with Kavanaugh's insistence that to read the story "correctly" we must be able to resist the impulse to identify with Delano. He remarks that,

> our initial "identification" with Delano depends as much, I think, on the formal patternings of the plot as on any supposed ideological affinity for the hero . . . The extravagantly melodramatic cast of Melville's narrative serves primarily to deflect us from the kinds of ideological questions so persuasively posed by Kavanaugh and others — thereby inducing in the reader what we might call a Delano-like complacency toward the text's ultimate intentionalities. (29)

Haegert explains this narrative strategy as an attempt to set up in the reader the expectation of a neat resolution to the "mystery," one that the narrative indefinitely withholds. Haegert examines the fictional deposition that comprises the second half of the story to show conclusively that the ambiguities never are resolved, or at least that there is no clear "true" account that serves to clear up all the questions, even though the story's generic markers lead us to expect such resolution.

In the tension between what we are led to expect and what we get (or don't get), Haegert finds the text's meaning. He believes that this discrepancy constitutes Melville's critique of narrative in general. He finds a "remarkable confluence, in *Benito Cereno,* of ideological critique and narrative open-endedness . . . For it is not only ambiguity or silence which occupies Melville's narrative, nor simply the ideological blindness of his central characters. Far more fundamental to the work's subversive movement is a deep-seated suspicion of the dynamics of narrative itself" (32).

The position put forward by Haegert is echoed in Dennis Pahl's "The Gaze of History in 'Benito Cereno.'" Pahl notes the absence of definitive "answers" and argues that the resulting ambiguity suggests that Melville is not interested in taking a position for or against Delano, but in revealing the unreliability of historical narrative. He argues that,

> we should consider the possibility that "Benito Cereno" is less interested in propounding a certain moral message than in exploring, very self-consciously, the precise ways in which narrative, and especially historical narrative, goes about constructing the illusion of moral truth. How indeed, we might ask, does Melville's text become a kind of meditation on the meaning of history, and on the history's ultimate desire to fashion moral, political, and epistemological truth? (173)

As another critic, Benjamin Reiss, puts it, the "sense that there is something left to know" (146) at the end has a very powerful impact. I would argue, however, that the narrative's refusal to satisfy the desire to know that it incites is part of a larger effort to leave the reader adrift, to tear the reader away from the secure moorings it lulls us into believing it will provide. My interest is in showing how this manipulation of the reader is accomplished and suggesting a theory as to why, at this particular moment in political and literary history, such an approach was both available and effective.

"Singularly Undistrustful": "Benito Cereno's" Inscribed Alliance Among Narrator, Character and Reader

"Benito Cereno's" narrator initially presents Delano as unreliable, but unreliable for all the wrong reasons: he is allegedly too innocent and trusting to perceive the kind of evil operating on board the *San Dominick*. In fact, it is Delano's intensive self-interested willingness to credit any version of reality, however improbable, that reinforces his economic and psychological security that leads him so dangerously astray in his interpretations of events. The narrator structures a reading response that likewise serves self-interest and vanity; readers are invited to see Delano's confusions as innocence and to view their own subsequent confusion through the same lens. American readers, the narrator suggests, are unfamiliar with the kinds of mysterious, exotic behaviors associated with both the Africans and the Spaniards on board the San Dominick. We are unable to fathom the horrors associated with both. Readers are not asked to believe Delano—indeed we are warned that he is a bit simple-minded—but to believe *in* him, in his essential good heartedness. But then, of course, we learn down what paths this alliance will lead us. There are two levels on which this narrative effort at forging an alliance takes place: first, the characterization of Delano himself, and second, the striking efforts of the narrator to explain or justify Delano's misunderstandings. The effects of this two-pronged effort are to make it extremely easy for an actual reader to fall into the position scripted for the reader within the text.

The narrator's first introduction of Delano establishes the fundamental dishonesty with which Delano is presented. The narrator describes Delano coming upon a strange ship in a lonely and desolate place, which, contrary to established custom, is flying no flag. Giving us the first erroneous hint that we are embarking on a pirate story, the narrator suggests that Delano should have been suspicious:

> Captain Delano's surprise might have deepened into some uneasiness had he not been a person of a singularly undistrustful good nature, not liable, except on extraordinary and repeated incentives, and hardly then, to indulge in personal alarms, any way involving the imputation of malign evil in man. Whether, in view of what humanity is capable, such a trait implies, along with a benevolent heart, more than ordinary quickness and accuracy of intellectual perception, may be left to the wise to determine. (162)

The narrator acknowledges that Delano gets it wrong, but he tempts us with an easy explanation, one that still allows us to respond to Delano positively, even though we know from the beginning that he is missing something crucial. Being "singularly undistrustful" (note, *not* "trusting"; the text abounds in such double negatives), seems on balance like a good thing, or at least not a bad thing, until we find out much later what mindset "singularly undistrustful" designates: Delano is singularly undistrustful of any information that serves to confirm his view of the world. Delano's "good nature" consists of believing himself good and innocent by nature and refusing to admit or even consider the possibility of his own implication in the systematic exploitation of Africans in the Americas.

A careful reading of this introduction reveals that it is more noncommittal than it first appears; it does not actually say that Delano has a benevolent heart, but merely that such might be one *possible* reading of this evidence. Kavanaugh observes that,

> the sentence can be read with the "whether" governing the phrase about a "benevolent heart," as well as that concerning Delano's "intellectual perception," leaving it uncertain "whether . . . Such a trait implies . . . a benevolent heart." Thus, the language of the text begins on the first page of the story as a complicated discourse of formal deference to Delano. (362–3)

This pattern of misleading wording recurs throughout the text. Kavanaugh reads it as "a necessary condition of a textual production that distantiates an ideology within the discourse of that ideology itself" (363). I read it as part of the narrator's ongoing efforts to mislead, to dupe actual readers into the passivity that characterizes Delano.

At the moments in which the narrative allows us to spend significant time inside Delano's head, we begin to understand what attributes and attitudes constitute his "good nature." He credits only that perceptual input that serves to confirm his set ideas about social order, ideas that elevate him over whatever "others" he encounters. This dynamic is particularly evident in the scene in which he watches an African mother with her child and experiences an overflowing of "benevolence" because he can use what he sees to dehumanize the Africans. Delano's sense of well being is contingent on the confirmation (or what he takes to be confirmation) of his prejudices:

> His attention has been drawn to a slumbering negress . . . lying, with youthful limbs carelessly disposed, under the lee of the bulwarks, like a doe in the shade of a woodland rock. Sprawling at her lapped breasts, was her wide-awake fawn, stark naked, its black little body half lifted from the deck, crosswise with its dam's; its hands, like two paws, clambering upon her; its mouth and nose ineffectually rooting to get at the mark; and meantime giving a vexatious half-grunt, blending with the composed snore of the negress.

> The uncommon vigor of the child at length roused the mother. She started up, at a distance facing Captain Delano. But as if not at all concerned at the attitude in which she had been caught, delightedly she caught the child up, with maternal transports, covering it with kisses.
> There's naked nature, now; pure tenderness and love, thought Captain Delano, well pleased. (198)

Delano's pleasure does not result from the mother-child tableaux, but from finding a seemingly secure place to ground himself. His experience on the ship has, up to this point, been a disorienting one because he cannot or will not see the reality of the slave revolt surrounding him as he relentlessly tries to fit what he does see into a narrative that will not challenge his fundamental assumptions about the world. In the African mother, he can find information he is willing to assimilate, but only because he finds in it a way to place himself above those he observes.

This scene reveals what is left out of Delano's "benevolence." The "natural" affection of the mother for the child pleases him, but it never occurs to him to ask what the fate of this mother and child might be. He still believes that he is onboard a functioning slave ship, but he does not pause to consider the implications of the system for the woman's "maternal transports."

Delano's fundamental belief about himself is that he is good and innocent. Delano thinks of himself as untainted, as child-like in his distance from the economic and political systems within which he operates:

> What I, Amasa Delano—Jack of the Beach as they called me when a lad—I, Amasa; the same that, ducksatchel in hand, used to paddle along the water-side to the school house made from the old hulk—I, little Jack of the Beach, that used to go berrying with cousin Nat and the rest; I to be murdered here at the ends of the earth . . . ? Too nonsensical to think of! Who would murder Amasa Delano? His conscience is clean. (203–4)

The last sentence of this passage is particularly important and potentially misleading. The "in view of what humanity is capable" opening has taught us to view with alarm the comfort Delano takes in concluding that if his conscience is clean, he will be safe. But the more serious question is whether his conscience *ought* to be clean, given both his attitudes toward the Africans and his structural investment in systems of oppression.

When Delano's thoughts are isolated, it seems pretty easy to recognize that he is a problematic character, that his presentation is ironic. However, much of the time we do not get Delano's thoughts directly, but mediated through the narrator, and the narrator's role through most of the text is principally to obfuscate. McLamore likens the narrator to a defense lawyer, and the analogy is an apt one. He describes the narrator as employing "lawyerly involutions of conditional phrases masquerading as indicatives or attributives with which contemporary legal and political operatives attempted to maintain order" (43). The narrator's efforts go toward rationalizing Delano's positions not, at least on an overt level, toward exposing them.

The first way that the narrator serves to bolster Delano's (mis)interpretations is through echoing his most egregious attitudes and reporting them neutrally. For instance, the narrator first introduces animalistic imagery when describing the blacks. The first description we get of Babo anticipates the later "Newfoundland dog" analogy (also the narrator's):

> By his side stood a black of small stature, in whose rude face, as occasionally, like a shepherd's dog, he

mutely turned it up into the Spaniard's, sorrow and affection were equally blended. (167)

Much of the text's racialism is communicated through the narrator's explanations. Descriptions of Babo's activities are frequently accompanied by commentary that does not contribute to an understanding of the scene; in fact, it does exactly the opposite — gives weight and justification to Delano's misreading. The narrator's explanation of Babo's "solicitousness" is an example:

Sometimes the negro gave his master his arm, or took his handkerchief out of his pocket for him; performing these and similar offices with that affectionate zeal which transmutes into something filial or fraternal acts in themselves but menial, and which has gained for the negro the repute of making the most pleasing body-servant in the world; one, too, whom a master need not be on stiffly superior terms with, but may treat with familiar trust; less a servant than a devoted companion. (169)

The narrator makes recourse to widely circulating racialist attitudes to provide cover for Delano's missing the point of what goes on between Cereno and Babo.

The narrator also joins Delano in overlooking the nature of the ship. Delano does not bother to imagine the ultimate fate of the slave mothers, and the narrator blithely mischaracterizes the tension and unrest aboard the slave ship by comparing it to a ship carrying *voluntary* immigrants to the New World:

The *San Dominick* was in the condition of a transatlantic emigrant ship, among whose multitude of living freight are some individuals, doubtless, as little troublesome as crates and bales; but the friendly remonstrances of such with their ruder companions are of not so much avail as the unfriendly arm of the mate. What the *San Dominick* wanted was, what the emigrant ship has, stern superior officers. But on these decks not so much as a fourth-mate was to be seen. (172)

The facts about the ship given here are accurate: there are no Spanish officers keeping order. But the interpretive framework is completely false. The *San Dominick* is *not* in any way similar to an emigrant ship, whose passengers might tend to get a little rowdy; it is a slave ship carrying human cargo held in perpetual servitude.

The clearest example of the narrator working to prevent apprehension of what is really going on is in the introduction to the shaving scene. This scene is particularly interesting because its menace comes through even if one does not, on a conscious level, realize what is happening. Babo holds the razor to Cereno's throat to encourage him to tell Babo's version of the story. Even Delano watches this performance with some discomfort at Cereno's obvious terror. The narrator, however, encourages us to view it through the lens of the supposedly devoted masterslave relationship between Cereno and Babo. It is once again introduced with reference to a general principle (and once again it is not only a racist principle but one that is utterly wrong for describing the situation) to which the particulars are applied. It is worth quoting at length because the set up has to be extensive given the misreading it must both foster and cover.

There is something in the negro which, in a peculiar way, fits him for avocations about one's person. Most negroes are natural valets and hair-dressers; taking to the comb and brush congenially as to the castinets, and flourishing them apparently with almost equal satisfaction. There is, too, a smooth tact about them in this employment, with a marvelous, noiseless, gliding briskness, not ungraceful in its way, singularly pleasing to behold, and still more so to be the manipulated subject of. And above all is the great gift of good-humor. Not the mere grin or laugh is here meant. Those were unsuitable. But a certain easy cheerfulness, harmonious in every glance and gesture; as though God has set the whole negro to some pleasant tune.

When to this is added the docility arising from the unaspiring contentment of a limited mind, and that susceptibility of bland attachment sometimes inhering in indisputable inferiors, one readily perceives why those hypochondriacs, Johnson and Byron — it may be, something like the hypochondriac Benito Cereno — took to their hearts, almost to the exclusion of the entire white race, their serving men, the negroes Barber and Fletcher. But if there be that in the negro which exempts him from the inflicted sourness of the morbid or cynical mind, how, in his most prepossessing aspects, must he appear to a benevolent one? When at ease with respect to exterior things, Captain Delano's nature was not only benign, but familiarly and humorously so. At home, he had often taken rare satisfaction in sitting in his door, watching some free man of color at his work or play. If on a voyage he chanced to have a black sailor, invariably he was on chatty and halfgamesome terms with him. In fact, like most men of a good, blithe heart, Captain Delano took to negroes, not philanthropically, but genially, just as other men to Newfoundland dogs. (212–3)

The first paragraph here sets out the general rule to which Babo's behavior will presently be applied. The next purports to explain Cereno's attachment to Babo, although the advocate/narrator here leaves a little wiggle room: "*it may be* something like the hypochondriac Benito Cereno" (emphasis mine). Of course, it is not the situation either that Cereno takes Babo to his heart, or for that matter that he is a hypochondriac, as the teller of the story clearly knows (unlike Delano who is genuinely, if unforgivably, deluded). Here is yet another of the red herrings thrown out by the narrator to encourage grave misreadings.

The narrator is a shadow figure in "Benito Cereno" who operates in the background, stirring the pot and adding murkiness that appears unnecessary to the plot (unless a crucial plot element is seen to be the creation of confusion, not just in Delano, but in the reader as well). As Eric Sundquist observes, the narrator plays a role of deception analogous to Babo's:

> We are as cunningly manipulated by the narrator as Benito Cereno is by Babo, to such an extent that the last tormenting image we are presented as Delano leaves the *San Dominick*, joined hand in hand with Cereno across the supporting and mediating figure of "the black's body," is appropriate as well to the tenuous relationship between the reader and Delano, joined but separated by the conspiring voice of the narrator exercising his authority in the very act of holding it in abeyance. (151)

The narrator fosters or even forces on the reader an identification with Delano, perhaps because Delano is a rather unappealing character when viewed on his own merits, through his own words.

"Left to the Wise": "Benito Cereno's" Contradictory Construction of the Reader

Melville opens his story by setting up the expectation that the reader should be wise and discerning, able to see beyond the allegedly innocent interpretations of Delano. Yet, as we have seen, tremendous narrative energy goes toward thwarting that "wise" reader, toward encouraging the reader to fill a subject position perilously close to Delano's. It is, of course, possible to argue that herein lies the challenge of the text; actual readers must be astute enough to resist the "temptations" of racism and struggle to stave off the

seductions of the narrator and Delano's self-serving misinterpretations. This reading, however, cannot fully account for the persuasive narrative voice; in this reading, Melville appears difficult simply for the sake of being difficult. However, the story ironically inscribes an ideal reader who will *not* initially get the story's full meaning. Usually when we use the term "ideal reader," it suggests a reader who fully apprehends what the text is about, "gets it" in all its complexity.[3] Instead, "Benito Cereno" structures and encourages misreadings so that the eventual discovery that one has been duped has the effect of revealing to the reader his or her complicity with Delano's most egregious and self-serving assumptions.

The emphasis "Benito Cereno" places on drawing in the reader places it in dialogue with the contemporary sentimental novel, albeit ironically. One of the principal narrative strategies of women's sentimental fiction, immensely popular at the time, was the structuring of emotional identification between the reader and the characters within a text. Melville references this tradition, borrows some of its strategies, but turns them ironic by betraying the reader who has entered this narrative compact and been willing to invest in it.

The play of narrative strategies within "Benito Cereno" can be made visible through the categories of "engaging" and "distancing" narrators that Robyn Warhol outlines in her study, *Gendered Interventions: Narrative Discourse in the Victorian Novel*. Warhol sets out two primary and opposing modes of narration, which tend to divide along gendered lines. Distancing narration is essentially ironic; the actual reader understands, or is strongly encouraged to understand, that he or she is not expected to identify with the narratee, the figure within the text who is the recipient of the narration. In engaging narration, on the other hand, all efforts are made to persuade the actual reader to occupy the position set out for the reader within the text. Warhol focuses on instances of direct address in defining the oppositional personas of engaging and distancing narrators, but the concept is a useful one beyond cases of direct address.

Although the narrator of "Benito Cereno" never addresses the reader as "you," the narrative pressure Melville's narrator puts on the reader implies an "engaging" text. What "Benito Cereno" does that is different from texts with either a clearly engaging or distancing narrator is blur the approaches, thus setting up the reader by forcing an engagement that is ultimately inappropriate. "Benito Cereno" borrows from sentimental narration its technique of structuring reader identification—the implicit assertion, "we all know this to be true," that modern readers tend to find annoying about sentimental narration—and turns it on its head. Readers' willingness to trust and agree with the narrator is their ultimate undoing. What both engaging and distancing forms of narration have in common is their secure situating of the reader; the reader understands that the expectation is either ironic resistance to, or honest identification with, the narratee's subjectivity. "Benito Cereno" withholds—or more precisely offers and then undercuts—that secure positionality for the reader, and is, thus, more confrontational toward its readers than texts that are clearly either distancing or engaging.

The possibility of reading "Benito Cereno" as in ironic dialogue with sentimental literature, particularly *Uncle Tom's Cabin,* has been recently observed by Sarah Robbins in her essay, "Gendering the History of the Antislavery Narrative." Robbins describes what she sees as an "appropriation of Stowe's familiar sentimental markers for a multi-layered ironic critique" (555). Through examining the serial publications within which both Stowe and Melville's fictions first appeared, Robbins establishes the clearly gendered conventions of *The National Era* and *Putnam's Monthly Magazine.* She argues that Melville's response to Stowe through "Benito Cereno" was part of an ongoing attack by male writers on the popular conventions of the female sentimental novel. Robbins contextualization of the publication of the two works is invaluable, as is her recognition of the extent to which Melville's story engages Stowe's; however, the ironic engagement is not constituted solely, or even primarily, through contrast between Melville and Stowe's narrative approaches, but through Melville's use, disingenuous as it is, of Stowe's narrative strategies.

Robbins views Melville's narrative approach as definitively what Warhol would describe as distancing, which is clearly and unambiguously ironic. She claims the narrator neglects to give the reader the kind of interpretive direction that is a defining characteristic of sentimental discourse.

> To keep his reader at the distance necessary for this manly critique, Melville used a narrative voice far less directive than Stowe's instructive maternal one. In her text, the frequently intruding female narrator provided a moral focus complementing those of properly "domesticated" characters . . . In Melville's tale, on the other hand, the reader was first cast adrift amid the muddled musings of the naïve captain, whose version of reality was only gradually problematized by the many verbal and physical hints of trouble he ignored . . . Unlike the explicit teacher-to-reader voices of domestic didactic authors . . . in other words, Melville's antislavery narrative pushed his readers to do their own interpreting. (553–4)

Melville's narrator is certainly not instructive in a positive way; most times the narrator's gloss on events is fundamentally misleading, as I demonstrated earlier. Delano is unquestionably muddled and unable to give the reader useful direction. However, the narrative does not push readers to do their own interpreting; in fact, it makes it very difficult for them to do so. If "Benito Cereno" encourages critical distance on Delano, why is critical distance so hard to achieve? Robbins addresses this problem in a footnote when she suggests that perhaps critics have been unable to distance themselves from Delano's perspective because they underestimate the ability of *Putnam's* readers to appreciate irony. However, few of "Benito Cereno's" critics have taken a reader-response approach to the text, which would thus privilege the readings of Melville's contemporaries. The narrator of "Benito Cereno" *does* provide a "moral focus," but it is the *wrong* moral focus.

The structuring of a reader's response is a central feature of antebellum sentimental literature. As I have argued at length elsewhere, Stowe's rhetorical strategy in *Uncle Tom's Cabin* depends on connections made between the emotional lives of readers and characters, particularly the slave characters, who are thus humanized through the analogy.[4] The limitations of an antislavery appeal premised on the argument that "they" are just like "us" are obvious, but there is another potentially dangerous outcome: emotional responses may be negative. An approach that privileges the reader's emotions presupposes of necessity that emotional identification is positive and will lead to greater apprehension of common humanity. Women's sentimental fiction in general (and *Uncle Tom's Cabin* in particular) grants great power to the realm of emotions, positing it as free from the manipulations that corrupt most discourse. This leap of faith is one which Melville is decidedly unwilling to make. His narrative structures emotional identification, but the emotions thus accessed consist of self-congratulatory complacency and dehumanizing condescension.

Melville does not, however, merely repudiate the "feminized" or "naïve" rhetoric of sentimentality. I believe that the final irony of "Benito Cereno" is the extent to which it borrows and extends the rhetorical strategy of targeting the reader, "getting under the skin," in order to make a powerful antislavery argument. Melville's reader may feel betrayed and misused, rather than encouraged and flattered like Stowe's, but there remains tremendous potential for the narrative integration of the inscribed reader to effect a strong reaction in the actual reader. We are as likely to feel bemused with Delano as to cry with Little Eva, and the power of the two narratives depends equally on their ability to get us to do so. Both texts leave the reader with the question, "how is this about me?" In the period following the passage of the Fugitive Slave Law, which sparked the writing of both texts, the issue of individual conscience was particularly timely. If the creation of Delano suggests that Melville was singularly pessimistic about the general state of the Northern American conscience, the appeal to the reader, coded and obscure as it is, and the power of the irony, deferred as its discovery may be, points to an appeal as intense as Stowe's, although one is opaque rather than transparent, contorted rather than straightforward.

Notes

1. Two classic texts of American literary criticism, Matthiessen's *American Renaissance* and Fiedler's *Love and Death in the American Novel*, both contain such misreadings of "Benito Cereno." For a more extended discussion of early readings of Delano, see Dillingham.
2. See McLamore (42).
3. For a brief definition of the concept of the ideal reader, see Gerald Prince's "Introduction to the Study of the Narratee." Prince claims that "an ideal reader would be one who would understand perfectly and would approve entirely the least of his words, the most subtle of his intentions" (9).
4. See "'The Magic of the Real Presence of Distress'" (15–18, 29–35 *et passim*). For a more general discussion of sentimentality in *Uncle Tom's Cabin*, see Jane Tompkins's *Sensational Designs*.

Works Cited

Dillingham, William B. *Melville's Short Fiction.* Athens: U of Georgia P, 1977.

Fiedler, Leslie. *Love and Death in the American Novel.* New York: Criterion Books, 1960.

Haegert, John. "Voicing Slavery Through Silence: Narrative Mutiny in Melville's *Benito Cereno. Mosaic* 26 (1993): 21–38.

Kavanaugh, James. "'That Hive of Subtlety': 'Benito Cereno' and the Liberal Hero." *Ideology and Classic American Literature.* Ed. Sacvan Bercovitch and Myra Jehlen. New York: Cambridge UP, 1986. 352–83.

Matthiessen, F. O. *American Renaissance: Art and Expression in the Age of Emerson and Whitman.* New York: Oxford UP, 1941.

McLamore, Richard. "Narrative Self-Justification: Melville and Amasa Delano." *Studies in American Fiction* 23 (1995): 35–53.

Melville, Herman. "Benito Cereno." *Billy Budd and Other Stories.* New York: Penguin, 1986.

O'Connell, Catharine. "'The Magic of the Real Presence of Distress': Sentimentality and Competing Rhetorics of Authority." *The Stowe Debate: Rhetorical Strategies in Uncle Tom's Cabin.* Ed. Mason Lowance, Jr., *et al.* Amherst: U of Massachusetts P, 1994. 13–36.

Pahl, Dennis. "The Gaze of History in 'Benito Cereno.'" *Studies in Short fiction,* 32 (1995): 171–83.

Prince, Gerald. "Introduction to the Study of the Narratee." *Reader-Response Criticism.* Ed. Jane Tompkins. Baltimore: Johns Hopkins UP, 1980.

Reiss, Benjamin. "Madness and Mastery in Melville's 'Benito Cereno.'" *Criticism* 38 (1996): 115–50.

Robbins, Sarah. "Gendering the History of the Antislavery Narrative: Juxtaposing Uncle Tom's Cabin and Benito Cereno, Beloved and Middle Passage." *American Quarterly* 49 (1997): 531–73.

Sundquist, Eric. *To Wake the Nations: Race in the Making of American Literature.* Cambridge: Harvard UP, 1993.

Tompkins, Jane. *Sensational Designs: The Cultural Work of American Fiction 1790–1860.* New York: Oxford UP, 1985.

Warhol, Robyn. *Gendered Interventions: Narrative Discourse in the Victorian Novel.* New Brunswick, NJ: Rutgers UP, 1989.

APPLICATION

In his essay on The Tempest, *Ole Skilleås suggests that audiences divided by a gap of centuries may have quite different responses. Annette Kolodny makes a similar case for the gender gap. Taking as her starting point Harold Bloom's version of intertextual reading, Kolodny objects that this account overlooks the fact that all interpretive strategies are "learned, historically determined, and thereby necessarily gender-inflected." What happens, she asks, to meanings "wandering around between texts" when we have two different groups of texts and two different groups of readers? This, she claims, was the situation when "The Yellow Wallpaper" appeared at the end of the nineteenth century, and Kolodny offers Gilman's work both as a story whose reception illustrates the politics of reading and as a story about the politics of reading. "Gilman's story represents not so much an object for the recurrent misreadings, or misprisions, of readers and critics (though this, of course, continues to occur) as an exploration, within itself, of the gender-inflected interpretive strategies responsible for our mutual misreadings, and even horrific misprisions, across sex lines. If neither male nor female reading audiences were prepared to decode properly 'The Yellow Wallpaper,' even less, Gilman understood, were they prepared to comprehend one another." Moving from Gilman's era to our own, Kolodny notes that Iser and others have begun to pay attention to the "meaning-making role of the reader," but laments that these critics "still manage so resolutely to ignore" the "crucial importance of the sex of the interpreter." Nevertheless Kolodny finds in the increasing availability of texts like "The Yellow Wallpaper" some cause to hope that a shared tradition is developing. The result must be a profound revision of the "canon" and with it a revision of our sensibilities. "Looked at this way, feminist appeals to revisionary reading . . . offer us all a potential enhancing of our capacity to read the world, our literary texts, and even one another, anew."*

A Map for Rereading: Or, Gender and the Interpretation of Literary Texts

Annette Kolodny

Reprinted by permission of the Johns Hopkins University Press from *New Literary History* 11:3 (1980): 451–67. Copyright 1980 by the University of Virginia.

Appealing particularly to a generation still in the process of divorcing itself from the New Critics' habit of bracketing off any text as an entity in itself, as though "it could be read, understood, and criticized entirely in its own terms,"[1] Harold Bloom has proposed a dialectical theory of influence between poets and poets, as well as between poems and poems which, in essence, does away with the static notion of a fixed or knowable text. As he argued in *A Map of Misreading* in 1975, "a poem is a response to a poem, as a poet is a response to a poet, or a person to his parent." Thus, for Bloom, "poems . . . are neither about 'subjects' nor about 'themselves.' They are necessarily about *other poems*."[2]

To read or to know a poem, according to Bloom, engages the reader in an attempt to map the psychodynamic relations by which the poet at hand has willfully misunderstood the work of some precursor (either single or composite) in order to correct, rewrite, or appropriate the prior poetic vision as his own. As first introduced in *The Anxiety of Influence* in 1973, the resultant "wholly different practical criticism . . . give[s] up the failed enterprise of seeking to 'understand' any single poem as an entity in itself" and "pursue[s] instead the quest of learning to read any poem as its poet's deliberate misinterpretation, *as a poet*, of a precursor poem or of poetry in general."[3] What one deciphers in the process of reading, then, is not any discrete entity but, rather, a complex relational event, "itself a synecdoche for a larger whole including other texts."[4] "Reading a text is necessarily the reading of a whole system of texts," Bloom explains in *Kabbalah and Criticism*, "and meaning is always wandering around between texts" (*KC*, pp. 107–8).

To help purchase assent for this "wholly different practical criticism," Bloom asserted an identity between critics and poets as coequal participants in the same "belated and all-but-impossible act" of reading (which, as he hastens to explain in *A Map of Misreading*, "if strong is always a misreading"—p. 3). As it is a drama of epic proportions, in Bloom's terms, when the ephebe poet attempts to appropriate and then correct a precursor's meaning, so, too, for the critic, his own inevitable misreadings or *misprisions* are no less heroic—nor any the less creative. "Poets' misinterpretations or poems" may be "more drastic than critics' misinterpretations or criticism," Bloom admits, but since he recognizes no such thing as "interpretations but only misinterpretations . . . all criticism" is

necessarily elevated to a species of "prose poetry" (*AI*, pp. 94–95). The critic's performance, thereby, takes place as one more "act of misprision [which] displaces an earlier act of misprision"—presumably the poet's or perhaps that of a prior critic; and, in this sense, the critic participates in that same act of "defensive warfare" before his own critical forebears, or even before the poet himself, as the poet presumably enacted before his poetic father/precursor (*KC*, pp. 125, 104, 108). Their legacy, whether as poetry or as "prose poetry" criticism, consequently establishes the strong survivors of these psychic battles as figures whom others, in the future, will need to overcome in their turn: "A poet is strong because poets after him must work to evade him. A critic is strong if his readings similarly provoke other readings."[5] It is unquestionably Bloom's most brilliant rhetorical stroke, persuading not so much by virtue of the logic of his argument as by the pleasure his (intended and mostly male) readership will take in the discovery that their own activity replicates the psychic adventures of The Poet, every critic's *figura* of heroism.[6]

What is left out of account, however, is the fact that whether we speak of poets and critics "reading" texts or writers "reading" (and thereby recording for us) the world, we are calling attention to interpretive strategies that are learned, historically determined, and thereby necessarily gender-inflected. As others have elsewhere questioned the adequacy of Bloom's paradigm of poetic influence to explain the production of poetry by women,[7] so now I propose to examine analogous limitations in his model for the reading—and hence critical—process (since both, after all, derive from his revisionist rendering of the Freudian family romance). To begin with, to locate that "meaning" which "is always wandering around between texts" (*KC*, pp. 107–8), Bloom assumes a community of readers (and, thereby, critics) who know that same "whole system of texts" within which the specific poet at hand has enacted his *misprision*. The canonical sense of a shared and coherent literary tradition is thereby essential to the utility of Bloom's paradigm of literary influence as well as to his notions of reading (and misreading). "What happens if one tries to write, or to teach, or to think or even to read without the sense of a tradition?" Bloom asks in *A Map of Misreading*. "Why," as he himself well understands, "nothing at all happens, just nothing. You cannot write or teach or think or even read without imitation, and what you imitate is what another person has done, that person's writing or teaching or thinking or reading. Your relation to what informs that person *is* tradition, for tradition is influence that extends past one generation, a carrying-over of influence" (*MM*, p. 32).

So long as the poems and poets he chooses for scrutiny participate in the "continuity that began in the sixth century B.C. when Homer first became a schoolbook for the Greeks" (*MM*, pp. 33–34), Bloom has a great deal to tell us about the carrying over of literary influence; where he must remain silent is where carrying over takes place among readers and writers who in fact have been, or at least have experienced themselves as, cut off and alien from that dominant tradition. Virginia Woolf made the distinction vividly over a half-century ago, in *A Room of One's Own,* when she described being barred entrance, because of her sex, to a "famous library" in which was housed, among others, a Milton manuscript. Cursing the "Oxbridge" edifice, "venerable and calm, with all its treasures safe locked within its breast," she returns to her room at the inn later that night, still pondering "how unpleasant it is to be locked out; and I thought how it is worse perhaps to be locked in; and, thinking of the safety and prosperity of the one sex and of the poverty and insecurity of the other and of the effect of tradition and of the lack of tradition upon the mind of a writer."[8] And, she might have added, on the mind of a reader as well. For while my main concern here is with reading (albeit largely and perhaps imperfectly defined), I think it worth noting that there exists an intimate interaction between readers and writers in and through which each defines for the other what s/he is about. "The effect . . . of the lack of tradition upon the mind of a writer" will communicate itself, in one way or another, to her readers; and, indeed, may respond to her readers' sense of exclusion from high (or highbrow) culture.

An American instance provides perhaps the best example. Delimited by the lack of formal or classical education, and constrained by the social and aesthetic norms of their day to conceptualizing "authorship as a profession rather than a calling, as work and not art,"[9] the vastly popular women novelists of the so-called feminine fifties often enough, and somewhat defensively, made a virtue of their sad necessities by invoking an audience of readers for whom aspirations to "literature" were as inappropriate as they were for the writer. As Nina Baym remarks in her recent study *Women's Fiction,* "often the women deliberately and even proudly disavowed membership in an artistic fraternity." "'Mine is a story for the table and arm-chair under the reading lamp in the livingroom, and not for the library shelves,'" Baym quotes Marion Harland from the introduction to Harland's autobiography; and then, at greater length, Baym cites Fanny Fern's dedicatory pages to her novel *Rose Clark:*

> When the frost curtains the windows, when the
> wind whistles fiercely at the key-hole, when
> the bright fire glows, and the tea-tray is removed,
> and father in his slippered feet lolls in his arm-
> chair; and mother with her nimble needle "makes
> auld claes look amaist as weel as new," and grand-
> mamma draws closer to the chimney-corner, and
> Tommy with his plate of chestnuts nestles content-
> edly at her feet; then let my unpretending story
> be read. For such an hour, for such an audience,
> was it written.
>
> Should any *dictionary on legs* rap inopportunely
> at the door for admittance, send him away to the
> groaning shelves of some musty library, where
> "literature" lies embalmed, with its stony eyes,
> fleshless joints, and ossified heart, in faultless
> preservation.[10]

If a bit overdone, prefaces like these nonetheless point up the self-consciousness with which writers like Fern and Harland perceived themselves as excluded from the dominant literary tradition and as writing for an audience of readers similarly excluded. To quote Baym again, these "women were expected to write specifically for their own sex and within the tradition of their woman's culture rather than within the Great Tradition. They never presented themselves as followers in the footsteps of Milton or Spenser."[11]

On the one hand, of course, increased literacy (if not substantially improved conditions of education) marked the generation of American women at mid-century, opening a vast market for a literature which would treat the contexts of their lives—the sewing circle rather than the whaling ship, the nursery instead of the lawyer's office—as functional symbols of the human condition.[12] On the other hand, while this vast new audience must certainly be credited with shaping the features of what then became popular women's fiction, it is also the case that the writers in their turn both responded to and helped to formulate their readers' tastes and habits. And both together, I would suggest, found this a means of accepting (or at least coping with) the barred entryway that was to distress Virginia Woolf so in the next century. But these facts of our literary history also suggest that from the 1850s on, in America at least, the meanings "wandering around between texts" were wandering around somewhat different groups of texts where male and female readers were concerned.[13] So that with the advent of women "who wished to be regarded as artists rather than careerists,"[14] toward the end of the nineteenth century, there arose the critical problem with which we are still plagued and which Bloom so determinedly ignores: the problem of reading any text as "a synecdoche for a larger whole including other texts" when that necessarily assumed "whole system of texts" in which it is embedded is foreign to one's reading knowledge.

The appearance of Kate Chopin's novel *The Awakening* in 1899, for example, perplexed readers familiar with her earlier (and intentionally "regional") short stories not so much because it turned away from themes or subject matter implicit in her earlier work, nor even less because it dealt with female sensuality and extramarital sexuality, but because her elaboration of those materials deviated radically from the accepted norms of women's fiction out of which her audience so largely derived its expectations. The nuances and consequences of passion and individual temperament, after all, fairly define the focus of most of her preceding fictions. "That the book is strong and that Miss Chopin has a keen knowledge of certain phases of feminine character will not be denied," wrote the anonymous reviewer for the Chicago *Times-Herald*. What marked an unacceptable "new departure" for this critic, then, was the impropriety of Chopin's focus on material previously edited out of the popular genteel novels by and about women which, somewhat inarticulately, s/he translated into the accusation that Chopin had "enter[ed] the overworked field of sex fiction."[15]

Charlotte Perkins Gilman's initial difficulty in seeing "The Yellow Wallpaper" into print repeated the problem, albeit in a somewhat different context: for her story located itself not as any deviation from a previous tradition of women's fiction but, instead, as a continuation of a genre popularized by Poe. And insofar as Americans had earlier learned to follow the fictive processes of aberrant perception and mental breakdown in *his* work, they should have provided Gilman, one would imagine, with a ready-made audience for *her* protagonist's progressively debilitating fantasies of entrapment and liberation. As they had entered popular fiction by the end of the nineteenth century, however, the linguistic markers for those processes were at once heavily male-gendered and highly idiosyncratic, having more to do with individual temperament than with social or cultural situations per se. As a result, it would appear that the reading strategies by which cracks in ancestral walls and suggestions of unchecked masculine willfulness were immediately noted as both symbolically and semantically relevant did not, for some reason, necessarily *carry over* to "the nursery at the top of the house" with its windows barred, nor even less to the forced submission of the woman who must "take great pains to control myself before" her physician husband.[16]

A reader today seeking meaning in the way Harold Bloom outlines that process might note, of course, a fleeting resemblance between the upstairs chamber in Gilman — with its bed nailed to the floor, its windows barred, and metal rings fixed to the walls — and Poe's evocation of the dungeon chambers of Toledo; in fact, a credible argument might be made for reading "The Yellow Wallpaper" as Gilman's willful and purposeful misprision of "The Pit and the Pendulum." Both stories, after all, involve a sane mind entrapped in an insanity-inducing situation. Gilman's "message" might then be that the equivalent revolution by which the speaking voice of the Poe tale is released to both sanity and freedom is unavailable to her heroine. No *deus ex machina*, no General Lasalle triumphantly entering the city, no "outstretched arm" to prevent Gilman's protagonist from falling into her own internal "abyss" is conceivable, given the rules of the social context in which Gilman's narrative is embedded. When gender is taken into account, then, so this interpretation would run, Gilman is saying that the nature of the trap envisioned must be understood as qualitatively different, and so too the possible escape routes.

Contemporary readers of "The Yellow Wallpaper," however, were apparently unprepared to make such connections. Those fond of Poe could not easily transfer their sense of mental derangement to the mind of a comfortable middle-class wife and mother;

and those for whom the woman in the home was a familiar literary character were hard-pressed to comprehend so extreme an anatomy of the psychic price she paid. Horace Scudder, the editor of *The Atlantic Monthly* who first rejected the story, wrote only that "I could not forgive myself if I made others as miserable as I have made myself!" (Hedges, p. 40). And even William Dean Howells, who found the story "chilling" and admired it sufficiently to reprint it in 1920, some twenty-eight years after its first publication (in *The New England Magazine* of May 1892), like most readers, either failed to notice or neglected to report "the connection between the insanity and the sex, or sexual role, of the victim" (Hedges, p. 41). For readers at the turn of the century, then, that "meaning" which "is always wandering around between texts" had as yet failed to find connective pathways linking the fanciers of Poe to the devotees of popular women's fiction, or the shortcut between Gilman's short story and the myriad published feminist analyses of the ills of society (some of them written by Gilman herself). Without such connective contexts, Poe continued as a well-traveled road, while Gilman's story, lacking the possibility of further influence, became a literary dead-end.

In one sense, by hinting at an audience of male readers as ill-equipped to follow the symbolic significance of the narrator's progressive breakdown as was her doctor-husband to diagnose properly the significance of his wife's fascination with the wallpaper's patternings; and by predicating a female readership as yet unprepared for texts which mirrored back, with symbolic exemplariness, certain patterns underlying their empirical reality, "The Yellow Wallpaper" anticipated its own reception. For insofar as writing and reading represent linguistically-based interpretive strategies—the first for the recording of a reality (that has, obviously, in a sense, already been "read") and the second for the deciphering of that recording (and thus also the further decoding of a prior imputed reality)—the wife's progressive descent into madness provides a kind of commentary upon, indeed is revealed in terms of, the sexual politics inherent in the manipulation of those strategies. We are presented at the outset with a protagonist who, ostensibly for her own good, is denied both activities and who, in the course of accommodating herself to that deprivation, comes more and more to experience her self as a text which can neither get read nor recorded.

In his doubly authoritative role as both husband and doctor, John not only appropriates the interpretive processes of reading—diagnosing his wife's illness and thereby selecting what may be understood of her "meaning"; reading to her, rather than allowing her to read for herself—but, as well, he determines what may get written and hence communicated. For her part, the protagonist avers, she does not agree with her husband's ideas: "Personally, I believe that congenial work, with excitement and change, would do me good." But given the fact of her marriage to "a physician of high standing" who "assures friends and relatives that there is really nothing the matter with one but temporary nervous depression—a slight hysterical tendency—what is one to do?" she asks. Since her husband (and by extension the rest of the world) will not heed what she says of herself, she attempts instead to communicate it to "this . . . dead paper . . . a great relief to my mind." But John's insistent opposition gradually erodes even this outlet for her since, as she admits, "it *does* exhaust me a good deal—having to be so sly about it, or else meet with heavy opposition" (p. 10). At the sound of his approach, following upon her first attempt to describe "those sprawling flamboyant patterns" in the wallpaper, she declares, "There comes John, and I must put this away,—he hates to have me write a word" (p. 13).

Successively isolated from conversational exchanges, prohibited free access to pen and paper, and thus increasingly denied what Jean Ricardou has called "the local exercise of syntax and vocabulary,"[17] the protagonist of "The Yellow Wallpaper" experiences the extreme extrapolation of those linguistic tools to the processes of perception and response. In fact, it follows directly upon a sequence in which: (1) she acknowledges that John's opposition to her writing has begun to make "the effort . . . greater than the relief"; (2) John refuses to let her "go and make a visit to Cousin Henry and Julia"; and (3) as a kind or punctuation mark to that denial, John carries her "upstairs and laid me on the bed, and sat by me and read to me till it tired my head." It is after these events, I repeat, that the narrator first makes out the dim shape lurking "behind the outside pattern" in the wallpaper: "it is like a woman stooping down and creeping" (pp. 21–22).

From that point on, the narrator progressively gives up the attempt to *record* her reality and instead begins to *read* it—as symbolically adumbrated in her compulsion to discover a consistent and coherent pattern amid "the sprawling outlines" of the wallpaper's apparently "pointless pattern" (pp. 20, 19). Selectively emphasizing one section of the pattern while repressing others, reorganizing and regrouping past impressions into newer, more fully realized configurations—as one might with any complex formal text—the speaking voice becomes obsessed with her quest for meaning, jealous even of her husband's or his sister's momentary interest in the paper. Having caught her sister-in-law "with her hand on it once," the narrator declares, "I know she was studying that pattern, and I am determined that nobody shall find it out but myself!" (p. 27). As the pattern changes with the changing light in the room, so too do her interpretations of it. And what is not quite so apparent by daylight becomes glaringly so at night: "At night in any kind of light, in twilight, candle light, lamplight, and worst of all by moonlight, it becomes bars! The outside pattern I mean, and the woman behind it is as plain as can be." "By daylight," in contrast (like the protagonist herself), "she is subdued, quiet" (p. 26).

As she becomes wholly taken up with the exercise of these interpretive strategies, so, too, she claims, her "life is very much more exciting now than it used to be. You see I have something more to expect, to look forward to, to watch" (p. 27). What she is watching, of course, is her own psyche writ large; and the closer she comes to "reading" in the wallpaper the underlying if unacknowledged patterns of her real-life experience, the less frequent becomes that delicate oscillation between surrender to or involvement in and the more distanced observation of developing meaning. Slowly but surely the narrative voice ceases to distinguish itself from the woman in the wallpaper pattern, finally asserting that "I don't want anybody to get that woman out at night but myself" (p. 31), and concluding with a confusion of pronouns that merges into a grammatical statement of identity:

> As soon as it was moonlight and that poor thing began to crawl and shake the pattern, I got up and ran to help her.
> *I* pulled and *she* shook, and *I* shook and *she* pulled, and before morning *we* had peeled off yards of that paper.   (p. 32, my italics)

She is, in a sense, now totally surrendered to what is quite literally her own text—or, rather, her self as text.

But in decoding its (or her) meaning, what she has succeeded in doing is discovering the symbolization of her own untenable and unacceptable reality. To escape that reality she attempts the destruction of the paper which seemingly encodes it: the pattern of bars entrapping the creeping woman. "'I've got out at last,' said I, 'in spite of you and Jane. I've pulled off most of the paper, so you can't put me back!'" (p. 36). Their paper pages may be torn and moldy (as is, in fact, the smelly wallpaper), but the meaning of texts is not so easily destroyed. Liberation here is liberation only into madness: for in decoding her own projections onto the paper, the protagonist had managed merely to reencode them once more, and now more firmly than ever, within.

With the last paragraphs of the story, John faints away—presumably in shock at his wife's now totally delusional state. He has repeatedly misdiagnosed, or misread, the heavily edited behavior with which his wife has presented herself to him; and never once has he divined what his wife sees in the wallpaper. But given his freedom to read (or, in this case, misread) books, people, and the world as he chooses, he is hardly forced to discover for himself so extreme a text. To exploit Bloom's often useful terminology once again, then, Gilman's story represents not so much an object for the recurrent misreadings, or misprisions, of readers and critics (though this, of course, continues to occur) as an exploration, within itself, of the gender-inflected interpretive strategies responsible for our mutual misreadings, and even horrific misprisions, across sex lines. If neither male nor female reading audiences were prepared to decode properly "The Yellow Wallpaper," even less, Gilman understood, were they prepared to comprehend one another.

It is unfortunate that Gilman's story was so quickly relegated to the backwaters of our literary landscape because, coming as it did at the end of the nineteenth century, it spoke to a growing concern among American women who would be serious writers: it spoke, that is, to their strong sense of writing out of nondominant or subcultural traditions (both literary and otherwise), coupled with an acute sensitivity to the fact that since women and men learn to read different worlds, different groups of texts are available to their reading and writing strategies. Had "The Yellow Wallpaper" been able to stand as a potential precursor for the generation of subsequent corrections and revisions, then, as in Bloom's paradigm, it might have made possible a form of fiction by women capable not only of commenting upon but even of overcoming that impasse. That it did not—nor did any other woman's fiction become canonical in the United States[18]—meant that, again and again, each woman who took up the pen had to confront anew her bleak premonition that, both as writers and as readers, women too easily became isolated islands of symbolic significance, available only to, and decipherable only by, one another.[19] If any Bloomian "meaning" wanders around between women's texts, therefore, it must be precisely this shared apprehension.

On the face of it such statements should appear nothing less than commonsensical, especially to those most recent theorists of reading who combine an increased attentiveness to the meaning-making role of the reader in the deciphering of texts with a recognition of the links between our "reading" of texts and our "reading" of the world and one another. Among them, Bloom himself seems quite clearly to understand this when, in *Kabbalah and Criticism,* he declares: "That which you are, that only can you read" (*KC,* p. 96). Extrapolating from his description of the processes involved in the reading of literary texts to a larger comment on our ability to take in or decipher those around us, Wolfgang Iser has lately theorized that "we can only make someone else's thought into an absorbing theme for ourselves, provided the virtual background of our own personality can adapt to it."[20] Anticipating such pronouncements in almost everything they have been composing for over a hundred years now, the women who wrote fiction, most especially, translated these observations into the structures of their stories by invoking that single feature which critics like Iser and Bloom still manage so resolutely to ignore: and that is, the crucial importance of the *sex* of the "interpreter" in that process which Nelly Furman has called "the active attribution of significance to formal signifiers."[21] Antedating both Bloom and Iser by over fifty years, for example, Susan Keating Glaspell's 1917 short story "A Jury of Her Peers" explores the necessary (but generally ignored) gender marking which *must* constitute any definition of "peers" in the complex process of unraveling truth or meaning.[22]

The opening paragraph of Glaspell's story serves, essentially, to alert the reader to the significations to follow: Martha Hale, interrupted at her kitchen chores, must drop "everything right where it was" in order to hurry off with her husband and the others. In so doing, "her eye made a scandalized sweep of her kitchen," noting with distress "that her kitchen was in no shape for leaving: her bread all ready for mixing, half the flour sifted and half unsifted." The point, of course, is that highly unusual circumstances demand this of her, and "it was no ordinary thing that called her away." When she seats herself "in the big two-seated buggy" alongside her impatient farmer husband, the sheriff and his wife, and the county attorney, the story proper begins.

All five drive to a neighboring farm where a murder has been committed—the farmer strangled, his wife already arrested. The men intend to seek clues to the motive for the crime, while the women are, ostensibly, simply to gather together the few necessities required by the wife incarcerated in the town jail. Immediately upon approaching the place, however, the very act of perception becomes sex-coded: the men look at the house only to talk "about what had happened," while the women note the geographical topography which makes it, repeatedly in the narrative, "a lonesome-looking place." Once inside, the men "'go upstairs first—then out to the barn and around there'" in their search for clues (even though the actual crime took place in the upstairs master bedroom), while the women are left to the kitchen and parlor. Convinced as they are of "the insignificance of kitchen things," the men cannot properly attend to what these might reveal and, instead, seek elsewhere for "'a clue to the motive,'" so necessary if the county attorney is to make his case. Indeed, it is the peculiar irony of the story that although the men never question their attribution of guilt to Minnie Foster, they nonetheless cannot meaningfully interpret this farm wife's world—her kitchen and parlor. And, arrogantly certain that the women would not even "'know a clue if they did come upon it,'" they thereby leave the discovery of the clues, and the consequent unraveling of the motive, to those who do, in fact, command the proper interpretive strategies.

Exploiting the information sketched into the opening, Glaspell has the neighbor, Mrs. Hale, and the sheriff's wife, Mrs. Peters, note, among the supposedly insignificant kitchen things, the unusual, and on a farm unlikely, remnants of kitchen chores left "half done," denoting an interruption of some serious nature. Additionally, where the men could discern no signs of "'anger—or sudden feeling'" to substantiate a motive, the women comprehend the implications of some "fine, even sewing" gone suddenly awry, "'as if she didn't know what she was about!'" Finally, of course, the very drabness of the house, the miserliness of the husband to which it attests, the old and broken stove, the patchwork that has become Minnie Foster's wardrobe—all these make the women uncomfortably aware that to acknowledge fully the meaning of what they are seeing is "'to get her own house to turn against her!'" Discovery by discovery, they destroy the mounting evidence—evidence which the men, at any rate, cannot recognize as such; and, sealing the bond between them as conspirators in saving Minnie Foster, they hide from the men the canary with its neck broken, the penultimate clue to the strangling of a husband who had so systematically destroyed all life, beauty, and music in his wife's environment.

Opposing against one another male and female realms of meaning and activity—the barn and the kitchen—Glaspell's narrative not only invites a semiotic analysis but, indeed, performs that analysis for us. If the absent Minnie Foster is the "transmitter" or "sender" in this schema, then only the women are competent "receivers" or "readers" of her "message," since they alone share not only her context (the supposed insignificance of kitchen things) but, as a result, the conceptual patterns which make up her world. To those outside the shared systems of quilting and knotting, roller towels and bad stoves, with all their symbolic significations, these may appear trivial, even irrelevant to meaning; but to those within the system, they comprise the totality of the message: in this case, a reordering of who in fact has been murdered and, with that, what has constituted the real crime in the story.

For while the two women who visit Minnie Foster's house slowly but surely decipher the symbolic significance of her action—causing her husband's neck to be broken because he had earlier broken her canary's neck—the narrative itself functions, for the reader, as a further decoding of what that symbolic action says about itself. The essential crime in the story, we come to realize, has been the husband's inexorable strangulation, over the years, of Minnie Foster's spirit and personality; and the culpable criminality is the complicity of the women who had permitted the isolation and the loneliness to dominate Minnie Foster's existence: "'I wish I had come over to see Minnie Foster sometimes,'" declares her neighbor guiltily. "'I can see now—' She did not put it into words."

"I wish you'd seen Minnie Foster," [says Mrs. Hale to the sheriff's wife] "when she wore a white dress with blue ribbons, and stood up there in the choir and sang."

The picture of that girl, the fact that she had lived neighbor to that girl for twenty years, and had let her die for lack of life, was suddenly more than she could bear.

"Oh, I *wish* I'd come over here once in a while!" she cried. "That was a crime! That was a crime! Who's going to punish that?"

The recognition is itself, of course, a kind of punishment. With it comes, as well, another recognition, as Mrs. Peters reveals experiences in her own life of analogous isolation, desperate loneliness, and brutality at the hands of a male. Finally they conclude: "'We all go through the same things—it's all just a different kind of the same thing! If it weren't—why do you and I *understand?* Why do we *know*—what we know this minute?'" By this point the narrative emphasis has shifted: To understand why it is that they know what they now know is for these women to recognize the profoundly sex-linked world of meaning which they inhabit; to discover how specialized is their ability to read that world is to discover anew their own shared isolation within it.

While neither the Gilman nor the Glaspell story necessarily excludes the male as reader—indeed, both in a way are directed specifically at educating him to become a better reader—they do, nonetheless, insist that, however inadvertently, he is a *different kind* of reader and that, where women are concerned, he is often an inadequate reader. In the first instance, because the husband cannot properly diagnose his wife or attend to her reality, the result is horrific: the wife descends into madness. In the second, because the men cannot even recognize as such the very clues for which they search, the ending is a happy one: Minnie Foster is to be set free, no motive having been discovered by which to prosecute her. In both, however, the same point is being made: lacking familiarity with the women's imaginative universe, that universe within which their acts are signs,[23] the men in these stories can neither read nor comprehend the meanings of the women closest to them—and this in spite of the apparent sharing of a common language. It is, in short, a fictive rendering of the dilemma of the woman writer. For while we may all agree that in our daily conversational exchanges men and women speak more or less meaningfully and effectively with one another, thus fostering the illusion of a wholly shared common language, it is also the case that where figurative usage is involved—that usage which often enough marks the highly specialized language of literature—it "can be inaccessible to all but those who share information about one another's knowledge, beliefs, intentions, and attitudes."[24] Symbolic representations, in other words, depend on a fund of shared recognitions and potential inference. For their intended impact to *take hold* in the reader's imagination, the author simply must, like Minnie Foster, be able to call upon a shared context with her audience; where she cannot, or dare not, she may revert to silence, to the imitation of male forms, or, like the narrator in "The Yellow Wallpaper," to total withdrawal and isolation into madness.

It may be objected, of course, that I have somewhat stretched my argument so as to conflate (or perhaps confuse?) *all* interpretive strategies with language processes, specifically *reading*. But in each instance, it is the survival of the *woman as text*—Gilman's narrator and Glaspell's Minnie Foster—that is at stake; and the competence of her reading audience alone determines the outcome. Thus, in my view, both stories intentionally function as highly specialized language acts (called "literature") which examine the difficulty inherent in deciphering other highly specialized realms of meaning—in this case, women's conceptual and symbolic worlds. And further, the intended emphasis in each is the inaccessibility of female meaning to male interpretation.[25] The fact that in recent years each story has increasingly found its way into easily available textbooks, and hence into the Women's Studies and American Literature classroom, to be read and enjoyed by teachers and students of both sexes happily suggests that their fictive premises are attributable not so much to necessity as to contingency.[26] Men can, after all, learn to apprehend the meanings encoded in texts by and about women—just as women have learned to become sensitive readers of Shakespeare and Milton, Hemingway and Mailer.[27] Both stories function, in effect, as a prod to that very process by alerting the reader to the fundamental problem of "reading" correctly within cohabiting but differently structured conceptual worlds.

To take seriously the implications of such relearned reading strategies is to acknowledge that we are embarking upon a revisionist rereading of our entire literary inheritance and, in that process, demonstrating the full applicability of Bloom's sec-

ond formula for canon-formation, "You are or become what you read" (*KC*, p. 96). To set ourselves the task of learning to read a wholly different set of texts will make of us different kinds of readers (and perhaps different kinds of people as well). But to set ourselves the task of doing this in a public way, on behalf of women's texts specifically, engages us—as the feminists among us have learned—in a challenge to the inevitable issue of "*authority* . . . in all questions of canon-formation" (*KC*, p. 100). It places us, in a sense, in a position analogous to that of the narrator of "The Yellow Wallpaper," bound, if we are to survive, to challenge the (accepted and generally male) authority who has traditionally wielded the power to determine what may be written and how it shall be read. It challenges fundamentally not only the shape of our canon of major American authors but, indeed, that very "continuity that began in the sixth century B.C. when Homer first became a schoolbook for the Greeks" (*MM*, pp. 33–34).

It is no mere coincidence, therefore, that readers as diverse as Adrienne Rich and Harold Bloom have arrived by various routes at the conclusion that *revision* constitutes the key to an ongoing literary history. Whether functioning as ephebe/poet or would-be critic, Bloom's reader, as "revisionist," "strives to *see* again, so as to esteem and *estimate* differently, so as then to *aim* "correctly'" (*MM*, p. 4). For Rich, "revision" entails "the act of looking back, of seeing with fresh eyes, of entering an old text from a new critical direction."[28] And each, as a result—though from different motives—strives to make the "literary tradition . . . the captive of the revisionary impulse" (*MM*, p. 36). What Rich and other feminist critics intended by that "re-visionism" has been the subject of this essay: not only would such revisionary rereading open new avenues for comprehending male texts but, as I have argued here, it would, as well, allow us to appreciate the variety of women's literary expression, enabling us to take it into serious account for perhaps the first time rather than, as we do now, writing it off as caprice or exception, the irregularity in an otherwise regular design. Looked at this way, feminist appeals to revisionary rereading, as opposed to Bloom's, offer us all a potential enhancing of our capacity to read the world, our literary texts, and even one another, anew.

To end where I began, then, Bloom's paradigm of poetic history, when applied to women, proves useful only in a negative sense: for by omitting the possibility of poet/mothers from his psychodynamic of literary influence (allowing the feminine only the role of Muse—as composite whore and mother), Bloom effectively masks the fact of an *other* tradition entirely—that in which women taught one another how to read and write about and out of their own unique (and sometimes isolated) contexts. In so doing, however, he points up not only the ignorance informing our literary history as it is currently taught in the schools, but, as well, he pinpoints (however unwittingly) what must be done to change our skewed perceptions: all readers, male and female alike, must be taught first to recognize the existence of a significant body of writing by women in America and, second, they must be encouraged to learn how to read it within its own unique and informing contexts of meaning and symbol. *Re-visionary rereading,* if you will. No more must we impose on future generations of readers the inevitability of Norman Mailer's "terrible confession . . .—I have nothing to say about any of the talented women who write today. I do not seem able to read them."[29] Nor should Bloom himself continue to suffer an inability to express useful "judgment upon . . . the 'literature of Women's Liberation.'"[30]

Notes

1. Albert William Levi, "*De Interpretatione:* Cognition and Context in the History of Ideas," *Critical Inquiry,* 3, No. 1 (Autumn 1976), 164.
5. Harold Bloom, *A Map of Misreading* (New York, 1975), p. 18 (hereafter cited as *MM*).
3. Bloom, *The Anxiety of Influence: A Theory of Poetry* (New York, 1973), p. 43 (hereafter cited as *AI*).
4. Bloom, *Kabbalah and Criticism* (New York, 1975), p. 106 (hereafter cited as *KC*). The concept is further refined in his *Poetry and Repression: Revisionism from Blake to Stevens* (New Haven, 1976), p. 26, where Bloom describes poems as "defensive processes in constant change, which is to say that poems themselves are *acts of reading.* A poem is a fierce, proleptic debate *with itself,* as well as with precursor poems."
5. *KC*, p. 125; by way of example, and with a kind of Apollonian modesty, Bloom demonstrates his own propensities for misreading, placing himself amid the excellent company of those other Super Misreaders, Blake, Shelley, C. S. Lewis, Charles Williams, and T. S. Eliot (all of whom misread Milton's Satan), and only regrets the fact "that the misreading of Blake and Shelley by Yeats is a lot

stronger than the misreading of Blake and Shelley by Bloom" (pp. 125–26).
6. In *Poetry and Repression,* p. 18, Bloom explains that "by 'reading' I intend to mean the work both of poet and of critic, who themselves move from dialectic irony to synecdochal representation as they confront the text before them."
7. See, for example, Joanne Feit Diehl's attempt to adapt the Bloomian model to the psychodynamics of women's poetic production in "'Come Slowly—Eden': An Exploration of Women Poets and Their Muse," *Signs,* 3, No. 3 (Spring 1978), 572–87; and the objections to that adaptation raised by Lillian Faderman and Louise Bernikow in their Comments, *Signs,* 4, No. 1 (Autumn 1978), 188–91 and 191–95, respectively. More recently, Sandra M. Gilbert and Susan Gubar have tried to correct the omission of women writers from Bloom's male-centered literary history in *The Madwoman in the Attic: The Woman Writer and the Nineteenth-Century Literary Imagination* (New Haven, 1979).
8. Virginia Woolf, *A Room of One's Own* (1928; rpt. Harmondsworth, 1972), pp. 9–10, 25–26.
9. Nina Baym, *Woman's Fiction: A Guide to Novels By and About Women in America 1820–1870* (Ithaca, 1978), p. 32.
10. See Baym, *Woman's Fiction,* pp. 32–33.
11. Ibid., p. 178.
12. I paraphrase rather freely here from some of Baym's acutely perceptive and highly suggestive remarks, p. 14.
13. The problem of audience is complicated by the fact that in nineteenth-century America distinct classes of so-called highbrow and lowbrow readers were emerging cutting across sex and class lines; and, for each sex, distinctly separate "serious" and "popular" reading materials were also being marketed. Full discussion, however, is beyond the scope of this essay. In its stead, I direct the reader to Henry Nash Smith's clear and concise summation in the introductory chapter to his *Democracy and the Novel: Popular Resistance to Classic American Writers* (New York, 1978), pp. 1–15.
14. Baym, p. 178.
15. From "Books of the Day," Chicago *Times-Herald* (1 June 1899), p. 9; excerpted in Kate Chopin, *The Awakening,* ed. Margaret Culley (New York, 1976), p. 149.
16. Charlotte Perkins Gilman, *The Yellow Wallpaper,* with Afterword by Elaine R. Hedges (New

1973), pp. 12, 11. Page references to this edition will henceforth be cited parenthetically in the text, with references to Hedges's excellent Afterword preceded by her name.

17. Jean Ricardou, "Composition Discomposed," tr. Erica Freiberg, *Critical Inquiry*, 3, No. 1 (Autumn 1976), 90.

18. The possible exception here is Harriet Beecher Stowe's *Uncle Tom's Cabin; or, Life Among the Lowly* (1852).

19. If, to some of the separatist advocates in our current wave of New Feminism, this sounds like a wholly acceptable, even happy circumstance, we must nonetheless understand that, for earlier generations of women artists, acceptance within male precincts conferred the mutually understood marks of success and, in some quarters, vitally needed access to publishing houses, serious critical attention, and even financial independence. That this was *not* the case for the writers of domestic fictions around the middle of the nineteenth century was a fortunate but anomalous circumstance. Insofar as our artist-mothers were separatist, therefore, it was the result of impinging cultural contexts and not (often) of their own choosing.

20. Wolfgang Iser, *The Implied Reader: Patterns of Communication in Prose Fiction from Bunyan to Beckett* (Baltimore, 1974), p. 293.

21. Nelly Furman, "The Study of Woman and Language: Comment on Vol. 3, No. 3," *Signs*, 4, No. 1 (Autumn 1978), 184.

22. First published in *Every Week* (15 March 1917), the story was then collected in *Best Short Stories of 1917*, ed. Edward O'Brien (London, 1917). My source for the text is Mary Anne Ferguson's *Images of Women in Literature* (Boston, 1973), pp. 370–85; for some reason the story was dropped from Ferguson's 1975 revised edition but, as will be indicated below, it is elsewhere collected. Since there are no textual difficulties involved, I have omitted page references to any specific reprinting.

23. I here paraphrase Clifford Geertz, *The Interpretation of Cultures* (New York, 1973), p. 13, and specifically direct the reader to the parable from Wittgenstein quoted on that same page.

24. Ted Cohen, "Metaphor and the Cultivation of Intimacy," *Critical Inquiry*, 5, No. 1 (Autumn 1978), 78.

25. It is significant, I think, that the stories do not suggest any difficulty for the women in apprehending the men's meanings. On the one hand this simply is not relevant to either plot; and on the other, since in each narrative the men clearly control the public realms of discourse, it would, of course, have been incumbent upon the women to learn to understand them. Though masters need not learn the language of their slaves, the reverse is never the case: for survival's sake, oppressed or subdominant groups always study the nuances of meaning and gesture in those who control them.

26. For example, Gilman's "The Yellow Wallpaper" may be found, in addition to the Feminist Press reprinting previously cited, in *The Oven Birds: American Women on Womanhood, 1820–1920*, ed. Gail Parker (Garden City, 1972), pp. 317–34; and Glaspell's "A Jury of Her Peers" is reprinted in *American Voices, American Women*, ed. Lee R. Edwards and Arlyn Diamond (New York, 1973), pp. 359–81.

27. That women may have paid a high psychological and emotional price for their ability to read men's texts is beyond the scope of this essay, but I enthusiastically direct the reader to Judith Fetterley's provocative study of the problem in her *The Resisting Reader: A Feminist Approach to American Fiction* (Bloomington, 1978).

28. Adrienne Rich, "When We Dead Awaken: Writing as Re-Vision," *College English*, 34, No. 1 (October 1972), 18; rpt. in *Adrienne Rich's Poetry*, ed. Barbara Charlesworth Gelpi and Albert Gelpi (New York, 1975), p. 90.

29. Norman Mailer, "Evaluations—Quick and Expensive Comments on the Talent in the Room," collected in his *Advertisements for Myself* (New York, 1966), pp. 434–35.

30. *MM*, p. 36. What precisely Bloom intends by the phrase is nowhere made clear; for the purposes of this essay, I have assumed that he is referring to the recently increased publication of new titles by women writers.

CHAPTER FOUR

Mimetic Criticism: Reality as Context

First follow NATURE, *and your Judgment frame*
By her just Standard, which is still the same

—Pope, *An Essay on Criticism*

We saw in a previous section how formal critics often come to locate part of the poem's value in its ability to represent the world. Despite this mimetic drift, formalists deserve their name because their theory emphasizes that fitting of the parts to the whole that produces a coherent poem. A theory that emphasizes instead the correspondence of the poem to external reality is more properly called "mimetic." Critics who adopt such a theory join the great tradition in Western literary criticism. Among the ancients, the idea that literature was mimetic was not so much an argued conclusion as it was the unchallenged premise on which all arguments were built. And with few exceptions that premise continued to control discussions of literature well into the eighteenth century. Even when historical concerns began to dominate the academic study of literature, these concerns were not seen as opposing mimetic criticism. It was assumed that great literature revealed truth; this was what justified interest in its author and the circumstances of its creation. On this point, the academic critic and the common reader often agreed, and the mimetic value terms are at once the most venerable and the most popular. For many readers, words like "real," "true," and "lifelike" are assumed to name incontestable literary values.

This assumption is illustrated in censorship controversies and even court cases where the prosecution is likely to argue the affective line that the work in question, in its language or the actions it portrays, has a harmful effect on its audience, while the defense may respond with the mimetic argument that the work gives an accurate picture of reality. After all, people say and do such things, and the author is simply reporting the facts of life. Thus, one side appeals to goodness, the other to truth. (Very seldom do such cases admit an appeal to beauty.) For mimeticists, though, truth is a higher good. And sometimes their argument wins. The famous decision that allowed James Joyce's *Ulysses* to be sold in the United States, for example, justified the work in part as an honest and accurate portrait of middle-class

Dubliners at the turn of the century. Those who objected to the book's "too poignant preoccupation with sex" were reminded that Joyce's "locale was Celtic and his season Spring."

This commitment to "realism" is also reflected in our tendency to claim a mimetic justification for changes in literary fashions and conventions. As drama, for instance, dropped the use of meter and adopted "natural" speech and carefully detailed settings and costumes to portray contemporary bourgeois characters, each development was hailed as making drama more "realistic." Yet Chekhov, for one, looked on plays that employed all these devices as "unrealistic" in their presentation of well-made plots and of characters who could concentrate their attention on a single theme or follow the thread of a complex conversation. In the name of realism, he introduced the meandering dialogue, the "irrelevant" remark, and with these mimetic devices he anticipated some of the conventions of the "theater of the absurd," conventions that are in turn defended as "true to life." Similarly, techniques of modern prose fiction such as the stream of consciousness or the rigorously limited point of view have usually been explained as attempts to portray reality more accurately. That one generation's realistic device should so often be the next generation's "mere convention" might lead us to suspect the entire line of argument. But the prevalence of this line illustrates the potency of the mimetic appeal. We incline to believe that if we can claim for a device, a technique, or a whole work a "realistic" purpose, we have provided an ultimate justification.

It follows that a poem's failure on these grounds may be cause for condemnation. On such mimetic principles, Plato, in history's most famous attack on poetry, banished the poet from the ideal state. Actually, Plato said several and sometimes contradictory things about poets in his various writings, and he also objected to poetry on the affective grounds that it feeds and waters the passions. But his best-known remarks occur in *Republic X,* where he attacks poetry because it gives us a false view of the world. His argument is of interest chiefly for the answers it has inspired.

In Plato's philosophy, the world most of us call "real," the world apprehended by the senses, is an imperfect manifestation of the true reality, the world of immutable ideas or forms, the Parmenidean stasis that stands behind the Heraclitean flux of the sensuous world and that can be apprehended only by the mind. The idea of the perfect circle, for example, is prior to and apart from all circles we may draw or see, and that idea is the standard against which any physical circle can be measured. Obviously, only the mind can know the idea of a circle, and the mind must know that idea independently of any drawn circle. Likewise, when we see a pencil protruding from a glass of water, our sense of sight tells us that the pencil is bent, but the mind, which understands the truth, corrects the false report. And so for all knowledge. The business of humanity is to use our reason to pierce the veil of illusion, to transcend the false reports of the senses, to escape from the shadowy knowledge of the cave and to come to know the real world of the ideal forms. What furthers that knowledge is good; what inhibits it is harmful. Poetry inhibits it.

To explain his point, Plato resorts, as he often does, to visual metaphor. We start with the idea of a bed. A kind of practical artist, the carpenter, copies the idea of the bed to produce a physical bed. This bed, though a mere "imitation" and necessarily imperfect because a translation of an idea into a physical medium, has nonetheless a practical use. But when a painter paints a picture of that bed, he makes an imitation of an imitation that has no practical use. Worse, by copying the physical bed, which was itself a copy of the real bed, the painter produces a work twice removed from reality and so leads us not toward the realm of true knowledge but in the opposite direction.

By this argument, one of the world's greatest image makers and symbol wielders banished poets from his perfect state. The irony did not go long unnoticed, and at least as early as Plotinus we find art defended on the same Platonic grounds that Plato had used to condemn it. Philosophers who manage to escape the cave and enter the transcendent realm of pure forms can communicate what they have discovered only by means of metaphor and symbol. To talk at all about such a realm, the thinker must perforce become, like Plato, a poet. Thus Shelley, in one of the best-known Platonic defenses of poetry, can claim that

> poets, or those who imagine and express this indestructible order, are not only the authors of language and of music, of dance and architecture, and statuary, and painting; they are the institutors of laws, and the founders of civil society, and the inventors of the arts of life, and the teachers, who draw into a certain propinquity with the beautiful and the true, that partial apprehension of the agencies of the invisible world which is called religion.

In other words, the artist's bed need not be a copy of the carpenter's. The artist's vision can penetrate to the ideal realm, and the artist's skill can translate that vision into the artistic symbol that is, if not quite the idea itself, something that can lead us to conceive the idea. Like Keats's urn, the artist's symbol mediates between the physical world of flux and the immutable, transcendent realm. Through synesthesia and paradox it takes us past the mode of sensuous apprehension toward the unheard melodies beyond the sounded notes, the static pattern behind the frenzied action. It allows us to contemplate that realm beyond appearances where beauty and truth are indeed one and the same. This realm is the reality that art imitates and that *only* art can imitate. Thus, despite Plato's argument in the *Republic,* Platonic philosophy has most often been used to defend poetry, and specifically on mimetic grounds.

But the earliest reply to Plato had been argued on a different basis. At any rate, Aristotle's *Poetics* has generally been thought to have as one of its purposes the attempt to refute Plato's charge by redefining the sense in which poetry imitates reality. *Mimesis* is Aristotle's key word, and not all he says about it in this fragmentary document seems entirely clear and consistent. But his central concepts are plain enough. Like Plato, Aristotle builds his poetics on his metaphysics, but in solider Aristotle's scheme the reality that art imitates is quite literally a different matter. "Form" is no longer something beyond the physical world. The material world we apprehend with our senses is the real world, and everything in it consists of matter that is formed in some way. This concept is easy enough to conceive if we think of man-made things like a bed, or a poem, and in fact Aristotle's concepts provide the basis for "formal" criticism. But when we think of the forms of living things, the forms that poems imitate rather than the forms they possess, we are apt to misunderstand. The true "form" of a living thing is that which it most characteristically is. The form of a man, for example, is best represented by a vigorous adult who has reached that stage toward which childhood develops and from which old age declines. The form of an acorn is not a small and somewhat spherical object but a full-grown, majestic oak tree.

Now there is a sense in which this true form is never realized in nature. Warping winds, poor soil, impatient lumberjacks, and a hundred other "accidents" may prevent the acorn from achieving its true form. So Aristotle develops his own split between form and appearance, and this split has important implications for his concept of mimesis. For one thing, it explains how it is possible for a mimetic art to represent men as "better than they are" or things "as they ought to be," just as a sculptor may study several models in order to "imitate" a form possessed by none of the models. More importantly, it explains how the artist must look past the accidents, the individual peculiarities, to discover the essential or characteristic form that underlies them. The artist gives us the essence of a character, a situation, an action. The artist shows us not what that person or this person did, but what such people do. In perceiving this essential form and then imitating it in the medium of art so that we may perceive it, the poet achieves "a more philosophical and a higher thing than history: for poetry tends to express the universal, history the particular." Both the poet and the historian tell us truths, but the poet tells the more important truths.

Here is a mimetic defense of poetry as cogent as the Platonic and even more influential. Between them, these defenses provided the philosophic foundations for nearly every mimetic theory of literature until the eighteenth century, and their influence is still felt in many ways in contemporary criticism. Despite their considerable differences, the Platonic and Aristotelian views of mimesis have at least one important similarity: that is, whether art is thought to pierce the illusory veil of sense to enter the transcendent realm of the true forms, or whether it is thought to penetrate the accidents of local particularity to perceive the essential and universal character of persons and actions, each system offers a view that separates appearance and reality. Consequently, each avoids a serious problem that troubles many mimetic theories. Generally, the more heavily we stress the congruence of the poem to reality, the more difficult it becomes to explain the formal coherence of the poem. But if the poem is congruent not with the shifty and chaotic world of appearance but instead with some transcendent or underlying reality, the usual tension between coherence and congruence is considerably relaxed, perhaps even dissolved. In the Platonic scheme especially, the coherence of the work of art can be explained on mimetic grounds as an imitation of the coherence of the real world of ideal forms, that realm where coherence and congruence, beauty and truth, are one and the same. In the Aristotelian view, the gap between appearance and reality is not so wide. But it is wide enough to allow us to see artistic imitation as a process that strips away the peculiar, local, and temporary to reveal the characteristic, general, and permanent; and this view also exempts the poem from any need to conform closely to the appearance of things.

When we contemplate, for example, Aristotle's favorite play, *Oedipus Tyrannus,* we notice that by the standards of circumstantial realism it is a confabulation of implausible premises, improbable coincidences, and impossible circumstances. In fact, the famous economy and symmetry of its structure are salient among the things that set it apart from the world of ordinary experience. But, Aristotle implicitly argues, precisely those same things throw into sharp relief the essential action and, hence, the essential meaning of the play. The coherence of the poem, achieved by pruning away the distracting and confusing details of life as we usually experience it, is exactly what allows us to perceive the poem's universal relevance, its correspondence to the form beneath appearances. So the Aristotelian concept of mimesis, too, is able to lessen, if it cannot entirely eliminate, the troublesome opposition between coherence and congruence, between formal unity and imitative accuracy.

Increasingly, however, modern thought has been dominated by what may be called a pervasive "empirical" view of reality, which says that the world apprehended by the senses, the confusing flux of felt experience, is the real world. Such a view makes it much more difficult to separate the poet's truth from the historian's, or from the psychologist's, the sociologist's, or the physical scientist's. One solution is simply to give up poetry's claims to truth and to defend it on entirely different, usually affective, grounds. I. A. Richards, we noticed, attempted to do precisely that. But this radical solution has not appealed to most modern critics, and Richards's denial of the referential function of poetic language was in turn denied even by the formalist critics, who accepted his analytical techniques. These critics and others vigorously asserted the truth of poetry on empirical grounds and even against the claims of empirical science, and in the process they brought about a rather startling shift of perspective.

Aristotle, we saw, argued that poetry, because it was not confined as history was to the unique acts of specific persons at particular times and places, could reveal a higher and more universal truth. Certainly the poem presents particular characters and particular actions, but these are represented in their essentials, and the purpose of artistic shaping is to reveal their general truth. Samuel Johnson, who was often a staunch mimeticist, was very much in this tradition when he had his character Imlac declare that it is not the business of poetry to "number the streaks of the tulip"; its business is rather "to examine, not the individual, but the species; to remark general properties and large appearances." Sir Joshua Reynolds, Johnson's contemporary and a famous painter, took a similar view when he claimed that the "disposition to abstractions, to generalizing and classification, is the great glory of the human mind." It was this kind of remark that prompted William Blake to write in his *marginalia* on Reynolds, "To generalize is to be an idiot." Blake strikes the modern note. Many twentieth-century attempts to assert the claims of poetic truth against those of scientific truth have taken the tack we noticed in the discussion of formal criticism. Science obviously deals in "general" truths. Newton's apple and Humpty-Dumpty obey the same "laws," which can be stated in compact formulas to describe an infinite number of specific cases. But, replies the literary critic, such description is too general. It provides an even ghostlier paradigm than the Platonic forms. It is too abstract to describe the heft and feel, the smell and sound and sight, of the world as we actually experience it. For that we need a more concrete medium, something, if not more simple, at least more sensuous and passionate. We need poetry.

In this way modern critics come very often to stress the solidity and particularity of the poetic symbol, the complexity and tensions of the poetic structure. In doing so, we should remember, they are simply putting the emphasis on the other side of the same concrete–universal coin that is the poem. Aristotle and centuries of later critics, defining poetry with reference to the historian's particularity, stressed its universality. Many modern critics, defining poetry with reference to the universality of science, have emphasized its particularity. Each emphasis is understandable. Hamlet is interesting because he is in some sense every man, but Everyman is less interesting than Hamlet.

This is simply to note that the paradox of the concrete–universal becomes even more paradoxical as our view of reality becomes more empirical. But the empirical critic's vision gains clarity and force if it can be integrated within a larger system of thought. Psychological critics, for example, though they often focus their attention on the author, and sometimes on the audience, will also frequently operate in the mimetic context. Whether followers of Freud, Jung, Lacan, Maslow, or some other leading figure, such critics bring to their reading a fully developed theory about the way people really behave, and why; and this theory provides a standard by which they can measure the accuracy of the poet's representations. Such critics are often pleased, but not at all surprised, to find that the great poets' vision of human nature agrees with their own. Freud, for instance, noticed that creative writers had anticipated many of his own discoveries. He named his famous "Oedipus complex" after a play by Sophocles, and he suggested its application to one by Shakespeare. In doing so, we should notice, he was practicing mimetic criticism, for he was claiming that these playwrights were perceptive students of reality whose intuitive grasp of human nature was later confirmed by more methodical and scientific observation. "Not I, but the poets, have discovered the unconscious." And when we respond to these poets we do so because at some level of consciousness we recognize the truth of their representations. This approach is fundamentally different from that of the historical scholar who tells us, for example, that *Hamlet* must be understood in the light of some long-forgotten Renaissance theory of psychology that Shakespeare accepted or assumed his audience accepted. To the mimetic critic of a psychoanalytic persuasion, there is nothing anachronistic in reading classical or Elizabethan drama in Freudian terms. The psychologist and the poet study the same nature, and the truth of their findings, not at all limited by time and place, is always referable to this same standard, "at once the source, and end, and test of art." And of science.

So any psychology, indeed, any systematic view of human behavior, can provide the basis for a mimetic criticism of literature. In our own century, one of the most influential systems of thought has been the Marxist. To be sure, Marxist critics have often analyzed the social and economic forces acting on writers, and they have frequently been very much concerned with literature's effects. But these genetic and affective concerns are often based on a mimetic criterion: the work is good to the extent that it accurately depicts the clash of class interests, the forces of economic determinism, the dialectic process of history, in brief, the social reality as the critic's particular interpretation of Marxism may conceive it.

In other words, critics operating within a system of thought can account for the function of literature and measure its truth in terms of a larger framework of ideas. This is a potential strength, but only to the extent that we are willing to accept the whole system that supports the criticism. In practice, the great majority of readers has found the mimetic standards of most systems too partial, too limited, to deal adequately with the abundance and variety of literature that the world has generally called great. What system is capacious enough to comprehend Homer's cosmology and Milton's, Dante's ethics and de Sade's, Assisi's flowers and Baudelaire's? Or, take him all in all, what system can contain Shakespeare alone? Perhaps this is why the largest number of mimetic critics—and this number would include most of us at one time or another—feel no need to claim allegiance to a particular system of thought. Apparently unaffiliated and eclectic, they appeal to empiricism in its root meaning, to our common sense and our common experience of the world, to provide the mimetic standard, and what they may lose in philosophic rigor they gain in flexibility and wider assent.

But even the most eclectic and flexible forms of mimetic criticism must encounter some basic difficulties that seem to inhere in the problematic relationship between art and "reality," and the more firmly the criticism is based on empirical premises, the more troublesome these difficulties will be. One of these difficulties may be expressed in the form of two related questions: How does the poem, in conforming to a reality already known, give us knowledge? Or, if the reality is not already known, how can we be sure the poem does in fact conform to it? We may praise a work by remarking that it is congruent to life as we know it: this is the way things look; this is how people really behave. But it is not clear why we want to have such representations. Because we already possess the standard by which we judge them—that is, because we already know the reality imitated sufficiently well to judge the accuracy of the imitation—in what sense can we be said to learn anything from the poem?

This is not easy to answer. Aristotle's remarks that people learn by imitation and that they enjoy learning are not especially helpful, because he doesn't explain in what way people learn from artistic representations, and the example he gives muddies the waters further. Drawing on visual metaphor, he says that only those who know the original that the painter imitates can derive pleasure from the comparison; those who lack that knowledge derive what pleasure they have from some other, apparently nonmimetic, source. A better answer is offered by Fra Lippo Lippi, in Browning's poem of that name, when he explains, again using the "realistic" painting as his example, that we look at things every day but we don't really see them until the artist's picture calls our attention to them. Then we say, "That's the very man!" but in fact we hadn't been fully aware of the life around us until the artist taught us to see it.

This line is promising, and a critical theory could be developed at some length in this direction. But when we inquire how the artist has achieved this result, we seem to be faced with the paradox that it has been achieved by altering the very reality the artist claims to imitate. The alteration may take the form of simply selecting or rearranging details to heighten our awareness and focus our vision, but it is, nonetheless, alteration. And when we start to argue that even the most "realistic" plot, the most "lifelike" characters and actions, have some degree of distortion, then on the same principle we might argue that the most elaborate plots, the most outlandish caricatures, the most fantastic fictions can be similarly justified. For they too could be called heightenings and intensifications of reality. And by such arguments the so-called realistic devices and modes of literature lose their special standing. If forms such as "realistic" drama or "naturalistic" fiction achieve their ends by departing from direct imitation in at least some respects, then those same ends might be as well attained by forms such as epic, romance, pastoral, and others that depart from direct imitation in most respects. This line of argument does promise to account for the great variety of literature, but because it locates the special function and force of art in its power to select from, rearrange, and otherwise distort reality, it doesn't seem appropriate to call such a line mimetic.

So the question of just how an arrangement of words can be said to imitate reality remains a rather difficult question to answer, and so does the question of why we should want such imitations. And the answers are made all the more difficult when "reality" is defined in empirical terms. A related problem, how to reconcile the poem's formal coherence with its mimetic function, is also made more difficult. As we noticed, only idealistic philosophies like the Platonic can fully achieve this reconciliation. As the conception of reality becomes more empirical, the problem grows more troublesome, because any selection from the flux of felt experience and any imposition of formal pattern must to some extent lessen the poem's correspondence to empirical reality. As we should expect, formalists have often complained that many types of mimetic criticism ignore the very things that make poems, poems. Whatever ideology or philosophy is used to provide the standard of "truth," none can very well account for the art of poetry, and all are inclined to separate form and meaning, to extract the paraphrasable content of the poem and to judge that as if the poem were a philosophic treatise or a religious or economic tract. And even when the mimetic critic is willing to acknowledge the formal aspects of the poem, to grant its difference from discursive argument, the mimetic context cannot itself provide the concepts that will allow an explication or account of these formal aspects. Thus, the opposition between artistic design and imitative accuracy troubles virtually all mimetic theories, and it especially troubles those with an empirical basis.

This same opposition, we noticed, puzzled formal critics, though they approached the problem from the other direction. In fact, we could locate both formal and mimetic critics somewhere on that imaginary line that connects the work of art with reality as we experience it outside of art. The difference between them is often a matter of emphasis. Mimetic critics are primarily concerned to measure the poem's congruence with reality and to judge it on that basis, but they can neither entirely overlook nor, on mimetic grounds, adequately account for the formal features of the poem that set it apart from the world of experience and from other forms of discourse. Conversely, formal critics stress the uniqueness of poetic language and the inseparability of form and content, and their analyses are designed to explicate the poem's formal coherence. Yet they usually insist as well on the referential function of poetic language, and they often find the meaning and value of the poem's "complexity" in its correspondence to the complex reality of life as we experience it. So for both the formal and the mimetic critic, despite their different starting points, coherence and congruence are always necessary, but seldom easily reconcilable, principles.

A third problem confronting all mimetic approaches is brought into focus by a more radical objection. When formalists complain that mimetic critics cannot deal with the form of the poem, they mean by "form" these particular words in this particular order. When intertextual critics make the same complaint, they mean by "form" all the literary conventions that make up the poem. This objection is more radical because the intertextual perspective sees the poem not as an imitation of life but as an imitation of other poems. This perspective threatens, therefore, to undermine the mimetic premise entirely, to simply deny the referential function of art.

The development of this line of criticism is the subject of the next chapter. Here we shall simply note some implications of this objection. The mimetic perspective seems to bring naturally to mind narrative and dramatic structures, particularly those that offer "rounded" characters and "realistic" settings and actions and that seem to invite comparison with life outside of books. The novel, for example, is sometimes thought to be synonymous with the techniques of "circumstantial realism," and the tendency of much recent fiction to abandon these techniques has been seen by some to herald "the death of the novel." But the intertextual critics remind us that even so-called realistic techniques are simply conventions, and they call our attention to the myriad forms that make up the bulk of literature, the romances and pastorals, the farces and burlesques, the chameleon satire, that can infiltrate any form, and the encyclopedic work, like *Ulysses,* that can contain most. They remind us, further, that to defend *Ulysses* as a faithful picture of middle-class Dublin life at the turn of the century in the spring of the year may be judicially useful, but it is critically myopic. And they remind us, finally, that it is very difficult to account for the many generic conventions and their endless permutations on mimetic grounds. Yet these are the salient features of literary form, in a fundamental sense of the term, and a theory's inability to account for them must be considered a serious weakness.

Mimetic critics, then, encounter some difficult problems. On the one hand, they must face the charge of reductivism because they cannot easily cope with literary "form" in either the formal or the intertextual senses of the term. On the other hand, their own context is replete with philosophical puzzles about the relationship between verbal structures and the "reality" these structures are supposed to imitate. Although most of these problems are very old, they are made especially difficult by the prevailing modern tendency to define "reality" in empirical terms. Still, as the very hoariness of the problems indicates, their existence has never drastically diminished the popularity of the mimetic context. From Aristophanes's day to Samuel

Johnson's, mimetic concerns dominated literary discussions, and these concerns have continued to play a major role in modern criticism.

Historical critics, of course, have always been centrally concerned with the representational aspects of literature. Anglo-American formalists, as we have seen, came to ground part of their theory of value in the poem's special ability to represent human experience. Freudians, Jungians, Marxists, Thomists, and other supporters of particular psychological or philosophical systems have perforce been interested in literature as a representation of human character and action, as have critics who focus on the issues of race, class, and gender as these are represented in literature. Indeed, as we will see, in the contexts of poststructural and cultural criticism, "representation" remains a central issue.

In other words, mimetic concerns, under a variety of names, continue to occupy much of our attention. There are good reasons why they should. The idea that literature in some way imitates life has been an axiom of Western thought from its earliest records, and while critics in some of our contexts have occasionally been willing to ignore that axiom, only certain kinds of structural and poststructural critics have been willing to deny it. Clearly, we are accustomed to thinking in mimetic terms. But more than habit may be involved. Almost any verbal representation, particularly one in narrative or dramatic form, seems to invite comparison with our nonliterary experience. Such comparison furnishes an obvious, an almost inevitable, point of reference for the viewer or reader, a standard automatically invoked whenever we remark the "consistency" of a character's behavior or the "plausibility" of an action. That is to say, our understanding of the characters and actions in literature seems to be at least partly, and almost by reflex, a matter of reference to the mimetic context.

Further, and perhaps most important, there is the large question of the value of literature. As we have seen, the attraction of mimetic theory has often been strongest here. To put it simply, if we can show that literature does, in some important ways, tell us the truth about experience, then the various forms of "scientific" thought can be met on their own ground and the vast enterprise connected with literature, and our own intense personal interest, can be given a widely accepted justification. Only the mimetic context promises to provide such justification.

Suggestions for Further Reading

Erich Auerbach, *Mimesis: The Representation of Reality in Western Literature* (1946), is a classic text; John D. Boyd, *The Function of Mimesis and Its Decline* (2nd ed., 1980), is a history of some of the key concepts. George Bisztray, *Marxist Models of Literary Realism* (1978), recounts the arguments among Marxist critics about this tricky term. Other explorations of "realism" include Ian Watt, *The Rise of the Novel* (1957), J. P. Sterne, *On Realism* (1973), Kathryn Hume, *Fantasy and Mimesis* (1984), Lilian R. Furst, *All Is True: The Claims and Strategies of Realist Fiction* (1995), and Arne Melberg, *Theories of Mimesis* (1996). Ernest Jones, *Hamlet and Oedipus* (1949), is a famous study asserting the psychological truth of Shakespeare's character on Freudian lines; Bernard Paris, *A Psychological Approach to Fiction* (1974), makes the case for mimetic criticism using a different psychological model. A. D. Nuttall, *A New Mimesis* (1983), Raymond Tallis, *In Defence of Realism* (1988), and Robert Alter, *The Pleasures of Reading in an Ideological Age* (1989), argue the viability of mimetic fiction in the face of structuralist and poststructuralist attacks.

Although feminist critics operate in most contexts, this diverse group may be cited here because their challenges to other forms of criticism, and to traditional ways of thinking about society, sex, and history, are often focused on questions of representation. The variety of feminist criticism is best illustrated in collections of essays. Elaine Showalter, ed., *The New Feminist Criticism* (1985), reprints 18 of the most influential essays published in the previous decade. The same editor's *Speaking of Gender* (1989) marks the more recent shift from "woman-centered feminism" to concern with socially constructed gender differences. An even fuller picture is offered by Robyn Warhol and Diane Herndl, eds., *Feminism: An Anthology of Literary Theory and Criticism* (1991), which reprints 58 essays originally published between 1975 and 1991, and by Mary Eagleton, ed., *Feminist Literary Theory: A Reader* (2nd ed., 1996), which reprints excerpts from a great number of essays. Toril Moi, *Sexual/Textual Politics* (1985), and Janet Todd, *Feminist Literary History* (1988), are two helpful studies of the development of feminist criticism. Also useful is Jane Gallop, *Around 1981* (1992), which constructs a history of feminist criticism by analyzing several anthologies of feminist essays published since 1972. Also see Diana Fuss, *Essentially Speaking: Feminism, Nature, and Difference* (1989), Eve Kosofsky Sedgwick, *Epistemology of the Closet* (1990), Judith Butler, *Gender Trouble: Feminism and the Subversion of Identity* (1990), and Teresa L. Ebert, *Ludic Feminism and After: Postmodernism, Desire, and Labor in Late Capitalism* (1996).

The Uses of Psychology

Bernard Paris

Critics have often applied psychological theories in the genetic context to get at the author's psyche, and in the affective context to get at the reader's. Bernard Paris argues that these theories can also be applied in the mimetic context to help us understand fictional characters, including "implied authors." Paris is fully aware of the objections to treating fictional characters as if they were real people, but he finds the arguments on the other side more persuasive, especially in the case of "realistic" novels where "representation" is the dominant mode. As his later work on Shakespeare indicates, Paris would include certain kinds of drama here as well. Citing such proponents of realism as Erich Auerbach, Georg Lukács, and Ian Watt, Paris claims that with the great novels of psychological realism "thematic and formal analysis can't begin to do justice to the psychological portraiture which is often the greatest achievement of these works." We need, instead, a mimetic criticism deploying the insights of modern psychology. Although he later argues specifically for the uses of "third force" psychology associated with such figures as Karen Horney and Abraham Maslow, Paris presents in his opening chapter a general defense of mimetic criticism and a rationale for applying psychological theories to fictional characters "as though they were real people."

Norman Holland finds it "hard to see how a psychology [can] deal with a work of art *qua* work of art," and observes that in practice psychoanalytic critics "do not."[1] Psychology cannot consider works of art in themselves, he argues, because psychology as such is concerned "not with literature, but with minds" (p. 293). "Any psychological system," therefore, "must deal, not with works of art in

Reprinted by permission of the author from Bernard Paris, *A Psychological Approach to Fiction*, pp. 1–13, 23–27. Copyright © 1974 by Indiana University Press. A part of the chapter has been omitted, and the notes have been renumbered.

isolation, but with works of art in relation to man's mind" (p. 151). The "three possible minds to which the psychological critic customarily refers" are the author's mind, a character's mind, and the audience's mind. It is only the study of the audience's mind, Holland feels, that can lead "to a bonafide method; the other two tend to confusion" (p. 294). I believe that there are two kinds of minds within realistic novels that can be studied in psychological terms: they are the minds of the implied authors and the minds of the leading characters.

Holland argues that "we should use psychology on our own real and lively reactions" to the work "rather than on the characters' fictitious minds" (p. 308). He feels that character study is useful and legitimate only when it is incorporated into our analysis of the audience's mind. Then it is seen to "identify 'latent impulses' of the characters which may be considered as stimuli to or projections of latent impulses of the audience" (p. 283). Character study is not legitimate when, as in most psychological criticism, it talks "about literary characters as though they were real people" (p. 296). Holland's strongest argument in support of this position is that "Homo Fictus and Homo Dramaticus do not so much what Homo Sapiens would do in similar circumstances, but what it is necessary for them to do in the logical and meaningful realities of the works of art in which they live" (pp. 305–306). The artist "hovers between *mimesis*, making like, and *harmonia*, the almost musical ordering of the events he depicts. . . . The psychoanalytic critic of character neglects the element of *harmonia*, the symbolic conceptions that must modify the mimetic" (p. 306). Other critics of literature have learned to avoid this mistake: ". . . as a plain matter of fact, most literary critics do not—any more—treat literary characters as real people" (p. 296).[2]

Holland is participating in what W. J. Harvey calls "the retreat from character" in modern criticism, a retreat which Harvey's book, *Character and the Novel*, is intended to halt. "What has been said about character" in the past forty years, Harvey observes, "has been mainly a stock of critical commonplaces used largely to dismiss the subject in order that the critic may turn his attention to other allegedly more important and central subjects—symbolism, narrative techniques, moral vision and the like."[3] In the criticism of realistic fiction this has been especially unfortunate, for "most great novels exist to reveal and explore character" (p. 23). There are many reasons for this retreat, Harvey continues, the most important of which is the rise of the New Criticism:

> The New Criticism was centrally concerned to apply close and rigorous analytical methods to lyric poetry; it is noticeable how ill at ease its practitioners have been when they have approached the bulky, diffuse and variegated world of the novel. What we might expect is in fact the case; the new critic, when dealing with fiction, is thrown back upon an interest in imagery, symbolism or structural features which have little to do with characterization. (p. 200)

The danger that the critic of novels must now be warned against is not the neglect of *harmonia*, but the neglect of *mimesis*; for *harmonia* has had its due of late, and "a mimetic intention" was, after all, "the central concern of the novel until the end of the nineteenth century" (p. 205).

No study of character should ignore the fact that characters in fiction participate in the dramatic and thematic structures of the works in which they appear and that the meaning of their behavior is often to be understood in terms of its function within these structures. The less mimetic the fiction, the more completely will the characters be intelligible in terms of their dramatic and thematic functions; and even in highly realistic fiction, the minor characters are to be understood more functionally than psychologically. But, as Harvey points out, the authors of the great realistic novels "display an appetite and passion for life which threatens to overwhelm the formal nature of their art" (pp. 187–188). There is in such novels "a surplus margin of gratuitous life, a sheer excess of material, a fecundity of detail and invention, a delighted submergence in experience for its own sake" (p. 188). The result is "that characterization often overflows the strict necessities of form" (p. 188). This is especially true in the characterization of the protagonists, of "those characters whose motivation and history are most fully established, who conflict and change as the story progresses . . ." (p. 56). What we attend to in the protagonist's story "is the individual, the unique and particular case. . . . We quickly feel uneasy if the protagonist is made to stand for something general and diffused; the more he *stands for* the less he *is*" (p. 67). Though such characters have their dramatic and thematic functions, they are "in a sense . . . end-products"; we often feel that "they are what the novel exists for; it exists to reveal them" (p. 56).

The retreat from character of which Harvey complains has been in part a reaction against reading plays, stories, impressionistic novels, and other tightly structured or basically symbolic works as though they were realistic fiction. This has frequently resulted, ironically, in the study of realistic novels as though they were tightly structured or basically symbolic forms. In our avoidance of what Northrop Frye would call a low-mimetic provincialism, we have often failed to do justice to the low-mimetic forms themselves.

Fortunately, the most recent trend in literary criticism has been to emphasize the qualities that distinguish the literary modes and kinds from each other. In the study of narrative art, we are learning to appreciate a variety of forms and effects; and this, in turn, is enabling us to grasp the distinctive characteristics of each form with greater precision.[4] We are coming to see, among other things, that character is central in many realistic novels and that much of the characterization in such fiction escapes dramatic and thematic analysis and can be understood only in terms of its mimetic function. A careful examination of the nature of realistic fiction as modern criticism is coming to conceive it will show that in certain cases it *is* proper to treat literary characters as real people and that only by doing so can we fully appreciate the distinctive achievement of the genre.

The diversity of aesthetic theories and of critical approaches is in part a reflection of the multiplicity of values to be found in literature and in part a product of the varying interests and temperaments with which different critics come to literature. Not all approaches are equally valid: the most satisfying kind of criticism is that which is somehow congruent with the work and which is faithful to the distribution of interests in the work itself. The approach employed here attempts to stress values which are inherently important in realistic fiction and to make these values more accessible to us than they hitherto have been.

The primary values of fiction can be described in a variety of terms; I shall classify them as mimetic, thematic, and formal. Fiction is mainly concerned with the representation, the interpretation, and the aesthetic patterning of experience.[5] In different works and in different fictional modes the distribution of emphasis varies; and in some works one of these interests may be far more important than the others. When a work concerns itself seriously with more than one of these interests, it must bring its various impulses into harmony if it is to be organically unified.

From the middle of the eighteenth to the beginning of the twentieth century, the novel attempted, by and large, to realize all of these values; but its primary impulse seems to have been the mimetic one. Henry James is reflecting not only his own taste, but the essential nature of the genre when he characterizes the novel as "a picture" and proclaims that "the only reason for the existence of a novel is that it does attempt to represent life."[6] It is not its interpretation of life or its formal perfection but its "air of reality (solidity of specification)" that James identifies as "the supreme virtue of a novel" (p. 14). Arnold Kettle distinguishes between the moral fable, which is dominated by "pattern" or "significance" and the novel, in which "pattern" is subordinate to "life." Despite a frequently strong commitment to thematic interests, the great realists, says Kettle, "are less consciously concerned with the moral significance of life than with its surface texture. Their talent is devoted first and foremost to getting life on to the page, to conveying across to their readers the sense of what life as their characters live it really feels like."[7]

The view of realistic fiction that we are developing is confirmed by such classic works on the subject as Ian Watt's *The Rise of the Novel* and Erich Auerbach's *Mimesis*. Formal interests cannot be paramount in a genre that, as Watt describes it, "works by exhaustive presentation rather than by elegant concentration."[8] Like E. M. Forster, Watt sees "the portrayal of 'life by time' as the distinctive role which the novel has added to literature's more ancient preoccupation with portraying 'life by values'" (p. 22). The domain of the novel is the individual and his social relationships, and it tends to present its subject less in terms of ethical categories than in terms of chronological and causal sequences. The distinctive characteristics of the novel are, for Watt, its emphasis upon the particular, its circumstantial view of life, and its full and authentic reporting of experience (pp. 31–32).

To our statement that the novel's primary impulse is a mimetic one, we must add the qualification that the reality imitated is not general nature or the world of Ideas, but the concrete and temporal reality of modern empirical thought. The novel came into being in a world dominated by secularism and individualism, a world in which men were losing their belief in the supernatural and institutional bases of life. "Both the philosophical and the literary innovations," says Watt, "must be seen as parallel manifestations of a larger change—that vast transformation of Western civilization since the Renaissance which has replaced the unified world picture of the Middle Ages with another very different one—one which presents us, essentially, with a developing but unplanned aggregate of particular individuals having particular experiences at particular times and at particular places" (p. 31).

For Erich Auerbach the foundations of modern realism are first, "the serious treatment of everyday reality, the rise of more extensive and socially inferior human groups to the position of subject matter for problematic-existential representation"; and, second, "the embedding of random persons and events in the general course of contemporary history, the fluid historical background."[9] Throughout *Mimesis* Auerbach is concerned with the contrast between the classical moralistic and the problematic existential ways of presenting reality. The distinction is basically between the representation of life in terms of fixed canons of style and of ethical categories which are a priori and static, and a stylistically mixed, ethically ambiguous portrayal which probes "the social forces underlying the facts and conditions" that it presents (p. 27). The problematic existential perception of reality, which *Mimesis* exists to celebrate, is one that is informed by the insights of Historicism. It is characterized by an awareness that "epochs and societies are not to be judged in terms of a pattern concept of what is desirable absolutely speaking but rather in every case in terms of their own premises"; by "a sense of historical dynamics, of the incomparability of historical phenomena and of their constant inner mobility"; and by a "conviction that the meaning of events cannot be grasped in abstract and general forms of cognition" (p. 391).

It is evident that in fiction employing the classical moralistic perspective, interpretation will outweigh and, indeed, govern representation, whereas in fiction written from a problematic existential point of view the mimetic impulse will be predominant. In many realistic novels, however, the classical moralistic perspective continues to exist alongside of, and often in disharmony with, the concrete, "serio-problematic" representation of life. Auerbach observes that Balzac, for example, "aspires to be a classical moralist" but that "this suits neither his style nor his temperament" (pp. 422–423). In his novels "the classically

moralistic element very often gives the impression of being a foreign body." It expresses itself in the narrator's "generalized apophthegms of a moral cast," which are "sometimes witty as individual observations," but which are often "far too generalized" and are sometimes "plain 'tripe'" (p. 422).

Realism for Auerbach means essentially social realism—the presentation of events in terms of the network of historical relations in which they exist and a concern for all of the forces at work, not simply for a limited, class-determined set of causes. His distinction between the categorical and the historistic views of experience applies just as readily to the presentation of character as it does to the rendering of society, though Auerbach himself has little to say about psychological realism. Representation is the primary interest of realistic fiction, and the two chief objects of representation are character and social milieu. Some novels are profoundly concerned with both character and society; others focus primarily on social or on psychological reality. Novels in which psychological realism predominates tend to present society from the point of view of the individual; novels of social realism often take a sociological rather than a psychological view of character.

Though realistic fiction is more concerned with mimesis than it is with theme and form the latter are, nonetheless, very important elements in the majority of novels. Indeed, one of the basic problems of the novel as a genre is that it attempts to integrate impulses which are disparate and often in conflict. The problematic existential portrayal of reality defies, by its very nature, authorial attempts at analysis and judgment. The great realists see and represent far more than they can understand. And, as Northrop Frye observes, "the realistic writer soon finds that the requirements of literary form and plausible content always fight against each other."[10] Form derives from generic conventions, and ultimately from mythic patterns, which are inherently unrealistic; realistic content obeys the laws of probability, of cause and effect, and belongs to a different universe of discourse. The integration of theme, form, and mimesis is an extremely difficult task.

Critics of realistic fiction, even some of those who best understand its nature, come to it demanding formal and thematic perfections which very few novels can achieve. The novel "may have a distinctive representational technique," says Ian Watt, "but if it is to be considered a valuable literary form it must also have, like any other literary form, a structure which is a coherent expression of all its parts" (p. 104). The novel, Watt feels, must "supplement its realism of presentation with a realism of assessment." If the interpretive element is weak "we shall be wholly immersed in the reality of the characters and their actions, but whether we shall be any wiser as a result is open to question" (p. 288). Arnold Kettle recognizes that "there are writers, and great ones, whose books have more vividness than wisdom, more vitality than significance"; but he feels that "the central core of any novel is what it has to say about life." Novels with more life than pattern, or in which life and pattern are not integrated, are wanting in the quality of their perception (pp. 14–16).

It is my impression that if we come to novels expecting moral wisdom and coherent teleological structures we are usually going to be disappointed. Such expectations are frequently aroused by the works themselves, and it is natural for the reader to want them fulfilled; but the mimetic impulse that dominates most novels often works against total integration and thematic adequacy. Even so, the novel is a valuable literary form. As Watt himself says, "In the novel, more perhaps than in any other literary genre, the qualities of life can atone for the defects of art . . ." (p. 301). The novel's weaknesses are in many cases the defects of its virtues, and its virtues are very great indeed. Some novels, of course, are integrated: they are usually those in which the interpretive element either is almost nonexistent or is incorporated into the mimesis. Such novels have coherent teleological structures, but they do not provide the kind of wisdom that Kettle, Watt, and many other critics seem to be looking for.

It is because they contain highly individualized characters or extremely detailed pictures of society that many novels lack total artistic integration. In novels of psychological realism (on which we shall focus here) there is a character-creating impulse which has its own inner logic and which tends to go its own way, whatever the implied author's formal and thematic intentions may be. As critics we demand, indeed, that the central characters of realistic fiction be like real people, that they have a life of their own beyond the control of their author. The novelist, says Harvey, "must accept his characters as asserting their human individuality and uniqueness in the face of all ideology (including his own limited point of view)" (p. 25). In realistic fiction, proclaims

Georg Lukács, "what matters is the picture conveyed by the work; the question to what extent this picture conforms to the views of the authors is a secondary consideration."[11] "A great realist," Lukács continues,

> . . . if the intrinsic artistic development of situations and characters he has created comes into conflict with his most cherished prejudices or even his most sacred convictions, will, without an instant's hesitation, set aside these his own prejudices and convictions and describe what he really sees, not what he would prefer to see. This ruthlessness towards their own subjective world-picture is the hall-mark of all great realists, in sharp contrast to the second-raters, who nearly always succeed in bringing their own *Weltanschauung* into "harmony" with reality. . . .
> (p. 11)

Lukács is chiefly concerned with the portrayal of social reality, but his observations apply also to the presentation of character:

> The characters created by the great realists, once conceived in the vision of their creator, live an independent life of their own; their comings and goings, their development, their destiny is dictated by the inner dialectic of their social and individual existence. No writer is a true realist—or even a truly good writer, if he can direct the evolution of his own characters at will.
> (p. 11)

The point I am trying to make has been most brilliantly developed by E. M. Forster, in his discussion of flat and round characters. "The novelist," he observes, "has a very mixed lot of ingredients to handle." He is telling a story ("life in time") which has a meaning ("life by values"). His story is "about human beings":

> The characters arrive when evoked, but full of the spirit of mutiny. For they have these numerous parallels with people like ourselves, they try to live their own lives and are consequently often engaged in treason against the main scheme of the book. They "run away," they "get out of hand": they are creations inside a creation, and often inharmonious towards it; if they are given complete freedom they kick the book to pieces, and if they are kept too sternly in check, they revenge themselves by dying, and destroy it by intestinal decay.[12]

What Forster has described here is the dilemma of the realistic novelist. If his characters are truly alive they will have a motivational life of their own and will tend to subvert the main scheme of the book. If he keeps his characters subordinated to their aesthetic and thematic functions, however, they will be lifeless puppets and his book will be flawed in a different and more serious way.

In their excellent book on narrative literature, Robert Scholes and Robert Kellogg recapitulate and refine many of our most recent insights into the nature of realistic fiction. Their division of characters into three types—aesthetic, illustrative, and mimetic—provides the best taxonomy that we have to date and offers a convenient way of formulating the thesis which I have been developing.

Characters should be understood in terms of the kind of function that they perform. Aesthetic types—"villains, ingénues, *ficelles,* choral characters, *nuntii,* and so on"—serve mainly to create formal patterns and dramatic impact. They have little inner depth or moral significance. Illustrative characters are most important in works governed by the classical moralistic perspective:

> Illustration differs from representation in narrative art in that it does not seek to reproduce actuality but to present selected aspects of the actual, essences referable for their meaning not to historical, psychological, or sociological truth but to ethical and metaphysical truth.

Illustrative characters

> . . . are concepts in anthropoid shape or fragments of the human psyche masquerading as whole human beings. Thus we are not called upon to understand their motivation as if they were whole human beings but to understand the principles they illustrate through their actions in a narrative framework. (p. 88)

Behind realistic fiction there is a strong "psychological impulse" that "tends toward the presentation of highly individualized figures who resist abstraction and generalization, and whose motivation is not susceptible to rigid ethical interpretation" (p. 101). When we encounter a fully drawn mimetic character "we are justified in asking questions about his motivation based on our knowledge of the ways in which real people are motivated" (p. 87).

There are aesthetic and illustrative types in realistic novels, of course, and in the central characters there is often a mixing of and a tension between illustrative, mimetic, and aesthetic functions. But in novels of psychological realism the main characters exist primarily as mimetic portraits whose intricacies escape the moral and symbolic meanings assigned to

them. Many aspects of their characterization which are of little formal or thematic interest become very significant when we see them as manifestations of the characters' inner being, as part of the author's unfolding of character for its own sake.

The great gift of the psychological realists, then, even of the most intellectually proficient and ethically sensitive of them, is not in the interpretation but in the representation of the experience of their characters. Their characters may have important functions in the thematic and formal structures of the works in which they exist, but thematic and formal analysis cannot begin to do justice to the psychological portraiture which is often the greatest achievement of these works, and it frequently blinds us to the fact that the experience represented does not always sustain the dramatic and thematic effects for which the work is striving.

Ortega y Gasset contends that all of the

> . . . psychological knowledge accumulated in the contemporary mind . . . is to no small degree responsible for the present failure of the novel. Authors that yesterday seemed excellent appear naive today because the present reader is a much better psychologist than the old author.[13]

This is true only if we judge the old authors primarily in terms of their analyses and assessments of their characters' behavior. Given the fact that the old authors were not necessarily gifted as analysts and moralists, that their value judgments were bound to be influenced by their own neuroses, and that the psychological theories available to them were inadequate to their insights, it was inevitable that their interpretations would be inferior to their representations of experience and that the beneficiaries of a more advanced psychological science would feel superior to them. If we do justice to their representations of character, however, we will see that they were excellent psychologists indeed, and that we need all of the resources of modern knowledge to understand and appreciate their achievement.

•   •   •

The question of what kind of illumination art—or, in our case, realistic fiction—*does* supply is too large to be dealt with completely here; but it is central to our concerns, and I shall attempt to offer a partial answer. If we have realism of presentation without realism of assessment, says Ian Watt, "we shall be wholly immersed in the reality of the characters and their actions, but whether we shall be any wiser as a result is open to question" (p. 288). Immersion in the inner reality of characters provides a kind of knowledge which is not wisdom, though it may be the basis of wisdom, and which realistic fiction is especially fitted to supply. If we understand by phenomenology the formulation of "an experience of the world, a contact with the world which precedes all" judgment and explanation,[14] we can say that highly mimetic fiction gives us a phenomenological knowledge of reality. It gives us an immediate knowledge of how the world is experienced by the individual consciousness and an understanding of the inner life in its own terms. It enables us to grasp from within the phenomena which psychology and ethics treat from without.

As Wayne Booth has observed, when we read novels in which there are deep inside views "that . . . give the reader an effect of living thought and sensation" (p. 324), we tend to abandon judgment and analysis. When we are immersed in the "indomitable mental reality" (p. 323) of a character, we adopt his perspective and experience his feelings as though they were our own. This kind of experience, which is one of the great gifts of fiction, is acceptable to Booth only when the character's perspective is, in his view, an ethically acceptable one. It is very dangerous, he feels, if the character's values are destructive, for then the reader is liable to be corrupted by his identification with unhealthy attitudes. I feel that Booth has overestimated both the danger which the reader is in and the effectiveness of rhetoric as a corrective, and that he has underestimated the value of deep inside views, though he admits that they "can be of immeasurable value in forcing us to see the human worth of a character whose actions, objectively considered, we would deplore" (p. 378). Robbe-Grillet's *The Voyeur* "does, indeed, lead us to experience intensely the sensations and emotions of a homicidal maniac. But is this," Booth asks, "really what we go to literature for?" (p. 384). My answer is, Yes.

We go to literature for many things, and not the least of them is the immediate knowledge that it gives to variously constituted human psyches. The novel makes its revelations not only through mimetic portraits of characters, but also, in many cases, through the picture that it creates of the implied author. As both Wayne Booth and Sheldon Sacks point out, when the implied author functions as interpreter, he often makes a multitude of particular judgments as his characters display their temperaments and confront their choices. This gives rise to "a much more detailed ordering of values" than we ever encounter in systematic philosophy. Even if we cannot accept the implied author's values as adequate either to his fictional world or to life outside, we have a marvellously rich portrayal of a particular kind of consciousness making ethical responses to a variety of human situations. Through the novel's rhetoric we become aware of the meaning which the characters' experience has for a mind like that of the implied author, and we enter thus into his subjective world.

What I am suggesting, then, is that if we view him as a fictional persona, as another dramatized consciousness, rather than as an authoritative source of values, the implied author, too, enlarges our knowledge of experience. What we have, in effect, is a deep inside view of *his* mind, a view which makes us phenomenologically aware of *his* experience of the world. When we see him as another consciousness, sometimes the most fascinating one in the book, it becomes more difficult to regret the technical devices by which he is revealed, even when they produce aesthetic flaws. To see him in this way we must set aside the fictional conventions which encourage us to invest him with the authority which Wayne Booth would like him to have; but it is essential to do so if we are to appreciate many great narrators whose wisdom we must question and whose obtrusiveness we must otherwise regret.

As long as we regard the implied author as a kind of god whose will we must understand but never question, it seems quite inappropriate to analyze him psychologically. His contradictions are manifestations of a higher harmony which we have not yet grasped; and his judgments, being right, require no explanation. When we see him as a dramatized consciousness whose values can be as subjective and as confused as those of an ordinary man, psychological analysis becomes a necessity.

I have tried to show by an analysis of the genre that it is often appropriate to study the characters and implied authors of realistic novels by a psychological method. In the interpretations of individual novels that will follow our discussion of Third Force psychology, I hope to demonstrate that the approach employed here helps us to appreciate some of fiction's most important values and to resolve some difficult critical problems.

I am aware, however, that the very arguments by which I have attempted to justify a psychological approach may seem to preclude it. I have argued that one of the chief interests of realistic fiction is a mimetic characterization which gives us a phenomenological grasp of experience in its immediacy and ambiguity and that the value of such characterization lies precisely in its continual resistance to the patterns by which the author has tried to shape and interpret it. It may be objected that the values of such characterization are incommensurate with any kind of analysis and that to intellectualize them is to destroy them. My reply must be that any criticism, whether it be psychological or not, is bound to operate with categories and abstractions which, if they are allowed to replace the values of literature, will destroy them. Criticism can make literature more accessible to us, but we must use it as a means to rather than as a substitute for the aesthetic encounter.

A common complaint about the psychological analysis of character is that it does violence to the literary values of fiction by reducing the novel to a case history, the character to his neurosis. We must recognize that literature and criticism belong to different universes of discourse. As Northrop Frye says, "the axiom of criticism must be, not that the poet does not know what he is talking about, but that he cannot talk about what he knows."[15] The function of criticism is to talk about what the artist knows, and to do that it must speak in the language of science and philosophy rather than in the language of art. But if we are aware of what we are doing this does not convert art into science or philosophy. Criticism points to a reality which is far more complex and of a different nature than itself; the values of which it speaks can be experienced only in the aesthetic encounter. All criticism is reductive. Psychological analysis is our best tool for talking about the intricacies of mimetic characterization. If properly conducted, it is less reductive than any other critical approach.

It is extremely valuable to bring literature and psychology together. The psychologist and the artist often know about the same areas of experience, but they comprehend them and present their knowledge in different ways. Each enlarges our awareness and satisfies our need to master reality in a way that the other cannot. The psychologist enables us to grasp certain configurations of experience analytically, categorically, and (if we accept his conceptions of health and neurosis) normatively. The novelist enables us to grasp these phenomena in other ways. Fiction lets us know what it is like to be a certain kind of person with a certain kind of destiny. Through mimetic portraits of character, novels provide us with artistic formulations of experience that are permanent, irreplaceable, and of an order quite different from the discursive formulations of systematic psychology. And, if we view him as a fictional persona, as a dramatized consciousness, the implied author, too, enlarges our knowledge of the human psyche.

Taken together, psychology and fiction give us a far more complete possession of experience than either can give us by itself. Psychology helps us to talk about what the novelist knows; fiction helps us to know what the psychologist is talking about.

Notes

1. *Psychoanalysis and Shakespeare* (New York, 1966), p. 151. Whenever the source is clear, page numbers will be given parenthetically in the text.
2. There is a slight modification of Holland's position in *The Dynamics of Literary Response* (New York, 1968), Chapter 10 ("Character and Identification"): "Psychoanalytic critics regularly apply psychological concepts from the world of everyday reality to characters who exist in a wholly different kind of world—it should not work but it does" (p. 267). My contention is that it should work, and it does.
3. (Ithaca, 1965), p. 192.
4. See especially, Robert Scholes and Robert Kellogg, *The Nature of Narrative* (New York, 1966); Northrop Frye, *The Anatomy of Criticism* (Princeton, 1957); Wayne C. Booth, *The Rhetoric of Fiction* (Chicago, 1961); and Sheldon Sacks, *Fiction and the Shape of Belief* (Berkeley and Los Angeles, 1964).
5. There is an element of interpretation in all representation, of course, in that representation is not mere copying but involves artistic selection for the purpose of creating a more effective mimetic portrait. When I distinguish between representation and interpretation, I am using "interpretation" to mean "analysis and judgment."
6. "The Art of Fiction," in *Myth and Method, Modern Theories of Fiction*, ed. James E. Miller, Jr. (Lincoln, 1960), pp. 24–25.
7. Arnold Kettle, *An Introduction to the English Novel* (Harper Torchbook ed.: New York, 1960), Vol. 1, p. 21.

8. (Berkeley and Los Angeles, 1965), p. 30.

9. *Mimesis, The Representation of Reality in Western Literature,* trans. by Willard Trask (Anchor Book ed.: New York, 1957), pp. 433–34.

10. "Myth, Fiction, and Displacement," in *Fables of Identity* (New York, 1963), p. 36.

11. *Studies in European Realism* (New York, 1964), p. 10.

12. *Aspects of the Novel* (London, 1927), Chapter 4.

13. *The Dehumanization of Art* (Anchor Book ed.: Garden City, 1956), p. 92.

14. Merleau-Ponty, quoted by Herbert Spiegelberg, *The Phenomenological Movement: A Historical Introduction* (The Hague, 1960), Vol. 2, p. 416.

15. *Anatomy of Criticism,* p. 5.

THEORY

Noting that much contemporary feminist criticism has passed beyond the "images of women" focus that was the movement's starting point, Josephine Donovan here returns to that focus to argue that the representation of women remains a key issue in feminist criticism. "Feminist criticism is rooted in the fundamental a priori intuition that women are seats of consciousness; are selves, not others." But in much literature, Donovan complains, and in much that is called the greatest, women are represented not as complex human beings and free moral agents but as stereotypes of good or evil, creatures whose function is simply to help or hinder the male hero's progress. In short, women are represented as others, not selves. This misrepresentation reflects the pervasive sexist bias of society; even worse, it serves to perpetuate that bias. In this context, misrepresentation is an intellectual error with serious moral consequences, and it must be combated by a serious moral criticism. On the one hand, then, the feminist critic must become a "negative" critic, a resisting reader who refuses to deny her own experience in order to identify with the fictional male hero and who refuses to accept the stereotype for the reality. On the other hand, the feminist critic must champion those works that do portray their characters, male and female, realistically, that is, as authentic, autonomous, and fully human beings. "Most literature that we call great expresses . . . universal, fundamental human experience." Looking back to the beginning of Western criticism in the mimetic theories of Plato and Aristotle, and glancing toward the work of Iris Murdoch, a modern student of Plato, Donovan puts the case for a feminist criticism that, by resisting false representations and praising true ones, will achieve a reconciliation of the Good and the True and become, thereby, a truly moral criticism.

Beyond the Net: Feminist Criticism as a Moral Criticism

Josephine Donovan

Reprinted by permission of the author from *Denver Quarterly* 17, 4 (1983): 40–57.

The death of a beautiful woman is the most poetical topic in the world.

—Edgar Allan Poe, "The Philosophy of Composition"

While feminist literary criticism has diversified considerably in the past few years, I wish in this article to return to the "images of women" approach that dominated feminist literary studies of the early 1970s and is still central to the pedagogy of Women's Studies in literature. Through the "images of women" approach the critic determines how women characters are presented in literature. Usually the critic discovers that the images are *Other*, and therefore that the literature is alien. The task may be labeled "negative criticism" if one wishes to adapt the dialectical terms of the Frankfurt school of Marxist criticism.[1] It is "negative" because the critic is in effect saying "no" to reified perceptions, structures, and models that have historically denied full humanity to women. This means looking "negatively" at much of Western literature. Here I wish to set down a theoretical moral basis for this critique.

Feminist criticism is rooted in the fundamental *a priori* intuition that women are seats of consciousness; are selves, not others. As Dorin Schumacher has pointed out, the dominant criticism of the past, which she labels "masculinist," has gone on the opposite assumption: "Man [is] self, or normative, and woman [is] other, or deviant."[2] Schumacher's analysis derives, of course (as any "images of women" criticism must, I believe), from Simone de Beauvoir's brilliant application of Existentialist phenomenology to women.

In her introduction to *The Second Sex*, Beauvoir, echoing Heidegger and Sartre, asserted that "Otherness is a fundamental category of human thought."[3] The fundamental duality between the Self and the Other "is as primordial as consciousness itself" (p. xvi). By the time Beauvoir was writing *The Second Sex*, Claude Lévi-Strauss had in fact identified (in *Les Structures élémentaires de la parenté*) the transition from "nature" to "culture" as one which required the development of a binary consciousness. Beauvoir seems to have been influenced by this thesis, so fundamental to structuralism.

Beauvoir perceived, moreover, that the Self-Other dichotomy quickly becomes expressed in political terms: it is the socially dominant group which establishes itself as Self, as the norm, the essential; while subordinate groups are Other, which means they are perceived as deviant, inessential, objects (p. xvii). In our society the masculine is the norm; the feminine, the aberrant.

Women in literature written by men are for the most part seen as Other, as objects, of interest only insofar as they serve or detract from the goals of the male protagonist. Such literature is alien from a female point of view because it denies her essential selfhood. Beauvoir cemented her point by citing a seventeenth-century critic, Poulain de la Barre: "All that has been written about women by men should be suspect, for the men are at once judge and party to the lawsuit" (p. xxii).

The primary assumption a critic in the "images of women" school must make is an evaluation of the *authenticity* of the female characters.[4] Authenticity is another concept borrowed from the Existentialists, in particular Heidegger, who meant by it whether an individual has a self-defined critical consciousness, as opposed to a mass-produced or stereotypical identity.[5] Sartre defined the latter as the *en-soi*, the *in-itself* or the object-self, as opposed to the authentic *pour-soi* or *for-itself,* which is the critical or reflective consciousness capable of forming projects.[6]

The concept of authenticity in feminist criticism is therefore not a free-floating, "impressionistic" notion, as has been suggested.[7] Judgments which evaluate a character's authenticity are rooted in the extensive body of Existentialist theory on the subject. Such judgments are made according to whether the character has a reflective, critical consciousness, whether s/he is a moral agent, capable of self-determined action, whether, in short, s/he is a Self, not an Other. Such judgments enable the feminist critic to determine the degree to which sexist ideology controls the text.[8] Sexist ideology necessarily promotes the concept of woman-as-object or woman-as-other. Sometimes the critic may note an interplay between the ideology and a critique of it expressed in the text (this is usually only in works written by women). Sometimes the critic has to supply the critique herself. Thus, one discovers that the "cult of true womanhood," a particular nineteenth-century American version of sexist ideology which essentially consigned women to true "otherhood," is embedded in scores of sentimentalist texts of the period. But one may also note ways in which the female authors somewhat subverted the ideology through plot and character.[9] Again one must stress that the feminist *a priori* is that women have in all historical periods been seats of consciousness and moral agents (i.e., selves), no matter how circumscribed their spheres or range of actions may have been. Any text which does not recognize the fundamental moral reality of women is sexist.

In order to illustrate how an author may create and exploit inauthentic female characters, thereby promulgating sexist ideology, I am first going to look at several contemporary films. In many of these we find visual examples of exploitation for aesthetic purposes, as in Poe's aesthetic excitement over the death of a beautiful woman. (I am not even addressing here the whole realm of pornographic treatment of women except to note that pornography is the ultimate objectification of women and represents the far end of the continuum of alien literature.)

Molly Haskell noted in her study of film images of women: "The conception of woman as idol, art object, icon and visual entity is . . . the first principle of the aesthetic of film as a visual medium."[10] Or, as Laura Mulvey, a Freudian feminist critic, pointed out:

> [In film] the determining male gaze projects its fantasy onto the female figure, which is styled accordingly. In their traditional exhibitionist role women are simultaneously looked at and displayed, with their appearance coded for strong visual and erotic impact so that they can be said to connote *to-be-looked-at-ness*.[11]

In other words, women characters in film are usually presented as objects or as *Other* to the male protagonist and for the pleasure of the male viewer. Such objectification is mitigated only when strong women film personalities take over the role, making of it something not intended by writer or director.

Some films of Ingmar Bergman provide excellent if subtle examples of the phenomenon of aesthetic exploitation of women characters. *Cries and Whispers* (1972) is a film which one might, on first viewing, hail as a sensitive portrayal of the lives of four women. The extraordinary visual beauty of the film is seductive enough to promote this judgment. However, on reflection one comes to realize that the women are used aesthetically as if they were on the same level of moral importance as the red decor of their surroundings. Like Poe, Bergman finds women's agonies aesthetically interesting because he sees them from without and not from within. He can visually appreciate the screams and agonized wriggling of Agnes.

But, as Constance Penley wrote in an important feminist critique of the film, the women's suffering is morally gratuitous. "Since the film is not about women coming to realizations of self-knowledge through their struggles, then their suffering must serve some other function."[12] That function is aesthetic.

I am using *aesthetic* here in the sense given it at least since Kant, that of a disinterested appreciation of a phenomenon that exists as a discrete entity in space and time, which is pleasing within these or because of these spatio-temporal coordinates. As we shall see, I believe that the imputed divorce between aesthetics and morals which this view entails is specious, masking as it does ideological exploitation of female figures. Nevertheless, aesthetics since the Renaissance has relied upon this divorce; spatio-temporal perspectives are the governing principle.[13] Consequently an artist like Bergman can treat his female figures as objects within a spatio-temporal continuum that are of use only insofar as they fit into the total aesthetic vision he has fashioned. In *Cries and Whispers* there is no moral resolution for the women characters because they are not conceived as moral creatures, as possessing authenticity. These women gain no wisdom. Their lot does not get any better. It gets worse. Theirs is a universe deprived of hope, a world that is irredeemably fallen; suffering is to no redemptive purpose. In *Cries and Whispers* that world, largely female, is damned to total alienation and meaningless suffering, saved only by the camera eye, an aesthetic redemption. One may argue that male protagonists in a modern world are also subjected to alienation and non-redemptive suffering; but female characters tend to be used more for aesthetic effects which divert attention from their moral existence.

Despite the fact that *Scenes from a Marriage* (1973) was touted as a "liberated" break-through in which male and female characters hold equal power, the woman character remains submissive to the end. She is unable to function autonomously, because Bergman does not allow her to. When tension between the couple escalates, it is the male character who is physically abusive. After a brutal scene in which the woman is kicked at length by her husband, she comes crawling back for more, and we, the audience, are expected to feel pity for her abuser because he lost his self-control and presumably his self-respect. The female character is used as a vehicle for the male's growth in self-awareness.

In *Face to Face* (1976) the female protagonist is even more limited. In this film Liv Ullmann plays a career/professional woman who is separated from her husband. As in most misogynist literature the unmated female is gratuitously abused because she has dared to attempt autonomy; she has rejected a male and refused to play the role of traditional wife-and-mother—which is the only acceptable female role in this misogynist vision because it is utterly passive and non-disruptive of predestined male triumph.[14]

The movie opens with the rape of the female protagonist. The experience precipitates her complete unravelment and breakdown. While the role is a tour de force for Liv Ullmann, the film provides no moral resolution to the great suffering that has been displayed. In no way is the enormity of the suffering justified. The sheer imbalance in the movie is the clue that Bergman relished aesthetically every nuance of the breakdown; that was sufficient cause for her suffering. Once again the suffering is viewed from without; it serves superficial aesthetic purposes. Ultimately such exploitation of suffering is an example of artistic bad faith, an author's immoral use of his characters. Unlike the great works of Western literature where suffering for the male protagonist leads to wisdom, to knowledge, to growth, or to positive social change, here the suffering is without meaning. Nor is there any catharsis for the female viewer (or the male viewer who may care for the protagonist). The only point of the movie is to show the marvelous acting *technique* of Liv Ullmann and filming *technique* of Bergman. But this is not art in its profoundest sense, for all great art is sustained by the integrity of a moral vision. It cannot depend on gratuitous suffering which is tantamount to torture. Later I will discuss what a feminist/humanist moral vision in art entails.

Another contemporary film which helps to illustrate my thesis is Woody Allen's *Interiors* (1978). Once again we have a visually seductive film, aesthetically very beautiful. All the frames are in aesthetic balance, and the colors of the interiors are aesthetically pleasing. But in the end the "interiors" of the characters are of no more moral substance than the house and apartment interiors they live in. This film, modeled whether consciously or not on Chekhov's masterwork *The Three Sisters*, attempts to portray and in some sense justify aesthetically the suffering of the female characters, primarily that of the mother-wife played by Geraldine Page. Once again the role is a tour de force for a supremely talented actress; but the overall resolution of the film is not satisfactory for the viewer who identifies with, or empathizes with, or simply cares for the central female character. Why is this the case? To answer this I must discuss the nature of aesthetic satisfaction.

The aesthetic dimension of literature and of film cannot be divorced from the moral dimension, as we have facilely come to assume under the influence of technique-oriented critical methodologies (New Criticism, for example). Since Aristotle, the aesthetic experience has in fact been understood as one which provides release, relief, catharsis, and the pleasure of wholeness. The events within this aesthetic frame may be horrible or violent but they are ultimately redeemed by the fact that they take their place within an order. This order cannot be a superficial order, i.e., it is not sufficient to simply frame a scene of grotesque suffering. It has to be placed within a moral order of great consequence. All the "great works" of Western literature intend and depend upon a moral order. The events of the work take their place within an order that satisfies one's sense of justice or one's sense of irony, which itself requires a belief in an order beyond the events of the work.

When one identifies too closely with a character's suffering in a work of art, or when that suffering is exploited to the point where it breaks the boundaries of appropriateness within the moral context of the work, the aesthetic continuity is dislocated; the suffering cannot be justified, morally or aesthetically.[15] So that when *Interiors* comes to its aesthetic ending (the three women are artistically arranged like beautiful motionless statues staring at the ocean), the resolution is not sufficient to justify the enormous suffering of the mother-wife character. No knowledge, no wisdom, no growth, no change has resulted. Passive reduction to beautiful objects is the resolution for those female characters who are still alive at the end of the film. This is not a sufficient moral resolution for the engaged spectator.

By contrast, Chekhov's play *The Three Sisters* exists on a plane far above the exploitation of female suffering seen in these contemporary films. The great themes of Chekhov's drama point to the vanity of human purposes and the corrosion of the human fabric through time. The male and the female characters equally suffer disillusionments and defeats inherent in the human condition. The strongest and most noble figure in the work, indeed, is a woman,

Olga. Chekhov clearly has full compassion and empathy for his female characters.

The great tragedies of Western literature intend the existence of a moral order that transcends and in some way justifies the evil and suffering that is occasioned in the text. As examples, consider *King Lear* and *Oedipus at Colonus*. The protagonist in each play experiences excruciating suffering. But the suffering is not morally meaningless. It is justified by the fact that wisdom and positive social change result (or have resulted in the case of Oedipus).

A powerful passage in Aeschylus's *Agammemnon* states this principle succinctly:

> Zeus, who guided men to think,
> who has laid it down that wisdom
> comes alone through suffering.
>
> • • •
>
> From the gods who sit in grandeur
> grace comes somehow violent.
> Trans. Richmond Lattimore

The tragic cycle of suffering, death, growth, rebirth fits into a universal human expectation of the death of vegetation in winter and its rebirth in the spring (the ancient ritual of the dying year god). Such mythic expectations are not sex-linked; they are universal. Most literature that we call great expresses such universal, fundamental human experiences.

In the case of *King Lear* and *Oedipus at Colonus*, suffering and evil are not hypostasized and projected onto a female Other, as they are in misogynist literature. It is true that Goneril and Regan, Lear's treacherous daughters, are irretrievably evil, but so is Edmund, the bastard son of Gloucester. Cordelia's honesty and loyalty are paralleled by Kent's faithful service to the mad Lear. Feminists (indeed, most viewers/readers) may regret that Shakespeare did not allow Cordelia to survive, along with Edgar, Gloucester's good son, and Kent; nevertheless, the dénoument goes beyond sexist scapegoating. Within the context of the play the deaths are morally and aesthetically necessary; they signify the expulsion of evil and error from the social body; they are necessary to the establishment of a viable moral order.[16] Similarly in *Oedipus at Colonus*, another work that concerns filial piety, Oedipus is assisted by his daughters Antigone and, to a lesser extent, Ismene in his final days. The charitable acts of the women are not the mechanical gestures of an Other, but are the acts of great compassion. That Shakespeare and Sophocles chose women—Cordelia and Antigone—

to exemplify the compelling power of love is not to be construed as sexist stereotyping. Rather, these women are simply humans moved to help a fallen figure in distress. Unfortunately, much of our literature does not reach this stage of grace.[17]

Much of our literature in fact depends upon a series of fixed images of women, stereotypes. These reified forms, surprisingly few in number, are repeated over and over again through much of Western literature. The objectified images have one thing in common, however: they define the woman insofar as she relates to, serves, or thwarts the interests of men.

In the Western tradition these stereotypes tend to fall into two categories, reflecting the endemic Manicheistic dualism in the Western world-view. Female stereotypes symbolize either the spiritual or the material, good or evil. Mary, the mother of Jesus, came through time to exemplify the ultimate in spiritual goodness, and Eve, the partner of Adam, the most sinister of evil physicality. The following diagram shows how this dualism is conceived:

spiritual	material
spirit/soul	body
virginal ideal	sex object
Mary	Eve
inspiration	seductress
good	evil

Under the category of the good-woman stereotypes, that is, those who serve the interests of the hero, are the patient wife, the mother/martyr, and the lady. In the bad or evil category are deviants who reject or do not properly serve men or his interests: the old maid/career woman, the witch/lesbian, the shrew or domineering mother/wife. Several works, considered archetypal masterpieces of the Western tradition, rely upon these simplistic stereotypes of women.

The *Odyssey* is not only the first masterwork of the Western tradition, it provides its archetypal sexist plot, depending as it does on a series of female stereotypes. The *Odyssey* relates the far-flung life adventures of a male hero on his return home to love and security. Tending the home during his twenty-year absence, faithful wife Penelope does little but fend off potential suitors and weave. It has been argued that Penelope matches her "wily" husband in character because she outwits the suitors, as he has outwitted various enemies (most of them women) on his journey. However, her role is so slight and her character so thinly developed that she remains little more than the stereotype of the patient wife.

On his travels, which have the ostensible goal of returning home, he is delayed by a series of female figures. As they present obstacles to his true course, they are seen as evil and fall into the category of "bad" woman. They are all sexual beings, as opposed to Penelope, and they successfully seduce Odysseus, thus delaying his proper progress.

His first encounter is with Calypso, an enchantress-seductress with whom he spends seven years, although he claimed he never gave consent in his heart (*Od.* IX). Next came Circe, a witch, whose brew turned Odysseus's men into pigs. Odysseus has a potion that renders him immune to her liquor, and so he can sleep with her for a year before moving on. Next come the sirens whose seductive songs threaten to delay him once again. Finally, there are Scylla and Charybdis, female monsters, who eat six crewmen.

There are other women in the *Odyssey*, but the central figures are these. They are defined solely in terms of whether they help or hinder the hero on his course. They are presented as wholly evil or wholly good, depending upon that role. Odysseus himself seems to bear no guilt or responsibility for his dallying. The fault, in this original statement of the double standard, is theirs.

Dante's *Commedia*, completed in 1321, is usually interpreted as an allegory of the soul's descent through hell and ascent through purgatory and into paradise. On his journey Dante is guided by various figures. In the *Inferno* and *Purgatorio* his guide is Virgil, who is usually interpreted as representing human reason. Female figures become especially evident in the *Paradiso*. Dante's primary guide in this section is Beatrice, an idealized version of an early romantic involvement he had supposedly had in real life (and which is described in an early work of the courtly love tradition, *La Vita Nuova*). Beatrice is the ultimate expression of the salvific woman, the muse, she who inspires the despairing artist. For this role she is promoted to the levels of highest significance in Dante's personal cosmos, which is extrapolated in the *Commedia* to be the moral cosmos of the Christian myth.

Also in the ultimate reaches of the *Paradiso* is a beatified Virgin Mary, the ultimate symbol in the work of love and grace. The *Commedia* presents, therefore, among other things, one of the greatest elaborations of the ideal spiritual woman, who is nevertheless defined (and in this case elevated to the ranks of ultimate goodness) in terms of her service to the male protagonist.[18]

Faust, completed in 1832 by Goethe, considered one of the greatest of the Western masterworks, also relies on a conception of woman as the inspiration for the man of genius. The final line of this massive dramatic poem is "das Ewig-Weibliche zieht uns hinan," translated: "The eternal feminine draws us upward." In this work the salvific female has been hypostasized as the ultimate inspirational and energizing force of the universe. A summary of the plot of this work will show that this force has been extrapolated from the sacrifice of a rather pathetic female figure, Margaret (or Gretchen).

Faust describes the reinspiration and therefore salvation of a scientist-scholar who has grown despondent and bored with the world. As the work opens, he is looking for something to recharge him. He turns to various means, one of which is a flirtation with a country maid named Gretchen whom he abandons pregnant. Eventually she kills her child, is imprisoned, and dies.

The unappealing philosophy underlying this work is that lesser people like Gretchen and most women are fuel for the great dynamic energy of the great male geniuses of history like Faust. Therefore the destruction of such "little people" is justified as a sacrifice to the greater good that a person like Faust represents in Goethe's dynamic universe. Faust is finally saved in Goethe's romantic version of the legend because he never gave up striving; his energy never ceased. And the reason he continued in a state of "becoming" or growth was due to the inspiration effected by various incarnations of womanhood, who are hypostasized finally as "das Ewig-Weibliche."

These works, central to the Western tradition— the *Odyssey*, the *Commedia*, and *Faust*—do not present the "inside" of women's experience. We learn little, if anything, of the women's own personal responses to events. They are simply vehicles for the growth and salvation of the male protagonist. The women are Other in Beauvoir's sense of the term, and therefore this literature must remain alien to the female reader who reads as a woman.

One can argue, of course, that a woman reader can suspend her femaleness and appreciate great works which have male protagonists (and objectified women) when the protagonists are wrestling with universal human problems. In other words, one can argue that one can transcend one's sex in appreciating a literary work.[19] To some extent I believe that this is indeed possible. One is certainly impelled when viewing or reading *Hamlet* to identify with, or simply to care for, the central character simply because he represents the active consciousness in the work. In *Hamlet* it would take a supreme act of the will to be more concerned about Ophelia, who is minor and whose appeal is largely aesthetic. The same is true for Penelope, Beatrice, and Gretchen.

The real question is not whether a woman *can* identify with the subjective consciousness or the self if it is male, but whether she *should,* given her own political and social environment. In other words, isn't it morally misleading to encourage a person who is barred from action to identify with an individual whose dilemma (in the case of Hamlet) is simply whether to act? Action, taking charge, is a choice that historically has been denied women and still is unavailable to them in many areas. Until, however, ideological socialization ceases, we as female readers cannot authentically transcend our sex. Such literature as treated in this article must remain alien. This does not mean that we should throw out or refuse to read these works, but that they should be read with a perspective that recognizes the sexism inherent in their moral vision.

All moral criticism of literature is based on the assumption that literature affects us, that it changes our attitudes and our behavior; in other words it assumes that literature can precipitate action, harmful or otherwise, in the "real" world. One of the oldest critical observations is Horace's comment that the purpose of art is to teach or to delight (*aut prodesse aut delectare*). Going back further, even Aristotle, often presented as the first technique-oriented critic (as opposed to Plato), couched his theory of mimesis in moral terms:

> Since the objects of imitation are men in action, and these men must be either of a higher or lower type (for moral character [ethos] mainly answers to these divisions, goodness and badness being the distinguishing marks of moral differences), it follows that we must represent men either as better than in real life, or as worse, or as they are (*Poetics* ii, 1; trans. S. H. Butcher).

It is clear in the rest of the *Poetics* that Aristotle prefers the form that imitates the actions of good men (tragedy). In his discussion of character (*ethos*) he

stipulates that the most important trait is "goodness." But Aristotle specifies further that "even a woman may be good, and also a slave; though the woman may be said to be an inferior being, and the slave quite worthless" (*Poetics* xv, 1). Thus, while moral criticism is quite old, the morality expressed has been for the most part sexist. Feminist criticism is a moral criticism which attempts to redress the balance.

John Gardner in *On Moral Fiction* has recently returned to the great moral tradition in criticism. An artistic medium is "good," he says,

> only when it has a clear positive moral effect, presenting valid models for imitation, eternal verities worth keeping in mind, and a benevolent vision of the possible which can inspire human beings toward virtue, toward life affirmation as opposed to destruction or indifference.[20]

Gardner is not talking about a facile didacticism. Instead, and rather courageously, given the epistemological quandary of contemporary ethics, he is trying to talk in everyday terms about values and literature.

Feminist criticism is moral because it sees that one of the central problems of Western literature is that in much of it women are not human beings, seats of consciousness. They are objects, who are used to facilitate, explain away, or redeem the projects of men. Western projects of redemption almost always depend upon a salvific woman. On the other hand, in some Western literature women are the objects, the scapegoats, of much cruelty and evil. Much Western thought and literature has failed to come to grips with the problem of evil because it facilely projects evil upon woman or other hypostasized "Others," such as the Jew, the Negro, thereby denying the reality of the contingent order.[21]

Feminist criticism becomes political when it asserts that literature, academic curricula, and the standards of critical judgment should be changed, so that literature will no longer function as propaganda furthering sexist ideology. The feminist critic recognizes that literature is an important contributing element to a moral atmosphere in which women are derrogated. Moreover, the feminist critic joins other critics of Western thinking in decrying the endemic Manicheism that projects evil upon the Other. Following is a discussion of some literary and ethical values which suggest a way beyond this cultural impasse.

"Moral action is action which affirms life," claims Gardner (p. 23). For a feminist, moral literature is one which affirms the life of women, as well as all other creatures. As Gardner points out, one of the most important criteria that a moral critic can use is to determine whether an author cares for his or her characters, or whether, as we have seen in our analysis of the films, s/he is simply using them for other purposes (pp. 84–85). A great writer must never "sink" to stereotype for even the most minor characters" (p. 109). "Beauty . . . should not be conceived only as a matter of the technique . . . but as the effect of emotional honesty as well . . ." (p. 145). These are fundamental criteria for the feminist critic.

Linguistic analysis and semiological studies can tell us much about how cultural ideologies are expressed in literary form. But only when style is studied in the context of the author's or the culture's moral view of women can it be of feminist significance. Unfortunately much formalist analysis in the past has relied on the convenient divorce between values and aesthetics described above. For this reason it has been able to evade the central evaluative issue that criticism must face: that of the moral stature of the work.

Criticism, by ignoring central questions of content, has become dehumanized in the same way as modern art did when it gave way to exclusively formal concerns. As Gardner notes,

> In all the arts, our criticism is for the most part inhumane. We are rich in schools which speak of how art "works" and avoid the whole subject of what work it ought to do. . . . Structuralists, formalists, linguistic philosophers who tell us that works of art are . . . simply objects for perception—all avoid on principle the humanistic question: who will the work of art help? (pp. 16–17)

Literature on its most profound level is a form of learning. We learn, we grow from the knowledge of life, of psychology, of human behavior and relationships that we discover in worthwhile works of art. The notion that art teaches is as old as criticism. But how it teaches is an equally old and perhaps unanswerable question.

Conversely, bad or immoral art can and does promote evil behavior, just as evil films promote evil acts. Again, as Iris Murdoch has noted, *how* art promotes behavior is a difficult question.[22] Gardner sees fiction as a kind of laboratory wherein moral ideas can be tested both by the author and the reader. The net effect of good literature on the reader should be moral growth, a learning of the effects of good and evil behavior. Much of Western literature does not provide women with such models of behavior and only provides the moral learning experience described above if she engages in inauthentic suspension of her female identity.

Tolstoy's *What Is Art?* is one of the best-known pieces of moral criticism. For all its faults it presents a view of art that is central to a moral critique. Art for Tolstoy is one of the highest forms of communication among humans:

> To evoke in oneself a feeling one has once experienced, and having evoked it in oneself, then, by means of movements, lines, colors, sounds, or forms expressed in words, so to transmit that feeling that others may experience the same feeling—that is the activity of art. Art is a human activity in this, that one . . . hands on to others feelings he has lived through, and that other people are infected by these feelings and also experience them.[23]

"It is a means of union" among peoples, "joining them together in the same feelings, and indispensable for the life and progress toward well-being of individuals and of humanity" (p. 52). Ultimately it is a religious idea of the good that art strives to communicate, according to Tolstoy. That art should be accessible to all, not just an elite, is one of his cardinal principles (p. 96).

Tolstoy argues that one may determine whether a work of art is worthwhile if it evokes "that feeling . . . of joy and of spiritual union with another (the author) and with others (those who are also infected by it)" (p. 139). Again, such spiritual union is hardly possible for a woman when the work involves the derogation of women. (Tolstoy himself was, of course, guilty of considerable misogyny.)

Like Gardner, Tolstoy specifies as one of the hallmarks of great literature a quality of emotional honesty, or what we might call integrity. Tolstoy's preference is for rural pre-industrial literature, the Greek epics, certain Biblical stories. Today, he would have probably loved a film like *Tree of Wooden Clogs* (1978) or, earlier, the short stories of Sarah Orne Jewett.

But it is British novelist Iris Murdoch who, in a series of essays, has developed the most appealing discussions of the moral purpose of art. Murdoch's view of art is that it is a form of education, that it promotes moral growth by helping us to *see* beyond the usual illusions and facile stereotypes by which we habitually organize the chaos of "reality." Following Simone Weil, Murdoch argues that our most serious moral weakness is our tendency to see by means of "fantasy mechanisms."

This concept derives from Simone Weil's notion of gravity, as discussed in *La Pesanteur et la grâce* (1948). In human relations, Weil argues, there are phenomena similar to "gravity" that function as if mechanically. These mechanisms describe the way the psyche orients itself in the world. For example, if one is abused, one has a tendency to retaliate in kind rather than absorb the injury. This injury-retaliation cycle tends to take the shape of a continuing mechanism; it functions almost as predictably as a physical phenomenon like gravity.

Similarly, Weil maintains, we tend to "fill the void" with an endless stream of fabrications, imaginings, myths, etc., which give us a feeling of significance. Sexist mythology promotes males' feelings of significance. These fantasies are stories which magically redeem one from the contingent order by denying its reality; they are false, or inauthentic, attempts at transcendence. The logic of this kind of thinking is deductive. The premises are assumed, and reality is pressed into a kind of unstated, defective syllogism: Women are unimportant; I am not a woman; Therefore I am important.

In "Diving into the Wreck," an early poem, Adrienne Rich wrote,

> the thing I came for:
> the wreck itself and not the story of the wreck
> the thing itself and not the myth.[24]

Such an approach points to the moral alternative described by Iris Murdoch. In wanting to get back to the "thing itself" Rich is attempting to get beyond (or under) the network of mythic confabulations we are enshrouded in. Getting back to the thing itself means not cramming it into a received syllogism; it means functioning by means of a kind of inductive logic (always considered women's strong point). It means starting not from mythic premises, but rather proceeding inductively from concrete, experiential realities, building and gathering knowledge from the events themselves. Women have been criticized in the past for their so-called inability to see the forest for the trees. But perhaps this "inability" is simply a resistance on the part of women to imposing mythic conceptions upon empirical events, knowing, as we do, how easily one's own reality, one's self, can be falsified by public myths.

Unlike Ludwig Wittgenstein, Murdoch does not despair of getting under this reified net of myths. She does not see us as irretrievably imprisoned behind linguistic and semiological barriers which keep us from the thing itself. Such entrapment is not a part of the human condition, Murdoch maintains; it is rather a condition we fall into out of moral weakness. In other words, while Wittgenstein (in the *Tractatus*) argues that the world is only that which we construct theoretically or mythically — and therefore a web of lies — Murdoch insists that we fall into the habit of mythic construction out of fear, weakness, or inertia. Murdoch proposes that we can get out of this epistemological trap by means of moral effort — by a redirection of the will and attention. Such a redirection can lead us to a moral knowledge of the real and of the good.

Murdoch's first novel illustrates concerns similar to Rich's of getting "under the net" (the novel's title), back to reality itself. Jake, the protagonist, is a good example of a person who has fallen into the habit of mythicizing; he continually fantasizes upon reality. His relationship with Anna is particularly illustrative: he constantly tries to see her in terms of various mythic paradigms (e.g., a fairy princess).

Anna herself (following in this regard Wittgenstein himself) has, by contrast, developed a philosophy of silence. Her position seems to be that at this stage of our moral development it is only through silence — only by "knowing the void" (Weil's concept) — that we can begin to see one another as we actually are. Only in this way can we overcome the psychic mechanisms that tend to make us construe people in terms of received myth. While the ending of the novel is somewhat irresolute, it is clear that Jake has moved away from the automatic mythicizing of the early sections toward the beginnings of an acceptance of the reality of the contingent world, of the reality of creatures other than himself and of their diversity. "It seemed," he reflects, "as if, for the first time, Anna really existed now as a separate being, and not as part of myself."[25]

Murdoch sees art and literature, in particular the novel, as an important vehicle for the liberation of people from "fantasy mechanisms." It can foster the growth of moral attention to contingent realities beyond the self and beyond self-promoting fantasies. An essay entitled "On 'God' and 'Good'" presents Murdoch's position most cogently. In this essay she argues that finally it is love that enables us to get under the mythic net, for love demands an awareness of realities beyond the self. The love Murdoch speaks of is, of course, not romantic love, which is itself a mythic mechanism, but rather an orientation toward the world that involves reverential attention. This kind of orientation can be developed and encouraged. It is not necessarily "natural"; at the same time it does not depend on supranatural intervention. It can be developed by a strengthening of our powers of attention, and we can decide to work at such strengthening. That is, we can choose to discipline our awareness; it is an act of will. Great artists exhibit such discipline and compel our awareness similarly. The discipline involves a focusing of the attention without:

> The direction of attention is, contrary to nature, outward, away from self which reduces all to a false unity, toward the great surprising variety of the world, and the ability to so direct attention is love.[26]

Murdoch borrowed the concept of attention from Simone Weil, as she acknowledges. Weil used the term to mean "the idea of a just and loving gaze directed upon an individual reality."[27] Such attention, Murdoch notes, is "the characteristic and proper mark of the active moral agent" (p. 34). Such attention counteracts such "states of illusion" as are fostered by stereotypic or mythic expectations (p. 37).

Seeing clearly through proper attentiveness brings one to proper conduct. It effects moral growth: "True vision occasions right conduct."

> The more the separateness and differentness of other people is realized, and the fact seen that another . . . has needs and wishes as demanding as one's own, the harder it becomes to treat a person as a thing (p. 66).

True liberation therefore lies in the capacity to apprehend realities beyond the self and its promotion:

> It is in the capacity to love, that is to see, that the liberation of the soul from fantasy consists. The freedom which is a proper human goal is the freedom from fantasy, that is the realism of compassion (p. 66).

Ideally, the work of great artists helps us to *see* reality in all its conflicting diversity and therefore to make choices that are truly responsible to the real contexts in which they are made.

In "The Sublime and the Good," Murdoch argues further that art and morals are rooted in the same impulse:

> The essence of both of them is love. Love is the perception of individuals. Love is the extremely difficult realization that something other than oneself is real. Love, and so art and morals, is the discovery of reality.[28]

Both intend the "non-violent apprehension of difference" (p. 54). Great novelists, she argues elsewhere, are not "afraid of the contingent." They display "a real apprehension of persons other than the author as having a right to exist and to have a separate mode of being which is important and interesting to themselves."[29]

Much of the literature of our Western tradition has not risen to such heights. Its male authors do not reach that "extremely difficult realization" that women, "something other than" themselves, exist, are real. Their works are morally insufficient, for they do not attend to the independent reality of women. This is a fundamental critique offered by an "images of women" approach to literature.

Notes

1. This article follows from the assumptions about feminist criticism as a negative criticism laid down in my "Afterword: Critical Re-Vision," *Feminist Literary Criticism: Explorations in Theory*, ed. Josephine Donovan (Lexington: University Press of Kentucky, 1975), p. 75.
2. "Subjectivities," *Feminist Literary Criticism*, p. 34.
3. *The Second Sex* (New York: Knopf, 1953), p. xviii. Other references will follow in the text.
4. As Marcia Holly pointed out in "Consciousness and Authenticity: Toward a Feminist Aesthetic," *Feminist Literary Criticism*, pp. 38–47.
5. See Martin Heidegger, *Being and Time*, trans. John MacQuarrie and Edward Robinson (New York: Harper, 1962), pp. 164–243.
6. Jean-Paul Sartre, *Being and Nothingness: An Essay in Phenomenological Ontology*, trans. Hazel E. Barnes (New York: The Citadel Press, 1966), pp. lxvi, 54, 535.
7. See Stuart Cunningham, "Some Problems of Feminist Literary Criticism," *Journal of Women's Studies in Literature*, 1, No. 2 (Spring, 1979), 159–78. Cunningham's thesis that more attention must be paid by American feminist critics to the role ideology plays in shaping stereotypes is, however, a useful suggestion.
8. Terry Eagleton explains Marxist and Freudian methodology in similar terms in *Criticism and Ideology* (London: Verso, 1978), pp. 91–101.
9. See Barbara Welter, "The Cult of True Womanhood: 1820–1860," *American Quarterly*, 18, No. 2, Pt. 1 (Summer, 1966), 151–74; Helen Papashvily, *All the Happy Endings* (New York: Harper, 1956);

and Nina Baym, *Woman's Fiction* (Ithaca: Cornell University Press, 1978).

10. *From Reverence to Rape: The Treatment of Women in the Movies* (New York: Penguin, 1974), p. 7.

11. "Visual Pleasure and Narrative Cinema," *Women and the Cinema: A Critical Anthology,* ed. Karyn Kay and Gerald Peary (New York: E. P. Dutton, 1977), p. 418.

12. "Cries and Whispers," *Movies and Methods: An Anthology,* ed. Bill Nichols (Berkeley: University of California Press, 1976), p. 207.

13. Erwin Panofsky's "Die Perspektive als 'symbolische Form,'" *Vorträge der Bibliothek Warburg 1924–1925* (Berlin: B. G. Tuebner, 1927), presents a brilliant discussion of the emergence of the mathematical paradigm as the governing aesthetic notion in the Renaissance.

14. See Katharine Rogers, *The Troublesome Helpmate: A History of Misogyny in Literature* (Seattle: University of Washington Press, 1966), pp. 201–57, for a brief history of attacks on the single woman.

15. Elsewhere I have argued that such is the case in Faulkner's *Light in August.* In that work the suffering and destruction of the spinster woman Joanna Burden, as well as her demoniacal evil, lead one to consider her existence improbable and beyond the pale of aesthetic and moral appropriateness (using once again Aristotelian criteria). When one character is so out of bounds, the whole moral and therefore the aesthetic universe of the work collapses. I noted that "it is impossible for a feminist to accept the aesthetic imperative of Faulkner's novel which requires that the author create an inauthentic woman and use her immorally for aesthetic ends" ("Feminism and Aesthetics," *Critical Inquiry,* 3, No. 3 [Spring, 1977], 608).

16. Even Cordelia exhibited the kind of moral intransigence that we associate with tragic hybris. One may argue whether she deserved her fate, but one cannot see her as doomed *because* she is a woman. I am relying here in part on A. C. Bradley's classic study, *Shakespearean Tragedy* (1904). Bradley does not see Cordelia as contributing to her fate, however, but rather as an innocent victim acci-dentally destroyed in the process of the expulsion of evil. For recent feminist analyses of Shakespeare see Carolyn Ruth Swift Lenz, Gayle Green, and Carol Thomas Neely (eds.), *The Woman's Part: Feminist Criticism of Shakespeare* (Urbana: University of Illinois Press, 1980).

17. The question of the extent to which tragedy as a *form* is inherently sexist would take us beyond the confines of this article. On the subject see Carol Gelderman, "The Male Nature of Tragedy," *Prairie Schooner,* 49, No. 3 (Autumn, 1975), 220–27.

18. Joan M. Ferrante presents a fully detailed analysis in *Woman as Image in Medieval Literature* (New York: Columbia University Press, 1975), Chap. 5.

19. I presented some of the ideas in the following two paragraphs in "Comment," *College English,* 38, No. 3 (November, 1976), 301–02.

20. *On Moral Fiction* (New York: Basic Books, 1978), p. 18. Further references will follow in the text.

21. See Jean-Paul Sartre's *Anti-Semite and Jew* (1956) and *Saint Genet* (1952), as well as Thomas Szasz, *The Manufacturer of Madness* (New York: Dell, 1970) for an exploration of this thesis. Szasz applies the concept of Otherness to witches, the insane, and homosexuals.

22. Iris Murdoch, *The Fire and the Sun: Why Plato Banished the Artists* (Oxford: Clarendon Press, 1977), p. 77.

23. Leo Tolstoy, *What Is Art?* trans. Aylmer Maude (Indianapolis: Bobbs-Merrill, 1960), p. 51. Further references will follow in the text.

24. *Diving into the Wreck—Poems 1971–72* (New York: W. W. Norton & Co., 1973), p. 23.

25. *Under the Net* (New York: Viking Press, 1954), p. 261.

26. "On 'God' and 'Good,'" in *The Sovereignty of Good* (New York: Schocken, 1971), p. 66.

27. Murdoch, "The Idea of Perfection," *The Sovereignty of Good,* p. 34. Further references follow in the text.

28. "The Sublime and the Good," *Chicago Review,* 13 (Autumn, 1959), p. 51. Further references follow in the text.

29. "The Sublime and the Beautiful Revisited," *Yale Review,* 69 (December, 1959), p. 257.

APPLICATION

In Bargains with Fate: Psychological Crises and Conflicts in Shakespeare and His Plays, *Bernard Paris continues his project of applying psychological theories to
fictional characters and to implied authors. In the selection that follows, Paris concentrates on the character of
Prospero, producing a reading of that character considerably at odds with Prospero's own estimate and with much
traditional criticism. In the selection from Paris in the
Theory section of this chapter, he had raised the possibility that in some literary works the mimetic impulse may
be in conflict with the thematic impulse. Paris finds just
such a conflict in* The Tempest. *There is a discrepancy,
he argues, between the play's thematic thrust and its representation of character. "When we understand Prospero's
psychological development, he seems different from the
figure celebrated by so many critics. Those who interpret*
The Tempest *as a story of magnanimity, forgiveness,
and reconciliation are responding correctly, I believe, to
Shakespeare's thematic intentions, whereas those who take
a more 'hard-nosed' view of the play are responding to the
psychological portrait of Prospero." As Paris sees it, those
who concentrate on the psychological portrait are going to
get closer to the play's real meaning.*

The Tempest is one of only two Shakespearean plays
whose plot, as far as we know, is entirely the author's invention. More than any other play, it is
Shakespeare's fantasy. What, we must ask, is it a fantasy of? What psychological needs are being met?
What wishes are being fulfilled? One way of approaching these questions is to look at the unrealistic
elements in the play, particularly Prospero's magic.
The function of magic is to do the impossible, to grant

The Tempest

Bernard Paris

Reprinted by permission of the author from *Bargains with
Fate: Psychological Crises and Conflicts in Shakespeare and His
Plays.* New York: Insight Books, 1991: 263–76. This selec-
tion is a retitled excerpt from Chapter 9, "*The Tempest:*
Shakespeare's Ideal Solution."

wishes that are denied to us in reality. What is his magic doing for Prospero? And for Shakespeare? What impossible dream does it allow to come true?

These questions can be approached from a variety of psychological perspectives. In Freudian theory, for instance, magic is associated with a belief in the omnipotence of thought, and it is employed in an effort to restore the delusions of grandeur that accompanied infantile megalomania. By giving him magical powers, Shakespeare grants Prospero the mastery of time, space, and matter that we once thought we enjoyed and that we still desire. In *Totem and Taboo*, Freud argued that man's conception of the universe has passed through three stages, the animistic, the religious, and the scientific:

> we have no difficulty in following the fortunes of the "omnipotence of thought" through all these phases. In the animistic stage man ascribes omnipotence to himself; in the religious he has ceded it to the gods, but without seriously giving it up, for he reserves to himself the right to control the gods by influencing them in some way or other in the interest of his wishes. In the scientific attitude toward life there is no longer any room for man's omnipotence; he has acknowledged his smallness and has submitted to death as to all other natural necessities in a spirit of resignation. (n.d., 115)

Most of Shakespeare's comedies and romances are written from a religious perspective; wishes are fulfilled through the cooperation or even the direct intervention of providential forces. Perhaps Northrop Frye, for whom domination by the pleasure principle is the glory of literature, calls *The Tempest* the "bedrock of drama" (1969, 67) because it is written from an animistic perspective. Prospero is indebted to "providence divine" for guiding him to the island and for placing his enemies within his reach, but to a large extent the powers given to the gods and to providence in the other romances are conferred here upon a human being. No doubt, the appeal of *The Tempest* lies, in part, in the directness and immediacy of its wish-fulfillment, in its regression to one of the earliest stages of primary-process thinking. One question we must ask, of course, is why Prospero gives up his magic. Is it a sign of movement to a religious or a scientific perspective?

This approach sheds a good deal of light upon the play, especially upon the ending, but it does not relate Prospero's magic to his personality and show us how it helps him to satisfy his specific psychological needs. Before he is overthrown, Prospero is a predominantly detached person. The detached person craves serenity, dislikes responsibility, and is averse to the struggle for power. His "two outstanding neurotic claims are that life should be . . . effortless and that he should not be bothered" (Horney 1950, 264). Prospero turns his responsibilities as duke over to his brother, rejects the pursuit of "worldly ends," and retires into his library, which is "dukedom large enough!" (II, ii). He immerses himself in a world of books, seeking glory not through the exercise of his office, which involves him in troublesome relations with other people, but through the pursuit of knowledge. As a result of his studies, he becomes "the prime duke, being so reputed / In dignity, and for the liberal arts / Without a parallel" (II, ii). He is not without ambition and a hunger for power, but he satisfies these needs in a detached way.

Prospero's study of magic is highly congruent with his personality. The detached person has an aversion to effort and places the greatest value upon freedom from constraint. Magic is a means of achieving one's ends without effort and of transcending the limitations of the human condition. It is a way of enforcing the claim that mind is the supreme reality, that the material world is subject to its dictates. Indeed, it symbolizes that claim. Through his withdrawal into the study of magic, Prospero is pursuing a dream of glory that is far more grandiose than any available to him as Duke of Milan. It is no wonder that he "prize[s]" his "volumes . . . above [his] dukedom." He becomes "transported / And rapt in secret studies" and grows a "stranger" to his state (I, ii).

Reality intrudes upon Prospero in the form of Antonio's plot, which leads to his expulsion from the dukedom. Although many critics have blamed Prospero for his neglect of his duties, Prospero does not seem to blame himself or to see himself as being responsible in any way for his fate. He interprets his withdrawal as a commendable unworldliness and presents his behavior toward his brother in a way that is flattering to himself:

> and my trust,
> Like a good parent, did beget of him
> A falsehood in its contrary as great
> As my trust was, which had indeed no limit,
> A confidence sans bound. (I, ii)

There are strong self-effacing tendencies in Prospero that lead him to think too well of his fellows and to bestow upon them a trust they do not deserve. Overtrustingness has disastrous consequences in the history plays and in the tragedies, but it has no permanent ill-effects in the comedies and romances. Prospero glorifies his excessive confidence in his brother and places the blame for what happens entirely upon Antonio's "evil nature." He seems to have no sense of how his own foolish behavior has contributed to his fate.

Antonio's betrayal marks the failure of Prospero's self-effacing bargain; his goodness to his brother, which he had expected to be repaid with gratitude and devotion, is used by Antonio to usurp the dukedom. This trauma is similar to those that precipitate psychological crises in the protagonists of the tragedies, crises from which none of them recover. Prospero's case is different because of his magic. Like the protagonists of the tragedies, Prospero is furious with those by whom he has been injured and craves a revenge that will assuage his anger and repair his idealized image. Unlike the characters in the realistic plays, however, he has a means of restoring his pride without being destructive to himself and others. He spends the next twelve years dreaming of his revenge and perfecting his magic in preparation for his vindictive triumph. *The Tempest* is the story of his day of reckoning.

Prospero has numerous objectives on this day, all of which he achieves through his magic. He wants to punish his enemies, to make a good match for his daughter, to get back what he has lost, to prove through his display of power that he was right to have immersed himself in his studies, and to demonstrate that he is the great man that he has felt himself to be, far superior to those who have humiliated him. The most important function of his magic, however, is that it enables him to resolve his psychological conflicts. Once he has been wronged, Prospero is caught between contradictory impulses. He is full of rage that he has a powerful need to express, but he feels that revenge is ignoble and that he will be as bad as his enemies if he allows himself to descend to their level. What Prospero needs is what Hamlet could not find and what Shakespeare is trying to imagine: a way of taking revenge and remaining innocent. This is a problem that only his magic can solve. *The Tempest* is above all a fantasy of innocent revenge. The revenge is Prospero's, but the fantasy is Shakespeare's, whose conflicting needs are similar to those of his protagonist.

The storm with which the play opens is an expression of Prospero's rage. It instills terror in his enemies and satisfies his need to make them suffer for what they have done to him. If the vindictive side of Prospero is embodied in the storm, his compassionate side is embodied in Miranda, who is full of pity for the suffering of the "poor souls" who seem to have "perish'd" (I, ii). Since Miranda is the product of Prospero's tutelage, she represents his ideal values, at least for a woman; and it is important to recognize that she is extremely self-effacing. When Prospero begins to tell the story of their past, her "heart bleeds / To think o' th' teen that I have turn'd you to"; and when he describes their expulsion, she exclaims, "Alack, what trouble / Was I then to you!" (I, ii). She wants to carry Ferdinand's logs for him, feels unworthy of his love, and swears to be his servant if he will not marry her (III, i). Like her father before his fall, she has an idealistic view of human nature. The "brave vessel" that has sunk "had no doubt some noble creature in her" (I, ii), and when she first sees the assembled company, she exclaims, "How beauteous mankind is! O brave new world / That has such people in't!" (V, i). Prospero is no longer so idealistic, but he has retained many of his self-effacing values and has instilled them in Miranda. He approves of her response to "the wrack, which touch'd / The very virtue of compassion in thee" (I, ii) and assures her that "There's no harm done." Through his "art" he has "So safely ordered" the storm that there is "not so much perdition as an hair / Betid to any creature in the vessel / Which thou heard'st cry." Miranda says that if she had "been any god of power" she would never have permitted the wreck to happen, and neither does Prospero. Through his magic, the wreck happens and does not happen. His magic permits him to satisfy his vindictive needs without violating the side of himself that is expressed by Miranda.[1] To further alleviate his discomfort with his sadistic behavior and Miranda's implied reproaches, Prospero claims that he has "done nothing but in care" of her and justifies his actions by telling the story of Antonio's perfidy.

Prospero's delight in the discomfiture of his enemies is revealed most vividly in his response to Ariel's account of his frightening behavior during the tempest. He asks Ariel if he has "Perform'd to point the tempest" he had commanded; and when Ariel replies that he has, Prospero's sadistic pleasure is evident: "My brave spirit! / Who was so firm, so

constant, that this coil / Would not infect his reason?"
His enthusiastic response inspires Ariel to elaborate:

> Not a soul
> But felt a fever of the mad and play'd
> Some tricks of desperation. All but mariners
> Plung'd in the foaming brine and quit the vessel,
> Then all afire with me. The King's son Ferdinand,
> With hair up-staring (then like reeds, not hair),
> Was the first man that leapt; cried "Hell is empty,
> And all the devils are here!" (I, ii)

Once again Prospero expresses his approval: "Why, that's my spirit!" Since Ariel has carried out his orders "To every article," we must assume that the madness and desperation Ariel describes are precisely what Prospero intended. He is pleased not only by the terror of his enemies, but also by that of Ferdinand, his future son-in-law. He is rather indiscriminate in his punishments, as he is later in his forgiveness.

Prospero can enjoy the terror of his victims because he has not injured them physically: "But are they, Ariel, safe?" Not only are they safe, but their garments are "fresher than before" (I, ii). In the history plays and the tragedies, revengers incur guilt and bring destruction upon themselves by doing physical violence to their enemies. Prospero is a cunning and sadistic revenger who employs his magic to inflict psychological violence upon his enemies while he shields them from physical injury and thereby preserves his innocence. In his mind, as long as no one is physically injured, "There's no harm done" (I, ii). Having everyone fear imminent destruction, including the good Gonzalo, having them run mad with terror at Ariel's apparitions, having Ferdinand and Alonso believe each other dead, such things, for Prospero, do not constitute harm.

Prospero's cruelty toward his enemies may not appear to say much about his character because it seems justified by their outrageous treatment of him. He is prone to react with aggression, however, whenever he can find a justification, however slight, for doing so.[2] He says he will put Ferdinand in chains and force him to drink sea water and to eat mussels, withered roots, and acorn husks, and he makes him remove thousands of logs, "lest too light winning" of Miranda "Make the prize light" (I, ii). This seems a weak excuse for his sadistic behavior. His pleasure with Ariel for his management of the tempest is followed by a scene in which he threatens to "rend an oak / And peg [him] in his knotty entrails till / [He] has howl'd away twelve winters" (I, ii). He even

threatens Miranda when she beseeches him to have pity upon Ferdinand: "Silence! One word more / Shall make me chide thee, if not hate thee" (I, ii).

Prospero is usually benevolent until he feels that his kindness has been betrayed or unappreciated, and then he becomes vindictive. He feels betrayed by Antonio, of course, and unappreciated by Ariel when that spirit presses for liberty. He justifies his enslavement of Ariel by reminding him that it was his "art" that freed him from Sycorax's spell, and he threatens him with torments similar to those Sycorax had inflicted if he continues to complain. Prospero's threats seem to me an overreaction. He will peg Ariel in the entrails of an oak merely for murmuring. Prospero makes enormous claims on the basis of his kindness, and if others do not honor these claims he becomes enraged. If he is ready to punish Ariel and to hate Miranda for very slight offenses, think of the vindictiveness that he must be feeling toward Antonio. Ariel is self-effacing and knows how to make peace with Prospero. He thanks him for having freed him and promises to "be correspondent to command / And do [his] spriting gently" (I, ii). This allows Prospero to become benevolent once again, and he promises to discharge Ariel in two days. Ariel then says what Prospero wants to hear: "That's my noble master!" This is the way Prospero insists upon being perceived. Indeed, his anger with Ariel when he murmurs derives partly from the fact that Ariel has threatened his idealized image by making him seem unkind.

Ariel plays Prospero's game, but Caliban does not. Prospero is initially very kind to Caliban; he strokes him, gives him treats, educates him, and lodges him in his cell. And Caliban initially reciprocates; he loves Prospero and shows him "all the qualities o' the isle" (I, ii). Prospero turns against Caliban, however, when he seeks to violate Miranda's honor, and from this point on he treats Caliban with great brutality. Here, too, Prospero overreacts. He is so enraged, I propose, because Caliban has repeated Antonio's crime, accepting Prospero's favors and repaying them with treachery. Prospero discharges onto him all the anger that he feels toward the enemies back home who, before the day of reckoning, are beyond his power. Even after he enslaves Caliban, Prospero expects him to behave submissively. He complains to Miranda that Caliban "never / Yields us kind answer," but then he summons Caliban in a way that reveals the unreasonableness of his expectation: "What, ho! slave! Caliban / Thou earth, thou!

Speak!" (II, ii). When Caliban responds to being treated like dirt by being bitterly resentful, Prospero takes this as a sign of his irreclaimable nature.

There is a major contradiction in Prospero's attitude toward Caliban. He feels that Caliban is subhuman, but he holds him morally responsible for his acts and he punishes him severely. If Caliban is subhuman, then he is not morally responsible and should simply be kept away from Miranda, a precaution Prospero could easily effect. If he is a moral agent, then he needs to be shown the error of his ways; but Prospero's punishments are merely designed to torture him and to break his spirit. The contradiction in Prospero's attitude results from conflicting psychological needs. He needs to hold Caliban responsible because doing so allows him to act out his sadistic impulses, but he also needs to regard Caliban as subhuman because this allows him to avoid feeling guilt. If Caliban is subhuman, he is not part of Prospero's moral community, and Prospero's behavior toward him is not subject to the shoulds and taboos that are operative in his relations with his fellow human beings. Caliban provides Prospero with a splendid opportunity for justified aggression, for being vindictive without losing his nobility.

Prospero's rationalization of his treatment of Caliban works so well that the majority of critics have accepted his point of view and have felt that Caliban deserves what he gets, though some have been sympathetic toward Caliban's suffering and uneasy about Prospero's behavior (Auden 1962, 129). Prospero is constantly punishing Caliban, not just for the attempted rape, but also for the much lesser crimes of surliness, resentment, and insubordination. When Caliban is slow in responding to Prospero's summons ("Slave! Caliban! / Thou earth, thou!"), Prospero calls him again in an even nastier way: "Thou poisonous slave, got by the devil himself / Upon thy wicked dam, come forth!" (I, ii). Caliban does not yield a "kind answer" but enters with curses: "As wicked dew as e'er my mother brush'd / With raven's feather from unwholesome fen / Drop on you both!" Prospero responds by promising horrible punishments:

> For this, be sure, to-night thou shalt have cramps,
> Side-stitches that shall pen thy breath up; urchins
> Shall, for that vast of night that they may work,
> All exercise on thee; thou shalt be pinch'd
> As thick as honeycomb, each pinch more stinging
> Than bees that made 'em.   (I, ii)

This is a very unequal contest, since Caliban's curses are merely words, an expression of ill-will, while Prospero has the power to inflict the torments he describes. Despite his "crime" in attempting Miranda (a natural act for an uncivilized being), Caliban seems to have reason for his resentment. He feels that the island is his (he was his "own king" before Prospero arrived), he has been turned into a drudge, and he is subject to vicious abuse. Prospero looks for penitence, submissiveness, and gracious service from Caliban and punishes him severely for his spirit of defiance. He seems to be trying to torture him into being a willing slave, like Ariel, and he is embittered by his lack of success.

Prospero and Caliban are caught in a vicious circle from which there seems to be no escape. The more Caliban resists what he perceives as Prospero's tyranny, the more Prospero punishes him; and the more Prospero punishes him, the more Caliban resists. He curses Prospero even though he knows that his spirits hear him and that he may be subject to retaliation — "yet I needs must curse" (II, ii). The need for this emotional relief must be powerful indeed in view of what may be in store for him:

> For every trifle are they set upon me;
> Sometimes like apes that mow and chatter at me,
> And after bite me; then like hedgehogs which
> Lie tumbling in my barefoot way and mount
> Their pricks at my footfall; sometime am I
> All wound with adders, who with cloven tongues
> Do hiss me into madness.   (II, ii)

It is remarkable that Caliban's spirit has not been broken as a result of such torments. And it is no wonder that Caliban seizes the opportunity he thinks is presented by Stephano and Trinculo to revolt against Prospero. "I am subject," he tells them, "to a tyrant, / A sorcerer, that by his cunning hath / Cheated me of the island" (III, ii). Is this far from the truth? He claims that Prospero's spirits "all do hate him / As rootedly as I." It is impossible to say whether or not this is true, but it might be. Even Ariel must be threatened with terrible punishments and reminded once a month of what Prospero has done for him.

Prospero does not need to use his magic to resolve inner conflicts in his relationship with Caliban because regarding Caliban as subhuman allows him to act out his vindictive impulses without guilt or restraint. The combination of his sadistic imagination and his magic makes him an ingenious torturer. He could have used his magic more benignly if he had regarded Caliban as part of his moral community, but this would have generated conflicts and deprived him of his scapegoat. (See Berger 1970, 261, on Caliban as scapegoat.) He insists, therefore, that Caliban is uneducable: "A devil, a born devil, on whose nature / Nurture can never stick! on whom my pains, / Humanely taken, all, all lost, quite lost!" (IV, i). His judgment is reinforced by Miranda, who abhors Caliban, in part, because his vindictiveness violates her self-effacing values, and by Caliban's plot, which seems to demonstrate his innate depravity. Since there is no point in being humane to a born devil, Prospero is free to "plague" him "to roaring."[3]

Many critics agree that Caliban is a hopeless case, but some are impressed by his sensitivity in "The isle is full of noises" speech (III, ii) and by his declaration that he will "seek for grace" (V, i) (see also Berger 1970, 255). His plot can be seen as a reaction to Prospero's abuse rather than as a sign that he is an "abhorred slave / Which any print of goodness wilt not take" (I, ii). Prospero must hold onto his image of Caliban as a devil in order to hold onto his idealized image of himself. If Caliban is redeemable, then Prospero has been a monster. The exchange of curses between Prospero and Caliban indicates that they have much in common. What Prospero hates and punishes in Caliban is the forbidden part of himself. His denial of moral status to Caliban is in part a rationale for his vindictive behavior and in part a way of denying the similarities that clearly exist between them. Prospero is doing to Caliban what Caliban would do to Prospero if he had the power.

Prospero is much more careful in his treatment of his fellow humans, some of whom strike us as being considerably more depraved than Caliban. Indeed, Prospero calls Caliban a devil but feels that Antonio and Sebastian "are worse than devils" (III, iii). Nonetheless, he regards them as fellow human beings and his shoulds and taboos are fully operative in relation to them. Not only does he conceal his vindictiveness from himself (and from many of the critics) by employing his magic to punish them without doing any "harm," but he justifies his treatment of them by seeing it as conducive to their moral growth. His object is not revenge but regeneration and reconciliation. Ariel articulates Prospero's perspective in the banquet scene. He accuses the "three men of sin" of their crimes against "good Prospero," threatens them with "ling'ring perdition," and indicates that they can escape Prospero's wrath only by "heart's sorrow / And

a clear life ensuing" (III, iii). Even as Prospero is knitting them up in "fits" and exulting in the fact that "they are now in [his] pow'r," he is being presented in a very noble light. He manages to take revenge in such a way that he emerges as the benefactor of his victims.

After he has tormented them so much that "the good old Lord Gonzalo" is in tears at the sight and even Ariel has "a feeling / Of their afflictions," Prospero relents, as he had intended to do all along:

> Though with their high wrongs I am struck to th'
>   quick,
> Yet with my nobler reason 'gainst my fury
> Do I take part. The rarer action is
> In virtue than in vengeance. They being penitent,
> The sole drift of my purpose doth extend
> Not a frown further.   (V, i)

Although Prospero is still furious with the evil three, his perfectionistic and self-effacing shoulds are stronger than his vindictive impulses. He releases them from his spell, in part, because his cruelty is making him uneasy and, in part, because his need for revenge has been assuaged by their suffering. He proclaims that "the rarer action is / In virtue than in vengeance," but he says this only after he has gotten a goodly measure of vengeance. He makes it seem that his only purpose has been to bring the men of sin to penitence, but that is hardly the case. This is a play not only about renouncing revenge but also about getting it.

There has been much debate over whether Prospero's enemies are indeed repentant. Prospero's forgiveness is made contingent upon penitence and a clear life after, but only Alonso seems to merit his pardon. Alonso displays his remorse again and again, but Sebastian and Antonio show no sign of repentance or promise of reformation. They have plotted against Prospero in the past; they try to kill Alonso during the course of the play; and they seem at the play's end still to be dangerous fellows. Many critics have speculated upon the likelihood of their continued criminality upon the return to Italy. In 1797, F. G. Waldron wrote a sequel to *The Tempest* in which Antonio and Sebastian betray Prospero during the voyage home and force him to retrieve his magic.

Why, then, does Prospero forgive them? It may be that he thinks they have repented, but I do not think he does. While Antonio is still under his spell, Prospero says, "I forgive thee, / Unnatural though thou art" (V, i); and when he has returned to full consciousness, Prospero forgives him again, in an even more contemptuous way:

> For you, most wicked sir, whom to call brother
> Would even infect my mouth, I do forgive
> Thy rankest fault—all of them . . .   (V, i)

As Bonamy Dobrée (1952) suggested, there is a nasty quality about Prospero's forgiveness. More like revenge than a movement toward reconciliation, it is a vindictive forgiveness that satisfies his need to express his scorn and bitterness while appearing to be noble. Antonio's undeservingness contributes to Prospero's sense of moral grandeur; the worse Antonio is, the more charitable is Prospero to forgive him. This is Prospero's perspective and that of the play's rhetoric; but from a psychological point of view, Prospero's forgiveness seems compulsive, indiscriminate, and dangerous. It is inappropriate to the practical and moral realities of the situation but necessary if Prospero is to maintain his idealized image.

For most of the play, Prospero's idealized image contains a combination of arrogant-vindictive and self-effacing traits that are reconciled by means of his magic. He needs to see himself as a humane, benevolent, forgiving man, and also as a powerful, masterful, dangerous man who cannot be taken advantage of with impunity and who will strike back when he has been injured. The first four acts of the play show Prospero satisfying his needs for mastery and revenge, but in ways that do not violate his perfectionistic and self-effacing dictates. By the end of act 4, he has achieved his objectives. He has knit up Antonio, Sebastian, and Alonso in his spell and has thwarted the plot of Caliban, Stephano, and Trinculo, with a final display of innocent delight in the torture of the conspirators. Prospero sets his dogs (two of whom are aptly named Fury and Tyrant) upon them, and tells Ariel to charge his "goblins that they grind their joints / With dry convulsions, shorten up their sinews / With aged cramps, and more pinch-spotted make them / Than pard or cat o' mountain" (IV, i). "At this hour," Prospero proclaims, "Lie at my mercy all mine enemies." From this point on, he becomes increasingly self-effacing. At the beginning of the next act, he gives up his vengeance and determines to renounce his magic. Once he gives up his magic, he has no choice but to repress his vindictive trends, for it was only through his magic that he was able to act them out innocently.

Prospero represses his vindictive side for a number of reasons. He has shown his power. Now, in order to satisfy his self-effacing shoulds, he must show his mercy. He cannot stop behaving vindictively until his anger has been partially assuaged, but he cannot continue once his enemies are in his power. That he is still angry is clear from the manner of his forgiveness, but the imperative to forgive is now more powerful than the need for revenge. Given his inner conflicts, Prospero is bound to feel uncomfortable about his aggressive behavior; and now that he has had his day of reckoning, his negative feelings about it become dominant. He regards revenge as ignoble and "abjures" his "rough magic" (V, i). His choice of words here is significant. He seems to feel ashamed of his magic (even as he celebrates its powers) and guilty for having employed it. Why else would he use the word "abjure," which means to disavow, recant, or repudiate? Whereas earlier he was able to enjoy his power, he now has a self-effacing response to it. He gives up his magic because he needs to place himself in an humble position and to show that he has not used his power for personal aggrandizement, but only to set things right, to bring about moral growth and reconciliation.

Although *Henry VIII* was yet to come, *The Tempest* is often read as Shakespeare's farewell to the theater, and Prospero is seen as his supreme embodiment of the artist figure. Though it is impossible to tell to what extent Prospero is Shakespeare's alter ego, there are some striking parallels. Prospero uses his magic and Shakespeare uses his art to attain mastery and to achieve disguised or innocent revenge. Shakespeare condemns or even kills off in his plays the kinds of people who have hurt him or of whom he is most afraid, but, like Prospero, he maintains a posture of benevolence and wisdom.[4] Again like Prospero, he seems after a certain point (*Timon*) to become more and more self-effacing; and he prematurely relinquishes his magic, perhaps because he, too, feels guilty about his exercise of power and needs to embrace "the blessedness of being little" (*Henry VIII*, IV, ii).

In the Epilogue, with his "charms . . . o'erthrown," Prospero adopts an extremely self-effacing posture. Since he can no longer "enchant," he can "be reliev'd" only by prayer,

> Which pierces so that it assaults
> Mercy itself and frees all faults.
> As you from crimes would pardon'd be,
> Let your indulgence set me free.

Prospero sees himself here not as the avenger, but as the guilty party, perhaps because of his revenge; and he tries to make a self-effacing bargain in which he judges not so that he will not be judged. We can now understand more fully his motives for forgiving the men of sin. Beneath his self-righteousness, Prospero has hidden feelings of guilt and fears of retribution. By refusing to take a more severe form of revenge, to which he certainly seems entitled, he protects himself against punishment. By forgiving others, he ensures his own pardon. Giving up his magic serves a similar purpose. It counteracts his feelings of pride and places him in a dependent, submissive position. Although Prospero's remarks in the Epilogue are partly a conventional appeal to the audience, he remains in character and expresses sentiments that are in keeping with his psychological development.

When we understand Prospero's psychological development, he seems different from the figure celebrated by so many critics. Those who interpret *The Tempest* as a story of magnanimity, forgiveness, and reconciliation are responding correctly, I believe, to Shakespeare's thematic intentions, whereas those who take a more "hard-nosed" view of the play are responding to the psychological portrait of Prospero. There is in this play, as in some others, a disparity between rhetoric and mimesis that generates conflicting critical responses and reflects the inner divisions of the author (see Paris 1991).

In his presentation of Prospero, Shakespeare employs a powerful rhetoric both of justification and of glorification. He employs numerous devices that justify Prospero's behavior toward Antonio, Sebastian, Alonso, Caliban, Ariel, Ferdinand, Stephano, and Trinculo—toward all the characters, in effect, whom Prospero treats harshly. Early in the play, there is some rhetoric of glorification and some rhetoric of justification toward the end, but by and large the justification occurs when Prospero is being punitive and the glorification occurs after he gives up his vengeance. We learn early in the play of Prospero's betrayal by his brother, of the dangers to which he was exposed, of Ariel's impatience, of Caliban's treachery, of the need to test Ferdinand, and of the continued perfidy of Antonio and Sebastian. All these things justify Prospero's harshness, as does Miranda's condemnation of Caliban and Ariel's acceptance of Prospero's reproaches. As the play progresses, Prospero is increasingly surrounded by a rhetoric of glorification. He is praised by Ariel ("my noble master")

and Ferdinand ("so rare a wonder'd father"), and he receives a tribute even from Caliban, who is impressed by his fineness and determines to "seek for grace." (Though Prospero cannot afford to recognize it, Caliban reforms when Prospero stops torturing him and holds out the prospect of pardon.)

The rhetoric of the play justifies the vindictive Prospero and glorifies the self-effacing one. It confirms Prospero's idealized image of himself as a kindly, charitable man who punishes others much less than they deserve and only for their own good. Meanwhile, the action of the play shows us a Prospero who is bitter, sadistic, and hungry for revenge. The disparity between rhetoric and mimesis is a reflection of Prospero's inner conflicts and of Shakespeare's. The rhetoric rationalizes and disguises Prospero's vindictiveness and celebrates his moral nobility.[5] Its function is similar to that of Prospero's magic. The magic enables Prospero to have his revenge and to remain innocent in his own eyes and in the eyes of the other characters. The magic and the rhetoric together enable Shakespeare to deceive himself and the audience as to Prospero's true nature.

Notes

1. Kahn observed that Prospero achieves "a brilliant compromise between revenge and charity, which allows him to have his cake and eat it too." The trials to which he subjects Antonio, Sebastian, and Alonso "would add up to a tidy revenge were they not sheer illusion . . . and were they not perpetrated for the sake of arousing 'heart-sorrow and a clear life ensuing.' They are and are not revenge" (1981, 223).

2. I am one of the relatively small number of critics who subscribe to what Harry Berger, Jr., calls "the hard-nosed" as opposed to the "sentimental" view of Prospero (1970, 279). See also Leech (1961), Abenheimer (1946), Auden (1962, 128–34), and Dobrée (1952).

3. In his response to my interpretation of *The Tempest* at the 1985 Florida Conference on Shakespeare's Personality, J. Dennis Huston pointed out that Prospero may have yet another motive for classifying Caliban as subhuman: "he does not have to recognize that he, like Antonio, has used raw power to usurp a kingdom belonging to another: if Caliban is really subhuman, he can hardly have valid claims to the island."

4. As A. D. Nuttall observed in his response to this chapter, "You can kill people in plays without hurting anyone."

5. David Sundelson observed that "much in the play that might pass for dissent only adds to Prospero's stature—the brief quarrel with Ariel, for example." He speaks of the "sanctioned narcissism of Prospero" (1980, 38, 39).

Works Cited

Abenheimer, K. M. "Shakespeare's *Tempest:* A Psychological Analysis." *Psychoanalytic Review* 33 (1946): 339–415.

Auden, W. H. *The Dyer's Hand.* New York: Random House, 1962.

Berger, Harry, Jr. "The Miraculous Harp: A Reading of Shakespeare's *Tempest.*" *Shakespeare Studies* 5 (1970): 254–83.

Dobrée, Bonamy. "The Tempest." *New Series of Essays and Studies* 5 (1952): 13–25.

Freud, Sigmund. *Totem and Taboo.* New York: Vintage Books, [n.d.].

Frye, Northrop. Introduction to *The Tempest.* In *Twentieth Century Interpretations of the Tempest.* Edited by Hallet Smith. Englewood Cliffs, NJ: Prentice-Hall, 1969.

Horney, Karen. *Neurosis and Human Growth: The Struggle Toward Self-Realization.* New York: Norton, 1950.

Kahn, Coppélia. *Man's Estate: Masculine Identity in Shakespeare.* Berkeley and Los Angeles: University of California Press, 1981.

Leech, Clifford. *Shakespeare's Tragedies.* London: Chatto & Windus, 1961.

Paris, Bernard J. *Character as a Subversive Force in Shakespeare: The History and the Roman Plays.* Rutherford, NJ: Fairleigh Dickinson University Press, 1991.

Sundelson, David. "So Rare a Wonder'd Father: Prospero's *Tempest.*" In *Representing Shakespeare: New Psychoanalytic Essays.* Edited by Murray M. Schwartz and Coppélia Kahn. Baltimore: Johns Hopkins University Press, 1980.

Pictures in Poetry: Keats's "Ode on a Grecian Urn"

Eva T. H. Brann

Eva T. H. Brann covers a remarkable amount of territory in her brief but suggestive essay. Touching on the origin and pervasiveness of the ut pictura poesis *trope, the concept of iconic poetry, the ekphrasitic tradition, and shifts in the meaning and value of terms like "mimesis" and "representation," her essay offers not only an analysis of Keats's poem but a brief sketch of one of the traditions from which it derives. As Brann rightly notes, "Ode on a Grecian Urn" is a central text for any exploration of these related ideas, for it's hard to think of another poem that more fully exploits paradoxes and synesthetic effects to force us to imagine beyond the bounds of language, to perceive motion in stasis, music in silence, eternity in time. While pushing the temporal medium of language into the visual artist's spatial realm, the poem insists that the visual artist can far excel the poet, even in the time-bound realm of narration. But this irony is undone by yet another when we remember that Keats accomplishes all this with mere words. We never see the urn, we only read the poem.*

By placing the poem in the tradition of iconic poetry, Brann prompts us to consider the puzzles that arise when we take seriously the long-standing belief that poetry is a mimetic art. Note, for instance, the complications of the term "form" in this context. And if language is the medium of poetic imitation, what are its modes, and what its objects? Is the "Ode," for example, an imitation of an urn, real or imagined, or is it an imitation of someone contemplating an urn? Further, by sketching a history of the iconic tradition, Brann prompts us to ask if we do indeed think differently today about the role of mimesis in both the visual and verbal arts, and if so, what accounts for this change?

Reprinted by permission of the author and the editor from *San Jose Studies* 14 (1988): 6–13.

I

Painting is poetry keeping silent; poetry is a talking picture.

This very ancient saying, attributed by Plutarch to the Greek poet Simonides, bears within it the seeds of a long critical tradition. That a painting should say something and that poetry should depict something is arguably the crux of the Western representational, mimetic mode.

Word and picture are here in an apparently mutual relation, "sister arts," in Dryden's words. Yet, since it is a poet who is making the observation, he puts it in terms of silence and speech, giving sound, the poet's element, a certain preeminence over sight, the painter's sense. Some half-millennium later Horace in *Art of Poetry* coined the phrase *Ut pictura poesis*, "poetry is like a picture." It is this simile, the literary half of the Simonidean metaphor, which enters the critical vocabulary as the watchword for the long-prevailing doctrine of pictorial poetry.

Behind this doctrine stands an oddly contradictory coupling of assumptions, namely that while poetry is the most serious of the arts, sight is the greatest of the senses. These assumptions are not grandly challenged until the 18th century, when Lessing in *Laocöon* directly criticizes Simonides's saying on the grounds that the visual arts and poetry differ not only in the manner but in the object of their imitation. The visual arts depict the pregnant moment while poetry tells of developing action; they have different temporalities. One might argue that by enforcing such specialization, Lessing is in fact preparing that rejection of the representational tradition itself which dominates the critical theory of our century. For how can either art form imitate the world if the one is debarred from telling a story and the other from depicting a shape?

II

The *Ut pictura poesis* tradition includes a very old, special, and fascinating strain. If poetry is to be *like* a picture then, by a natural transition, it might very appropriately be *about* a picture. That is to say, the descriptive power of words, their magical capacity for evoking visual images, might well be applied to visions which are themselves artful, namely to paintings and sculptures. Indeed, there is no purer way of insuring that poetry will be strictly picture-like than to make it speak about a picture.

Such descriptions of visual works in poetry are nowadays called "iconic." The source of this term is a writer of the second century, Philostratus the Elder, who (along with several others) wrote "images," *eikones* or "icons" in Greek, prose pieces describing with the utmost pictorial vividness real or imaginary works of graphic art, images of images as it were. These descriptions were meant to return the compliment of the painters who had, of course, painted literary themes all along: Homer's *Odyssey*, for example, had begun to be illustrated on pottery in the eighth century B.C. and was still the subject of wall paintings in Roman times. Ben Jonson translates a dictim of Philostratus showing the spirit of this enterprise: "Whosoever loves not pictures is injurious to Truth and all the wisdom of Poetry."

This direct way of realizing the *Ut pictura poesis* principle may be a minor strain in the tradition, but it has at least four great instances. One, coeval with poetry itself, occurs in one of Homer's descriptive passages, the one in Book XVIII of the *Iliad* depicting the shield made for Achilles by the divine metalsmith Hephaestus. What Achilles carries before him as he leaps onto his final field of battle is quite simply the world—heaven, sea, land, war, peace. For all that is depicted upon the shield by means of precious inlays. There is no subsequent iconic passage of equal grandeur.

A second famous ancient case is the only antique full-length pastoral novel, *Daphnis and Chloe* (of uncertain date). Longus wrote it after having seen in the grove of the Nymphs "a most beautiful sight, a painted image," which he so admired that he was seized by a desire to write in response to the painting" (*antigrapsai tei grammei*—significantly the Greek words for writing and a painting are the same—both are "graphic"). So he searched out an interpreter of the visual work and set about writing his four books of woodland romance, in prose to be sure, but poetic in spirit.

A third, medieval, case of iconic poetry is the description of the three bas-reliefs showing scenes of humility in Canto X of Dante's *Purgatory*. He refers to these reliefs as "visible speech," thereby giving force to the whole of Simonides's metaphor: Because the pictures speak silently through sight, the poem can render them visible through speech. It has been pointed out that the presence of iconic poetry exclusively in Purgatory—it occurs in no other region— has remarkable significance; for it marks Purgatory as a place without true nature or present reality, where all is either past or future, either memory or imagination: the place of images *par excellence* (De Sanctis in Hagstrum, 1958).

III

Finally, a modern, indeed a Romantic poem, Keats's "Ode on a Grecian Urn" of 1819, is both as canonical and as original a case of the "iconic" genre as one might hope to find. Keats's urn combines elements from real marble vases, such as that of Sosibos in the Louvre which Keats had seen in drawings by Piranese, with the front-and-back picture panel arrangement common in classical Attic pottery (Bowra, 1950). Thus Keats produces an "image," indeed an image of an image, in the Philostratan tradition. It is likely that he was aware, if not of this sub-genre specifically, then at least of the lively *Ut pictura poesis* debate of his time.

He goes even further. He adds an epigram, as it were. The urn, "a friend of man," addresses us with oracular speech: "Beauty is truth, truth beauty." An epigram is a metric inscription affixed to a picture or statue or grave monument by way of breaking through the muteness of the images to make them "speaking pictures"; often the utterance is in the first person — the work itself speaks. The epigrammatic tradition goes back to the Archaic period in Greece. In reviving this ancient practice, evidently quite deliberately (Spitzer, 1962), Keats adds a wonderful complication: In the outer stanzas the urn as a whole, as an incarnate *memento mori,* is personally addressed, and it in turn responds in *propria persona.* In the three inside stanzas it becomes a quiet bearer of obstinately mute "speaking pictures" which at first seem to rebuff the poet's wildly passionate questioning with their silent frozen messages.

The silence of those middle scenes is a betwixt-and-between silence. Later on, painting will be valued for its principled speechlessness. Ortega y Gasset makes explicit the post-Romantic view:

> All the marvelousness of painting rests on its dual condition: its will to express and its resolve to stay silent . . . Like a spring it depresses itself in its muteness in order to be able to bounce back with the suggestion of ineffable things.

On the other hand, the antique urn itself, that "Sylvan historian," depicts its scenes with that silently articu-

late classical clarity, a sharp vividness, whose rhetorical counterpart (called *enargeia*) was greatly valued in the very tradition which thought of speech as highly visual; for example Plutarch praises Thucydides, who is like the urn a historian, for the vivid clarity, the *enargeia* of his descriptions.

Keats sees in the mute stasis of the urn's pictures neither only the serene clarity of antiquity, nor only the tense ineffability of modernity, but a quality of silence which, for a moment, bridges these two. It is the epitome of Romanticism, namely the silence of a rapture fixed in endless *prolongation,* which is depicted in the pale marble painting of the ever-unconsummated love chase on the front panel of the vase. Can one imagine a better device for expressing the Romantic coalescence of "forever" and "not yet," of clear shape and misty longing, than that of "iconic" poetry, the translation into moving speech of a frozen visual moment?

There is yet another, even deeper facet of Romanticism which Keats's "icon" serves to convey. It is the broaching of the boundaries between art and life. That breakthrough comes when the view shifts to the back, where a sacrifice is depicted. The poet wanders off the vase to view and to muse about the empty little city with its vacant acropolis, the city which the celebrants had left one morning long ago for the altar in the woods, only to be caught in a static enchantment forever. Any romantic wanderer about an antique site, one where the place is very much present but the people very much gone, will be familiar with Keats's romantic sense: They must be somewhere!

IV

One might say that the *Ut pictura poesis* tradition has a complex culmination in the ode: Here is a poem addressing an urn and describing the pictures upon it, pictures which in turn induce visions of a world behind them; moreover, in the end the urn itself gives voice and responds to the poet's questioning — responds delphically, though not, as some claim, vapidly.

What the urn says, presumably as the moral to what it shows, is, to be sure, not original. The association of beauty and truth comes through Shaftsbury into Akenside's famous poem-essay of 1744, *The Pleasures of the Imagination;* and their identity, which is implied in Keats's two converses, is to be found in

Schelling's aesthetic philosophy. Nonetheless, the urn's oracle is very much Keats's own answer to certain doubts about what we would call the "reality" of the imagination.

Two years before the writing of the ode, on November 22, 1817, Keats had written to his friend Benjamin Bailey in order to "end all your troubles as to that of your momentary start about the authenticity of the imagination." (Forman, 1952) "What the imagination seizes as Beauty must be truth," Keats advises him, "whether it existed before or not," for all the imaginative passions are "creative of essential Beauty." "The imagination may be compared to Adam's dream. [The reference is to *Paradise Lost*.]—He awoke and found it truth." So the first member of the epigram, "Beauty is Truth," encapsulates this poet's long-standing answer to the question: What existence is behind the images of the imagination? It is that passionate imagining itself bestows existence.

The converse member, "truth is beauty," is the poet's answer to the question: Is meaning ultimately in visions or in thoughts? In the same letter, in the context of his "favorite speculation," Keats raises a problem which was indeed his lifelong preoccupation: Whether the way to truth can possibly be by "consequitive reasoning," that is, by thought and philosophy, or whether, as the poet is inclined to think, it is through the sensory imagination. The urn's dictum that truth is beauty is a concise resolution, fitting its visible source. It is in the Philostratan tradition which allies pictures and truth. Truth is essentially in imaginative vision, not in words. The crown of this Romantic artfulness is that this reflection comes from the urn, after all, not in the form of a properly engraved epigram but emanates, an unspoken truth, from the vision of the vase itself.

So the convertibility of beauty and truth, far from being an accident of vapid phrase-making, serves as a resting point for Keats's passionate poetic speculation: The objects "seized" by the imagination are actual, and what is ultimately actual has a visual character, "—that is all ye know on earth and all ye need to know," adds the poet, seconding the vase. Here the modest old critical doctrine of *Ut pictura poesis*, that poetry is essentially visualizable, has been elevated to a grand piece of metaphysics. Truthful words, that is to say, poetic words, are essentially about significant visions, "silent forms," such as can "tease us out of thought / As doth eternity." For in eternity, in the "empyreal hereafter," Keats intimates, there are to be found the preexistent prototypes of the visionary imagination—"another favorite speculation of mine."

V

The "Ode on a Grecian Urn" marks the grand climax of the iconic technique; for its enabling doctrine, that "poetry is like a picture," comes to an end when imitation, mimesis, no longer drives either the visual or the poetic arts. And that happens from the Romantic period onward, when non-mimetic theories of the imagination begin to gain currency. The sisters part; music, if any, is the new preferred sibling to literature. Indeed the typical iconic *tour de force* of our century is the verbal rendition of real or invented musical compositions, such as is found in the novels of Proust or Mann. What painters peculiarly value in painting is now no longer its visual communicativeness, its silent poetry, but its silence simply:

> I confess my predilection for the silent arts . . .
> Words are indiscreet; they break in on your tranquility, solicit your attention, arouse discussion.
> (Delacroix.)

And what poets value in painting is the same; when they write about painting it is not to describe it but to express its silence:

> Where the poet was lucky his poem will speak the silence of painting; it too will say nothing more than: It is so, it is as it is.   (Nemerov.)

Thus, after nearly two and a half millennia, language and visual imagining draw apart; for their mutuality depended on the understanding that visual arts depict *something*, the very thing the poetic arts describe. And that is just what neither artists or critics any longer take for granted.

Works Cited

Bowra, C. M. *The Romantic Imagination.* Oxford University Press: Oxford, 1950.

Delacroix, Eugene. *Journal,* trans. Walter Pach (New York, 1948).

Forman, Maurice B. *The Letters of John Keats.* Oxford University Press: Oxford, 1952.

Hagstrum, Jean H. *The Sister Arts: The Tradition of Literary Pictorialism and English Poetry from Dryden to Gray.* The University of Chicago Press: Chicago, 1958.

Nemerov, Howard. "On Poetry and Painting, with a Thought of Music," in *The Language of Images,* ed. W. J. T. Mitchell. The University of Chicago Press: Chicago, 1980.

Spitzer, Leo. "'The Ode on a Grecian Urn,' or Content vs. Metagrammar," in *Essays on English and American Literature.* Princeton University Press: Princeton, 1962.

Vendler, Helen. *The Odes of John Keats.* Harvard University Press: Cambridge, 1983.

APPLICATION

The Topicality of Depravity in "Benito Cereno"

Allan Moore Emery

Allan Moore Emery raises a crucial question in mimetic criticism: Should a literary work represent the historical situation at the time of its creation or more universal themes and actions that transcend the work's time and place of origin? The oldest and strongest forms of mimeticism, dating back to Plato and Aristotle, have assumed the second answer. John Ellis follows this line when he argues that a work becomes "literature" only when we read it as transcending its origin, and Josephine Donovan continues the line when she asserts that "most literature that we call great expresses . . . universal, fundamental human experience." But this view, always at odds with the older historicism, has come under direct attack in recent decades from neo-Marxists, New Historians, feminists, post-colonialists, and other cultural critics who view all claims of transcendence and universality with deep suspicion and whose project is to situate the work in its original context and to reveal there its (often unconscious) political and social meaning. From these perspectives, attempts to universalize the work are really attempts to repress its true import. Is Joseph Conrad's Heart of Darkness, *for example, to be read as a comment on European colonization in nineteenth-century Africa or as a revelation of the darkness in every human heart? While the second reading seems to include the first, it also robs the first of any real force. If everyone is always guilty, no one need feel particularly guilty, and our response is not savage indignation but tragic resignation.*

Emery offers to adjudicate a similar controversy around "Benito Cereno": Is the story a comment on slavery in the 1850s, or is it a representation of universal human depravity? Emery favors the second view, finding that the tale expresses an almost Swiftian irony: "'Benito Cereno' offers a choice of negative alternatives: a life of cheerful obliviousness or an awareness [of evil] incompatible with life." But this vision, Emery argues, grows out of Melville's deep concern with a number of topical issues, including slavery and racism. Finally, then, Emery offers a version of the concrete-universal paradox. "'Benito Cereno' may be more topical than most tales, but it is also more immense, presuming to comment on the nature of man and his continuing tendency to misbehave."

Over the past half-century, Herman Melville's "Benito Cereno" has evoked a kaleidoscopic critical response to which no brief summary could do perfect justice. Nevertheless, one might cast most of the story's commentators into two camps: (1) those who read the tale as a powerful portrait of human depravity, with a sadistic Babo as the prime embodiment of evil, an obtuse Delano as Melville's figure of naive optimism, and a doomed Cereno as his contrasting symbol of moral awareness;[1] and (2) those who view the tale as a stern indictment of American slavery, complete with an amply prejudiced Delano, a guilt-ridden Cereno, and a sympathetic (or even heroic) Babo, driven to violence by an insufferable bondage.[2] The "depravity" critics appear to have a preponderance of textual evidence on their side: certainly Babo's "heroism" is difficult to document. Moreover, they appreciate Melville's penchant for "universal" themes. Yet their opponents recall, with equal rightness, his habitual reference to contemporary issues (slavery included) and note as well that "Benito Cereno" appeared in 1855, at a time when slavery was a subject of considerable concern to Melville's audience.

Indeed, these critics imply that slavery was *so* important to mid-century America that a Melville tale published in 1855, featuring slaves and treating depravity rather than slavery, would represent a flouting of historical obligation: a work in which Melville ignored the topicality of his own materials in striving to prove some large "literary" point. To reformulate the suggestion: either "Benito Cereno" treats slavery—or else the author stands convicted of an irresponsible (if temporary) disregard for his own times. Perhaps, however, the "depravity" party should neither quit the field nor admit the charge of authorial fecklessness,[3] for their dilemma is actually false: if "Benito Cereno" treats human depravity, it does so for specific historical reasons. In other words, one need not turn away from history in order to appreciate Melville's universal theme, nor need one adopt an abolitionist reading in order to rescue

Melville's tale from "irrelevant" generality. For his depravity emphasis was itself thoroughly topical.

Alert as always to social injustice, Melville did allude to American slavery in his tale—but infrequently, and mainly as a local instance of a far-flung phenomenon. Amasa Delano, Melville's representative American, attempts to buy Babo at one point (p. 168); eventually he also "[grinds] the prostrate negro" (p. 236).[4] Yet even such impressive details fail to demonstrate an authorial preoccupation with America's peculiar institution. Delano's truthful assertion that "slavery breeds ugly passions in man" (p. 211) seems universally applicable, especially given Babo's original enslavement at the hands of blacks (p. 149). Moreover, the tableau carved upon the stern-piece of the *San Dominick* shows "a dark satyr in a mask, holding his foot on the prostrate neck of a writhing figure, likewise masked" (p. 115). While this image predicts the embarrassing behavior of the "benevolent" Delano, it also depicts Babo's oppression of Cereno and Babo's own earlier subjugation of blacks *and* whites. Melville's masks serve, then, to make the *San Dominick* symbolic of a worldwide oppression (indicative of a global depravity)—with American slavery as non-"peculiar" illustration.[5]

Nor do the prejudices of Delano prove Melville's overriding concern with the perceptual underpinnings of American slavery. To be sure, Delano's Caucasian confidence that blacks are "stupid" (p. 180) becomes ludicrous in light of a day's events: far from having the "limited mind" of an "indisputable inferior" (p. 200), Babo is the "uncommonly intelligent" (p. 215) owner of a remarkably resourceful brain.[6] Yet if the blacks of the *San Dominick* are smarter than Delano thinks, they are also more fiendish: Delano's chief limitation is not, one remembers, a tendency to intellectual snobbery but a refusal to recognize the presence of "malign evil in man" (p. 110). Though he fails to accurately estimate the black I.Q., he fails, more precisely, to appreciate the "subtlety" (p. 270) of black men in whom intelligence is conjoined to "malignity," in whom "sophistication" (p. 119) merely enhances the ability to oppress. Eminently perceptual, Delano's mistake nevertheless underlines not so much the bigotry of Americans as the calculated cruelty of mankind.

Melville's readers should not suppose, however, that he casually chose blacks to exemplify human viciousness, disregarding the importance of race in 1855. On the contrary, Melville's focus on black ferocity represents an acknowledgment rather than an evasion of American intellectual history. One clue to the topical context of "Benito Cereno" is Delano's emphasis on the "docility" (pp. 149, 200, 220), "cheerfulness" (p. 200), and "affection" (pp. 120, 123) of blacks; another is Melville's revelatory ending, which, more than heightening our sympathy for Babo[7] or increasing our respect for black intelligence, serves to demolish the notion of black amiability. For by 1855 this notion was hardly unique to Delano. In "Prospects of American Slavery," an article appearing in the influential *Christian Examiner* near the time Melville's tale was composed,[8] one reads: "We . . . point, first, to the affectionate, patient, docile, tractable disposition of the African race,—tolerant of burdens, not apt to harbor deep animosity, . . . and won by the slightest kindness to a grateful and confiding affection. . . . [We point as well] to the example of the British West Indies, which, whatever else they prove, show that violence and hostility are the last things to be dreaded from the blacks when they come to feel their strength. . . .[9] Similar remarks graced Harriet Beecher Stowe's phenomenally popular *Uncle Tom's Cabin*, first published in book form in 1852: "[One day] the negro race, no longer despised and trodden down, will, perhaps, show forth some of the . . . most magnificent revelations of human life. Certainly they will, in their gentleness, their lowly docility of heart, their aptitude to repose on a superior mind and rest on a higher power, their childish simplicity of affection, and facility of forgiveness."[10] One could hardly imagine views more akin to those of Delano—or less consistent with the evidence of "Benito Cereno." Apparently Melville was acquainted with contemporary arguments for black docility[11] and sought to attack them by means of his naive protagonist and bloodcurdling plot.

Melville found may proofs of black "violence and hostility"—and few signs of Negro "gentleness"—in Amasa Delano's *Narrative of Voyages and Travels* (1817).[12] Yet in altering his source for literary purposes, Melville actually heightened the barbarity of Babo and company. According to Delano's *Narrative*, the blacks of the *Tryal* refrained from murder after Cereno signed a document promising them safe passage to Senegal;[13] on Melville's *San Dominick*, the mate Raneds is killed "for a chance gesture" long after the agreement is reached (p. 255). Likewise, only the *San Dominick* sports a grisly "figure-head" (p. 239): according to the *Narrative*, Alexandro Aranda believed his blacks were "tractable";[14] in "Benito Cereno," his bones belie that idea. When embellish-ing his source Melville also highlighted particular instances of black depravity with ironic assertions regarding its opposite. Typical is his disquisition on the Negro as "body-servant" (pp. 123–24), which anticipates the disclosure that Jose, Aranda's personal attendant, brutally "stabbed his master" after Aranda had been "dragged half-lifeless to the deck" (pp. 259–60).[15] Melville's account of Negroes as "natural valets and hair-dressers" (p. 199) becomes similarly suspect once one discovers that Babo was not simply barberous in Melville's shaving scene (pp. 196–210).

Furthermore, Melville changed both the date of Delano's adventure and the name of Cereno's vessel so as to invoke the violent slave revolt which occured on the isle of Santo Domingo in 1799.[16] He invented as well those six "Ashantees" (pp. 143, 161, 165, 221) whose hatchet wielding an ironic author attributes to "the peculiar love in negroes of uniting industry with pastime" (p. 119)—but whose actual function and particular "fury" are described in Cereno's deposition (pp. 253, 256, 260). Not coincidentally, the Ashantees of West Africa were famous for their ferocity: like the South African "Caffres" also mentioned by Melville (p. 170), they had frequently faced white troops in battle.[17] Finally, too, Melville expanded the character of Atufal, strangely thought by some critics to be Melville's symbol of the noble black man, ignobly enchained.[18] While Delano praises Atufal's "royal spirit" and "general docility" (pp. 148–49) and finds the "chained" Negro a comforting sight (p. 231), he is obviously laboring under a misconception. Atufal is nothing less than Babo's "right hand man" (p. 256), and his chains are a charade. If he has a particular symbolic role, he most likely hints at the power of America's blacks to break their bonds, to imitate Nat Turner, to stun those innocent Americans comfortably convinced of the "tractability" of slaves.[19]

Yet Melville's most artful assault on the concept of black contentedness is his continuing emphasis on black musicianship. Perhaps he saw "Negro Minstrelsy," an article praising black music, in the January 1855 number of *Putnam's Magazine*. The author remarked upon "the lightness and prevailing good humor of . . . negro songs," insisting that "a true [negro] melody is seldom sentimental, and never melancholy. And this," he added, "results directly from the character and habits of the colored race. No hardships or troubles can destroy, or even check their happiness and levity."[20] Having read this or some equally dubious declaration, Melville included in "Benito Cereno" a number of details designed to question both the "lightness" of Negro music and the natural "levity" of blacks. At one point, for example, he applauds the Negro's "great gift of good-humor," discovering in the darker race "a certain easy cheerfulness, harmonious in every glance and gesture; as though God had set the whole negro to some pleasant tune" (p. 200). Elsewhere, however, he nullifies this stereotype by noting that the favorite tunes of Aranda's blacks are anything *but* pleasant. The four grizzled Negroes who, unbeknown to Delano, keep order on the *San Dominick,* emit "a continuous, low, monotonous chant; droning and druling away like so many gray-headed bag-pipers playing a funeral march" (pp. 118–19). And the black females of the *San Dominick* form an even gloomier chorus during and after the revolt on their vessel. Cereno eventually explains: "In the various acts of murder, [the negresses] sang songs and danced—not gaily, but solemnly; and before the engagement with the boats, as well as during the action, they sang melancholy songs to the negroes, and . . . this melancholy tone was more inflaming than a different one would have been, and was so intended . . . " (p. 261).[21] Significant, too, is Melville's passing observation that the murderous Francesco, a person of "good voice," once sang "in the Valparaiso churches" (p. 249). From all these facts, one draws the appropriate conclusion: that, contrary to the claims of *Putnam's,* Negro "minstrelsy" precludes neither melancholy nor maleficence.

Melville did not, then, underline the barbarity of Babo's blacks out of a "literary" disregard for racial implication, or a casual conflation of blackness with evil, but in direct response to the contemporary image of the Negro as more "docile," "cheerful," and "harmonious" than other men: to Melville, black depravity was a matter of "topical" concern. Yet so, too, was white depravity. Aware that the revelations of his tale might instill in the minds of his readers attitudes even more dangerous than Delano's, Melville embedded in "Benito Cereno" considerable evidence of the fact that depravity is an essential attribute of all men rather than the private failing of an individual race.[22] Especially noteworthy are his comparison of Cereno's black barber to a "Nubian sculptor finishing off a white statue-head" (p. 209) and his subsequent likening of Atufal to "one of those sculptured porters of black marble guarding the porches of Egyptian

tombs" (p. 220). These references accompany Delano's reflection that Babo, a "full-blooded African," seems "not unconscious of inferiority" to Francesco, Cereno's mulatto steward (pp. 211–12). A pivotal conversation is also nearby:

> Captain Delano observed with interest that while the complexion of the mulatto was hybrid, his physiognomy was European—classically so.
>
> "Don Benito," whispered he, "I am glad to see this usher-of-the-goldenrod of yours; the sight refutes an ugly remark once made to me by a Barbadoes planter; that when a mulatto has a regular European face, look out for him; he is a devil. But see, your steward here has features more regular than King George's of England; and yet there he nods, and bows, and smiles; a king, indeed—the king of kind hearts and polite fellows. What a pleasant voice he has, too."
>
> "He has, Señor."
>
> "But tell me, has he not, so far as you have known him, always proved a good, worthy fellow?" said Captain Delano, pausing, while with a final genuflexion the steward disappeared into the cabin; "come, for the reason just mentioned, I am curious to know."
>
> Francesco is a good man," [somewhat] sluggishly responded Don Benito, like a phlegmatic appreciator, who would neither find fault nor flatter.
>
> "Ah, I thought so. For it were strange, indeed, and not very creditable to us white-skins, if a little of our blood mixed with the African's, should, far from improving the latter's quality, have the sad effect of pouring vitriolic acid into black broth; improving the hue, perhaps, but not the wholesomeness."
>
> "Doubtless, doubtless, Señor, but"—glancing at Babo—"not to speak of negroes, your planter's remark I have heard applied to the Spanish and Indian intermixtures in our provinces." (pp. 212–13)

Moments later, as Delano and Cereno continue their conversation over a bottle of Canary, the Spaniard alludes "to the different constitution of races, enabling one to offer more resistance to certain maladies than another" (pp. 215–16).

Melville's references (by way of Delano and Cereno) to Francesco's "hybrid" complexion, the moral "wholesomeness" of white "blood," and "the different constitution of races" suggest he was aware of mid-century American interest in "ethnology," or the study of racial characteristics; his references to Egyptian and Nubian sculpture point specifically to Josiah Nott's and George Gliddon's *Types of*

Mankind, a massive and much-touted ethnological compendium published in 1854 and extensively reviewed in the pages of *Putnam's.*[23] Nott was a Southern physician, well acquainted (so he thought) with the various deficiencies of the Negro; Gliddon was a retired Egyptologist, eager to buttress Nott's racist arguments with archaeological evidence. In particular, Gliddon sought to demonstrate that the "types" of men existing in the nineteenth century were no recent development; hence he included reproductions of numerous Egyptian (and Nubian) paintings and sculptures, some of blacks and some of whites, but all proving the antiquity of racial differences.[24] Meanwhile, Nott explored the racial implications of human "hybridity." Sharing Cereno's medical opinion, he noted that mulattoes, like pure-bred Negroes, enjoyed "extraordinary exemption from yellow fever" when brought to Southern cities. At the same time, he anticipated the views of Delano by insisting that even "a small trace of white blood in the negro improves him in intelligence and morality."[25]

Apparently, however, Melville doubted the validity of Nott's ethnological claims, for the case of Francesco suggests that the intermingling of races does not always produce results favorable to the notion of white preeminence. From Cereno's deposition one learns that, throughout the mutiny, Francesco was "in all things, the creature and tool of the negro Babo" (p. 260); thus Delano was wrong to accuse the "full-blooded African" of a racial inferiority complex. Moreover, Cereno had good reason for "sluggishly" praising Francesco. As Melville's Barbadoes planter might have predicted, the "worthy" mulatto was "of the first band of revolters" against Cereno's rule (p. 260), his morals having been un-"improved" by the dash of white blood in his veins. Melville's earlier reference to "a Lima intriguante's one sinister eye peering across the Plaza from the Indian loophole of her dusk *saya-y-manta*" (p. 111) and his later mention of Lima's "Plaza" and "Rimac bridge" (p. 270) imply that his own view of human "hybridity" may have derived in part from an 1851 *Harper's* article which contained not only detailed accounts of both the "*saya y manto*" and Lima's architecture but also an assertion regarding what Cereno, careful not to comment on Negroes, calls the "Spanish and Indian intermixtures in our provinces." Wrote the author: "As a general rule the mixed races, which constitute about a third of the population of Lima, inherit the vices without the virtues of the pure races from which they sprung."[26] No Delanovian optimist, he might have said the same for Francesco.

Yet if the mulatto's career discredits the notion of white-blood-as-better, then so does the behavior of Babo's "full-blooded" foes, the vindictive Spaniards of "Benito Cereno." The original Delano explained that he was forced to "exercise authority" over Cereno's crewmen in order to "prevent them from cutting to pieces and killing" their black enemies, following the recapture of the *San Dominick.*[27] Melville's Delano is less successful at averting bloodshed. In his deposition Cereno insists that "beside the negroes killed in the action, some were killed after the capture and re-anchoring at night, when shackled to the ring-bolts on deck; that these deaths were committed by the [Spanish] sailors, ere they could be prevented" (p. 263). Nor are Cereno's seamen alone in demonstrating Spanish depravity. In both Delano's *Narrative* and "Benito Cereno," the authorities of Lima flagrantly advertise their own savagery by abusing the bodies of blacks they have lately killed (pp. 269–70).[28]

More significant for Melville—and more disturbing for his readers—may have been the behavior of Delano's Americans, who likewise indulge in "white-blooded" brutality when seizing the *San Dominick.*[29] The original Delano admitted that the results of American victory were "truly horrid": "Some of [the negroes] had part of their bowels hanging out, and some with half their backs and thighs shaved off." "This," he proudly proclaimed, "was done with our boarding lances, which were always kept exceedingly sharp, and as bright as a gentleman's sword."[30] Melville similarly notes that many of Babo's blacks were "mangled" during the American attack, "their wounds—mostly inflicted by the long-edged sealing-spears, resembling those shaven ones of the English at Preston Pans, made by the poled scythes of the Highlanders" (pp. 245–46). By implication, the actions of Delano's compatriots are in keeping with prior examples of white savagery (unconfined to the Spanish). Consider, too, this mention of a militant exchange: "Upon the second volley, . . . [the negroes] hurtled their hatchets. One took off a sailor's fingers. Another struck the whale-boat's bow, . . . remaining stuck in the gunwale like a woodman's axe. Snatching it, quivering from its lodgment, the mate hurled it back. The returned gauntlet now stuck in the ship's broken quarter-gallery, and so remained" (p. 242). Here white truculence precisely mirrors black truculence—a doubling later reemphasized when "sealing-spears and cutlasses [cross] hatchets and hand-spikes" (p. 244). Clearly the shout of the invader (p. 244) and the motto of the *San Dominick* (pp. 115–16, 239) speak true; if Babo's blacks are guilty of viciousness, then Delano's whites are all too willing to "follow their lead."

No other detail of "Benito Cereno" so eloquently bespeaks the author's emphasis on universal depravity, unless it be his subsequent notation that the black women of the *San Dominick* were party to the Spanish massacre.[31] Midway through the story, Delano perceives a "slumbering negress" (p. 174) and remarks: "There's naked nature, now; pure tenderness and love" (p. 175). He then proceeds to eulogize all the ladies on board: "He was gratified with their manners: like most uncivilized women, they seemed at once tender of heart and tough of constitution; equally ready to die for their infants or fight for them. Unsophisticated as leopardesses; loving as doves. Ah! thought Captain Delano, these, perhaps, are some of the very women whom Ledyard saw in Africa, and gave such a noble account of" (p. 175). The actual words of the explorer, John Ledyard, were these: "I have observed among all nations, that the women . . . are the same kind, civil, obliging, humane, tender beings. . . . They do not hesitate, like men, to perform a hospitable or generous action; not haughty, nor arrogant, nor supercilious, but full of courtesy, and fond of society; industrious, economical, ingenuous, more liable . . . to err than man, but . . . also more virtuous, and performing more good actions than he."[32] Melville's story casts doubt, however, on both the perspicacity of Ledyard and the sexual suppositions of Delano, for whereas the *Narrative* merely noted that "the negresses of age, were knowing to the revolt, and influenced the death of their master,"[33] a less reticent Melville declares in the deposition that "the negresses . . . testified themselves satisfied at the death of their master, Don Alexandro; that, had the negroes not restrained them, they would have tortured to death, instead of simply killing, the Spaniards slain by command of the negro Babo . . ." (pp. 260–61). Apparently Melville found the idea of female "generosity" as dubious as the notion of black docility. His tale implies that Delano and Ledyard have erred in thinking that violence and brutality are foreign to *any* segment of humanity since, finally, these traits are as much a part of "naked human nature" as "tenderness and love."

In other words, despite the opinion of Cereno, there is one "malady" to which no "race" offers more "resistance" than another. Humanity is depraved to a man—and woman—or so goes the lesson of "Benito Cereno." Yet Melville also derived several other "lessons" from this one—all of them significantly topical. Perhaps his ubiquitous animal imagery had its contemporary relevance, for example; midcentury ethnologists were fond, after all, of stressing the animalism of blacks. Nott compared Negroes to "wild horses, cattle, asses, and other brutes," insisting that the intellectual gap between blacks and chimpanzees was no greater than that between Negroes and "Teutonic" types; for him, the "lower races of mankind" formed "connecting links in the animal kingdom."[34] Moreover, Delano appears to side with Nott when he likens Babo to a "shepherd's dog" (p. 120), his favorite black female to a "doe" with "fawn" (p. 174), and one group of blacks to a "social circle of bats," inhabiting a "subterraneous sort of den" (pp. 193–94). Melville, too, sounds vaguely Nottish when comparing Babo's blacks to "cawing crows" (p. 240) and when peering into their "wolf-like" mouths (p. 245). If "Benito Cereno" supports Nott's contention that blacks are "brutish" (in a moral sense), it also challenges Nott's central thesis by underscoring the brutishness of whites, by exalting no race above another, by treating all men (and women) as equal partners in the "animal kingdom."

Melville's story may contradict as well both the pre-Darwinian evolutionists, who, while noting man's animal origins, also viewed him as clearly superior to beasts, and their orthodox opponents, who commonly emphasized man's spiritual "specialness." Trusting in both evolution and Scripture, the *Putnam's* reviewer of *Types* took issue with Nott over the question of Negro animality, asserting that "a man is a man all the world over, and nowhere a monkey or a hippopotamus, and whatever his rank in the scale of human being he is entitled to every consideration that properly pertains to man, as separated from ape, baboon, bat, or any other creature that appears to be making a wonderful effort towards his standard." For this writer, man was "inconvertably separated from every other organism, by his anatomy, his physiology, his mind and his heart, which [placed] him, in his lowest forms, at the head of creation."[35] Perhaps Melville read these words, for "Benito Cereno" has something to say about man's pretensions to preeminence of "heart." Observing a general human depravity, Melville simply hinted that God's "noblest" work, the hero of evolution, had clay feet. Man might or might not be better-looking than the baboon, but surely any ape (or bat, or wolf) could meet his moral "standard." And apart from Delano, the human animal might rank high intellectually; but, morally speaking, all "forms" of man were significantly "low" enough.

Like Melville's focus on black savagery, his broader concern with a universal depravity had, then, its contemporary cause — or, rather, causes. For, indeed, another of Delano's remarks invokes a third intellectual context. Assuming that "stupid" blacks could not have independently conspired against him, Delano goes on to conclude that Cereno and Babo could hardly be in cahoots: "Who ever heard of a white," he thinks, "so far a renegade as to apostatize from his very species almost, by leaguing in against it with negroes?" (p. 180). Evidently Melville realized that, for all its "Egyptian" eccentricities, *Types of Mankind* was no isolated phenomenon, being one of many contributions to a mid-century debate regarding the "unity" of the human race.[36] The English ethnologist, James Prichard, had portrayed the race as a single "species" in two influential works of the 1840s, citing men's common origin (in Adam) and the ability of diverse races to produce fertile "hybrids."[37] The American Presbyterian minister, Thomas Smyth, had sided with Prichard in *The Unity of the Races,* published in 1850; Smyth was opposed by Robert Knox in *The Races of Men* (1850) and, in 1854, by Nott and Gliddon, who meant by "types" the various species to which mankind belonged.[38] The "unity" debate also raged on the magazine front. Readers of "Benito Cereno" (*Putnam's,* 1855) had seen "Is Man One or Many?" in the *Putnam's* number for July 1854, and "Are All Men Descended from Adam?" in the number for January 1855. Meanwhile, *Harper's,* to which Melville likewise subscribed, ran consecutive editorials in September and October of 1854 asking "Is the Human Race One or Many?" and "Are We One or Many?" Thus as he began to compose "Benito Cereno," Melville was everywhere confronted with the question of mankind's "oneness."

That fact helps to explain his emphasis on human viciousness. The earlier *Putnam's* article joined Nott and Gliddon in affirming the multiple origin of races, yet insisted that men were united in having an opportunity for salvation denied to lesser creatures; the second suggested that men were inextricably related by a common parentage. Both *Harper's* articles based arguments for unity on Scriptural grounds. And Melville? In "Benito Cereno" he, too, enlisted on the side of unity — but without the enthusiasm of his allies. Suspicious of contemporary insistences on the moral superiority of whites, the sweet-temperedness of blacks, and the saving virtues of women, he apparently wished to underline the unity-in-depravity of all human beings. Delano assumes that men are of different "species almost"; Nott and Gliddon stressed the "moral and intellectual peculiarities" of races.[39] But Melville's tale proves a single point beyond all else: that when it comes to his remarkable capacity for wrongdoing, man is all too undeniably "one."

Understanding this point — and the interwoven historical roots of "Benito Cereno" — one more fully appreciates the essential dichotomy of the tale: the opposition between Cereno, who knows what depraved men can do, and Delano, who owes his survival to his inability to perceive the truth. Speaking to Cereno after his escape, Delano explains: "[My good-nature, compassion, and charity] enabled me to get the better of momentary distrust, at times when acuteness might have cost me my life. . ." (pp. 266–67). Cereno concurs, noting in his deposition "the generosity and piety of Amasa Delano incapable of sounding such wickedness" (p. 261). In other words, throughout his stay on the *San Dominick,* Delano exhibits the same kindly obtuseness Melville discovered in him at outset (p. 110). More important, even after Babo has leaped in his direction (p. 236) and a "flash of revelation" has occurred (p. 237), even after Cereno has testified and the facts of the *San Dominick* are known, Delano *still* refuses to "see" what has been "revealed" to him. Ultimately, he urges Cereno not to "moralize" upon the past (p. 267) — not to seek, that is, the moral implications of his experience. Granted a glimpse of naked human nature, Delano has nevertheless managed to keep his eyes shut. Cereno, on the other hand, has had an eyeful, and it will prove his undoing, much as Bartleby's vision of human limitation spells his inevitable end. For, like "Bartleby," "Benito Cereno" offers a choice of negative alternatives: a life of cheerful obliviousness or an awareness incompatible with life. Having seen his best friend murdered, having felt Babo's fresh-stropped razor pass along the flesh of his own throat, Cereno knows the one thing Captain Delano will never know — "of what humanity is capable" (p. 110). His is a knowledge to die from.

If Delano's primary function is to embody, then, certain naive notions typical of Melville's age, Cereno's is to present Melville's own view of humanity—or, rather, to approximate that view. For, in the end, Cereno makes an understandable mistake: he too closely identifies depravity with blacks. Having observed neither the American attack on the *San Dominick* nor the subsequent Spanish atrocities, and unable to control his fear of Babo, he finally insists that "the negro" has cast the "shadow" of death upon him (p. 268). Cereno might have learned a profounder lesson from his misfortunes. Whatever Babo may represent for the Spanish captain, he was obviously meant to typify the "malign" potential in every man. "Snakishly writhing up" from the bottom of Delano's boat (p. 237), he is far more than a homicidal black: he is the devilish symbol of *all* the depravity—black, white, male, and female—to be found aboard the *San Dominick*. Cereno's private fixation should not obscure Melville's "larger" point. In "Benito Cereno," "the negro" stands for all mankind.

The author of such a firmly integrationist tale should scarcely be charged with racism. Nor should he be accused of slighting the topical in his haste to proclaim the universal. For if Melville did not produce in "Benito Cereno" an exhaustive treatment of the slavery question, he did consider a host of contemporary issues—and a bevy of prevailing stereotypes. Indeed, he had little time for slavery, being frankly too busy with race. Yet Melville likewise sought to transcend the level of historical particulars. "Benito Cereno" may be more topical than most tales, but it is also more immense, presuming to comment on the nature of man and his continuing tendency to misbehave. It is a work thoroughly in touch with the 1850s—and yet likely to remain relevant as the 1980s fade.

Notes

1. See, for example, Stanley T. Williams, "'Follow Your Leader': Melville's 'Benito Cereno'," *Virginia Quarterly Review*, 23 (1947), 61–76; Rosalie Feltenstein, "Melville's 'Benito Cereno'," *American Literature*, 19 (1947), 245–55; and Richard Harter Fogle, "The Monk and the Bachelor: Melville's *Benito Cereno*," *Tulane Studies in English*, 3 (1952), 155–78, rpt. *Melville's Shorter Tales* (Norman: Univ. of Oklahoma Press, 1960), pp. 116–47.
2. Most persuasive are Joseph Schiffman, "Critical Problems in Melville's 'Benito Cereno'." *Modern Language Quarterly*, 11 (1950), 317–24; Allen Guttmann, "The Enduring Innocence of Captain Amasa Delano," *Boston University Studies in English*, 5 (1961), 35–45; David D. Galloway, "Herman Melville's *Benito Cereno*: An Anatomy," *Texas Studies in Literature and Language*, 9 (1967), 239–52; Joyce Adler, "Melville's *Benito Cereno*: Slavery and Violence in the Americas," *Science and Society*, 38 (1974), 19–48, rpt. *War in Melville's Imagination* (New York: New York Univ. Press, 1981), pp. 88–110; and Glenn C. Altschuler, "Whose Foot on Whose Throat? A Reexamination of Melville's *Benito Cereno*," *CLA Journal*, 18 (1975), 383–92.
3. For versions of this admission, see F. O. Matthiessen, *American Renaissance* (New York: Oxford Univ. Press, 1941), p. 508; Margaret Jackson, "Melville's Use of a Real Slave Mutiny in 'Benito Cereno'," *CLA Journal*, 4 (1960), 92; and Kingsley Widmer, "The Perplexity of Melville: *Benito Cereno*," *Studies in Short Fiction*, 5 (1968), 231–32.
4. Parenthetical citations are to *The Piazza Tales* (New York: Dix and Edwards, 1856). Melville's tale first appeared in the numbers of *Putnam's Monthly Magazine* for October, November, and December of 1855.
5. See Kermit Vanderbilt, "'Benito Cereno': Melville's Fable of Black Complicity," *Southern Review*, 12 (1976), 317–18.
6. For a reading of "Benito Cereno" as a defense of black intelligence, see Richard E. Ray, "'Benito Cereno': Babo as Leader," *American Transcendental Quarterly*, No. 7 (1970), 31–37.
7. For commiserative treatments of Babo, see Schiffman, Guttmann, Galloway, and Ray; Warren D'Azevedo, "Revolt on the San Dominick," *Phylon*, 32 (1956), 129–40; Ray B. Browne, *Melville's Drive to Humanism* (Lafayette, Ind.: Purdue Univ. Studies, 1971), pp. 168–88; and Marvin Fisher, *Going Under: Melville's Short Fiction and the American 1850s* (Baton Rouge: Louisiana State Univ. Press, 1977), pp. 104–17.
8. In "The Chronology of Melville's Short Fiction, 1853–1856," *Harvard Library Bulletin*, 28 (1980), 391–403, Merton M. Sealts, Jr., offers convincing evidence that "Benito Cereno" was "probably composed during the winter of 1854–1855."
9. *Christian Examiner*, 57 (Sept. 1854), 226.
10. *Uncle Tom's Cabin; or, Life Among the Lowly* (Boston: John P. Jewett, 1852), I, 259. A similar passage appeared in Stowe's *Key to Uncle Tom's Cabin* (Boston: Jewett, 1854), p. 41.

11. For a discussion of these arguments, see George Fredrickson, *The Black Image in the White Mind* (New York: Harper and Row, 1971), pp. 97–129. Fredrickson notes Stowe's emphasis on black docility.

12. Harold Scudder identified Melville's source in "Melville's *Benito Cereno* and Captain Delano's Voyages," *PMLA*, 43 (1928), 502–32.

13. See Amasa Delano, *A Narrative of Voyages and Travels, in the Northern and Southern Hemispheres: Comprising Three Voyages Round the World; together with a Voyage of Survey and Discovery, in the Pacific Ocean and Oriental Islands* (Boston: E. G. House, 1817; rpt. New York: Praeger, 1970), p. 337.

14. P. 334. Melville incorporated this detail into "Benito Cereno" (p. 250).

15. See Margaret M. Vanderhaar, "A Re-Examination of 'Benito Cereno,'" *American Literature*, 40 (1968), 186. Delano's *Narrative* declared simply that Jose "advised the other negroes to kill his master, Don Alexandro" (p. 340); Melville contributed the "stabbing" anecdote.

16. See H. Bruce Franklin, "'Apparent Symbol of Despotic Command': Melville's *Benito Cereno*," *New England Quarterly*, 34 (1961), 471–72, rpt. *The Wake of the Gods: Melville's Mythology* (Stanford: Stanford Univ. Press, 1963), p. 145. Perhaps Melville saw an 1854 *Putnam's* article describing the violent history of Santo Domingo. See "Hayti and the Haytians," *Putnam's*, 3 (Jan. 1854), 53–62. According to Merton Sealts, *Melville's Reading: A Check-List of Books Owned and Borrowed* (Madison: Univ. of Wisconsin Press, 1966), p. 87, Melville "probably subscribed" to *Putnam's*, to which he contributed a number of tales, including "Benito Cereno."

17. The Ashantees had defeated a British force in 1824; the bloodiest of the "Kaffir Wars" occurred in the early 1850s. For a contemporary account of the "powerful and fierce Ashantees," see J. C. Brent, "Leaves from an African Journal," *Knickerbocker*, 33 (May 1849), 403–04.

18. See, for example, Galloway, p. 248 and D'Azevedo, p. 130.

19. See Adler, p. 47 and Altschuler, p. 389.

20. "Negro Minstrelsy—Ancient and Modern," *Putnam's*, 5 (Jan. 1855), 74.

21. Delano's *Narrative* states: "In the act of murder, and before that of the engagement of the ship, [the negresses] began to sing, and were singing a very melancholy song during the action, to excite the courage of the negroes. . ." (p. 341). Melville added emphases of his own.

22. Two critics overlook this evidence when accusing the author of an unconscious racism. See Sidney Kaplan, "Herman Melville and the American National Sin," *Journal of Negro History*, 42 (1957), 12–27; and Joseph Schiffman, *Three Shorter Novels of Herman Melville* (New York: Harper, 1962), p. 235.

23. See *Types of Mankind: or, Ethnological Researches, based upon the Ancient Monuments, Paintings, Sculptures, and Crania of Races, and upon their Natural Geographical, Philological, and Biblical History* (Philadelphia: Lippincott, 1854); "Is Man One or Many?" *Putnam's*, 4 (July 1854), 1–14; and Carolyn L. Karcher, *Shadow Over the Promised Land: Slavery, Race, and Violence in Melville's America* (Baton Rouge: Louisiana State Univ. Press, 1980), pp. 128–30.

24. *Types*, pp. 141–79, 246–71.

25. *Types*, pp. 68, 373.

26. "Lima and the Limanians," *Harper's Monthly*, 3 (Oct. 1851), 606. According to Sealts, *Melville's Reading*, p. 64, Melville subscribed to *Harper's* throughout his tale-writing years. Significantly, Melville's first mention of the *saya* (by name) occurs in *Pierre*, which he was writing at the time the Lima article appeared. See *Pierre, or The Ambiguities*, ed. Harrison Hayford, Hershel Parker, and G. Thomas Tanselle (Evanston and Chicago: Northwestern Univ. Press and the Newberry Library, 1971), p. 149. Moreover, Melville's own "Town-Ho's Story" appeared in the same number of *Harper's* as the Lima article, making his familiarity with that number more likely.

27. *Narrative*, p. 328.

28. See Delano, p. 347; Guy A. Cardwell, "Melville's Gray Story: Symbols and Meaning in 'Benito Cereno'," *Bucknell Review*, 8 (1959), 166; and Max Putzel, "The Source and the Symbols of Melville's 'Benito Cereno'," *American Literature*, 34 (1962), 194.

29. See Vanderhaar, p. 190.

30. Delano, p. 328.

31. See Feltenstein, p. 254.

32. Quoted in "American Travelers," *Putnam's*, 5 (June 1855), 565. When moving "Benito Cereno" from *Putnam's* to *The Piazza Tales*, Melville substituted Ledyard's name for that of Mungo Park, an English explorer. See Egbert S. Oliver, "Explanatory Notes" to *The Piazza Tales* (New York:

Hendricks House, 1948), pp. 235–36. In "Mungo Park and Ledyard in Melville's *Benito Cereno*," *English Language Notes*, 3 (1965), 122–23. Seymour Gross suggests that the substitution resulted from Melville's reading of "About Niggers," *Putnam's*, 6 (Dec. 1855), 608–12, where he could have learned that Ledyard, and not Park, was the original source of those views which interested him. "American Travelers" contained the same information.

33. Delano, p. 341.

34. *Types*, pp. 260, 457.

35. "Is Man One or Many?" pp. 5–6, 14.

36. William Stanton traces the history of this debate in *The Leopard's Spots: Scientific Attitudes Toward Race in America, 1815–59* (Chicago: Univ. of Chicago Press, 1960).

37. See *The Natural History of Man: Comprising Inquiries into the Modifying Influences of Physical and Moral Agencies on the Different Tribes of the Human Family* (London: H. Bailliere, 1843); and *Researches into the Physical History of Mankind*, 5 vols. (London: Houlston and Stoneman, 1847–51).

38. See *The Unity of the Races Proved to be the Doctrine of Scripture, Reason, and Science* (New York: G. P. Putnam, 1850); *The Races of Men; a fragment* (Philadelphia: Lea and Blanchard, 1850); and *Types*, pp. 81, 465. For reviews of Smyth, see the *Literary World*, 6 (1 June 1850), 533–34; *Harper's*, 1 (July 1850), 284–85; and "Is Man One or Many?" pp. 2–3. A review of Knox appeared in the *Literary World*, 7 (7 Dec. 1850), 453–54. See Sealts, *Melville's Reading*, p. 75, for Melville's acquaintance with the *Literary World*.

39. See *Types*, p. 50.

APPLICATION

In their influential book, The Madwoman in the Attic, *Sandra M. Gilbert and Susan Gubar examine the images of women in several nineteenth-century literary works by women writers with an eye both to the accuracy of the images and to their effects. As Josephine Donovan explains, the "images of women" criticism is often "negative" because "the critic is in effect saying 'no' to refined perceptions, structures, and models that have historically denied full humanity to women." The situation is complicated, of course, when the images are those presented by women writers. For example, Gilbert and Gubar attribute the pervasive scenes of imprisonment and escape in these texts to the conflicting pressures society placed on all women. "For it is, after all, through the violence of the double that the female author enacts her own raging desire to escape male houses and male texts, while at the same time it is through the double's violence that this anxious author articulates for herself the costly destructiveness of anger repressed until it can no longer be contained." Thus, Gilbert and Gubar claim, male authors' images of imprisonment and escape are crucially different being "metaphysical and metaphorical" whereas those of female authors are "social and actual" because "women authors . . . reflect the literal reality of their own confinement in the constraints they depict." On all these points, Gilbert and Gubar find "The Yellow Wallpaper" a "paradigmatic tale which (like* Jane Eyre) *seems to tell the story that all literary women would tell if they could speak their 'speechless woe'."*

"The Yellow Wallpaper"

Sandra M. Gilbert and Susan Gubar

Reprinted by permission from Sandra M. Gilbert and Susan Gubar, *The Madwoman in the Attic*. New Haven: Yale University Press, 1979: 85–92. Copyright 1979 by Yale University Press. The title of the excerpt has been added.

Dramatizations of imprisonment and escape are so all-pervasive in nineteenth-century literature by women that we believe they represent a uniquely female tradition in this period. Interestingly, though works in this tradition generally begin by using houses as primary symbols of female imprisonment, they also use much of the other paraphernalia of "woman's place" to enact their central symbolic drama of enclosure and escape. Ladylike veils and costumes, mirrors, paintings, statues, locked cabinets, drawers, trunks, strong-boxes, and other domestic furnishing appear and reappear in female novels and poems throughout the nineteenth century and on into the twentieth to signify the woman writer's sense that, as Emily Dickinson put it, her "life" has been "shaven and fitted to a frame," a confinement she can only tolerate by believing that "the soul has moments of escape/When bursting all the doors/She dances like a bomb abroad."[1] Significantly, too, the explosive violence of these "moments of escape" that women writers continually imagine for themselves returns us to the phenomenon of the mad double so many of these women have projected into their works. For it is, after all, through the violence of the double that the female author enacts her own raging desire to escape male houses, and male texts, while at the same time it is through the double's violence that this anxious author articulates for herself the costly destructiveness of anger repressed until it can no longer be contained.

As we shall see, therefore, infection continually breeds in the sentences of women whose writing obsessively enacts this drama of enclosure and escape. Specifically, what we have called the distinctively female diseases of anorexia and agoraphobia are closely associated with this dramatic/thematic pattern. Defining themselves as prisoners of their own gender, for instance, women frequently create characters who attempt to escape, if only into nothingness, through the suicidal self-starvation of anorexia. Similarly, in a metaphorical elaboration of bulimia, the disease of overeating which is anorexia's complement and mirror-image (as Marlene Boskind-Lodahl has recently shown),[2] women writers often envision an "outbreak" that transforms their characters into huge and powerful monsters. More obviously, agoraphobia and its complementary opposite, claustrophobia, are by definition associated with the spatial imagery through which these poets and novelists express their feelings of social confinement and their yearning for spiritual escape. The paradigmatic female story, therefore—the story such angels in the house of literature as Goethe's Makarie and Patmore's Honoria were in effect "forbidden" to tell—is frequently an arrangement of the elements most readers will readily remember from Charlotte Brontë's *Jane Eyre*. Examining the psychosocial implications of a "haunted" ancestral mansion, such a tale explores the tension between parlor and attic, the psychic split between the lady who submits to male dicta and the lunatic who rebels. But in examining these matters the paradigmatic female story inevitably considers also the equally uncomfortable spatial options of expulsion into the cold outside or suffocation in the hot indoors, and in addition it often embodies an obsessive anxiety both about starvation to the point of disappearance and about monstrous inhabitation.

Many nineteenth-century male writers also, of course, used imagery of enclosure and escape to make deeply felt points about the relationship of the individual and society. Dickens and Poe, for instance, on opposite sides of the Atlantic, wrote of prisons, cages, tombs, and cellars in similar ways and for similar reasons. Still, the male writer is so much more comfortable with his literary role that he can usually elaborate upon his visionary theme more consciously and objectively than the female writer can. The distinction between male and female images of imprisonment is—and always has been—a distinction between, on the one hand, that which is both metaphysical and metaphorical, and on the other hand, that which is social and actual. Sleeping in his coffin, the seventeenth-century poet John Donne was piously rehearsing the constraints of the grave in advance, but the nineteenth-century poet Emily Dickinson, in purdah in her white dress, was anxiously living those constraints in the present. Imagining himself buried alive in tombs and cellars, Edgar Allan Poe was letting his mind poetically wander into the deepest recesses of his own psyche, but Dickinson, reporting that "I do not cross my Father's ground to any house in town," was recording a real, self-willed, self-burial. Similarly, when Byron's Prisoner of Chillon notes that "my very chains and I grew friends," the poet himself is making an epistemological point about the nature of the human mind, as well as a political point about the tyranny of the state. But when Rose Yorke in *Shirley* describes Caroline Helstone as living the life of a toad enclosed in a block of marble, Charlotte Brontë is speaking through her about her own deprived and constricted life, and its real conditions.[3]

Thus, though most male metaphors of imprisonment have obvious implications in common (and many can be traced back to traditional images used by, say, Shakespeare and Plato), such metaphors may have very different aesthetic functions and philosophical messages in different male literary works. Wordsworth's prison-house in the "Intimations" ode serves a purpose quite unlike that served by the jails in Dickens's novels. Coleridge's twice-five miles of visionary greenery ought not to be confused with Keats's vale of soul-making, and the escape of Tennyson's Art from her Palace should not be identified with the resurrection of Poe's Ligeia. Women authors, however, reflect the literal reality of their own confinement in the constraints they depict, and so all at least begin with the same unconscious or conscious purpose in employing such spatial imagery. Recording their own distinctively female experience, they are secretly working through and within the conventions of literary texts to define their own lives.

While some male authors also use such imagery for implicitly or explicitly confessional projects, women seem forced to live more intimately with the metaphors they have created to solve the "problem" of their fall. At least one critic does deal not only with such images but with their psychological meaning as they accrue around houses. Noting in *The Poetics of Space* that "the house image would appear to have become the topography of our inmost being," Gaston Bachelard shows the ways in which houses, nests, shells, and wardrobes are in us as much as we are in them.[4] What is significant from our point of view, however, is the extraordinary discrepancy between the almost consistently "felicitous space" he discusses and the negative space we have found. Clearly, for Bachelard the protective asylum of the house is closely associated with its maternal features, and to this extent he is following the work done on dream symbolism by Freud and on female inner space by Erikson. It seems clear too, however, that such symbolism must inevitably have very different implications for male critics and for female authors.

Women themselves have often, of course, been described or imagined as houses. Most recently Erik Erikson advanced his controversial theory of female "inner space" in an effort to account for little girls' interest in domestic enclosures. But in medieval times, as if to anticipate Erikson, statues of the Madonna were made to open up and reveal the holy family hidden in the Virgin's inner space. The female womb has certainly, always and everywhere, been a child's first and most satisfying house, a source of food and dark security, and therefore a mythic paradise imaged over and over again in sacred caves, secret shrines, consecrated huts. Yet for many a woman writer these ancient associations of house and self seem mainly to have strengthened the anxiety about enclosure which she projected into her art. Disturbed by the real physiological prospect of enclosing an unknown part of herself that is somehow also not herself, the female artist may, like Mary Shelley, conflate anxieties about maternity with anxieties about literary creativity. Alternatively, troubled by the anatomical "emptiness" of spinsterhood, she may, like Emily Dickinson, fear the inhabitations of nothingness and death, the transformation of womb into tomb. Moreover, conditioned to believe that as a house she is herself owned (and ought to be inhabited) by a man, she may once again but for yet another reason see herself as inescapably an object. In other words, even if she does not experience her womb as a kind of tomb or perceive her child's occupation of her house/ body as depersonalizing, she may recognize that in an essential way she has been defined simply by her purely biological usefulness to her species.

To become literally a house, after all, is to be denied the hope of that spiritual transcendence of the body which, as Simone de Beauvoir has argued, is what makes humanity distinctively human. Thus, to be confined in childbirth (and significantly "confinement" was the key nineteenth-century term for what we would now, just as significantly, call "delivery") is in a way just as problematical as to be confined in a house or prison. Indeed, it might well seem to the literary woman that, just as ontogeny may be said to recapitulate phylogeny, the confinement of pregnancy replicates the confinement of society. For even if she is only metaphorically denied transcendence, the woman writer who perceives the implications of the house/body equation must unconsciously realize that such a trope does not just "place" her in a glass coffin, it transforms her into a version of the glass coffin herself. There is a sense, therefore, in which, confined in such a network of metaphors, what Adrienne Rich has called a "thinking woman" might inevitably feel that now she has been imprisoned within her own alien and loathsome body.[5]

Once again, in other words, she has become not only a prisoner but a monster.

As if to comment on the unity of all these points — on, that is, the anxiety-inducing connections between what women writers tend to see as their parallel confinements in texts, houses, and maternal female bodies — Charlotte Perkins Gilman brought them all together in 1890 in a striking story of female confinement and escape, a paradigmatic tale which (like *Jane Eyre*) seems to tell *the* story that all literary women would tell if they could speak their "speechless woe." "The Yellow Wallpaper," which Gilman herself called "a description of a case of nervous breakdown," recounts in the first person the experiences of a woman who is evidently suffering from a severe postpartum psychosis.[6] Her husband, a censorious and paternalistic physician, is treating her according to methods by which S. Weir Mitchell, a famous "nerve specialist," treated Gilman herself for a similar problem. He has confined her to a large garret room in an "ancestral hall" he has rented, and he has forbidden her to touch pen to paper until she is well again, for he feels, says the narrator, "that with my imaginative power and habit of story-making, a nervous weakness like mine is sure to lead to all manner of excited fancies, and that I ought to use my will and good sense to check the tendency."

The cure, of course, is worse than the disease, for the sick woman's mental condition deteriorates rapidly. "I think sometimes that if I were only well enough to write a little it would relieve the press of ideas and rest me," she remarks, but literally confined in a room she thinks is a one-time nursery because it has "rings and things" in the walls, she is literally locked away from creativity. The "rings and things," although reminiscent of children's gymnastic equipment, are really the paraphernalia of confinement, like the gate at the head of the stairs, instruments that definitively indicate her imprisonment. Even more tormenting, however, is the room's wallpaper: a sulphurous yellow paper, torn off in spots, and patterned with "lame uncertain curves" that "plunge off at outrageous angles" and "destroy themselves in unheard of contradictions." Ancient, smoldering, "unclean" as the oppressive structures of the society in which she finds herself, this paper surrounds the narrator like an inexplicable text, censorious and overwhelming as her physician husband, haunting as the "hereditary estate" in which she is trying to survive. Inevitably she studies its sui-

cidal implications — and inevitably, because of her "imaginative power and habit of story-making," she revises it, projecting her own passion for escape into its otherwise incomprehensible hieroglyphics. "This wall-paper," she decides, at a key point in her story,

> has a kind of sub-pattern in a different shade, a particularly irritating one, for you can only see it in certain lights, and not clearly then.
>
> But in the places where it isn't faded and where the sun is just so — I can see a strange, provoking, formless sort of figure, that seems to skulk about behind that silly and conspicuous front design.

As time passes, this figure concealed behind what corresponds (in terms of what we have been discussing) to the facade of the patriarchal text becomes clearer and clearer. By moonlight the pattern of the wallpaper "becomes bars! The outside pattern I mean, and the woman behind it is as plain as can be." And eventually, as the narrator sinks more deeply into what the world calls madness, the terrifying implications of both the paper and the figure imprisoned behind the paper begin to permeate — that is, to *haunt* — the rented ancestral mansion in which she and her husband are immured. The "yellow smell" of the paper "creeps all over the house," drenching every room in its subtle aroma of decay. And the woman creeps too — through the house, in the house, and out of the house, in the garden and "on that long road under the trees." Sometimes, indeed, the narrator confesses, "I think there are a great many women" both behind the paper and creeping in the garden,

> and sometimes only one, and she crawls around fast, and her crawling shakes [the paper] all over. . . . And she is all the time trying to climb through. But nobody could climb through that pattern — it strangles so; I think that is why it has so many heads.

Eventually it becomes obvious to both reader and narrator that the figure creeping through and behind the wallpaper is both the narrator and the narrator's double. By the end of the story, moreover, the narrator has enabled this double to escape from her textual/architectural confinement: "I pulled and she shook, I shook and she pulled, and before morning we had peeled off yards of that paper." Is the message of the tale's conclusion mere madness? Certainly the righteous Doctor John — whose name links him to the anti-hero of Charlotte Brontë's *Villette* —

has been temporarily defeated, or at least momentarily stunned. "Now why should that man have fainted?" the narrator ironically asks as she creeps around her attic. But John's unmasculine swoon of surprise is the least of the triumphs Gilman imagines for her madwoman. More significant are the madwoman's own imaginings and creations, mirages of health and freedom with which her author endows her like a fairy godmother showering gold on a sleeping heroine. The woman from behind the wallpaper creeps away, for instance, creeps fast and far on the long road, in broad daylight. "I have watched her sometimes away off in the open country," says the narrator, "creeping as fast as a cloud shadow in a high wind."

Indistinct and yet rapid, barely perceptible but inexorable, the progress of that cloud shadow is not unlike the progress of nineteenth-century literary women out of the texts defined by patriarchal poetics into the open spaces of their own authority. That such an escape from the numb world behind the patterned walls of the text was a flight from disease into health was quite clear to Gilman herself. When "The Yellow Wallpaper" was published she sent it to Weir Mitchell, whose strictures had kept her from attempting the pen during her own breakdown, thereby aggravating her illness, and she was delighted to learn, years later, that "he had changed his treatment of nervous prostration since reading" her story. "If that is a fact," she declared, "I have not lived in vain."[7] Because she was a rebellious feminist besides being a medical iconoclast, we can be sure that Gilman did not think of this triumph of hers in narrowly therapeutic terms. Because she knew, with Emily Dickinson, that "Infection in the sentence breeds," she knew that the cure for female despair must be spiritual as well as physical, aesthetic as well as social. What "The Yellow Wallpaper" shows she knew, too, is that even when a supposedly "mad" woman has been sentenced to imprisonment in the "infected" house of her own body, she may discover that, as Sylvia Plath was to put it seventy years later, she has "a self to recover, a queen."[8]

Notes

1. J. 512 ("The Soul has Bandaged moments—") in *The Poems of Emily Dickinson,* ed. Thomas Johnson, 3 vols. (Cambridge, Mass.: The Belknap Press of Harvard University Press, 1955).

2. Marlene Boskind-Lodahl, "Cinderella's Stepsisters: A Feminist Perspective on Anorexia Nervosa and Bulimia," *Signs* 2, no. 2 (Winter 1976): 342–56.

3. *The Letters of Emily Dickinson,* ed. Thomas Johnson, 3 vols. (Cambridge, Mass.: The Belknap Press of Harvard University Press, 1958), 2:460; Byron, "The Prisoner of Chillon," lines 389–893; Brontë, *Shirley* (New York: Dutton, 1970), p. 316.

4. Gaston Bachelard, *The Poetics of Space,* trans. Maria Jolas (Boston: Beacon, 1970), p. xxxii.

5. *Adrienne Rich's Poetry,* ed. Barbara Charlesworth Gelpi and Albert Gelpi (New York: Norton, 1975), p. 12: "A thinking woman sleeps with monsters. The beak that grips her, she becomes" ("Snapshots of a Daughter-in-Law," #3).

6. Charlotte Perkins Gilman, *The Yellow Wallpaper* (Old Westbury: The Feminist Press, 1973).

7. *The Living of Charlotte Perkins Gilman* (New York: Harper and Row, 1975), p. 121.

8. "Stings," *Ariel* (New York: Harper and Row, 1966), p. 62.

CHAPTER FIVE

Intertextual Criticism: Literature as Context

Be Homer's *Works your* Study, *and* Delight,
Read them by Day, *and meditate by* Night
          —Pope, *An Essay on Criticism*

Poems do not imitate life; they imitate other poems. This is the central idea of the perspective I have labeled "intertextual criticism," a perspective that says the poem can best be understood by seeing it in the larger contexts of the linguistic and literary conventions it employs. Unless we know these, says the intertextualist, we can't know the poem at all.

Not all of the many critics who have adopted this perspective consider themselves members of the same critical school, and perhaps only a few would answer to the name I have given to their approach. I can only plead that no other term would meet with greater recognition. And this is odd because the approach itself has a history as old and as rich as any other. But this approach has never had a widely accepted label, and often it has had no label at all. Northrop Frye states the case, and the problem, in an essay on *Lycidas*:

> In the writing of *Lycidas* there are four creative principles of particular importance. . . . One is convention, the reshaping of the poetic material which is appropriate to this subject. Another is genre, the choosing of the appropriate form. A third is archetype, the use of appropriate, and therefore recurrently employed, images and symbols. The fourth, for which there is no name, is the fact that the forms of literature are autonomous: that is, they do not exist outside of literature. Milton is not writing an obituary: he does not start with Edward King and his life and times, but with the conventions and archetypes that poetry requires for such a theme.

This fourth principle, "for which there is no name," includes the other three; to name it is to name the entire context. But critics have failed to agree on an appropriate label.

To supply this lack, some have tried to promote one of the other words to the status of cover term, and each label tells us something about the interests of this perspective. So we hear, for example, of "genre criticism," and clearly any conception of genre does fall within this context. But as a cover term, "genre criticism" has two drawbacks. First, it suggests to many minds a rigid and even hierarchic conception of discrete forms and a concern with arid distinctions parodied in Polonius's pedantic taxonomy: "tragedy, comedy, history, pastoral, pastoral-comical, historical-pastoral, tragical-historical, tragical-comical-historical-pastoral." This reaction may be prejudice, but it is strong enough to erode the usefulness of the term. More importantly, the concept "genre" is itself reducible to an indefinite number of conventions by which we recognize the various "kinds" of literature. Consequently, many critics can operate in this context without being directly concerned with "genre" in the usual sense of the word.

The word "archetype" offers another possibility, and Frye himself is often called an "archetypal" or a "myth" critic. Some justification exists for these terms if they are understood to have the special meanings Frye sometimes gives them. Unfortunately, Frye uses the term "myth" in several senses and, even more confusing, it has long been used to label critical approaches very different from his own. "Archetype" presents similar problems. Frye's sense of "recurrently employed images and symbols" clearly fits the context I am describing here, though, like "genre," it too seems reducible to "convention." But the chief difficulty is that "archetype" inevitably suggests to many readers the very different Jungian sense of the word. The fact that Frye is still often classed with "myth" critics or with "archetypal" critics of a Jungian persuasion shows that these labels are likely to cause confusion.

There remains, then, the basic term "convention." Archetype, in Frye's sense, and "genre" as well, are simply elaborations of this more fundamental concept. And a concern with the conventional aspects of art is indeed the characteristic feature of the criticism we are here describing. All art, in this view, is conventional, and any work of art can be understood only by those who know the conventions it employs. So it would be both accurate and appropriate to call this approach "conventional" criticism. I can think of only one disadvantage to this name: the obvious and fatal one that "conventional" criticism, like "conventional" wisdom, will be taken to mean the dull, the ordinary, the uninspired, and that would be neither accurate nor appropriate. Convention, nevertheless, remains the key concept. Our understanding of a particular work is an analogical process by which we measure its conformity to the linguistic and literary conventions we know. The conformity is never absolute; in this sense each work is "unique." Yet, if the work were truly unique, if it used no conventions we knew, it would be simply unintelligible. This is the primary reason I have labeled the approach to literature by way of its conventional elements an "intertextual" approach.

The term has achieved some currency, particularly in connection with the related terms "semiotics" and "structuralism," which we'll need to glance at again later in this introduction. Here I simply note that "semiotics" and "structuralism" are used to describe movements in several intellectual fields besides literary criticism. That is, they are both more and less than approaches to literature. But when structuralists or semioticians do concentrate on literature, they are primarily concerned with the conventional and self-referential aspects of the art, with literature as a system of signs. So "intertextual" is an appropriate cover term for most semiotic and structural, and even for much "poststructural," criticism.

But I use "intertextual" here in an even wider yet fairly obvious sense. While interest in structuralism and semiotics is a relatively recent phenomenon, especially among English-speaking critics, interest in "intertextual" relations, under a variety of cover terms, is very old and very widespread. In this broad sense of the term, whenever critics focus on the conventional elements of literature and relate the poem not to "reality" but, by analogy, to other poems, they are practicing "intertextual" criticism.

The term understood in this sense helps to clarify the crucial distinction between the genetic and the generic perspectives. Studies that attempt to trace the literary influences on a particular poem have long been a staple of genetic or historical criticism. As the words "genetic" and "influence" imply, such studies seek the causes of poems and necessarily operate in chronological sequence. With a tradition as diffuse as that of the pastoral and with an author as learned as Milton, tracing the sources of a poem like *Lycidas* becomes difficult and frustrating. The difficulty results from the vast number of parallels that exist for many features of the poem. The frustration follows from our inability to know precisely which of these parallels Milton had in mind when he wrote. But when we shift from the genetic to the intertextual perspective, the difficulty evaporates. We need to know pastoral conventions to understand *Lycidas,* and therefore we need to know other pastoral poems, but it makes little difference on this view whether we know only those pastoral poems that Milton knew. For that matter, our knowledge of later poems in the genre may be quite as helpful as our knowledge of earlier ones. Yet clearly no one would argue that Arnold's "Thyrsis," say, or Shelley's "Adonais" in any way "influenced" Milton's poem.

Similarly, our comprehension of the *Aeneid* is improved when we read it with *Paradise Lost* in mind, and our understanding of the *Iliad* is conditioned by our reading of Virgil's epic, even though the "lines of influence" in each case run in the opposite direction. And the process operates when there are no clear lines of influence at all. The question of how much Shakespeare could have known about Sophocles's drama is, on this view, less important than the reciprocal illumination that results when their plays are compared. The relationships in all these instances are not genetic but generic, not diachronic but synchronic, not causal but analogical. Robert Frost, though he probably never used the term, has furnished a succinct description of intertextual reading: "A poem is best read in the light of all the other poems ever written. We read A the better to read B (we have to start somewhere; we may get very little out of A). We read B the better to read C, C the better to read D, D the better to go back and get something out of A. Progress is not the aim, but circulation. The thing is to get among the poems where they hold each other apart in their places as the stars do" (*Selected Prose,* New York, 1966, pp. 96–97).

"Intertextual" criticism, then, is something neither new nor strange, and the idea that our understanding of literature depends on a knowledge of its conventions may often go unremarked because it goes, as we say, without saying. But quite as often, one suspects, it goes unsaid because it is *unseen.* A curious thing about conventions is that the more firmly established they are, the less likely we are to notice them. Scarcely any visitor to a museum remarks the absence of octagonal paintings, and few concertgoers in the West notice departures from five-tone or quarter-tone scales. Literary critics have often displayed a similar inattention to literary convention.

Perhaps for this reason, much of the history of intertextual criticism is to be found in the observations and, above all, in the practice of the poets themselves. It now seems clear, for example, that the *Iliad* and the *Odyssey,* those songs of "Homer" that for us stand at the beginning of Western literature, achieved their final form only at the end of several centuries of oral heroic poetry. During these illiterate centuries, the characters, the actions, the meter, and the hundreds of formulaic phrases that make up these poems were gradually developed, refined, and transmitted from poet to poet. How much of either poem can be attributed to an individual genius is quite impossible to determine and, for the intertextualist, quite unnecessary to determine. But the image of the self-effacing lyre-smiter, the Phemios or the blind Demodokos, who must quite sincerely invoke the aid of Memory's daughters, is very much to the point. For what these bards must remember are all the other poems on the same themes and all the formulae with which they will build their own at each performance. They tell the old stories in the old way, and their success consists in doing well what many others have done before.

Traditional poets may be self-effacing, but their art is very important. That art is sometimes called the "collective memory" of the tribe, but it is really more like the tribe's collective imagination. The epic poem, under the guise of re-creating the distant past, actually creates a world of more heroic characters and more significant actions than those its hearers know from life. So the worlds of Achilles and Odysseus, far from mirroring the lives of their listeners, provide an image of greatness, an imagined standard, against which those lives can be measured. The mirror may tell us what we are; memory may tell us what we were; but only the imagination can tell us what we might be. It is the function of art to provide these imagined worlds, and to the extent that artists work with the materials of this world, they must not copy but transform those materials. "All the world," said Mallarmé, "exists in order to make a book," a bit of "decadent aestheticism" anticipated many centuries earlier by Homer's Phaiakian king, who gives the poet's game away when he reminds the weeping Odysseus that the whole tragic action of Troy had been fashioned by the gods "so that it might become a song for future generations."

Most often, however, what the poets transform is not the raw material of life but the conventions of their medium. And this is why, says the intertextualist, only an absurdly small proportion of the world's literature can be accounted for on "mimetic" principles. It is not the mimetic but the conventional elements in art that enable us to understand it, and the great poets from Homer to the present have always known this. Pope pictures Virgil as closing up the barren leaves of art to turn directly to nature as the model for his Roman epic, only to discover that Homer had already produced the faithful copy. In actuality, it is very unlikely that Virgil ever contemplated any such thing; and neither did Pope. Virgil follows Homer at every turn because he wants his readers to know that the *Aeneid* is a heroic poem, and that meant for him, as it means for us, a poem that looks like the *Iliad* and the *Odyssey.* He also follows Homer at every turn because he wants his readers to know how profoundly his vision differs from Homer's. In other words, Virgil carefully copies the Homeric poems because much of the meaning of his work depends on our marking these comparisons. And there is reason to believe that "Homer" relates to his predecessors in the same way. For the same reasons, Milton takes pains to copy Homer and Virgil in *Paradise Lost,* and Pope, in turn, draws on all these in *The Rape of the Lock.*

The last is, of course, a mock heroic. But from the intertextual perspective, all poems are to some degree "mock" forms. That is, it may be readily admitted that Pope's *Rape of the Lock* will not be very meaningful to anyone who doesn't understand the conventions of heroic poetry and that the reader who comes to the poem with a knowledge of the epics of Homer and Virgil and Milton is better equipped than one who brings only a knowledge of Pope's life, or of Arabella Fermor's. But a knowledge of the conventions of heroic poetry is equally indispensable, says the intertextual critic, to our understanding of the "primary" works. And this knowledge can be gained only by studying heroic poems.

And so with every other form or "genre." It can be said that Pope, like Milton, never sat down to write a poem; he always wrote some "kind" of poem. All poets must do this, the intertextualist claims, but not all poets have been equally conscious of the fact. One of the few things that makes Wordsworth's 1800 "Preface" to the *Lyrical Ballads* a truly revolutionary critical document is his inclination to talk about poetry with no reference to generic type and with little reference to convention, except for those conventions he wishes to extirpate. Somehow the term "decorum" has become attached to those conventions, and the poor reputation of the word dates from about this time. This represents a clear and symptomatic decline from the term's earlier meaning of "suitability," specifically that suiting of image, diction, style, and tone to theme and subject that Milton had in mind when he pronounced "decorum" to be "the grand masterpiece to observe," a pronouncement that makes sense only in the context of some conception of genre and convention.

The intertextual critic will point out, of course, that Wordsworth's poems, despite his critical theory, are quite as conventional as any others. But the tendency to overlook this fact is by no means limited to Wordsworth. Perhaps, as some have argued, the modern emphasis on individualism and "originality" has served to further obscure the conventional and communal elements in literature. At any rate, it is the case that until fairly recently modern critical theory has tended to play down the role of convention. Yet most readers remain at least dimly aware that many of the masterpieces of Western literature, including the works of Virgil, Dante, Chaucer, Shakespeare, and Milton, are profoundly "conventional" poems, though we may prefer to call them "highly allusive" instead; and few works require a greater knowledge of literary conventions than do such modernist masterpieces as *The Waste Land* and *Ulysses.* This interdependence is not really surprising, argues the intertextual critic, for poetry, being an art, must go on rediscovering, re-creating, and recombining the conventions of that art if it is to exist at all. And poetry must continue to do so even when critical theory takes little notice of the fact and even when its readers come less and less to share similar assumptions and similar training.

This last is a serious difficulty, and for the past two hundred years, as the number of readers has increased several times over but the number trained as Pope and Milton were trained has steadily declined, poets have lamented their plight. Yeats, like Blake before him, tried to solve the problem by making of his own poems an interlocking set of images and symbols, a sounding box in which the individual poem may resonate. Eliot complained that the modern poet and his readers lacked anything like the extensive system of attitudes and symbols that Dante shared with his audience, but then proceeded to write poetry nearly as allusive as Dante's. Each solution illustrates the intertextualist's point: the poet can speak only through the conventions of poetry.

In his famous essay "Tradition and the Individual Talent" (1917), Eliot asserted that "honest criticism and sensitive appreciation are directed not upon the poet but upon the poetry," and the essay has been often cited as an opening shot in the formalists' battle against genetic criticism. But the formalists largely ignored, and their theory cannot easily deal with, the chief thesis of that essay in which Eliot explained that "no poet, no artist of any art, has his complete meaning alone." He urged both the poet and the critic to develop what he called a "historical sense," which "involves a perception, not only of the pastness of the past, but of its presence; the historical sense compels a man to write not merely with his own generation in his bones, but with a feeling that the whole of the literature of Europe from Homer and within it the whole of the literature of his own country has a simultaneous existence and composes a simultaneous order." While we may hesitate to call this synchronic view a "historical" sense, Eliot's vision of all the works of Western literature, not strung out in fixed sequence but arranged in some kind of conceptual space to form a context for the understanding of each poem, is precisely the vision of intertextual criticism.

From this perspective, the intertextual critic offers to explain a central fact that nearly everyone recognizes but that no other theory can adequately account for: people who have read a lot of poetry can generally interpret a given poem better than people who have not. We noticed in particular that critics operating in the formal and mimetic contexts find this phenomenon difficult to explain, and for the simple reason that these contexts have no way of dealing with literary convention. The problem goes much deeper than "allusion." In discussing formalism, I remarked that formalists sometimes appear to confront the poem armed only with their wits and a dictionary. But this immensely oversimplifies the case. In the first place, if the poem is in English, any reader has already more or less — and it is always more or less — mastered several systems of conventions that make up "written English." That certain marks should stand for certain sounds and that these sounds should stand for things, actions, and relationships are matters quite arbitrary and peculiar to each language. In English, for example, we depend almost exclusively on word order to signal meaning, and we are required to describe a certain spatial relationship by saying, "the cat is on the mat" rather than "the mat is on the cat." These devices are not the result of our perception of the world; they are purely conventional elements. But unless one has mastered these conventions, one cannot understand even the simplest English sentence.

Now poems, says the analogist, present analogous cases. But to explain literary conventions by analogy to linguistic conventions somewhat clouds the issue, for a poem is in the first place a system of linguistic conventions, the "system" itself being one of the conventional elements. It differs from other utterances in the same language, the intertextual critic would argue, by also employing a number of supra-linguistic conventions peculiar to or characteristic of literature. This fact explains, incidentally, why poems are and are not translatable. Linguistic conventions and the literary conventions most closely bound to them, such as meter, rhythm, and rhyme, are notoriously difficult to reproduce in another language. But devices of structure and plot, techniques of character representation, and a vast reservoir of images and symbols are conventions that most of the Western literatures, at least, have in common, and these easily cross linguistic boundaries. But, like the conventions of language, they have meaning only to those who have learned them. As Eliot says in the same essay, the literary tradition "cannot be inherited, and if you want it you must obtain it by great labour."

This idea that literary conventions must be learned is a crucial point that sets intertextual critics apart from most "myth" critics. The latter, whatever their psychological or anthropological affiliation, are generally affectivists who locate the power of poems in special patterns or symbols that have the ability to appeal directly and forcefully to our subconscious minds. They may, like the Jungians, account for this power on the basis of some theory of inherited racial memory, or like the Freudians, they may feel that the essential similarity of human experience offers sufficient explanation. In either case they are concerned only with certain special poetic "conventions" (though they would surely find that word too slight) and, as we noticed in the discussion of reader-response criticism, while their view offers an apparently plausible explanation of why some of us respond intensely to certain works, it offers no explanation at all of why many of us do not. Intertextual critics, by contrast, though not necessarily denying that certain symbols may have special potency, feel no need to locate the power of myths or symbols in the unconscious or in the extraliterary.

Like the conventions of language, literary conventions are arbitrary, and they must, therefore, be learned. From this perspective, readers who fail to respond to *King Lear,* say, or to *Moby Dick,* are not psychologically defective; they simply don't know how to read well enough.

It is the fundamental task of literary criticism to teach them, first by explaining what they need to know and then by showing how they may most efficiently acquire that knowledge. What they need to know, of course, are the conventions of literature, and here the only singing school is studying the monuments themselves. That is, in the intertextual view, the study of literature cannot be based on psychology, anthropology, sociology, or biography, nor can it be grounded in religious, economic, or political history. None of these contexts can directly tell us much about how literary conventions carry meaning. For similar reasons, the traditional genetic categories of author, period, and nation often prove less than ideal organizing forms for the study of literature. From the intertextual perspective, the best context for the understanding of any poem is all the other poems that employ similar conventions. These may or may not include poems by the same author or from the same historical period, but they are almost never limited to these, and they are seldom limited to the writings of a single nation or a single language.

This range suggests that in practice the intertextual study of literature may best be organized along generic lines, lines that keep our attention on conventional elements and that cut across national, temporal, and linguistic boundaries. The problem, again, is how to arrange this vast body of simultaneously existing works so that it may be most efficiently studied. Or, in terms of our definition of criticism, the problem is how to assure that the relevant information can be brought to bear on whatever work we have placed at the center of our attention. Generic concepts are helpful here, but generic distinctions are not. The critical task is not to define tragedy, or pastoral, or epic, but to assemble for our understanding the most useful comparisons. With large works, like *The Faerie Queen* or *Paradise Lost,* this purpose very quickly takes us beyond "generic" concerns to a contemplation of the vast networks of conventional images, symbols, and patterns of action that give such poems their multileveled meanings and their astonishing richness. In this view, the reader of *Ulysses* may need to know very little about Dublin in the springtime, but a great deal about Western literature since Homer's time.

To be sure, nothing short of a total knowledge of all literature will guarantee that one will come to a given poem with all the relevant conventions in mind. But it's not difficult to imagine a course of study by which readers could acquire much of what the intertextual critics claim they must know to understand most works in the Western tradition. Such a study would concentrate early and long on the classical languages and literatures. It would emphasize the *Iliad* and the *Odyssey;* the plays of Aeschylus, Sophocles, Euripides, and Aristophanes; the dialogues of Plato. It would include some Greek lyrics, Plautus and Terence, Virgil and Ovid and Horace. It would very likely include Dante's *Commedia,* and it would certainly include intensive study of the Bible. Above all, it would conceive of Western literature as a unit, and it would largely ignore national boundaries. Obviously, this course of study resembles, in content if not in methodology, the curriculum of "liberal" education as that phrase was generally understood before the twentieth century. And this resemblance is not surprising, for readers who follow this curriculum would be learning the conventions of literature in much the same way that the poets they want to read had learned them. As the intertextual critic sees it, these works, quite aside from their intrinsic merit, form the "grammar" and the basic "vocabulary" of European literary language, and consequently a knowledge of them is as indispensable to readers of Barth and Borges, Pynchon and Joyce, Eliot and Stevens as it is to readers of Spenser or Milton or Pope. For all art, says the intertextualist, is conventional.

This is the fundamental tenet. And the intertextualist can demonstrate it with even the briefest example. Consider, as a case in point, another Blake lyric, "The Sick Rose":

> O Rose, thou art sick.
> The invisible worm
> That flies in the night
> In the howling storm
>
> Has found out thy bed
> Of crimson joy,
> And his dark secret love
> Does thy life destroy.

To the intertextual critic, it seems pointless to look to Blake's life for the meaning of these words, and equally pointless to examine the responses of readers, until we know which readers have the best responses. Furthermore, although the poem, short as it is, exhibits a complex structure and a high degree of formal coherence, these in themselves do not account for the referential sense of the words. Now, ordinarily referential meaning implies correspondence to the world of nonverbal experience. Yet as a botanical description, Blake's poem is, like most poems, negligible if not downright ridiculous. But the intertextual critic argues that the real frame of reference for poetic language is not the world of nonverbal experience but the world of poetry, the world that literature creates and is.

If, ignoring considerations of rhythm and rhyme, we substitute "tulip" for "rose," "insect" for "invisible worm," "dawn" for "night," and so forth, we can construct a poem that would not only be equally coherent, but that would present at least as accurate a picture of the nonverbal world. As a poem, though, it would be a very poor thing, for it would lack the extensive range of conventional associations that Blake's words have. The rose, for example, has been long established in the Western tradition as a symbol of beauty. This is not a matter of perception or "aesthetics" in the basic sense. Under the aspect of eternity, we may suppose, all plants are equally beautiful, and many people may prefer tulips to roses in their vases. But not in their verses. The convention is too strong. One thinks of the *Romance of the Rose*, of Dante's Rose of Heaven, of Eliot's rose garden, of Waller's lovely rose and Housman's withered rose and Thomas's crooked rose, and on and on through a hundred other poems great and small. The only limit is our reading and our memory. And "worm," whatever its relation to real roses, has a similarly extensive literary pedigree. It calls to mind those snakes and serpents that slither through countless other poems and that have, whatever their possible psychological sources, a necessarily sinister resonance because of the pervasive influence of the Bible, a resonance reinforced here by the conventional associations of "invisible," "night," "howling storm," "dark," and "secret." Most of us do not need a Freudian analyst to tell us that "bed of joy" has sexual associations, nor that "crimson" in this context is "multivalent."

Indeed, the whole poem is wonderfully multivalent, or "plurisignificant." We can construct upon it a coherent "religious" reading, an equally coherent "sexual" reading, and any number of other readings within or around these. Short as it is, the poem can support pages of relevant commentary and not be exhausted because it is a coherent arrangement of elements that were already highly charged with poetic—

that is, with "conventional" — significance. Blake didn't invent these associations any more than he invented the dictionary definitions of his words. His business as a poet was to be unusually sensitive to the conventional associations of words and to have the genius to combine deftly these already charged particles to create that supercharged verbal structure that is his poem. But that poem, the intertextualist reminds us, is fully available only to readers who have mastered the relevant conventions of literature. "The Sick Rose" has eight lines; *Paradise Lost* has 10,565. We begin to see what Eliot meant by "great labour." Happily, most of this labor consists of reading poems.

This, then, is a sketch of the intertextual critic's argument, and even skeptical readers might grant that it has much to recommend it. But they might also feel that the perspective raises some difficult questions. Consider, for example, the question of the poem's relationship to the world. We have noticed that the mimetic critic, by definition, and the formal critic, often more hesitantly, locate the value of poetry in its correspondence to reality, however subtly such correspondence is defined and qualified. And this "reality" is usually the empiricist's reality, the world of experience. This mimetic grounding causes difficulties, but because correspondence to reality is the definition of "truth" in most commonsense views, poetry's claim to mimetic accuracy, to "truth-revealing" powers, seems to many critics to offer the only stable ground for poetic value. Yet the intertextual critic, by arguing that poems imitate other poems and not the world of experience, appears to surrender that claim at the outset. Literature becomes, as I. A. Richards had said it was, a system of purely hypothetical or "pseudo" statements.

But in defense of this position, the intertextualist can urge two arguments that were not so readily available in Richards's affective context. The first argument, interestingly, simply accepts the empirical view of "truth." The poem does provide cognitive knowledge, but knowledge of imagined worlds. By showing us not what life is but in what ways it could be better or worse, poetry becomes, in Matthew Arnold's phrase, a "criticism of life." For the only standard by which we can measure actuality must be an imagined standard. The characters and actions we find in literature are, in this view, less imitations of things than things to be imitated, or shunned, images of desire or aversion. This, I assume, is what Northrop Frye means when he says that one of the functions of art is to provide the "goals of work" for civilization. Looked at this way, what we call civilization is our collective attempt to create, from the world of nature we find, something approximating the world we imagine. And in this sense, life does indeed imitate art. As that arch-antimimeticist, Oscar Wilde, reminds us, nature has good intentions, but she can't carry them out.

This argument meets the empiricists on their own ground because it assumes that the correspondence definition of truth holds and that the world experienced outside of art is the "real" world. Only now, paradoxically, the value of literature seems to inhere not in its correspondence to that world but in its difference from it. This reversal, admittedly, offers as many evaluative difficulties as does the correspondence standard. But such a view is at least better able to account for the many forms of literature, and it would serve to counter the modern, mimetic prejudice against forms such as epic, romance, and pastoral that flaunt their "unrealistic" conventions.

And yet, the more we contemplate the conventional aspects of poems, the more it appears that all verbal constructs are to a high degree conventional. Carried to its logical conclusion, such a view undercuts empiricism itself. It does so not by denying the existence of "reality" but by denying that it can be known apart from the structure of the mind that knows it. Perception, as Kant perceived, is itself creation, and to the extent that art organizes our perceptions, we can understand the more profound implications of Wilde's remark that "life imitates art far more than art imitates life." This begins to sound like Kant's structuralist answer to the empiricism that Hume had pushed to its logical and paradoxical limits, and while the intertextual perspective in criticism does not require any particular philosophical orientation, it is not surprising that many intertextual critics should feel comfortable with what we might call, broadly speaking, a "structuralist" outlook. At any rate, it is typical of neo-Kantian philosophers, such as Ernst Cassirer, and of structuralist thinkers, such as Ferdinand de Saussure and Claude Lévi-Strauss and their many followers in literary criticism, to emphasize the conventional, symbolic, and self-referential elements in all systems of thought. In such philosophies the empiricist's truth of correspondence tends to disappear. There is instead only truth of coherence.

In other words, the truth of any statement must be judged not by its correspondence to empirical reality, for this correspondence cannot be directly known, but by its coherence, its ability to fit into the system of other statements that we have already accepted as "true." And there is not only one system; there are several. Mathematics, for instance, appears to some thinkers to be a clear example of such a system of complex and totally coherent relationships that, as a system, is congruent with, or corresponds to, nothing at all outside mathematics. By analogy, what we call "history" and "sociology" and "physics" are also self-contained systems. For in this view even the physicists, the hardest of the "hard" scientists, cannot tell us if a statement corresponds to reality. They can only tell us, in the first place, if the terms of that statement have any meaning within the universe of discourse we call physics and, in the second, if the statement is consistent with other statements that constitute that universe of discourse.

And so with all systems of thought. Clearly it is beyond the scope of this book to explore such large philosophic questions as whether truth is a matter of coherence or of correspondence. But we can at least note briefly a few of the consequences for literary criticism that are implied in a "structuralist" view of the mind's relationship to the world. Such a view suggests, in the first place, that no system of thought has a firm empirical base and that all are imaginative constructs. It follows that the critic who adopts this view is in a very different position than Richards was, for Richards denied truth of correspondence to poetry but granted it to science; the "coherence" theory denies truth of correspondence to everybody. Further, whereas mimetic critics operating with the empirical or correspondence model have difficulty separating poems from other kinds of discourse because they assume that all verbal constructs are "imitations" of reality, critics operating on the coherence model have the same difficulty for the opposite reason. If all verbal structures are imaginative structures, then what we call poems can again differ from other types of discourse only in degree, not in kind.

But though defining poetry from this perspective may be difficult, it is also unnecessary. We need instead to define criticism, that system of discourse that is centrally concerned with the conventional elements of symbolic or metaphorical structures. This shift of perspective eliminates two problems that sometimes trouble critics. On the one hand, if all verbal structures are metaphorical or symbolic, literary critics need not worry about getting "out of their field" if they comment on, say, the writings of Xenophon or Thucydides, Gibbon or Hume, Mill or Marx, nor need they worry too much whether biography or autobiography is within their ken. Their business is metaphor wherever they find it, and they find it everywhere. On the other hand, the literary critic, understood in this sense, has no reason to object to the historian, the psychologist, the economist, or anyone else making statements about poems. For the statements they make would not be literary criticism simply because they were about poems; their statements would continue to be history, psychology, economics, or whatever the discipline being applied was named.

To put the matter differently, it is not a question of what we study but of *how* we study. In this view, literary criticism has often appeared confused because critics have tried to define their subject of study by their object of study. They have tried to set poems apart from other verbal structures, and then they have tried to borrow their methodology—their way of seeing the object—from some other discipline. By this route we get such terms as "sociological criticism," "psychological criticism," and "historical criticism." From the perspective we are exploring here, this attempt is nonsense. One cannot borrow an approach or a methodology from another discipline, because the approach or methodology *is* the discipline. Disciplines are ways of seeing, not things to be seen; subjects, not objects. And what literary critics must master is not a definition of their object, but the discipline of criticism, which involves a systematic knowledge of the conventions from which metaphoric or symbolic forms are created and through which they can be understood.

These, I believe, are a few of the consequences that follow from accepting what I have called a "structuralist" view of criticism, but one doesn't need to get to this view by way of that label, nor is the critic who wishes to adopt an intertextual perspective compelled also to adopt this view of the mind and all that it seems to entail. As we have seen, even an empiricist can operate comfortably in the intertextual context.

But whatever their philosophic orientation may be, critics who employ the intertextual approach to literature will face some conceptual difficulties. One of these is the problem of circularity. We saw one version of this circularity in formalist theory, which holds that any part of the work can be understood and evaluated only in terms of the whole work, although (necessarily) that whole can be known only through its parts. In intertextual criticism, a similar difficulty returns on a larger scale. A particular poem can be understood only by someone who understands its conventions, but these conventions must be learned by studying similar poems, and a reading of each of these requires in turn a knowledge of conventions. But this problem, like the formalist's circularity, is less serious in practice than in theory, and again the parallel to language is instructive. We can understand, and even produce, new utterances in English because, through a complex, little understood, and never quite completed process, we have learned the conventions of our language, and this learning was gained by attending to other utterances in English. Thus the continuous interplay between convention and particular construct presents little practical difficulty at this level, however mysterious it may be to logic.

But this interplay points to a more serious problem, and that is the tendency of intertextual criticism to lose its focus on the individual work in question. Granted, this loss of focus is a problem mainly when criticism is defined, as in this book, as having as its primary goal the interpretation of particular poems. But if we hold to this conception—and most critics do—then the inclination of intertextual criticism to dissolve the particular work into an aggregate of conventions opens the approach to the charge of reductivism. If all poems are conventional, what makes some poems more effective than others? Does *Paradise Lost* have more, or better, conventions than Blackmore's *Prince Arthur*? Does *Lycidas* employ a greater number of conventional elements than lesser pastorals? Or does the better poem simply employ its conventions more effectively? Surely the latter is the case, the formalists would answer.

And, while they must grant the reader's need to know the conventions used in any poem, formalists will persist in regarding such knowledge as no different in kind from a knowledge of dictionary definitions. A dictionary and *Hamlet,* they might argue, consist of conventional meanings just as a marble quarry and the Parthenon consist of stone: the particular arrangement makes all the difference.

This analogy, as the intertextualists will remind us, is greatly complicated by the fact that in literature, as in architecture, the arrangement itself is largely a matter of convention. Nevertheless, formalists, the *intra*textualists, will continue to insist on the importance of "form" in their sense of the term, the special meaning that results from these particular words in this particular order, and so they will try to pull the reader's attention along the horizontal axis to the center of our diagram while the intertextual critics pull the reader's attention toward the larger context of literary and linguistic conventions. As long as the understanding of the particular poem remains the primary, if not the ultimate, goal of criticism, this tension is difficult to relax. But it is also relatively easy to live with, and the formal and intertextual perspectives are probably more compatible than other combinations that might be formed among our contexts. Still, in spite of this compatibility, or perhaps because of it, the formalist's complaint that intertextual criticism has difficulty keeping a clear and useful focus on the individual poem is one of the most troublesome objections to the intertextual approach.

It is not, of course, the only objection. Mimetic critics, for example, will point out that if it is hard to see why we should value a poem simply because of its fidelity to empirical reality, it is also hard to see why we should value some departures from that standard more than others. Reader-response critics will want to know why some conventions, or some uses of conventions, will produce greater or lesser emotional impact, and genetic critics, even if they grant the importance of the conventional and communal elements in literature, will continue to maintain that some conception of "authorial" meaning is necessary to provide a standard for valid interpretation. Only this, they insist, will allow us to separate what the poem does mean from what it could mean.

The intertextual perspective, in short, has not resolved all the issues. It has, however, gained many adherents. In the English-speaking world, Northrop Frye's influence alone has been considerable; it has helped to create, as it has profited from, a climate of opinion that finds many literary theorists interested in philosophers like Ernst Cassirer or art critics like E. H. Gombrich, who emphasize the role of convention in all art and thought. And on the continent, and increasingly in Britain and the United States, the concepts of structuralism and semiotics, long applied in the fields of linguistics and anthropology, have been employed to elucidate the conventional elements in literary structures. This climate may also account in part for the enthusiastic reception given the work of Mikhail Bakhtin. Though much of that work was done in the first half of the century, its impact was slight before the 1970s; since then, though, Bakhtin's influence has been strong, and several of his key terms, like "dialogic," "heteroglossia," "polyglossia," "chronotope," and "carnival" have been frequently adopted. For Bakhtin, carnival reflected the "lived life" of medieval and early modern peoples. In carnival, official authority and high culture were jostled "from below" by elements of satire, parody, irony, mimicry, bodily humor, and grotesque display. This jostling from below served to keep society open, to liberate it from deadening, because univocal, authority. In "carnivalesque" literature, epitomized by the writings of Rabelais, these same elements jostle the univocal and elevated language of "high" art and high society, and to the same effect. The result is a many-voiced, multileveled, polymodal "novel" whose inclusiveness is similarly liberating.

As early as 1929, in his study of Dostoevsky, Bakhtin had seen the "novel" as the heteroglossic form *par excellence,* an antigeneric genre that undercut the authority of the single voice traditionally found in the lyric or epic. For Bakhtin, the "novel" was a kind of literary equivalent to carnival. As such, it could be traced back not only to Rabelais and Cervantes but, as he shows in "From the Pre-History of Novelistic Discourse," all the way to Hellenistic literature where "monoglossia," the myth of one language, had to give way to the reality of "polyglossia," the clash and mixture of many languages. Bakhtin, then, is interested in the historical development of literary forms and in their interaction with social forces. His concept of the "chronotope" assumes that each era has its own way of perceiving and representing time and space, and his concepts like "carnival" and "heteroglossia" assume close connections between language, literature, and ideology. An apostle of heterogeneity, Bakhtin argues that all periods are characterized by competing ideologies, competing social forces, and, intimately bound to these, competing voices. For these reasons he could be placed as well in my final context, where his influence has also been strong.

But this may serve to remind us that the intertextual context doesn't represent a single school of thought. Like the other contexts, it includes various schools and movements as well as unaffiliated individuals, some of whom may feel uncomfortable in the company I have assigned them, and many of whom may want to argue with parts of the position I have sketched. Our concern, however, is with basic orientations to the literary work, and on this principle I have classed together those critics who, despite their many differences, share a central interest in the conventional aspects of literature. This interest defines the perspective and sets it apart from the others we have considered. And, while the objections to this perspective are not negligible, the critics who adopt it enjoy some real advantages. They, like the formal and the mimetic critics, find it possible to discuss the meaning of poems without appealing to the psyches of particular authors or particular readers, and so they avoid most of the difficulties that trouble genetic and reader-response approaches. By orienting the poem toward the world of poetic convention rather than toward the world of empirical reality, they eliminate the problems that haunt mimetic attempts to explain how verbal constructs can "imitate" this reality, or why we should want them to. And by arguing that poems imitate other poems and take their meaning from these literary relationships, they can account for literary form in the sense that the "formal" critics cannot. Finally, and this is by no means the least of their strengths, the intertextual critics' theory will explain, as no other theory will, why a study of poetry should help one understand poems.

Suggestions for Further Reading

In the English-speaking world, Northrop Frye, though he was an intertextualist *avant la lettre,* has been the most influential figure in this context, and *Anatomy of Criticism* (1957) is the fullest expression of his views. Among his later books, *The Educated Imagination* (1964) is a brief introduction to his main ideas. Studies more self-consciously "structural" or "semiotic" include Roland Barthes, *Elements of Semiology* (1967); Edward Said, *Beginnings* (1975); Umberto Eco, *A Theory of Semiotics* (1975); Seymour Chatman, *Story and Discourse* (1978); Tzvetan Todorov, *Introduction to Poetics* (1981);

Gerard Genette, *Figures of Literary Discourse* (1982); A. J. Greimas, *On Meaning: Selected Writings in Semiotic Theory* (1987); and Michael Riffaterre, *Fictional Truths* (1990). Adena Rosmarin, *The Power of Genre* (1985), analyzes several influential concepts of genre.

E. H. Gombrich, *Art and Illusion* (1961), is a study of perception and convention in the visual arts that has influenced literary theory. The fictional structuring of "historical" narrative is treated in Hayden White, *Metahistory* (1973); Paul Fussell, *The Great War and Modern Memory* (1975); and Frank Kermode, *The Genesis of Secrecy* (1979). Mikhail Bakhtin's work may be represented by *The Dialogic Imagination: Four Essays* (1981); Bakhtin's complex career and ideas are given a book-length exposition in Gary Saul Morson and Caryl Emerson, *Bakhtin: Creation of a Prosaics* (1990).

For the entire context, three interpretive works in recommended order of reading: Terence Hawkes, *Structuralism and Semiotics* (1977); Jonathan Culler, *Structuralist Poetics* (1975); and Robert Scholes, *Semiotics and Interpretation* (1982). Michael Worton and Judith Still, eds., *Intertextuality: Theories and Practices* (1990), and Jay Clayton and Eric Rothstein, eds., *Influence and Intertextuality in Literary History* (1991), are useful collections of essays. Udo J. Hebel, *Intertextuality, Allusion, and Quotation: An International Bibliography* (1989), is a well-indexed, multilingual, 2,033-entry bibliography.

THEORY

The Critical Path

Northrop Frye

Northrop Frye's influential writings provided a rationale for intertextual criticism well before structuralist and semiotic critics came to be widely known in the English-speaking world. In the retrospective opening chapter to The Critical Path, *Frye describes the critical scene when he began to write, and he explains why the genetic, formal, and reader-response contexts seemed to him not quite the right bases for the study of literature, each being too limited and extraliterary: "I felt that no critic had given his full attention to what seemed to me the first operation of criticism: trying to see what meaning could be discovered in works of literature from their context in literature." Frye's exploration of this context led to his concentration on "conventions, genres, and recurring image groups," which he called "archetypal" criticism. It also led to the charge that such intertextual criticism lacks social relevance. Frye goes on to suggest that since literature provides the "models" or "goals of work" for civilization, literary study has a great deal of social relevance, and this relevance is most clearly understood by the kind of criticism that can see literature as a whole in its social context.*

The phrase "The Critical Path" is, I understand, a term in business administration, and was one that I began hearing extensively used during the preparations for the Montreal Expo of 1967. It associated itself in my mind with the closing sentences of Kant's *Critique of Pure Reason*, where he says that dogmatism and skepticism have both had it as tenable philosophical positions, and that "the critical path is alone open." It also associated itself with a turning point in my own development. About twenty-five years ago, when still in middle life, I lost my way in the dark wood of Blake's prophecies, and looked around for some path that would get me out of there. There were many paths, some well trodden and equipped with signposts, but all pointing in what for me were the wrong directions. They directed me to the social conditions of Blake's time, to the history of the occult tradition, to psychological factors in Blake's mind, and other subjects quite valid in themselves. But my task was the specific one of trying to crack Blake's symbolic code, and I had a feeling that the way to that led directly through literature itself. The critical path I wanted was a theory of criticism which would, first, account for the major phenomena of literary experience, and, second, would lead to some view of the place of literature in civilization as a whole.

Following the bent that Blake had given me, I became particularly interested in two questions. One was: What is the total subject of study of which criticism forms part? I rejected the answer: "Criticism is a subdivision of literature," because it was such obvious nonsense. Criticism is the theory of literature, not a minor and non-essential element in its practice. This latter notion of it is not surprising in outsiders, or in poets, but how a critic himself can be so confused about his function as to take the same view I could not (and cannot yet) understand. Of course criticism has a peculiar disability in the number of people who have drifted into it without any vocation for it, and who may therefore have, however unconsciously, some interest in keeping it theoretically incoherent.

Literary criticism in its turn seemed to be a part of two larger but undeveloped subjects. One was the unified criticism of all the arts; the other was some area of verbal expression which had not yet been defined, and which in the present book is called mythology. The latter seemed more immediately promising: the former I felt was the ultimate destiny of the subject called aesthetics, in which (at least at that time) relatively few technically competent literary critics appeared to be much interested. I noticed also the strong centrifugal drift from criticism toward social, philosophical and religious interests, which had set in at least as early as Coleridge. Some of this seemed to me badly motivated. A critic devoting himself to literature, but without any sense of his distinctive function, is often tempted to feel that he can never be anything more than a second-class writer or thinker, because his work is derived from

the work of what by his postulates are greater men. I felt, then, that a conception of criticism was needed which would set the critic's activity in its proper light, and that once we had that, a critic's other interests would represent a natural expansion of criticism rather than an escape from it.

The other question was: How do we arrive at poetic meaning? It is a generally accepted principle that meaning is derived from context. But there are two contexts for verbal meaning: the imaginative context of literature, and the context of ordinary intentional discourse. I felt that no critic had given his full attention to what seemed to me to be the first operation of criticism: trying to see what meaning could be discovered in works of literature from their context in literature. All meaning in literature seemed to be referred first of all to the context of intentional meaning, always a secondary and sometimes the wrong context. That is, the primary meaning of a literary work was assumed to be the kind of meaning that a prose paraphrase could represent. This primary meaning was called the "literal" meaning, a phrase with a luxuriant growth of semantic tangles around it which I have discussed elsewhere and return to more briefly here.

When I first began to write on critical theory, I was startled to realize how general was the agreement that criticism had no presuppositions of its own, but had to be "grounded" on some other subject. The disagreements were not over that, but over the question of what the proper subjects were that criticism ought to depend on. The older European philological basis, a very sound one, at least in the form in which it was expounded by August Boeckh and others in the nineteenth century, had largely disappeared in English-speaking countries. In some places, notably Oxford, where I studied in the thirties, it had declined into a much narrower conception of philology. This was partly because the shifting of the centre of literary study from the Classical to the modern languages had developed a prejudice, derived from one of the more bizarre perversions of the work ethic, that English literature at least was a merely entertaining subject, and should not be admitted to universities unless the main emphasis fell on something more beneficial to the moral fibre, like learning the classes of Old English strong verbs. In most North American universities the critical establishment rested on a mixture of history and philosophy, evidently on the assumption that every work of literature is what Sir Walter Raleigh said *Paradise Lost* was, a monument to dead ideas. I myself was soon identified as one of the critics who took their assumptions from anthropology and psychology, then still widely regarded as the wrong subjects. I have always insisted that criticism cannot take presuppositions from elsewhere, which always means wrenching them out of their real context, and must work out its own. But mental habits are hard to break, especially bad habits, and because I found the term "archetype" an essential one, I am still often called a Jungian critic, and classified with Miss Maud Bodkin, whose book I have read with interest, but whom, on the evidence of that book, I resemble about as closely as I resemble the late Sarah Bernhardt.

The reason for this rather silly situation was obvious enough. As long as the meaning of a poem, let us say for short, is sought primarily within the context of intentional discourse, it becomes a document, to be related to some verbal area of study outside literature. Hence criticism, like Los Angeles, becomes an aggregate of suburbs, with no central area in literature itself. One of these suburbs is the biographical one, where the literary work is taken to be a document illustrating something in the writer's life. The most fashionable time for this approach was the nineteenth century, and its strongest proponent Carlyle, for whom great poetry could only be the personal rhetoric of a great man. The theory demands that Shakespeare, for instance, should be an obviously and overwhelmingly great man, which is why so much nineteenth-century critical energy was expended in trying to invent a sufficiently interesting biography for Shakespeare out of fancied allusions in the poetry. This misguided industry has now largely been restricted to the sonnets, where, as Mutt says in *Finnegans Wake*, "he who runes may rede it on all fours." Carlyle's essay on Shakespeare, in *Heroes and Hero-Worship*, comes as close to pure verbiage, to rhetoric without content, as prose sentences can in the nature of things get. Something seems to be wrong with the theory, at least in this form. One is better off with Goethe, but even there the sense of personal greatness may be connected less with the quality of the poetry than with the number of things Goethe had been able to do besides writing poetry.

I am not talking here about real biography, but about the assumption that the poet's life is the essential key to the deeper understanding of the poetry. It often happens that interesting literature is produced by an uninteresting man, in the sense of one who disappoints us if we are looking for some kind of culture-hero. In fact it happens so often that there is clearly no correlation between the ability to write poetry and any other ability, or, at least, it is clearly absurd to assume that every real poet must be a certain kind of person. Hence the formula "this poem is particularly notable for the way in which it throws light on," etc., soon ceases to carry much conviction for all but a selected group of poets. Something else, more deeply founded in a wider literary experience, is needed for critical understanding.

In these days, a biographical approach is likely to move from the manifest to the latent personal content of the poem, and from a biographical approach properly speaking to a psychological one. At the present time and place this means very largely a Freudian, or what I think of as a Luther-on-the-privy, approach. A considerable amount of determinism enters at this stage. All documentary conceptions of literature are allegorical conceptions of it, and this fact becomes even more obvious when poems are taken to be allegories of Freudian repressions, unresolved conflicts, or tensions between ego and id, or, for another school, of the Jungian process of individuation. But what is true of allegorical poetry is equally true of allegorical criticism: that allegory is a technique calling for tact. Tact is violated when the whiteness of Moby Dick is explained as a Lockian *tabula rasa*, or when Alice in Wonderland is discussed in terms of her hypothetical toilet training, or when Matthew Arnold's line in *Dover Beach*, "Where ignorant armies clash by night," is taken as a covert reference to the copulation of his parents. One is reminded of the exempla from natural history made by medieval preachers. According to Richard Rolle in the fourteenth century, the bee carries earth in its feet to ballast itself when it flies, and thereby reminds us of the Incarnation, when God took up an earthly form. The example is ingenious and entertaining, and only unsatisfying if one happens to be interested in bees.

If we tire of the shadow-play of explaining real poems by assumed mental states, we may be driven to realize that the ultimate source of a poem is not so much the individual poet as the social situation from which he springs, and of which he is the spokesman and the medium. This takes us into the area of historical criticism. Here again no one can or should deny the relevance of literature to history, but only rarely in historical criticism is there any real sense of the fact that literature is itself an active part of the historical process. Poets are assumed to have a sensitive litmus-paper response to social trends, hence literature as a whole is taken to be something that the historical process acts on, and we have still not escaped from a documentary and allegorical procedure.

Once more, some historical critics, like the biographical ones, will want to go from manifest to latent social content, from the historical context of the poem to its context in some unified overview of history. Here again determinism, the impulse to find the ultimate meaning of literature in something that is not literature, is unmistakable. At the time of which I am speaking, a generation ago, a conservative Catholic determinism was fashionable, strongly influenced by Eliot, which adopted Thomism, or at least made references to it, as the summit of Western cultural values, and looked down benignantly on everything that followed it as a kind of toboggan slide, rushing through nominalism, Protestantism, liberalism, subjective idealism, and so on to the solipsism in which the critic's non-Thomist contemporaries were assumed to be enclosed. Marxism is another enlarged historical perspective, widely adopted, and perhaps inherently the most serious one of them all. Literature is a part of a social process; hence that process as a whole forms the genuine context of literature. Theoretically, Marxism takes a social view of literature which is comprehensive enough to see it within this genuine context. In practice, however, Marxism operates as merely one more determinism, which avoids every aspect of literature except one allegorical interpretation of its content.

All these documentary and external approaches, even when correctly handled, are subject to at least three limitations which every experienced scholar has to reckon with. In the first place, they do not account for the literary form of what they are discussing. Identifying Edward King and documenting Milton's attitude to the Church of England will throw no light on *Lycidas* as a pastoral elegy with specific Classical and Italian lines of ancestry. Secondly, they do not account for the poetic and metaphorical language of the literary work, but assume its primary meaning to be a non-poetic meaning. Thirdly, they do not account for the fact that the genuine quality of a poet is often in a negative relation to the chosen context. To understand Blake's *Milton* and *Jerusalem* it is useful to know something of his quarrel with Hayley and his sedition trial. But one also needs to be aware of the vast disproportion between these minor events in a quiet life and their apocalyptic transformation in the poems. One should also know enough of criticism, as well as of Blake, not to ascribe the disproportion to paranoia on Blake's part. Similarly, a scholar may write a whole shelf of books about the life of Milton studied in connexion with the history of this time, and still fail to notice that Milton's greatness as a poet has a good deal to do with his profound and perverse misunderstanding of the history of his time.

By the time I began writing criticism, the so-called "new criticism" had established itself as a technique of explication. This was a rhetorical form of criticism, and from the beginning rhetoric has meant two things: the figuration of language and the persuasive powers of an orator. New criticism dealt with rhetoric in the former sense, and established a counterweight to the biographical approach which treated poetry as a personal rhetoric. The great merit of explicatory criticism was that it accepted poetic language and form as the basis for poetic meaning. On that basis it built up a resistance to all "background" criticism that explained the literary in terms of the non-literary. At the same time, it deprived itself of the great strength of documentary criticism: the sense of context. It simply explicated one work after another, paying little attention to genre or to any larger structural principles connecting the different works explicated.

The limitations of this approach soon became obvious, and most of the new critics sooner or later fell back on one of the established documentary contexts, generally the historical one, although they were regarded at first as anti-historical. One or two have even been Marxists, but in general the movement, at least in America, was anti-Marxist. Marxists had previously condemned the somewhat similar tendency in Russian criticism called "formalism," because they realized that if they began by conceding literary form as the basis for literary significance, the assumptions on which Marxist bureaucracies rationalized their censorship of the arts would be greatly weakened. They would logically have to end, in fact, in giving poets and novelists the same kind of freedom that they had reluctantly been compelled to grant to the physical scientists.

More recently, Marshall McLuhan has placed a formalist theory, expressed in the phrase "the medium is the message," within the context of a neo-Marxist determinism in which communication media play the same role that instruments of production do in more orthodox Marxism. Professor McLuhan drafted his new mosaic code under a strong influence from the conservative wing of the new critical movement, and many traces of an earlier Thomist determinism can be found in *The Gutenberg Galaxy*. An example is the curiously exaggerated distinction he draws between the manuscript culture of the Middle Ages and the book culture of the printed page that followed it.

It seemed to me obvious that, after accepting the poetic form of a poem as its primary basis of meaning, the next step was to look for its context within literature itself. And of course the most obvious literary context for a poem is the entire output of its author. Just as explication, by stressing the more objective aspect of rhetoric, had formed a corrective to the excesses of biographical criticism, so a study of a poet's whole work might form the basis of a kind of "psychological" criticism that would operate within literature, and so provide some balance for the kind that ends in the bosom of Freud. Poetry is, after all, a technique of communication; it engages the conscious part of the mind as well as the murkier areas, and what a poet succeeds in communicating to others is at least as important as what he fails to resolve for himself.

We soon become aware that every poet has his own distinctive structure of imagery, which usually emerges even in his earliest work, and which does not and cannot essentially change. This larger context of the poem within its author's entire "mental landscape" is assumed in all the best explication — Spitzer's, for example. I became aware of its importance myself, when working on Blake, as soon as I realized that Blake's special symbolic names and the like did form a genuine structure of poetic imagery and not, despite his use of the word, a "system" to which he was bound like an administrator to a computer. The structure of imagery, however, as I continued to study it, began to show an increasing number of similarities to the structures of other poets. Blake had always been regarded as a poet with a "private symbolism" locked up in his own mind, but this conception of him was so fantastically untrue that overcoming it carried me much further than merely correcting a mistaken notion of Blake.

I was led to three conclusions in particular. First, there is no private symbolism: the phrase makes no

sense. There may be private allusions or associations that need footnotes, but they cannot form a poetic structure, even if the poet himself is a psychotic. The structure of the poem remains an effort at communication, however utterly it may fail to communicate. Second, as just said, every poet has his own structure of imagery, every detail of which has its analogue in that of all other poets. Third, when we follow out this pattern of analogous structures, we find that it leads, not to similarity, but to identity. Similarity implies uniformity and monotony, and any conclusion that all poets are much alike, in whatever respect, is too false to our literary experience to be tenable. It is identity that makes individuality possible: poems are made out of the *same* images, just as poems in English are all made out of the same language. This contrast of similarity and identity is one of the most difficult problems in critical theory, and we shall have to return to it several times in this book.

I was still not satisfied: I wanted a historical approach to literature, but an approach that would be or include a genuine history of literature, and not simply the assimilating of literature to some other kind of history. It was at this point that the immense importance of certain structural elements in the literary tradition, such as conventions, genres, and the recurring use of certain images or image-clusters, which I came to call archetypes, forced itself on me. T. S. Eliot had already spoken of tradition as a creative and informing power operating on the poet specifically as a craftsman, and not vaguely as a merely cultivated person. But neither he nor anyone else seemed to get to the point of identifying the factors of that tradition, of what it is that makes possible the creation of new works of literature out of earlier ones. The new critics had resisted the background approach to criticism, but they had not destroyed the oratorical conception of poetry as a personal rhetoric.

And yet convention, within literature, seemed to be a force even stronger than history. The difference between the conventions of medieval poets writing in the London of Richard II and those of Cavalier poets writing in the London of Charles II is far less than the difference in social conditions between the two ages. I began to suspect that a poet's relation to poetry was much more like a scholar's relation to his scholarship than was generally thought. Whatever one is producing, the psychological processes involved seem much the same. The scholar cannot be a scholar until he immerses himself in his subject, until he attaches his own thinking to the body of what is thought in his day about that subject. A scholar, *qua* scholar, cannot think for himself or think at random: he can only expand an organic body of thought, add something logically related to what he or someone else has already thought. But this is precisely the way that poets have always talked about their relation to poetry. From Homer onward, poets have continually insisted that they were simply places where something new in literature was able to take its own shape.

From here it is clear that one has to take a step. Criticism must develop a sense of history within literature to complement the historical criticism that relates literature to its non-literary historical background. Similarly, it must develop its own form of historical overview, on the basis of what is inside literature rather than outside it. Instead of fitting literature into a prefabricated scheme of history, the critic should see literature as a coherent structure, historically conditioned but shaping its own history, responding to but not determined in its form by an external historical process. This total body of literature can be studied through its larger structural principles, which I have just described as conventions, genres and recurring image-groups or archetypes. These structural principles are largely ignored by most social critics. Their treatment of literature, in consequence, is usually superficial, a matter of picking things out of literary works that seem interesting for non-literary reasons.

When criticism develops a proper sense of the history of literature, the history beyond literature does not cease to exist or to be relevant to the critic. Similarly, seeing literature as a unity in itself does not withdraw it from a social context: on the contrary, it becomes far easier to see what its place in civilization is. Criticism will always have two aspects, one turned toward the structure of literature and one turned toward the other cultural phenomena that form the social environment of literature. Together, they balance each other: when one is worked on to the exclusion of the other, the critical perspective goes out of focus. If criticism is in proper balance, the tendency of critics to move from critical to larger social issues becomes more intelligible. Such a movement need not, and should not, be due to a dissatisfaction with the narrowness of criticism as a discipline, but should be

simply the result of a sense of social context, a sense present in all critics from whom one is in the least likely to learn anything.

There was another difficulty with new criticism which was only a technical one, but still pointed to the necessity for a sense of context. Whenever we read anything there are two mental operations we perform, which succeed one another in time. First we follow the narrative movement in the act of reading, turning over the pages and pursuing the trail from top left to bottom right. Afterwards, we can look at the work as a simultaneous unity and study its structure. This latter act is the critical response properly speaking: the ordinary reader seldom needs to bother with it. The chief material of rhetorical analysis consists of a study of the poetic "texture," and such a study plunges one into a complicated labyrinth of ambiguities, multiple meanings, recurring images, and echoes of both sound and sense. A full explication of a long and complex work which was based on the reading process could well become much longer, and more difficult to read, than the work itself. Such linear explications have some advantages as a teaching technique, but for publishing purposes it is more practical to start with the second stage. This involves attaching the rhetorical analysis to a deductive framework derived from a study of the structure, and the context of that structure is what shows us where we should begin to look for our central images and ambiguities.

The difficulty in transferring explication from the reading process to the study of structure has left some curious traces in new critical theory. One of them is in Ransom, with his arbitrary assumption that texture is somehow more important for the critic than structure; another is again in McLuhan, who has expanded the two unresolved factors of explication into a portentous historical contrast between the "linear" demands of old printed media and the "simultaneous" impact of the new electronic ones. The real distinction however is not between different kinds of media, but between the two operations of the mind which are employed in every contact with every medium. There is a "simultaneous" response to print; there is a "linear" response to a painting, for there is a preliminary dance of the eye before we take in the whole picture; music, at the opposite end of experience, has its score, the spatial presentation symbolizing a simultaneous understanding of it. In reading a newspaper there are two preliminary linear operations: the glance over the headlines and the following down of a story.

This point is crucial for critical theory, because the whole prose-paraphrase conception of "literal" meaning is based on an understanding which is really pre-critical. It is while we are striving to take in what is being presented to us that we are reducing the poetic to the intentional meaning, attending to what the work explicitly says rather than to what it is. The pre-critical experience of literature is wordless, and all criticism which attempts to ground itself on such experience tends to assume that the primary critical act is a wordless reaction, to be described in some metaphor of immediate and nonverbal contact, such as "taste." Verbal criticism, in this view, is a secondary operation of trying to find words to describe the taste. Students who have been encouraged to think along these lines often ask me why I pay so little attention to the "uniqueness" of a work of literature. It may be absurd that "unique" should become a value-term, the world's worst poem being obviously as unique as any other, but the word brings out the underlying confusion of thought very clearly. Criticism is a structure of knowledge, and the unique as such is unknowable; uniqueness is a quality of experience, not of knowledge, and of precisely the aspect of experience which cannot form part of a structure of knowledge.

A better word, such as "individuality," would raise deeper problems. The basis of critical knowledge is the direct experience of literature, certainly, but experience as such is never adequate. We are always reading *Paradise Lost* with a hangover or seeing *King Lear* with an incompetent Cordelia or disliking a novel because some scene in it connects with something suppressed in our memories, and our most deeply satisfying responses are often made in childhood, to be seen later as immature overreacting. The right occasion, the right mood, the right state of development to meet the occasion, can hardly coincide more than once or twice in a lifetime. Nevertheless, the conception of a definitive experience in time seems to be the *hypothesis* on which criticism is based. Criticism, surely, is designed to reconstruct the kind of experience that we could and should have had, and thereby to bring us into line with that experience, even if the "shadow" of Eliot's *The Hollow Men* has forever darkened it. As a structure of knowledge, then, criticism, like other structures of knowledge, is in one sense a monument to a failure of experience, a tower of Babel or one of the "ruins of time" which, in Blake's phrase, "build mansions in eternity." Hence the popularity of the evaluative or taste-criticism which seems to point backwards to a greater intensity of response than the criticism itself can convey. It corresponds to a popular view of poetry itself, that whatever the poet writes down is merely salvaged from an original "inspiration" of a much more numinous kind. There is a real truth here, though it needs to be differently stated.

There are two categories of response to literature, which could be well described by Schiller's terms naive and sentimental, if used in his sense but transferred from qualities inherent in literature to qualities in the experience of it. The "naive" experience is the one we are now discussing, the linear, participating, pre-critical response which is thrown forward to the conclusion of the work as the reader turns pages or the theatre audience expectantly listens. The conclusion is not simply the last page or spoken line, but the "recognition" which, in a work of fiction particularly, brings the end into line with the beginning and pulls the straight line of response around into a parabola. A pure, self-contained pleasure of participating response is the end at which all writers aim who think of themselves as primarily entertainers, and some of them ignore, resist, or resent the critical operation that follows it.

Such pleasure is however a state of innocence rarely attained in adult life. Many of us have "favorite" authors who set up for us a kind of enclosed garden in which we can wander in a state of completely satisfied receptivity. But for each reader there are very few of these, and they are usually discovered and read fairly early. The sense of guilt about reading "escape" literature is a moral anxiety mainly derived from a feeling that it is a substitute for an unattained experience, and that if escape literature really did what it professes to do it would not be escape literature. As a rule our pleasure in direct response is of a more muted and disseminated kind. It arises from a *habit* of reading or theatre-going, and much of this pleasure comes from a greatly enlarged kind of expectation, extending over many works and many years. Instead of trying to operate the gambling machine of an ideal experience, which may never pay off, we are building something up, accumulating a total fund of experience, each individual response being an investment in it.

It is a central function of criticism to explain what is going on in the habit of reading, using "reading" as a general term for all literary experience. If reading formed simply an unconnected series of experiences, one novel or poem or play after another, it would have the sense of distraction or idle time-filling about it which so many of those who are afraid of leisure believe it to have. The real reader knows better: he knows that he is entering into a coherent structure of experience, and the criticism which studies literature through its organizing patterns of convention, genre and archetype enables him to see what that structure is. Such criticism can hardly injure the "uniqueness" of each experience: on the contrary, it rejects the evaluating hierarchy that limits us to the evaluator's reading list, and encourages each reader to accept no substitutes in his search for infinite variety. It is simply not true that the "great" writers supply all the varieties of experience offered by the merely "good" ones: if Massinger is not a substitute for Shakespeare, neither is Shakespeare a substitute for Massinger.

Still less does the study of the recurring structural patterns of literature lead the reader to the conviction that literature is everywhere much alike. For such study, as just said, does not keep bringing the student back to similar points, but to the same point, to the sense of an identity in literary experience which is the objective counterpart to his own identity. That variety and novelty can be found only at the place of identity is the theme of much of the most influential writing in our century, of the Eliot Quartets with their garlic and sapphires clotting a bedded axletree, of the Pound Cantos which insist on "making it new" but remain at the center of the "unwobbling pivot," of that tremendous hymn to the eternal newness of the same which is *Finnegans Wake*. Twentieth-century criticism which does not understand a central theme of the literature of its own time can hardly be expected to make much sense of the literature of the past.

This brings us to the "sentimental" type of response, which starts where criticism starts, with the unity of the work being read. In modern literature there has been a strong emphasis on demanding a response from the reader which minimizes everything "naive," everything connected with suspense or expectation. This emphasis begins in English literature

with the Blake Prophecies, *Milton* and *Jerusalem* particularly, which avoid the sense of linear narration and keep repeating the central theme in an expanding series of contexts. Fiction tends increasingly to abolish the teleological plot which keeps the reader wondering "how it turns out"; poetry drops its connective tissue of narrative in favor of discontinuous episodes; in Mallarmé and elsewhere it even avoids the centrifugal movement of naming or pointing to objects thought of as external to the poem. The emphasis, though it starts with unity, is not on unity for its own sake, but on intensity, a word which brings us back to the conception of an ideal experience. Hopkins with his "inscape" and "instress," Proust with his instants of remembrance and recognition, Eliot with his timeless moments at the world's axis, and a host of more recent writers with their mystiques of orgasm, drugs, and quasi-Buddhist moments of enlightenment, are all talking about a form of ideal experience, which in one way or another seems to be the real goal of life. The ideal experience itself, for the shrewder of these writers at least, never occurs, but with intense practice and concentration a deeply satisfying approximation may occur very rarely. The curious link with religion—for even writers who are not religious still often employ religious terminology or symbolism in this connexion, as Joyce and Proust do—indicates that this direct analogy of ideal experience is typically the way of the mystic or saint rather than the artist—"an occupation for the saint," as Eliot calls it, though he immediately adds that it cannot be in any sense an occupation.

Traditional Christian thought had an explanation for the dilemma of experience which at least made sense within its own postulates. According to it, Adam was capable of a preternatural power of experience before his fall, and we have lost this capacity. Our structures of reason and imagination are therefore analogical constructs designed to recapture, within the mental processes that belong to our present state, something of a lost directness of apprehension. Thus Milton can define education as "an attempt to repair the ruin of our first parents by regaining to know God aright." Similar language continues in our day. Proust concludes his colossal analysis of experience by saying that the only paradises are lost paradises; Yeats, in a much more light-hearted way, tells us in "Solomon and the Witch," anticipating the more recent orgasm cults, that a single act of perfect intercourse would restore the unfallen world. In this view, literature, philosophy and religion at least are all articulate analogies of an experience that goes not only beyond articulateness, but beyond human capacity as well.

The Christian fallen world is only one form of a conception which has run through human imagination and thought from earliest times to the present, according to which the existing world is, so to speak, the lower level of being or reality. Above it is a world which may not exist (we do not actually know that it exists even if we seem to have an experience of it), but is not nothing or non-existence; is not a merely ideal world, because it can act as an informing principle of existence, and yet cannot convincingly be assigned to any intermediate category of existence, such as the potential. This world, related by analogy to the intelligible world of the philosopher and scientist, the imaginable world of the poet, and the revealed world of religion, is increasingly referred to in our day by the term "model." In religion, as noted, this model world is usually projected as an actually existing world created by God, though at present out of human reach. In philosophy it appears in such concepts as Aristotle's final cause, and in the more uninhibited structures of the poets it is the idealized world of romance, pastoral, or apocalyptic vision. As such it suggests a world with which we should wish to identify ourselves, or something in ourselves, and so it becomes the world indicated by the analogy of ideal experience just mentioned.

A direct experience or apprehension of such a world would be a microcosmic experience, an intelligence or imagination finding itself at the centre of an intelligible or imaginable totality, and so experiencing, for however brief an instant, without any residue of alienation. It would thus also be an experience of finally attained or recovered identity. Most of us, at least, never reach it directly in experience if it is attainable in experience at all, but only through one of the articulated analogies, of which literature is

a central one. Whatever it is, it represents the end of our critical path, though we have not as yet traversed the path.

As we proceed to do this, we must keep to a middle way between two uncritical extremes. One is the centrifugal fallacy of determinism, the feeling that literature lacks a social reference unless its structure is ignored and its content associated with something non-literary. No theory is any good unless it explains facts, but theory and facts have to be in the same plane. Psychological and political theories can explain only psychological and political facts; no literary facts can be explained by anything except a literary theory. I remember a student, interested in the Victorian period, who dismissed several standard critical works in that area as "totally lacking in any sense of social awareness." I eventually learned that social awareness, for him, meant the amount of space given in the book, whatever the announced subject, to the Chartist movement. Chartism and similar social movements have their relevance to literature, certainly; but literature is all about something else, even when social protest is its explicit theme.

The other extreme is the centripetal fallacy, where we fail to separate criticism from the pre-critical direct experience of literature. This leads to an evaluating criticism which imposes the critic's own values, derived from the prejudices and anxieties of his own time, on the whole literature of the past. Criticism, like religion, is one of the sub-academic areas in which a large number of people are still free to indulge their anxieties instead of studying their subject. Any mention of this fact is apt to provoke the response: "Of course you don't understand how important our anxieties are." I understand it sufficiently to have devoted a good deal of this essay to the subject of social anxiety and its relation to genuine criticism. We note that the two fallacies mentioned above turn out to be essentially the same fallacy, as opposed extremes so often do.

THEORY

Structuralism and Literature

Jonathan Culler

Like Northrop Frye, Jonathan Culler believes we must see the individual poem within the context of literature if we are to understand it fully, and especially if we are to know how we understand it. Structuralism, as Culler views it, offers in the first place "not a new way of interpreting literary works, but an attempt to understand how it is that works do have meaning for us." So structuralist critics speak of genres and conventions and of the "system" or "institution" of literature. And they frequently take our understanding of language as the base and analogy for our understanding of literature. They may also show, as Culler does, considerable sympathy for some forms of reader-response criticism, for they will be much concerned with what the reader needs to know to attain "literary competence." At the same time, because structuralists define the competent reader as one who has mastered the relevant conventions, the number of readings they accept as competent must be considerably restricted. But this definition of competence is also the structuralists' great strength, for their theory offers a rationale for literary study as a discipline through which one can progressively come to know the conventions of literature. Structuralism, then, presents the intertextual context as the fundamental context, the one that ultimately grounds our understanding. Yet although Culler initially stresses the distinction between this generalized understanding and the interpretation of particular poems, he suggests at the end of his essay how the structuralist view may also facilitate specific interpretations.

My main purpose here is to show that despite its more extreme manifestations structuralism is not an abstruse or recondite theory but that, on the contrary, a structuralist approach to literature is directly relevant to the practical study and teaching of

Reprinted by permission from Hilda Schiff, ed., *Contemporary Approaches to English Studies*, pp. 59–76. Copyright © 1977 by Barnes & Noble Books, Totowa, N.J.

literature. Further, I am going to assume from the first that the teaching of literature involves a concern with the fact that the objects of study are literary works rather than simply documents about interpersonal relations, and that students are supposed to learn about literature and how to read it, rather than about life and how to live.

There are, of course, good reasons for using literary works as ways of finding out about the possibilities of human experience: the images they offer are both more complex and less embarrassing to discuss than, say, another individual's account of relationships with parents or friends. And I think there would be much to be said from a structuralist or semiological point of view about the way in which attention of this kind tries to organize our world; but that is not what I am concerned with here. I shall assume that studying literature and teaching literature involve the development and mastery of special operations and procedures which are required for the reading of literature, as opposed to the reading of other kinds of texts.

First I shall try to explain what structuralism is and why it is especially relevant to the study of literature. Then I shall outline a structuralist approach to literature, both in general and with respect to several examples. But I should like to emphasize from the outset that I am not proposing a structuralist "method" of interpretation: structuralism is not a new way of interpreting literary works, but an attempt to understand how it is that works do have meaning for us.

First, then, what is structuralism? Roland Barthes once defined it, in its "most specialized and consequently most relevant version," as a method for the study of cultural artefacts derived from the methods of contemporary linguistics.[1] Now there are two possible ways of using linguistic methods in the study of literature. The first would be to describe in linguistic terms the language of literary texts. Many critics speak eloquently of the benefits of this approach, but it is not, I think, what Barthes meant by his definition nor is it the kind of structuralism with which I am concerned here. The second approach would be to take linguistics as a model which indicates how one might go about constructing a poetics which stands to literature as linguistics stands to language. In other words, one takes linguistics as an analogy which indicates how other cultural artefacts should be studied. For this kind of structural-

ism only a few fundamental principles of linguistics are directly relevant, of which the most important is Ferdinand Saussure's distinction between *langue* and *parole*.

La langue, the linguistic system, is what one knows when one knows English. *La parole,* specific utterances or speech arts, are instances of language, *la langue.* Saussure argued that *la langue,* the linguistic system, was the proper object of linguistics, and he went on to say that "dans la langue il n'y a que des différences, sans termes positifs." In the linguistic system there are only differences, with no positive terms. Study of *la langue* is an attempt to determine the nature of a system of relations, oppositions, and differences which makes possible *la parole.* In learning a language we master a linguistic system which makes actual communication possible, and the linguist's task is to describe and to make explicit what it is we have mastered.[2]

Taking this as a point of departure we can say that structuralism and its close relation semiology are based on two fundamental insights: first, that social and cultural phenomena do not have essences but are defined by a network of relations, both internal and external; and, secondly, that in so far as social and cultural phenomena, including literature, have meaning they are signs.

If one wished to distinguish between structuralism and semiology (and the reasons for the distinction are historical rather than logical), one could do so in these terms: structuralism studies the structures or systems of relations by which cultural objects are defined and distinguished from one another; semiology studies cultural objects as signs that carry meanings. But I think that it is extremely important *not* to make the distinction, not to try to separate the two enterprises, since one entails the other where a profitable study of literature is concerned. If the two are separated one risks either discovering patterns of relations and oppositions which are irrelevant in that they have no sign function (this is the danger of the kind of linguistic analysis best represented by Roman Jakobson[3]), or else investigating signs on a one-to-one basis without due regard to the systems of convention which produce them (this is the danger of a limited semiological approach).

The task of structural analysis, we may then say, is to formulate the underlying systems of convention which enable cultural objects to have meaning for us. In this sense structuralism is not hermeneutic: it is

not a method for producing new and startling interpretations of literary works (although in another
sense which I shall mention below it *is* hermeneutic).
It asks, rather, how the meanings of literary works
are possible.

I should perhaps digress for a moment at this
point to correct a frequent misapprehension about
the relative status of literary theory and critical interpretation. It is common to speak of interpretations
of particular works as though they were the central
activity of literary criticism and to think of literary
theory as something peripheral and altogether secondary, but of course the truth is quite the reverse.
Interpretations of authors and works are wholly par-
asitic on the activity of reading literature: the critic
who writes about an author is simply producing a
more thorough and perhaps more perceptive version
of what readers of literature do for themselves. But
to enquire about the *nature* of literature, a theoretical
task, is to ask what is involved in reading something
as literature, and this is to tackle questions which are
fundamental to anyone engaged in critical interpretation in that implicit answers are necessarily presupposed both by the activity of reading literature,
and by the development of a discipline concerned
with the study of literature as an institution.

The best way to ease oneself into this structuralist
perspective is to take linguistics as a model and to
think of the relationship between an utterance and
the speaker/hearer. A sentence which I utter comes
to you as a series of physical events, a sequence of
sounds which we might represent by a phonetic
transcription. You hear this sequence of sounds and
give it a meaning. The question linguistics asks is
how is this possible, and the answer, of course, is that
you bring to the act of communication an immense
amount of implicit, subconscious knowledge. You
have assimilated the phonological system of English
which enables you to relate these physical sounds to
the abstract and relational phonemes of English; you
have assimilated a grammatical system, so complex
that we are only beginning to understand it, which
enables you to assign a structural description to the
sentence, to ascertain the relations among its parts,
and to recognize it as grammatically well-formed,
even though you have never heard it before; and finally, your knowledge of the semantic component of
the language enables you to assign an interpretation
to this string of sounds. Now we may say, if we wish,

that the phonological and syntactic structure and the
meaning are *properties* of the utterance, so long as we
remember that they are properties of the utterance
only with respect to the complex grammar which
speakers of English have assimilated. Without the
complex knowledge brought to the communicative
act, they have none of these properties.

Moving from language to literature, we find an
analogous situation. Imagine someone who knows
English but has no knowledge of literature and indeed no acquaintance with the concept of literature.
If presented with a poem he would be quite baffled.
He would understand words and sentences, certainly, but he would not know what this strange
thing was; he would not, quite literally, know what
to do with this curious linguistic construction. What
he lacks is a complex system of knowledge that experienced readers have acquired, a system of conventions and norms which we might call "literary
competence." And we can say that just as the task of
linguistics is to make explicit the system of a language which makes linguistic communication possible, so in the case of literature a structuralist poetics
must enquire what knowledge must be postulated to
account for our ability to read and understand literary works.

Lest you be skeptical about the importance of this
implicit knowledge that we bring to the act of reading poetry, let me offer a simple and crude example.
Take a perfectly ordinary sentence, such as "Yesterday I went into town and bought a lamp," and set it
down on a page as a poem:

> Yesterday I
> Went into town and bought
> A lamp.

The words remain the same, and if meanings change
it is because we approach the poem with different expectations and interpretative operations. What sort
of things happens? First of all, "Yesterday" takes on
a different force: it no longer refers to a particular
day but to the set of possible yesterdays and serves
primarily to set up a temporal opposition within the
poem (between present and recent past). This is due
to our conventions about the relationship of poems
to the moment of utterance. Secondly, we expect the
lyric to capture a moment of some significance, to be
thematically viable; and we thus apply to "lamp"
and "bought" conventions of symbolic extrapola-

tion. The traditional associations of *lamp* are obvious; *buying* we can take as one mode of acquisition as opposed to others; and we thus acquire potential thematic material. Thirdly, we expect a poem to be a unified whole and thus we must attempt to interpret the fact that this poem ends so swiftly and inconclusively. The silence at the end can be read as a kind of ironic comment, a blank, and we can set up an opposition between the action of buying a lamp, the attempt to acquire light, and the failure to tell of any positive benefits which result from yesterday's action. This general structure can, of course, support a variety of paraphrases, but any interpretation of the poem is likely to make use of these three elementary operations enshrined in any institution of poetry. The conventions of the lyric create the possibility of new and supplementary meanings.

Note also, and this is important, that though in one sense these meanings are in the poem — they are public, can be argued about, and do not depend upon individual subjective associations — in another sense, which is more important given the current critical climate, they are not *in* the poem. They depend on operations performed by readers (and assumed by poets).

Though this may seem obvious, there are good reasons for insisting on it. What we still call the New Criticism, in its desire to free the text from a controlling authorial intention, wanted to convince us that meanings could be there in the language of the text. The poem was to be thought of as complete in itself, a harmonious totality, not unlike an autonomous self-sufficient natural organism. Despite the salutary effects of this Coleridgean line of criticism, which I should not in the least want to deny, it was perhaps inevitable that it should lead to the notion that the critic or reader, like a good empiricist, approaches the poem without preconceptions and attempts to appreciate fully what is there. Such a notion leads to a theoretical impasse, to a hopeless attempt to show how the language of poetry itself differs from the language of prose or everyday speech.

Structuralism leads us to think of the poem not as a self-contained organism but as a sequence which has meaning only in relation to a literary system, or rather, to the "institution" of literature which guides the reader. The sense of a poem's completeness is a function of the totality of the interpretive process, the result of the way we have been taught to read poems.

And to avoid misunderstanding I should perhaps emphasize that, though it is preferable to talk about reading rather than writing, we are dealing with conventions which are assumed by the writer. He is not just setting words down on paper but writing a poem. Even when he is in revolt against the tradition, he still knows what is involved in reading and writing poems; and when he chooses among alternative words or phrases, he does so as a master of reading.

Although this notion of a literary system or of literary competence may be anathema to many, the reasons which lead one to postulate it are quite convincing. First of all, the claims of schools and universities to offer literary training cannot be lightly dismissed: it is, alas, only too clear that knowledge of English and a certain experience of the world do not suffice to make someone a perceptive reader of literature. Something else is required, something which literary training is designed to provide. And a poetics ought to be able to go some way towards specifying what is supposed to be learned. We presume, after all, to judge a student's progress towards literary competence: our examinations are not designed merely to check whether he or she has read and remembered certain books but to test his or her progress as a reader of literature. And that presumption suggests that there is something to be learnt here.

Secondly, it seems obvious that the study of one work facilitates the study of the next. We gain not only points of comparison but a sense of how to read — general formal principles and distinctions that have proved useful, questions which one addresses to certain kinds of texts, a sense of what one is looking for. We can speak if we like of extrapolating from one work to another, so long as we do not thereby obscure the fact that it is precisely this extrapolation which requires explanation. If we are to make any sense of the process of literary education we must assume, as Northrop Frye says, the possibility of "a coherent and comprehensive theory of literature . . . some of which the student unconsciously learns as he goes along, but the main principles of which are as yet unknown to us."[4]

What are the obstacles to this kind of enterprise? First, critics are accustomed to think of their task as that of producing new and subtler interpretations of literary works, and to ask them to attend to what must be taken for granted by experienced readers of literature cannot but seem an impoverishment of the

critical enterprise. Just as most people are more interested in using their language than in trying to determine the nature of their linguistic competence, so
most critics are more interested in exercising their
understanding of literature than in investigating
what it involves. But of course in the first case we do
not deceive ourselves that those engaged in using
their linguistic competence are thereby participating
in the study of language, whereas in the second case
critics have succeeded in making us believe that their
discussion of individual works constitutes the study
of literature. This notion is a significant obstacle; but
if we are at all concerned with the nature of literature
itself, and if we recognize the desirability of understanding what it is that we expect our students to
learn, we would do well to grant poetics its proper
status at the centre of literary studies.

The second obstacle seems more serious: the difficulty of determining what will count as evidence
for literary competence, evidence about the assumptions and operations of reading. It might seem that
critics differ so widely in their interpretations as to
undermine any notion of a general literary competence. But I should stress first of all that this is not, in
fact, an obstacle which must be overcome initially,
but a matter which will resolve itself in practice.
Since what one is trying to do is to determine the
conventions and operations which will account for
certain effects, one begins by specifying what effects
in fact one is attempting to explain, and then constructs models to account for them. As it is obvious
that there is a range of acceptable readings for any
poem, what one attempts to discover are the operations which account for this range of readings. In
the case of the brief poem which I discussed above, I
assumed that the sentence had different possible
meanings when set down as a poem rather than as a
prose statement, and offered some crude hypotheses
to explain why this should be so. If you think that it
is not so, if the meanings do not strike you as acceptable in terms of your own literary competence,
you will reject the hypotheses and the explanation
as false. The only danger, in other words, is that
you will find what I have to say irrelevant because
I am trying to account for facts which you do not
accept. However, even if one were to succeed only
in describing in an explicit fashion one's own literary competence, that would be a significant achievement. And because literary competence is the result
of an interpersonal experience of reading and dis-

cussion, any account of it will doubtless cover much
common ground.

Moreover it cannot be emphasized too strongly
that some kind of literary competence is presupposed
by everyone who discusses or writes about literature.
Any critic who claims to offer more than a purely personal and idiosyncratic response to a text is claiming
that his interpretation derives from operations of
reading that are generally accepted, that it is possible
to convince readers of its validity because there are
shared points of departure and common notions of
how to read, and that both critic and audience know
what counts as evidence for a reading, what can be
taken for granted, and what must be explicitly argued for. What I am asking is that we try to grasp
more clearly this common basis of reading and thus
to make explicit the conventions which make literature possible.

A structuralist approach starts by stressing the artificiality of literature, the fact that though literature
may be written in the language of information it is
not used in the "language-game" of giving information. It is obvious, for example, that by convention
the relationship of speaker to utterance is different
when we are dealing with a poem and with another
speech act. The poet does not stand in the same relation to a lyric as to a letter he has written, even if
the poem be Ben Jonson's "Inviting a Friend to Supper." This initial strangeness, this artifice, is the primary fact with which we have to deal, and we can
say that the techniques of reading are ways of simultaneously cherishing and overcoming this strangeness—ways of "naturalizing" the text and making it
something of a communication. To naturalize a
text—I use this word in preference to what some of
the French theorists call *vraisemblablisation*—is to
transform it so that it can be assimilated to an order
of *vraisemblance*. This is absolutely basic to the reading of literature, and a simple example would be the
interpretation of metaphor. When Shelley writes
"my soul is an enchanted boat" we must, in order to
"understand" this, naturalize the figure; we must
perform a semantic transformation on "enchanted
boat" so as to bring it under a particular order of
vraisemblance, which here we might call "possible
characteristics of the soul." Of course, the fact that
understanding involves more than translation of this
kind must be stressed: we must preserve the distance
traversed in the act of translation as a sign in its own
right. Here, for example, we have a sign of a partic-

ular lyric posture, of the poetical character, of the inadequacy of ordinary discourse, and so on.

Now there are various levels at which we can naturalize, various sets of conventions which can be brought into play. And of course these change with the institution of literature itself, so that once a style or mode of discourse becomes established it is pos-sible to naturalize a poem as a comment upon this literary mode. When we read Lewis Carroll's "A-Sitting on a Gate" as a parody of Wordsworth's "Resolution and Independence" we naturalize the former and make its strange features intelligible as commentary upon the latter.

The conventions of literature guide the process of naturalization and provide alternatives to what might be called "premature naturalization." This is a direct move from poem to utterance which ignores the former's specifically literary characteristics, as if we were to naturalize Donne's "The Good Morrow" by saying: the poet was in bed with his mistress one morning when the sun rose and, being still befuddled with drink, he uttered this statement in the hope that the sun would go away and shine elsewhere. If one had no knowledge of the institution of literature this is what one might be tempted to do, but even the least advanced student knows that this is an inappropriate step, that he must naturalize at another level which takes into account some of the conventions of literature. The protest to the sun is itself a figure; the situation of the utterance of a poem is a fiction which must be incorporated in our interpretation. We are likely to naturalize "The Good Morrow" as a love poem which uses this situation as an image of energy and annoyance, and hence as a figure for a strong, self-sufficient passion.

This ought at least to indicate what I mean by naturalization: it is the process of making something intelligible by relating it to what is already known and accepted as *vraisemblable*. We are guided in this process by various codes of expectations which we ought to try to make explicit. In discussing prose fiction Roland Barthes identifies five different codes, but I shall mention just two by way of example.[5]

What Barthes calls the semic code is an especially good case of literary conventions which produce intelligibility. As we go through a novel we pick out items which refer to the behaviour of characters and use them, as we say, to create character. Generally this involves considerable semantic transformation. Cultural stereotypes enable us to move from descriptions of dress or behaviour to qualities of persons, and we admit in fiction moves which we would not accept in ordinary circumstances. We do not believe that there is a real correlation between perfect or blemished complexions and perfect or blemished moral character, but certain *genres* permit inferences of this kind. We do not believe that blonde women as a class have different qualities from brunettes as a class, but the conventions of literature provide us with a set of opposed qualities with which the opposition between a blonde and a dark heroine may be correlated. Indeed, in order to see literature as an agent of moral education, as Christopher Butler has urged, we have to assume that literature will provide us with models of personality and ways of relating action to motive which are not the fruit of our ordinary experience; one of the things a reader of literature learns, that is to say, is how to construct personalities out of the notations that the text offers. He acquires mastery of the semic code.

The symbolic code is one of the oddest and most difficult to discuss. It is also the code with which students have the greatest difficulty, and both students and teachers ought to attempt to gain clearer notions of what it involves than we have at present. What governs the perception and interpretation of symbols? There are obviously a few symbols, consecrated by tradition, which seem to bear an intrinsic meaning, but most potential symbols are defined by complex relations with a context. The rose, for example, can lead in a variety of directions, and within each of these semantic fields (religion, love, nature) its significance will depend on its place in an oppositional structure. Sun and moon can signify almost anything, provided the opposition between them is preserved. Although, as I say, this code is poorly understood, it seems clear that symbolic extrapolation is a teleological process with a set of goals which limit the range of plausible interpretations and specify what kind of meanings serve as adequate *terminii ad quem* [ends or boundaries]. For example, there is a rule of generalization: to be told that in a phrase like "shine on my bowed head, O moon" the moon symbolizes "the quarterly production quota set by the district manager" is bathetic. We quickly learn that there is a set of semantic oppositions, such as life and death, simplicity and complexity, harmony and strife, reality and appearance, body and soul, certainty and doubt, imagination and intellect, which are culturally marked as in some way "ultimate" and hence as goals in the process of symbolic extrapolation. But we ought to be able to say a good deal more about this process which we expect students to master.

After these sketchy indications of the problems involved, I should like to turn by way of example to the kind of fundamental expectations concerning poetry which govern the operation of codes and the process of naturalization. We might start with a short poem by William Carlos Williams:

> This Is Just to Say
>
> I have eaten
> the plums
> that were in
> the icebox
>
> and which
> you were probably
> saving
> for breakfast
>
> Forgive me
> they were delicious
> so sweet
> so cold

The fact that this is printed on a page as a poem brings into play our expectations concerning poetry (as sentences in a novel it would, of course, be read differently), the first of which we might call the convention of distance and impersonality. Although at one level the sentences are presented as a note asking forgiveness for eating plums, since poetry is by convention detached from immediate circumstances of utterance we deprive it of this pragmatic function, retaining simply the reference to a context as an implicit statement that this kind of experience is important, worthy of poetry. By doing this we avoid the premature naturalization which says, "the poet ate the plums and left this note on the table for his wife, writing it as verse because he was a poet."

Starting then with the assumption that this is not a pragmatic utterance but a lyric in which a fictional "I" speaks of eating plums, we are faced with the question of what to do with this object, how to structure it. We expect poems to be organic wholes and we possess a variety of models of wholeness: the simplest is the binary opposition which is given a temporal dimension (not X but Y); another is the unresolved opposition (neither X nor Y but both simultaneously); next there is the dialectical resolution of a binary opposition; and finally, remaining with

simple models of wholeness, the four-term homology (X is to Y as A is to B) or the series closed and summed up by a transcendent final term. In studying this poem we need to apply a model of completeness so as to secure an opening up of the poem and to establish a thematic structure into which we can fit its elements, which thus become sets of features subject to thematic expansion. Our elementary model of the opposition can here take the thematic form of rule and transgression: the plums were to be saved for breakfast but they have been eaten. We can then group various features on one side or the other: on the side of "eating" we have "delicious," "sweet" and "cold," stressed by their final position (this is a conventional rule) and implying that eating plums was indeed worth it; on the other side we have the assumed priority of domestic rules about eating (one recognizes them and asks for forgiveness), the reference to "breakfast," the orderly life represented by the hypostatization of meal-times. The process of thematic interpretation requires us to move from facts towards values, so we can develop each thematic complex, retaining the opposition between them. Thus we have the valuing of immediate sensuous experience, as against an economy of order and saving, which is also valued, though transgressed.

Then, presumably, the question we must ask ourselves is whether this structure is complete: whether the opposition is a simple one, a move from X to Y, or whether the attitude of the poem is in fact more complex and requires us to call upon other models. And here we can take account of what we earlier set aside — the fact that the poem masquerades as a note asking forgiveness. We can say that the poem itself acts as a mediating force, recognizing the priority of conventions (by the act of writing a note) but also seeking absolution. We can also give a function at this level to the deictics, the "I" and "you" which we had set aside, taking the relationship as a figure of intimacy, and say that the note tries to bring this realm of immediate sensuous experience into the realm of interpersonal relations, where there will be tension, certainly, but where (as the abrupt ending of the poem implies) there is hope that intimacy and understanding will resolve the tension.

Although I have been naming and paraphrasing, what I am producing is, of course, a thematic structure which could be stated in various ways. The claim is simply that in interpreting a poem like this we are implicitly relying on assumptions about poetry and structural models without which we could not proceed: that our readings of the poem (which will, of course, differ) depend upon some common interpretive operations.

Interpretation might generally stop here, but if we think about the fact that these sentences are presented as a poem we can go a step further by asking "why?" Why should this sort of banal statement be a poem? And here, by an elementary reversal which is crucial to the reading of modern poetry, we can take banality of statement as a statement about banality and say that the world of notes and breakfast is also the world of language, which must try to make a place for this kind of immediate experience which sounds banal and whose value can only be hinted at. This, we could go on to say, is why the poem must be so sparse and apparently incomplete. It must produce, as it were, a felt absence, a sense of missing intensity and profundity, so that in our desire to read the poem and to make it complete we will supply what the poem itself dare not claim: the sense of significance.

Let me turn now to a poem of a rather different kind, one which is usually read as a political statement and act of engagement, Blake's "London."

I wander through each chartered street,
Near where the chartered Thames does flow,
And mark in every face I meet
Marks of weakness, marks of woe.

In every cry of every Man,
In every Infant's cry of fear,
In every voice, in every ban,
The mind-forged manacles I hear.

How the Chimney-sweeper's cry
Every black'ning Church appalls;
And the hapless Soldier's sigh
Runs in blood down Palace walls.

But most thro' midnight streets I hear
How the youthful Harlot's curse
Blasts the new-born Infant's tear,
And blights with plagues the Marriage hearse.

I don't want to suggest that this isn't a political poem, but I would like to impress upon you how much work we must do in order to make it a political statement and what a variety of extremely artificial conventions we must call upon in order to read it in this way.

The poem is organized as a list of things seen and heard: I mark marks; I hear manacles; I hear how. . . . And it is obvious from the outset that the things heard or seen are bad (marks of weakness, marks of woe, manacles, blasts and blights). This gives us our initial opposition between the perceiving subject and the objects of perception and provides a thematic centre which helps us to organize details. We may start with the assumption, based on the convention of unity, that we have a series which will cohere at some level (the second stanza with its repetitions of "every" is ample warrant for that). But it is quite difficult to produce this coherence. In the third stanza we can try to collate the two propositions in order to discover their common subject: I hear how the cry of the sweep and the sigh of the soldier act upon the church or palace. This gives us a sound (which fits into the series of "marks" which the "I" perceives), an actor (who, our cultural model tells us, counts among the oppressed), and an institution which they affect. The opposition between institution and oppressed is one whose parameter we know: the possibilities are those of protest and submission, the results the indifference or guilt of the institution. And in fact the structure which Blake has established is ambiguous enough to preclude our really knowing which to choose here. One critic, citing historical evidence, argues that the sigh of the soldier is the murmur of possible rebellion and that the visionary can already see the blood on palace walls in a native version of the French Revolution. But we can also say, in an alternative naturalization, that the palace is bloody because it is responsible for the blood of soldiers whom it commands. Both readings, of course, are at some distance from the "sigh running in blood," but we are sufficiently accustomed to such interpretive operations for this not to worry us.

What, though, of the chimney-sweep? One might assume that the Church is horrified ("appalled") at the conditions of child labour, but the convention of coherence invariably leads critics to reject this reading and to emphasize that "appall" means to make pale or (since by convention puns are permitted when relevant) to cast a pall over and to weaken the Church's moral authority. The "black'ning" church either becomes black, with guilt as well as soot, or makes things black by its indifference and hypocrisy; and the cry of the sweep changes its colour either by making it pale or by casting a pall of metaphorical soot over it. Our ability to perform these acts of semantic transference, moving "black" and "soot" around from sweep to church to its moral character, works as a kind of proof of the poem, a demonstration that there is a rich logical coherence and semantic solidarity here. The point, however, is that the lines do not carry an obvious meaning; they cannot be naturalized as an intimation of oppression without the help of a considerable amount of condensation and displacement.

The last stanza too has an initial strangeness which is difficult to naturalize. The speaker hears how a harlot's curse blasts a tear. We could, of course, read this as a harlot cursing at the fact that her own baby is crying, but since this is to be the climax of the poem we are constrained to reject this interpretation as premature naturalization. Indeed, such is the force of conventional expectations that no commentary I have read cites this reading, though it is the most obvious. To produce unity we must discover mind-forged manacles, and the best candidate for manacling is the infant. If we are to allow his tear to be blasted we must perform semantic operations on it: the tear can be an expression of protest and feeling, of innocence also perhaps, which is cursed and manacled not so much by the curse of the harlot (and again we become involved in semantic transfers) as by her existence. Her curse becomes her sign or mark and thus fits into the series of sounds which the narrator hears. By another transfer we can say that the infant himself is cursed, as he becomes an inhabitant of this world of harlots and charters. Similarly, in the last line we can transfer epithets to say that it is marriage itself which is blighted, so that the wedding carriage becomes a hearse, through the existence of the harlot. We could, of course, work out a causal relationship here (marriage is weakened if husbands visit harlots), but the level of generality at which the poem operates suggests that this will make coherence difficult. "London " is not after all a description of specific social evils, and that, if we read the poem as a protest, is a fact with which we must now contend.

We must ask, in other words, what we are to say about the fact that the poem goes some way towards defeating our expectations: the cries are not cries of misery only but every cry of every man, even the shouts of street vendors. What are we to make, shall we say, of this odd semiotic procedure and of the interpretive requirements which the poem imposes

upon us? There is a great distance which the reader must traverse in order to get from the language of the text to political protest. What does this signify? And the answer is, I think, that here, in the kind of reading which the poem requires, we have a representation of the problems of the visionary state. The distance between every cry and mind-forged manacles is great, so great that there is a possible ambiguity about whose mind is manacled. The speaker "marks marks"; is it because he is "marking" that he sees marks? He perceives, after all, the same thing in every street cry, in every face. In order to make sense of this we must construct an identity for the "I" of the poem; we must postulate the figure of a visionary who sees what no one else sees, who can traverse these distances and read signs whose meaning is obscure to other observers. The city is not itself aware of its problems, its grief. The gap between appearance and awareness is presented, we can say, as the greatest terror of London. The true misery of manacles forged in the mind lies in the fact that they restrict the perception of misery and that no one else, not even the reader until the poem has forced him to exercise his symbolic imagination, can see the blood run down palace walls.

This has been a laboured account of what seems required if we are to read the poem as we do. It is not a structuralist interpretation for it agrees, except for the last paragraph, with customary readings of the poem. If it seems different, that is because it tries to make explicit some of the operations which we are accustomed to taking for granted. Some of these operations are highly conventional; they involve a special logic of literary interpretation, and it is not at all strange that critics prefer to take them for granted. But I think that if we are concerned with the nature of literature itself, or with dispelling the popular notion of the interpretation of literary texts as involving a complex guessing game, it is important to think more explicitly about the operations which our interpretations presuppose.

I think also, and my final remarks on "London" were designed to provide some hint of this, that the last stage in our interpretation of a poem ought to be one which returns dialectically to its source, which takes into consideration the kind of naturalization and the interpretive conventions which the poem has compelled us to use, and which asks what these demands signify. For finally the meaning of a poem will lie in the kinds of operations which it forces us to perform, in the extent to which it resists or complies with our expectations about literary signs. It is in this sense that the structuralist poetics can be hermeneutic. If we become accustomed to thinking of literature as a set of interpretive norms and operations, we will be better equipped to see (and this is crucial in the case of the most modern and difficult texts) how and where the work resists us, and how it leads to that questioning of the self and of received modes of ordering the world which has always been the result of the greatest literature.

My readers, says the narrator at the end of *A la recherche du temps perdu*, will become "les propres lecteurs d'eux-mêmes." In my book, he says, they will read themselves and their own limits. How better to facilitate a reading of the self than by gaining a sense of the conventions of intelligibility that define the self, than by trying to make explicit one's sense of order and disorder, of the significant and the insignificant, of the naturalized and the bizarre? In its resolute artificiality, literature challenges the limits we set to the self as an agent of order and allows us to accede, painfully or joyfully, to an expansion of self. But that requires, if it is to be fully accomplished, a measure of awareness of the modes of ordering which are the components of one's culture, and it is for that reason that I think a structuralist poetics has a crucial role to play, not only in advancing an understanding of literature as an institution but also in promoting the richest experience of reading.

Notes

1. "Science versus Literature," *Times Literary Supplement*, 28 September 1967, p. 897.
2. See F. de Saussure, *Course in General Linguistics*, London, Fontana, 1974.
3. See Roman Jakobson, *Questions de poétique*, Paris, Seuil, 1973. For discussion see Culler, *Structuralist Poetics*, chapter III.
4. *Anatomy of Criticism*, New York, Atheneum, 1965, p. 11.
5. Roland Barthes, *S/Z*, Paris, Sevil, 1970.

APPLICATION

Shakespeare's *The Tempest*

Northrop Frye

In the course of his long career, Northrop Frye frequently wrote about The Tempest. *The late essay that follows is his most extensive commentary on the play. He begins, typically, by addressing questions of genre, claiming that Shakespeare's final romances are the "genuine culmination" of his career, the plays wherein he "reaches the bedrock of drama, the musical, poetic, and spectacular panorama of magic and fantasy in which there is no longer tragedy or comedy, but an action passing through tragic and comic moods to a conclusion of serenity and peace." Appropriately, from Frye's point of view, these transcendent dramatic structures are built from the crudest and most primitive materials, and* The Tempest, *particularly, has aspects of mystery, magic, and fairy tale. All such terms, of course, imply a contrasting "reality" as a point of reference, but it is precisely that sense of reality that is put in question by the action of the play.*

Although Frye touches in passing on issues like the magus as modern scientist or Caliban as oppressed colonial, for him the center of the play is this conflict between illusion and reality. In our earlier selection from The Critical Path, *Frye remarks on the importance of the conception of an "unfallen" world, a world most of us can experience only through the "articulated analogies" of literature, especially in the "idealized world of romance, pastoral, or apocalyptic vision." Such a vision, the end or goal of our literary experience, is fittingly supplied in Shakespeare's last great work. Yet the play's movement from illusion to reality is paradoxical, and "it seems highly significant that this vision of the reality of nature from which we have fallen away can be attained only through some kind of theatrical illusion." That is to say, only through some kind of "articulated analogy" that art, and only art, can supply. At this level, only the imagination can deliver the real world.*

Reprinted by permission of the estate of Northrop Frye from *The Northrop Frye Newsletter* 2 (Summer 1990): 19–27.

In Shakespeare's day, if a cultivated person had been asked what a comedy was, he would probably have said that it was a play which depicted people in the middle and lower ranks of society, observed their foibles and follies, and was careful not to diverge too far from what would be recognized as credible, if not necessarily plausible, action. This was Ben Jonson's conception of comedy, supported by many prefaces and manifestos, and is illustrated by the general practice of English comic writers down to our own day. But the earlier Elizabethan dramatists—Peele, Greene, Lyly—wrote in a very different idiom of comedy, one which introduced themes of romance and fantasy, as well as characters from higher social ranks. The first fact about Shakespeare, considered as a writer of comedy, is that he followed the older practice and ignored the Jonsonian type of comedy, even in plays which are later than Jonson's early ones.

One reason for this is not hard to see. Observing men and manners on a certain level of credibility demands a degree of sophistication, whereas the fairy tale plots of Peele's *Old Wives' Tale* and Lyly's *Endymion* appeal to a more childlike desire to see a show and be told a story, without having to think about whether the story is "true to life" or not. The child wants primarily to know what comes next; he may not care so much about the logic of its relation to what it follows. If the adult completely loses this childlike response, he loses something very central to the dramatic experience, and Shakespeare was careful never to lose it as a playwright. Jonson tends to scold his audiences for not being mature enough to appreciate him: Shakespeare says (in the epilogue to *Twelfth Night*), "We'll strive to please you every day," and never fails to include some feature or incident that is incredible, that belongs to magic, fairyland, folktale, or farce rather than to the observation of men and manners. In Jonsonian comedy the play is intended to be a transparent medium for such observation: we learn about life through the comedy. In Shakespearean comedy the play is opaque: it surrounds us and wraps us up, with nothing to do but to see and hear what is passing. This does not mean that an unusual or unfamiliar type of story is wanted: again, the simple and childlike response is to the familiar and conventional, new variants of well-loved stories that have been told many times before. Shakespeare's comedies are all very different from one another, but he understands this response well enough to keep repeating his comic devices.

Further, not only does Shakespeare adhere to the pre-Jonsonian type of comedy, but he moves closer to it as he goes on. The plays are classified by the First Folio as comedies, histories, and tragedies, but criticism has isolated a fourth genre, that of romance, to which Shakespeare devoted his main attention in his last years. We have also come to realize that the romances are not a relaxation or letdown after the strenuous efforts of *King Lear* or *Macbeth*, as often used to be said, but are the genuine culmination of Shakespeare's dramatic achievement. These are the plays in which Shakespeare reaches the bedrock of drama, the musical, poetic, and spectacular panorama of magic and fantasy in which there is no longer tragedy or comedy, but an action passing through tragic and comic moods to a conclusion of serenity and peace.

We notice that the plays that seem most to have influenced Shakespeare in writing the romances were much cruder than those of Peele or Lyly. One of them was *Mucedorus*, a play of the 1590s revived around 1609, which clearly held the affections of the reading public as well as playgoers, as it went through seventeen editions in about eighty years. It is a very simple-minded play about a prince who goes in disguise to another country to woo a princess, and who gains her after baffling a cowardly villain and rescuing her and himself from a wild man in a forest. There is a prologue in which two figures named "Comedy" and "Envy" engage in a sharp dispute about the shape of the forthcoming action, the former promising a happy ending and the latter many pitfalls along the way. In another early play, *The Rare Triumphs of Love and Fortune*, which features a magician and his daughter, like *The Tempest*, we begin with an assembly of gods and a debate between Fortuna and Venus, again over the character of the story that is to follow.

From such unlikely (as it seems to us) sources, Shakespeare drew hints for an expanding stage action that can include not only all social levels from royalty to clowns, but gods and magicians with superhuman powers as well. The romances end happily, or at any rate quietly, but they do not avoid the tragic: *The Winter's Tale* in particular passes through and contains a complete tragic action on its way to a more festive conclusion, and *Cymbeline*, which has at least a token historical theme (Cymbeline was a real king of Britain, and his coins are in the British Museum), is actually classified as a tragedy in the Folio.

Such plays are "tragicomedies," a genre that not only Shakespeare but Beaumont and Fletcher were popularizing from about 1607 onward. In the preface to Fletcher's *Faithful Shepherdess* (ca. 1609), it is said that in a tragicomedy a god is "lawful," i.e., superhuman agents can be introduced with decorum.

But to expand into a divine world means reducing the scale of the human one. The jealousy of Leontes and Posthumus is quite as unreasonable as that of Othello, but it is not on the gigantic human scale of Othello's: we see it from a perspective in which it seems petty and ridiculous as well. The form of the romance thus moves closer to the puppet show, which again, as Goethe's *Wilhelm Meister* reminds us, is a form of popular drama with a strong appeal to children, precisely because they can see that the action is being manipulated. The debates of Comedy and Envy in *Mucedorus,* and of Venus and Fortuna in *The Rare Triumphs* introduce us to another approach to the manipulating of action. Here we are told that the play to follow is connected with certain genres, and that characters who personify these genres are taking a hand in the action. The notion of Comedy as a character in the action of a comedy may seem strange at first, but is deeply involved in the structure of Shakespearean comedy. Let us look at a comedy of Shakespeare that many people have found very puzzling, *Measure for Measure,* from this point of view.

In *Measure for Measure,* Vincentio, the Duke of Vienna (which Shakespeare seems to have thought of as an Italian town), announces his departure, leaving his deputy Angelo in charge to tighten up laws against sexual irregularity. Everything goes wrong, and Angelo, who sincerely wants to be an honest and conscientious official, is not only impossibly rigorous, condemning to death young Claudio for a very trifling breach of the law, but is thrown headlong by his first temptation, which is to seduce Claudio's sister Isabella when she comes to plead for his life. The action leads up to the dialogue of the condemned Claudio and his sister in prison. Claudio's nerve breaks down under the horror of approaching death, and he urges Isabella to yield to Angelo. Isabella, totally demoralized by her first glimpse of human evil, and, perhaps, by finding herself more attracted to Angelo and his proposal than she would ever have thought possible, explodes in a termagant fury. She says: "I'll pray a thousand prayers for thy death"—

hardly a possible procedure for any Christian, though Isabella wants to be a cloistered nun. Everything is drifting toward a miserable and total impasse, when the disguised Duke steps forward. The rhythm abruptly changes from blank verse to prose, and the Duke proceeds to outline a complicated and very unplausible comic plot, complete with the naive device known as the "bed trick," substituting one woman for another in the dark. It is clear that this point is the "peripety" or reversal of the action, and that the play falls into the form of a diptych, the first half tragic in direction and the second half comic. Vincentio has the longest speaking part of any character in Shakespearean comedy: a sure sign that he has the role of a subdramatist, a deputy producer of the stage action. *Measure for Measure,* then, is not a play about the philosophy of government or sexual morality or the folly of trying to legislate people into virtue. It is a play about the relation of the structure of comedy to these things. The Duke's actions make no kind of realistic sense, but they make structural dramatic sense, and only the structure of comedy, intervening in human life, can bring genuine repentance out of Angelo and genuine forgiveness out of Isabella.

In *The Winter's Tale* the action also forms a diptych, and again we have first a tragic movement proceeding toward chaos and general muddle. This action comprises Leontes's jealousy, the disappearance of his wife Hermione, the death of his son Mamillius, the exposing of the infant Perdita, and the devouring of Antigonus, who exposes her, by a bear. Then a shepherd and his son enter the action: as in *Measure for Measure,* the rhythm immediately changes from blank verse to prose. The shepherd finds the infant and the son sees the death of Antigonus, and the shepherd's remark, "Thou mettest with things dying, I with things new born," emphasizes the separating into two parts of the total action. This separating of the action is referred to later on in a recognition scene, not presented but reported in the conversation of some gentlemen: "all the instruments that aided to expose the child were even then lost when it was found." Such phrases indicate that the real dividing point in the action is the finding of Perdita at the end of the third act, not the sixteen years that are said to elapse before the fourth act begins. In the final scene of the play Paulina, the widow of Antigonus, says to Hermione, who is pretending to be a statue: "our Perdita is found." This is the formula that first draws speech from Hermione. Paulina, though an agent of the comic structure of the second half of the play, is not its generator: that appears to be some power connected with the Delphic oracle, which had previously announced that Leontes would live without an heir "if that which is lost be not found."

In *The Tempest* there is no clearly marked peripety or reversal of action. The reason is that the entire play is a reversal of an action which has taken place before the play begins. This concentration on the second half of a total dramatic action accounts for many features of *The Tempest*. It is quite a short play, which is why Prospero's role has fewer lines than Vincentio's, though he dominates the action even more completely. Again, we are constantly aware of the passing of a brief interval of time, an interval of a few hours, very close to the period of time we spend in watching the play. The dramatic action is generated by Prospero and carried out by Ariel, whose role is parallel to that of Pauline in *The Winter's Tale*. But because only the second or rearranging half of the action is presented, the characters have no chance to mess up their lives in the way that Angelo and Leontes do. The theme of frustrated aggressive action recurs several times: when Ferdinand tries to draw his sword on Prospero, when Antonio and Sebastian attempt to murder Alonso and Gonzalo, and later to attack Ariel, and when Stephano's conspiracy is baffled. Prospero's magic controls everything, and the effect is of an audience being taken inside a play, so that they not only watch the play but, so to speak, see it being put on.

Ordinarily, in our dramatic experience, this sense of a play being created before our eyes is one that we can only get when we are watching an action that seems to be partly improvised on the spot, where we know the general outline of the story but not its particulars. Various devices such as Brecht's "alienating" techniques and the Stanislavski method of acting attempt to create such a feeling in modern audiences. In Shakespeare's day this type of improvising action appeared in the *commedia dell' arte,* which was well known in England, and influenced Shakespeare in all periods of his production. Some of the sketchy plot outlines (*scenari*) of this type of play have been preserved, and we note that they feature magicians, enchanted islands, reunions of families, clown scenes (*lazzi*), and the like. Such *scenari* are probably as close

as we shall ever get to finding a general source for *The Tempest.*

Not only does Prospero arrange the action, but we are seldom allowed to forget that it is specifically a dramatic action that is going on. Prospero orders Ariel to disguise himself as a nymph of the sea, while remaining invisible to everyone else. In reading the play, we might wonder what point there is in dressing up so elaborately if he is to remain invisible, but in the theater we realize at once that he will not be invisible to us. Again, an illusory banquet is presented to and snatched away from the Court Party, and Ariel, as a harpy, makes a somber speech condemning the "three men of sin." It is an impressive and oracular speech, but we hardly notice this because Prospero immediately undercuts it, coming forward to commend Ariel on doing a good actor's job. The opposite emphasis comes in the epilogue, when Prospero says:

> As you from crimes would pardon'd be,
> Let your indulgence set me free.

The epilogue represents only the convention of asking the audience to applaud the play, so we hardly notice how grave the tone is. Yet it is clear that the restructuring of the lives of the characters in the play is being said to be a deeply serious operation, with an application in it for ourselves. We have not merely been watching a fairy tale, we feel, but participating in some kind of mystery. What kind of mystery?

The Tempest is almost a comic parody of a revenge tragedy, in which there is repentance, forgiveness, and reconciliation instead of revenge. The characters are divided into three groups and each is put through ordeals, illusions, and a final awakening to some kind of self-knowledge. There is hardly a character in the play who is not believed by other characters to be dead, and in the final recognition scene there is something very like a sense that everyone is being raised from the dead, as there is with Hermione in the last scene of *The Winter's Tale*. Prospero actually claims the power of raising the dead in his renunciation speech, and he also pretends that Miranda was drowned in the storm he raised.

The Court Party goes through a labyrinth of "forthrights and meanders" with strange shapes appearing and disappearing around them, but nevertheless they finally arrive at a state of self-recognition where

Gonzalo is able to say that each has found himself "when [formerly] no man was his own." Gonzalo himself is on the highest moral level of the Court Party: in contrast to Antonio and Sebastian, he finds the island a pleasant place and his garments fresh, and he is excluded from Ariel's condemnation of the "three men of sin." Alonso comes next: his repentance and his gaining of self-awareness seem equally genuine, and he is clearly the focus of Prospero's regenerative efforts. Next is Sebastian, a weak and ineffectual person who does what the stronger characters around him suggest that he do. In the final scene he seems quite cheerful, and we feel that, while nothing very profound has happened to him, he will be as easily persuaded to virtue as to vice. Antonio, who speaks only once in the last scene, in reply to a direct question, is a more doubtful quantity. Stephano, Trinculo, and Caliban go through a kind of parody of the Court Party ordeals and illusions, yet they too reach some level of self-awareness. Stephano is reconciled to losing his imaginary kingdom, and Caliban, who has emerged as much the most intelligent of the three, is apparently ready to be weaned from idolatry, and so to take the first step in self-knowledge himself.

To the extent that people are acquiring self-knowledge, then, they seem to be taking their places in a moral hierarchy. Yet as we look further into it, it seems to be less a moral hierarchy than an imaginative one. They move from illusion to reality as the play presents these categories. What is illusion? Primarily, it is what such people as Antonio consider reality. As soon as Alonso falls asleep, Antonio starts a plot to murder him: this is *Realpolitik,* the way things are done in the real world. Similarly, he takes a very "realistic" view of the island, in contrast to Gonzalo's. But the play itself moves toward a reversal of this view of reality. Antonio's one remark in the last scene is that Caliban is a "plain fish" — one of several indications that living on his level is symbolically living under water. The illusions in the mazy wanderings of the Court Party are more real than Antonio's life without conscience.

What, then, is reality, as the play presents it? That is more difficult, and Prospero seems to agree with T. S. Eliot that whatever reality is, humankind cannot bear very much of it. But just as "reality" for Antonio turns out to be illusion, so perhaps what is illusion on the much higher level of Ferdinand and Miranda might turn out to be closer to reality. The masque put

on for their benefit by Prospero is a vision of the highest form of "reality" in our cultural tradition: the vision of what in Christianity is called "unfallen" nature, the original world before the fall, the model divine creation that God observed and saw to be good. The dance of nymphs and August reapers seems to suggest the "perpetual spring" which is a traditional attribute of Paradise, and the three goddesses of earth, sky, and rainbow suggest the newly washed world after Noah's flood, when the curse was lifted from the ground and a regularity of seasons was promised. The vision, however, is one of a renewed power and energy of nature rather than simply a return to a lost Paradise: a sense of a "brave new world" appropriate as a wedding offering to a young and attractive couple. And it seems highly significant that this vision of the reality of nature from which we have fallen away can be attained only through some kind of theatrical illusion.

The action of the play, then, moves from illusion to reality in a paradoxical way. What we think of as reality is illusion: not all of us are realistic in the criminal way that Antonio is, but, as Prospero's great speech at the end of the masque says, in our world everything that we call real is merely an illusion that lasts a little longer than some other illusions. At the other end, what we think of as real can come to us only as a temporary illusion, specifically a dramatic illusion. This is what the wedding masque symbolizes in the play: the masque is presented to Ferdinand and Miranda, but the whole play is being presented to us, and we must be sure that we omit no aspect of it.

The play keeps entirely within the order of nature: there are no gods or oracles, though Alonso expects them, and Prospero's magic operates entirely within the four elements below the moon. Sycorax, like other witches, could draw down the moon, i.e., bring "lunatic" influences to bear on human life, but this is not Prospero's interest, though it may be within his power. In the action that took place before the play began, when Prospero was Duke of Milan, his brother Antonio had become the *persona* or dramatic mask of the absentminded Prospero, and gradually expanded until he became "absolute Milan," the entire Duke, until Prospero and the infant Miranda vanished into another world in an open boat (for Milan, like Bohemia in *The Winter's Tale,* appears to have a seacoast). On the enchanted island this dramatic action goes into reverse, Prospero expanding into the real Duke of Milan and Antonio shrinking to a kind of discarded shell. Prospero's life in Milan is what passes for real life in our ordinary experience: the action of *The Tempest* presents us with the aspect of nature which is real but, like the dark side of the moon, constantly hidden from us. We note in passing the folktale theme of the struggle of brothers, the rightful heir exiled only to return later in triumph.

The feeling that the play is some kind of mystery or initiation, then, is a quite normal and central response to it. The connection between drama and rites of initiation probably goes back to the Old Stone Age. In classical times there were several mystery religions with dramatic forms of initiation, the most celebrated being those of Eleusis, near Athens, which were held in honor of the earth goddess Demeter, the Roman Ceres who is the central figure in Prospero's masque. In the eighteenth century Bishop Warburton suggested that the sixth book of the *Aeneid*, depicting Aeneas's journey to the lower world, was a disguised form of Eleusinian initiation, and in 1921 Colin Still, in *Shakespeare's Mystery Play*, applied a similar theory to *The Tempest*. He noted that the route of the Court Party, from Tunis in Africa to the coast of Italy, paralleled the route of Aeneas from Carthage, and the otherwise pointless identification of Tunis with Carthage made by Gonzalo in Act II, along with the equally pointless amusement of Antonio and Sebastian, seems to be emphasizing the parallel. I suspect that Colin Still's book was an influence on T. S. Eliot's *Waste Land*, published the next year, though Eliot does not mention Still before his preface to Wilson Knight's *Wheel of Fire* in 1930.

Colin Still, recognizing that Shakespeare could have had no direct knowledge of classical mystery rites, ascribed the symbolic coincidences he found with *The Tempest* to an inner "necessity," to the fact that the imagination must always talk in some such terms when it gets to a sufficient pitch of intensity. I should add only that the "necessity" is specifically a necessity of dramatic structure. We can see this more clearly if we turn to a dramatic form which not only did not influence Shakespeare but was nowhere in his cultural tradition, the No play of Japan. In a No play what usually happens is that two travelers encounter a ghost who was a famous hero in his former life, and who re-creates the story of his exploits in this ghostly world, which is also presented as a world of reconciliation and mutual understanding. This type of drama is linked to Buddhist beliefs in a

world intervening between death and rebirth, but we do not need such beliefs to make imaginative sense of No plays. We do recognize in them, however, a very powerful and integral dramatic structure. When we enter the world of *The Tempest*, with its curious feeling of being a world withdrawn from both death and birth, we recognize again that that world is being specifically identified with the world of the drama.

As often in Shakespeare, the characters in *The Tempest* are invited to a meeting to be held after the play in which the puzzling features of their experiences will be explained to them. This seems a curious and unnecessary convention, but it is true to the situation of drama, where the audience always knows more about what is going on than the characters do, besides being in a greater state of freedom, because they are able to walk out of the theater. Each character in *The Tempest*, at the beginning of the play, is lost in a private drama of his own. This is true even of Prospero, in the long dialogues he holds with Miranda, Ariel, and Caliban in Act I, mainly for the benefit of the audience. Through the action of the play, a communal dramatic sense gradually consolidates, in which all the characters identify themselves within the same drama, a drama which the audience is finally invited to enter.

The Tempest, like its predecessor *The Winter's Tale*, is both comedy and romance. In the tradition of comedy that Shakespeare inherited from Plautus and Terence, what typically happens is that a young man and a young woman wish to get married, that there is parental opposition, and that this opposition is eventually evaded and the marriage takes place. Comedy thus moves toward the triumph of youth over age, and toward the vision of the renewal and rebirth of nature which such a triumph symbolizes, however little of nature there may be in a Roman comedy. In *The Tempest*, the conventionally comic aspect of the play is represented by the marriage of Ferdinand and Miranda. Prospero puts up a token opposition to this marriage, apparently because it is customary for fathers to do so, and he forces Ferdinand into the role of servant, as part of the token tests and ordeals which traditionally make the suitor worthy of his mistress.

The corresponding comic element in *The Winter's Tale* centered on the successful marriage of Florizel and Perdita in the teeth of strenuous parental opposition. Florizel temporarily renounces his princely heritage and exchanges garments with the thief Autolycus, just as Ferdinand takes over Caliban's role as a bearer of logs. Here again the renewal of nature is a part of the theme, more explicitly because of the romance element in the play. The great sheep-shearing festival in the fourth act of *The Winter's Tale* is a vision of the power of nature extending through four seasons, that being probably what the dance of the twelve satyrs symbolizes. Nature has it all her own way throughout this scene, and Perdita, the child of nature, announces that she will have nothing to do with "bastard" flowers adulterated by art. Nor will she listen to Polixenes's sophisticated idealism about art as being really nature's way of improving nature. The traditional symbol of the domination of art over nature, Orpheus, whose music could command animals and plants, appears only in parody, in connection with the ballads of Autolycus.

But this triumph of nature and its powers of renewal and rebirth, with its center of gravity in the future, is only the lesser recognition in the play. The main emphasis comes not on the successful wooing of the younger pair, but, as usual in Shakespearean romance, on the reintegrating of the world of their elders. The greater recognition scene takes place in a world of art, Paulina's chapel, where we are told that we are being presented with a work of sculpture and painting, where music is heard, where references to the art of magic are made. In the vision of the triumph of art, the emphasis is not on renewal and rebirth but on resurrection, the transformation from death to life. And just as the vision of nature's renewal and rebirth relates primarily to the future, so the triumph of art and resurrection relates primarily to the past, where the words of the oracle, spoken sixteen years earlier, are brought to life in the present, and where old sins and blunders are healed up. In his essay *The Decay of Lying,* Oscar Wilde says of music that it "creates for one a past of which one has been ignorant, and fills one with a sense of sorrows that have been hidden from one's tears." Perhaps it is the function of all art to "create a past" in this sense of revealing to us the range of experience that our timid senses and reasonings largely screen out. The power of nature gives us a hope that helps us to face the future: the power of art gives us a faith that helps us to face the past.

The Tempest is concerned even more than *The Winter's Tale* with the triumph of art, and much less with the triumph of nature. This is mainly because Prospero is a magus figure: in Elizabethan English "art" meant mostly magic, as it does here. Prospero renounces his magic at the end of the play: this was conventional, for while magic was a great attraction as dramatic entertainment, it was a highly suspicious operation in real life; hence all dramatic magicians were well advised to renounce their powers when the play drew to a close. But there is more to Prospero's renunciation of magic than this. We recall the deep melancholy of his "our revels now are ended" speech at the end of the masque, and his somber comment on Miranda's enthusiasm for her brave new world: "'tis new to thee." In the world of reality that we can reach only through dramatic illusion, the past is the source of faith and the future the source of hope. In the world of illusion that we take for reality, the past is only the no longer and the future only the not yet: one vanishes into nothingness and the other, after proving itself to be much the same, vanishes after it.

As a magus, Prospero is fulfilling the past, reliving and restructuring his former life as Duke of Milan. To do so, he must take an obsessive interest in time: "the very minute bids thee ope thine ear," he says to Miranda, referring to astrology, and he later tells her that the fortunes of all the rest of his life depend on his seizing the present moment. Antonio's urging the same plea on Sebastian later is a direct parody of this. Prospero's anxiety about time interpenetrates very curiously with his anxieties as a theatrical producer, making sure that Ariel comes in on cue and that his audience is properly attentive and impressed. Such strain and such anxiety cannot go on for long, and all through the play Prospero, no less than Ariel, is longing for the end of it.

Prospero's magic summons up the romantic enthusiasm for magic with which the sixteenth century had begun, in Agrippa and Paracelsus and Pico della Mirandola and the legendary Faust. It continued for most of the next century, and among contemporary scholars Frances Yates in particular has speculated about its curious relation to Shakespeare's romances. But this vision of a power and wisdom beyond human scope seems to be passing away when Ariel is released and melts into the thin air from whence he came. Whether magic was a reality or a dream, in either case it could only end as dreams do. In Shakespeare's day magic and science were very imperfectly separated, and today, in a postscientific age when they seem to be coming together again, the magus figure has revived in contemporary fiction, with much the same dreams attached to it. Such a return may make *The Tempest* more "relevant" to us today, but if so, the weariness and disillusionment of Prospero are equally "relevant."

Just as the mere past, the vanishing age, seems to be summed up in the figure of Ariel, so the mere future, the yet-to-vanish new age, seems to be summed up in the figure of Caliban. Caliban's name seems to echo the "cannibals" of Montaigne's famous essay, a passage from which forms the basis for Gonzalo's reverie about an ideal commonwealth in Act II. Around the figure of Caliban, again, there are many phrases indicating Shakespeare's reading in contemporary pamphlets dealing with the first English efforts to settle on the American coast. Every editor of *The Tempest* has to record this fact, while pointing out that Prospero's island is in the Mediterranean, not the Atlantic, and has nothing to do with the New World. Still, the historical situation of *The Tempest*, coming at the end of an age of speculative magic and at the beginning of an age of colonization in the New World, seems to give Caliban a peculiar and poignant resonance. Caliban is the shape of things to come in the future "real" world, not a brave new world of hope, but, for the most part, a mean and cruel world, full of slavery and greed, of which many Calibans will be the victims.

Of course, we had rather have the past of faith and the future of hope than the past of dream and the future of nightmare, but what choice have we? This is perhaps another way of asking what *The Tempest*, as dramatic illusion, has to give us in the way of reality. When Shakespeare touches on such subjects he is apt to bury what he says in unlikely places, passages of dialogue that the eye and ear could easily pass over as mere "filler." We find such a passage in the inane babble of Antonio and Sebastian at the beginning of the second act. Sebastian's response to a narrow escape from drowning is a kind of giggling hysteria, and Antonio falls in with this mood and encourages it, because he knows what he wants to do with Sebastian later on. In the course of the dialogue Gonzalo, who is speaking with a wisdom and insight not his own, assures the others that "Tunis was Carthage." We pick up the implication that *The Tempest*, as explained, is repeating the experience of Aeneas voyaging from Carthage to Italy to build a new Troy, and presenting an imaginative moment, at once retrospective and prospective, in the history of the third Troy, as England was conventionally supposed to be. The dialogue goes on:

> ANT. What impossible matter will he make easy next?
> SEB. I think he will carry this island home in his pocket, and give it his son for an apple.
> ANT. And, sowing the kernels of it in the sea, bring forth more islands.

Gonzalo never claims to make impossible matters easy, but Prospero can do so, and by implication Shakespeare himself can. And it is Shakespeare who gives us, as members of his audience, his island, as one would give a child an apple, but with the further hope that we will not stop with eating the apple, but will use its seeds to create for ourselves new seas and even more enchanted islands.

"Silence and Slow Time": Pastoral *Topoi* in Keats's Odes

Lore Metzger

Working on the assumption that the frame of reference for "Ode on a Grecian Urn" is not the world of plastic art but the world of literary convention, Lore Metzger places the poem in the context of pastoral poetry, and specifically in the context of the classical topos *of the decorated cup awarded to the triumphant poet. "Theocritus's prize cup in* Idyll I *set the pattern for variations on the theme by Virgil, Spenser, Milton, Pope, and Keats."* Variations *on the theme is the key term, for the task of the intertextual critic is to show how the work uses conventions to create meaning, how it manipulates the* topoi *or commonplace themes to make its singular statement. Invoking Schiller's distinction between the naive and the sentimental poet (compare the use of the same contrast in the essays by Douglas Wilson and Northrop Frye), Metzger finds Keats definitely evinces the divided consciousness of the self-aware, sentimental poet. "In some of his odes Keats the classicist deployed pastoral* topoi *to give allusive resonance to his personal debates, while Keats the romanticist exploited the tensions and dissonances that surfaced in his confrontations with literary tradition." "Ode on a Grecian Urn" is a signal instance of this divided consciousness, for it is not simply a poem that employs pastoral conventions, it is a poem about them. Like Eva T. H. Brann, Metzger sees the "Ode" as the self-conscious end of a tradition, a poem aware of its double vision. "Like the urn, pastoral* topoi *are silent survivors from the past until poets endow them with new life by engaging them in dynamic debate, interrogating them, and assimilating them into the armory of the mind." But for poets of Keats's era, and since, this assimilation has become problematical. "Keats's odes point up the problem and suggest one solution for the modern poet: intensifying the dissonance between the*

---

ideal pastoral ethos and the alienating consciousness of the contemporary world." But only an intertextual criticism, a criticism fully aware of the pastoral conventions, will be able to register this dissonance.

When Keats abandoned *Hyperion,* he scuttled with it the heavy load of classical myth that he had been unable to mold into his own shifting moods and perspectives. Yet, stymied though he felt in the spring of 1819 by the "over-powering idea of our dead poets" (*Letters* 2:116), he did not ruthlessly reject all literary precursors. He knew that (in Yeats's words) "A style is found by sedentary toil/And by the imitation of great masters" (*Ego Dominus Tuus* 65–66). Like other Romantics, Keats insisted on his right to enlarge the neoclassic canon of "great masters," to test a wide spectrum of masterpieces and to allow the masterpieces to test him. When he turned to experimenting with the Pindaric ode, he evolved both his own stanzaic form and his own repertoire of *topoi* by testing literary models, imprinting on them his own design. Like Schiller, he remained to the end of his life a romantic classicist who believed that he could find his "true voice of feeling" (*Letters* 2:167) and yet temper its Dionysian intensity with Apollonian knowledge and order. In some of his odes Keats the classicist deployed pastoral *topoi* to give allusive resonance to his personal debates, while Keats the romanticist exploited the tensions and dissonances that surfaced in his confrontations with literary tradition.

•   •   •

In his *Ode to Psyche* Keats devoted his visionary and verbal powers to reviving a pagan goddess. In his *Ode on a Grecian Urn* he used his poetic resources to animate a marble sculpture, making mute antiquity speak to him and to his time. Whereas the poet could provide for Psyche an immortal shrine, he confronts in the marble urn a nearly immortal object that exposes his own mortality. The two odes illustrate Keats's maxim "that eve[r]ly point of thought is the centre of an intellectual world—the two uppermost thoughts in a Man's mind are the two poles of his World he revolves on them and every thing is southward or northward to him through their means" (*Letters* 1:243). In both odes the thought at the center of the poet's intellectual world is the question of the *Fall of Hyperion:* What is the poet's role in the modern world? Keats sets out to explore the aesthetic and moral certainties and uncertainties of realms made of

language and of marble. He may have been inspired by a real work of art, but I am not going to contribute to the conjectures whether the Borghese Vase or the Townley or the Sosibios Vase or the Holland House Urn or any other piece of chiseled marble was the prototype for Keats's urn.[1] Here I am concerned only with his incorporation and reinterpretation of the classical *topos* of the decorated cup awarded as a prize in a bucolic singing contest.

Theocritus's prize cup in *Idyll I* set the pattern for variations on the theme by Virgil, Spenser, Milton, Pope, and Keats.[2] Theocritus vividly presents the sculptured details. Encircled by tendrils of ivy and framed by acanthus, the panels depict nonpastoral scenes: a coy woman toying with two suitors, an old fisherman sinuously gathering up his net, two foxes plundering a vineyard and raiding the knapsack of the boy on guard, who is absorbed in braiding a cricket cage. These panels contain (in both senses of the word) the nonpastoral world of competition, hardship, cruelty, and deception, as it intrudes on Theocritus's pastoral arbor. What matters, as Thomas Rosenmeyer points out, is that "these echoes of the world beyond the pleasance" are stilled, "frozen into sculptured beauty, hemmed in by the ivy frame that winds around the lip of the cup. Within the poem, their life force is minimal" (91). Keats reverses Theocritus's strategy: instead of stilling the disturbing forces of the world beyond the pastoral bower, he freezes the pastoral world and reduces it to a single sculptured panel on his imaginary urn. But if he thus miniaturizes the pastoral realm, he vastly enlarges the scope of the cup itself; it is no longer a prize awarded either for singing a specially requested song, as in Theocritus, or for winning a singing match, as in Virgil. Keats prunes away the pastoral setting, shepherd-poets, and the pastoral occasion of his predecessors to allow his cup to fill all the space and time of his poem. His poem is not an ameobean eclogue containing the ecphrastic motif of a prize cup but a lyric debate, an ode on a Grecian urn. The speaker stations the urn squarely on the center of his mental stage, never letting it out of his sight, speaking to it and for it. He sings by his own eyes inspired, carrying on a lyric dialogue with the imaginary carved figures and engaging in a friendly contest with the urn itself. Keats's persona is at once spectator and actor, distant observer and empathic participant in the scenes he visualizes. And of course he is first and foremost the poet who translates into his verbal medium the marble object that exists only in and through his words, just as Psyche's temple exists only as a verbal construct. Yet his pictorial skill is so fine that readers speak of the urn as if it existed solidly in space, as if they could actually turn it or walk around it to look at the different panels. The panels include both pastoral and nonpastoral scenes, yet even an image of Dionysian frenzy does not prevent Keats from making his urn as a whole the bearer of the pastoral and Apollonian ideals of tranquility and order, equanimity and immutability.

The urn immediately evokes a compliment from its apostrophizing beholder: silent historian though it is, it can "express/A flowery tale more sweetly" than the poet's rhyme (3–4). The speaker awards the palm to his sister art before even challenging it to a contest. Nevertheless, the agon between poetry and plastic art emerges as a quiet undercurrent in the poem, with the poet playing the roles of both contestants and of the umpire. Does he immediately pronounce the urn as superior to the poet as a teller of tales because it is more truly pastoral, more truly a naive mimesis of the Arcadian world of resonant *silvae*? The epithet "silvan" recalls Virgil's ubiquitous forests and thickets that form the echoing groves of pastoral singers: "non canimus surdis, respondent omnia silvae" [we do not sing to the deaf, the woods echo everything — Ed.] (*Eclogue* 10:8). Virgil's "muse is *silvestris*," says Phillip Damon, "because the forest is one of the natural echo chambers which his conception of the pastoral genre seems to require. . . . Songs are badly sung outside the forest" (282). Even the prize cups staked in *Eclogue* 3 are made of beechwood (*fagina*), linking them closely to the forest setting of the singing contest. Keats's "Silvan historian" silently encodes these echoes of a naive pastoral mood, which are antithetical to the sentimental speaker's divided sensibility.

The sentimental poet is immediately provoked to myriad questions and speculations about the sensuous reality that the urn unquestioningly embodies:

> What leaf-fringed legend haunts about thy shape
> Of deities or mortals, or of both,
>   In Tempe or the dales of Arcady?
> What men or gods are these? What maidens loth?
> What mad pursuit? What struggle to escape?
> What pipes and timbrels? What wild ecstasy?
> (5–10)

Not the classical sculptor but only the modern poet is teased into distinguishing between gods and mortals. Only the poet feels the need to name the pastoral valleys as Tempe or Arcady. But has he named them appropriately, or has he imposed his own nostalgia for Arcadian tranquility on the marble landscape? And is the dissonant Dionysian intensity of the "mad pursuit" and "struggle to escape" his own or the urn's? He quickly dissolves his perception of such "wild ecstasy" into an Arcadian pleasance of eternal spring and a happy piper serenading his youthful beloved. The poet dwells far more exuberantly on this pastoral tableau than on either the Dionysian panel that precedes it or that of a religious procession that follows, yet the whole "Attic shape" (41) strikes the speaker as "Cold pastoral" (45). Apparently all the sculptured depictions of happy spring, with its boughs that never shed their leaves and the love "For ever warm and still to be enjoyed" (26), are painful reminders that such serenity is available only as still life, existence frozen into art and not as lived experience. In this agon between life and art, the poet lends his imaginative resources to realizing unreality — the sweetness of unheard melodies and the happiness of unconsummated love:

> Fair youth beneath the trees, thou canst not leave
> Thy song, nor ever can those trees be bare;
>   Bold lover, never, never canst thou kiss,
> Though winning near the goal — yet do not grieve:
> She cannot fade, though thou hast not thy bliss,
>   For ever wilt thou love, and she be fair!
> (15–20)

For the moment the speaker's imagination is so fully absorbed by the pastoral scene on the urn that he offers the chiseled lover consoling advice. The contest between art and life, sculpture and poetry, has reached a moment of equipoise. But increasingly the speaker's tone becomes plaintive as he meditates on lovers that cannot age, trees that will not shed their leaves, unheard melodies that, like unconsummated love, will never grow stale. He tries to persuade himself that these timeless and lifeless states are preferable to timebound human passion "That leaves a heart high-sorrowful and cloyed, / A burning forehead, and a parching tongue" (29–30). He seems to arrive at the weak conclusion that moments of true harmony and happiness are accessible only as "Cold pastoral" and that the only refuge from painful mortality lies in the silent immortality of the urn.

This conclusion is, however, open also to a stronger interpretation: that the speaker can bear the world "full of Misery and Heartbreak, Pain, Sickness and oppression" (*Letters* 1:281) as long as this world includes marble urns, artifices of eternity that order violent *and* tranquil, distressing *and* re-creative symbols into a *concordia discors*. Neither the pure harmony of pastoral inspiration nor the echoing green bower can, for this speaker, offer restorative spots of time. Only dissonant "Cold pastoral" can help the mind uncover moments of arresting beauty within the world of pain and flux. Keats concludes his unresolved contests between naive and sentimental modes of feeling, between plastic art and lyric poetry, between the stillness of pastoral joy and the bittersweet intensity of mutable existence, as the Pygmalion-like speaker gives life and voice to the urn. Generously and ironically, he lets the timeless piece of sculpture have the last word, addressed to timebound generations of men. With its commonplace epigram, the urn triumphs over the poet.[3] But since the whole debate has been a psychomachia, in which Keats brilliantly incorporated the motif of a pastoral contest with its prize cup, since he made the cup itself a participant in his contest, the poet-umpire has nothing to award to the victor. His Greek urn must be its own award.

Keats's debate with an imaginary urn may serve as a fit emblem for the Romantic poets' recuperation of pastoral motifs and perspectives. Like the urn, pastoral *topoi* are silent survivors from the past until poets endow them with new life by engaging them in dynamic debate, interrogating them, and assimilating them into their armory of the mind. But deploying them in forays into uncharted territories became increasingly problematical. Keats's odes point up the problem and suggest one solution for the modern poet: intensifying the dissonance between an ideal pastoral ethos and the alienating consciousness of the contemporary world. The poet then experiences the Wordsworthian double consciousness of the self as the speaking subject and of the earlier self as the subject about which the speaker speaks, but he can no longer trust that the traces of the earlier self,

> Those shadowy recollections,
>   Which, be they what they may,
> Are yet the fountain light of all our day,
> Are yet a master light of all our seeing. . . .
>   (*Intimations of Immortality* 150–53)

The Wordsworthian belief in an Arcadia of the soul whose emanations could permeate the fibers of adult life and change the fabric of society became a dubious ideology.

Notes

1. See Jack 215–21 for a full discussion of Keats's visual sources.
2. See Rosenmeyer 305–6, note 54 for references to the wide-ranging adaptations of the *topos* of the prize cup.
3. After reviewing the principal divergent judgments of Keats's famous apothegm, Sperry concludes that "what it offers us is a sublime commonplace" (278). I think it offers just a commonplace.

Works Cited

Damon, Phillip. *Modes of Analogy in Ancient and Medieval Verse.* Berkeley: University of California Press, 1973.

Jack, Ian. *Keats and the Mirror of Art.* Oxford: Clarendon Press, 1967.

Keats, John. *The Letters of John Keats, 1814–1821.* Edited by Hyder Edward Rollins. 2 vols. Cambridge: Harvard University Press, 1958.

Rosenmeyer, Thomas G. *The Green Cabinet: Theocritus and the European Pastoral Lyric.* Berkeley: University of California Press, 1969.

Sperry, Stuart M. *Keats the Poet.* Princeton: Princeton University Press, 1973.

After sketching some of the many and profound disagreements about the meaning of "Benito Cereno," Charles Swann suggests that the larger mysteries surrounding the story "can only be understood when seen in terms of the novella's form and genre: in other words, "Benito Cereno" is a mystery story in the conventional sense." More specifically, Swann argues that "a recognition of the importance of narrative form and literary genre will at least improve our definitions of the complexities that confront the reader, and will help us see how the story relates to the history and politics that it springs from and is so deeply about." Thus, rather than seeing these literary connections as leading away from the story's political implications, Swann proposes a reading that will foreground the story's involvement in history and politics and that may, like Catharine O'Connell's reader-response analysis, end by convicting the reader of being "at the least, an (unconscious) accomplice of an ideology he may consciously repudiate." "I am trying to show that serious political meanings are being mediated through the form of the mystery story—and that many of the critical problems have to be reformulated when "Benito Cereno" is located within the genre." In reformulating these problems, Swann offers a counter-argument to those like Kaplan who believe the story makes blacks the representatives of vice, but also to those who see them as the symbols of virtue. Neither reading, Swann argues, has truly understood the story's mystery.

Whodunnit? Or, Who Did What? "Benito Cereno" and the Politics of Narrative Structure

Charles Swann

Reprinted by permission from David Nye, ed. *American Studies in Transition.* Odense: Odense University Press, 1985: 199–234. Copyright 1985 by Odense University Press.

I

The tale entitled "Benito Cereno" is most painfully interesting, and in reading it we became nervously anxious for the solution of the mystery it involves.[1]

"Benito Cereno" is a mystery story. I don't mean to appear to be suggesting that it is to be interpreted by metaphysical appeals to religious *cum* mystical notions of the mysteries of iniquity. (Mysteries of inequity are, however, more to the point). Nor do I mean merely that its meanings are ambiguous or ambivalent, though a concern with ambiguity and ambivalence is obviously present — obviously enough for the short novel to have generated an extraordinarily large amount of criticism which has notoriously quarrelled over interpretations and evaluations. That it appears ambiguous should not be surprising for Melville was obviously concerned with the problematics of meaning as the most cursory reading of *Moby Dick* indicates, and Melville overtly signalled that concern in the title of his next novel: *Pierre Or, The Ambiguities.* But the fact that the central debate (about a narrative that contains a slave revolt of all things) has revolved around the question of Melville's (or the narrative's) attitude to slavery and race should appear surprising when the novella is seen in its historical contexts (whether those contexts are defined as the general political situation, or Melville's literary career), for if there was one question that people were taking sides on in the 1850s in the United States it was slavery, and if evidence is taken from Melville's other pre-war writings, it is clear that he was antislavery in more than merely the racial context — if puzzled about the ways in which racial and other forms of oppression could be abolished. And the Supplement to *Battle-Pieces* seems clear enough:

Those of us who always abhorred slavery as an atheistical iniquity, gladly we join in the exulting chorus of humanity over its downfall. But we should remember that emancipation was accomplished not by deliberate legislation; *only through agonized violence could so mighty a result be effected.* (My emphasis)

These mysteries are, of course, important. But I want to argue that they can only be understood when seen in terms of the novella's form and genre: in other words, "Benito Cereno" is a mystery story in the conventional sense — the sense in which Chandler used the term when attempting to define different types of crime stories:

to indicate that type of story in which the search is not for a specific criminal, but for a raison d'être, a meaning in character and relationship, what the hell went on, rather than who done it. The story can be violent or calm, brutal or elegant, and there is always something to be discovered before the thing makes sense.[2]

I don't want to claim that this is an entirely original point, nor that calling "Benito Cereno" a mystery story in this semi-technical sense offers a final solution to the difficulties of the tale. I do want to argue that a recognition of the importance of narrative form and literary genre will at least improve our definitions of the complexities that confront the reader, and will help us to see how the story relates to the history and politics that it springs from and is so deeply about.

The narrative suspense that is one key element of the mystery-story genre is deployed in such a way as to foreground history and politics yet to make those terms problematic — problematic because "Benito Cereno" is not a conventional detective story. It lacks the explanatory authority the detective provides — however morally or politically ambiguous that figure was at that early moment in the genre's history. That is why I insist on calling it a mystery story — for it is a detective story where the reader on reading and, crucially, *rereading* the story has to learn not only to be the detective who could have solved the crime, but to decide what the crime was and who the real criminal is. Kermode, in an article which has many suggestive comments on novels of detection, quotes Raymond Queneau as asking for "'an ideal detective story' in which not only does the criminal remain unknown but one has no clear idea whether there has even been a crime or who the detective is." Charles Rycroft suggests that "the reader is not only the detective; he is also the criminal" and "in the ideal detective story the detective . . . would discover that he himself is the criminal for whom he has been seeking."[3] Both might have found "Benito Cereno" a suggestive text with still more radical implications. These are points I shall return to — but I want now to suggest that the rereader/detective may, as he learns the meanings of the clues both cultural and narrative, have to indict himself in his avatar as first reader as criminal, or at the least, as an (unconscious) accomplice of an ideology he may consciously repudiate.

II

One of the points which lurked behind much debate at the conference* was the question of the canon — how it has been established, how it is maintained, and what implications its existence has for questions of literary value. (Just which titles and authors constitute the canon was not really discussed: I would argue that it is less stable a construct than others took it to be and that this is particularly true of American literature. And — at least in the case of the novel — connections with popular genres are almost always importantly present.) That Melville is *now* part of the canon, however, is sufficiently clear but his emergence as a "classic" is a modern (even in some readings a modernist) phenomenon and the history of his reputation should make it crystal clear that "the canon" is the product of historical forces — however history is to be defined here. Obviously a history of (educational) institutions would be central; less obviously and more problematically we may have to rebuke history (in the form of past readers) for obtuseness. This is at least potentially a political point for it may involve seeing Melville as subversive, as challenging conventional ideas about the literary, about value. His contemporaries' valuation of Melville as the man who lived among cannibals, as very largely the author of *Typee* and *Omoo,* and the subsequent long neglect (amply evidenced by what was not in print) provide an exemplary instance for debate about canon formation and the formulation of questions about literary value.[4] "Benito Cereno" provides an example of this process. Published in *Putnam's* after an unenthusiastic reader's report, reprinted in *The Piazza Tales* (which were poorly reviewed and sold badly), it was not republished until the rediscovery of Melville. Since then it has appeared as a story which has seemed to demand interpretation and resist interrogation to such an extent that over merely the last half century it has given rise to an extraordinarily large amount of criticism and polemic even allowing for criticism as a growth industry and American criticism of American literature as a boom area.

I don't intend to rehearse the whole debate because most of it can be boiled down, like blubber, to

two or three main positions against which I want to position my argument that all are flawed by their failure to ask the right questions, to see the real problems that each position contains, united as they are by a shared implicit or explicit "liberal" ideology. However diverse the recent interpretations, it doesn't take any ingenuity to discover areas of consensus: all accept, for example, that one can't be overtly racist, none feel the need to explain why slavery is wrong — though it is only fair to note that the formalist readings "permit" a racist reading.[5] (Whatever else the criticism shows, it demonstrates how strong the "community" of critical discourse is — which defines the sayable.) The first interpretation is that "Benito Cereno" is a metaphysical meditation on the mysteries of iniquity and that these meanings are deployed through a conventional ahistorical colour symbolism. As Cardwell puts it with acid clarity:

> By interpretation of this kind the story falls . . . into a coherent, orderly pattern of meaning. Don Benito is pure good; Babo is pure evil; and Delano sees the essential nature of the world clearly, and sees it as a perfect dichotomy.

But one can only claim that "Slavery is not the issue here; the focus is upon evil in action" if one uses myth/symbol criticism to evade questions of politics and morality — if the historical moment of the narrative's production is denied and Melville's other statements about slavery and racism ignored. The elimination of any consideration of narrative sequence in favour of static symbolic antitheses, the conversion of characters into abstract moral quantities, convert it into a mythic fable, a technical exercise in moral speculation totally removed from social morality. Second: that Melville is (in this story at least) an apologist for racism and/or slavery — or that, and this is more problematic a point and more valid a reading) that the story can be so read without obvious distortion. This interpretation has been reluctantly assented to by good liberals like Matthiessen, unable to celebrate a literature dependent on metaphysical abstraction, well aware that formalist readings are essentially reactionary:

> the embodiment of good in the pale Spanish captain and of evil in the mutinied African crew, though pictorially and theatrically effective, was unfortunate in raising unanswered questions. Although the Negroes were savagely vindictive and drove a terror of blackness into Cereno's heart,

---

*This paper was first presented at the Faborg Conference on American Studies in Transition, June 1984 — ED.

the fact remains that they were slaves and that evil thus had originally been done to them. Melville's failure to reckon with this fact within the limits of his narrative, makes its tragedy, for all its prolonged suspense, comparatively superficial.

The judgement might stand if "Benito Cereno" were not an historical fiction (as its first sentence should have indicated to so intelligent a reader) where history is internalized within the fictional narrative in the form of clues which need to be decoded — and if the function of the suspense form had not been ignored. (One might also ask if there is not a place for a literature of questions?) A stronger version of this position is Kaplan's in his lengthy piece "Herman Melville and the American National Sin":

> It is Babo, the prototype of innate depravity, who, like an unrepentant villain, an Iago indeed, gazes "unabashed" from his death's head of unfathomably malign subtlety at the goodness he murdered. For Melville, in his story, Babo was a victor in the malign sense only . . .
>
> [L]ooked at objectively, the tale seems . . . an "artistic sublimation" not . . . of anti-slaveryism, but rather of notions of black primitivism dear to the hearts of slavery's apologists, a sublimation in fact of all that was sleazy, patronizing, backward and fearful in the works that preceded it. It is to put the matter too mildly perhaps to say, as Charles Neider does, that "Melville glosses over extenuating circumstances in his effort to blacken the blacks and whiten the whites, to create poetic images of pure evil and pure virtue," so that the result is "sometime unfortunate in the feelings it arouses against the Negro" . . .
>
> [I]n "Benito Cereno," the fear and doubt of slave-revolt proclaimed in *Mardi* and implied in *White-Jacket* were . . . transmuted into hatred of the "ferocious pirates" of the *San Dominick*.[6]

My rejection of Kaplan's "reluctant conclusion" is, in a sense, this article. But the points he (and Neider) raise must be answered, not bypassed or suppressed. Here I would simply note that he has not asked why slavery is wrong — and agree (indeed, insist) that there is nothing in the story to forbid a Southern planter of the 1850s from having most of his prejudices and fears of his black slaves reinforced. (Only rape fantasies are omitted.) However, a dialectical reading turns the argument back on Kaplan: what the Southerner then has to *exclude* is the fantasy of paternalism, of the happy black singing as he toils in the cotton fields. The fuller the assent to this reading

the heavier the price: the fantasy of the Southerner's virtue may be sustained (as Cereno continues to insist on his innocence) — but his confidence in his slaves' assent to that self-definition, and in his own security cannot be. Melville's strategy towards the Southern reader may be more subtle and radical than mere open moral rebuke could be. We usually have defenses against our overt opponents — and by the 1850s the slavocracy had had a large amount of practice in erecting them. But, ironically, to endorse one half of what was a profoundly divided attitude towards the slave is potentially unbalancing and secretly subversive. To agree with this reading of the Negro is to limit belief in the usefulness of one's benevolence, in the existence of gratitude and thus increases oppression, unmasks the ideology, makes conflict and rebellion more likely. As Melville wrote in *White-Jacket* (Ch. XXXV), "It is next to idle at the present day, merely to denounce an iniquity. Be ours, then, a different task."

To argue that Melville allows for "misreading" and even in this misreading (which locates the origins of the evil in the wrong place and misdefines its nature) maintains his subversive intended effect is not to suggest that the Southerner is the principal addressee: "Benito Cereno's" appearance in the anti-slavery *Putnam's* is sufficient proof that he or she is to be found elsewhere. The problem of the Northern liberal reader I shall attempt to discuss later. The left-liberals constitute my third category with their argument that Melville is clearly anti-slavery, anti-racist and for insurrection — and that he is to be approved for his correct attitudes. Carolyn Karcher and Marvin Fisher have offered the strongest version of this position as one would expect of critics who are self-consciously products of the 1960s and 70s. As Fisher puts it: "the story . . . becomes a kind of underground revenge tragedy of a 'bad dude' who was 'offed' because he 'had it all together.'"[7] They claim that experience of the Civil Rights movement, of the Black Muslims, of the political claims of the Third World advantages our readings. This, or something like this, is, I must confess, the conclusion I want to think correct — but for all their intelligence and their historical knowledge (especially true of Karcher), in their haste to claim Melville for liberal democratic radicalism they evade the difficulties of the story, suppressing the objections raised by Matthiessen and Kaplan. Whatever else we are getting, it isn't a reading of the text which recognizes the ways in which it resists easy incorporation into a liberal politics. In their tendency to read the text through contemporary spectacles, slavery gets less attention than racism—which, when taken with the worthy liberalism that is a reaction to racism, means that we get a (sentimental) rhetoric where the portrayal of a black as anything other than virtuous is likely to be defined as racist. (One critic has even complained that the blacks in *White-Jacket* are given funny names—which is to ask for propaganda rather than critical mimesis). This can too easily lead to an inverted racism which unintentionally patronizes in its refusal to give full moral responsibility to the black, which refuses to see that the history of the political structures of slavery and racism are not necessarily related. (Of course there may always be a strong understandable tendency for slaveholders to salve their consciences by defining their slaves as of another race, as less than fully human—but the reverse does not hold. It is perfectly possible to be an ardent abolitionist and a racist—as the history of American abolition repeatedly if regrettably shows.) This leads to another problem with this kind of reading: given this (uncritical) valuation of the blacks' means and ends, how is Delano to be situated? To define him as stupid or morally imperceptive for failing to see the true state of affairs aboard the *San Dominick*—isn't this to be in danger of devaluing Babo's magnificent work as actor-manager—and the performance of the supporting cast? It isn't the Southerner alone who is in danger of falling into an ironic trap. But the most serious gap in this kind of reading is the failure to confront the problems resulting from one unquestionable piece of historical information modern readers do have: our knowledge of the source from which Melville took his story—one (if only one) certain origin.

III

That Ch. XVIII of Amasa Delano's *Narrative of Voyages and Travels* (Boston, 1817) was the primary source for "Benito Cereno" has been known since 1929; it has not generally been accepted, however, that an exploration of the relations between the two is crucial for an understanding of what kind of story it is. Yet given Melville's obsessive interest in the relations between "fact" and "fiction," given the meditations on the difficult relations between realities and realisms in *The Confidence-Man*, given the implausibility of the story—an implausibility located not in the fact of a slave revolt but in the convincing willed miming of servitude and the enforced miming of mastery—the fact that there is a source and that it is true is, surely, crucial. I regret that Melville did not keep the note to which he refers in a letter to his publishers (which presumably authenticated the narrative much as the preface to *Israel Potter* does) when the title of the book changed from *Benito Cereno and Other Sketches* to *The Piazza Tales*. If he had, he would have eliminated the time-wasting response of one kind of reader—that the story *cannot* be true—though obviously a contrary argument can be mounted. The questions "Could it happen? Is it possible?" could then be read as constituting much of the intended response to the narrative. But, of course, the point is not constituted as a question but as a (negative) assertion—"The story must be rejected because it is unrealistic: what it tells could not have happened, could not happen." And that is to allow the reader to ally himself with the legal tribunal who "inclined to the opinion that the deponent . . . raved of some things which could never have happened"—except that for "deponent" such a reader would say "author" (as, of course, some did of *Typee*). However, we cannot read like that today: the story *qua* paraphrasable report is in one obviously crucial sense history—something that actually happened—and the fact that Melville expanded and restructured an original is *now* an inescapable part of our reading.[8] I want to argue that it is not just that we cannot or should not want to escape that knowledge but that an adequate reading of the story of "Benito Cereno" is dependent on a reading of Delano's narrative.

Most of the specific, detailed changes have, naturally enough, been noted by critics drawing attention to the changes that support a specific case. But those detailed changes when looked at cumulatively don't seem to me to give any great comfort to either the formalists or the left liberals. They can, however, seem to provide melancholy evidence for the case so reluctantly mounted by Kaplan. The formalist anti-historical, "apolitical" readings are condemned by the very evidence they adduce. One must agree that Melville transforms the direct, plain style of the original into a language which contains metaphor and insists on a symbolic reading, which makes the prose more "significant," complicating the relation to the referent (or, at least, multiplying the referents). But the nature of the symbolization needs to be taken into account: the symbols are, crucially, cultural/ historical. To take one obvious example, the name of the Spanish ship is changed from the Tryal (a name which would have served Melville perfectly well if metaphysical moral debate had been his major concern and odd enough to call attention to itself) to the San Dominick. Our knowledge of that clue enables us to decode the multilayered signal thus: San Dominick → Santo Domingo → black slave revolt *and* San Dominick → Dominicans (Black Friars/Jacobins) → Black Jacobins.[9] The actions of the blacks are thus placed in an historical context and situated politically. The "thickening" of the prose is a way of generalizing and historicizing the story, of converting it from an interesting tale where the interest lies in its oddness into one which has representative, typical significance, changing it from chronicle to history.

However, this is only to argue for the centrality of history as a subject of the story: it is not to say anything about Melville's attitude towards that history. There can be no doubt that the changes made seem in general to go against the liberal reading of the story: the blacks are blackened and Benito Cereno as a self-conscious moral agent is morally better in Melville's text than he is in the original. Benito Cereno in the original, for example, tries to stab a slave. Delano immediately caught hold of him, took away his dirk, and threatened him

> with the consequences of my displeasure, if he attempted to hurt one of them. Thus I was obliged to be continually vigilant, to prevent them from using violence towards these wretched creatures.

He also tries to do Delano out of his salvage rights and clearly is alive and well and entirely unbroken by the experience when Delano sails away. In the original the idea of deception is Cereno's — "to appease and quiet" the blacks.[10] In Melville's version, it is Babo's. Perhaps most important is the fate of Aranda. In the original he is killed because the blacks felt that they "could not otherwise obtain their liberty," but, that done, he is then disposed of overboard. In Melville's tale,

> the negro Babo came to the place where the deponent was, and told him that he had determined to kill his master . . . both because he and his companions could not otherwise be sure of their liberty, and that to keep the seamen in subjection, he wanted to prepare a warning of what road they should be made to take did they or any of them oppose him; and that, by means of the death of Don

Alexandro, that warning would best be given . . . (p. 293)

> During the three days which followed, the deponent, uncertain what fate had befallen the remains of Don Alexandro, frequently asked the negro Babo where they were, and, if still on board, whether they were to be preserved for interment ashore, entreating him so to order it; that the negro Babo answered nothing till the fourth day, when at sunrise, the deponent coming on deck, the negro Babo showed him a skeleton, which had been substituted for the ship's proper figure-head — the image of Christopher Colon, the discoverer of the New World; that the negro Babo asked him whose skeleton that was, and whether, from its whiteness, he should not think it a white's; that upon discovering his face, the negro Babo, coming close, said words to this effect: "Keep faith with the blacks from here to Senegal, or you shall in spirit, as now in body, follow your leader". . . (p. 295)

No matter whether we infer cannibalism either because of our fantasies or because of Melville's (cf. *Typee*), or even because of mere practicality (how else can one get clean white bones after a mere three days?), it is clear that something unspeakably nasty happens down in the hold:

> Yan was the man who . . . willingly prepared the skeleton . . . in a way the negroes afterwards told the deponent, but which he, so long as reason is left him, can never divulge. (p. 301)

It is Melville who invents this space for horror, this opportunity for anti-black fears, as it is Melville who repetitiously hammers home the negritude of Babo. No matter how we may defend the action as effective terrorism or as witty symbolism, Melville chose to present a Cereno who thinks of himself as "innocent . . . the most pitiable of all men" (p. 306), and a Babo who is not only a rebel but a sadistic terrorist.[11]

That the blacks are blackened and the whites whitewashed is, then, unquestionable: the question as to why is more problematic (except, of course, for the narrow formalist) — but it seems to me to be dependent on the most radical, important and neglected change between source and novella. (It is also the most obvious — at least to the dedicated reader of mystery stories.) In the original there is no narrative suspense, no narrative secret. The story is told at least three times: first, there is the impersonal authority of the ship's log — a couple of pages long; second, we have Delano's recollections; third, we are given the court documents which include Delano's testimony (supported by his midshipman) as well as that of Benito Cereno. The shifting points of view have considerable interest in raising questions of narrative authority. But, in essence, we know the story after half a page—insofar as the story is constituted by the slave revolt and the dramatic deceiving of Delano.

Melville tells the reader towards the end of "Benito Cereno" that narrative suspense realized through a disruption of narrative sequence has been a deliberate and necessary strategy:

> Hitherto the nature of this narrative, besides rendering the intricacies in the beginning unavoidable, has more or less required that many things, instead of being set down in the order of occurrence, should be retrospectively or irregularly given; this last is the case with the following passages, which will conclude the account. (p. 304)

But what does Melville mean here? The story did not *have* to be told this way. The evidence of the source proves that it is a willed choice by the author to structure the narrative this way—to begin with a statement that insists on history, on a time and a place, to continue into a mystery story, to provide an apparent solution with Benito Cereno's legal deposition and to "conclude" with two scenes, two further "clues": first the conversation on board ship before the trial between Delano and Cereno (which suggests that Cereno may be a criminal who is unconscious of his guilt) and, second, the account of Babo's behavior after his defeat and his final fate—an account which returns us to the beginning of the story to reread, to discover the clues which we must then learn to decode to see what the solution—what, indeed, the problem—is.

On first reading, what is happening (or, perhaps, that should read what has happened or even what will have happened)[12] is concealed as we follow Delano through, watching him, watching with him, as he tries to interpret what seems to be happening—with considerable if biassed intelligence (as I shall try to show later). We *may* guess on that first (forgotten?) reading what the real state of affairs is aboard the San Dominick, but we do not, cannot know—until the leap into the boat:

> All this, with what preceded, and what followed, occurred with such involutions of rapidity, that past, present, and future seemed one. (p. 283)

History, narrative, even temporality seem to be collapsed into an instantaneous moment of confusion and seeming revelation—which moves into the construction of narrative as Delano, in understanding what is going on, discovers another narrative which replaces the tale that Cereno has so repeatedly told him and tried to establish as a realistic and coherent story all through that dreary threatening day:

> That moment, across the long-benighted mind of Captain Delano, a flash of revelation swept, illuminating, in unanticipated clearness, his host's whole mysterious demeanour, with every enigmatic event of the day, as well as the entire past voyage of the San Dominick. (p. 284)

If we accept Chandler's so-called "Casual Notes on the Mystery Novel" as authoritatively informative, Melville's achievement is to be celebrated:

> The mystery novel must have enough essential simplicity of structure to be explained easily when the time comes. The ideal denouement is the one in which everything is made clear in a brief flash of action.

This is precisely what we get as Babo aims with a dagger "at the heart of his master, his countenance lividly vindictive, expressing the centred purpose of his soul" (p. 283):

> A writer who can achieve this once is to be congratulated. The explanation need not be short . . . and often cannot be short. The important thing is that it should be interesting in itself, something that the reader is anxious to hear, not a story with a new or unrecognizable set of characters . . . The solution, once revealed, must seem to have been inevitable.
> (pp. 64, 65)

Chandler's comments don't stop here in their usefulness. It may be, for example, that an alert reader has intuited the correct "solution" (but how hard this is to say with confidence and honesty: so many of such intuitions are possible conclusions that flash across one's mind as one anticipates—much as, in a different kind of novel, one speculates on who the hero/heroine will marry). But Chandler has an answer:

> The mystery must elude a reasonable intelligent reader. This, and the problem of honesty are two of the most baffling elements in mystery writing. Some of the best detective stories do not elude an intelligent reader to the end . . . But it is one thing

to guess the final solution and quite another to be able to justify the guess by reasoning. (p. 65)

This deals nicely with the irritating and otherwise irrefutable claim of the kind of reader who claims (and perhaps believes) that he had "really" known what was going on all along. More important is Chandler's comment that "the point of the mystery story" is "that it is two stories in one: the story of what happened and the story of what appeared to have happened." (p. 68) That this is suggestive for a formal analysis of the structure of "Benito Cereno" is, I hope, clear. That this definition has implications for the question of political content will, I hope, emerge later.

By using Chandler I am trying to show that serious political meanings are being mediated through the form of the mystery story—and that many of the conventional critical problems have to be reformulated when "Benito Cereno" is located within the genre. Those critics who mention the mystery story element have done so apologetically. A not unfair version goes like this: "Benito Cereno" may look very like a detective story with Delano as a Watson minus Holmes, but, of course, Melville is an artist and "Benito Cereno" is literature; therefore, it is much better than any mere detective story could be. This élitism is more serious than might at first appear. The mystery story element (which is to say the very form of the story) is repressed as we are taken off into the empyrean of "literature" with apologies for having debased Melville by mentioning his work in the same breath as a low, vulgar popular form. However, we do now have the very real advantage that the mystery story is no longer something that academics have to apologize for reading or writing about (or are coyly amusing about reading or writing—what might be called the Oxford don syndrome). There are two not always complementary reasons for this: first, the growing academic respectability of an interest in and respect for popular culture, and second, the obsession with narrative theory—and the mystery story is a wonderful way of starting to think about narrative.

IV

The mystery/detective story, involving as it does so clearly questions of crime and punishment, confronts questions of authority in society. It is not necessarily on the side of "duly constituted" authority—though

it very frequently has been. Its author may not *consciously* engage with questions about the sources and legitimacy of (social) authority (in other words with history and society) but a full reading of such stories will necessarily need to do so. (Those critics who claim that the detective story is not "political" are to a man or woman conservative who see a conservative world view as "natural.") One form of that alliance between the authority of the detective and conservative notions of social order can be seen in Poe's mystery fiction. Richard Godden has made the connections apparent in an excellent article "Edgar Allan Poe and the Detection of Riot"[13]—which, in the connections it makes between problems of social order thrown up by Jacksonian rioting and Poe's detective fiction as responding to this, in its analysis of the relations between Poe's work and southern conservatism, suggests a fascinating and revealing contrast between his attitude to law and order and Melville's. (The contrast is at its clearest when "Benito Cereno" is set against Poe's work—though "Bartleby" might be another radical mystery story whose radicalism is revealed in opposition to Poe—with as problematic a "crime" as in "Benito Cereno" and as well-meaning a detective.) I don't want to repeat Godden's argument here which seems to me to be quite conclusive in its broad outlines but only to add a confirmatory footnote—starting from the explicit connection between the authority of Poe's detective and the fear of riot that appears in "The Mystery of Mary Rogêt." This, of course, was Poe's fictive treatment of a real case, the death of Mary Cecilia Rogers near New York, and, as such, the story is a useful parallel and contrast. Poe competes with reality, with history, and attempts in his commitment to the "ideal" to write the future, to anticipate authority: Melville meditates on history, *interprets* it, *re*writes it. And, ironically, in that rewriting he is the more prescient than Poe.

In Poe's story the reward for the "conviction of the assassin . . . stood at no less than thirty thousand francs." This, the narrator tells us, "will be regarded as an extraordinary sum when we consider the *humble condition of the girl and the great frequency in large cities of such atrocities* as the one described." (My emphasis.) There is, however, good reason for this enormous reward for the solution of a commonplace murder of an insignificant and commonplace individual. The "prejudice which always exists in Paris against the Police" had given "vent to itself in several *émeutes*" — so the Prefect of Police and a committee of no doubt solid citizens had made up the sum and the Prefect calls in the undoubtedly aristocratic Dupin to help him. The fact that *"émeute"* translates as riot needs no comment: it is the fear of social disorder, not the desire for justice which originates the reward. "The Mystery of Marie Rogêt" would seem to bear out H. Bruce Franklin's contention only too neatly:

> The narrative of the detective appears only after the consolidation of bourgeois power. The bourgeoisie, having emerged from its origin as an illegitimate, even outlaw class, now begins to view the question of crime and criminals from the point of view of the establishment, of law and order.[14]

Poe seems to feel no need to ask *why* a prejudice against the police should exist. It is internalized within his narrative as something "natural" and inevitable. He does not ponder the possibility that the lower orders may legitimately feel that the police are unconcerned by the fate of an unimportant girl of uncertain sexual morals. It is symptoms, not causes, that the story registers. Order must be preserved — and if the police have to buy the services of a decadent aristocrat to preserve that order and their reputation, then it is a price well worth the paying.

That question of social order so explicitly raised in this story is equally present in Poe's other detective fiction. In "The Murders in the Rue Morgue," the analogue for the mob is, in Godden's words "an ape with a razor, loose in a street called Charnal," while detective Dupin is, in Poe's words, "of an excellent — indeed of an illustrious family." In "The Purloined Letter," adultery in the highest places must be condoned and concealed so that social order can be preserved. (Interestingly, Dupin distracts the attention of D — when he changes the letters by getting a man to shoot off a musket, sure that this would guarantee the "screams" and "shoutings of a mob.") In "The Gold-Bug" Legrand solves the riddle of Captain Kidd's secret code, and, by finding the pirate's stolen hoard, recovers his proper social status:

> He was of an ancient Huguenot family, and had once been wealthy; but a series of misfortunes had reduced him to want. To avoid the mortification consequent upon his disasters, he left New Orleans, the city of his forefathers . . .

The story starts from a problem in nature (the identity of the gold-bug) but it moves into dealing with questions of the meaningless insect: "This bug is to make my fortune . . . to reinstate me in my family possessions." History is manipulated by Poe into the recovery of lost treasure — which is equivalent to a kind of pre-history: "There was no American money." But while Legrand may retrieve the means by which he may publicly display his social status, in one way he has maintained it all along. Even at his lowest point.

> he was usually accompanied by an old negro . . . who had been manumitted before the reverses of the family, but who could not be induced, neither by threats nor by promises, to abandon what he considered his right of attachment upon the footsteps of his young "Massa Will."

This, of course, is the relationship that Babo so brilliantly parodies. Legrand is, as it were, a successful Cereno — and the narrator of "The Gold-Bug" and Delano have points in common as they both try to make sense of a character. Both stories are concerned with the recovery of social order and status — but "Benito Cereno" radically questions the terms by which that order is violently maintained as is indicated by the narrative disruption that follows the trial and with the silent interrogatory gaze of Babo that concludes the tale.

V

Here I must quarrel with Godden's argument that not only is Poe's detective fiction anti-democratic but that the genre is essentially and necessarily authoritarian:

> Getting to the end of "Murders in the Rue Morgue" (or *Farewell, My Lovely*) has less than one might imagine to do with discovering who did it, or even how it was done or why; instead, it revolves around justifying our initial and simple acceptance of the detective's authority over fact and time — that is, over history. It may be objected that the whole point about detective fiction is that it has narrative pace . . . — a great deal goes on, but only because something is going on repeatedly, as the reader proves to himself, time and time again, that he has taken out a good contract with the Ultimate in Authority. (p. 207)

Hammett's work, *Trent's Last Case*, the reflections on the genre in Butor's *Passing Time* — all these in their differing ways should have made Godden realize that while one strand of the history of the genre may be conservative, there is another where the detective can be used to expose the structure of power in the society, where the discovery of corruption is not particular but general. Even the school of Mayhem Parva (the butler dunnit and the body-is-in-the-library school) must include the notion that anyone *may* be guilty—even the faithful retainer. It may be objected that the guilt of the butler means a class security ("At least it's not one of us"), and that the opening up of potential guilt is more apparent than real—that the solution, the ending of the novel, is so strong that any wider implications are introduced only to be rejected. But the point remains that no class or category are self-evidently guiltless (to say nothing of the other guilty secrets which are revealed on the way to the solution of the principal crime). To generalize from Poe and Chandler is to generalize from only one "history": There is undoubtedly a radical history beginning from Godwin's *Caleb Williams*—and the origins of the detective story spring from the ambivalent Vidocq:

> it was Vidocq who "first struck the European imagination as the detective". . . because he embodied in one person both the thief-taker and the thief. Vidocq's importance rested in his nature as the archetypal ambiguous figure of the criminal who is also a hero. The . . . doubt about whether a particular character is hero or villain is an essential feature of the crime story, and Vidocq embodied it in his own person. (Symons, pp. 30, 29)

I am not suggesting any direct influence—but Melville did acquire *Caleb Williams* in 1849 and, we learn from *White-Jacket,* had either read or read of Vidocq (Ch. XLIV).

To claim that the detective has an improper authority over a history that seems reduced to repetition is surely perverse—unless Godden wants to take a radically skeptical attitude towards any historiographical project. One of the detective's key roles is analogous to the historian's task—it is precisely to construct/discover a true, secular narrative to replace the false story (even the amnesia) which the criminal has tried to establish. (And one might add that the Ultimate in Authority is, surely, ultimately, a creative power—which is just what the detective is not—and what the criminal may be.) To discover how the crime was done and why, to define the crime

as a crime, can be a radical criticism. Ann Douglas puts the point as it relates to Melville nicely and provocatively:

> Melville defined the test which every formidable American author in his day and since has had to impose on himself: how to exploit and resist the crude American material which both enriches and impoverishes the writer; how to take the exact measure of the reader who belongs to and is that material, how to know him utterly and intimately without being absorbed by him . . . Increasingly over the course of Melville's career, his protagonists—Ishmael, Pierre, Captain Amasa Delano, the lawyer in "Bartleby, the Scrivener" come to mind—become proto-detectives, and Melville's own undoubtedly hostile conception of the American writer's task becomes exactly that of imagining his society's crime without enacting it.

She also makes the interesting if debatable point of *White-Jacket* that

> Melville is suggesting, in profound opposition to the tendencies of his culture, that the real "plot" on shipboard—and in the American society which shipboard life for Melville always symbolizes—is essentially political and class-oriented.
>
> This is a difficult problem but Melville was perhaps the first major American author to sense that the essential question for the American writer and intellectual was whether he was going to subscribe to what would be the Freudian or what would be the Marxist analysis of his culture—whether he would focus on personality or on societal structures as causal agents. It is worth noting that in all the narratives from which (American) women are excluded . . . Melville is interested primarily in questions of class: the clash between employer and employed, master and slave, government and soldier.[15]

As so often, Cooper seems to have been forgotten—and shouldn't (American) read (white, middle-class American)? More importantly, can the two categories be so easily separated? Isn't Douglas ignoring the Marxist commitment to the dialectic? Even if Pierre is an appallingly poor "proto-detective" (at least insofar as the question of the true identity of Isabel is concerned), the novel brings class and sex together in an interestingly poisonous mix. The infuriated contemporary reviewer was quite right when he said that, in *Pierre,* Melville was no "gentleman," who strikes with an "impious . . . hand at the very foundations of society." (Unfortunately, he was also right to describe that hand as "weak.") Commentary like this makes one understand why, in the short fiction of the 1850s, while Melville continued and extended that attack, giving an almost systematic critical perspective on most of the central institutions of the day (the law, the church, the home, industrialism, etc.), he mediated that criticism through irony and indirection. (When that protective irony slipped as it did in "The Two Temples," the story was rejected.) The destruction of confidence in these institutions is attempted through a whole bag of confidence tricks. Inextricably linked with the social criticism are experiments in narrative form — experiments which leave the successful reader (the rereader, that is to say) as a producer of meanings. (I must emphasize I mean the production of determinate meanings — not speculative invention: the meanings are produced in collaboration with the author. One example of this production is the episode when Babo appears on deck with a razor-cut on his cheek: we are never told that Babo cuts himself in order to sustain the drama for Delano. But on re-reading this cannot be doubted: any other interpretation would be a mis-reading.) The reader has to be the kind of detective who will read the deep narrative that underlies the harmless-seeming surface. Charvat in any excellent and historically informed piece suggests that, from *Mardi* on Melville,

> shifted to a kind of internal dialectic which gave the reader no choice. He involved him in the very processes of thought, made him collaborate in exploratory, speculative thinking which is concerned not with commitment but with possibility. It is the one kind of thinking that the general reader will not tolerate, and the nineteenth century reader, when he detected it, declared it subversive.[16]

Perhaps that "he" given the dominance of the female in the consumption of magazine material should read "s/he" — and whether "commitment" is so entirely absent (except in the sense of commitment to one's prejudices) is open to debate. But the point about subversion is clearly true — the genuinely affronted cries of the reviewers of *Pierre* is evidence enough of that. "The Paradise of Bachelors and the Tartarus of Maids" is an excellent example of the politicization of sex/the sexualization of politics, of social criticism enacted through a dialectical narrative structure. (How *did* Melville get this sexualization of "Signs of the Times" past Mrs. Grundy?) The

"dyptych" definition of this type of tale is inadequate in that it stresses the pictorial at the expense of the story/ies: the two elements set up a narrative tension — though we must construct very largely the "bridging" narrative and be prepared to read backwards as well as forwards. "Paradise" alone could not be read confidently as a criticism of those jolly bachelors — but rather as a celebration of the good (if self-indulgent) life. And the dehumanization/desexualization of the factory girls is felt the more because we construct the connection between the two worlds, the connections between class and sexual oppression.

VI

The "dyptych" definition does have the advantage of emphasizing the sequential apprehension of such narrative "bridges." I referred earlier (p. 13) to Chandler's suggestive point about the double narrative of the mystery story. He was drawing on Mary Roberts Rinehart, and her comment helps illuminate the more complex narrative structure of "Benito Cereno" — what might be called its "layering," a form in which two stories are being told simultaneously:

> the crime story . . . consists of two stories. One is known only to the criminal and to the author himself . . . The other story is the story which is told. It is capable of great elaboration and should, when finished, be complete in itself. It is necessary, however, to connect the two stories throughout the book. This is done by allowing a bit, here and there, of the hidden story to appear. It may be a clue, it may be another crime.

I want to suggest that this structure has its political implications. On first reading, one apparent structuring principle of the story (until the leap into the boat) is built around an opposition between Delano and Cereno and what they represent — the United States *versus* Spain, the North *versus* the South, Protestantism *versus* Catholicism, Democracy *versus* Aristocracy etc. etc. But with the revelation of the true state of affairs aboard the *San Dominick*, with the full emergence of "the hidden story" we see a consequent explicit alliance between Delano and Cereno. The binary oppositions we see are more apparent than real, are elided with the entry of the story of rebellion and revolt, with the emergence of Babo and the others in their chosen identities — and what they stand for: Africa, Paganism, etc. It is the entry of a third term and—to follow Fisher however a-historically—the third world. What follows that leap is a narrative which both involves the action which recaptures the ship (felt by both Delano and Cereno to be "natural") and re-establishes white control, and Cereno's story to the court which emphasizes white control over "historiography." (This is ironically undercut, however—note the repetition of the phrase "all this is believed, because the negroes have said it.") But that alliance between the two captains we realize on re-reading has always been latent (at the same time as we see the "bits" of the "hidden story" appearing—whether as clues or crimes). It is Cereno's belief in this alliance which permits his leap of faith.

The alliance is made manifest in the scene which comes between the deposition and the deaths of Babo and Cereno. That interpolation is a way of fore-grounding the terms of that alliance and of examining how complete the mutual understanding is, of speculating about the future:

> the two captains had many cordial conversations—their *fraternal* unreserve in singular contrast with former withdrawments.
> Again and again it was repeated, how hard it had been to enact the part forced on the Spaniard by Babo. (p. 304. My emphasis)

Whether shame or guilt generates the repetition is left open—as is the question why Cereno should have found the part so hard to play. In one sense, no role should have been easier. One irony of the story is that the revolt is in part enacted as a drama in which the characters play the parts that history has assigned them. It is notorious that this scene ends with Delano's incomprehension of Cereno's suffering silence. For those that hope that class rule and white supremacy will be broken this failure of fraternal understanding is hardly to be regretted—and Delano's appeal to nature has its satisfying narrative irony if we remember the authorial voice some thirty pages earlier, imagining the sea telling Cereno "that, sulk as he might, and go mad with it, nature cared not a jot; since, whose fault was it, pray?" (p. 278). It's a good question—if one that the reader is left to answer.

The story as a whole enacts the re-establishment of history—history as (criminal?) authority—which suppresses the utopian/nostalgic narrative the blacks aim to establish but cannot or will not publicly speak. Babo's (willed) silence guarantees that his discourse

will not be incorporated: Cereno *cannot* go further than "the negro" as a clue to his silence. The future of that history was a question of some centrality for the 1850s. The ending of "Benito Cereno" is open, problematic—not out of a liberal pluralism but because the history that Melville was living through is alive to just this set of issues. Will the North collaborate with the South to maintain a social order based on slavery (whether wage or chattel slavery: capitalism or feudalism)? Will the Union be preserved—and if so on what terms? Mild-mannered and otherwise law-abiding liberals became "revolutionary" lawbreakers on this very issue. Melville was in a remarkable position to *know* what was going on. His father-in-law to whom he had dedicated *Typee* in his role as "Chief Justice of the Commonwealth of Massachusetts" was not only one of the most massively influential figures in the history of the American judiciary but was also involved in the key fugitive slave law cases:

> The Chief Justice was a noted, strong opponent to slavery and expressed his opinion privately, in print and appropriate judicial opinions. Yet in the great *causes celebres* involving fugitive slaves, Shaw came down hard for an unflinching application of the harsh and summary law.[17]

One doesn't have to accept Cover's extremely persuasive suggestion that Vere's dilemma was modelled on Shaw's to see that Melville must have known about the whole debate, the dramatic tension between law and morals, public and private codes—and the question whether it was right to resort to violence.

While "Benito Cereno" comes from and reflects on the debates and conflicts of the 1850s, it stretches out from that history to offer itself as a meditation on the problematics of a certain kind of revolutionary situation, on American history (by which I mean the history of the Americas and therefore necessarily the history of Europe and Africa). This is an ambitious claim to make but it can be justified if we follow up the Santo Domingo reference and read that as an historical clue as well as a clue to the plot aboard ship—and if we take Genovese's points:

> By the end of the eighteenth century, the historical content of the slave revolts shifted decisively from attempts to secure freedom from slavery to attempts to overthrow slavery as a social system. The great black revolution in Saint-Domingue marked the turning-point. To understand this epoch-making shift, the revolts in the United States, or in any other

country, must be viewed in a hemispheric, indeed world, context.

"The role which the great Negro Toussaint, called l'Ouverture, played in the history of the United States," W. E. B. DuBois wrote almost eighty years ago, as might be written even now . . . "has seldom been appreciated." Developing a line of thought opened by Henry Adams, he argued that the revolution in Saint-Domingue enormously strengthened the antislavery movement in England and prepared the way for its flowering in America; that it ended Napoleon's dream of an American empire and led him to the sale of Louisiana, which doubled the size of the United States; and that it influenced, perhaps decisively, the decision of the southern states to close the African slave trade. In these as in so many ways, Haiti became, in the words Raul Castro used for Cuba in our own day, a small country with a big revolution.[18]

And "Benito Cereno" a small story with a big subject. If *White-Jacket* was subtitled *The World in a Man-of-War*, then the subtitle of "Benito Cereno" would be *World History in a Slave-Ship*.

But Melville doesn't lose touch with the hopes and anxieties of the contemporary situation — and the structure of the story speaks very precisely of and to those concerns. As a Northern abolitionist put it:

I have wondered in times past, when I have been so weak-minded as to submit my chin to the razor of a colored brother, as his sharp steel grazed my skin, the patience of the negro shaving the white man for many years, yet kept the razor outside of the throat . . .
    Behind all these years of shrinking and these long years of cheerful submission . . . there may lie a dagger and a power to use it when the time comes . . . We forget the heroes of Santo Domingo . . .

Santo Domingo was in no danger of being forgotten. As Mary Chesnut says, it was "indelibly printed" on the mind of the South — only there the blacks were seen as "the black terror" rather than as revolutionary heroes:

The image of black violence and retribution, drawn not only from Nat Turner, but from memories of what had occurred in Santo Domingo, continued to haunt the Southern imagination . . . In moments of candor, Southerners admitted their suspicion that duplicity, opportunism and potential rebelliousness lurked behind the mask of Negro affability.[19]

Melville's story is mimetic of social consciousness on both sides: whites fear what lies behind the blacks' servile smiles — blacks may "serve" but even if they do not overtly revolt, they play the role of slave rather than authentically live it. Here we can see how appropriate the form of "Benito Cereno" is for its theme: the problem of duplicity, of false meanings, of masks accompanied by the threat of hidden violence is precisely the problem that the mystery story needs and addresses.

VII

It is the basic theory of all mystery writing that at some stage of the proceedings the reader could, given the necessary acuteness, have closed the book and revealed the essence of the denouement. But this implies more than mere possession of the facts; it implies that the ordinary lay reader could honestly be expected to draw the right conclusion from these facts. The reader cannot be charged with special and rare knowledge . . . For if such were necessary, the reader did not in fact have the materials for the solution, he merely had the unopened packages they came in. (p. 66)

Chandler raises a number of important questions here — questions, for example, about our apprehension of narrative structure, questions about the "common reader" and the whole problem of audience. But his comment is particularly useful in focusing attention on what the necessary information is for the reader of "Benito Cereno." The relevant knowledge, I want to argue, is not that of (say) "special and rare" Oriental poisons but rather a different *kind* of knowledge — social (political) knowledge. This is, of course, to open up the difficult questions of the knowledge we (need to) bring to the text — and the knowledge we can (perhaps) acquire from literature — to suggest that "Benito Cereno" has a didactic dimension. This has to lead on to the vexed question of Delano. Half the brickbats thrown at him seem to me to have been motivated by our embarrassed irritation at sharing his failure, our annoyance at following him up the garden path so neatly constructed by Babo accompanied by a tendency to discuss him as though he were a literary critic or a detective — an Empson or a Holmes safely ensconced in a book-lined study with time to ratiocinate and re-examine the evidence. To claim that he should have solved the case — isn't that to confuse life and art, captaincy and criticism? To claim that Delano should have seen through the production that Babo has mounted is to get very close to saying that Babo's was somehow a flawed drama, that it wasn't really good enough to fool an acute white (which is to allow racism in through the back door). This can impale the liberal on the horns of a dilemma. The way out of this problem is to ask what knowledge is required (that Delano lacks) to see the true state of affairs and at the same time to ask how far Delano is in the "god-like" position of the classic detective.

One problem he has which differentiates him from such a figure is that he does not *know* that a "crime" has been committed. (Nor do we—on first reading—and the fact that we neither get a "confession" from Babo nor a verdict from the court suggests that Melville is leaving the question open.) Delano has to detect that there is something to detect. The detective usually only starts acting after the originating event (the murder, say) has been discovered. Delano enters after that origin but without knowing what the beginnings of that narrative are and faced by a plausible cover story—though he constructs the real narrative with remarkable speed when he gets the right clue. To define him as stupid is itself stupid: if Delano is not a "real" detective, he is a remarkably good detective's assistant—if the reader accepts that role. To take one example, he "speculates" on the peculiarities of the captain and crew:

> First, the affair of the Spanish lad assailed with a knife by the slave boy; an affair winked at by Don Benito. Second, the tyranny in Don Benito's treatment of Atufal, the black; as if a child should lead a bull of the Nile by the ring in his nose. Third, the trampling of the sailor by the two negroes; a piece of insolence passed over without so much as a reprimand. Fourth, the cringing submission to their master of all the ship's underlings, mostly blacks; as if by the least inadvertence they feared to draw down his despotic displeasure. (p. 258)

Melville even uses Delano to nudge the reader still further:

> If Don Benito's story was, throughout, an invention, then every soul on board, down to the youngest negress, was his carefully drilled recruit in the plot: an incredible inference. And yet, if there was ground for mistrusting his veracity, that inference was a legitimate one. (pp. 245–6)

Delano fails for one reason—racism in one of its formulations.

> The whites . . . by nature were the shrewder race . . . But if the whites had dark secrets concerning Don Benito, could then Don Benito be any way in complicity with the blacks? But they were too stupid. Besides, who ever heard of a white so far a renegade as to apostatize from his very species almost, by leaguing in against it with negroes? (p. 254)

The liberal reader on returning to this passage must ask himself a painful question: if he failed to solve the mystery, wasn't the reason that he (however unconsciously) shares (or, hopefully, shared) Delano's racism? (Or at least that he was willing to accept this kind of racism as a "reliable" part of the narrative.) The knowledge he needed was not only that blacks are intelligent but that slaves are always ready to rebel. If I am right, then the reader has had to learn to be the detective—and to indict himself as criminal. There is, however, a danger that he may commit a worse crime. Whatever else white readers learn, we can no longer believe that blacks are stupid. But that definition may only be displaced to be replaced by a vision of the blacks as satanically clever.

Insofar as "Benito Cereno" is a *detective* story, it is one of a peculiar kind best described by Grossvogel (in *Mystery and Its Fictions*)—as a detective story where "detective" is adjectival since there is no detective to invite identification. (We may identify with Delano on first reading but in subsequent readings we distance ourselves from him—sometimes unfairly and try to situate him within the total narrative.) Such a story, Grossvogel argues, then invites the reader to participate in the unfolding of the story, to play the "game" actively rather than through the passivity of a demonstration. (The relevance of this to Charvat's description of Melville's literary strategy needs no comment.) It is a deliberately risky strategy—but Melville's point is that passive demonstration, simplistic moral assertion is likely to be counterproductive. To repeat that suggestive passage from *White-Jacket* (Ch. XXXV), "It is next to idle, at the present day, merely to denounce an iniquity. Be ours, then, a different task." It is a strategy with two (or more) moves. If the definition of the blacks as stupid children is replaced by a definition of them as evil, we are faced with a choice. Either one is left with a racist metaphysics and repression is the only political response—or the genetic question has to be asked: why are the slaves "evil"? Either way, the liberal view that the oppressed are the salt of the earth, with its sentimentality about the morality of the lowly has to be repudiated. "Benito Cereno," then, is to be read as rejecting the ideology of such works as *Uncle Tom's Cabin Or, Life Among The Lowly* — that T. W. Higginson acidly and accurately placed: "If it be the normal tendency of bondage to produce saints like Uncle Tom, let us all offer ourselves at auction immediately." A definition of the oppressed and exploited as uniquely virtuous is to risk feeling that they may be better off that way — and it's the greater a risk if one is committed to any form of otherworldliness such as Christianity. The point is — or should be — simple: slavery damages your moral health — whether you are a slaveowner or slave. As Equiano wrote,

> When you make men slaves you deprive them of half their virtue, you set them in your own conduct an example of fraud, rapine, and cruelty, and compel them to live with you in a state of war.[20]

But, of course, it is a particularly hard point for the (middle-class) liberal fully to internalize. It is difficult if one calls for justice for a class not to believe that the members of that class "deserve" justice — that they are morally worthy in terms of one's own moral discourse (a discourse which doesn't want them to be threatening). It is this truth that Melville is fully seized of and, in "Benito Cereno," successfully narratizes:

> It is to no purpose that you apologetically appeal to . . . general depravity . . . Depravity in the oppressed is no apology for the oppressor; but rather an additional stigma to him, as being, in a large degree, the effect, and not the cause and justification of oppression. (*White-Jacket*, Ch. XXXIV)

As Bell says,

> This is the classic revolutionary ideology; that all evil, finally, is social evil — that the evil unleashed by revolution is ultimately the product of the tyranny against which revolution is launched.[21]

and Babo's witty cruelty is justified for this is the ideology that informs "Benito Cereno."

"Ah, this slavery breeds ugly passions in man."

The function, then, of this mystery story is to enable us to read this sentence — to re-read the whole story in order to set it in the right, hidden narrative. All through "Benito Cereno" sentences change their meanings on re-reading. On first reading, we follow Delano (with the plausible "evidence" of Babo's cut cheek) in contextualizing it as referring to the guilt of the master. Another partial reading would say it is about the corruption of the slave — but Melville's di-

alectical narrative established that it is about their mutual (but not identical) corruption:

Slavery breeds ugly passions in *man.*

Notes

1. Anon. *Knickerbocker,* Sept. 1856, reprinted in Watson G. Branch (ed.), *Melville: The Critical Heritage* (London and Boston: Routledge and Kegan Paul, 1974), p. 359. C. L. R. James, *Mariners, Renegades and Castaways: The Story of Herman Melville and the World We Live In* (New York: C. L. R. James, 1953), p. 134.
2. Dorothy Gardiner and K. S. Walker (eds.), *Raymond Chandler Speaking* (New York: Houghton Mifflin, 1962), p. 57. Subsequent references will be placed parenthetically in the text.
3. Frank Kermode, *Essays on Fiction 1971–82* (London: Routledge and Kegan Paul, 1983), p. 61. Quoted in Julian Symons in *Bloody Murder: From the Detective Story to the Crime Novel* (Harmondsworth, Middlesex: Penguin, 1974), p. 13.
4. Fitzgerald, the other author who appeared under the heading of "the classic," has never really suffered from this problem. Valuations of *The Great Gatsby,* for example, have varied over the years — but Fitzgerald's work (whether seen as great or merely good) has been consistently regarded as worthy of serious critical debate — in a word (however problematic that word) as literature.
5. It would be interesting to read an analysis of the story by an overt racist or believer in slavery. George Fitzhugh's *Cannibals All* (1859) is a text which suggests how such a reading might be constituted.
6. Guy Cardwell, "Melville's Gray Story: Symbols and Meaning in 'Benito Cereno'," Bucknell Review VII (May 1959), p. 161. F. O. Matthiessen, *American Renaissance* (London and New York: Oxford University Press, 1968), p. 476. Sidney Kaplan, "Herman Melville and the American National Sin: The Meaning of 'Benito Cereno'," *Journal of Negro History,* XLI (October 1956), pp. 311–38, and XLII (January 1957), pp. 11–37, p. 27.
7. Marvin Fisher, *Going Under: Melville's Short Fiction and the American 1850s* (Baton Rouge and London: Louisiana State University Press, 1977), p. 107. Carolyn L. Karcher, *Shadow Over The Promised Land: Slavery, Race, and Violence in Melville's America,*

(Baton Rouge and London: Louisiana State University Press, 1980).

8. I have used this widely available edition: *Billy Budd, Sailor and Other Stories*, Selected and Edited with an Introduction by Harold Beaver (Harmondsworth, Middlesex: Penguin, 1967). All references will be placed parenthetically in text. The editor quotes long passages from Delano in the notes. The other paperback editions I have seen (such as Berthoff's) all mention the source—so the knowledge is hardly reserved for the scholarly community.

9. There is no need to explain how I get from San Dominick to Dominicans but perhaps I should explain that while the Dominicans were known as Black Friars in England, they were known as Jacobins in France—and the political Jacobins were so called because they met in an ex-convent of the Dominicans. I have argued this at more length in a note "The San Dominick, Blackfriars, and Jacobins" (*Journal of American Studies*, Vol. 19, No. 1, Spring 1985).

10. Amasa Delano, *A Narrative of Voyages and Travels in the Northern and Southern Hemispheres* (Boston: E. G. House, 1817), pp. 328, 336.

11. Indeed, the introduction of the possibility of cannibalism apparently plays into Southern hands: "According to the South Carolina novelist William Gilmore Simms, the Negro came from a continent where he was a cannibal, destined . . . to eat his fellow, or be eaten by him. 'Southern slavery brought him to a land in which he suffers no risk of life or limb other than that to which his owner is equally subjected' and had . . . elevated 'his mind and morals',," in G. M. Frederickson, *The Black Image in the White Mind* (New York and London, Harper and Row, 1979), p. 52.

12. See Robert Champigny, *What Will Have Happened: A Philosophical and Technical Essay on Mystery Stories* (Bloomington and London: Indiana University Press, 1977) for a defense of this term, and for an extremely stimulating (and frequently irritating) study of the genre.

13. Richard Godden, "Edgar Allan Poe and the Detection of Riot," *Literature and History*, Vol. 8 no. 2, Autumn 1982, p. 206.

14. H. Bruce Franklin, *The Victim as Criminal and Artist* (New York: Oxford University Press, 1978), p. 223.

15. Ann Douglas, *The Feminization of American Culture* (New York: Knopf, 1977), pp. 283, 288.

16. William Charvat, *The Profession of Authorship in America, 1800–1870* (Ohio State University Press, 1968), p. 268.

17. Robert M. Cover, *Justice Accused: Antislavery and the Judicial Process* (New Haven and London: Yale University Press, 1975), pp. 4–5.

18. E. D. Genovese, *From Rebellion to Revolution: Afro-American Slave Revolts in the Making of the Modern World* (New York: Vintage Books, 1981), pp. 3, 93. The cruelty of Babo of course has to be set against the cruelty of his punishment. This could not be dismissed as Spanish sadism: "The slaveholders of Louisiana who in 1811 spiked rebel heads to decorate the river road from New Orleans to Major André's plantation had not unleashed some early frontier temper that later generations would repudiate. In 1856 the slaveholders of Tennessee repeated the performance with a slight variation: they carried the impaled heads in a parade. And, unlike the Louisianians of 1811, they had not even confronted slaves in arms; their victims had only fallen under suspicion of insurrectionary design" (pp. 106–7).

19. Tilden G. Edelstein, *Strange Enthusiasm: A Life of Thomas Wentworth Higginson* (New Haven and London: Yale University Press, 1968), p. 211. George M. Frederickson, op. cit., p. 53. Higginson was writing for the converted in *The Liberator*—and attempting to cheer them up in 1858. Despite the eery parallelism with Melville, Higginson disliked his work. One of Melville's additions to the story was the blacks "cleaning" the hatchets—a "device . . . uniting deceit and defense." I can't help speculating that this would have recalled to the contemporary reader the widely reported attempt to break the fugitive slave Burns out of Boston jail in 1854. Higginson bought a dozen handaxes for this enterprise—getting (God bless Boston) a five per cent discount for cash. A number of blacks were involved in this adventure.

20. Quoted by Genovese (op. cit.), p. 109. I ought to add that many of Higginson's other comments about this text were less dismissive. *Equiano's Travels*, abridged and edited by Paul Edwards (London and Ibadan: Heinemann, 1967), p. 73. First published 1789. Equiano goes on to ask

"Are you not hourly in fear of an insurrection? Nor would it be surprising: for when '—No peace is given/To us enslav'd, but custody severe;/And stripes and arbitrary punishment/Inflicted—What peace can we return?/ But to our power, hostility and hate;/Untam'd reluctance, and revenge, though slow./Yet ever plotting how the conqueror least/May reap his conquest, and may least rejoice/In doing what we most in suffering feel.'" That use of Milton's rebel angel voice is—interesting.

21. M. D. Bell, *The Development of American Romance: The Sacrifice of Relation* (Chicago and London: University of Chicago Press, 1980), pp. 201–2.

APPLICATION

Convention Coverage or How to Read Your Own Life

Jean E. Kennard

Just as Annette Kolodny poses a feminist challenge to Harold Bloom's intertextual reading in Chapter 3, Jean E. Kennard here questions the theories of Frye, Culler, Bloom, Barthes, and intertextualists in general by probing this context's key concept: literary convention. What most intertextual theories ignore, she claims, is the degree to which literary conventions are influenced by the life—as opposed to the literary—experiences of different groups of readers. While a literary text may remain stable over time, the experiences of readers, and hence their understanding of "conventions," may vary considerably. Kennard cites "The Yellow Wallpaper" as a case in point. "I suggest that when we look at why it was possible for Elaine Hedges to read The Yellow Wallpaper *as a feminist work in 1973, for this reading to become accepted, for Gilman's novella to find a place in a revised canon of American literature, we are looking at series of conventions available to readers of the 1970s which were not available to those of 1892." To illustrate her case, Kennard points out how recent readings, such as those by Kolodny and by Gilbert and Gubar, differ profoundly from earlier readings of the story as a gothic thriller yet largely agree among themselves. Something more than literary experience seems to be involved: "We have to come to the text as to any text, as Culler says, with certain expectations based on our previous literary experience. But the ability to read the narrator's confinement in a room as symbolic of the situation of women in a patriarchal society depends on an agreement, on a literary convention, which, I suggest, was formed from contemporary experience both literary and extra literary." Kennard then analyzes a cluster of meanings associated with patriarchy, madness, space, and quest to show that with all these concepts the conventions have changed considerably over the course of the twentieth century, and they have changed, Kennard argues, because earlier conventions came to be seen as false to the experience of certain interpretive communities and therefore oppressive. "Convention" remains the key concept, but in Kennard's analysis, it turns out to be more problematic than most intertextual theories had assumed.*

I must have reread Northrop Frye's *Anatomy of Criticism*—or at least many parts of it—several times since the first reading fifteen years ago. Yet despite this familiarity, when I looked at it again this spring, I found myself uncomfortable with a couple of sentences which had never troubled me before: "All humor demands agreement that certain things, such as a picture of a wife beating her husband in a comic strip, are conventionally funny. To introduce a comic strip in which a husband beats his wife would distress the reader, because it would mean learning a new convention."[1]

My objection had nothing to do with Frye's basic concept of a convention as an agreement which allows art to communicate. I agreed with this definition which he had developed more fully earlier: "The contract agreed on by the reader before he can start reading is the same thing as a convention."[2] I was also in sympathy with a critical approach based upon the response of the reader. Nor did my objection concern the question of humor, which, it is perhaps worth noting, I was quite able to ignore even though it was Frye's primary focus.

My distress as a reader was with his example. I was uncomfortable with a discussion of wife beating as an even potentially acceptable source of humor. To talk about it as a new convention seemed insensitive. My discomfort extended, though more diffusely, to the idea of considering any form of violence amusing. I had a strong feeling that the picture of a wife beating her husband was no longer funny; in other words, that other people (that is, people I knew) would no longer find it funny. I granted, however, that it was at one time "conventionally funny" and realized that I had probably accepted it as such when I first read Frye. The indication of that acceptance was a failure to notice or remember the example.

For me, obviously, a convention had changed, and some of the reasons at least seemed apparent. Such extraliterary experiences as talking with friends who worked with battered women, an increased awareness of violence in every city I visited, together with reading feminist scholarship, had led me to formulate values which resisted the convention Frye named. I no longer agreed to find it funny.

I start with this quotation from Frye and my response to it as a reader because, while providing a useful definition of convention (that is, one that I agree with), it raises some interesting questions (that is, the ones I want to consider here): How and when do literary conventions change? To what extent can the sources of these changes be other than literary?

These questions are, of course, part of the broader issue of the relationship between literary conventions and life. I am using the term *life* to mean any experience other than that of reading literature, realizing that the peculiarity of this exclusion is part of the question. As my discussion of Frye's quotation suggests, I believe the questions can be most usefully addressed through an approach which has been rather loosely defined as reader-response criticism. Since I am a feminist critic, my interest in these issues is to understand their usefulness, if any, to feminist literary criticism and to feminist concerns generally. In saying this I believe I am admitting to as much but to no more bias than that of any other critic.

It is against a naive equation of literature with life that Frye is arguing when he emphasizes the importance of the literary tradition: "Poetry can only be made out of other poems; novels out of other novels. Literature shapes itself, and is not shaped externally . . . it is possible for a story of the sea to be archetypal, to make a profound imaginative impact on a reader who has never been out of Saskatchewan."[3] While some contemporary critics might point out that the impact would no doubt be different on a reader who lived in Maine, many would agree with Frye's basic assumption that reading and writing involve an understanding of literary conventions and that in order to read (or write) one has to have read. This assumption lies behind Harold Bloom's work on influences,[4] for example, and behind Roland Barthes's discussion of the "intertextual."[5] Geoffrey Hartman points out that "we must read the writer as a reader";[6] Nelly Furman that "the writer's work can also be construed as the product of a prior reading."[7]

For Jonathan Culler the literary conventions we learn from reading are a set of expectations—of significance, of metaphorical coherence, of thematic unity—which we impose on the text; the ability to apply these conventional procedures in reading other works constitutes a reader's "literary competence":

"To read a text as literature is not to make one's mind a *tabula rasa* and approach it without preconceptions; one must bring to it an implicit understanding of the operations of literary discourse which tells one what to look for."[8] But Culler does not account for why readers who have learned the same literary strategies will read the same texts differently nor why the same readers will read the same texts differently at different times.

In an attempt to answer these questions, Stanley Fish introduces the notion of "interpretive communities," groups of readers who share certain interpretive strategies (who agree to apply particular literary conventions).[9] He gives as his examples psychoanalytic critics, Robertsonians, and numerologists. According to Fish, readers may move from one "interpretive community" to another and may belong to more than one at any one time. Fish believes that interpretive communities create the texts they read—write rather than read them[10]—by selectively applying certain conventional procedures, a position more radical than that of many other reader-response critics. He allows for the possibility of an endless series of interpretations of any one work.

Fish does not, however, examine the process of or the reasons for "ways of interpreting" being "forgotten or supplanted, or complicated or dropped from favor";[11] and although he certainly allows for extraliterary influences on changing conventions, he does not claim to be primarily interested in discussing them. His emphasis is on the lack of a fixed text: "When any of these things happens," he continues, "there is a corresponding change in texts, not because they are being read differently but because they are being written differently."[12] He does not examine what conditions are necessary to make "these things happen" nor what results from texts changing.

I suggest that any account of changes in literary conventions will have to consider nonliterary as well as literary influences. The fact that the word *convention* has meaning in both literary and nonliterary contexts alone suggests this connection. Raymond Williams, while agreeing with the definition of convention I have been employing so far,[13] begins his discussion of the term with a reminder of its origins in a nonliterary context: "The meaning of convention was originally an assembly and then, by derivation, an agreement. Later the sense of agreement was extended to tacit agreement and thence to custom. An adverse sense developed, in which a convention was seen as no more than as old rule, or somebody else's rule, which it was proper and often necessary to disregard."[14]

The interrelation of literary conventions and life is suggested also in the parallels between the history of the word in this nonliterary sense and the process of growth and decline literary conventions undergo. In 1899 readers of Kate Chopin's *The Awakening* reacted with bewilderment expressed as anger when Edna Pontellier rejected her husband, took a lover, and left the family house because they had at that point no agreement that (1) leaving her house and husband and taking a lover can indicate a woman is searching for self-fulfillment, and (2) this search for self-fulfillment should be approved. By the time Sue Kaufman published *Diary of a Mad Housewife* (1967), Joyce Carol Oates *Do With Me What You Will* (1973), Erica Jong *Fear of Flying* (1974), and Doris Lessing *The Summer Before the Dark* (1974), agreement on these interpretations had taken place among a sufficient number of readers to make the novels readily understood. A convention had been established. Yet by 1977 when Marilyn French published *The Women's Room,* she talked of this convention as "an old rule," "a convention of the women's novel" which she intended to break.[15] When does bewilderment become boredom? When did we begin to talk of "just another mad housewife novel"? By what process does the convention become too conventional?

As my example suggests, when a convention is an agreement on the meaning of a symbolic gesture in a literary context rather than agreement to use a specific interpretive strategy, to seek metaphorical coherence, for example, the question of value is made more obvious. This is not to say that interpretive strategies are neutral and do not in themselves imply certain moral values, only that these values become clearer when we are considering what Frye has called "associative clusters" or archetypes. His example is a good illustration of this: "When we speak of 'symbolism' in ordinary life we usually think of such learned cultural archetypes as the cross or the crown, or of conventional associations, as of white with purity or green with jealousy."[16] When we consider changes in literary conventions, we are considering changes in our agreements on both how we shall interpret and how we shall evaluate that interpretation. These changes are certainly influenced, then, by aspects of our cultural context which are not specifically literary.

Norman Holland claims readers imprint every text with their own "identity themes";[17] and, although there may be limitations to his definition of identity,[18] in any consideration of changes in reading conventions some attention must be paid to the subjective judgment of the individual reader. Nelly Furman recognizes the reader as "a carrier of perceptual prejudices";[19] Annette Kolodny argues convincingly that gender often affects the ability to read specific texts.[20] "That which you are, that only can you read," claims Bloom.[21] And here we come full circle since "what we are" is compounded of our experiences, literary and nonliterary.

Let me sum up the assumptions I have been discussing so far and from which I shall be arguing in the latter part of this article. Any interpretation/reading of any text (whether or not the text is to any extent fixed) is dependent on two things: one, the literary conventions known to the reader at the time — these conventions include both reading strategies and associative clusters of meaning; two, the choices the reader makes to apply or not any one of these conventions — these choices are dependent on what the reader is at the time. It is a question, then, of what the individual reader chooses to notice or to ignore at the time of reading, and this idea raises the specter of a multiplicity of unchallengeable readings and the end of our discipline as we have known it. I shall attempt to exorcise the specter later.

If a convention is that which allows literature to be read, then readings of the same texts separated by many years should be instructive on the question of changes in contentions. It is here that the work of feminist scholars can be extremely helpful. This is partly because we see as one of our major tasks the rereading of earlier works, both those well established in the traditional literary canon and those previously excluded from it.[22] In the past ten years feminist scholarship has provided us with a large number of new readings which have resurrected such neglected works as Charlotte Perkins Gilman's *The Yellow Wallpaper* (1892) and Kate Chopin's *The Awakening* (1899) and radically changed our view of entire centuries. Sandra Gilbert and Susan Gubar's *The Madwoman in the Attic*, for example, has completely reinterpreted the women writers of the nineteenth century.[23] Feminist rereadings are also helpful in understanding changes in conventions for two other reasons: one, they are often unusually radical in their divergence from earlier readings;[24] two, they

represent the views of a clearly defined "interpretive community."

Though feminist critics have successfully employed many different methodologies, the alliance between feminist criticism and reader-response criticism seems to have been particularly fruitful. In the past three years Judith Fetterley's *The Resisting Reader*,[25] Annette Kolodny's "A Map for Rereading: Or, Gender and the Interpretation of Literary Texts"[26] and "Dancing Through the Minefield: Some Observations on the Theory, Practice and Politics of Feminist Criticism," Gilbert and Gubar's *The Madwoman in the Attic*, and Nelly Furman's "Textual Feminism" have all demonstrated the usefulness of reader-response criticism to feminists.[27] In my own footnotes to this article I have already found reason to refer to four of these texts. This connection is not surprising, of course, since rereading is to such a large extent our enterprise, and we might be expected therefore to be concerned with many of the same questions about the process of reading and the nature of audiences.

Despite radical reinterpretations, feminist critics have on the whole remained on the conservative side with regard to the question of the "fixed text." If the implication is not always that a feminist rereading reveals the only "correct" meaning of a text, it is usually assumed that it reveals what has always been there but not previously seen. Elaine Showalter claims feminist criticism "has allowed us to see meaning in what has previously been empty space. The orthodox plot recedes, and another plot, hitherto submerged in the anonymity of the background, stands out in bold relief like a thumbprint."[28] Sandra Gilbert and Susan Gubar talk of "literary works that are in some sense palimpsestic, works whose surface designs conceal or obscure deeper, less accessible (and less socially acceptable) levels of meaning" (p. 91). Annette Kolodny, in an article which discusses and allows for a plurality of interpretations, talks of a male critic's possible inability when reading women's writing "to completely decipher its intended meaning" (p. 456).

It is perhaps because feminist critics have usually held to the notions of a fixed text and of discovering rather than of creating meaning that we have not examined the question of why our rereadings, our discoveries, took place when they did. I suggest that when we look at why it was possible for Elaine Hedges to read *The Yellow Wallpaper* as a feminist work in 1973, for this reading to become accepted, for Gilman's novella to find a place in a revised canon of American literature, we are looking at a series of conventions available to readers of the 1970s which were not available to those of 1892. It is an examination of these conventions that I intend to undertake here in order to see whether it allows us to hypothesize in any way about how literary conventions change.

My suggestion that it is the literary conventions of the 1970s that allowed feminist readings of *The Yellow Wallpaper* does not necessarily imply anything about Gilman's intention. It is essentially irrelevant to my concern here—though in other contexts important—whether or not this meaning was, as Gilbert and Gubar claim, "quite clear to Gilman herself" (p. 91). I am using *The Yellow Wallpaper* as an example, realizing that other works would perhaps be equally fruitful,[29] because of the similarity in the readings which have taken place since 1973 and because of the vast discrepancy between these readings and previous ones. I shall draw on four feminist readings: Elaine Hedges's "Afterword" to the Feminist Press edition of the text; Annette Kolodny's in "A Map for Rereading"; Sandra Gilbert and Susan Gubar's in *The Madwoman the Attic;* and my own. Although these interpretations emphasize different aspects of the text, they do not conflict with each other.

In its time and until the last eight years, *The Yellow Wallpaper* was read, when it was read at all, "as a Poesque tale of chilling horror,"[30] designed "to freeze our blood,"[31] praised, when it was praised, for the detail with which it recorded developing insanity. Even as late as 1971 Seon Manley and Gogo Lewis included it in a collection entitled *Ladies of Horror: Two Centuries of Supernatural Stories by the Gentle Sex* and introduced it with the following words: "There were new ideas afloat: perhaps some of the horrors were in our own minds, not in the outside world at all. This idea gave birth to the psychological horror story and *The Yellow Wallpaper* by Charlotte Perkins Gilman shows she was a mistress of the art."[32]

No earlier reader saw the story as in any way positive. When Horace Scudder rejected it for publication in *The Atlantic Monthly,* he explained that he did not wish to make his readers as miserable as the story had made him. As Elaine Hedges points out, "No one seems to have made the connection between insanity and the sex, or sexual role of the vic-

tim, no one explored the story's implications for male-female relationships in the nineteenth century" (p. 41).

Feminist critics approach *The Yellow Wallpaper* from the point of view of the narrator. "As she tells her story," says Hedges, "the reader has confidence in the reasonableness of her arguments and explanations" (p. 49). The narrator is seen as the victim of an oppressive patriarchal social system which restricts women and prevents their functioning as full human beings. The restrictions on women are symbolized by the narrator's imprisonment in a room with bars on the window, an image the narrator sees echoed in the patterns of the room's yellow wallpaper. "The wallpaper," claims Hedges, symbolizes "the morbid social situation" (p. 52). Gilbert and Gubar talk of "the anxiety-inducing connections between what women writers tend to see as their parallel confinements in texts, houses and maternal female bodies" and describe the wallpaper as "ancient, smoldering, 'unclean' as the oppressive structures of the society in which she finds herself" (p. 90). The women the narrator "sees" in the wallpaper and wants to liberate are perceived to be "creeping." "Women must creep," says Hedges, "the narrator knows this" (p. 53). I see the indoor images of imprisonment echoed in the natural world of the garden with its "walls and gates that lock, and lots of separate little houses for the gardeners and people" (p. 11). Like so many other women in literature, the only access to nature the narrator has is to a carefully cultivated and confined garden. Gilbert and Gubar point out that in contrast the idea of "open country" is the place of freedom (p. 91).

The representative of the repressive patriarchal society is the narrator's husband John, "a censorious and paternalistic physician" (p. 89), as Gilbert and Gubar call him. John has "a doubly authoritative role as both husband and doctor" (p. 457), Kolodny points out. The description of John as rational rather than emotional, as a man who laughs at what cannot be put down in figures, emphasizes his position as representative of a male power which excludes feeling and imagination. Indeed, the first sentence in the story which suggests a feminist reading to me is a comment on John's character: "John laughs at me, of course, but one expects that in marriage" (p. 9).

John's treatment of his wife's mental illness is isolation and the removal of all intellectual stimulation, "a cure worse than the disease" (p. 89), as Gilbert and

Gubar call it. Feminist critics see the narrator's being deprived of an opportunity to write, the opportunity for self-expression, as particularly significant. Kolodny (p. 457) and Gilbert and Gubar (p. 89) remind us that the narrator thinks of writing as a relief. Hedges sees the narrator as someone who "wants very much to work" (p. 49). By keeping her underemployed and isolated, John effectively ensures his wife's dependence on him. She must remain the child he treats her as. Hedges draws attention to the fact that he calls her "blessed little goose" and his "little girl" and that the room she stays in was once a nursery (p. 50). For Hedges, John is "an important source of her afflictions" (p. 49).

The narrator experiences her victimization as a conflict between her own personal feelings, perceived by feminist critics as healthy and positive, and the patriarchal society's view of what is proper behavior for women. Since, like so many women up to the present day, she has internalized society's expectations of women, this conflict is felt as a split within herself. Early in the story the words "Personally, I" (p. 10) are twice set against the views of John and her brother. Nevertheless, she also continues to judge her own behavior as John does. "I get unreasonably angry with John sometimes" (p. 11), she explains; "I cry at nothing, and cry most of the time" (p. 19). As Hedges points out, this split is symbolized by the woman behind the wallpaper: "By rejecting that woman, she might free the other imprisoned woman within herself" (p. 53). The narrator's madness is perceived by Hedges and others as a direct result of societally induced confusion over personal identity. If the images of women as child or cripple, as prisoner, even as fungus growth in Gilman's story are "the images men had of women, and hence that women had of themselves," Hedges writes, "it is not surprising that madness and suicide bulk large in the work of late nineteenth-century women writers" (p. 54).

The most radical aspect of the feminist reading of *The Yellow Wallpaper* lies in the interpretation of the narrator's descent into madness as a way to health, as a rejection of and escape from an insane society. Gilbert and Gubar describe her as sinking "more and more deeply into what the world calls madness" (p. 90). They see her "imaginings and creations" as "mirages of health and freedom" (p. 91). Hedges stresses this aspect of the story. She describes the narrator as "ultimately mad and yet, throughout her descent into madness, in many ways more sensible than the people who surround and cripple her" (p. 49). "In her mad-sane way she has seen the situation of women for what it is," Hedges continues, and so "madness is her only freedom" (p. 53).

It is the interpretation of madness as a higher form of sanity that allows feminist critics finally to read this story as a woman's quest for her own identity. Deprived of reading material, she begins to read the wallpaper. "Fighting for her identity, for some sense of independent self, she observes the wallpaper" (pp. 50–51), writes Hedges. More sophisticatedly, Kolodny claims the narrator "comes more and more to experience herself as a text which can neither get read nor recorded" (p. 457). Both Kolodny and Gilbert and Gubar emphasize that the narrator creates meaning in the wallpaper in her need to find an image of herself which will affirm the truth of her own situation and hence her identity. Kolodny writes: "Selectively emphasizing one section of the pattern while repressing others, reorganizing and regrouping past impressions into newer, more fully realized configurations—as one might with any formal text—the speaking voice becomes obsessed with her quest for meaning" (p. 458). Gilbert and Gubar describe the narrator's creation of meaning as a reversal of the wallpaper's implications: "Inevitably she studies its suicidal implications—and inevitably, because of her 'imaginative power and habit of story-making,' she revises it, projecting her own passion for escape into its otherwise incomprehensible hieroglyphics" (p. 90). Although the narrator is not seen to emerge either from madness or marriage at the end of the novella, her understanding of her own situation and, by extension, the situation of all women can be read as a sort of triumph. This triumph is symbolized by the overcoming of John, who is last seen fainting on the floor as his wife creeps over him.

In order to read the novel this way, much must be assumed that is not directly stated, much must be ignored that is. There is no overt statement, for example, that invites us to find a socially induced cause for the narrator's madness, to assume that her situation is that of all women. There is perhaps even a certain perversity in claiming that a mentally deranged woman crawling around an attic floor is experiencing some sort of victory. It is also true that if the narrator claims she thinks writing would relieve her mind, she also says it tires her when she tries (p. 16). Since she so often contradicts herself, we are free to believe her only when her comments support our reading. Much is made in the novella of the color yellow; feminist readings do little with this. Despite all these objections, which could probably be continued indefinitely, it is the feminist reading I teach my students and which I believe is the most fruitful. In pointing out the "weaknesses" in my own reading, I am only providing the sort of evidence that could be used to counter any interpretation of the story. I am interested in why we read it as we do, not whether we are correct in doing so.

In order to read/write the story or any story in a feminist or in any other way, we are, of course, dependent on some interpretive strategies, some reading conventions which, if not fixed, have remained relatively so for a long period of time. The ability to see the narrator's confinement in a room as symbolic, for example, comes from other reading; we have learned to symbolize. We have come to the text as to any text, as Culler says, with certain expectations based on our previous literary experience.

But the ability to read the narrator's confinement in a room as symbolic of the situation of women in a patriarchal society depends on an agreement, on a literary convention, which, I suggest, was formed from contemporary experience—both literary and extraliterary. The feminist reading of *The Yellow Wallpaper* depends on the knowledge of a series of "associative clusters" of meaning which have been employed sufficiently frequently in contemporary literature for us to accept them as conventions. The existence of these conventions in the 1970s accounts both for the new reading and for its widespread acceptance. In saying this I am not claiming that any one reader had read any particular works or been exposed to specific experiences.

The conventions I refer to overlap each other but are associated with four basic concepts: patriarchy, madness, space, quest. The concept of patriarchy or of male power appears most frequently in contemporary fiction in the characters of men, often husbands, who are unimaginative, compartmentalized, obsessively rational and unable to express their feelings. The prototype for these figures—like so much else in contemporary feminist thought—comes from Virginia Woolf, from the character of Mr. Ramsay in *To the Lighthouse* (1927). These men are to be found

everywhere in contemporary fiction by women, particularly in the fiction of the seventies. Norm in French's *The Women's Room,* Brooke Skelton in Margaret Laurence's *The Diviners* (1974), and the narrator's father in *Surfacing* are three examples of the type. As husbands they are unquestioning representatives of the status quo. As a result their wives, usually the protagonists of the novels, begin to feel they are being treated as children or as dolls. Ibsen's image of a wife as doll is conventional in this fiction—for example, Joyce Carol Oates's *Do With Me What You Will*—and occurs also in poetry. In Margaret Atwood's "After I Fall Apart" the speaker talks of herself as a broken doll gradually being mended;[33] in Sylvia Plath's "The Applicant" the speaker, as doll, applies for a position as wife.[34]

In fiction the female protagonist gradually learns to recognize the universality of her experience, conceives in some fashion of the notion of patriarchy, and "slams the door" on her past. In such "early" feminist works as Erica Jong's *Fear of Flying* or Doris Lessing's *The Summer Before the Dark,* the agent of her freedom is another man, a lover. This is the contemporary version of the nineteenth-century convention of the two suitors which I explored in my book *Victims of Convention.*[35] In the older convention the maturity of the female protagonist is measured by her choice of a "right" suitor, one who represents the novelist's views, over a "wrong" suitor, one whose views parallel the heroine's own initial weaknesses. She marries the right suitor and the novel ends. In the contemporary version the husband has become the "wrong" suitor, the representative of patriarchal restrictions; the lover represents freedom. It was the contemporary version of the convention that Marilyn French described herself as breaking when she set out to explore in *The Women's Room* what really happens after the heroine walks out.

John in *The Yellow Wallpaper* can easily be read as an example of the husband as patriarch; his well-meaning but misguided efforts to help his wife as the result of a view of women as less than adult. He is also a doctor and that compounds the situation. Recent nonfiction, both popular magazines and books, has challenged the conventional notion of the good doctor and emphasized the fact that the traditional treatment of women, particularly in childbirth, exists for the convenience of the medical profession, not for the health of their patients. Two highly influential feminist studies, Adrienne Rich's *Of Woman Born* (1976) and Mary Daly's *Gyn/Ecology* (1978), make this point. Traditional medicine is indicted for treating women as objects, for committing the basic sin of patriarchy. Just as the antidote for the compartmentalization of traditional medicine is seen to be holistic medicine, the values implied by the indictment of patriarchy are those considered implicit in matriarchy: nurturance, collaboration, emotion, unity. It is here that feminist values and those of the sixties counterculture overlap.

The concept of madness is related to patriarchy since female madness is read as a result of patriarchal oppression. Gilbert and Gubar point out that "recently, in fact, social historians like Jessie Bernard, Phyllis Chesler, Naomi Weissten, and Pauline Bart have begun to study the ways in which patriarchal socialization literally makes women sick, both physically and mentally" (p. 53). The observation that many women novelists and poets experienced mental breakdowns, that many of those who did committed suicide, is made frequently in feminist scholarship since 1970. "Suicides and spinsters / all our kind!" writes Erica Jong in "Dear Colette," "Even decorous Jane Austen / never marrying, / & Sappho leaping, / & Sylvia in the oven, / & Anna Wickham, Tsvetaeva, Sara Teasdale, / & pale Virginia floating like Ophelia, / & Emily alone, alone, alone."[36]

In seventies' fiction by women, madness or some form of mental disturbance became a conventional representation of the situation of women in a patriarchal society. Kate Brown, in Lessing's *The Summer Before the Dark*, looks back on her married life and decides she has acquired not virtues but a form of dementia. In Sue Kaufman's *Diary of a Mad Housewife*, Tina Balser subscribes to the notion that her failure to perform as the perfect wife means she is going mad. In Joyce Carol Oates's *Do With Me What You Will*, Elena's total passivity so well fulfills the desires of her husband that he does not consider her, as the reader (this reader at least) does, mentally ill. Again, the same convention occurs in the poetry — for example, Jong's "Why I Died"[37] or Carol Cox's "From the Direction of the Mental Institution."[38]

The appropriateness of this convention (our willingness to agree to it) is probably a coalescence of two aspects of experience. First, women frequently feel mad because their own reality/feeling is in conflict with society's expectations. This is often expressed in literature as the sense of being "split." The protagonists of Sylvia Plath's *The Bell Jar* (1963), Margaret Laurence's *The Diviners*, Margaret Atwood's *Surfacing*, and Rita Mae Brown's *Rubyfruit Jungle* (1973) are among many who describe this sensation. The nameless narrator of *Surfacing* says, "I'd allowed myself to be cut in two;"[39] her head (her rationality) is no longer attached to her body (her emotions). Morag Gunn in *The Diviners* experiences an increased sense of "being separated from herself."[40] So feminist critics can readily identify the narrator of *The Yellow Wallpaper*'s division of herself in two as an example of this split. The need to assert the female personal voice as a way to reestablish wholeness or health results from an awareness of the split. When Gilman's narrator asserts "Personally, I," I personally read it with this knowledge in mind.[41]

Second, women who try to express difference (do not submit to patriarchal expectations) are frequently called "crazy." Alice Munro's short story "The Office," in which a woman who rents an office to write in is considered mad, is a good illustration of this,[42] as is Ellen Goodman's column in the *Boston Globe* on the occasion of Martha Mitchell's death, "Here's To All The Crazy Ladies."

Another aspect of this "associated cluster" of meanings is the Laingian notion of madness as a form of higher sanity, as an indication of a capacity to see truths other than those available to the logical mind. An extension of the tradition of the wise fool, this concept was reinforced by a vision-seeking drug culture in the sixties and occurs frequently in literature by both women and men. Such novels as Ken Kesey's *One Flew Over the Cuckoo's Nest* (1962), in which inhabitants of a mental institution are seen to be saner than their doctors, and Doris Lessing's *Briefing For a Descent into Hell* (1971), in which the reader must choose between the reality of the institutionalized protagonist and that of his doctors, are typical examples. The work of Doris Lessing is perhaps the best illustration of the use of this concept, which is first fully developed in her novel *The Four-Gated City* (1969). Here Martha Quest identifies herself with the apparently mad wife of her lover Mark and comes to hear voices from a world validated as superior at the end of the novel. Carol P. Christ describes Lynda, the wife, as being "destroyed by psychologists who called her powers madness."[43] Especially useful to feminist writers since it defines the established society as less perceptive than she who is called deviant, the concept is conventional enough by 1973 for

Elaine Hedges to talk of "her mad-sane way" and speak volumes (particularly those of Doris Lessing) to her readers.

It is significant that the central experience of *The Four-Gated City* takes place during two weeks in which Martha and Lynda remain enclosed in Lynda's room and, like the narrator of *The Yellow Wallpaper*, crawl around its perimeter. The conventions associated with space, particularly with rooms, are central to a feminist reading of *The Yellow Wallpaper*. Although still indicative in a contemporary fiction by women of the limitations of women's sphere, a convention French employs in the first—the toilet—scene of *The Women's Room*, rooms are also claimed as independent space (with or without the five hundred pounds a year Woolf told us was also necessary). "You keep me in" has become "I keep you out." This dual use of the conventions associated with rooms, which as Gilbert and Gubar remind us are also representative of female bodies, can be seen in two short stories: Doris Lessing's "To Room 19"[44] and the Munro story "The Office" I referred to earlier. In the former a woman rents a hotel room in which to be alone and is forced to invent a lover to protect her space; in the latter a woman is accused of sexual promiscuity when she rents an office in which to work. The association between independent space and women's creative work—a connection we make in reading *The Yellow Wallpaper*—is, of course, established clearly by Woolf in *A Room of One's Own* (1929).

The concept of space also includes the question of women in relationship to nature, too large a subject to fully explore here, and which only peripherally affects the reading of *The Yellow Wallpaper*. It is interesting to note, though, that Gilbert and Gubar read the narrator's double's escape into open country as "not unlike the progress of nineteenth-century women out of the texts defined by patriarchal poetics into the open spaces of their own authority" (p. 91). Traditionally women have been identified with nature, a convention which has effectively precluded, in American literature at least, the possibility of female protagonists interacting with nature in the way male protagonists have. This applies to the wilderness rather than to such tamed natural environments as gardens, and to the American wilderness rather than, for example, to the Canadian where female protagonists do not find the space already occupied by the heroes of Hemingway, Faulkner, and Steinbeck. The possibilities for the boy in Faulkner's "The Bear," who sees the

woods as both mistress and wife, to find himself in nature by confronting a bear are simply not open to women. No American woman novelist has written a novel like Marian Engel's *Bear* (1976) in which a female character has her version of the same experience.

For this reason, perhaps, women on spiritual quests—I come to my final concept—do not journey horizontally in contemporary American literature, do not cross wildernesses like frontier heroes, despite the actualities of frontier history. We appear to quest vertically: we dive and surface or we fly. Carol P. Christ's recent book, *Diving Deep and Surfacing*, examines some of these motifs in the novels of Doris Lessing and Margaret Atwood and in Adrienne Rich's *Diving into the Wreck* (1973) and *The Dream of a Common Language* (1978). *Surfacing* is a particularly interesting example since the protagonist begins by searching for her father horizontally, which involves a long journey by road and an exploration of the woods, but she only finds him when she dives. Christ does not examine the flying metaphor, which is obvious in the titles of Erica Jong's *Fear of Flying* and Kate Millett's *Flying* (1974).

The aspect of the quest concept which we need to reread *The Yellow Wallpaper*, however, has more to do with a different convention. To see the narrator as a quester for self-fulfillment is to agree to grant her our trust (to see her as the accurate perceiver of reality), which we do partly because she is female, partly because she speaks to us directly (though we have the choice here of opting for the unreliable narrator convention), and partly because we agree to read madness as sanity. Both Gilbert and Gubar and Kolodny see her as searching for her identity, her place, in the wallpaper and call this "reading." The convention we are using here is that suggested by Adrienne Rich in "Diving into the Wreck." We are aware of the "book of myths / in which our names do not appear," recognize the need for a literary past which reflects "the thing itself and not the myth,"[45] and examine our literary history with this in mind. Again, the convention has two aspects: one, literature is seen as lying about women, and our truths remain unwritten or suppressed, as Tillie Olsen explains in *Silences* (1978); two, the literature we have been given is seen as a quarry which must be mined to produce the truths we need. So Jane Clifford in Gail Godwin's *The Old Woman* (1974) hunts fiction to find the character she most resembles; so Maxine Hong Kingston's narrator in *The Woman Warrior* (1976) translates the legends of her Chinese past into workable myths for her American present and learns to say "I" and "Here"; so Morag Gunn learns that whether or not her adopted father Christie's tales of her Scottish ancestors were true is unimportant since they have given her the "strength of conviction." So the narrator of *The Yellow Wallpaper* can be read as reading her own text in (into) the patterns of the wallpaper.

What does this examination of the contemporary conventions necessary for rereading *The Yellow Wallpaper* demonstrate about the way literary conventions change? I suggest that these conventions can all be seen as responses to, changes in, conventions which had become oppressive to the feminist "interpretive community." By oppressive I mean both dishonest, suggesting an idea contrary to the view of experience called reality by the interpretive community, and inadequate, not able to provide a form in which to express that view of experience. If a conventional view is seen as dishonest, then the convention is often reversed. So a gothic treatment of female madness which exploits the reader's sadistic impulses (pleasure in another's pain) and sees women as basically unstable (hysterical) is reversed in two ways in the contemporary conventions associated with madness: the woman's mental disease is seen to be the fault of society (patriarchy) rather than her own; madness is read as sanity. The conventional associations of space function in the same way. Reversal here takes the form of changing a negative evaluation to a positive one. In other literature by women we have seen women writers adopt the supposedly negative slurs directed at them: they have written poems which celebrate themselves as witches, lesbians, Amazons;[46] they have deliberately exploited the confessional mode for which their writing had been condemned;[47] they have emphasized the "insignificant" kitchen imagery of their own lives.[48] This is a tactic also used by other victims of discrimination: "Black is beautiful"; "gay is good."

Reversal may take the form of exposing the implications of an old convention by changing the point of view, often by changing the gender of the participants. Erica Jong's *Fear of Flying*, for example, was considered original at the time of publication because it made men rather than women sex objects. Similarly, in a recent film *Nine to Five*, a male is held captive by his female employees. Poems in which male poets are rewritten from the female point of view employ this same procedure. See, for example, Mona Van Duyn's "Leda" and "Leda Reconsidered,"[49] Julie Randall's "To William Wordsworth from Virginia,"[50] Judith Rechter's "From Fay Wray to the King."[51]

When experience cannot be expressed in the available literary conventions, new conventions appear to develop. I say "appear" because these new conventions could perhaps be described as occupying the gaps left by the old. At all events they are not totally unrelated to what has gone before. So the conventions associated with diving, surfacing, and flying as forms of quest may seem to be new until they are recognized as vertical alternatives to a traffic jam on the horizontal. Woman's search for her own story, which ends in its creation, is a response to the absence of that story in literary history.

To fully test my hypothesis that literary conventions change when their implications conflict with the vision of experience of a new "interpretive community" would require going beyond the feminist rereading I have examined here, and more space than I have. It can certainly be demonstrated, though, that changes in literary conventions are frequently justified in the name of a greater truth to present reality, to "life." "Is life like this? Must novels be like this?" asks Virginia Woolf as she builds her case against the fictional conventions of "realistic" novels in favor of a truth to the reality of the mind, to the stream of consciousness: "If he [a writer] could write what he chose and not what he must, if he could base his work upon his own feeling and not upon convention, there would be no plot, no comedy, no tragedy, no love interest or catastrophe in the accepted sense. . . . Life is not a series of gig lamps symmetrically arranged."[52] In Lessing's *A Proper Marriage* Martha Quest complains: "In the books, the young and idealistic girl gets married, has a baby — she at once turns into something quite different; and she is perfectly happy to spend her whole life bringing up children with a tedious husband."[53] This convention no longer represents life as Martha knows it; it has clearly become "someone else's rule" which it is now "necessary to disregard."

The appeal to "real life" is not limited to the twentieth century. In the sixteenth century Marguerite de Navarre is already concerned that the "flowers of rhetoric" not hide "the truth of history."[54] Nor is it limited to female writers. Ford Madox Ford appeals in the same way as Virginia Woolf to perceived experience as he explains why he and Conrad began changing a fictional convention: "It became very early evident to us that what was the matter with the Novel, and the British novel in particular, was that it went straight forward, whereas in your gradual making acquaintanceship with your fellows you never do go straight forward. . . . We agreed that the general effect of a novel must be the general effect that life makes on mankind."[55]

The problem with appealing to the "general effect life makes" is that we do not all agree on what is lifelike. When we talk about "reality," we are really talking about a writer's or a reader's vision of experience, the way s/he needs to see it. Conventions change according to our needs as readers or, if we accept Fish's views, as groups of readers, as "interpretive communities." It follows, then, that conventions are always to some extent outmoded, always "old rules," lagging necessarily behind the vision they are designed to express. Once we can identify "a mad housewife novel," it is already too late to write another one successfully.

This view of literary conventions can prove useful to feminist critics. The fact that the conventions we use to reread the literary past are already dying should remind us that the remaking of the literary canon is a process and must remain ongoing; it is not a goal to be achieved. New texts will appear hidden in the old in answer to new needs, in response to new conventions. These texts in turn will affect that "real life" experience which forces changes in conventions.[56]

Like the narrators of *The Yellow Wallpaper* and *The Woman Warrior,* like Morag Gunn, we project ourselves into the text's "otherwise incomprehensible hieroglyphics." The value of our rereadings lies not in their "correctness" nor in our ability to demonstrate their intentionality but, like Christie's tales, in their ability to enrich our present by providing us with that book of myths in which our names do appear. To do this they do not need to be "true," merely satisfying. As Morag Gunn says to her daughter Pique when she asks whether the stories she was told as a child really happened: "'Some did and some didn't, I guess. It doesn't matter a damn, don't you see?'"[57]

The idea that we invent rather than discover new meanings does not lessen the importance of the rereading enterprise.[58] To remind ourselves that we all create the conventions that allow us to read the text is to grant our readings as much authority — or as little — as any other. Indeed, it provides us with an answer to those frequent accusations of bias. Feminists and other clearly defined interpretive communities are no more biased than any other readers; our biases are simply more readily identifiable and often more acknowledged.

Nor should this notion raise what Walter Benn Michaels has called "the fear of subjectivity" among Anglo-American literary critics, the fear that "if there were no determinate meanings, the interpreter's freedom could make a text anything it wanted."[59] In theory (some theories) we as individual readers can choose to make of the text anything we wish, but in practice we do not do so. This is not only because we read by means of the conventions shared by our interpretive communities and are, as Fish has pointed out, programmed by our experience: "To the list of made or constructed objects we must add ourselves, for we no less than the poems and assignments we see are the product of social and cultural patterns of thought."[60] It is equally, or perhaps alternatively, because we always surrender some part of the individual freedom we do have in order to seek affirmation for our reading from our interpretive community. If our reading is not accepted, it will not satisfy us, that is, comfort us by providing that sense of community we read for in the first place. In reading we seek a coming together, a convention.

Notes

1. Northrop Frye, *Anatomy of Criticism: Four Essays* (1957; rpt. Princeton, 1971), p. 225.
2. Frye, p. 76. Cf. p. 99: "The problem of convention is the problem of how art can be communicable."
3. Frye, pp. 97 and 99.
4. See, e.g., Harold Bloom, "The Breaking of Form," in *Deconstruction and Criticism,* ed. Geoffrey Hartman (New York, 1979), p. 3: "The truest sources, again necessarily, are in the powers of poems *already written,* or rather, *already read.*"
5. See, e.g., Roland Barthes, "From Work to Text," in *Image-Music-Text,* ed. and tr. Stephen Heath (New York, 1977), p. 160: "The citations which go to make up a text are anonymous, untraceable, and yet *already read:* they are quotations without inverted commas."
6. Geoffrey Hartman, "Words, Wish, Worth: Wordsworth," in *Deconstruction and Criticism,* p. 187.

7. Nelly Furman, "Textual Feminism," in *Woman and Language in Literature and Society,* ed. Sally McConnell-Ginet, Ruth Borker, and Nelly Furman (New York, 1980), p. 49.

8. Jonathan Culler, "Literary Competence," in *Structuralist Poetics* (Ithaca, 1975). Rpt. in *Reader-Response Criticism: From Formalism to Post-Structuralism,* ed. Jane P. Tompkins (Baltimore, 1980), p. 102. Cf. Annette Kolodny, "Dancing Through the Minefield: Some Observations on the Theory, Practice and Politics of a Feminist Literary Criticism," *Feminist Studies,* 6, No. 1 (Spring 1980), 10: "What we have really come to mean when we speak of competence in reading historical texts, therefore, is the ability to recognize literary conventions which have survived through time."

9. Stanley E. Fish, "Interpreting the *Variorum*," *Critical Inquiry,* 2 (Spring 1976), 465–85.

10. Fish, p. 483: "In other words these strategies exist prior to the act of reading and therefore determine the shape of what is read." Cf. Furman, p. 52: "Furthermore the reader is not a passive consumer, but an active producer of a new text."

11. Fish, p. 484.

12. Fish, p. 484.

13. Raymond Williams, *Marxism and Literature* (Oxford, 1977), p. 179: "For it is of the essence of a convention that it ratifies an assumption or a point of view so that the work can be made and received."

14. Williams, p. 173.

15. Quoted in "Breaking the Conventions of the Women's Novel," *Boston Globe,* 28 Nov. 1977, p. 15.

16. Frye, p. 102.

17. Norman Holland, "Unity Identity Text Self," *PMLA,* 90, No. 5 (October 1975), 818: "All readers create from the fantasy seemingly 'in' the work fantasies to suit their several character structures. Each reader in effect, recreates the work in terms of his own identity theme."

18. Jonathan Culler points out that Holland is working with a simplified notion of personal identity, that people "are not harmonious wholes whose every action expresses their essence or is determined by their ruling 'identity theme.'" "Prolegomena to a Theory of Reading," in *The Reader in the Text: Essays on Audience and Interpretation,* ed. Susan R. Sulieman and Inge Crosman (Princeton, 1980), p. 53.

19. Furman, p. 52.

20. Kolodny, p. 12.

21. Harold Bloom, *Kabbalah and Criticism* (New York, 1975), p. 76.

22. All feminist critics agree on the importance of this enterprise. The most frequently cited reference on the subject is Adrienne Rich's call for "revisioning" our literary past in "When We Dead Awaken: Writing as Re-Vision," *College English,* 34, No. 1 (October 1978), 18.

23. Sandra Gilbert and Susan Gubar, *The Madwoman in the Attic: The Woman Writer and the Nineteenth-Century Literary Imagination* (New Haven, 1979). Since this work will be cited frequently, all subsequent page references will be indicated in the text.

24. Hélène Cixous's comments provide the strongest explanation for this. See "The Laugh of the Medusa," tr. Keith Cohen and Paula Cohen, *Signs,* 1, No. 4 (Summer 1976), 875–93: "A feminine text cannot fail to be more than subversive. It is volcanic; as it is written it brings about an upheaval of the old property crust, carrier of masculine investments; there's no other way."

25. Judith Fetterley, *The Resisting Reader: A Feminist Approach to American Fiction* (Bloomington, 1978).

26. Annette Kolodny, "A Map for Rereading: Or, Gender and the Interpretation of Literary Texts," *New Literary History,* 11, No. 3 (Spring 1980), 451–67. Since this article will be cited frequently, all subsequent page references will be indicated in the text.

27. What is surprising and annoying is that reader-response critics so rarely recognize the similarities or refer to the work of feminist critics. Even two recent collections, both with extensive bibliographies and both edited by women, make no mention of feminist criticism: Tompkins, ed., *Reader-Response Criticism,* and Suleiman and Crosman, eds., *The Reader of the Text.*

28. Elaine Showalter, "Review Essay," *Signs,* 1, No. 2 (Winter 1975), 435.

29. Kate Chopin's *The Awakening* is the obvious second choice. Conventions available to readers differ for other reasons than time, of course. An interesting illustration of the influence of geography is Margaret Atwood's novel *Surfacing* (New York, 1972), which was read in the United States as a feminist statement and in Canada as a statement about Canadian nationalism.

30. Elaine R. Hedges, "Afterword," in Charlotte Perkins Gilman's *The Yellow Wallpaper* (New York, 1973), p. 39. Since this work will be cited

frequently, all subsequent page references will be indicated in the text.

31. William Dean Howells, ed., *The Great Modern American Stories* (New York, 1920), p. vii.

32. Interestingly, the work is classified as "Juvenile Literature" under the Library of Congress classification system.

33. Atwood, "After I Fell Apart," in *The Animals in That Country* (Boston, 1968).

34. Sylvia Plath, *Ariel* (New York, 1966).

35. Jean E. Kennard, *Victims of Convention* (Hamden, Conn., 1978).

36. Erica Jong, *Loveroot* (New York, 1968).

37. Jong, *Half-Lives* (New York, 1973).

38. In *Mountain Moving Day,* ed. Elaine Gill (New York, 1973).

39. *Surfacing,* p. 129.

40. *The Diviners* (Toronto, 1974), p. 263.

41. The use of the first person in feminist criticism is related to this notion. See Suzanne Juhasz, "The Critic as Feminist: Reflections on Women's Poetry, Feminism and the Art of Criticism," *Women's Studies,* 5 (1977), 113–27; Sandra Gilbert, "Life Studies, or, Speech After Long Silence: Feminist Critics Today," *College English,* 40 (1979), 849–63; Jean E. Kennard, "Personally Speaking: Feminist Critics and the Community of Readers," *College English,* 43 (1981), 140–45.

42. Alice Munro, *Dance of the Happy Shades* (Toronto, 1968).

43. Carol P. Christ, *Diving Deep and Surfacing: Women Writers on Spiritual Quest* (Boston, 1980), p. 64.

44. Doris Lessing, *A Man and Two Women and Other Stories* (New York, 1963).

45. Adrienne Rich, *Diving into the Wreck* (New York, 1973), p. 24.

46. See, e.g., Susan Sutheim, "For Witches," and Jean Tepperman, "Witch," in *No More Masks,* ed. Florence Howe and Ellen Bass (New York, 1973),

pp. 297 and 333. *Amazon Poetry,* ed. Elly Bulkini and Joan Larkin (New York, 1975).

47. See, e.g., Kate Millett's *Flying* (New York, 1974) and Kolodny's article on critical responses to it, "The Lady's Not for Spurning: Kate Millett and the Critics," *Contemporary Literature,* 17, No. 4 (1976), 541–62.

48. See, e.g., Tillie Olsen's "I Stand Here Ironing," in *Tell Me A Riddle* (New York, 1961). Also Jong's "The Woman Who Loved to Cook," in *Half-Lives;* Nikki Giovanni's "Woman Poem," in *Black Feeling, Black Talk, Black Judgement* (New York, 1970).

49. Mona Van Duyn, *To See, To Take* (New York, 1970).

50. In *No More Masks,* p. 158.

51. *No More Masks,* p. 257.

52. Virginia Woolf, "Modern Fiction," in *The Common Reader* (London, 1951).

53. Doris Lessing, *A Proper Marriage* (1952; rpt. New York, 1970), p. 206.

54. Marguerite de Navarre, *The Heptameron,* tr. Walter K. Kelly (London, n.d.), p. 9.

55. Quoted in Jocelyn Baines, *Joseph Conrad: A Critical Biography* (London, 1960), pp. 136–37.

56. Cf. Christ, pp. 4–5: "In a very real sense, there is no experience without stories. There is a dialectic between stories and experience. Stories give shape to experience, experience gives rise to stories."

57. *The Diviners,* p. 350.

58. Cf. Nelly Furman's discussion of textual criticism in "Textual Feminism."

59. Walter Benn Michaels, "The Interpreter's Self: Pierce on the Cartesian Subject," *Georgia Review,* 31 (1977), 383–402.

60. Fish, *Is There a Text in This Class? The Authority of Interpretive Communities* (Cambridge, Mass., 1980), p. 332.

CHAPTER SIX

Poststructural Criticism: Language as Context

Others for Language *all their Care express*
  —Pope, *An Essay on Criticism*

In the earlier chapters of this book I have defined and illustrated five contexts for criticism, five ways of looking at the literary work to decide what it means. And I have claimed that these contexts are the fundamental grounds for interpretation because questions of meaning must first be decided within one of these contexts before the significance of that meaning can be gauged. Perhaps the wary reader was inclined to accept this distinction, and the contexts themselves, only provisionally. This same reader may have noticed that occasionally the symmetrical diagram mapped some asymmetrical concepts. The mimetic context, for example, does not go exactly on all fours with the others because it seems to offer a standard for evaluating rather than determining meanings. Not surprisingly, then, the discussion of mimeticism opened easily to the larger concerns of significance.

All similes limp, as the proverb has it, and if the inclusion of the mimetic context has hobbled my metaphor, it has allowed us to at least touch upon some ideas that have been central to thinking about art from the time of ancient Greece. It has also allowed us to touch upon some difficult conceptual problems. For not only will explorers in this context soon encounter such large questions as what is "truth" and what is "reality"; they will also quickly meet the related question of how truth or reality, however it may be defined, can be presented, or represented, in language. And even to state the case this way may beg the question because it assumes that there is a truth or reality independent of language that is to be represented by means of language.

But this is merely to say that the problems of the mimetic context appear sooner rather than later. Explorers on the vertical axis of our diagram will eventually encounter their own puzzles. The author, that solid center of genetic meaning who is the object as well as the subject of biography, gradually diminishes to the vanishing point as one pursues the day, the hour, the instant when the "real" poem was fully present to the author's consciousness. And that same apparently solid center expands, diffuses, and quite evaporates again as one pursues in the opposite direction the forces, the ideas, the "spirit of the age" that made the author that made the work. In either case the center and origin of meaning in genetic criticism, the meaner, disappears, and only language remains. Attempts to center meaning in the reader, we have noticed, will encounter parallel problems. Critics who report the behavior of actual readers offer us an embarrassing variety of different meanings; those who try to ground interpretation in some version of an ideal reader tend to shift the argument to one of the other contexts. And neither those critics who claim to interpret poems, nor those who claim merely to interpret readers, are ever free from the web of words.

Whatever line we follow then, it seems that thought finally reaches an impasse and begins to turn back on itself. Obviously these problems do not stop us from interpreting, because we cannot read at all without interpreting. But if we pause to face the problems, we may be moved to wonder how far our practice of interpreting, and our confidence in that practice, depends on our ability to suppress these problems, to become blind to the impasses. We have discovered often enough, as we moved from context to context, from argument to argument, that critics who were very clear-sighted in spotting the difficulties of other approaches appeared to be rather less perceptive about their own perceptions. Because metaphors in such discussions turn frequently to the visual, we may say we have here several variations on an old problem: it is very difficult to examine the lens you see with, to look *at* the instrument you are looking *through*.

But the visual metaphor, like all metaphors, may obscure as well as enlighten. For one constant in all these paradoxes and impasses is that they appear to arise from the nature of language itself. If language is our instrument of thought, as it is certainly our instrument of expression, then we are always in the position of trying to think about language in language. And if, as some philosophers maintain, we can escape this predicament (though the etymology of "predicament" offers little encouragement here), we must then fall into another, for we must at any rate talk about language in language, and even at this level the potential for confusion is high.

The problems of language, then, haunt all our contexts. But the formal and intertextual critics have often seemed to be most fully aware of these problems and to have wrestled most strenuously with them. We recall that the formalist usually begins by separating the language of poetry from other kinds of language. The words of a poem may be quite ordinary—as, for example, in "London" or "The Sick Rose"—but the contextual pressures within the poem itself create tensions, ambiguities, paradoxes, ironies, in short, special meanings that arise from this unique and supercharged arrangement of words. Furthermore, elements that would be irrelevant and distracting in conversation or in a laboratory report—such as rhythm, rhyme, meter, image, metaphor, and symbol—all combine in the poem to *form* meaning. As a consequence of these synergistic pressures, quite ordinary words become extraordinary language as their extensive and intensive meanings fuse in tensive balance. The result, the formalist argues, is an indissoluble unity of form and content that can express important truths, truths that cannot be stated, or rather, imaged, in any other pattern of words.

We have already examined many aspects of this argument; here we should note three points in particular. First, by asserting the truth-telling or referential function of the poem, the formalists purchase a powerful argument for poetic value, but at a price. For now they must deal with all the difficulties of the mimetic context, most centrally the (re)presentational problems noted earlier. And the formalists' claim that the poem is a special kind of verbal structure that is in some mysterious way

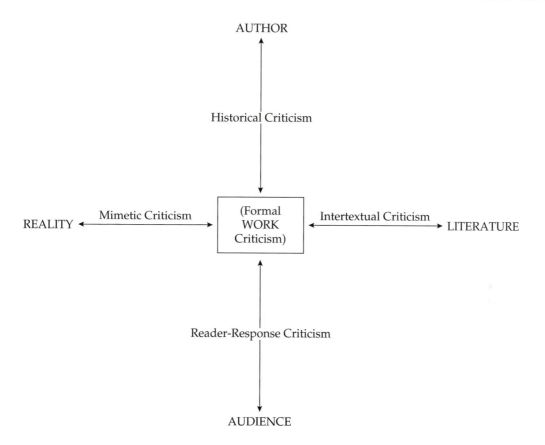

AUTHOR

Historical Criticism

REALITY ← Mimetic Criticism → (Formal WORK Criticism) ← Intertextual Criticism → LITERATURE

Reader-Response Criticism

AUDIENCE

peculiarly suited to capture the complexities of nonverbal reality is a claim that has not been accepted by all students of language.

Second, as we saw earlier, the formalists threaten to undercut their own mimetic ground when they emphasize the poem's apparently nonreferential qualities of unity and coherence. But are unity and coherence really features of the poem, or are they simply functions of the critics' own rage for order? And can the formalists escape the relativism of reader-response criticism by appealing to the "text" as a stable origin and center of meaning? Or does the radically metaphorical nature of poetic language, the same metaphorical nature that the formalists have always taken as a starting point, undercut this claim? For one could argue that precisely because poetic language is radically metaphorical, it is radically indeterminate. That is, poetic language will always elude readings that seek to impose upon it a complete unity or to determine exactly its range of meanings. Other equally coherent readings will always be possible, and instead of a stable center for determinate meaning, the text becomes, from this perspective, a network for the free play of an indefinite number of meanings.

And this argument leads to the third point. For if these are the consequences of taking very seriously the metaphorical or "rhetorical" nature of poetic language, what follows if we examine closely, with a formalist's trained eye for implied image and submerged metaphor, the "nonpoetic" language used in other forms of discourse, and we discover that this language too—in fact, all language—is radically metaphorical or rhetorical? One thing that will follow is that the formalists' enabling distinction between "poetic" and "nonpoetic" language will begin to get fuzzy. If the language explaining a poem is itself poetic, then the poet and the critic, the poem and the commentary, will begin to blur and meld in an unsettling way, all the more unsettling because here, too, the conclusion that shakes the formalist's premises appears to follow directly from those premises.

Now the intertextual critics, and particularly those most committed to a structuralist perspective, have recognized some of these difficulties. By taking the system of language as their base and model, they acknowledge more fully than do critics in any other context the central place of language in all matters of interpretation. Furthermore, by stressing the self-referential nature of the system, they are able to defer (indefinitely, some would argue) the problems of mimesis or correspondence. "Meanings" are generated and deciphered within the self-contained system of signs. In this view we humans are essentially structuring or signifying animals, and our entire culture—the foods we eat, the clothes we wear, the sounds we utter—is a system of sign systems, a layering of codes. Hence the broad claim that all the world, at least as it can be known to *homo significans,* is "text," and all understanding, all deciphering, is "intertextual."

This is, of course, a radical structuralist's view of the world. Not all intertextual critics feel compelled to extend the notion of "text" this far. Yet even if we confine ourselves to more traditional literary problems, the intertextual emphasis on system or code seems to have wide explanatory power. Perhaps most importantly it offers to explain how readers may come to know literature in the same way that they progressively come to know their own language. At least by analogy, then, we can talk of the "language" of poetry, or of painting, of architecture, of music, and so forth. In each medium the competent "readers"—and, perforce, the competent artists—would be those who had mastered the conventions, the "language," of their art. From this perspective, the study of poetry could become the coherent, progressive discipline that Frye and others have called for, and "literary criticism" would be the name of that discipline.

Thus, intertextual critics offer their perspective as the interpretive context *par excellence,* for they undertake to show not simply what a particular poem means but how it is possible for a poem to carry meaning at all and how it is possible for the competent reader to understand that meaning. Consequently, they would argue that my diagram is misleading. In place of a number of perspectives set at equal distance from the work and from each other, with the formalist perspective apparently closer or more central than the rest, the intertextual critics would image a pyramid with the intertextual perspective at the base, since to understand anything in language at all, they would claim, is to understand "intertextually," that is, within a system of conventional signs. In other words, the textual meaning that formalists claim as their ground is in turn grounded on intertextual meaning. And so is every other kind of meaning.

But how solid is that ground? One suggestion of sponginess appears when we try to separate the "literary" elements in a work from the "nonliterary" elements. "The Sick Rose" is a poem in English. It would mean little to a highly competent reader of French poetry who knew no English. But it would also mean little to a native speaker of English who knew nothing about poetry and who happened to be in search of gardening instruction. And if we set about learning the language of poetry — that system of conventions somehow independent of particular linguistic systems, although always expressed within one of them — is there any principle of limitation we could apply? Or will the right side of our diagram expand indefinitely until we are driven once more to the position of the radical structuralist and must see the strands of any text interwoven with the strands of all texts? If so, then again the world becomes "text," no clear line can be drawn between one kind of text and another kind, or between one text and another text, and the meaning of any individual text becomes radically indeterminate because potentially limitless. In this view, intertextual meaning seems not merely a rather spongy ground for textual meaning but a quicksand that threatens to submerge the individual poem in a slough of signs.

This threat may not be as serious as it sounds as long as the individual reader can supply the focus. But it is not easy to see how readers are going to keep their feet on this ground either. We may be, as the structuralists claim, structuring animals. But it is at least as true to say that we are structured animals, as much products as producers of systems, as much creatures as creators of our structures. Language once again supplies the paradigm. Any language is a system of systems — phonological, morphological, syntactical, lexical. Those who know the phonemes of English, for example, can immediately structure the speech sounds they hear into clusters of sounds, grouping together as one "sound" all variations that never contrast meanings in English (paying no attention, say, to the change from aspirated to unaspirated "p" in the word *pip*) but sharply distinguishing differences in sound that are significant in the system (such as the voicing of the initial consonant that changes *pip* to *bip*). We say that English listeners "structure" the sounds they hear, but only to the extent that those sounds conform to the independent and impersonal structure of English. And if the English phonemic system is the only one they know, listeners will quite automatically "hear" any language the same way, which means that they will miss some significant sounds when listening to a different language. So it would be as accurate to say that English has structured their hearing, has formed their perceptions. In this respect, surely, we are much less creators than we are creatures of "our" language.

And language, to repeat, is the paradigm case, the simple instance of structured humanity. If our analogy holds, the idea of what qualifies one as a competent hearer of English could be expanded to explain what makes one a competent reader of *Hamlet* by showing how much of the system of English and how much of the system of "literature" such a reader would need to master — or be mastered by. Such an explanation would be immensely complex, yet at any point within these multi-layered and interlocking systems the paradigm case would apply: readers could read only according to the way they had been structured. Thus the idea of the sturdy, autonomous "ego" controlling meaning as it reads begins to sink into the same slough of signs.

Another troublesome feature of structures emerges when we try to think of their origin and development. For if the "system" must be already in place before any element in that system can have meaning, it is difficult to conceive of an origin or starting point. The problem here is not the infinite regress of the diachronic vision where each cause must have its prior cause, *ad infinitum*, but the impossibility of regressing at all. For try as we might to image in its pristine isolation the first meaningful utterance, the first systemless "sign" around which the system could form, imagination fails us. There can be no meaning, no sign, except within the system that confers meaning. So the system must be already there at the beginning; it must be always already there. In short, from this perspective we can't very well account for the phenomenon of change at all, and this thoroughly synchronic vision seems to throw up new versions of the ancient paradoxes propounded by Zeno the Eleatic that appeared to show that change itself was but an illusion.

So the intertextual line, too, ends in paradox and puzzle. We start with the plausible view that meaning takes place within a conventional system, with "ordinary language" serving as the paradigm, and we construct on this ground a vision of literary criticism as a progressive and coherent discipline that might explain the system of literature as linguistics explains the system of language. Yet these premises, which promise to explain much, seem to lead logically to larger and more radical claims and to some puzzling problems. The very notion of "intertextuality," while showing how texts can have meaning, seems to undercut any way of delimiting meaning. For while it is easy to see that meaning must be limited by context, it is hard to see how context can be limited. Furthermore, the idea of structure begins to double-back on itself in odd ways if one pushes the structuralist premises far enough. At the end of the line, the coder and decoder of the message come to appear not as autonomous creators and masters of structures they employ but, at least in part, as creatures structured by the codes, employees of the system, with the notion of the autonomous ego itself being merely a device of language. The difficulty we have in thinking of the origin of the system, of imaging that first, lonely, "sign," may be a symptom of this condition. This is, perhaps, a strange conclusion to structuralist thought, but it is one that appears to follow logically from structuralist assumptions.

We may say, then, that even those critics who have wrestled most strenuously with the problems of language have come off with nothing better than a draw. Their own premises seem to carry implications that, when fully unfolded, serve to undercut those premises. To demonstrate that this is always the case is the main task or project of the "deconstructive" critics. The chief figure here, and the man who has provided the name and many of the key terms for the movement, is the French philosopher Jacques Derrida. Derrida's way of working—he will not call it a method—is to concentrate his considerable analytical powers on a particular text, usually a piece of discursive or "philosophical" prose, and to deconstruct or "unbuild" that text to show how it was constructed, to reveal its underlying metaphorical base. In this description, Derrida appears to practice some combination of formal and structural analysis, and that appearance is not entirely misleading, for Derrida could be called a superformalist or a superstructuralist, a reader who is willing to push the assumptions of the formal and structural perspectives to their logical, and paradoxical, conclusions. Above all else, he is a philosopher who takes the problems of language seriously and who argues that Western "metaphysics" from Plato to the present has contrived to ignore or suppress those problems. As Derrida sees it, metaphysicians have typically thought of truth or ultimate reality as something above or beyond language. They have then sought, or simply assumed, an "unproblematic" language, a transparent medium that would contain or express this truth, a "philosophical discourse" that would rise above the ambiguities of ordinary language and the obscuring rhetoricity of poetry. By subjecting "philosophical" texts to careful, formal analysis, Derrida seeks to show that there is no such language. All philosophical texts, all texts of any kind, he argues, are radically metaphorical or "poetic," and thus the very nature of language undoes the metaphysicians' attempts to get through or beyond language, to convey their thoughts directly without imposing an intervening screen of rhetoric.

Some philosophers who have been acutely aware of these problems have tried to circumvent this screening effect by claiming to concentrate on those moments when the objects of thought were most fully "present" to the thinker, and the speaker of those thoughts most fully "present" to his or her hearers. Socrates's famous distrust of writing is a case in point. These attempts, according to Derrida, have led to the widespread and mistaken "privileging" of speech over writing, which has led in turn to Derrida's already notorious reversal of that priority, his counter-privileging of writing and the science of "grammatology." By such reversals and transpositions, Derrida wants to decenter our thought so we can see how it was centered in the first place. In the case of speech and writing, for example, the paradoxical position that writing is prior to speech becomes more understandable when we notice that by "writing" Derrida means something like the system of language, and in this he shows himself a thoroughgoing structuralist as well as a thoroughgoing formalist. For, as we have noted, the necessary condition for any meaningful utterance is that it be structured according to a system that is, in Derrida's phrase, "always already" in place and quite independent of the speaker—already "written," one might say.

As a formalist, then, Derrida deconstructs the text to reveal its metaphorical basis, its inherent rhetoricity, conditions necessarily at odds with the idea of philosophical prose as a transparent, undistorting medium for presenting nonverbal reality. As a structuralist, he deconstructs the text to show how it is structured by the system of language, a condition that once again limits the control of the speaker or author. Furthermore, as a radical structuralist, he subjects the concept of "structure" to the same deconstructive analysis. This maneuver is illustrated in his reading of the structural anthropologist Claude Lévi-Strauss in the essay "Structure, Sign, and Play," which follows in this section. Here Derrida reveals at the "center" of structuralist thought an insoluble paradox: structuralists argue that they can critique empiricism because any knowledge empirically derived can be recognized as knowledge only within a system already in place; yet structuralists simultaneously argue that their own understanding of the system was empirically derived and can, therefore, be altered by new empirical discoveries. In other words, the structuralists claim to operate outside structure while claiming that such operation is impossible. And both claims are necessary to their enterprise.

This paradox haunts our attempts to think about structure at any and all levels. It is surely lurking in the tension we noted between the formalist's "empirical" view of form as the unique possession of the individual poem and the intertextualist's "structural" view of form as what the poem shares with other poems. For to make critical statements at all, each must accommodate the other's viewpoint. At a higher level of abstraction, the paradox is central to the long-playing debate between those who claim that truth is a matter of empirically discovered correspondence to "the way things are" and those who claim that truth is a matter of coherence, of conformity to a system of beliefs already in place. For empiricists must finally defend their view on the ground that it is consistent with our other beliefs, whereas their opponents must finally argue that the coherence theory does indeed correspond to "the way things are."

Closer to hand, the reader can discover a convenient example of the problem in the design of this book, because it should now be apparent that our program—to examine four target texts from different perspectives, and to measure the usefulness of these perspectives by what they revealed about the texts—could be pursued only by ignoring this empiricist–structuralist paradox. If we assume we can apply, say, a formal approach to *The Tempest*, and then a historical approach, an intertextual approach, and so forth, and see which approach works best, or see to what extent each "works," we implicitly claim that we possess already a standard of critical adequacy independent of any approach. We will know what "works" when we see it. This is the empiricist view, and our willingness to accept this as the commonsense view shows our empirical bias. Yet if we must always read some way, within some context, then the structuralist view reasserts itself, for if we can never know the poem apart from some approach, then we can never use the "poem" to test the adequacy of an approach. We may prefer one context to another, but we could never point to the poem to ground that preference, could never claim one perspective was more "illuminating" than another, for the idea of what counted as illumination would itself be determined within the context we were defending. By such reasoning we simultaneously undercut our structures while revealing our inability to do without them.

These, then, are some of the consequences of deconstructive thought. As the sample essay illustrates, Derrida is difficult to paraphrase or summarize. Because he claims to approach each text on its own terms, even if only to show that these terms are not what the author thought they were, he claims to be something of an empiricist himself. Yet he knows full well that he cannot escape the dilemma he reveals in Lévi-Strauss's thought. Furthermore, because he is acutely aware of the metaphorical nature of language and of our tendency to overlook that nature, he has adopted a strategy of changing his key terms, his key metaphors, from book to book, or even from essay to essay, to prevent them hardening into unexamined starting points. By such shifts and dodges he hopes to keep his readers alive to the rhetorical basis of his own language and to remind us that he doesn't offer a method or a system. Rather, he offers a way of reading that focuses our attention on the problematic nature of language and that deconstructs the methods and systems of others.

Yet despite his claim to offer no method, or perhaps because of it, Derrida's way of reading has attracted a number of followers, especially in the field of literary criticism. On this side of the Atlantic, three of the most prominent figures associated with deconstruction are Paul de Man, Geoffrey Hartman, and J. Hillis Miller. Each of these men was an established critic before adopting the name and some of the aims of deconstruction, and each has a different emphasis and practices a different kind of deconstructive analysis. Hartman, for example, has been most concerned with the theoretical implications of the movement for the entire enterprise of criticism, often celebrating the ludic and "liberating" elements in deconstruction. Miller shares some of these interests but tends to downplay theory and to focus, like a good formalist, on specific texts. For him, deconstruction is yet one more critical perspective that may help him in his attempt to get at what he calls "the oddity of literary language." This focus on individual texts is even more intense in the work of Paul de Man, whose patient, probing, careful analyses are in some ways ideal formalist readings.

As even these few examples show, deconstruction is hardly a unified school of criticism, and given Derrida's starting point, that is scarcely surprising. Nonetheless, the work of Derrida and his followers has been much discussed and often imitated in the past three decades, so much so that we may soon have in print a deconstructive reading of most major literary texts. And this seems, in some ways, a rather strange prospect. After all, it might be exciting and liberating to argue, as Derrida does, that "philosophical" texts are radically metaphorical or tropical, that they have not achieved a truth-bearing medium free from the distortions of rhetoric or poetry, but it can hardly be news that poems are radically metaphorical or rhetorical. The formal and intertextual critics have asserted that all along. And up to a certain point, the deconstructive critic always performs some version of formal or intertextual analysis.

But it is the mark of the deconstructive critics not to stop at any certain point. As formalists—and the rigorous analyses of Paul de Man may be taken as exemplary here—they will be concerned with the rhetorical or tropical nature of the text's language, but they will not start with the formalist assumption of unity or coherence. Instead, given their view of language, they will work from the opposite assumption and will seek to show how the rhetoricity of the text will undo or undercut any single or unified meaning. Thus the language of the poem, sharing with all language a radically rhetorical nature, shares too the condition of being radically undecidable or indeterminate. Ironically, de Man, starting from this assumption, occasionally comes to re-distinguish and re-privilege specifically "poetic" language as the only language aware of its own condition. The poem, by frankly announcing itself as a rhetorical or metaphorical structure, rather than trying to conceal this condition as "nonpoetic" language does, becomes the only truly honest language. This seems to be the deconstructivists' version of the old idea that poets never lie because they never affirm. In this version, the poet's language affirms only that it lies—which at least puts it one up on everybody else's language.

As formalists, then, the deconstructive critics keep all the formalist assumptions, except the central one that coherence and unity are the defining features of poetry. Likewise, as intertextualists, they accept most of the structuralist assumptions: the poem is an utterance encoded in a system of signs, a *parole* in the *langue* of literature; the text is a dense fabric of threads stretching out to other texts. The exemplary figure here might be Roland Barthes as he carries his structuralist enterprise to its elaborate and playful conclusion in *S/Z*, a book-length reading of a Balzac short story in terms of several layered codes. Looked at one way, the book is the apogee of structuralism. Yet one gets the impression that these codes lack the firmness that the typical structuralist would want. It seems they could easily be more or fewer or other than they are, and rather than revealing a "competent" reader who has mastered a system of literary codes firmly controlling large but determinate meanings, the book displays instead a subtle and playful intelligence exulting in the creation of signs, "codes," and alternative versions of the story he is "reading." As intertextualists then, deconstructive critics accept the main structuralist assumptions, but refuse to accept the limits that the concepts of structure or system are generally thought to impose.

In other words, the relationship between structuralism and "poststructuralism" is complex. Poststructuralism is sometimes simply another name for deconstruction, but even in this restricted sense it is potentially confusing. As Derrida's critique of Lévi-Strauss illustrates, in important ways deconstruction is not so much a break from structuralism as an extension of it. Structuralist thinkers had already applied the linguistic model to all cultural phenomena, had already "textualized" the world. And in the process they had gone some way toward decentering the "individuals" who were supposed to control these all-encompassing semiological systems. Yet structuralist thought is characterized, as the term "structure" implies, by an emphasis on order, form, and limit. Authors and readers may be less in control than they imagine, but the system, the structure, remains always in place to stabilize meaning. It is exactly this stability that the deconstructive critique of structure destabilizes, revealing a system that guarantees only free play, a ceaseless slide of signifiers, an endless deferral of meaning with all possible points of fixity—origin, telos, center, circumference—now deconstructed. And this critique, we should remember, takes place at the level of language itself, the foundation and paradigm of structuralist thought.

Deconstructive criticism, then, is poststructural in at least three senses: it comes after structuralism; it deconstructs the central concept of "structure"; yet at the same time it continues many of the key ideas of structuralism, among them the ideas that humans are signifying creatures, that human culture is a system of sign systems, and that the source and pattern for these systems is language.

While Derrida and other deconstructive critics have concentrated their analyses on literary and philosophical texts, other writers have applied these ideas and these analytical strategies to different layers of cultural coding. If, as the structuralists claim, all culture is a language, then the deconstructive critique of language will similarly destabilize all cultural codes. With that realization, language, as Derrida has put it, "invaded the universal problematic." Poststructuralism, then, may be more broadly defined as the application of a deconstructive language model to all aspects of culture and thought.

While poststructuralism in this expanded sense has received considerable play in recent Anglo-American criticism, French thinkers have clearly been the leaders in this context, and three of the most influential have been Jacques Lacan, Jean-François Lyotard, and Jean Baudrillard. None of these writers is primarily a "literary" critic in the usual sense of the term; each developed his views independently of Derridean deconstruction; and they disagree among themselves about much. Yet their areas of agreement are more important, and their influences have been very much in the same direction. They agree, for example, that most modern philosophy from Descartes to the present has been built on the false premise that philosophy could provide a foundation for knowledge solid enough to support totalizing or universal claims. Instead, they are inclined to accept the views of skeptical thinkers such as Nietzsche and Heidegger who argue that all perspectives are partial and all representation inevitably mediated and distorted by language. They agree, too, that the autonomous, rational, unified "individual" posited by most philosophical systems is a fiction, and they are inclined to speak instead of the decentered, fragmented, and linguistically constructed "subject." Above all, they agree that language in its problematicized form is the key to understanding subjects, objects, history, and culture.

For Jacques Lacan, language is not only the base and model for all cultural formations, it is the element that literally creates and structures our psychic life. A psychoanalyst, Lacan rewrites Freud in terms of language. As the child enters the "Symbolic Order," the "pure desire" of prelinguistic existence is dominated, channeled, and repressed. "The law of man has been the law of language" (*Ecrits* 61). The result is the linguistically created "subject," including both conscious and unconscious levels. Further, the unconscious thus created is structured by language on the pattern of language. Conflating Freud's "displacement" and "condensation" with "metaphor" and "metonymy," Lacan reads the unconscious as one reads a literary language. But then, for the poststructuralist, all language is literary language.

Lyotard comes at the problematic of language from a philosophical background. Adopting aspects of Nietzsche's critique, he rejects all foundationalist and essentialist modes of thought and he parallels, on a political level, Derrida's concept of "dissemination," the insight that signification always eludes and exceeds structural constraints. For Lyotard, political struggle is very much a matter of language and depends on our using deconstructive strategies to decenter and undermine the "dominant" discourses. The goal, however, cannot be to replace one dominant discourse with another, but rather to maintain a multiplicity of discourses.

If Lyotard's extension of the poststructuralist critique of language to political discourses ends in a vision of a pluralist utopia, Baudrillard's further extension of that critique takes on a distinctly dystopian cast. While Lacan saw the unconscious as structured like a language and Lyotard subsumed politics to discourse theory, the early Baudrillard explained economics on the model of language. Deconstructing the Marxist distinctions between base and superstructure, use value and exchange value, he pictured the economy as an endless circulation of signs with no values that could be grounded outside the system. In effect, exchange value was the only value. Here again we replace foundational systems of thought, like those of Freud or Marx, which claim to get beneath superficial appearances to reveal the real meaning, the real forces, underneath, with something resembling the deconstructivist language model. In the later work of Baudrillard this model, now extended to the entire textualized world, to all aspects of culture, yields the vision of "hyperreality." We live, says Baudrillard, in a postmodern age of "radical semiurgy," an era of proliferated signs where the boundaries between sign and signified have "imploded" and the very basis of the "real" has simply disappeared. "Life" imitates "art," Disneyland becomes the exemplar, and the entire world is simulacra, signs without referents. "Whoever lives by meaning dies by meaning."

An extreme view, certainly, though one that was perhaps implicit all along in the poststructural critique of language and representation. Once the deconstructive view of language was combined with the structuralist idea that language is the model for all cultural formations, the road was open to Baudrillard's hyperreality. To be sure, not all poststructuralists have been willing to go as far as Baudrillard, but most have worked to extend the critique of language and representation to various aspects of culture. In the process, they have profoundly influenced the way we think about language, literature, philosophy, politics, and the psyche. Their terminology, their analytical strategies, and their key ideas have been adopted and adapted by writers in all these fields, often by writers who in important ways disagree with them.

We will see some of these influences and disagreements in the next chapter. If we focus now on the more limited area of "literary" study as it is usually defined, we can say that on one level poststructural criticism offers a way of reading texts that combines and extends formal and intertextual analysis, but with the crucial differences noted above. On another level, and perhaps more importantly, it offers a metacritical and skeptical critique of all contexts and systems and theories of reading. By subjecting language to deconstructive analysis, poststructuralists remind us that our constructs are, after all, constructs and that the metaphors we think with are, after all, metaphors. By following the premises of our interpretative systems to their paradoxical conclusions, they remind us that we often achieve our insights by turning a blind eye to those impasses where our line of thought turns back upon itself. We will, of course, go on thinking and speaking in metaphors, for we have no other way to think or speak. And we will go on interpreting in one context or another, for we have no other ways to interpret. But if we have absorbed the lessons of poststructural thought, we will suspect that our practices rest on very shaky theoretical foundations. Language has indeed "invaded the universal problematic."

Suggestions for Further Reading

For deconstruction the work of Jacques Derrida is central; Peggy Kamuf, ed., *A Derrida Reader* (1991) offers a convenient selection. Roland Barthes, *S/Z* (1970) shows this protean writer in one of his poststructuralist phases. Some representative texts by American critics associated with deconstruction are Paul de Man, *Blindness and Insight* (1983); Shoshana Felman, *What Does a Woman Want?* (1993); Geoffrey Hartman, *Criticism in the Wilderness* (1980); Barbara Johnson, *The Critical Difference* (1980); and J. Hillis Miller, *The Linguistic Moment from Wordsworth to Stevens* (1985). Four explanatory works on deconstruction, in recommended order of reading: G. Douglas Atkins, *Reading Deconstruction, Deconstructive Reading* (1983), Christopher Norris, *Deconstruction: Theory and Practice* (rev. ed. 1991); Jonathan Culler, *On Deconstruction* (1982), and Vincent Leitch, *Deconstruction: An Advanced Introduction* (1983). Lacan's work can be sampled in *Ecrits: A Selection* (1977), Lyotard's in Andrew Benjamin, ed., *The Lyotard Reader* (1989), and Baudrillard's in Mark Poster, ed., *Jean Baudrillard: Selected Writings* (1988). The variety of poststructuralist practice is illustrated in collections like Josue V. Harari, ed., *Textual Strategies: Perspectives in Post-Structural Criticism* (1979) and Richard Machin and Christopher Norris, eds., *Post-Structural Readings of English Poetry* (1987). Anthony Easthope, *British Post-Structuralism* (1988), and Art Berman, *From the New Criticism to Deconstruction* (1988) examine the impact of poststructuralist thought on, respectively, British and American criticism. Nick Mansfield, *Subjectivity: Theories of the Self from Freud to Haraway* (2000) is a helpful discussion of this key concept in poststructuralist thought.

THEORY

When Jacques Derrida presented his "Structure, Sign, and Play" at a conference on the "Sciences of Man" at Johns Hopkins University in 1966, it marked the entrance of deconstruction onto the Anglo-American literary scene. While no single essay can fully represent Derrida's thought, or capture his shifting terminology, this influential paper shows some aspects of that thought in operation and introduces a number of terms—supplementarity, presence, différance—which have become part of the lexicon of poststructural criticism. It also displays Derrida's characteristic way of going to work. Examining the thought of Claude Lévi-Strauss, probably the world's best-known structural anthropologist, Derrida deconstructs structuralism itself. Since deconstructivists are often called "poststructuralists," it is worth noticing that this name is potentially misleading. For although Derrida's critique proceeds by uncovering an irreducible contradiction built into structuralist thought, he does not claim to pass beyond structuralism nor to replace it with another, contradiction-free system of thought. Rather, the critique of structuralism presented here is exemplary. All systems of thought are subject to a similar deconstruction because we cannot very well think of a centerless system, one that does not claim to be grounded finally on some presence, foundation, origin (archè), or end (telos) beyond freeplay. Each of the "contexts" of this book, for example, proposes a locus or ground for meaning (author, text, audience, reality, literature), and all are open to the same critique. As long as we continue to interpret interpretation, structure, sign, and freeplay in the hope of finding an end where interpretation itself can come to rest, we are, Derrida concludes, deluded by our habits of mind and language.

Structure, Sign, and Play in the Discourse of the Human Sciences[1]

Jacques Derrida

Perhaps something has occurred in the history of the concept of structure that could be called an "event" if this loaded word did not entail a meaning which it is precisely the function of structural—or structuralist—thought to reduce or to suspect. But let me use the term "event" anyway, employing it with caution and as if in quotation marks. In this sense, this event will have the exterior form of a *rupture* and a *redoubling*.

It would be easy enough to show that the concept of structure and even the word "structure" itself are as old as the *epistèmè*—that is to say, as old as western science and western philosophy—and that their roots thrust deep into the soil of ordinary language, into whose deepest recesses the *epistèmè* plunges to gather them together once more, making them part of itself in a metaphorical displacement. Nevertheless, up until the event which I wish to mark out and define, structure—or rather the structurality of structure—although it has always been involved, has always been neutralized or reduced, and this by a process of giving it a center or referring it to a point of presence, a fixed origin. The function of this center was not only to orient, balance, and organize the structure—one cannot in fact conceive of an unorganized structure—but above all to make sure that the organizing principle of the structure would limit what we might call the *freeplay* of the structure. No doubt that by orienting and organizing the coherence of the system, the center of a structure permits the freeplay of its elements inside the total form. And even today the notion of a structure lacking any center represents the unthinkable itself.

Nevertheless, the center also closes off the freeplay it opens up and makes possible. *Qua* center, it is the point at which the substitution of contents, elements, or terms is no longer possible. At the center, the permutation or the transformation of elements (which may of course be structures enclosed within a structure) is forbidden. At least this permutation has always remained *interdicted*[2] (I use this word deliberately). Thus it has always been thought that the center, which is by definition unique, constituted that very thing within a structure which governs the structure, while escaping structurality. This is why classical thought concerning structure could say that the center is, paradoxically, *within* the structure and *outside* it. The center is at the center of the totality, and yet, since the center does not belong to the totality (is not part of the totality), the totality *has its center elsewhere*. The center is not the center. The concept of centered structure—although it represents coherence itself, the condition of the *epistèmè* as philosophy or science—is contradictorily coherent. And, as always, coherence in contradiction expresses the force of a desire. The concept of centered structure is in fact the concept of a freeplay based on a fundamental ground, a freeplay which is constituted upon a fundamental immobility and a reassuring certitude, which is itself beyond the reach of the freeplay. With this certitude anxiety can be mastered, for anxiety is invariably the result of a certain mode of being implicated in the game, of being caught by the game, of being as it were from the very beginning at stake in the game.[3] From the basis of what we therefore call the center (and which, because it can be either inside or outside, is as readily called the origin as the end, as readily *archè* as *telos*), the repetitions, the substitutions, the transformations, and the permutations are always *taken* from a history of meaning [*sens*]—that is, a history, period—whose origin may always be revealed or whose end may always be anticipated in the form of presence. This is why one could perhaps say that the movement of any archeology, like that of any eschatology, is an accomplice of this reduction of the structurality of structure and always attempts to conceive of structure from the basis of a full presence which is out of play.

If this is so, the whole history of the concept of structure, before the rupture I spoke of, must be thought of as a series of substitutions of center for center, as a linked chain of determinations of the center. Successively, and in a regulated fashion, the center receives different forms or names. The history of metaphysics, like the history of the West, is the history of these metaphors and metonymies. Its matrix—if you will pardon me for demonstrating so little and for being so elliptical in order to bring me more quickly to my principal theme—is the determination of being as *presence* in all the senses of this word. It would be possible to show that all the names related to fundamentals, to principles, or to the center have always designated the constant of a presence—*eidos, archè, telos, energeia, ousia* (essence, existence, substance, subject), *aletheia*, transcendentality, consciousness, or conscience, God, man, and so forth.

The event I called a rupture, the disruption I alluded to at the beginning of this paper, would presumably have come about when the structurality of structure had to begin to be thought, that is to say, repeated, and this is why I said that this disruption was repetition in all of the senses of this word. From then on it became necessary to think the law which governed, as it were, the desire for the center in the constitution of structure and the process of signification prescribing its displacements and its substitutions for this law of the central presence—but a central presence which was never itself, which has always already been transported outside itself in its surrogate. The surrogate does not substitute itself for anything which has somehow pre-existed it. From then on it was probably necessary to begin to think that there was no center, that the center could not be thought in the form of a being-present, that the center had no natural locus, that it was not a fixed locus but a function, a sort of nonlocus in which an infinite number of sign-substitutions came into play. This moment was that in which language invaded the universal problematic; that in which, in the absence of a center or origin, everything became discourse—provided we can agree on this word—that is to say, when everything became a system where the central signified, the original or transcendental signified, is never absolutely present outside a system of differences. The absence of the transcendental signified extends the domain and the interplay of signification *ad infinitum*.

Where and how does this decentering, this notion of the structurality of structure, occur? It would be somewhat naïve to refer to an event, a doctrine, or an author in order to designate this occurrence. It is no doubt part of the totality of an era, our own, but still it has already begun to proclaim itself and begun to *work*. Nevertheless, if I wished to give some sort of indication by choosing one or two "names," and by recalling those authors in whose discourses this occurrence has most nearly maintained its most radical formulation, I would probably cite the Nietzschean critique of metaphysics, the critique of the concepts of being and truth, for which were substituted the concepts of play, interpretation, and sign (sign without truth present); the Freudian critique of self-presence, that is, the critique of consciousness, of the subject, of self-identity and of self-proximity or self-possession; and, more radically, the Heideggerean destruction of metaphysics, of onto-theology, of the determination of being as presence. But all these destructive discourses and all their analogues are trapped in a sort of circle. This circle is unique. It describes the form of the relationship between the history of metaphysics and the destruction of the history of metaphysics. *There is no sense* in doing without the concepts of metaphysics in order to attack metaphysics. We have

no language—no syntax and no lexicon—which is alien to this history; we cannot utter a single destructive proposition which has not already slipped into the form, the logic, and the implicit postulations of precisely what it seeks to contest. To pick out one example from many: the metaphysics of presence is attacked with the help of the concept of the *sign*. But from the moment anyone wishes this to show, as I suggested a moment ago, that there is no transcendental or privileged signified and that the domain or the interplay of signification has, henceforth, no limit, he ought to extend his refusal to the concept and to the word sign itself—which is precisely what cannot be done. For the signification "sign" has always been comprehended and determined, in its sense, as sign-of, signifier referring to a signified, signifier different from its signified. If one erases the radical difference between signifier and signified, it is the word signifier itself which ought to be abandoned as a metaphysical concept. When Lévi-Strauss says in the preface to *The Raw and the Cooked*[4] that he has "sought to transcend the opposition between the sensible and the intelligible by placing [himself] from the very beginning at the level of signs," the necessity, the force, and the legitimacy of his act cannot make us forget that the concept of the sign cannot in itself surpass or bypass this opposition between the sensible and the intelligible. The concept of the sign is determined by this opposition: through and throughout the totality of its history and by its system. But we cannot do without the concept of the sign, we cannot give up this metaphysical complicity without also giving up the critique we are directing against this complicity, without the risk of erasing difference [altogether] in the self-identity of a signified reducing into itself its signifier, or, what amounts to the same thing, simply expelling it outside itself. For there are two heterogenous ways of erasing the difference between the signifier and the signified: one, the classic way, consists in reducing or deriving the signifier, that is to say, ultimately in *submitting* the sign to thought; the other, the one we are using here against the first one, consists in putting into question the system in which the preceding reduction functioned: first and foremost, the opposition between the sensible and the intelligible. The *paradox* is that the metaphysical reduction of the sign needed the opposition it was reducing. The opposition is part of the system, along with the reduction. And what I am saying here about the sign can be extended to all the concepts and all the sentences of metaphysics, in particular to the discourse on "structure." But there are many ways of being caught in this circle. They are all more or less naïve, more or less empirical, more or less systematic, more or less close to the formulation or even to the formalization of this circle. It is these differences which explain the multiplicity of destructive discourses and the disagreement between those who make them. It was within concepts inherited from metaphysics that Nietzsche, Freud, and Heidegger worked, for example. Since these concepts are not elements or atoms and since they are taken from a syntax and a system, every particular borrowing drags along with it the whole of metaphysics. This is what allows these destroyers to destroy each other reciprocally—for example, Heidegger considering Nietzsche, with as much lucidity and rigor as bad faith and misconstruction, as the last metaphysician, the last "Platonist." One could do the same for Heidegger himself, for Freud, or for a number of others. And today no exercise is more widespread.

What is the relevance of this formal schéma when we turn to what are called the "human sciences"? One of them perhaps occupies a privileged place—ethnology. One can in fact assume that ethnology could have been born as a science only at the moment when a de-centering had come about: at the moment when European culture—and, in consequence, the history of metaphysics and of its concepts—had been *dislocated,* driven from its locus, and forced to stop considering itself as the culture of reference. This moment is not first and foremost a moment of philosophical or scientific discourse, it is also a moment which is political, economic, technical, and so forth. One can say in total assurance that there is nothing fortuitous about the fact that the critique of ethnocentrism—the very condition of ethnology—should be systematically and historically contemporaneous with the destruction of the history of metaphysics. Both belong to a single and same era.

Ethnology—like any science—comes about within the element of discourse. And it is primarily a European science employing traditional concepts, however much it may struggle against them. Consequently, whether he wants to or not—and this does not depend on a decision on his part—the ethnologist accepts into his discourse the premises of ethnocentrism at the very moment when he is employed in denouncing them. This necessity is irreducible; it is not a historical contingency. We ought to consider very carefully all its implications. But if nobody can escape this necessity, and if no one is therefore responsible

for giving in to it, however little, this does not mean that all the ways of giving in to it are of an equal pertinence. The quality and the fecundity of a discourse are perhaps measured by the critical rigor with which this relationship to the history of metaphysics and to inherited concepts is thought. Here it is a question of a critical relationship to the language of the human sciences and a question of a critical responsibility of the discourse. It is a question of putting expressly and systematically the problem of the status of a discourse which borrows from a heritage the resources necessary for the deconstruction of that heritage itself. A problem of *economy* and *strategy.*

If I now go on to employ an examination of the texts of Lévi-Strauss as an example, it is not only because of the privilege accorded to ethnology among the human sciences, nor yet because the thought of Lévi-Strauss weighs heavily on the contemporary theoretical situation. It is above all because a certain choice has made itself evident in the work of Lévi-Strauss and because a certain doctrine has been elaborated there, and precisely in a *more or less explicit manner,* in relation to this critique of language and to this critical language in the human sciences.

In order to follow this movement in the text of Lévi-Strauss, let me choose as one guiding thread among others the opposition between nature and culture. In spite of all its rejuvenations and its disguises, this opposition is congenital to philosophy. It is even older than Plato. It is at least as old as the Sophists. Since the statement of the opposition—*physis/nomos, physis/technè*—it has been passed on to us by a whole historical chain which opposes "nature" to the law, to education, to art, to technics—and also to liberty, to the arbitrary, to history, to society, to the mind, and so on. From the beginnings of his quest and from his first book, *The Elementary Structures of Kinship,*[5] Lévi-Strauss has felt at one and the same time the necessity of utilizing this opposition and the impossibility of making it acceptable. In the *Elementary Structures,* he begins from this axiom or definition: that belongs to nature which is *universal* and spontaneous, not depending on any particular culture or on any determinate norm. That belongs to culture, on the other hand, which depends on a system of *norms* regulating society and is therefore capable of *varying* from one social structure to another. These two definitions are of the traditional type. But, in the very first pages of the *Elementary Structures,* Lévi-Strauss, who has begun to give these concepts an acceptable standing, encounters what he calls a *scandal,* that is to say, something which no longer tolerates the nature/culture opposition he has accepted and which seems to require *at one and the same time* the predicates of nature and those of culture. This scandal is the *incest-prohibition.* The incest-prohibition is universal; in this sense one could call it natural. But it is also a prohibition, a system of norms and interdicts; in this sense one could call it cultural.

> Let us assume therefore that everything universal in man derives from the order of nature and is characterized by spontaneity, that everything which is subject to a norm belongs to culture and presents the attributes of the relative and the particular. We then find ourselves confronted by a fact, or rather an ensemble of facts, which, in the light of the preceding definitions, is not far from appearing as a scandal: the prohibition of incest presents without the least equivocation, and indissolubly linked together, the two characteristics in which we recognized the contradictory attributes of two exclusive orders. The prohibition of incest constitutes a rule, but a rule, alone of all the social rules, which possesses at the same time a universal character (p. 9).

Obviously there is no scandal except in the *interior* of a system of concepts sanctioning the difference between nature and culture. In beginning his work with the *factum* of the incest-prohibition, Lévi-Strauss thus puts himself in a position entailing that this difference, which has always been assumed to be self-evident, becomes obliterated or disputed. For, from the moment that the incest-prohibition can no longer be conceived within the nature/culture opposition, it can no longer be said that it is a scandalous fact, a nucleus of opacity within a network of transparent significations. The incest-prohibition is no longer a scandal one meets with or comes up against in the domain of traditional concepts; it is something which escapes these concepts and certainly precedes them— probably as the condition of their possibility. It could perhaps be said that the whole of philosophical conceptualization, systematically relating itself to the nature/culture opposition, is designed to leave in the domain of the unthinkable the very thing that makes this conceptualization possible: the origin of the prohibition of incest.

I have dealt too cursorily with this example, only one among so many others, but the example nevertheless reveals that language bears within itself the necessity of its own critique. This critique may be undertaken along two tracks, in two "manners." Once the limit of nature/culture opposition makes itself felt, one might want to question systematically and rigorously the history of these concepts. This is a first action. Such a systematic and historic questioning would be neither a philological nor a philosophical action in the classic sense of these words. Concerning oneself with the founding concepts of the whole history of philosophy, deconstituting them, is not to undertake the task of the philologist or of the classic historian of philosophy. In spite of appearances, it is probably the most daring way of making the beginnings of a step outside of philosophy. The step "outside philosophy" is much more difficult to conceive than is generally imagined by those who think they made it long ago with cavalier ease, and who are in general swallowed up in metaphysics by the whole body of the discourse that they claim to have disengaged from it.

In order to avoid the possibly sterilizing effect of the first way, the other choice—which I feel corresponds more nearly to the way chosen by Lévi-Strauss—consists in conserving in the field of empirical discovery all these old concepts, while at the same time exposing here and there their limits, treating them as tools which can still be of use. No longer is any truth-value attributed to them; there is a readiness to abandon them if necessary if other instruments should appear more useful. In the meantime, their relative efficacy is exploited, and they are employed to destroy the old machinery to which they belong and of which they themselves are pieces. Thus it is that the language of the human sciences criticizes *itself.* Lévi-Strauss thinks that in this way he can separate *method* from *truth,* the instruments of the method and the objective significations aimed at by it. One could almost say that this is the primary affirmation of Lévi-Strauss; in any event, the first words of the *Elementary Structures* are: "One begins to understand that the distinction between state of nature and state of society (we would be more apt to say today: state of nature and state of culture), while lacking any acceptable historical signification, presents a value which fully justifies its use by modern sociology: its value as a methodological instrument."

Lévi-Strauss will always remain faithful to this double intention: to preserve as an instrument that whose truth-value he criticizes.

On the one hand, he will continue in effect to contest the value of the nature/culture opposition. More than thirteen years after the *Elementary Structures, The Savage Mind*[6] faithfully echoes the text I have just quoted: "The opposition between nature and culture which I have previously insisted on seems today to offer a value which is above all methodological." And this methodological value is not affected by its "ontological" non-value (as could be said, if this notion were not suspect here): "It would not be enough to have absorbed particular humanities into a general humanity; this first enterprise prepares the way for others . . . which belong to the natural and exact sciences: to reintegrate culture into nature, and finally, to reintegrate life into the totality of its physio-chemical conditions" (p. 327).

On the other hand, still in *The Savage Mind*, he presents as what he calls *bricolage*[7] what might be called the discourse of this method. The *bricoleur*, says Lévi-Strauss, is someone who uses "the means at hand," that is, the instruments he finds at his disposition around him, those which are already there, which had not been especially conceived with an eye to the operation for which they are to be used and to which one tries by trial and error to adapt them, not hesitating to change them whenever it appears necessary, or to try several of them at once, even if their form and their origin are heterogeneous—and so forth. There is therefore a critique of language in the form of *bricolage*, and it has even been possible to say that *bricolage* is the critical language itself. I am thinking in particular of the article by G. Genette, "Structuralisme et Critique littéraire," published in homage to Lévi-Strauss in a special issue *L'Arc* (no. 26, 1965), where it is stated that the analysis of *bricolage* could "be applied almost word for word" to criticism, and especially to "literary criticism."[8]

If one calls *bricolage* the necessity of borrowing one's concepts from the text of a heritage which is more or less coherent or ruined, it must be said that every discourse is *bricoleur*. The engineer, whom Lévi-Strauss opposed to the *bricoleur*, should be the one to construct the totality of his language, syntax, and lexicon. In this sense the engineer is a myth. A subject who would supposedly be the absolute origin of his own discourse and would supposedly construct it "out of nothing," "out of whole cloth," would be the creator of the *verbe*, the *verbe* itself. The notion of the engineer who had supposedly broken with all forms of *bricolage* is therefore a theological idea; and since Lévi-Strauss tells us elsewhere that *bricolage* is mythopoetic, the odds are that the engineer is a myth produced by the *bricoleur*. From the moment that we cease to believe in such an engineer and in a

discourse breaking with the received historical discourse, as soon as it is admitted that every finite discourse is bound by a certain *bricolage*, and that the engineer and the scientist are also species of *bricoleurs* then the very idea of *bricolage* is menaced and the difference in which it took on its meaning decomposes.

This brings out the second thread which might guide us in what is being unraveled here.

Lévi-Strauss describes *bricolage* not only as an intellectual activity but also as a mythopoetical activity. One reads in *The Savage Mind*, "Like *bricolage* on the technical level, mythical reflection can attain brilliant and unforeseen results on the intellectual level. Reciprocally, the mythopoetical character of *bricolage* has often been noted" (p. 26).

But the remarkable endeavor of Lévi-Strauss is not simply to put forward, notably in the most recent of his investigations, a structural science of knowledge of myths and of mythological activity. His endeavor also appears—I would say almost from the first—in the status which he accords to his own discourse on myths, to what he calls his "mythologicals." It is here that his discourse on the myth reflects on itself and criticizes itself. And this moment, this critical period, is evidently of concern to all the languages which share the field of the human sciences. What does Lévi-Strauss say of his "mythologicals"? It is here that we rediscover the mythopoetical virtue (power) of *bricolage*. In effect, what appears most fascinating in this critical search for a new status of the discourse is the stated abandonment of all reference to a *center*, to a *subject*, to a privileged *reference*, to an origin, or to an absolute *archè*. The theme of this de-centering could be followed throughout the "overture" to his last book, *The Raw and the Cooked*. I shall simply remark on a few key points.

1. From the very start, Lévi-Strauss recognizes that the Bororo myth which he employs in the book as the "reference-myth" does not merit this name and this treatment. The name is specious and the use of the myth improper. This myth deserves no more than any other its referential privilege:

> In fact the Bororo myth which will from now on be designated by the name *reference-myth* is, as I shall try to show, nothing other than a more or less forced transformation of other myths originating either in the same society or in societies more or less far removed. It would therefore have been legitimate to choose as my point of departure any representative of the group whatsoever. From this point

of view, the interest of the reference-myth does not depend on its typical character, but rather on its irregular position in the midst of a group (p. 10).

2. There is no unity or absolute source of the myth. The focus or the source of the myth are always shadows and virtualities which are elusive, unactualizable, and nonexistent in the first place. Everything begins with the structure, the configuration, the relationship. The discourse on this acentric structure, the myth, that is, cannot itself have an absolute subject or an absolute center. In order not to short change the form and the movement of the myth, that violence which consists in centering a language which is describing an acentric structure must be avoided. In this context, therefore it is necessary to forgo scientific or philosophical discourse, to renounce the *epistèmè* which absolutely requires, which is the absolute requirement that we go back to the source, to the center, to the founding basis, to the principle, and so on. In opposition to *epistèmic* discourse, structural discourse on myths — *mythological* discourse — must itself be *mythomorphic*. It must have the form of that of which it speaks. This is what Lévi-Strauss says in *The Raw and the Cooked,* from which I would now like to quote a long and remarkable passage:

> In effect the study of myths poses a methodological problem by the fact that it cannot conform to the Cartesian principle of dividing the difficulty into as many parts as are necessary to resolve it. There exists no veritable end or term to mythical analysis, no secret unity which could be grasped at the end of the work of decomposition. The themes duplicate themselves to infinity. When we think we have disentangled them from each other and can hold them separate, it is only to realize that they are joining together again, in response to the attraction of unforeseen affinities. In consequence, the unity of the myth is only tendential and projective; it never reflects a state or a moment of the myth. An imaginary phenomenon implied by the endeavor to interpret, its role is to give a synthetic form to the myth and to impede its dissolution into the confusion of contraries. It could therefore be said that the science or knowledge of myths is an *anaclastic,* taking this ancient term in the widest sense authorized by its etymology, a science which admits into its definition the study of the reflected rays along with that of the broken ones. But, unlike philosophical reflection, which claims to go all the way back to its source, the reflections in question here concern rays without any other than a virtual focus. . . . In wanting to imitate the spontaneous movement of mythi-

cal thought, my enterprise, itself too brief and too long, has had to yield to its demands and respect its rhythm. Thus is this book, on myths itself and in its own way, a myth.

This statement is repeated a little farther on (p. 20): "Since myths themselves rest on second-order codes (the first-order codes being those in which language consists), this book thus offers the rough draft of a third-order code, destined to insure the reciprocal possibility of translation of several myths. This is why it would not be wrong to consider it a myth: the myth of mythology, as it were." It is by this absence of any real and fixed center of the mythical or mythological discourse that the musical model chosen by Lévi-Strauss for the composition of his book is apparently justified. The absence of a center is here the absence of a subject and the absence of an author: "The myth and the musical work thus appear as orchestra conductors whose listeners are the silent performers. If it be asked where the real focus of the work is to be found, it must be replied that its determination is impossible. Music and mythology bring man face to face with virtual objects whose shadow alone is actual. . . . Myths have no authors" (p. 25).

Thus it is at this point that ethnographic *bricolage* deliberately assumes its mythopoetic function. But by the same token, this function makes the philosophical or epistemological requirement of a center appear as mythological, that is to say, as a historical illusion.

Nevertheless, even if one yields to the necessity of what Lévi-Strauss has done, one cannot ignore its risks. If the mythological is mythomorphic, are all discourses on myths equivalent? Shall we have to abandon any epistemological requirement which permits us to distinguish between several qualities of discourse on the myth? A classic question, but inevitable. We cannot reply — and I do not believe Lévi-Strauss replies to it — as long as the problem of the relationships between the philosopheme or the theorem, on the one hand, and the mytheme or the mythopoem(e), on the other, has not been expressly posed. This is no small problem. For lack of expressly posing this problem, we condemn ourselves to transforming the claimed transgression of philosophy into an unperceived fault in the interior of the philosophical field. Empiricism would be the genus of which these faults would always be the species. Trans-philosophical concepts would be transformed into philosophical naïvetés. One could give many examples to demonstrate this risk: the concepts of sign, history, truth, and so forth. What I want to emphasize is simply that the passage beyond philosophy does not consist in turning the page of philosophy (which usually comes down to philosophizing badly), but in continuing to read philosophers *in a certain way*. The risk I am speaking of is always assumed by Lévi-Strauss and it is the very price of his endeavor. I have said that empiricism is the matrix of all the faults menacing a discourse which continues, as with Lévi-Strauss in particular, to elect to be scientific. If we wanted to pose the problem of empiricism and *bricolage* in depth, we would probably end up very quickly with a number of propositions absolutely contradictory in relation to the status of discourse in structural ethnography. On the one hand, structuralism justly claims to be the critique of empiricism. But at the same time there is not a single book or study by Lévi-Strauss which does not offer itself as an empirical essay which can always be completed or invalidated by new information. The structural schemata are always proposed as hypotheses resulting from a finite quantity of information and which are subjected to the proof of experience. Numerous texts could be used to demonstrate this double postulation. Let us turn once again to the "Overture" of *The Raw and the Cooked*, where it seems clear that if this postulation is double, it is because it is a question here of a language on language:

> Critics who might take me to task for not having begun by making an exhaustive inventory of South American myths before analyzing them would be making a serious mistake about the nature and the role of these documents. The totality of the myths of a people is of the order of the discourse. Provided that this people does not become physically or morally extinct, this totality is never closed. Such a criticism would therefore be equivalent to reproaching a linguist with writing the grammar of a language without having recorded the totality of the words which have been uttered since that language came into existence and without knowing the verbal exchanges which will take place as long as the language continues to exist. Experience proves that an absurdly small number of sentences . . . allows the linguist to elaborate a grammar of the language he is studying. And even a partial grammar or an outline of a grammar represents a valuable acquisition in the case of unknown languages. Syntax does not wait until it has been possible to enumerate a theoretically unlimited series of events before becoming manifest, because syntax consists in the body of rules which presides over the generation of these events. And it is precisely a syntax of South American mythology that I wanted to outline. Should new texts appear to enrich the mythical discourse, then this will provide an opportunity to check or modify the way in which certain grammatical laws have been formulated, an opportunity to discard certain of them and an opportunity to discover new ones. But in no instance can the requirement of a total mythical discourse be raised as an objection. For we have just seen that such a requirement has no meaning (pp. 15–16).

Totalization is therefore defined at one time as *useless*, at another as *impossible*. This is no doubt the result of the fact that there are two ways of conceiving the limit of totalization. And I assert once again that these two determinations coexist implicitly in the discourses of Lévi-Strauss. Totalization can be judged impossible in the classical style: one then refers to the empirical endeavor of a subject or of a finite discourse in a vain and breathless quest of an infinite richness which it can never master. There is too much, more than one can say. But nontotalization can also be determined in another way: not from the standpoint of the concept of finitude as assigning us to an empirical view, but from the standpoint of the concept of *freeplay*. If totalization no longer has any meaning, it is not because the infinity of a field cannot be covered by a finite glance or a finite discourse, but because the nature of the field — that is, language and a finite language — excludes totalization. This field is in fact that of *freeplay*, that is to say, a field of infinite substitutions in the closure of a finite ensemble. This field permits these infinite substitutions only because it is finite, that is to say, because instead of being an inexhaustible field, as in the classical hypothesis, instead of being too large, there is something missing from it: a center which arrests and founds the freeplay of substitutions. One could say — rigorously using that word whose scandalous signification is always obliterated in French — that this movement of the freeplay, permitted by the lack, the absence of a center or origin, is the movement of *supplementarity*. One cannot determine the center, the sign which *supplements*[9] it, which takes its place in its absence — because this sign adds itself, occurs in addition, over and above, comes as a *supplement*.[10] The movement of signification adds something, which results in the fact that there is always more, but this addition is a floating one because it comes to perform a vicarious function, to supplement a lack on the part of the signified. Although Lévi-Strauss in his use of the word supplementary never emphasizes as I am doing here the two directions of meaning which are so strangely compounded within it, it is not by chance that he uses this word twice in his "Introduction to the Work of Marcel Mauss,"[11] at the point where he is speaking of the "superabundance of signifier, in relation to the signifieds to which this superabundance can refer":

> In his endeavor to understand the world, man therefore always has at his disposition a surplus of signification (which he portions out amongst things according to the laws of symbolic thought—which it is the task of ethnologists and linguists to study). This distribution of a *supplementary* allowance [*ration supplémentaire*]—if it is permissible to put it that way—is absolutely necessary in order that on the whole the available signifier and the signified it aims at may remain in the relationship of complementarity which is the very condition of the use of symbolic thought (p. xlix).

(It could no doubt be demonstrated that this *ration supplémentaire* of signification is the origin of the *ratio* itself.) The word reappears a little farther on, after Lévi-Strauss has mentioned "this floating signifier, which is the servitude of all finite thought":

> In other words—and taking as our guide Mauss's precept that all social phenomena can be assimilated to language—we see in *mana, Wakau, oranda* and other notions of the same type, the conscious expression of a semantic function, whose role it is to permit symbolic thought to operate in spite of the contradiction which is proper to it. In this way are explained the apparently insoluble antinomies attached to this notion. . . . At one and the same time force and action, quality and state, substantive and verb, abstract and concrete, omnipresent and localized—*mana* is in effect all these things. But is it not precisely because it is none of these things that *mana* is a simple form, or more exactly, a symbol in the pure state, and therefore capable of becoming charged with any sort of symbolic content whatever? In the system of symbols constituted by all cosmologies, *mana* would simply be a *valeur symbolique zéro*, that is to say, a sign marking the necessity of a symbolic content *supplementary* [my italics] to that with which the signified is already loaded, but which can take on any value required, provided only that this value still remains part of

the available reserve and is not, as phonologists put it, a group-term.

Lévi-Strauss adds the note:

> Linguists have already been led to formulate hypotheses of this type. For example: "A zero phoneme is opposed to all the other phonemes in French in that it entails no differential characters and no constant phonetic value. On the contrary, the proper function of the zero phoneme is to be opposed to phoneme absence." (R. Jakobson and J. Lutz, "Notes on the French Phonemic Pattern," *Word*, vol. 5, no. 2 [August, 1949], p. 155). Similarly, if we schematize the conception I am proposing here, it could almost be said that the function of notions like *mana* is to be opposed to the absence of signification, without entailing by itself any particular signification (p. 1 and note).

The *superabundance* of the signifier, its *supplementary* character, is thus the result of a finitude, that is to say, the result of a lack which must be *supplemented*.

It can now be understood why the concept of freeplay is important in Lévi-Strauss. His references to all sorts of games, notably to roulette, are very frequent, especially in his *Conversations*,[12] in *Race and History*,[13] and in *The Savage Mind*. This reference to the game or freeplay is always caught up in a tension.

It is in tension with history, first of all. This is a classical problem, objections to which are now well worn or used up. I shall simply indicate what seems to me the formality of the problem: by reducing history, Lévi-Strauss has treated as it deserves a concept which has always been in complicity with a teleological and eschatological metaphysics, in other words, paradoxically, in complicity with that philosophy of presence to which it was believed history could be opposed. The thematic of historicity, although it seems to be a somewhat late arrival in philosophy, has always been required by the determination of being as presence. With or without etymology, and in spite of the classic antagonism which opposes these significations throughout all of classical thought, it could be shown the concept of *epistèmè* has always called forth that of *historia,* if history is always the unity of a becoming, as tradition of truth or development of science or knowledge oriented toward the appropriation of truth in presence and self-presence, toward knowledge in consciousness-of-self.[14] History has always been conceived as the movement of a resumption of history, a diversion between two presences. But if it is legitimate to suspect this concept of history, there is a risk, if it is reduced without an express statement of the problem I am indicating here, of falling back into an ahistoricism of a classical type, that is to say, in a determinate moment of the history of metaphysics. Such is the algebraic formality of the problem as I see it. More concretely, in the work of Lévi-Strauss it must be recognized that the respect for structurality, for the internal originality of the structure, compels a neutralization of time and history. For example, the appearance of a new structure, of an original system, always comes about—and this is the very condition of its structural specificity—by a rupture with its past, its origin, and its cause. One can therefore describe what is peculiar to the structural organization only by not taking into account, in the very moment of this description, its past conditions: by failing to pose the problem of the passage from one structure to another, by putting history into parentheses. In this "structuralist" moment, the concepts of chance and discontinuity are indispensable. And Lévi-Strauss does in fact often appeal to them as he does, for instance, for that structure of structures, language, of which he says in the "Introduction to the Work of Marcel Mauss" that it "could only have been born in one fell swoop":

> Whatever may have been the moment and the circumstances of its appearance in the scale of animal life, language could only have been born in one fell swoop. Things could not have set about signifying progressively. Following a transformation the study of which is not the concern of the social sciences, but rather of biology and psychology, a crossing over came about from a stage where nothing had a meaning to another where everything possessed it (p. xlvi).

This standpoint does not prevent Lévi-Strauss from recognizing the slowness, the process of maturing, the continuous toil of factual transformations, history (for example, in *Race and History*). But, in accordance with an act which was also Rousseau's and Husserl's, he must "brush aside all the facts" at the moment when he wishes to recapture the specificity of a structure. Like Rousseau, he must always conceive of the origin of a new structure on the model of catastrophe—an overturning of nature in nature, a natural interruption of the natural sequence, a brushing aside *of* nature.

Besides the tension of freeplay with history, there is also the tension of freeplay with presence. Freeplay is the disruption of presence. The presence of an element is always a signifying and substitutive reference inscribed in a system of differences and the movement of a chain. Freeplay is always an interplay of absence and presence, but if it is to be radically conceived, freeplay must be conceived of before the alternative of presence and absence; being must be conceived of as presence or absence beginning with the possibility of freeplay and not the other way around. If Lévi-Strauss, better than any other, has brought to light the freeplay of repetition and the repetition of freeplay, one no less perceives in his work a sort of ethic of presence, an ethic of nostalgia for origins, an ethic of archaic and natural innocence, of a purity of presence and self-presence in speech[15]—an ethic, nostalgia, and even remorse which he often presents as the motivation of the ethnological project when he moves toward archaic societies—exemplary societies in his eyes. These texts are well known.

As a turning toward the presence, lost or impossible, of the absent origin, this structuralist thematic of broken immediateness is thus the sad, *negative*, nostalgic, guilty, Rousseauist facet of the thinking of freeplay of which the Nietzschean *affirmation*—the joyous affirmation of the freeplay of the world and without truth, without origin, offered to an active interpretation—would be the other side. *This affirmation then determines the non-center otherwise than as loss of the center.* And it plays the game without security. For there is a *sure* freeplay: that which is limited to the *substitution of given and existing, present*, pieces. In absolute chance, affirmation also surrenders itself to *genetic* indetermination, to the *seminal* adventure of the trace.[16]

There are thus two interpretations of interpretation, of structure, of sign, of freeplay. The one seeks to decipher, dreams of deciphering, a truth or an origin which is free from freeplay and from the order of the sign, and lives like an exile with the necessity of interpretation. The other, which is no longer turned toward the origin, affirms freeplay and tries to pass beyond man and humanism, the name man being the name of that being who, throughout the history of metaphysics or of ontotheology—in other words, through the history of all of his history—has dreamed of full presence, the reassuring foundation, the origin and the end of the game. The second interpretation of interpretation, to which Nietzsche showed us the way, does not seek in ethnography, as Lévi-Strauss wished, the "inspiration of a new humanism" (again from the "Introduction to the Work of Marcel Mauss").

There are more than enough indications today to suggest we might perceive that these two interpretations of interpretation—which are absolutely irreconcilable even if we live them simultaneously and reconcile them in an obscure economy—together shared the field which we call, in such a problematic fashion, the human sciences.

For my part, although these two interpretations must acknowledge and accentuate their difference and define their irreducibility, I do not believe that today there is any question of *choosing*—in the first place because here we are in a region (let's say, provisionally, a region of historicity) where the category of choice seems particularly trivial; and in the second, because we must first try to conceive of the common ground, and the *différance* of this irreducible difference.[17] Here there is a sort of question, call it historical, of which we are only glimpsing today the *conception, the formation, the gestation, the labor.* I employ these words, I admit, with a glance toward the business of childbearing—but also with a glance toward those who, in a company from which I do not exclude myself, turn their eyes away in the face of the as yet unnameable which is proclaiming itself and which can do so, as is necessary whenever a birth is in the offing, only under the species of the non-species, in the formless, mute, infant, and terrifying form of monstrosity.

Notes

1. "La Structure, le signe et le jeu dans le discours des sciences humaines." The text which follows is a translation of the revised version of M. Derrida's communication. The word "jeu" is variously translated here as "play," "interplay," "game," and "stake," besides the normative translation "freeplay." All footnotes to this article are additions by the translator.
2. *Interdite:* "forbidden," "disconcerted," "confounded," "speechless."
3. "... qui naît toujours d'une certaine manière d'être impliqué dans le jeu, d'être pris au jeu, d'être comme être d'entrée de jeu dans le jeu."
4. *Le cru et le cuit* (Paris: Plon, 1964).

5. *Les structures élémentaires de la parenté* (Paris: Presses Universitaires de France, 1949).
6. *La pensée sauvage* (Paris: Plon, 1962).
7. A *bricoleur* is a jack-of-all trades, someone who potters about with odds-and-ends, who puts things together out of bits and pieces.
8. Reprinted in: G. Genette, *Figures* (Paris: Editions du Seuil, 1966), p. 145.
9. The point being that the word, both in English and French, means "to supply a deficiency," on the one hand, and "to supply something additional," on the other.
10. "... ce signe s'ajoute, vient en sus, en *supplément.*"
11. "Introduction à l'oeuvre de Marcel Mauss," in: Marcel Mauss, *Sociologie et anthropologie* (Paris: Presses Universitaires de France, 1950).
12. Presumably: G. Charbonnier, *Entretiens avec Claude Lévi-Strauss* (Paris: Plon-Julliard, 1961).
13. *Race and History* (Paris: UNESCO Publications, 1958).
14. "... l'unité d'un devenir, comme tradition de la vérité dans la présence et la présence à soi, vers le savoir dans la conscience de soi."
15. "... de la présence à soi dans la parole."
16. "Tournée vers la présence, perdue ou impossible, de l'origine absente, cette thématique structuraliste de l'immédiateté rompue est donc la face triste, *négative,* nostalgique, coupable, rousseauiste, de la pensée du jeu dont *l'affirmation* nietzschéenne, l'affirmation joyeuse du jeu du monde et de l'innocence du devenir, l'affirmation d'un monde de signes sans faute, sans vérité, sans origine, offert à une interprétation active, serait l'autre face. *Cette affirmation détermine alors le* non-centre *autrement que comme perte du centre.* Et elle joue sans sécurité. Car il y a un jeu *sûr:* celui qui se limite à la *substitution* de piéces *données et existantes, présentes.* Dans le hasard absolu, l'affirmation se livre aussi à l'indétermination *génétique,* à l'aventure *séminale* de la trace."
17. From *différer,* in the sense of "to postpone," "put off," "defer." Elsewhere Derrida uses the word as a synonym for the German *Aufschub:* "postponement," and relates it to the central Freudian concepts of *Verspätung, Nachträglichkeit,* and to the "*détours* to death" of *Beyond the Pleasure Principle* by Sigmund Freud (Standard Edition, ed. James Strachey, vol. XIX, London, 1961), Chap. V.

Semiology and Rhetoric

Paul de Man

*After reviewing some recent forms of criticism that as-
sume a continuity between grammar and rhetoric or
figurative language, Paul de Man proceeds to challenge
that assumption. Citing Kenneth Burke, Charles Sanders
Peirce, and Jacques Derrida as others who have questioned
that continuity, he begins with the playful example of a
"rhetorical" question as it might be viewed by an "archie
Debunker," moves on to a deconstructive reading of four
lines by Yeats, and ends with an extended analysis of
a passage from Proust. In each case, his reading argues
that rhetoric undoes grammar, and vice versa. Having
sketched an immense deconstructive project for criticism
along the lines suggested by his analyses, de Man cautions
us that the superior status this project seems to confer on
the philosopher-critic is an illusion. The poet has always
been there first and the task of the deconstructive critic
is to follow closely, like a good formalist, the text the poet
has given him. "Poetic writing is the most advanced and
refined mode of deconstruction," de Man insists and, as
he demonstrates, it demands the closest of close readers.
But such readers will discover not the formalist's unity
and coherence but the text's propensity to deconstruct
itself. "Literature," he concludes, "as well as criticism—
the difference between them being delusive—are condemned (or privileged) to be forever the most rigorous
and, consequently, the most unreliable language in terms
of which man names and modifies himself."*

To judge from various recent publications, the
spirit of the times is not blowing in the direction
of formalist and intrinsic criticism. We may no longer
be hearing too much about relevance but we keep
hearing a great deal about reference, about the nonverbal "outside" to which language refers, by which
it is conditioned and upon which it acts. The stress
falls not so much on the fictional status of literature—

Reprinted by permission from *Diacritics* 3 (Fall 1973): 27–33.

a property now perhaps somewhat too easily taken for granted—but on the interplay between these fictions and categories that are said to partake of reality, such as the self, man, society, "the artist, his culture and the human community," as one critic puts it. Hence the emphasis on hybrid texts considered to be partly literary and partly referential, on popular fictions deliberately aimed towards social and psychological gratification, on literary autobiography as a key to the understanding of the self, and so on. We speak as if, with the problems of literary form resolved once and forever, and with the techniques of structural analysis refined to near-perfection, we could now move "beyond formalism" towards the questions that really interest us and reap, at last, the fruits of the ascetic concentration on techniques that prepared us for this decisive step. With the internal law and order of literature well policed, we can now confidently devote ourselves to the foreign affairs, the external politics of literature. Not only do we feel able to do so, but we owe it to ourselves to take this step: our moral conscience would not allow us to do otherwise. Behind the assurance that valid interpretation is possible, behind the recent interest in writing and reading as potentially effective public speech acts, stands a highly respectable moral imperative that strives to reconcile the internal, formal, private structures of literary language with their external, referential and public effects.

I want, for the moment, to consider briefly this tendency in itself, as an undeniable and recurrent historical fact, without regard for its truth or falseness or for its value as desirable or pernicious. It is a fact that this sort of thing happens, again and again, in literary studies. On the one hand, literature cannot merely be received as a definite unit of referential meaning that can be decoded without leaving a residue. The code is unusually conspicuous, complex and enigmatic; it attracts an inordinate amount of attention to itself and this attention has to acquire the rigor of a method. The structural moment of concentration on the code for its own sake cannot be avoided and literature necessarily breeds its own formalism. Technical innovations in the methodical study of literature only occur when this kind of attention predominates. It can legitimately be said, for example, that, from a technical point of view, very little has happened in American criticism since the innovative works of New Criticism. There certainly have been numerous excellent books of criticism

since, but in none of them have the techniques of description and interpretation evolved beyond the techniques of close reading established in the thirties and the forties. Formalism, it seems, is an all-absorbing and tyrannical muse; the hope that one can be at the same time technically original and discursively eloquent is not borne out by the history of literary criticism.

On the other hand—and this is the real mystery—no literary formalism, no matter how accurate and enriching in its analytic powers, is ever allowed to come into being without seeming reductive. When form is considered to be the external trappings of literary meaning or content, it seems superficial and expendable. The development of intrinsic, formalist criticism in the twentieth century has changed this model: form is now a solipsistic category of self-reflection and the referential meaning is said to be extrinsic. The polarities of inside and outside have been reversed, but they are still the same polarities that are at play: internal meaning has become outside reference and the outer form has become the intrinsic structure. A new version of reductiveness at once follows this reversal: formalism nowadays is mostly described in an imagery of imprisonment and claustrophobia: the "prison house of language," "the impasse of formalist criticism," etc. Like the grandmother in Proust's novel ceaselessly driving the young Marcel out into the garden, away from the unhealthy inwardness of his closeted reading, critics cry out for the fresh air of referential meaning. Thus, with the structure of the code so opaque, but the meaning so anxious to blot out the obstacle of form, no wonder that the reconciliation of form and meaning would be so attractive. The attraction of reconciliation is the elective breeding-ground of false models and metaphors; it accounts for the metaphorical model, of literature as a kind of box that separates an inside from an outside, and the reader or critic as the person who opens the lid in order to release into the open what was secreted but inaccessible inside. It matters little whether we call the inside of the box the content or the form, the outside the meaning or the appearance. The recurrent debate opposing intrinsic to extrinsic criticism stands under the aegis of an inside/outside metaphor that is never being seriously questioned.

Metaphors are much more tenacious than facts and I certainly don't expect to dislodge this age-old model in one short expository talk. I merely wish to speculate on a different set of terms, perhaps less simple in their differential relationship than the strictly polar, binary opposition between inside and outside and therefore less likely to enter into the easy play of chiasmic reversals. I derive these terms (which are as old as the hills) pragmatically from the observation of developments and debates in recent critical methodology.

One of the most controversial among these developments coincides with a new approach to poetics or, as it is called in Germany, poetology, as a branch of general semiotics. In France, a semiology of literature comes about as the outcome of the long-deferred but all the more explosive encounter of the nimble French literary mind with the category of form. Semiology, as opposed to semantics, is the science or study of signs as signifiers; it does not ask what words mean but how they mean. Unlike American New Criticism, which derived the internalization of form from the practice of highly self-conscious modern writers, French semiology turned to linguistics for its model and adopted Saussure and Jakobson rather than Valéry or Proust for its masters. By an awareness of the arbitrariness of the sign (Saussure) and of literature as an autotelic statement "focused on the way it is expressed" (Jakobson) the entire question of meaning can be bracketed, thus freeing the critical discourse from the debilitating burden of paraphrase. The demystifying power of semiology, within the context of French historical and thematic criticism, has been considerable. It demonstrated that the perception of the literary dimensions of language is largely obscured if one submits uncritically to the authority of reference. It also revealed how tenaciously this authority continues to assert itself in a variety of disguises, ranging from the crudest ideology to the most refined forms of aesthetic and ethical judgment. It especially explodes the myth of semantic correspondence between sign and referent, the wishful hope of having it both ways, of being, to paraphrase Marx in the German Ideology, a formalist critic in the morning and a communal moralist in the afternoon, of serving both the technique of form and the substance of meaning. The results, in the practice of French criticism, have been as fruitful as they are irreversible. Perhaps for the first time since the late eighteenth century, French critics can come at least somewhat closer to the kind of linguistic awareness that never ceased to be operative in its poets and novelists and that forced all of them including Sainte Beuve to write their main works "contre Sainte Beuve." The distance was never so considerable in England and the United States, which does not mean, however, that we may be able, in this country, to dispense with a preventative semiological hygiene altogether.

One of the most striking characteristics of literary semiology, as it is practiced today, in France and elsewhere, is the use of grammatical (especially syntactical) structures conjointly with rhetorical structures without apparent awareness of a possible discrepancy between them. In their literary analyses, Barthes, Genette, Todorov, Greimas and their disciples all simplify and regress from Jakobson in letting grammar and rhetoric function in perfect continuity, and in passing from grammatical to rhetorical structures without difficulty of interruption. Indeed, as the study of grammatical structures is refined in contemporary theories of generative, transformational and distributive grammar, the study of tropes and of figures (which is how the term rhetoric is used throughout this paper, and not in the derived sense of comment or of eloquence or persuasion) becomes a mere extension of grammatical models, a particular subset of syntactical relations. In the recent *Dictionnaire encyclopédique des sciences du language*, Ducrot and Todorov write that rhetoric has always been satisfied with a paradigmatic view over words (words substituting for each other), without questioning their syntagmatic relationship (the contiguity of words to each other). There ought to be another perspective, complementary to the first, in which metaphor, for example, would not be defined as a substitution but as a particular type of combination. Research inspired by linguistics or, more narrowly, by syntactical studies, has begun to reveal this possibility—but it remains to be explored. Todorov, who calls one of his books a *Grammar of the Decameron*, rightly thinks of his own work and that of his associates as first explorations in the elaboration of a systematic grammar of literary modes, genres and also of literary figures. Perhaps the most perceptive work to come out of this school, Genette's studies of figural modes, can be shown to be assimilations of rhetorical transformations or combinations to syntactical, grammatical patterns. Thus a recent study, now printed in *Figures III* and entitled *Metaphor and Metonomy in Proust*, shows the combined presence, in a wide and astute selection of passages, of paradigmatic, metaphorical figures with syntagmatic, metonymic structures. The combination of both is treated descriptively and nondialectically without suffering the possibility of logical tensions.

One can ask whether this reduction of figure to grammar is legitimate. The existence of grammatical structures, within and beyond the unit of the sentence in literary texts is undeniable, and their description and classification are indispensable. The question remains if and how figures of rhetoric can be included in such a taxonomy. This question is at the core of the debate going on, in a wide variety of apparently unrelated forms, in contemporary poetics, but I do not plan to make clear the connection between this "real" problem and the countless pseudo-problems that agitate literary studies. The historical picture of contemporary criticism is too confused to make the mapping out of such a topography a useful exercise. Not only are these questions mixed in and mixed up within particular groups or local trends, but they are often co-present, without apparent contradiction, within the work of a single author.

Neither is the theory of the question suitable for quick expository treatment. To distinguish the epistemology of grammar from the epistemology of rhetoric is a redoubtable task. On an entirely naïve level, we tend to conceive of grammatical systems as tending towards universality and as simply generative, i.e. as capable of deriving an infinity of versions from a single model (that may govern transformations as well as derivations) without the intervention of another model that would upset the first. We therefore think of the relationship between grammar and logic, the passage from grammar to propositions, as being relatively un-problematic: no true propositions are conceivable in the absence of grammatical consistency or of controlled deviation from a system of consistency no matter how complex. Grammar and logic stand to each other in a dyadic relationship of unsubverted support. In a logic of acts rather than of statements, as in Austin's theory of speech acts, that has had such strong influence on recent American work in literary semiology, it is also possible to move between speech acts and grammar without difficulty. The performance of what is called illocutionary acts such as ordering, questioning, denying, assuming etc. within the language is congruent with the grammatical structures of syntax in the corresponding imperative, interrogative, negative, optative sentences. "The rules for illocutionary acts," writes Richard Ohman in a recent paper, "determine

whether performance of a given act is well-executed, in just the same way as *grammatical* rules determine whether the product of a locutionary act—a sentence—is well formed [. . .]. But whereas the rules of grammar concern the relationships among sound, syntax, and meaning, the rules of illocutionary acts concern relationships among people" ("Speech, Literature, and the Space in between," *New Literary History* IV, No. 1 [Autumn 1972]; p. 50). And since rhetoric is then conceived exclusively as persuasion, as actual action upon others (and not as an intralinguistic figure or trope), the continuity between the illocutionary realm of grammar and the perlocutionary realm of rhetoric is self-evident. It becomes the basis for a new rhetoric that, exactly as is the case for Todorov and Genette, would also be a new grammar.

Without engaging the substance of the question, it can be pointed out, without having to go beyond recent and American examples, and without calling upon the strength of an age-old tradition, that the continuity here assumed between grammar and rhetoric is not borne out by theoretical and philosophical speculation. Kenneth Burke mentions *Deflection* (which he compares structurally to Freudian displacement), defined as "any slight bias or even unintended error," as the rhetorical basis of language, and deflection is then conceived as a dialectical subversion of the consistent link between sign and meaning that operates within grammatical patterns; hence Burke's well-known insistence on the distinction between grammar and rhetoric. Charles Sanders Peirce who, with Nietzsche and Saussure, laid the philosophical foundation for modern semiology, stressed the distinction between grammar and rhetoric in his celebrated and so suggestively unfathomable definition of the sign. He insists, as is well known, on the necessary presence of a third element, called the interpretant, within any relationship that the sign entertains with its object. The sign is to be interpreted if we are to understand the idea it is to convey, and this is so because the sign is not the thing but a meaning derived from the thing by a process here called representation that is not simply generative, i.e. dependent on a univocal origin. The interpretation of the sign is not, for Peirce, a meaning but another sign; it is a reading, not a decodage, and this reading has, in its turn, to be interpreted into another sign, and so on *ad infinitum*. Peirce calls this process by means of which "one sign gives birth to another" pure rhetoric, as distinguished from pure grammar, which postulates the possibility of un-problematic, dyadic meaning and pure logic, which postulates the possibility of the universal truth of meanings. Only if the sign engendered meaning in the same way that the object engenders the sign, that is, by representation, would there be no need to distinguish between grammar and rhetoric.

These remarks should indicate at least the existence and the difficulty of the question, a difficulty which puts its concise theoretical exposition beyond my powers. I must retreat therefore into a pragmatic discourse and try to illustrate the tension between grammar and rhetoric in a few specific textual examples. Let me begin by considering what is perhaps the most commonly known instance of an apparent symbiosis between a grammatical and a rhetorical structure, the so-called rhetorical question, in which the figure is conveyed directly by means of a syntactical device. I take the first example from the sub-literature of the mass media: asked by his wife whether he wants to have his bowling shoes laced over or laced under, Archie Bunker answers with a question: "What's the difference?" Being a reader of sublime simplicity, his wife replies by patiently explaining the difference between lacing over and lacing under, whatever this may be, but provokes only ire. "What's the difference" did not ask for difference but means instead "I don't give a damn what the difference is." The same grammatical pattern engenders two meanings that are mutually exclusive: the literal meaning asks for a concept (difference) whose existence is denied by the figurative meaning. As long as we are talking about bowling shoes, the consequences are relatively trivial; Archie Bunker, who is a great believer in the authority of origins (as long, of course, as they are the right origins) muddles along in a world where literal and figurative meanings get in each other's way, though not without discomforts. But suppose that it is a *de*-bunker rather than a "Bunker," and a de-bunker of the arche (or origin), an archie Debunker such as Nietzsche or Jacques Derrida for instance, who asks the question "What is the Difference"—and we cannot even tell from his grammar whether he "really" wants to know "what" the difference is or is just telling us that we shouldn't even try to find it. Confronted with the question of the difference between grammar and rhetoric, grammar allows us to ask the question, but the sentence by means of which we ask it may deny the very possibility of asking. For what is the use of asking, I ask, when we cannot even authoritatively decide whether a question asks or doesn't ask?

The point is as follows. A perfectly clear syntactical paradigm (the question) engenders a sentence that has at least two meanings of which the one asserts and the other denies its own illocutionary mode. It is not so that there are simply two meanings, one literal and the other figural, and that we have to decide which one of these meanings is the right one in this particular situation. The confusion can only be cleared up by the intervention of an extra-textual intention, such as Archie Bunker putting his wife straight; but the very anger he displays is indicative of more than impatience; it reveals his despair when confronted with a structure of linguistic meaning that he cannot control and that holds the discouraging prospect of an infinity of similar future confusions, all of them potentially catastrophic in their consequences. Nor is this intervention really a part of the mini-text constituted by the figure which holds our attention only as long as it remains suspended and unresolved. I follow the usage of common speech in calling this semiological enigma "rhetorical." The grammatical model of the question becomes rhetorical not when we have, on the one hand, a literal meaning and on the other hand a figural meaning, but when it is impossible to decide by grammatical or other linguistic devices which of the two meanings (that can be entirely contradictory) prevails. Rhetoric radically suspends logic and opens up vertiginous possibilities of referential aberration. And although it would perhaps be somewhat more remote from common usage, I would not hesitate to equate the rhetorical, figural potentiality of language with literature itself. I could point to a great number of antecedents to this equation of literature with figure; the most recent reference would be to Monroe Beardsley's insistence in his contribution to the *Essays* to honor William Wimsatt, that literary language is characterized by being "distinctly above the norm in ratio of implicit (or, I would say rhetorical) to explicit meaning" (p. 37).

Let me pursue the question of rhetorical question through one more example. Yeats's poem "Among School Children," ends with the famous line: "How can we know the dancer from the dance?" Although there are some revealing inconsistencies within the commentaries, the line is usually interpreted as stating, with the increased emphasis of a rhetorical device, the potential unity between form and experience, between creator and creation. It could be said that it denies the discrepancy between the sign and the referent from which we started out. Many elements in the imagery and the dramatic development of the poem strengthen this traditional reading; without having to look any further than the immediately preceding lines, one finds powerful and consecrated images of the continuity from part to whole that makes synecdoche into the most seductive of metaphors: the organic beauty of the tree, stated in the parallel syntax of a similar rhetorical question, or the convergence, in the dance, of erotic desire with musical form:

> O chestnut tree, great rooted blossomer
> Are you the leaf, the blossom or the bole?
> O body swayed to music, O brightening glance
> How can we know the dancer from the dance?

A more extended reading, always assuming that the final line is to be read as a rhetorical question, reveals that the thematic and rhetorical grammar of the poem yields a consistent reading that extends from the first line to the last and that can account for all details in the text. It is equally possible, however, to read the last line literally rather than figuratively, as asking with some urgency the question we asked at the beginning of this talk within the context of contemporary criticism: *not* that sign and referent are so exquisitely fitted to each other that all difference between them is at times blotted out but, rather, since the two essentially different elements, sign and meaning, are so intricately intertwined in the imagined "presence" that the poem addresses, how can we possibly make the distinctions that would shelter us from the error of identifying what cannot be identified? The clumsiness of the paraphrase reveals that it is not necessarily the literal reading which is simpler than the figurative one, as was the case in our first example; here, the figural reading, which assumes the question to be rhetorical is perhaps naïve, whereas the literal reading leads to greater complications of theme and statement. For it turns out that the entire scheme set up by the first reading can be undermined or deconstructed, in the terms of the second, in which the final line is read literally as meaning that, since the dancer and the dance are not the same, it might be useful, perhaps even desperately necessary—for the question can be given a ring of urgency, "Please tell me, how *can* I know the dancer from the dance"—to tell them apart. But this will replace the reading of each symbolic detail by a divergent interpretation. The oneness of trunk, leaf and blossom, for example, that would have appealed to Goethe, would find itself replaced by the much less reassuring Tree of Life from the Mabinogion that appears in the poem "Vacillation," in which the fiery blossom and the earthly leaf are held together, as well as apart, by the crucified and castrated God Attis, of whose body it can hardly be said that it is "not bruised to pleasure soul." This hint should suffice to suggest that two entirely coherent but entirely incompatible readings can be made to hinge on one line, whose grammatical structure is devoid of ambiguity, but whose rhetorical mode turns the mood as well as the mode of the entire poem upside down. Neither can we say, as was already the case in the first example, that the poem simply has two meanings that exist side by side. The two readings have to engage each other in direct confrontation, for the one reading is precisely the error denounced by the other and has to be undone by it. Nor can we in any way make a valid decision as to which of the readings can be given priority over the other; none can exist in the other's absence. There can be no dance without a dancer, no sign without a referent. On the other hand, the authority of the meaning engendered by the grammatical structure is fully obscured by the duplicity of a figure that cries out for the differentiation that it conceals.

Yeats's poem is not explicitly "about" rhetorical questions but about images or metaphors, and about the possibility of convergence between experiences of consciousness such as memory or emotions—what the poem calls passion, piety and affection—and entities accessible to the senses such as bodies, persons or icons. We return to the inside/outside model from which we started out and which the poem puts into question by means of a syntactical device (the question) made to operate on a grammatical as well as on a rhetorical level. The couple grammar/rhetoric, certainly not a binary opposition since they in no way exclude each other, disrupts and confuses the neat antithesis of the inside/outside pattern. We can transfer this scheme to the act of reading and interpretation. By reading we get, as we say, inside a text that was first something alien to us and which we now make our own by an act of understanding. But this understanding becomes at once the representation of an extra-textual meaning; in Austin's terms, the illocutionary speech act becomes a perlocutionary actual act—in Frege's terms, *Bedeutung* becomes *Sinn*. Our recurrent question is whether this transformation is semantically controlled along grammatical or along rhetorical lines. Does the metaphor of reading really unite outer meaning with inner understanding, action with reflection, into one single totality? The assertion is powerfully and suggestively made in a passage from Proust that describes the experience of reading as such a union. It describes the young Marcel, near the beginning of Combray, hiding in the closed space of his room in order to read. The example differs from the earlier ones in that we are not dealing with a grammatical structure that also functions rhetorically but have instead the representation, the dramatization, in terms of the experience of a subject, of a rhetorical structure—just as in many other passages, Proust dramatizes tropes by means of landscapes or descriptions of objects. The figure here dramatized is that of metaphor, an inside/outside correspondence as represented by the act of reading. The reading scene is the culmination of a series of actions taking place in enclosed spaces and leading up to the "dark coolness" of Marcel's room.

> I had stretched out on my bed, with a book, in my room which sheltered, trembling, its transparent and fragile coolness against the afternoon sun, behind the almost closed blinds through which a glimmer of daylight had nevertheless managed to push its yellow wings, remaining motionless between the wood and the glass, in a corner, poised like a butterfly. It was hardly light enough to read and the sensation of the light's splendor was given me only by the noise of Camus [. . .] hammering dusty crates; resounding in the sonorous atmosphere that is peculiar to hot weather, they seemed to spark off scarlet stars; and also by the flies executing their little concert, the chamber music of summer: evocative not in the manner of a human tune that, heard perchance during the summer, afterwards reminds you of it; it is connected to summer by a more necessary link: born from beautiful days, resurrecting only when they return, containing some of their essence, it does not only awaken their image in our memory; it guarantees their return, their actual, persistent, unmediated presence.
> The dark coolness of my room related to the full sunlight of the street as the shadow relates to the ray of light, that is to say it was just as luminous and it gave my imagination the total spectacle of the summer, whereas my senses, if I had been on a walk, could only have enjoyed it by fragments; it matched my repose which (thanks to the adven-

tures told by my book and stirring my tranquility) supported, like the quiet of a motionless hand in the middle of a running brook the shock and the motion of a torrent of activity. (*Swann's Way*. Paris: Pléiade, 1954; p. 83. Author's translation.)

From the beginning of the passage, inwardness is valorized positively as something desirable that has to protect itself against the intrusion of outside forces, but that nevertheless has to borrow, as it were, some of its constitutive properties from the outside. A chain of binary properties is set up and antithetically differentiated in terms of the inside/outside polarity: properties of coolness, darkness, repose, silence, imagination and totality, associated with inwardness, contrast with the heat, the light, the activity, the sounds, the senses and the fragmentation that govern the outside. By the act of reading, these static oppositions are put in motion, thus allowing for the play of substitutions by means of which the claim for totalization can be made. Thus, in a beautifully seductive effect of chiaroscuro, mediated by the metaphor of light as a poised butterfly, the inner room is convincingly said to acquire the amount of light necessary to reading. In the wake of this light, warmth can also enter the room, incarnate in the auditive synaesthesia of the various sounds. According to the narrator, these metaphorical substitutions and reversals render the presence of Summer in the room more complete than the actual experience of Summer in the outside world could have done. The text achieves this synthesis and comments on it in normative terms, comparable to the manner in which treatises of practical rhetorics recommend the use of one figure in preference to another in a given situation: here it is the substitutive totalization by metaphor which is said to be more effective than the mere contiguity of metonymic association. As opposed to the random contingency of metonymy ("par hasard"), the metaphor is linked to its proper meaning by, says Proust, the "necessary link" that leads to perfect synthesis. In the wake of this synthesis, the entire conceptual vocabulary of metaphysics enters the text: a terminology of generation, of transcendental necessity, of totality, of essence, of permanence, and of unmediated presence. The passage acts out and asserts the priority of metaphor over metonymy in terms of the categories of metaphysics and with reference to the act of reading.

The actual test of the truth of the assertion comes in the second paragraph when the absurd mathematical ratio set up at the beginning has to be verified by a further substitution. This time, what has to be exchanged are not only the properties of light and dark, warm and cool, fragment and totality (part and whole), but the properties of action and repose. The full seduction of the text can only come into being when the formal totalization of light and dark is completed by the transfer from rest to action that represents the extratextual, referential moment. The text asserts the transfer in the concluding sentence: "The dark coolness of my room [. . .] supported, like the quiet of a motionless hand in the middle of a running brook, the shock and the motion of a torrent of activity." The verb "to support" here carries the full weight of uniting rest and action ("repos et activité"), fiction and reality, as firmly as the base supports the column. The transfer, as is so often the case in Proust, is carried out by the liquid element of the running brook. The natural, representational connotation of the passage is with coolness, so particularly attractive within the predominant summer-mood of the entire *Recherche*. But coolness, it will be remembered, is one of the characteristic properties of the "inside" world. It cannot therefore by itself transfer us into the opposite world of activity. The movement of the water evokes a freshness which in the binary logic of the passage is associated with the inward, imaginary world of reading and fiction. In order to accede to action, it would be necessary to capture one of the properties belonging to the opposite chain such as, for example, warmth. The mere "cool" action of fiction cannot suffice: it is necessary to reconcile the cool immobility of the hand with the heat of action if the claim made by the sentence is to stand up as true. The transfer is carried out, always within the same sentence, when it is said that repose supports "a torrent of activity." The expression *"torrent d'activité"* is not, or no longer, a metaphor in French: it is a cliché, a dead, or sleeping metaphor that has lost the suggestive, connotative values contained in the word "torrent." It simply means "a great deal of activity," the amount of activity that is likely to agitate one to the point of getting hot. Heat is thus surreptitiously smuggled into the passage from a cold source, closing the ring of antithetical properties and allowing for their exchange and substitution: from the moment tranquility can be active and warm without losing its cool and its distinctive quality of repose, the fragmented experience of reality can become whole without losing its quality of being real.

The transfer is made to seem convincing and seductive by the double play on the cliché "torrent of activity." The proximate, contiguous image of the brook awakens, as it were, the sleeping beauty of the dozing metaphor which, in its common use, had become the metonymic association of two words united by sheer habit and no longer by the inner necessity, the necessary link of a transcendental signification. "Torrent" functions in a double semantic register: in its reawakened literal meaning it relays the attribute of coolness that is actually part of the running water, whereas in its figural non-meaning it designates the quantity of activity connotative of the contrary property of warmth.

The rhetorical structure of this sentence is therefore not simply metaphorical. It is at least doubly metonymic, first because the coupling of words, in a cliché, is not governed by the necessary link that reveals their potential identity but by the contingent habit of proximity; second, because the reawakening of the metaphorical term "torrent" is carried out by a statement that happens to be in the vicinity, but without there being any necessity for the proximity on the level of the referential meaning. The most striking thing is that this doubly metonymic structure is found in a text that also contains highly seductive and successful metaphors (as in the chiaroscuro effect of the beginning, or in the condensation of light in the butterfly image) and that explicitly asserts the superiority of metaphor over metonymy in terms of metaphysical categories.

That these metaphysical categories do not remain unaffected by such a reading would become clear from an inclusive reading of Proust's novel or would become even more explicit in a language-conscious philosopher, such as Nietzsche who, as a philosopher, has to be concerned with the epistemological consequences of the kind of rhetorical seductions exemplified by the Proust passage. It can be shown that the systematic critique of the main categories of metaphysics undertaken by Nietzsche in his late work, the critique of the concepts of causality, of the subject, of identity, of referential and revealed truth, etc. occurs along the same pattern of deconstruction that was operative in Proust's text; and it can also be shown that this pattern exactly corresponds to Nietzsche's description, in texts that precede *The Will to Power* by more than fifteen years, of the structure of the main rhetorical tropes. The key to this critique of metaphysics, which is itself a recurrent gesture throughout the history of thought, is the rhetorical model of the trope or, if one prefers to call it that, literature. It turns out that, in these innocent-looking didactic exercises we are in fact playing for very sizable stakes.

It is therefore all the more necessary to know what is linguistically involved in a rhetorically conscious reading of the type here undertaken on a brief fragment from a novel and extended by Nietzsche to the entire text of post-Hellenic thought. Our first examples dealing with the rhetorical questions were rhetorizations of grammar, figures generated by syntactical paradigms, whereas the Proust example could be better described as a grammatization of rhetoric. By passing from a paradigmatic structure based on substitution, such as metaphor, to a syntagmatic structure based on contingent association such as metonymy, the mechanical, repetitive aspect of grammatical forms is shown to be operative in a passage that seemed at first sight to celebrate the self-willed and autonomous inventiveness of a subject. Figures are assumed to be inventions, the products of a highly particularized individual talent, whereas no one can claim credit for the programmed pattern of grammar. Yet, our reading of the Proust passage shows that precisely when the highest claims are being made for the unifying power of metaphor, these very images rely in fact on the deceptive use of semiautomatic grammatical patterns. The deconstruction of metaphor and of all rhetorical patterns such as mimesis, paranomasis or personification that use resemblance as a way to disguise differences, takes us back to the impersonal precision of grammar and of a semiology derived from grammatical patterns. Such a deconstruction puts into question a whole series of concepts that underlie the value judgments of our critical discourse: the metaphor of primacy, of genetic history and, most notably, of the autonomous power to will of the self.

There seems to be a difference, then, between what I called the rhetorization of grammar (as in the rhetorical question) and the grammatization of rhetoric, as in the deconstructive readings of the type sketched out in the passage from Proust. The former end up in indetermination, in a suspended uncertainty that was unable to choose between two modes of reading, whereas the latter seems to reach a truth, albeit by the negative road of exposing an error, a false pretense. After the deconstructive reading of the Proust passage, we can no longer believe the assertion made

in this passage about the intrinsic, metaphysical superiority of metaphor over metonymy. We seem to end up in a mood of negative assurance that is highly productive of critical discourse. The further text of Proust's novel, for example, responds perfectly to an extended application of this de-constructive pattern: not only can similar gestures be repeated throughout the novel, at all the crucial articulations or all passages where large aesthetic and metaphysical claims are being made—the scenes of involuntary memory, the workshop of Elstir, the septette of Vinteuil, the convergence of author and narrator at the end of the novel—but a vast thematic and semiotic network is revealed that structures the entire narrative and that remained invisible to a reader caught in naïve metaphorical mystification. The whole of literature would respond in similar fashion, although the techniques and the patterns would have to vary considerably, of course, from author to author. But there is absolutely no reason why analyses of the kind here suggested for Proust would not be applicable, with proper modifications of technique, to Milton or to Dante or to Hölderlin. This will in fact be the task of literary criticism in the coming years.

It would seem that we are saying that criticism is the deconstruction of literature, the reduction to the rigors of grammar of rhetorical mystifications. And if we hold up Nietzsche as the philosopher of such a critical deconstruction, then the literary critic would become the philosopher's ally in his struggle with the poets. Criticism and literature would separate around the epistemological axis that distinguishes grammar from rhetoric. It is easy enough to see that this apparent glorification of the critic-philosopher in the name of truth is in fact a glorification of the poet as the primary source of this truth; if truth is the recognition of the systematic character of a certain kind of error, then it would be fully dependent on the prior existence of this error. Philosophers of science like Bachelard or Wittgenstein are notoriously dependent on the aberrations of the poets. We are back at our unanswered question: does the grammatization of rhetoric end up in negative certainty or does it, like the rhetorization of grammar, remain suspended in the ignorance of its own truth or falsehood?

Two concluding remarks should suffice to answer the question. First of all, it is not true that Proust's text can simply be reduced to the mystified assertion (the superiority of metaphor over metonymy) that our reading deconstructs. The reading is not "our" reading, since it uses only the linguistic elements provided by the text itself; the distinction between author and reader is one of the false distinctions that the deconstruction makes evident. The deconstruction is not something we have added to the text but it constituted the text in the first place. A literary text simultaneously asserts and denies the authority of its own rhetorical mode and by reading the text as we did, we were only trying to come closer to being as rigorous a reader as the author had to be in order to write the sentence in the first place. Poetic writing is the most advanced and refined mode of deconstruction; it may differ from critical or discursive writing in the economy of its articulation, but not in kind.

But if we recognize the existence of the deconstructive moment as constitutive of all literary language we have surreptitiously reintroduced the categories that this deconstruction was supposed to eliminate and that have merely been displaced. We have, for example, displaced the question of the self from the referent into the figure of the narrator, who then becomes the *signifié* of the passage. It becomes again possible to ask such naïve questions as what Proust, or Marcel's, motives may have been in thus manipulating language: was he fooling himself, or was he represented as fooling himself and fooling us into believing that fiction and action are as easy to unite, by reading, as the passage asserts? The pathos of the entire section, which would have been more noticeable if the quotation had been a little more extended, the constant vacillation of the narrator between guilt and well-being, invites such questions. They are absurd questions, of course, since the reconciliation of fact and fiction occurs itself as a mere assertion made in the text, and is thus productive of more text at the moment when it asserts its decision to escape from textual confinement. But even if we free ourselves of all false questions of intent and rightfully reduce the narrator to the status of a mere grammatical pronoun, without which the deconstructive narrative could not come into being, this subject remains endowed with a function that is not grammatical but rhetorical, in that it gives voice, so to speak, to a grammatical syntagm. The term voice, even when used in a grammatical terminology as when we speak of the passive or interrogative voice is, of course, a metaphor inferring by analogy the intent of the subject from the structure of the predicate. In the case of the deconstructive discourse that we call literary, or rhetorical, or poetic, this creates a distinctive complication illustrated by the Proust passage. The deconstructive reading revealed a first paradox: the passage valorizes metaphor as being the "right" literary figure, but then proceeds to constitute itself by means of the epistemologically incompatible figure of metonymy. The deconstructive critical discourse reveals the presence of this delusion and affirms it as the irreversible mode of its truth. It cannot pause there however. For if we then ask the obvious and simple next question, whether the rhetorical mode of the text in question is that of metaphor or metonymy, it is impossible to give an answer. Individual metaphors, such as the chiaroscuro effect or the butterfly, are shown to be subordinate figures in a general clause whose syntax is metonymic; from this point of view, it seems that the rhetoric is superseded by a grammar that deconstructs it. But this metonymic clause has as its subject a voice whose relationship to this clause is again metaphorical. The narrator who tells us about the impossibility of metaphor is himself, or itself, a metaphor, the metaphor of a grammatical syntagm whose meaning is the denial of metaphor stated, by antiphrasis, as its priority. And this subject-metaphor is, in its turn, open to the kind of deconstruction to the second degree, the rhetorical deconstruction of psycholinguistics, in which the more advanced investigations of literature are presently engaged, against considerable resistance.

We end up therefore, in the case of the rhetorical grammatization of semiology, just as in the grammatical rhetorization of illocutionary phrases, in the same state of suspended ignorance. Any question about the rhetorical mode of a literary text is always a rhetorical question which does not even know whether it is really questioning. The resulting pathos is an anxiety (or bliss, depending on one's momentary mood or individual temperament) of ignorance, not an anxiety of reference—as becomes thematically clear in Proust's novel when reading is dramatized, in the relationship between Marcel and Albertine, not as an emotive reaction to what language does, but as an emotive reaction to the impossibility of knowing what it might be up to. Literature as well as criticism—the difference between them being delusive—are condemned (or privileged) to be forever the most rigorous and, consequently, the most unreliable language in terms of which man names and modifies himself.

APPLICATION

The many and various interpretations of The Tempest, *several of which are noted in Stephen J. Miko's first footnote, could furnish a striking illustration of Stanley Fish's "interpretive communities" in action. But Miko's reading of the play is poststructural in another sense, for while each of these interpretations shows a strategy for determining meaning, this text, as Miko sees it, remains radically indeterminate. Thus the various interpretations point not to "some hinted idea to which the variety can be subordinated," but instead to "the multiplicity and possibly deliberate inconclusiveness of Shakespeare's last plays." A text's unity and coherence, the poststructuralists argue, are largely a function of the critic's will to order, his or her willingness to turn a blind eye to elements that won't fit the critic's reading. As Miko puts it, "the neatness of this (and possibly any) work of art largely depends on how strongly one insists on details that seem to violate a defined, usually conventional pattern." Miko's own reading insists strongly on precisely those details. The play's inconclusiveness may "possibly" be deliberate; what's true of this play may "possibly" be true of any. Miko is appropriately tentative about large claims, beyond the claim that this play is appropriately tentative. By tugging firmly at the play's "loose ends," he produces a reading which, by a deManian paradox, finds the text's meaning in its very inconclusiveness. "All the mirrors are chipped and cracked," and "the main point, to which Shakespeare consistently returns, is that attempts to match words and things, wishes and realities, inevitably leave disjunctions."*

Tempest

Stephen J. Miko

Reprinted by permission from *ELH* 49 (1982): 1–17. Copyright © 1982 by The Johns Hopkins University Press.

How beauteous mankind is! O brave new world,
That has such people in't!

V,i,183–4

Many ironies sit here. Except for the most obvious one, residing in the gap between Miranda's innocence and our knowledge that some of these beauties are attempted homicides, there is little agreement either about what they are or how far they go. Miranda speaks from a tableau, just revealed by a magician to those who astonish her, and who have just been released by the same magician from a charmed circle. They are astonished too. The language of miracle and wonder is appropriate on both sides; a father is reunited with his son, gains a daughter, reconciles himself with conscience. Yet the magician who managed all this says almost nothing about the "strange maze" which he has led these wanderers through. He calls their miracles "accidents," which he promises to make "seem probable," along with the story of his life. Later, after the play is over. To clear the way for thinking ("every third thought") of his grave. The ironies I speak of multiply as these elements are heightened into contrasts.

To harp on ironies is to harp on (possible) problems. The range of disagreement as to how to take this play is itself astonishing.[1] If Miranda's world is, demonstrably, neither brave nor new, what degree of mockery may be lurking here? To complicate matters further, this last scene, especially by virtue of being a last scene, has given rise to talk about mystery. That has in turn led to talk of symbol, allegory, and mysticism. Something cryptic appears to most critics to be going on, and the usual (but certainly not universal) response has been to fill in Shakespeare's meaning with religious and moral hierarchies. Yet anything thought cryptic may also be an invitation to ask questions about explanations, to wonder, finally, whether explanation itself may be mocked in Prospero's promises to tell all some other time some other place.

What we have just noticed is at least an obvious manipulation of most of the characters into a position where they must be astonished, and, further, must behave themselves. Moral correction is another matter. So is forgiveness. The new world is most obviously new in being rearranged; rearrangement took place in careful isolation, on an island, with the help of a lot of magic and tricks. Yet the trickster is willingly giving up his magic powers to return, with-

out notable enthusiasm, to rule Milan by conventional methods. He takes with him two unredeemed villains, one redeemed villain, a loyal retainer, two humiliated buffoons, and a wholly conventional romantic couple. He leaves behind both his magic emissary and his enslaved monster, probably, after Prospero himself, the two most intriguing characters of the play. There is not much agreement about what these final groupings mean, and very little sense that Prospero has *solved* anything. Both his future and Caliban's seem open questions — it is not even clear that Caliban will remain. What is clear is that Prospero has succeeded in his manipulations of bodies (if not destinies) and that he is packing up his tricks. Perhaps the playwright is also packing up his tricks, completing his play by completing its island actions, rounding them out but not (because of their very nature) fully resolving them. Once one looks at what finally happens to the various characters and the themes they embody, it is difficult to accept either Prospero's or Shakespeare's manipulations as a series of exalted gestures, part of a symbolic package that points toward (even if it doesn't actually show) a grand, coherent, or transcendent completion of Shakespeare's highest art. Neither is it possible to read the play as "just a play," without meanings of various symbolic kinds, in fact many kinds. I propose, then, to look at the play as if it is, in a stronger sense than is usually conceded, experimental. Shakespeare may be experimenting with the very assumptions that lead us to expect poetic justice, symbolic neatness, and "resolved" endings for plays. I think, in fact, that he is demonstrating the limits of all three sets of expectation.

II Loose Ends

Does this play have loose ends or not? Those who lean toward heavily symbolic readings tend to think not; those who favor character analysis and even moral analysis tend to think it does. I belong to the second group, though my reasons perhaps differ from those most often given or implied. The neatness of this (and possibly any) work of art largely depends on how strongly one insists on details that seem to violate a defined, usually conventional pattern. For example, isn't Antonio an embarrassment to the dominant moral pattern of the play? Unlike Alonzo he shows no repentance whatever, and some question the sincerity of Prospero's forgiving him.[2]

In the same vein, does Caliban's intention to "seek for grace" represent a lurch upward toward moral stature? Both show stubborn resistance to redemption, or even to claims that the *tone* of the ending is grandly affirmative. Yet one can always insist that exceptions prove the rule: Antonio and Caliban only show us that moral ideals exist in an imperfect world—all the more are just, forgiving, philosopher-magician-kings required. And from a certain comfortable distance this may do; why should we want to find a loose end in what can be seen as a reflection (though inverted) of the need for grace, or help, or even a civilized culture to keep evil (both natural and unnatural) in check?[3] One ready answer is that these reflections just as easily suggest something very different, though not exactly contradictory. In these stubborn characters we may also see limits: to Prospero's power and all that it may represent, including Shakespeare's power in art, or *the* power of art.

Probably more than any of Shakespeare's other plays, *The Tempest* leaves "reflection" a live metaphor. It has even been read as a kind of cypher to contemporary biographical, political, or religious events, quite beside the theories of more general symbolic construction alluded to already.[4] I do not propose another attempt to sort these theories out, but to note that this variety must mean something—not, I think, some hinted idea to which the variety can be subordinated, but something about the multiplicity and possibly the deliberate inconclusiveness of Shakespeare's last plays. However we evaluate these many interpretations, we can consistently infer that the play which occasions such riches must itself be rich and strange. Both the richness and strangeness are functions, it seems to me, of Shakespeare's testing, or at least playing with, the limits of his—and maybe anyone's—playmaking, including powerful gestures of affirmation while affirming, in Sidney's sense, nothing. In short, there are loose ends indeed, of the most fundamental sort: the art and magic of playmaking questions both its matter (the themes) and its own power, affirming only in understood, limited ways.

What, then, are these affirmations? Beside the usual "romance" themes of forgiveness, reconciliation, and regeneration I would put a list that has a negative cast, because it derives from ironic perspectives: men and their desires need checking and ordering, a process which makes (limited) fulfillment of desire possible, and may even transform coarse emotion into something higher (or at least more interesting); "natural" is a profoundly ambiguous term, but all good (and, less clearly, most evil) is an art that nature makes; true love requires civilizing (another kind of limiting); plays and the art of making them are special, deliberately artificial distortions of the "real" world, meant less to teach than to present interesting, sometimes heartening, analogies; art is no avenue to higher realms but a modest (yet at best very impressive) image of man's desires reflected back through his intelligence, which shapes and approves selectively; and even spectacular magic art has very little consequence in the world "outside." I think all these points are made by the play—are, in fact, its central affirmations. I don't see how such things could be asserted in a play without, at least in the most conventional senses, loose ends. The failure to carry out fully the pattern of moral correction may be seen, then, as just the most obvious refusal to make this play neat. If my list is accurate, the cast of mind dominating the play is neither tragic, nor, in the celebratory sense, comic; it is skeptical, yet genial.

III Prospero: Theurgist, Mage, Goetist, Trickster, Stage Manager

This is Prospero's play, with no very close parallel in Shakespeare. Whatever symbolic freight we make visible, Prospero is either carrying it or managing the carrying. It is no doubt obvious already that my emphasis will drift from left to right on the scale listed above: although we are surely impressed by Prospero's ability to disintegrate and reassemble ships, quick-dry (and even freshen) costumes, cast spells, put on spirit-masques, and pinch out punishments, there are hints throughout the play that invite us—quite inconclusively—to subordinate this power, this Art, to something approaching hypnosis, the creation of dream states for moral psychotherapy. The magic lore that creeps into the play is capable of causing embarrassment both to those who prefer the notion that they all just dreamt the tempest and the transportations and those who say magic is magic, usually invoking John Dee and insisting that at least it's white.[5] To be very short on this issue, transportations are not likely dreamt if you actually end up in other places, alive when you thought you had drowned, and we can hardly doubt that Ariel and company exist. On the other hand all this power results in only one indisputable conversion (Alonzo), the tempest is also obviously *inside* most of the characters, the magic shows are dispensable and vanish without trace or consequence, the selves everyone finds when released from trance are much the same as they were earlier, and we can't be sure that Prospero isn't embroidering a little—the Ovidian list including raising the dead (V,i,41–50) embarrasses almost everyone. We seem to be put repeatedly in the position of trying to decide what the magic means before we can say what it is. And that meaning, or those meanings, are all extensions of Prospero.

It may be helpful to descend for a while into the unambiguous. Although I think that Prospero's magic tricks shift in emphasis from magic to tricks, and that this shift is emblematic of much else in the play's movement, some solid "facts" about Prospero are given us, mostly in the usual first act history, and much also follows from them.

Besides an enormously powerful magician—the play begins, of course, with the ship disintegrating in Prospero's tempest—Prospero is an overprotective father and an uneasy, apparently disillusioned idealist. His exile is a consequence both of the natural evil in his brother and his own retreat from ducal responsibility into studies—magic and the liberal arts. He takes blame for his condition, claiming to have brought out the evil in Antonio and to have lived too much in his mind (his dream?). Once the initial hardship of the journey was overcome, his magic books and powers made him a god of his island, displacing Caliban. So for a dozen years Prospero has been running everything, even, it would appear, the local weather. He has not seen fit to tell his daughter her own early history or his, and he has failed only in redeeming—making human, more-or-less—his "devil-whelp." His child at fifteen is the very type of virginal virtue, full of sympathy for fellow creatures she has never seen but has apparently learned of from books and paternal instruction. The preservation of her innocence—of evil, especially sexual evil—has been a central concern, nearly foiled by Caliban's attempted rape. Now that the outside world must again be confronted (Prospero cannot neglect this providential opportunity to master his enemies), Miranda gets her history in careful doses, with considerable solicitousness for the shock to her delicate system and to her credulity.

A few obvious inferences follow easily from this list: first, we can expect no real trouble in any plans Prospero has to control the movements of his ene-

mies; if he can do tempests, he can do most anything. Second, the single but striking failure with Caliban gives basis for a more fundamental sort of anxiety: Prospero's power does not extend to minds or souls, so we may wonder how much external manipulation can touch natural evil, which we soon discover also continues in Antonio and Sebastian. What effect, then, can Prospero's external powers have on internal (moral, spiritual) states? The whole plot seems to hinge on this question, yet it is begged early on. What in fact transpires is a series of scenes illustrating Prospero's control, especially of two kinds: the testing of goodness and the interruption—not the correction or extinction—of evil. In short, a series of magic shows allowing the characters to *show themselves*. The metaphor of "finding" a self is, I believe, ironic well before the end of the play.

How we take these shows inevitably depends on how much we take them, either in themselves or by various allusive procedures, to have symbolic or allegorical meanings—and, in turn, whether these meanings arrange themselves into consistent pictures, or lessons, or larger "wholes." Even more fundamentally, what we construct as interpretation depends directly on how serious we think Shakespeare was in presenting *his* shows, or, more narrowly, what sort of seriousness is appropriate to them.

What follows will reveal at least two assumptions about this seriousness: first, that the easiest way to encompass the divergent earnestness of so many critics is to assume that their earnestness led to their divergence; second, the play's failure to achieve an unambiguous resolution, its resistance to any available version of a neat, closed form, suggests that games with closed form may be going on, and the mode of these may be playful (yet not *without* seriousness). *The Tempest* is more like a comedy than a tragedy, neat in very abstract ways only (the much-noticed unities at last observed), yet lacking in mysteries that resonate, either ethical, religious, or aesthetic.

By this thinking, then, a central point (or meaning) of Prospero's magic is that it defines moral limits by illustrating (mostly) psychological obduracy, including Prospero's own. If we do read his behavior as stubborn and reluctant to leave his island kingdom, we may also without strain read it as a preference for art (and dream) over "reality." But that cannot in turn be assumed to be *Shakespeare's* preference.[6] If Prospero's art is a type (in any sense) of Art, the most obvious inference is not that Shakespeare yearns for a dream world, but that Art comes from one, or constitutes one, and that any effects Art has on the world "outside" must include recognizing this. Perhaps drowning the book and breaking the staff enact not the rejection of Art but of ideas that Art can, even in its own realm, control the desires it reflects. Even as *model* Art rejects Absolutes. Prospero is not, apparently, very happy about this; Shakespeare may or may not have been, but he certainly accepted limits gracefully elsewhere, although he tested them constantly. In this play and also, strikingly, in *The Winter's Tale* they become part of the subject matter.

Insofar as this play is "about" art it requires a broad acceptance of artificiality. The sequence of Prospero's magic shows illustrates an increased willfulness and arbitrariness, moving from the impressive tempest to a nuptial masque introduced as a "vanity" and petulantly interrupted (although essentially over) and then to a tableau imitating an emblem book (the chess game).[7] The villains and their burlesque counterparts, once their homicidal intents are recognized and foiled on stage, receive magical punishments mostly out of sight, all repetitive of the early demonstrations of power over bodies (freeze them and pinch them), descending into mud and horsepiss—although it has been noted that the island reveals no other sign of horses. I doubt that any audience can worry, once Ariel saves Alonzo and Gonzalo, that evil may triumph after all, especially with Ariel's constant reassurances and effortless ubiquity. Yet the point does not seem to be to mock evil or reduce it by parody, but to show us, as many have noticed, that it's *always there*, fully preventable only in a magical world, where it may become the occasion for jokes.[8] What is most directly mocked is stupidity and narrow egotism, the traditional targets of comedy, yet unlike what happens in most comedy the mockery does not convincingly triumph; the magical garden continues to harbor real snakes.

So Prospero's magic is limited in several ways: it does not touch man's inner nature; its use descends into stage shows and trickery; it must be put aside fully to confront the "real" world (outside island and play). We can read it, then, as emblematic of good intentions, whose goodness is compromised by self-indulgence, but more fundamentally compromised by the necessary element of illusion in equating art with magic—not only Prospero's illusion, but ours.[9] Shakespeare's art both uses and criticizes such equations, as I hope will be made clearer by some closer looks.

IV Art, Magic, and Illusion

I have suggested that Prospero is a manager of shows. He runs versions of a living theatre, both producing and directing—although the latter function is often Ariel's—to test, to punish, and to convert. Those tested, however, don't need it: Ferdinand carries logs absurdly to prove he respects virginity; no real temptation is allowed him. Miranda (we must strain to include her) has her sympathy and new love tested through the same log-carrying; she offers to help, properly anguished over "her" Ferdinand's suffering. Both pass, foregone conclusions. Ferdinand, in fact, is so without passion some critics don't like him; his protestations that his honor won't melt appear comic. All those whose conversions are sought resist but one, and we easily doubt Alonzo's need for all the browbeating and lying he gets, especially the repeated "news," cheerfully delivered by the play's only teacher of sympathy, that his son is dead.[10] Both the tests and conversions, then, degenerate into punishments. So the putative intent of most of Prospero's shows fails to coincide with their results. Prospero is apparently caught in moral justifications that fail to fit his shows because they were not really, or mainly, or purely, moral shows.

What are they then? Obviously enough, they are entertainments. But for whom, and to what point? That is not easy to answer. Or there are several, perhaps not fully consistent, answers.

First, they are for Prospero. A vanity of his art, a demonstration of control, and perhaps a demonstration of longing to stay on the island. Like Leontes in *The Winter's Tale* Prospero enjoys making the world over to fit his dreams. The log-carrying and the harpied banquet seem obvious instances of a father punishing bad children by whatever dramatic expedient may occur to him. Only in the former the children are not bad at all, so that Prospero has to apologize for these activities, and in the latter the bad children are too bad to be affected. We can understand and even approve, however, Prospero's tours de force: to freeze swords in the air, taunt villains (and credulous Gonzalo) with disappearing acts, and mock the folly of airslicing. The victims are also, of course, an audience, forced to appreciate

Prospero's power, only the point, even for this audience, seems to be more showmanship than power. Everyone's dreams have to be subordinate to Prospero's dreams, however arbitrary. Behavior is controlled largely by controlling perception, emphasizing that the world is as it is seen.

For the next audiences, Prospero and then us, the shows flirt, even through their allusions, with the idea that art itself is to some important degree arbitrary.[11] We are also made conscious that, if we are not to take log-carrying with the seriousness of a "real" test, nor dismiss it as a wholly arbitrary entertainment, it may be part of a literary or dramatic game Shakespeare is playing with us, this time with Prospero as the "forced" actor. The curious combination of Prospero's real power and real impotence, both functions of his involvement in his own magical (here read "imaginative") world, seems an excellent—and once one notices this pattern, inevitable—metaphor for the powers and limits of Shakespeare's own imaginative world, and by not too forced an extension, art in general. Art affirms nothing largely in the sense that Prospero's magic "comes to" nothing: As Alonzos we may want, inspired by renewed consciousness of guilt, or reawakened goodness, or any other *already resident* characteristic, to act, "led" to this action by art. But if this is causation, it is indirect, crucially dependent on our being largely "there" already. Meanwhile, shows go on, and we must learn not to expect too much of them, or, if we do, suffer Prospero's moodiness and unresolved state, or possibly even Alonzo's wish for suicide. In art or in magic shows black may be white, emblems may appear as realities, wishes may become harpies, but they are all spirits that vanish into thin air, and we forget this at the cost (at least) of being bemired in our folly.

Prospero's (and the play's) most famous speech (IV,i,147–158) takes these ideas a step further. As the spirit masque, so the world, meaning our world, or any world known to men. This burst of eloquence, variously noticed as a curious intrusion or a striking change of tone seems, depending on how we read it, to ally this play with tragedy, to provide a metaphysical dimension hardly hinted at before, to undercut all of Prospero's efforts before or after, to change our perspective on *The Tempest* by enforcing a new degree of detachment. My general argument has been that all these things are already there in the various forms of inconclusiveness we have been noting—although I would play down tragic undertones. This speech is indeed central, but it need not be taken with the sadness and weariness that Prospero apparently feels during its delivery.

It is tempting to read it at a discount. Prospero is obviously in a funk, which is not adequately justified by the reason he gives for introducing the "strange, hollow, and confused noise" that cuts off the show. If the "minute of their plot" is almost come, the drama of their entry is curiously attenuated, leaving room for Ariel to be amusing in his description of the helpless plotters, left dancing up to their chins in a filthy mantled pool. And Prospero's subsequent mutterings about the "born devil" hardly sound a grave note either, less even than Caliban's threat of driving a nail into his head did earlier. Yet Prospero seems genuinely upset, as his daughter notices, and if it is not about threats of evildoing, it is most likely about the content of that eloquent speech. The masque, a creation of Prospero's imagination, is interrupted by another creation of his imagination—in short, by the thought that the whole world is no more stable or meaningful than the imagination which "creates" it.

This is indeed metaphysics, but our consciousness that a troubled brain is here expressing itself warns us not to leap at once into Tragic Apprehension; it is just this reminder that Prospero needs to prepare to detach himself from a world where his dreams are everything, yet "amount" to nothing. And there is a positive side to this gloomy view of the ephemerality of things: if we are such stuff as dreams are made on, we make ourselves by dreaming, and much of "the world" too. Our lovers are an obvious case in point; Ferdinand really would do anything for his Miranda, and he very likely really believes, as he says just before the interruption, that "So rare a wonder'd father and a wise / Makes this place paradise." What the naive Ferdinand doesn't yet know (and let him take his time finding out) is that the wisdom and the paradise are both also dreams, already infected beyond repair.

We, on the other hand, are expected to know these things by now, and to be reminded pointedly, here, by Prospero. If this speech undercuts both the moral gravity and magical powers of the play—and even, I would argue, undercuts itself—it is not a violent change or misplaced comment on what has been going on all along. Both here and in *The Winter's Tale* Shakespeare has been setting up his audience for reflections of this kind, which include consciousness of deliberate artifice, especially as it reveals the gap, sometimes trivial but always present, between desire and act, dream and the real world.

The last act collects these matters for us. For instance, Prospero's famous lesson in sympathy, noted by the Arden editor as a "gnomic and vital idea":

> Yet with my nobler reason 'gainst my fury
> Do I take part: the rarer action is
> In virtue than in vengeance: they being penitent,
> The sole drift of my purpose doth extend
> Not a frown further.   (V,i,27–31)

This is in response to Ariel's vivid description of the three villains distracted, wept over by Gonzalo. How can we ignore that two of the three are *not* (even in the slightest degree) penitent? They merely have temporarily boiled brains, a result of Prospero's art. Yet the rarer action *is* in virtue, even if helped along by a delusion grown out of a wish. As art is. The irony points both back into the play and at us, who are also wishers for powers like Prospero's, and perhaps too ready to give them to Shakespeare.

Or, even more strikingly, this speech a little further on, after the major speech abjuring magic. It has often been read with great solemnity.

> Most cruelly
> Didst thou, Alonzo, use me and my daughter:
> Thy brother was a furtherer in the act.
> Thou art pinch'd for't now, Sebastian. Flesh and blood,
> You, brother mine, that entertain'd ambition,
> Expell'd remorse and nature; whom, with Sebastian,—
> Whose inward pinches therefore are most strong,—
> Would here have kill'd your king; I do forgive thee,
> Unnatural though thou art.   (V,i,71–79)

Not, "unnatural hast thou been." The gesture of forgiveness, which we have no reason to think phony, rebounds off Sebastian's consistent (unnatural) malice, although Prospero wants in the same breath to insist that the pinching was "inward"—which must mean, pinching of conscience, the agenbite of inwit. But it wasn't, and Prospero knows it, hence the ambivalence in the speech, shortly followed up by further admission that remorse and nature remain expelled.[12] So we have another show, with some of the actors playing the parts Prospero has "written," others just walking through them, deliberately dis-

tracted. They want to write their own parts, and do. Prospero doesn't like to admit this, but surely *we* should. Nor do we need to deny that there is a serious moral lesson here, only the emphasis of the play seems as much on ill-fitting yet necessary illusions as on either the fallen world or, especially, on grand regenerations and moral uplift.

We are further reminded that this isle is full of subtleties that distort the taste and encumber belief (perhaps fatally). Gonzalo, with his usual blindness to subtleties of any kind, unwittingly blurts out a few lines that summarize much of what has been going on:

> All torment, trouble, wonder and amazement
> Inhabits here: some heavenly power guide us
> Out of this fearful country!   (V,i,104–6)

Heavenly power is indeed needed, since the fearful country is, variously, the magical illusions, the imagination, and the mind and soul. Nothing is there that they didn't bring, nor will they leave these things there when they go—except Ariel, and perhaps Caliban. Gonzalo will find wonder and amazement at home too, Antonios will replace them with wisecracks and plots, and Prosperos will retire, along with Alonzos, chastened by overreaching.

Prospero, despite his inability not to frown at the recalcitrants, appears to be having a good time, as he promised himself earlier, gloating that they were all at his mercy. If he can't properly be a heavenly power, he can at least run the show his way, even teasing lugubrious Alonzo:

> ALONZO: When did you lose your daughter?
> Prospero: In this last tempest.   (V,i,152–3)

Their trances and boiled brains, not very effectual morally, are just the thing to reduce them to an ideal audience for a chess game. And the chess game, suggestive as you please of elegant aristocracy, suggests also isolation, especially the sort necessary to maintain the protestations of romantic love. Miranda's wondering expletives are echoed, as Kermode especially notices, by Caliban, both of them much taken by elegant attire:

> O Setebos, these be brave spirits indeed!
> How fine my master is!   (V,i,261–2)

Prospero's mild retort to his enthusiastic daughter fits as well here.

> 'Tis new to thee.

V Art, Nature, and Caliban

O ho, O ho! would't had been done!
Thou didst prevent me; I had peopled else
This isle with Calibans.

Perhaps Shakespeare has. As many critics emphasize, Caliban is an appealing demi-devil, whose shape, though deformed in some unspecified way, is human. E. E. Stoll has with particular relish laid out the psychology of the "brute," who loves his sensual pleasures and is more amoral than immoral, and who may be allowed an imagination — *must* be allowed one, if we refuse to dismiss his lyrical speech on dream-inducing music (III,ii,133–40) as out of character.[13] Few besides Stoll are willing to stop here, however, including me.

With many others I think Caliban should be promoted from a natural man, or a brute man, to Natural Man, and maybe even Us. I don't of course mean we all secretly yearn to rape virgins or murder our bosses, but that Caliban's attempts to understand enough to control his own life have obvious similarities to the rest of the cast, to Prospero, to any playmaker, and to us. In short I would play down the contrasts — which are certainly there in the play — to the idealized romantic and moral paradigms which Miranda and Ferdinand keep assuring us they live by, and which Prospero pays rather ambivalent service to, and emphasize instead that our sympathy with and pleasure in this brute qualifies, if not refutes, Prospero's rants about him and makes any strict belief that nurture will never stick false. At least Caliban has learned that gods don't reside in bottles and that his admiration — and even, he says once, love — for his master isn't all inverted into resentment and hatred, nails or no nails. If not redeemed into goodness, Caliban is very likely to know much better what to do when the next batch of civilized creatures visit him. And the gift of language is far from stagnant in him, either for cursing or celebrating.

Like everyone else in the play, Caliban lives, or tries to live, in illusions that the play shows inadequate. In this context he specially emphasizes that illusions, even fond dreams of evildoing, are *natural*, opening wide the door to a popular paradox (or would-be paradox) of Shakespeare's time as well as to modern philosophizing on the mysteries of "natural" man — in both cases fallen and hoping to rise.

Polixenes's argument with Perdita in *The Winter's Tale* (IV,iv,85–100) is sufficient footnote here to contemporary debate on the natural and the artificial, and applications to notions of the noble savage may be pursued extensively in D. G. James's *Dream of Prospero*. The basic point, as I take it anyhow, is that good and evil are built into most of us (perhaps all — I'm holding out Miranda), and most of us are capable of being better — especially of being taught to be better. This may finally mean better at moral action or better at imagining — two activities ideally connected, but in practice sometimes opposed, since desire inevitably remains in the picture. Moral art as well as the art of illusion are natural, so the common split in the word's use — unnatural acts being either magical or immoral — are not contradictions but isolations in a hierarchy under the rubric of Polixenes, "the art that nature makes." That brothers can kill each other is unnatural only from the point of view of someone who insists that natural always means moral — an unusually rigid or didactic playwright, for example. Even the innocent Miranda knows better, when she comforts her father over Antonio's evildoing in Act One. And the other use of "unnatural" in this play, the unnatural events that Prospero has brought about, remain unnatural only as we remain ignorant of what's in those magic books, or, if larger mysteries are preferred, what providential forces brought the boat into range of the tempest. Yet it seems odd to call providence unnatural. God must be allowed His own magic tricks, and so must Shakespeare. We have room to choose how earnestly we receive either.[14]

The main point, to which I think Shakespeare consistently returns, is that attempts to match words and things, wishes and realities, inevitably leave disjunctions, especially for those who insist on neatness and univocality. Shakespeare most certainly did not, and Caliban's "puzzling" bursts of poetry point this up. Perhaps his uncertain future does too. In trying to be a junior Prospero he got minor tortures and a large wallow — and a little more common sense. Prospero proper got everyone at his mercy, a son-in-law, and his city back — all three rather qualified victories, and basic, fundamental evil is just untouched.

Neither Caliban nor his master could typecast; nature wouldn't have it. That nature wouldn't is one of the play's main messages, one of its "truths about life," one of its loose ends. Art, like life, orders by acts of wishing and willing and above all imagining; the results are bound to be a little messy. They can be neat only if will dominates all.

I hope this makes it clearer why I think of *The Tempest* as experimental, tentative among its wonderful reconciliations. It is tempting, but I think too neat, to identify Caliban with some sort of reality principle, evil itself, or perhaps original sin. Auden seems closer to the truth in making Caliban both the interrogating audience and a voice which becomes, finally, Shakespeare's own—after a kind of reverse metamorphosis from Ariel, the soaring spirit collapsed into the undeniable body.[15] If as I believe Shakespeare will not allow either unequivocal idealization or consistent, "realistic" parody, all the characters are mirrors of us, especially as we are all artist-dreamers, and all the mirrors are chipped and cracked.

Notes

1. The extremes in the range of interpretation may be represented by Colin Still's *The Timeless Theme* (London, 1936) and E. E. Stoll's "The Tempest," *PMLA* 47 (1932). The former finds the whole play an allegory, the latter denies any secondary meanings whatever. Between them there is considerable variety, but the central division seems to be between those who take the play as a serious and coherent moral or religious statement and those who find it problematic, ironic, or otherwise resistant to allegorical interpretations. The majority still favor what I call the earnest view—that Shakespeare is in this play culminating (or even summarizing) his career, probably saying farewell to the stage, making a symbolic statement of unusual economy, resonance, and power. The minority offer various more skeptical readings, tend to be critical of Prospero, find ambiguities or loose ends, and generally find the play not fully explained by symbolic patterns. Representative of the majority are Derek Traversi, *Shakespeare: The Last Phase* (Stanford, 1955), R. G. Hunter, *Shakespeare's Comedy of Forgiveness* (New York, 1955), D. G. James, *The Dream of Prospero* (Oxford, 1967); Frank Kermode, Arden Edition to *The Tempest* (London, 1954); G. Wilson Knight, *The Shakespearean Tempest* (Oxford 1932). Representatives of the minority are Bonamy Dobree in *Twentieth Century Interpretations of The Tempest*, ed. Hallet Smith (Englewood Cliffs, 1969); Harry Berger's "Miraculous Harp: A Reading of Shakespeare's *Tempest*," *Shakespeare Studies V* 1970; and Clifford Leech, *Shakespeare's Tragedies* (London, 1950). Berger's essay overlaps most with my own, although it focuses more intensely on Prospero's psychology.

   Norman Rabkin's comments on Shakespeare's consciousness of art and artifice in *Shakespeare and the Common Understanding* (New York, 1967) also resemble mine, but he differs strikingly in the seriousness with which he responds to symbolic patterns and to tone generally. My own emphasis here is on a much more relaxed view of the play, with special interest in the way Shakespeare's last plays remind us of limits: of dreams, desires, acts, and particularly the ordering action of art. All subsequent references to these authors will be to the works already cited, unless otherwise noted.

2. Dobree and Berger, for example.

3. These last few sentences crudely summarize the views of D. G. James. I found this a fascinating and helpful book, although James's elegiac view of the play is almost a polar opposite to mine.

4. See especially Robert Graves, *Poetic Unreason* (New York, 1968).

5. D. G. James (Chapter II) insists that there are "two tempests," the first an illusion, but no one I have read is quite willing to claim all the play's action is somehow just "dreamt." If there is a prevalent view about the "actual" force of Prospero's powers, it seems to be that they do indeed exceed what we now mean by magician's tricks, yet most critics proceed without much troubling over this to discussing what the magic may mean in the play. James sees Prospero's rejection of it as the rejection by the seventeenth century of magical explanations in favor of the new science. See C. J. Sisson, "The Magic of Prospero," *Shakespeare Survey* II (1958), for a neat summary of Elizabethan notions, legal and philosophical, concerning black and white magic.

6. Harry Berger argues these points strongly.

7. In "New Uses of Adversity: Tragic Experience in *The Tempest*," Stephen Orgel has the reading most plausibly claiming that the masque is functional. For him it represents, as masques traditionally do, a world outside time and also, as a masque of Ceres omitting winter, a natural order shaped by man's idealization (the imagination). In short, it is a version of Prospero's imagined wishes, so that "Prospero's interruption is full of a consciousness

of the dangers not only of the conspiracy he has forgotten but also of the imaginative world that has tempted him to forget it." This reading appears to me to reinforce my own, even though Orgel takes the idea of suffering more seriously than I do throughout. Orgel notes at the play's ending some of the loose ends I do, but for him they represent tragic implications. His essay appeared in *In Defense of Reading*, Richard Poirier and Reuben Brower, eds. (New York, 1962).

8. See R. G. Hunter, who thinks the evil *is* reduced, against Harry Berger.

9. All the more extreme symbolic readings, especially Still's, appear to want to assert metamorphic powers (acting on us) in *The Tempest*. In my view the play mocks them.

10. Although we feel much less cruelty here, Alonzo's punishments resemble Isabel's in *Measure for Measure*, where the Duke requires her to forgive her brother's executioner before he tells her there was no execution.

11. For the banquet scene, for example, R. G. Hunter favors an interrupted communion, finding this a more precise analogy than a symbol of deceitful desire (such as Northrop Frye, in his introduction to the *Pelican Shakespeare*) or allusion to Christ's temptation (such as Kermode in his introduction to the Arden Shakespeare). I prefer the more general sort of suggestion (Frye's), since to insist on close Christian parallels would require precisely the narrowness of didactic focus which I would argue against. My point is simply that the scene invites various interpretations without requiring one "right" reading.

12. Sebastian does make one pious remark—"O most high miracle"—but this hardly constitutes an obvious change of heart. He also says Prospero is possessed by the devil, and Prospero's remarks to Antonio don't seem to suppose a conversion. If we are to believe, as Gonzalo appears to, that everyone has found himself and become virtuous too, Shakespeare has strikingly left out reassurances we might reasonably expect, especially if we bear in mind his usual attention to such loose ends in his comedies.

13. See also John Wain, who sees in Caliban underprivileged people everywhere. Wain's essay appears in Hallett Smith's anthology, *Twentieth Century Interpretations of The Tempest*.

14. Again, this whole argument can be conceived as a game exploring limits, as I try to elaborate in a companion essay on *The Winter's Tale*. I don't think J. M. Murry got it quite right when he argued that Polixenes—and Shakespeare—were saying that "Where man's art improves nature, it is nature's art in man; where it makes nature worse, it is man's art alone." The problem is in calling "man's art alone" unnatural, as usage both in Shakespeare's time and ours amply illustrates. Are elaborately synthetic poisons unnatural? Man makes them by natural wit from natural elements. Is evil unnatural? It is the profoundest urge of some human creatures, as Shakespeare's tragedies fully show. To shift the terms in the way I favor is merely to call attention, as I think Shakespeare does often, to man's tendency to use the label unnatural for things he doesn't like, want, or understand. Here he meets his own limits—of, naturally enough, taste, desire, and knowledge, and finally, if he acts, in what he produces—like plays.

15. *The Sea and The Mirror*. I am not sure I understand all that Caliban is meant to be here, and I think Shakespeare stops short of Auden's apparently religious solution, but I find most of Caliban's musings close to mine. Especially this, where he speaks as audience:

> You yourself, we seem to remember, have spoken of the conjured spectacle as 'a mirror held up to nature,' a phrase misleading in its aphoristic sweep but indicative at least of one aspect of the relationship between the real and the imagined, their mutual reversal of value, for isn't the essential artistic strangeness to which your citation of the sinisterly biased image would point just this: that on the far side of the mirror the general will to compose, to form at all costs a felicitous pattern becomes the *necessary cause* of any particular effort to live or act or love or triumph or vary, instead of being as, in so far as it emerges at all, it is on this side their *accidental effect*?

> It seems to me that Shakespeare has in this play also included the second perspective, that of accidental effect.

Resisting the Aesthetic

Barbara Jones Guetti

Just as Paul de Man opens his analysis of "Among School Children" by taking the speaker's "rhetorical" questions "literally," so Barbara Jones Guetti proposes to read Keats's questions to the urn "not as rhetorical exclamations but as sincere and urgent demands for information." "It is because he doesn't understand the urn, does not know how to read the message it once conveyed . . . that Keats has to respond to it as what we would call an 'aesthetic object.'" The poem, then, is not a description of the urn but a description of an attempt to "read" the urn. The conflict between grammar and rhetoric, or figurative language, that figures in de Man's "Semiology and Rhetoric" and is refigured in his "Resisting the Aesthetic" as a conflict between the aesthetic and the literary, is central to Guetti's poststructural reading. Like de Man, she performs a formal analysis, a close reading, but, also like de Man, she expects the text to resist attempts to unify its meanings. Thus Guetti opposes to harmonizing formalism a poststructural analysis that discovers in the Ode "both an aesthetic resistance to the literary . . . and a literary resistance to such aesthetic 'solutions' or evasions."

In "Semiology and Rhetoric," Archie Bunker's question "What's the difference?" [*Allegories* 9] leads de Man into a discussion of some crucial—and, he insists, undecidable—differences between, as he puts it, *grammar* and *rhetoric*, which implicitly raise questions about competing kinds of verbal authority. In the "Resistance to Theory" essay, we find de Man stubbornly and, it would seem, quite gleefully repeating his by then notorious view of literature as the area where crucial differences (between grammar and rhetoric, literal and figurative statements, and so forth) are continually undermined. There he diag-

Reprinted by permission of The Johns Hopkins University Press from *Diacritics* 17 (Spring 1987): 34–40, 45. Parts of the essay have been omitted.

noses not only external resistances to "literary theory" as he defines it, but the internal resistances that any theoretician, or simply any especially engaged reader, may have to the activity of reading itself: "reading," he says, instead of "leading to the knowledge of an entity (such as language)" is "an unreliable process of knowledge production," since what it produces are "consistently defective models of language's impossibility to be a model language" [19]. Such readings do not reach a satisfactory conclusion but instead, characteristically, break off, as does the exemplarily defective reading de Man offers, in the same essay, of Keats's unfinished epic, *The Fall of Hyperion.* "Just as Keats had to break off his narrative, the reader has to break off his understanding at the very moment when he is most directly engaged and summoned by the text" [16–17].

De Man's work constantly encourages such venturesome and hazardous textual encounters. In this respect, it resembles the work of three other exemplary critics or readers who have affected the kind of reading I am about to engage in here: Kenneth Burke, William Empson, and Jacques Derrida. As I go along, I will implicitly be responding to criticisms of de Man's work by Gerald Graff and Frank Lentricchia. Both have cast de Man, incorrectly as nearly as I can tell, in the role of literary formalist *par excellence.* They see him as a superlatively cagey defender of institutional and literary cages, prison houses and ivory towers. I was genuinely amazed—having been a Burke fan even before I encountered Paul de Man thirty years ago—to find that Lentricchia, in presenting a case for Burke in *Criticism and Social Change,* seemed unable to do so without adopting the strategy of allowing de Man to function there as a scapegoat, precisely in the Burkian sense. We seem to have an example here of exactly the kind of methodological (as opposed to merely personal) blindness de Man diagnosed in *Blindness and Insight:* even though Lentricchia prefers to envision a critical struggle (or *agon*) between two opponents to whom he assigns proper names ("Burke" and "de Man"), it is remarkable that he is led to perform, apparently quite unselfconsciously, the kind of symbolic ritual Burke has so often discerned in a wide variety of texts. The issues at stake seem to be ones that cannot be so easily resolved by naming (or calling) names: to my mind, it is no longer simply or self-evidently possible to "know the difference" between a de Manian, a Burkian, an Empsonian or perhaps even a Derridian

reading. I can only attempt at the outset to take my distance from those whose confident claims to know (and hence to resolve) such differences I do not presume to share.

In answer to Gerald Graff's accusation that de Man is superlatively complacent in embracing what Graff refers to as textual "undecidability," let me just call attention to another passage from "Resistance to Theory" in which de Man comments on the particular dilemma posed by the title of Keats's *The Fall of Hyperion:* "it matters a great deal how we read the title, as an exercise not only in semantics, but in what the text actually does to us. . . . One could hardly expect to find solace in this 'fearful symmetry' between the author's and reader's plight since, at this point, the symmetry is no longer a formal but an actual trap, and the question no longer 'merely' theoretical" [16–17]. Here as elsewhere de Man, far from just residing comfortably in a doctrine of textual "undecidability," isolates a particular kind of undecidability: the question is whether we are reading a literary text that tells the story of a fall undergone by a fictional character, named Hyperion, or whether, as readers, we are participating in a process figuratively expressed as the "fall of Hyperion," but which is literally duplicated in our actual experience as readers of this or any other (literary) text. Such questions are far from superficial. For they refer to the one real activity we can all be sure we are actually engaged in, whatever else one may affirm or deny about the nature of the community we constitute.

So much for the preliminaries. Let us now turn to Keats's "Ode on a Grecian Urn." This is a poem that has become so familiar, so extensively commented upon, that it may appear by now to be virtually unreadable: whether you love it or hate it, it has acquired the status of a sacred cow in our culture. William Empson makes this complaint as he attempts to read the Ode in *The Structure of Complex Words:* "It seems clear that we have to imagine what went on in the mind of Keats, as he wondered what the pot can have meant—we, it is understood, being those who have lost our innocence in the matter by reading the contradictory babble of the critics" [371]. Empson's effort to demystify the urn by calling it "the pot" as he does throughout his reading indicates the particular challenge posed by such canonized works to any reader. In this case, the challenge is compounded by the fact that not only the poem, but the object it purports to describe—the urn—has been canonized, or appears to be canonized within the poem, especially when we remember—and how could we fail to?—the famous final slogan, "Beauty is Truth, Truth Beauty," which appears to have been formulated precisely in order to be quotable, or infinitely repeatable outside the immediate context of the poem. In fact, critical controversy has tended to focus not so much on the meaning of these lines, as on whether they belong in this (or any) actual poem: whether this oracle, or slogan, or punch line, isn't all too serenely self-sufficient ("That is all ye know on earth and all ye need to know") to belong, properly, to a poem which is manifestly about struggle, sacrifice, and the frustrating disjunction between the "heat" of human desires and the "cold" repose of works of art. Cleanth Brooks's effort, in *The Well-Wrought Urn*, to contextualize those final lines with reference to the rest of the poem, and to defend them as "dramatic" writings rather than as ideological doctrine, is an especially notable example of such readings.

I'm not, however, going to attempt even a sketchy summary of all the variant readings of the poem; instead I want to consider a point that none of the innumerable readings I've come across has made—at least, none has done so emphatically enough. Virtually no critics have thought of reading the questions Keats addresses to the urn literally—that is, not as rhetorical exclamations, but as sincere and urgent demands for information—and therefore it has not occurred to anyone that Keats is, as de Man would put it, attempting to read, rather than to imagine, the urn. It has been noticed that the poem is composed primarily as a series of questions; a corollary of this formal strategy, perhaps, is that this ode does not give us the kind of concretely sensuous description of its object that we may have come to expect from Keats on the basis of his other poems. As in the case of a poem by Victor Hugo which de Man analyzes in his essay on Riffaterre [*Resistance* 27–51], the apparent "object" of Keats's poem (the urn) is not so much "described" as it is "addressed." What happens, then, if we take these questions as serious, literal questions, to which Keats would really like to know the answer: "what men or gods are these?"

Here I am borrowing a strategy used by de Man in his early and late readings of Yeats's "Among School Children," when he suggests that we can read the final question of that poem, "How can we know the dancer from the dance?" not as a rhetorical ques-

tion, asserting the unity of part and whole, form and experience, creator and creation, but as a literal question, "Please tell me how to know the dancer from the dance," which begs to be released from just such delusive affirmations of unity [*The Rhetoric of Romanticism* 200–202]. De Man insists that these two ways of reading the final question are drastically incompatible: "one reading is precisely the error denounced by the other and has to be undone by it" ["Semiology and Rhetoric," *Allegories* 12]. Now if, following de Man's example, we take the questions addressed to the urn by Keats as real questions, we begin to see that Keats doesn't know the very things about the urn that would have been of the utmost importance to the people who made it, things which would have "made a difference" to them: he doesn't know whether it depicts men or gods; he doesn't know whether it is a ritual object, or, if it is, what is the precise nature of the ritual: "Who are these coming to the sacrifice?" And I would argue that what gives the urn its special status for Keats is precisely this problem: that the urn "matters" to Keats because of his ignorance about it.

This reading can be supported by further evidence from some of Keats's other poems about Greek culture. We may recall that "On First Looking into Chapman's Homer" is about reading Homer in translation, not in the original. Yet another sonnet, "To Homer," begins, "Standing aloof in giant ignorance / Of thee I hear . . ." in lines whose grammatical ambiguity makes it impossible to tell whether the "ignorance" belongs to "thee" (Homer) or to "I" (Keats): the rest of the poem is emphatically about blindness and insight ("Aye, on the shores of darkness there is light"), but the illumination attributed to the blind Homer may refer as well to the unbridgeable distance that separates Keats from Greek culture [Keats 261]. An early sonnet, "How many bards gild the lapses of time," also suggests that poems from the past reach Keats, in the present, only vaguely and distantly, like the "unnumbered sounds" of nature that surround him. This lack of precision, distinction, or, as the poem puts it, "number" enables Keats to respond to the ancient bards, and to the sounds of the evening, as an unspecified "pleasing music," precisely because no sound is distinguishable from any other: "and thousand others more, / That distance of recognizance bereaves, / Make pleasing music, and not wild uproar" [82]. The negative implications of "bereavement" here are at odds with the poem's otherwise reassuring assertions that the poet's "distance" from Greek culture is pleasant and soothing. I would suggest that a similar "bereavement of recognizance" occurs in the "Ode on a Grecian Urn," and that the poem, far from being an assertion of the eternal values of art regardless of time or history, is a meditation on how the loss of meaning in the course of history creates aesthetic masterworks, such as the urn. It is because he doesn't understand the urn, does not know how to read the message it once conveyed ("What leaf-fringed legend *haunts* about thy shape / Of deities, or mortals, or of both?") that Keats has to respond to it as what we would call an "aesthetic object."

In this context, Paul de Man's remarks about aesthetics in "The Resistance to Theory" are relevant:

Whenever [the] autonomous potential of language can be revealed by analysis, we are dealing with literariness and, in fact, with literature as the place where this negative knowledge about the reliability of linguistic utterance is made available. The ensuing foregrounding of material, phenomenal aspects of the signifier creates a strong illusion of aesthetic seduction at the very moment when the actual aesthetic function has been, at the very least, suspended. . . . Literature involves the voiding, rather than the affirmation, of aesthetic categories. One of the consequences of this is that, whereas we have traditionally been accustomed to reading literature by analogy with the plastic arts and with music, we now have to recognize the necessity of a non-perceptual, linguistic moment in painting and music, and learn to *read* pictures rather than to *imagine* meaning. [10]

In the reading I am proposing, the "Ode on a Grecian Urn" enacts a complex process, stemming from Keats's initial failure to *read* the urn. One consequence of this failure is an "affirmation of aesthetic categories" which, however, remains tentative—for it "succeeds" or "works" only by expressing, at the same time, the "negative knowledge about the reliability of linguistic utterance" which de Man calls "literary."

Let's try to clarify this by going back once more to the poem, and to its especially rich opening lines: "Thou still unravished bride of quietness, / Thou foster-child of silence and slow time" [252]. It is remarkable that nearly all critics—among them, Burke, Empson and de Man—tend to leave these lines unread. This is especially surprising in view of the extraordinary weight of figural meaning they bear:

why have such ingenious readers resisted such a rich load of interpretable ore? Like the questions in the poem, the lines appear to have been dismissed, even by readers who should know better, as "mere rhetoric," elaborate ways of exclaiming over the urn, without saying much about it. The reading I am developing enables me to translate these lines, fairly crudely, into a statement—although I should hasten to add that having done so, I will still be perplexed by certain conflicts implied in the figures. As often happens in Empsonian paraphrase, a dogged pursuit of the plainest sort of sense will make it possible to specify some crucial ambiguities. The translation, at any rate, goes something like this: "Urn, I can't possibly understand you, because I can't understand what you originally may have meant: (you are like a "still unravished bride") what I see before me is not the original produced by the Greeks, but a by-product ("foster-child") of the passage of time, which has erased your original meaning." I would then go on to establish a scenario for the ensuing action of the poem, as follows: "Since, not understanding these things, I can't even be sure what ceremonious function you may have had, I will have to improvise a ceremony that will do justice to my way of apprehending you. In the long run, I will accept the only answer you can legitimately give to my impatient and perhaps improper questions."

Now, although this translation works well insofar as it makes fairly consistent sense out of some highly "overwrought" figural language, some interesting resistances turn up the minute we return to the actual figures. Let's re-examine "still unravished bride of quietness." As far as I know, the only person who has attempted a serious commentary on these lines is William Faulkner, a large part of whose complete works might be defined as extended readings of "still unravished bride" as personified by such characters as Caddie Compson, Addie Bundren, and Rosa Coldfield—not to mention Temple Drake and Big Ben the bear. (An especially explicit reference to Keats occurs in "The Bear" in *Go Down Moses* 296–97.) What makes this bride, in all her manifestations, so tantalizingly unapproachable is not merely the metaphorical equation of sexual consummation with knowledge—in itself a standard and familiar figure—but the curious conflict that is set up between legitimate and illegitimate forms of sexual activity. The phrase "still unravished bride of quietness" falls into two alternative meanings that resist the kind of reconciliation that critics such as Cleanth Brooks have found in the paradoxical language ("Cold Pastoral") elsewhere in the poem. The problem is, bluntly, that "ravish" doesn't go with "bride." If we were simply told that the urn had contracted an unconsummated marriage to quietness, we would be dealing with a fairly simple figural reversal of values, expressed in an allegory, thus: loss of meaning ("bride of quietness") has its compensation in the preservation of purity, of a formal "aesthetic" integrity that resists paraphrase, and does not need to be "understood." In this case one could read the figure as an assertion that the urn, in her "marriage" to quietness, had achieved something thought to be even more fulfilling than sexual consummation. But "unravished" seriously interferes with the coherence of this little allegorical story: a "ravisher" could not be the bride's husband (especially if the husband is "quietness"), but would have to be someone who intruded on this legitimate, if fruitless, union: a rival, an interloper. And images of rape proliferate in the last lines of the stanza: "What maidens loth? What mad pursuit? What struggle to escape?" So if Keats is saying that the urn is no longer susceptible to understanding, because it has been married to quietness and adopted by its foster-parents, "silence and slow time" (who presumably gave the bride away), he still envisions *any* understanding of the urn (even that of the Greeks themselves) as a violation, a rape, and indeed he goes on to read the figures of men (or gods) on the urn as being, originally, stories of such a rape. Instead of simply lamenting, nostalgically, the loss of meaning that an artifact might have if "read" in the appropriate context of its culture, Keats appears to be celebrating the urn's escape, to quote de Man in the passage already cited, from "the place where [the] negative knowledge about the reliability of linguistic utterance is made available." We may imagine, regretfully, a "lost" story that would explain the urn, and could be read from it: "What leaf-fringed legend haunts about thy shape?" But if we could actually read such a story, far from being transported back to the truth of Ancient Greek culture, we might instead find ourselves, like the Greeks who actually made the pot, back in the uncomfortable literary terrain which is not so much a "realm of gold" as, according to Paul de Man, a place where "sign and meaning can never coincide" [*Blindness and Insight* 17], a place not of "pleasing music" but of "wild uproar," in the words of the early Keats sonnet previously cited.

Keats wrote a poem to his friend John Hamilton Reynolds, March 1818, about a year before he composed the Odes, which depicts a grotesque jumble of private nightmares mingled with historical and literary allusions:

> Dear Reynolds, as last night I lay in bed,
> There came before my eyes that wonted thread
> Of shapes, and shadows and remembrances,
> That every other minute vex and please:
> Things all disjointed came from north and south,
> Two witches' eyes above a cherub's mouth,
> Voltaire with casque and shield and Habergeon,
> And Alexander with his nightcap on—
> Old Socrates atying his cravat
> And Hazlitt playing with Miss Edgeworth's cat . . .
> [265–66]

In an effort, as he puts it, to "escape these visitings" from what we might call a threateningly uncensored literary realm, Keats begins to sketch early drafts of the Ode, as in these lines: "The sacrifice goes on: the pontiff knife / Gleams in the sun, the milk-white heifer lows, / The pipes go shrilly, the libation flows . . ." but such images keep lapsing back into the kind of endlessly unresolved Gothic fictions produced by Miss Edgeworth and Mrs. Radcliffe: the classic Greek landscape is continually invaded by maddeningly romantic structures:

> The doors all look as if they oped themselves,
> The windows as if latched by fays and elves—
> And from them comes a silver flash of light
> As from the westward of a summer's night;
> Or like a beauteous woman's large blue eyes
> Gone mad through olden songs and poesies . . .
> [266]

What Keats complains of, in this poem, is a potentially endless proliferation of stories out of stories, signs out of other signs which, for Paul de Man, characterizes "literariness," "metaphoricity" or "figuration." I quote now from de Man's early discussion of Empson's *Seven Types of Ambiguity*:

> Instead of setting up an adequation between two experiences, and thereby fixing the mind on the repose of an established equation, [metaphor] deploys the initial experience into an infinity of associated experiences that spring from it. In the manner of a vibration spreading in infinitude from its center, metaphor is endowed with the capacity to situate the experience at the heart of a universe that it generates. It provides the ground rather than

the frame, a limitless anteriority that permits the limiting of a specific entity. Experience sheds its uniqueness and leads instead to a dizziness of the mind. Far from referring back to an object that would be its cause, the poetic sign sets in motion an imaging activity that refers to no object in particular. The "meaning" of the metaphor is that it does not "mean" in any definite manner ["The Dead-End of Formalist Criticism," *Blindness and Insight* 235].

Or, as Keats put it in his sonnet "On Seeing the Elgin Marbles": "Such dim-conceived glories of the brain / Bring round the heart an indescribable feud; / So do these wonders a most dizzy pain . . ." [89].

If we return, now, to the first stanza of the Ode we may perhaps begin to see more clearly an ambivalence, or "undecidability" in the poem that is quite different from the "paradoxes" and not-so-fearful "symmetries" often celebrated in New Critical readings of the poem, such as that of Cleanth Brooks. Instead we find a more indescribable, and perhaps less easily resolvable, feud between Keats's desire to "know" the urn, to understand what it says (expressed, as we have seen, in the strongest sexual terms) and his suspicion that any such access to the meanings the urn once actually had in its culture would in fact seriously threaten its status as a distinct "form," or "shape," or coherent aesthetic object. It is safer, and far "sweeter," to imagine what the "flowery tale" depicted on the urn might have said than it could be actually to read it: the unreadable urn — like the poetry of Homer and other bards mentioned in the sonnets previously cited — takes on the status of a natural object: "Sylvan historian, who canst thus express / A flowery tale more sweetly than our rhyme." What de Man says of Hölderlin's metaphor, "Words like flowers . . ." (*Worte, wie blumen*), clearly applies here: "The metaphor requires that we begin by forgetting all we have previously known about words. . . . Unlike words, which originate like something else ('like flowers'), flowers originate like themselves; they are literally what they are, definable without the assistance of metaphor" ["The Intentional Structure of the Romantic Image," *The Rhetoric of Romanticism* 3–4]. Yet a certain hesitancy on Keats's part as to the validity of such "flowery tales" may be indicated in the oxymoron, "Sylvan historian." Despite such efforts to forget "all we have previously known about words," the urn must at very least recount the history of this forgetting: it persistently reminds us of what it can no longer say.

Such scruples, however, appear to have been eradicated in the second and third stanzas of the Ode, which offer declarations in the place of questions: "Heard melodies are sweet, but those unheard are sweeter." The change in tone is indeed quite striking; the previously hesitant, inquiring speaker now begins to lay down the law, commanding the pipes to "play on," and telling the figures on the urn what they can and cannot do: offering instructions, admonitions, advice:

> Bold lover, never, never canst thou kiss,
> Though winning near the goal — yet, do not grieve;
> She cannot fade, though thou hast not thy bliss,
> Forever wilt thou love, and she be fair!

It is fairly obvious that these instructions are intended, also, for the readers of Keats's poem, who are, however, being instructed at this point not to "read" the poem, but rather to permit its language to evoke for them something that is not susceptible to "reading" at all. The words in the poem, in other words — in Keats's words — "tease" us, as the girl teases her "forever panting" lover, constantly holding out the bait of an object that is constituted by the failure of our efforts to reach it. We have here, indeed, a classic stance of what is meant by "auto-referentiality": what Keats chooses to see depicted on the urn — the silent piper, the frustrated lover — refers to the obligatory activity required for proper aesthetic reception. The lover is to the girl as we are to the urn: what is imagined as being portrayed on the pot "refers" to our efforts to imagine the pot.

But something a bit different happens in stanza four: "Who are these coming to the sacrifice?" As he begins to ask these new questions — which might be called questions about what was just happening in the previous stanza: who, after all, are we who look at the urn? what sort of sacrifice are we making? — Keats also violates the very aesthetic "rules" which obtained in the previous stanzas. The questions he starts to ask are not so much about what's on the urn, as about what's missing from it: what has been omitted, what must be sacrificed if we are to remain obedient to his previous instructions. The ceremony we see, with its glamorous sacrificial object ("that heifer lowing at the skies / And all her silken flanks with garlands dressed" — a sacred cow if there ever was one!) does not so much "refer to" or "represent" or even substitute for, as *conceal* the empty town that has been left desolate by these ritual celebrations:

What little town, by river or sea shore,
   Or mountain-built with peaceful citadel,
      Is emptied of this folk, this pious morn?

And, little town, thy streets forever more
   Will silent be; and not a soul to tell
      Why thou art desolate, can e'er return.

In a critique of this poem included in the introduction to the Signet Edition, Paul de Man remarks: "the poet of the Odes would hardly be able to evoke the happy world on the Urn if he were himself the creature 'lowing at the skies' about to be sacrificed" [xxxi]. But I see, in the contrast between the beribboned heifer the urn overtly displays, and the desolate town it represses and conceals, an acknowledgment, on Keats's part, of the mundane everyday costs entailed by the splendid ritual he seems to be recommending. The loss Keats alludes to in this stanza is not simply imposed by the passage of time, not merely a historical message that cannot be recovered by future generations; it is the high price that is paid whenever we sacrifice what de Man calls "the literary" in favor of "the aesthetic." The poem cannot tell us which option to choose, but it can and does express the option quite clearly. In order to do so, Keats must violate the aesthetic decorum he has previously recommended: he not only reads, but "reads into" the urn, making up a story about something the urn does not display — a story which tells us that a story will never be told — in what I would call a distinctly literary, as opposed to an aesthetic gesture.

In the "Epistle to Reynolds" I cited earlier, Keats imagines the terror of not being able to communicate his highest "visions" to his closest "friends":

An echo of sweet music doth create
A fear in the poor herdsman who doth bring
His beasts to trouble the enchanted spring:
He tells of the sweet music and the spot
To all his friends, and they believe him not.   [267]

He goes on to express a wish that he could convey to his contemporaries more "sublime" material than the manifestly Freudian fantasies that have been plaguing him throughout the poem, dreams which "shadow our own soul's daytime / In the dark void of night." He laments his inability to "philosophize" or "moralize," to discover an appropriate way of legislating his ungovernable imaginative activity:

     O never will the prize,
High reason, and the lore of good and ill,
Be my reward. Things cannot to the will
Be settled, but they tease us out of thought.

Or is it that imagination brought
Beyond its proper bound, yet still confined —
Lost in a sort of Purgatory blind —
Cannot refer to any standard law
Of either earth or heaven? — It is a flaw
In happiness to see beyond our bourn —
It forces us in summer skies to mourn:
It spoils the singing of the nightingale. [267–68]

Adumbrating both the urn, and the nightingale, which, as we know, are companion-pieces, the passage indicates how much Keats longed for the kind of authoritative, systematic union of grammar, logic, rhetoric, ethics, epistemology and aesthetics which, according to Paul de Man, is continually threatened by literary theory. (De Man's article, "Resistance to Theory," was quite understandably deemed unsuitable by the Modern Language Association, who had commissioned it for their guidebook, *Introduction to Scholarship in Modern Languages and Literatures*, because it systematically demonstrated the theoretical impossibility of providing such a package: see *Resistance* 3.) Reading these lines, "Things cannot by the will be settled, but they tease us out of thought," forward to their final version in the Ode, we may discover in Keats's poem both an aesthetic resistance to the literary, in the "silent form" of the urn, and a literary resistance to such aesthetic "solutions" or evasions: "Thou, silent form, does tease us out of thought. / As doth eternity." This phrase, no less then Hölderlin's "Words, like flowers," is a curious simile. The urn "teases us out of thought as *doth eternity*." It offers us the appearance of a timeless, eternal "object" — very much as the term, or signifier, "eternity," permits us to think we are thinking our way outside time or history. As Edgar Allen Poe said of the similar term, "infinity": "It stands for the possible attempt at an impossible conception . . . [it] is thus the representative but of the *thought of a thought*" [*Selected Prose, Poetry and Eureka* 496–97]. The Urn, despite what commentators, including Paul de Man, have said, does not function as a commemorative, funeral object: far from containing the ashes of the dead, it instructs us to forget, to remain ignorant of its meanings, referents or origins. What it offers us does not even "belong," properly, to the Greeks or to any particular culture: the same poem could have been written about any human artifact whose historical identity has been erased, so that we could no longer know the answer to the questions Keats keeps asking about it. The urn tells us all it knows, and it knows nothing more than it is able to say. But if the ritual language that most appropriately celebrates the urn is self-referential, laying down the grammatical and logical rules which constitute such eternal artifacts, or "silent forms," the poem also tries to tell us of other silences, of "other woes (even) than ours," about what de Man refers to as a "residue of indetermination" [15], the persistent questions that must continue to haunt any text even (or especially) after it has been thoroughly decoded.

Works Cited

Brooks, Cleanth. *The Well-Wrought Urn.* New York: Harcourt Brace, 1947.

Burke, Kenneth. *A Grammar of Motives.* New York: Prentice-Hall, 1945.

de Man, Paul. *Allegories of Reading.* New Haven and London: Yale University Press, 1979.

———. *Blindness and Insight: Essays in the Rhetoric of Contemporary Criticism.* Second edition, revised. Minneapolis: University of Minnesota Press, 1983.

———. *The Rhetoric of Romanticism.* New York: Columbia University Press, 1984.

Empson, William. *The Structure of Complex Words.* Norfolk, Connecticut: New Directions, 1951.

Faulkner, William. *Go Down, Moses.* New York: Random House: Vintage Books, 1973.

Fish, Stanley. *Is There a Text in this Class? The Authority of Interpretive Communities.* Cambridge, Mass.: Harvard University Press, 1982.

Graff, Gerald. *Literature Against Itself.* Chicago and London: University of Chicago Press, 1979.

Keats, John. *The Selected Poetry of Keats.* Edited by Paul de Man. New York: New American Library: Signet Editions, 1966. Page references to Keats are to this edition.

Lentricchia, Frank. *Criticism and Social Change.* Chicago and London: University of Chicago Press, 1984.

Poe, Edgar Allen. *Selected Prose, Poetry and Eureka.* Edited with an introduction by W. H. Auden. New York: Rinehart, 1970.

The New Psychoanalysis and Literary Criticism

Elizabeth Wright

I have suggested that poststructuralism may be defined broadly as the application of the deconstructive view of language to all aspects of culture and thought. The "new psychoanalysis" is a case in point. After describing the features of this language-centered approach to psychoanalysis, Elizabeth Wright proposes to test its uses for literary criticism, drawing especially on "Lacan's theory of the subject and its attendant myths" and "Derrida's method of treating language as a decentered system that can have no univocal meaning." Wright admits that at first glance Melville's text appears to offer little to the psychoanalytic critic, but in the end her close reading discovers much. "For the psychoanalytic critic an approach based on a decentering of language is constructive, for it will seek out those nodal points in a text where a desire for lost meaning manifests itself." While Wright is unwilling to reject entirely the referential aspect of language, she concludes that the new psychoanalysis has proven its usefulness for literary criticism. "Lacanian and Derridean theory has enabled me to see patterns which undermine the stable meaning of the text, which I might not have seen and would certainly not have been able to make clear to myself otherwise."

Psychoanalytic literary criticism has been, and one presumes will continue to be, under constant attack from literary critics. The main objection has always been that it reduces the work to a narrow set of configurations which do not do justice to the complexity of the text. The ambiguities of the text are said to go far beyond such a crude schematization. At best it was grudgingly admitted that a psychoan-

Reprinted by permission of the Duke University Press from Elizabeth Wright, "The New Psychoanalysis and Literary Criticism: A Reading of Hawthorne and Melville," *poetics today*, 3:2 (1982): 89–91, 96–105. Copyright 1982 by the Porter Institute for Poetics and Semiotics. All rights reserved. Parts of the essay dealing with Hawthorne have been omitted and notes have been renumbered.

alytic interpretation might be allowed to stand as one possible interpretation among many. But this kind of concession is far from acceptable to the new movement and it is not hard to see why. The new movement is not especially interested in the elucidation of individual works, except inasmuch as they can help to validate its findings: that literature, far from presenting a unified consciousness, shows up the divisions of the self. Literary critics, on the other hand, are committed to the concept of ambiguity as product of an omniscient authorial consciousness, which undermines any notion of a work without a stable center. The old psychoanalytic criticism is really on the orthodox side, for it trades on an omniscient authorial *unconscious*, which smuggled in "whispered meanings" (I refer to the title of a recent book by one of its pioneers, Simon Lesser [1977]). This approach could be vastly entertaining and very subtle—witness D. H. Lawrence's *Studies in Classic American Literature*—but too often it was boringly clear. Sometimes, however, one is assailed by a regressive longing for examples of its boring clarity. In the end most of us would rather be mystified by the work than by the explanation.

Reading a text is no longer considered an innocent activity. Post-structuralist criticism undermines the notion that the text contains a stable meaning. The author's intention is not only not recoverable but was never where he might have thought it was in the first place. The critic can at best transform the text so as to realize his experience of the author's experience, the author himself being engaged in an act of interpretation. It is a matter of sorting out what Paul de Man calls "Blindness and Insight" (1971), that is, to show how the falsifications of lived experience as narrated by the ego-bound literary self, the self that says "I," differ from the revelations of the existent subject, the self that falls outside the conscious discourse.

What, then, is the new psychoanalytic critic looking for? Fiction is what the subject, whether writer or reader, flies to in an attempt to reconstitute his lost wholeness, only to discover that language is the very thing which betrays him, since it is what he acquired to symbolize his lack. Hence his desire to make the word fit the world will be constantly undercut. What the critic can search for is the breakdown of this wholeness, as it reveals itself in a structural intentionality which does not reside in a latent or manifest content, but cuts across the two. This structuration,

as distinct from structure, will act as a countertext, and is to be distinguished from the old subtext of psychoanalytic criticism in that it lacks a center. The term "structuration" suggests that the text can be caught in the act of producing itself, whereas the term "structure" suggests a closed, unified, stable artifact.

All this is a domesticated and drastically summarized account of what has been debated elsewhere at considerable length around the writing of the leading poststructuralists in general and Lacan and Derrida in particular. It has to be said that their ambition is far from wishing to be a means of furnishing us with an improved practical criticism. But their use of literary texts to help establish their theory of language more than justifies us in asking what their theory can do to further our understanding of the literary text. Such use as I shall make of Lacan and Derrida, Lacan's theory of the subject and its attendant myths, Derrida's method of treating language as a decentered system that can have no univocal meaning, need not be taken as a declaration of any absolute commitment. I would rather describe my position by analogy with one current philosophy of science. Imre Lakatos characterizes scientific advance by its proceeding on a central body of unquestioned assumptions, a "hard core" of presuppositions, rendered "irrefutable" by the methodological decision of the protagonists" (1970: 133). Like the scientists in the research program who hold the central tenets of their theory, I shall take the basic doctrine for granted in order to test it for its fruitfulness in the reading of literary texts. To clarify my use of this analogy (for I do not wish to suggest that I am undertaking a scientific inquiry), I might say that I am accepting Lacan's rereading of Freud as a postulate, in order to see what results from its application. But I am not making any claim that I am myself free from prejudice, for my very method depends on the assumption that an objective stance is not possible.

When modern psychoanalytic criticism uses the oedipal model it usually shows how this model operates across a number of texts. I would like to see if the new method can be made to work on an individual text in a way that neither reduces the text to clinical material nor robs it of all referential status. In order to make it easier for myself I have selected two texts which belong to the time shortly before psychoanalysis came into being. Hawthorne's "Young Goodman Brown" (1835) and Melville's "Benito Cereno" (1856) have been much praised for their ambiguity, and I propose to look at these texts for their ambivalence. I hope the concept of ambivalence that I am working with will emerge in the course of my discussion, but if I had to give a quick indication I would say that I am looking at ironies which do not depend on the matching of intentional perspectives of author, author-surrogate, and reader in the text. My readings will therefore strive to disregard the stable ambiguities of the text and search instead for those nodal points in the text which seem to reveal desire by meaning more than they say. These parts then need a new arrangement which suggests this surplus meaning without spelling it out and giving the text a nervous breakdown. Each story poses a different problem for the psychoanalytic critic: "Young Goodman Brown" seems to have too much psychoanalytic material, while "Benito Cereno" seems not to have enough. One might be taken as an example of the classic fantastic text, hesitating between a real and imaginary world; the other as an example of the classic realist text, unmistakably set in the empirical world.

•   •   •

"Benito Cereno"[1] presents a more difficult problem for the psychoanalytic critic. On the face of it, all material is lacking and indeed I know of no psychoanalytic interpretation. I will again give a brief outline of its narrative stances, and then a brief outline of the plot. No such outline can be entirely impartial but it will at least recall the story. The events of "Benito Cereno" are seen first and chiefly through the eyes of its central character, Captain Delano. They are then seen through the eyes of the title figure, Benito Cereno, through the insertion of another text, or pre-text. Melville uses a written source for his story, an extract from a narrative by the historical Captain Delano published in 1817 (Melville, 1972: 29). This extract is the deposition of Captain Cereno and much of it, though not all, is quoted verbatim. The story ends with an epilogue, accounting for the fates of the main characters. The plot is as follows: The American Captain Delano sights a ship which is apparently in difficulties, and offers to help its Spanish Captain Cereno and his mainly Negro crew, including the special aide to the captain, the Negro Babo. Delano is puzzled by something odd in the relationship between the two. The plot is resolved when Delano discovers, as he is about to return to his own ship, that the few whites on the Spanish ship are the surviving victims of a Negro revolt, in the course of which the

owner and most of his Spanish crew were slain. The ship is finally recaptured after a fight, and the inserted deposition is allowed to recap the events and fill in the missing details. There follows the execution of Babo and subsequent death of Cereno. Delano is left, thanking providence.

Again I would like to cut across these narrative stances, and examine narrative structures instead. Where "Young Goodman Brown" revealed its image structure in a series of sound-scapes, this text reveals itself in what one might punningly call a series of "see-scapes," both in setting and structure. Captain Delano is a man who believes in "ever-watchful Providence" (p. 199). Something is certainly watching him, but is it providence? At the outset of the story Captain Delano is viewing a strange ship through a telescope:

> With no small interest Captain Delano continued to watch her — a proceeding not much facilitated by the vapors partly mantling the hull, through which the far matin light from her cabin streamed equivocally enough; much like the sun — by this time hemisphered on the rim of the horizon, and apparently, in company with the strange ship entering the harbor — which, wimpled by the same low, creeping clouds, showed not unlike a Lima intrigante's one sinister eye peering across the Plaza from the Indian loophole of her dusk *saya-y-manta* (p. 142).

Here is a triple image of a gaze covertly watching him: the porthole light shining "equivocally" through the sea mist is like the sun half coming out of the clouds, and the sun in turn is "not unlike" the single eye of a female intriguer, wearing a *saya-y-manta*, a dress and hooded cloak of the time, the hood so disposed by the wearer that one eye and the mouth were always covered. Delano continues to look through his glass, not knowing he is observed by his object. At the same time, the reader, now alerted, will have his eye on the gaze and engage in a dialectic of interpretation.

In that most difficult of difficult seminars, "Of the Gaze as *Objet Petit a*," Lacan, as I understand it, criticizes Sartre for not sufficiently considering the subjectivity of the self. In Lacan's view, Sartre accepts self and Other as givens and only allows the self to change through the ethical experience of shame. Just because the Other is objectifying the "annihilating subject" (the one looking through the keyhole), this does not mean that the latter's subjectivity is cancelled out. It is not the annihilating subject that is surprised into shame, but "the subject sustaining himself in a function of desire" (Lacan, 1977a: 84–85). What happens is a replacement of one function of desire by another. One set of intentions has to be abandoned and another set accepted; a misconstruction is understood. This notion must be seen in the context of the communication model of psychoanalysis, the countertransference phenomenon, and of Lacan's rejection of the analyst as "subject-who-is-supposed-to-know," but it also applies to author and critic. It is particularly relevant in the context of a story whose chief reflecting consciousness, Delano, turns the world into comfortable objects and in which all intersubjective relationships are conspicuous by their absence. For it is precisely the inability to interact with the Other which is at the center of the two sets of master-slave relationships so tortuously intertwined.

Before showing how these relationships are constituted, I would like to place them in the context of the narrative from which Melville selected the deposition which he inserted in his story. In the historical Amasa Delano's narrative, Cereno's deposition is in a different context, caught up in the issue of certain financial matters between the two captains. It turns out that this Delano, though generous (like his fictional counterpart), has considerable difficulty in getting proper compensation for his pains from the apparently not-so-noble Cereno. This slightly decenters the revolt, but it is nevertheless there in all its drama. Melville has extracted only Cereno's deposition from the narrative but has been criticized for unduly lengthening his tale with a document hardly differing from its counterpart. Some differences turn out to be interesting. Firstly, in the source text Babo is not a single dominant figure, but shares the scene with "the negro Mure" and "the negro Jose" as fellow-perpetrators of the crimes. Secondly, two significant episodes, one concerning the slave-owner Don Aranda, the other concerning the behavior of the Negresses during the revolt, have been rewritten by means of omission and addition, respectively. Yet in its overall effect the historical narrative at first seems to share a certain imbalance with Melville's. Where Melville's version in the story demonizes the slaves, the historical account takes their revolt and defeat for granted; hence both cases suggest a measure of white superiority. Yet in Melville's case the insertion of the white man's long written indictment into the story, where the black, "seeing all was over [he] uttered no sound" (p. 222), makes its own structural comment on such superiority.

I would now like to look at a key episode to see how the two master-slave relationships function and interlock. Here are two extracts from the long shaving scene, engaging Babo and Cereno in a ritual of which Delano is spectator. The whole scene, indeed the whole story, is built on this double perspective of the happy and wholesome primitive, and of the threatening and alien savage:

> There is something in the Negro which, in a peculiar way, fits him for avocations about one's person. Most Negroes are natural valets and hairdressers, taking to the comb and brush congenially as to the castinets, and flourishing them apparently with almost equal satisfaction. There is, too, a smooth tact about them in this employment, with a marvelous, noiseless, gliding briskness, not ungraceful in its way, singularly pleasing to behold, and still more so to be the manipulated subject of. And above all is the great gift of good humor. Not the mere grin or laugh is here meant. Those were unsuitable. But a certain easy cheerfulness, harmonious in every glance and gesture, as though God had set the whole Negro to some pleasant tune (p. 184).

> Setting down his basin, the Negro searched among the razors, as for the sharpest, and, having found it, gave it an additional edge by expertly stropping it on the firm, smooth, oily skin of his open palm; he then made a gesture as if to begin, but midway stood suspended for an instant, one hand elevating the razor, the other professionally dabbling among the bubbling suds on the Spaniard's lank neck. Not unaffected by the close sight of the gleaming steel, Don Benito nervously shuddered; his usual ghastliness was heightened by the lather, which lather, again, was intensified in its hue by the contrasting sootiness of the Negro's body. Altogether the scene was somewhat peculiar, at least to Captain Delano, nor, as he saw the two thus postured, could he resist the vagary that in the black he saw a headsman, and in the white a man at the block. But this was one of those antic conceits, appearing and vanishing in a breath, from which, perhaps, the best-regulated mind is not always free (p. 186).

These two aspects of the same scene show how Babo is at one and the same time domesticated by Delano's paternalism and demonized by Cereno's dread. Yet this dual response springs from the very situation of Babo, who is simultaneously slave and master. Here

I find Lacan's version of Hegel's master-slave dialectic useful. Whereas Lacan rereads Sartre optimistically, he rereads Hegel pessimistically. According to Hegel, the slave rediscovers himself in labor (1971: 239). Lacan on the other hand argues that the slave is not in his labor,

> he *is* in the anticipated moment of the master's death, from which moment he will begin to live, but in the meantime he identifies himself with the master as dead, and as a result of this he is himself already dead. Nevertheless he makes an effort to deceive the master by the demonstration of the good intentions manifested in his labour (1968: 79).

The uncanny force of the shaving scene resides in the slave's actions being both signifier of his good intentions to Delano, the new master, and at the same time signifier of his bad ones to Cereno, his old master, whose death is the moment he anticipates. His behavior throughout the long episode on board registers this dual message before the uncomprehending Delano. And this is also true for the labor that is taking place all over the ship, such as that of the oakum-pickers, who "accompanied the task with a continuous, low, monotonous chant; droning and druling away like so many grey-headed bagpipers playing a funeral march," and that of the hatchet-polishers, who "neither spoke to others, nor breathed a whisper among themselves, but sat intent upon their task, except at intervals, when, with the peculiar love in Negroes of uniting industry with pastime, two and two they sideways clashed their hatchets together, like cymbals, with a barbarous din" (p. 146). These activities function both as images of necessary labor in the view of the new master and as images of alienated labor in anticipation of the old master's death.

Delano clings to only one signified, not because he lacks a sense of evil, as some critics have suggested (Fogle, 1962: 119), but because he is caught in a series of imaginary identifications. In this series he is one stage ahead of Babo, his illusory self, who can neither say the word "I" nor "thou" nor "he," who says "a black man's slave was Babo, who now is the white's" (p. 160), instead of saying "I was once his slave and now I'm yours." For Babo, the other is wholly alien, for he has as yet no self-image, not even a false one, since he has not even seen the self in the other, as has Delano. He is in that very beginning of the mirror phase, as Lacan has it, when:

> the "I" is precipitated in a primordial form, before it is objectified in the dialectic with the other, and before language restores to it, in the universal, its function as a subject (1977b: 2).

Babo is reduced to that primitive mode of domination, the fixing or objectifying of the other by means of the gaze, or "evil eye" of envy, mentioned by Freud in his essay, "The Uncanny" (1953–1973: vol. 17, 240). Hence, "He spoke no word. He only rested his eye on his master's" (p. 193), or "the black with one arm still encircled the master, at the same time keeping his eye fixed on his face" (p. 152).

Delano on his part creates Babo as his symmetrical opposite and loves himself in this image of self-completion. Whereas Babo has no word, Delano overpredicates himself:

> "What, I, Amasa Delano—Jack of the Beach, as they called me when a lad—I, Amasa, the same that, ducksatchel in hand, used to paddle along the waterside to the schoolhouse made from the old hulk—I, little Jack of the Beach, that used to go berrying with cousin Nat and the rest—I to be murdered here at the ends of the earth on board a haunted pirate ship by a horrible Spaniard? Too nonsensical to think of! Who would murder Amasa Delano? His conscious is clean. There is someone above (p. 177).

Delano's refusal to see difference is grounded in an idealization of another's incompleteness: he loves Babo's naïveté as image of the lack of difference, as the completeness which Delano himself wants to possess. This refusal goes beyond the plot level into the image structure of the text and hence perhaps beyond the perspective of Delano. An interesting example is a scene observed by Delano:

> His attention had been drawn back to a slumbering negress, partly disclosed through the lacework of some rigging, lying, with youthful limbs carelessly disposed, under the lee of the bulwarks, like a doe in the shade of a woodland rock. Sprawling at her lapped breasts, was her wide-awake fawn, stark naked, its black little body half lifted from the deck, crosswise with its dam's; its hands, like two paws, clambering upon her; its mouth and nose ineffectually rooting to get at the mark; and meantime giving a vexatious half-grunt, blending with the composed snore of the negress.
>
> The uncommon vigour of the child at length roused the mother. She started up, at a distance facing Captain Delano. But as if not at all concerned at the attitude in which she had been caught, delightedly she caught the child up, with maternal transports, covering it with kisses.

> There's naked nature, now; pure tenderness
> and love, thought Captain Delano, well pleased
> (pp. 172–73).

This is no mere scene, but a Lacanian scenario, in which a demand for food is about to be transformed into a demand for love.[2] Delano sees only "naked nature," when what he is observing is the infant beginning its journey from nature to culture. The blindly groping creature is seeking to satisfy its hunger, its biological need, but the cry of desire for the mother is shaping the human infant's future, transforming its animal need for food into a human need for love, and preparing it for that moment of separation when it will symbolize its lack of being in language. Delano, however, sees only the fullness of maternal presence. His excessive faith in "ever-watchful Providence," coupled with his firm belief in "naked nature" can be seen as analogous to Goodman Brown's battle cry: "With heaven above and Faith below, I will yet stand firm against the devil" (p. 94).

But the inserted deposition savagely refutes Delano's idealized vision of womanhood. I quote a shortened version:

> The negresses [. . .] had the negroes not restrained them [they] would have tortured to death, instead of simply killing, the Spaniards slain by command of the Negro Babo [. . .] in the various acts of murder, they sang songs and danced — not gaily, but solemnly [. . .] and that this melancholy tone was more inflaming than a different one would have been, and was so intended (pp. 217–18).

This is usually taken as evidence that Melville introduced his idyll into the text in order to ironize Delano, not an unreasonable assumption when one remembers that the Captain's ship is called *Bachelor's Delight*. Yet there is something gratuitous about attributing a special savagery to the Negro women. Delano's idyllic view is already made questionable by the fact that he is looking not at a picture of nature free from all restraints, but of nature in slavery.[3] The viewpoint retains its ambivalence because the image of the idyll, what we might call its Madonna aspect, poetically survives its subsequent destruction, and this implicates both author and reader.

The world of "Benito Cereno" is, apart from the cited example, an all male world, and yet it is a world without a father. There are metaphors of paternal absence, such as "providence," "someone above," "the Prince of Heaven," and there is a dead father-figure, in both a metaphorical sense and a literal one, since the skeleton of the unfortunate "leader" is very much present, being tied to the mast of the *San Dominick*. The murder of Aranda, once owner of the slaves and leader of the whites, does take on the mythical coloring of that great misdeed with which, according to Freud's account in *Totem and Taboo*, society began, or as he later conceded, was imagined to have begun. It was a crime only to be repeated symbolically, "again and again in the sacrifice of the totem animal, whenever, as a result of the changing conditions of life, the cherished fruit of the crime, appropriation of the paternal attributes — threatened to disappear" (Freud, 1953–1973: vol. 13, 145). Here the crime is symbolically repeated in the text, by a "son" who has been denied the word "father," and whose only resource is to steal the word. In the end the consequences are fatal for Babo when he is brought to justice.

> Seeing all was over, he uttered no sound, and could not be made to. His aspect seemed to say: since I cannot do deeds, I will not speak words (p. 221).

Babo has taken a word he can never give back, both because he cannot use it and take part in the symbolic order of language by becoming a free father, and because he has destroyed the image he wanted to become. For by his own act of cannibalism, the incorporation of the "father's" remains in a grotesque totemic feast, he is in effect saying: "I wish to become a father whom a son can kill." The main text does not speak of this cannibalistic act and the inserted deposition account barely does so:

> Yan was the man who, by Babo's command, willingly prepared the skeleton of Don Alexandro, in a way the Negroes afterwards told the deponent, but which he, so long as reason left him, can never divulge (p. 217).[4]

In this whole act must lie the source of Cereno's superstitious dread and fear of being touched by Babo, the violator of the taboo. Cereno is part of the psychic and artistic structure of the text at a level which transcends the more referential, in that he and Babo can be seen as the "sons" sharing that ambivalence of the emotions inherent in this scenario, of which Freud speaks in *Totem and Taboo*:

> They hated the father, who presented such a formidable obstacle to their craving for power and their sexual desires; but they loved and admired him too (1953–1973: vol. 13, 143).

The aristocratic and effete Don Benito Cereno, the very antithesis of machismo, is the social and psychic representative of one who has come into power without earning it. His narcissism is stripped away as he has to mime his own mastership on the *San Dominick* after having relived retrospectively the murder of the father. His inability to forget, his melancholy and death, completes the textual configuration, in which the patronizing and paternalistic Delano is merely repeating the part played by Don Alexandro Aranda, the benevolent despot and owner of the *San Dominick*, before his downfall. Together the three contestants form a triple consciousness of various stages of incomplete awareness caught up in a vicious circle, all blighted by their lack of a concept of true authority.

Finally, here is a remarkable passage which combines the text's literary and psychoanalytic status. It is a nodal point in both senses of the term, as metaphor for writing and as that point, where, as in a dream, chains of meaning intersect. The passage occurs where Delano is watching an old sailor as he is working strands of rope into a large knot:

> Captain Delano crossed over to him and stood in silence surveying the knot, his mind, by a not uncongenial transition, passing from its own entanglements to those of the hemp. For intricacy, such a knot he had never seen in an American ship, nor indeed any other. The old man looked like an Egyptian priest making Gordian knots for the temple of Ammon. The knot seemed a combination of double-bowline-knot, treble-crown-knot, backhanded-well-knot, knot-in-and-out-knot, and jamming knot.
>
> At last, puzzled to comprehend the meaning of such a knot, Captain Delano addressed the knotter: "What are you knotting there, my man?"
>
> "The knot," was the brief reply, without looking up.
>
> "So it seems; but what is it for?"
>
> "For someone else to undo," muttered back the old man, plying his fingers harder than ever, the knot being now nearly completed.
>
> While Captain Delano stood watching him, suddenly the old man threw the knot towards him, saying in broken English — the first heard in the ship — something to this effect: "Undo it, cut it, quick." It was said slowly, but with such condensation of rapidity, that the long, slow words in Spanish, which had preceded and followed, almost operated as covers to the brief English between.
>
> For a moment, knot in hand, and knot in head, Captain Delano stood mute, while, without further heeding him, the old man was now intent upon other ropes. Presently there was a slight stir behind Captain Delano. Turning, he saw the chained Negro, Atufal, standing quietly there. The next moment the old sailor rose, muttering, and, followed by his subordinate Negroes, removed to the forward part of the ship, where in the crowd he disappeared.
>
> An elderly Negro, in a clout like an infant's, and with a pepper-and-salt head and a kind of attorney air, now approached Captain Delano. In tolerable Spanish, and with a good-natured knowing wink, he informed him that the old knotter was simplewitted, but harmless, often playing his odd tricks. The Negro concluded by begging the knot, for of course the stranger would not care to be troubled with it. Unconsciously, it was handed to him. With a sort of congé, the Negro received it, and, turning his back, ferreted into it like a detective customhouse officer after smuggled laces. Soon, with some African words equivalent to pshaw, he tossed the knot overboard (pp. 175–76).

At the level of the Spanish sailor's gestural utterance the knot is an image for words not being interpreted, Delano's misconstructions, and it also contains words not being read, a message from the sailor. So it is metaphorical and literal at the same time. But there is also a metaknot, where the knot is an image of *all* Delano's misconstructions, *one* of which is not understanding the message of the knot. Hence the knot is also an image of itself, both as metaphor (which fails to be understood) and as literal message, the hidden letter (which fails to be read). And finally, insofar as the knot is an image of the whole story as riddle for the reader to undo, the "old knotter [...] simple-witted, but harmless, often playing his odd tricks" can thereby be seen as an author-image, and the throwing away of the knot a joke on the reader. And at this point one wonders who has out-deconstructed whom.

Deconstructionists understandably treasure images of language reflecting on itself, for such images show that language in trying to map the world is itself part of what it is trying to map. In order to get out of itself language needs a speaker who has neither to repeat the other's word automatically, as Babo does, nor repeat his own meaning, as Delano does. This can only lead to the kind of paradox in which Cereno is locked, who has to speak the master's language as a slave.

In my analyses I have tried to produce a coherent set of ambivalences which are not part of a subtext but go across the surface and the depth of the text. It seems to me that a linguistically oriented psychoanalytic criticism can analyze structures in a meaning-ful, or, should I say, a meaningless way, whether or not the implied ideology of the method is accepted. For the psychoanalytic critic an approach based on a decentering of language is constructive, for it will seek out those nodal points in a text where a desire for lost meaning manifests itself. The structures of ambivalence reveal such desire at the same time as they illuminate the text's literary aspect, even if from a biased point of view.

The question naturally arises why we should bother ourselves about unstable meanings. What do we gain from proving that an author is ambivalent, and he did not know he meant it when he said it? It seems that on the one hand we are taking a share of the credit away from him, but on the other hand we are also giving him credit for an act of living com-munication. Instead of treating the author virtually as an egoist we are treating him as a subject whom we could enlighten. We do this not by gleefully un-covering hidden meanings, but by helping new meanings to grow, meanings of which he had only a blurred view, because no one can project perfectly and infinitely into the future. Nevertheless, we should remember that it is the creative activity of the artist that has produced the text from which we can gen-erate such a wealth of meanings.

If meanings can grow, they are not wholly consti-tuted by the language in which they appear. I am not denying that the meanings of words are governed by the text, but we must not engage in games of verbal association and then forget their relevance to the world at large. I cannot accept what seems to be a post-structuralist credo, the contention that there is no reality outside the text and that we must therefore ignore the referential aspect. My readings have taken into account that Hawthorne's double-bind images are grounded in the historical fact of puritanism, and Melville's master/slave repetition in the American and Spanish conquest of the native. But it is better to let this context emerge rather than stress the obvious. Psychoanalysis is not the only treatment that can give the text a nervous breakdown.

Lacanian and Derridean theory has enabled me to see patterns which undermine the stable meaning of the text, which I might not have seen and would cer-tainly not have been able to make clear to myself otherwise. The result for me is inseparable from the method by which I have arrived at it. I have taken the two together because psychoanalytic theory alone does not pay sufficient attention to the work's literary status, as, for example, its neglect of self-reference in the text. Lacan and Derrida are in agree-ment in throwing doubt upon the idealization of the sign, and this is more important for my purpose than the differences between them. To idealize the sign is wholly to believe in the completeness of meaning, to ignore what Derrida calls *différance* and Lacan calls "lack." What for Derrida is the sliding of meaning is for Lacan the failure to find. In both these concepts is implied a fundamental revision of psychoanalysis away from its positivist bent.

People are hostile to psychoanalytic theory be-cause they already have theories on how families work and have learned to rely on the quotidian use of such terms as father, mother and child. They go by what they call "intuition," forgetting that good intu-ition is only a theory that worked out right. But there is a limit to the explicability which any theory has, and the time comes when its cliché sense is ex-hausted and we cannot get beyond it because it will not give us any more. It seems to me that the so-called "French Connection" (Hartman, 1978: 86) has fruitfully utilized such a moment in the development of Freudian psychoanalytic theory.

Notes

1. All subsequent references are to Melville, 1961.
2. For Lacan's theory of the relation between need, demand and desire, see "The Significance of the Phallus" (Lacan, 1977b: 281–91, especially 286–87).
3. In the historical narrative, the Cereno text differs in not making the behavior of the Negresses a de-liberate act of cruelty: "The negresses of age, were knowing to the revolt, and influenced the death of their master . . . that in the act of murder, and before that of the engagement of the ship, they began to sing, and were singing a very melan-choly song during the action, to excite the courage of the negroes." (Melville, 1972: 29).
4. This again is a rewriting of the historical narra-tive, where the body of Aranda is simply thrown overboard, and where there is no account of a skeleton episode and no fixing of the skeleton as a totem to the ship's mast.

Works Cited

Crews, Frederick C. *The Sins of the Fathers: Hawthorne's Psychological Themes*. New York: Oxford UP, 1966.

de Man, Paul. *Blindness and Insight.* New York: Oxford UP, 1971.

Fogle, Richard Harter. "Benito Cereno," in: Richard Chase, ed. *Melville.* Englewood Cliffs, New Jersey: Prentice-Hall, 1962. 116–124.

Freud, Sigmund. *The Standard Edition of the Complete Psychological Works,* ed. James Strachey. London: Hogarth Press, 1953–1973.

Hartman, Geoffry H. "Psychoanalysis and the French Connection," in: Geoffry H. Hartman, ed. *Psychoanalysis and the Question of the Text.* Baltimore and London: Johns Hopkins UP, 1978. 86–113.

Hawthorne, Nathaniel. "Young Goodman Brown," in: *The Celestial Railroad and Other Stories.* New York and Toronto: New English Library, 1963 (1835). 87–114.

Hegel, G. W. F. *The Phenomenology of Mind,* trans. J. B. Baillie. London: Allen and Unwin, 1971 (1807).

Lacan, Jacques. "The Function of Language in Psychoanalysis," in: *The Language of the Self,* trans. Anthony Wilden. New York: Delta, 1968. 3–87.

———. *The Four Fundamental Concepts of Psychoanalysis,* trans. Alan Sheridan. London: Hogarth Press, 1977a.

———. *Écrits,* trans. Alan Sheridan. London: Tavistock, 1977b.

Lakatos, Imre. "Falsification and Methodology of Scientific Research Programmes," in: Imre Lakatos and Alan Musgrave, eds. *Criticism and the Growth of Knowledge.* Cambridge: Cambridge UP, 1970. 91–195.

Lesser, Simon O. *The Whispered Meanings.* Amherst: Massachusetts UP, 1977.

Levin, David. "Shadows of Doubt: Specter Evidence in Hawthorne's 'Young Goodman Brown'," in: Thomas E. Connolly, ed. *Nathaniel Hawthorne: Young Goodman Brown.* Columbus, Ohio: Charles E. Merrill, 1968. 96–104.

Melville, Herman. "Benito Cereno," in: *Billy Budd and Other Tales.* New York and Toronto: New English Library, 1961 (1856). 141–223.

———. *Benito Cereno and Particulars of the Capture of the Spanish Ship Tryal, at the Island of St. Maria, with Documents relating to that Affair, by Amasa Delano,* Lawrance Thompson ed. Barre, Massachusetts: The Imprint Society, 1972 (1817).

Rahv, Philip. *Literature and the Sixth Sense.* New York: Houghton Mifflin, 1979.

Thomas, Dylan. "Return Journey," in: *Miscellany One.* London: Dent, 1974. 101–118.

APPLICATION

Reader, Text, and Ambiguous Referentiality in "The Yellow Wall-Paper"

Richard Feldstein

Richard Feldstein begins his essay on "The Yellow Wall[-]paper" by detailing numerous, if apparently minor, inconsistencies in the text. Despite these "loose ends," he finds that a critical consensus has been reached on two central points: "John is the story's antagonist and the narrator/protagonist succumbs to a progressive form of madness." Against this consensus Feldstein proposes an ironic counter-reading: "If we read 'The Yellow Wall-Paper' ironically and not simply as a case history of one woman's mental derangement, the narrator's madness becomes questionable, and the question of madness itself, an issue raised as a means of problematizing such a reading." In this reading, John becomes a representative of "realism" who finds himself pitted against ironic discourse: "The wall-paper becomes an overdetermined construct destabilizing signification. Like the wall-paper, the text itself shifts, a signifier generating possibilities of interpretation while providing for a metacritique of its textuality." Like Stephen J. Miko reading The Tempest, *Feldstein highlights differences and inconsistencies, not with a view to harmonizing these but rather to show that univocal readings are achieved only by suppressing the differences. Thus Feldstein concludes, with a nod to both Lacan and Derrida, "Text as question formulates an inconclusiveness that attends enigma generated in part by the hyphen between wall and paper—a sign of difference and reminder of text as Other to which we look for closure, a means of satisfying unsatisfiable desires."*

A Critical Consensus

Critics who have written on "The Yellow Wall-Paper" disagree on the most basic issues pertaining to the text. Is it a short story or a novella; should we underline its title or place it in quotation marks? The 1899 edition presents a novella format, but, in fact, "The Yellow Wall-Paper" first appeared as a short story in 1892.[1] There is also disagreement among critics about the writer's name: is it Charlotte Perkins, Charlotte Stetson, Charlotte Perkins Stetson, Charlotte Gilman, Charlotte Perkins Gilman, or Charlotte Perkins Stetson Gilman? Although each name relates to a phase in the writer's life, many commentators have arbitrarily chosen one designation to use normatively when discussing the writer's life and work. Ironically, this confusion over text's and writer's names was in part generated by Charlotte Perkins Gilman herself, who was anything but consistent in the names she used or the way she spelled *wall-paper*. If Gilman had the advantage of our perspective, she might have been pleased by this confusion of textual identity (is *wall-paper* one word or two) and amused by the critics' befuddlement over her name. Even without a historical perspective, however, she might have predicted such bafflement, possibly foresaw the manipulation of the names of the fathers—Perkins, Stetson, Gilman—as a means of destabilizing the process of signification by presenting a proliferation of signifiers that ironically generate a paucity of signifieds.

Meanwhile, Gilman's editors have repeatedly altered the spelling of *wall-paper*, the overdetermined signifier that refers to both the title and the image of protean change featured in the story. The Feminist Press edition would have us believe that Gilman hyphenated the compound in the narrative but gave it in the title of the short story as *Wallpaper*.[2] But the original manuscript presents a different configuration: the use of *wall-paper* shifts arbitrarily, in defiance of any unvarying pattern of logic. The initial five references are *wallpaper, wall paper, wall-paper, wall paper, wall-paper*; its spelling then becomes more ambiguous because *wall-paper* then appears twice, hyphenated at the end of both lines; the final five references construct the indeterminate pattern of *wall-paper, wall paper, wall-paper, paper*, and *wall paper*.[3] Editors of the *New England Magazine*, where the story first appeared, could not abide such "confusion," so they altered the spelling to impose uniformity of tex-

tual reference. The title remained "The Yellow Wall-Paper," and the narrative reference still provided the ambiguous alteration of *wall-paper* and *wall paper*, but now there was a perceptible, though random, pattern of word usage: initially, there are three references to *wall-paper*; then, inexplicably, *wallpaper* appears five times before the pattern reverses itself and *wall-paper* is used four times. The next time the story was published, in 1899, Small, Maynard & Company consistently presented the compound as *wall paper*. Today, the version in *The Norton Anthology of Literature by Women* imposes the counterconsistency of *wallpaper*.[4] From Gilman's original manuscript, however, it is apparent that the word(s) *wall(-)paper* were conceived as a shifter calculated to create ambiguity about a referent that resists analysis, even as the narrator resists her husband's diagnosis and prescription for cure.

Despite such confusion, a critical consensus has developed on two issues central to "The Yellow Wall-Paper": John is the story's antagonist and the narrator/protagonist succumbs to a progressive form of madness. There is almost universal agreement that John is a turn-of-the-century patriarchal physician whose diagnosis of "a slight hysterical tendency" imprisons his wife within the prescription for her cure (10). Colluding with his brother and the likes of Weir Mitchell, John prescribes the placebo-like "rest cure," which discourages work and isolates the patient from society. But the doctor who hypocritically pretends to be a neutral observer is emotionally implicated in the transference between husband and wife. Thus compromised, he relies on a realistic credo, openly scoffing "at any talk of things not to be felt and seen and put down in figures," a position he authorizes while policing his wife, making certain that her behavior complies with the regime suggested by his diagnosis (9). To counter these tactics, the narrator constructs representational strategies that privilege the spatial image over its analysis, modernist strategies that inform the imagist anthologies of the early twentieth century. Implementing this aesthetic through her writing and later through a purposeful acting out, the narrator produces a feminist counterdiscourse that opposes John's dualistic nineteenth-century empiricism with its dyads of good/evil, right/wrong, and, most relevant to this story, rational/irrational.

We can measure John's success in subjugating the narrator by the number of critics who direct our attention to the question of woman's madness as a central issue of the text. Critics generally agree that the narrator's condition deteriorates after she stops writing in her journal and becomes obsessed with the wall-paper. After the narrator substitutes a fixation with the wall-paper for her previous interests, she becomes protective toward the paper and the fantasized double(s) who inhabit it, eventually going so far as to threaten that "no person touches this paper but me,—not *alive*" (33). Because she recognizes these double(s) as fellow victims of a phallic system that resembles the wall-paper's restrictive outside pattern, the narrator believes that her projections might share a common psychogenesis with her: "I wonder if they all come out of the wall-paper as I did?" (35). Commentators who assert that the narrator's madness is genuine not only point to this quotation but to a list of other disconcerting facts to make their case—the narrator gnaws on her bedstead, crawls around the room with her shoulder against a long smooch in the paper, thinks about throwing herself out of a window, and determines that a rope is necessary to apprehend her double(s), who have escaped the wall-paper to creep over the lawn. Commentators who consider these actions conclusive evidence of madness find it difficult to accept Gilman's protagonist as a feminist, especially since she seems incapable of fending off insidious forms of surveillance.

In a recent issue of *Tulsa Studies in Women's Literature* there is a debate among three feminist critics—Paula Treichler, Karen Ford, and Carol Neely—which provides a representative sampling of critical opinion. Declaring that the narrator's final "confinement, infantilization, trivalization, banishment from discourse, [and] madness" are a triumph for patriarchy rather than a statement of feminism, Carol Neely argues that we should view that act of crawling at the end of the story not as "a victory for the narrator but as her defeat." As for the wall-paper itself, Neely considers that important symbol to be representative of patriarchal discourse "as perceived by women who look at it close up for [too] long."[5] Karen Ford also wonders what value the wall-paper holds for feminists; if it is "a new vision of women," she asks, "why is the narrator tearing it down?" Like Neely, Ford criticizes the narrator for "creeping as though she, like its [the wallpaper's] designs, is lame." On the question of madness, she concurs with Neely that no matter how "dignified and victorious these reso-

lutions into madness and death may seem in relation to the compromised life of marriage and motherhood, they are not ultimately acceptable because suicide is not a viable alternative to a fulfilling life."[6] If one reads the short list of critical articles on "The Yellow Wall-Paper," it becomes apparent that on such issues Neely and Ford speak for the majority of critics who have analyzed the story.

In this issue of *Tulsa Studies*, Neely and Ford were responding to an essay written by Paula Treichler, "Escaping the Sentence: Diagnosis and Discourse in 'The Yellow Wallpaper,'" which appeared a year before.[7] Neely's and Ford's essays are followed by Treichler's rebuttal, "The Wall behind the Yellow Wallpaper: Response to Carol Neely and Karen Ford." Although Treichler concedes that both scholars' "interpretations of the yellow wallpaper metaphor are logical and persuasive," in an adept display of counterlogic, she notes that the text remains "an open and contested terrain" of language "which different people and groups inhabit, and 'work over' in many different ways." Treichler believes in an overdetermined conceptual space, in "multiple discourses," evolved in "multiple contexts," and thus she warns against an either-or reductionism, claiming that "women's discourse is never truly 'alternative' but rather inhabits the same terrain as the 'patriarchal discourse' it challenges." According to her reading, regression from linguistic expression to visual captation is not solely an act of compliance because it allows for the establishment of a counterdiscourse on "a highly policed terrain in which attempts at counterdiscourse are discouraged or forbidden."[8] This politicized regression through which the narrator endeavors to liberate the women of the wall-paper allows her to work through a conflict not previously visualized because of its unacceptability to consciousness. If we consider this important political dimension of the narrator's acting out, her "regression" can be framed by quotation marks to indicate the possibility of an ironic interpretation.

An Ironic Reading of the Wall(-)Paper

If we read "The Yellow Wall-Paper" ironically and not simply as a case history of one woman's mental derangement, the narrator's madness becomes questionable, and the question of madness itself, an issue raised as a means of problematizing such a reading. Reconfigured, the text becomes an allegorical statement of difference, pitting John, an antagonist and a proponent of realism who condemns his wife as a stricken romantic, against a nameless protagonist whose ironic discourse opposes the empirical gaze of the nineteenth-century American realist to a modern, not romantic, configuration—the wall-paper as gestalt—with its shifting significations born of the intermixture of figure and ground. The wall-paper is given to protean changes of shape from the sun or moonlight reflecting on it. Combine this mutability with another variable: the wall-paper is a mirroring screen for the protagonist's projections, and the paper becomes an overdetermined construct destabilizing signification. Like the wall-paper, the text itself shifts, a signifier generating possibilities of interpretation while providing for a metacritique of its textuality.

From the standpoint of American realism, the narrator's obsession with the wall-paper constitutes a regression from a linguistic presentation, the one she would write if John would allow her "work," to an imaginary reconfiguration, an identification with mirror images in the paper as gestalt. From John's perspective, the narrator is a hapless romantic, a "little girl," a "blessed little goose," in other words, a regressed creature (23). Read ironically, however, her "regression" becomes purposeful—a cunning craziness, a militant, politicized madness by which the narrator resists the interiorization of authority. Through gestural comment, in a pantomime of subversion, the protagonist carefully enacts a series of reversals by exerting what little control she can as the madwoman in the nursery: she feigns sleep at night, sleeps during the day; she refuses to eat when eating is prescribed; she pretends not to write while writing a stratified discourse, literally a "writing" of the body, the sinuous crawl of an Eve/Satan composite commenting on the androcentric myth of the Fall. All the while the protagonist, though appearing to regress, maintains a level of ironic distance from her object of commentary.

From this point of view, the conclusion that the narrator of "The Yellow Wall-Paper" has a nervous breakdown, an oft-given answer to the difficulties posed by the text, becomes suspect. Although Gilman herself in *The Living of Charlotte Perkins Gilman* states that "The Yellow Wall-Paper" is a story about a woman's "nervous breakdown," later in her autobiography, she asserts another, more didactic purpose for having written the story: to prevent medical practitioners from prescribing "the rest cure" for "hyster-

ical" patients.[9] In other words, Gilman consciously conceived "The Yellow Wall-Paper" from conflicting impulses; one accepted the narrator as simply "mad" and the other politicized the question of woman's madness and its "cure." Born of this conflict is a feminist text using modernist strategies in opposition to the prevailing literary theory of the period, American realism, which foreclosed examination of the complexities and inconsistencies posed by not only Gilman herself but a multilevel textuality that enunciates ambiguity. From this ironic perspective, to read "The Yellow Wall-Paper" as simply a flat representation of one woman's progressive descent into insanity is to diagnose the protagonist's case by means of the empirical ontology championed by the protagonist's doctor husband John, her doctor brother, and the *sujet supposé savoir*, Doctor Weir Mitchell.

Within the time frame of the story the protagonist comes to a modernist realization, that the field of representation is as important as that which is represented. This lesson is learned only after she pleads with John to acknowledge her illness as serious, but he dismisses her symptoms as the product of an overactive imagination. As physician and husband, John consolidates his authority to undermine the protagonist's confidence in her intuitive understanding of her illness. No matter how often she pleads for John's sympathy, once he claims that "she shall be as sick as she pleases," her case history is judged on the basis of his opinion and that of a consulting physician, if John decides that step is necessary (24). Once she understands this patriarchal logic, the nameless protagonist rechannels her effort into the symbolic sphere to counter John's simplistic notion of transparent reality.

We are then left asking if there is a therapeutic value in such acting out. More specifically, is there therapeutic value in the narrator's crawling as a means to shock her husband? To answer these questions, we need to consider the context. In most cases, patients who distrust their analysts terminate analysis. Unsatisfied Dora dumps Freud, who found it difficult to analyze the countertransference. But the protagonist in "The Yellow Wall-Paper" remains a captive to her husband, secluded in a room with barred windows, beyond a "gate at the head of the stairs," under the watchful eyes of John and Jennie (14). While other patients simply withdraw from analysis, the nameless protagonist must either file for divorce (as Gilman did in her lifetime) or find another effective means to register her dissatisfaction with the inequity of their relationship. Mindful of John's desire to misread her symptoms, the narrator chooses to act out, visualizing her experience, highlighting the common predicament she shares with other women victimized by patriarchy. She thus stages herself in the field of representation.

Within this context we observe the narrator creeping. Round a circle she goes, brushing against the paper that stains all who touch it. Prohibited from writing in her journal, the narrator embodies herself as a stylus writing the line, her body being written in the process. Round she goes, drawing the circle of certainty, diagrammatically constructing the binding process of obsession. When John discovers this activity, he faints. After he is revived, would he characterize her ritual as one of the narrator's many fixations with the wall-paper or with the women in it? If he did so, John's condemnation would not dissuade the narrator from recognizing that he exhibits his own fixations, especially the claim to a definitive diagnosis of her case, articulated with a fixed certainty that feigns objectivity while denying the countertransference. He thus constitutes an incontrovertible truth, a facet of the real he withholds from the symbolic order, dialectical transformation, and the network of free association.

The act of creeping is also a culminating illustration of the protagonist's disaffection with her husband. By the end of the story, she demonstrates the power to "see through" John when he pretends "to be loving and kind" (34). Her dissatisfaction with him becomes such that she wishes he "would take another room!" (31). Kept secluded for weeks on end in their country estate and banished for protracted periods to her bedroom, the protagonist decides to seek like revenge, if only for an instant, by locking John out of their bedroom. After fetching the key from under the plantain leaf, John goes to their bedchamber and enters an unidealized, contested space of intersubjectivity he finds confronting. John is confronted with the narrator's invocation of the Fall, in which woman works in tandem with Satan to violate knowledge. According to this myth, the fallen Eve/Satan composite combines to oust humanity from the garden, sentencing it, in Lacanian parlance, to a confrontation with its limitations as barred subjects forever separated from the Other. In the narrator's enactment of the Fall, woman is yet again blamed for the interpenetration of desire and knowledge. By creeping, the narrator draws attention to the misogynist nature of this condemnation, which

presupposes that knowledge maintains a safe haven or conceptual space not permeated with desire.

An Attendant Inclusiveness

It is of less consequence whether an interpretation is ironic if we conflate the identity of the narrator with that of the protagonist in the story. Until recently, critics have not distinguished between the protagonist who stops writing in her journal and the narrator who produces that journal, which becomes our narrative, an effective example of counterdiscourse with political implications for feminists. If the protagonist and the narrator are one character, the narrator's journal poses a contradiction to the theory that the protagonist stopped writing when she regressed from the linguistic to the imaginary level of articulation. This problem, however, has been brushed over while critics place the narrator at an impossible interface: as an extension of the protagonist in the narrative and/or as a representation of the biological author, Charlotte Perkins Gilman. To accept the later conflation is to misread the symbolic for the real, a dimension that cannot be grasped through a dramatico-thematic explication.

An equation is made between the narrator and the protagonist early in "The Yellow Wall-Paper." At the end of the first segment the narrator writes, "We have been here two weeks, and I haven't felt like writing before, since that first day" (13). From this statement and others we are led to believe that we now read what she once wrote. Later in the story the narrator reinforces the impression that she is identical to the protagonist, explaining, "I am sitting by the window now, up in this atrocious nursery, and there is nothing to hinder my writing as much as I please, save lack of strength" (13). This set of quotations indicates that Gilman expended some effort to establish the link between the narrator/journalist and the protagonist in the story. As events unfold, however, John continues to debunk his wife's "imaginative power and habit of story-making" (15) so that she decides the effort needed to oppose her husband is "greater than the relief" she gets from writing (21). About two-thirds of the way through, the narrative records that the protagonist becomes too absorbed in her contemplation of the wall-paper to make reference to her need to write. It is this redirection of interest which leaves us with the seemingly irreconcilable contradiction I have described: if the protagonist stops writing, how do we explain the completion of her journal? To ask Paula Treichler's question: how do we understand a narrative that "is unfolding in an impossible form?"[10]

We could invent many conclusions to explain the radical disjuncture created by the characterological splitting of narrator/narrated. For instance, we could deny the split by concluding that after the protagonist creeps over her husband and the story ends, she writes her recollection of the final scene in her journal. We could also deny the narrator/narrated division by arguing for a chronological transposition in which the protagonist writes the second segment of her narrative after the fact, in effect providing us with documentation of her recovery. The last scenario most obviously parallels the accounts we have of Gilman's own life, how she divorced her husband, left her child with him, and then wrote "The Yellow Wall-Paper." If we reject a psychobiographical reading, however, and insist instead that the text be treated as a linguistic artifact, we are free to reconstruct traces of an ever-changing, inconsistent narrative in the same way that the protagonist grafts onto the wallpaper a gestalt with fluid boundaries.

The account the narrator provides is a written transcription inexplicably interrupted and succeeded by a spoken account in which she relates details of her life to a hypothetical audience of confidants. For as the story concludes, we confront yet another contradiction when the narrator asserts she is speaking to us, not writing in her journal, as she had previously explained: "I have found out a funny thing, but I shan't *tell* it this time!" (31, my emphasis). This statement, which equates narrative technique with a verbal recounting of events, is like a question asking how it should be read. It is especially significant because of the protagonist's previously stated concern for being allowed to write, a point of pique in the first half of the story, a mute issue in the second. No matter how we choose to read this contradiction, however, it will remain unassimilable to an interpretation of the text. Whichever reading we choose to affix univocal meaning onto a purposely ambiguous text will impose a thematic reduction that should be resisted, just as Gilman resisted Weir Mitchell's diagnosis and her protagonist resisted John's phallocentric assessment of her situation.

The aim of this essay is to raise a feminist question cast in post-modernist terms: did Charlotte Perkins Gilman, grounding her critique in gender difference, use modernist techniques to form a disjunctive text that plays on the question of identity when emphasizing the narrator/narrated split that presents one entity as two? Could it be possible that Gilman intended the narrator to be both the same as and different from the protagonist, just as she believes the protagonist to be the same as and different from her double(s), the imprisoned other(s) in the wallpaper? From this perspective one slides into two with the shifting of signification. If we look back to the original manuscript of "The Yellow Wall-Paper," we are reminded that Gilman confused the issue of whether wall-paper was one word, two conjoined by a hyphen, or two separate words, whether this central referent — the paper — already a screen for the protagonist's projections, could become more ambiguous, a lure for transposition by critics and anthologists alike.

Besides foregrounding the modernist concern with self-reflexivity, Gilman's presentation of the wall-paper as mirror depicts the intrapsychic splitting and the consequent objectification of fantasy which produces what Lacan calls *méconnaissance*.[11] Lacan explains that in the mirror stage the child develops the ability to differentiate itself from its projective image, a developmental achievement of zero to one (awareness of "self") and one to two (distinction between subject and other). Like Lacan's infant, the creeping narrator is faced with overcoming a motor incapacity when she peers into the looking glass (actual or not), and like this infant, the reader faces a text that reflects itself as a literary artifact through the differentiation of the text's spelling from the wall(?)paper cited in the narrative. Like the infant and the narrator, we reassemble bits and pieces of perception into a unified configuration that fictionalizes analysis even as it calls attention to the stage where the first fictions were formed. Thus, we are left to *identify* with the object of our choice: with the protagonist, whose loss of boundaries causes us to experience a similar loss of identity, with the narrator, whose prose writes itself as a presence absent from most critics' deliberations, with both or neither of these narrative constructs. We configure our own fictions.

The use of text as mirror problematizes interpretation because it produces a doubling that, like the reductio ad absurdum of irony, resists the easy answer or definitive diagnosis. "The Yellow Wall-Paper," however, does not merely present a text that mirrors itself, since the story/novella also insists on its status as a question, a hesitation that replicates the narrative it recounts. In this way the text maintains a difference that remains unassimilable to a theoretical perspective that would reassemble it for its own advantage. This strategy of resistance is similar to the one Todorov describes as *fantastic* in a book by the same name.[12] The fantastic presents a textual resistance that induces us to suspend our judgment when interpreting an event as representative of either the supernatural (the women in the wall-paper are ghosts) or the uncanny (the protagonist projects self-aspects to form her double[s]). The fantastic exists, then, suspended between these dimensions, a contradiction to both, a pause or hesitation that, through its inconclusiveness, questions the validity of our assertions. If we apply Todorov's theory of the fantastic to "The Yellow Wall-Paper," we have yet another reason to suspend our judgment, especially since the protagonist acknowledges, as early as the second paragraph, the possibility of a supernatural interpretation — these "secure ancestral halls" are haunted (9). Such a conservative interpretation, which privileges the supernatural manifestation of gothic romanticism while discarding historical and cultural analysis, should not be confused with Todorov's notion of the fantastic, which delights in the ambiguity articulated in expressed difference.

Stated another way, "The Yellow Wall-Paper" is more a writerly than a readerly text, which Gilman designed to challenge her readers to produce, not merely consume. Gilman's protagonist, who configures a text from her vision of the wall-paper, illustrates a means of reading that allows for a play of difference, just as her protagonist allows for the play of sun and moon off the wall-paper's surface. This is how Gilman's text presents itself to us, an ambiguous, double referent, cast in the interrogative mode, a gestalt of changing patterns. Text as question formulates an inconclusiveness that attends enigma generated in part by the hyphen between wall and paper — a sign of difference and reminder of text as Other to which we look for closure, a means of satisfying unsatisfiable desires.

Notes

1. Charlotte Perkins Gilman, *The Yellow Wall Paper* (Boston: Small, Maynard, 1899); Gilman, "The Yellow Wall-Paper," *New England Magazine* 5 (1891–92), 647–56.

2. Gilman, *The Yellow Wallpaper* (New York: Feminist Press, 1973). For ease of referral, all subsequent references, unless otherwise noted, are to this edition of the text.

3. Gilman, "The Yellow Wall-Paper," Schlesinger Library, Radcliffe College, Charlotte Perkins Gilman Collection, Folder 221.

4. Gilman, *The Yellow Wallpaper,* in *The Norton Anthology of Literature by Women,* ed. Sandra M. Gilbert and Susan Gubar (New York: Norton, 1985), 1148–61.

5. Carol Thomas Neely, "Alternative Women's Discourse," *Tulsa Studies in Women's Literature* 4 (1985), 316.

6. Karen Ford, "'The Yellow Wallpaper' and Women's Discourse," *Tulsa Studies in Women's Literature* 4 (1985), 310, 311, 313.

7. Paula A. Treichler, "Escaping the Sentence: Diagnosis and Discourse in 'The Yellow Wallpaper,'" *Tulsa Studies in Women's Literature* 3 (1984), 61–77.

8. Paula A. Treichler, "The Wall behind the Yellow Wallpaper: Response to Carol Neely and Karen Ford," *Tulsa Studies in Women's Literature* 4 (1985), 324, 325, 327.

9. Gilman, *The Living of Charlotte Perkins Gilman* (New York: Arno-Hawthorne Books, 1972), 118–21.

10. Treichler, "Escaping the Sentence," 73.

11. See Jacques Lacan, "The Mirror Stage as Formative of the Function of the I as Revealed in Psychoanalytic Experience," in *Ecrits: A Selection,* trans. Alan Sheridan (New York: Norton, 1977), 1–7.

12. Tzvetan Todorov, *The Fantastic: A Structural Approach to a Literary Genre,* trans. Richard Howard (Ithaca: Cornell University Press, 1975).

CHAPTER SEVEN

Historical Criticism II: Culture as Context

The Face of Nature we no more Survey
—Pope, *An Essay on Criticism*

The most notable trend in recent literary theory has been a turn to historical criticism. I stress the term "theory," for much critical practice, we should remember, has continued to be historical in the senses used in the first chapter of this book. Genetic studies that investigate an author's life and times to determine what that author might have meant in a given work continue to be produced in large numbers. But the recent turn toward history is not quite a return to genetic criticism. The newer historians, though reacting against the ahistorical thrust of much contemporary theory, are new precisely because they have absorbed many ideas from these ahistorical approaches.

The reaction was probably predictable. Ever since formalism challenged the then-dominant genetic criticism, the chief theoretical debates have been among competing forms of ahistorical, or even antihistorical, theories. Reader-response critics, for example, have usually been content to study the responses of contemporary readers. Mimetic critics—and often formalists are mimetic critics in this respect—have usually argued that literature imitates universal human nature and conveys timeless truths. Intertextual critics, especially those most influenced by structuralist thought, have generally pictured literature as a synchronic system of simultaneously present works. To be sure, none of these contexts, except perhaps formalism in its Anglo-American versions, is inherently ahistorical. Reception aesthetics, for example, traces reader responses over different historical periods. Mimesis can accommodate imitation of historically contingent as well as timeless conditions. And intertextual studies—Bakhtin's work comes to mind—can have a diachronic as well as a synchronic basis. Even so, the emphasis in all these contexts has been heavily ahistorical.

This is also true of poststructuralist criticism, which has occasionally been antihistorical as well. Deconstructive critics have often pushed formalist and structuralist arguments to their logical, or illogical, conclusions, pointing up irreducible tensions in the work or tracing the strands by which that work is woven into the larger text that is the only world man-the-signifier can know. In the process, they have strongly emphasized the ahistorical bent of these approaches. But deconstruction has also offered a more direct challenge to historical criticism. By calling into question the very concepts of origin, telos, and cause, deconstruction has threatened to deconstruct the historian's as well as the metaphysician's enterprise.

In sum, historical criticism has been decidedly on the margins of most theoretical debates in the last half-century, so much so that some historical critics have claimed that virtually all the critical controversies since the New Criticism are merely in-house squabbles among competing formalisms. Against this background, the call for a "return to history" is sometimes taken as a vindication of genetic criticism in its various forms. But the kinds of historical criticism that have moved to the center in recent theoretical discussions are not those that have simply rejected the ahistorical approaches. Among these newer historical criticisms one can identify a few loosely formed groups or "interpretive communities." Somewhat confusingly, the New Historicism is the name for one of these groups. Others call their own work "sociological poetics" or "cultural studies" or "cultural criticism." Much of this work has been influenced by Marxist thought, and Marxist critics who have in turn been influenced by structuralism, deconstruction, and postmodernism might also be included here among the poststructuralist historians. In addition, the turn to history can be seen in the work of many feminist critics and in the growing number of studies that focus on the issues of race, ethnicity, and postcolonialism.

This turn to history, then, includes a large and diverse group of critics. But they share several concerns, and often the things that unite them are the things they have taken over from formalism, structuralism, and poststructuralism. One of these is an emphasis on "textuality" and the problems of "representation." They agree that no text can offer a transparent window to historical fact. On the contrary, all texts must be scrutinized with formalist rigor and with a formalist's eye to the implications of even the smallest textual features. Further, many of the newer historians have accepted the poststructuralist deconstruction of the "self," the "individual," the "autonomous ego," which they associate with "liberal humanism," and they speak instead of the "subject," a social or linguistic construct. Most also accept the deconstruction of such long-standing oppositions as that between the literary and the nonliterary, or that between high and popular culture, and they are inclined to collapse the disciplinary walls that are built on such oppositions. They agree with the genetic critics that we need to look at the historical causes of literary productions, but they would add that we need also to look at their historical consequences. And we need to look, too, they would say, at the "situatedness" of the historian; we need to be aware of how much of our present we carry into our investigations of the past. Most generally, and most importantly, the newer historians have absorbed the poststructuralists' skepticism toward any universalizing or totalizing claims, and they are adept at using the techniques of deconstruction to argue that nearly everything we may have thought was "natural"—from the superiority of Shakespeare's poetry to one's sexual or racial identity—is actually a social and historically contingent construction.

The New Historicism is a case in point. It's not clear how many people apply this label to themselves. Stephen Greenblatt, who is often cited as the leading New Historicist, prefers to call his work "cultural poetics," and an anthology of *The New Historicism* (Veeser) reveals several points of disagreement or differing emphases among figures such as Greenblatt, Louis Montrose, Joel Feinman, and Catherine Gallagher, all critics associated with the movement. But the assumptions they share are numerous and important. Some of these can be traced to the influence of the French historian/philosopher/sociologist/"archeologist," Michel Foucault. Foucault's work is hard to classify because one of his goals was to erase or blur such classifications. His project was to examine the intricately structured power relations that obtain in a society at a given time, to show how that society constructs, defines, and thus controls its members. Most often, Foucault argues, society maintains control by making its constructed categories, say, of "crime" or "madness" or "sexuality," appear to be natural, things given rather than made, and so beyond question or change. Yet such constructs do change over time, as historical study can show us, thus leading us to suspect the "naturalness" of our own constructs. Nevertheless, in tracing the changes in power relations, Foucault is not claiming to offer a history that moves from origin to end, or from worse to better. Neither does he see power as a necessarily oppressive force from which we must be liberated or even from which we could be liberated, for Foucault is impressed by society's ability to absorb opposition and to maneuver those who would challenge existing power relations into actually supporting the status quo. In other words, Foucault often shows considerable respect — too much respect, his critics say — for the totalizing power of society. He is also keenly aware of the difficulties of seeing the past except through the lenses, the constructs, of the present. Yet these difficulties make the historian's task not less but more necessary, not an impossibility but the only possibility. If we can find no transcendent standpoint and no "natural," nonhistorical anchors for our key ideas ("madness" really means . . . "sexuality" truly is . . .), all we can do is conduct archeological expeditions, patiently constructing the genealogies of these ideas from the sedimented layers of the past. Our key ideas, in other words, have no essence; they have only a history.

Several of Foucault's interests can be seen in the work of Greenblatt and other New Historicists. Like Foucault, they think of history in terms of power relations and they are fascinated by the "circulation" of power within society. They also traverse traditional disciplinary boundaries, collapsing distinctions between the literary and the nonliterary, between the foreground and the background. And they are deeply suspicious of any appeals to "universal" truths or "natural" behavior. Greenblatt, who has worked chiefly with the English Renaissance, positions his "cultural poetics" between the two extremes of earlier kinds of literary history: on the one hand, studies that paint with a broad brush the main ideas of an "age" and then find those ideas directly reflected in the period's chief literary works and, on the other, highly specialized studies that turn every work into a political allegory. Instead, Greenblatt produces what anthropologists like Clifford Geertz have called "thick descriptions," linking literary works with contemporary cultural phenomena in sometimes startling ways — King Lear with a now-obscure attack on exorcism, for example. Like Foucault, Greenblatt has been chided by more politically committed critics for describing power relations as a mysterious and agentless totality. Other critics have complained that his work represents an abandonment of "literary" criticism, though it could equally be argued that it represents the extension of literary criticism to all aspects of culture. Either way, the question depends on a distinction of little concern to Greenblatt, for whom "literature" is simply a "part of the system of signs that constitutes a given culture."

Jerome McGann is another writer who has tried to steer criticism toward a more historical course. In several books and essays dealing mainly with the English Romantic poets, McGann has argued the need for a "sociological poetics" that will go beyond the formalist's ahistorical focus on the text but also beyond the genetic critic's focus on the author and even beyond the wider but still "literary" focus of traditional literary history. Only a social history, he asserts, can fully elucidate the poem's "network of social relations." Acknowledging a debt to Marxism, Russian Formalism, and the work of Bakhtin, McGann calls for a criticism that will explicate all the stages of a poem's "socializations," starting with the material conditions of its place and mode of publication and going on to trace not only its original reception but also the history of its reception over time. For our present responses "are clearly tied to this entire historical development, whether we are aware of it or not" (*Inflections* 54).

While both McGann's "sociological poetics" and Greenblatt's "cultural poetics" would considerably broaden the scope of literary study, neither includes all the diverse practices that cluster under the labels "Cultural Studies" or "Cultural Criticism." Here again one of the chief goals of those who accept these labels is to traverse disciplinary and departmental boundaries, so it's not surprising that they resist attempts to define and thus rebound them. Indeed, "traversing" and "resisting" are terms that figure prominently in the lexicon of Cultural Studies. If we try to shackle this Proteus by applying the traditional schema of sources, techniques, and ends, we can say that British Cultural Criticism begins with the work of Raymond Williams, Richard Hoggart, and E. P. Thompson in the 1950s and 1960s. This work, strongly influenced by Marxism, questioned the distinctions between "high" and popular culture and argued that working-class culture, generally misunderstood and undervalued, was a proper subject for serious study. While never abandoning this class-conscious and egalitarian origin, Cultural Studies in their British, American, and Continental forms have subsequently been heavily influenced by the same structuralist and poststructuralist ideas that have changed the intellectual landscape in many fields. They have also been heavily influenced by the competing voices that have put issues of gender, race, and ethnic identity on the agenda alongside or ahead of social class. So today the cultural critic will apply the techniques of poststructural criticism to any and all cultural phenomena from opera to sporting events, from classical drama to television shows, from museum exhibits to graffiti. Clearly "culture" in this context is defined expansively.

But while there is no limit to the objects of cultural study, cultural critics, despite their antidisciplinary stance, usually share similar goals. Above all, the end of their inquiry is to show what kind of "cultural work" the object under scrutiny has done, or is doing, or could be made to do. Like Foucault, the cultural critic is concerned with relations of power within society. But even more than the New Historicists, cultural critics are likely to stress the present implications of their studies and to see their own work, even when it's focused on the past, as an intervention into current political arrangements. Almost always that intervention is in opposition to existing power structures and designed to empower groups historically disadvantaged. Along these lines, the thrust of many recent studies of popular culture has been to point up the element of political "resistance" to be found not only in such phenomena as "skinhead" or "punk" groups but also in the ways the apparently passive audiences of mass-appeal entertainments convert these to their own purposes. Such studies often show the influence of the Italian Marxist Antonio Gramsci, who described the "hegemonic" power of the prevailing ideology, but who also stressed the possibilities of local or "micropolitical" opposition to this power, and of Bakhtin, whose idea of the "carnivalesque" emphasizes the oppositional role of popular culture.

This activist agenda figures in other distinguishing features of cultural criticism. For example, the urge to collapse distinctions between high and popular culture, between canonical and noncanonical literature, between one field of study and another, is motivated not only by skepticism about the ontological status of these distinctions but perhaps more by the belief that such distinctions serve to maintain the existing power relations in society. Similarly, cultural critics' objections to terms such as "humanism" and "universal truth" rest not so much on epistemological grounds as on the fact that these terms have historically been used to privilege the views of one small group—white males of European descent, who have had the power to impress their own image on the "human" and the "universal." Hence the worry among cultural critics that they are themselves in danger of becoming a recognized discipline, or even an academic department, or that they may inadvertently establish a canonical countercanon. An institutionalized opposition is always something of an oxymoron.

Quite consistently, therefore, cultural critics have joined other poststructuralist historians in stressing the inquirer's need for self-awareness. As we attempt to investigate cultural phenomena across geographical, temporal, and class boundaries, we need to know what cultural baggage we carry with us and how we acquired it. One result of this emphasis has been a number of investigations into literary study itself as a cultural practice. What gets defined as "literature," what texts get assigned in schools and colleges, what kinds of topics get discussed in classes and in standard exams? And who decides the answers to these questions? In short, what social forces influence reading practices and what are the social consequences of these practices? Not surprisingly, feminist cultural critics have led the way in raising these questions, but they have been joined by many others who have been concerned to point out the economic and social class implications of literary study, especially as it has been organized in the schools.

In these and other ways, the Marxist influence in cultural criticism has remained strong, as it has in most of the newer historicisms. Although relatively few in these groups may call themselves simply "Marxist" ("cultural materialist" is a favored name among some British cultural critics), many acknowledge that Marxist ideas have shaped their thinking. But influences run in both directions, and Marxist critics have also had to confront the powerful challenges of formalism, structuralism, and poststructuralism. So we should include in this latest turn to history the work of writers such as Terry Eagleton and Fredric Jameson, two leading Marxist critics who have appropriated many poststructuralist concepts. Both eschew simple dichotomies like base versus superstructure or form versus content, both use formalist and poststructuralist techniques to investigate the ideological implications of literary forms, and both find the relations between literary texts and their social contexts multidirectional and highly complex. Of the two, Jameson is the more difficult theorist. Indeed, some readers have complained that his absorption of other critical approaches has been so comprehensive and his account of social and literary relations so refined that his Marxism has been obscured. Nevertheless, Jameson has continued to insist that the Marxist view of history remains the unboundable "horizon" that bounds all other critical approaches.

In addition to these loosely defined groups and practices, the latest turn to history includes the work of a large number of unaffiliated or multiaffiliated critics who may disagree about much but who agree that literary studies must become more historical and more engaged with "real-world" problems. I include here the growing number of writers who have made issues of gender, race, and postcolonialism the focus of their work. This focus almost demands some kind of historical approach, and in recent years these approaches, too, have been strongly influenced by poststructuralist thought. Feminist critics, for example, have been quick to see the uses of poststructuralist analysis for deconstructing oppressive stereotypes and undermining patriarchal power. But feminist perspectives have in turn been subjected to the same kind of analysis by those who find some feminist work complicit in maintaining the dominant heterosexual ideology and by those who would assert the importance of race or class over gender as the crucial social determinant. And just as feminist criticism has questioned the "representation" of women in literary works, these other voices have critiqued the representation of homosexuals, African Americans, native Americans, and other colonized peoples, questioning not only the images that purport to represent these groups but also the authority of those who claim to speak as their representatives.

Such studies have often asked as well in what language these representatives should speak. In the context of theories that stress the decisive influence of language upon thought, this issue becomes central for colonized voices. Again following the pattern of feminists who questioned the adequacy of "patriarchal" language to represent them, minority and Third-World critics have examined both the problems and the subversive potentials entailed in adopting the colonizer's language. Most often, of course, that language has been English, which has been imposed not only on millions within the British Isles but on hundreds of millions around the globe. Given the intimate connections between language and culture, a merging of the poststructuralist emphasis on language with the historicist emphasis on culture has seemed inevitable.

The New Historicism, "sociological poetics," cultural criticism, revisionist Marxism, studies of race, gender, ethnicity, and postcolonialism, the social history of literary study—a mixed bag, and a shapeless one. Yet as different as these practices are, they all represent a turn to history, and the history they turn to is markedly different in many ways from the kinds of history explored in the opening chapter. What sets these newer practices apart, as we have seen, is the extent to which they reflect the assumptions and techniques of formal and poststructural criticism. In fact, we might use "poststructuralist history" as a convenient cover term for this entire context.

The complaint, then, that there is little new in the newer histories is easily answered. But the charge that what's new isn't historical may have more substance. This charge has been leveled both by undeconstructed Marxists and by unreconstructed geneticists. The latter, for example, have continued to object to the extreme historical relativism that would see readers as largely limited to their own cultural horizons. The virtues of self-awareness, they argue, can become vices if the recognition of one's supposedly "inescapable" biases becomes an excuse not to try to escape them. More seriously, if we are really in thrall to our own perspective, we can't really "do" history at all. Finding this position epistemologically dubious as well as self-defeating, genetic critics continue to claim that with care and effort we can reconstruct with reasonable accuracy the perspectives of people who lived in other times and places. Yet the model these critics invoke of an independent subject observing an independent, but knowable, object is a model that has been under heavy attack in virtually all critical contexts from reader-response criticism to deconstruction.

From another direction, some Marxists have objected to New Historical practice on the grounds that its "thick descriptions" can be historically disabling in two ways. On the one hand, disclosure of surprising links between the most disparate elements in a society (e.g., between witchcraft and "high" art) may imply power relationships at once so intricate and so agentless as to render futile any attempts to change them. On the other hand, these "thick descriptions" are like snapshots or stills that present a detailed picture of a society at a point in time but that offer no way to move from one time frame to another. In short, the method is synchronic rather than diachronic. Having no way to explain changes from one period to another, it is not really "historical" at all, certainly not in any Marxist sense of the term. In both cases the problem is an inability to establish a cause-and-effect relationship. Yet while it is difficult to think of doing history without some sense of causality, it is also difficult to think of any causal links that poststructural analysis couldn't dissolve.

These and similar objections point to a basic problem — the very assumptions and techniques that define poststructuralist history also make it difficult to do poststructuralist history. This raises the suspicion that poststructuralist history may be not a new element but a highly unstable compound in which historicist and sometimes interventionist elements mix incompletely with formal and deconstructive elements. To change the metaphor, many of the practices in this context appear to involve a two-stage operation in which deconstructive analysis is brought in for the ground-clearing demolition work, then moved safely off-site when the reconstruction work begins.

If, for example, you want to open the "canon" to previously marginalized works, you will find it useful to deconstruct the binary opposition of center and margin and to subject the process of canon formation to a demystifying analysis that will show all claims for literary value to be historically contingent. But these procedures will make it equally difficult to justify any alternative reading lists. If you want to dissolve the limiting stereotypes of, say, the "feminine," or the "African American," deconstruction and historical genealogy will be effective solvents. But if you then want to reconstruct the "feminine" or the "African American" as a characteristic form of writing or as a site for exposing and opposing oppression, it's not clear how your reconstruction will be able to resist these same solvents. If your task is to decenter the bourgeois "individual" of capitalism, or the autonomous "ego" of ego psychology, or the independent "self" of liberal humanism, here again deconstruction and Foucauldian archeology will be useful tools. But in a society populated entirely by socially constructed "subject formations in transit," it's not apparent where you will be able to fix the responsibility for anyone's actions. In the same way, the need of subaltern groups to form strong bonds of self-recognition and group identity finds ambiguous aid from poststructuralist analysis. Though such analysis will delegitimize the claims of any group currently holding power, it also threatens to delegitimize any proposed substitutions, undercut any "essentialist" definitions around which oppositional groups might unite, and fracture any basis for solidarity. Where in such a world will socially (de)constructed subjects find the "justice" that is their goal?

Many of the internal stresses in this amalgam I have labeled poststructuralist history center on the embattled term "representation." The fact that "representation" is a key word both for poststructuralists and for most of the newer historians obscures the point that it means something rather different in each context. For poststructuralists, as we have seen, "representation" is primarily a linguistic and epistemological problem. Working from the model of structural linguistics, they argue that signifiers inevitably slide, meaning is always deferred, and true "representation" ever eludes us. For poststructuralist historians, who focus on power relations in society and on issues of class, gender, and race, "representation" is also the central issue. More exactly, subaltern groups of all types have echoed the feminists' complaint that the main problem is "misrepresentation." As Edward Said has put it, the task of the "oppositional" critic is to understand and ultimately to change the "ideological power of misrepresentation." Such a critic must expose those works that misrepresent women or gays or people of color and laud those works that tell it like it is, or was. "Oppositional" critics, then, have a considerable stake in the possibility of accurate representation, and, indeed, they will often value highly works of "social realism" that purport to offer a direct mimesis of social conditions. In short, for the oppositional critic, misrepresentation is largely a result, as well as a cause, of maldistributed power in society. For the poststructuralist, it is an inherent condition of human language. Any group whose goal is the undistorted self-representation of all groups will find an uncomfortable ally in a theory that rules out the possibility of undistorted representation. And since all critics who claim to be "historical," whether oppositional or not, have a similar stake in the possibility of accurate representation, "poststructuralist" history is necessarily a highly problematic concept.

Once again, then, we find that our context consists of a cluster of critical practices marked by apparently inherent and irreducible tensions. This will come as no surprise to those who have absorbed the lessons of deconstruction, and despite much talk about the blindness that enables insight, many poststructuralist historians are keenly aware of the tensions within their own work. At the same time, they are unwilling to abandon either the "worldly" thrust of their history or the textual thrust of poststructural analysis. Whether or not they think of themselves as "oppositional" critics, they agree on the two chief points that are the source of these tensions: literary study must become more historical, and historical study must become more poststructural.

Certainly they agree that the sociohistorical connections between the text and the world, the sense of a text as the product of social causes as well as the producer of social effects, has been too much neglected in literary study. For these critics, the formal concentration on the isolated text, the intertextual focus on literary relations, and the poststructural emphasis on the linguistically constructed universe are merely progressively larger cells in the prisonhouse of language. Yet given the right twist, each of these contexts offers useful insights for those who would see the literary work in its cultural contexts. Such critics will remind us that Derrida's famous remark, "there is nothing outside the text," though often seen as isolating the text from the world, could also be seen as an invitation to read the whole world as text and so open all aspects of culture to poststructuralist "literary" analysis.

Therein lies the promise, and the problem. As we have seen, the analytical strategies of poststructural criticism can indeed open up cultural issues in exciting and disturbing ways. They are especially effective for dismantling foundationalist and essentialist arguments, for demolishing totalizing claims, for deconstructing ideologies, for delegitimizing power, and generally for demonstrating that nearly everything called universal, timeless, and natural is really local, historically contingent, and socially constructed. So poststructuralist history, perhaps more than most kinds of historical study, offers to free us from the past. But as we have also seen, poststructuralist analysis constantly threatens to subvert any historical project, to deconstruct any political agenda, and to reenclose any inquiry in the endless loop of sliding signifiers. The challenge, then, as in our other contexts, is to harness the energy in these tensions and to channel it to productive uses. The burgeoning number of studies in this context indicates that, at the moment, this energy is considerable.

Suggestions for Further Reading

For the New Historicism, Michel Foucault's work, represented by Paul Rabinow, ed., *The Foucault Reader* (1984), is an important influence. Stephen Greenblatt, *Shakespearean Negotiations: The Circulation of Social Energy in Renaissance England* (1988), and Catherine Gallager, *The Industrial Reformation of English Fiction: Social Discourse and Narrative Form, 1832–1867* (1988), are two examples of New Historical practice. H. Aram Veeser, ed., *The New Historicism* (1989) contains a few essays by these and other writers illustrating the New Historicism along with several essays critiquing it. Another useful collection is Jeffrey N. Cox and Larry J. Reynolds, eds., *New Historical Literary Study* (1993). Brook Thomas, *The New Historicism and Other Old-Fashioned Topics* (1991), is a series of essays probing the movement's key concepts. Catherine Gallagher and Stephen Greenblatt, *Practicing New Historicism* (2000), offers six exemplary essays and an introduction in which the authors trace the rise of new historicism and insist that "new historicism is not a repeatable methodology or a literary critical program." Jerome J. McGann's work is represented by *The Beauty of Inflections: Literary Investigations in Historical Method and Theory* (1985).

Three founding texts of British cultural studies are Richard Hoggart, *The Uses of Literacy: Changing Patterns in English Mass Culture* (1958); Raymond Williams, *The Long Revolution* (1961); and E. P. Thompson, *The Making of the English Working Class* (1963). Contemporary "cultural materialism" is illustrated in Alan Sinfield, *Literature, Politics, and Culture in Postwar Britain* (1989), and Jonathan Dollimore and Alan Sinfield, eds., *Political Shakespeare: New Essays in Cultural Materialism* (1985). The diverse practices of contemporary cultural studies are displayed in Lawrence Grossberg et al., eds., *Cultural Studies* (1992), which prints 40 essays by cultural critics from most parts of the English-speaking world. John Story, ed., *What Is Cultural Studies? A Reader* (1996), reprints 22 essays that offer to define, rather than to illustrate, the aims of cultural studies. Patrick Brantlinger, *Crusoe's Footprints: Cultural Studies in Britain and America* (1990), is a sympathetic but probing analysis of the various movements within cultural studies. See also Michael Berube, *Public Access: Literary Theory and American Cultural Politics* (1994).

Terry Eagleton, *Criticism and Ideology: A Study in Marxist Literary Theory* (1978), and Fredric Jameson, *The Political Unconscious: Narrative as a Socially Symbolic Act* (1981), are representative of the work of these two prolific authors. Jameson's ideas receive a helpful exposition in William C. Dowling, *Jameson, Althusser, Marx: An Introduction to "The Political Unconscious"* (1984). More general studies of Marxist thought and its relation to contemporary literary theory are Michael Ryan, *Marxism and Deconstruction* (1982); Martin Jay, *Marxism and Totality* (1984); and John Frow, *Marxism and Literary History* (1986). Eagleton's *Ideology* (1991) is a book-length examination of this key concept. Chris Bullock and David Peck, eds., *A Guide to Marxist Literary Criticism* (1980), is a useful bibliography. Terry Eagleton and Drew Milne, eds., *Marxist Literary Theory: A Reader* (1996) is a collection of representative essays from Marx to the present.

The subversive possibilities of taking over or "deterritorializing" the colonizer's language are explored in studies like Gilles Deleuze and Felix Guattari, *Kafka: Toward a Minor Literature* (1975), and Henry Louis Gates, Jr., *The Signifying Monkey: A Theory of Afro-American Literary Criticism* (1988). The concerns of feminist, Third-World, and poststructuralist criticism intersect in the work of Gayatri Spivak, *In Other Worlds: Essays in Cultural Politics* (1987). Homi K. Bhabha, *The Location of Culture* (1994) argues that the insights of poststructuralism can be employed to further a postcolonial critique. Edward Said, *The World, the Text, and the Critic* (1983), calls for a "worldly" criticism that will emphasize the text's, and the critic's, interaction with history and society. Issues of postcolonial literature and criticism are treated in Bill Ashcroft, Gareth Griffiths, and Helen Tiffin, *The Empire Writes Back* (1989), and in Padmini Mongia, ed., *Contemporary Postcolonial Theory: A Reader* (1996).

Jane Tomkins, *Sensational Designs* (1985), Russell Reising, *The Unusable Past* (1986), and John Guillory, *Cultural Capital* (1993), discuss questions of canon formation. Literary study as an institutional practice is viewed from an American perspective in Gerald Graff, *Professing Literature* (1987) and from a British perspective in Chris Baldick, *The Social Mission of English Criticism, 1848–1932* (1983); Ian Hunter, *Culture and Government* (1988); and Brian Doyle, *English and Englishness* (1989).

THEORY

Literature and History

Terry Eagleton

In the first chapter of his Marxism and Literary Criticism, *Terry Eagleton asserts that critical explanation should mean grasping literary forms, styles, and meaning "as products of a particular history." In opposition, then, to those critics who claim that great literature transcends the circumstances of its creation, the Marxist critic will stress its ties to those circumstances. The result will be a historical criticism, but one very different from the author-centered, intentionalist criticism we saw in the first chapter. From the Marxist perspective, authors are likely to be profoundly unaware of the true significance of their work, for they generally lack the "revolutionary understanding of history" that permits the Marxist critic to explain the literary work's relationship to the "ideology" of its age. Eagleton defines ideology here as "the way men live out their roles in class-society, the values, ideas and images which tie them to their social functions and so prevent them from having a true knowledge of society as a whole." Ideology, in this sense (see Eagleton's* Ideology *[1991] for a fuller discussion of this key term), is something like "false consciousness," and Eagleton stresses his point that the literary work's relation to the ideology of its age is likely to be much more complicated than the "vulgar Marxist" will generally allow, neither simply supporting that ideology nor directly challenging it. A truly "scientific" criticism, Eagleton claims, will "seek to explain the literary work in terms of the ideological structure of which it is a part, yet which it transforms in its art."*

Marx, Engels and Criticism

If Karl Marx and Frederick Engels are better known for their political and economic rather than literary writings, this is not in the least because they regarded literature as insignificant. It is true, as Leon Trotsky remarked in *Literature and Revolution* (1924), that "there are many people in this world who think as revolutionists and feel as philistines"; but Marx and Engels were not of this number. The writings of Karl Marx, himself the youthful author of lyric poetry, a fragment of verse-drama and an unfinished comic novel much influenced by Laurence Sterne, are laced with literary concepts and allusions; he wrote a sizeable unpublished manuscript on art and religion and planned a journal of dramatic criticism, a full-length study of Balzac, and a treatise on aesthetics. Art and literature were part of the very air Marx breathed, as a formidably cultured German intellectual in the great classical tradition of his society. His acquaintance with literature, from Sophocles to the Spanish novel, Lucretius to potboiling English fiction, was staggering in its scope; the German workers' circle he founded in Brussels devoted an evening a week to discussing the arts, and Marx himself was an inveterate theatre-goer, declaimer of poetry, devourer of every species of literary art from Augustan prose to industrial ballads. He described his own works in a letter to Engels as forming an "artistic whole," and was scrupulously sensitive to questions of literary style, not least his own; his very first pieces of journalism argued for freedom of artistic expression. Moreover, the pressure of aesthetic concepts can be detected behind some of the most crucial categories of economic thought he employs in his mature work.[1]

Even so, Marx and Engels had rather more important tasks on their hands than the formation of a complete aesthetic theory. Their comments on art and literature are scattered and fragmentary, glancing allusions rather than developed positions.[2] This is one reason why Marxist criticism involves more than merely restating cases set out by the "sociology of literature." The sociology of literature concerns itself chiefly with what might be called the means of literary production, distribution and exchange in a particular society—how books are published, the social composition of their authors and audiences, levels of literacy, the social determinants of "taste." It also examines literary texts for their "sociological" relevance, raiding literary works to abstract from them themes of interest to the social historian. There has been some excellent work in this field,[3] and it forms one aspect of Marxist criticism as a whole; but taken by itself it is neither particularly Marxist nor particularly critical. It is, indeed, for the most part a suitably tamed, degutted version of Marxist criticism, appropriate for Western consumption.

Marxist criticism is not merely a "sociology of literature," concerned with how novels get published and whether they mention the working class. Its aim is to *explain* the literary work more fully; and this means a sensitive attention to its forms, styles and meanings.[4] But it also means grasping those forms, styles and meanings as the products of a particular history. The painter Henri Matisse once remarked that all art bears the imprint of its historical epoch, but that great art is that in which this imprint is most deeply marked. Most students of literature are taught otherwise: the greatest art is that which timelessly transcends its historical conditions. Marxist criticism has much to say on this issue, but the "historical" analysis of literature did not of course begin with Marxism. Many thinkers before Marx had tried to account for literary works in terms of the history which produced them;[5] and one of these, the German idealist philosopher G. W. F. Hegel, had a profound influence on Marx's own aesthetic thought. The originality of Marxist criticism, then, lies not in its historical approach to literature, but in its revolutionary understanding of history itself.

Base and Superstructure

The seeds of that revolutionary understanding are planted in a famous passage in Marx and Engels's *The German Ideology* (1845–6):

> The production of ideas, concepts and consciousness is first of all directly interwoven with the material intercourse of man, the language of real life. Conceiving, thinking, the spiritual intercourse of men, appear here as the direct efflux of men's material behaviour . . . we do not proceed from what men say, imagine, conceive, nor from men as described, thought of, imagined, conceived, in order to arrive at corporeal man; rather we proceed from the really active man . . . Consciousness does not determine life: life determines consciousness.

A fuller statement of what this means can be found in the Preface to *A Contribution to the Critique of Political Economy* (1859):

> In the social production of their life, men enter into definite relations that are indispensable and independent of their will, *relations of production* which correspond to a definite stage of development of their material productive *forces*. The sum total of these relations of production constitutes the economic structure of society, the real foundation, on which rises a legal and political superstructure and to which correspond definite forms of social consciousness. The mode of production of material life conditions the social, political and intellectual life process in general. It is not the consciousness of men that determines their being, but on the contrary, their social being that determines their consciousness.

The social relations between men, in other words, are bound up with the way they produce their material life. Certain "productive forces"—say, the organisation of labour in the middle ages—involve the social relations of villein to lord we know as feudalism. At a later stage, the development of new modes of productive organisation is based on a changed set of social relations—this time between the capitalist class who owns those means of production, and the proletarian class whose labour-power the capitalist buys for profit. Taken together, these "forces" and "relations" of production form what Marx calls "the economic structure of society," or what is more commonly known by Marxism as the economic "base" or "infrastructure." From this economic base, in every period, emerges a "superstructure"—certain forms of law and politics, a certain kind of state, whose essential function is to legitimate the power of the social class which owns the means of economic production. But the superstructure contains more than this: it also consists of certain "definite forms of social consciousness" (political, religious, ethical, aesthetic and so on), which is what Marxism designates as *ideology*. The function of ideology, also, is to legitimate the power of the ruling class in society; in the last analysis, the dominant ideas of a society are the ideas of its ruling class.[6]

Art, then, is for Marxism part of the "superstructure" of society. It is (with qualifications we shall make later) part of a society's ideology—an element in that complex structure of social perception which ensures that the situation in which one social class has power over the others is either seen by most members of the society as "natural," or not seen at all. To understand literature, then, means understanding the total social process of which it is part. As the Russian Marxist critic George Plekhanov put it: "The social mentality of an age is conditioned by that age's social relations. This is nowhere quite as evident as in the history of art and literature."[7] Literary works are not mysteriously inspired, or explicable simply in terms of their author's psychology. They are forms of perception, particular ways of seeing the world; and as such they have a relation to that dominant way of seeing the world which is the "social mentality" or ideology of an age. That ideology, in turn, is the product of the concrete social relations into which men enter at a particular time and place; it is the way those class-relations are experienced, legitimized and perpetuated. Moreover, men are not free to choose their social relations; they are constrained into them by material necessity—by the nature and stage of development of their mode of economic production.

To understand *King Lear, The Dunciad* or *Ulysses* is therefore to do more than interpret their symbolism, study their literary history and add footnotes about sociological facts which enter into them. It is first of all to understand the complex, indirect relations between those works and the ideological worlds they inhabit—relations which emerge not just in "themes" and "preoccupations," but in style, rhythm, image, quality and (as we shall see later) *form*. But we do not understand ideology either unless we grasp the part it plays in the society as a whole—how it consists of a definite, historically relative structure of perception which underpins the power of a particular social class. This is not an easy task, since an ideology is never a simple reflection of a ruling class's ideas; on the contrary, it is always a complex phenomenon, which may incorporate conflicting, even contradictory, views of the world. To understand an ideology, we must analyze the precise relations between different classes in a society; and to do that means grasping where those classes stand in relation to the mode of production.

All this may seem a tall order to the student of literature who thought he was merely required to discuss plot and characterization. It may seem a confusion of literary criticism with disciplines like politics and economics which ought to be kept separate. But it is, nonetheless, essential for the fullest explanation of any work of literature. Take, for example, the great Placido Gulf scene in Conrad's *Nostromo*. To evaluate the fine artistic force of this episode, as Decoud and Nostromo are isolated in utter darkness on the slowly sinking lighter, involves us in subtly placing the scene within the imaginative vision of the novel as a whole. The radical pessimism of that vision (and to grasp it fully we must, of course, relate *Nostromo* to the rest of Conrad's fiction) cannot simply be accounted for in terms of "psychological" factors in Conrad himself; for individual psychology is also a *social* product. The pessimism of Conrad's world view is rather a unique transformation into art of an ideological pessimism rife in his period—a sense of history as futile and cyclical, of individuals as impenetrable and solitary, of human values as relativistic and irrational, which marks a drastic crisis in the ideology of the Western bourgeois class to which Conrad allied himself. There were good reasons for that ideological crisis, in the history of imperialist capitalism throughout this period. Conrad did not, of course, merely anonymously reflect that history in his fiction; every writer is individually placed in society, responding to a general history from his own particular standpoint, making sense of it in his own concrete terms. But it is not difficult to see how Conrad's personal standing, as an "aristocratic" Polish exile deeply committed to English conservatism, intensified for him the crisis of English bourgeois ideology.[8]

It is also possible to see in these terms why that scene in the Placido Gulf should be artistically fine. To write well is more than a matter of "style"; it also means having at one's disposal an ideological perspective which can penetrate to the realities of men's experience in a certain situation. This is certainly what the Placido Gulf scene does; and it can do it, not just because its author happens to have an excellent prose-style, but because his historical situation allows him access to such insights. Whether those insights are in political terms "progressive" or "reactionary" (Conrad's are certainly the latter) is not the point—anymore than it is to the point that most of the agreed major writers of the twentieth century—Yeats, Eliot, Pound, Lawrence—are political conservatives who each had truck with fascism. Marxist criticism, rather than apologising for the fact, explains it—sees that, in the absence of gen-

uinely revolutionary art, only a radical conservatism, hostile like Marxism to the withered values of liberal bourgeois society, could produce the most significant literature.

Literature and Superstructure

It would be a mistake to imply that Marxist criticism moves mechanically from "text" to "ideology" to "social relations" to "productive forces." It is concerned, rather, with the *unity* of these "levels" of society. Literature may be part of the superstructure, but it is not merely the passive reflection of the economic base. Engels makes this clear, in a letter to Joseph Bloch in 1890:

> According to the materialist conception of history, the determining element in history is *ultimately* the production and reproduction in real life. More than this neither Marx nor I have ever asserted. If therefore somebody twists this into the statement that the economic element is the *only* determining one, he transforms it into a meaningless, abstract and absurd phrase. The economic situation is the basis, but the various elements of the superstructure—political forms of the class struggle and its consequences, constitutions established by the victorious class after a successful battle, etc.—forms of law—and then even the reflexes of all these actual struggles in the brains of the combatants: political, legal, and philosophical theories, religious ideas and their further development into systems of dogma—also exercise their influence upon the course of the historical struggles and in many cases preponderate in determining their *form*.

Engels wants to deny that there is any mechanical, one-to-one correspondence between base and superstructure; elements of the superstructure constantly react back upon and influence the economic base. The materialist theory of history denies that art can *in itself* change the course of history; but it insists that art can be an active element in such change. Indeed, when Marx came to consider the relation between base and superstructure, it was art which he selected as an instance of the complexity and indirectness of that relationship:

> In the case of the arts, it is well known that certain periods of their flowering are out of all proportion to the general development of society, hence also to the material foundation, the skeletal structure, as it were, of its organisation. For example, the Greeks

compared to the moderns or also Shakespeare. It is even recognised that certain forms of art, e.g. the epic, can no longer be produced in their world epoch-making, classical stature as soon as the production of art, as such, begins; that is, that certain significant forms within the realm of the arts are possible only at an undeveloped stage of artistic development. If this is the case with the relation between different kinds of art within the realm of art, it is already less puzzling that it is the case in the relation of the entire realm to the general development of society. The difficulty consists only in the general formulation of these contradictions. As soon as they have been specified, they are already clarified.⁹

Marx is considering here what he calls "the unequal relationship of the development of material production . . . to artistic production." It does not follow that the greatest artistic achievements depend upon the highest development of the productive forces, as the example of the Greeks, who produced major art in an economically undeveloped society, clearly evidences. Certain major artistic forms like the epic are only *possible* in an undeveloped society. Why then, Marx goes on to ask, do we still respond to such forms, given our historical distance from them?

> But the difficulty lies not in understanding that the Greek arts and epic are bound up with certain forms of social development. The difficulty is that they still afford us artistic pleasure and that in a certain respect they count as a norm and as an unattainable model.

Why does Greek art still give us aesthetic pleasure? The answer which Marx goes on to provide has been universally lambasted by unsympathetic commentators as lamely inept:

> A man cannot become a child again, or he becomes childish. But does he not find joy in the child's naiveté, and must he himself not strive to reproduce its truth at a higher stage? Does not the true character of each epoch come alive in the nature of its children? Why should not the historic childhood of humanity, its most beautiful unfolding, as a stage never to return, exercise an eternal charm? There are unruly children and precocious children. Many of the old peoples belong in this category. The Greeks were normal children. The charm of their art for us is not in contradiction to the undeveloped stage of society on which it grew. [It] is its result, rather, and is inextricably bound up,

rather, with the fact that the unripe social conditions under which it arose, and could alone rise, can never return.

So our liking for Greek art is a nostalgic lapse back into childhood—a piece of unmaterialistic sentimentalism which hostile critics have gladly pounced on. But the passage can only be treated thus if it is rudely ripped from the context to which it belongs—the draft manuscripts of 1857, known today as the *Grundrisse*. Once returned to that context, the meaning becomes instantly apparent. The Greeks, Marx is arguing, were able to produce major art not *in spite of* but *because of* the undeveloped state of their society. In ancient societies, which have not yet undergone the fragmenting "division of labour" known to capitalism, the overwhelming of "quality" by "quantity" which results from commodity-production and the restless, continual development of the productive forces, a certain "measure" or harmony can be achieved between man and Nature—a harmony precisely dependent upon the *limited* nature of Greek society. The "childlike" world of the Greeks is attractive because it thrives within certain measured limits—measures and limits which are brutally overridden by bourgeois society in its limitless demand to produce and consume. Historically, it is essential that this constricted society should be broken up as the productive forces expand beyond its frontiers; but when Marx speaks of "striv[ing] to reproduce its truth at a higher stage," he is clearly speaking of the communist society of the future, where unlimited resources will serve an unlimitedly developing man.¹⁰

Two questions, then, emerge from Marx's formulations in the *Grundrisse*. The first concerns the relation between "base" and "superstructure"; the second concerns our own relation in the present with past art. To take the second question first: how can it be that we moderns still find aesthetic appeal in the cultural products of past, vastly different societies? In a sense, the answer Marx gives is no different from the answer to the question: How is it that we moderns still respond to the exploits of, say, Spartacus? We respond to Spartacus or Greek sculpture because our own history links us to those ancient societies; we find in them an undeveloped phase of the forces which condition us. Moreover, we find in those ancient societies a primitive image of "measure" between man and Nature which capitalist society necessarily destroys, and which socialist society can reproduce at an incomparably higher level. We ought, in other words, to think of "history" in wider terms than our own contemporary history. To ask how Dickens relates to history is not just to ask how he relates to Victorian England, for that society was itself the product of a long history which includes men like Shakespeare and Milton. It is a curiously narrowed view of history which defines it merely as the "contemporary moment" and relegates all else to the "universal." One answer to the problem of past and present is suggested by Bertolt Brecht, who argues that "we need to develop the historical sense . . . into a real sensual delight. When our theatres perform plays of other periods they like to annihilate distance, fill in the gap, gloss over the differences. But what comes then of our delight in comparisons, in distance, in dissimilarity—which is at the same time a delight in what is close and proper to ourselves?"[11]

The other problem posed by the *Grundrisse* is the relation between base and superstructure. Marx is clear that these two aspects of society do not form a *symmetrical* relationship, dancing a harmonious minuet hand-in-hand throughout history. Each element of a society's superstructure—art, law, politics, religion—has its own tempo of development, its own internal evolution, which is not reducible to a mere expression of the class struggle or the state of the economy. Art, as Trotsky comments, has "a very high degree of autonomy"; it is not tied in any simple one-to-one way to the mode of production. And yet Marxism claims too that, in the last analysis, art is determined by that mode of production. How are we to explain this apparent discrepancy?

Let us take a concrete literary example. A "vulgar Marxist" case about T. S. Eliot's *The Waste Land* might be that the poem is directly determined by ideological and economic factors—by the spiritual emptiness and exhaustion of bourgeois ideology which springs from that crisis of imperialist capitalism known as the First World War. This is to explain the poem as an immediate "reflection" of those conditions; but it clearly fails to take into account a whole series of "levels" which "mediate" between the text itself and capitalist economy. It says nothing, for instance, about the social situation of Eliot himself—a writer living an ambiguous relationship with English society, as an "aristocratic" American expatriate who became a glorified City clerk and yet identified deeply with the conservative-traditionalist, rather than bourgeois-commercialist, elements of English

ideology. It says nothing about that ideology's more general forms—nothing of its structure, content, internal complexity, and how all these are produced by the extremely complex class-relations of English society at the time. It is silent about the form and language of *The Waste Land*—about why Eliot, despite his extreme political conservatism, was an *avant-garde* poet who selected certain "progressive" experimental techniques from the history of literary forms available to him, and on what ideological basis he did this. We learn nothing from this approach about the social conditions which gave rise at the time to certain forms of "spirituality," part-Christian, part-Buddhist, which the poem draws on; or of what role a certain kind of bourgeois anthropology (Fraser) and bourgeois philosophy (F. H. Bradley's idealism) used by the poem fulfilled in the ideological formation of the period. We are unilluminated about Eliot's social position as an artist, part of a self-consciously erudite, experimental élite with particular modes of publication (the small press, the little magazine) at their disposal; or about the kind of audience which that implied, and its effect on the poem's style and devices. We remain ignorant about the relation between the poem and the aesthetic theories associated with it—of what role that aesthetic plays in the ideology of the time, and how it shapes the construction of the poem itself.

Any complete understanding of *The Waste Land* would need to take these (and other) factors into account. It is not a matter of *reducing* the poem to the state of contemporary capitalism; but neither is it a matter of introducing so many judicious complications that anything as crude as capitalism may to all intents and purposes be forgotten. On the contrary: all of the elements I have enumerated (the author's class-position, ideological forms and their relation to literary forms, "spirituality" and philosophy, techniques of literary production, aesthetic theory) are directly relevant to the base/superstructure model. What Marxist criticism looks for is the unique *conjuncture* of these elements which we know as *The Waste Land*.[12] No one of these elements can be conflated with another: each has its own relative independence. *The Waste Land* can indeed be explained as a poem which springs from a crisis of bourgeois ideology, but it has no simple correspondence with that crisis or with the political and economic conditions which produced it. (As a poem, it does not of course *know itself* as a product of a particular ideological crisis, for if it did it would cease to exist. It needs to translate that crisis into "universal" terms—to grasp it as part of an unchanging human condition, shared alike by ancient Egyptians and modern man.) *The Waste Land*'s relation to the real history of its time, then, is highly *mediated*; and in this it is like all works of art.

Literature and Ideology

Frederick Engels remarks in *Ludwig Feuerbach and the End of Classical German Philosophy* (1888) that art is far richer and more "opaque" than political and economic theory because it is less purely ideological. It is important here to grasp the precise meaning for Marxism of "ideology." Ideology is not in the first place a set of doctrines; it signifies the way men live out their roles in class-society, the values, ideas and images which tie them to their social functions and so prevent them from a true knowledge of society as a whole. In this sense *The Waste Land* is ideological: it shows a man making sense of his experience in ways that prohibit a true understanding of his society, ways that are consequently false. All art springs from an ideological conception of the world; there is no such thing, Plekhanov comments, as a work of art entirely devoid of ideological content. But Engels's remark suggests that art has a more complex relationship to ideology than law and political theory, which rather more transparently embody the interests of a ruling class. The question, then, is what relationship art has to ideology.

This is not an easy question to answer. Two extreme, opposite positions are possible here. One is that literature is *nothing but* ideology in a certain artistic form—that works of literature are just expressions of the ideologies of their time. They are prisoners of "false consciousness," unable to reach beyond it to arrive at the truth. It is a position characteristic of much "vulgar Marxist" criticism, which tends to see literary works merely as reflections of dominant ideologies. As such, it is unable to explain, for one thing, why so much literature actually *challenges* the ideological assumptions of its time. The opposite case seizes on the fact that so much literature challenges the ideology it confronts, and makes this part of the definition of literary art itself. Authentic art, as Ernst Fischer argues in his significantly entitled *Art Against Ideology* (1969), always transcends the ideological limits of its time, yielding us insight into the realities which ideology hides from view.

Both of these cases seem to me too simple. A more subtle (although still incomplete) account of the relationship between literature and ideology is provided by the French Marxist theorist Louis Althusser.[13] Althusser argues that art cannot be reduced to ideology: it has, rather, a particular *relationship* to it. Ideology signifies the imaginary ways in which men experience the real world, which is, of course, the kind of experience literature gives us too—what it feels like to live in particular conditions, rather than a conceptual analysis of those conditions. However, art does more than just passively reflect that experience. It is held within ideology, but also manages to distance itself from it, to the point where it permits us to "feel" and "perceive" the ideology from which it springs. In doing this, art does not enable us to *know* the truth which ideology conceals, since for Althusser "knowledge" in the strict sense means *scientific* knowledge—the kind of knowledge of, say, capitalism which Marx's *Capital* rather than Dickens's *Hard Times* allows us. The difference between science and art is not that they deal with different objects, but that they deal with the same objects in different ways. Science gives us conceptual knowledge of a situation; art gives us the experience of that situation, which is equivalent to ideology. But by doing this, it allows us to "see" the nature of that ideology, and thus begins to move us towards that full understanding of ideology which is scientific knowledge.

How literature can do this is more fully developed by one of Althusser's colleagues, Pierre Macherey. In his *Pour une Théorie de la Production Littéraire* (1966), Macherey distinguishes between what he terms "illusion" (meaning, essentially, ideology), and "fiction." Illusion—the ordinary ideological experience of men—is the material on which the writer goes to work; but in working on it he transforms it into something different, lends it a shape and structure. It is by giving ideology a determinate form, fixing it within certain fictional limits, that art is able to distance itself from it, thus revealing to us the limits of that ideology. In doing this, Macherey claims, art contributes to our deliverance from the ideological illusion.

I find the comments of both Althusser and Macherey at crucial points ambiguous and obscure; but the relation they propose between literature and ideology is nonetheless deeply suggestive. Ideology, for both critics, is more than an amorphous body of free-floating images and ideas; in any society it has a certain structural coherence. Because it possesses such relative coherence, it can be the object of scientific analysis; and since literary texts "belong" to ideology, they too can be the object of such scientific analysis. A scientific criticism would seek to explain the literary work in terms of the ideological structure of which it is part, yet which it transforms in its art: it would search out the principle which both ties the work to ideology and distances it from it.

Notes

1. See M. Lifshitz, *The Philosophy of Art of Karl Marx* (London, 1973). For a naively prejudiced but reasonably informative account of Marx and Engels's literary interests, see P. Demetz, *Marx, Engels and the Poets* (Chicago, 1967).

2. See Karl Marx and Frederick Engels, *On Literature and Art* (New York, 1973), for a compendium of these comments.

3. See especially L. Schücking, *The Sociology of Literary Taste* (London, 1944); R. Escarpit, *The Sociology of Literature* (London, 1971); R. D. Atlick, *The English Common Reader* (Chicago, 1957); and R. Williams, *The Long Revolution* (London, 1961). Representative recent works have been D. Laurenson and A. Swingewood, *The Sociology of Literature* (London, 1972), and M. Bradbury, *The Social Context of English Literature* (Oxford, 1971). For an account of Raymond Williams's important work, see my article in *New Left Review* 95 (January–February, 1976).

4. Much non-Marxist criticism would reject a term like "explanation," feeling that it violates the "mystery" of literature. I use it here because I agree with Pierre Macherey, in his *Pour une Théorie de la Production Littéraire* (Paris, 1966), that the task of the critic is not to "interpret" but to "explain." For Macherey, "interpretation" of a text means revising or correcting it in accordance with some ideal norm of what it should be; it consists, that is to say, in refusing the text *as it is*. Interpretative criticism merely "redoubles" the text, modifying and elaborating it for easier consumption. In saying *more* about the work, it succeeds in saying *less*.

5. See especially Vico's *The New Science* (1725); Madame de Staël, *Of Literature and Social Institutions* (1800); H. Taine, *History of English Literature* (1863).

6. This, inevitably, is a considerably over-simplified account. For a full analysis, see N. Poulantzas, *Political Power and Social Classes* (London, 1973).

7. Quoted in the Preface to Henri Arvon's *Marxist Aesthetics* (Ithaca, 1970).

8. On the question of how a writer's personal history interlocks with the history of his time, see J. P. Sartre, *The Search for a Method* (London, 1963).

9. Introduction to the *Grundrisse* (Harmondsworth, 1973).

10. See Stanley Mitchell's essay on Marx in Hall and Walton (eds.), *Situating Marx* (London, 1972).

11. Appendices to the "Short Organum on the Theatre," in J. Willett (ed.), *Brecht on Theatre: The Development of an Aesthetic* (London, 1964).

12. To put the issue in more complex theoretical terms: the influence of the economic "base" on *The Waste Land* is evident not in a direct way, but in the fact that it is the economic base which in the last instance determines the state of development of each element of the superstructure (religious, philosophical and so on) which went into its making, and moreover determines the structural interrelations between those elements, of which the poem is a particular conjuncture.

13. In his "Letter on Art in reply to André Daspre," in *Lenin and Philosophy* (London, 1971). See also the following essay on the abstract painter Cremonini.

THEORY

Catherine Belsey's "Literature, History, Politics" touches on a number of this context's chief concerns: literature versus Literature, classical versus revisionary Marxism, the constructed "subject" versus the autonomous "ego," criticism as an institution, the fluidity of disciplinary boundaries, the study of the past as an intervention in current power relations. The institution of literary criticism, Belsey complains, is still dominated by the formal-mimetic belief that literature represents universal truths. The dominance of this belief is clearly demonstrated, she feels, by standard examination questions, just as the power of the institution is demonstrated by the existence of such examinations. But when we claim to read trans-historically, we may reveal only that we are totally bound by our own horizons. The antidote is "history," but not traditional literary history. "When the institution of literary criticism in Britain invokes history, whether as world picture or as long-lost organic community, it is ultimately in order to suppress it, by showing that in essence things are as they have always been." Structuralism, though it seemed to challenge the critical establishment, has turned out to be little help in this regard, for it largely continued the dominance of the synchronic view and so served to further suppress history and politics. And American deconstruction, Belsey claims, for all its supposed radicalism, has had much the same effect. But in the work of other poststructuralists—and especially in the work of Foucault—Belsey sees the promise of a new history, a "poststructuralist history" that will be "explicitly partial, from a position and on behalf of a position" and whose effect will be "to locate the present in history and in process."

One of the first steps toward truly historicizing literary study is to take a historical view of literary study itself, and Belsey notes that in recent years this kind of analysis has done much to expose the ideological

Literature, History, Politics[1]

Catherine Belsey

Reprinted by permission of the author and publisher from *Literature and History* 9 (Spring 1983): 17–27.

assumptions of the institution of literary criticism, and to "relativize its claims to universality." But, says Belsey, as we strive to unite literature, history, and politics, to undermine literary study "as currently constituted," and to "challenge the category of Literature"—all worthy goals, she agrees—we do not need to ignore "literary" texts entirely. The study of even canonical texts can further these goals if we go about it in the right ways. We can, for example, extend the concept of "intertextuality" to include the "nonliterary" and thereby encounter "the discourses themselves in their uncertainty, their instability, their relativity." Further, while admitting that we can read any text any way, Belsey feels that "fictional" texts "offer a space for the problematisation of the knowledge they invoke" in ways that other kinds of texts do not. She hastens to add that she is not trying to "privilege literature (and certainly not Literature) but only to allow it a certain specificity which identifies its use-value in the construction of the history of the present." "The construction of the history of the present" might stand as a brief description of the goals of most poststructural historians. If we can see how power relations that offer themselves as natural and timeless have in fact been historically constructed, we may feel empowered to change them. This kind of poststructural history, this way of uniting literature, history, and politics, is "a stake through the heart of Eternal Man, and the world of practice as well as theory is consequently laid open to effective political action."

To bring these three terms together is hardly to do anything new. *Literature and History* has been doing it since its inception; the Essex Conference volumes do it; Raymond Williams has spent his life doing it; historians like E. P. Thompson and Christopher Hill, glancing sideways at literature, have frequently done it; a venerable tradition of Marxist criticism all over Europe does it. Less marginally, as far as the institution of literary criticism in Britain is concerned, T. S. Eliot, F. R. Leavis and E. M. W. Tillyard did it when they constructed between them a lost Elizabethan utopia where thought and feeling were one, where the native rhythms of speech expressed in poetry the intuitive consciousness of an organic community, and everyone recognised in the principle of order the necessity of submission to the proper authorities, social and divine.

And yet paradoxically to bring these three terms together *explicitly* is still to scandalise the institution of literary criticism, because it is to propose a rela-

tionship between the transcendent (literature), the contingent (history) and the merely strategic (politics). The institution is dedicated to the infinite repetition of the best that has been thought and said in the world, and this luminous heritage, however shaded by the Discarded Image of medieval ideas, or the Victorian Frame of Mind, stands ready to be released from history by the apparatus criticus which the academic profession supplies, and to reappear resplendent before every new generation of student-critics. The model for the institution's conception of history as a kind of perpetual present, and its conviction of the vulgarity of politics, is Arnold's essay, "The Study of Poetry," where it is clear from the "touchstones" Arnold invokes that great poetry from Homer to Milton, despite minor differences of language and setting, has always taught the same elegiac truth, that this world is inevitably a place of sorrow and that the only heroism is a solitary resignation of the spirit.

The sole inhabitant of the universe of literature is Eternal Man (and the masculine form is appropriate), whose brooding, feeling presence precedes, determines and transcends history as it precedes and determines the truths inscribed in the English syllabus, the truths examination candidates are required to reproduce. "'When we read Chaucer's early poems we feel the author's awareness of how complex and involved the events and circumstances of life are, of how they defy any single interpretation.' Discuss." (Oxford Honour School of English Language and Literature, "Chaucer and Langland," 1980.) Miraculously, Chaucer's awareness of the complexity of it all precisely resembles mine, ours, everyone's. Every liberal's, that is, in the twentieth century: a modern "recognition" is rendered eternal by literary criticism. Examination questions, the ultimate location of institutional power, identify the boundaries of the discipline, and define what it is permissible to "discuss," as they so invitingly and misleadingly put it (Davies, 1982, p. 39). "'The sense of a peculiarly heightened personal dignity is at the centre of Donne's work.' (Alvarez) *Either* discuss with reference to Donne or describe the sense of personal dignity in any other writer of the period." (Oxford Honour School . . . , "English Literature from 1600 to 1740," 1980.) Or any other writer of any other period, perhaps, because it is a reading from the present, from a position of liberal humanism, which finds the sense of personal dignity at issue wherever it looks.

Historians have been quite clear, at least since Eric Hobsbawm's seminal articles were published in *Past and Present* in 1954, that the seventeenth century was a period of general crisis. That general crisis has apparently no repercussions whatever for the literature of the period as it is defined in the broad run of examinations at O Level, at A Level and in the universities. Where the crisis is glimpsed, it is instantly depoliticised: "'Courtly poetry without a court.' What do the Cavalier poets gain or lose by the decline and final absence of a Court? Discuss one or more poets." (Cambridge English Tripos, Part II, "Special Period, 1616–60," 1981.) Had the question asked what was gained or lost from the collapse of the Court by agricultural labourers, by an emerging feminism or by radical politics, the answer might have mattered. But that would be history. What matters in English is the implications of the Revolution of the 1640s for the Cavalier poets. Alternatively, the crisis is personalised as the idiosyncratic interest of an individual: "'Throughout *Paradise Lost* Milton's concern is to present and investigate a crisis of authority.' Discuss." (Oxford Honour School . . . , "Spenser and Milton," 1980.) What it is not possible to say in answer to that question is how a crisis of authority is at the heart of *Paradise Lost,* not as a matter for the author's investigation, but as a source of fragmentation within the poem and the writing of the poem. It is precisely the location of authority—in God and in the human will, in the subjectivity of the narrator and in a signification which is outside the narrator and appeals to all human cultures—or rather, it is these contradictory locations of authority which insist on the inadequacy of any reading of the poem that looks for "Milton's concern" as a guide to its possible meanings. And among these possible meanings is the limits of what can be said about authority in a period when authority is in crisis.

When the institution of literary criticism in Britain invokes history, whether as world picture or as long-lost organic community, it is ultimately in order to suppress it, by showing that *in essence* things are as they have always been. The function of scholarship, as of conventional criticism, is finally to reinstate the continuity of felt life which the ignorance of a trivialising society obscures. No history: no politics. Because if there has never been change at a fundamental level, there are no rational grounds for commitment to change. No politics—or rather, no overt politics, since there is, of course, no political neutral-ity in the assertion of an unchanging essential human nature.

The radical theoretical work of the last twenty years has not always confronted the suppression of history and politics in literary criticism. Structuralism, widely regarded, when it began to appear in Britain in the sixties and early seventies, as the beginning of the end of civilization as we know it, quite failed to challenge the institution on this central issue. Saussure's *Course in General Linguistics* is a remarkably plural text. Insofar as its readers confined themselves to its discovery of an opposition which precisely replicated the classic liberal opposition between the individual and society, structuralism offered no threat to the equilibrium of the free West. Fired by the concept of the difference between *langue* and *parole,* which permitted utterance within the permutations already authorized by the language-system, the structuralists set off in quest of similar timeless enabling systems in other spheres, the form of all societies, the pattern of all narrative, the key to all mythologies. It was the signifying system itself which was held to lay down, long before the drama of history was inscribed in it, the elementary structures of culture and of subjectivity (Lacan, 1977, p. 148). Structuralism thus proclaimed Eternal Man and the suppression of history with a new and resounding authority. Ironically, Saussure's analysis of language as a system of differences was invoked to initiate the elimination of all difference.

But it was also Saussure's work, in conjunction with the Marxist analysis of ideology, which permitted Roland Barthes on behalf of anarchism to identify Eternal Man as the product and pivot of bourgeois mythology (Barthes, 1972, p. 140), and subsequently to repudiate the structuralist equalization of all narrative "under the scrutiny of an indifferent science" (Barthes, 1975, p. 3). This was possible because one of the effects of the *Course in General Linguistics* was to relativise meaning by detaching it from the world outside language. Insofar as the value of a specific sign differs from one language to another, and insofar as language is the condition of meaning and thought, meaning and thought differ from one language to another, one culture to another. As linguistic habits alter, cultures are transformed. Difference, history, change reappear.

They disappear again, however, in American deconstructionism, which nails its colours to the free play of the eternal signifier. Here all writing and all speech is fiction in a timeless present without presence, and the subject celebrates its own non-being in an infinite space where there is no room for politics. Deconstructionism has nothing to say about the relationship between literature and history, or the political implications of either. Nothing explicit, that is.

What is at stake here is the elision of the signified. Saussure distinguished three terms of orders—the signifier (the sound or written image), the signified (the meaning) and the referent (the thing in the world). A certain elusiveness in Saussure's theory concerning the relationship between meaning and *intention* prompted Derrida's deconstruction of Saussure's phono-centrism, and in the interests of contesting the notion of a pure, conceptual intelligibility, a "truth in the soul" which precedes the signifier (Derrida, 1976, p. 15), Derrida in that context treats as suspect, as he puts it, the difference between signifier and signified (p. 14). The order of the signified is subsumed under "presence," which is understood indiscriminately as concept, intention or referent, so that meaning, being and truth are collapsed together. Elsewhere Derrida's notion of *différence* does not eliminate the possibility of signification. Meaning exists, neither as being nor as truth, but as linguistic difference, textually produced, contextually deferred (Derrida, 1973, pp. 129–60). But the opening pages of *Grammatology* invite vulgar deconstructionists to take it that there is no such thing as meaning, and in consequence, since meaningless language is literally unthinkable, that words mean whatever you want them to mean. This *Looking-Glass* reasoning leads at best to an anarchic scepticism, the celebration of undecidability as an end in itself, and at worst to the reinstatement of the mirror phase, where the critic-subject at play rejoices in its own linguistic plenitude. In the constant and repeated assertion of the evaporation of meaning there is no place to analyse the contest for meaning, and therefore no politics, and there is no possibility of tracing changes of meaning, the sliding of the signified, in history.

It was at this point in the debate that political post-structuralism began to turn more insistently to the work of Foucault. (It was also, perhaps, at this point in the debate that Foucault's own work became more explicitly political.) Foucault goes beyond Derridean scepticism to the extent that he identifies the relationship between meaning (or discourse-as-knowledge) and power. Conceding that language does not map the world, but distinguishing signified from referent

and intention, knowledge from what is true (because guaranteed by being or by things), Foucault reinstates politics in a post-structuralist world which, despite the heroic efforts of Althusser, could not support the concept of science. *I, Pierre Rivière . . .* documents Pierre Rivière's murder in 1835 of his mother, his sister and his brother. It is made clear that the meaning of Pierre's memoir exceeds any single reading of it, since reading always takes place from a position and on behalf of a position. The question is not, "what is the *truth* of Pierre Rivière's behaviour?," "was he *really* mad?" but "from what positions, inscribed in what knowledge, did the contest between the legal and the medical professions for control of Pierre Rivière take place?" And in addition, "what possibilities of a reading of these documents are available now which were not available in the 1830s?" From the perspective of the present, the records of Pierre Rivière's act of unauthorized resistance can be read as a part of the history of the present, because they demonstrate the social and discursive construction of a deviant and at the same time permit him to speak. The "humanitarian" practice which confines the criminally insane for life silences them even more effectively than execution, since whatever they say is rendered inaudible, "mad."

Foucault's work politicizes the polyphony of the signified. The plurality of meaning is not exclusively a matter of infinite play, as recent history demonstrates. Meanings produce practices and generate behaviour. It was explicitly in a contest for the meaning of "aggression"—as colonialism, as theft, or as violence—that British and Argentine soldiers killed and mutilated each other in the South Atlantic, both sides using might to establish that might is not right. In this as in all other just wars it was evident that the letter kills. While the American deconstructionists play, Reagan is preparing to reduce us all to radioactive rubble to preserve our freedom. The control of meanings—of freedom, democracy, the American way of life—the control of these meanings is political power, but it is a mistake to suppose that the abolition of the signified is the abolition of power. On the contrary, deconstructionalism collaborates with the operations of meaning-as-power precisely insofar as it protests that there is no such thing.

Foucault's work brings together two of my three terms, history and politics, in its analysis of the ways in which power produces new knowledges. It is a history of ideas in which ideas are understood as generating practices, a history of discourses in which discourses define and are reproduced in institutions. It offers a challenge to classical Marxist politics to the extent that it refuses to find a central and determining locus of power in the mode of production, and a challenge to empiricist history in its refusal to treat documents as transparent. In a sense we needed both challenges. Whatever the inadequacies of Althusserian Marxism, it was impossible for a post-structuralist politics subsequently to retreat from the decentring concept of overdetermination. To attribute a relative autonomy to ideology was to open up the possibility of a history of the forms in which people become conscious of their differences and begin to fight them out. These forms are precisely the classical superstructural forms of law, metaphysics, aesthetics, and so on, but with the addition of those areas where struggle has become increasingly pressing in the twentieth century—sexuality, the family, subjectivity. The theory of relative autonomy, however vulnerable in itself, permitted attention within Marxism to these areas as sites of struggle.

But if post-structural politics implied the dispersal of history into new areas, it also implied a historiography which was both more and less than the transcription of lost experience. To take a single example of the problem, Lawrence Stone's book, *The Family, Sex and Marriage in England, 1500–1800*, published in 1977, is extremely welcome insofar as it tackles precisely one of those areas which politics (specifically, in this instance, feminist politics) had brought to prominence. But Stone's vocabulary of "evidence," "sources," "documents" and "sampling" define the historian's quarry, however elusive, as something anterior to textuality, revealed through its expression in the mass of diaries, memoirs, autobiographies and letters cited. History is seen as the recovered presence of pure, extra-discursive, representative experience, "how it (usually) felt." What Stone produces in consequence is a smooth, homogeneous evolution, with overlapping strata for enhanced verisimilitude, from the open lineage family of the late middle ages to the affective nuclear family in the seventeenth and eighteenth centuries. But the affective nuclear family begins to be glimpsed in discourse in the mid-sixteenth century, and there is evidence (if evidence is what is at stake) that this concept of a private realm, in which power is exercised invisibly for the public good, defines itself in this period in opposition to a control of marriage exercised directly but precariously by the sovereign as head of the church. What Stone's quest for the representative experience behind the documents eliminates is the *politics* of the history of the family, precisely the issue which put it on the feminist map, the contest for power, which is also a contest for meaning in its materiality, the struggle about the meaning and practice of family life.

Representative experience is understood to be whatever a lot of people said they felt, and it is held to be the origin of, and to issue in, representative behaviour. This notion of the "fit" between documented feelings and recorded behaviour relegates to the margins of history any feelings or behaviour which were not dominant. Struggle thus becomes marginal, always the province, except in periods of general struggle, of the idiosyncratic few. But more important, modes of resistance to what was dominant are ignored if they could not be formulated in so many words, were not allowed a voice, were not experienced as resistance or can be defined as deviant. Stone makes no space, for instance, for a consideration of witchcraft as a practice of offering women a form of power which was forbidden precisely by orthodox concepts of the family.

The point is worth dwelling on because Stone is by no means an isolated case. Even among those radical historians for whom struggle is heroic, if still idiosyncratic, the quest for experience and the belief that documents are ultimately transparent remain common. But documents do not merely transcribe experience: to the extent that they inevitably come from a context where power is at stake, they are worth analysis not as access to something beyond them, not as evidence of how it felt, but as themselves locations of power and resistance to power.

A post-structuralist history needs to re-examine Stone's mass of documents (and perhaps others), and to address to them a different series of questions. These include the following (borrowed, in modified form, from Foucault):

What are the modes and conditions of these texts?

Where do they come from; who controls them; on behalf of whom?

What possible subject positions are inscribed in them?

What meanings and what contests for meaning do they display?

(cf. Foucault, 1977, p. 138)

The answers to these questions give us a different history of the family, sex and marriage. This is the history not of an irrecoverable experience, but of meanings, of the signified in its plurality, not the referent in its singular but imaginary presence. It is, therefore, a history of struggle and, in consequence, a political history.

Such a history is not offered as objective, authoritative, neutral or true. It is not outside history itself, or outside the present. On the contrary, it is part of history, part of the present. It is irreducibly textual, offering no place outside discourse from which to interpret or judge. It is explicitly partial, from a position and on behalf of a position. It is not culturally relative in so far as relativism is determinist and therefore a-political: "I think like this because my society thinks like this." But its effect is to relativise the present, to locate the present in history and in process.

Foucault's work gives us a methodology for producing our own history and politics, a history which is simultaneously a politics, but it has little to say about my third term, literature. Literature is not a knowledge. Literary criticism is a knowledge, produced in and reproducing an institution. Some of the most important and radical work of the last decade has been devoted to analysis of the institution of literary criticism, challenging its assumptions, exposing its ideological implications and relativising its claims to universality and timelessness.[2] One of the central concerns of this work has been the interrogation of the idea of literature itself as "the central coordinating concept of the discourse of literary criticism, supplying the point of reference to which relationships of difference and similarity within the field of writing are articulated" (Bennett, 1981, p. 139). Tony Bennett's point here is an important one. "Literature" signifies as an element in a system of differences. It is that which is *not* minor, popular, ephemeral or trivial, as well as that which is not medicine, economics, history or, of course, politics. "Literature" designates a value and a category.

That conjunction—of value and category—issues in English departments as we know them, and generates, I have argued, the continuous production and reproduction of hierarchies of subjectivity (Belsey, 1982). We need, therefore, as Tony Bennett argues, to call into question both the category—the autonomy of literary studies—and the value—Literature as distinct from its residue, popular fiction. We need to

replace the quest for value by an "analysis of the social contestation of value" (Bennett, 1981, p. 143).

Work on the institution of literary criticism is centrally concerned with the reception of literary texts, with the text as site of the range of possible meanings that may be produced during the course of its history, and with the knowledges inscribed in both dominant and radical discourses. Its importance seems to me to be established beyond question. Here is a field of operations which brings together literature, history and politics in crucial ways, undermining the power of the institution and challenging the category of Literature.

The effect of this project, in other words, is to de-centre literary criticism, to displace "the text," the "primary material," from its authoritative position at the heart of the syllabus, to dislodge the belief in the close reading of the text as the critic's essential and indispensable skill. Quite whether we can afford to dispose of the literary text altogether is not usually made clear, but it seems implicit in the project that we can do without it for most of the time. What is to be read closely is criticism, official reports on the teaching of English, examination papers, and all the other discursive displays of institutional power.

But before we throw out the Arden Shakespeares and the Penguin English Library (in order to make a space for the Critical Heritage and the Newbolt Report), I want to propose a way of recycling the texts, on the grounds that work on the institution is not the only way of bringing together literature, history and politics, of undermining literary studies as currently constituted, or of challenging the category of Literature. I want to argue in favour of at least one additional way of doing all those things (in the hope of forestalling one of those fierce bouts of either-orism which periodically dissipate the energies of the left).

Literature (or fiction: the fields defined by the two words are not necessarily co-extensive: what about Bacon's *Essays*, Donne's sermons, the "Epistle to Dr. Arbuthnot," *The Prelude*? But perhaps we read these texts as fiction now, so the term will perhaps serve to modify the ideological implications of Literature)—literature or fiction is not a knowledge, but it is not only a site where knowledge is produced. It is also the location of a range of knowledges. In this sense the text always exceeds the history of its reception. While on the one hand meaning is never single, eternally inscribed in the words on the page, on the other hand readings do not spring unilaterally out of the subjectivities (or the ideologies) of readers. The text is not an empty space, filled with meaning from outside itself, any more than it is the transcription of an authorial intention, filled with meaning from outside language. As a signifying practice, writing always offers raw material for the production of meanings, the signified in its plurality, on the understanding, of course, that the signified is distinct from the intention of the author (pure concept) or the referent (a world already constituted and re-presented).

The intertextual relations of the text are never purely literary. Fiction draws not only on other fiction but on the knowledges of its period, discourses in circulation which are themselves sites of power and the contest for power. In the case of *Macbeth*, for instance, the Victorian fable of vaulting ambition and its attendant remorse and punishment is also a repository of Reformation Christianity, morbid, demonic, apocalyptic; of the Jacobean law of sovereignty and succession; of Renaissance medicine; and of Stuart history. Equally, since narrative fiction depends on impediments (where there are no obstacles to be overcome there's no story), *Macbeth* depends on resistance to those knowledges, on what refuses or escapes them: on witchcraft seen as a knowledge which repudiates Christian knowledge, on regicide, madness, suicide, as evasions of a control which is thereby shown to be precarious. A political and historical reading of *Macbeth* might analyze these discourses, not in the manner of Tillyard, as a means of a deeper understanding of the text, and at the same time a lost golden world where nature itself rose up to punish resistance to the existing order, but on the contrary, as a way of encountering the discourses themselves in their uncertainty, their instability, their relativity.

Narrative necessarily depends on the establishment within the story of fictional forms of control and resistance to control, norms and the repudiation of norms. And in the period to which English departments are centrally committed, from the Renaissance to the present, the criterion of verisimilitude, towards or against which fiction has consistently pressed, has necessitated that these concepts of control and normality be intelligible outside fiction itself. Thus, sovereignty, the family, subjectivity are defined and redefined in narrative fiction, problematised and reproblematised. *Macbeth* (again) offers, in the scene with Lady Macduff, an early instance of the emerging concept of the affective nuclear family—a

private realm of domestic harmony shown as vulnerable to crisis in a public and political world which is beginning to be perceived as distinct from it. It presents, on the other hand, the fragmentation of the subject, Macbeth, under the pressure of a crisis in which the personal and the political are still perceived as continuous.

In *Critical Practice* I tried to distinguish between three kinds of texts, which I identified as declarative, imperative and interrogative. The declarative text imparts "knowledge" (fictional or not) to the reader, the imperative text (propaganda) exhorts, instructs or orders the reader, and the interrogative text poses questions by enlisting the reader in contradiction (Belsey, 1980, pp. 90 ff.). It now seems to me that this classification may have been excessively formalistic, implying that texts can unilaterally determine their reception by the reader. As we know, a reading practice which actively seeks out contradiction can *produce* as interrogative a text which has conventionally been read as declarative. Nonetheless, the categories may be useful if they enable us to attribute a certain kind of specificity to literary/fictional texts. The danger of formalism is to be set against the structuralist danger of collapsing all difference. That there is a formal indeterminacy does not mean that we can never speak of form, any more than the polyphony of "freedom" prevents us from condemning police states. In the period of *Macbeth* many of the available written texts are imperative—sermons, tracts, pamphlets, marked as referring to a given external reality, and offering the reader a position of alignment with one set of values and practices and opposition to others (divorce, for instance, or patriarchal sovereignty). Fictional (declarative or interrogative) texts, by contrast, marked as alluding only indirectly to "reality," informing without directly exhorting, offer a space for the problematisation of the knowledges they invoke in ways which imperative texts cannot risk.[3] Radically contradictory definitions of marriage in a divorce pamphlet inevitably reduce its propaganda-value: plays, on the contrary, can problematise marriage without affecting the coherence of the story.

To say this is not, I hope, to privilege literature (and certainly not Literature) but only to allow it a certain specificity which identifies its use-value in the construction of the history of the present. A vest is not a sock, but it is not in consequence obvious that one is better than the other. On the basis of this specificity which is neither privilege nor autonomy, I want to urge that lyric poetry, read as fiction, is also worth recycling. Sexuality and subjectivity are the twin themes of the lyric, and since any text longer than, say, an imagist poem, moves towards argument or narrative, and therefore toward crisis, similar definitions and problematisations of these areas of our history offer themselves for analysis here. Sexuality, gender, the subject are not fixed but slide in history, and this sliding is available to an analysis which repudiates both the quarry of an empiricist history (experience, the world) and the quarry of conventional criticism (consciousness, the author).

The quest is for, say, the subject in its meanings. The word, "I," the fixed centre of liberal humanism, may always *designate* the speaker, but it *means* something new in the late sixteenth century, and something new again in the early nineteenth century. Equally, sexuality is not given but socially produced. We don't have access to the eighteenth-century experience of sexuality, but we can analyse the contest in that period for its meaning. It may be the case that the size of household in Britain has not changed much since the middle ages (Laslett, 1977), but the meaning of the family, institutionally and in practice, has changed fundamentally—and can therefore change again. This kind of analysis is a stake through the heart of Eternal Man, and the world of practice as well as theory is consequently laid open to effective radical political action.

The reading practice implied by this enterprise—the production of a political history from the raw material of literary texts—is a result of all that post-structuralism has urged about meaning: its often marginal location, its disunity and discontinuity, as well as its plurality. In this way the text reappears, but not as it "really is," or "really was." On the contrary, this is the text as it never was, though it was never anything else—dispersed, fragmented, produced, politicized. The text is no longer the centre of a self-contained exercise called literary criticism. It is one of the places to begin to assemble the political history of the present.

I say "to begin" because it is immediately apparent that such a history is not bounded by the boundaries of Literature or literature. Literary value becomes irrelevant: political assassination is problematised in Pickering's play, *Horestes* (1567) as well as in *Hamlet*. Equally, the subject is a legal and a psychoanalytic category just as much as a literary one; the family is

defined by medical and religious discourses as well as by classic realist texts. And so the autonomy of literature begins to dissolve, its boundaries to waver as the enterprise unfolds. The text does not disappear, though the canon does; and fiction is put to work for substantial political ends which replace the mysterious objectives of aesthetic satisfaction and moral enrichment.

Two projects, related but distinct, immediately present themselves. The first is the synchronic analysis of a historical moment, starting possibly but not inevitably from literary texts. This has perhaps been the project of the Essex conferences, focussed on a series of crises (1848, 1936, 1642, 1789), and subtitled, "the Sociology of Literature." The Essex volumes have made available some excellent work, but if the projected archaeology did not materialise in its entirety, there are reasons for this which have little to do with the value or the practicality of the project itself. I suspect that one of these reasons was that the project was not shared by all participants. (There is no reason why it should have been: it makes no exclusive claims.) Ideally the project is a collective one, but it's not easy to work collectively if you meet only once a year. It's also a long-term project involving deliberate and patient analysis, and it may be that the conference paper is not an ideal place for its presentation and discussion.

But if the Essex conferences have not achieved everything that was hoped for, they have produced work which in various ways suggests important directions for the future.[4] And in addition, there is a second and analogous project—what Foucault sporadically calls a genealogy because it traces change without invoking a single point of origin (Foucault, 1977, pp. 139–64, etc.). This is a diachronic analysis of specific discontinuities—in sovereignty, gender, the subject, for instance. And where else should we begin this analysis but by looking at fiction, poetry, autobiography? If we start with the texts on the syllabus—because they are available and for no other very specific reason—we shall not end with them, because the enquiry inevitably transgresses the boundaries of the existing discipline.

The proposal is to reverse the Leavisian enterprise of constructing (inventing) a lost organic world of unfallen orality, undissociated sensibility and uncontested order. In fact, in so far as it concerns the sixteenth and seventeenth centuries, the kind of archaeology I have in mind uncovers a world of violence, disorder and fragmentation. The history of the present is not a history of a fall from grace but of the transformations of power and resistances to power. The claim is not that such a history, or such a reading of literary texts, is more accurate, but only that it is more radical. No less partial, it produces the past not in order to present an ideal of hierarchy, but to relativise the present, to demonstrate that since change has occurred in those areas which seem most intimate and most inevitable, change in those areas is possible for us.

According to Foucault, who invents the verb "to fiction" in order to undermine his own use of the word "truth," "one 'fictions' a history starting from a political reality that renders it true, one 'fictions' a politics that doesn't as yet exist starting from a historical truth" (Foucault, 1979, pp. 74–75). I want to add this: the literary institution has "fictioned" a criticism which uncritically protests its own truth; we must instead "fiction" a literature which renders up our true history in the interests of a politics of change.

Notes

1. I am grateful for the comments of Francis Barker and Chris Weedon on an earlier draft of this essay.
2. See for example the work of Renée Balibar; Francis Mulhern, *The Moment of Scrutiny* (London: NLB, 1979); Tony Bennett, *Formalism and Marxism* (London: Methuen, 1979); Peter Widdowson ed., *Re-Reading English* (London: Methuen, 1982); the LTP (Literature Teaching Politics) conferences and journal.
3. I am indebted for this idea to Simon Barker.
4. See particularly in the *1642* volume (ed. Francis Barker *et al.*) essays by Francis Barker, Peter Hulme, Christine Berg and Philippa Berry.

Bibliography

Barker, Francis *et al.* 1642: *Literature and Power in the Seventeenth Century.* University of Essex, 1981.

Barthes, Roland. *Mythologies.* Annette Lavers, London: Cape, 1972.

Barthes, Roland. *S/Z.* Richard Miller, London: Cape, 1975.

Belsey, Catherine. *Critical Practice.* London: Methuen, 1980.

Belsey, Catherine. "Re-Reading the Great Tradition." *Re-Reading English.* Peter Widdowson, ed. London: Methuen, 1982, pp. 121–35.

Bennett, Tony. "Marxism and Popular Fiction." *Literature and History,* VII. 1981, pp. 138–65.

Davies, Tony. "Common Sense and Critical Practice: Teaching Literature." *Re-Reading English.* Peter Widdowson, ed. London: Methuen, 1982, pp. 32–43.

Derrida, Jacques. *Speech and Phenomena.* David B. Allison, Evanston, Ill.: Northwestern U.P., 1973.

Derrida, Jacques. *Of Grammatology.* Gayatri Chakravorty Spivak, Baltimore and London: Johns Hopkins U.P., 1976.

Foucault, Michel. *Language, Counter-Memory, Practice.* Donald Bouchard, ed. Oxford: Blackwell, 1977.

Foucault, Michel, ed. *I, Pierre Rivière. . . .* Harmondsworth: Penguin, 1978.

Foucault, Michel. *Power, Truth, Strategy.* Meaghan Morris and Paul Patton, eds. Sydney: Feral Publications, 1979.

Lacan, Jacques. *Ecrits.* Alan Sheridan, London: Tavistock, 1977.

Laslett, Peter. *Family Life and Illicit Love in Earlier Generations.* Cambridge: Cambridge U.P., 1977.

Stone, Lawrence. *The Family, Sex and Marriage in England, 1500–1800.* London: Weidenfeld and Nicolson, 1977.

Culture

Stephen Greenblatt

*Stephen Greenblatt is a leading figure in the "New His-
toricism." But he prefers to call his own work "cultural
poetics," and we have seen others in this context who call
themselves cultural historians, cultural materialists, and
cultural critics. Why, asks Greenblatt, should the term
"culture" be useful to students of literature? Characteristically, he immediately transforms the question: "how can
we get the concept of culture to do more work for us?"
Reading culture in Foucault's terms as a system of constraints and freedoms, Greenblatt proposes a set of "cultural questions" we could ask about a literary work. The
answers will be "historical," but they will require a poststructural history quite different from the author-centered
history explored in the first chapter. Greenblatt's questions
will certainly lead us to investigate what Eagleton calls
the "ideology" of an age, though not necessarily with all
of Eagleton's Marxist assumptions. And they will also
get us into some of the territory that Catherine Belsey
maps out. At first glance, though, Greenblatt's program
looks less radical than Belsey's. Greenblatt stresses the
importance of formal analysis, talks unabashedly about
"great literature," and seems to argue that we should
take the past on its, rather than on our, terms. But he
also points out that cultural poetics will quickly dissolve
the formalist's distinction between what's "within" and
what's "outside" the text and will just as quickly dissolve the distinction between "high" and "popular" culture. Further, though he admits his own writings may
have given the impression that art simply reinforces the
boundaries of its culture, he recognizes that art sometimes
challenges these boundaries, becoming thereby a "trans-
gressive force" that may open the way to intervention in
our own cultural scene. "If it is the task of cultural criticism to decipher the power of Prospero, it is equally its*

Reprinted by permission from Frank Lentricchia and
Thomas McLaughlin, eds. *Critical Terms for Literary Study.*
Chicago: University of Chicago Press, 1995: 225–232. Copy-
right © 1995 by the University of Chicago Press.

task to hear the accents of Caliban." Having explained how a concept of culture can be useful to students of literature, Greenblatt reminds us that the initial question was backward, noting that "in a liberal education broadly conceived, it is literary study that is the servant of cultural education."

The term "culture" has not always been used in literary studies, and indeed the very concept denoted by the term is fairly recent. "Culture or Civilization," wrote the influential anthropologist Edward B. Tylor in 1871, "taken in its wide ethnographic sense, is that complex whole which includes knowledge, belief, art, morals, law, custom, and any other capabilities and habits acquired by man as a member of society." Why should such a concept be useful to students of literature?

The answer may be that it is not. After all, the term as Tylor uses it is almost impossibly vague and encompassing, and the few things that seem excluded from it are almost immediately reincorporated in the actual use of the word. Hence we may think with a certain relief that at least "culture" does not refer to material objects — tables, or gold, or grain, or spinning wheels — but of course those objects, as used by men and women, are close to the center of any particular society, and we may accordingly speak of such a society's "material culture." Like "ideology" (to which, as a concept, it is closely allied), "culture" is a term that is repeatedly used without meaning much of anything at all, a vague gesture toward a dimly perceived ethos: aristocratic culture, youth culture, human culture. There is nothing especially wrong with such gestures — without them we wouldn't ordinarily be able to get through three consecutive sentences — but they are scarcely the backbone of an innovative critical practice.

How can we get the concept of culture to do more work for us? We might begin by reflecting on the fact that the concept gestures toward what appear to be opposite things: *constraint* and *mobility*. The ensemble of beliefs and practices that form a given culture function as a pervasive technology of control, a set of limits within which social behavior must be contained, a repertoire of models to which individuals must conform. The limits need not be narrow — in certain societies, such as that of the United States, they can seem quite vast — but they are not infinite, and the consequences for straying beyond them can be severe. The most effective disciplinary techniques

practiced against those who stray beyond the limits of a given culture are probably not the spectacular punishments reserved for serious offenders — exile, imprisonment in an insane asylum, penal servitude, or execution — but seemingly innocuous responses: a condescending smile, laughter poised between the genial and the sarcastic, a small dose of indulgent pity laced with contempt, cool silence. And we should add that a culture's boundaries are enforced more positively as well: through the system of rewards that range again from the spectacular (grand public honors, glittering prizes) to the apparently modest (a gaze of admiration, a respectful nod, a few words of gratitude).

Here we can make our first tentative move toward the use of culture for the study of literature, for Western literature over a very long period of time has been one of the great institutions for the enforcement of cultural boundaries through praise and blame. This is most obvious in the kinds of literature that are explicitly engaged in attack and celebration: satire and panegyric. Works in these genres often seem immensely important when they first appear, but their power begins quickly to fade when the individuals to whom the works refer begin to fade, and the evaporation of literary power continues when the models and limits that the works articulated and enforced have themselves substantially changed. The footnotes in modern editions of these works can give us the names and dates that have been lost, but they cannot in themselves enable us to recover a sense of the stakes that once gave readers pleasure and pain. An awareness of culture as a complex whole can help us to recover that sense by leading us to reconstruct the boundaries upon whose existence the works were predicated.

We can begin to do so simply by a heightened attention to the beliefs and practices implicitly enforced by particular literary acts of praising or blaming. That is, we can ask ourselves a set of cultural questions about the work before us:

What kinds of behavior, what models of practice, does this work seem to enforce?

Why might readers at a particular time and place find this work compelling?

Are there differences between my values and the values implicit in the work I am reading?

Upon what social understandings does the work depend?

Whose freedom of thought or movement might be constrained implicitly or explicitly by this work?

What are the larger social structures with which these particular acts of praise or blame might be connected?

Such questions heighten our attention to features of the literary work that we might not have noticed, and, above all, to connections among elements within the work. Eventually, a full cultural analysis will need to push beyond the boundaries of the text, to establish links between the text and values, institutions, and practices elsewhere in the culture. But these links cannot be a substitute for close reading. Cultural analysis has much to learn from scrupulous formal analysis of literary texts because those texts are not merely cultural by virtue of reference to the world beyond themselves; they are cultural by virtue of social values and contexts that they have themselves successfully absorbed. The world is full of texts, most of which are virtually incomprehensible when they are removed from their immediate surroundings. To recover the meaning of such texts, to make any sense of them at all, we need to reconstruct the situation in which they were produced. Works of art by contrast contain directly or by implication much of this situation within themselves, and it is this sustained absorption that enables many literary works to survive the collapse of the conditions that led to their production.

Cultural analysis then is not by definition an extrinsic analysis, as opposed to an internal formal analysis of works of art. At the same time, cultural analysis must be opposed on principle to the rigid distinction between that which is within a text and that which lies outside. It is necessary to use whatever is available to construct a vision of the "complex whole" to which Tylor referred. And if an exploration of a particular culture will lead to a heightened understanding of a work of literature produced within that culture, so too a careful reading of a work of literature will lead to a heightened understanding of the culture within which it was produced. The organization of this volume makes it appear that the analysis of culture is the servant of literary study, but in a liberal education broadly conceived it is literary study that is the servant of cultural understanding.

I will return to the question of extrinsic as opposed to intrinsic analysis, but first we must continue to pursue the idea of culture as a system of constraints.

The functioning of such a system is obvious in poems like Pope's "Epistle to Doctor Arbuthnot" or Marvell's "Horatian Ode" on Cromwell, works that undertake to excoriate dullness as embodied in certain hated individuals and celebrate civic or military virtue as embodied in certain admired individuals. Indeed culture here is close to its earlier sense of "cultivation"—the internalization and practice of a code of manners. And this sense extends well beyond the limits of satire and panegyric, particularly for those periods in which manners were a crucial sign of status difference.

Consider, for example, Shakespeare's *As You Like It*, where Orlando's bitter complaint is not that he has been excluded from his patrimony—Orlando accepts the custom of primogeniture by which his brother, as the eldest son, inherits virtually all the family property—but rather that he is being prevented from learning the manners of his class: "My father charged you in his will to give me a good education: you have train'd me like a peasant, obscuring and hiding from me all gentleman-like qualities." Shakespeare characteristically suggests that Orlando has within him an innate gentility that enables him to rise naturally above his boorish upbringing, but he equally characteristically suggests that Orlando's gentility needs to be shaped and brought to fruition through a series of difficult trials. When in the Forest of Arden the young man roughly demands food for his aged servant Adam, he receives a lesson in courtesy: "Your gentleness shall force / More than your force moves us to gentleness." The lesson has a special authority conferred upon it by the fact that it is delivered by the exiled Duke, the figure at the pinnacle of the play's social order. But the entire world of *As You Like It* is engaged in articulating cultural codes of behavior, from the elaborate, ironic training in courtship presided over by Rosalind to the humble but dignified social order by which the shepherds live. Even the simple country wench Audrey receives a lesson in manners from the sophisticated clown Touchstone: "bear your body more seeming, Audrey." This instruction in the management of the body, played no doubt for comic effect, is an enactment in miniature of a process of acculturation occurring everywhere in the play, and occurring most powerfully perhaps on an almost subliminal level, such as the distance we automatically keep from others or the way we position our legs when we sit down. Shakespeare wittily parodies this process—for example, in Touchstone's elaborate rule-book for insults—but he also participates in it, for even as his plays represent characters engaged in negotiating the boundaries of their culture, the plays also help to establish and maintain those boundaries for their audiences.

Art is an important agent then in the transmission of culture. It is one of the ways in which the roles by which men and women are expected to pattern their lives are communicated and passed from generation to generation. Certain artists have been highly self-conscious about this function. The purpose of his vast romance epic, *The Faerie Queene,* writes the Renaissance poet Edmund Spenser, is "to fashion a gentleman or noble person in virtuous and gentle discipline." The depth of our understanding of such a project, extended over a complex plot involving hundreds of allegorical figures, depends upon the extent of our grasp of Spenser's entire culture, from its nuanced Aristotelian conception of moral hierarchies to its apocalyptic fantasies, from exquisite refinement at court to colonial violence in Ireland. Most precisely, we need to grasp the way in which this culture of mixed motives and conflicting desires seemed to Spenser to generate an interlocking series of models, a moral order, a set of ethical constraints ranged against the threat of anarchy, rebellion, and chaos.

To speak of *The Faerie Queene* only in terms of the constraints imposed by culture is obviously inadequate, since the poem itself, with its knights and ladies endlessly roaming an imaginary landscape, is so insistent upon mobility. We return to the paradox with which we started: if culture functions as a structure of limits, it also functions as the regulator and guarantor of movement. Indeed the limits are virtually meaningless without movement; it is only through improvisation, experiment, and exchange that cultural boundaries can be established. Obviously, among different cultures there will be a great diversity in the ratio between mobility and constraint. Some cultures dream of imposing an absolute order, a perfect stasis, but even these, if they are to reproduce themselves from one generation to the next, will have to commit themselves, however tentatively or unwillingly, to some minimal measure of movement; conversely, some cultures dream of an absolute mobility, a perfect freedom, but these too have always been compelled, in the interest of survival, to accept some limits.

What is set up, under wildly varying circumstances and with radically divergent consequences, is a structure of improvisation, a set of patterns that

have enough elasticity, enough scope of variation, to accommodate most of the participants in a given culture. A life that fails to conform at all, that violates absolutely all the available patterns, will have to be dealt with as an emergency—hence exiled, or killed, or declared a god. But most individuals are content to improvise, and, in the West at least, a great many works of art are centrally concerned with these improvisations. The novel has been particularly sensitive to the diverse ways in which individuals come to terms with the governing patterns of culture; works like Dickens's *Great Expectations* and Eliot's *Middlemarch* brilliantly explore the ironies and pain, as well as the inventiveness, of particular adjustments.

In representing this adjustment as a social, emotional, and intellectual education, these novels in effect thematize their own place in culture, for works of art are themselves educational tools. They do not merely passively reflect the prevailing ratio of mobility and constraint; they help to shape, articulate, and reproduce it through their own improvisatory intelligence. This means that, despite our romantic cult of originality, most artists are themselves gifted creators of variations upon received themes. Even those great writers whom we regard with special awe, and whom we celebrate for their refusal to parrot the clichés of their culture, tend to be particularly brilliant improvisers rather than absolute violaters or pure inventors. Thus Dickens crafted cunning adaptations of the melodramatic potboilers of his times; Shakespeare borrowed most of his plots, and many of his characters, from familiar tales or well-rehearsed historical narratives; and Spenser revised for his own culture stories first told, and told wonderfully, by the Italian poets Ariosto and Tasso.

Such borrowing is not evidence of imaginative parsimony, still less a symptom of creative exhaustion—I am using Dickens, Shakespeare, and Spenser precisely because they are among the most exuberant, generous, and creative literary imaginations in our language. It signals rather a further aspect of the cultural mobility to which I have already pointed. This mobility is not the expression of random motion but of *exchange.* A culture is a particular network of negotiations for the exchange of material goods, ideas, and—through institutions like enslavement, adoption, or marriage—people. Anthropologists are centrally concerned with a culture's kinship system—its conception of family relationships, its prohibitions of certain couplings, its marriage rules—and with its narratives—its myths, folktales, and sacred stories. The two concerns are linked, for a culture's narratives, like its kinship arrangements, are crucial indices of the prevailing codes governing human mobility and constraint. Great writers are precisely masters of these codes, specialists in cultural exchange. The works they create are structures for the accumulation, transformation, representation, and communication of social energies and practices.

In any culture there is a general symbolic economy made up of the myriad signs that excite human desire, fear, and aggression. Through their ability to construct resonant stories, their command of effective imagery, and above all their sensitivity to the greatest collective creation of culture—language—literary artists are skilled at manipulating this economy. They take symbolic materials from one zone of the culture and move them to another, augmenting their emotional force, altering their significance, linking them with other materials taken from a different zone, changing their place in a larger social design. Take, for example, Shakespeare's *King Lear*: the dramatist borrows an often-told pseudo-historical account of an ancient British king, associates with it his society's most severe anxieties about kinship relations on the one hand and civil strife on the other, infuses a measure of apocalyptic religious expectation mingled paradoxically with an acute skepticism, and returns these materials to his audience, transformed into what is perhaps the most intense experience of tragic pleasure ever created. A nuanced cultural analysis will be concerned with the various matrices from which Shakespeare derives his materials, and hence will be drawn outside the formal boundary of the play—toward the legal arrangements, for example, the elderly parents in the Renaissance made with their children, or toward child-rearing practices in the period, or toward political debates about when, if ever, disobeying a legitimate ruler was justified, or toward predictions of the imminent end of the world.

The current structure of liberal arts education often places obstacles in the way of such an analysis by separating the study of history from the study of literature, as if the two were entirely distinct enterprises, but historians have become increasingly sensitive to the symbolic dimensions of social practice, while literary critics have in recent years turned with growing interest to the social and historical dimensions of symbolic practice. Hence it is more possible, both in terms of individual courses and of overall programs of study, for students to reach toward a sense of the complex whole of a particular culture. But there is much to be done in the way of cultural analysis even without an integrated structure of courses, much that depends primarily on asking fresh questions about the possible social functions of works of art. Indeed even if one begins to achieve a sophisticated historical sense of the cultural materials out of which a literary text is constructed, it remains essential to study the ways in which these materials are formally put together and articulated in order to understand the cultural work that the text accomplishes.

For great works of art are not neutral relay stations in the circulation of cultural materials. Something happens to objects, beliefs, and practices when they are represented, reimagined, and performed in literary texts, something often unpredictable and disturbing. That "something" is the sign both of the power of art and of the embeddedness of culture in the contingencies of history. I have written at moments as if art always reinforces the dominant beliefs and social structures of its culture, as if culture is always harmonious rather than shifting and conflict-ridden, and as if there necessarily is a mutually affirmative relation between artistic production and the other modes of production and reproduction that make up a society. At times there is precisely such an easy and comfortable conjunction, but it is by no means necessary. The ability of artists to assemble and shape the forces of their culture in novel ways so that elements powerfully interact that rarely have commerce with one another in the general economy has the potential to unsettle this affirmative relation. Indeed in our own time most students of literature reserve their highest admiration for those works that situate themselves on the very edges of what can be said at a particular place and time, that batter against the boundaries of their own culture.

Near the end of his career Shakespeare decided to take advantage of his contemporaries' lively interest in New World exploration. His play *The Tempest* contains many details drawn from the writings of adventurers and colonists, details that are skillfully displaced onto a mysterious Mediterranean island and interwoven with echoes from Virgil's *Aeneid*, from other art forms such as the court masque and pastoral tragicomedy, and from the lore of white magic. The play reiterates the arguments that Europeans made about the legitimacy and civilizing force of their presence in the newly discovered lands; indeed it intensifies those arguments by conferring upon Prospero the power not only of a great prince who has the right to command the forces of this world but of a wizard who has the ability—the "Art" as the play terms it—to command supernatural forces as well. But the intensification has an oddly discordant effect: the magical power is clearly impressive but its legitimacy is less clear.

As magician Prospero resembles no one in the play so much as Sycorax, the hated witch who had preceded him as the island's ruler. The play, to be sure, does not endorse a challenge to Prospero's rule, any more than Shakespeare's culture ever encouraged challenges to legitimate monarchs. And yet out of the uneasy matrix formed by the skillful interweaving of cultural materials comes an odd, discordant voice, the voice of the "savage and deformed slave" Caliban:

> This island's mine, by Sycorax my mother,
> Which thou tak'st from me. When thou cam'st first
> Thou strok'st me, and made much of me; wouldst
>   give me
> Water with berries in't; and teach me how
> To name the bigger light, and how the less,
> That burn by day and night: and then I lov'd thee,
> And show'd thee all the qualities o'th'isle,
> The fresh springs, brine-pits, barren place and fertile:

> Curs'd be I that did so! All the charms
> Of Sycorax, toads, beetles, bats, light on you!
> For I am all the subjects that you have,
> Which first was mine own King: and here you sty me
> In this hard rock, whiles you do keep from me
> The rest o'th'island.

Caliban, of course, does not triumph: it would take different artists from different cultures—the postcolonial Caribbean and African cultures of our own times—to rewrite Shakespeare's play and make good on Caliban's claim. But even within the powerful constraints of Shakespeare's Jacobean culture, the artist's imaginative mobility enables him to display cracks in the glacial front of princely power and to record a voice, the voice of the displaced and oppressed, that is heard scarcely anywhere else in his own time. If it is the task of cultural criticism to decipher the power of Prospero, it is equally its task to hear the accents of Caliban.

Suggested Readings

Bakhtin, Mikhail. *Rabelais and His World.* 1968.
Benjamin, Walter. *Illuminations.* 1968.
Elias, Norbert. *The Civilizing Process.* 1978.
Geertz, Clifford. *The Interpretation of Cultures.* 1973.
Williams, Raymond. *Culture and Society, 1780–1950.* 1958.

Nymphs and Reapers Heavily Vanish: The Discursive Con-texts of *The Tempest*

Francis Barker and Peter Hulme

Francis Barker and Peter Hulme agree with Catherine Belsey's complaint that traditional literary history is usually less concerned with "history" than with the "eternal" which serves to abolish history, and like Belsey they offer to show "how the relationship between text and historical context can be more adequately formulated." To set the stage, they present a brief overview of some other approaches and, citing historians like Hirsch as well as intertextual and poststructural critics, they survey some of the same ground this book has covered. Like Garson and Dock in the essays that follow, they are concerned not only with the text at the moment of its creation, but also with the history of its interpretation, and they propose to "critique" this history, that is, not simply to identify the inadequacies of rival interpretations but "to explain why such readings come about and what ideological role they play." Defining "discourse" as "the field in and through which texts are produced" and hyphenating "con-texts" to deconstruct the text/context hierarchy, Barker and Hulme then set forth their thesis: "The ensemble of fictional and lived practices, which for convenience we will simply refer to here as 'English colonialism', provides The Tempest's dominant discursive con-texts." Their reading, then, accords with Stephen Greenblatt's advice to "hear the accents of Caliban," and it is in many ways a representative example of the many cultural materialist and postcolonial readings of The Tempest that have appeared in recent decades. In contesting such readings, both Russ McDonald and Paul Yachnin explicitly reference Barker and Hulme's essay, as they implicitly appeal to E. D. Hirsch's criterion: "it is necessary to establish that the context invoked is the most probable context." So the arguments continue.

Reprinted by permission from John Drakakis, ed. *Alternative Shakespeares*, Methuen & Co., 1985: 191–205.

I

No one who has witnessed the phenomenon of mid-summer tourism at Stratford-upon-Avon can fail to be aware of the way in which "Shakespeare" functions today in the construction of an English past: a past which is picturesque, familiar and untroubled. Modern scholarly editions of Shakespeare, amongst which the Arden is probably the most influential, have seemed to take their distance from such mythologising by carefully locating the plays against their historical background. Unfortunately such a move always serves, paradoxically, only to highlight in the foregrounded text preoccupations and values which turn out to be not historical at all, but eternal. History is thus recognised and abolished at one and the same time. One of the aims of this essay is to give a closer account of this mystificatory negotiation of "history," along with an examination of the ways in which the relationship between text and historical context can be more adequately formulated. Particular reference will be made to the way in which, in recent years, traditional notions of the historical sources of the text have been challenged by newer analyses which employ such terms as "intertextuality" and "discourse." To illustrate these, a brief exemplary reading will be offered of The Tempest. But to begin with, the new analyses themselves need setting in context.

II

The dominant approach within literary study has conceived of the text as autotelic, "an entity which always remains the same from one moment to the next";[1] in other words a text that is fixed in history and, at the same time, curiously free of historical limitation. The text is acknowledged as having been produced at a certain moment in history; but that history itself is reduced to being no more than a background from which the single and irreducible meaning of the text is isolated. The text is designated as the legitimate object of literary criticism, *over against* its contexts, whether they be arrived at through the literary-historical account of the development of particular traditions and genres or, as more frequently happens with Shakespeare's plays, the study of "sources." In either case the text has been separated from a surrounding ambit of other texts over which it is given a special pre-eminence.

In recent years, however, an alternative criticism, often referred to as "structuralist" and "poststruc-turalist," has sought to displace radically the primacy of the autotelic text by arguing that a text indeed "cannot be limited by or to . . . the originating moment of its production, anchored in the intentionality of its author."[2] For these kinds of criticism exclusive study of the moment of production is defined as narrowly "historicist" and replaced by attention to successive *inscriptions* of a text during the course of its history.[3] And the contextual background—which previously had served merely to highlight the profile of the individual text—gives way to the notion of *intertextuality,* according to which, in keeping with the Saussurean model of language, no text is intelligible except in its differential relations with other texts.[4]

The break with the moment of textual production can easily be presented as liberatory; certainly much work of importance has stemmed from the study of inscription. It has shown for example that texts can never simply be *encountered* but are, on the contrary, repeatedly constructed under definite conditions: The Tempest read by Sir Walter Raleigh in 1914 as the work of England's national poet is very different from The Tempest constructed with full textual apparatus by an editor critic such as Frank Kermode, and from the "same" text inscribed institutionally in that major formation of "English Literature" which is the school or university syllabus and its supporting practices of teaching and examination.[5]

If the study of the inscription and reinscription of texts has led to important work of historical description, it has also led to the formulation of a political strategy in respect of literary texts, expressed here by Tony Bennett when he calls for texts to be "articulated with new texts, socially and politically mobilised in different ways within different class practices."[6] This strategy also depends, therefore, on a form of intertextuality which identifies in all texts a potential for new linkages to be made and thus for new political meanings to be constructed. Rather than attempting to derive the text's significance from the moment of its production, this politicised intertextuality emphasises the present use to which texts can now be put. This approach undercuts itself, however, when, in the passage from historical description to contemporary rearticulation, it claims for itself a radicalism which it cannot then deliver. Despite speaking of texts as always being "installed in a field of struggle,"[7] it denies to itself the very possibility of combating the dominant orthodoxies. For if, as the logic of Bennett's argument implies, "the text" were wholly dissolved into an indeterminate miscellany of inscriptions, then how could any confrontation between different but contemporaneous inscriptions take place: what would be the ground of such a contestation?[8] While a genuine difficulty in theorising "the text" does exist, this should not lead inescapably to the point where the only option becomes the voluntaristic ascription to the text of meanings and articulations derived simply from one's own ideological preferences. This is a procedure only too vulnerable to pluralistic incorporation, a recipe for peaceful co-existence with the dominant readings, not for a contestation of those readings themselves. Struggle can only occur if two positions attempt to occupy the same space, to appropriate the "same" text; "alternative" readings condemn themselves to mere irrelevance.

Our criticism of this politicised intertextuality does not however seek to reinstate the autotelic text with its single fixed meaning. Texts are certainly not available for innocent, unhistorical readings. Any reading must be made *from* a particular position, but is not *reducible* to that position (not least because texts are not infinitely malleable or interpretable, but offer certain constraints and resistances to readings made of them). Rather, different readings struggle with each other on the site of the text, and all that can count, however provisionally, as knowledge of a text, is achieved through this discursive conflict. In other words, the onus on new readings, especially radical readings aware of their own theoretical and political positioning, should be to proceed by means of a *critique* of the dominant readings of a text.

We say critique rather than simply criticism, in reference to a powerful radical tradition which aims not merely to disagree with its rivals but to *read their readings:* that is, to identify their inadequacies and to explain why such readings come about and what ideological role they play.[9] Critique operates in a number of ways, adopting various strategies and lines of attack as it engages with the current ideological formations, but one aspect of its campaign is likely to have to remain constant. Capitalist societies have always presupposed the naturalness and universality of their own structures and modes of perception, so, at least for the foreseeable future, critiques will need to include an *historical* moment, countering capitalism's self-universalisation by reasserting the rootedness of texts in the contingency of history. It is on this particular ground that what we have been referring to as alternative criticism runs the risk of surrendering unnecessarily. As we emphasised earlier, the study of successive textual inscriptions continues to be genuinely important, but it must recognised that attention to such inscriptions is not logically dependent on the frequent presupposition that *all* accounts of the moment of production are either crudely historicist or have recourse to claims concerning authorial intentionality. A *properly* political intertextuality would attend to successive inscriptions without abandoning that no longer privileged but still crucially important *first* inscription of the text. After all, only by maintaining our right to make statements that we can call "historical" can we avoid handing over the very notion of history to those people who are only too willing to tell us "what really happened."

III

In order to speak of the Shakespearean text as an historical utterance, it is necessary to read it with and within series of *con-texts*.[10] These con-texts are the precondition of the plays' historical and political signification, although literary criticism has operated systematically to close down that signification by a continual process of occlusion. This may seem a strange thing to say about the most notoriously bloated of all critical enterprises, but in fact "Shakespeare" has been force-fed behind a high wall called Literature, built out of the dismantled pieces of other seventeenth-century discourses. Two particular examples of the occlusive process might be noted here. First, the process of occlusion is accomplished in the production of critical meaning, as is well illustrated by the case of Caliban. The occlusion of his political claims—one of the subjects of the present essay—is achieved by installing him at the very centre of the play, but only as the ground of a nature/art confrontation, itself of undoubted importance for the Renaissance, but here, in Kermode's account, totally without the historical contextualisation that would locate it among the early universalising forms of incipient bourgeois hegemony.[11] Secondly, source criticism, which might *seem* to militate against autotelic unity by relating the text in question to other texts, in fact only obscures such relationships. Kermode's paragraphs on "The New World" embody the hesitancy with which Shakespearean scholarship has approached the problem. Resemblances between the *language* of the Bermuda pamphlets and that of *The Tempest* are brought forward as evidence that Shakespeare "has these documents in mind" but, since this must remain "inference" rather than "fact," it can only have subsidiary importance, "of the greatest interest and usefulness," while clearly not "fundamental to [the play's] structure of ideas." Such "sources" are then reprinted in an appendix so "the reader may judge of the verbal parallels for himself," and the matter closed.[12]

And yet such closure proves premature since, strangely, source criticism comes to play an interestingly crucial role in Kermode's production of a site for *The Tempest*'s meaning. In general, the fullness of the play's unity needs protecting from con-textual contamination, so "sources" are kept at bay except for the odd verbal parallel. But occasionally, and on a strictly *singular* basis, that unity can only be protected by recourse to a notion of source as explanatory of a feature otherwise aberrant to that posited unity. One example of this would be Prospero's well-known irascibility, peculiarly at odds with Kermode's picture of a self-disciplined, reconciliatory white magician, and therefore to be "in the last analysis, explained by the fact that [he] descend[s] from a bad-tempered giant-magician."[13] Another would be Prospero's strange perturbation which brings the celebratory masque of Act IV to such an abrupt conclusion, in one reading (as we will demonstrate shortly) the most important scene in the play, but here explained as "a point at which an oddly pedantic concern for classical structure causes it to force its way through the surface of the play."[14] In other words the play's unity is constructed only by shearing off some of its "surface" complexities and explaining them away as relevant survivals or unfortunate academicisms.

Intertextuality, or con-textualisation, differs most importantly from source criticism when it establishes the necessity of reading *The Tempest* alongside congruent texts, irrespective of Shakespeare's putative knowledge of them, and when it holds that such congruency will become apparent from the constitution of discursive networks to be traced independently of authorial "intentionality."

IV

Essential to the historico-political critique which we are proposing here are the analytic strategies made possible by the concept of *discourse*. Intertextuality

has usefully directed attention to the relationship *between* texts: discourse moves us towards a clarification of just what kinds of relationship are involved.[15]

Traditionally *The Tempest* has been related to other texts by reference to a variety of notions: *source*, as we have seen, holds that Shakespeare was influenced by his reading of the Bermuda pamphlets. But the play is also described as belonging to the *genre* of pastoral romance and is seen as occupying a particular place in the *canon* of Shakespeare's works. Intertextuality has sought to displace work done within this earlier paradigm, but has itself been unable to break out of the practice of connecting text with text, of assuming that single texts are the ultimate objects of study and the principal units of meaning.[16] Discourse, on the other hand, refers to the *field* in and through which texts are produced. As a concept wider than "text" but narrower than language itself (Saussure's *langue*), it operates at the level of the enablement of texts. It is thus not an easy concept to grasp because discourses are never simply observable but only approachable through their effects just as, in a similar way, grammar can be said to be *at work* in particular sentences (even those that are ungrammatical), governing their construction but never fully present "in" them. The operation of discourse is implicit in the regulation of what statements can and cannot be made and the forms that they can legitimately take. Attention to discourse therefore moves the focus from the interpretative problem of meaning to questions of instrumentality and function. Instead of *having* meaning, statements should be seen as *performative of* meaning; not as possessing some portable and "universal" content but, rather, as instrumental in the organisation and legitimation of power-relations—which of course involves, as one of its components, control over the constitution of meaning. As the author of one of the first modern grammars said, appropriately enough in 1492, "language is the perfect instrument of empire."[17] Yet, unlike grammar, discourse functions effectively precisely because the question of codifying its rules and protocols can never arise: the utterances it silently governs speak what appears to be the "natural language of the age." Therefore, from within a given discursive formation no general rules for its operation will be drawn up except against the ideological grain; so the constitution of the discursive fields of the past will, to some degree, need comprehending through the excavatory work of historical study.

To initiate such excavation is of course to confront massive problems. According to what we have said above, each individual text, rather than a meaningful unit in itself, lies at the intersection of different discourses which are related to each other in a complex but ultimately hierarchical way. Strictly speaking, then, it would be meaningless to talk about the unity of any given text—supposedly the intrinsic quality of all "works of art." And yet, because literary texts *are* presented to us as characterised precisely by their unity, the text must still be taken as a point of purchase on the discursive field—but in order to demonstrate that, athwart its alleged unity, the text is in fact marked and fissured by the interplay of the discourses that constitute it.

V

The ensemble of fictional and lived practices, which for convenience we will simply refer to here as "English colonialism," provides *The Tempest*'s dominant discursive con-texts.[18] We have chosen here to concentrate specifically on the figure of usurpation as the nodal point of the play's imbrication into this discourse of colonialism. We shall look at the variety of forms under which usurpation appears in the text, and indicate briefly how it is active in organising the text's actual diversity.[19]

Of course conventional criticism has no difficulty in recognising the importance of the themes of legitimacy and usurpation for *The Tempest*. Indeed, during the storm-scene with which the play opens, the issue of legitimate authority is brought immediately to the fore. The boatswain's peremptory dismissal of the nobles to their cabins, while not, according to the custom of the sea, strictly a mutinous act, nonetheless represents a disturbance in the normal hierarchy of power relations. The play then proceeds to recount or display a series of actual or attempted usurpations of authority: from Antonio's successful palace revolution against his brother, Prospero, and Caliban's attempted violation of the honour of Prospero's daughter—accounts of which we hear retrospectively; to the conspiracy of Antonio and Sebastian against the life of Alonso and, finally, Caliban's insurrection, with Stephano and Trinculo, against Prospero's domination of the island. In fact it could be argued that this series *is* the play, insofar as *The Tempest* is a dramatic action at all. However, these rebellions, treacheries, mutinies and conspiracies, referred to here collectively as usurpation, are not *simply* present in the text as extractable "Themes of the Play."[20] Rather, they are differentially embedded there, figural traces of the text's anxiety concerning the very matters of domination and resistance.

Take for example the play's famous *protasis*, Prospero's long exposition to Miranda of the significant events that predate the play. For Prospero, the real beginning of the story is his usurpation twelve years previously by Antonio, the opening scene of a drama which Prospero intends to play out during *The Tempest* as a comedy of restoration. Prospero's exposition seems unproblematically to take its place as the indispensable prologue to an understanding of the present moment of Act I, no more than a device for conveying essential information. But to see it simply as a neutral account of the play's prehistory would be to occlude the contestation that follows insistently throughout the rest of the first act, of Prospero's version of true beginnings. In this narration the crucial early days of the relationship between the Europeans and the island's inhabitants are covered by Prospero's laconic "Here in this island we arriv'd" (I.ii.171). And this is all we would have were it not for Ariel and Caliban. First Prospero is goaded by Ariel's demands for freedom into recounting at some length how his servitude began, when, at their first contact, Prospero freed him from the cloven pine in which he had earlier been confined by Sycorax. Caliban then offers his compelling and defiant counter to Prospero's single sentence when, in a powerful speech, he recalls the initial mutual trust which was broken by Prospero's assumption of the political control made possible by the power of his magic. Caliban, "Which first was mine own King," now protests that "here you sty me / In this hard rock, whiles you do keep from me / The rest o'th' island" (I.ii.344–6).

It is remarkable that these contestations of "true beginnings" have been so commonly occluded by an uncritical willingness to identify Prospero's voice as direct and reliable authorial statement, and therefore to ignore the lengths to which the play goes to dramatise its problems with the proper beginning of its own story. Such identification hears, as it were, only Prospero's play, follows only his stage directions, not noticing that Prospero's play and *The Tempest* are not necessarily the same thing.[21]

But although different beginnings are offered by different voices in the play, Prospero has the effective power to impose his construction of events on the others. While Ariel gets a threatening but nevertheless expansive answer, Caliban provokes an entirely different reaction. Prospero's words refuse engagement with Caliban's claim to original sovereignty ("This island's mine, by Sycorax my mother. Which thou tak'st from me," I.ii.333–4). Yet Prospero is clearly disconcerted. His sole—somewhat hysterical—response consists of an indirect denial ("Thou most lying slave," I.ii.346) and a counter accusation of attempted rape ("thou didst seek to violate / The honour of my child," I.ii.349–50), which together foreclose the exchange and serve in practice as Prospero's only justification for the arbitrary rule he exercises over the island and its inhabitants. At a stroke he erases from what we have called Prospero's play all trace of the moment of his reduction of Caliban to slavery and appropriation of his island. For, indeed, it could be argued that the series of usurpations listed earlier as constituting the dramatic action all belong to that play alone, which is systematically silent about Prospero's own act of usurpation: a silence which is curious, given his otherwise voluble preoccupation with the theme of legitimacy. But, despite his evasiveness, this moment ought to be of decisive *narrative* importance since it marks Prospero's self-installation as ruler, and his acquisition, through Caliban's enslavement, of the means of supplying the food and labour on which he and Miranda are completely dependent: "We cannot miss him: he does make our fire, / Fetch in our wood, and serves in offices / That profit us" (I.ii.313–15). Through its very occlusion of Caliban's version of proper beginnings, Prospero's disavowal is itself performative of the discourse of colonialism, since this particular reticulation of denial of dispossession with retrospective justification for it, is the characteristic trope by which European colonial regimes articulated their authority over land to which they could have no conceivable legitimate claim.[22]

The success of this trope is, as so often in these cases, proved by its subsequent invisibility. Caliban's "I'll show thee every fertile inch o'th' island" (II.ii.148) is for example glossed by Kermode with "The colonists were frequently received with this kindness, though treachery might follow," as if this were simply a "fact" whose relevance to *The Tempest* we might want to consider, without seeing that to speak of "treachery" is already to interpret, from the position of colonising power, through a purported "descrip-

tion." A discursive analysis would indeed be alive to the use of the word "treachery" in a colonial context in the early seventeenth century, but would be aware of how it functioned for the English to explain to themselves the *change* in native behaviour (from friendliness to hostility) that was in fact a *reaction* to their increasingly disruptive presence. That this was an explanatory trope rather than a description of behaviour is nicely caught in Gabriel Archer's slightly bemused comment: "They are naturally given to treachery, howbeit we could not finde it in our travell up the river, but rather a most kind and loving people."[23] Kermode's use of the word is of course by no means obviously contentious: its power to shape readings of the play stems from its continuity with the grain of unspoken colonialist assumptions.

So it is not just a matter of the occlusion of the play's initial colonial moment. Colonialist legitimation has always had then to go on to tell its own story, inevitably one of native violence: Prospero's play performs this task within *The Tempest*. The burden of Prospero's play is already deeply concerned with producing legitimacy. The purpose of Prospero's main plot is to secure recognition of his claim to the usurped duchy of Milan, a recognition sealed in the blessing given by Alonso to the prospective marriage of his own son to Prospero's daughter. As part of this, Prospero reduces Caliban to a role in the supporting sub-plot, as instigator of a mutiny that is programmed to fail, thereby forging an equivalence between Antonio's initial *putsch* and Caliban's revolt. This allows Prospero to annul the memory of his failure to prevent his expulsion from the dukedom, by repeating it as a mutiny that he will, this time, forestall. But, in addition, the playing out of the colonialist narrative is thereby completed: Caliban's attempt—tarred with the brush of Antonio's supposedly self-evident viciousness—is produced as final and irrevocable conformation of the natural treachery of savages.

Prospero can plausibly be seen as a playwright only because of the control over the other characters given him by his magic. He can freeze Ferdinand in mid-thrust, immobilise the court party at will, and conjure a pack of hounds to chase the conspirators. Through this physical control he seeks with considerable success to manipulate the mind of Alonso. Curiously though, while the main part of Prospero's play runs according to plan, the sub-plot provides the only real moment of drama when Prospero calls a sudden halt to the celebratory masque, explaining, aside:

> I had forgot that foul conspiracy
> Of the beast Caliban and his confederates
> Against my life: the minute of their plot
> Is almost come.   (IV.i.139–42)

So while, on the face of it, Prospero has no difficulty in dealing with the various threats to his domination, Caliban's revolt proves uniquely disturbing to the smooth unfolding of Prospero's plot. The text is strangely emphatic about this moment of disturbance, insisting not only on Prospero's sudden vexation, but also on the "strange hollow, and confused noise" with which the Nymphs and Reapers—two lines earlier gracefully dancing—now "heavily vanish"; and the apprehension voiced by Ferdinand and Miranda:

> FERDINAND: This is strange: your father's in some
>   passion
>   That works him strongly.
> MIRANDA: Never till this day
>   Saw I him touch'd with anger, so distemper'd.
>   (IV.i.143–5)

For the first and last time Ferdinand and Miranda speak at a distance from Prospero and from his play. Although this disturbance is immediately glossed over, the hesitation, occasioned by the sudden remembering of Caliban's conspiracy, remains available as a site of potential fracture.

The interrupted masque has certainly troubled scholarship, introduced a jarring note into the harmony of this supposedly most highly structured of Shakespeare's late plays. Kermode speaks of the "apparently inadequate motivation" for Prospero's perturbation,[24] since there is no obvious reason why he should so excite himself over an easily controllable insurrection.

What then is the meaning of this textual excess, this disproportion between apparent cause and effect? There are several possible answers, located at different levels of analysis. The excess obviously marks the recurrent difficulty that Caliban causes Prospero—a difficulty we have been concerned to trace in some detail. So, at the level of character, a psychoanalytic reading would want to suggest that Prospero's excessive reaction represents his disquiet at the irruption into consciousness of an unconscious anxiety concerning the grounding of his legitimacy,

both as producer of his play and, *a fortiori*, as governor of the island. The by now urgent need for action forces upon Prospero the hitherto repressed contradiction between his dual roles as usurped and usurper. Of course the emergency is soon contained and the colonialist narrative quickly completed. But, nonetheless, if only for a moment, the effort invested in holding Prospero's play together as a unity is laid bare.

So, at the formal level, Prospero's difficulties in staging his play are themselves "staged" by the play that we are watching, this moment presenting for the first time the possibility of distinguishing between Prospero's play and *The Tempest* itself.

Perhaps it could be said that what is staged here in *The Tempest* is Prospero's anxious determination to keep the sub-plot of his play in its place. One way of distinguishing Prospero's play from *The Tempest* might be to claim that Prospero's carefully established relationship between main and sub-plot is reversed in *The Tempest*, whose *main* plot concerns Prospero's anxiety over his *sub*-plot. A formal analysis would seem to bear this out. The climax of Prospero's play is his revelation to Alonso of Miranda and Ferdinand playing chess. This is certainly a true *anagnorisis* for Alonso, but for us a merely theatrical rather than truly dramatic moment. *The Tempest*'s dramatic climax, in a way its only dramatic moment at all, is, after all, this sudden and strange disturbance of Prospero.

But to speak of Prospero's anxiety being staged by *The Tempest* would be, on its own, a recuperative move, preserving the text's unity by the familiar strategy of introducing an ironic distance between author and protagonist. After all, although Prospero's anxiety over his sub-plot may point up the *crucial* nature of that "sub" plot, a generic analysis would have no difficulty in showing that *The Tempest* is ultimately complicit with Prospero's play in treating Caliban's conspiracy in the fully comic mode. Even before it begins, Caliban's attempt to put his political claims into practice is arrested by its implication in the convention of clownish vulgarity represented by the "low-life" characters of Stephano and Trinculo, his conspiracy framed in a grotesquerie that ends with the dubiously amusing sight of the conspirators being hunted by dogs, a fate, incidentally, not unknown to natives of the New World. The shakiness of Prospero's position is indeed staged, but in the end his version of history remains *authoritative*, the larger play acceding as it were to the containment of the conspirators in the safely comic mode, Caliban allowed only his poignant and ultimately vain protests against the venality of his co-conspirators.

That this comic closure is necessary to enable the European "reconciliation" which follows hard on its heels—the patching up of a minor dynastic dispute within the Italian nobility—is, however, itself symptomatic of the text's own anxiety about the threat posed to its decorum by its New World materials. The lengths to which the play has to go to achieve a legitimate ending may then be read as the quelling of a fundamental disquiet concerning its own functions within the projects of colonialist discourse.

No adequate reading of the play could afford not to comprehend *both* the anxiety and the drive to closure it necessitates. Yet these aspects of the play's "rich complexity" have been signally ignored by European and North American critics, who have tended to listen exclusively to Prospero's voice: after all, he speaks their language. It has been left to those who have suffered colonial usurpation to discover and map the traces of that complexity by reading in full measure Caliban's refractory place in both Prospero's play and *The Tempest*.25

VI

We have tried to show, within the limits of a brief textual analysis, how an approach via a theory of discourse can recognise *The Tempest* as, in a significant sense, a play imbricated within the discourse of colonialism; and can, at the same time, offer an explanation of features of the play either ignored or occluded by critical practices that have often been complicit, whether consciously or not, with a colonialist ideology.

Three points remain to be clarified. To identify dominant discursive networks and their mode of operation within particular texts should by no means be seen as the end of the story. A more exhaustive analysis would go on to establish the precise articulation of discourses within texts: we have argued for the discourse of colonialism as the articulatory *principle* of *The Tempest*'s diversity but have touched only briefly on what other discourses are articulated and where such linkages can be seen at work in the play.

Then again, each text is more than simply an *instance* of the operation of a discursive network. We have tried to show how much of *The Tempest*'s com-

plexity comes from its *staging* of the distinctive moves and figures of colonialist discourse. Discourse is always performative, active rather than ever merely contemplative; and, of course, the mode of the theatre will also inflict it in particular ways, tending, for example, through the inevitable (because structural) absence of any direct authorial comment, to create an effect of distantiation, which exists in a complex relationship with the countervailing (and equally structural) tendency for audiences to identify with characters presented—through the language and conventions of theatre—as heroes and heroines. Much work remains to be done on the articulation between discursive performance and mode of presentation.

Finally, we have been concerned to show how *The Tempest* has been severed from its discursive con-texts through being produced by criticism as an autotelic unity, and we have tried therefore to exemplify an approach that would engage with the fully dialectical relationship between the detail of the text and the larger discursive formations. But nor can theory and criticism be exempt from such relationships. Our essay too must engage in the discursive struggle that determines the history within which the Shakespearean texts will be located and read: it matters what kind of history that is.

Notes

1. E. D. Hirsch, *Validity in Interpretation* (New Haven, CT, 1967), p. 46.
2. T. Bennett, "Test and History" in Peter Widdowson (ed.), *Re-Reading English* (London, 1982), pp. 223–36, p. 227; drawing on the argument of Jacques Derrida, "Signature, event context," *Glyph*, 1 (1977), 172–98.
3. For the theory behind the concept of inscription see Renée Balibar, *Les Français fictifs: le raport des styles littérares au français national* (Paris, 1974) and "National language, education, literature," in F. Barker et al. (eds.), *The Politics of Theory* (Colchester, 1983), pp. 79–99; P. Macherey and R. Balibar, "On literature as an ideological form: Some Marxist hypotheses," *Oxford Literary Review*, 3 (1978), 43–58; and Tony Davies, "Education, ideology and literature," *Red Letters*, 7 (1978), 4–15. For an accessible collection of essays which put this theory to work on the corpus of English literature, see Widdowson, *Re-Reading English*.

4. Intertextuality is a term coined by Julia Kristeva in 1970, from her reading of the seminal work of Mikhail Bakhtin.

5. For Raleigh's *Tempest* see Terence Hawkes, "Swisser-Swatter: Making a Man of English Letters," in *Alternative Shakespeares,* ed. John Drakakis (London, 1985), pp. 226–46; Kermode is editor of the Arden edition of *The Tempest* (1964); on the formation of "English" see Davies, "Education, ideology and literature."

6. Bennett, "Text and History," p. 224.

7. Ibid., p. 229.

8. Stanley Fish, *Is There a Text in this Class? The Authority of Interpretive Communities* (Cambridge, MA, 1980), p. 165, whose general argument is similar to Bennett's, admits that in the last analysis he is unable to answer the question: what are his interpretative acts interpretations *of?*

9. Marx's work was developed out of his critique of the concepts of classical political economy that had dominated economic thought in the middle of the nineteenth century. We choose here to offer a critique of Kermode's introduction to the Arden because of the *strengths* of his highly regarded and influential work.

10. Con-texts with a hyphen, to signify a break from the inequality of the usual text/context relationship. Con-texts are themselves *texts* and must be *read with:* they do not simply make up a background.

11. Kermode, Arden edition, p. lxiii.

12. Ibid., p. xxviii.

13. Ibid., p. lxiii.

14. Ibid., p. lxxv.

15. Colin MacCabe, "On Discourse," *Economy and Society,* 8 (1979), 279–307 offers a helpful guide through some of discourse's many usages. The concept of discourse at work in the present essay draws on Michel Foucault's investigation of the discursive realm. A useful introduction to his theorisation of discourse is provided by Foucault's essays. His most extended theoretical text is *The Archaeology of Knowledge* (London, 1972). However, a less formal and in many ways more suggestive treatment of discourse is practised and, to a certain extent theorised, in his early works on "madness" and in more recent studies of the prison and of sexuality, where discourse is linked with both the institutional locations in which it circulates and the power functions it performs. For a cognate approach to discourse see the theory of "utterance"—developed by Valentin Volosinov, *Marxism and the Philosophy of Language* (New York, 1973).

16. On the weakness of Kristeva's own work in this respect see J. Culler "Jacques Derrida," in J. Sturrock (ed.), *Structuralism and Since* (London, 1981), pp. 105–7.

17. Antonio de Nebrija, quoted in Lewis Hanke, *Aristotle and the American Indians* (Bloomington, IN, 1959), p. 8.

18. In other words we would shift the emphasis from the futile search for the texts Shakespeare "had in mind" to the establishment of significant patterns within the larger discursive networks of the period. The notion of "English colonialism" can itself be focused in different ways. The widest focus would include present con-texts, the narrowest would concentrate on the con-texts associated with the initial period of English colonisation of Virginia, say 1585 to 1622. In the first instance many of the relevant texts would be found in the contemporary collections of Hakluyt (1903–5) and Purchas (1905–7). For congruent approaches see James Smith, *"The Tempest,"* in *Shakespearian and Other Essays* (Cambridge, 1974, pp. 159–261; Charles Frey, *"The Tempest* and the New World," *Shakespeare Quarterly,* 30 (1979), pp. 29–41; Stephen Greenblatt, *Renaissance Self-Fashioning: From More to Shakespeare* (Chicago, 1980), ch. 4; and Peter Hulme, "Hurricanes in the Caribbees: The Constitution of the Discourse of English Colonialism," in Francis Barker et al. (eds.), *1642: Literature and Power in the Seventeenth Century* (Colchester, 1981), pp. 55–83.

19. See Macherey, "On literature as an ideological form." Macherey characterises the literary text not as unified but as plural and diverse. Usurpation should then be regarded not as the centre of a unity but as the principle of a diversity.

20. Kermode's second heading (Arden edition, p. xxiv).

21. This is a weak form of the critical fallacy that, more chronically, reads Prospero as an autobiographical surrogate for Shakespeare himself.

22. This trope is studied in more detail in Peter Hulme, *"Of the caniballes": The Discourse of European Colonialism* (forthcoming), Chs. 3 and 4. See

also Francis Jennings, *The Invasion of America: Indians, Colonialism and the Cant of Conquest* (New York, 1976).

23. Gabriel Archer, "The Description of the now discovered river and county of Virginia . . ." (1607), in D. Quinn et al. (eds.), *New American World*, vol. 5 (London, 1979).

24. Kermode, Arden edition, p. lxxv.

25. See for example George Lamming, *The Pleasures of Exile* (1960, New York, 1984). Aimé Césaire's rewriting of the play, *Une Tempête: D'Après 'la Tempête' de Shakespeare — Adaptation pour un théâtre nègre* (Paris, 1969), has Caliban as explicit hero. For an account of how Caliban remains refractory for contemporary productions of *The Tempest* see Trevor R. Griffiths, "'This Island's Mine': Caliban and Colonialism," *Yearbook of English Studies*, 13 (1983), 159–80.

Bodily Harm: Keats's Figures in the "Ode on a Grecian Urn"

Marjorie Garson

Marjorie Garson clearly has little sympathy for John Ellis's argument that our agreement to read a text as transcending the circumstances of its creation is exactly what confers its status as literature. Like the other critics in this context, Garson views claims to transcendence with suspicion, and she sees our well-documented willingness to read Keats's poem this way as a cause for complaint. On this point, most historians might agree. But one has only to compare Garson's reading of the poem as "a discourse of sexual and cultural appropriation" with Allen C. Austin's intentionalist interpretation to realize that there are very different kinds of history. Although Garson's project is to place the poem firmly within the circumstances of its creation, she has little interest in discovering Keats's conscious intentions. Rather, she finds the poem's real meaning in the social and political circumstances that are not directly addressed, in what got left out of this "expensive torso," or, to change the metaphor, in the international and sexual politics that were repressed into the poem's "political unconscious." And she is concerned as well with the history of criticism on the text, a history that she feels has continued the poem's original repression of its political content. On both counts, Garson offers a historical reading that brings together literature, history, and politics in a way that Catherine Belsey would approve.

Keats's "Ode on a Grecian Urn" is constructed upon two principal rhetorical figures. Beginning with a triple apostrophe—"Thou still unravish'd bride," "Thou foster-child," "Sylvan historian"—and going on to apostrophize "ye soft pipes," "Fair youth," "Bold lover," "happy boughs," "happy melodist," "happy love," "mysterious priest," "little town," and, in the last stanza, the urn itself again ("O Attic shape," "silent form," "Cold Pastoral")—the speaker

Reprinted by permission from *English Studies in Canada* 17 (1991): 37–51.

addresses directly just about every noun in the poem, with the exception of the female victims of its action, the maiden — or maidens — in the first design and the heifer led to the sacrifice in the second. Keats's second important figure is the rhetorical question. The poem moves in the first stanza into a series of such questions:

> What leaf-fring'd legend haunts about thy shape . . . ?
>   What men or gods are these? What maidens loth?
> What mad pursuit? What struggle to escape?
>   What pipes and timbrels? What wild ecstasy?[1]

And it continues, in the fourth stanza, around to the other side of the urn: "Who are these coming to the sacrifice?" To what altar is the heifer being led? From what town has the procession come?

Apostrophe is an address to the absent as if present, the inanimate as if animate; a rhetorical question is one to which no answer is expected. These are figures of power.[2] To use them is to address someone who cannot talk back — a strategy that ensures not only that you will have the last word, but that your discourse will manifest a high degree of "literariness" (Scholes). Indeed, Keats's poem announces its aspirations to literariness in every way. To write an ode was to appropriate the language of cultural power; to write an ecphrastic poem was in 1819 to employ a fashionable form with distinct academic and class associations.[3] What better genre could be chosen by a young poet ardently hoping for membership in a pantheon from which his detractors had sought to exclude him at least partly on grounds of social class?[4] A successful attempt to capture in words a cultural icon like the urn would win him permanent place of honour in a culture that had invested heavily in such artefacts and in the values they had been made to stand for.

The attempt was, of course, inordinately successful. Praised for its "Greekness" in the nineteenth century (Rhodes 6), the "Ode on a Grecian Urn" has in the twentieth been accorded uncontrovertible classic status: the status of an art object that, liberated from the exigencies of history, at once embodies and laments the permanent paradoxes of the human condition, of time and eternity, love and death, art and life, finally dissolving them in a totalizing formula that reaches beyond the material into a transcendental realm of Platonic Idealism. The poem becomes what it beholds: like the urn, like Stephen Dedalus's basket, it is a "rhythmic" whole bounded by an invisible line that cuts it off from its background, renders it a self-sufficient object of aesthetic contemplation (Joyce 212) — and, in the 1940s, the ideal focus of New Critical attention.

This impression of universality and of aesthetic self-sufficiency owes much no doubt to the West's construction of the "Grecian." The nineteenth century tended to project upon the Greeks a wholeness, harmony, and radiance, a balance and *integritas* (Joyce 212) that more modern cultures are felt irrevocably to have lost. From Schlegel, who began the first of his Lectures in Dramatic Art and Literature by asserting that "The whole of their art and their poetry is expressive of the consciousness of this harmony of all their faculties" (1.12), to Arnold, who praised the Greek "idea of beauty and of a human nature perfect on all its sides" (5.99), and who found Greek art, sculpture, drama, architecture, character, and culture to be marked by the same "high symmetry" (10.71), there was a tendency to agree that "They regarded the whole; we regard the parts" (Arnold 1.5). The desired wholeness is often implicitly female: indeed, it became a commonplace to describe the peculiar quality of Greek art under the metaphor of chastity (Aske 163 n73).

This mythic and ahistorical construction of Greekness may well have continued even to the present day to shape readers' responses to Keats's poem. Leo Spitzer, in an influential and relentlessly Platonic reading of the ode, argues that the speaker is wrong to sully the urn with quasi-historical questions, which, however, she eludes successfully, her "unbroken flawless totality, rising again before his eyes, reborn as a perfect whole!" (82). More recent readings, though more willing to draw attention to the insufficiency of the urn's Platonic message, continue nevertheless to use Spitzer's critique of the speaker as a starting point and to stay, as he does, within the poem itself, ignoring its political and social context and responding to the urn as "a self-contained anonymous world, complete in itself, which asks an emphatic identification supremely free both of factual inquiry and of self-interest" (in the words of Helen Vendler, 121). David Simpson, for example, who distinguishes, like Spitzer, between poet and speaker, uses the distinction to arrive at a destination of the poem as the poet's "metacommentary" — as a text that "involves the reading mind in a confrontation with and refinement of its own . . . ambitions" (8).[5] Though Spitzer takes the urn's Platonic message "straight" — as a

valid definition of what we should look to art for—
and Simpson takes it ironically, both assume that the
point of the poem is the chastening of the speaker,
who learns that he cannot get what he demands,
both locate the poem's irony within its own circular
structure, emphasizing in particular the problems
raised by the ambiguous ending, and both treat the
poem as self-referential—dealing with the poetic act
itself. The self-referentiality of both the urn and the
poem has indeed become a critical cliché.[6] Keats's
ode is so successful a critical icon not only because it
dramatizes the link between wholeness and Greekness that has apparently been of the first importance
in Western European constitution of the self, but also
because it seems peculiarly amenable to organicist
criteria of aesthetic worth that in one way or another
have been dominant since it was written.

But this impression of self-sufficiency and circularity—of a wholeness at once radiant and "rhythmic"—depends on the poem's insulation from the
historical moment of its production. The urn's seam-
less surface tends to conceal that it is constructed
of historical materials—made up of fragments of an
appropriated culture. Greek style, borrowed and
vulgarized, had been popular in England for some
time when Keats wrote his ode: it has been plausibly
suggested that Josiah Wedgwood's extremely canny
and profitable exploitation of Grecian motifs could
have contributed to its imagery (Robinson).[7] Scholars interested in more culturally prestigious sources
have attempted, without success, to discover one
specific urn that Keats might have seen and used
as his model. Ian Jack has concluded that Keats probably drew on a number of museum-pieces that he had
seen, or seen drawings of, and constructed a composite ideal urn from their details. He suggests that
its marmoreality might have come from the Portland Vase or the Townley Vase, the figures in the first
three stanzas from the Borghese Vase as illustrated
by Piranesi, and the "heifer lowing at the skies" from
a fragment of the South Frieze of the Parthenon
(Jack 217–19).

The frieze from the Parthenon is one of the Elgin
Marbles, on display in the British Museum from
1816, which Keats saw for the first time in 1817. The
history of their acquisition is not irrelevant to a reading of his ode. From the middle of the seventeenth
century, the stones of Greece had become increasingly vulnerable to souvenir-hunters—cheerful van-
dals like John Bacon Sawrey Morritt, who in 1795

complacently described the progress of the workmen
he had hired in Athens, "hammering down the Cen-
taurs and Lapithae, like Charles's mayor and alder-
men in the 'School for Scandal'" (Webb 204). This
kind of amateur depredation was to serve as a justification for the much larger-scale devastation that
was to follow. At the turn of the century, Lord Elgin,
the British ambassador to Constantinople—with the
complicity of the Turks, whose dependence on the military support of their British allies against Napoleon
made them vulnerable to British pressure, and in
emulation of the French, whose recent acquisitions
of *objets d'art* the British were anxious to equal[8]—
had the Parthenon denuded and the fragments sent
to England.[9]

Lord Elgin's original purpose was to ornament
his own Scottish estate; his subsequent claim—that
he was attempting to preserve the antiquities from
the indifference of a Turkish administration unable
to prevent their destruction—has been echoed by
his defenders ever since. Not everyone, however, has
accepted it. Byron, in the first instalment of *Childe
Harold* and in "The Curse of Minerva," mounted a
bitter personal attack upon him, and his criticisms
were soon echoed in other quarters. A ravaged culture is metaphorically female: it was as natural for
Byron to describe "fair Greece" mourned as lovers
mourn "the dust they lov'd" (*CH* 2.15), an Athena
undefended by her powerless sons (*CH* 2.12), a
weeping Minerva, her altars "violated" ("Minerva"
99), her walls "insulted" by Elgin's carved name
(106), her shrines "pollute[d]" by that of his adul-
terous wife (119)[10] as for popular rumour to report
that when one Caryatid was removed from the
Erechtheum, those that remained lamented "their
ravished sister" with wailing that could be heard
throughout the town (St. Clair 212). The notion of the
female assaulted and offended informs the language
of one of the speakers in the House of Commons debate of 1816, who, arguing against the government's
purchase of the marbles, protested that he "was not
so enamoured of those headless ladies as to forget
another lady, which was justice" (Hitchens 132).
Such voices have never been entirely silenced: because of the unique symbolic status of the Parthenon,
British possession of the Elgin Marbles has remained
a vexed question. In the meantime the tickets under
the fragments in the British Museum testify graphically to the appropriation and dismemberment of a
culture: "The heads of the Lapith and Centaur . . . are

now in Copenhagen"; "Part of the Centaur's head is in Würzburg"; "The head of the Lapith is in the Louvre and that of the Centaur in Athens"; "The Centaur's head and right arm and the Lapith's right knee are in Athens" (St. Clair 274).

The painter Benjamin Haydon, who introduced Keats to the exhibition—where he was more than once seen by Severn, "rapt in revery" (Sharp 32)—was involved in the public squabble occasioned by the English government's purchase of the marbles. Heydon, who passionately defended Lord Elgin, responded fervently to the pathos of fragmented bodies, as he records in his *Autobiography:*

> As the light streamed across the room and died away into obscurity, there was something solemn and awful in the grand forms and heads and trunks and fragments of mighty temples and columns that lay scattered about in sublime insensibility—the remains, the only actual remains, of a mighty people.
> (1.107)

The description assimilates the fragments to architectural ruins (while suppressing the fact that Lord Elgin himself was responsible for their ruinous condition), and also implies that the Greek people who generated them had in effect ceased to exist—a defence of Britain's retention of them used to this day (Hitchens 102–04). Behind the parts, however, Haydon saw a conceptual whole: a miraculous "combination of nature and idea," a set of "principles which the common sense of the English people would understand" (*Autobiography* 1.67). He envisaged the exhibition doing for him what it was widely believed likely to do for English art and architecture as a whole—stimulating a new age of creativity. Other enthusiasts went further, prophesying for England development not only artistic but economic and industrial as well (Hitchens 133). Happily, the dissolution of one culture seemed to promise a new moment of integration for another.

The consensus seems to be that the renaissance never took place, either in Haydon or in the British art world generally. The marbles arrived too late to influence the shape of many public monuments (Whinney 209) or to envigorate neo-classical history-painting (Rothenberg 445), and although motifs inspired by them dot the London landscape, no major artistic or architectural flowering resulted from their acquisition (St. Clair 264–67, Hitchens 85–89). The principal artistic legacy of Elgin's acquisition is not anything that happened in the visual and plastic arts,

but the poems inspired by Keats's exposure to them: the two sonnets "On Seeing the Elgin Marbles" and "To B. R. Haydon"—the latter an ardent tribute to the man Keats believed was largely responsible for persuading the nation to buy the collection—and, chiefly, the "Ode on a Grecian Urn."

The poem, then, is written not in a historical vacuum, but in the face of a national act of appropriation that seemed to promise England benefits not only spiritual but also material, and in the context of a political debate of which Keats was fully aware.[11] The ode, however, tends apparently to suppress both the appropriation and the debate. The urn, serenely isolated in a purely aesthetic space, is—like an object in a museum—"liberated" (in both the standard and the colloquial senses of the word) from its national and cultural context. It could be argued that the question "What men or gods are these?" draws attention to the provenance of the urn in a potentially topical way. Indeed, Jerome McGann, who reminds us that the ode was first published in the *Annals of the Fine Arts,* suggests that twentieth-century condescension toward earlier researchers who attempted to discover what particular urn Keats might have seen is misplaced, and observes that they were merely "attempting to answer many of the same questions which the poet raises in the poem: as if, should they be able to find that original urn, they might then be able to see *in fact* what men or gods Keats was speaking of" ("Keats" 1010). However, even critics who have sought the urn have not tended to give the poem a political reading. And for good reason. The poem does not really want to know what men or gods these are, for any archaeological answer would defeat the claim to universality upon which it bases its own appropriation of Greekness. It poses its questions so that they are not really questions, to make sure that they are not really answered. The rhetoric successfully excludes the very political issues the opening questions might seem to raise.[12] To show how this happens I want to look closely at the way a reader responds to the poem as she moves through it line by line.

The ode arouses two kinds of generic expectations: while it announces itself as a lyric poem, it also promises to tell a story. The urn presents a legend that is to be investigated; she is a sylvan historian who will tell a flowery tale. We read the poem, then, at the nexus of two hermeneutics: the poetics of the lyric and the codes of narrative. The promise that there is a story to be unfolded tells us to read the questions that follow as clues to that story. In Barthes's terminology, the questions become part of the proairetic code (Barthes 19). As the speaker interrogates the urn, we interrogate the poem: his questions serve as our answers. What we learn is that the urn has god-like male figures on it, and maidens; there is pursuit and struggle; musical instruments are depicted in the scene. The only question that emerges for the *reader* at the end of the last stanza—"What is going on here?"—directs attention *toward* the urn, not away from it into its historical context. And that question—though a real one for the reader, at the end of the first stanza—is already a pseudo-question for the speaker, who could not formulate it the way he does unless he had in fact already answered it. (You cannot ask "what mad pursuit?" unless you have already interpreted the action as a pursuit and thereby identified both pursuer and pursued.) It is clear by the end of the first stanza that the speaker knows, if not all he needs to know, at least all he is ever going to know about the urn, given the kinds of questions he is choosing to ask: they remain questions for us only because he has not yet unfolded their answers. The perfect hermeneutic circle, the urn will never provide an answer he himself has not already produced. That the figure whose words are thus appropriated is a woman is neither surprising nor irrelevant to the ode's design and effect.

Indeed the poem suppresses not only its international but its sexual politics. Because all the questions in the first stanza have been cast in the same syntactical form, they conceal the fact that the nature of the inquiry shifts around line 9.[13] The urn cannot itself tell the questioner who the figures are. However, it can and does tell him why the men are pursuing and the women attempting to escape. The scene depicts a sexual assault, as the elaboration upon it in the second stanza makes clear. By blandly absorbing the first stanza's pseudo-questions into the sequence of earlier, more genuinely problematical queries ("What men or gods are these? What maidens loth?"), by implying that, similar as they are syntactically, the questions all have similar ontological status, a common degree of "un-answerability," the speaker positions himself as an innocent, startled observer, and veils his complicity in the narrative the urn relates, and in his interpretation of it. *He* does not know what these men can be doing; he does not know why the women are "loth" to engage in it. By the time he

has figured it out, the violence of the scene has been filtered out, and the emphasis has switched from gang rape—a group of men pursuing maidens, plural—to the poignant dilemma of a single lover.[14]

We can trace the way the narrator moves from putative ignorance in the first stanza to his confident reading of the image in the second stanza. It is via the concept of silent music. The phrase "What pipes and timbrels?" prepares for the shift into a locus of interpretative license. Only the spiritual ear of the sensitive observer, we are told, can "hear" the silent music the pipes and timbrels play. By the time we have surrendered this power of hearing to the narrator (and, as sensitive individuals ourselves, identified with him in his sensitivity), we have also surrendered to him the right to read the imagery in the way he chooses. Along with him, we identify with the "bold lover" as subject, and position the maiden as the object of desire. The wildness and rapid movement of the scene as first described has frozen into a static paradigm of permanent deferral. The foregrounding of such Derridean *angst* represses, however, the poem's sexual politics. The idea that the lover's fulfilment would involve the maiden's "sacrifice" has been dropped, and we are allowed to respond to the pathos that an as-yet-unravished female may arouse in the male imagination.

Among Keats's readers the sympathy is usually for the would-be ravisher, not for the potential victim. Even critics who have made a point of the femaleness of the urn itself have often remained complacent about the sexual power-structure adumbrated in the opening scenario.[15] Speaking to the question of Keats's "belatedness," Harold Bloom sympathizes with the "vulnerability" of the speaker in the ode, "who contemplates a world of values he cannot appropriate for his own" ("Keats" 137); Martin Aske, whose Bloomian reading of the poetry constructs a Keats with his nose pressed against a sweet-shop window, attempting in vain to possess the classics, emphasizes the poignant situation of the man who has "dared to approach the urn in the guise of a bold lover," but whose "romance with antiquity can never be consummated" (116). Certainly the poem's central trope emphasizes the poignancy of a female not yet possessed, not yet sacrificed. The action stops just before the youth touches the maiden, before the heifer reaches the altar, and the urn itself is memorably addressed as a "still unravish'd bride" (indeed, this oxymoronic lady tends to displace the "maidens loth" in the minds of many readers). The proposed rape of the personified urn has come to be read as a metaphor of the critical or interpretative act, the assumption being that the poem's irony is a self-contained and controlled irony, that it is at the expense of the narrator, and that the desire to possess is rightly thwarted when at the end of the poem "she" emerges unscathed from the frenzied advances of her "explainer-ravisher" (Hartman 102). I am suggesting, on the other hand, that the reluctance of the frantic maidens might be kept in mind, and that the metaphor of rape is more applicable to Keats's own project than the poem's serene and enigmatic ending might suggest. It is a question whether the poem—which moves in space and in time as the urn does not—undoes the stillness, and completes the ravishment suspended in the first line; whether the poet, who certainly has designs upon her, does not in fact succeed in approaching her for his own purposes.

The urn's chastity is connected with her expressive silence. A foster child, she is to be seen and not heard; a virginal bride, she is a metaphorical female body, complete, circular, intact.[16] In Stephen Dedalus's terms, she embodies wholeness, harmony, and radiance (Joyce 212); in Lacanian terms, she is the mirror-stage self, constituted in the Imaginary by identification with the body of the mother and figured in dreams by the walled-in fortress or arena—like the mountain citadel in the fourth stanza (Lacan 1–7).[17] Yet her perfect silence apparently needs to be supplemented with male words. In writing an ecphrastic poem, the poet himself necessarily violates, in speaking for her, the chastity expressed by that silence. The appropriation of the female by the male, however, is displaced by a more familiar and less political antithesis: that between body and spirit. The urn, we are told, speaks silently to the spiritual ear, rather than coarsely to the material one. With becoming modesty, the speaker pays tribute to her silence and her music, while even as he does so displacing them with his words.

To translate the three-dimensional urn into language is to destroy its circularity, since one of the scenes has to be described first. Stripping the "legend" off the circular surface of the urn and running it comic-strip-wise precipitates its "still" images into time. It gives the poem a plot that the rules of narrative constrain us to read: the poem moves from love on the one side of the urn toward death on the other—as the lover himself would do, liberated

from the urn's surface. The male—the lover—is "kinetic," the female—his object—"static" (Joyce 205). His role is to love—hers is forever, perfectly, to *be*: "For ever wilt thou love, and she be fair!"

A poem, however, cannot be, but must mean. The very process of "translating" the urn into words *enacts* the dissolution also *described* at the end of the third stanza, which itemizes representative parts of the male body after intercourse:

> a heart high-sorrowful and cloy'd,
> A burning forehead, and a parching tongue.

The list, implicitly inclusive, displaces, however, the part that is really in question. Postcoital disillusionment is dissolution: this is Lacan's *corps morcelé*, but it belongs to the female object as well as to the male subject. Indeed, the parodic blazon—by appropriating for the male body the very *topos* by which the female body is conventionally constituted in the male imagination—foregrounds the factitiousness of all such constructs. Woman as a collection of fetished body-parts (fetishized precisely by an act of displacement that the poem here repeats), woman as a radiant whole: these are interdependent linguistic productions, both equally illusory.[18] The poem knows that bodily integrity—male *or* female—is an illusion: the very figure that contrasts life on the urn to "real" life outside the realm of art deconstructs the urn's static wholeness, the quality upon which the contrast between "her" and us is based. The ode, by enacting the fall into language, undercuts the Romantic artist's claim to unmediated vision[19] as well as the male fantasy of possessing female wholeness, and reveals the link between that claim and that fantasy.

The failure is deferred by a final gambit. The narrator moves around to the other side of the urn and tries again. The questions in the fourth stanza repeat the swerve away from history. The first question—"Who are these coming to the sacrifice?"—is one that conceivably could be answered by McGann's researchers, in that it deals with what is on the urn and could have an historical answer. The second question—"Toward what green altar . . . ?"—evidently moves off the urn and into the imagined "green world" (Frye 182) of an idealized past (for if the altar were *on* the urn, it would not be green). The third question leads into the poem's most sublime excursus:

> What little town by river or sea shore,
>   Or mountain-built with peaceful citadel,
>   Is emptied of this folk, this pious morn?

And, little town, thy streets for evermore
    Will silent be; and not a soul to tell
        Why thou art desolate, can e'er return.

The little town is not on the urn—it exists only in the speaker's mind, a "desolate," perhaps, but charming paradox: a sign of human culture, impossibly outside of history. The lines have an indefinable pathos—a pathos at once overdetermined and displaced. "Desolate" is indeed a kind of transferred epithet: the sympathy is less for the personified town itself than for human beings—for the members of the procession, perhaps, who can never go home again, who have been ejected from their own finite lives onto the surface of the urn, into the realm of art, rather the way Porphyro and Madeline are ejected at the end of "The Eve of St. Agnes" (Rajan 136); but especially for the narrator, who has appropriated the urn, forced it to speak, and in possessing it has lost it; who has tried in vain to move deeper into the desired silence, toward an object unsullied by representation.

The town's silence is the suppression of history; yet the figure undercuts itself. In speaking of the town, the narrator speaks to her; by apostrophizing her, he calls her into being; he tells her history even as he laments her citizens' inability to tell it. The dream of the pristine citadel is undone even as it is expressed. The town, like the urn, is the Other of desire, never to be possessed, always to be resymbolized. There is no "return" to this place of origin: this is a mythical *integritas,* to which the narrator, no more than the frozen figures, can ever find the way back. The fictionality of the little town draws attention to itself, suspends our suspension of disbelief and initiates the return—signalled in the stanza's last word—to the pure ventriloquism of the last stanza.

For even as the poem asserts that no return is possible, the *word* "return" effects a return—performs, with wonderful succinctness, the same function as the homologous "forlorn" at the end of the penultimate stanza in the "Ode to a Nightingale" (O'Rourke 42), bringing the narrator suddenly back from fantasy to the time of speaking. The concluding stanza is in every way a "return." By repeating the figure of apostrophe with which the poem began, and by extracting from the urn its neatly chiastic aphorism, "Beauty is truth, truth beauty," Keats imposes on the poem at least a rhetorical circularity, a decisive sense of closure, and gives it a properly sonorous conclusion.

But the voicing of this conclusion is notoriously problematical. To see the urn's fragment of direct discourse as itself enclosed in an apostrophe is to obviate the debate about where precisely the closing quotation marks ought to be placed[20]—for, since the narrator is telling the urn what statement she makes, *all* the words are his. Indeed, the gender of this bride is undecidable. On the one hand the urn is a woman—a cave-like body with an oracular voice, a tease who speaks in riddles, who claims to be whole, and who offers a man *everything*—"all ye need"—"All ye need to *know*—"know" in the archaic sexual sense? On the other hand, the words she speaks are a man's: her statement that "Beauty is truth, truth beauty" takes its authority from Plato, and from the tradition he has fathered. The meaning of the famous five words has been endlessly debated, but is less important than their rhetorical *effect.* The statement functions as a sign that indicates "This is a poem within the Platonic tradition: this is a mainstream production." Even as Keats dramatizes the insufficiency of the Platonic message (if we agree that this is indeed what he is doing), he positions himself within the Platonic field. By the very act of saying she is complete, is whole, is one, the urn proves she is split, divided, factitious—that she differs from herself. The split enacts the problem of sexual and cultural appropriation. But for that very reason, it has a perennial appeal to a culture still deeply permeated by the same desires. The ending feels somewhat forced and arbitrary, yet rhetorically it is most successful. In calling attention, by its very arbitrariness, to the existential paradoxes in Keats's project, it masks the political paradoxes.

The dream of cultural possession is the dream of appropriating the wholeness of the Other, as nineteenth-century characterizations of "Greekness" make clear—a dream of supplementing our lack with a borrowed *integritas.* On the psychological level such a project cannot succeed; on the political level, on the other hand, it may. The English appropriated Greek culture and the ideal of Greekness in a highly selective and opportunistic way, making it serve social and cultural ends that were in the widest sense thoroughly political. Keats's project has as its prototype the very historical process that made the urn accessible to him in the first place—the process of cultural and national appropriation. Though the lover cannot seize the maiden, Keats can seize the urn: the lover's failure to possess masks Keats's stunning success. While the poem can be read as deconstructing the very ambition that gave rise to it, its rhetoric has tended apparently to conceal the specifically political nature of this ambition.

My reading of the ode has been an attempt to think in a new way about, as Roger Poole has put it, "What has got left out of this poem to make of it the particularly expensive torso that it is" (Bloom, "Breaking" 15). I am also interested in what has got left out of the traditional readings of the poem, by critics whose totalizing interpretations ignore its most radical irony. This is the irony of a text that, voicing its awareness that life cannot appropriate the static perfection of art, nevertheless speaks—with apparent complacency to which generations of readers have complacently responded—a discourse of sexual and cultural appropriation. The ode's stunning currency as a cultural icon—its exemplary canonicity—is perhaps worth thinking about in the context of the history and the politics it has tended so thoroughly to repress.

Notes

1. Quotations from the ode are from Keats, 372–73. The allusion in my title is to the novel by Atwood.
2. See Culler on apostrophe as the essential lyric figure; see Johnson on the ways in which a woman's use of this figure foregrounds the issue of power.
3. Jack, 215, notes that the subject for the Oxford Prize Poem, for about ten years running, was some work of art.
4. Byron's satire (*Don Juan* 11.60) on the cockney poet who "without Greek/Contrived to talk about the Gods of late" makes explicit the link between class, education, and the right to things Greek and to a place in the literary canon. On Keats's sensitivity to the political associations of verse form, see Keach. On his political opinions, see also the other papers in "Keats and Politics: A Forum" in *Studies in Romanticism* 25:2 (1986). The consensus here seems to be that Keats was an idealistic liberal, though Bewell, noting his unease with the liberal language of progress, suggests that he identified less with any specific body of political thought than with the political outsider.
5. Simpson cites Spitzer, Cleanth Brooks, Stuart Sperry, and Morris Dickstein as distinguishing in various ways between poet and speaker, and identifies most closely with the position of Harold Bloom (201–02n). Bloom reads the urn's words

ironically, insisting that Keats himself is "the only genuine forerunner of the representative post-Romantic sensibility" precisely because he is under no illusions about the "finality of human life and death" or about the mind's power to transcend experience ("Keats" 138). O'Rourke sees the poet's and speaker's separate points of view eventually converging when the speaker discovers that an urn cannot answer the questions that a poem can formulate.

6. Harding (100), for example, cites Vendler (133): "The urn can speak of nothing but itself, and its self-referentiality is nowhere clearer than in the interior completeness of its circular epigram"; Mansell describes the poet, "making love" to an urn whose "self-sufficient, self-referential circularity" remains "unbroken" (243), as onanistic. The only critic I have seen who emphasizes that the poem is "implicated in . . . political and social contradictions" (104–05) is Watkins, who argues that it participates in the oppression of women and who also notes the relevance of the controversy about the Elgin marbles.
7. Robinson overstates his case, and Jack, who concedes that he considered Wedgwood Ware as a possible inspiration of Keats's ode, dismisses "much" of his argument (284–85). But while Jack has shown that Keats would not have *had* to rely on this very popular commodity for his Grecian imagery, Robinson's evidence that Keats would have been surrounded by Wedgwood Ware and might very well have appreciated it and been influenced by its general style remains plausible. Jack's distaste for Robinson's line of argument seems to me symptomatic of the critical bias that I am suggesting still tends to inform the reading of Keats's poetry.
8. Haydon succinctly makes a point that continues to be made by Elgin's defenders: "Buonaparte would have had them the moment he had the power (*Diary* 1.87–88).
9. For accounts of Lord Elgin's acquisition of the marbles, see Smith and St. Clair. Hitchens (57–59), in a critique of Smith, sums up the case against Elgin.
10. See also the sympathetic review of *Childe Harold's Pilgrimage* in the *Critical Quarterly*, March 1812, 185–86. For an account of Byron's influence on public opinion, see St. Clair, 188–202.
11. Watkins makes this point (117–18).

12. McGann observes that Romantic poems "tend to develop different sorts of artistic means with which to occlude and disguise their own involvement in a certain nexus of historical relations" (*Ideology* 82).

13. Vendler also proceeds by differentiating between the opening questions and the later ones, although her distinctions and conclusions differ from mine.

14. So different is the tone of the two stanzas that it has sometimes been assumed that Keats is describing two different scenes. Vendler distinguishes sharply between the "mad pursuit" and the "contrasting entirely idyllic portrait" (141). On the other hand, Baker argues convincingly, from the link implied in "soft pipes," that stanza two represents a detail of the first scene "brought into sharper focus," its "sexual gusto . . . etherealised" (175–76).

15. Neither Baker nor Waldoff, for example, makes any distinction between the enthusiasm of the pursuers and that of the pursued, Baker characterizing the scene as one of "lustful joy" (176), and Waldoff assuming the "erotic excitement" of both "the bold lover" and the "maidens overwrought" (135). Watkins on the other hand notes that nothing suggests that the female figures participate in the "wild ecstasy" (108).

16. Readers who respond to this suggestion tend not to see it as at all problematical. For an ardent evocation of "the feminine form in all its vital richness—woman the eternal, holding deep within her the sum of all," see Patterson 53–54.

17. Hartman's essay expresses his nostalgia for the object not yet soiled by overexplanation, and focusses on the urn as an exemplary image that retains its virginal plenitude by resisting interpretation. The essay mirrors the poem, taking shape, via a quotation from Robbe-Grillet (105), around the two images used by Keats, the woman and the city, and imbuing them with mythic resonance.

18. Barthes elucidates the interconnection: the blazon, expressing as sequence what is to be apprehended as totality, is constructed like the sentence, which "can never constitute a *total*." "The blazon expresses the belief that a *complete* inventory can reproduce a *total* body," but "language undoes the body, returns it to the fetish" (113–14).

19. A number of recent studies, though proceeding from very different premises, have suggested that a certain type of irony—the self-conscious questioning of the ontological status of the poet's own claims—is the definitive mark of the Romantic project. See Simpson; McGann, *Ideology;* Mellor; Rajan.

20. Summarized by Stillinger, "Who Says What."

Works Cited

Arnold, Matthew. *The Complete Prose Works.* Ed. R. H. Super. 11 vols. Ann Arbor: U of Michigan P, 1960–.

Aske, Martin. *Keats and Hellenism: An Essay.* Cambridge: Cambridge UP, 1985

Atwood, Margaret. *Bodily Harm.* Toronto: McClelland, 1981.

Baker, Jeffrey. *John Keats and Symbolism.* Sussex: Harvester, 1986.

Barthes, Roland. *S/Z.* Trans. Richard Miller. Preface Richard Howard. New York: Hill, 1974.

Bewell, Alan J. "The Political Implication of Keats's Classicist Aesthetics." *Studies in Romanticism* 25 (1986): 220–29.

Bloom, Harold. "The Breaking of Form." Harold Bloom et al., *Deconstruction and Criticism.* New York: Seabury, 1979. 1–37.

———. "Keats and the Embarrassments of Poetic Tradition." *The Ringers in the Tower: Studies in Romantic Tradition.* Chicago: U of Chicago P, 1971. 131–42.

Byron, George Gordon, Baron. *The Complete Poetical Works.* Ed. Jerome J. McGann. 5 vols. Oxford: Clarendon, 1980–.

Culler, Jonathan. "Apostrophe." *Diacritics* 7:4 (Winter 1977): 59–69. Rpt. in *The Pursuit of Signs: Semiotics, Literature, Deconstruction.* Ithaca, NY: Cornell UP, 1981. 135–54.

Frye, Northrop. *Anatomy of Criticism: Four Essays.* Princeton, NJ: Princeton UP, 1957.

Harding, Anthony John. "Speech, Silence, and the Self-Doubting Interpreter in Keats's Poetry." *Keats-Shelley Journal* 35 (1986): 83–103.

Hartman, Geoffrey H. "History Writing as Answerable Style." *The Fate of Reading and Other Essays.* Chicago: U of Chicago P, 1975. 101–13.

Haydon, Benjamin Robert. *The Autobiography and Memoirs of Benjamin Robert Haydon (1786–1846).* Ed. Tom Taylor. Introd. Aldous Huxley. 2 vols. London: Davies, 1926.

———. *The Diary of Benjamin Robert Haydon.* Ed. Willard B. Pope. 5 vols. Cambridge, MA: Harvard UP, 1960.

Hitchens, Christopher. *The Elgin Marbles: Should they be returned to Greece?* With essays by Robert Browning and Graham Binns. London: Chatto, 1987.

Jack, Ian. *Keats and the Mirror of Art.* Oxford: Clarendon, 1967.

Johnson, Barbara. "Apostrophe, Animation, and Abortion." *Diacritics* 16:1 (Spring 1986): 29–39.

Joyce, James. *A Portrait of the Artist as a Young Man.* Ed. Chester G. Anderson. New York: Viking, 1968.

Keach, William. "Cockney Couplets: Keats and the Politics of Style." *Studies in Romanticism* 25 (1986): 182–96.

Keats, John. *Poems of John Keats.* Ed. Jack Stillinger. Cambridge, MA: Belknap P of Harvard UP, 1978.

Lacan, Jacques. "The mirror stage as formative of the function of the I as revealed in psychoanalytic experience." *Écrits: A Selection.* Trans. Alan Sheridan. New York: Tavistock, 1977.

Mansell, Darrel. "Keats's Urn: 'On' and On." *Language and Style* 7 (1974): 235–44.

McGann, Jerome J. "Keats and the Historical Method in Literary Criticism." *Modern Language Notes* 94 (1979): 988–1032.

———. *The Romantic Ideology: A Critical Investigation.* Chicago: U of Chicago P, 1983.

Mellor, Anne K. *English Romantic Irony.* Cambridge, MA: Harvard UP, 1980.

O'Rourke, James. "Persona and Voice in the 'Ode on a Grecian Urn'." *Studies in Romanticism* 26 (1987): 27–48.

Patterson, Charles I. "Passion and Permanence in Keats's 'Ode on a Grecian Urn'." *Twentieth-Century Interpretations of Keats's Odes.* Ed. Jack Stillinger. 48–57.

Rajan, Tilottama. *Dark Interpreter: The Discourse of Romanticism.* Ithaca, NY: Cornell UP, 1980.

Rhodes, Jack Wright. *Keats's Major Odes: An Annotated Bibliography of the Criticism.* London: Greenwood, 1984.

Robinson, Dwight E. "Ode on a 'New Etrurian' Urn: A Reflection of Wedgwood Ware in the Poetic Imagery of John Keats." *Keats-Shelley Journal* 12 (1963): 11–35.

Rothenberg, Jacob. *"Descensus Ad Terram": The Acquisition and Reception of the Elgin Marbles.* New York: Garland, 1977.

St. Clair, William. *Lord Elgin and the Marbles.* London: Oxford UP, 1967.

Schlegel, August Wilhelm von. *A Course of Lectures on Dramatic Art and Literature.* Trans. John Black. 2 vols. London: Baldwin, 1815.

Scholes, Robert. "Towards a Semiotics of Literature." *Semiotics and Interpretation.* New Haven: Yale UP, 1982. 17–36.

Sharpe, William. *The Life and Letters of Joseph Severn.* London: Sampson, 1892.

Simpson, David. *Irony and Authority in Romantic Poetry.* London: Sampson, 1892.

Smith, A. H. "Lord Elgin and his Collection." *Journal of Hellenic Studies* 36 (1916): 163–372.

Spitzer, Leo. "The 'Ode on a Grecian Urn,' or Content vs. Metagrammar." *Essays on English and American Literature.* Ed. Anna Hatcher. Princeton, NJ: Princeton UP, 1962. 67–97.

Stillinger, Jack. *The Hoodwinking of Madeline and Other Essays on Keats's Poems.* Urbana: U of Illinois P, 1971.

———. "Who Says What to Whom at the End of *Ode on a Grecian Urn?*" *Twentieth-Century Interpretations.* Ed. Stillinger. 113–14. Rpt. and expanded as Appendix III in *The Hoodwinking of Madeline,* 167–73.

———. ed. *Twentieth-Century Interpretations of Keats's Odes. A Collection of Critical Essays.* Englewood Cliffs: Prentice, 1968.

Vendler, Helen. *The Odes of John Keats.* Cambridge, MA: Belknap P of Harvard UP, 1983.

Waldoff, Leon. *Keats and the Silent Work of Imagination.* Urbana: U of Illinois P, 1985.

Watkins, Daniel P. "'Coming to the Sacrifice': *Ode on a Grecian Urn.*" *Keats's Poetry and the Politics of the Imagination.* Rutherford: Fairleigh Dickinson UP, 1989. 104–20.

Webb, Timothy. *English Romantic Hellenism, 1700–1824.* New York: Barnes, 1982.

Whinney, Margaret. *Sculpture in Britain: 1530–1830.* Pelican History of Art. Harmondsworth: Penguin, 1964.

The Legal Fictions of Herman Melville and Lemuel Shaw

Brook Thomas

Brook Thomas speaks for most of the critics in this context when he argues that "the ambiguity of literary texts might better be understood in terms of an era's social contradictions rather than in terms of the inherent qualities of literary language or rhetoric and, conversely, that a text's ambiguity can help us expose the contradictions masked by an era's dominant ideology." He also speaks for most when he disowns any "positivist" need to prove direct lines of influence and when he remarks the tendency of psychological readings to deflect our attention from political and social issues. "I compare Shaw to Melville not to reduce Melville's politics to psychology but to prevent a political study from neglecting the political implications of psychology, to remind us—as the title of Fredric Jameson's book The Political Unconscious *reminds us—that psychological questions always have political implications." For Thomas, as for Eagleton, "ideology" is the key concept, and his study of Melville's stories is designed to demonstrate "their relationship to the dominant ideology of their times, especially their capacity to allow us to see the contradictions in that ideology, contradictions that they themselves cannot avoid." Thus by reading "Benito Cereno" in the context of Lemuel Shaw's legal writings, Thomas claims to uncover the story's "political unconscious" and to show how its ambiguities reveal the ideological conflicts of its age.*

I have three aims in this essay. (1) I want to offer an example of an interdisciplinary historical inquiry combining literary criticism with the relatively new field of critical legal studies. (2) I intend to use this historical inquiry to argue that the ambiguity of literary texts might better be understood in terms of an era's social contradictions rather than in terms of the inherent qualities of literary language or rhetoric and, conversely, that a text's ambiguity can help us expose the contradictions masked by an era's dominant ideology. (3) I try to prove my assertion by applying my method to Herman Melville's "Benito Cereno," a work that deals with the law and lawyers and is widely acknowledged as ambiguous.[1] I will base my critical inquiry into this story on Melville's relationship with his father-in-law, Lemuel Shaw, who, while sitting as the chief justice of the Supreme Judicial Court of Massachusetts from 1830 to 1860, wrote some of the most important opinions in what Roscoe Pound has called "the formative era of American law."[2]

Before I get started, I should clarify what this study does not entail. By using Shaw and his legal decisions in conjunction with Melville's fiction, I am not conducting a positivistic influence study. My method will not depend on the positivist assumption that Shaw's legal opinions can be used to illuminate Melville's texts only when his direct knowledge of Shaw's opinions can be proved. Nor will I limit myself to a traditional psychoanalytic reading: my emphasis is on political and social issues, and too often these issues are deflected by translating them into psychological ones. At the same time, I recognize that critics concerned with political and social issues too often neglect questions raised by a writer's individual situation. I compare Shaw to Melville not to reduce Melville's politics to psychology but to prevent a political study from neglecting the political implications of psychology, to remind us — as the title of Fredric Jameson's book *The Political Unconscious* reminds us — that psychological questions always have political implications.

If, for instance, psychological critics refer to the early death of his father to explain Melville's fascination with paternal authority figures who abandon their "children," I would argue that given the patriarchal structure of authority in both his family and society, Melville's fascination inevitably has political implications. That Melville, fatherless for years, finally acquired a father-*in-law* who was the most important figure upholding the law in the Commonwealth of Massachusetts presents almost too neat a coincidence for anyone interested in studying the politics of their relationship, for it suggests that part of the power of Melville's works can be explained by his unique personal situation. It is, after all, important that it was Melville's father-in-law who made such important legal decisions. When Melville wrote stories about the law, he was no doubt influenced by

the fact that his father-in-law was a famous judge. Even so, that personal relationship is significant for me because of what it reveals about the dominant ideology of Melville's times, an ideology that his father-in-law's court decisions both reflected and helped to shape.

This emphasis on ideology is what moves my study beyond a positivistic influence study. When I cite Shaw's legal opinions, I usually do so not to imply that Melville had direct knowledge of them; I cite them because they are the best evidence we have of Shaw's way of thinking about political matters, a way of thinking shared by many people in power during the antebellum period. It is not so important to prove that Melville had detailed knowledge of any one of Shaw's opinions as it is to demonstrate that he had some sense of the opinions behind the opinions. What my interdisciplinary method offers, therefore, is not so much a new interpretation that extracts a long-hidden meaning from Melville's stories, as a demonstration of their relationship to the dominant ideology of their times, especially their capacity to allow us to see the contradictions in that ideology, contradictions that they themselves cannot avoid.

As such, my investigation into the ideological implications of Melville's stories agrees basically, if not totally, with Louis Althusser's understanding of literature's relation to ideology. Althusser rejects the view that submission to the laws of art made a writer like Balzac abandon his own political convictions and generate telling social criticism despite his conservative beliefs. "On the contrary," Althusser argues, "*only because he retained them could he produce his work,* only because he stuck to his political ideology could he produce *in it* this internal 'distance' which gives us a critical 'view' of it." Art does not escape ideology, for Althusser, but what it "makes us see . . . is the *ideology* from which it is born, in which it bathes, from which it detaches itself as art, and to which it *alludes*."[3]

I will start by reading "Benito Cereno" in conjunction with Shaw's fugitive slave decisions, for if there was one issue which dramatically revealed contradictions in the American legal system, it was slavery. Shaw's decisions will help us better understand Melville's only direct treatment of slavery, at the same time that Melville's fictional account of a slave uprising will help us expose the inconsistencies within Shaw's decisions.

Prior to the Fugitive Slave Act of 1850, Shaw went out of his way (with one exception) to find loopholes in the existing Fugitive Slave Act of 1793. Shaw's desire to help runaway blacks achieve their freedom whenever possible grew out of his personal abhorrence of slavery. Shaw's reputation as an opponent of slavery was so strong that in an 1845 decision, Judge Nevius of New Jersey questioned whether Shaw's personal beliefs might have biased his opinions on slavery: "It is no matter of surprise that Chief Justice Shaw, entertaining the opinions he did upon this question of slavery, should have found it repugnant to the spirit of [the] Constitution" (*JA*, p. 58 n). Given Shaw's antislavery reputation, it was a matter of considerable surprise to some that he reversed himself and supported the new 1850 fugitive slave law.

The new fugitive slave law was part of Daniel Webster's compromise to hold the country together. Yet it was widely known that prior to 1850 no fugitive slave had been returned from Boston, the seat of much of Webster's support. Thus strong political pressure was exerted on Webster's friends (Shaw was one) to enforce the new law, in order to counter Southern charges that Massachusetts was ruled by abolitionists. Their first chance to prove their loyalty to the union came in February 1851, when a black named Shadrach was apprehended in Boston. But to the dismay of Southerners and Webster supporters, Shadrach escaped from the courthouse, aided by an unruly crowd of antislavery forces. Thus, on 3 April 1851, when Thomas Sims was taken into custody, officials made certain that he was brought to "justice." Curtailed by a state law from holding an accused runaway slave in a state jail, officials locked Sims in the federal courthouse and barricaded the door with chains. As abolitionists were quick to point out, the chains produced a highly symbolic scene the next day when Judge Shaw had to bow beneath them in order to enter a court of justice. In his decision Shaw himself felt fettered by the existing law of the land. When asked to rule on the constitutionality of the 1850 law, Shaw upheld it in a decision that for a decade was regarded as the highest authority on the issue. Free to proceed, the federal commissioner ordered the return of Sims to slavery, and, guarded by three hundred armed men, Sims was delivered to a ship and sent on his way south.

Shaw's decisions in the 1850s were not necessarily inconsistent with his earlier stand against slavery.

In his pre-1850 decisions, Shaw never transgressed what he deemed the letter of the law. When the 1850 law tightened the loopholes which had allowed him to decide in favor of blacks, he saw no recourse but to decide as he did. Equally important, his decisions revealed principles he stated as early as 1820. Discussing the Missouri Compromise, Shaw had used abolitionist language to denounce slavery, but he added that immediate emancipation might cause misery. Furthermore, he felt the most important consideration was the "moral" necessity to hold the union together.

That Shaw saw maintaining the union in moral terms helps clarify a common misunderstanding about the conflict between antislavery forces and their opponents. Persuaded by powerful antislavery rhetoric, we often see the conflict as one between defenders of rule by secular authority—man-made law manifested in positive law—and proponents of rule by sacred authority—divine law manifested in private conscience. To a certain extent this statement of the conflict is accurate, but it is important to recognize that Shaw and many members of the legal profession also saw their secular responsibility in sacred terms. Preserving the union was a moral imperative because the United States was not merely one government among many but the hope of mankind: it, above all others, guaranteed the absolute and entire supremacy of the law. If abolitionists claimed that the country was not worth saving because its passage of laws like the Fugitive Slave Act violated its sacred mission, Shaw felt that unless the union *was* saved its sacred mission could never be fulfilled. To obey the act of 1850 would not only reaffirm the sacred principle of rule by law, which made the union worth preserving, it would also support a law that everyone knew was designed specifically to keep the country united. Thus, those who praised Shaw's *Sims* decision praised it because it declared that rule by law would prevail over the violence threatening to tear the country apart. Associated with blackness, that violence could easily be linked with satanic forces.

Those in power feared a violent slave uprising that might threaten the peace of the country and the sanctity of the law; this is evinced by the response to the Shadrach escape. The escape was reported as an example of "negro insurrection"; Secretary of State Webster labeled it "a case of treason"; President Fillmore called a special cabinet meeting to discuss the crisis; on the Senate floor Henry Clay asked whether "a government of white men was to be yielded to by a government of blacks."[4] For those so threatened, Shaw's decision in the *Sims* case signaled a victory for the forces of light over the forces of violence and darkness. The problem that the slavery issue posed for people who saw America's mission as furthering the cause of enlightenment—which, as I have argued, included both Shaw *and* antislavery factions—was that it was not always clear which were the forces of light and which of darkness.

This is, of course, precisely the dilemma facing readers of "Benito Cereno." Melville confronts us with a story which starts as a world full of grays only to transform into a world divided between blacks and whites, where the whites who seem to be in power are not and where a violent slave uprising, masterminded by a black man described in satanic terms, is squelched by an American captain who, because he is oblivious, appears innocent. A history of conflicting interpretations has arisen because the story provides no authoritative point of view to help us determine whether the blacks, the whites, or neither fight for an enlightened cause. This is not to say that Melville does not offer points of view which can traditionally be considered authoritative. To be sure, the two points of view through which the events of the story are filtered would conventionally be accepted as authoritative: first, the personal authority of a ship's captain; second, the impersonal authority of a legal deposition. But the authority of both of these points of view is undercut. The deficiencies of the legal deposition prompt us to examine the nature of justice guaranteed by the rule by law held so sacred by Justice Shaw. But first we need to review the limitations of Captain Delano's personal point of view.

Despite the many conflicting interpretations of the story, almost all readers agree that it exposes the narrowness of Captain Delano's innocent point of view. His innocent, straightforward reading of the events aboard the *San Dominick* turns out to be a complete misreading, a misreading that ironically saves him. As Don Benito Cereno, the *San Dominick's* captain, tells him toward the end of the tale, if he had accurately interpreted the state of affairs aboard ship, he would have faced instant death. As a result, both he and Don Benito attribute his salvation to Providence; the reader, however, can see that Captain Del-

ano's salvation results as much from his prejudice as from a providential concern for the innocent. Or put another way, his innocence is riddled with prejudice. As kind as Captain Delano seems to the Africans, he is unable to decipher the bizarre events on board ship because the possibility that Africans rather than Europeans could be in power is incomprehensible to him. When he sees blacks and whites, he immediately relegates blacks to a subservient role. He can think of blacks as only valets, hairdressers, or body servants. The true extent of Captain Delano's kindness to blacks is apparent when we learn that "like most men of good, blithe heart, Captain Delano took to negroes, not philanthropically, but genially, just as other men to Newfoundland dogs" (p. 265).

If the reader has not realized the limitations of Captain Delano's point of view, they are further emphasized in the story's second half, when the events are recounted from the point of view of the legal deposition. As opposed to Captain Delano's partial account of events, the legal point of view purports to offer an impartial account. But there are hints in the text that even the legal point of view might be partial, although in a much more subtle manner than Captain Delano's "innocent" prejudice.[5] First, the "document" Melville includes from the proceedings is "selected, from among many others, for partial translation" (p. 289). We do not receive all of the documents or even a complete translation of the one we do receive. Second, the selected document contains Don Benito's deposition, including testimony originally "held dubious" because of his "not undisturbed" state of mind (p. 289). Third, the final decision on what evidence is accepted as authoritative is made by a tribunal none of whose members witnessed any of the events under litigation. Rather than bringing us closer to the actual events, the legal point of view in one sense removes us even further from them. Finally, nowhere is the Africans' position voiced, a point I will return to later.

Despite the questionable accuracy of the legal point of view, many readers accept its authority. What the authority of the law legitimates becomes poignantly clear in the story's final paragraph. Certainly, one of the most heinous acts that Babo, the leader of the slave uprising, commits is using the decaying body of the slaveowner Don Alexandro Aranda as the *San Dominick's* figurehead. But that act of violence is no worse than the one committed against Babo during his execution. "Dragged to the gibbet at the tail of a mule, the black met his voiceless end. The body was burned to ashes; but for many days, the head, that hive of subtlety, fixed on a pole in the Plaza, met, unabashed, the gaze of the whites" (p. 307). Babo's bleached skull, like the bleached bones of Don Alexandro, had been put on display to ensure obedience. The law, however, has the power to sanction an act that outside the law is censured as inhumane. Violence is justified when backed by the authority of the law, condemned as brutal and satanic when not. Rule by law, supposedly the only safeguard against the irrationality of violence, depends upon violence or the threat of violence to maintain itself, whether it be the suppression of the African's revolt or the armed enforcement, by three hundred men, of Sims's return to slavery.

Of course, it could be objected that Melville's story is a fictional account of the proceedings of a legal tribunal in Peru, with no bearing on American law and its treatment of the slavery issue. But the *Amistad* case, a case sometimes cited as a source for "Benito Cereno," suggests otherwise. In 1839 forty-nine Africans bloodily seized control of the Spanish ship *Amistad* and tried to return to Africa. The ship was captured off Long Island by the American Navy. The lawsuit that followed involved two Americans filing for salvage; the Spanish owners demanding the ship's cargo, including the Africans; and the Africans claiming their freedom. The United States Government intervened on behalf of the Spaniards, citing a treaty between Spain and the United States promising to restore merchandise rescued from the hands of robbers or pirates. Justice Joseph Story, a Massachusetts judge similar in ideology to Shaw, wrote the opinion of the United States Supreme Court which granted the Africans their freedom. Arguing that the treaty did not apply since under Spanish law the Africans had been unlawfully enslaved and hence were not property, this notably conservative judge went so far as to concede the right of the Africans to rebel in their circumstances. "We may lament the dreadful acts by which they asserted their liberty, and took possession of the *Amistad*, but they cannot be deemed pirates or robbers in the sense of the law of nations" (*JA*, p. 112).[6]

In granting the Africans their freedom, the *Amistad* decision seems to manifest the concern the American legal system had for slaves. But Story was careful to point out that the Africans' rebellion was justified only on the high seas. If it had occurred within the United States, under American law, the legal questions would have been different. It was, for instance, the same Justice Story—an antislavery man himself—who ruled a year later in *Prigg* v. *The State of Pennsylvania* that according to United States law the Fugitive Slave Act of 1793 was constitutional and that state laws conflicting with it were unconstitutional. Story's decision was the one that Shaw cited to send Sims back to slavery. These cases indicate that, as far as slavery was concerned, American law was more repressive than "the law of nations." The action of "Benito Cereno" would seem to bear this out.

For anyone who considers the United States a progressive country, there is a certain irony in a plot in which a representative of the democratic United States (Captain Delano) returns Africans to slavery after they have achieved their freedom from a representative of the decaying, feudal power of Spain (Don Benito). Read as a political allegory, the story marks the ascendancy of the United States to its role as a new, more effective, imperialist power. The moment of ascendancy occurs in the boat departing from the *San Dominick*, when Captain Delano uses his hand to hold down Don Benito while simultaneously, with his foot, holding down Babo, who is "snakishly writhing up from the boat's bottom" (p. 283)—which recalls the symbolic sternpiece described at the beginning of the story, often cited as an emblem for exploitation.[7]

Melville's story even suggests one motive generating the rise of the United States to power. Boarding the *San Dominick* to put down the black insurrection, the sailors of Captain Delano's ship, the *Bachelor's Delight*, are spurred on by a promise that they will be economically rewarded, since Don Benito has declared the cargo lost and for their taking. One of the most valuable cargoes on the *San Dominick* is, of course, human beings. Thus, while mistakenly killing two of the remaining Spanish crew members, the Americans take great care not "to kill or maim the negroes" (p. 286).

The economic interest impelling the American sailors is paralleled by the economic interest which promoted the passage of the Fugitive Slave Act of 1850. That act was the product of an affiliation of the cotton spinners of the North and the cotton producers of the South, or as Charles Sumner put it, "the lords of the loom and the lords of the lash" (*LC*, p. 86). In the name of national unity and loyalty to the Constitution, Boston "Cotton Whigs" protected their financial interests. Indeed, parts of the Boston merchant class were outright supporters of the South and its peculiar institution. That Shaw's decisions upholding the return of fugitive slaves aided the commercial interests of Boston merchants was readily noticed by his critics. One abolitionist accused Shaw of being as morally reprehensible as a "slave pirate on the African coast" (*LC*, p. 82). Probably more accurate, Richard Henry Dana wrote in his journal after the *Shadrach* case that Shaw's conduct "shows how deeply seated, so as to affect, unconsciously I doubt not, good men like him, in this selfish hunkerism of the property interest on the slave question" (*LC*, p. 91). Similarly, Captain Delano, a good, honest man serving on a merchant ship, aids in the exploitation of human beings for commercial interests, unconsciously I doubt not, helping to make the new United States' democracy as exploitive as the feudal system it replaced. The exploitive power of the United States promises to be more difficult to unmask than even that of the cunning Babo, since it is disguised by the benevolence, goodwill, and spirit of equality that both Captain Delano and Justice Shaw embody.

While it would be too crude to identify Shaw with Captain Delano, it is important to point out that these two good, fair-minded men from Massachusetts reenslave blacks who had achieved freedom. Furthermore, we can discover in Shaw the same sort of prejudice masked by condescending kindness toward blacks that we found in Captain Delano. The case providing the best evidence is not a slave decision but one which endorsed segregation in Boston public schools. In *Roberts* v. *The City of Boston* (1849), Shaw proclaimed the famous separate-but-equal doctrine that was adopted by the federal courts until it was overruled in 1954. Arguing that the prejudice which existed "is not created by law, and probably cannot be changed by law," Shaw went on to reveal his own prejudice in deciding the law, stating that while all were equal under the law, some were more equal than others.[8]

Commenting on Shaw's stand on the Fugitive Slave Act, Judge Benjamin Thomas remarked that Shaw "was so simple, honest, upright, and straightforward, it never occurred to him there was any way around, over, under, or through the barrier of the Constitution" (*LC*, p. 102). But Shaw's hidden prejudice toward blacks suggests another reason why he saw no way around the Constitution. Just as Captain Delano's prejudiced point of view gives way to a legalistic point of view which legitimates the repression of the black revolt, so Shaw's prejudiced attitude becomes embodied in the law and therefore legitimated.

As I have argued, however, the thrust of Melville's story undercuts the authority of both the personal and the legal points of view. I could go on to claim that this undercutting invites us to read the story from a point of view not overtly contained within its pages. That alternative perspective, it could be argued, of necessity goes beyond and challenges the two presented in the story. But the problem with this argument is that not all readers construct an alternative perspective. Because Melville formulates no alternative himself, he allows readers either sharing Captain Delano's prejudices or believing in the objectivity of legal documents to accept the version of the story closest to their own perspective. Even readers holding neither view can argue that because the alternative, antislavery point of view is not explicitly supplied in the story, it cannot be attributed to it. In fact, if a reader insists on locating a point of view *within* the story, he can only conclude that Melville presented a story from a proslavery perspective. While one reader can argue that it is precisely through presenting proslavery prejudices that Melville undercuts them, another can argue that Melville's technique reinforces them. Ultimately, then, "Benito Cereno" subverts its own power of subversion. Readers who see the text undercutting the proslavery perspectives within it cannot propose their own antislavery perspective as an impartial and complete account of the text, because their perspective is based solely on an absence.

A number of liberal and radical critics have tried to fill this absence by propounding the point of view most obviously missing: Babo's.[9] Indeed, when they tell the story from Babo's viewpoint, they eliminate the ambiguity of the story by turning it into an antislavery tract. But it is precisely Babo's point of view that Melville does not offer. Instead, we are confronted by Babo's mysterious silence. That silence makes Babo the most difficult character to assess, a difficulty compounded because Babo's power is so great that he also silences Don Benito, the only character seemingly capable of understanding him. Rather than deciding whether Melville is sympathetic or not toward Babo, I would agree with those critics who consider silence as Melville's comment on him. But unlike those who conclude from Melville's silence that the story is about indeterminacy, I contend that the text's silences and ambiguities can be explained in terms of the historical contradictions which slavery posed to "enlightened" whites such as Melville and Shaw.

The most simple explanation of Babo's silence is to see it in terms of the silencing of blacks throughout antebellum America. Not only were blacks generally repressed; specifically, the Fugitive Slave Act of 1850 refused to accept testimony of accused slaves in proceedings against them. But to consider Babo's silence merely as Melville's comment on the silencing of blacks in American society would be far too simple. Psychological critics who see Babo as a frightening product of Melville's psyche, a character whose Iago-like silence indicates Melville's inability to comprehend him, are not irresponsibly imposing their own reading onto the text. Babo is indeed frightening to a white audience; he is not at all sympathetic like Harriet Beecher Stowe's Uncle Tom. And Babo is indeed a creature of Melville's imagination, an essential part of his imaginary narrative treating the complexity of the slavery issue.

In *The Political Unconscious*, Jameson has argued that most writers, when confronted with a historical issue as complex as slavery, adopt a "strategy of containment" whereby their imagined narrative gives historical contradictions an illusory resolution.[10] Babo has often been read as a vital part of Melville's strategy of containment. Sidney Kaplan, for instance, sees Babo's portrayal as a retreat from Melville's "democratic" treatment of blacks in *Moby-Dick* because Babo reinforces every antiblack fear of his 1855 audience. That audience could read the story as a warning against indulging in lax discipline and naive trust in blacks, since such indulgence encourages a rebellion producing violence worse than that maintaining slavery.[11] The story's conclusion would indicate, accordingly, that Melville supports Shaw's rule by law, no matter how flawed, as a necessary defense against the violence threatened by Babo.

But if Babo is part of Melville's imagined resolution, Melville's resolution does not actually resolve anything. While rule by law seems to have settled all questions about the events aboard the *San Dominick* and transformed its violent chaos into rational order

by eliminating Babo, Babo continues to cast a shadow over the world of the book. As a true representative of the repressed, Babo cannot be contained. He marks the return of the repressed not only in Freud's psychological sense but also in the political sense. At the same time that he is the embodiment of the dark, irrational forces repressed by Melville's psyche, forces which in the culture at large only the legal system seems able to control, he is also the repressed black, who, denied voice by that very legal system, has no way to speak but through violence. He is a figure whom Melville, in examining slavery, must represent, but for whom, as the alien other, Melville can provide no voice.

Another factor complicates Melville's treatment of slavery: Melville does not share the secure confidence of most critics of slavery that the Northern alternative is unambiguously better. Southerners countered Northern attacks on slavery by arguing that their system was only a more explicit version of the exploitation occurring daily in the Northern "wage-slave" system. Melville, while opposed to all forms of exploitation, seems to have recognized a limited truth to the Southern response. In *White-Jacket*, for instance, Melville is not unequivocally sympathetic to Guinea's plight as a slave. Instead, he uses Guinea's slavery to comment on the slavery of the "free" men enlisted in the navy. It is in "Bartleby, the Scrivener," however, that we find Melville's most poignant account of how the lords of the loom and their commercial friends on Wall Street held their workers in bondage much as the lords of the lash held their slaves.

Like "Benito Cereno," "Bartleby" is haunted by a figure whose silence—although different from Babo's—has produced endless critical controversies. Once again that silence can help us discover contradictions in Shaw's legal ideology, while his legal ideology can help us understand the causes of that silence. If in "Benito Cereno" we saw how a general belief in the paramount necessity of rule by law could have led whites theoretically sympathetic to blacks to support the slave economy of the South, in "Bartleby" we will see how the specific individualist basis of Shaw's legal system could have led those full of benevolence and charity to support the wage-slave economy of the North. We will also see the dilemma of a writer who senses the injustice of that system but does not feel capable of offering alternative, affirmative visions to combat its injustice.

●   ●   ●

Notes

1. See Herman Melville, "Benito Cereno," *"Billy Budd, Sailor" and Other Stories,* ed. Harold Beaver (Harmondsworth, 1967); all further references to this work will be included in the text.

2. See Roscoe Pound, *The Formative Era of American Law* (Boston, 1938). For discussions of Melville and Lemuel Shaw, see Charles Roberts Anderson, *Melville in the South Seas,* Columbia University Studies in English and Comparative Literature, no. 138 (New York, 1966), pp. 432–33; Charles H. Foster, "Something in Emblems: A Reinterpretation of *Moby-Dick,*" *New England Quarterly* 34 (Mar. 1961): 3–35; Robert L. Gale, "Bartleby — Melville's Father-in-Law," *Annali sezione germanica, Istituto Universitario Orientale di Napoli* 5 (Dec. 1962): 57–72; Keith Huntress, "'Guinea' of *White-Jacket* and Chief Justice Shaw," *American Literature* 43 (Jan. 1972): 639–41; Carolyn L. Karcher, *Shadow over the Promised Land: Slavery, Race, and Violence in Melville's America* (Baton Rouge, La., 1980), pp. 9–11 and 40; John Stark, "Melville, Lemuel Shaw, and 'Bartleby,'" in *Bartleby, the Inscrutable: A Collection of Commentary on Herman Melville's Tale "Bartleby the Scrivener,"* ed. M. Thomas Inge (Hamden, Conn., 1979), pp. 166–73; and Robert M. Cover, *Justice Accused: Antislavery and the Judicial Process* (New Haven, Conn., 1975); all further references to this work, abbreviated *JA,* will be included in the text.

3. Louis Althusser, "A Letter on Art in Reply to André Daspre," *"Lenin and Philosophy" and Other Essays,* trans. Ben Brewster (New York, 1971), pp. 225, 222.

4. *New York Journal of Commerce,* Daniel Webster, Henry Clay, quoted in Leonard W. Levy, *The Law of the Commonwealth and Chief Justice Shaw: The Evolution of American Law, 1830–1860* (Cambridge, Mass., 1957), pp. 89, 90; all further references to this work, abbreviated *LC,* will be included in the text.

5. See Allen Guttmann, "The Enduring Innocence of Captain Amasa Delano," *Boston University Studies in English* 5 (Spring 1961): "The official and attested view of the matter, the view put forth by Don Benito and ingenuously accepted by Captain Delano, is *the very thing which Melville is subverting.* With its legalistic pretensions of objectivity, the deposition misses the truth as widely as did Delano in his completest innocence" (p. 42). See also Edgar A. Dryden, *Melville's Thematics of Form: The Great Art of Telling the Truth* (Baltimore, 1968).

6. See *The "Amistad" Case* (New York, 1968). Sidney Kaplan discusses the *Amistad* affair and also another important case, the *Creole* affair, in relationship to "Benito Cereno" (see "Herman Melville and the American National Sin: The Meaning of 'Benito Cereno'," *Journal of Negro History* 42 [Jan. 1957]: 14–16).

7. There is not space here to enter into the long critical debate about the meaning of this emblem. For points of view with which I share sympathy, see Joyce Sparer Adler, *War in Melville's Imagination* (New York, 1981), p. 108, and Edward S. Grejda, *The Common Continent of Men: Racial Equality in the Writings of Herman Melville* (Port Washington, N.Y., 1974), p. 144.

8. Shaw, quoted in *Jim Crow in Boston: The Origin of the Separate but Equal Doctrine,* ed. Levy and Douglas L. Jones (New York, 1974), p. 230. Edwin Haviland Miller notes a similarity between Captain Delano and Shaw in passing (see *Melville* [New York, 1975], p. 299).

9. Karcher argues throughout *Shadow over the Promised Land* that Melville's strategy in the 1850s was to adopt a proslavery point of view in order to undercut it. The most radical Melville is the working-class Melville proposed by H. Bruce Franklin (see "Herman Melville: Artist of the Worker's World," in *Weapons of Criticism: Marxism in America and the Literary Tradition,* ed. Norman Rudich [Palo Alto, Calif., 1976], pp. 287–310).

10. See Fredric Jameson, *The Political Unconscious: Narrative as a Socially Symbolic Act* (Ithaca, N.Y., 1981).

11. See Kaplan, "Herman Melville and the American National Sin."

APPLICATION

In some respects, Julie Bates Dock's essay seems to bring us full circle. Certainly, careful textual and biographical scholarship are the staples of traditional literary history, and Dock deploys both to good effect. But if part of the project of the newer history is to cast a critical eye on the institution of literary study itself, Dock's essay could be cited as an exemplary work in this context. Looking closely at the history of commentary on "The Yellow Wallpaper," Dock discovers an eagerness to accept "facts" that have no firm foundation, a tendency to overlook certain kinds of evidence, a willingness to repeat assertions as if they were demonstrations, and in general a desire to believe a narrative in which Gilman's story is initially misunderstood, repressed, and then largely forgotten only to be rediscovered in 1973 as a "paradigmatic" feminist text and thereafter progressively illuminated and finally canonized. Dock illustrates her case by pointing to a number of the best-known studies of Gilman's story, including those by Kennard, Kolodny, and Gilbert and Gubar. But the purpose of her critique is not simply to discover error and bias but to account for it, to explain, as Barker and Hulme phrase it, "why such readings come about and what ideological role they play." Thus Dock attributes the oversights she catalogs not to mere carelessness but to the "need" of feminist critics to construct their story of heroic resistance and eventual triumph. Ironically, their insight into the ideology they opposed was enabled by their blindness to their own. As we might expect, it remains the task of other critics to discover this blindness.

"But One Expects That": Charlotte Perkins Gilman's "The Yellow Wallpaper" and the Shifting Light of Scholarship

Julie Bates Dock with Daphne Ryan Allen, Jennifer Palais, and Kristen Tracy

In the two decades since the Feminist Press issued a slim volume containing a text of "The Yellow Wallpaper" with an afterword by Elaine R. Hedges, Charlotte Perkins Gilman's remarkable work has found a secure place in contemporary literary studies. Omitting "The Yellow Wallpaper" from an American literature anthology has become almost as unthinkable as leaving out "The Raven" or "Civil Disobedience." The story appears not just in those weighty, two-volume collections of American literature but also in textbooks for courses in women's studies and genre studies and in dozens of introductory literature texts for undergraduates.[1] It has been analyzed by literary historians of every stripe, although feminist critics still lead the way in championing Gilman's achievement.

By now, scholars have accumulated a wealth of information about Gilman's life in general and about "The Yellow Wallpaper" in particular. Some "facts" have become common knowledge as critics have built on one another's work. But those "facts" need reassessment as scholars increasingly acknowledge that literary criticism is as grounded in historical biases as the literature it seeks to interpret.

Most of the pioneering work on "The Yellow Wallpaper" occurred during the 1970s and early 1980s, when scholars like Ellen Moers, Elaine Showalter, and Sandra Gilbert and Susan Gubar were challenging what they perceived to be a patriarchal literary canon and arguing for the centrality of politics in literature and literary criticism.[2] In 1985 Gayle Greene and Coppélia Kahn aptly characterized "the two major foci of feminist scholarship: deconstructing dominant male patterns of thought and social practice; and reconstructing female experience previously hidden or overlooked" (6). Just as this deconstructive project led critics to weigh some textual elements more heavily than they did others, it led them to privilege some kinds of scholarship over others. Susan S. Lanser has persuasively argued that feminist criticism from the 1960s until the mid-1980s was "collusive with ideology"—specifically, with the ideology of a white, middle-class, heterosexual, female academy.[3] Lanser points out that feminist criticism has "embraced contradictory theories of literature, proceeding as if men's writings were ideological sign systems and women's writings were representations of truth, reading men's or masculinist texts with resistance and women's or feminist texts with empathy" (422).

Like Lanser, we believe that it is necessary to revisit feminist scholars' widely accepted readings of "The Yellow Wallpaper." We too wonder whether critics have replicated the activity of the narrator: she reads and rereads the text "until she finds what she is looking for—no less and no more." Critics "may have reduced the text's complexity to what [they] need most: [their] own image reflected back to [them]" (Lanser 420). In this essay, we look at how that description applies to scholarship on Gilman's story. Since the story's "rediscovery" in 1973, the transmission of the text has suffered: recent editions offer variations in wording at several critical points and in the location and number of the section breaks that signal the narrator's successive diary entries. Moreover, many received "facts" on which interpretations of "The Yellow Wallpaper" have been built—including Gilman's valiant struggle to get her story into print, the original audience's reading of it as a ghost story, and the irate reception it received from the male medical community—do not hold up well under scrutiny. These commonly accepted ideas regarding the work's publication and reception histories reveal the ways critics of the 1970s introduced or overlooked evidence. The struggle to gain a foothold for women writers in literary studies and in the academy often took precedence over textual criticism and archival research into letters and reviews. A study of the textual, publication, and reception histories of "The Yellow Wallpaper" demonstrates how shifts in criticism from one era to another cast different light on the evidence surrounding the story.

Modern Misidentification of Texts

The textual history of "The Yellow Wallpaper" since 1973 illustrates changing critical priorities in the academy. The Feminist Press edition of that year gave the story wider currency than ever before, although there had already been ten reprintings since the initial publication in 1892.[4] Hedges's lengthy afterword aligned "The Yellow Wallpaper" with other "deliberate dramatic indictments, by women writers, of the crippling social pressures imposed on women" (*Wallpaper* 55), thereby positioning it in the feminist literary tradition then being charted by Moers, Showalter, Gilbert and Gubar, and others. Hedges's edition can justly claim to be the starting point for the renewed interest in Gilman and her work. Indeed, it has become the Feminist Press's "all-time best-seller," with over 200,000 copies sold (Feminist Press 16).

But what is that edition? The copyright page claims it is a "[r]eprint of the 1899 ed. published by Small, Maynard, Boston." However, collation shows that it reprints the 1892 *New England Magazine* text and adds a few variants of its own. Some are typos with little significance — "phospsites" for "phosphites" (10) — but toward the end of the story two entire sentences are omitted. The 1892 *New England Magazine* text reads:

> I see her in that long shaded lane, creeping up and down. I see her in those dark grape arbors, creeping all around the garden.
>
> I see her on that long road under the trees, creeping along, and when a carriage comes she hides under the blackberry vines.   (654)

Through what was probably a compositor's eyeskip, the first two sentences beginning "I see her" were dropped, and only the last line was included (30–31).[5]

Hedges's edition prompted so much interest in Gilman that in 1980 Pantheon issued *The Charlotte Perkins Gilman Reader*, edited by Ann Lane, a collection that made more of Gilman's work available to a wide and eager audience. A note implies that Lane's reprinting of "The Yellow Wallpaper" derives from the 1892 *New England Magazine* version; instead, Lane reprints the 1933 *Golden Book* magazine version, which contains many anomalies of wording, as well as section breaks that differ from those in the 1892 and 1899 texts. While Hedges's edition is erroneously labeled a reprint of the 1899 edition, Lane's is incorrectly billed as the 1892 text when it appears in numerous college anthologies.[6]

Apparently neither Hedges nor Lane ensured that they were reprinting the editions they claimed to have used or that their texts transmitted the editions they used without error. This seeming carelessness suggests that Hedges's and Lane's scholarly priorities lay elsewhere. In fact, traditional textual scholarship in the manner of Fredson Bowers had been practiced by increasingly fewer scholars since the heyday of the Center for Editions of American Authors in the 1960s, and general literary critics in the succeeding decades privileged theoretical and political concerns. By the beginning of the 1990s, however, textual studies was newly energized by Jerome McGann's thoughtful *Critique of Modern Textual Criticism* (1983) and by discussions that it prompted in literary circles. Feminist scholars argued — and pub-

lishers agreed — that women authors deserved scholarly editions of their own.

The story's 1992 centennial saw the publication of Catherine Golden's *The Captive Imagination: A Casebook on "The Yellow Wallpaper."* In promotional material the Feminist Press called this "companion to the feminist classic" a "critical edition," a phrase Golden repeats in her introduction (19). According to a footnote (24), the edition reprints the 1899 text and reproduces for the first time the illustrations from the 1892 magazine.[7] However, a close look confirms that the text is simply a reissue of Hedges's edition, including every typo. Moreover, the omitted lines are restored in a footnote, after Golden asserts, "Here, the 1892 edition of 'The Yellow Wallpaper' includes the following passage" (38). She misleadingly informs readers that the 1899 edition omits the lines and that the 1892 edition contains them, when no such variance exists. The only text to omit those lines is Hedges's. Although Golden claims the authority of the term *critical edition*, she did not prepare what textual scholars would recognize by that label, for she did not collate various versions of the text. Nonetheless, the effort to identify her edition with criticism as a critical edition and to include information about textual variants suggests that textual criticism had higher priority in the 1980s than in the early 1970s.

Other publishers besides the Feminist Press have given editions of women's works a prominent place in their annual lists. Oxford University Press's Women's Classics Series, New York University Press's Early American Women Writers Series, and Rutgers University Press's American Women Writers Series are only some of the projects to make available long-out-of-print writings by women. Rutgers University Press's recent series Women Writers: Texts and Contexts includes a volume on "The Yellow Wallpaper." Along with a biographical introduction, a chronology, background readings, bibliography, and critical essays, the book contains "the authoritative text of the story itself," according to the jacket, a text that the editors, Thomas L. Erskine and Connie L. Richards, claim is "[f]rom *New England Magazine*, January 1892" (29). Apparently aware of the discrepancies between Hedges's and Lane's texts, Erskine and Richards seem to have tried to split the difference between the two. When variants arise, they choose now from one text, now from the other, giving no rationale for their choices. They restore the lines missing from Hedges's text but also include words added in the 1933 text Lane reprinted. What Erskine and Richards have created, then, is a text that never was, a text that includes the most words, if not necessarily the right ones.

Despite their problems, these texts bear witness to textual criticism's rise in status within the academy. Misidentification of texts apparently mattered little to Hedges and Lane, but a decade or so after publication of their editions, Golden as well as Erskine and Richards paid homage to the idea (if not the actuality) of critical editions and authoritative texts.

Textual Variants and Diary Entries

In an age when the hyphen in "wall-paper" receives its share of critical ink as a "signifier" (see Feldstein), even a minor textual variant has potential consequences for literary interpretation. And some of the variants that have crept into "The Yellow Wallpaper" are far from minor, especially those that bear on gender issues in the story. In the discussion of variants that follows, we take the 1892 *New England Magazine* text, the first printing of the story, to be the most authoritative and make it the basis for our comparisons. Gilman's manuscript has no necessary textual priority, for she would have expected editors to regularize punctuation in accordance with standards of her day. Moreover, Gilman offered no objection to the minor variations from her manuscript, as far as we have been able to discover. In the absence of evidence that Gilman opposed printing-house changes, the first printing stands as the version that best embodies the story Gilman presented to her contemporaries.

The first important variant, and the one most resonant with meaning, comes in the fifth paragraph. After declaring that there is "something queer" about the house, the narrator remarks, "John laughs at me, of course, but one expects that in marriage." Texts that follow Lane's, which reproduces the 1933 *Golden Book* version, print the following: "John laughs at me, of course, but one expects that." Omitting "in marriage" radically transforms the line. Why would one "expect that"? Does John laugh at the narrator because she is genuinely funny? because he thinks her a silly little woman? because she feels the house is creepy? because John is a jerk? The reader cannot know.

Other Gilman scholars do not know either, and some have attempted to clarify this ambiguity by adding loaded phrases such as "in [him]" (Parker, *Oven* 317), "in men" (Wells 177), and "in man" (Oates 154). The first addition suggests that John laughs at the narrator for reasons related to his own character.

In the second and third, the narrator engages in obvious male bashing, which, though perhaps amusing, sets a definite tone for the rest of the story. More important, these two changes distort the author's focus; Gilman is bashing marriage in particular, not men in general.

At the close of the story there is another intriguing variant. After John pounds ineffectually at her locked door, the narrator reports, "Now he's crying for an axe" (35). Textual descendants of the 1933 *Golden Book* version render the line, "Now he's crying to Jennie for an axe."[8] The 1892 wording, which allows readers to imagine that John is literally crying, undermines his masculinity and shows his wife gaining the upper hand, at least emotionally. In the variant reading, he cries out because he needs an axe quickly in a serious situation. Furthermore, Jennie becomes John's overt accomplice in repressing the narrator. While this interpretation may be valid (other evidence in the story suggests that Jennie acts as jailer in John's absence), it does not arise from Gilman's original wording in this line.

Another class of variants involves section breaks, often regarded as typographical trivia but vital to this particular work. The story is presented as if it were the narrator's private journal, and the section breaks demarcate entries.[9] Gilman uses these breaks to depict the narrator's circumstances as well as her mental state. The narrator must break off writing in her secret journal each time she hears her husband or sister-in-law draw near. She signals their approach by announcing, for example, "There comes John, and I must put this away,—he hates to have me write a word" (13) or "There's sister on the stairs!" (18). These disruptions put her at the mercy of those who wish to suppress her writing. Later section breaks illustrate mood fluctuations. Before one break the narrator is enthusiastic and protective because she suspects that Jennie is interested in the wallpaper: "But I know she was studying that pattern, and I am determined that nobody shall find it out but myself!" (27). Before another she is disgusted by the paper: "If those heads were covered or taken off it would not be half so bad" (30). The breaks that follow such statements act as an emotional barometer as the narrator immerses herself in contemplation of the wallpaper.

The breaks Gilman indicated in her manuscript were accurately reproduced in all the editions published during her lifetime except the last two. The tradition changed with the 1933 *Golden Book* version,[10] which eliminated seven of the original breaks, associating phrases that had never been presented together before. These alterations change the narrator's character. For instance, all editions published before 1933 insert a break between the two sentences "I will take a nap, I guess" and "I don't know why I should write this" (20–21). When the break is deleted, the narrator appears indecisive. Until this point, readers might see her as emotional and fanciful but never ambivalent—she is constant in her need to discover the wallpaper's secrets.

The *Golden Book* adds five new breaks, which also affect interpretation. One is inserted between John's question "Can you not trust me as a physician when I tell you so?" and the narrator's internal response "So of course I said no more on that score, and we went to sleep before long" (24–25). A break between these related sentences makes little sense, except perhaps to show eccentric behavior in the narrator, who seems to be pausing between journal entries before she completes a thought. But the 1892 *New England Magazine* text shows the narrator completing her thoughts unless she is interrupted and forced to stop writing.

The number of section breaks is as vexed a question as the placement of them. Gilman's manuscript divides "The Yellow Wallpaper" into twelve sections, but texts published after 1973 have offered fewer and fewer diary entries without altering the story's length. Hedges's edition preserves the original number of entries, but instead of signaling the beginning of each new section typographically (with an enlarged capital or with a combination of large and small capitals, as in earlier editions), it simply uses a blank line to separate sections. Two of the original breaks fall at page breaks (20–21, 22–23), and they are not reproduced in editions based on Hedges's text. Thus Golden can state that "the story is comprised of ten diary-like entries" (12), for by the time she transmits the text those two end-of-page section breaks have disappeared. Moreover, texts based on Golden's edition will likely reduce the story to nine "diary-like entries," since the break after the narrator's remark that "[t]here is a week more, and I think that will be enough" (28) falls at the bottom of a page and before an illustration in her edition.

Erskine and Richards's "authoritative text" picks and chooses between the traditions of section breaks in Hedges's 1973 version and in the 1933 *Golden Book* version handed down through Lane's *Gilman Reader.*

This newest academic edition presents a story composed of only six sections. If critics are right in thinking that the section breaks define diary entries and have some interpretive values (Janice Haney-Peritz even refers to them as "movements" [266]), then scholars should preserve all the breaks that Gilman authorized and only those breaks.

It would certainly help critics make sense of these variants if Gilman's own pen could be linked to a post-1892 edition, especially since the *Golden Book* version was published during her lifetime and with her permission. But a study of the section breaks in that version quickly banishes this hope. Each story printed in the *Golden Book* uses the same format: there are two columns a page; an enlarged capital begins each new section; and every full page of text contains one and only one enlarged capital. Moreover, the capitals are spaced so that each two-page spread has the ornaments balanced in opposite corners, if possible. While this design made the pages visually appealing, it also forced the editors to create extra breaks when the original text lacked appropriate ones and to delete breaks when they occurred too close to the end of a page or too near one another. The section breaks in this story thus became a design feature and no longer separated diary entries. The Gilman Papers at the Schlesinger Library at Radcliffe College contain a clipping of the *Golden Book* version with half a dozen corrections. Five of the six restore original breaks that have been erroneously closed up, but none of the added section breaks are deleted.[11] Given this evidence, Gilman's involvement in or approval of the *Golden Book* version seems unlikely.

Although the possibility cannot be entirely ruled out, there is no immediate evidence that Gilman edited or approved any version of "The Yellow Wallpaper" printed during her lifetime. In her autobiography she makes passing reference to the 1899 and 1920 printings but indicates no personal supervision. Because of the sheer volume and pace of her writing after 1890, she was probably not intimately involved with editing and printing every text. Nor did she give special attention to the story that now marks her place in literary history. She told William Dean Howells that she considered "The Yellow Wallpaper" to be not "literature" but merely a story that had "a purpose," as all her other writings did (*Living* 121).

The variety of forms in which the story has been presented suggests that editors have been concerned less with textual evidence than with other kinds of evidence, most notably autobiography. Many feminist critics have relied heavily and sometimes carelessly on *The Living of Charlotte Perkins Gilman*. The autobiographical nature of "The Yellow Wallpaper" and the compelling story Gilman tells of her life provide ample incentive for critics to seek clues to "The Yellow Wallpaper" in *The Living*. Then, too, Gilman's version of her life has often confirmed critics' visions of literary history. Furthermore, two decades ago autobiography was considered a more trustworthy source of evidence and a less problematic form of discourse than it is today. However, distortion inevitably occurs when the subject of scholarly study becomes the sole source of evidence.

He Says, She Says

Scholars have wrestled with two well-known versions of the publication history of "The Yellow Wallpaper," Gilman's and Howells's. By now, a standard interpretation of the divergent accounts has been accepted, in part because it has been so often repeated. How critics have come to terms with these conflicting versions — the way they have resolved the "he says, she says" conundrum — reveals shifts in emphasis within the academy.

Everyone seems to agree that Gilman first sent the story to the noted editor Howells, who had praised her earlier work. On receiving the unsolicited story in early October 1890, Howells sent it to Horace Scudder, then editor of the *Atlantic,* with a note telling Scudder, "It's pretty blood curdling, but strong, and is certainly worth reading" (Howells, Letter).[12] Scudder rejected the story, saying, according to Howells's account, "that it was so terribly good that it ought never to be printed" (Howells, *Stories* vii). In her autobiography, Gilman recalls Scudder's informing her that the story made him "miserable." At this point, accounts of the story's fate begin to differ fundamentally. Gilman claims in *The Living* that she then gave the manuscript to Henry Austin, a commercial literary agent, who eventually placed the story with *New England Magazine*. She reprints her peevish letter to the magazine's editor in which she demands to know if he pays his contributors. Her indignation reaches its apex when she relates that Austin apparently pocketed her profits from the publication (119). In contrast, Howells recalls that after learning of Scudder's rejection, "I could not rest until I had cor-

rupted the editor of *The New England Magazine* into publishing it" (*Stories* vii).

Faced with these conflicting accounts, most feminist critics have sided with Gilman in her dismissal of Howells. Of the critics in Golden's recent collection who discuss Howells's role in the story's publication, three ignore his claim altogether. Others take Gilman's account at face value, despite its inaccurate dates and titles. Among the earliest feminist critics to write on this question, Gail Parker chided Howells in 1972 for his "misgivings" about the story and claimed he "was really the enemy" of American feminists ("Introduction" 85, 89). Hedges later offered more-measured criticism of Howells's "limitations" ("Afterword" 125). Gradually, critics began to cast Gilman in a heroic mold, asserting, as Conrad Shumaker did in 1985, that after Scudder's rejection "Gilman persevered" and got the story published (242). Golden scolds Howells for what she calls his "self-congratulatory tone" and his "belief" that he had something to do with the story's acceptance (55). The most recent collection of essays on "The Yellow Wallpaper" proposes a handy compromise between Howells's version and Gilman's: "Gilman hired Henry Austin, a literary agent, who finally placed the story, with Howells's intervention and support, in *New England Magazine* in 1892" (Erskine and Richards 7).

Many feminist critics of the 1970s accepted — and perhaps even required — a publication history that cast Gilman in the role of beleaguered heroine. Later feminist critics did not question their predecessors' work and lent their own authority to this history. Now that the court of critical opinion has recognized the value of Gilman's work, scholars can ask what evidence exists to support either version of events. If Howells scholars are correct in characterizing him as an honest and modest autobiographer, it would seem unlikely that he invented the episode or exaggerated his own contribution to the story's publication.[13] Nevertheless, Howells's claim to have "corrupted" the editor of *New England Magazine* provides ample reason for further investigation. In fact, that editor was Edwin Doak Mead, a first cousin of Howells's wife, Elinor. Mead had benefited from Howells's patronage: just when Howells had become influential as the assistant editor of the *Atlantic Monthly,* he brought the seventeen-year-old Mead to Boston from New Hampshire (Mann 442). If Howells exerted personal pressure on Mead, he may well have been reluctant to elaborate publicly on his machinations. This reluctance would account for his coy reference nearly three decades later to a form of "corruption." It is also possible that Gilman either did not know or forgot about Howells's claim that he had a hand in the story's publication. According to Joanne B. Karpinski's study of Gilman's relationship with Howells, Gilman's "failure to credit Howells . . . follow[ed] a pattern of denying the actual contributions of those who, in Gilman's opinion, ought to have done more" (228).

.The story of a heroic woman author fighting valiantly in defiance of a thwarting male editorial presence makes for great drama, capped as it is with a male agent's theft of the profit that should have gone to the woman who would later write *Women and Economics*. Elizabeth Ammons comments accurately, though without any apparent irony, that this outcome "seems almost unbelievably fitting" (42). Perhaps the "unbelievable" should not be believed — at least not without corroborating evidence.

Despite all the ink that has been expended on subjectivity in autobiography (see, e.g., Spengemann; Jelinek), Gilman scholars have not always challenged the subject's authority. As early as 1975, Beate Schöpp-Schilling reprimanded her peers for relying "exclusively on Gilman's own interpretation of her life." She explained that memoirs "can never be taken at face value for autobiographical statements combine fact *and* fiction" (285). A few years later, Juliann E. Fleenor warned against "reading an autobiography as a factual transcription of a life rather than as a literary form" (236). *The Living*, Fleenor points out, presents "the heroine of the autobiography [as] an injured woman." Gilman carefully crafts her self-portrait for her readers, "even to the point of omitting or misrepresenting some events" (Fleenor 240).

These cautions notwithstanding, leading Gilman scholars have based their interpretations of Gilman's life and work on her own accounts. Lane, for instance, notes that much of the information she relies on in her biography of Gilman "comes filtered through Charlotte's pen." In the preface of *To Herland*, Lane tries to assert the neutrality of that filter, saying that Gilman "largely restrained her impulse to reshape her story by relying greatly on diaries and letters" (xiii). But diaries and letters are among the forms of discourse in which authors "reshape" their stories for their own purposes. Lane later acknowledges that "there is much in [*The Living*] as in all autobi-

ographies, of fiction, of self-deception, of purposeful misleading, of a refashioned and recrafted life, of a persona created for the occasion" (353), but by this point Lane has given her readers more than 350 pages of biography heavily dependent on Gilman's version of her life.

Gilman's version of events may someday be substantiated, but not until scholars move outside her own discourse for support. If Gilman did rely on diaries and letters in writing her autobiography, what do those documents show? In a recent edition of Gilman's diaries, Denise D. Knight identifies Austin not as Henry Austin but as Alfred Austin, editor of the *National Review* (432).[14] Perhaps Gilman's extant correspondence includes letters to Henry and Alfred Austin or the one from Horace Scudder? Is the actual letter to the editor of *New England Magazine* as self-righteous and accusatory as the one Gilman includes in *The Living*? Gilman mistakenly gives May 1891 as the publication date of "The Yellow Wallpaper," but that date is closer to the publication of her first piece for *New England Magazine*, "The Giant Wistaria" (June 1891). Is it not likely that she would inquire about the journal's payment policies after the publication of her first story rather than her second? And if Henry Austin did act as her agent with *New England Magazine*, perhaps he absconded with the payment for "Wistaria," not for "Wallpaper." There is no way to resolve these questions without looking beyond Gilman's own claims.

The point here is not to determine whether Gilman's or Howells's version of events is correct. Hers has the satisfying shape of well-crafted drama, while his can be backed by a preponderance of circumstantial evidence but nothing more. But what Lanser notes about earlier feminists' contradictory behavior toward men's and women's literary texts seems equally true for documentary evidence: critics have treated men's testimony with "resistance" and women's with "empathy."

Ghosts and Male Murderers

Just as the story's publication history has become part of the Gilman legend, entrenched ideas about the work's initial reception as a ghost story or as a story that male doctors sought to suppress have contributed substantially to the feminist mythology surrounding Gilman. When Hedges reintroduced "The Yellow Wallpaper" to the literary world, she remarked that "in its time . . . the story was read essentially as a Poe-esque tale of chilling horror" (39). Gilman herself made the analogy with Poe (*Living* 119), and the chilling qualities of the tale did draw the attention of its early readers: writing in the *Conservator* in 1899, Anne Montgomerie praises the story for its "perfect crescendo of horror" (61), while an anonymous Baltimore reviewer notes that the piece "has a touch of ghastliness" ("Question"). Similarly, Howells points to the story's ability to "freeze our young blood" and remarks, "I shiver over it as much as I did when I first read it in manuscript" (*Stories* vii). Many readers of the story have been troubled by its powerful subject matter, but there is a definite distinction between a tale of horror and a tale of ghosts.

Pioneering feminist critics of Gilman's work blurred this distinction, but editors of college anthologies crystallized interpretation into adamantine fact. Lane first suggested that "'The Yellow Wallpaper' ha[d] often been reprinted as a horror story," pointing to Howells's 1920 anthology (Lane, *Gilman Reader* xvii). However, Howells's *Great Modern American Stories* can be regarded as a collection of horror stories only if the term's definition is stretched to include Mark Twain's "The Celebrated Jumping Frog of Calaveras County," Bret Harte's "Outcasts of Poker Flat," and Mary E. Wilkins Freeman's "The Revolt of 'Mother.'" Lane goes on to assert that "horror writer H. P. Lovecraft called ['The Yellow Wallpaper'] one of the great 'spectral tales' in American literature," but her footnote for this quotation merely offers "thanks to Paul Buhle for providing this piece of information" (xvii, xli).

Golden follows up on this lead and supports Lane's claim: "As recently as 1973, horror writer H. P. Lovecraft included ['The Yellow Wallpaper'] as a 'classic example in subtly delineating the madness which crawls over a woman dwelling in the hideously papered room' in a collection titled *Supernatural Horror in Literature*" (Golden 3). Lovecraft's book is not a recent "collection" of supernatural tales, however, but a critical study of horror tales in world literature that was published in 1945 and reprinted in 1973.[15] Lovecraft mentions Gilman only in passing, praising her for "ris[ing] to a classic level" in her delineation of madness (72).

The outlines of the reception myth suggested in collections of Gilman's work have been solidified in college anthologies. A 1993 Macmillan anthology flatly states that "'The Yellow Wallpaper' was initially read as a ghost story in the tradition of Edgar Allan Poe" (Rubenstein and Larson 387). Similarly, the study questions in the *Heath Introduction to Fiction* tell students that "'The Yellow Wallpaper' was long thought to be a simple 'ghost story'" (Clayton 234). Likewise, the instructor's guide for the original edition of the widely used *Heath Anthology of American Literature* suggests that teachers ask students to consider why the story has "been read as a gothic thriller rather than a story about the sexual politics of marriage" (Stanford 349).[16]

Modern critics, beginning with Hedges, seem to imply that "The Yellow Wallpaper" has been read either as a horror story or as a story of sexual politics, more specifically that the late-nineteenth-century audience read it as horror but that the enlightened readers of a century later see it accurately. Hedges contends, and others repeat her assertion, that "no one seems to have made the connection between the insanity and the sex, or sexual role, of the victim, no one explored the story's implications for male-female relationships in the nineteenth century" (41).[17] Yet reviews demonstrate that the story's first readers did recognize its indictments of marriage and of the treatment of women, although these discussions do not use modern terminology. Three reviews of the 1899 Small, Maynard edition identify the cause of the narrator's insanity as her husband, a man whom one reviewer calls a "blundering, well-intentioned male murderer" (Rev. of "The Yellow Wallpaper," *News*). Another, writing in *Time and the Hour*, declares the edition "a book to keep away from the young wife," presumably because the "story is calculated to prevent girls from marrying." Henry B. Blackwell, writing in the *Woman's Journal* in 1899, ascribes the narrator's madness to "the effort of her husband" and recommends that the book be "widely perpetuated and circulated." Ironically, it is Blackwell, a male reviewer, who argues most forcefully that the narrator's madness results not from any hereditary condition or extraordinary ill-treatment but from the average wife's narrow and isolated life:

Nothing more graphic and suggestive has ever been written to show why so many women go crazy, especially farmers' wives, who live lonely, monotonous lives. A husband of the kind described in this little sketch once said that he could not account for his wife's having gone insane — "for," said he, "to my certain knowledge she has hardly left her kitchen and bedroom in 30 years."

Moreover, Shumaker observes that Howells for one "understood quite clearly the source of the story's effect" and asserts that the story was unpopular because, as Howells recognized, it "struck too deeply and effectively at traditional ways of seeing the world and woman's place in it" (251). Shumaker's voice has gone unheeded by feminist critics such as Haney-Peritz, who prefer to generalize about a "male line of response" (262).

Jean E. Kennard contends that a feminist reading could not emerge until audiences grasped certain literary conventions—particularly those associated with "patriarchy, madness, space, [and] quest" (78)—but her premise that "no earlier reader saw the story as in any way positive" (75) obscures the tensions and complexities in Gilman's text, particularly the gender constructions in play between the story and its original readers. To misunderstand these early readers' language of horror as the language of the supernatural is to misinterpret their efforts to read politically in their own times. The story of a female writer driven mad, in part by her husband, was a horrifying subject. Reviewers recognized its subversive undercurrents and treated the story with caution. Their comments may sometimes gloss over the radical social commentary of the story, but the evidence indicates that they saw Gilman's feminist message.

"Why do you think readers became aware of [the] social and psychological reality [of 'The Yellow Wallpaper'] only so recently?" the editor of one recent college anthology asks students (Clayton 234). To reword that question in the current context, Why do critics seem to need oppositional myth-frames in literary history to legitimize the study of a remarkable piece of writing? What is gained by identifying "The Yellow Wallpaper" as a hitherto victimized piece of literature? One answer lies in the academy's built-in bias in favor of the new: scholars engaged in enlarging knowledge privilege new interpretations, new facts, new documents. There would be scant pleasure in unearthing a nineteenth-century story if the original audience read it exactly as twentieth-century readers do. The thrill comes in finding the gem that others have overlooked. Critics must differentiate themselves from earlier readers, not just for self-gratification but also to validate the importance of the find.

Another answer comes from the way criticism is embedded in the ideological constructs of its time. Feminist critics of the 1970s garnered evidence to confirm their version of literary history as a patriarchal exclusion of women writers. This version is not necessarily incorrect but, rather, incomplete. Examination of another legend about the initial reception of "The Yellow Wallpaper" indicates what happens when critics stop looking for evidence after they find "facts" that validate their interpretations.

Perilous Doctors

One of the best-rubbed chestnuts of Gilman criticism concerns the hostility Gilman faced from her contemporary audience, especially from the male-dominated medical community. According to Gilman, "The Yellow Wallpaper" made a "tremendous impression" (*Living* 119) and even elicited a letter of protest from a Boston physician. Hedges first called modern critics' attention to the warning of "a doctor" that such stories were "perilous stuff" (*Wallpaper* 61, 41), and others have followed her lead. Golden describes how one "protester, an anonymous male physician, argued to censure the story of 'deadly peril'" (4); Jeffrey Berman notes the "anger and ill will" of the Boston physician (236); and Haney-Peritz places this doctor at the head of "a long line of male readers" (261).

The source for these reports is—once again—the author herself. In "Why I Wrote 'The Yellow Wallpaper,'" Gilman describes the correspondent as "a Boston physician," adding that "he said" stories like hers "ought not to be written." Twenty-two years later, she reprinted the letter in her autobiography as evidence of the hostility the story initially faced (*Living* 120).

A look at the *Boston Evening Transcript* for 8 April 1892 undercuts Gilman's cry of male censorship. A letter to the editor entitled "Perilous Stuff" indeed proposes that the vivid portrayal of a woman's mental deterioration is inappropriate subject matter for publication. "Should such stories be allowed to pass without protest, without severest censure?" the writer demands. But the letter includes not the slightest suggestion of the writer's sex or occupation. Its language merely implies that the writer has a close relationship with a mentally ill person: "The story can hardly, it would seem, give pleasure to any reader, and to many, whose lives have been touched through the nearest ties by this dread disease, it must bring the keenest pain" (M. D.). This distress seems more characteristic of a spousal, parental, or sibling relationship than of a doctor-patient relationship, and certainly either sex is capable of such sensitivity. But the writer's identity remains a mystery, for the letter is signed "M. D." The space between the two letters signals that they are initials of a proper name, which could belong as easily to a woman as to a man.

In *The Living*, Gilman chooses to interpret the initials as a doctor's signature. When she reprints the letter, she closes up the space between the initials, presenting the writer as an "M.D." Changing "the nearest ties" to the "dearest ties," either by mistake or by design, she obscures the implication that the writer and the patient are related. She follows the letter with that of "another doctor," thereby confirming the erroneous impression she has created.

In relying on Gilman's account without checking the original newspaper, critics have failed to consider how Gilman's expectations or motives may have colored her perception and transmission of the letter. Since her story seems designed to criticize common medical practices toward women and the mentally ill, Gilman may have anticipated an angry response from offended doctors and husbands and seen only what she expected to see when she read the letter. Moreover, if the writer were a male doctor, he would further exemplify men's attempts to suppress women's creative expression, like the male editors who tried to suppress Gilman's story and the husband who tries to suppress the narrator's writing. By providing support for arguments about women's struggles throughout literary history, this tale of a censorious male doctor served the purposes of critics following Hedges's lead in the 1970s as fully as it had Gilman's.

Mitchell's Conversion

The real villain in the history of "The Yellow Wallpaper" is not an anonymous male physician or even Howells but the celebrated neurologist S. Weir Mitchell, under whose supervision Gilman endured the famous rest cure. What better closure for that troubled history than for Mitchell, influenced by Gilman's fiction, to alter his cure and mend his evil ways. Not surprisingly, the story of this apt conclusion originates in Gilman's accounts. In three successive versions, the author fleshes out the details of the story's effect and heightens her sense of mission in writing it.

An early typescript history of the story refers generally to "an eminent specialist" who "state[d] that he had changed his treatment of neurasthenia since reading it" (Gilman, "History").[18] Gilman's second version, "Why I Wrote 'The Yellow Wallpaper,'" which was published in the *Forerunner* in 1913, elaborates on the response of a "noted specialist," to whom Gilman says she sent a copy of her story. Though he "never acknowledged it," he must have received it, for she notes that "[m]any years later [she] was told that the great specialist had admitted to friends of his that he had altered his treatment of neurasthenia since reading *The Yellow Wallpaper*." The purpose of the story, she adds in this account, was "to save people from being driven crazy, and it worked."

In her autobiography, published after a lapse of two more decades, Gilman repeats the tale:

> But the real purpose of the story was to reach Dr. S. Weir Mitchell and convince him of the error of his ways. I sent him a copy as soon as it came out, but got no response. However, many years later, I met some one who knew close friends of Dr. Mitchell's who said he had told them that he had changed his treatment of nervous prostration since reading "The Yellow Wallpaper." If that is a fact, I have not lived in vain.   (*Living* 121)

Thus Gilman decides that her "real purpose" was to reach Mitchell, whom she here first identifies by name. Moreover, his "friends" become "close friends," lending weight to this third-hand report of the story's effect. In this final retelling Gilman falls back on melodramatic clichés—"the error of his ways," "I have not lived in vain"—as if to cast herself as the noble heroine who reforms the wicked villain.

One after another, Gilman's biographers and critics reiterate her assertions without commentary or challenge.[19] Even Berman, whose article about the "unrestful cure" provides well-researched information about Mitchell's medical contributions, repeats her report that Mitchell changed his cure, quotes her remark about "sav[ing] people from being [driven] crazy," and adds, "No work of literature can accomplish more than this" (237). We have found no evidence to support Gilman's version of events other than her memoirs. Discussions of Mitchell's career never mention Gilman's course of treatment or her famous short story. Mitchell's published letters contain no hint that he altered his thinking about the rest cure; on the contrary, as late as 1908 he wrote to Andrew Carnegie that he wanted to build a hospital for "Rest Treatment for the Poor." Far from abandoning his methods, Mitchell proposed to extend them beyond the middle and upper classes, some sixteen years after Gilman's story appeared (Robson 344).

Critical Watchfulness

Hedges recently pointed to "an early critical investment" on the part of feminist critics "in finding some degree of triumph" in "The Yellow Wallpaper." Her remarks focused on whether the narrator's madness at the story's close constitutes success or failure ("'Out'" 326). That same problematic that Lanser describes as ideological collusion needs to be extended to the gathering and assessment of evidence (422). The dramatic story of Saint Charlotte and the evil Doctor Mitchell, the indignant outcry of the "Boston physician," the misreading of a searing indictment of marriage as a mere ghost story, the hostility of the male-dominated literary marketplace, the heroic struggles of the undaunted woman author— these notions went unchallenged because they meshed with what those seeking to recover Gilman from obscurity expected and hoped to find. Later critics operating from within the same frame of reference failed to challenge the prevailing wisdom.

American literature would certainly be the poorer without "The Yellow Wallpaper," but an understanding of such stories and of the culture that produced them requires careful scrutiny of assumptions made by critics and by texts and writers of the past. Of course, Gilman's story is not the only text that bears the marks of invested scholarship. A similar effect has doubtless occurred not only for other authors and texts "rediscovered" by feminist critics but also perhaps for any works recovered when textual and scholarly exactitude was not a critical priority. It seems inevitable that critics seeking recognition for previously ignored, forgotten, or suppressed individuals or groups—women, gay men and lesbians, writers of color, to name a few—should channel their energies single-mindedly toward a compelling political struggle. Less obvious, but no less common, are biases that attend the induction of a young author into the pantheon of acknowledged masters. Young writers typically portray themselves as battling hostility from the critical establishment or suffering neglect in their own lands. For example, Theodore Dreiser's tale of the vexed publication history of *Sister Carrie* offers contours remarkably similar to those of Gilman's story.[20] Once battles for recognition have been won, however, critical notions that have served as rallying cries need to shift. Motives and methods—of authors and of scholars who study them—need to be reassessed, along with the evidence that undergirds literary interpretation. The cycle of revaluation will continue as long as the vitality of literary texts endures. But one expects that in scholarship.

Notes

1. "The Yellow Wallpaper" appears in the most recent American literature anthologies published by Harcourt (1st ed., 1991), Harper (2nd ed., 1993), Heath (2nd ed., 1994), Macmillan (5th ed., 1993), Norton (4th ed., 1994), and Prentice (1st ed., 1991). The story can also be found in textbooks marketed for courses in women's studies, for example, *American Women Writers: Diverse Voices in Prose since 1845*, edited by Eileen Barrett and Mary Cullinan (St. Martin's, 1992) and *Rediscoveries: American Short Stories by Women, 1800–1916*, edited by Barbara H. Solomon (Mentor, 1994). Recent introductory fiction anthologies that reprint "The Yellow Wallpaper" include *Fictions*, edited by Joseph F. Trimmer and C. Wade Jennings (Harcourt, 1989); *Short Fiction: Classic and Contemporary*, edited by Charles H. Bohner (Prentice, 1989); *Lives and Moments*, edited by Hans Ostrom (Holt, Rinehart, 1991); *The Longwood Introduction to Fiction*, edited by Sven Birkerts (Allyn, 1992); *Fiction 100* (Macmillan, 1992) and *Fiction 50* (Macmillan, 1993), both edited by James H. Pickering; *The Situation of the Story*, edited by Diana Young (Bedford, 1993); *Fiction's Many Worlds*, edited by Charles E. May (Heath, 1993); *Stories: An Anthology and an Introduction*, edited by Eric S. Rabkin (Harper, 1995); and *The Story and Its Writer*, edited by Ann Charters (Bedford, 1995).

2. For a cogent summary of how Moers's *Literary Woman* (1976), Showalter's *A Literature of Their Own* (1977), and Gilbert and Gubar's *The Madwoman in the Attic* (1979) "strive to define a distinctively female tradition in literature" in contrast to the patriarchal male tradition, see Moi 50–69.

3. Lanser examines six studies of "The Yellow Wallpaper" published between 1973 and 1986, but she traces the theoretical positions of academic feminist criticism in the United States back to the 1960s.

4. Contrary to the belief that the story was "quickly relegated to the backwaters of our literary landscape," as Kolodny claims (459), it saw print in mainstream publications far more than might be expected for a "suppressed" literary work.

5. Unless otherwise indicated, references to "The Yellow Wallpaper" are to Hedges's text, since it is the most widely available.

6. Among the anthologies listed in note 1, those edited by Barrett and Cullinan; Trimmer and Jennings; Bohner; Ostrom; Birkerts; Young; and Charters reprint Lane's version of the story. That version is also reprinted in several of the American literature anthologies listed in note 1: those published by Harper, Macmillan, and Norton.

7. The final illustration showing the narrator crawling over her prostrate husband is reversed in this volume (41). Golden analyzes the illustrations at some length but gives no reason for the reversal (4–6).

8. Evidence points to the *Golden Book* as the source for the reading. There the variant reads "to Jenny," although John's sister's name is spelled "Jennie" elsewhere in the story. Subsequent versions regularize the spelling as "Jennie" in this line.

9. Several critics have explored the contradictions inherent in this form. See, for instance, Treichler; Haney-Peritz.

10. This version was reprinted in 1934 in *A Book of the Short Story*.

11. The clipping is located in folder 260. The erroneous date "October 1934" is inscribed in ink on the first page in what looks to be Gilman's hand. The six corrections, which seem to be in pencil, unfortunately are not distinctive enough to indicate whose hand they represent.

12. This letter is quoted by permission of the Houghton Library at Harvard University.

13. On Howells's "high standard of honesty" in his memoirs, see, for example, Lynn 39–40, 320; Cady 204–08.

14. Knight offers no evidence to support this identification, but the discrepancy is worth noting.

15. Golden implies that Lovecraft played an active part in the publication of the 1973 volume; since he died in 1937, this assertion is probably not true (though with a writer of the supernatural, one is never sure).

16. The instructor's guide accompanying the newly issued second edition softens this approach, saying that the story "seems not to have been read as it is read today, as a critique of marriage and of medical treatment of women." The guide then evokes Poe, asking whether "The Yellow Wallpaper" might have "been perceived as similar to a Poe story" (Alberti 423–24).

17. "Not until 1973," says Lane, "was it read from a feminist perspective" (*Gilman Reader* xvii). She repeats this claim in her 1990 biography of Gilman, *To Herland and Beyond*, declaring that Hedges's afterword is the "first feminist reading" and that the story "was originally seen as a horror story" (130). Golden echoes Lane: "Howells did not remark in his very brief introduction that 'The Yellow Wallpaper' also 'wanted [more than] two generations' for its feminist thrust or its polemical intent to be appreciated" (7).

18. A hand-printed note, signed with the initials of Gilman's daughter Katherine Beecher Stetson Chamberlin, claims that the undated typescript is a "[n]ote left by C.P.G." The typescript seems to have served as the basis for "Why I Wrote 'The Yellow Wallpaper.'" The typescript is quoted by permission of the Schlesinger Library at Radcliffe College.

19. Golden anthologizes the work of half a dozen critics who lend credence to Gilman's account by failing to comment on it. See Golden 8; Parker, "Introduction" 84; Gilbert and Gubar 147; Treichler 199–200; Berman 237. Jacobus alone notes that the story is "hearsay" and describes Mitchell as a "surrogate for the absent father whom Gilman also tried to 'convert' through her writing" (278).

20. The Norton Critical Edition of *Sister Carrie* reprints Dreiser's preface to the 1932 Modern Library edition, along with other documents that contribute to what Donald Pizer labels "the legend of the suppression of *Sister Carrie*" (465).

Works Cited

Alberti, John, ed. *Instructor's Guide for the* Heath Anthology of American Literature. 2nd ed. Lexington: Heath, 1994.

Ammons, Elizabeth. *Conflicting Stories: American Women Writers at the Turn into the Twentieth Century*. New York: Oxford UP, 1991.

Berman, Jeffrey. "The Unrestful Cure: Charlotte Perkins Gilman and 'The Yellow Wallpaper.'" Golden 211–41.

B[lackwell], H[enry] B. Rev. of "The Yellow Wallpaper." *Woman's Journal* 17 June 1899: 187.

Cady, Edwin H. *The Realist at War: The Mature Years, 1885–1920, of William Dean Howells.* Syracuse: Syracuse UP, 1958.

Clayton, John J., ed. *Heath Introduction to Fiction.* 4th ed. Lexington: Heath, 1992.

Erskine, Thomas L., and Connie L. Richards, eds. *"The Yellow Wallpaper."* Women Writers: Texts and Contexts. New Brunswick: Rutgers UP, 1993.

Feldstein, Richard. "Reader, Text, and Ambiguous Referentiality in 'The Yellow Wall-Paper.'" Golden 307–18.

Feminist Press. Publications catalog. Spring 1994.

Fleenor, Juliann E. "The Gothic Prism: Charlotte Perkins Gilman's Gothic Stories and Her Autobiography." *The Female Gothic.* Ed. Fleenor. Montreal: Eden, 1983. 227–41.

Gilbert, Sandra, and Susan Gubar. "From *The Madwoman in the Attic: The Woman Writer and the Nineteenth-Century Literary Imagination.*" Golden 145–48.

Gilman, Charlotte Perkins. *The Living of Charlotte Perkins Gilman: An Autobiography.* 1935. Introd. Ann J. Lane. Madison: U of Wisconsin P, 1990.

———. "Why I Wrote 'The Yellow Wallpaper.'" *Forerunner* Oct. 1913: 271.

———. "The Yellow Wallpaper." *New England Magazine* Jan. 1892: 647–56.

———. *The Yellow Wallpaper.* Boston: Small, 1899.

———. "The Yellow Wallpaper." *Golden Book* Oct. 1933: 363–73.

———. "The Yellow Wall Paper." *A Book of the Short Story.* Ed. E. A. Cross. New York: American Book Co., 1934. 400–13.

———. "The Yellow Wall Paper—Its History and Reception—Note Left by C.P.G." Ts. Folder 221. Charlotte Perkins Gilman Papers. Schlesinger Lib., Radcliffe Coll.

Golden, Catherine, ed. *The Captive Imagination: A Casebook on "The Yellow Wallpaper."* New York: Feminist, 1992.

Green, Gayle, and Coppélia Kahn, eds. *Making a Difference Feminist Literary Criticism.* London: Methune, 1985.

Haney-Peritz, Janice. "Monumental Feminism and Literature Ancestral House: Another Look at 'The Yellow Wallpaper.'" Golden 261–76.

Hedges, Elaine R. "Afterword." Golden 123–36.

———. "'Out at Last'? 'The Yellow Wallpaper' after Two Decades of Feminism Criticism." Golden 319–33.

———, ed. *The Yellow Wallpaper.* New York: Feminist, 1973.

Howells, William Dean, ed. *The Great Modern American Stories: An Anthology.* New York: Boni, 1920.

———. Letter to Horace Scudder. 5 Oct. 1890. bMS Am 1784.1 (92). Houghton Lib., Harvard Univ.

Jacobus, Mary. "An Unnecessary Maze of Sign-Reading." Golden 277–95.

Jelinek, Estelle C., ed. *Women's Autobiography: Essays in Criticism.* Bloomington: Indiana UP, 1980.

Karpinski, Joanne B. "When the Marriage of True Minds Admits Impediments: Charlotte Perkins Gilman and William Dean Howells." *Patrons and Protégées: Gender, Friendship, and Writing in Nineteenth-Century America.* Ed. Shirley Marchalonis. New Brunswick: Rutgers UP, 1988. 212–34.

Kennard, Jean E. "Convention Coverage: or, How to Read Your Own Life." *New Literary History* 13 (1981): 69–88.

Knight, Denise D., ed. *The Diaries of Charlotte Perkins Gilman.* 2 vols. Charlottesville: UP of Virginia, 1994.

Kolodny, Annette. "A Map for Rereading: or, Gender and the Interpretation of Literary Texts." *New Literary History* 11 (1980): 451–67.

Lane, Ann J., ed. *The Charlotte Perkins Gilman Reader: "The Yellow Wallpaper" and Other Fiction.* New York: Pantheon, 1980.

———. *To Herland and Beyond: The Life and Work of Charlotte Perkins Gilman.* New York: Pantheon, 1990.

Lanser, Susan S. "Feminist Criticism, 'The Yellow Wallpaper,' and the Politics of Color in America." *Feminist Studies* 15 (1989): 415–41.

Lovecraft, H[oward] P[hillips]. *Supernatural Horror in Literature.* New York: Abramson, 1945. Introd. E. F. Bleiler. New York: Dover, 1973.

Lynn, Kenneth. *William Dean Howells: An American Life.* New York: Harcourt, 1970.

Mann, Arthur. "Edwin Doak Mead." *Dictionary of American Biography.* Vol. 9. Pt. 2. Supp. 2. 442–43.

M. D. "Perilous Stuff." *Boston Evening Transcript* 8 Apr. 1892: 6.

Moi, Toril. *Sexual/Textual Politics: Feminist Literary Theory.* London: Routledge, 1985.

M[ontgomerie], A[nne]. Rev. of "The Yellow Wallpaper." *Conservator* June 1899: 60–61.

Oates, Joyce Carol, ed. *The Oxford Book of American Short Stories.* Oxford: Oxford UP, 1992.

Parker, Gail. "From the Introduction to *The Oven Birds: American Women on Womanhood, 1820–1920.*" Golden 83–98.

———, ed. *The Oven Birds: American Women on Womanhood, 1820–1920.* Garden City: Doubleday, 1972.

Pizer, Donald, ed. *Sister Carrie.* by Theodore Dreiser. Norton Critical Edition. 2nd ed. New York: Norton, 1991.

"A Question of 'Nerves.'" Rev. of "The Yellow Wallpaper." 10 June [1899]. Folder 301. Charlotte Perkins Gilman Papers. Schlesinger Lib., Radcliffe Coll.

Robson, Anna. *Weir Mitchell: His Life and Letters.* New York: Duffield, 1930.

Rubenstein, Roberta, and Charles R. Larson, eds. *Worlds of Fiction.* New York: Macmillan, 1993.

Schöpp-Schilling, Beate. "'The Yellow Wallpaper': A Rediscovered 'Realistic' Story." *American Literary Realism* 8 (1975): 284–85.

Shumaker, Conrad. "'Too Terribly Good to Be Printed': Charlotte Gilman's 'The Yellow Wallpaper.'" Golden 242–52.

Spengemann, William C. *Forms of Autobiography: Episodes in the History of a Literary Genre.* New Haven: Yale UP, 1980.

Stanford, Judith A., ed. *Instructor's Guide for the* Heath Anthology of American Literature. Lexington: Heath, 1990.

Treichler, Paula A. "Escaping the Sentence: Diagnosis and Discourse in 'The Yellow Wallpaper.'" Golden 191–210.

Wells, Carolyn, ed. *American Mystery Stories.* N.p.: Oxford UP, 1927.

Rev. of "The Yellow Wallpaper." *Time and the Hour* 17 June 1899. Folder 301. Charlotte Perkins Gilman Papers. Schlesinger Lib., Radcliffe Coll.

Rev. of "The Yellow Wallpaper." *News* [Newport, RI] 27 Jan. [1905?]. Folder 301. Charlotte Perkins Gilman Papers. Schlesinger Lib., Radcliffe Coll.

APPENDIX A

A Text of "Ode on a Grecian Urn"

John Keats

The text of "Ode on a Grecian Urn" presents few problems—until the last two lines, where it presents a major one. Readers may encounter three different ways of punctuating these lines. The earliest printed version of the poem uses no quotation marks at all. The 1820 *Lamia* text, which is reproduced here, puts only the aphorism, "Beauty is truth, truth beauty," in quotation marks. Some modern editions, however, put the entire last two lines in quotation marks. While there is no direct textual ancestor for this practice, it can be defended on the grounds that the earliest transcriptions of the poem seem to show the final two lines as a single thought.

Much has been written about the implications of these different forms of punctuation. The main possibilities are these: (1) If the entire final sentence is a quote, it must be read as the urn's statement to the audience. (2) If only "Beauty is truth, truth beauty" is quoted, we may still feel that the urn speaks the entire sentence and the quotation marks merely point up the epigrammatic character of the apothegm; but this form of punctuation opens the possibility that the last line and a half are said not by the urn but by the speaker of the poem. If so, we must then decide to whom this commentary is delivered. If the speaker turns toward the audience—"that is all you, reader, need to know"—then the urn's message is reinforced by the commentator. But if we envision the speaker turning toward the urn at the end—"that is all you, urn, need to know"—then the implication is that living people need to know other things, and this radically changes the meaning of the poem. (3) Leaving the quotation marks out altogether seems to leave all possibilities open. (The reader will find a fuller discussion of these possibilities along with an account of the textual evidence in Jack Stillinger, "Who Says What to Whom at the End of the *Ode on a Grecian Urn*" in *The Hoodwinking of Madeline,* Urbana: University of Illinois Press, 1971: 167–73.)

This textual puzzle and its implications are worth contemplating. For one thing, we may be moved to think about the relationship between textual scholarship and critical interpretation. We generally assume it is the textual scholar's job to deliver the text and the reader's job to interpret it, even when the scholar and the reader are the same person. But as this example shows, very often interpretation determines the text. We decide what the first forty-eight lines mean and punctuate the final two accordingly.

Yet the more we ponder these shifting and disappearing quotation marks, the more we may be led to wonder about the status of the entire text. Is "Keats's" poem truly presented (or truly represented) by these black marks printed on a white page? Are these not transcriptions of earlier transcriptions of a now-vanished autograph that was itself an inscription of—what? Shall we give ear at this point to those who claim that all writing is a secondary encoding of the primary language code, which is speech? Did the autograph then inscribe a representation of the poem in Keats's ear? And was that in turn merely a representation of the real poem in his mind, which was beyond language either written or spoken? Where, in short, is the "real" poem? In the author's mind? In the reader's? Somehow within yet outside of all minds? Is it potential or actual? Ideal or material?

These questions are implicit in any text, even the simplest, but they are posed insistently in Keats's far from simple poem. With its play between the visual and the verbal arts, its complex synesthetic effects, its frenzied stasis and its silent music, the "Ode" may serve to tease us into thought about some of the fundamental problems of literary interpretation.

Ode on a Grecian Urn

1

Thou still unravish'd bride of quietness,
 Thou foster-child of silence and slow time,
Sylvan historian, who canst thus express
 A flowery tale more sweetly than our rhyme;
What leaf-fring'd legend haunts about thy shape   5
 Of deities or mortals, or of both,
  In Tempe or the dales of Arcady?
  What men or gods are these? What maidens loth?
What mad pursuit? What struggle to escape?
  What pipes and timbrels? What wild ecstasy?   10

2

Heard melodies are sweet, but those unheard
 Are sweeter; therefore, ye soft pipes, play on;
Not to the sensual ear, but, more endear'd,
 Pipe to the spirit ditties of no tone;
Fair youth, beneath the trees, thou canst not leave   15
 Thy song, nor ever can those trees be bare;
  Bold lover, never, never canst thou kiss,
Though winning near the goal—yet, do not grieve;
  She cannot fade, though thou hast not thy bliss,
For ever wilt thou love, and she be fair!   20

3

Ah, happy, happy boughs! that cannot shed
 Your leaves, nor ever bid the spring adieu;
And, happy melodist, unwearied,
 For ever piping songs for ever new;

More happy love! more happy, happy love!   25
    For ever warm and still to be enjoy'd,
        For ever panting, and for ever young;
All breathing human passion far above,
    That leaves a heart high-sorrowful and cloy'd,
        A burning forehead, and a parching tongue.   30

4

Who are these coming to the sacrifice?
    To what green altar, O mysterious priest,
Lead'st thou that heifer lowing at the skies,
    And all her silken flanks with garlands drest?
What little town by river or sea shore,   35
    Or mountain-built with peaceful citadel,
        Is emptied of this folk, this pious morn?
And, little town, thy streets for evermore
    Will silent be; and not a soul to tell
        Why thou art desolate, can e'er return.   40

5

O Attic shape! Fair attitude! with brede
    Of marble men and maidens overwrought,
With forest branches and the trodden weed;
    Thou, silent form, dost tease us out of thought
As doth eternity: Cold Pastoral!   45
    When old age shall this generation waste,
        Thou shalt remain, in midst of other woe
    Than ours, a friend to man, to whom thou say'st,
"Beauty is truth, truth beauty," — that is all
        Ye know on earth, and all ye need to know.   50

APPENDIX B

"Benito Cereno"

Herman Melville

This text of "Benito Cereno" and the explanatory notes are reprinted by permission from Perkins, George and Perkins, Barbara, eds., The American Tradition in Literature, *9th ed. New York: McGraw-Hill, 1999, vol. 1: 1601–1650. The text is that of Melville's* Piazza Tales, *1856.*

In the year 1799, Captain Amasa Delano, of Duxbury, in Massachusetts, commanding a large sealer[1] and general trader, lay at anchor with a valuable cargo, in the harbor of St. Maria—a small, desert, uninhabited island toward the southern extremity of the long coast of Chili. There he had touched for water.

On the second day, not long after dawn, while lying in his berth, his mate came below, informing him that a strange sail was coming into the bay. Ships were then not so plenty in those waters as now. He rose, dressed, and went on deck.

The morning was one peculiar to that coast. Everything was mute and calm; everything gray. The sea, though undulated into long roods of swells, seemed fixed, and was sleeked at the surface like waved lead that has cooled and set in the smelter's mould. The sky seemed a gray surtout. Flights of troubled gray fowl, kith and kin with flights of troubled gray vapors among which they were mixed, skimmed low and fitfully over the waters, as swallows over meadows before storms. Shadows present, foreshadowing deeper shadows to come.

To Captain Delano's surprise, the stranger, viewed through the glass, showed no colors; though to do so upon entering a haven, however uninhabited in its shores, where but a single other ship might be lying, was the custom among peaceful seamen of all nations. Considering the lawlessness and loneliness of the spot, and the sort of stories, at that day, associated with those seas, Captain Delano's surprise might have deepened into some uneasiness had he not been a person of a singularly undistrustful good nature, not liable, except on extraordinary and repeated incentives, and hardly then, to indulge in personal alarms, any way involving the imputation of malign evil in man. Whether, in view of what humanity is capable, such a trait implies, along with a benevolent heart, more than ordinary quickness and accuracy of intellectual perception, may be left to the wise to determine.

But whatever misgivings might have obtruded on first seeing the stranger, would almost, in any seaman's mind, have been dissipated by observing that, the ship, in navigating into the harbor, was drawing too near the land; a sunken reef making out off her bow. This seemed to prove her a stranger, indeed, not only to the sealer, but the island; consequently, she could be no wonted freebooter on that ocean. With no small interest, Captain Delano continued to watch

---

1. Seal-hunting ship.

her — a proceeding not much facilitated by the vapors partly mantling the hull, through which the far matin[2] light from her cabin streamed equivocally enough; much like the sun — by this time hemisphered on the rim of the horizon, and, apparently, in company with the strange ship entering the harbor — which, wimpled by the same low, creeping clouds, showed not unlike a Lima intriguante's one sinister eye peering across the Plaza from the Indian loop-hole of her dusk *saya-y-manta*.[3]

It might have been but a deception of the vapors, but, the longer the stranger was watched the more singular appeared her manœuvres. Ere long it seemed hard to decide whether she meant to come in or no — what she wanted, or what she was about. The wind, which had breezed up a little during the night, was now extremely light and baffling, which the more increased the apparent uncertainty of her movements.

Surmising, at last, that it might be a ship in distress, Captain Delano ordered his whale-boat to be dropped, and, much to the wary opposition of his mate, prepared to board her, and, at the least, pilot her in. On the night previous, a fishing-party of the seamen had gone a long distance to some detached rocks out of sight from the sealer, and, an hour or two before daybreak, had returned, having met with no small success. Presuming that the stranger might have been long off soundings, the good captain put several baskets of the fish, for presents, into his boat, and so pulled away. From her continuing too near the sunken reef, deeming her in danger, calling to his men, he made all haste to apprise those on board of their situation. But, some time ere the boat came up, the wind, light though it was, having shifted, had headed the vessel off, as well as partly broken the vapors from about her.

Upon gaining a less remote view, the ship, when made signally visible on the verge of the leaden-hued swells, with the shreds of fog here and there raggedly furring her, appeared like a white-washed monastery after a thunder-storm, seen perched upon some dun cliff among the Pyrenees. But it was no purely fanciful resemblance which now, for a moment, almost led Captain Delano to think that nothing less than a ship-load of monks was before him.

Peering over the bulwarks were what really seemed, in the hazy distance, throngs of dark cowls; while, fitfully revealed through the open port-holes, other dark moving figures were dimly described, as of Black Friars[4] pacing the cloisters.

Upon a still nigher approach, this appearance was modified, and the true character of the vessel was plain — a Spanish merchantman of the first class, carrying negro slaves, amongst other valuable freight, from one colonial port to another. A very large and, in its time, a very fine vessel, such as in those days were at intervals encountered along that main; sometimes superseded Acapulco treasure-ships, or retired frigates of the Spanish king's navy, which, like superannuated Italian palaces, still, under a decline of masters, preserved signs of former state.

As the whale-boat drew more and more nigh, the cause of the peculiar pipe-clayed aspect of the stranger was seen in the slovenly neglect pervading her. The spars, ropes, and great part of the bulwarks, looked woolly, from long unacquaintance with the scraper, tar, and the brush. Her keel seemed laid, her ribs put together, and she launched, from Ezekiel's Valley of Dry Bones.[5]

In the present business in which she was engaged, the ship's general model and rig appeared to have undergone no material change from their original warlike and Froissart pattern.[6] However, no guns were seen.

The tops[7] were large, and were railed about with what had once been octagonal network, all now in sad disrepair. These tops hung overhead like three ruinous aviaries, in one of which was seen perched, on a ratlin,[8] a white noddy, a strange fowl, so called from its lethargic, somnambulistic character, being frequently caught by hand at sea. Battered and mouldy, the castellated forecastle seemed some ancient turret, long ago taken by assault, and then left to decay. Toward the stern, two high-raised quarter galleries — the balustrades here and there covered with dry, tindery sea-moss — opening out from the unoccu-

---

2. Morning.

3. Hooded tunic and mantle.

---

4. Dominican friars, called "Black Friars" because of the black mantle worn for preaching.

5. Ezekiel xxxvii: 1–4.

6. Jean Froissart (c. 1337–1410?) chronicled the first half of the Hundred Years' War.

7. Platforms on the masts.

8. Thin ropes woven into ladders.

pied state-cabin, whose dead-lights,[9] for all the mild weather, were hermetically closed and calked — these tenantless balconies hung over the sea as if it were the grand Venetian canal. But the principal relic of faded grandeur was the ample oval of the shield-like stern-piece, intricately carved with the arms of Castile and Leon,[1] medallioned about by groups of mythological or symbolical devices; uppermost and central of which was a dark satyr in a mask, holding his foot on the prostrate neck of a writhing figure, likewise masked.

Whether the ship had a figure-head, or only a plain beak, was not quite certain, owing to canvas wrapped about that part, either to protect it while undergoing a re-furbishing, or else decently to hide its decay. Rudely painted or chalked, as in a sailor freak, along the forward side of a sort of pedestal below the canvas, was the sentence, *"Seguid vuestro jefe,"* (follow your leader); while upon the tarnished headboards, near by, appeared, in stately capitals, once gilt, the ship's name, "SAN DOMINICK," each letter streakingly corroded with tricklings of copper-spike rust; while, like mourning weeds, dark festoons of sea-grass slimily swept to and fro over the name, with every hearse-like roll of the hull.

As, at last, the boat was hooked from the bow along toward the gangway amidship, its keel, while yet some inches separated from the hull, harshly grated as on a sunken coral reef. It proved a huge bunch of conglobated[2] barnacles adhering below the water to the side like a wen — a token of baffling airs and long calms passed somewhere in those seas.

Climbing the side, the visitor was at once surrounded by a clamorous throng of whites and blacks, but the latter outnumbering the former more than could have been expected, negro transportation-ship as the stranger in port was. But, in one language, and as with one voice, all poured out a common tale of suffering; in which the negresses, of whom there were not a few, exceeded the others in their dolorous vehemence. The scurvy, together with the fever, had swept off a great part of their number, more especially the Spaniards. Off Cape Horn they had narrowly escaped shipwreck; then, for days together, they had lain tranced without wind; their provisions were low; their water next to none; their lips that moment were baked.

While Captain Delano was thus made the mark of all eager tongues, his one eager glance took in all faces, with every other object about him.

Always upon first boarding a large and populous ship at sea, especially a foreign one, with a nondescript crew such as Lascars[3] or Manilla men, the impression varies in a peculiar way from that produced by first entering a strange house with strange inmates in a strange land. Both house and ship — the one by its walls and blinds, the other by its high bulwarks like ramparts — hoard from view their interiors till the last moment: but in the case of the ship there is this addition; that the living spectacle it contains, upon its sudden and complete disclosure, has, in contrast with the blank ocean which zones it, something of the effect of enchantment. The ship seems unreal; these strange costumes, gestures, and faces, but a shadowy tableau just emerged from the deep, which directly must receive back what it gave.

Perhaps it was some such influence, as above is attempted to be described, which, in Captain Delano's mind, heightened whatever, upon a staid scrutiny, might have seemed unusual; especially the conspicuous figures of four elderly grizzled negroes, their heads like black, doddered willow tops, who, in venerable contrast to the tumults below them, were couched, sphinx-like, one on the starboard cat-head,[4] another on the larboard, and the remaining pair face to face on the opposite bulwarks above the main-chains. They each had bits of unstranded old junk[5] in their hands, and, with a sort of stoical self-content, were picking the junk into oakum,[6] a small heap of which lay by their sides. They accompanied the task with a continuous, low, monotonous chant; droning and druling away like so many gray-headed bag-pipers playing a funeral march.

The quarter-deck rose into an ample elevated poop, upon the forward verge of which, lifted, like the oakum-pickers, some eight feet above the gen-

9. Covers for portholes, used in storms.

1. Old Spanish kingdoms.

2. Formed into a ball.

3. East Indian sailors.

4. A beam projecting from the bow of a ship to assist in raising the anchor. One is on the starboard (right) side, another on the larboard (left).

5. Old rope.

6. Strands of hemp fiber, used in caulking the seams of a ship.

eral throng, sat along in a row, separated by regular spaces, the cross-legged figures of six other blacks; each with a rusty hatchet in his hand, which, with a bit of brick and a rag, he was engaged like a scullion in scouring; while between each two was a small stack of hatchets, their rusted edges turned forward awaiting a like operation. Though occasionally the four oakum-pickers would briefly address some person or persons in the crowd below, yet the six hatchet-polishers neither spoke to others, nor breathed a whisper among themselves, but sat intent upon their task, except at intervals, when, with the peculiar love in negroes of uniting industry with pastime, two and two they sideways clashed their hatchets together, like cymbals, with a barbarous din. All six, unlike the generality, had the raw aspect of unsophisticated Africans.

But that first comprehensive glance which took in those ten figures, with scores less conspicuous, rested but an instant upon them, as, impatient of the hubbub of voices, the visitor turned in quest of whomsoever it might be that commanded the ship.

But as if not unwilling to let nature make known her own case among his suffering charge, or else in despair of restraining it for the time, the Spanish captain, a gentlemanly, reserved-looking, and rather young man to a stranger's eye, dressed with singular richness, but bearing plain traces of recent sleepless cares and disquietudes, stood passively by, leaning against the main-mast, at one moment casting a dreary, spiritless look upon his excited people, at the next an unhappy glance toward his visitor. By his side stood a black of small stature, in whose rude face, as occasionally, like a shepherd's dog, he mutely turned it up into the Spaniard's, sorrow and affection were equally blended.

Struggling through the throng, the American advanced to the Spaniard, assuring him of his sympathies, and offering to render whatever assistance might be in his power. To which the Spaniard returned for the present but grave and ceremonious acknowledgments, his national formality dusked by the saturnine mood of ill-health.

But losing no time in mere compliments, Captain Delano, returning to the gangway, had his basket of fish brought up; and as the wind still continued light, so that some hours at least must elapse ere the ship could be brought to the anchorage, he bade his men return to the sealer, and fetch back as much water as the whale-boat could carry, with whatever soft bread the steward might have, all the remaining pumpkins on board, with a box of sugar, and a dozen of his private bottles of cider.

Not many minutes after the boat's pushing off, to the vexation of all, the wind entirely died away, and the tide turning, began drifting back the ship helplessly seaward. But trusting this would not long last, Captain Delano sought, with good hopes, to cheer up the strangers, feeling no small satisfaction that, with persons in their condition, he could — thanks to his frequent voyages along the Spanish main — converse with some freedom in their native tongue.

While left alone with them, he was not long in observing some things tending to heighten his first impressions; but surprise was lost in pity, both for the Spaniards and blacks, alike evidently reduced from scarcity of water and provisions; while long-continued suffering seemed to have brought out the less good-natured qualities of the negroes, besides, at the same time, impairing the Spaniard's authority over them. But, under the circumstances, precisely this condition of things was to have been anticipated. In armies, navies, cities, or families, in nature herself, nothing more relaxes good order than misery. Still, Captain Delano was not without the idea, that had Benito Cereno been a man of greater energy, misrule would hardly have come to the present pass. But the debility, constitutional or induced by hardships, bodily and mental, of the Spanish captain, was too obvious to be overlooked. A prey to settled dejection, as if long mocked with hope he would not now indulge it, even when it had ceased to be a mock, the prospect of that day, or evening at furthest, lying at anchor, with plenty of water for his people, and a brother captain to counsel and befriend, seemed in no perceptible degree to encourage him. His mind appeared unstrung, if not still more seriously affected. Shut up in these oaken walls, chained to one dull round of command, whose unconditionality cloyed him, like some hypochondriac abbot he moved slowly about, at times suddenly pausing, starting, or staring, biting his lip, biting his fingernail, flushing, paling, twitching his beard, with other symptoms of an absent or moody mind. This distempered spirit was lodged, as before hinted, in as distempered a frame. He was rather tall, but seemed never to have been robust, and now with nervous suffering was almost worn to a skeleton. A tendency to some pulmonary complaint appeared to have been lately confirmed. His voice was like that of one with lungs half gone—hoarsely suppressed, a husky whisper. No wonder that, as in this state he tottered about, his private servant apprehensively followed him. Sometimes the negro gave his master his arm, or took his handkerchief out of his pocket for him; performing these and similar offices with that affectionate zeal which transmutes into something filial or fraternal acts in themselves but menial; and which has gained for the negro the repute of making the most pleasing body-servant in the world; one, too, whom a master need be on no stiffly superior terms with, but may treat with familiar trust; less a servant than a devoted companion.

Marking the noisy indocility of the blacks in general, as well as what seemed the sullen inefficiency of the whites, it was not without humane satisfaction that Captain Delano witnessed the steady good conduct of Babo.

But the good conduct of Babo, hardly more than the ill-behavior of others, seemed to withdraw the half-lunatic Don Benito from his cloudy languor. Not that such precisely was the impression made by the Spaniard on the mind of his visitor. The Spaniard's individual unrest was, for the present, but noted as a conspicuous feature in the ship's general affliction. Still, Captain Delano was not a little concerned at what he could not help taking for the time to be Don Benito's unfriendly indifference towards himself. The Spaniard's manner, too, conveyed a sort of sour and gloomy disdain, which he seemed at no pains to disguise. But this the American in charity ascribed to the harassing effects of sickness, since, in former instances, he had noted that there are peculiar natures on whom prolonged physical suffering seems to cancel every social instinct of kindness; as if, forced to black bread themselves, they deemed it but equity that each person coming nigh them should, indirectly, by some slight or affront, be made to partake of their fare.

But ere long Captain Delano bethought him that, indulgent as he was at the first, in judging the Spaniard, he might not, after all, have exercised charity enough. At bottom it was Don Benito's reserve which displeased him; but the same reserve was shown towards all but his faithful personal attendant. Even the formal reports which, according to sea-usage, were, at stated times, made to him by some petty underling, either a white, mulatto or black, he hardly had patience enough to listen to, without betraying contemptuous aversion. His man-

ner upon such occasions was, in its degree, not unlike that which might be supposed to have been his imperial countryman's, Charles V.,[7] just previous to the anchoritish retirement of that monarch from the throne.

This splenetic disrelish of his place was evinced in almost every function pertaining to it. Proud as he was moody, he condescended to no personal mandate. Whatever special orders were necessary, their delivery was delegated to his body-servant, who in turn transferred them to their ultimate destination, through runners, alert Spanish boys or slave boys, like pages or pilot-fish[8] within easy call continually hovering round Don Benito. So that to have beheld this undemonstrative invalid gliding about, apathetic and mute, no landsman could have dreamed that in him was lodged a dictatorship beyond which, while at sea, there was no earthly appeal.

Thus, the Spaniard, regarded in his reserve, seemed the involuntary victim of mental disorder. But, in fact, his reserve might, in some degree, have proceeded from design. If so, then here was evinced the unhealthy climax of that icy though conscientious policy, more or less adopted by all commanders of large ships, which, except in signal emergencies, obliterates alike the manifestation of sway with every trace of sociality; transforming the man into a block, or rather into a loaded cannon, which, until there is call for thunder, has nothing to say.

Viewing him in this light, it seemed but a natural token of the perverse habit induced by a long course of such hard self-restraint, that, notwithstanding the present condition of his ship, the Spaniard should still persist in a demeanor, which, however harmless, or, it may be, appropriate, in a well-appointed vessel, such as the San Dominick might have been at the outset of the voyage, was anything but judicious now. But the Spaniard, perhaps, thought that it was with captains as with gods: reserve, under all events, must still be their cue. But probably this appearance of slumbering dominion might have been but an attempted disguise to conscious imbecility—not deep policy, but shallow device. But be all this as it might, whether Don Benito's manner was designed or not,

_____

7. Charles V (1500–1558), king of Spain, spent his last years in a monastery.

8. Pilot fish often accompany sharks, seeming to guide them.

the more Captain Delano noted its pervading reserve, the less he felt uneasiness at any particular manifestation of that reserve towards himself.

Neither were his thoughts taken up by the captain alone. Wonted to the quiet orderliness of the sealer's comfortable family of a crew, the noisy confusion of the San Dominick's suffering host repeatedly challenged his eye. Some prominent breaches, not only of discipline but of decency, were observed. These Captain Delano could not but ascribe, in the main, to the absence of those subordinate deck-officers to whom, along with higher duties, is intrusted what may be styled the police department of a populous ship. True, the old oakum-pickers appeared at times to act the part of monitorial constables to their countrymen, the blacks; but though occasionally succeeding in allaying trifling outbreaks now and then between man and man, they could do little or nothing toward establishing general quiet. The San Dominick was in the condition of a transatlantic emigrant ship, among whose multitude of living freight are some individuals, doubtless, as little troublesome as crates and bales; but the friendly remonstrances of such with their ruder companions are of not so much avail as the unfriendly arm of the mate. What the San Dominick wanted was, what the emigrant ship has, stern superior officers. But on these decks not so much as a fourth-mate was to be seen.

The visitor's curiosity was roused to learn the particulars of those mishaps which had brought about such absenteeism, with its consequences; because, though deriving some inkling of the voyage from the wails which at the first moment had greeted him, yet of the details no clear understanding had been had. The best account would, doubtless, be given by the captain. Yet at first the visitor was loth to ask it, unwilling to provoke some distant rebuff. But plucking up courage, he at last accosted Don Benito, renewing the expression of his benevolent interest, adding, that did he (Captain Delano) but know the particulars of the ship's misfortunes, he would, perhaps, be better able in the end to relieve them. Would Don Benito favor him with the whole story.

Don Benito faltered; then, like some somnambulist suddenly interfered with, vacantly stared at his visitor, and ended by looking down on the deck. He maintained this posture so long, that Captain Delano, almost equally disconcerted, and involuntarily almost as rude, turned suddenly from him, walking forward to accost one of the Spanish seamen for the desired information. But he had hardly gone five paces, when, with a sort of eagerness, Don Benito invited him back, regretting his momentary absence of mind, and professing readiness to gratify him.

While most part of the story was being given, the two captains stood on the after part of the main-deck, a privileged spot, no one being near but the servant.

"It is now a hundred and ninety days," began the Spaniard, in his husky whisper, "that this ship, well officered and well manned, with several cabin passengers—some fifty Spaniards in all—sailed from Buenos Ayres bound to Lima, with a general cargo, hardware, Paraguay tea and the like—and," pointing forward, "that parcel of negroes, now not more than a hundred and fifty, as you see, but then numbering over three hundred souls. Off Cape Horn we had heavy gales. In one moment, by night, three of my best officers, with fifteen sailors, were lost, with the main-yard; the spar snapping under them in the slings,[9] as they sought, with heavers,[1] to beat down the icy sail. To lighten the hull, the heavier sacks of mata were thrown into the sea, with most of the water-pipes[2] lashed on the deck at the time. And this last necessity it was, combined with the prolonged detentions afterwards experienced, which eventually brought about our chief causes of suffering. When——"

Here there was a sudden fainting attack of his cough, brought on, no doubt, by his mental distress. His servant sustained him, and drawing a cordial from his pocket placed it to his lips. He a little revived. But unwilling to leave him unsupported while yet imperfectly restored, the black with one arm still encircled his master, at the same time keeping his eye fixed on his face, as if to watch for the first sign of complete restoration, or relapse, as the event might prove.

The Spaniard proceeded, but brokenly and obscurely, as one in a dream.

——"Oh, my God! rather than pass through what I have, with joy I would have hailed the most terrible gales; but——"

His cough returned and with increased violence; this subsiding, with reddened lips and closed eyes he fell heavily against his supporter.

---

9. Restraining lines.

1. Bars.

2. Water casks.

"His mind wanders. He was thinking of the plague that followed the gales," plaintively sighed the servant; "my poor, poor master!" wringing one hand, and with the other wiping the mouth. "But be patient, Señor," again turning to Captain Delano, "these fits do not last long; master will soon be himself."

Don Benito reviving, went on; but as this portion of the story was very brokenly delivered, the substance only will here be set down.

It appeared that after the ship had been many days tossed in storms off the Cape, the scurvy broke out, carrying off numbers of the whites and blacks. When at last they had worked round into the Pacific, their spars and sails were so damaged, and so inadequately handled by the surviving mariners, most of whom were become invalids, that, unable to lay her northerly course by the wind, which was powerful, the unmanageable ship, for successive days and nights, was blown northwestward, where the breeze suddenly deserted her, in unknown waters, to sultry calms. The absence of the water-pipes now proved as fatal to life as before their presence had menaced it. Induced, or at least aggravated, by the more than scanty allowance of water, a malignant fever followed the scurvy; with the excessive heat of the lengthened calm, making such short work of it as to sweep away, as by billows, whole families of the Africans, and a yet larger number, proportionably, of the Spaniards, including, by a luckless fatality, every remaining officer on board. Consequently, in the smart west winds eventually following the calm, the already rent sails, having to be simply dropped, not furled, at need, had been gradually reduced to the beggars' rags they were now. To procure substitutes for his lost sailors, as well as supplies of water and sails, the captain, at the earliest opportunity, had made for Valdivia, the southernmost civilized port of Chili and South America; but upon nearing the coast the thick weather had prevented him from so much as sighting that harbor. Since which period, almost without a crew, and almost without canvas and almost without water, and, at intervals, giving its added dead to the sea, the San Dominick had been battle-dored[3] about by contrary winds, inveigled by currents, or grown weedy in calms. Like a man lost in woods, more than once she had doubled upon her own track.

"But throughout these calamities," huskily continued Don Benito, painfully turning in the half embrace of his servant, "I have to thank those negroes you see, who, though to your inexperienced eyes appearing unruly, have, indeed, conducted themselves with less of restlessness than even their owner could have thought possible under such circumstances."

Here he again fell faintly back. Again his mind wandered; but he rallied, and less obscurely proceeded.

"Yes, their owner was quite right in assuring me that no fetters would be needed with his blacks; so that while, as is wont in this transportation, those negroes have always remained upon deck—not thrust below, as in the Guineamen[4]—they have, also, from the beginning, been freely permitted to range within given bounds at their pleasure."

Once more the faintness returned—his mind roved—but, recovering, he resumed:

"But it is Babo here to whom, under God, I owe not only my own preservation, but likewise to him, chiefly, the merit is due, of pacifying his more ignorant brethren, when at intervals tempted to murmurings."

"Ah, master," sighed the black, bowing his face, "don't speak of me; Babo is nothing; what Babo has done was but duty."

"Faithful fellow!" cried Captain Delano. "Don Benito, I envy you such a friend; slave I cannot call him."

As master and man stood before him, the black upholding the white, Captain Delano could not but bethink him of the beauty of that relationship which could present such a spectacle of fidelity on the one hand and confidence on the other. The scene was heightened by the contrast in dress, denoting their relative positions. The Spaniard wore a loose Chili jacket of dark velvet; white small-clothes and stockings, with silver buckles at the knee and instep; a high-crowned sombrero, of fine grass; a slender sword, silver mounted, hung from a knot in his sash—the last being an almost invariable adjunct, more for utility than ornament, of a South American gentleman's dress to this hour. Excepting when his occasional nervous contortions brought about disarray, there

---

3. Tossed back and forth like a shuttlecock by a battledore, or paddle.

4. Slavers trading with Guinea, on the west coast of Africa.

was a certain precision in his attire curiously at variance with the unsightly disorder around; especially in the belittered Ghetto, forward of the mainmast, wholly occupied by the blacks.

The servant wore nothing but wide trowsers, apparently, from their coarseness and patches, made out of some old topsail; they were clean, and confined at the waist by a bit of unstranded rope, which, with his composed, deprecatory air at times, made him look something like a begging friar of St. Francis.[5]

However unsuitable for the time and place, at least in the blunt-thinking American's eyes, and however strangely surviving in the midst of all his afflictions, the toilette of Don Benito might not, in fashion at least, have gone beyond the style of the day among South Americans of his class. Though on the present voyage sailing from Buenos Ayres, he had avowed himself a native and resident of Chili, whose inhabitants had not so generally adopted the plain coat and once plebeian pantaloons; but, with a becoming modification, adhered to their provincial costume, picturesque as any in the world. Still, relatively to the pale history of the voyage, and his own pale face, there seemed something so incongruous in the Spaniard's apparel, as almost to suggest the image of an invalid courtier tottering about London streets in the time of the plague.

The portion of the narrative which, perhaps, most excited interest, as well as some surprise, considering the latitudes in question, was the long calms spoken of, and more particularly the ship's so long drifting about. Without communicating the opinion, of course, the American could not but impute at least part of the detentions both to clumsy seamanship and faulty navigation. Eying Don Benito's small, yellow hands, he easily inferred that the young captain had not got into command at the hawse-hole,[6] but the cabin-window; and if so, why wonder at incompetence, in youth, sickness, and gentility united?

But drowning criticism in compassion, after a fresh repetition of his sympathies, Captain Delano, having heard out his story, not only engaged, as in the first place, to see Don Benito and his people supplied in their immediate bodily needs, but, also, now

further promised to assist him in procuring a large permanent supply of water, as well as some sails and rigging; and, though it would involve no small embarrassment to himself, yet he would spare three of his best seamen for temporary deck officers; so that without delay the ship might proceed to Conception, there to refit for Lima, her destined port.

Such generosity was not without its effect, even upon the invalid. His face lighted up; eager and hectic, he met the honest glance of his visitor. With gratitude he seemed overcome.

"This excitement is bad for master," whispered the servant, taking his arm, and with soothing words gently drawing him aside.

When Don Benito returned, the American was pained to observe that his hopefulness, like the sudden kindling in his cheek, was but febrile and transient.

Ere long, with a joyless mien, looking up towards the poop, the host invited his guest to accompany him there, for the benefit of what little breath of wind might be stirring.

As, during the telling of the story, Captain Delano had once or twice started at the occasional cymballing of the hatchet-polishers, wondering why such an interruption should be allowed, especially in that part of the ship, and in the ears of an invalid; and moreover, as the hatchets had anything but an attractive look, and the handlers of them still less so, it was, therefore, to tell the truth, not without some lurking reluctance, or even shrinking, it may be, that Captain Delano, with apparent complaisance, acquiesced in his host's invitation. The more so, since, with an untimely caprice of punctilio, rendered distressing by his cadaverous aspect, Don Benito, with Castilian[7] bows, solemnly insisted upon his guest's preceding him up the ladder leading to the elevation; where, one on each side of the last step, sat for armorial supporters and sentries two of the ominous file. Gingerly enough stepped good Captain Delano between them, and in the instant of leaving them behind, like one running the gauntlet, he felt an apprehensive twitch in the calves of his legs.

But when, facing about, he saw the whole file, like so many organ-grinders, still stupidly intent on their work, unmindful of everything beside, he could not but smile at his late fidgety panic.

---

5. A Franciscan friar.

6. Hole for cables. Don Benito's hands show that he did not begin as a common seaman, but went to sea in a position of authority.

---

7. Courtly.

Presently, while standing with his host, looking forward upon the decks below, he was struck by one of those instances of insubordination previously alluded to. Three black boys, with two Spanish boys, were sitting together on the hatches, scraping a rude wooden platter, in which some scanty mess had recently been cooked. Suddenly, one of the black boys, enraged at a word dropped by one of his white companions, seized a knife, and, though called to forbear by one of the oakum-pickers, struck the lad over the head, inflicting a gash from which blood flowed.

In amazement, Captain Delano inquired what this meant. To which the pale Don Benito dully muttered, that it was merely the sport of the lad.

"Pretty serious sport, truly," rejoined Captain Delano. "Had such a thing happened on board the Bachelor's Delight, instant punishment would have followed."

At these words the Spaniard turned upon the American one of his sudden, staring, half-lunatic looks; then, relapsing into his torpor, answered, "Doubtless, doubtless, Señor."

Is it, thought Captain Delano, that this hapless man is one of those paper captains I've known, who by policy wink at what by power they cannot put down? I know no sadder sight than a commander who has little of command but the name.

"I should think, Don Benito," he now said, glancing towards the oakum-picker who had sought to interfere with the boys, "that you would find it advantageous to keep all your blacks employed, especially the younger ones, no matter at what useless task, and no matter what happens to the ship. Why, even with my little band, I find such a course indispensable. I once kept a crew on my quarterdeck thrumming[8] mats for my cabin, when, for three days, I had given up my ship—mats, men, and all—for a speedy loss, owing to the violence of a gale, in which we could do nothing but helplessly drive before it."

"Doubtless, doubtless," muttered Don Benito.

"But," continued Captain Delano, again glancing upon the oakum-pickers and then at the hatchet-polishers, near by, "I see you keep some, at least, of your host employed."

"Yes," was again the vacant response.

"Those old men there, shaking their pows[9] from their pulpits," continued Captain Delano, pointing to the oakum-pickers, "seem to act the part of old dominies[1] to the rest, little heeded as their admonitions are at times. Is this voluntary on their part, Don Benito, or have you appointed them shepherds to your flock of black sheep?"

"What posts they fill, I appointed them," rejoined the Spaniard, in an acrid tone, as if resenting some supposed satiric reflection.

"And these others, these Ashantee[2] conjurors here," continued Captain Delano, rather uneasily eyeing the brandished steel of the hatchet-polishers, where, in spots, it had been brought to a shine, "this seems a curious business they are at, Don Benito?"

"In the gales we met," answered the Spaniard, "what of our general cargo was not thrown overboard was much damaged by the brine. Since coming into calm weather, I have had several cases of knives and hatchets daily brought up for overhauling and cleaning."

"A prudent idea, Don Benito. You are part owner of ship and cargo, I presume; but none of the slaves, perhaps?"

"I am owner of all you see," impatiently returned Don Benito, "except the main company of blacks, who belonged to my late friend, Alexandro Aranda."

As he mentioned this name, his air was heartbroken; his knees shook; his servant supported him.

Thinking he divined the cause of such unusual emotion, to confirm his surmise, Captain Delano, after a pause, said: "And may I ask, Don Benito, whether—since awhile ago you spoke of some cabin passengers—the friend, whose loss so afflicts you, at the outset of the voyage accompanied his blacks?"

"Yes."

"But died of the fever?"

"Died of the fever. Oh, could I but——"

Again quivering, the Spaniard paused.

"Pardon me," said Captain Delano, lowly, "but I think that, by a sympathetic experience, I conjecture, Don Benito, what it is that gives the keener edge to your grief. It was once my hard fortune to lose, at sea, a dear friend, my own brother, then supercargo.[3]

---

8. Weaving.

9. Heads.

1. Religious leaders.

2. Ashanti, a West African people.

3. The officer on a ship who represents the owners.

Assured of the welfare of his spirit, its departure I could have borne like a man; but that honest eye, that honest hand—both of which had so often met mine—and that warm heart; all, all—like scraps to the dogs—to throw all to the sharks! It was then I vowed never to have for fellow-voyager a man I loved, unless, unbeknown to him, I had provided every requisite, in case of a fatality, for embalming his mortal part for interment on shore. Were your friend's remains now on board this ship, Don Benito, not thus strangely would the mention of his name affect you."

"On board this ship?" echoed the Spaniard. Then, with horrified gestures, as directed against some spectre, he unconsciously fell into the ready arms of his attendant, who, with a silent appeal toward Captain Delano, seemed beseeching him not again to broach a theme so unspeakably distressing to his master.

This poor fellow now, thought the pained American, is the victim of that sad superstition which associates goblins with the deserted body of man, as ghosts with an abandoned house. How unlike are we made! What to me, in like case, would have been a solemn satisfaction, the bare suggestion, even, terrifies the Spaniard into this trance. Poor Alexandro Aranda! what would you say could you here see your friend—who, on former voyages, when you, for months, were left behind, has, I dare say, often longed, and longed, for one peep at you—now transported with terror at the least thought of having you anyway nigh him.

At this moment, with a dreary grave-yard toll, betokening a flaw, the ship's forecastle bell, smote by one of the grizzled oakum-pickers, proclaimed ten o'clock, through the leaden calm; when Captain Delano's attention was caught by the moving figure of a gigantic black, emerging from the general crowd below, and slowly advancing towards the elevated poop. An iron collar was about his neck, from which depended a chain, thrice wound round his body; the terminating links padlocked together at a broad band of iron, his girdle.

"How like a mute Atufal moves," murmured the servant.

The black mounted the steps of the poop, and, like a brave prisoner, brought up to receive sentence, stood in unquailing muteness before Don Benito, now recovered from his attack.

At the first glimpse of his approach, Don Benito had started, a resentful shadow swept over his face;

and, as with the sudden memory of bootless[4] rage, his white lips glued together.

This is some mulish mutineer, thought Captain Delano, surveying, not without a mixture of admiration, the colossal form of the negro.

"See, he waits your question, master," said the servant.

Thus reminded, Don Benito, nervously averting his glance, as if shunning, by anticipation, some rebellious response, in a disconcerted voice, thus spoke:—

"Atufal, will you ask my pardon, now?"

The black was silent.

"Again, master," murmured the servant, with bitter upbraiding eying his countryman, "Answer, master, he will bend to master yet."

"Answer," said Don Benito, still averting his glance, "say but the one word, *pardon*," and your chains shall be off."

Upon this, the black, slowly raising both arms, let them lifelessly fall, his links clanking, his head bowed; as much as to say, "no, I am content."

"Go," said Don Benito, with inkept and unknown emotion.

Deliberately as he had come, the black obeyed.

"Excuse me, Don Benito," said Captain Delano, "but this scene surprises me; what means it, pray?"

"It means that that negro alone, of all the band, has given me peculiar cause of offense. I have put him in chains; I——"

Here he paused; his hand to his head, as if there were a swimming there, or a sudden bewilderment of memory had come over him; but meeting his servant's kindly glance seemed reassured, and proceeded:—

"I could not scourge such a form. But I told him he must ask my pardon. As yet he has not. At my command, every two hours he stands before me."

"And how long has this been?"

"Some sixty days."

"And obedient in all else? And respectful?"

"Yes."

"Upon my conscience, then," exclaimed Captain Delano, impulsively, "he has a royal spirit in him, this fellow."

"He may have some right to it," bitterly returned Don Benito, "he says he was king in his own land."

---

4. Profitless.

"Yes," said the servant, entering a word, "those slits in Atufal's ears once held wedges of gold; but poor Babo here, in his own land, was only a poor slave; a black man's slave was Babo, who now is the white's."

Somewhat annoyed by these conversational familiarities, Captain Delano turned curiously upon the attendant, then glanced inquiringly at his master; but, as if long wonted to these little informalities, neither master nor man seemed to understand him.

"What, pray, was Atufal's offense, Don Benito?" asked Captain Delano; "if it was not something very serious, take a fool's advice, and, in view of his general docility, as well as in some natural respect for his spirit, remit him his penalty."

"No, no, master never will do that," here murmured the servant to himself, "proud Atufal must first ask master's pardon. The slave there carries the padlock, but master here carries the key."

His attention thus directed, Captain Delano now noticed for the first time, that, suspended by a slender silken cord, from Don Benito's neck, hung a key. At once, from the servant's muttered syllables, divining the key's purpose, he smiled and said: — "So, Don Benito — padlock and key — significant symbols, truly."

Biting his lip, Don Benito faltered.

Though the remark of Captain Delano, a man of such native simplicity as to be incapable of satire or irony, had been dropped in playful allusion to the Spaniard's singularly evidenced lordship over the black; yet the hypochondriac seemed some way to have taken it as a malicious reflection upon his confessed inability thus far to break down, at least, on a verbal summons, the entrenched will of the slave. Deploring this supposed misconception, yet despairing of correcting it, Captain Delano shifted the subject; but finding his companion more than ever withdrawn, as if still sourly digesting the lees of the presumed affront above-mentioned, by-and-by Captain Delano likewise became less talkative, oppressed against his own will, by what seemed the secret vindictiveness of the morbidly sensitive Spaniard. But the good sailor, himself of a quite contrary disposition, refrained, on his part, alike from the appearance as from the feeling of resentment, and if silent, was only so from contagion.

Presently the Spaniard, assisted by his servant, somewhat discourteously crossed over from his guest; a procedure which, sensibly enough, might have been allowed to pass for idle caprice of ill-humor, had not master and man, lingering around the corner of the elevated skylight, began whispering together in low voices. This was unpleasing. And more; the moody air of the Spaniard, which at times had not been without a sort of valetudinarian stateliness, now seemed anything but dignified; while the menial familiarity of the servant lost its original charm of simple-hearted attachment.

In his embarrassment, the visitor turned his face to the other side of the ship. By so doing, his glance accidentally fell on a young Spanish sailor, a coil of rope in his hand, just stepped from the deck to the first round of the mizzen-rigging. Perhaps the man would not have been particularly noticed, were it not that, during his ascent to one of the yards, he, with a sort of covert intentness, kept his eye fixed on Captain Delano, from whom, presently, it passed, as if by a natural sequence, to the two whisperers.

His own attention thus redirected to that quarter, Captain Delano gave a slight start. From something in Don Benito's manner just then, it seemed as if the visitor had, at least partly, been the subject of the withdrawn consultation going on — a conjecture as little agreeable to the guest as it was little flattering to the host.

The singular alternations of courtesy and ill-breeding in the Spanish captain were unaccountable, except on one of two suppositions — innocent lunacy, or wicked imposture.

But the first idea, though it might naturally have occurred to an indifferent observer, and, in some respect, had not hitherto been wholly a stranger to Captain Delano's mind, yet, now that, in an incipient way, he began to regard the stranger's conduct something in the light of an intentional affront, of course the idea of lunacy was virtually vacated. But if not a lunatic, what then? Under the circumstances, would a gentleman, nay, any honest boor, act the part now acted by his host? The man was an imposter. Some low-born adventurer, masquerading as an oceanic grandee; yet so ignorant of the first requisites of mere gentlemanhood as to be betrayed into the present remarkable indecorum. That strange ceremoniousness, too, at other times evinced, seemed not uncharacteristic of one playing a part above his real level. Benito Cereno — Don Benito Cereno — a sounding name. One, too, at that period, not unknown, in the surname, to supercargoes and sea captains trading along the Spanish Main, as belonging to one of the most enterprising and extensive mercantile families in all those provinces; several members of it having titles; a sort of Castilian Rothschild,[5] with a noble brother, or cousin, in every great trading town of South America. The alleged Don Benito was in early manhood, about twenty-nine or thirty. To assume a sort of roving cadetship in the maritime affairs of such a house, what more likely scheme for a young knave of talent and spirit? But the Spaniard was a pale invalid. Never mind. For even to the degree of simulating mortal disease, the craft of some tricksters had been known to attain. To think that, under the aspect of infantile weakness, the most savage energies might be couched — those velvets of the Spaniard but the silky paw to his fangs.

From no train of thought did these fancies come; not from within, but from without; suddenly, too, and in one throng, like hoar frost; yet as soon to vanish as the mild sun of Captain Delano's good-nature regained its meridian.

Glancing over once more towards his host — whose side-face, revealed above the skylight, was now turned towards him — he was struck by the profile, whose clearness of cut was refined by the thinness, incident to ill-health, as well as ennobled about the chin by the beard. Away with suspicion. He was a true off-shoot of a true hidalgo[6] Cereno.

Relieved by these and other better thoughts, the visitor, lightly humming a tune, now began indifferently pacing the poop, so as not to betray to Don Benito that he had at all mistrusted incivility, much less duplicity; for such mistrust would yet be proved illusory, and by the event; though, for the present, the circumstance which had provoked that distrust remained unexplained. But when that little mystery should have been cleared up, Captain Delano thought he might extremely regret it, did he allow Don Benito to become aware that he had indulged in ungenerous surmises. In short, to the Spaniard's black-letter[7] text, it was best, for a while, to leave open margin.[8]

Presently, his pale face twitching and overcast, the Spaniard, still supported by his attendant, moved over towards his guest, when, with even more than his usual embarrassment, and a strange sort of intriguing intonation in his husky whisper, the following conversation began: —

"Señor, may I ask how long you have lain at this isle?"

"Oh, but a day or two, Don Benito."

"And from what port are you last?"

"Canton."[9]

"And there, Señor, you exchanged your sealskins for teas and silks, I think you said?"

"Yes. Silks, mostly."

"And the balance you took in specie,[1] perhaps?"

Captain Delano, fidgeting a little, answered —

"Yes; some silver; not a very great deal, though."

"Ah — well. May I ask how many men have you, Señor?"

Captain Delano slightly started, but answered —

"About five-and-twenty, all told."

"And at present, Señor, all on board, I suppose?"

"All on board, Don Benito," replied the Captain, now with satisfaction.

"And will be to-night, Señor?"

At this last question, following so many pertinacious ones, for the soul of him Captain Delano could not but look very earnestly at the questioner, who, instead of meeting the glance, with every token of craven discomposure dropped his eyes to the deck; presenting an unworthy contrast to his servant, who, just then, was kneeling at his feet, adjusting a loose shoe-buckle; his disengaged face meantime, with humble curiosity, turned openly up into his master's downcast one.

The Spaniard, still with a guilty shuffle, repeated his question:

"And — and will be to-night, Señor?"

"Yes, for aught I know," returned Captain Delano — "but nay," rallying himself into fearless truth, "some of them talked of going off on another fishing party about midnight."

"Your ships generally go — go more or less armed, I believe, Señor?"

"Oh, a six-pounder or two, in case of emergency," was the intrepidly indifferent reply, "with a small stock of muskets, sealing-spears, and cutlasses, you know."

---

5. Rothschild: a member of a great German banking family.

6. Spanish nobleman.

7. A typeface that imitates medieval lettering.

8. Delano made no marginal notes; he suspended judgment.

---

9. In China, now called Guangzhou.

1. Coin.

As he thus responded, Captain Delano again glanced at Don Benito, but the latter's eyes were averted; while abruptly and awkwardly shifting the subject, he made some peevish allusion to the calm, and then, without apology, once more, with his attendant, withdrew to the opposite bulwarks, where the whispering was resumed.

At this moment, and ere Captain Delano could cast a cool thought upon what had just passed, the young Spanish sailor, before mentioned, was seen descending from the rigging. In act of stooping over to spring inboard to the deck; his voluminous, unconfined frock, or shirt, of course woolen, much spotted with tar, opened out far down the chest, revealing a soiled under-garment of what seemed the finest linen, edged, about the neck, with a narrow blue ribbon, sadly faded and worn. At this moment the young sailor's eye was again fixed on the whisperers, and Captain Delano thought he observed a lurking significance in it, as if silent signs, of some Freemason[2] sort, had that instant been interchanged.

This once more impelled his own glance in the direction of Don Benito, and, as before, he could not but infer that himself formed the subject of the conference. He paused. The sound of the hatchet-polishing fell on his ears. He cast another swift side-look at the two. They had the air of conspirators. In connection with the late questionings, and the incident of the young sailor, these things now begat such return of involuntary suspicion, that the singular guilelessness of the American could not endure it. Plucking up a gay and humorous expression, he crossed over to the two rapidly, saying:—"Ha, Don Benito, your black here seems high in your trust; a sort of privy-counselor, in fact."

Upon this, the servant looked up with a good-natured grin, but the master started as from a venomous bite. It was a moment or two before the Spaniard sufficiently recovered himself to reply; which he did, at last, with cold constraint:—"Yes, Señor, I have trust in Babo."

Here Babo, changing his previous grin of mere animal humor into an intelligent smile, not ungratefully eyed his master.

Finding that the Spaniard now stood silent and reserved, as if involuntarily, or purposely giving hint that his guest's proximity was inconvenient just then,

Captain Delano, unwilling to appear uncivil even to incivility itself, made some trivial remark and moved off; again and again turning over in his mind the mysterious demeanor of Don Benito Cereno.

He had descended from the poop, and, wrapped in thought, was passing near a dark hatchway, leading down into the steerage, when, perceiving motion there, he looked to see what moved. The same instant there was a sparkle in the shadowy hatchway, and he saw one of the Spanish sailors, prowling there, hurriedly placing his hand in the bosom of his frock, as if hiding something. Before the man could have been certain who it was that was passing, he slunk below out of sight. But enough was seen of him to make sure that he was the same young sailor before noticed in the rigging.

What was that which so sparkled? thought Captain Delano. It was no lamp—no match—no live coal. Could it have been a jewel? But how come sailors with jewels?—or with silk-trimmed under-shirts either? Has he been robbing the trunks of the dead cabin-passengers? But if so, he would hardly wear one of the stolen articles on board ship here. Ah, ah—if, now, that was, indeed, a secret sign I saw passing between this suspicious fellow and his captain awhile since; if I could only be certain that, in my uneasiness, my senses did not deceive me, then—

Here, passing from one suspicious thing to another, his mind revolved the strange questions put to him concerning his ship.

By a curious coincidence, as each point was recalled, the black wizards of Ashantee would strike up with their hatchets, as in ominous comment on the white stranger's thoughts. Pressed by such enigmas and portents, it would have been almost against nature had not, even into the least distrustful heart, some ugly misgivings obtruded.

Observing the ship, now helplessly fallen into a current, with enchanted sails, drifting with increased rapidity seaward; and noting that, from a lately intercepted projection of the land, the sealer was hidden, the stout mariner began to quake at thoughts which he barely durst confess to himself. Above all, he began to feel a ghostly dread of Don Benito. And yet, when he roused himself, dilated his chest, felt himself strong on his legs, and coolly considered it—what did all these phantoms amount to?

Had the Spaniard any sinister scheme, it must have reference not so much to him (Captain Delano) as to his ship (the Bachelor's Delight). Hence

---

2. A secret fraternal society.

the present drifting away of the one ship from the other, instead of favoring any such possible scheme, was, for the time, at least, opposed to it. Clearly any suspicion, combining such contradictions, must need be delusive. Beside, was it not absurd to think of a vessel in distress—a vessel by sickness almost dismanned of her crew—a vessel whose inmates were parched for water—was it not a thousand times absurd that such a craft should, at present, be of a piratical character; or her commander, either for himself or those under him, cherish any desire but for speedy relief and refreshment? But then, might not general distress, and thirst in particular, be affected? And might not that same undiminished Spanish crew, alleged to have perished off to a remnant, be at that very moment lurking in the hold? On heart-broken pretense of entreating a cup of cold water, fiends in human form had got into lonely dwellings, nor retired until a dark deed had been done. And among the Malay pirates, it was no unusual thing to lure ships after them into their treacherous harbors, or entice boarders from a declared enemy at sea, by the spectacle of thinly manned or vacant decks, beneath which prowled a hundred spears with yellow arms ready to upthrust them through the mats. Not that Captain Delano had entirely credited such things. He had heard of them—and now, as stories, they recurred. The present destination of the ship was anchorage. There she would be near his own vessel. Upon gaining that vicinity, might not the San Dominick, like a slumbering volcano, suddenly let loose energies now hid?

He recalled the Spaniard's manner while telling his story. There was a gloomy hesitancy and subterfuge about it. It was just the manner of one making up his tale for evil purposes, as he goes. But if that story was not true, what was the truth? That the ship had unlawfully come into the Spaniard's possession? But in many of its details, especially in reference to the more calamitous parts, such as the fatalities among the seamen, the consequent prolonged beating about, the past sufferings from obstinate calms, and still continued suffering from thirst; in all these points, as well as others, Don Benito's story had corroborated not only the wailing ejaculations of the indiscriminate multitude, white and black, but likewise—what seemed impossible to be counterfeit—the very expression and play of every human feature, which Captain Delano saw. If Don Benito's story was, throughout, an invention, then

every soul on board, down to the youngest negress, was his carefully drilled recruit in the plot: an incredible inference. And yet, if there was ground for mistrusting his veracity, that inference was a legitimate one.

But those questions of the Spaniard. There, indeed, one might pause. Did they not seem put with much the same object with which the burglar or assassin, by day-time, reconnoitres the walls of a house? But, with ill purposes, to solicit such information openly of the chief person endangered, and so, in effect, setting him on his guard; how unlikely a procedure was that? Absurd, then, to suppose that those questions had been prompted by evil designs. Thus, the same conduct, which, in this instance, had raised the alarm, served to dispel it. In short, scarce any suspicion or uneasiness, however apparently reasonable at the time, which was not now, with equal apparent reason, dismissed.

At last he began to laugh at his former forebodings; and laugh at the strange ship for, in its aspect, someway siding with them, as it were; and laugh, too, at the odd-looking blacks, particularly those old scissors-grinders, the Ashantees; and those bedridden old knitting women, the oakum-pickers; and almost at the dark Spaniard himself, the central hobgoblin of all.

For the rest, whatever in a serious way seemed enigmatical, was now good-naturedly explained away by the thought that, for the most part, the poor invalid scarcely knew what he was about; either sulking in black vapors, or putting idle questions without sense or object. Evidently, for the present, the man was not fit to be intrusted with the ship. On some benevolent plea withdrawing the command from him, Captain Delano would yet have to send her to Conception, in charge of his second mate, a worthy person and good navigator—a plan not more convenient for the San Dominick than for Don Benito; for, relieved from all anxiety, keeping wholly to his cabin, the sick man, under the good nursing of his servant, would, probably, by the end of the passage, be in a measure restored to health, and with that he should also be restored to authority.

Such were the American's thoughts. They were tranquilizing. There was a difference between the idea of Don Benito's darkly preordaining Captain Delano's fate, and Captain Delano's lightly arranging Don Benito's. Nevertheless, it was not without something of relief that the good seaman presently perceived his whale-boat in the distance. Its absence had been prolonged by unexpected detention at the sealer's side, as well as its returning trip lengthened by the continual recession of the goal.

The advancing speck was observed by the blacks. Their shouts attracted the attention of Don Benito, who, with a return of courtesy, approaching Captain Delano, expressed satisfaction at the coming of some supplies, slight and temporary as they must necessarily prove.

Captain Delano responded; but while doing so, his attention was drawn to something passing on the deck below: among the crowd climbing the landward bulwarks, anxiously watching the coming boat, two blacks, to all appearances accidentally incommoded by one of the sailors, violently pushed him aside, which the sailor someway resenting, they dashed him to the deck, despite the earnest cries of the oakum-pickers.

"Don Benito," said Captain Delano quickly, "do you see what is going on there? Look!"

But, seized by his cough, the Spaniard staggered, with both hands to his face, on the point of falling. Captain Delano would have supported him, but the servant was more alert, who, with one hand sustaining his master, with the other applied the cordial. Don Benito restored, the black withdrew his support, slipping aside a little, but dutifully remaining within call of a whisper. Such discretion was here evinced as quite wiped away, in the visitor's eyes, any blemish of impropriety which might have attached to the attendant, from the indecorous conferences before mentioned; showing, too, that if the servant were to blame, it might be more the master's fault than his own, since, when left to himself, he could conduct thus well.

His glance called away from the spectacle of disorder to the more pleasing one before him, Captain Delano could not avoid again congratulating his host upon possessing such a servant, who, though perhaps a little too forward now and then, must upon the whole be invaluable to one in the invalid's situation.

"Tell me, Don Benito," he added, with a smile— "I should like to have your man here, myself—what will you take for him? Would fifty doubloons be any object?"

"Master wouldn't part with Babo for a thousand doubloons," murmured the black, overhearing the offer, and taking it in earnest, and with the strange vanity of a faithful slave, appreciated by his master, scorning to hear so paltry a valuation put upon him by a stranger. But Don Benito, apparently hardly yet completely restored, and again interrupted by his cough, made but some broken reply.

Soon his physical distress became so great, affecting his mind, too, apparently, that, as if to screen the sad spectacle, the servant gently conducted his master below.

Left to himself, the American, to while away the time till his boat should arrive, would have pleasantly accosted some one of the few Spanish seamen he saw; but recalling something that Don Benito had said touching their ill conduct, he refrained; as a shipmaster indisposed to countenance cowardice or unfaithfulness in seamen.

While, with these thoughts, standing with eye directed forward towards that handful of sailors, suddenly he thought that one or two of them returned the glance and with a sort of meaning. He rubbed his eyes, and looked again; but again seemed to see the same thing. Under a new form, but more obscure than any previous one, the old suspicions recurred, but, in the absence of Don Benito, with less of panic than before. Despite the bad account given of the sailors, Captain Delano resolved forthwith to accost one of them. Descending the poop, he made his way through the blacks, his movement drawing a queer cry from the oakum-pickers, prompted by whom, the negroes, twitching each other aside, divided before him; but, as if curious to see what was the object of this deliberate visit to their Ghetto, closing in behind, in tolerable order, followed the white stranger up. His progress thus proclaimed as by mounted kings-at-arms, and escorted as by a Caffre[3] guard of honor, Captain Delano, assuming a good-humored, off-handed air, continued to advance; now and then saying a blithe word to the negroes, and his eye curiously surveying the white faces, here and there sparsely mixed in the blacks, like stray white pawns venturously involved in the ranks of the chessmen opposed.

While thinking which of them to select for his purpose, he chanced to observe a sailor seated on the deck engaged in tarring the strap of a large block, a

---

3. Kafir: the name used by Europeans for Bantu-speaking people of South Africa, or for black Africans generally.

circle of blacks squatted round him inquisitively eying the process.

The mean employment of the man was in contrast with something superior in his figure. His hand, black with continually thrusting it into the tar-pot held for him by a negro, seemed not naturally allied to his face, a face which would have been a very fine one but for its haggardness. Whether this haggardness had aught to do with criminality, could not be determined; since, as intense heat and cold, though unlike, produce like sensations, so innocence and guilt, when, through causal association with mental pain, stamping any visible impress, use one seal — a hacked one.

Not again that this reflection occurred to Captain Delano at the time; charitable man as he was. Rather another idea. Because observing so singular a haggardness combined with a dark eye, averted as in trouble and shame, and then again recalling Don Benito's confessed ill opinion of his crew, insensibly he was operated upon by certain general notions which, while disconnecting pain and abashment from virtue, invariably link them with vice.

If, indeed, there be any wickedness on board this ship, thought Captain Delano, be sure that man there has fouled his hand in it, even as now he fouls it in the pitch. I don't like to accost him. I will speak to this other, this old Jack here on the windlass.

He advanced to an old Barcelona tar, in ragged red breeches and dirty night-cap, cheeks trenched and bronzed, whiskers dense as thorn hedges. Seated between two sleepy-looking Africans, this mariner, like his younger shipmate, was employed upon some rigging — splicing a cable — the sleepy-looking blacks performing the inferior function of holding the outer parts of the ropes for him.

Upon Captain Delano's approach, the man at once hung his head below its previous level; the one necessary for business. It appeared as if he desired to be thought absorbed, with more than common fidelity, in his task. Being addressed, he glanced up, but with what seemed a furtive, diffident air, which sat strangely enough on his weather-beaten visage, much as if a grizzly bear, instead of growling and biting, should simper and cast sheep's eyes. He was asked several questions concerning the voyage — questions purposely referring to several particulars in Don Benito's narrative, not previously corroborated by those impulsive cries greeting the visitor on first coming on board. The questions were briefly answered, confirming all that remained to be confirmed of the story. The negroes about the windlass joined in with the old sailor; but, as they became talkative, he by degrees became mute, and at length quite glum, seemed morosely unwilling to answer more questions, and yet, all the while, this ursine[4] air was somehow mixed with his sheepish one.

Despairing of getting into unembarrassed talk with such a centaur, Captain Delano, after glancing round for a more promising countenance, but seeing none, spoke pleasantly to the blacks to make way for him; and so, amid various grins and grimaces, returned to the poop, feeling a little strange at first, he could hardly tell why, but upon the whole with regained confidence in Benito Cereno.

How plainly, thought he, did that old whiskerando yonder betray a consciousness of ill desert. No doubt, when he saw me coming, he dreaded lest I, appraised by his Captain of the crew's general misbehavior, came with sharp words for him, and so if I err not, was one of those who seemed so earnestly eying me here awhile since. Ah, these currents spin one's head round almost as much as they do the ship. Ha, there now's a pleasant sort of sunny sight; quite sociable, too.

His attention had been drawn to a slumbering negress, partly disclosed through the lace-work of some rigging, lying, with youthful limbs carelessly disposed, under the lee of the bulwarks, like a doe in the shade of a woodland rock. Sprawling at her lapped breasts, was her wide-awake fawn, stark naked, its black little body half lifted from the deck, crosswise with its dam's; its hands, like two paws, clambering upon her; its mouth and nose ineffectually rooting to get at the mark; and meantime giving a vexatious half-grunt, blending with the composed snore of the negress.

The uncommon vigor of the child at length roused the mother. She started up, at a distance facing Captain Delano. But as if not at all concerned at the attitude in which she had been caught, delightedly she caught the child up, with maternal transports, covering it with kisses.

There's naked nature, now; pure tenderness and love, thought Captain Delano, well pleased.

This incident prompted him to remark the other negresses more particularly than before. He was

---

4. Bearlike.

gratified with their manners: like most uncivilized women, they seemed at once tender of heart and tough of constitution; equally ready to die for their infants or fight for them. Unsophisticated as leopardesses; loving as doves. Ah! thought Captain Delano, these, perhaps, are some of the very women whom Ledyard[5] saw in Africa, and gave such a noble account of.

These natural sights somehow insensibly deepened his confidence and ease. At last he looked to see how his boat was getting on; but it was still pretty remote. He turned to see if Don Benito had returned; but he had not.

To change the scene, as well as to please himself with a leisurely observation of the coming boat, stepping over into the mizzen-chains, he clambered his way into the starboard quarter-gallery — one of those abandoned Venetian-looking water-balconies previously mentioned — retreats cut off from the deck. As his foot pressed the half-damp, half-dry seamosses matting the place, and a chance phantom cats-paw — an islet of breeze, unheralded, unfollowed — as this ghostly cats-paw came fanning his cheek; as his glance fell upon the row of small, round dead-lights — all closed like coppered eyes of the coffined — and the state-cabin door, once connecting with the gallery, even as the dead-lights had once looked out upon it, but now calked fast like a sarcophagus lid; and to a purple-black tarred-over, panel, threshold, and post; and he bethought him of the time, when that state-cabin and this state-balcony had heard the voices of the Spanish king's officers, and the forms of the Lima viceroy's daughters had perhaps leaned where he stood — as these and other images flitted through his mind, as the cats-paw through the calm, gradually he felt rising a dreamy inquietude, like that of one who alone on the prairie feels unrest from the repose of the noon.

He leaned against the carved balustrade, again looking off toward his boat; but found his eye falling upon the ribbon grass, trailing along the ship's waterline, straight as a border of green box; and parterres of sea-weed, broad ovals and crescents, floating nigh and far, with what seemed long formal alleys between, crossing the terraces of swells, and sweeping round as if leading to the grottoes below. And overhanging all was the balustrade by his arm, which, partly stained with pitch and partly embossed with moss, seemed the charred ruin of some summerhouse in a grand garden long running to waste.

Trying to break one charm, he was but becharmed anew. Though upon the wide sea, he seemed in some far inland country; prisoner in some deserted château, left to stare at empty grounds, and peer out at vague roads, where never wagon or wayfarer passed.

But these enchantments were a little disenchanted as his eye fell on the corroded main-chains. Of an ancient style, massy and rusty in link, shackle and bolt, they seemed even more fit for the ship's present business than the one for which she had been built.

Presently he thought something moved nigh the chains. He rubbed his eyes, and looked hard. Groves of rigging were about the chains; and there, peering from behind a great stay, like an Indian from behind a hemlock, a Spanish sailor, a marlingspike in his hand, was seen, who made what seemed an imperfect gesture towards the balcony, but immediately, as if alarmed by some advancing step along the deck within, vanished into the recesses of the hempen forest, like a poacher.

What meant this? Something the man had sought to communicate, unbeknown to any one, even to his captain. Did the secret involve aught unfavorable to his captain? Were those previous misgivings of Captain Delano's about to be verified? Or, in his haunted mood at the moment, had some random, unintentional motion of the man, while busy with the stay, as if repairing it, been mistaken for a significant beckoning.

Not unbewildered, again he gazed off for his boat. But it was temporarily hidden by a rocky spur of the isle. As with some eagerness he bent forward, watching for the first shooting view of its beak, the balustrade gave way before him like charcoal. Had he not clutched an outreaching rope he would have fallen into the sea. The crash, though feeble, and the fall, though hollow, of the rotten fragments, must have been overheard. He glanced up. With sober curiosity peering down upon him was one of the old oakum-pickers, slipped from his perch to an outside boom; while below the old negro, and, invisible to him, reconnoitering from a port-hole like a fox from the mouth of its den, crouched the Spanish sailor again. From something suddenly suggested by the man's air, the mad idea now darted into Captain

5. John Ledyard (1751–1789), whose observations appeared in *Proceedings of the Association for Promoting the Discovery of the Interior Parts of Africa* (1790).

Delano's mind, that Don Benito's plea of indisposition, in withdrawing below, was but a pretense: that he was engaged there maturing his plot, of which the sailor, by some means gaining an inkling, had a mind to warn the stranger against; incited, it may be, by gratitude for a kind word on first boarding the ship. Was it from foreseeing some possible interference like this, that Don Benito had, beforehand, given such a bad character of his sailors, while praising the negroes; though, indeed, the former seemed as docile as the latter the contrary? The whites, too, by nature, were the shrewder race. A man with some evil design, would he not be likely to speak well of that stupidity which was blind to his depravity, and malign that intelligence from which it might not be hidden? Not unlikely, perhaps. But if the whites had dark secrets concerning Don Benito, could then Don Benito be any way in complicity with the blacks? But they were too stupid. Besides, who ever heard of a white so far a renegade as to apostatize from his very species almost, by leaguing in against it with negroes? These difficulties recalled former ones. Lost in their mazes, Captain Delano, who had now regained the deck, was uneasily advancing along it, when he observed a new face; an aged sailor seated cross-legged near the main hatchway. His skin was shrunk up with wrinkles like a pelican's empty pouch; his hair frosted; his countenance grave and composed. His hands were full of ropes, which he was working into a large knot. Some blacks were about him obligingly dipping the strands for him, here and there, as the exigencies of the operation demanded.

Captain Delano crossed over to him, and stood in silence surveying the knot; his mind, by a not uncongenial transition, passing from its own entanglements to those of the hemp. For intricacy, such a knot he had never seen in an American ship, nor indeed any other. The old man looked like an Egyptian priest, making Gordian knots for the temple of Ammon.[6] The knot seemed a combination of double-bowline-knot, treble-crown-knot, back-handed-well-knot, knot-in-and-out-knot, and jamming-knot.

At last, puzzled to comprehend the meaning of such a knot, Captain Delano addressed the knotter: —

"What are you knotting there, my man?"

"The knot," was the brief reply, without looking up.

"So it seems; but what is it for?"

"For some one else to undo," muttered back the old man, plying his fingers harder than ever, the knot being now nearly completed.

While Captain Delano stood watching him, suddenly the old man threw the knot towards him, saying in broken English — the first heard in the ship — something to this effect: "Undo it, cut it, quick." It was said lowly, but with such condensation of rapidity, that the long, slow words in Spanish, which had preceded and followed, almost operated as covers to the brief English between.

For a moment, knot in hand, and knot in head, Captain Delano stood mute; while, without further heeding him, the old man was now intent upon other ropes. Presently there was a slight stir behind Captain Delano. Turning, he saw the chained negro, Atufal, standing quietly there. The next moment the old sailor rose, muttering, and, followed by his subordinate negroes, removed to the forward part of the ship, where in the crowd he disappeared.

An elderly negro, in a clout like an infant's, and with a pepper and salt head, and a kind of attorney air, now approached Captain Delano. In tolerable Spanish, and with a good-natured, knowing wink, he informed him that the old knotter was simple-witted, but harmless; often playing his odd tricks. The negro concluded by begging the knot, for of course the stranger would not care to be troubled with it. Unconsciously, it was handed to him. With a sort of congé,[7] the negro received it, and, turning his back, ferreted into it like a detective custom-house officer after smuggled laces. Soon, with some African word, equivalent to pshaw, he tossed the knot overboard.

All this is very queer now, thought Captain Delano, with a qualmish sort of emotion; but, as one feeling incipient sea-sickness, he strove, by ignoring the symptoms, to get rid of the malady. Once more he looked off for his boat. To his delight, it was now again in view, leaving the rocky spur astern.

The sensation here experienced, after at first relieving his uneasiness, with unforeseen efficacy soon began to remove it. The less distant sight of that well-

---

6. Alexander the Great was acclaimed as a god after a visit to the Egyptian oracle of Ammon. According to legend, in a visit to Phrygia he cut the Gordian knot and later fulfilled the prophecy that whoever untied it would become king of all Asia.

---

7. Bow of leave-taking.

known boat—showing it, not as before, half blended with the haze, but with outline defined, so that its individuality, like a man's was manifest; that boat, Rover by name, which, though now in strange seas, had often pressed the beach of Captain Delano's home, and, brought to its threshold for repairs, had familiarly lain there, as a Newfoundland dog; the sight of that household boat evoked a thousand trustful associations, which, contrasted with previous suspicions, filled him not only with lightsome confidence, but somehow with half humorous self-reproaches at his former lack of it.

"What, I, Amasa Delano—Jack of the Beach, as they called me when a lad—I, Amasa; the same that, duck-satchel in hand, used to paddle along the water-side to the school-house made from the old hulk—I, little Jack of the Beach, that used to go berrying with cousin Nat and the rest; I to be murdered here at the ends of the earth, on board a haunted pirate-ship by a horrible Spaniard? Too nonsensical to think of! Who would murder Amasa Delano? His conscience is clean. There is some one above. Fie, fie, Jack of the Beach! you are a child indeed; a child of the second childhood, old boy; you are beginning to dote and drule, I'm afraid."

Light of heart and foot, he stepped aft, and there was met by Don Benito's servant, who, with a pleasing expression, responsive to his own present feelings, informed him that his master had recovered from the effects of his coughing fit, and had just ordered him to go present his compliments to his good guest, Don Amasa, and say that he (Don Benito) would soon have the happiness to rejoin him.

There now, do you mark that? again thought Captain Delano, walking the poop. What a donkey I was. This kind gentlemen who here sends me his kind compliments, he, but ten minutes ago, dark-lantern in hand, was dodging round some old grind-stone in the hold, sharpening a hatchet for me, I thought. Well, well; these long calms have a morbid effect on the mind, I've often heard, though I never believed it before. Ha! glancing towards the boat; there's Rover; good dog; a white bone in her mouth. A pretty big bone though, seems to me.—What? Yes, she has fallen afoul of the bubbling tide-rip there. It sets her the other way, too, for the time. Patience.

It was now about noon, though, from the grayness of everything, it seemed to be getting towards dusk.

The calm was confirmed. In the far distance, away from the influence of land, the leaden ocean seemed laid out and leaded up, its course finished, soul gone, defunct. But the current from landward, where the ship was, increased; silently sweeping her further and further towards the tranced waters beyond.

Still, from his knowledge of those latitudes, cherishing hopes of a breeze, and a fair and fresh one, at any moment, Captain Delano, despite present prospects, buoyantly counted upon bringing the San Dominick safely to anchor ere night. The distance swept over was nothing; since, with a good wind, ten minutes' sailing would retrace more than sixty minutes, drifting. Meantime, one moment turning to mark "Rover" fighting the tide-rip, and the next to see Don Benito approaching, he continued walking the poop.

Gradually he felt a vexation arising from the delay of his boat; this soon merged into uneasiness; and at last—his eye falling continually, as from a stage-box into the pit, upon the strange crowd before and below him, and, by-and-by, recognizing there the face—now composed to indifference—of the Spanish sailor who had seemed to beckon from the main-chains—something of his old trepidations returned.

Ah, thought he—gravely enough—this is like the ague: because it went off, it follows not that it won't come back.

Though ashamed of the relapse, he could not altogether subdue it; and so, exerting his good-nature to the utmost, insensibly he came to a compromise.

Yes, this is a strange craft; a strange history, too, and strange folks on board. But—nothing more.

By way of keeping his mind out of mischief till the boat should arrive, he tried to occupy it with turning over and over, in a purely speculative sort of way, some lesser peculiarities of the captain and crew. Among others, four curious points recurred:

First, the affair of the Spanish lad assailed with a knife by the slave boy; an act winked at by Don Benito. Second, the tyranny in Don Benito's treatment of Atufal, the black; as if a child should lead a bull of the Nile by the ring in his nose. Third, the trampling of the sailor by the two negroes; a piece of insolence passed over without so much as a reprimand. Fourth, the cringing submission to their master, of all the ship's underlings, mostly blacks; as if by the least inadvertence they feared to draw down his despotic displeasure.

Coupling these points, they seemed somewhat contradictory. But what then, thought Captain Delano, glancing towards his now nearing boat—what then? Why, Don Benito is a very capricious commander.

But he is not the first of the sort I have seen; though it's true he rather exceeds any other. But as a nation—continued he in his reveries—these Spaniards are all an odd set; the very word Spaniard has a curious, conspirator, Guy-Fawkish[8] twang to it. And yet, I dare say, Spaniards in the main are as good folks as any in Duxbury, Massachusetts. Ah good! At last "Rover" has come.

As, with its welcome freight, the boat touched the side, the oakum-pickers, with venerable gestures, sought to restrain the blacks, who, at the sight of three gurried[9] water-casks in its bottom, and a pile of wilted pumpkins in its bow, hung over the bulwarks in disorderly raptures.

Don Benito, with his servant, now appeared; his coming, perhaps, hastened by hearing the noise. Of him Captain Delano sought permission to serve out the water, so that all might share alike, and none injure themselves by unfair excess. But sensible, and, on Don Benito's account, kind as this offer was, it was received with what seemed impatience; as if aware that he lacked energy as a commander, Don Benito, with the true jealousy of weakness, resented as an affront any interference. So, at least, Captain Delano inferred.

In another moment the casks were being hoisted in, when some of the eager negroes accidentally jostled Captain Delano, where he stood by the gangway; so that, unmindful of Don Benito, yielding to the impulse of the moment, with good-natured authority he bade the blacks stand back; to enforce his words making use of a half-mirthful, half-menacing gesture. Instantly the blacks paused, just where they were, each negro and negress suspended in his or her posture, exactly as the word had found them—for a few seconds continuing so—while, as between the responsive posts of a telegraph, an unknown syllable ran from man to man among the perched oakum-pickers. While the visitor's attention was fixed by this scene, suddenly the hatchet-polishers half rose, and a rapid cry came from Don Benito.

Thinking that at the signal of the Spaniard he was about to be massacred, Captain Delano would have sprung for his boat, but paused, as the oakum-pickers, dropping down into the crowd with earnest exclamations, forced every white and every negro back, at the same moment, with gestures friendly and familiar, almost jocose, bidding him, in substance, not be a fool. Simultaneously the hatchet-polishers resumed their seats, quietly as so many tailors, and at once, as if nothing had happened, the work of hoisting in the casks was resumed, whites and blacks singing at the tackle.

Captain Delano glanced towards Don Benito. As he saw his meagre form in the act of recovering itself from reclining in the servant's arms, into which the agitated invalid had fallen, he could not but marvel at the panic by which himself had been surprised, on the darting supposition that such a commander, who, upon a legitimate occasion, so trivial, too, as it now appeared, could lose all self-command, was, with energetic iniquity, going to bring about his murder.

The casks being on deck, Captain Delano was handed a number of jars and cups by one of the steward's aids, who, in the name of his captain, entreated him to do as he had proposed—dole out the water. He complied, with republican impartiality as to this republican element, which always seeks one level, serving the oldest white no better than the youngest black; excepting, indeed, poor Don Benito, whose condition, if not rank, demanded an extra allowance. To him, in the first place, Captain Delano presented a fair pitcher of the fluid; but, thirsting as he was for it, the Spaniard quaffed not a drop until after several grave bows and salutes. A reciprocation of courtesies which the sight-loving Africans hailed with clapping of hands.

Two of the less wilted pumpkins being reserved for the cabin table, the residue were minced upon the spot for the general regalement. But the soft bread, sugar, and bottled cider, Captain Delano would have given the white alone, and in chief Don Benito; but the latter objected; which disinterestedness not a little pleased the American; and so mouthfuls all around were given alike to whites and blacks; excepting one bottle of cider, which Babo insisted upon setting aside for his master.

Here it may be observed that as, on the first visit to the boat, the American had not permitted his men to board the ship, neither did he now; being unwilling to add to the confusion of the decks.

Not uninfluenced by the peculiar good-humor at present prevailing, and for the time oblivious of any but benevolent thoughts, Captain Delano, who, from recent indications, counted upon a breeze within an

---

8. Guy Fawkes was executed in 1606 for his part in a conspiracy to blow up the Houses of Parliament.

9. Slimy; coated with fish offal.

hour or two at furthest, dispatched the boat back to the sealer, with orders for all the hands that could be spared immediately to set about rafting casks to the watering-place and filling them. Likewise he bade word be carried to his chief officer, that if, against present expectation, the ship was not brought to anchor by sunset, he need be under no concern; for as there was to be a full moon that night, he (Captain Delano) would remain on board ready to play the pilot, come the wind soon or late.

As the two Captains stood together, observing the departing boat — the servant, as it happened, having just spied a spot on his master's velvet sleeve, and silently engaged rubbing it out — the American expressed his regrets that the San Dominick had no boats; none, at least, but the unseaworthy old hulk of the long-boat, which, warped as a camel's skeleton in the desert, and almost as bleached, lay potwise inverted amid-ships, one side a little tipped, furnishing a subterraneous sort of den for family groups of the blacks, mostly women and small children; who, squatting on old mats below, or perched above in the dark dome, on the elevated seats, were described, some distance within, like a social circle of bats, sheltering in some friendly cave; at intervals, ebon flights of naked boys and girls, three or four years old, darting in and out of the den's mouth.

"Had you three or four boats now, Don Benito," said Captain Delano, "I think that, by tugging at the oars, your negroes here might help along matters some. Did you sail from port without boats, Don Benito?"

"They were stove in the gales, Señor."

"That was bad. Many men, too, you lost then. Boats and men. Those must have been hard gales, Don Benito."

"Past all speech," cringed the Spaniard.

"Tell me, Don Benito," continued his companion with increased interest, "tell me, were these gales immediately off the pitch of Cape Horn?"

"Cape Horn? — who spoke of Cape Horn?"

"Yourself did, when giving me an account of your voyage," answered Captain Delano, with almost equal astonishment at this eating of his own words, even as he ever seemed eating his own heart, on the part of the Spaniard. "You yourself, Don Benito, spoke of Cape Horn," he emphatically repeated.

The Spaniard turned, in a sort of stooping posture, pausing an instant, as one about to make a plunging exchange of elements, as from air to water.

At this moment a messenger-boy, a white, hurried by, in the regular performance of his function carrying the last expired half hour forward to the forecastle, from the cabin time-piece, to have it struck at the ship's large bell.

"Master," said the servant, discontinuing his work on the coat sleeve, and addressing the rapt Spaniard with a sort of timid apprehensiveness, as one charged with a duty, the discharge of which, it was foreseen, would prove irksome to the very person who had imposed it, and for whose benefit it was intended, "Master told me never mind where he was, or how engaged, always to remind him, to a minute, when shaving-time comes. Miguel has gone to strike the half-hour afternoon. It is *now* master. Will master go into the cuddy?"

"Ah — yes," answered the Spaniard, starting, as from dreams into realities; then turning upon Captain Delano, he said that ere long he would resume the conversation.

"Then if master means to talk more to Don Amasa," said the servant, "why not let Don Amasa sit by master in the cuddy, and master can talk, and Don Amasa can listen, while Babo here lathers and strops."

"Yes," said Captain Delano, not unpleased with this sociable plan, "yes, Don Benito, unless you had rather not, I will go with you."

"Be it so, Señor."

As the three passed aft, the American could not but think it another strange instance of his host's capriciousness, this being shaved with such uncommon punctuality in the middle of the day. But he deemed it more than likely that the servant's anxious fidelity had something to do with the matter; inasmuch as the timely interruption served to rally his master from the mood which had evidently been coming upon him.

The place called the cuddy was a light deck-cabin formed by the poop, a sort of attic to the large cabin below. Part of it had formerly been the quarters of the officers; but since their death all the partitionings had been thrown down, and the whole interior converted into one spacious and airy marine hall; for absence of fine furniture and picturesque disarray of odd appurtenances, somewhat answering to the wide, cluttered hall of some eccentric bachelor-squire in the country, who hangs his shooting-jacket and tobacco-pouch on deer antlers, and keeps his fishing-rod, tongs, and walking-stick in the same corner.

The similitude was heightened, if not originally suggested, by glimpses of the surrounding sea; since, in one aspect, the country and the ocean seem cousins-german.

The floor of the cuddy was matted. Overhead, four or five old muskets were stuck into horizontal holes along the beams. On one side was a claw-footed old table lashed to the deck; a thumbed missal[1] on it, and over it a small, meagre crucifix attached to the bulk-head. Under the table lay a dented cutlass or two, with a hacked harpoon, among some melancholy old rigging, like a heap of poor friars' girdles. There were also two long, sharp-ribbed settees of Malacca cane, black with age, and uncomfortable to look at as in-quisitors' racks, with a large, misshapen arm-chair, which, furnished with rude barber's crotch at the back, working with a screw, seemed some grotesque engine of torment. A flag locker was in one corner, open, exposing various colored bunting, some rolled up, others half unrolled, still others tumbled. Oppo-site was a cumbrous washstand, of black mahogany, all of one block, with a pedestal, like a font, and over it a railed shelf, containing combs, brushes, and other implements of the toilet. A torn hammock of stained grass swung near; the sheets tossed, and the pillow wrinkled up like a brow, as if whoever slept here slept but illy, with alternate visitations of sad thoughts and bad dreams.

The further extremity of the cuddy, overhanging the ship's stern, was pierced with three openings, windows or port-holes, according as men or cannon might peer, socially or unsocially, out of them. At present neither men nor cannon were seen, though huge ring-bolts and other rusty iron fixtures of the wood-work hinted of twenty-four-pounders.

Glancing towards the hammock as he entered, Captain Delano said, "You sleep here, Don Benito?"

"Yes, Señor, since we got into mild weather."

"This seems a sort of dormitory, sitting-room, sail-loft, chapel, armory, and private closet all together, Don Benito," added Captain Delano, looking round.

"Yes, Señor; events have not been favorable to much order in my arrangements."

Here the servant, napkin on arm, made a motion as if waiting his master's good pleasure. Don Benito signified his readiness, when, seating him in the Malacca arm-chair, and for the guest's convenience drawing opposite one of the settees, the servant com-menced operations by throwing back his master's collar and loosening his cravat.

There is something in the negro which, in a pecu-liar way, fits him for avocations about one's person. Most negroes are natural valets and hair-dressers; taking to the comb and brush congenially as to the castinets, and flourishing them apparently with al-most equal satisfaction. There is, too, a smooth tact about them in this employment, with a marvelous, noiseless, gliding briskness, not ungraceful in its way, singularly pleasing to behold, and still more so to be the manipulated subject of. And above all is the great gift of good-humor. Not the mere grin or laugh is here meant. Those were unsuitable. But a certain easy cheerfulness, harmonious in every glance and gesture; as though God had set the whole negro to some pleasant tune.

When to this is added the docility arising from the unaspiring contentment of a limited mind, and that susceptibility of bland attachment sometimes inher-ing in indisputable inferiors, one readily perceives why those hypochondriacs, Johnson and Byron—it may be, something like the hypochondriac Benito Cereno—took to their hearts, almost to the exclusion of the entire white race, their serving men, the ne-groes, Barber and Fletcher.[2] But if there be that in the negro which exempts him from the inflicted sour-ness of the morbid or cynical mind, how, in his most prepossessing aspects, must he appear to a benevo-lent one? When at ease with respect to exterior things, Captain Delano's nature was not only benign, but fa-miliarly and humorously so. At home, he had often taken rare satisfaction in sitting in his door, watching some free man of color at his work or play. If on a voyage he chanced to have a black sailor, invariably he was on chatty and half-gamesome terms with him. In fact, like most men of a good, blithe heart, Captain Delano took to negroes, not philanthropi-cally, but genially, just as other men to Newfound-land dogs.

Hitherto, the circumstances in which he found the San Dominick had repressed the tendency. But in the cuddy, relieved from his former uneasiness, and,

---

1. Prayer book.

2. Frank Barber was a black servant to Samuel Johnson. Byron's white valet, William Fletcher, seems here confused with the black servant of a friend who sometimes traveled with him.

for various reasons, more sociably inclined than at any previous period of the day, and seeing the colored servant, napkin on arm, so debonair about his master, in a business so familiar as that of shaving, too, all his old weakness for negroes returned.

Among other things, he was amused with an odd instance of the African love of bright colors and fine shows, in the black's informally taking from the flag-locker a great piece of bunting of all hues, and lavishly tucking it under his master's chin for an apron.

The mode of shaving among the Spaniards is a little different from what it is with other nations. They have a basin, specifically called a barber's basin, which on one side is scooped out, so as accurately to receive the chin, against which it is closely held in lathering; which is done, not with a brush, but with soap dipped in the water of the basin and rubbed on the face.

In the present instance salt-water was used for lack of better; and the parts lathered were only the upper lip, and low down under the throat, all the rest being cultivated beard.

The preliminaries being somewhat novel to Captain Delano, he sat curiously eying them, so that no conversation took place, nor, for the present, did Don Benito appear disposed to renew any.

Setting down his basin, the negro searched among the razors, as for the sharpest, and having found it, gave it an additional edge by expertly strapping it on the firm, smooth, oily skin of his open palm; he then made a gesture as if to begin, but midway stood suspended for an instant, one hand elevating the razor, the other professionally dabbling among the bubbling suds on the Spaniard's lank neck. Not unaffected by the close sight of the gleaming steel, Don Benito nervously shuddered; his usual ghastliness was heightened by the lather, which later, again, was intensified in its hue by the contrasting sootiness of the negro's body. Altogether the scene was somewhat peculiar, at least to Captain Delano, nor, as he saw the two thus postured, could he resist the vagary, that in the black he saw a headsman, and in the white a man at the block. But this was one of those antic conceits, appearing and vanishing in a breath, from which, perhaps, the best regulated mind is not always free.

Meantime the agitation of the Spaniard had a little loosened the bunting from around him, so that one broad fold swept curtain-like over the chair-arm to the floor, revealing, amid a profusion of armorial bars and ground-colors—black, blue, and yellow—

a closed castle in a blood-red field diagonal with a lion rampant in a white.

"The castle and the lion," exclaimed Captain Delano—"why, Don Benito, this is the flag of Spain you use here. It's well it's only I, and not the King, that sees this," he added, with a smile, "but"—turning towards the black—"it's all one, I suppose, so the colors be gay," which playful remark did not fail somewhat to tickle the negro.

"Now, master," he said, readjusting the flag, and pressing the head gently further back into the crotch of the chair; "now, master," and the steel glanced nigh the throat.

Again Don Benito faintly shuddered.

"You must not shake so, master. See, Don Amasa, master always shakes when I shave him. And yet master knows I never yet have drawn blood, though it's true, if master will shake so, I may some of these times. Now master," he continued. "And now, Don Amasa, please go on with your talk about the gale, and all that; master can hear, and, between times, master can answer."

"Ah yes, these gales," said Captain Delano; "but the more I think of your voyage, Don Benito, the more I wonder, not at the gales, terrible as they must have been, but at the disastrous interval following them. For here, by your account, have you been these two months and more getting from Cape Horn to St. Maria, a distance which I myself, with a good wind, have sailed in a few days. True, you had calms, and long ones, but to be becalmed for two months, that is, at least, unusual. Why, Don Benito, had almost any other gentlemen told me such a story, I should have been half disposed to a little incredulity."

Here an involuntary expression came over the Spaniard, similar to that just before on the deck, and whether it was the start he gave, or a sudden gawky roll of the hull in the calm, or a momentary unsteadiness of the servant's hand, however it was, just then the razor drew blood, spots of which stained the creamy lather under the throat: immediately the black barber drew back his steel, and, remaining in his professional attitude, back to Captain Delano, and face to Don Benito, held up the trickling razor, saying, with a sort of half humorous sorrow, "See, master—you shook so—here's Babo's first blood."

No sword drawn before James the First of England, no assassination in that timid King's presence, could have produced a more terrified aspect than was now presented by Don Benito.

Poor fellow, thought Captain Delano, so nervous he can't even bear the sight of barber's blood; and this unstrung, sick man, is it credible that I should have imagined he meant to spill all my blood, who can't endure the sight of one little drop of his own? Surely, Amasa Delano, you have been beside yourself this day. Tell it not when you get home, sappy Amasa. Well, well, he looks like a murderer, doesn't he? More like as if himself were to be done for. Well, well, this day's experience shall be a good lesson.

Meantime, while these things were running through the honest seaman's mind, the servant had taken the napkin from his arm, and to Don Benito had said — "But answer Don Amasa, please, master, while I wipe this ugly stuff off the razor, and strop it again."

As he said the words, his face was turned half round, so as to be alike visible to the Spaniard and the American, and seemed, by its expression, to hint, that he was desirous, by getting his master to go on with the conversation, considerately to withdraw his attention from the recent annoying accident. As if glad to snatch the offered relief, Don Benito resumed, rehearsing to Captain Delano, that not only were the calms of unusual duration, but the ship had fallen in with obstinate currents; and other things he added, some of which were but repetitions of former statements, to explain how it came to pass that the passage from Cape Horn to St. Maria had been so exceedingly long; now and then mingling with his words, incidental praises, less qualified than before, to the blacks, for their general good conduct. These particulars were not given consecutively, the servant, at convenient times, using his razor, and so, between the intervals of shaving, the story and panegyric went on with more than usual huskiness.

To Captain Delano's imagination, now again not wholly at rest, there was something so hollow in the Spaniard's manner, with apparently some reciprocal hollowness in the servant's dusky comment of silence, that the idea flashed across him, that possibly master and man, for some unknown purpose, were acting out, both in word and deed, nay, to the very tremor of Don Benito's limbs, some juggling play before him. Neither did the suspicion of collusion lack apparent support, from the fact of those whispered conferences before mentioned. But then, what could be the object of enacting this play of the barber before him? At last, regarding the notion as a whimsy, insensibly suggested, perhaps, by the theatrical aspect of Don Benito in his harlequin ensign, Captain Delano speedily banished it.

The shaving over, the servant bestirred himself with a small bottle of scented waters, pouring a few drops on the head, and then diligently rubbing; the vehemence of the exercise causing the muscles of his face to twitch rather strangely.

His next operation was with comb, scissors, and brush; going round and round, smoothing a curl here, clipping an unruly whisker-hair there, giving a graceful sweep to the temple-lock, with other impromptu touches evincing the hand of a master; while, like any resigned gentleman in barber's hands, Don Benito bore all, much less uneasily, at least, than he had done the razoring; indeed, he sat so pale and rigid now, that the negro seemed a Nubian sculptor finishing off a white statue-head.

All being over at last, the standard of Spain removed, tumbled up, and tossed back into the flag-locker, the negro's warm breath blowing away any stray hair which might have lodged down his master's neck; collar and cravat readjusted; a speck of lint whisked off the velvet lapel; all this being done; backing off a little space, and pausing with an expression of subdued self-complacency, the servant for a moment surveyed his master, as, in toilet at least, the creature of his own tasteful hands.

Captain Delano playfully complimented him upon his achievement; at the same time congratulating Don Benito.

But neither sweet waters, nor shampooing, nor fidelity, nor sociality, delighted the Spaniard. Seeing him relapsing into forbidding gloom, and still remaining seated, Captain Delano, thinking that his presence was undesired just then, withdrew, on pretense of seeing whether, as he had prophesied, any signs of a breeze were visible.

Walking forward to the main-mast, he stood awhile thinking over the scene, and not without some undefined misgivings, when he heard a noise near the cuddy, and turning, saw the negro, his hand to his cheek. Advancing, Captain Delano perceived that the cheek was bleeding. He was about to ask the cause, when the negro's wailing soliloquy enlightened him.

"Ah, when will master get better from his sickness; only the sour heart that sour sickness breeds made him serve Babo so; cutting Babo with the razor, because, only by accident, Babo had given master one little scratch; and for the first time in so many a day, too. Ah, ah, ah," holding his hand to his face.

It is possible, thought Captain Delano; was it to wreck in private his Spanish spite against this poor friend of his, that Don Benito, by his sullen manner, impelled me to withdraw? Ah, this slavery breeds ugly passions in man.— Poor fellow!

He was about to speak in sympathy to the negro, but with a timid reluctance he now re-entered the cuddy.

Presently master and man came forth; Don Benito leaning on his servant as if nothing had happened.

But a sort of love-quarrel, after all, thought Captain Delano.

He accosted Don Benito, and they slowly walked together. They had gone but a few paces, when the steward— a tall, rajah-looking mulatto, orientally set off with a pagoda turban formed by three or four Madras handkerchiefs wound about his head, tier on tier— approaching with a salaam, announced lunch in the cabin.

On their way thither, the two captains were preceded by the mulatto, who, turning round as he advanced, with continual smiles and bows, ushered them on, a display of elegance which quite completed the insignificance of the small bareheaded Babo who, as if not unconscious of inferiority, eyed askance the graceful steward. But in part Captain Delano imputed his jealous watchfulness to that peculiar feeling which the full-blooded African entertains for the adulterated one. As for the steward, his manner if not bespeaking much dignity or self-respect, yet evidenced his extreme desire to please; which is doubly meritorious, as at once Christian and Chesterfieldian.[3]

Captain Delano observed with interest that while the complexion of the mulatto was hybrid, his physiognomy was European— classically so.

"Don Benito," whispered he, "I am glad to see this usher-of-the-golden-rod[4] of yours; the sight refutes an ugly remark once made to me by a Barbadoes planter; that when a mulatto has a regular European face, look out for him; he is a devil. But see, your steward here has features more regular than

King George's of England; and yet there he nods, and bows, and smiles; a king, indeed— the king of kind hearts and polite fellows. What a pleasant voice he has, too!"

"He has, Señor."

"But tell me, has he not, so far as you have known him, always proved a good, worthy fellow?" said Captain Delano, pausing, while with a final genuflexion the steward disappeared into the cabin; "come, for the reason just mentioned, I am curious to know."

"Francesco is a good man," a sort of sluggishly responded Don Benito, like a phlegmatic appreciator, who would neither find fault nor flatter.

"Ah, I thought so. For it were strange, indeed, and not very creditable to us white skins, if a little of our blood mixed with the African's, should, far from improving the latter's quality, have the sad effect of pouring vitriolic acid into black broth; improving the hue, perhaps, but not the wholesomeness."

"Doubtless, doubtless, Señor, but"— glancing at Babo— "not to speak of negroes, your planter's remark I have heard applied to the Spanish and Indian intermixtures in our provinces. But I know nothing about the matter," he listlessly added.

And here they entered the cabin.

The lunch was a frugal one. Some of Captain Delano's fresh fish and pumpkins, biscuit and salt beef, the reserved bottle of cider, and the San Dominick's last bottle of Canary.[5]

As they entered, Francesco, with two or three colored aids, was hovering over the table giving the last adjustments. Upon perceiving their master they withdrew, Francesco making a smiling congé, and the Spaniard, without condescending to notice it, fastidiously remarking to his companion that he relished not superfluous attendance.

Without companions, host and guest sat down, like a childless married couple, at opposite ends of the table, Don Benito waving Captain Delano to his place, and, weak as he was, insisting upon that gentleman being seated before himself.

The negro placed a rug under Don Benito's feet, and a cushion behind his back, and then stood behind, not his master's chair, but Captain Delano's. At first, this a little surprised the latter. But it was soon evident that, in taking his position, the black was still

---

3. Combining Christian humility and worldly good breeding— Philip Stanhope, Lord Chesterfield (1694–1773), became a famous advocate of courtly manners after his letters to his son were published.

4. An usher (an attendant leading a dignitary) frequently carries a rod indicative of his office.

5. Wine from the Canary Islands.

true to his master; since by facing him he could the more readily anticipate his slightest want.

"This is an uncommonly intelligent fellow of yours, Don Benito," whispered Captain Delano across the table.

"You say true, Señor."

During the repast, the guest again reverted to parts of Don Benito's story, begging further particulars here and there. He inquired how it was that the scurvy and fever should have committed such wholesale havoc upon the whites, while destroying less than half of the blacks. As if this question reproduced the whole scene of plague before the Spaniard's eyes, miserably reminding him of his solitude in a cabin where before he had had so many friends and officers round him, his hand shook, his face became hueless, broken words escaped; but directly the sane memory of the past seemed replaced by insane terrors of the present. With starting eyes he stared before him at vacancy. For nothing was to be seen but the hand of his servant pushing the Canary over towards him. At length a few sips served partially to restore him. He made random reference to the different constitution of races, enabling one to offer more resistance to certain maladies than another. The thought was new to his companion.

Presently Captain Delano, intending to say something to his host concerning the pecuniary part of the business he had undertaken for him, especially—since he was strictly accountable to his owners—with reference to the new suit of sails, and other things of that sort; and naturally preferring to conduct such affairs in private, was desirous that the servant should withdraw; imagining that Don Benito for a few minutes could dispense with his attendance. He, however, waited awhile; thinking that, as the conversation proceeded, Don Benito, without being prompted, would perceive the propriety of the step.

But it was otherwise. At last catching his host's eye, Captain Delano, with a slight backward gesture of his thumb, whispered, "Don Benito, pardon me, but there is an interference with the full expression of what I have to say to you."

Upon this the Spaniard changed countenance; which was imputed to his resenting the hint, as in some way a reflection upon his servant. After a moment's pause, he assured his guest that the black's remaining with them could be of no disservice; because since losing his officers he had made Babo (whose original office, it now appeared, had been captain of the slaves) not only his constant attendant and companion, but in all things his confidant.

After this, nothing more could be said; though, indeed, Captain Delano could hardly avoid some little tinge of irritation upon being left ungratified in so inconsiderable a wish, by one, too, for whom he intended such solid services. But it is only his querulousness, thought he; and so filling his glass he proceeded to business.

The price of the sails and other matters was fixed upon. But while this was being done, the American observed that, though his original offer of assistance had been hailed with hectic animation, yet now when it was reduced to a business transaction, indifference and apathy were betrayed. Don Benito, in fact, appeared to submit to hearing the details more out of regard to common propriety, than from any impression that weighty benefit to himself and his voyage was involved.

Soon, his manner became still more reserved. The effort was vain to seek to draw him into social talk. Gnawed by his splenetic mood, he sat twitching his beard, while to little purpose the hand of his servant, mute as that on the wall, slowly pushed over the Canary.

Lunch being over, they sat down on the cushioned transom; the servant placing a pillow behind his master. The long continuance of the calm had now affected the atmosphere. Don Benito sighed heavily, as if for breath.

"Why not adjourn to the cuddy," said Captain Delano; "there is more air there." But the host sat silent and motionless.

Meantime his servant knelt before him, with a large fan of feathers. And Francesco coming in on tiptoes, handed the negro a little cup of aromatic waters, with which at intervals he chafed his master's brow; smoothing the hair along the temples as a nurse does a child's. He spoke no word. He only rested his eye on his master's, as if, amid all Don Benito's distress, a little to refresh his spirit by the silent sight of fidelity.

Presently the ship's bell sounded two o'clock; and through the cabin windows a slight ripping of the sea was discerned; and from the desired direction.

"There," exclaimed Captain Delano, "I told you so, Don Benito, look!"

He had risen to his feet, speaking in a very animated tone, with a view the more to rouse his companion. But though the crimson curtain of the stern-window near him that moment fluttered against his pale cheek, Don Benito seemed to have even less welcome for the breeze than the calm.

Poor fellow, thought Captain Delano, bitter experience has taught him that one ripple does not make a wind, any more than one swallow a summer. But he is mistaken for once. I will get his ship in for him, and prove it.

Briefly alluding to his weak condition, he urged his host to remain quietly where he was, since he (Captain Delano) would with pleasure take upon himself the responsibility of making the best use of the wind.

Upon gaining the deck, Captain Delano started at the unexpected figure of Atufal, monumentally fixed at the threshold, like one of those sculptured porters of black marble guarding the porches of Egyptian tombs.

But this time the start was, perhaps, purely physical. Atufal's presence, singularly attesting docility even in sullenness, was contrasted with that of the hatchet-polishers, who in patience evinced their industry; while both spectacles showed, that lax as Don Benito's general authority might be, still, whenever he chose to exert it, no man so savage or colossal but must, more or less, bow.

Snatching a trumpet which hung from the bulwarks, with a free step Captain Delano advanced to the forward edge of the poop, issuing his orders in his best Spanish. The few sailors and many negroes, all equally pleased, obediently set about heading the ship towards the harbor.

While giving some directions about setting a lower stu'n'-sail, suddenly Captain Delano heard a voice faithfully repeating his orders. Turning, he saw Babo, now for the time acting, under the pilot, his original part of captain of the slaves. This assistance proved valuable. Tattered sails and warped yards were soon brought into some trim. And no brace or halyard was pulled but to the blithe songs of the inspirited negroes.

Good fellows, thought Captain Delano, a little training would make fine sailors of them. Why see, the very women pull and sing too. These must be some of those Ashantee negresses that make such capital soldiers, I've heard. But who's at the helm. I must have a good hand there.

He went to see.

The San Dominick steered with a cumbrous tiller, with large horizontal pullies attached. At each pulley-end stood a subordinate black, and between them, at the tiller-head, the responsible post, a Spanish sea-

man, whose countenance evinced his due share in the general hopefulness and confidence at the coming of the breeze.

He proved the same man who had behaved with so shame-faced an air on the windlass.

"Ah,—it is you, my man," exclaimed Captain Delano—"well, no more sheep's-eyes now;—look straight forward and keep the ship so. Good hand, I trust? And want to get into the harbor, don't you?"

The man assented with an inward chuckle, grasping the tiller-head firmly. Upon this, unperceived by the American, the two blacks eyed the sailor intently.

Finding all right at the helm, the pilot went forward to the forecastle, to see how matters stood there.

The ship now had way enough to breast the current. With the approach of evening, the breeze would be sure to freshen.

Having done all that was needed for the present, Captain Delano, giving his last orders to the sailors, turned aft to report affairs to Don Benito in the cabin; perhaps additionally incited to rejoin him by the hope of snatching a moment's private chat while the servant was engaged upon deck.

From opposite sides, there were, beneath the poop, two approaches to the cabin; one further forward than the other, and consequently communicating with a longer passage. Marking the servant still above, Captain Delano, taking the nighest entrance—the one last named, and at whose porch Atufal still stood—hurried on his way, till, arrived at the cabin threshold, he paused an instant, a little to recover from his eagerness. Then, with the words of his intended business upon his lips, he entered. As he advanced toward the seated Spaniard, he heard another footstep, keeping time with his. From the opposite door, a salver in hand, the servant was likewise advancing.

"Confound the faithful fellow," thought Captain Delano; "what a vexatious coincidence."

Possibly, the vexation might have been something different, were it not for the brisk confidence inspired by the breeze. But even as it was, he felt a slight twinge, from a sudden indefinite association in his mind of Babo with Atufal.

"Don Benito," said he, "I give you joy; the breeze will hold, and will increase. By the way, your tall man and time-piece, Atufal, stands without. By your order, of course?"

Don Benito recoiled, as if at some bland satirical touch, delivered with such adroit garnish of apparent good breeding as to present no handle for retort.

He is like one flayed alive, thought Captain Delano; where may one touch him without causing a shrink?

The servant moved before his master, adjusting a cushion; recalled to civility, the Spaniard stiffly replied: "you are right. The slave appears where you saw him, according to my command; which is, that if at the given hour I am below, he must take his stand and abide my coming."

"Ah now, pardon me, but that is treating the poor fellow like an ex-king indeed. Ah, Don Benito," smiling, "for all the license you permit in some things, I fear lest, at bottom, you are a bitter hard master."

Again Don Benito shrank; and this time, as the good sailor thought, from a genuine twinge of his conscience.

Again conversation became constrained. In vain Captain Delano called attention to the now perceptible motion of the keel gently cleaving the sea; with lack-lustre eye, Don Benito returned words few and reserved.

By-and-by, the wind having steadily risen, and still blowing right into the harbor, bore the San Dominick swiftly on. Rounding a point of land, the sealer at distance came into open view.

Meantime Captain Delano had again repaired to the deck, remaining there some time. Having at last altered the ship's course, so as to give the reef a wide berth, he returned for a few moments below.

I will cheer up my poor friend, this time, thought he.

"Better and better, Don Benito," he cried as he blithely re-entered: "there will soon be an end to your cares, at least for a while. For when, after a long, sad voyage, you know, the anchor drops into the haven, all its vast weight seems lifted from the captain's heart. We are getting on famously, Don Benito. My ship is in sight. Look through this side-light here; there she is; all a-taunt-o! The Bachelor's Delight, my good friend. Ah, how this wind braces one up. Come, you must take a cup of coffee with me this evening. My old steward will give you as fine a cup as ever any sultan tasted. What say you, Don Benito, will you?"

At first, the Spaniard glanced feverishly up, casting a longing look towards the sealer, while with mute concern his servant gazed into his face. Suddenly the old ague of coldness returned, and dropping back to his cushions he was silent.

"You do not answer. Come, all day you have been my host; would you have hospitality all on one side?"

"I cannot go," was the response.

"What? it will not fatigue you. The ships will lie together as near as they can, without swinging foul. It will be little more than stepping from deck to deck; which is but as from room to room. Come, come, you must not refuse me."

"I cannot go," decisively and repulsively repeated Don Benito.

Renouncing all but the last appearance of courtesy, with a sort of cadaverous sullenness, and biting his thin nails to the quick, he glanced, almost glared, as his guest, as if impatient that a stranger's presence should interfere with the full indulgence of his morbid hour. Meantime the sound of the parted waters came more and more gurglingly and merrily in at the windows; as reproaching him for his dark spleen; as telling him that, sulk as he might, and go mad with it, nature cared not a jot; since, whose fault was it, pray?

But the foul mood was now at its depth, as the fair wind at its height.

There was something in the man so far beyond any mere unsociality or sourness previously evinced, that even the forbearing good-nature of his guest could no longer endure it. Wholly at a loss to account for such demeanor, and deeming sickness with eccentricity, however extreme, no adequate excuse, well satisfied, too, that nothing in his own conduct could justify it, Captain Delano's pride began to be roused. Himself became reserved. But all seemed one to the Spaniard. Quitting him, therefore, Captain Delano once more went to the deck.

The ship was now within less than two miles of the sealer. The whale-boat was seen darting over the interval.

To be brief, the two vessels, thanks to the pilot's skill, ere long in neighborly style lay anchored together.

Before returning to his own vessel, Captain Delano had intended communicating to Don Benito the smaller details of the proposed services to be rendered. But, as it was, unwilling anew to subject himself to rebuffs, he resolved, now that he had seen the San Dominick safely moored, immediately to quit her, without further allusion to hospitality or business. Indefinitely postponing his ulterior plans, he would regulate his future actions according to future circumstances. His boat was ready to receive him; but his host still tarried below. Well, thought Captain Delano, if he has little breeding, the more need to show mine. He descended to the cabin to bid a ceremonious, and, it may be, tacitly rebukeful adieu. But to his great satisfaction, Don Benito, as if he began to feel the weight of that treatment with which his slighted guest had, not indecorously, retaliated upon him, now supported by his servant, rose to his feet, and grasping Captain Delano's hand, stood tremulous; too much agitated to speak. But the good augury hence drawn was suddenly dashed, by his resuming all his previous reserve, with augmented gloom, as, with half-averted eyes, he silently reseated himself on his cushions. With a corresponding return of his own chilled feelings, Captain Delano bowed and withdrew.

He was hardly midway in the narrow corridor, dim as a tunnel, leading from the cabin to the stairs, when a sound, as of the tolling for execution in some jail-yard, fell on his ears. It was the echo of the ship's flawed bell, striking the hour, drearily reverberated in this subterranean vault. Instantly, by a fatality not to be withstood, his mind, responsive to the portent, swarmed with superstitious suspicions. He paused. In images far swifter than these sentences, the minutest details of all his former distrusts swept through him.

Hitherto, credulous good-nature had been too ready to furnish excuses for reasonable fears. Why was the Spaniard, so superfluously punctilious at times, now heedless of common propriety in not accompanying to the side his departing guest? Did indisposition forbid? Indisposition had not forbidden more irksome exertion that day. His last equivocal demeanor recurred. He had risen to his feet, grasped his guest's hand, motioned toward his hat; then, in an instant, all was eclipsed in sinister muteness and gloom. Did this imply one brief, repentant relenting at the final moment, from some iniquitous plot, followed by remorseless return to it? His last glance seemed to express a calamitous, yet acquiescent farewell to Captain Delano forever. Why decline the invitation to visit the sealer that evening? Or was the Spaniard less hardened than the Jew, who refrained not from supping at the board of him whom the same night he meant to betray?[6] What imported all those day-long enigmas and contradictions, except they were intended to mystify, preliminary to some stealthy blow? Atufal, the pretended rebel, but punctual shadow, that moment lurked by the threshold

without. He seemed a sentry, and more. Who, by his own confession, had stationed him there? Was the negro now lying in wait?

The Spaniard behind—his creature before: to rush from darkness to light was the involuntary choice.

The next moment, with clenched jaw and hand, he passed Atufal, and stood unharmed in the light. As he saw his trim ship lying peacefully at anchor, and almost within ordinary call; as he saw his household boat, with familiar faces in it, patiently rising and falling on the short waves by the San Dominick's side; and then, glancing about the decks where he stood, saw the oakum-pickers still gravely plying their fingers; and heard the low, buzzing whistle and industrious hum of the hatchet-polishers, still bestirring themselves over their endless occupation; and more than all, as he saw the benign aspect of nature, taking her innocent repose in the evening; the screened sun in the quiet camp of the west shining out like the mild light from Abraham's[7] tent; as charmed eye and ear took in all these, with the chained figure of the black, clenched jaw and hand relaxed. Once again he smiled at the phantoms which had mocked him, and felt something like a tinge of remorse, that, by harboring them even for a moment, he should, by implication, have betrayed an atheist doubt of the ever-watchful Providence above.

There was a few minutes' delay, while, in obedience to his orders, the boat was being hooked along to the gangway. During this interval, a sort of saddened satisfaction stole over Captain Delano, at thinking of the kindly offices he had that day discharged for a stranger. Ah, thought he, after good actions one's conscience is never ungrateful, however much so the benefited party may be.

Presently, his foot, in the first act of descent into the boat, pressed the first round of the side-ladder, his face presented inward upon the deck. In the same moment, he heard his name courteously sounded; and, to his pleased surprise, saw Don Benito advancing—an unwonted energy in his air, as if, at the last moment, intent upon making amends for his recent discourtesy. With instinctive good feeling, Captain Delano, withdrawing his foot, turned and reciprocally advanced. As he did so, the Spaniard's nervous eagerness increased, but his vital energy

---

6. Judas sat with Jesus at the Last Supper (Matthew xxvi).

7. A reference to the promise of God's blessing to humanity, as expressed to Abraham (Genesis xxii–xxviii).

failed; so that, the better to support him, the servant, placing his master's hand on his naked shoulder, and gently holding it there, formed himself into a sort of crutch.

When the two captains met, the Spaniard again fervently took the hand of the American, at the same time casting an earnest glance into his eyes, but, as before, too much overcome to speak.

I have done him wrong, self-reproachfully thought Captain Delano; his apparent coldness has deceived me; in no instance had he meant to offend.

Meantime, as if fearful that the continuance of the scene might too much unstring his master, the servant seemed anxious to terminate it. And so, still presenting himself as a crutch, and walking between the two captains, he advanced with them towards the gangway; while still, as if full of kindly contrition, Don Benito would not let go the hand of Captain Delano, but retained it in his, across the black's body.

Soon they were standing by the side, looking over into the boat, whose crew turned up their curious eyes. Waiting for a moment for the Spaniard to relinquish his hold, the now embarrassed Captain Delano lifted his foot, to overstep the threshold of the open gangway; but still Don Benito would not let go his hand. And yet, with an agitated tone, he said, "I can go no further; here I must bid you adieu. Adieu, my dear, dear Don Amasa. Go—go!" suddenly tearing his hand loose, "go, and God guard you better than me, my best friend."

Not unaffected, Captain Delano would now have lingered; but catching the meekly admonitory eye of the servant, with a hasty farewell he descended into his boat, followed by the continual adieus of Don Benito, standing rooted in the gangway.

Seating himself in the stern, Captain Delano, making a last salute, ordered the boat shoved off. The crew had their oars on end. The bowsmen pushed the boat a sufficient distance for the oars to be lengthwise dropped. The instant that was done, Don Benito sprang over the bulwarks, falling at the feet of Captain Delano; at the same time calling towards his ship, but in tones so frenzied, that none in the boat could understand him. But, as if not equally obtuse, three sailors, from three different and distant parts of the ship, splashed into the sea, swimming after their captain, as if intent upon his rescue.

The dismayed officer of the boat eagerly asked what this meant. To which, Captain Delano, turning a disdainful smile upon the unaccountable Spaniard, answered that, for his part, he neither knew or cared; but it seemed as if Don Benito had taken it into his head to produce the impression among his people that the boat wanted to kidnap him. "Or else—give way for your lives," he wildly added, starting at a clattering hubbub in the ship, above which rang the tocsin[8] of the hatchet-polishers; and seizing Don Benito by the throat he added, "this plotting pirate means murder!" Here, in apparent verification of the words, the servant, a dagger in his hand, was seen on the rail overhead, poised, in the act of leaping, as if with desperate fidelity to befriend his master to the last; while, seemingly to aid the black, the three white sailors were trying to clamber into the hampered bow. Meantime, the whole host of negroes, as if inflamed at the sight of their jeopardized captain, impended in one sooty avalanche over the bulwarks.

All this, with what preceded, and what followed, occurred with such involutions of rapidity, that past, present, and future seemed one.

Seeing the negro coming, Captain Delano had flung the Spaniard aside, almost in the very act of clutching him, and, by the unconscious recoil, shifting his place, with arms thrown up, so promptly grappled the servant in his descent, that with dagger presented at Captain Delano's heart, the black seemed of purpose to have leaped there as to his mark. But the weapon was wrenched away, and the assailant dashed down into the bottom of the boat, which now, with disentangled oars, began to speed through the sea.

At this juncture, the left hand of Captain Delano, on one side, again clutched the half-reclined Don Benito, heedless that he was in a speechless faint, while his right foot, on the other side, ground the prostrate negro; and his right arm pressed for added speed on the after oar, his eye bent forward, encouraging his men to their utmost.

But here, the officer of the boat, who had at last succeeded in beating off the towing sailors, and was now, with face turned aft, assisting the bowsman at his oar, suddenly called to Captain Delano, to see what the black was about; while a Portuguese oarsman shouted to him to give heed to what the Spaniard was saying.

---

8. Alarm bell.

Glancing down at his feet, Captain Delano saw the freed hand of the servant aiming with a second dagger—a small one, before concealed in his wool—with this he was snakishly writhing up from the boat's bottom, at the heart of his master, his countenance lividly vindictive, expressing the centred purpose of his soul; while the Spaniard, half-choked, was vainly shrinking away, with husky words, incoherent to all but the Portuguese.

That moment, across the long-benighted mind of Captain Delano, a flash of revelation swept, illuminating, in unanticipated clearness, his host's whole mysterious demeanor, with every enigmatic event of the day, as well as the entire past voyage of the San Dominick. He smote Babo's hand down, but his own heart smote him harder. With infinite pity he withdrew his hold from Don Benito. Not Captain Delano, but Don Benito, the black, in leaping into the boat, had intended to stab.

Both the black's hands were held, as, glancing up towards the San Dominick, Captain Delano, now with scales dropped from his eyes, saw the negroes, not in misrule, not in tumult, not as if frantically concerned for Don Benito, but with mask torn away, flourishing hatchets and knives, in ferocious piratical revolt. Like delirious black dervishes, the six Ashantees danced on the poop. Prevented by their foes from springing into the water, the Spanish boys were hurrying up to the topmost spars, while such of the few Spanish sailors, not already in the sea, less alert, were descried, helplessly mixed in, on deck, with the blacks.

Meantime Captain Delano hailed his own vessel, ordering the ports up, and the guns run out. But by this time the cable of the San Dominick had been cut; and the fag-end, in lashing out, whipped away the canvas shroud about the beak, suddenly revealing, as the bleached hull swing round towards the open ocean, death for the figure-head, in a human skeleton; chalky comment on the chalked words below, *"Follow your leader."*

At the sight, Don Benito, covering his face, wailed out: "'Tis he, Aranda! my murdered, unburied friend!"

Upon reaching the sealer, calling for ropes, Captain Delano bound the negro, who made no resistance, and had him hoisted to the deck. He would then have assisted the now almost helpless Don Benito up the side; but Don Benito, wan as he was, refused to move, or be moved, until the negro should have been first put below out of view. When, presently assured that it was done, he no more shrank from the ascent.

The boat was immediately dispatched back to pick up the three swimming sailors. Meantime, the guns were in readiness, though, owing to the San Dominick having glided somewhat astern of the sealer, only the aftermost one could be brought to bear. With this, they fired six times; thinking to cripple the fugitive ship by bringing down her spars. But only a few inconsiderable ropes were shot away. Soon the ship was beyond the gun's range, steering broad out of the bay; the blacks thickly clustering round the bowsprit, one moment with taunting cries towards the whites, the next with upthrown gestures hailing the now dusky moors of ocean—cawing crows escaped from the hand of the fowler.

The first impulse was to slip the cables and give chase. But, upon second thoughts, to pursue with whale-boat and yawl seemed more promising.

Upon inquiring of Don Benito what fire-arms they had on board the San Dominick, Captain Delano was answered that they had none that could be used; because, in the earlier stages of the mutiny, a cabin-passenger, since dead, had secretly put out of order the locks of what few muskets there were. But with all his remaining strength, Don Benito entreated the American not to give chase, either with ship or boat; for the negroes had already proved themselves such desperadoes, that, in case of a present assault, nothing but a total massacre of the whites could be looked for. But, regarding this warning as coming from one whose spirit had been crushed by misery the American did not give up his design.

The boats were got ready and armed. Captain Delano ordered his men into them. He was going himself when Don Benito grasped his arm.

"What! have you saved my life, Señor, and are you now going to throw away your own?"

The officers also, for reasons connected with their interests and those of the voyage, and a duty owing to the owners, strongly objected against their commander's going. Weighing their remonstrances a moment, Captain Delano felt bound to remain; appointing his chief mate—an athletic and resolute man, who had been a privateer's-man—to head the party. The more to encourage the sailors, they were told, that the Spanish captain considered his ship good as lost; that she and her cargo, including some gold and silver, were worth more than a thousand dubloons. Take her, and no small part shall be theirs. The sailors replied with a shout.

The fugitives had now almost gained an offing. It was nearly night; but the moon was rising. After hard, prolonged pulling, the boats came up on the ship's quarters, at a suitable distance laying upon their oars to discharge their muskets. Having no bullets to return, the negroes sent their yells. But, upon the second volley, Indianlike, they hurtled their hatchets. One took off a sailor's fingers. Another struck the whale-boat's bow, cutting off the rope there, and remaining stuck in the gunwale like a woodman's axe. Snatching it, quivering from its lodgment, the mate hurled it back. The returned gauntlet now stuck in the ship's broken quarter-gallery, and so remained.

The negroes giving too hot a reception, the whites kept a more respectful distance. Hovering now just out of reach of the hurtling hatchets, they, with a view to the close encounter which must soon come, sought to decoy the blacks into entirely disarming themselves of their most murderous weapons in a hand-to-hand fight, by foolishly flinging them, as missiles, short of the mark, into the sea. But, ere long, perceiving the stratagem, the negroes desisted, though not before many of them had to replace their lost hatchets with hand-spikes; an exchange which, as counted upon, proved, in the end, favorable to the assailants.

Meantime, with a strong wind, the ship still clove the water; the boats alternately falling behind, and pulling up, to discharge fresh volleys.

The fire was mostly directed towards the stern, since there, chiefly, the negroes, at present, were clustering. But to kill or maim the negroes was not the object. To take them, with the ship, was the object. To do it, the ship must be boarded; which could not be done by boats while she was sailing so fast.

A thought now struck the mate. Observing the Spanish boys still aloft, high as they could get, he called to them to descend to the yards, and cut adrift the sails. It was done. About this time, owing to causes hereafter to be shown, two Spaniards, in the dress of sailors, and conspicuously showing themselves, were killed; not by volleys, but by deliberate marksman's shots; while, as it afterwards appeared, by one of the general discharges. Atufal, the black, and the Spaniard at the helm likewise were killed. What now, with the loss of the sails, and loss of leaders, the ship became unmanageable to the negroes.

With creaking masts, she came heavily round to the wind; the prow slowly swinging into view of the boats, its skeleton gleaming in the horizontal moonlight, and casting a gigantic ribbed shadow upon the water. One extended arm of the ghost seemed beckoning the white to avenge it.

"Follow your leader!" cried the mate; and one on each bow, the boats boarded. Sealing-spears and cutlasses crossed hatchets and hand-spikes. Huddled upon the long-boat amidships, the negresses raised a wailing chant, whose chorus was the clash of the steel.

For a time, the attack wavered; the negroes wedging themselves to beat it back; the half-repelled sailors, as yet unable to gain a footing, fighting as troopers in the saddle, one leg sideways flung over the bulwarks, and one without, plying their cutlasses like carters' whips. But in vain. They were almost overborne, when, rallying themselves into a squad as one man, with a huzza, they sprang inboard, where, entangled, they involuntarily separated again. For a few breaths' space, there was a vague, muffled, inner sound, as of submerged sword-fish rushing hither and thither through shoals of blackfish. Soon, in a reunited band, and joined by the Spanish seamen, the whites came to the surface, irresistibly driving the negroes toward the stern. But a barricade of casks and sacks, from side to side, had been thrown up by the mainmast. Here the negroes faced about, and though scorning peace or truce, yet fain would have had respite. But, without pause, overleaping the barrier, the unflagging sailors again closed. Exhausted, the blacks now fought in despair. Their red tongues lolled, wolf-like, from their black mouths. But the pale sailors' teeth were set; not a word was spoken; and, in five minutes more, the ship was won.

Nearly a score of the negroes were killed. Exclusive of those by the balls, many were mangled; their wounds—mostly inflicted by the long-edged sealing-spears, resembling those shaven ones of the English at Preston Pans,[9] made by the poled scythes of the Highlanders. On the other side, none were killed, though several were wounded; some severely, including the mate. The surviving negroes were temporar-

---

9. The Battle of Prestonpans in 1745 was part of the ill-fated campaign to win the English throne for Charles Edward Stuart (Bonnie Prince Charlie).

ily secured, and the ship, towed back into the harbor at midnight, once more lay anchored.

Omitting the incidents and arrangements ensuing, suffice it that, after two days spent in refitting, the ships sailed in company for Conception, in Chili, and thence for Lima, in Peru; where, before the vice-regal courts, the whole affair, from the beginning, underwent investigation.

Though, midway on the passage, the ill-fated Spaniard, relaxed from constraint, showed some signs of regaining health with freewill; yet, agreeably to his own foreboding, shortly before arriving at Lima, he relapsed, finally become so reduced as to be carried ashore in arms. Hearing of his story and plight, one of the many religious institutions of the City of Kings opened an hospitable refuge to him, where both physician and priest were his nurses, and a member of the order volunteered to be his one special guardian and consoler, by night and by day.

The following extracts, translated from one of the official Spanish documents, will, it is hoped, shed light on the preceding narrative, as well as, in the first place, reveal the true port of departure and true history of the San Dominick's voyage, down to the time of her touching at the island of St. Maria.

But, ere the extracts come, it may be well to preface them with a remark.

The document selected, from among many others, for partial translation, contains the deposition of Benito Cereno; the first taken in the case. Some disclosures therein were, at the time, held dubious for both learned and natural reasons. The tribunal inclined to the opinion that the deponent, not undisturbed in his mind by recent events, raved of some things which could never have happened. But subsequent depositions of the surviving sailors, bearing out the revelations of their captain in several of the strangest particulars, gave credence to the rest. So that the tribunal, in its final decision, rested its capital sentences upon statements which, had they lacked confirmation, it would have deemed it but duty to reject.

I, DON JOSE DE ABOS AND PADILLA, His Majesty's Notary for the Royal Revenue, and Register of this Province, and Notary Public of the Holy Crusade of this Bishopric, etc.

Do certify and declare, as much as is requisite in law, that, in the criminal cause commenced the twenty-fourth of the month of September, in the year seventeen hundred and ninety-nine, against the negroes of the ship San Dominick, the following declaration before me was made:

Declaration of the first witness, DON BENITO CERENO.

The same day, and month, and year, His Honor, Doctor Juan Martinez de Rozas, Councilor of the Royal Audience of this Kingdom, and learned in the law of this Intendency,[1] ordered the captain of the ship San Dominick, Don Benito Cereno, to appear; which he did in his litter, attended by the monk Infelez; of whom he received the oath, which he took by God, our Lord, and a sign of the Cross; under which he promised to tell the truth of whatever he should know and should be asked;—and being interrogated agreeably to the tenor of the act commencing the process, he said, that on the twentieth of May last, he set sail with his ship from the port of Valparaiso, bound to that of Callao; loaded with the produce of the country beside thirty cases of hardware and one hundred and sixty blacks, of both sexes, mostly belonging to Don Alexandro Aranda, gentleman, of the city of Mendoza; that the crew of the ship consisted of thirty-six men, beside the persons who went as passengers; that the negroes were in part as follows:

[*Here, in the original, follows a list of some fifty names, descriptions, and ages, compiled from certain recovered documents of Aranda's, and also from recollections of the deponent, from which portions only are extracted.*][2]

—One, from about eighteen to nineteen years, named José, and this was the man that waited upon his master, Don Alexandro, and who speaks well the Spanish, having served him four or five years; . . . a mulatto, named Francesco, the cabin steward, of a good person and voice, having sung in the Valparaiso churches, native of the province of Buenos Ayres, aged thirty-five years. . . . A smart negro, named Dago, who had been for many years a grave-digger among the Spaniards, aged forty-six years. . . . Four old negroes, born in Africa, from sixty to seventy, but sound, calkers by trade, whose names are as follows:—the first was named Muri, and he was killed (as was also his son named Diamelo); the second, Nacta; the third, Yola, likewise killed; the

---

1. District.

2. The brackets and ellipses throughout are Melville's.

fourth Ghofan; and six full-grown negroes, aged from thirty to forty-five, all raw, and born among the Ashantees—Matiluqui, Yan, Lecbe, Mapenda, Yambaio, Akim; four of whom were killed; . . . a powerful negro named Atufal, who being supposed to have been a chief in Africa, his owner set great store by him. . . . And a small negro of Senegal, but some years among the Spaniards, aged about thirty, which negro's name was Babo; . . . that he does not remember the names of the others, but that still expecting the residue of Don Alexandro's papers will be found, will then take due account of them all, and remit to the court; . . . and thirty-nine women and children of all ages.

[*The catalogue over, the deposition goes on.*]

. . . That all the negroes slept upon deck, as is customary in this navigation, and none wore fetters, because the owner, his friend Aranda, told him that they were all tractable; . . . that on the seventh day after leaving port, at three o'clock in the morning, all the Spaniards being asleep except the two officers on the watch, who were the boatswain, Juan Robles, and the carpenter, Juan Bautista Gayete, and the helmsman and his boy, the negroes revolted suddenly, wounded dangerously the boatswain and the carpenter, and successively killed eighteen men of those who were sleeping upon deck, some with hand-spikes and hatchets, and others by throwing them alive overboard, after tying them; that of the Spaniards upon deck, they left about seven, as he thinks, alive and tied, to manœuvre the ship, and three or four more, who hid themselves, remained also alive. Although in the act of revolt the negroes made themselves masters of the hatchway, six or seven wounded went through it to the cockpit, without any hindrance on their part; that during the act of revolt, the mate and another person, whose name he does not recollect, attempted to come up through the hatchway, but being quickly wounded, were obliged to return to the cabin; that the deponent resolved at break of day to come up the companionway, where the negro Babo was, being the ringleader, and Atufal, who assisted him, and having spoken to them, exhorted them to cease committing such atrocities, asking them, at the same time, what they wanted and intended to do, offering, himself, to obey their commands; that notwithstanding this, they threw, in his presence, three men, alive and tied,

overboard; that they told the deponent to come up, and that they would not kill him; which having done, the negro Babo asked him whether there were in those seas any negro countries where they might be carried, and he answered them, No; that the negro Babo afterwards told him to carry them to Senegal, or to the neighboring islands of St. Nicholas; and he answered, that this was impossible, on account of the great distance, the necessity involved of rounding Cape Horn, the bad condition of the vessel, the want of provisions, sails, and water; but that the negro Babo replied to him he must carry them in any way; that they would do and conform themselves to everything the deponent should require as to eating and drinking; that after a long conference, being absolutely compelled to please them, for they threatened to kill all the whites if they were not, at all events, carried to Senegal, he told them that what was most wanting for the voyage was water; that they would go near the coast to take it, and thence they would proceed on their course; that the negro Babo agreed to it; and the deponent steered towards the intermediate ports, hoping to meet some Spanish or foreign vessel that would save them; that within ten or eleven days they saw the land, and continued their course by it in the vicinity of Nasca; that the deponent observed that the negroes were now restless and mutinous, because he did not effect the taking in of water, the negro Babo having required, with threats, that it should be done, without fail, the following day; he told him he saw plainly that the coast was steep, and the rivers designated in the maps were not to be found, with other reasons suitable to the circumstances; that the best way would be to go to the island of Santa Maria, where they might water easily, it being a solitary island, as the foreigners did; that the deponent did not go to Pisco, that was near, nor make any other port of the coast, because the negro Babo had intimated to him several times, that he would kill all the whites the very moment he should perceive any city, town, or settlement of any kind on the shores to which they should be carried: that having determined to go to the island of Santa Maria, as the deponent had planned, for the purpose of trying whether, on the passage or near the island itself, they could find any vessel that should favor them, or whether he could escape from it in a boat to the neighboring coast of Arruco, to adopt the necessary means he immediately changed his course, steering for the island; that the negroes Babo and Atufal held daily conferences, in which they discussed what was necessary for their design of returning to Senegal, whether they were to kill all the Spaniards, and particularly the deponent; that eight days after parting from the coast of Nasca, the deponent being on the watch a little after day-break, and soon after the negroes had their meeting, the negro Babo came to the place where the deponent was, and told him that he had determined to kill his master, Don Alexandro Aranda, both because he and his companions could not otherwise be sure of their liberty, and that to keep the seamen in subjection, he wanted to prepare a warning of what road they should be made to take did they or any of them oppose him; and that, by means of the death of Don Alexandro, that warning would best be given; but, that what this last meant, the deponent did not at the time comprehend, nor could not, further than that the death of Don Alexandro was intended; and moreover the negro Babo proposed to the deponent to call the mate Raneds, who was sleeping in the cabin, before the thing was done, for fear, as the deponent understood it, that the mate, who was a good navigator, should be killed with Don Alexandro and the rest; that the deponent, who was the friend, from youth, of Don Alexandro, prayed and conjured, but all was useless; for the negro Babo answered him that the thing could not be prevented, and that all the Spaniards risked their death if they could attempt to frustrate his will in this matter, or any other; that, in this conflict, the deponent called the mate, Raneds, who was forced to go apart, and immediately the negro Babo commanded the Ashantee Martinqui and the Ashantee Lecbe to go and commit the murder; that those two went down with hatchets to the berth of Don Alexandro; that, yet half alive and mangled, they dragged him on deck; that they were going to throw him overboard in that state, but the negro Babo stopped them; bidding the murder be completed on the deck before him, which was done, when, by his orders, the body was carried below, forward; that nothing more was seen of it by the deponent for three days; . . . that Don Alonzo Sidonia, an old man, long resident at Valparaiso, and lately appointed to a civil office in Peru, whither he had taken passage, was at the time sleeping in the berth opposite Don Alexandro's; that awakening at his cries, surprised by them, and at the sight of the negroes with their bloody hatchets in their hands, he threw himself into the sea through a window which was near him, and was drowned, without it being in the power of the deponent to assist or take him up; . . . that a short time after killing Aranda, they brought upon deck his german-cousin, of middle-age, Don Francisco Masa, of Mendoza, and the young Don Joaquin, Marques de Aramboalaza, then lately from Spain, with his Spanish servant Ponce, and the three young clerks of Aranda, José Mozairi, Lorenzo Bargas, and Hermenegildo Gandix, all of Cadiz; that Don Joaquin and Hermenegildo Gandix, the negro Babo, for purposes hereafter to appear, preserved alive; but Don Francisco Masa, José Mozairi, and Lorenzo Bargas, with Ponce the servant, beside the boatswain, Juan Robles, the boatswain's mates, Manuel Viscaya and Roderigo Hurta, and four of the sailors, the negro Babo ordered to be thrown alive into the sea, although they made no resistance, nor begged for anything else but mercy; that the boatswain, Juan Robles, who knew how to swim, kept the longest above water, making acts of contrition, and, in the last words he uttered, charged this deponent to cause mass to be said for his soul to our Lady of Succor: . . . that, during the three days which followed, the deponent, uncertain what fate had befallen the remains of Don Alexandro, frequently asked the negro Babo where they were, and, if still on board, whether they were to be preserved for interment ashore, entreating him so to order it; that the negro Babo answered nothing till the fourth day, when at sunrise, the deponent coming on deck, the negro Babo showed him a skeleton, which had been substituted for the ship's proper figure-head—the image of Christopher Colon, the discoverer of the New World; that the negro Babo asked him whose skeleton that was, and whether, from its whiteness, he should not think it a white's; that, upon discovering his face, the negro Babo, coming close, said words to this effect: "Keep faith with the blacks from here to Senegal, or you shall in spirit, as now in body, follow your leader," pointing to the prow; . . . that the same morning the negro Babo took by succession each Spaniard forward, and asked him whose skeleton that was, and whether, from its whiteness, he should not think it a white's; that each Spaniard covered his face; that then to each the negro Babo repeated the words in the first place said to the deponent; . . . that they (the Spaniards), being then assembled aft, the negro Babo harangued them, saying that he had now done all; that the deponent (as navigator for the negroes) might pursue his course, warning him and all of them that they should, soul and body, go the way of Don Alexandro, if he saw them (the Spaniards) speak or plot anything against them (the negroes)—a threat which was repeated every day; that, before the events last mentioned, they had tied the cook to throw him overboard, for it is not known what thing they heard him speak, but finally the negro Babo spared his life, at the request of the deponent; that a few days after, the deponent, endeavoring not to omit any means to preserve the lives of the remaining whites, spoke to the negroes of peace and tranquillity, and agreed to draw up a paper, signed by the deponent and the sailors who could write, as also by the negro Babo, for himself and all the blacks, in which the deponent obliged himself to carry them to Senegal, and they not to kill any more, and he formally to make over to them the ship, with the cargo, with which they were for that time satisfied and quieted. . . . But the next day, the more surely to guard against the sailors' escape, the negro Babo commanded all the boats to be destroyed but the long-boat, which was unseaworthy, and another, a cutter in good condition, which knowing it would yet be wanted for towing the water casks, he had it lowered down into the hold.

•   •   •

[*Various particulars of the prolonged and perplexed navigation ensuing here follow, with incidents of a calamitous calm, from which portion one passage is extracted, to wit:*]
—That on the fifth day of the calm, all on board suffering much from the heat, and want of water, and five having died in fits, and mad, the negroes became irritable, and for a chance gesture, which they deemed suspicious—though it was harmless—made by the mate, Raneds, to the deponent in the act of handing a quadrant, they killed him; but that for this they afterwards were sorry, the mate being the only remaining navigator on board, except the deponent.

•   •   •

—That omitting other events, which daily happened, and which can only serve uselessly to recall past misfortunes and conflicts, after seventy-three days' navigation, reckoned from the time they sailed from Nasca, during which they navigated under a scanty allowance of water, and were afflicted with the calms before mentioned, they at last arrived at the island of Santa Maria, on the seventeenth of the month of August, at about six o'clock in the afternoon, at which hour they cast anchor very near the American ship, Bachelor's Delight, which lay in the same bay, commanded by the generous Captain Amasa Delano; but at six o'clock in the morning, they had already descried the port, and the negroes became uneasy, as soon as at distance they saw the ship, not having expected to see one there; that the negro Babo pacified them, assuring them that no fear need be had; that straightway he ordered the figure on the bow to be covered with canvas, as for repairs, and had the decks a little set in order; that for a time the negro Babo and the negro Atufal conferred; that the negro Atufal was for sailing away, but the negro Babo would not, and, by himself, cast about what to do; that at last he came to the deponent, proposing to him to say and do all that the deponent declares to have said and done to the American captain;

•   •   •

that the negro Babo warned him that if he varied in the least, or uttered any word, or gave any look that should give the least intimation of the past events or present state, he would instantly kill him, with all his companions, showing a dagger, which he carried hid, saying something which, as he understood it, meant that the dagger would be alert as his eye; that the negro Babo then announced the plan to all his companions, which pleased them; that he then, the better to disguise the truth, devised many expedients, in some of them uniting deceit and defense; that of this sort was the device of the six Ashantees before named, who were his bravoes; that them he stationed on the break of the poop, as if to clean certain hatchets (in cases, which were part of the cargo), but in reality to use them, and distribute them at need, and at a given word he told them; that, among other devices, was the device of presenting Atufal, his right hand man, as chained, though in a moment the chains could be dropped; that in every particular he informed the deponent what part he was expected to enact in every device, and what story he was to tell on every occasion, always threatening him with instant death if he varied in the least: that, conscious that many of the negroes would be turbulent, the negro Babo appointed the four aged negroes, who were calkers, to keep what domestic order they could on the decks; that again and again he harangued the Spaniards and his companions, informing them of his intent, and of his devices, and of the invented story that this deponent was to tell; charging them lest any of them varied from that story; that these arrangements were made and matured during the interval of two or three hours, between their first sighting the ship and the arrival on board of Captain Amasa Delano; that this happened about half-past seven o'clock in the morning, Captain Amasa Delano coming in his boat, and all gladly receiving him; that the deponent, as well as he could force himself, acting then the part of principal owner, and a free captain of the ship, told Captain Amasa Delano, when called upon, that he came from Buenos Ayres, bound to Lima, with three hundred negroes; that off Cape Horn, and in a subsequent fever, many negroes had died; that also, by similar casualties, all the sea officers and the greatest part of the crew had died.

·   ·   ·

[*And so the deposition goes on, circumstantially recounting the fictitious story dictated to the deponent by Babo, and through the deponent imposed upon Captain Delano; and also recounting the friendly offers of Captain Delano, with other things, but all of which is here omitted. After the fictitious story, etc, the deposition proceeds:*]

·   ·   ·

—that the generous Captain Amasa Delano remained on board all the day, till he left the ship anchored at six o'clock in the evening, deponent speaking to him always of his pretended misfortunes, under the fore-mentioned principles, without having had it in his power to tell a single word, or give him the least hint, that he might know the truth and state of things: because the negro Babo, performing the office of an officious servant with all the appearance of submission of the humble slave, did not leave the deponent one moment; that this was in order to observe the deponent's actions and words, for the negro Babo understands well the Spanish; and besides, there were thereabout some others who were constantly on the watch, and likewise understood the Spanish; . . . that upon one occasion, while deponent was standing on the deck conversing with Amasa Delano, by a secret sign the negro Babo drew him (the deponent) aside, the act appearing as if originating with the deponent; that then, he being drawn aside, the negro Babo proposed to him to gain from Amasa Delano full particulars about his ship, and crew, and arms; that the deponent asked "For what?" that the negro Babo answered he might conceive; that, grieved at the prospect of what might overtake the generous Captain Amasa Delano, the deponent at first refused to ask the desired questions, and used every argument to induce the negro Babo to give up this new design; that the negro Babo showed the point of his dagger; that, after the information had been obtained the negro Babo again drew him aside, telling him that that very night he (the deponent) would be captain of two ships, instead of one, for that, great part of the American's ship's crew being to be absent fishing, the six Ashantees, without any one else, would easily take it; that at this time he said other things to the same purpose; that no entreaties availed; that, before Amasa Delano's coming on board, no hint had been given touching the capture of the American ship: that to prevent this project the deponent was powerless; . . . —that in some things his memory is confused, he cannot distinctly recall every event; . . . —that as soon as they had cast anchor at six of the clock in the evening, as has before been stated, the American Captain took leave, to return to his vessel; that upon a sudden impulse, which the deponent believes to have come from God and his angels, he, after the farewell had been said, followed the generous Captain Amasa Delano as far as the gunwale, where he stayed, under pretense of taking leave, until Amasa Delano should have been seated in his boat; that on shoving off, the deponent sprang from the gunwale into the boat, and fell into it, he knows not how, God guarding him; that—

·   ·   ·

[*Here, in the original, follows the account of what further happened at the escape, and how the San Dominick was retaken, and of the passage to the coast; including in the recital many expressions of "eternal gratitude" to the "generous Captain Amasa Delano." The deposition then proceeds with recapitulatory remarks, and a partial renumeration of the negroes, making record of their individual part in the past events, with a view to furnishing, according to command of the court, the data whereon to found the criminal sentences to be pronounced. From this portion is the following;*]

—That he believes that all the negroes, though not in the first place knowing to the design of revolt, when it was accomplished, approved it. . . . That the negro, José, eighteen years old, and in the personal service of Don Alexandro, was the one who communicated the information to the negro Babo, about the state of things in the cabin, before the revolt; that this is known, because, in the preceding midnight, he used to come from his berth, which was under his master's, in the cabin, to the deck where the ringleader and his associates were, and had secret conversations with the negro Babo, in which he was several times seen by the mate; that, one night, the mate drove him away twice; . . . that this same negro José was the one who, without being commanded to do so by the negro Babo, as Lecbe and Martinqui were, stabbed his master, Don Alexandro, after he had been dragged half-lifeless to the deck; . . . that the mulatto steward, Francesco, was of the first band of revolters, that he was in all things, the creature and tool of the negro Babo; that, to make his court, he, just before a repast in the cabin, proposed, to the negro Babo, poisoning a dish for the generous Captain Amasa Delano; this is known and believed, because the negroes have said it; but that the negro Babo, having another design, forbade Francesco; . . . that the Ashantee Lecbe was one of the worst of them; for that, on the day the ship was retaken, he assisted in the defense of her, with a hatchet in each hand, with one of which he wounded, in the breast, the chief mate of Amasa Delano, in the first act of boarding; this all knew; that, in sight of the deponent, Lecbe struck, with a hatchet, Don Francesco Masa, when, by the negro Babo's orders, he was carrying him to throw him overboard, alive, beside participating in the murder, before mentioned, of Don Alexandro Aranda, and others of the cabin-passengers; that, owing to the fury with which the Ashantees fought in the engagement with the boats, but this Lecbe and Yan survived; that Yan was bad as Lecbe; that Yan was the man who, by Babo's command, willingly prepared the skeleton of Don Alexandro, in a way the negroes afterwards told the deponent, but which he, so long as reason is left him, can never divulge; that Yan and Lecbe were the two who, in a calm by night, riveted the skeleton to the bow; this also the negroes told him; that the negro Babo was he who traced the inscription below it; that the negro Babo was the plotter from first to last; he ordered every murder, and was the helm and keel of the revolt; that Atufal was his lieutenant in all; but Atufal, with his own hand, committed no murder, nor did the negro Babo; . . . that Atufal was shot, being killed in the fight with the boats, ere boarding; . . . that the negresses, of age, were knowing to the revolt, and testified themselves satisfied at the death of their master, Don Alexandro; that, had the negroes not restrained them, they would have tortured to death, instead of simply killing, the Spaniards slain by command of the negro Babo; that the negresses used their utmost influence to have the deponent made away with; that, in the various acts of murder, they sang songs and danced—not gaily, but solemnly; and before the engagement with the boats, as well as during the action, they sang melancholy songs to the negroes, and that this melancholy tone was more inflaming than a different one would have been, and was so intended; that all this is believed, because the negroes have said it,—that of the thirty-six men of the crew, exclusive of the passengers (all of whom are now dead), which the deponent had knowledge of, six only remained alive, with four cabin-boys and ship-boys, not included with the crew; . . .—that the negroes broke an arm of one of the cabin-boys and gave him strokes with hatchets.

[*Then follow various random disclosures referring to various periods of time. The following are extracted;*]

—That during the presence of Captain Amasa Delano on board, some attempts were made by the sailors, and one by Hermenegildo Gandix, to convey hints to him of the true state of affairs; but that these attempts were ineffectual, owing to fear of incurring death, and, furthermore, owing to the devices which offered contradictions to the true state of affairs, as well as owing to the generosity and piety of Amasa Delano incapable of sounding such wickedness; . . . that Luys Galgo, a sailor about sixty years of age, and formerly of the king's navy, was one of those who sought to convey tokens to Captain Amasa Delano; but his intent, though undiscovered, being suspected, he was, on a pretense, made to retire out of sight, and at last into the hold, and there was made away with. This the negroes have since said; . . . that one of the ship-boys feeling, from Captain Amasa Delano's presence, some hopes of release, and not having enough prudence, dropped some chance-word respecting his expectations, which being overheard and understood by a slave-boy with whom he was eating at the time, the latter struck him on the head with a knife, inflicting a bad wound, but of which the boy is now healing; that likewise, not long before the ship was brought to anchor, one of the seamen, steering at the time, endangered himself by letting the blacks remark some expression in his countenance, arising from a cause similar to the above; but this sailor, by his heedful after conduct, escaped; . . . that these statements are made to show the court that from the beginning to the end of the revolt, it was impossible for the deponent and his men to act otherwise than they did; . . . — that the third clerk, Hermenegildo Gandix, who before had been forced to live among the seamen, wearing a seaman's habit, and in all respects appearing to be one for the time; he, Gandix, was killed by a musket ball fired through mistake from the boats before boarding; having in his fright run up the mizzen-rigging, calling to the boats — "don't board," lest upon their boarding the negroes should kill him; that this induced the Americans to believe he some way favored the cause of the negroes, they fired two balls at him, so that he fell wounded from the rigging, and was drowned in the sea; . . . — that the young Don Joaquin, Marquis de Aramboalaza, like Hermenegildo Gandix, the third clerk, was degraded to the office and appearance of a common seaman; that upon one occasion when Don Joaquin shrank, the negro Babo commanded the Ashantee Lecbe to take tar and heat it, and pour it upon Don Joaquin's hands; . . . — that Don Joaquin was killed owing to another mistake of the Americans but one impossible to be avoided as upon the approach of the boats, Don Joaquin, with a hatchet tied edge out and upright to his hand, was made by the negroes to appear on the bulwarks; whereupon, seen with arms in his hands and in a questionable attitude, he was shot for a renegade seaman; . . . — that on the person of Don Joaquin was found a secreted jewel, which, by papers that were discovered, proved to have been meant for the shrine of our Lady of Mercy in Lima; a votive offering, beforehand prepared and guarded, to attest his gratitude, when he should have landed in Peru, his last destination, for the safe conclusion of his entire voyage from Spain; . . . — that the jewel, with the other effects of the late Don Joaquin, is in the custody of the brethren of the Hospital de Sacerdotes, awaiting the disposition of the honorable court; . . . — that, owing to the condition of the deponent, as well as the haste in which the boats departed from the attack, the Americans were not forewarned that there were, among the apparent crew, a passenger and one of the clerks disguised by the negro Babo; . . . — that, beside the negroes killed in the action, some were killed after the capture and reanchoring at night, when shackled to the ring-bolts on deck; that these deaths were committed by the sailors, ere they could be prevented. That so soon as

informed of it, Captain Amasa Delano used all his authority, and, in particular with his own hand, struck down Martinez Gola, who, having found a razor in the pocket of an old jacket of his, which one of the shackled negroes had on, was aiming it at the negro's throat; that the noble Captain Amasa Delano also wrenched from the hand of Bartholomew Barlo a dagger, secreted at the time of the massacre of the whites, with which he was in the act of stabbing a shackled negro, who, the same day, with another negro, had thrown him down and jumped upon him; . . . — that, for all the events, befalling through so long a time, during which the ship was in the hands of the negro Babo, he cannot here give account; but that, what he has said is the most substantial of what occurs to him at present, and is the truth under the oath which he has taken; which declaration he affirmed and ratified, after hearing it read to him.

He said that he is twenty-nine years of age, and broken in body and mind; that when finally dismissed by the court, he shall not return home to Chili, but betake himself to the monastery on Mount Agonia without; and signed with his honor, and crossed himself, and, for the time, departed as he came, in his litter, with the monk Infelez, to the Hospital de Sacerdotes.

DOCTOR ROZAS.   BENITO CERENO.

If the Deposition have served as the key to fit into the lock of the complications which preceded it, then, as a vault whose door has been flung back, the San Dominick's hull lies open to-day.

Hitherto the nature of this narrative, besides rendering the intricacies in the beginning unavoidable, has more or less required that many things, instead of being set down in the order of occurrence, should be retrospectively, or irregularly given; this last is the case with the following passages, which will conclude the account:

During the long, mild voyage to Lima, there was, as before hinted, a period during which the sufferer a little recovered his health, or, at least in some degree, his tranquillity. Ere the decided relapse which came, the two captains had many cordial conversations — their fraternal unreserve in singular contrast with former withdrawments.

Again and again it was repeated, how hard it had been to enact the part forced on the Spaniard by Babo.

"Ah, my dear friend," Don Benito once said, "at those very times when you thought me so morose and ungrateful, nay, when, as you now admit, you half thought me plotting your murder, at those very times my heart was frozen; I could not look at you, thinking of what, both on board this ship and your own, hung, from other hands, over my kind benefactor. And as God lives, Don Amasa, I know not whether desire for my own safety alone could have nerved me to that leap into your boat, had it not been for the thought that, did you, unenlightened, return to your ship, you, my best friend, with all who might be with you, stolen upon, that night, in your hammocks, would never in this world have wakened again. Do but think how you walked this deck, how you sat in this cabin, every inch of ground mined into honey-combs under you. Had I dropped the least hint, made the least advance towards an understanding between us, death, explosive death—yours as mine—would have ended the scene."

"True, true," cried Captain Delano, starting, "you have saved my life, Don Benito, more than I yours; saved it, too, against my knowledge and will."

"Nay, my friend," rejoined the Spaniard, courteous even to the point of religion. "God charmed your life, but you saved mine. To think of some things you did—those smilings and chattings, rash pointings and gesturings. For less than these, they slew my mate, Raneds; but you had the Prince of Heaven's safe-conduct through all ambuscades."

"Yes, all is owing to Providence, I know: but the temper of my mind that morning was more than commonly pleasant, while the sight of so much suffering, more apparent than real, added to my good-nature, compassion, and charity, happily interweaving the three. Had it been otherwise, doubtless, as you hint, some of my interferences might have ended unhappily enough. Besides, those feelings I spoke of enabled me to get the better of momentary distrust, at times when acuteness might have cost me my life, without saving another's. Only at the end did my suspicions get the better of me, and you know how wide of the mark they then proved."

"Wide, indeed," said Don Benito, sadly; "you were with me all day; stood with me, sat with me, talked with me, looked at me, ate with me, drank with me; and yet, your last act was to clutch for a monster, not only an innocent man, but the most pitiable of all men. To such degree may malign machina-

tions and deceptions impose. So far may even the best man err, in judging the conduct of one with the recesses of whose condition he is not acquainted. But you were forced to it; and you were in time undeceived. Would that, in both respects, it was so ever, and with all men."

"You generalize, Don Benito; and mournfully enough. But the past is passed; why moralize upon it? Forget it. See, yon bright sun has forgotten it all, and the blue sea, and the blue sky; these have turned over new leaves."

"Because they have no memory," he dejectedly replied; "because they are not human."

"But these mild trades[3] that now fan your cheek, do they not come with a human-like healing to you? Warm friends, steadfast friends are the trades."

"With their steadfastness they but waft me to my tomb, Señor," was the foreboding response.

"You are saved," cried Captain Delano, more and more astonished and pained; "you are saved: what has cast such a shadow upon you?"

"The negro."

There was silence, while the moody man sat, slowly and unconsciously gathering his mantle about him, as if it were a pall.

There was no more conversation that day.

But if the Spaniard's melancholy sometimes ended in muteness upon topics like the above, there were others upon which he never spoke at all; on which, indeed, all his old reserves were piled. Pass over the worst, and, only to elucidate, let an item or two of these be cited. The dress, so precise and costly, worn by him on the day whose events have been narrated, had not willingly been put on. And that silver-mounted sword, apparent symbol of despotic command, was not, indeed, a sword, but the ghost of one. The scabbard, artificially stiffened, was empty.

As for the black—whose brain, not body, had schemed and led the revolt, with the plot—his slight frame, inadequate to that which it held, had at once yielded to the superior muscular strength of his captor, in the boat. Seeing all was over, he uttered no sound, and could not be forced to. His aspect seemed to say, since I cannot do deeds, I will not speak words. Put in irons in the hold, with the rest, he was carried to Lima. During the passage, Don Benito did

---

3. Trade winds.

not visit him. Nor then, nor at any time after, would he look at him. Before the tribunal he refused. When pressed by the judges he fainted. On the testimony of the sailors alone rested the legal identity of Babo.

Some months after, dragged to the gibbet at the tail of a mule, the black met his voiceless end. The body was burned to ashes; but for many days, the head, that hive of subtlety, fixed on a pole in the Plaza, met, unabashed, the gaze of the whites; and across the Plaza looked towards St. Bartholomew's church, in whose vaults slept then, as now, the recovered bones of Aranda: and across the Rimac bridge looked towards the monastery, on Mount Agonia without; where, three months after being dismissed by the court, Benito Cereno, borne on the bier, did, indeed, follow his leader.

1855, 1856

The Yellow Wallpaper

Charlotte Perkins Gilman

This text of "The Yellow Wallpaper" is reprinted from the story's first publication in the January 1892 issue of the New England Magazine. *I have corrected a few obvious misprints, but I have retained all other features of that text, including the inconsistent hyphenation of "wall-paper." In the title, however, in deference to current usage, I have dropped the hyphen. For the authority of the 1892 text, see the essay by Julie Bates Dock in Chapter 7.*

It is very seldom that mere ordinary people like John and myself secure ancestral halls for the summer.

A colonial mansion, a hereditary estate, I would say a haunted house, and reach the height of romantic felicity—but that would be asking too much of fate!

Still I will proudly declare that there is something queer about it.

Else, why should it be let so cheaply? And why have stood so long untenanted?

John laughs at me, of course, but one expects that in marriage.

John is practical in the extreme. He has no patience with faith, an intense horror of superstition, and he scoffs openly at any talk of things not to be felt and seen and put down in figures.

John is a physician, and *perhaps*—(I would not say it to a living soul, of course, but this is dead paper and a great relief to my mind—) *perhaps* that is one reason I do not get well faster.

You see he does not believe I am sick!

And what can one do?

If a physician of high standing, and one's own husband, assures friends and relatives that there is really nothing the matter with one but temporary nervous depression—a slight hysterical tendency— what is one to do?

My brother is also a physician, and also of high standing, and he says the same thing.

So I take phosphates or phosphites—whichever it is, and tonics, and journeys, and air, and exercise, and am absolutely forbidden to "work" until I am well again.

Personally, I disagree with their ideas.

Personally, I believe that congenial work, with excitement and change, would do me good.

But what is one to do?

I did write for a while in spite of them; but it *does* exhaust me a good deal—having to be so sly about it, or else meet with heavy opposition.

I sometimes fancy that in my condition if I had less opposition and more society and stimulus—but John says the very worst thing I can do is to think about my condition, and I confess it always makes me feel bad.

So I will let it alone and talk about the house.

The most beautiful place! It is quite alone, standing well back from the road, quite three miles from the village. It makes me think of English places that you read about, for there are hedges and walls and gates that lock, and lots of separate little houses for the gardeners and people.

There is a *delicious* garden! I never saw such a garden—large and shady, full of box-bordered paths, and lined with long grape-covered arbors with seats under them.

There were greenhouses, too, but they are all broken now.

There was some legal trouble, I believe, something about the heirs and co-heirs; anyhow, the place has been empty for years.

That spoils my ghostliness, I am afraid, but I don't care—there is something strange about the house—I can feel it.

I even said so to John one moonlight evening, but he said what I felt was a *draught,* and shut the window.

I get unreasonably angry with John sometimes. I'm sure I never used to be so sensitive. I think it is due to this nervous condition.

But John says if I feel so, I shall neglect proper self-control; so I take pains to control myself—before him, at least, and that makes me very tired.

I don't like our room a bit. I wanted one downstairs that opened on the piazza and had roses all over the window, and such pretty old-fashioned chintz hangings! but John would not hear of it.

He said there was only one window and not room for two beds, and no near room for him if he took another.

He is very careful and loving, and hardly lets me stir without special direction.

I have a schedule prescription for each hour in the day; he takes all care from me, and so I feel basely ungrateful not to value it more.

He said we came here solely on my account, that I was to have perfect rest and all the air I could get. "Your exercise depends on your strength, my dear," said he, "and your food somewhat on your appetite; but air you can absorb all the time." So we took the nursery at the top of the house.

It is a big, airy room, the whole floor nearly, with windows that look all ways, and air and sunshine galore. It was nursery first and then playroom and gymnasium, I should judge; for the windows are barred for little children, and there are rings and things in the walls.

The paint and paper look as if a boys' school had used it. It is stripped off—the paper—in great patches all around the head of my bed, about as far as I can reach, and in a great place on the other side of the room low down. I never saw a worse paper in my life.

One of those sprawling flamboyant patterns committing every artistic sin.

It is dull enough to confuse the eye in following, pronounced enough to constantly irritate and provoke study, and when you follow the lame uncertain curves for a little distance they suddenly commit suicide—plunge off at outrageous angles, destroy themselves in unheard of contradictions.

The color is repellant, almost revolting; a smouldering unclean yellow, strangely faded by the slow-turning sunlight.

It is a dull yet lurid orange in some places, a sickly sulphur tint in others.

No wonder the children hated it! I should hate it myself if I had to live in this room long.

There comes John, and I must put this away,—he hates to have me write a word.

    *   *   *   *   *   *

We have been here two weeks, and I haven't felt like writing before, since that first day.

I am sitting by the window now, up in this atrocious nursery, and there is nothing to hinder my writing as much as I please, save lack of strength.

John is away all day, and even some nights when his cases are serious.

I am glad my case is not serious!

But these nervous troubles are dreadfully depressing.

John does not know how much I really suffer. He knows there is no *reason* to suffer, and that satisfies him.

Of course it is only nervousness. It does weigh on me so not to do my duty in any way!

I meant to be such a help to John, such a real rest and comfort, and here I am a comparative burden already!

Nobody would believe what an effort it is to do what little I am able,—to dress and entertain, and order things.

It is fortunate Mary is so good with the baby. Such a dear baby!

And yet I *cannot* be with him, it makes me so nervous.

I suppose John never was nervous in his life. He laughs at me so about this wall-paper!

At first he meant to repaper the room, but afterwards he said that I was letting it get the better of me, and that nothing was worse for a nervous patient than to give way to such fancies.

He said that after the wall-paper was changed it would be the heavy bedstead, and then the barred windows, and then the gate at the head of the stairs, and so on.

"You know the place is doing you good," he said, "and really, dear, I don't care to renovate the house just for a three months' rental."

"Then do let us go downstairs," I said, "there are such pretty rooms there."

Then he took me in his arms and called me a blessed little goose, and said he would go down cellar, if I wished, and have it whitewashed into the bargain.

But he is right enough about the beds and windows and things.

It is an airy and comfortable room as any one need wish, and, of course, I would not be so silly as to make him uncomfortable just for a whim.

I'm really getting quite fond of the big room, all but that horrid paper.

Out of one window I can see the garden, those mysterious deep-shaded arbors, the riotous old-fashioned flowers, and bushes and gnarly trees.

Out of another I get a lovely view of the bay and a little private wharf belonging to the estate. There is a beautiful shaded lane that runs down there from the house. I always fancy I see people walking in these numerous paths and arbors, but John has cautioned me not to give way to fancy in the least. He says that with my imaginative power and habit of story-making, a nervous weakness like mine is sure to lead to all manner of excited fancies, and that I ought to use my will and good sense to check the tendency. So I try.

I think sometimes that if I were only well enough to write a little it would relieve the press of ideas and rest me.

But I find I get pretty tired when I try.

It is so discouraging not to have any advice and companionship about my work. When I get really well, John says we will ask Cousin Henry and Julia down for a long visit; but he says he would as soon put fireworks in my pillow-case as to let me have those stimulating people about now.

I wish I could get well faster.

But I must not think about that. This paper looks to me as if it *knew* what a vicious influence it had!

There is a recurrent spot where the pattern lolls like a broken neck and two bulbous eyes stare at you upside down.

I get positively angry with the impertinence of it and the everlastingness. Up and down and sideways they crawl, and those absurd, unblinking eyes are everywhere. There is one place where two breaths didn't match, and the eyes go all up and down the line, one a little higher than the other.

I never saw so much expression in an inanimate thing before, and we all know how much expression they have! I used to lie awake as a child and get more entertainment and terror out of blank walls and plain furniture than most children could find in a toy-store.

I remember what a kindly wink the knobs of our big, old bureau used to have, and there was one chair that always seemed like a strong friend.

I used to feel that if any of the other things looked too fierce I could always hop into that chair and be safe.

The furniture in this room is no worse than inharmonious, however, for we had to bring it all from downstairs. I suppose when this was used as a play-room they had to take the nursery things out, and no wonder! I never saw such ravages as the children have made here.

The wall-paper, as I said before, is torn off in spots, and it sticketh closer than a brother—they must have had perseverance as well as hatred.

Then the floor is scratched and gouged and splintered, the plaster itself is dug out here and there, and this great heavy bed which is all we found in the room, looks as if it had been through the wars.

But I don't mind it a bit—only the paper.

There comes John's sister. Such a dear girl as she is, and so careful of me! I must not let her find me writing.

She is a perfect and enthusiastic housekeeper, and hopes for no better profession. I verily believe she thinks it is the writing which made me sick!

But I can write when she is out, and see her a long way off from these windows.

There is one that commands the road, a lovely shaded winding road, and one that just looks off over the country. A lovely country, too, full of great elms and velvet meadows.

This wallpaper has a kind of sub-pattern in a different shade, a particularly irritating one, for you can only see it in certain lights, and not clearly then.

But in the places where it isn't faded and where the sun is just so—I can see a strange, provoking, formless sort of figure, that seems to skulk about behind that silly and conspicuous front design.

There's sister on the stairs!

*   *   *   *   *   *

Well, the Fourth of July is over! The people are all gone and I am tired out. John thought it might do me good to see a little company, so we just had mother and Nellie and the children down for a week.

Of course I didn't do a thing. Jennie sees to everything now.

But it tired me all the same.

John says if I don't pick up faster he shall send me to Weir Mitchell in the fall.

But I don't want to go there at all. I had a friend who was in his hands once, and she says he is just like John and my brother, only more so!

Besides, it is such an undertaking to go so far.

I don't feel as if it was worth while to turn my hand over for anything, and I'm getting dreadfully fretful and querulous.

I cry at nothing, and cry most of the time.

Of course I don't when John is here, or anybody else, but when I am alone.

And I am alone a good deal just now. John is kept in town very often by serious cases, and Jennie is good and lets me alone when I want her to.

So I walk a little in the garden or down that lovely lane, sit on the porch under the roses, and lie down up here a good deal.

I'm getting really fond of the room in spite of the wallpaper. Perhaps *because* of the wallpaper.

It dwells in my mind so!

I lie here on this great immovable bed—it is nailed down, I believe—and follow that pattern about by the hour. It is as good as gymnastics, I assure you. I start, we'll say, at the bottom, down in the corner over there where it has not been touched, and I determine for the thousandth time that I *will* follow that pointless pattern to some sort of a conclusion.

I know a little of the principle of design, and I know this thing was not arranged on any laws of radiation, or alternation, or repetition, or symmetry, or anything else that I ever heard of.

It is repeated, of course, by the breadths, but not otherwise.

Looked at in one way each breadth stands alone, the bloated curves and flourishes—a kind of "debased Romanesque" with *delirium tremens*—go waddling up and down in isolated columns of fatuity.

But, on the other hand, they connect diagonally, and the sprawling outlines run off in great slanting waves of optic horror, like a lot of wallowing sea-weeds in full chase.

The whole thing goes horizontally, too, at least it seems so, and I exhaust myself in trying to distinguish the order of its going in that direction.

They have used a horizontal breadth for a frieze, and that adds wonderfully to the confusion.

There is one end of the room where it is almost intact, and there, when the crosslights fade and the sun shines directly upon it, I can almost fancy radiation after all,—the interminable grotesques seem to form around a common centre and rush off in headlong plunges of equal distraction.

It makes me tired to follow it. I will take a nap I guess.

*   *   *   *   *   *

I don't know why I should write this.

I don't want to.

I don't feel able.

And I know John would think it absurd. But I *must* say what I feel and think in some way—it is such a relief!

But the effort is getting to be greater than the relief.

Half the time now I am awfully lazy, and lie down ever so much.

John says I mustn't lose my strength, and has me take cod liver oil and lots of tonics and things, to say nothing of ale and wine and rare meat.

Dear John! He loves me very dearly, and hates to have me sick. I tried to have a real earnest reasonable talk with him the other day, and tell him how I wish he would let me go and make a visit to Cousin Henry and Julia.

But he said I wasn't able to go, nor able to stand it after I got there; and I did not make out a very good case for myself, for I was crying before I had finished.

It is getting to be a great effort for me to think straight. Just this nervous weakness I suppose.

And dear John gathered me up in his arms, and just carried me upstairs and laid me on the bed, and sat by me and read to me till it tired my head.

He said I was his darling and his comfort and all he had, and that I must take care of myself for his sake, and keep well.

He says no one but myself can help me out of it, that I must use my will and self-control and not let any silly fancies run away with me.

There's one comfort, the baby is well and happy, and does not have to occupy this nursery with the horrid wallpaper.

If we had not used it, that blessed child would have! What a fortunate escape! Why, I wouldn't have a child of mine, an impressionable little thing, live in such a room for worlds.

I never thought of it before, but it is lucky that John kept me here after all, I can stand it so much easier than a baby, you see.

Of course I never mention it to them any more — I am too wise, — but I keep watch of it all the same.

There are things in that paper that nobody knows but me, or ever will.

Behind that outside pattern the dim shapes get clearer every day.

It is always the same shape, only very numerous.

And it is like a woman stooping down and creeping about behind that pattern. I don't like it a bit. I wonder — I begin to think — I wish John would take me away from here!

*   *   *   *   *   *

It is so hard to talk with John about my case, because he is so wise, and because he loves me so.

But I tried it last night.

It was moonlight. The moon shines in all round just as the sun does.

I hate to see it sometimes, it creeps so slowly, and always comes in by one window or another.

John was asleep and I hated to waken him, so I kept still and watched the moonlight on that undulating wallpaper till I felt creepy.

The faint figure behind seemed to shake the pattern, just as if she wanted to get out.

I got up softly and went to feel and see if the paper *did* move, and when I came back John was awake.

"What is it, little girl?" he said. "Don't go walking about like that — you'll get cold."

I thought it was a good time to talk, so I told him that I really was not gaining here, and that I wished he would take me away.

"Why, darling!" said he, "our lease will be up in three weeks, and I can't see how to leave before.

"The repairs are not done at home, and I cannot possibly leave town just now. Of course if you were in any danger, I could and would, but you really are better, dear, whether you can see it or not. I am a doctor, dear, and I know. You are gaining flesh and color, your appetite is better, I feel really much easier about you."

"I don't weigh a bit more," said I, "nor as much; and my appetite may be better in the evening when you are here, but it is worse in the morning when you are away!"

"Bless her little heart!" said he with a big hug, "she shall be as sick as she pleases! But now let's improve the shining hours by going to sleep, and talk about it in the morning."

"And you won't go away?" I asked gloomily.

"Why, how can I dear? It is only three weeks more and then we will take a nice little trip of a few days while Jennie is getting the house ready. Really dear you are better!"

"Better in body perhaps —" I began, and stopped short, for he sat up straight and looked at me with such a stern, reproachful look that I could not say another word.

"My darling," said he, "I beg of you, for my sake and for our child's sake, as well as for your own, that you will never for one instant let that idea enter your mind! There is nothing so dangerous, so fascinating, to a temperament like yours. It is a false and foolish fancy. Can you not trust me as a physician when I tell you so?"

So of course I said no more on that score, and we went to sleep before long. He thought I was asleep first, but I wasn't, and lay there for hours trying to decide whether that front pattern and the back pattern really did move together or separately.

*   *   *   *   *   *

On a pattern like this, by daylight, there is a lack of sequence, a defiance of law, that is a constant irritant to a normal mind.

The color is hideous enough, and unreliable enough, and infuriating enough, but the pattern is torturing.

You think you have mastered it, but just as you get well underway in following, it turns a back-somersault and there you are. It slaps you in the face, knocks you down, and tramples on you. It is like a bad dream.

The outside pattern is a florid arabesque, reminding one of a fungus. If you can imagine a toadstool in joints, an interminable string of toadstools, budding and sprouting in endless convolutions — why, that is something like it.

That is, sometimes!

There is one marked peculiarity about this paper, a thing nobody seems to notice but myself, and that is that it changes as the light changes.

When the sun shoots in through the east window—I always watch for that first long, straight ray—it changes so quickly that I never can quite believe it.

That is why I watch it always.

By moonlight—the moon shines in all night when there is a moon—I wouldn't know it was the same paper.

At night in any kind of light, in twilight, candlelight, lamplight, and worst of all by moonlight, it becomes bars! The outside pattern I mean, and the woman behind it is as plain as can be.

I didn't realize for a long time what the thing was that showed behind, that dim sub-pattern, but now I am quite sure it is a woman.

By daylight, she is subdued, quiet. I fancy it is the pattern that keeps her so still. It is so puzzling. It keeps me quiet by the hour.

I lie down ever so much now. John says it is good for me, and to sleep all I can.

Indeed he started the habit by making me lie down for an hour after each meal.

It is a very bad habit I am convinced, for you see I don't sleep.

And that cultivates deceit, for I don't tell them I'm awake—O no!

The fact is I am getting a little afraid of John.

He seems very queer sometimes, and even Jennie has an inexplicable look.

It strikes me occasionally, just as a scientific hypothesis,—that perhaps it is the paper!

I have watched John when he did not know I was looking, and come into the room suddenly on the most innocent excuses, and I've caught him several times *looking at the paper!* And Jennie too. I caught Jennie with her hand on it once.

She didn't know I was in the room, and when I asked her in a quiet, a very quiet voice, with the most restrained manner possible, what she was doing with the paper—she turned around as if she had been caught stealing, and looked quite angry—asked me why I should frighten her so!

Then she said that the paper stained everything it touched, that she had found yellow smooches on all my clothes and John's, and she wished we would be more careful!

Did not that sound innocent? But I know she was studying that pattern, and I am determined that nobody shall find it out but myself!

* * * * * *

Life is very much more exciting now than it used to be. You see I have something more to expect, to look forward to, to watch. I really do eat better, and am more quiet than I was.

John is so pleased to see me improve! He laughed a little the other day, and said I seemed to be flourishing in spite of my wall-paper.

I turned it off with a laugh. I had no intention of telling him it was *because* of the wall-paper—he would make fun of me. He might even want to take me away.

I don't want to leave now until I have found it out. There is a week more, and I think that will be enough.

* * * * * *

I'm feeling ever so much better! I don't sleep much at night, for it is so interesting to watch developments; but I sleep a good deal in the daytime.

In the daytime it is tiresome and perplexing.

There are always new shoots on the fungus, and new shades of yellow all over it. I cannot keep count of them, though I have tried conscientiously.

It is the strangest yellow, that wall-paper! It makes me think of all the yellow things I ever saw—not beautiful ones like buttercups, but old foul, bad yellow things.

But there is something else about that paper—the smell! I noticed it the moment we came into the room, but with so much air and sun it was not bad. Now we have had a week of fog and rain, and whether the windows are open or not, the smell is here.

It creeps all over the house.

I find it hovering in the dining-room, skulking in the parlor, hiding in the hall, lying in wait for me on the stairs.

It gets into my hair.

Even when I go to ride, if I turn my head suddenly and surprise it—there is that smell!

Such a peculiar odor, too! I have spent hours in trying to analyze it, to find what it smelled like.

It is not bad—at first, and very gentle, but quite the subtlest, most enduring odor I ever met.

In this damp weather it is awful, I wake up in the night and find it hanging over me.

It used to disturb me at first. I thought seriously of burning the house—to reach the smell.

But now I am used to it. The only thing I can think of that it is like is the *color* of the paper! A yellow smell.

There is a very funny mark on this wall, low down, near the mopboard. A streak that runs round the room. It goes behind every piece of furniture, except the bed, a long, straight, even *smooch*, as if it had been rubbed over and over.

I wonder how it was done and who did it, and what they did it for. Round and round and round — round and round and round — it makes me dizzy!

*   *   *   *   *   *

I really have discovered something at last.

Through watching so much as night, when it changes so, I have finally found out.

The front pattern *does* move — and no wonder! The woman behind shakes it!

Sometimes I think there are a great many women behind, and sometimes only one, and she crawls around fast, and her crawling shakes it all over.

Then in the very bright spots she keeps still, and in the very shady spots she just takes hold of the bars and shakes them hard.

And she is all the time trying to climb through. But nobody could climb through that pattern — it strangles so; I think that is why it has so many heads.

They get through, and then the pattern strangles them off and turns them upside down, and makes their eyes white!

If those heads were covered or taken off it would not be half so bad.

*   *   *   *   *   *

I think that woman gets out in the daytime!

And I'll tell you why — privately — I've seen her!

I can see her out of every one of my windows!

It is the same woman, I know, for she is always creeping, and most women do not creep by daylight.

I see her in that long shaded lane, creeping up and down. I see her in those dark grape arbors, creeping all around the garden.

I see her on that long road under the trees, creeping along, and when a carriage comes she hides under the blackberry vines.

I don't blame her a bit. It must be very humiliating to be caught creeping by daylight!

I always lock the door when I creep by daylight. I can't do it at night, for I know John would suspect something at once.

And John is so queer now, that I don't want to irritate him. I wish he would take another room! Besides, I don't want anybody to get that woman out at night but myself.

I often wonder if I could see her out of all the windows at once.

But, turn as fast as I can, I can only see out of one at one time.

And though I always see her, she *may* be able to creep faster than I can turn!

I have watched her sometimes away off in the open country, creeping as fast as a cloud shadow in a high wind.

*   *   *   *   *   *

If only that top pattern could be gotten off from the under one! I mean to try it, little by little.

I have found out another funny thing, but I shan't tell it this time! It does not do to trust people too much.

There are only two more days to get this paper off, and I believe John is beginning to notice. I don't like the look in his eyes.

And I heard him ask Jennie a lot of professional questions about me. She had a very good report to give.

She said I slept a good deal in the daytime.

John knows I don't sleep very well at night, for all I'm so quiet!

He asked me all sorts of questions, too, and pretended to be very loving and kind.

As if I couldn't see through him!

Still, I don't wonder he acts so, sleeping under this paper for three months.

It only interests me, but I feel sure John and Jennie are secretly affected by it.

*   *   *   *   *   *

Hurrah! This is the last day, but it is enough. John to stay in town over night, and won't be out until this evening.

Jennie wanted to sleep with me — the sly thing! but I told her I should undoubtedly rest better for a night all alone.

That was clever, for really I wasn't alone a bit! As soon as it was moonlight and that poor thing began to crawl and shake the pattern, I got up and ran to help her.

I pulled and she shook, I shook and she pulled, and before morning we had peeled off yards of that paper.

A strip about as high as my head and half around the room.

And then when the sun came and that awful pattern began to laugh at me, I declared I would finish it to-day!

We go away to-morrow, and they are moving all my furniture down again to leave things as they were before.

Jennie looked at the wall in amazement, but I told her merrily that I did it out of pure spite at the vicious thing.

She laughed and said she wouldn't mind doing it herself, but I must not get tired.

How she betrayed herself that time!

But I am here, and no person touches this paper but me,—not *alive!*

She tried to get me out of the room—it was too patent! But I said it was so quiet and empty and clean now that I believed I would lie down again and sleep all I could; and not to wake me even for dinner—I would call when I woke.

So now she is gone, and the servants are gone, and the things are gone, and there is nothing left but that great bedstead nailed down, with the canvas mattress we found on it.

We shall sleep downstairs to-night, and take the boat home to-morrow.

I quite enjoy the room, now it is bare again.

How those children did tear about here!

This bedstead is fairly gnawed!

But I must get to work.

I have locked the door and thrown the key down into the front path.

I don't want to go out, and I don't want to have anybody come in, till John comes.

I want to astonish him.

I've got a rope up here that even Jennie did not find. If that woman does get out, and tries to get away, I can tie her!

But I forgot I could not reach far without anything to stand on!

This bed will *not* move!

I tried to lift and push it until I was lame, and then I got so angry I bit off a little piece at one corner— but it hurt my teeth.

Then I peeled off all the paper I could reach standing on the floor. It sticks horribly and the pattern just enjoys it! All those strangled heads and bulbous eyes and waddling fungus growths just shriek with derision!

I am getting angry enough to do something desperate. To jump out of the window would be admirable exercise, but the bars are too strong even to try.

Besides I wouldn't do it. Of course not. I know well enough that a step like that is improper and might be misconstrued.

I don't like to *look* out of the windows even— there are so many of those creeping women, and they creep so fast.

I wonder if they all come out of that wall-paper as I did?

But I am securely fastened now by my well-hidden rope—you don't get *me* out in the road there!

I suppose I shall have to get back behind the pattern when it comes night, and that is hard!

It is so pleasant to be out in this great room and creep around as I please!

I don't want to go outside. I won't, even if Jennie asks me to.

For outside you have to creep on the ground, and everything is green instead of yellow.

But here I can creep smoothly on the floor, and my shoulder just fits in that long smooch around the wall, so I cannot lose my way.

Why there's John at the door!

It is no use, young man, you can't open it!

How he does call and pound!

Now he's crying for an axe.

It would be a shame to break down that beautiful door!

"John dear!" said I in the gentlest voice, "the key is down by the front steps, under a plantain leaf!"

That silenced him for a few moments.

Then he said—very quietly indeed, "Open the door, my darling!"

"I can't," said I. "The key is down by the front door under a plantain leaf!"

And then I said it again, several times, very gently and slowly, and said it so often that he had to go and see, and he got it of course, and came in. He stopped short by the door.

"What is the matter?" he cried. "For God's sake, what are you doing!"

I kept on creeping just the same, but I looked at him over my shoulder.

"I've got out at last," said I, "in spite of you and Jane. And I've pulled off most of the paper, so you can't put me back!"

Now why should that man have fainted? But he did, and right across my path by the wall, so that I had to creep over him every time!

INDEX